2009- 1A

America's History

Read with confidence. Study effectively.

America's History is carefully designed to help you read, study, and excel, whether your goal is a quick review before class or preparing for an exam. Use the tools in your book to succeed in your history course.

Review the book as a whole

- **The part structure** showcases different eras in American history and helps you focus on important developments and major changes over time. Each part begins with a brief essay and a timeline that establish the main themes and events of the era. Each part includes three or more chapters, and each chapter focuses on one or more of the major part themes.

- **Chapter titles and section headings** provide signposts to help you navigate the textbook. Each chapter is organized into several clearly labeled main sections emphasizing main points and showing how individual events and long-term developments connect.

- **Documents** at the back of the book include the Declaration of Independence and United States Constitution. The **Appendix** includes additional tables and figures illustrating long-term changes in American society and government.

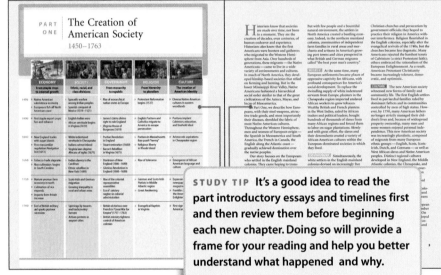

> **STUDY TIP** It's a good idea to read the part introductory essays and timelines first and then review them before beginning each new chapter. Doing so will provide a frame for your reading and help you better understand what happened and why.

Read each chapter

- **A chapter outline** on the first page of every chapter lists the major headings and subheadings.

- **Review questions** follow every main section of the chapter and draw your attention to the key issues. If you are able to answer these questions, you've understood that section.

- **Key terms** and concepts are highlighted in the narrative and listed for quick review in the **Glossary** at the end of the book. Consult the **index** to locate specific people and events.

> **STUDY TIP** Dates in titles and headings are important. Often a particular date or year isn't as important as understanding the related sequence of events. Chronology frequently determines significance — why something matters.

> **STUDY TIP** Examine the outline as you begin each chapter — it is your roadmap to that chapter's organization and main themes.

■ **Illustrations** have been selected to reinforce main points. They include numerous maps, artwork and photographs, figures, and tables. Frequently a map or a picture is more effective than words alone in explaining or emphasizing a particular development.

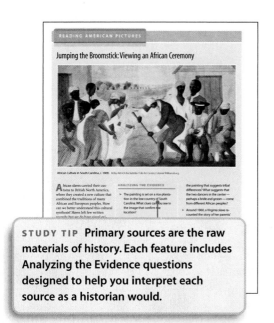

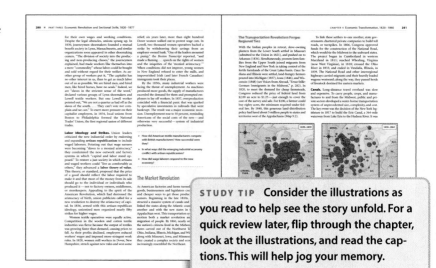

STUDY TIP Primary sources are the raw materials of history. Each feature includes Analyzing the Evidence questions designed to help you interpret each source as a historian would.

STUDY TIP Consider the illustrations as you read to help see the story unfold. For a quick review later, flip through the chapter, look at the illustrations, and read the captions. This will help jog your memory.

■ **Boxed features** are a central element of each chapter. They present primary sources as a way to experience the immediacy of the past through the words and perspectives of those who lived it. The features — Comparing American Voices, Reading American Pictures, and Voices from Abroad — emphasize important developments in the narrative.

Review at the end of the chapter

■ **A summary** concludes each chapter and highlights the main chapter themes.

■ **Connections** immediately following the summary link the chapter's main themes back to the part introduction and provide a bridge to the next chapter.

■ **Chapter review questions** ask you to relate the themes presented in the different sections of the chapter. They model the types of broad questions your instructor might ask on an exam.

■ **Timelines** help you keep the chronology of events straight.

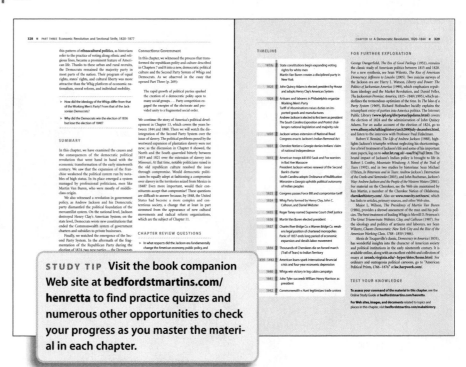

STUDY TIP Visit the book companion Web site at bedfordstmartins.com/henretta to find practice quizzes and numerous other opportunities to check your progress as you master the material in each chapter.

America's History

Sixth Edition

James A. Henretta
University of Maryland

David Brody
University of California, Davis

Lynn Dumenil
Occidental College

Bedford / St. Martin's
Boston • New York

For Bedford/St.Martin's
Executive Editor for History: Mary Dougherty
Director of Development for History: Jane Knetzger
Senior Developmental Editor: William J. Lombardo
Senior Production Editor: Bridget Leahy
Senior Production Supervisor: Joe Ford
Executive Marketing Manager: Jenna Bookin Barry
Editorial Assistants: Holly Dye and Amy Leathe
Production Assistants: Amy Derjue and Lidia MacDonald-Carr
Copyeditors: Barbara Bell and Lisa Wehrle
Text Design: Catherine Hawkes, Cat and Mouse Design
Indexer: EdIndex
Photo Research: Pembroke Herbert and Sandi Rygiel/Picture Research Consultants & Archives
Cover Design: Donna Lee Dennison
Cover Art: Joining of the Rails (Meeting of the Engines) at Promontory Summit, Utah, on May 10, 1869.
 Photograph by Charles Roscoe Savage, from the Central Pacific Railroad Photographic History Museum,
 http://CPRR.org; The Union Pacific Railroad Topographical Map. Library of Congress.
Cartography: Mapping Specialists Limited
Composition: TechBooks
Printing and Binding: R.R. Donnelley & Sons Company

President: Joan E. Feinberg
Editorial Director: Denise B. Wydra
Director of Marketing: Karen Melton Soeltz
Director of Editing, Design, and Production: Marcia Cohen
Managing Editor: Elizabeth M. Schaaf

Library of Congress Control Number: 2006940027

Manufactured in the United States of America.

1 0 9
f e

For information, write: Bedford/St. Martin's, 75 Arlington Street, Boston, MA 02116
(617-399-4000)

ISBN-10: 0–312–44350–1 ISBN-13: 978–0–312–44350–4 (combined edition)
ISBN-10: 0–312–45285–3 ISBN-13: 978–0–312–45285–8 (Vol. 1)
ISBN-10: 0–312–45286–1 ISBN-13: 978–0–312–45286–5 (Vol. 2)
ISBN-10: 0–312–46548–3 ISBN-13: 978–0–312–46548–3 (high school edition)

Acknowledgments

Acknowledgments and copyrights can be found at the back of the book on pages C-1–C-4, which constitute an extension of the copyright page.

ONE OF THE GIFTS OF textbook writing is the second and third chances it affords. Where else, after all, does the historian have the opportunity to revisit work and strive, on a regular basis, to make it better? Relishing the opportunity, we have, with each edition, sharpened the narrative, refined arguments, restructured chapters, and incorporated fresh scholarship. In this, the sixth edition, we pick up that task again, only this time with a more ambitious goal. We want to bring *America's History* into the twenty-first century. *America's History* was conceived nearly thirty years ago and built into it were assumptions — both intellectual and pedagogical — that, for this edition, we have reconsidered. On the intellectual side, this has led us to a thorough rethinking and recasting of our post-1945 chapters. On the pedagogical side, it has led us to a back-to-basics approach, utilizing an array of learning tools that we are confident will engage and instruct today's students. On both counts, *America's History* will strike instructors as quite new. But we have not departed from the core idea with which we began — to write a comprehensive text that has explanatory power and yet is immediately accessible to every student who enrolls in the survey course.

From the very inception of *America's History*, we set out to write a *democratic* history, one that would convey the experiences of ordinary people even as it recorded the accomplishments of the great and powerful. We focus not only on the marvelous diversity of peoples who became American but also on the institutions — political, economic, cultural, and social — that forged a common national identity. And we present these historical trajectories in an integrated way, using each perspective to make better sense of the others. In our discussion of government and politics, diplomacy and war, we show how they affected — and were affected by — ethnic groups and economic conditions, intellectual beliefs and social changes, and the religious and moral values of the times. Just as important, we place the American experience in a global context. We trace aspects of American society to their origins in European and African cultures, consider the American Industrial Revolution within the framework of the world economy, and plot the foreign relations of the United States as part of an ever-shifting international system of imperial expansion, financial exchange, and diplomatic alliances. In emphasizing the global context, we want to remind students that America never existed alone in the world; that other nations experienced developments comparable to our own; and that, knowing this, we can better understand, through comparative discussions at opportune moments, what was distinctive and particular to the American experience.

In these eventful times, college students — even those who don't think much about America's past or today's news — have to wonder about 9/11 or the Iraq war or the furor over illegal immigration: How did that happen? This question is at the heart of historical inquiry. And in asking it, the student is thinking historically. In *America's History* we aspire to satisfy that student's curiosity. We try to ask the right questions — the big ones and the not-so-big — and then write history that illuminates the answers. We are writing narrative history, but harnessed to historical argument, not simply a retelling of "this happened, then that happened."

Structure

One way of overcoming the student's sense that history is just one-damn-thing-after-another is to show her that American history is constituted of distinct periods or eras that give it shape and meaning. Accordingly, we devised early on a six-part structure, corresponding to what we understood to be the major phases of American development. Part Six, carrying the story from 1945 to the present, stood somewhat apart because it was, by definition, unfinished. In earlier editions, that made sense, but as we move into the twenty-first century, it becomes increasingly clear that we have entered a new phase of American history, and that the era that began in 1945 has ended. So now we have a fully realized Part Six, which we call the Age of Cold War Liberalism, 1945–1980, and a new Part Seven, with the breaking point at 1980 signaling the advent of a conservative America in an emerging post–Cold War world. Students who know only this new age will find in Part Six a coherent narrative history of the times of their parents and grandparents. In Part Seven, they will find an account of an era truly their own, carried to the present with a full chapter on the post-2000 years.

Given the importance of the part structure in the text's scheme, we have taken pains to provide students with the aids to comprehension they need to benefit fully from this organization. Each part begins with a two-page overview. First, a **thematic timeline** highlights the key developments in politics, the economy, society, culture, and foreign affairs; then these themes are fleshed out in a corresponding **part essay**. Each part essay focuses on the crucial engines of historical change—in some eras primarily economic, in others political or diplomatic—that created new conditions of life and transformed social relations. The part organization, encapsulated in the thematic timelines and opening essays, helps students understand the major themes and periods of American history, to see how bits and pieces of historical data acquire significance as part of a larger pattern of development.

The individual chapters are similarly constructed with student comprehension in mind. A **chapter outline** gives readers an overview of the text discussion, followed by a **thematic introduction** that orients them to the central issues and ideas of the chapter. Then, at the end of the chapter, we remind students of important events in a **chapter timeline** and reiterate the themes in an **analytic summary**. The summaries have been thoroughly revised, with the aim of underlining as concretely as possible the main points of the chapter. In addition, we have added a new feature, **Connections**, that enables students to take a longer view, to see how the chapter relates to prior and forthcoming chapters. We are also more attentive to the need of students for effective study aids. Within each chapter, we now append focus questions to each section, and at the chapter's end, a set of study questions. And where students are likely to stumble, we provide a **glossary** that defines the **key concepts** bold faced in the text where first mentioned.

Features: Back to Basics

In keeping with our back-to-basics approach, *America's History* has rebuilt its features program around primary sources, providing students with an opportunity to experience the past through the words and perspectives of those who lived it and, equally important, to encounter historical evidence and learn how to extract meaning from it. The cornerstone of this program is the two-page **Comparing American Voices** feature that appears in every chapter. Each contains several primary sources—excerpts from letters, diaries, autobiographies, and public testimony—offering varying, often conflicting, views on a single event or theme discussed in the chapter. An introduction establishes the historical context, generally with reference to the chapter, and headnotes identify and explain the provenance of the individual documents. These are followed by a series of questions—under the heading Analyzing the Evidence—that focus the student's attention on revealing aspects of the documents and show her how historians—herself included—can draw meaning from contemporary evidence. Instructors will find in Comparing American Voices a major resource for inducting beginning students into the processes of historical analysis. Carried over from the previous edition is **Voices from Abroad,** featuring first-person testimony by foreign visitors and observers, but now also equipped with questions like those in Comparing American Voices, and with a similar pedagogical intent.

America's History has always been noted for its rich offering of maps, figures, and pictures that help students visualize the past. Over 120 **full-color maps** encourage a geographic perspective, many of them with annotations that call out key points. All the maps are cross-referenced in the narrative text, as are the tables and figures. Nearly 40 percent of the **art** and **photographs** are new to this edition, selected to reflect changes in the text and to underscore chapter themes. Most appear in full color, with unusually **substantive captions** that actively engage students with the image and encourage them to analyze visuals as primary documents. To advance further this pedagogical aim, we have developed a new feature that we call **Reading American Pictures**, a full page in each chapter devoted to the visual study of one or more carefully selected contemporary paintings, cartoons, or photographs. These are introduced by a discussion of the context in which they were produced and followed by questions designed to prompt students to treat them as another form of historical evidence. We anticipate that the exercise will provoke lively classroom discussion. In our pedagogical program focusing on primary sources, Reading American Pictures is offered as the visual counterpart to Comparing American Voices and Voices from Abroad.

Textual Changes

Of all the reasons for a new edition, of course, the most compelling is to improve the text itself. Good narrative history is primarily a product of good sentences and good paragraphs. So our labors have been mostly in the trenches, so to speak, in a line-by-line striving for the vividness and human presence that are hallmarks of narrative history. We are also partisans of economical writing, by necessity if we are to incorporate what's new in the field and in contemporary affairs while holding *America's History* to a manageable length. This is a challenge we welcome, believing as we do that brevity is the best antidote to imprecise language and murky argument. Of the more substantive changes, a notable one arose from the refocusing of our features program on primary sources. Whereas previous editions contained boxed essays on American Lives, we have now integrated those stories of ordinary and notable Americans into the narrative, much expanding and enlivening its people-centered approach.

Within chapters we have been especially attentive to chronology, which sometimes involved a significant reordering of material. In Part Two (1776–1820), chapters 6 and 7 now provide a continuous political narrative from the Declaration of Independence to the Era of Good Feelings. In Part Three (1820–1877), feedback from instructors persuaded us to consolidate our treatment of the pre–Civil War South into a single, integrated chapter. In Part Four (1877–1914), our chapter on Gilded Age politics has been reorganized to improve chronology and placed after the chapter on the city so as to provide students with a seamless transition to the Progressive era. In Part Five (1914–1945), the three chapters on the 1920s, the Great Depression, and the New Deal have been melded into two crisper, more integrated chapters. All of the chapters in Part Six (1945–1980) and the new Part Seven (1980–2006) have been thoroughly reworked as part of our rethinking of the post-1945 era. In the companion Chapters 26 and 27, we now offer a thematic treatment of the 1950s, while Chapters 28 and 29 provide a coherent narrative account of liberalism's triumph under Kennedy and Johnson and its dramatic decline after 1968. Part Seven represents a much expanded coverage of the post-1980 years, with new chapters devoted to social and economic developments and America since 2000. Altogether, these organizational changes represent the biggest shake-up of *America's History* since its inception.

The revising process also affords us a welcome opportunity to incorporate fresh scholarship. In Part One, we have added new material on life in Africa, the slave trade, the emergence of an African American ethnicity, and on such non-English ethnic colonial groups as the Scots Irish and the Germans. In Chapter 11, we have a completely new section on urban popular culture (masculinity, sexuality, minstrel shows, and racism) drawing on recent advances in cultural history, inventive scholarship that also informs Chapter 18 (on the late-nineteenth-century city) and several twentieth-century chapters, including in Chapter 27 our treatment of consumer culture in the 1950s. Chapter 16 contains fresh information about the impact of farming on the ecosystem of the Great Plains. In Chapter 20, the opening section has been recast to incorporate recent insights into the middle-class impulse behind progressivism, and a new section treats the industrial strife that reoriented progressivism toward the problem of the nation's labor relations. Of the many revisions in the post-1945 chapters, perhaps the most notable derive from the opening of Soviet archives, which allows us at last to see the Cold War from both sides of the Iron Curtain, and also to amend our assessment of the impact of communism on American life. In addition, Part Six contains fresh material on the civil rights movement, on the Vietnam War, and on the revival of American conservatism. Even richer are the additions to Part Seven, "Entering a New Era: Conservatism, Globalization, Terrorism, 1980–2006," especially in the treatment of social movements and the information technology revolution in Chapter 31, and a completely new post-2000 Chapter 32, which, unlike all the preceding chapters, relies not on secondary sources, but primarily on a reading of the contemporary press and the public record.

Supplements

For Students

Documents to Accompany** America's History, **Sixth Edition. Edited by Melvin Yazawa, University of New Mexico (Volume 1), and Kevin Fernlund, University of Missouri, St. Louis (Volume 2), this primary source reader is designed to accompany *America's History*, Sixth Edition, and offers a chorus of voices from the past to enrich the study of U.S. history. Both celebrated figures and ordinary people, from Frederick Douglass to mill workers, demonstrate the diversity of America's history while putting a human face on historical experience. A wealth of speeches, petitions, advertisements, and posters paint a vivid picture of the social and political life of the time, providing depth and breadth to the textbook discussion. Brief introductions set each document in context, while questions for analysis help link the individual source to larger historical themes.

NEW *E-Documents to Accompany* America's History, *Sixth Edition*. The most robust gathering of primary sources to accompany any U.S. history survey text is now available online. *E-Documents to Accompany* America's History, *Sixth Edition* is perfect for adding an electronic dimension to your class or integrating with your existing online course.

Online Study Guide at bedfordstmartins.com/henretta. The popular Online Study Guide for *America's History* is a free and uniquely personalized learning tool to help students master themes and information presented in the textbook and improve their historical skills. Assessment quizzes let students evaluate their comprehension and provide them with customized plans for further study through a variety of activities. Instructors can monitor students' progress through the online Quiz Gradebook or receive e-mail updates.

Maps in Context: A Workbook for American History. Written by historical cartography expert Gerald A. Danzer (University of Illinois, Chicago), this skill-building workbook helps students comprehend essential connections between geographic literacy and historical understanding. Organized to correspond to the typical U.S. history survey course, *Maps in Context* presents a wealth of map-centered projects and convenient pop quizzes that give students hands-on experience working with maps. Available free when packaged with the text.

NEW *The Bedford Glossary for U.S. History*. This handy supplement for the survey course gives students clear, concise definitions of the political, economic, social, and cultural terms used by historians and contemporary media alike. The terms are historically contextualized to aid comprehension. Available free when packaged with the text.

NEW *History Matters: A Student Guide to U.S. History Online.* This new resource, written by Alan Gevinson, Kelly Schrum, and Roy Rosenzweig (all of George Mason University), provides an illustrated and annotated guide to 250 of the most useful Web sites for student research in U.S. history as well as advice on evaluating and using Internet sources. This essential guide is based on the acclaimed "History Matters" Web site developed by the American Social History Project and the Center for History and New Media. Available free when packaged with the text.

Bedford Series in History and Culture. Over 100 titles in this highly praised series combine first-rate scholarship, historical narrative, and important primary documents for undergraduate courses. Each book is brief, inexpensive, and focused on a specific topic or period. Package discounts are available.

Historians at Work Series. Brief enough for a single assignment yet meaty enough to provoke thoughtful discussion, each volume in this series examines a single historical question by combining unabridged selections by distinguished historians, each with a different perspective on the issue, with helpful learning aids. Package discounts are available.

Trade Books. Titles published by sister companies Farrar, Straus and Giroux; Henry Holt and Company; Hill and Wang; Picador; and St. Martin's Press are available at deep discounts when packaged with Bedford/St. Martin's textbooks. For more information, visit bedfordstmartins.com/tradeup.

Critical Thinking Modules at bedfordstmartins.com/historymodules. This Web site offers over two dozen online modules for interpreting maps, audio, visual, and textual sources, centered on events covered in the U.S. history survey. An online guide correlates modules to textbook chapters.

Research and Documentation Online at **bedfordstmartins.com/resdoc.** This Web site provides clear advice on how to integrate primary and secondary sources into research papers, how to cite sources correctly, and how to format in MLA, APA, *Chicago,* or CBE style.

The St. Martin's Tutorial on Avoiding Plagiarism at **bedfordstmartins.com/plagiarismtutorial.** This online tutorial reviews the consequences of plagiarism and explains what sources to acknowledge, how to keep good notes, how to organize research, and how to integrate sources appropriately. This tutorial includes exercises to help students practice integrating sources and recognize acceptable summaries.

Bedford Research Room at **bedfordstmartins.com/researchroom.** The Research Room, drawn from Mike Palmquist's *The Bedford Researcher,* offers a wealth of resources — including interactive tutorials, research activities, student writing samples, and links to hundreds of other places online — to support students in courses across the disciplines. The site also offers instructors a library of helpful instructional tools.

For Instructors

Instructor's Resource Manual. Written by Jason Newman (Cosumnes River College, Los Rios Community College District), the *Instructor's Resource Manual for AMERICA'S HISTORY,* Sixth Edition, provides both first-time and experienced instructors with valuable teaching tools — annotated chapter outlines, lecture strategies, in-class activities, discussion questions, suggested writing assignments, and related readings and media — to structure and customize their American history course. The manual also offers a convenient, chapter-by-chapter guide to the wealth of supplementary materials available to instructors teaching *America's History.*

Computerized Test Bank. A fully updated Test Bank CD-ROM offers over 80 exercises for each chapter, allowing instructors to pick and choose from a collection of multiple-choice, fill-in, map, and short and long essay questions. To aid instructors in tailoring their tests to suit their classes, every question includes a textbook page number so instructors can direct students to a particular page for correct answers. Also, the software allows instructors to edit both questions and answers to further customize their texts. Correct answers and model responses are included.

Transparencies. This set of over 160 full-color acetate transparencies of all maps and selected images in the text helps instructors present lectures and teach students important map-reading skills.

Book Companion Site at **bedfordstmartins.com/henretta.** The companion Web site gathers all the electronic resources for *America's History,* including the Online Study Guide and related Quiz Gradebook, at a single Web address, providing convenient links to lecture, assignment, and research materials such as PowerPoint chapter outlines and the digital libraries at Make History.

NEW Make History at **bedfordstmartins.com/makehistory.** Comprising the content of our five acclaimed online libraries — Map Central, the U.S. History Image Library, DocLinks, HistoryLinks, and PlaceLinks — Make History provides one-stop access to relevant digital content including maps, images, documents, and Web links. Students and instructors alike can search this free, easy-to-use database by keyword, topic, date, or specific chapter of *America's History* and can download any content they find. Instructors using *America's History* can also create entire collections of content and store them online for later use or post their collections to the Web to share with students.

Instructor's Resource CD-ROM. This disc provides instructors with ready-made and customizable PowerPoint multimedia presentations built around chapter outlines, maps, figures, and selected images from the textbook. The disc also includes all maps and selected images from the textbook in jpeg format, the *Instructor's Resource Manual* in pdf format, and a quick-start guide to the Online Study Guide.

Course Management Content. E-content is available for *America's History* in Blackboard, WebCT, and other platforms. This e-content includes nearly all of the offerings from the book's Online Study Center as well as the book's test bank.

Videos and Multimedia. A wide assortment of videos and multimedia CD-ROMs on various topics in American history is available to qualified adopters.

NEW *The AP U.S. History Teaching Toolkit for America's History, Sixth Edition.* Written by AP experts Jonathan Chu (University of Massachusetts, Boston) and Ellen W. Parisi (Williamsville East High School and D'Youville College), this entirely new AP resource is the first comprehensive history resource for AP teachers. The *AP U.S. History Teaching ToolKit* provides materials to teach the basics of and preparation for the AP U.S. history examination, including entire DBQs. The *ToolKit* also includes a wealth of materials that address the course's main challenges, especially coverage, pacing, and methods for conveying the critical knowledge and skills that AP students need.

NEW *AP U.S. History Testbank for America's History, Sixth Edition.* Written by Ellen W. Parisi (Williamsville East High School and D'Youville College) specifically for AP teachers and students, the *AP U.S. History Test Bank* is designed to help students recall their textbook reading and prepare for the format and difficulty level of the AP exam. Each chapter of *America's History*, Sixth Edition, has a twenty-question multiple-choice quiz and five AP-style questions that mimic the exam questions. Each major part of *America's History* has a corresponding test containing fifty AP-style questions, which can be used for both student self-testing and in-class practice exams. All multiple-choice questions include five distracters.

Acknowledgments

We are very grateful to the following scholars and teachers who reported on their experiences with the fifth edition or reviewed chapters of the sixth edition. Their comments often challenged us to re-think or justify our interpretations and always provided a check on accuracy down to the smallest detail.

Elizabeth Alexander, *Texas Wesleyan University*
Marjorie Berman, *Red Rocks Community College*
Rebecca Boone, *Lamar University*
Michael L. Cox, *Barton County Community College*
Glen Gendzel, *Indiana University-Perdue*
Jessica Gerard, *Ozarks Technical Community College*
Martin Halpern, *Henderson State University*
Yvonne Johnson, *Central Missouri State University*
Sanford B. Kanter, *San Jacinto College South*
Anthony Kaye, *Penn State University*
William J. Lipkin, *Union County College*
Daniel Littlefield, *University of South Carolina*
James Meriwether, *California State University, Bakersfield*
William Moore, *University of Wyoming*
Allison Parker, *SUNY Brockport*
Phillip Payne, *St. Bonaventure University*
Louis W. Potts, *University of Missouri, Kansas City*
Yasmin Rahman, *University of Colorado at Boulder*
Kim Richardson, *Community College at Jacksonville*
Howard Rock, *Florida International University*
Donald W. Rogers, *Central Connecticut State University*
Jason Scott Smith, *University of New Mexico*
David Steigerwald, *The Ohio State University, Marion*
David G. Thompson, *Illinois Central College*
Christine S. White, *San Jacinto College South*

We also extend our thanks and gratitude to our high school colleagues and college instructors associated with the College Board who commented on *America's History* and reviewed the new AP supplements tailored specifically for our textbook.

Tom Alleman, *Carbon High School*
Margaret Bramlett, *St. Paul's Episcopal School*
Cameron Flint, *Cloverleaf High School*
Tim Greene, *Jersey Shore Senior High School*
Jonathan Lurie, *Rutgers University*
Jackie McHargue, *Duncanville High School*
Christine Madsen, *Flintridge Prep School*
Louisa Moffitt, *Marist School*
Joseph J. O'Neill, *Mount Saint Charles Academy*
La Juana J. Reban Coleman, *NMHU Center at Rio Rancho*
Rex Sanders, *A & M Consolidated High School*
Mary van Weezel, *Lakeland Regional High School*
Joe Villano, *Marist College (retired)*

As the authors of *America's History*, we know better than anyone else how much this book is the work of other hands and minds. We are grateful to Mary Dougherty and Jane Knetzger, who oversaw the project, and William Lombardo, who used his extensive knowledge and critical skills as a well-trained historian to edit our text and suggest a multitude of improvements. As usual, Joan E. Feinberg has been generous in providing the resources we needed to produce the sixth edition. Bridget Leahy did more than we had a right to expect in producing an outstanding volume. Karen Melton Soeltz and Jenna Bookin Barry in the marketing department have been instrumental in helping this book reach the classroom. We also thank the rest of our editorial and production team for their dedicated efforts: Amy Leathe, Holly Dye, Amy Derjue, and Lidia MacDonald-Carr; Pembroke Herbert and Sandi Rygiel at Picture Research Consultants and Archives; and Sandy Schechter. Finally, we want to express our appreciation for the invaluable assistance of Patricia Deveneau and Jason Newman, whose work contributed in many ways to the intellectual vitality of this new edition of *America's History*.

James A. Henretta
David Brody
Lynn Dumenil

CONTENTS

PART FOUR

A Maturing Industrial Society, 1877–1914 *484*

16 The American West *487*

17 Capital and Labor in the Age of Enterprise, 1877–1900 *519*

18 The Industrial City: Building It, Living in It *551*

19 Politics in the Age of Enterprise, 1877–1896 583

20 The Progressive Era, 1900–1914 611

21 An Emerging World Power, 1877–1914 641

PART SIX
The Age of Cold War Liberalism, 1945–1980 *798*

MAPS

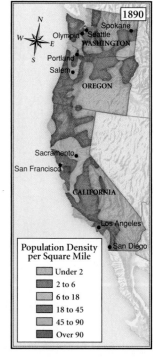

FIGURES AND TABLES

SPECIAL FEATURES

ABOUT THE AUTHORS

JAMES A. HENRETTA is Priscilla Alden Burke Professor of American History at the University of Maryland, College Park. He received his undergraduate education at Swarthmore College and his Ph.D. from Harvard University. He has taught at the University of Sussex, England; Princeton University; UCLA; Boston University; as a Fulbright lecturer in Australia at the University of New England; and at Oxford University as the Harmsworth Professor of American History. His publications include *The Evolution of American Society, 1700–1815: An Interdisciplinary Analysis; "Salutary Neglect": Colonial Administration under the Duke of Newcastle; Evolution and Revolution: American Society, 1600–1820; The Origins of American Capitalism;* and an edited volume, *Republicanism and Liberalism in America and the German States, 1750–1850.* His most recent publication is a long article, "Charles Evans Hughes and the Strange Death of Liberal America," (*Law and History Review,* 2006), derived from his ongoing research on The Liberal State in New York, 1820–1975.

DAVID BRODY is Professor Emeritus of History at the University of California, Davis. He received his B.A., M.A., and Ph.D. from Harvard University. He has taught at the University of Warwick in England, at Moscow State University in the former Soviet Union, and at Sydney University in Australia. He is the author of *Steelworkers in America; Workers in Industrial America: Essays on the 20th Century Struggle;* and *In Labor's Cause: Main Themes on the History of the American Worker.* His most recent book is *Labor Embattled: History, Power, Rights* (2005). He has been awarded fellowships from the Social Science Research Council, the Guggenheim Foundation, and the National Endowment for the Humanities. He is past president (1991–1992) of the Pacific Coast branch of the American Historical Association.

LYNN DUMENIL is Robert Glass Cleland Professor of American History at Occidental College in Los Angeles. She is a graduate of the University of Southern California and received her Ph.D. from the University of California, Berkeley. She has written *The Modern Temper: American Culture and Society in the 1920s* and *Freemasonry and American Culture: 1880–1930.* Her articles and reviews have appeared in the *Journal of American History;* the *Journal of American Ethnic History: Reviews in American History;* and the *American Historical Review.* She has been a historical consultant to several documentary film projects and is on the Pelzer Prize Committee of the Organization of American Historians. Her current work, for which she received a National Endowment for the Humanities Fellowship, is on World War I, citizenship, and the state. In 2001–2002 she was the Bicentennial Fulbright Chair in American Studies at the University of Helsinki.

America's History

PART ONE | The Creation of American Society

1450–1763

ECONOMY	SOCIETY	GOVERNMENT	RELIGION	CULTURE
From staple crops to internal growth	Ethnic, racial, and class divisions	From monarchy to republic	From hierarchy to pluralism	The creation of American identity

	ECONOMY	SOCIETY	GOVERNMENT	RELIGION	CULTURE
1450	▶ Native American subsistence economy ▶ Europeans fish off North American coast	▶ Sporadic warfare among Indian peoples ▶ Spanish conquest of Mexico (1519–1521)	▶ Rise of monarchical nation-states in Europe	▶ Protestant Reformation begins (1517)	▶ Diverse Native American cultures in eastern woodlands
1600	▶ First staple export crops: furs and tobacco	▶ English-Indian wars ▶ African servitude begins in Virginia (1619)	▶ James I claims divine right to rule England ▶ Virginia House of Burgesses (1619)	▶ English Puritans and Catholics migrate to America to escape persecution	▶ Puritans implant Calvinism, education, and freehold ideal
1640	▶ New England trades with sugar islands ▶ First mercantilist regulation: Navigation Act (1651)	▶ White indentured servitude in Chesapeake ▶ Indians retreat inland ▶ Virginia laws deprive Africans of rights (1671)	▶ Puritan Revolution in England ▶ Stuart restoration (1660) ▶ Bacon's Rebellion in Virginia (1675)	▶ Puritans in Massachusetts Bay quash "heresy" ▶ Religious liberty in Rhode Island	▶ Aristocratic aspirations in Chesapeake region
1680	▶ Tobacco trade stagnates ▶ Rice cultivation begins in South Carolina	▶ Indian slavery in the Carolinas ▶ Ethnic rebellion in New York (1689)	▶ Dominion of New England (1686–1689) ▶ Glorious Revolution in England (1688–1689)	▶ Rise of tolerance	▶ Emergence of African American language and culture
1720	▶ Mature yeoman farm economy in north ▶ Cultivation of rice expands ▶ Imports from Britain increase	▶ Scots-Irish and German migration ▶ Growing inequality in rural and urban areas	▶ Rise of the colonial representative assemblies ▶ Era of salutary neglect in colonial administration	▶ German and Scots-Irish Pietists in Middle Atlantic region ▶ Great Awakening	▶ Expansion of colleges, newspapers, and magazines ▶ Franklin and the American Enlightenment
1760	▶ End of British military aid sparks postwar recession	▶ Uprisings by tenants and backcountry farmers ▶ Artisan protests in seaport cities	▶ Britain victorious over French in "Great War for Empire" (1757–1763) ▶ British ministry tightens control of American colonies	▶ Evangelical Baptists in Virginia	▶ First signs of an American identity

Historians know that societies are made over time, not born in a moment. They are the creation of decades, even centuries, of human endeavor and experience. Historians also know that the first Americans were hunters and gatherers who migrated to the Western Hemisphere from Asia. Over hundreds of generations, these migrants—the Native Americans—came to live in a wide variety of environments and cultures. In much of North America, they developed kinship-based societies that relied on farming and hunting. But in the lower Mississippi River Valley, Native Americans fashioned a hierarchical social order similar to that of the great civilizations of the Aztecs, Mayas, and Incas of Mesoamerica.

In Part One, we describe how Europeans, with their steel weapons, attractive trade goods, and most importantly their diseases, shredded the fabric of most Native American cultures. Throughout the Western Hemisphere, men and women of European origin—the Spanish in Mesoamerica and South America, the French in Canada, the English along the Atlantic coast—gradually achieved domination over the native peoples.

Our story focuses on the Europeans who settled in the English mainland colonies. They came hoping to transplant their traditional societies, cultures, and religious beliefs in the soil of the New World. But things did not work out exactly as they planned. In learning to live in the new land, English, Germans, and Scots-Irish created societies in British North America that differed from those of their homelands in their economies, social character, political systems, religions, and cultures. Here, in brief, is the story of that transformation as we explain it in Part One.

ECONOMY Many European settlements succeeded as economic ventures. Traditional Europe was made up of poor, overcrowded, and unequal societies that periodically suffered devastating famines. But with few people and a bountiful natural environment, the settlers in North America created a bustling economy. Indeed, in the northern mainland colonies, communities of independent farm families in rural areas and merchants and artisans in America's growing port towns and cities prospered in what British and German migrants called "the best poor man's country."

SOCIETY At the same time, many European settlements became places of oppressive captivity for Africans, with profound consequences for America's social development. To replace the dwindling supply of white indentured servants from Europe, planters in the Chesapeake region imported enslaved African workers to grow tobacco. Wealthy British and French planters in the West Indies, aided by African traders and political leaders, bought hundreds of thousands of slaves from many African regions and forced them to labor on sugar plantations. Slowly and with great effort, the slaves and their descendants created a variety of African American cultures within the European-dominated societies in which they lived.

GOVERNMENT Simultaneously, the white settlers in the English mainland colonies devised an increasingly free and competitive political system. The first migrants transplanted authoritarian institutions to America and, until 1689, English authorities intervened frequently in their economic and political affairs. Thereafter, local governments and representative assemblies became more important and created a tradition of self-rule that would spark demands for political independence from Britain in the years following the conclusion of the Great War for Empire in 1763.

RELIGION The American experience profoundly changed religious institutions and values. Many migrants left Europe because of conflicts among rival Christian churches and persecution by government officials; they hoped to practice their religion in America without interference. Religion flourished in the English colonies, especially after the evangelical revivals of the 1740s, but the churches became less dogmatic. Many Americans rejected the harshest tenets of Calvinism (a strict Protestant faith); others embraced the rationalism of the European Enlightenment. As a result, American Protestant Christianity became increasingly tolerant, democratic, and optimistic.

CULTURE The new American society witnessed new forms of family and community life. The first English settlers lived in patriarchal families ruled by dominant fathers and in communities controlled by men of high status. However, by 1750, many American fathers no longer strictly managed their children's lives and, because of widespread property ownership, many men and some women enjoyed personal independence. This new American society was increasingly pluralistic, composed of migrants from many European ethnic groups—English, Scots, Scots-Irish, Dutch, and Germans—as well as West African slaves and Native American peoples. Distinct regional cultures developed in New England, the Middle Atlantic colonies, the Chesapeake, and the Carolinas. Consequently, an overarching American identity based on the English language, English legal and political institutions, and shared experiences emerged very slowly.

Thus, the story of the English colonial experience is both depressing and uplifting. On the one hand, Europeans and their diseases destroyed many Native American peoples and European slaveowners held an increasing number of African Americans in bondage. On the other hand, white migrants enjoyed unprecedented opportunities for economic security, political freedom, and spiritual fulfillment.

OCEANVS OCCIDENTALIS

GROWLAND

Notuegia   Datia   Iuetia

Li uonia

Littouia

Tartaria p rotu

Ifarrufa

Oxiaflus

Dana   Poce   Polonia   Rufia   Tartaria

Saxonia   Germani

Bohe   Valachia   Ruffia

Colchis   albania

Matehircanū

Hi   nia

An   an

Anglia   Gallia   Arabia   Venetia   Grc   Mare macor   Asia minor   Armenia maior   Hircania   Parthia

Hilpania   Mare   Mediterraneum   Tigris   &   Eufrates   mefopotania   affiria   Ba nia   Rudiana

Barbaria   Africa   tunefe   Grene   Algeri   Egiptus   arabiade ferra   Caldea   Persia   Sin9 Perfi   Camari   Canale   arabafce   Indus

Fortunate   Libia interior   Arabia felix

Iabella   Ifpagniola

Gigāc   Brafil   bacot

Ethiopia   Mare   Lurt   peritbos   Cambia   fetani

AFRICA   Viride   fā   mu   de   ginoa   Rtode   pet   cit   ingradelj   ncipe   Ethio   pia   Nilus   fl   Garfula   nogadafa

Gonne   cis   Requnā   meli   Gluri   Melinda

Equinocialis Crculus   mon   bafa   qui   loa

Canut   s.crucis   Mons Lune   monfanbiqui

AMERICA   Rjode magni congo

mons niger

bona fpe   rania

Allepaguo   de s.pauli   Tropicus Capricorni   cabo   Madaga   fcar   MA

1 Worlds Collide: Europe, Africa, and America

1450–1620

"BEFORE THE FRENCH CAME AMONG us," an elder of the Natchez people of Mississippi explained, "we were men . . . and we walked with boldness every road, but now we walk like slaves, which we shall soon be, since the French already treat us . . . as they do their black slaves." Before the 1490s, the Natchez and the other native peoples of the Western Hemisphere knew nothing about the light-skinned inhabitants of Europe and the dark-complexioned peoples of Africa. But Portuguese merchants seeking gold, ivory, and slaves had been trading along the west coast of Africa for fifty years. When Christopher Columbus, a European searching for a sea route to Asia, encountered the peoples of the Western Hemisphere in 1492, the destinies of four continents quickly became intertwined. On his second voyage, Columbus carried a cargo of enslaved Africans, initiating the centuries-long trade that would produce a multitude of triracial societies in the Americas.

As the Natchez elder knew well, the resulting mixture of peoples was based on exploitation, not equality. But by the time he urged his people to resist, the French intruders were too numerous and strong. With the help of Indian allies, they killed hundreds of Natchez rebels and sold the survivors into slavery on the sugar plantations of the West Indies. And the fate of the Natchez was not unique. In the three centuries following

◄ **Orbis Typus Universalis**

This map of the world, drawn by German cartographer Martin Waldseemüller in 1507, was one of the first to use *America* as the name of the New World. Only the northwestern area of present-day Brazil and a few (mislocated) Caribbean islands appear on Waldseemüller's map. Europeans had yet to comprehend the size and shape of the Western Hemisphere.
John Carter Brown Library, Brown University.

Columbus's voyage, many Native American peoples came under the domination of the Spanish, Portuguese, French, English, and Dutch who colonized the Western Hemisphere and used African slaves to work their agricultural plantations.

How did this happen? How did Europeans become leaders in world trade and extend their influence across the Atlantic? What made Native Americans vulnerable to conquest by European adventurers? And what led to the transatlantic trade in African slaves? In the answers to these questions lie the origins of the United States and the dominance of people of European descent in the modern world.

Native American Societies

When the Europeans arrived, most Native Americans — about 40 million — lived in Mesoamerica (present-day Mexico and Guatemala) and along the western coast of South America (present-day Peru); another 7 million resided in lands to the north, in what is now the United States and Canada. Some Native peoples lived in simple hunter-gatherer or agricultural communities governed by kin ties, but most lived in societies ruled by warrior-kings and priests. In Mesoamerica and Peru, Indian peoples created civilizations whose art, religion, society, and economy were as complex as those of Europe and the Mediterranean.

The First Americans

According to the elders of the Navajo people, history began when their ancestors emerged from under the earth; for the Iroquois, the story of their Five Nations began when people fell from the sky. But most twenty-first-century anthropologists and historians believe that the first inhabitants of the Western Hemisphere were migrants from Asia. Some came by water; most probably came by land. Strong archaeological and genetic evidence suggests that in the last Ice Age, which began about twenty thousand years ago, small bands of tribal hunters followed herds of game across a 100-mile-wide land bridge between Siberia and Alaska. An

oral history of the Tuscarora Indians, who settled in present-day North Carolina, tells of a famine in the Old World and a journey over ice toward where "the sun rises," a trek that brought their ancestors to a lush forest with abundant food and game.

Most anthropologists would argue that the main migratory stream from Asia lasted from about fifteen thousand to nine thousand years ago, after which the glaciers melted and the rising ocean waters submerged the land bridge and created the Bering Strait (Map 1.1). Around eight thousand years ago, a second movement of peoples, now traveling by water across the narrow strait, brought the ancestors of the Navajos and the Apaches to North America. A third migration around five thousand years ago introduced the forebears of the Aleut and Inuit peoples, the "Eskimos." Subsequently, the peoples of the Western Hemisphere were largely cut off from the rest of the world for three hundred generations.

For many centuries, the first Americans lived as hunter-gatherers, subsisting on the abundant wildlife and vegetation. Gradually, as the larger species of animals — mammoths, giant beaver, and horses — died out because of overhunting and climatic change, hunters became adept at killing more-elusive game — rabbits, deer, and elk. By about 3000 B.C., some Native American peoples in the region near present-day Mexico had begun to farm. They planted beans, squash, and maize (corn), as well as tomatoes, potatoes, and manioc (cassava) — crops that would eventually enrich the food supply of the entire world. In fact, the Indians gradually bred maize into an extremely nutritious plant that had a higher yield per acre than did wheat, barley, or rye, the staple cereals of Europe. They also learned to plant beans and squash together with corn, a mix of crops that provided a nourishing diet and kept the soil fertile. The resulting agricultural surplus made urban society possible, laying the economic foundation for populous and wealthy societies in Mexico, Peru, and the Mississippi River Valley (Map 1.2).

The Mayas and the Aztecs

The flowering of civilization in Mesoamerica began around 700 B.C. among the Olmec people, who lived along the Gulf of Mexico. Subsequently, the Mayas of the Yucatán Peninsula of Mexico and the neighboring rain forests of Guatemala built large urban centers that relied on elaborate systems of water storage and irrigation. By A.D. 300, more than 20,000 people were living in the Mayan city of Tikal [*tee-kall*]. Most were farmers, whose labor had built the city's huge stone temples. An elite class claiming

Inca Cup

This painted wooden drinking cup (*q'iru*) shows how the Incas, who ruled a great sixteenth-century empire in present-day Peru (see Map 1.5), made use of history and tradition. Around A.D. 1000, the Tiwanaku people ruled an empire in the highlands of Peru; one of the central motifs of their culture was a sacred staircase symbolizing heavens, earth, and the underworld. By placing that Tiwanaku motif on the central band of this cup and combining its symbol with their own — the man with the staff, shield, and headdress — the Incas grounded their claim of royal authority in the prestige of the Tiwanaku. Courtesy, National Museum of the American Indian, Smithsonian Institution.

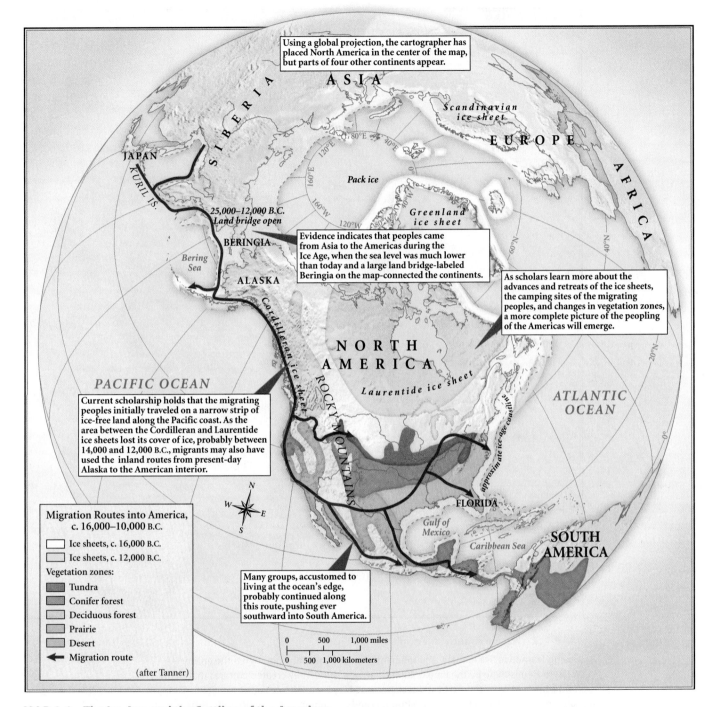

Using a global projection, the cartographer has placed North America in the center of the map, but parts of four other continents appear.

ASIA

SIBERIA

Scandinavian ice sheet

EUROPE

AFRICA

JAPAN

KURIL IS.

Pack ice

25,000–12,000 B.C. Land bridge open

Greenland ice sheet

BERINGIA

Bering Sea

Evidence indicates that peoples came from Asia to the Americas during the Ice Age, when the sea level was much lower than today and a large land bridge-labeled Beringia on the map-connected the continents.

ALASKA

As scholars learn more about the advances and retreats of the ice sheets, the camping sites of the migrating peoples, and changes in vegetation zones, a more complete picture of the peopling of the Americas will emerge.

Cordilleran ice sheet

PACIFIC OCEAN

NORTH AMERICA

Laurentide ice sheet

ATLANTIC OCEAN

approximate ice-age coastline

Current scholarship holds that the migrating peoples initially traveled on a narrow strip of ice-free land along the Pacific coast. As the area between the Cordilleran and Laurentide ice sheets lost its cover of ice, probably between 14,000 and 12,000 B.C., migrants may also have used the inland routes from present-day Alaska to the American interior.

ROCKY MOUNTAINS

FLORIDA

N
W   E
S

Gulf of Mexico

Caribbean Sea

SOUTH AMERICA

Migration Routes into America, c. 16,000–10,000 B.C.

☐ Ice sheets, c. 16,000 B.C.
☐ Ice sheets, c. 12,000 B.C.

Vegetation zones:
■ Tundra
■ Conifer forest
☐ Deciduous forest
■ Prairie
■ Desert
← Migration route

(after Tanner)

Many groups, accustomed to living at the ocean's edge, probably continued along this route, pushing ever southward into South America.

0   500   1,000 miles
0   500   1,000 kilometers

MAP 1.1 The Ice Age and the Settling of the Americas

Some sixteen thousand years ago, a sheet of ice covered much of Europe and North America. Making use of a broad bridge of land connecting Siberia and Alaska, hunting peoples from Asia migrated to North America in search of woolly mammoths and other large game animals, and ice-free habitats. By 10,000 B.C., the descendants of these migrant peoples had moved south to present-day Florida and central Mexico. In time, they would settle as far south as the tip of South America and as far east as the Atlantic coast of North America.

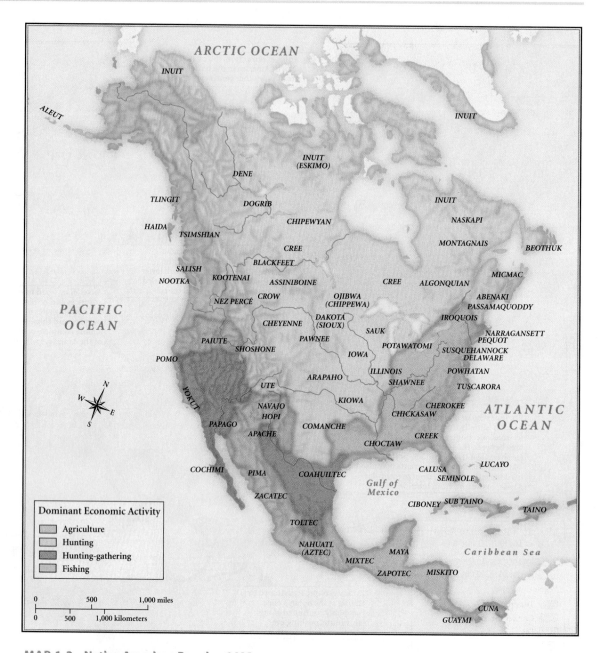

MAP 1.2 Native American Peoples, 1492

Having learned to live in many environments, Native Americans populated the entire Western Hemisphere by the time Columbus arrived there. They created cultures that ranged from centralized agriculture-based societies (the Mayas and the Aztecs), to societies that combined farming and hunting (the Iroquois and Algonquins), to seminomadic tribes of hunter-gatherers (the Micmacs and Ottowas). Their diversity — of tradition, language, and tribal identity — in large part prevented Native Americans from uniting to resist the European invaders.

descent from the gods ruled Mayan society and lived in splendor on goods and taxes extracted from peasant families. Drawing on the religious and artistic traditions of the Olmecs, Mayan artisans decorated temples and palaces with depictions of jaguars, warrior-gods, and complex religious ritu-

als. Mayan astronomers created a calendar that recorded historical events and accurately predicted eclipses of the sun and the moon. And Mayan scholars developed hieroglyphic writing to record royal lineages and wars and other noteworthy events. These skills in calculation and writing enhanced the authority of the class of warriors and priests that ruled Mayan society, and they provided the people with a sense of history and identity. By facilitating the movement of goods and ideas, they also increased the prosperity of Mayan society and the complexity of its culture.

Beginning around 800, Mayan civilization went into decline. Evidence suggests that a two-century-long drought led to an economic crisis and prompted overtaxed peasants to desert the temple cities and retreat to the countryside. By 900, many religious centers had been abandoned. The few Mayan city-states that remained intact would vigorously resist the Spanish invaders in the 1520s.

A second major Mesoamerican civilization developed in the highlands of Mexico around the city of Teotihuacán [*tee-o-ti-hue-kon*], with its magnificent Pyramid of the Sun. At its zenith, about A.D. 500, Teotihuacán had more than one hundred temples, some four thousand apartment buildings, and a population of at least 100,000. By 800, the city was failing, the likely victim of both long-term drought and the recurrent invasions of seminomadic warrior peoples. Eventually one of these invading peoples, the Aztecs, established an even more extensive empire.

The Aztecs entered the great central valley of Mexico from the north and settled on an island in Lake Texcoco. There, in 1325, they began to build a new city, Tenochtitlán [*ten-och-tit-lan*], Mexico City today. The Aztecs learned the ways of the resident peoples, mastered their complex irrigation systems and written language, and established an elaborate culture with a hierarchical social order. Priests and warrior-nobles ruled over twenty **clans** of free Aztec commoners who farmed communal land. The nobles also used huge numbers of non-Aztec slaves and serfs to labor on their private estates.

An aggressive people, the Aztecs soon subjugated most of central Mexico. Their rulers demanded both economic and human tribute from scores of subject peoples, sacrificing untold thousands of men and women to ensure fertile fields and the daily return of the sun.

Aztec merchants forged trading routes that crisscrossed the empire, and imported furs, gold, textiles, food, and obsidian from as far north as the Rio Grande and as far south as present-day Panama. By 1500, Tenochtitlán had grown into a metropolis, with magnificent palaces and temples and more than 200,000 inhabitants — making it far larger than most European cities. Aztec artisans worked in stone, pottery, cloth, leather, and especially obsidian, a hard volcanic glass used to make sharp-edged weapons and tools. The splendor of the city and its elaborate crafts dazzled both subject peoples and Spanish soldiers. "These great towns and pyramids and buildings arising from the water, all made of stone, seemed like an enchanted vision," marveled one Spaniard. The Aztecs' strong institutions, military power, and wealth posed a formidable challenge to any adversary, at home or from afar.

The Indians of the North

The societies north of the Rio Grande generally were less complex and less coercive than those to the south. They lacked occupational diversity, social hierarchy, and strong state institutions. Most northern peoples lived in self-governing tribes made up of clans, groups of related families that traced their lineage to a real or legendary common ancestor. Clan elders and local chiefs set war policy, conducted ceremonies, and resolved personal feuds. They also made social policy — banning marriage between members of the same clan, for example, to prevent inbreeding — and disciplined those who violated that policy and other customs. But elders and chiefs usually did not form a distinct ruling class; instead, they ruled with limited powers through a kinship system of government that was local and worked by consent.

The culture of these lineage-based societies did not encourage the accumulation of material goods. Individual ownership of land was virtually unknown: As a French missionary among the Iroquois noted, they "possess hardly anything except in common." The elders would urge members to share food and other scarce goods, encouraging an ethic of reciprocity rather than one of accumulation. "You are covetous, and neither generous nor kind," the Micmac Indians of Nova Scotia would tell acquisitive French fur traders in the late 1600s. "As for us, if we have a morsel of bread, we share it with our neighbor."

The Hopewell Culture. Over the centuries, some Indian peoples did become materialistic, engaging in trade or conquest (see Reading American Pictures, "Maize for Blankets: Indian Trading Networks on the Great Plains," p. 10). By A.D. 100, the vigorous Hopewell people of present-day Ohio had increased their food supply by domesticating plants, organized themselves in large villages, and set up a trading network that stretched from present-day Louisiana to Wisconsin. They imported obsidian from the Yellowstone region of the Rocky Mountains, copper from the Great Lakes, and pottery and marine shells from the Gulf of Mexico. The Hopewells built large burial mounds and surrounded them with extensive circular, rectangular,

Maize for Blankets: Indian Trading Networks on the Great Plains

Tom Lovell, *Trade Among Indian Peoples.* Courtesy of Abell-Hanger Foundation and of the Permian Basin Petroleum Museum, Library and Hall of Fame of Midland, Texas, where the painting is on permanent display.

In most Native American societies, there were no merchants, store-keepers, or traders. Yet, as the text explains, many Indian peoples exchanged goods with their neighbors and often acquired wares produced in distant lands. Those "wares" included captives taken in battle, who were put to work as slaves or integrated into the society through marriage or adoption. This 1973 painting offers a historical reconstruction of the commerce in goods at the fortified Towa pueblo of Cicúye (in what is Pecos, New Mexico, today), which stands on a high mountain pass between the Rio Grande Valley and the Great Plains (and looms in the background to the left). The Towa people are trading with Apaches.

ANALYZING THE EVIDENCE

➤ Why did the location of the Pecos pueblo make it a major trading post? One clue comes from a Spanish explorer who visited Pecos in 1541 with Francisco Vásquez de Coronado's expedition (see Chapter 2). He reported that Indians from the Great Plains exchanged "*cueros de Cíbola* [bison hides] and deer skins" for the "maize and blankets" produced by the Pueblo peoples. Do you see any other pueblo products in this painting?

➤ What do the clothing, material goods, and lodgings of the two peoples — the Towas and the Apaches — tell us about their respective ways of life?

➤ How have the Apaches transported their goods to Pecos? Based on what you have read in the text, can you explain why no horses are shown in the painting, which is set in A.D. 1500?

➤ Look closely at what the men and women are doing. What does the painting tell you about gender roles in Native American societies?

The Great Serpent Mound

Scholars long believed that the serpent was the work of Adena peoples (500 B.C.–A.D. 200) because of its proximity to an Adena burial site. Recent research places the mound at a much later date (A.D. 950–1200) and, because of the serpent imagery, ties it to the culture of Mississippian peoples. The head of the serpent is aligned with the sunset of the summer solstice, an event of great religious significance to a sun worshipping culture. © Richard A. Cooke/Corbis.

or octagonal earthworks that in some cases still survive. Skilled Hopewell artisans fashioned striking ornaments to bury with the dead: copper beaten into intricate designs, mica cut into the shape of serpents or human hands, and stone pipes carved to represent frogs, hawks, bears, and other spiritually powerful beings. For unknown reasons, the elaborate trading network of the Hopewells gradually collapsed around 400.

The Southwestern Peoples and Environmental Decline. A second complex culture developed among the Pueblo peoples of the Southwest — the Hohokams, Mogollons, and Anasazis. By A.D. 600, Hohokam [*ho-ho-kam*] people in the high country along the border of present-day Arizona and New Mexico were using irrigation to grow two crops a year, fashioning fine pottery in red-on-buff designs, and worshiping their gods on Mesoamerican-like platform mounds; by 1000, they were living in elaborate multiroom stone structures called **pueblos**. To the east, in the Mimbres Valley of present-day New Mexico, the

Mogollon [*mo-gee-yon*] people developed a distinctive black-on-white pottery. And by A.D. 900, to the north, the Anasazi (or Ancestral Pueblo) people had become master architects. They built residential-ceremonial villages in steep cliffs, a pueblo in Chaco Canyon that housed one thousand people, and 400 miles of straight roads. But the culture of the Pueblo peoples gradually collapsed after 1150, as soil exhaustion and extended droughts disrupted maize production and prompted the abandonment of Chaco Canyon and other communities. The descendants of these peoples — including the Acomas, Zunis, and Hopis — later built strong but smaller village societies better suited to the dry and unpredictable climate of the American Southwest.

Mississippian Culture. The last large-scale culture to emerge north of the Rio Grande was the Mississippian. By about A.D. 800, the farming technology of Mesoamerica had reached the Mississippi River Valley, perhaps carried by Mayan refugees from the war-torn Yucatán Peninsula. By planting new strains of maize and beans, the Mississippian peoples produced an agricultural surplus that allowed them to live in small, fortified temple cities, where they developed a robust culture. By 1150, the largest city, Cahokia [*ka-ho-kee-ah*], near present-day St. Louis, boasted a population of 15,000 to 20,000 and more than one hundred temple mounds, one of them as large as the great Egyptian pyramids. Here, too, as in Mesoamerica, the tribute paid by peasant farmers supported a privileged class of nobles and priests who waged war against neighboring chiefdoms, patronized artisans, and claimed descent from the sun god.

By 1350, the Mississippian civilization was in rapid decline. The large population had overburdened the environment, depleting nearby forests and herds of deer. The Indians also fell victim to tuberculosis and other deadly urban diseases. Still, Mississippian institutions and practices endured for centuries.

When Spanish conquistador Hernán de Soto invaded the region in the 1540s, he found the Apalachee [*ap-a-la-chee*] and Timucua [*tee-moo-kwa*] Indians living in permanent settlements under the command of powerful chiefs. "If you desire to see me, come where I am," a chief told de Soto, "neither for you, nor for any man, will I set back one foot." A century and a half later, French traders and priests found the Natchez people living in a society rigidly divided among hereditary chiefs, two groups of nobles and honored people, and a bottom class of peasants. "Their chiefs possess all authority," a Frenchman noted. "They distribute their favors and presents at will." Undoubtedly influenced by Mesoamerican rituals, the Natchez marked the death of a chief by sacrificing his wives and burying their remains in a ceremonial mound (see Voices from Abroad, "Father Le Petite: The Customs of the Natchez, 1730," p. 13).

Iroquois Women at Work, 1724

As this European engraving suggests, Iroquois women were responsible for growing food crops. Several of the women at the top are hoeing the soil into small hillocks, while others are planting corn and beans. The lower section shows other women tapping sugar maples and boiling the sweet sap to make maple syrup. The woman at the left is probably grinding corn into flour. Later she would add water to make flat patties for baking. Newberry Library, Chicago.

Father Le Petite

The Customs of the Natchez, 1730

The beliefs and institutions of the Mississippians (A.D. 1000–1450) survived for centuries among the native peoples of the Southeast, and helped them resist the attacks of Spanish conquistador Hernán de Soto in the 1540s. Mississippian customs lasted longest among the Natchez people, who lived in present-day Mississippi. A fine description of their society appears in a letter written around 1730 by Father Le Petite, one of the hundreds of Jesuit priests who lived among the Indians in the French colonies of Louisiana and Canada. Here, Father Le Petite accurately describes several Indian customs to his religious superiors in France. However, he misunderstands the reasons why the chief is succeeded by his sister's son rather than his own son. In a matrilineal society, lines of descent and inheritance pass through women, not men.

My Reverend Father, The peace of Our Lord.

This Nation of Savages inhabits one of the most beautiful and fertile countries in the World, and is the only one on this continent which appears to have any regular worship. Their Religion in certain points is very similar to that of the ancient Romans. They have a Temple filled with Idols, which are different figures of men and of animals, and for which they have the most profound veneration. Their Temple in shape resembles an earthen oven, a hundred feet in circumference. They enter it by a little door about four feet high, and not more than three in breadth. Above on the outside are three figures of eagles made of wood, and painted red, yellow, and white. Before the door is a kind of shed with folding-doors, where the Guardian of the Temple is lodged; all around it runs a circle of palisades [pointed wooden stakes], on which are seen exposed the skulls of all the heads which their Warriors had brought back from the battles in which they had been engaged with the enemies of their Nation. . . .

The Sun is the principal object of veneration to these people; as they cannot conceive of anything which can be above this heavenly body, nothing else appears to them more worthy of their homage. It is for the same reason that the great Chief of this Nation, who knows nothing on the earth more dignified than himself, takes the title of brother of the Sun, and the credulity of the people maintains him in the despotic authority which he claims. To enable them better to converse together, they raise a mound of artificial soil, on which they build his cabin, which is of the same construction as the Temple. When a great Chief dies, his many wives are killed and are buried with him and personal goods in a great ceremonial mound.

The old men prescribe the Laws for the rest of the people, and one of their principles is . . . the immortality of the soul, and when they leave this world they go, they say, to live in another, there to be recompensed or punished.

In former times the Nation of the *Natchez* was very large. It counted sixty Villages and eight hundred Suns or Princes; now it is reduced to six little Villages and eleven Suns. [Its] Government is hereditary; it is not, however, the son of the reigning Chief who succeeds his father, but the son of his sister, or the first Princess of the blood. This policy is founded on the knowledge they have of the licentiousness of their women. They are not sure, they say, that the children of the chief's wife may be of the blood Royal, whereas the son of the sister of the great Chief must be, at least on the side of the mother.

SOURCE: Reuben Gold Thwaites, ed., *The Jesuit Relations and Allied Documents* (Cleveland: Murrow Brothers, 1900), 68: 121–135.

ANALYZING THE EVIDENCE

➤ Which of Le Petite's remarks suggest a link between the Natchez and the Aztecs of Mesoamerica? How might this link have been established?

➤ Given what you have learned about the Native American population decline, how would you explain that sixty Natchez villages had been reduced to six?

The Eastern Woodland Peoples. The cultures of the native peoples of eastern North America were diverse. Like the Natchez, the Creeks, Choctaws, and Chickasaws who lived in present-day Alabama and Mississippi had once been organized in powerful chiefdoms. However, the devastating epidemics of European diseases introduced by de Soto's expedition in the 1540s killed a majority of their populations and destroyed their traditional institutions. The survivors of the various chiefdoms intermarried and settled in smaller and less powerful agricultural communities.

In these Muskogean-speaking societies — and among the Algonquian-speaking peoples who lived farther north and to the east, in present-day Virginia — farming became the work of women. While the men hunted and fished, the women used flint hoes to raise corn, squash, and beans. Because of the importance of farming, a **matrilineal** system developed among many eastern Indian peoples, including the Five Nations of the Iroquois, who lived in present-day New York State. Women cultivated the fields around semipermanent settlements and passed the use rights to the fields to their daughters. In these matrilineal societies, the father stood outside the main lines of descent and authority; the principal responsibility for child raising fell on the mother and her brothers, who often lived with their sisters rather than with their wives. Among these farming peoples, religious rituals centered on the agricultural cycle. The Iroquois, for example, celebrated green corn and strawberry festivals. Although the eastern Indian peoples of 1500 ate a balanced diet of meat and vegetables, they enjoyed few material comforts and their populations grew slowly.

When Europeans intruded into their lives, most eastern woodland Indians lived in relatively small kinship-based societies. The strong city-states that had once flourished in the Southwest and in the Mississippi River Valley had vanished. Consequently, there were no great Indian empires or religious centers here — as there were in Mesoamerica — that could sustain a campaign of military and spiritual resistance to European invaders. "When you command, all the French obey and go to war," the Chippewa chief Chigabe [*chig-ah-bee*] remarked to a French general, but "I shall not be heeded and obeyed by my nation." Because household and lineage were the basis of his society, Chigabe explained, "I cannot answer except for myself and for those immediately allied to me."

> What were the major similarities and differences between the civilizations of Mesoamerica and the Mississippian culture to the north?

> How did the climate affect the rise and decline of various Native peoples?

> How were eastern woodland Indian societies organized and governed?

Europe Encounters Africa and the Americas, 1450–1550

In 1400, few observers would have predicted that Europeans would dominate the trade of Africa and become overlords of the Western Hemisphere. One thousand years after the fall of the great Roman empire, Europe remained a mosaic of small and relatively weak kingdoms. Moreover, around 1350, a vicious epidemic from the subcontinent of India — the Black Death — had killed one-third of Europe's population. Peoples in other regions had stronger economies and governments and seemed more likely to seize control of world commerce. In 1417, for example, a large Chinese fleet had traveled thousands of miles to trade along the eastern coast of Africa; and Muslim merchants controlled all of Europe's trade with Asia.

European Agricultural Society

In 1450, there were just a few large cities in Western Europe: Only Paris, London, and Naples had as many as 100,000 residents. Most Europeans were **peasants** who lived in small agricultural communities. Peasant families usually owned or leased a small dwelling in the village center and had the right to farm the surrounding fields. The fields were open — not divided by fences or hedges — which made cooperative farming a necessity. The community decided which crops to grow, and every family followed its dictates. Because output was limited and there were few good roads, most trade was local. Neighboring families exchanged surplus grain and meat and bartered their farm products for the services of local millers, weavers, and blacksmiths. Most peasants yearned to be **yeomen**, to own enough land to support their families in comfort, but relatively few achieved that goal.

The Seasonal Cycle and the Peasants' Lot. For European peasants, as for Native Americans, the rhythm of life followed the seasons. The agricultural year began in late March, when the ground thawed and dried and the villagers began the exhausting work of spring plowing and then planting

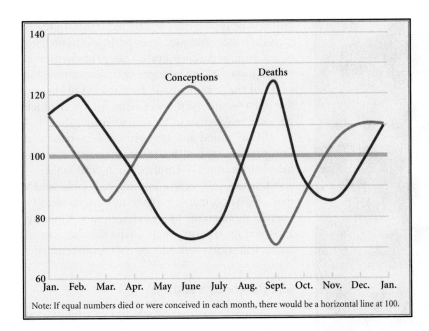

FIGURE 1.1 The Rhythm of Rural Life

The annual cycle of nature profoundly affected the life of European peasants for many centuries. Each year the death rate soared in February (from viruses) and September (from fly-borne dysentery). Early summer was the healthiest season, the time of the fewest deaths and the most conceptions (as measured by births nine months later).

wheat, rye, and oats. During these busy months, men sheared the thick winter wool of their sheep, which the women washed and spun into yarn. In June, peasants cut the first crop of hay and stored it as winter fodder for their livestock. During the summer, life was more relaxed, and families had the time to repair their houses and barns. Fall brought the strenuous harvest, followed by solemn feasts of thanksgiving and riotous bouts of merry-making. As winter approached, peasants slaughtered excess livestock and salted or smoked the meat. During the cold months, they threshed grain and wove textiles, visited friends and relatives, and celebrated the winter solstice or the birth of Christ. Just before the farming cycle began again in the spring, they held carnivals, celebrating with drink and dance the end of the long winter night. Even births and deaths followed the seasons: More successful conceptions took place in early summer than any other time of the year. And many rural people died in January and February, victims of viral diseases and then again in August and September, casualties of epidemics of fly-borne dysentery (Figure 1.1).

For most peasants, survival meant constant labor, breaking the soil with primitive wooden plows or harvesting hay and grain with small hand sickles. In the absence of high-quality seeds, chemical fertilizers, and pesticides, output was pitifully small—less than one-tenth of present-day yields. The margin of existence was also small, and that corroded family relationships. Malnourished mothers fed their babies sparingly, calling them

"greedy and gluttonous," and many newborn girls were "helped to die" so that their older brothers would have enough to eat. Disease killed about half of all peasant children before the age of twenty-one. Indeed, when the Black Death ravaged Europe, it took the lives of millions. Even in less dangerous times, assault, murder, and rape were woven into the fabric of daily life, and hunger was a constant companion. "I have seen the latest epoch of misery," a French doctor reported as famine and plague struck. "The inhabitants . . . lie down in a meadow to eat grass, and share the food of wild beasts."

Often destitute, usually exploited by landlords and nobles, many peasants simply accepted their condition. Others hoped for a better life for themselves and their children. It was the peasants of Spain, Germany, and Britain who would supply the majority of white migrants to the Western Hemisphere.

Hierarchy and Authority

In traditional societies—Mesoamerican or European—authority came from above. In Europe, kings and princes owned vast tracts of land, forcibly conscripted men for military service, and lived in splendor off the labor of the peasantry. Yet monarchs were far from supreme: Local nobles also owned large estates and controlled hundreds of peasant families. Collectively, these nobles challenged royal authority with both their military power and their legislative institutions, such as the French *parlements* and the English House of Lords.

Artisan Family

Work was slow and output was limited in the preindustrial world, and survival required the efforts of all family members. Here a fifteenth-century French woodworker planes a panel of wood while his wife twists flax fibers into linen yarn for the family's clothes and their young son cleans up wood shavings from the workshop floor. Giraudon/Art Resource, New York.

Just as kings and nobles ruled society, so men governed families. Rich or poor, the man was the head of the house, his power justified by the teachings of the Christian church. As one English clergyman put it, "The woman is a weak creature not embued with like strength and constancy of mind"; consequently, law and custom "subjected her to the power of man." Once she married, an Englishwoman assumed her husband's surname and had to submit, under threat of legally sanctioned physical "correction," to his orders. Moreover, she surrendered to her husband the legal right to all her property. Her sole protection: When he died, she received a **dower**, usually the use during her lifetime of one-third of the family's land and goods.

Men also controlled the lives of their children, who usually were required to work for their father into their middle or late twenties. Then landowning peasants would give land to their sons and dowries to their daughters and choose marriage partners of appropriate wealth and status. In many regions, fathers bestowed most of their land on their eldest son, a practice known as **primogeniture**, which forced many younger children to join the ranks of the roaming poor. In this kind of society, few men — and even fewer women — had much personal freedom or individual identity.

Hierarchy and authority prevailed in traditional European society both because of the power of established institutions — family, church, and village — and because, in a violent and unpredictable world, they offered ordinary people a measure of security. Carried by migrants to America, these institutions and need for security would shape the character of family and society well into the eighteenth century.

The Power of Religion

For centuries, the Roman Catholic Church served as the great unifying institution in Western Europe. The pope in Rome stood at the head of a vast religious hierarchy of cardinals, bishops, and priests. Catholic books and theologians preserved Latin, the great language of classical scholarship, and Christian dogma provided a common understanding of God, the world, and human history. Equally important, the Church provided a bulwark of authority and discipline. Every village had a church, and the holy shrines that dotted the byways of Europe were reminders of the Church's power and teachings.

Christian doctrine penetrated deeply into the everyday lives of peasants. Originally, most Europeans were **pagans**. Like the Indians of North America, they were animists: They believed that unpredictable spiritual forces governed the natural world and that those spirits had to be paid ritual honor. As Christianity spread, priests taught the peasants that spiritual power came from outside nature, from God, a supernatural being, who had sent his divine son, Jesus Christ, into the world to save humanity from its sins. The Church also devised a religious calendar that transformed pagan agricultural festivals into Christian holy days. Thus the winter solstice, which for pagans marked the return of the sun, became the feast of Christmas, to mark the birth of Christ. To avert famine and plague, Christianized peasants no longer made ritual offerings to nature; instead, they offered prayers to Christ and the saints.

The Church also taught that Satan, a lesser and evil supernatural being, was constantly challenging God by tempting people to sin. If a devout Christian fell mysteriously ill, the cause might be an evil spell cast by a witch in league with Satan. If prophets spread **heresies**, — doctrines that were inconsistent with the teachings of the Church — they

Christ's Crucifixion

The German painter Grünewald rendered this graphic portrayal of Christ's death on the cross and subsequent burial. It was meant to remind believers not only of Christ's sacrifice but also of the ever-present prospect of their own death. The panel to the left depicts the martyr Saint Sebastian, killed by dozens of arrows; the panel to the right probably portrays the abbot of the monastery in Isenheim, Germany, that commissioned the altarpiece. Musée Unterlinden, Colmar, Colmar-Giraudon/Art Resource.

were surely the tools of Satan. Suppressing false doctrines became an obligation of Christian rulers. So did combating Islam, a religion that like Christianity proclaimed a single god (monotheism). Following the death in A.D. 632 of the prophet Muhammad, the founder of Islam, the newly converted Arab peoples of the Mediterranean used force and persuasion to spread the Muslim faith into sub-Saharan Africa, India, and Indonesia, and deep into Spain and the Balkan regions of Europe. Between 1096 and 1291, Christian armies undertook a series of Crusades to halt this advance and win back the holy lands where Christ had lived.

The crusaders had some military successes against the Muslims, but their most profound impact was on European society. Religious warfare intensified Europe's Christian identity and prompted the persecution of Jews and their expulsion from many European countries. The Crusades also broadened the intellectual and economic horizons of the privileged classes of Western Europe, who absorbed the scholarship of the Arab world and set out to capture the Arab-dominated trade routes that stretched from Constantinople to Beijing and from the Mediterranean to the East Indian seas (Maps 1.3 and 1.4).

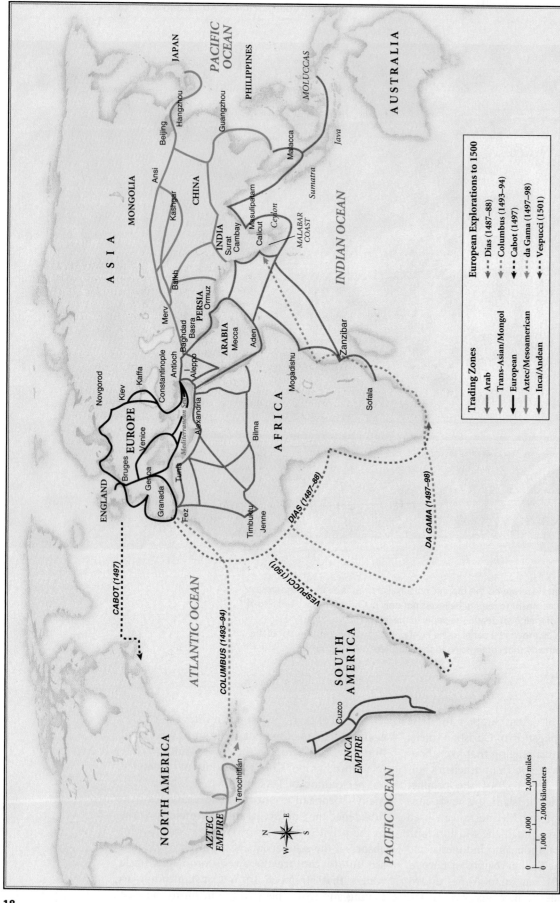

MAP 1.3 The Eurasian Trade System and European Maritime Ventures, c. 1500

For centuries, the Mediterranean Sea was the meeting point for the commerce of Europe, North Africa, and Asia — via the Silk Road from China and the Spice Trade from India. During the 1490s, Portuguese, Spanish, and Dutch monarchs and merchants subsidized maritime explorers who discovered new trade routes and challenged the commercial primacy of the Muslim-dominated Mediterranean.

Trading Zones

- Arab
- Trans-Asian/Mongol
- European
- Aztec/Mesoamerican
- Inca/Andean

European Explorations to 1500

- Dias (1487–88)
- Columbus (1493–94)
- Cabot (1497)
- da Gama (1497–98)
- Vespucci (1501)

Astronomers at Istanbul (Constantinople), 1581
Arab and Turkish scholars transmitted ancient texts and learning to Europeans during the Middle Ages and provided much of the geographical and astronomical knowledge European explorers used during the sixteenth century, the great Age of Discovery. University Library, Istanbul, Turkey & Bridgeman Art Library.

The Renaissance Changes Europe, 1300–1500

Stimulated by exposure to Arab society, first Italy and then the countries of northern Europe recovered from the Black Death and experienced a rebirth of cultural life and economic energy. Arabs had access to the silks and spices of the East and had acquired magnetic compasses, water-powered mills, and mechanical clocks, mostly from the Chinese. Moreover, Arab scholars carried on the legacy of Byzantine civilization, which had preserved the great achievements of the Greeks and

Romans in medicine, philosophy, mathematics, astronomy, and geography. The Crusades exposed Europeans to Byzantine and Arab learning and reacquainted them with the achievements of classical antiquity.

Innovations in Economics, Art, and Politics. The Renaissance had the most profound impact on the upper classes. Merchants from the Italian city-states of Venice, Genoa, Florence, and Pisa dispatched ships to Alexandria, Beirut, and other eastern Mediterranean ports, where they purchased goods from China, India, Persia, and Arabia, and sold them throughout Europe. The enormous profits from this commerce created powerful merchants, bankers, and textile manufacturers who conducted trade, lent vast sums of money, and spurred technological innovation in silk and wool production. These Italian moneyed elites ruled their city-states as **republics**, with no prince or king. They celebrated **civic humanism**, an **ideology** that praised public virtue and service to the state and in time profoundly influenced European and American conceptions of government.

Perhaps no other age in European history has produced such a flowering of artistic genius. Michelangelo, Andrea Palladio, and Filippo Brunelleschi designed and built great architectural masterpieces, while Leonardo da Vinci, Jacopo Bellini, and Raphael produced magnificent religious paintings, setting styles and standards that have endured into the modern era.

This creative energy inspired Renaissance rulers. In *The Prince* (1513), Niccolò Machiavelli offered unsentimental advice on how monarchs could increase their political power. The kings of Western Europe followed his advice, creating royal law courts and bureaucracies to reduce the power of the landed classes and forging alliances with merchants and urban artisans. Monarchs allowed merchants to trade throughout their realms, granted privileges to the artisan organizations called **guilds**, and safeguarded commercial transactions in royal law courts, thereby encouraging domestic manufacturing and foreign trade. In return, kings and princes extracted taxes from towns and loans from merchants to support their armies and officials. This mutually enriching alliance of monarchs and merchants propelled Europe into its first age of overseas expansion.

Prince Henry and Maritime Expansion. Under the direction of Prince Henry (1394–1460), Portugal led a surge of maritime commercial expansion. Prince Henry was the third son of King João I of Portugal and his English wife, Philippa of Lancaster. In 1415, as a young soldier of the Crusading Order of Christ, he instigated a successful attack on the Muslim port of Ceuta in northern Morocco, where he learned of Arab merchants' rich trade in gold and slaves across the Sahara Desert. In his search for a maritime route to the sources of this trade in West Africa, Henry patronized Renaissance thinkers and drew on the work of Arab and Italian geographers. In 1420, he founded a center for oceanic navigation and astronomical observation at Sagres, in the south of Portugal. There he oversaw the making of more precise maps and

Prince Henry of Portugal

As the third son of the king, Henry stood little chance of succeeding to the throne. So he devoted his energies to Christian crusades against the Moors and to maritime explorations. In the 1430s, his mariners finally rounded Cape Bojador and began to trade with the peoples of sub-Saharan Africa. The Granger Collection, New York.

pushed forward the development of the caravel, a three-masted ship with two regular sails and one lateen (triangular) sail for maneuverability. Most important, Henry urged his captains to find a way around Cape Bojador in North Africa, a region of fierce winds and treacherous currents, and to explore the feared "Sea of Darkness" to the south. Eventually Henry's mariners sailed far into the Atlantic, where they discovered and colonized the Madeira and Azore Islands; and from there they explored the sub-Saharan African coast. By 1435, Portuguese sea captains had reached the coast of Sierra Leone, where they exchanged salt, wine, and fish for African ivory and gold. By the 1440s, they were trading in humans as well, the first Europeans to engage in the long-established and extensive African trade in slaves. By the time he died, Henry had succeeded in his mission of enhancing Portugal's wealth through maritime commerce with West Africa.

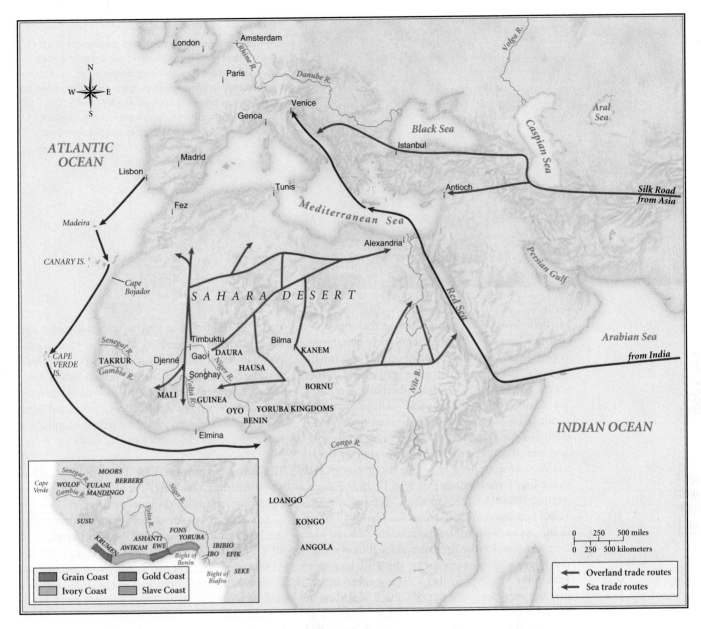

MAP 1.4   West Africa and the Mediterranean in the Fifteenth Century

Trade routes across the Sahara Desert had long connected West Africa with the Mediterranean. Gold, ivory, and slaves moved north and east; fine textiles, spices, and the Muslim faith traveled south. Beginning in the 1430s, the Portuguese opened up maritime trade with the coastal regions of West Africa, which were home to many peoples and dozens of large and small states. Within a decade, they would take part in the slave trade there.

West African Society and Slavery

Vast and diverse, West Africa stretches along the coast from present-day Senegal to Angola. In the 1400s, tropical rain forest covered much of the coast, but a series of great rivers—the Senegal, Gambia, Volta, Niger, and Congo—provided relatively easy access to the woodlands and savannas of the interior, where

most people lived. There were few coastal cities because there was little seaborne trade (Map 1.4).

West African Life. Most West Africans lived in extended families in small villages and farmed modest plots. Normally, the men cleared the land and the women planted and harvested the crops. On the plains, farmers grew millet and cotton, and

Fulani Village in West Africa

Around 1550, the Fulani people conquered the lands to the south of the Senegal River. To protect themselves from subject peoples and neighboring tribes, the Fulanis constructed fortified villages like the one shown here. The Fulanis were originally nomadic herders and, as the enclosed pasture shows, continued to keep livestock. Notice the cylindrical houses of mud brick with their thatched roofs. Frederic Shoberl, ed., *The World in Miniature: Africa*, 4 vols. (London: Ackermann, 1821).

set their livestock out to graze; the forest peoples planted yams and harvested oil-rich palm nuts. Forest dwellers exchanged palm oil and kola nuts, a highly valued stimulant, for the textiles and leather goods produced by savanna dwellers. Similarly, merchants collected valuable salt, which was produced along the coast and mined in great deposits in the Sahara, and traded it for iron, gold, and manufactures along the Niger and other rivers.

West Africans lived in diverse ethnic groups and spoke four basic languages, each with many dialects. Among West Atlantic–speakers, the Fulani and Wolof peoples were most numerous. Mande-speakers in the upper Niger region included the Malinke and Bambara peoples; the Yorubas and the Ibos of southern Nigeria spoke varieties of the Kwa language. Finally, the Mossis and other Voltaic-speakers inhabited the area along the upper Volta River. Most of these peoples lived in societies that were similar to those of the Mayas and Aztecs—socially stratified states ruled by kings and princes. Some lived in city-states that produced high-quality metal, leather, textiles, and pottery. Other West Africans dwelled in stateless societies organized by household and lineage, much like those of the eastern woodland Indians.

Spiritual beliefs varied greatly. West Africans who lived immediately south of the Sahara—the Fulanis in Senegal, Mande-speakers in Mali, and the Hausas in northern Nigeria—learned about Islam from Arab merchants and missionaries. Although some worshiped only the Muslim god, Allah, most recognized a number of other gods and the spirits they believed lived in the earth, in animals, and in plants. Many Africans also believed their kings had divine attributes and that they were able to contact the spirit world. They also treated their ancestors with great respect, partly because they believed that

the dead resided in a nearby spiritual realm and could intercede in their lives. Most West African peoples had secret societies, such as the Poro for men and the Sande for women, that united people from different lineages and clans. These societies educated their members in sexual practices, conducted adult initiation ceremonies, and used public humiliation to enforce codes of conduct and morality.

The European Impact. Early European traders had a positive impact on West Africa by introducing new plants and animals. Portuguese merchants brought coconuts from East Africa, oranges and lemons from the Mediterranean, pigs from Western Europe, and, after 1492, maize, manioc, and tomatoes from the Americas. Portuguese merchants also expanded existing African trade networks. From small, fortified trading posts on the coast, they shipped metal products, manufactures, and slaves along the coast and to inland regions, and took gold, ivory, and pepper in return. For much of the inland trade, the Portuguese relied on Africans: Portuguese ships could travel just 150 miles up the slow-flowing Gambia and lesser distances on the other rivers. Yellow fever, malaria, and dysentery quickly struck down Europeans who spent time in the interior of West Africa, often killing as many as half of them each year.

As they traded with Africans, Portuguese adventurers continued their quest for an ocean route to Asia. In 1488, Bartholomeu Dias rounded the Cape of Good Hope, the southern tip of Africa; ten years later, Vasco da Gama reached India. Although the Arab, Indian, and Jewish merchants who controlled the trade along India's Malabar Coast tried to exclude him, da Gama acquired a highly profitable cargo of cinnamon and pepper, spices used to flavor and preserve meat. To capture the trade in spices and Indian textiles, da Gama returned to India in 1502 with twenty-one fighting vessels, which outmaneuvered and outgunned the Arab fleets. Soon the Portuguese government set up fortified trading posts for its merchants at key points around the Indian Ocean, in Indonesia, and along the coast of Asia to China and Japan. In a transition that laid the foundation for the momentous growth of European wealth and power, the Portuguese used the route around Africa to replace Arabs as the leaders in world commerce.

African Slavery. Portuguese traders joined African states and Arab merchants in the slave trade. Bonded labor — slavery, serfdom, indentured servitude — was the norm in most premodern societies, and in Africa it took the form of slavery. Some people were held in bondage as security for debts; others were sold into servitude by their kin, often in exchange for food in times of famine; many others were captured in wars. Most slaves worked as agricultural laborers or served in slave armies. And most were treated as property. Sometimes their descendants were allowed to became members of society, usually with a low class or caste status; but others endured hereditary bondage. Sonni Ali, the ruler from 1464 to 1492 of the powerful upper-Niger Islamic kingdom of Songhay, personally owned twelve "tribes" of hereditary agricultural slaves, many of them seized in raids against stateless peoples.

A significant number of West Africans became **trade slaves**, sold as agricultural workers by one kingdom to another, or carried overland in caravans by Arab traders to the Mediterranean region. When the great Tunisian traveler Ibn Battua returned to North Africa from the Kingdom of Mali around 1350, he trekked across the Sahara with a caravan of six hundred female slaves, who were destined for domestic service or concubinage in North Africa, Egypt, and the Ottoman Empire. Some decades later, the first Portuguese in Senegambia found that the Wolof king, who stood at the head of a horse-mounted warrior aristocracy, "supports himself by raids which result in many slaves. . . . He employs these slaves in cultivating the land allotted to him; but he also sells many to the [Arab] merchants in return for horses and other goods."

To exploit this trade, Portuguese merchants established forts at small port cities — first at Elmina in 1482 and later at Gorée, Mpinda, and Loango — where they bought gold and slaves from African princes and warlords. Initially, they carried a few thousand African slaves each year to work on sugar plantations in the Cape Verde Islands, the Azores, and the Madeira Islands; they also sold slaves in Lisbon, which soon had a black population of 9,000. After 1550, the maritime slave trade expanded enormously as Europeans set up sugar plantations in the newly discovered lands of Brazil and the West Indies.

Europeans Explore America

Explorers financed by the Spanish monarchs, King Ferdinand of Aragon and Queen Isabel of Castile, discovered the Western Hemisphere for Europeans. As Renaissance rulers, Ferdinand and Isabel saw national unity and foreign commerce as the keys to power and prosperity. Married in an arranged match to combine their Christian kingdoms, the young rulers (r. 1474–1516) completed the centuries-long *reconquista*. In 1492, their armies captured Granada, the last Islamic state in Western Europe. Using Catholicism to build a sense of "Spanishness," they launched the brutal Inquisition against suspected Christian heretics and expelled or forcibly converted thousands of Jews and Muslims.

Simultaneously, Ferdinand and Isabel sought trade and empire, and enlisted the services of Christopher Columbus, a mariner from Genoa. Misinterpreting the findings of Italian geographers, Columbus believed that the Atlantic Ocean, long feared by Arab merchants as a 10,000-mile-wide "green sea of darkness," was a much narrower channel of water separating Europe from Asia. Although dubious about Columbus's theory, Ferdinand and Isabel arranged financial backing from Spanish merchants and charged Columbus with finding a western route to Asia and carrying Christianity to its peoples.

Columbus set sail in three small ships in August 1492. Six weeks later, after a perilous voyage of 3,000 miles, he disembarked on an island in the present-day Bahamas. Believing he had reached Asia — "the Indies," in fifteenth-century parlance — Columbus called the native inhabitants Indians and the islands the West Indies. Surprised by the rude living conditions of the native people, Columbus expected them to "easily be made Christians." With ceremony and solemnity, he bestowed the names of the Spanish royal family and Catholic holy days on the islands, thereby intending to claim them for Spain and for Christendom. Columbus then explored the neighboring Caribbean islands and demanded tribute from the local Taino [*tie-no*], Arawak [*r-a-wak*], and Carib peoples. Buoyed by the natives' stories of rivers of gold lying "to the west," Columbus left forty men on the island of Hispaniola (present-day Haiti and the Dominican Republic) and returned triumphantly to Spain.

Although Columbus brought back no gold, the Spanish monarchs supported three more voyages over the next twelve years. During those expeditions, Columbus began the colonization of the

West Indies, transporting more than a thousand Spanish settlers — all men — and hundreds of domestic animals. He also began the transatlantic trade in slaves, carrying Indians to bondage in Europe and Africans to work as artisans and farmers in the new Spanish settlements. Because Columbus failed to find either golden treasures or great kingdoms, his death in 1506 went virtually unnoticed.

A German geographer soon labeled the "new" continents "America" in honor of a Genoese explorer, Amerigo Vespucci (see the Waldseemüller map, p. 4). Vespucci, who had explored the region around 1500, denied that it was Asia and called it a *nuevo mundo*, a "new world." For its part, the Spanish crown continued to call the continents *Las Indias* ("the Indies") and wanted to make them a new Spanish world.

The Spanish Conquest

Spanish adventurers ruled the peoples of the Indies with an iron hand. After subduing the Arawaks and Tainos on Hispaniola, the Spanish probed the mainland for gold and slaves. In 1513, Juan Ponce de León explored the coast of Florida and gave the peninsula its name. That same year, Vasco Núñez de Balboa crossed the Isthmus of Darien (Panama) and became the first European to see the Pacific Ocean. Rumors of rich Indian kingdoms in the interior encouraged other Spaniards, including hardened veterans of the *reconquista,* to launch an invasion. They also had the support of the Spanish monarchs, who offered successful conquistadors (conquerors) titles, and vast estates and Indian laborers to farm them.

Cortés, Malinche, and the Fall of the Aztecs.
Hernán Cortés (1485–1547) conquered an empire and destroyed a civilization. Cortés came from a family of minor gentry in Spain and, seeking military adventure and material gain, sailed to Santo Domingo in 1506. Ambitious and charismatic, he distinguished himself in battle, putting down a revolt and serving in the conquest of Cuba. These exploits, and marriage to a well-connected Spanish woman, won Cortés an extensive Cuban estate and a series of administrative appointments.

Eager to increase his fortune, Cortés jumped at the chance in 1519 to lead an expedition to the mainland. He landed with six hundred men near the Mayan settlement of Potonchan, which he quickly overpowered. Then Cortés got lucky. The defeated Mayas presented him with twenty slave women to serve as servants and concubines, among them Malinali, a young woman of noble birth. Not only was she "of pleasing appearance and sharp-witted and outward-going" — the words of a Spanish soldier; she also spoke Nahuatl, the Aztecs' lan-

Malinche and Cortés

In this Aztec pictograph (c. 1540), Cortés is shown with Malinche (Mariana in Spanish), his Nahuatl-speaking interpreter, advisor, and mistress. Signifying her dual identity as an Indian and a European, Malinche wears native clothes but holds a rosary. Bibliothèque Nationale de France, Paris.

guage. Cortés took her as his mistress and interpreter, and soon she became his guide. When the Spanish leader learned from Malinali the extent of the Aztec empire, his goal became power rather than plunder. He would depose its king, Moctezuma [*mok-tah-zoo-mah*], and take over his realm.

Of Malinali's motives for helping Cortés there is no record. Like his Spanish followers, she may have been dazzled by his powerful personality. Or, more likely, she may have calculated that Cortés was her best hope for escaping slavery and reclaiming her noble status. Whatever her reasons, Malinali's loyalty to her new master was complete. As the Spanish marched on the Aztec capital of Tenochtitlán in 1519, she risked her life by warning Cortés of a surprise attack in the city of Cholula and served as his translator as he negotiated his way into the Aztec capital. "Without her," concluded Bernal Díaz del Castillo, the Spanish chronicler of the conquest, we would "have been unable to surmount many difficulties."

Awed by the military prowess of the Spanish invaders, Moctezuma received Cortés with great ceremony, only to become his captive. When the emperor's supporters tried to expel the invaders, they faced superior European military technology. The sight of the Spaniards in full metal armor, with guns that shook the heavens and inflicted devastating wounds, made a deep impression on the Aztecs, who knew how to purify gold but not how to produce iron tools or weapons. Moreover, the Aztecs had no wheeled carts or cavalry, and their warriors, fighting on foot with flint- or obsidian-tipped spears and arrows, were no match for mounted Spanish conquistadors wielding steel swords and aided by vicious attack dogs. Although heavily outnumbered and suffering great losses, Cortés and his men were able to fight their way out of the Aztec capital.

The Aztec emperor could easily have crushed the Spanish invaders if he had ruled a united empire. But many Indian peoples hated the Aztecs, and Cortés deftly exploited their anger. With the help of Malinali, now known by the honorific Nahuatl name Malinche, he formed military alliances with the subject peoples whose wealth had been appropriated by Aztec nobles and whose people had been sacrificed to the Aztec sun god. The Aztec empire collapsed, the victim not of superior military technology but of a vast internal rebellion instigated by the wily Cortés (see Comparing American Voices, "The Spanish Conquest of Mexico," pp. 26–27).

The Impact of Disease. The Spanish also had a silent ally — disease. Separated from the Eurasian land mass for thousands of years, the inhabitants of the Americas had no immunities to common European diseases. A massive smallpox epidemic lasting seventy days ravaged Tenochtitlán following the Spanish exodus, "striking everywhere in the city," according to an Aztec source, and killing Moctezuma's brother and thousands more. "They could not move, they could not stir. . . . Covered, mantled with pustules, very many people died of them." Subsequent outbreaks of smallpox, influenza, and measles killed hundreds of thousands of Indians and sapped the morale of the survivors. Exploiting this demographic weakness, Cortés quickly extended Spanish rule over the Aztec empire. His lieutenants then moved against the Mayan city-states in the Yucatán Peninsula, eventually conquering them as well.

In 1524, Francisco Pizarro led a Spanish military expedition toward Peru, home of the rich and powerful Inca empire, which stretched 2,000 miles along the Pacific coast of South America. To govern this far-flung empire, the Inca rulers had laid 24,000 miles of roads and built dozens of administrative centers, carefully constructed of finely crafted stone. A semidivine Inca king ruled the empire with the help of a hierarchical bureaucracy staffed by noblemen, many of them the king's relatives. By the time Pizarro and his small force of 168 men and 67 horses finally reached Peru in 1632, half of the Inca population had died from European diseases spread by Indian traders. Weakened militarily and fighting over succession to the throne, the Inca nobility was easy prey for Pizarro's army. In the mere space of

sixteen years, Spain had become the master of the wealthiest and most populous regions of the Western Hemisphere (Map 1.5).

The Ecological Legacy of the Conquest. The Spanish invasion changed life forever in the Americas. Disease and warfare wiped out virtually all of the Indians of Hispaniola — at least 300,000 people. In Peru, the population plummeted from 9 million in 1530 to fewer than 500,000 a century later. Mesoamerica suffered the greatest losses: In 1500, it boasted a population of 30 million; by 1650, its Native American population had fallen to just 3 million — one of the great demographic disasters in world history.

Once the conquistadors had triumphed, the Spanish monarchs quickly created an elaborate bureaucratic empire. From its headquarters in Madrid, the Council of the Indies issued laws and decrees to viceroys and other Spanish officials in America. Still, the conquistadors and their descendants remained powerful because they held ***encomiendas,*** royal grants that gave them legal control of the labor of the native population. They ruthlessly exploited the surviving Native Americans, forcing them to raise crops and cattle both for local consumption and for export to Europe. The Spaniards also permanently altered the natural environment by introducing grains and grasses that supplanted the native flora. Horses, once native to the Western Hemisphere but long extinct, spread quickly and widely across the Americas, and dramatically changed the way of life of many Indian peoples, especially on the Great Plains of North America.

The Spanish conquest had a significant ecological impact on Europe and Africa as well. In a process historians call the **Columbian Exchange,** the food products of the Western Hemisphere — especially maize, potatoes, manioc, sweet potatoes, and tomatoes — were transferred to the peoples of other continents, significantly increasing agricultural yields and population growth worldwide. A less welcome gift was the virulent strain of syphilis Columbus's crew members took back to Europe with them. Similarly, the livestock and crops — and weeds and human diseases — of Africa and Eurasia became part of life in the Americas. Nor was that all. The gold and silver that had formerly honored Aztec gods now gilded the Catholic churches of Europe and flowed into the countinghouses of Spain, making that nation the richest and most powerful in Europe.

By 1550, the once magnificent civilizations of Mexico and Peru lay in ruins. "Of all these wonders" — the great city of Tenochtitlán, the bountiful irrigated fields, the rich orchards, the

The Spanish Conquest of Mexico

How could a Spanish force of six hundred men take control of an empire of 20 million people? That the Spaniards had horses, guns, and steel swords certainly gave them a military advantage. Still, a concerted attack by the armies of the Aztecs and their allies would have overwhelmed the invaders as they initially approached the Mexican capital. Why did the Aztecs wait months to attack Cortés and his men?

These documents, which describe Cortés's initial entry into Tenochtitlán, come from the memoir of a participant and an oral history. Consider them first as *sources:* How trustworthy are they? In what ways might they be biased? Then think about their *content:* Where do the accounts agree? What key events do they identify?

FRIAR BERNARDINO DE SAHAGÚN
Aztec Elders Describe the Behavior of Moctezuma

During the 1550s, Friar Bernardino de Sahagún published The Florentine Codex: General History of New Spain. *According to Sahagún, the authors of the codex were Aztec elders who lived through the conquest. They told their stories to Sahagún in a repetitive style, according to the conventions of Aztec oral histories, and he translated them into Spanish.*

Moctezuma enjoyed no sleep, no food, no one spoke to him. Whatsoever he did, it was as if he were in torment. Ofttimes it was as if he sighed, became weak, felt weak.... Wherefore he said, "What will now befall us? Who indeed stands [in charge]? Alas, until now, I. In great torment is my heart; as if it were washed in chili water it indeed burns." And when he had so heard what the messengers reported, he was terrified, he was astounded.... Especially did it cause him to faint away when he heard how the gun, at [the Spaniards'] command, discharged: how it resounded as if it thundered when it went off. It indeed bereft one of strength; it shut off one's ears. And when it discharged, something like a round pebble came forth from within. Fire went showering forth; sparks went blazing forth. And its smoke smelled very foul; it had a fetid odor which verily wounded the head. And when [the shot] struck a mountain, it was as if it were destroyed, dissolved ... as if someone blew it away.

All iron was their war array. In iron they clothed themselves. With iron they covered their heads. Iron were their swords. Iron were their crossbows. Iron were their shields.

Iron were their lances. And those which bore them upon their backs, their deer [horses], were as tall as roof terraces.

And their bodies were everywhere covered; only their faces appeared. They were very white; they had chalky faces; they had yellow hair, though the hair of some was black.... And when Moctezuma so heard, he was much terrified. It was as if he fainted away. His heart saddened; his heart failed him. ... [But] he made himself resolute; he put forth great effort; he quieted, he controlled his heart; he submitted himself entirely to whatsoever he was to see, at which he was to marvel.... [Moctezuma then greets Cortés, as described above.]

And when [the Spaniards] were well settled, they thereupon inquired of Moctezuma as to all the city's treasure ... the devices, the shields. Much did they importune him; with great zeal they sought gold.... Thereupon were brought forth all the brilliant things; the shields, the golden discs, the devils' necklaces, the golden nose crescents, the golden leg bands, the golden arm bands, the golden forehead bands.

SOURCE: Friar Bernardino de Sahagún, *Florentine Codex: General History of New Spain,* trans. Arthur J. O. Anderson and Charles E. Dibble (Santa Fe and Salt Lake City: School of American Research and University of Utah Press, 1975), 12: 17–20, 26.

BERNAL DÍAZ DEL CASTILLO
Cortés and Moctezuma Meet

Bernal Díaz was an unlikely chronicler of great events. Born poor, he went to America as a common soldier in 1514 and served under conquistadors in Panama and Cuba. In 1519, he joined Cortés's expedition, fought in many battles, and, as a reward, received an estate in present-day Guatemala. In his old age, Díaz wrote The True History of the Conquest of New Spain, *a compelling memoir written from a soldier's perspective. In fresh and straightforward prose, he depicts the conquest as a divinely blessed event that saved the non-Aztec peoples of Mexico from a barbarous regime.*

The Great Moctezuma had sent these great Caciques in advance to receive us, and when they came before Cortés they bade us welcome in their language, and as a sign of peace, they touched their hands against the ground. . . .

When we arrived near to Mexico, . . . the Great Moctezuma got down from his litter, and those great Caciques supported him with their arms beneath a marvelously rich canopy of green coloured feathers with much gold and silver embroidery . . . which was wonderful to look at. The Great Moctezuma was richly attired according to his usage, and he was shod with sandals, the soles were of gold and the upper part adorned with precious stones. . . .

Many other Lords walked before the Great Moctezuma, sweeping the ground where he would tread and spreading cloths on it, so that he should not tread on the earth. Not one of these chieftains dared even to think of looking him in the face, but kept their eyes lowered with great reverence. . . .

When Cortés was told that the Great Moctezuma was approaching, and he saw him coming, he dismounted from his horse, and when he was near Moctezuma, they simultaneously paid great reverence to one another. Moctezuma bade him welcome and our Cortes replied through Doña Marina [Malinche, Cortés's Indian mistress and interpreter] wishing him very good health. . . . And then Cortes brought out a necklace which he had ready at hand, made of glass stones, . . . which have within them many patterns of diverse colours, these were strung on a cord of gold and with musk so that it should have a sweet scent, and he placed it round the neck of the Great Moctezuma. . . .

Then Cortés through the mouth of Doña Marina told him that now his heart rejoiced having seen such a great Prince, and that he took it as a great honour that he had come in person to meet him. . . .

Thus space was made for us to enter the streets of Mexico, without being so much crowded. But who could now count the multitude of men and women and boys who were in the streets and in canoes on the canals, who had come out to see us. It was indeed wonderful. . . . Coming to think it over it seems to be a great mercy that our Lord Jesus Christ was pleased to give us grace and courage to dare to enter into such a city; and for the many times He has saved me from danger of death . . . I give Him sincere thanks. . . .

They took us to lodge in some large houses, where there were apartments for all of us, for they had belonged to the father of the Great Moctezuma, who was named Axayaca. . . .

Cortés thanked Moctezuma through our interpreters, and Moctezuma replied, "Malinche, you and your brethren are in your own house, rest awhile," and then he went to his palaces, which were not far away, and we divided our lodgings by companies, and placed the artillery pointing in a convenient direction, and the order which we had to keep was clearly explained to us, and that we were to be much on the alert, both the cavalry and all of us soldiers. A sumptuous dinner was provided for us according to their use and custom, and we ate it at once. So this was our lucky and daring entry into the great city of Tenochtitlan Mexico on the 8th day of November the year of our Saviour Jesus Christ, 1519.

SOURCE: Bernal Díaz del Castillo, *The True History of the Conquest of New Spain*, trans. A. P. Maudslay (1632; London: Routledge, 1928), 272–275.

ANALYZING THE EVIDENCE

➤ Díaz's account is a memoir written long after the event. What effect does that have on the structure and tone of his writing? How is the Aztec description, as translated by Sahagún, different in those respects?

➤ Why does Moctezuma pay "great reverence" to Cortés? Why does Cortés return the honor? What is the strategy of each leader?

➤ How does Díaz explain the Spaniards' easy entry into Tenochtitlán? What explanation do the Aztec elders suggest? Why do you think they are different?

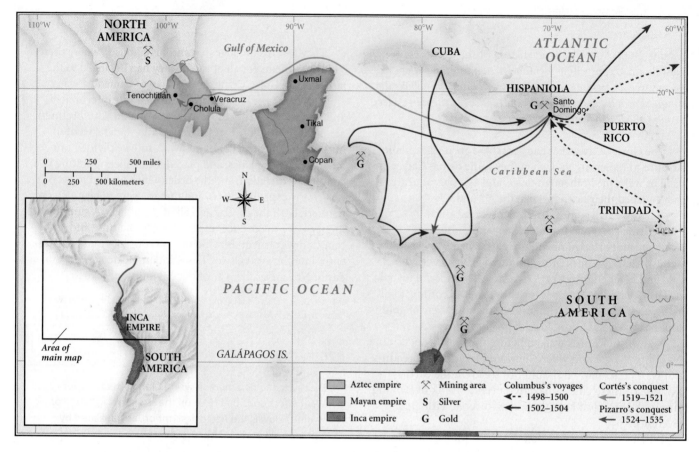

MAP 1.5 The Spanish Conquest of the Great Indian Civilizations

The Spanish first invaded and settled the islands of the Caribbean. Rumors of a golden civilization led to Cortés's invasion of the Aztec empire in 1519. By 1535, other Spanish conquistadors had conquered the Mayan temple cities and the Inca empire in Peru, completing one of the great conquests in world history.

overflowing markets — "all is overthrown and lost, nothing left standing," recalled Bernal Díaz, who had been a young soldier in Cortés's army. Moreover, the surviving Indian peoples lost a vital part of their cultural identity when Spanish priests suppressed their worship of traditional gods and converted them to Catholicism. As early as 1531, an Indian convert reported a vision of a dark-skinned Virgin Mary, later known as the Virgin of Guadalupe, a Christian version of the "corn mother" who traditionally protected the maize crop.

A new society took shape on the lands emptied by disease and exploitation. Between 1500 and 1650, no fewer than 350,000 Spaniards migrated to Mesoamerica and western South America. More than 75 percent of the Spanish settlers were men, and many of them took Indian women as wives or mistresses. Consequently, a substantial mixed-race population, called **mestizos**, quickly appeared, along with an elaborate race-based **caste system**. Around 1800, near the end of the colonial era,

Spanish America stretched from the tip of South America to the northern border of present-day California. It contained about 17 million people: a dominant caste of 3.2 million Spaniards; 5.5 million people of mixed Indian and European race and cultural heritage; 1.0 million African slaves; and 7.5 million Indians, who lived mostly on marginal lands. For the original Native American peoples, the consequences of the European invasion that began in 1492 were tragic and irreversible.

➤ Compare and contrast the main characteristics of traditional European society and West African society. How were they each similar to and different from Native American societies?

➤ Why and how did Portugal and Spain pursue overseas commerce and conquest?

➤ What was the impact of the Columbian Exchange on the Americas, Europe, and Africa?

The Protestant Reformation and the Rise of England

Even as Catholic fervor prompted the forced conversion of the Indians in America and the Muslims and Jews in Spain, Christianity ceased to be a unifying force in European society. During the early sixteenth century, new religious doctrines preached by Martin Luther and other reformers divided Europe between Catholic and Protestant states and plunged the continent into a century-long series of religious wars. During these conflicts, France replaced Spain as the most powerful European state, and Holland and England emerged as Protestant nations determined to colonize the Western Hemisphere.

The Protestant Movement

Over the centuries, the Catholic Church had become a large and wealthy institution. Renaissance popes and cardinals used the Church's wealth to patronize the arts, and some clerics used their power for personal gain. Pope Leo X (r. 1513–1521) received half a million ducats (about $20 million in 2006 dollars) a year from the sale of religious offices. Corruption at the top encouraged ordinary priests and monks to seek economic or sexual favors. One English reformer denounced the clergy as a "gang of scoundrels" who should be "rid of their vices or stripped of their authority," but he was ignored. Other critics of the Church, such as Jan Hus of Bohemia, were executed as heretics.

In 1517, Martin Luther, a German monk and professor at the university in Wittenberg, took up the cause of reform. His *Ninety-five Theses* condemned many Catholic practices, including **indulgences**, certificates that allegedly pardoned sinners from punishment in the afterlife. Outraged by Luther's charges, the pope dismissed him from the Church, and the Holy Roman Emperor, King Charles I of Spain (r. 1516–1556), threatened Luther with punishment. However, the princes of northern Germany, who were resisting the emperor's authority for political reasons, protected Luther from arrest, thus allowing the Protestant movement to survive.

Luther took issue with Roman Catholic doctrine in three major respects. First, he rejected the belief that Christians could secure salvation through good deeds or the purchase of indulgences; instead, Luther argued that people could be saved only by grace, which came as a free gift from God. Second, the German reformer downplayed the role of the clergy and the pope as mediators between God and the people, and proclaimed a much more democratic outlook. "Our baptism consecrates us all without exception and makes us all priests." Third, Luther said that believers must look to the Bible — not to Church officials or doctrine — as the ultimate authority in matters of faith. And so that every literate German could read the Bible, for centuries only available in Latin, he translated it into German.

Peasants as well as princes heeded Luther's attack on authority and, to his dismay, mounted social protests of their own. In 1524, many German peasants rebelled against their manorial lords. Fearing social revolution, Luther urged obedience to established political institutions and condemned the teachings of the Anabaptists (who rejected the baptism of infants) and other new groups of religious dissidents. Assured of Luther's social conservatism, most princes in northern Germany embraced his teachings and broke from Rome, thereby gaining the power to appoint bishops and control the Church's property within their domains. To restore Catholic doctrine and his political authority, the Holy Roman Emperor dispatched armies to Germany, setting off a generation of warfare. Eventually, the Peace of Augsburg (1555) divided Germany into Lutheran states in the north and Catholic principalities in the south.

John Calvin, a French theologian in Geneva, Switzerland, established the most rigorous Protestant regime. Even more than Luther, Calvin stressed human weakness and God's omnipotence. His *Institutes of the Christian Religion* (1536) depicted God as an awesome and absolute sovereign who governed the "wills of men so as to move precisely to that end directed by him." Calvin preached the doctrine of **predestination**, the idea that God chooses certain people for salvation before they are born and condemns the rest to eternal damnation. In Geneva, he set up a model Christian community, eliminating bishops and placing spiritual power in the hands of ministers chosen by the congregation. Ministers and pious laymen ruled the city, prohibiting frivolity and luxury and imposing religious discipline. "We know," wrote Calvin, "that man is of so perverse and crooked a nature, that everyone would scratch out his neighbor's eyes if there were no bridle to hold them in." Calvin's authoritarian doctrine won converts all over Europe; it became the theology of the Huguenots in France, the Reformed churches in Belgium and Holland, and the Presbyterians and Puritans in Scotland and England (Map 1.6).

In England, King Henry VIII (r. 1509–1547) initially opposed Protestantism. However, in 1534, when the pope refused to annul his marriage to the Spanish princess Catherine of Aragon, Henry broke

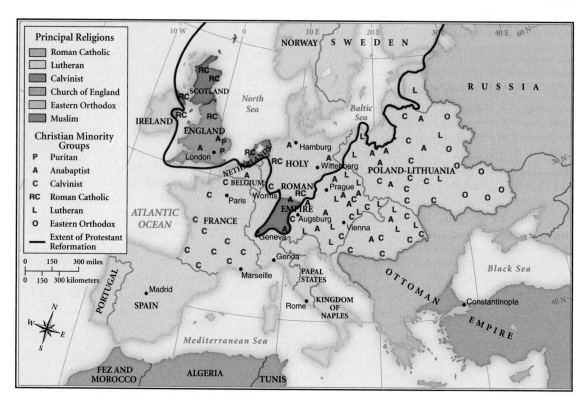

MAP 1.6 Religious Diversity in Europe, 1600

By 1600, Europe was permanently divided among rival churches. Catholicism remained dominant in the south; but Lutheran princes and monarchs ruled northern Europe, and Calvinism had strongholds in Switzerland, Holland, and Scotland. By persecuting radical religious sects, legally established churches — both Protestant and Catholic — encouraged the migration of sect members to America.

with Rome and placed himself at the head of a national church, the Church of England, which promptly granted the king an annulment. Henry made few changes in Catholic doctrine, organization, and ritual, but he did allow the spread of Protestant beliefs and teachings. Faced with popular pressure for greater reform, Henry's daughter and successor, Queen Elizabeth I (r. 1558–1603), approved a Protestant confession of faith that incorporated both the Lutheran doctrine of salvation by grace and the Calvinist belief in predestination. To satisfy traditionalists, Elizabeth retained the Catholic ritual of Holy Communion — now conducted in English rather than Latin — as well as the hierarchy of bishops and archbishops.

Elizabeth's compromises angered radical Protestants, who condemned the power of bishops as "anti-Christian and devilish and contrary to the Scriptures." These reformers were inspired by the presbyterian system pioneered in Calvin's Geneva and developed by John Knox for the Church of Scotland. In Scotland, congregations elected lay elders

(presbyters) who helped ministers and participated in the synods (councils) that decided Church doctrine. By 1600, at least five hundred ministers in the Church of England wanted to eliminate bishops and install a presbyterian form of church government.

Other radical English Protestants called themselves "unspotted lambs of the Lord" or Puritans. These extraordinarily devout Calvinists wanted to "purify" the Church of England of all Catholic teachings and magical or idolatrous practices. Puritans refused to burn incense or to appeal to dead saints for their intervention; a carefully argued sermon was the focus of their service. Puritans placed special emphasis on the "conversion experience," the felt infusion of God's grace, and the "calling," the duty to serve God in one's ordinary life and work. To ensure that all men and women had direct access to God's commands in the Bible, they encouraged literacy and Bible-study. Finally, most Puritans wanted authority over spiritual and financial matters to rest primarily with local congregations. Eventually, thousands of English Puritans would migrate to

A Dutch Merchant Family
This painting of Pierre de Moucheron and his family by Dutch artist Cornelius de Zeeuw captures both the prosperity and the severe Calvinist ethos of sixteenth-century Holland. It also depicts the character of the traditional patriarchal family, in which status reflected a rigid hierarchy of gender and age. Rijksmuseum, Amsterdam.

North America and establish churches there based on these radical Protestant doctrines.

The Dutch and English Challenge Spain

Luther's challenge to Catholicism in 1517 came just two years before Cortés began his conquest of the Aztec empire, and the two events became linked. Gold and silver from Mexico and later Peru made Spain the wealthiest nation in Europe and King Philip II (r. 1556–1598) its most powerful ruler. In addition to Spanish America, Philip presided over wealthy city-states in Italy, the commercial and manufacturing provinces of the Spanish Netherlands (present-day Holland and Belgium), and, after 1580, Portugal and all its possessions in America, Africa, and the East Indies. "If the Romans were able to rule the world simply by ruling the Mediterranean," a Spanish priest boasted, "what of the man who rules the Atlantic and Pacific oceans, since they surround the world?"

Philip's Wars and Spain's Decline. Philip, an ardent Catholic, tried to root out Islam in North Africa and Protestantism in the Netherlands and in England. He failed in both efforts. A massive Spanish fleet defeated a Turkish armada at Lepanto in the eastern Mediterranean in 1571, freeing 15,000 Christian galley slaves, but Muslims continued to rule nearby Morocco and Algiers. To the north, the Spanish-controlled Netherlands had grown wealthy from trade with the vast Portuguese empire and from weaving wool and linen. These provinces had also become hotbeds of Calvinism. To protect their Calvinist faith and political liberties, the Dutch and Flemish revolted against Spain in 1566. In 1581, after fifteen years of war and with the help of other Protestant states, the seven northern provinces declared their independence, becoming the Dutch Republic (or Holland).

Elizabeth I of England helped the Dutch cause by dispatching six thousand troops to Holland. She also supported military expeditions to extend direct English rule over Gaelic-speaking Catholic regions of Ireland. Calling the Irish "wild savages," English troops brutally massacred thousands, prefiguring the treatment of Indians in America. In 1588, to meet Elizabeth's challenge, Philip sent the Spanish Armada—130 ships and thirty thousand men—against England. Philip intended to restore Catholicism to England and Ireland and then wipe out Calvinism in Holland. But he failed utterly when English ships and a fierce storm destroyed the Spanish fleet.

Shrugging off this defeat, Philip continued to spend his American gold on religious wars. This ill-advised policy diverted resources from industrial investment in Spain and weakened its economy. Oppressed by high taxes on agriculture and fearful

of military service, more than 200,000 residents of Castile, the richest region of Spain, migrated to America. By the time of Philip's death in 1598, Spain was in serious decline.

As mighty Spain faltered, tiny Holland prospered — the economic miracle of the seventeenth century. Amsterdam emerged as the financial capital of northern Europe, and the Dutch Republic replaced Portugal as the dominant trader in Indonesia and West Africa. Dutch merchants also looked across the Atlantic: They created the West India Company, which invested in sugar plantations in Brazil and established the fur-trading colony of New Netherland along the Hudson River in North America.

Elizabeth's Mercantile Policies. England also emerged as a European power in the sixteenth century, its economy stimulated by an increase in population, from 3 million in 1500 to 5 million in 1630. Equally important, its royal government supported the expansion of commerce and manufacturing. English merchants had long supplied European weavers with high-quality wool; by around 1500, they had created their own textile industry. That industry relied on **outwork**: Merchants bought wool from the owners of great estates and then hired landless peasants to spin and weave the wool into cloth. The government helped textile entrepreneurs by setting low rates for wages, and it helped merchants by awarding monopoly privileges in foreign markets. Queen Elizabeth granted monopolies to the Levant Company (Turkey) in 1581, the Guinea Company (Africa) in 1588, and the East India Company (India) in 1600.

This system of state-assisted manufacturing and trade became known as **mercantilism**. By encouraging domestic manufacturing, Elizabeth hoped to reduce imports and increase exports, giving England a favorable balance of trade. The queen and her advisors wanted gold and silver to flow into the country in payment for English goods, stimulating further economic expansion and enriching the merchant community. Increased trade also meant greater revenues from import duties, which swelled the royal treasury and enhanced the power of the national government. By 1600, Elizabeth's mercantile policies had laid the foundations for overseas colonization. Now the English, as well as the Dutch, had the merchant fleets and wealth needed to challenge Spain's domination of the Western Hemisphere, and strong social and economic reasons for doing so.

The Social Causes of English Colonization

England sent more than merchant fleets and manufactures to America. The rapid growth of the English population also provided a large body of settlers, many fleeing economic hardship. The massive expenditure of American gold and silver by Philip II had doubled the money supply of Europe and sparked a major economic upheaval known today as the **Price Revolution** (Figure 1.2).

The landed nobility in England was the first casualty of the Price Revolution. Aristocrats customarily rented out their estates on long leases for fixed rents, which gave them a secure income and plenty

Figure 1.2 Inflation and Living Standards in Europe, 1400–1700

As American gold and silver poured into Europe after 1520 and was minted into money, people used it to bid up the price of grain. Grain remained in short supply because Europe's population almost doubled between 1500 and 1700, from 68 million to 120 million. The increased supply of money in combination with the increased demand for goods led to the Price Revolution.

As the graph shows, from 1500 through 1630, grain prices rose more quickly than wages. Thus real wages — what wages actually purchase — fell from a high point in about 1430 to a low point in about 1650. As real wages rose after 1650, people lived better.

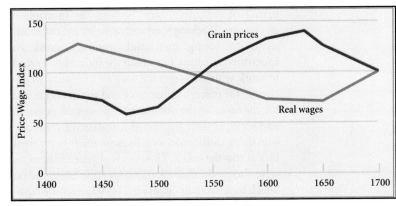

The base period for the graph is 1700: That is, the price and wage levels in 1700 have the index value of 100. In 1630, the index for grain was about 140, which means that grain cost about 40 percent more relative to wages than it would cost in 1700.

of leisure. As one English nobleman put it, "We eat and drink and rise up to play and this is to live like a gentleman." Then inflation struck. In less than two generations, the price of goods more than tripled while the nobility's income from rents barely increased. As the income of the aristocracy fell, that of the **gentry** and the yeomen rose. The gentry, who were nonnoble landholders with substantial estates, kept pace with inflation by renting land on short leases at higher rates. Yeomen, described by a European traveler as "middle people of a condition between gentlemen and peasants," owned small farms that they worked with family help. As wheat prices tripled, yeomen used the profits to build larger houses and provide their children with land.

As always, economics influenced politics. As nobles lost wealth, the influence of their branch of Parliament, the House of Lords, weakened. At the same time, members of the rising gentry entered the House of Commons, the political voice of the propertied classes. Supported by the yeomen, the gentry demanded new rights and powers for the Commons, among them control of taxation. Thus the Price Revolution encouraged the rise of representative institutions in which rich commoners and small property owners had a voice. This development had profound consequences for English — and American — political history.

The Price Revolution likewise transformed the lives of peasants, who made up three-fourths of the English population (Figure 1.3). The economic stimulus of Spanish gold spurred the expansion of the textile industry. To increase the supply of wool, profit-minded landlords and wool merchants persuaded Parliament to pass **enclosure acts**, laws that allowed owners to fence in the open fields that surrounded many peasant villages and put sheep to graze on them. Those peasant families who were

dispossessed of their lands lived on the brink of poverty, spinning and weaving wool or working as wage laborers on farms. Wealthy men had "taken farms into their hands," an observer noted in 1600, "whereby the peasantry of England is decayed and become servants to gentlemen."

In 1600, Europe experienced the first of a series of remarkably long and cold winters, a phenomenon that lasted a century and was known as the Little Ice Age. The resulting crop failures brought soaring grain prices and social discontent. "Thieves and rogues do swarm the highways," warned one

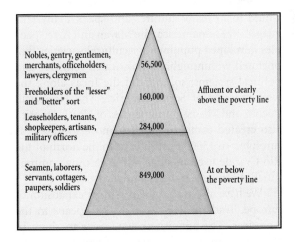

Figure 1.3 The Structure of English Society, 1688

This famous chart, the work of Gregory King (1648–1712), an early statistician, shows the results of centuries of aristocratic rule. A small privileged elite perches atop the thin pyramid, and a mass of poor working people forms its base. Most English families (some 849,000 according to King) lived at or below the poverty line and, according to King, were "Decreasing the Wealth of the Kingdom." In fact, the labor of the poor produced much of the wealth owned by the 500,500 families in the higher reaches of society.

justice of the peace, "and bastards be multiplied in parishes." Seeking food and security, tens of thousands of young men and women signed an **indenture**, a contract in which the individual agreed to work without wages for four or five years in exchange for passage to America and room and board for the term of the contract. Dispossessed peasants and weavers, their livelihood threatened by a recession in the cloth trade, were likewise ready to try their luck across the ocean. Thousands of yeomen families were also on the move, looking for affordable land on which to settle their children. This large-scale migration of English yeomen families and impoverished laborers would lead to a new collision with Indian peoples, this time in North America.

> ➤ How did Protestant religious doctrine differ from that of Roman Catholicism?
>
> ➤ Why did Spain lose its position as the dominant European power?
>
> ➤ What factors prompted the large-scale migration of English men and women to America?

SUMMARY

In this chapter we have seen that the first human inhabitants of the Western Hemisphere were hunter-gatherers from Asia. Their descendants would form many cultures and speak many languages. In Mesoamerica, the Mayan and Aztec peoples developed populous agricultural societies that operated within highly sophisticated religious and political systems; so, too, did the Incas along the western coast of South America. The Hopewell, Pueblo, and Mississippian peoples of North America also created complex societies and elaborate cultures; but in 1500, most Indians to the north of the Rio Grande lived in small self-governing communities of foragers, hunters, and farmers.

We have also traced the maritime expansion of Europe. Trade initially brought Europeans to the Americas. The Spanish crown, eager to share in Portugal's mercantile success, financed expeditions to uncover new trade routes to Asia. When Christopher Columbus revealed a "new world" to Europeans in 1492, Spanish adventurers undertook to conquer it. By 1535, conquistadors had destroyed the wealthy civilizations of Mesoamerica and Peru and introduced diseases that would kill millions of Native Americans. And through the exchange of crops, animals, and plants, they fundamentally altered the ecology of much of the world.

Population growth, religious warfare, and American gold and silver transformed European society in the sixteenth century. As the costs of religious warfare sapped Spain's strength, the rise of strong and purposeful governments in Holland, France, and England, along with a class of increasingly powerful merchants, enhanced the economies of those countries and whetted their appetite for overseas expansion.

Connections: Society

In the essay opening Part One (p. 3), we noted that

> Europeans, with their steel weapons and their diseases, shredded the fabric of most Native American cultures.

In this chapter, you've read the first part of that story — the Spanish invasion of Mesoamerica and South America. In Chapter 2, we compare the interaction of Native Americans with various European peoples: the Spanish in New Mexico and Florida; the French in Louisiana; and the Dutch and English in the Northeast. The chapter concludes with an analysis of Native Americans in New England as of 1700. Later chapters explain how and why Native Americans continued to shape the history of the eastern seaboard, even as their numbers and strength underwent a sharp decline. Part One concludes with the Great War for Empire (1754–1763). That war was known in the British colonies as the French and Indian War, and rightly so: It was fought by Native Americans to defend their lands from Anglo-American settlers.

The coming of those settlers to the Chesapeake region and New England between 1600 and 1675, and their initial wars with the Native peoples, will be a major theme of Chapter 2.

CHAPTER REVIEW QUESTIONS

> ➤ How do you explain the different ways in which the Indian peoples of Mesoamerica and North America developed?
>
> ➤ What made Native American peoples vulnerable to conquest by European adventurers?
>
> ➤ What led to the transatlantic trade in African slaves?
>
> ➤ What was mercantilism? How did this doctrine shape the policies of European monarchs to promote domestic manufacturing and foreign trade?
>
> ➤ How did Europeans become leaders in world trade and extend their influence across the Atlantic?

TIMELINE

13,000–3000 B.C.	Asian migrants reach North America
3000 B.C.	Farming begins in Mesoamerica
A.D. 100–400	Flourishing of Hopewell culture
300	Rise of Mayan civilization
500	Zenith of Teotihuacán civilization
600	Pueblo cultures emerge
632–1100	Arab people adopt Islam and spread its influence
800–1350	Development of Mississippian culture
1096–1291	Crusades link Europe with Arab learning
1300–1450	Italian Renaissance
1325	Aztecs establish capital at Tenochtitlán
1440s	Portugal enters trade in African slaves
1492	Christopher Columbus makes first voyage to America
1513	Juan Ponce de León explores Florida
1517	Martin Luther sparks Protestant Reformation
1519–1521	Hernán Cortés conquers Aztec empire
1520–1650	Price Revolution
1532–1535	Francisco Pizarro vanquishes Incas
1534	Henry VIII establishes Church of England
1536	John Calvin publishes *Institutes of the Christian Religion*
1550–1630	English crown endorses mercantilism
	Parliament passes enclosure acts
1556–1598	Reign of Philip II, King of Spain
1558–1603	Reign of Elizabeth I, Queen of England
1560s	Puritan movement begins in England
1588	English and storms defeat Spanish Armada

FOR FURTHER EXPLORATION

Kenneth Pomeranz, *The Great Divergence: Europe, China, and the Making of the Modern World Economy* (2000), examines the settlement of America from the perspective of world history. Brian M. Fagan, *The Great Journey: The People of Ancient America* (1987), and Alvin M. Josephy Jr., ed., *America in 1492: The World of the Indian Peoples Before the Arrival of Columbus* (1991), offer a panorama of early Indian societies, and are more reliable than Charles C. Mann, 1491: *New Revelations of the Americas Before Columbus* (2005). For the European background of colonization, begin with George Huppert, *After the Black Death* (2nd ed., 1998), a highly readable study of Western Europe's recovery from the devastating epidemic of the mid-fourteenth century. William D. Phillips, with Carla Rahn Phillips, discusses European expansion in *The Worlds of Christopher Columbus* (1992), an engaging biography that describes the enormous consequences of Columbus's voyages. Two interesting Public Broadcasting Service (PBS) videos examine the ancient civilizations of Mesoamerica: *Odyssey: Maya Lords of the Jungle* (1 hour) and *Odyssey: The Incas* (1 hour). For additional information, log on to "1492: An Ongoing Voyage" (**www.loc.gov/exhibits/1492/intro.html**), which surveys the native cultures of the Western Hemisphere and offers full-color images of artifacts and art. Material on an early Indian civilization in the Southwest is available at "Sipapu: The Anasazi Emergence into the Cyber World" (**sipapu.gsu.edu/**).

Peter Laslett, *The World We Have Lost* (3rd ed., 1984), paints a vivid portrait of society in seventeenth-century England; important recent studies include Andrew McRae, *God Speed the Plough* (2002), and Ethan Shagan, *Popular Politics and the English Reformation* (2003). "Martin Luther" (**www.luther.de/e/index. html**) offers biographies of the leading figures of the Protestant Reformation and striking images of the era. Giles Milton, *Nathaniel's Nutmeg: Or, the True and Incredible Adventures of the Spice Trader Who Changed the Course of History* (1999), tells the rousing tale of international seagoing competition among European powers for control of the spice trade and, subsequently, the New World. Also see the BBC's interactive Web site on the history of navigation (**www.bbc.co.uk/history/discovery/exploration/navigation_animation.shtml**), which made that competition possible.

TEST YOUR KNOWLEDGE

To assess your command of the material in this chapter, see the Online Study Guide at **bedfordstmartins.com/henretta**.

For Web sites, images, and documents related to topics and places in this chapter, visit **bedfordstmartins.com/makehistory**.

T·B   9

2

The Invasion and Settlement of North America

1550–1700

ESTABLISHING COLONIES IN NORTH AMERICA was not for the faint of heart. First came a long voyage over stormy, dangerous waters, a trip that took many lives. Of three hundred migrants to New France in 1663, for example, seventy died en route. Those who survived, although weakened by spoiled food and shipboard diseases, immediately had to build shelter and plant crops. Many also faced hostile Indian peoples. "We neither fear them or trust them," declared Puritan settler Francis Higginson; instead, he went on, they relied on "our musketeers." Still, despite great risks and uncertain rewards, English, French, and Spanish migrants by the tens of thousands crossed the Atlantic during the seventeenth century. They were either driven by poverty and religious persecution at home or drawn by the promise of land, gold, or — according to one pious migrant — promoting "the Christian religion to such People as yet live in Darkness."

For Native Americans, the European invasion was a catastrophe. Whether they came as settlers, missionaries, or fur traders, the white-skinned people brought new diseases and religions that threatened the Indians' lives, lands, and cultures. "Our fathers had plenty of deer and skins, . . . and our coves were full of fish and fowl," Narragansett chief Miantonomi reminded the Montauk people in 1642, "but these English having gotten our land . . . their cows and horses eat the grass, and their

◀ **A European View of Virginia**

Many Europeans received their first impressions of America from the engravings of Theodore de Bry (1528–1598), who published an illustrated edition of Thomas Hariot's *A briefe and true report of the new found land of Virginia* in 1590. De Bry based his famous engravings on the paintings of John White, who had accompanied the English expedition to Roanoke. Whereas White pictured the Indians in realistic and casual poses, de Bry rendered them as sculpturelike figures with muscular bodies and European faces. William L. Clements Library, University of Michigan.

hogs spoil our clam banks, and we shall all be starved." Miantonomi called for united resistance: "We [are] all Indians [and must] say brother to one another, . . . otherwise we shall all be gone shortly." The Narragansett leader's unsuccessful plea foretold the course of North American history: The European invaders would advance, and the Indian peoples would be dispossessed.

The Rival Imperial Models of Spain, France, and Holland

In Mesoamerica, the Spanish seized the Indians' lands, converted them to Catholicism, and made them dig for gold and farm large estates. In the more sparsely populated eastern regions of North America, French and Dutch merchants created fur-trading colonies, and the native peoples retained their lands and political autonomy (Table 2.1). Whatever the Europeans' mission, all across the continent Indian peoples diminished in numbers and soon rebelled.

New Spain: Colonization and Conversion

In their ceaseless quest for gold, Spanish explorers penetrated deeply into the southern and western areas of what would become the United States. In the 1540s, Francisco Vásquez de Coronado searched in vain for the fabled seven golden cities of Cíbola; what he discovered instead were the southern reaches of the Grand Canyon, the Pueblo peoples of the Southwest, and the grasslands of present-day Kansas. Simultaneously, Hernán de Soto and a force of six hundred cut a bloody swath across the Southeast, doing battle with the Apalachees (in what is northern Florida today) and the Coosas (in northern Alabama) but finding no gold (Map 2.1).

By the 1560s, Spanish officials gave up the search for Indian gold and focused on the defense of their empire. Roving English "sea dogs" were plundering Spanish treasure ships and Caribbean seaports, and French Protestants were settling in Florida despite Spain's claim to the land there. Following King Philip II's order to cast out the trespassing Frenchmen "by the best means," Spanish troops massacred three hundred members of the "evil Lutheran sect" near the mouth of the St. John River. To safeguard the route of the treasure fleet, in 1565 Spain established a fort at St. Augustine, making it the first permanent European settlement in the future United States. Raids by the Calusas and Timucuas wiped out a dozen other Spanish military outposts in Florida, and Algonquins destroyed Jesuit religious missions along the east coast, one as far north as the Chesapeake Bay.

TABLE 2.1 European Colonies in North America before 1660

Colony	Date	First Settlement	Type	Religion	Chief Export/ Economic Activity
New Spain	1520	Mexico City	Royal	Catholic	Gold, silver, grain, hides
New France	1608	Quebec	Royal	Catholic	Furs
New Netherland	1613	Fort Orange (Albany)	Corporate	Dutch Reformed	Furs
New Sweden	1628	Fort Christina	Corporate	Lutheran	Furs, farming
English Colonies					
Virginia	1607	Jamestown	Corporate (merchant)	Anglican	Tobacco
Plymouth	1620	Plymouth	Corporate (religious)	Separatist Puritan	Mixed farming, livestock
Massachusetts Bay	1629	Boston	Corporate	Puritan	Mixed farming, livestock
Maryland	1634	St. Mary's	Proprietary (religious)	Catholic	Tobacco, grain
Connecticut	1635	Hartford	Corporate (religious)	Puritan	Mixed farming, livestock
Rhode Island	1636	Providence	Corporate (religious)	Separatist Puritan	Mixed farming, livestock

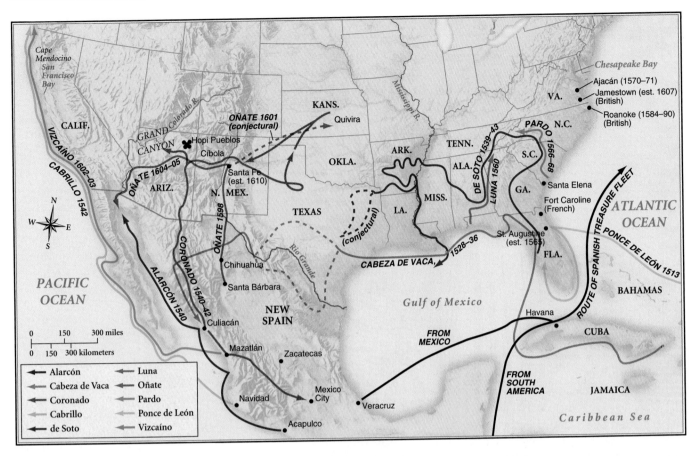

MAP 2.1 New Spain Looks North, 1513–1610

The search for gold drew Spanish explorers first to Florida and then deep into the present-day United States. When the wide-ranging expeditions of Hernán de Soto and Francisco Vásquez de Coronado failed to find gold or flourishing Indian civilizations, authorities in New Spain limited settlements in the northern territories to St. Augustine in Florida (to protect the treasure fleet) and Santa Fe in the upper Rio Grande Valley.

Franciscan Missions. These military setbacks prompted the Spanish crown to adopt a new policy toward the Indian peoples, one of Christianization. The Comprehensive Orders for New Discoveries, issued in 1573, placed responsibility for pacification of new lands primarily in the hands of missionaries, not conquistadors. Over the next century, dozens of Franciscan friars set up missions among the Apalachees in Florida and the Pueblo peoples in the lands they named Nuevo México. Although the friars often learned Indian languages, they systematically attacked the natives' culture. And their methods were anything but peaceful. Protected by Spanish soldiers, missionaries whipped Indians who continued to practice **polygamy,** smashed their religious idols, and severely punished those who worshiped traditional gods. On one occasion, forty-seven "sorcerers" in Nuevo México were whipped and sold into slavery.

For the Franciscans, religious conversion, cultural assimilation, and forced labor went hand in hand. They encouraged the Indians to talk, cook, dress, and walk like Spaniards. They ignored Spanish laws that protected the native peoples, and allowed privileged Spanish landowners (*encomenderos*) in New Mexico to extract goods and forced labor from the native population. The missions also depended on Indian workers to grow crops and carry them to market, often on their backs.

Popé and the Pueblo Revolt of 1680. Native Americans initially tolerated the Franciscans because they feared military reprisals and hoped to learn the friars' spiritual secrets. But when Christian prayers failed to protect their communities from European diseases, droughts, and raids by nomadic Apaches and Pawnees, many Pueblo people returned to their ancestral religions. Thus, the people of Hawikuh refused to become "wet-heads" (as the Indians called baptized Christians) "because with the water of baptism they would have to die."

In 1598, the tense relations between Indians and Spaniards in New Mexico exploded into open

La V:M: Maria de Iesus de Agreda. Predicando à los Chichimecos del Nuebo-mexico. Anttº de Cafno fº

warfare. An expedition of five hundred Spanish soldiers and settlers led by Juan de Oñate seized corn and clothing from the Pueblo peoples and murdered or raped those who resisted. When Indians of the Acoma pueblo retaliated by killing eleven soldiers, the Spanish troops destroyed the pueblo and murdered five hundred men and three hundred women and children. Faced with bitterly hostile native peoples, most of the settlers left New Mexico. In 1610, the Spanish returned, founded the town of Santa Fe, and reestablished the system of missions and forced labor. Over the next two generations, European diseases, forced tribute, and raids by nomadic plains Indians reduced the population of Pueblo peoples from 60,000 to just 17,000.

As a prolonged drought threatened the survivors with extinction, the Indian shaman Popé called for the Pueblo peoples to expel the Spaniards and "return to the laws of their ancients." He "who

shall kill a Spaniard will get an Indian women for a wife," Popé promised, and be "free from the labor . . . performed for the religious and the Spaniards." In 1680, in a carefully coordinated rebellion, Popé and his followers from two dozen pueblos killed more than four hundred Spaniards and forced the remaining fifteen hundred colonists (and five hundred Pueblo and Apache slaves) to flee 300 miles to El Paso. Repudiating Christianity, the Pueblo peoples desecrated churches and tortured and killed twenty-one missionaries. They burned "the seeds which the Spaniards sowed," planted "only maize and beans, which were the crops of their ancestors," and rebuilt the sacred kivas, the round stone structures in which they had long worshiped. Like those who would later lead Native American resistance, Popé marched forward while looking backward, hoping to restore the traditional religion and way of life.

It was not to be. A decade later, Spain reasserted control over most of the Pueblo peoples. The oppressed Natives rebelled again in 1696, only to be subdued. Exhausted by a generation of warfare, they agreed to a compromise that allowed them to practice their own religion and ended forced labor. In return, they accepted a dependent position in New Mexico and helped the Spanish defend their settlements and farms there against attacks by nomadic Apaches and Comanches.

Spain had maintained its northern empire, but it failed to convert and assimilate the Indian peoples. Some Natives had married Spaniards and their offspring formed a bicultural mestizo population. However, most Pueblo Indians continued to practice the old ways. As a Franciscan friar admitted, "They are still drawn more by their idolatry and infidelity than by the Christian doctrine."

The situation in Florida was equally disappointing to Spanish officials. Raids by the English in Carolina in the early 1700s destroyed most of the Spanish missions there, and killed or enslaved most Catholic converts. These setbacks persuaded Spanish officials to delay the settlement of the distant northern province of California until the 1760s. For the time being, Santa Fe and St. Augustine stood as vulnerable defensive northern outposts of Spain's American empire.

New France: Furs, Souls, and Warfare

Far to the northeast, the French were likewise trying to convert the native peoples to Catholicism. In the 1530s, Jacques Cartier had claimed the lands bordered by the Gulf of St. Lawrence for France. By the 1580s, hundreds of ships from many nations were arriving annually off the coast of Newfoundland to catch fish, whales, and seals. However, the first permanent settlement came only in 1608, when Samuel de Champlain founded Quebec. The small French fur-trading post was struggling in 1627, when Cardinal Richelieu, chief minister of King Louis XIII (r. 1610–1643), transferred control of the region to the Company of One Hundred Associates. The company agreed to send out four thousand settlers but fell well short of that target. Then, in 1662, King Louis XIV (r. 1643–1714) turned New France into a royal colony and began subsidizing the migration of indentured servants there. Those who signed indentures would serve a term of thirty-six months, be paid a yearly salary, and eventually receive a leasehold farm — terms far more generous than those for indentured servants in the English colonies.

Still, despite brutal famines in France, few Frenchmen and -women migrated to New France. This reluctance puzzled a contemporary observer, who asked: "Is it possible that peasants are so afraid of losing sight of the village steeple, that they would rather languish in their misery and poverty?" In fact, various state policies and laws discouraged migration. In his fervor to expand France's boundaries, Louis XIV drafted tens of thousands of potential migrants into military service. The Catholic monarch also barred Huguenots (French Calvinist Protestants) from migrating to New France. Moreover, the French legal system gave peasants strong rights to their village lands, which they were loathe to give up. Finally, most French people thought of New France (also called Canada, from the Huron-Iroquois word for village) as a cold and forbidding place, "a country at the end of the world." Of the 27,000 men and women who migrated to New France before 1760, almost two-thirds eventually returned to France. In 1698, the European population of the colony was only 15,200; by contrast, there were 100,000 residents in English settlements at that time.

Lacking settlers, New France became a vast enterprise for acquiring furs, which were in great demand in Europe to make felt hats and fur garments. To secure plush beaver pelts from the Huron Indians, who controlled trade north of the Great Lakes, Champlain provided them with blankets and iron utensils. He also gave them guns to fight the expansionist-minded Five Nations of the Iroquois of New York (see Voices from Abroad, "Samuel de Champlain: Going to War with the Hurons," p. 42). Searching for new sources of furs to the west, explorer Jacques Marquette reached the Mississippi River in present-day Wisconsin in 1673 and traveled as far south as Arkansas. Then, in 1681, Robert de La Salle traveled down the majestic river to the Gulf of Mexico, trading as he went. As a French priest noted with disgust, La Salle and his associates hoped "to buy all the Furs and Skins of the remotest Savages, who, as they thought, did not know their Value; and so enrich themselves in one single voyage." To honor Louis XIV, La Salle named the region Louisiana; it would include the thriving port of New Orleans on the Gulf of Mexico, which was established in 1718.

The Rise of the Iroquois. Despite their small numbers, the French had a disastrous impact. By unwittingly introducing European diseases, they triggered epidemics that killed from 25 percent to 90 percent of many Indian peoples. Moreover, by bartering guns for furs, the French sparked a series of deadly wars. The Five Iroquois Nations were the prime aggressors. From their strategic geographical location in central New York, the Iroquois could obtain guns and goods from Dutch merchants at

Samuel de Champlain

Going to War with the Hurons

Although Samuel de Champlain is best known as the founder of Quebec, he was primarily a soldier and an adventurer. After fighting in the French religious wars, Champlain joined the Company of New France and set out to create a French empire in North America. In 1603, he traveled down the St. Lawrence River as far as Quebec. He then lived for several years in the company's failed settlement in Maine before returning to Quebec in 1608. To ensure French access to the western fur trade, Champlain joined the Hurons in a raid against the Iroquois in 1609, which he later described in a book of his American adventures.

Pursuing our route, I met some two or three hundred savages, who were encamped in huts near a little island called St. Eloi. . . . We made a reconnaissance, and found that they were tribes of savages called Ochasteguins [Hurons] and Algonquins, on their way to Quebec to assist us in exploring the territory of the Iroquois, with whom they are in deadly hostility. . . . [We joined with them and] went to the mouth of the River of the Iroquois [the Richelieu River, where it joins the St. Lawrence River], where we stayed two days, refreshing ourselves with good venison, birds, and fish, which the savages gave us.

In all their encampments, they have their Pilotois, or Ostemoy, a class of persons who play the part of soothsayers, in whom these people have faith. One of these builds a cabin, surrounds it with small pieces of wood and covers it with his robe: after it is built, he places himself inside, so as not to be seen at all, when he seizes and shakes one of the posts of his cabin, muttering some words between his teeth, by which he says he invokes the devil, who appears to him in the form of a stone, and tells them whether they will meet their enemies and kill many of them. . . . They frequently told me that the shaking of the cabin, which I saw, proceeded from the devil, who made it move, and not the man inside, although I could see the contrary. . . . They told me also that I should see fire come out from the top, which I did not see at all.

Now, as we began to approach within two or three days' journey of the abode of our enemies, we advanced only at night. . . . By day, they withdraw into the interior of the woods, where they rest, without straying off, neither making any noise, even for the sake of cooking, so as not to be noticed in case their enemies should by accident pass by. They make no fire, except in smoking, which amounts to almost nothing. They eat baked Indian meal, which they soak in water, when it becomes a kind of porridge. . . .

In order to ascertain what was to be the result of their undertaking, they often asked me if I had had a dream, and seen their enemies, to which I replied in the negative. . . . [Then one night] while sleeping, I dreamed that I saw our enemies, the Iroquois, drowning near a mountain, within sight. When I expressed a wish to help them, our allies, the savages, told me we must let them all die. . . . This, upon being related [to our allies], gave them so much confidence that they did not doubt any longer that good was to happen to them. . . .

[After our victory over the Iroquois,] they took one of the prisoners, to whom they made a harangue, enumerating the cruelties which he and his men had already practiced toward them without any mercy, and that, in like manner, he ought to make up his mind to receive as much. They commanded him to sing, if he had courage, which he did; but it was a very sad song.

Meanwhile, our men kindled a fire; and, when it was well burning, they brand, and burned this poor creature gradually, so as to make him suffer greater torment. Sometimes they stopped, and threw water on his back. Then they tore out his nails, and applied fire to the extremities of his fingers and private member. Afterwards, they flayed the top of his head, and had a kind of gum poured all hot upon it.

SOURCE: Samuel de Champlain, *Voyages of Samuel de Champlain, 1604–1618*, ed. W. L. Grant (New York: Charles Scribner's Sons, 1907), 79–86.

ANALYZING THE EVIDENCE

➤ How do you account for the differences between the Hurons' and Champlain's perceptions of the soothsayer's hut? What does it suggest about their respective views of the world?

➤ Having read this passage, what would you say was the role of dreams in Huron culture?

➤ At the beginning of this passage, Champlain refers to the Indians as savages. Would the torture he describes help to explain that characterization? How do you think a modern anthropologist would explain the Indians' custom of torturing war captives?

Albany and quickly attack other Indian peoples by water. Iroquois warriors moved to the east along the Mohawk River as far as New England, and south along the Delaware and Susquehanna Rivers as far as the Carolinas. They traveled north via Lake Champlain and the Richelieu River to Quebec. And they journeyed west via the Great Lakes and the Allegheny-Ohio river system to exploit the rich fur-bearing lands of the upper Mississippi River Valley.

The rise of the Iroquois was breathtakingly rapid, just as their subsequent decline was tragically sobering. In 1600, the Iroquois numbered about 30,000 and lived in large towns of 500 to 2,000 inhabitants. Over the next two decades, they organized themselves in a confederation of Five Nations: Senecas, Cayugas, Onondagas, Oneidas, and Mohawks. Partly in response to a virulent smallpox epidemic in 1633, which cut their number by a third, the Iroquois waged a devastating series of wars against the Hurons (1649), Neutrals (1651), Eries (1657), and Susquehannocks — all Iroquoian-speaking peoples. They razed the villages and killed most of the men, cooking and eating their flesh to gain access to their spiritual powers. They took thousands of women and children as captives, adopting them into Iroquois lineages and clans in formal ceremonies. These rituals transferred to the captives the names of the Iroquois dead, along with their social roles and duties. The Hurons simply ceased to exist as a distinct people and culture. Those who survived the Iroquois raids migrated westward and joined other remnant peoples to form a new tribe, the Wyandots.

These triumphs gave the Iroquois control of the fur trade with the French in Quebec and the Dutch in New Amsterdam. Equally important, they changed the character of Iroquois society. By 1657, adopted prisoners made up as much as half of the population of many Iroquois communities. Cultural diversity within the confederacy increased further when the Five Nations made peace with the French and allowed Jesuit missionaries to live among them. As the Jesuits won converts, Iroquois villages split into bitter religious factions. Many Christian Indians moved to French-sponsored mission towns, and tradition-minded Iroquois took control of the Five Nations.

During the 1670s, those traditionalists repudiated their ties with the French and formed an alliance, called the Covenant Chain, with English officials in New York. Seeking furs to sell to merchants in Albany, they embarked on a new series of western "beaver wars." Iroquois warriors pushed a dozen Algonquian-speaking peoples allied with the French — Ottawas, Foxes, Sauks, Kickapoos, Miamis, and Illinois — out of their traditional lands north of the Ohio River and into a multitribal region west of Lake Michigan (in present-day Wisconsin). The Iroquois' victory came at a high cost: more than 2,200 warriors dead. To end the bloodshed, in 1701 the Iroquois made treaties with the French as well as the English, a diplomatic maneuver that brought peace for two generations.

The Jesuit Missions. The French priests who sought converts, first among the Hurons and then among their Iroquois conquerors, were members of the Society of Jesus (or Jesuits), a Catholic religious order founded to combat the Protestant Reformation. Between 1625 and 1763, hundreds of French Jesuits lived among the Indian peoples of the Great Lakes region. These priests — to a greater extent than the Spanish Franciscan monks — came to understand and respect the Indians' values. One Jesuit noted the Huron belief that "our souls have desires which are inborn and concealed, yet are made known by means of dreams." For their part, many Indian peoples initially welcomed the French "Black Robes" as powerful spiritual beings with magical secrets, among them the ability to forge iron. But when prayers to the Christian god did not protect them from disease or attack, they grew skeptical. A Peoria chief charged that a priest's "fables are good only in his own country; we have our own [religious beliefs], which do not make us die as his do." In the face of epidemics and droughts, some Indian peoples vented their anger on French missionaries and fur traders. "If you cannot make rain, they speak of nothing less than making away with you," lamented one Jesuit.

Whatever the limits of their spiritual powers, the French Jesuits did not exploit the labor of the Indian peoples. Moreover, they tried to keep brandy, which wreaked havoc among the natives, from becoming a bargaining chip in the French fur trade. Finally, the Jesuits won converts by adapting Christian beliefs to the Indians' needs. In the 1690s, for example, they introduced the cult of the Virgin Mary to the young women of the Illinois people. Its emphasis on chastity reinforced the Algonquian belief that unmarried women were "masters of their own body."

Still, despite the Jesuits' efforts, the French fur-trading system brought cultural devastation to the Indian peoples of the Great Lakes region. Epidemics killed tens of thousands, and Iroquois warriors murdered thousands more. Nor did the Iroquois escape unscathed. In 1666 and again in the 1690s, French armies invaded their land, burned villages and cornfields, and killed many warriors. "Everywhere there was peril and everywhere mourning," recalled an oral Iroquois legend.

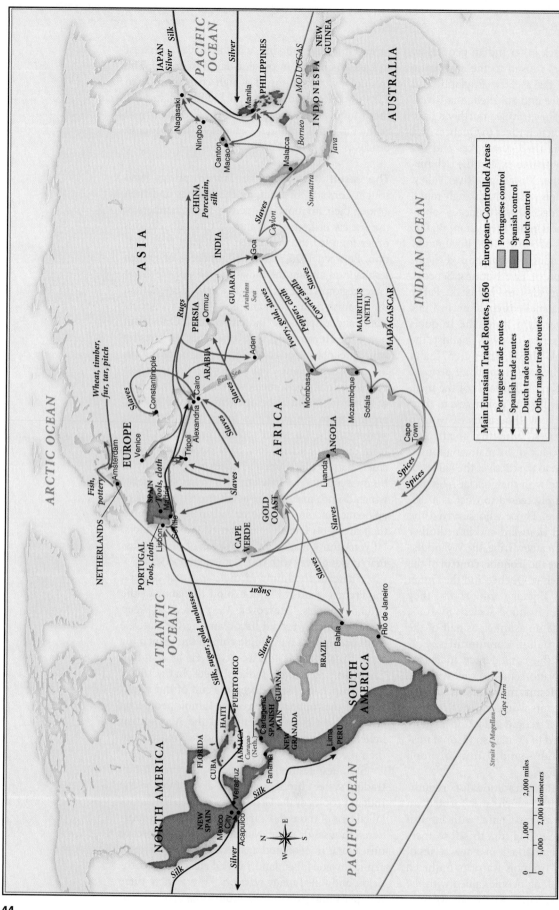

MAP 2.2 The Eurasian Trade System and European Spheres of Influence, 1650

Between 1550 and 1650, Spanish, Portuguese, and Dutch merchants took control of the maritime trade routes between Europe and India, Indonesia, and China. They also created the South Atlantic system (see Chapter 3), which carried slaves, sugar, and manufactured goods between Europe, Africa, and the valuable plantation settlements in Brazil and the Caribbean Islands. (To trace long-term changes in trade and empires, see Map 1.3 on p. 18 and Map 5.1 on p. 139.)

New Netherland: Commerce and Conquest

By 1600, Holland had emerged as the financial and commercial hub of northern Europe. Exploiting the country's strategic location — at the mouth of the great Rhine River and near the Baltic sea — enterprising Dutch merchants controlled the trade in western and northern Europe. In addition, Dutch entrepreneurs dominated the European banking, insurance, and textile industries; and its merchants owned more tons of shipping and employed more sailors than did the combined fleets of England, France, and Spain. Indeed, the Dutch managed much of the world's commerce. During their struggle for independence from Spain (and its Portuguese dependency), the Dutch seized Portuguese forts in Africa, Brazil, and Indonesia, which gave them control of the Atlantic trade in slaves and the Indian Ocean commerce in East Indies spices and Chinese silks (Map 2.2).

In 1609, Dutch merchants, long active in the Baltic and Russian fur trade, dispatched an Eng-lishman, Henry Hudson, to locate a new source of supply in North America. After Hudson explored the river that bears his name, the merchants set up a fur-trading post at Fort Orange (Albany). In 1621, the Dutch government chartered the West India Company and gave it a monopoly over the American fur trade and the West African slave trade. Three years later, the company founded the town of New Amsterdam on Manhattan Island, and made it the capital of New Netherland.

The new colony did not thrive. The population of the Dutch Republic was small — just 1.5 million people, compared to 5 million in Britain and 20 million in France — and relatively prosperous. Consequently, few Dutch settlers moved to the fur-trading posts, which made them vulnerable to rival European nations. To encourage migration, the West India Company granted huge estates along the Hudson River to wealthy Dutchmen with the proviso that each proprietor settle fifty tenants on the land within four years or lose his grant. By 1646, only one proprietor, Kiliaen Van

New Amsterdam, c. 1640

As the wooden palisade suggests, New Amsterdam was a fort-like trading post at the edge of a vast land populated by alien Indian peoples. It was also a pale miniature version of Amsterdam, a city with many canals. The first settlers built houses in the Dutch style, with their gable ends facing the street (notice the two middle houses), and excavated a canal across lower Manhattan Island (New York City's Canal Street today). Library of Congress.

Rensselaer, had succeeded. In 1664, New Netherland had just 5,000 residents, and fewer than half of them were Dutch.

Although the colony failed to attract settlers, it flourished as a fur-trading enterprise. In 1633, Dutch traders at Fort Orange exported thirty thousand beaver and otter pelts. Their success reflected their practice of offering high-quality goods at relatively low prices and the policy of peace they adopted toward the powerful Iroquois. Dutch settlers near New Amsterdam were more aggressive. They seized prime farming land from their Algonquian-speaking neighbors and took over the Indians' trading network, in which corn and wampum from Long Island were exchanged for furs from Maine. The Algonquins responded with force. In the 1640s, in a bloody two-year war, more than two hundred Dutch residents and one thousand Indians died, many of them women, children, and elderly men. During the fighting, the Dutch formed an alliance with the Mohawks, a longtime foe of the Algonquins. Thereafter, the Mohawks controlled Indian access to Albany, and the Mohawk dialect became the language of business in the small fur-trading outpost.

After the crippling Indian war of the 1640s, the West India Company largely ignored New Netherland, focusing instead on the profitable trade in African slaves to sugar plantations in Brazil. In New Amsterdam, Dutch officials ruled shortsightedly. Governor Peter Stuyvesant rejected the demands of English Puritan settlers on Long Island for a representative system of government and alienated the colony's increasingly diverse population of Dutch, English, and Swedish migrants. It is not surprising, then, that the residents of New Amsterdam offered little resistance to English invaders in 1664.

Initially, the Duke of York, the overlord of the new English colony of New York, ruled with a mild hand: He allowed the Dutch residents to retain their property, legal system, and religious institutions. That changed after a Dutch assault in 1673, which momentarily recaptured the colony. In retaliation, the duke's governor, Edmund Andros, shut down the Dutch courts, imposed English law, and demanded an oath of allegiance. Dutch residents avoided the English courts, settling disputes by arbitration, and resisted cultural assimilation by speaking Dutch, marrying among themselves, and worshipping at the Dutch Reformed Church. Once dominant over the Algonquins, the Dutch had themselves become a subject people. As a group of Anglicans noted in 1699, New York "seemed rather like a conquered Foreign Province held by the terror of a Garrison, than an English colony."

> ► How were Spanish, French, and Dutch colonial strategies similar? How did they differ? In what ways were the similarities and differences reflected in the nations' settlements in the New World?

> ► Why did the Five Nations of the Iroquois unite? What were the goals of the confederation? How successful were the Iroquois in achieving those goals?

The English Arrive: The Chesapeake Experience

Unlike their European rivals, the English founded populous colonies in North America. Settlers in the Chesapeake Bay region used force to take possession of Indian lands. They created a society based on tobacco that brought wealth to certain prominent families who ruthlessly pursued their dreams of wealth by exploiting the labor of English indentured servants and African slaves.

Settling the Tobacco Colonies

The first English settlements in North America were organized by minor nobles in the 1580s and by merchants and religious dissidents after 1600. Although the English monarch and ministry approved these ventures, they neither directed nor controlled them. This meant that English colonies, unlike the state-supervised Spanish and French settlements, enjoyed considerable autonomy.

In part because they lacked the direct support of the English government, the ventures of the 1580s were abject failures. Sir Humphrey Gilbert's settlement in Newfoundland collapsed for lack of financing, and Sir Ferdinando Gorges's colony along the coast of Maine floundered because of the harsh climate. Sir Walter Raleigh's three expeditions to North Carolina likewise ended in disaster when the colony on Roanoke Island vanished without a trace. (Roanoke is still known today as the "lost colony.")

Following these failures, merchants took charge of English expansion and, like the French and Dutch, initially focused on trade with the native population. In 1606, King James I (r. 1603–1625) granted to the Virginia Company of London all the

Carolina Indians Fishing, 1585

The artist John White was one of the English settlers in Sir Walter Raleigh's ill-fated colony on Roanoke Island, and his watercolors provide a rich visual record of Native American life. Here the Indians who resided near present-day Albemarle Sound in North Carolina are harvesting a protein-rich diet of fish from its shallow waters. Trustees of the British Museum.

The manner of their fishing.

lands stretching from present-day North Carolina to southern New York. To honor the memory of Elizabeth I, the never-married "Virgin Queen," the company's directors named the region Virginia and promised to "propagate the [true] Christian religion" among the "infidels and Savages" (Map 2.3).

The Jamestown Settlement. Commerce was the Virginia Company's primary goal. The first expedition, in 1607, was limited to male traders — no women, farmers, or ministers — who were the employees or "servants" of the company. The company directed them to procure their own food and to ship gold, exotic crops, and Indian merchandise to England. Some of the traders were young gentlemen with personal ties to the company's shareholders: a bunch of "unruly Sparks, packed off by their Friends to escape worse Destinies at home." Others were cynical men bent on turning a quick profit: All they wanted, one of them said, was to "dig gold, refine gold, load gold."

But there was no gold, and the traders were ill equipped to deal with the new environment. Arriving in Virginia after an exhausting four-month voyage, they settled in May on a swampy, unhealthy peninsula, which they named Jamestown in honor of the king. Because they lacked access to fresh water and refused to plant crops, they quickly died off; only 38 of the 120 traders were alive nine months later. Death rates remained high. By 1611, the Virginia Company had dispatched 1,200 settlers to Jamestown, but fewer than half had survived. "Our men were destroyed with cruell diseases, as Swellings, Fluxes, Burning Fevers, and by warres,"

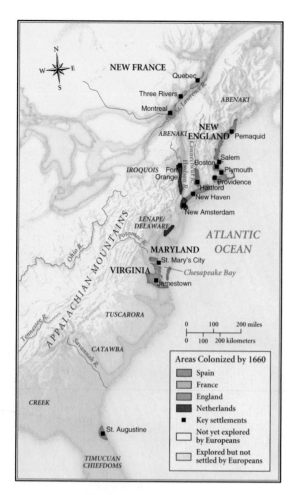

MAP 2.3 Eastern North America, 1650

By 1650, four European nations had permanent settlements along the eastern coast of North America, but only England had substantial numbers of settlers, some 25,000 in New England and another 15,000 in the Chesapeake region. The Europeans also had a presence in the interior, as colonial authorities established diplomatic relations with neighboring Indian peoples and as French and Dutch fur traders carried European goods — and diseases — to distant tribes.

reported one of the settlement's leaders, "but for the most part they died of meere famine."

At first the local Indians were suspicious of the settlers, perhaps because they remembered the violent end to a mission established in the 1570s by Spanish Jesuit missionaries. However, Powhatan, chief of the Algonquian-speaking peoples of the region, treated the English traders as potential allies and a source of valuable goods. A "grave majestical man," according to explorer John Smith, Powhatan allowed his followers — some fourteen thousand people in all — to exchange their corn for English cloth and iron hatchets. To integrate the newcomers peacefully into his chiefdom, Powhatan arranged a

marriage between his daughter Pocahontas and John Rolfe, an English colonist. His tactic failed in part because Rolfe had imported tobacco seed from the West Indies and cultivated the crop, which fetched a high price in England. Eager to become rich by planting tobacco, thousands of English settlers embarked for Virginia. Now Powhatan accused the English of coming "not to trade but to invade my people and possess my country."

To foster the flow of migrants, the Virginia Company instituted new policies. In 1617, it allowed individual settlers to own land, granting one hundred acres to every freeman and allowing those who imported servants to claim an additional fifty acres for every one. The company also issued a "great Charter" that created a system of representative government. The House of Burgesses, which first convened in 1619, could make laws and levy taxes, although the governor and the company council in England could veto its acts. By 1622, land ownership, self-government, and a judicial system based on "the lawes of the realme of England" had attracted some 4,500 new recruits. Virginia was on the verge of becoming a settler colony.

Opechancanough and the Indian Revolt of 1622.
The influx of land-hungry English migrants sparked all-out revolt by the Indian peoples. The uprising was led by a mysterious chief named Opechancanough, who was Powhatan's brother and successor. Some evidence suggests that Opechancanough was taken to Spain as a young man and converted to Catholicism, and that when he returned to Virginia as part of a Jesuit mission, he killed the missionaries. It is certain that thirty years later, in 1609, Opechancanough personally confronted the English invaders, capturing Captain John Smith but sparing his life. Subsequently, the Indian chief "stood aloof" from the English settlers and "would not be drawn to any Treaty." In particular, he resisted proposals to take Indian children from their parents so that they might be "brought upp in Christianytie." When Opechancanough became the main chief in 1621, he assumed a new name, Massatamohtnock, and a new mission: "Before the end of two moons," he told the chief of the Potomacks, "there should not be an Englishman in all their Countries."

Massatamohtnock almost succeeded. In 1622, he coordinated a surprise attack by twelve Indian tribes that killed 347 English settlers, nearly a third of the white population. The English fought back by seizing the Indians' fields and food and, after a decade of intermittent fighting, finally secured the safety of the colony. The victorious settlers sold captured warriors into slavery, "destroy[ing] them who sought to

John Smith and Chief Opechancanough

The powerful Indian chief Opechancanough towers over English explorer John Smith. This engraving depicts the confrontation between the two men in 1609 over English access to Indian supplies of food; the scenes in the background depict the major uprising led by Opechancanough — now called Massatamohtnock — in 1622. Library of Congress.

C: Smith taketh the King of Pamavnkee prisoner 1608

destroy us," and took control of "their cultivated places . . . possessing the fruits of others' labour."

Shocked by the Indian uprising, James I revoked the charter of the Virginia Company and, in 1624, made Virginia a royal colony. Now the king and his ministers appointed the governor and a small advisory council. James retained the House of Burgesses but stipulated that his Privy Council, a committee of leading ministers, must ratify all legislation. The king also decreed the legal establishment of the Church of England, which meant that all property owners had to pay taxes to support its clergy. These institutions — a royal governor, an elected assembly, and an established Anglican church — became the model for royal colonies throughout English America.

Lord Baltimore Settles Catholics in Maryland.

A second tobacco-growing colony developed in neighboring Maryland, but with a different set of insti-

tutions. King Charles I (r. 1625–1649), James's successor, was secretly sympathetic toward Catholicism and had a number of Catholic friends. In 1632, he granted the lands bordering the vast Chesapeake Bay to Cecilius Calvert, a Catholic aristocrat who carried the title Lord Baltimore. As the proprietor of Maryland (named for Queen Henrietta Maria, the king's wife), Baltimore could sell, lease, or give the land away as he pleased. He also had the authority to appoint public officials and to found churches and appoint ministers.

Lord Baltimore wanted Maryland to become a refuge for Catholics, who were subject to persecution in England. In 1634, twenty gentlemen, mostly Catholics, and two hundred artisans and laborers, mostly Protestants, established St. Mary's City, which overlooked the mouth of the Potomac River. To minimize religious confrontations, the proprietor instructed the governor (his brother, Leonard Calvert) to allow "no scandall nor offence to be given to any of the Protestants" and to "cause

All Acts of Romane Catholicque Religion to be done as privately as may be."

Maryland's population grew quickly because the Calverts imported scores of artisans and offered ample grants of land to wealthy migrants. But political conflict constantly threatened the colony's stability. When Governor Calvert violated the charter by governing without the "Advice, Assent, and Approbation" of the freemen, they elected a representative assembly. The assembly insisted on the right to initiate legislation, which Lord Baltimore grudgingly granted. Anti-Catholic agitation by Protestant settlers also endangered Maryland's religious mission. To protect his coreligionists, who remained a minority, Lord Baltimore persuaded the assembly to enact the Toleration Act (1649), which granted all Christians the right to follow their own religious beliefs and hold church services.

Tobacco and Disease. In Maryland, as in Virginia, tobacco quickly became the basis of the economy. Indians had long used tobacco as a medicine and a stimulant, and the English came to crave the nicotine it contained. By the 1620s, they were smoking, chewing, and snorting tobacco with abandon. James I initially condemned tobacco as a "vile Weed" whose "black stinking fumes" were "baleful to the nose, harmful to the brain, and dangerous to the lungs." But the king's attitude changed as taxes on imported tobacco bolstered the royal treasury.

European demand for tobacco set off a forty-year economic boom in the Chesapeake region. "All our riches for the present do consist in tobacco," a planter remarked in 1630. Exports rose from about 3 million pounds in 1640 to 10 million pounds in 1660. Newly arrived planters moved up the river valleys, establishing large plantations a good distance from one another but easily reached by water.

Despite the economic boom, life in the Chesapeake colonies was harsh. The scarcity of towns deprived settlers of community (Map 2.4). Families were equally scarce because there were few women settlers, and marriages often ended with the death of a young spouse. Pregnant women were especially vulnerable to malaria, which was spread by the mosquitoes that flourished in the warm climate (Table 2.2). Many mothers died after bearing a first or second child, so that orphaned children (along with unmarried young men) formed a large segment of the society. Sixty percent of the children born in Middlesex County, Virginia, before 1680, lost one or both of their parents by the time they were thirteen. Although 15,000 English migrants arrived in Virginia between 1622 and 1640, the population during that period rose only from 2,000 to 8,000.

The Tobacco Economy

Most farmers in Virginia — poor and rich — raised tobacco. Wealthy planters used indentured servants and slaves, like those pictured here, to grow and process the crop. The workers cured the tobacco stalks by hanging them for several months in a well-ventilated shed; then they stripped the leaves and packed them tightly into large plantation-made barrels, or hogsheads, for shipment to Europe. Library of Congress.

Masters, Servants, and Slaves

Despite the difficulty of life in the Chesapeake region, the prospect of owning land lured migrants there. By 1700, more than 100,000 Englishmen and -women had come to Virginia and Maryland, most as indentured servants. English shipping registers reveal their backgrounds. Three-quarters of the 5,000 indentured servants who embarked from the port of Bristol were young men, many of them displaced by the enclosure of their village lands (see Chapter 1). They came to Bristol searching for work; and, once there, they were persuaded by merchants and sea captains to sign labor contracts. The indentures bound the men — and a much smaller number of women — to work for a master in the Chesapeake

MAP 2.4 River Plantations in Virginia, c. 1640

The first migrants settled in widely dispersed plantations — and different disease environments — along the James River. The growth of the tobacco economy promoted this pattern: Wealthy planter-merchants would trade with English ship captains from their riverfront plantations. Consequently, few substantial towns or trading centers developed in the Chesapeake region.

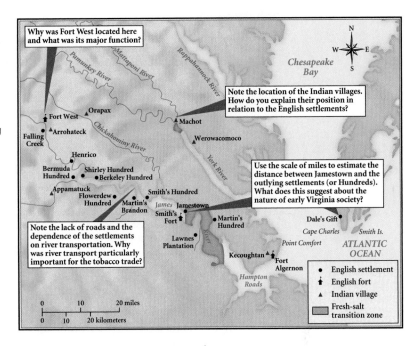

colonies for four or five years, after which they would be free to marry and work for themselves.

Indentured Life. For merchants, servants were valuable cargo: Their contracts fetched high prices from Chesapeake planters. For the plantation owners, they were an incredible bargain. During the tobacco boom, a male servant could produce five times his purchase price in a single year. To ensure maximum production, most masters ruled their servants strictly, beating them for bad behavior and withholding permission to marry. If servants ran away or became pregnant, masters went to court to increase the term of their service. Female servants were especially vulnerable to abuse. As a Virginia law of 1692 stated, "dissolute masters have gotten their maids with child; and yet claim the benefit of their service." Planters got rid of uncooperative servants by selling their contracts to new masters. As one Englishman remarked in disgust, in Virginia "servants were sold up and down like horses."

Most indentured servants did not escape from poverty. Half the men died before completing the term of their contract, and another quarter

TABLE 2.2 Environment, Disease, and Death in Virginia, 1618–1624

Zones of James River Estuary	Colony Population in Zone (percent)	Annual Mortality in Zone (percent)	Proportion of All Deaths in Colony (percent)
Freshwater	28.5	16.7	6.9
Freshwater/saltwater	49.3	27.1	64.6
Saltwater	22.2	23.3	18.4

Early Virginia was a deadly place. Historians estimate that at least 28 percent of the population died each year, most of typhoid fever and dysentery (the "bloody flux"). Only a constant stream of migrants allowed the population of the colony to grow at all. Most settlers lived along the James River estuary, but their location along the river determined their chance of survival. The most dangerous environment was the zone with a mix of freshwater and salt water. The influx of salt water during the dry summer months trapped human and animal waste from upriver and contaminated the water and its fish, oysters, and crabs. The year-round saltwater zone was the next most deadly, both because of fecal contamination and because of salt poisoning from drinking brackish well water.

SOURCE: Adapted from Carville V. Earle, "Environment, Disease, and Mortality in Early Virginia," in *The Chesapeake in the Seventeenth Century*, ed. Thad W. Tate and David L. Ammerman (New York: W. W. Norton, 1979), table 3.

TABLE 2.3 Indentured Servants in the Chesapeake Labor Force, 1640–1700

Decade Ending	White Population	White Population in Labor Force (percent)	White Labor Force	White Servant Population	White Servants in Labor Force (percent)
1640	8,000	75	6,000	1,790	30
1660	24,000	66	15,800	4,300	27
1680	55,600	58	32,300	5,500	17
1700	85,200	46	38,900	3,800	10

The population of the Chesapeake increased more than tenfold between 1640 and 1700, and its character changed significantly. As more women migrated to Virginia and bore children, the percentage of the population in the labor force fell dramatically, from 75 percent to 46 percent. So did the region's reliance on indentured servants: In 1640, white servants made up about 30 percent of the labor force; by 1700, they accounted for just 10 percent.

SOURCE: Adapted from Christopher Tomlins, "Reconsidering Indentured Servitude" (unpublished paper, 2001), table 3.

although freed remained poor. Only a quarter acquired the property and respectability they had been looking for (Table 2.3). Female servants generally fared better. Men in the Chesapeake had grown "very sensible of the Misfortune of Wanting Wives," so many female servants married well-established men. By migrating to the Chesapeake, these few — and very fortunate — men and women escaped a life of landless poverty in England.

African Laborers. Fate was equally mixed for the first African workers in the Chesapeake colonies. In 1619, John Rolfe noted that "a Dutch man of warre . . . sold us twenty Negars." But for a generation, the number of Africans in the region remained small. About 400 Africans lived in the Chesapeake colonies in 1649, just 2 percent of the population; by 1670, only 5 percent of the population was black. Although many Africans served their English masters for life, they were not legally enslaved. English **common law** did not acknowledge **chattel slavery,** the ownership of a human being as property. Moreover, some of these African workers came from the Kingdom of Kongo, where Portuguese missionaries had converted the king to Christianity, and they had some knowledge of European ways. By calculation, hard work, or conversion to Christianity, many of these first African laborers found a way to escape their bondage. Some ambitious African freemen in the Chesapeake region even purchased slaves, bought the labor contracts of white servants, or married Englishwomen.

This mobility for Africans came to an end in the 1660s with the collapse of the tobacco boom. Tobacco had once sold for 24 pence a pound; now it fetched just a tenth of that. The "low price of Tobacco requires it should bee made as cheap as possible," declared Virginia planter Nicholas Spencer, and "blacks can make it cheaper than whites." As the English-born elite imported fewer English servants and more African slaves, Chesapeake legislatures grew more conscious of race and enacted laws undercutting the status of blacks. By 1671, the Virginia House of Burgesses had forbidden Africans to own guns or join the militia. It also had barred them — "tho baptized and enjoying their own Freedom" — from buying the labor contracts of white servants and from winning their freedom by converting to Christianity. Being black was now a mark of inferior legal status, and slavery was becoming a permanent and hereditary condition. As an English clergyman observed, "These two words, Negro and Slave had by custom grown Homogeneous and convertible."

The Seeds of Social Revolt

As the tobacco boom went bust in the 1660s, long-standing social conflicts flared into political turmoil. The drop in tobacco prices stemmed primarily from an imbalance in the market: A rapid increase in production was outstripping limited demand. But it also reflected Parliament's decision in 1651 to pass the Act of Trade and Navigation and to add new provisions in 1660 and 1663. The Navigation Acts allowed only English or colonial-owned ships to enter American ports, thereby excluding Dutch merchants, who paid the highest prices for tobacco, sold the best goods, and provided the cheapest shipping services. They also required the colonists to ship tobacco and other "enumerated articles" (including sugar) only to England, where monarchs continually raised import duties, stifling the profitability of the market. By the 1670s, tobacco planters were getting just a penny a pound for their crop.

Despite low prices, tobacco exports from the region doubled between 1670 and 1700. The reason was simple: As the Chesapeake region's population increased, so did the number of planters. Lacking another cash crop, they planted tobacco, which provided yeomen families with just enough to scrape by. Worse off were newly freed indentured servants, who could not earn enough to buy tools and seed or to pay the fees required to claim their fifty-acre head rights. Many ex-servants had to sell their labor again, either by signing new indentures or becoming wage workers or tenant farmers.

Increasingly, an elite of planter-merchants dominated the Chesapeake colonies. Like the English gentry, they prospered from the ownership of large estates that they leased to the growing population of former servants. Many well-to-do planters also became commercial middlemen and moneylenders. They set up retail stores and charged commissions for shipping the tobacco produced by yeomen farmers to merchants in England. This elite accumulated nearly half the land in Virginia by securing grants from royal governors. In Maryland, well-connected Catholic planters were equally powerful; by 1720, one of those planters, Charles Carroll, owned 47,000 acres of land, which he farmed with the labor of scores of tenants, indentured servants, and slaves.

Bacon's Rebellion

As these aggressive planter-entrepreneurs confronted a multitude of young, landless laborers, political and social conflict rocked Virginia during the 1670s. This violent struggle left a contradictory legacy: a decrease in class conflict among whites and greater reliance on black slaves, which greatly intensified hostility between Europeans and Africans.

The Corrupt Regime of Governor William Berkeley. William Berkeley first served as governor of Virginia between 1642 and 1652, and played a key role in suppressing a second major Indian uprising in 1644. Appointed governor again in 1660, Berkeley bestowed large land grants on members of his council. The councilors promptly exempted their lands from taxation and appointed their friends as local justices of the peace and county judges. To suppress dissent in the House of Burgesses, Berkeley bought off legislators with land grants and lucrative appointments as sheriffs, tax collectors, and estate appraisers. Unrest increased when the corrupt Burgesses changed the voting system to exclude landless freemen, who by now constituted half the adult white men in the colony. Property-holding yeomen retained the vote; but frustrated by falling tobacco prices, rising taxes, and political corruption, they were no longer willing to support Berkeley and the landed gentry.

An Indian conflict lit the flame of social rebellion. When the English intruded into Virginia in 1607 there were 30,000 Native Americans living there; by 1675, the number of Indians had dwindled to a mere 3,500. By comparison, the number of Europeans had multiplied to 38,000 and the number of Africans to about 2,500. Most Indians lived on treaty-guaranteed territory along the frontier, land that was now coveted by impoverished white **freeholders** and aspiring tenants. They demanded that the natives be expelled or exterminated. Opposition came from wealthy planters along the seacoast, who wanted a ready supply of tenant farmers and wage laborers, and from Berkeley and the planter-merchants, who traded with the Native Americans for furs.

Fighting broke out late in 1675, when a band of Virginia militiamen murdered thirty Indians. Defying Berkeley's orders, a larger force of one thousand militiamen then surrounded a fortified Susquehannock village and killed five chiefs who had come out to negotiate. The Susquehannocks, recent migrants from present-day northern Pennsylvania, retaliated by raiding outlying plantations and killing three hundred whites. To avoid an Indian war, Berkeley proposed a defensive military strategy—a series of frontier forts to deter Indian intrusions. The settlers dismissed this scheme as useless. They also questioned Berkeley's motivation, insisting his plan was simply a plot by planters and merchants to impose high taxes and take "all our tobacco into their own hands."

Nathaniel Bacon, Rebel Leader. Nathaniel Bacon emerged as the leader of the rebels. A young English migrant, Bacon had settled on a frontier estate and his English connections had secured him an appointment to the governor's council. Because of his considerable wealth and commanding personal presence, Bacon also commanded the respect of his neighbors. When Berkeley refused to grant Bacon a military commission to lead an attack on nearby Indians, the headstrong planter marched a force of frontiersmen against the Indians anyway and slaughtered some of the peaceful Doeg people. Condemning the frontiersmen as "rebels and mutineers," Berkeley expelled Bacon from the council and had him arrested. But Bacon's men quickly won his release and forced the governor to hold legislative elections. The newly elected House of Burgesses enacted far-reaching political reforms that curbed the powers of the governor and the council and restored voting rights to landless freemen.

These much-needed reforms came too late. Bacon remained bitter toward Berkeley, and the poor farmers and indentured servants that he now led resented years of exploitation by wealthy planters and arrogant justices of the peace. As one yeoman rebel complained, "A poor man who has only his labour to maintain himself and his family pays as much [in taxes] as a man who has 20,000 acres." Backed by four hundred armed men, Bacon issued a "Manifesto and Declaration of the People" that

Nathaniel Bacon

Condemned as a rebel and a traitor in his own time, Nathaniel Bacon emerged in the late nineteenth century as an American hero, a harbinger of the Patriots of 1776. This stained-glass window probably was designed by famed jeweler and glassmaker Tiffany & Co. of New York. It was installed in a Virginia church, endowing Bacon with semisacred status. The Association for the Preservation of Virginia Antiquities.

demanded the death or removal of all Indians and an end to the rule of wealthy "parasites." "All the power and sway is got into the hands of the rich," Bacon proclaimed, as his army burned Jamestown to the ground and plundered the plantations of Berkeley's allies. When Bacon died suddenly of dysentery in October 1676, the governor took his revenge, dispersing the rebel army, seizing the estates of well-to-do rebels, and hanging twenty-three men.

Bacon's Rebellion was a pivotal event in the history of Virginia and the Chesapeake. Thereafter, landed planters retained their dominance by curbing corruption and appointing ambitious yeomen to public office. They appeased the lower social orders by cutting taxes and supporting white expansion onto Indian lands. Most important, the uprising confirmed the planters' growing reliance on African

slaves. To forestall another rebellion by poor whites, Chesapeake planters turned away from indentured servants; in 1705, the Burgesses explicitly legalized chattel slavery, and planters began importing thousands of African laborers. Those fateful decisions committed subsequent generations of Americans to a social system based on racial exploitation.

> ➤ What were the special characteristics of the population of Virginia in the seventeenth century and what accounted for them?

> ➤ What were the various systems of forced labor that took hold in the Chesapeake colonies?

> ➤ Compare the Indian uprising in Virginia in 1622 with Bacon's Rebellion in 1675. What were the consequences of each for Virginia's economic and social development?

Puritan New England

As the scramble for wealth escalated in the Chesapeake, 500 miles to the north Puritan settlers created colonies with a strong moral dimension. Between 1620 and 1640, thousands of Puritans fled to America in what was both a worldly quest for land and a spiritual quest to preserve the "pure" Christian faith. By distributing land broadly, the Puritans set out to build a society of independent farm families. And by establishing a "holy commonwealth" in America, they hoped to reform the Church of England. Although sharp conflicts over religious dogma ultimately led to the founding of a number of different colonies, all New England Puritans defined their mission in spiritual terms. Indeed, their "errand into the wilderness" gave a moral dimension to American history that survives today.

The Puritan Migration

New England differed from other European colonies in America. Unruly male adventurers founded New Spain and Jamestown, and male traders dominated life in New France and New Netherland. By contrast, the leaders of the Plymouth and Massachusetts Bay colonies were pious Protestants, and the settlers there included women and children as well as men (Map 2.5).

The Pilgrims. The Pilgrims who settled in Plymouth were religious separatists, Puritans who had left the Church of England. When King James I threatened to drive Puritans "out of the land, or else do worse," the Pilgrims left England and lived among Dutch Calvinists in Holland. Subsequently,

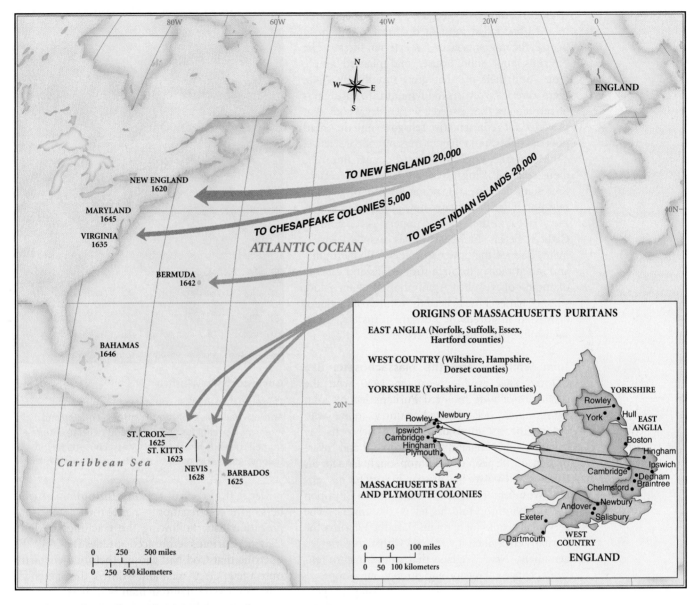

MAP 2.5   The Puritan Migration to America, 1620–1640

Forty-five thousand Puritans left England between 1620 and 1640, but they created religious societies only in the New England colonies of Plymouth, Massachusetts Bay, and Connecticut. Within New England, migrants from the three major centers of English Puritanism — Yorkshire, East Anglia, and the West Country — commonly settled among those from their own region. They named American communities after their English towns of origin and practiced their traditional regional customs. Thus settlers from Rowley in Yorkshire transplanted their system of open-field agriculture to Rowley in Massachusetts Bay.

thirty-five of these exiles resolved to migrate to America to maintain their English identity. Led by William Bradford and joined by sixty-seven migrants from England, they sailed to America in 1620 aboard the *Mayflower* and settled near Cape Cod in southeastern Massachusetts. Lacking a royal charter, they created their own covenant of government, the Mayflower Compact, to "combine ourselves together into a civill body politick." The Compact, the first American constitution, used the

Puritans' self-governing religious congregation as the model for its political structure.

The first winter in Plymouth tested the Pilgrims. Like the early settlers in Virginia, the Pilgrims faced hunger and disease: Of the 102 migrants who arrived in November, only half survived until spring. But then Plymouth became a healthy and thriving community. The cold climate inhibited the spread of mosquito-borne diseases, and the Pilgrims' religious discipline established a strong work ethic. Moreover, because a smallpox epidemic in 1618 had killed most of the local Wampanoag people, the migrants faced few external threats. The Pilgrims built solid houses and planted ample crops, and their number grew rapidly. By 1640, there were 3,000 settlers in Plymouth. To ensure political stability, they issued a written legal code that provided for representative self-government, broad political rights, and religious freedom of conscience.

Meanwhile, England plunged deeper into religious turmoil. King Charles I repudiated certain Protestant doctrines, including the role of grace in salvation. English Puritans, now powerful in Parliament, accused the king of "popery"—of holding Catholic beliefs. In 1629, Charles dissolved Parliament, claimed the power to rule by "divine right," and raised money through royal edicts and the sale of monopolies. When Archbishop William Laud, whom Charles chose to head the Church of England, dismissed hundreds of Puritan ministers, thousands of Puritans fled to America.

John Winthrop and the Massachusetts Bay Colony. That exodus began in 1630 with the departure of nine hundred Puritans led by John Winthrop, a well-educated country squire who became the first governor of the Massachusetts Bay colony. Calling England morally corrupt and "overburdened with people," Winthrop sought land for his children and a place in Christian history for his people. "We must consider that we shall be as a City upon a Hill," Winthrop told his fellow passengers. "The eyes of all people are upon us." Like the Pilgrims, the Puritans envisioned a reformed Christian society, a genuinely "New" England that would inspire religious change in England and throughout Europe.

Winthrop and his associates established the government of the Massachusetts Bay Colony in the town of Boston. They transformed their **joint-stock corporation**, the General Court of shareholders, into a representative political system with a governor, council, and assembly. To ensure rule by the godly, the Puritans limited the right to vote and hold office to men who were church members. Ignoring the policy of religious tolerance in Plymouth Colony, they established Puritanism as the state-supported religion, barred other faiths from conducting services, and used the Bible as a legal guide. "Where there is no Law," the colony's government declared, magistrates should rule "as near the law of God as they can." Over the next decade, about ten thousand Puritans migrated to the colony, along with ten thousand others fleeing hard times in England.

In establishing churches, New England Puritans tried to recreate the simplicity of the first Christians. They eliminated bishops and placed

Governor John Winthrop

This portrait, painted in the style of Flemish artist Anthony Van Dyke, captures Winthrop's gravity and intensity. His religious orthodoxy and belief in elite rule shaped the early history of the Massachusetts Bay Colony. Courtesy American Antiquarian Society, Worcester.

power in the hands of the laity, the ordinary members of the congregation—hence their name, Congregationalists. Following the teachings of John Calvin, Puritans embraced predestination, the doctrine that God had chosen (before their birth) only a few "elect" men and women, the Saints, for salvation. Many church members lived in great anxiety, uncertain that God had selected them.

Puritans dealt with this uncertainty in three ways. Some congregations stressed the conversion experience, the intense spiritual sensation of being born again upon receiving God's grace. Other Puritans focused on preparation, the confidence in salvation that came from years of spiritual guidance from their ministers. Still others believed that God considered the Puritans his chosen people, the new Israelites, who would be saved if they obeyed his laws (see Reading American Pictures, "Skeletons and Angels: Exploring Colonial New England Cemeteries," p. 58).

Roger Williams and Rhode Island. To maintain God's favor, the Puritan magistrates of Massachusetts Bay purged their society of religious dissidents. One target was Roger Williams, the minister of the Puritan church in Salem, a coastal town north of Boston. Williams endorsed the Pilgrim's separation of church and state in Plymouth, condemning the legal establishment of Congregationalism in Massachusetts Bay. He taught that political magistrates had authority over only the "bodies, goods, and outward estates of men," not their spiritual lives. Moreover, the Salem minister questioned the Puritans' seizure of Indian lands. The magistrates banished him from the colony in 1636.

Williams and his followers settled about fifty miles south of Boston, founding the town of Providence on land purchased from the Narragansett Indians. Other religious dissidents settled nearby at Portsmouth and Newport. In 1644, the settlers obtained a corporate charter from Parliament for a new colony — Rhode Island — with full authority "to rule themselves." In Rhode Island as in Plymouth, there was no legally established church: Every congregation was independent, and individuals could worship God as they pleased.

Anne Hutchinson. Puritan magistrates in Massachusetts Bay also felt their authority threatened by Anne Hutchinson, the wife of a merchant and a mother of seven who worked as a midwife. Hutchinson held weekly prayer meetings for women in her house and accused various Boston clergymen of placing too much emphasis on good behavior. Recalling Martin Luther's rejection of indulgences, Hutchinson denied that salvation could be earned through good deeds. She insisted that there was no "covenant of works," that God bestowed salvation through the "covenant of grace." Moreover, Hutchinson declared that God "revealed" divine truth directly to the individual believer, a doctrine the Puritan magistrates denounced as heretical.

The magistrates also resented Hutchinson because of her sex. Like other Christians, Puritans believed that both men and women could be saved, but gender equality stopped there. They believed that women were inferior to men in earthly affairs, and so instructed married women: "Thy desires shall bee subject to thy husband, and he shall rule over thee." They likewise denied women significant roles within the church. According to John Robinson, a Pilgrim minister, women "are debarred by their sex from ordinary prophesying, and from any other dealing in the church wherein they take authority over the man." Puritan women could not be ministers or lay preachers, and they had no vote in the congregation.

In 1637, the magistrates put Hutchinson on trial for teaching that inward grace freed an individual from the rules of the church. Hutchinson defended her views with great skill; even Winthrop admitted that she was "a woman of fierce and haughty courage." But the judges scolded her for not attending to "her household affairs, and such things as belong to women" and found her guilty of holding heretical views. Banished, she followed Roger Williams into exile in Rhode Island.

These coercive policies in Winthrop's colony, along with the desire for better farm land, prompted some Puritans to migrate to the Connecticut River Valley. In 1636, pastor Thomas Hooker and his congregation established the town of Hartford, and other Puritans settled along the river at Wethersfield and Windsor. In 1662, they secured a charter from King Charles II (r. 1660–1685) for a self-governing colony. Like Massachusetts Bay, the Connecticut plan of government provided for a legally established church and an elected governor and assembly; however, it granted voting rights to most propertyowning men, not just church members as in the original Puritan colony.

The English Puritan Revolution. As Puritan migrants established colonies in America, England fell into a religious war. When Archbishop Laud imposed a Church of England prayer book on Presbyterian Scotland in 1642, a Scottish army invaded England. Thousands of English Puritans (and hundreds of American Puritans) joined the invaders, demanding reform of the established church and greater authority for Parliament. After several years of civil war, the parliamentary forces led by Oliver Cromwell were victorious. In 1649, Parliament executed King Charles I, proclaimed a republican commonwealth, and banished bishops and elaborate rituals from the Church of England.

The Puritan triumph was short-lived. Popular support for the Commonwealth ebbed, especially after 1653, when Cromwell took dictatorial control. After his death in 1658, moderate Protestants and a resurgent aristocracy restored the monarchy and the hierarchy of bishops. For many Puritans, Charles II's accession in 1660 represented the victory of the Antichrist, the false prophet described in the final book of the New Testament.

For the Puritans in America, the restoration of the monarchy began a new phase of their "errand into the wilderness." They had come to New England to preserve the "pure" Christian church, expecting to return to Europe in triumph. When the failure of the English Revolution dashed that sacred mission, Puritan ministers exhorted their congregations to create a holy society in America.

Puritanism and Witchcraft

Like Native Americans, Puritans believed that the physical world was full of supernatural forces. Devout Christians saw signs of God's (or Satan's) power in blazing stars, birth defects, and other unusual events. Noting that the houses of many ministers "had been

Skeletons and Angels: Exploring Colonial New England Cemeteries

Susanna Jayne, died 1776, Marblehead, Massachusetts.
Peabody Essex Museum, Salem, Massachusetts.

Elder Robert Murray, died December 13, 1790, Old Hill Burial Ground,
Newburyport, Massachusetts. From the collection of photographs *New England
Gravestones*, vol. 1772–1778, copyright Jenn Marcelais.

Before 1800, New England was a much healthier place than Europe. As the text explains, most Puritan infants who survived past one year—especially before 1730—lived into their sixties. Yet when historians ventured into American cemeteries, they found that Puritan gravestones often depicted death in terrifying terms. Surprisingly, after 1730, as epidemics ravaged growing colonial cities and densely populated farming towns, and death rates rose, the images on gravestones became less frightening. How do we reconcile the statistical and visual evidence?

ANALYZING THE EVIDENCE

➤ Look at Susanna Jayne's gravestone. Why do you think the Puritans used such terrifying images? Do those images carry a religious message? What clues can you find on the stone about Puritan culture?

➤ How does Elder Murray's gravestone reflect the changing image of death in the eighteenth century? How would you relate this shift in imagery to changes in Puritan religious beliefs?

➤ The angel curved on the 1790 gravestone bears Elder Murray's face. It was not uncommon to reproduce an image of the person who had died on his or her grave-stone. Why do you think a family would choose to use a personal image on a gravestone? Could you argue that the need to personalize a gravestone reflects the rise of American individualism? Why or why not?

➤ There are thousands of antique gravestone in New England cemeteries, the work of scores of carvers, and you can find photographs of many of them on the Web. One good resource is **www.gravematter. com**. What patterns do you see in the images? How would a historian prove that a hypothesis — for example, the use of personal images on gravestones increased with the rise of individualism — is sound?

smitten with Lightning," Cotton Mather, a prominent Puritan theologian, wondered "what the meaning of God should be in it."

This belief in "spirits" stemmed in part from Christian teachings—the Catholic belief in miracles, for example, and the Protestant faith in grace. It also reflected a pagan influence. When Samuel Sewall, a well-educated Puritan merchant and judge, moved into a new house, he fended off evil spirits by driving a metal pin into the floor. Thousands of ordinary Puritan farmers followed the pagan astrological charts—they were printed in almanacs—to determine the best times to plant crops, marry, and make other important decisions.

Zealous ministers attacked these beliefs and practices as "superstition" and condemned the "cunning" individuals who claimed special powers as healers or prophets. Indeed, many Christians believed these conjurers were Satan's "wizards" or "witches." The people of Andover, one of the Massachusetts Bay settlements, "were much addicted to sorcery," claimed one observer, and "there were forty men in it that could raise the Devil as well as any astrologer." Between 1647 and 1662, civil authorities in New England hanged fourteen people for witchcraft, mostly older women accused of being "double-tongued" or of having "an unruly spirit."

The most dramatic episode of witch-hunting occurred in Salem in 1692. It began when several young girls experienced strange seizures and then accused various neighbors of bewitching them. When judges at the trials allowed the use of "spectral" evidence—visions seen only by the girls—the accusations spun out of control. Eventually, Massachusetts Bay authorities arrested and tried 175 people for the crime of witchcraft and executed nineteen of them. The causes of this mass hysteria were complex and are still debated. Some historians point to group rivalries: Many of the accusers were the daughters or servants of poor farmers in a rural area of Salem, whereas many of the alleged witches were wealthier church members or their friends. Because eighteen of those put to death were women, other historians claim the trials and executions were part of the broader Puritan effort to subordinate women. Still other scholars focus on political instability in Massachusetts Bay in the early 1690s (see Chapter 3) and fears raised by recent Indian attacks in nearby Maine, in which the parents of some of the young accusers had been killed.

Whatever the cause, the Salem witch-hunts marked a turning point. Many settlers were horrified by the executions, a response that discouraged additional legal prosecutions. Another reason for the demise of witchcraft accusations in New England was the influence of the European Enlightenment,

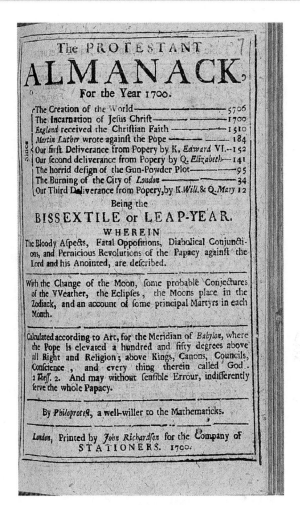

The Protestant Almanack, 1700

The conflict between Protestants and Catholics took many forms. To reinforce the religious identity of English Protestants, the Company of Stationers published a yearly almanac that charted not only the passage of the seasons but also the "Pernicious Revolutions of the Papacy against the Lord and his Anointed." By permission of the Syndics of Cambridge University Library.

a major intellectual movement that began around 1675 and promoted a rational, scientific view of the world. Increasingly, educated people explained accidents and sudden deaths by reference to the "laws of nature." In contrast to Cotton Mather (1663–1728), who believed that lightning might be a supernatural sign, Benjamin Franklin and other well-read men of the next generation would conceive of lightning as a natural phenomenon.

A Yeoman Society, 1630–1700

In building their communities, New England Puritans consciously rejected the feudal practices of traditional European society. They had "escaped out of the pollutions of the world," declared the

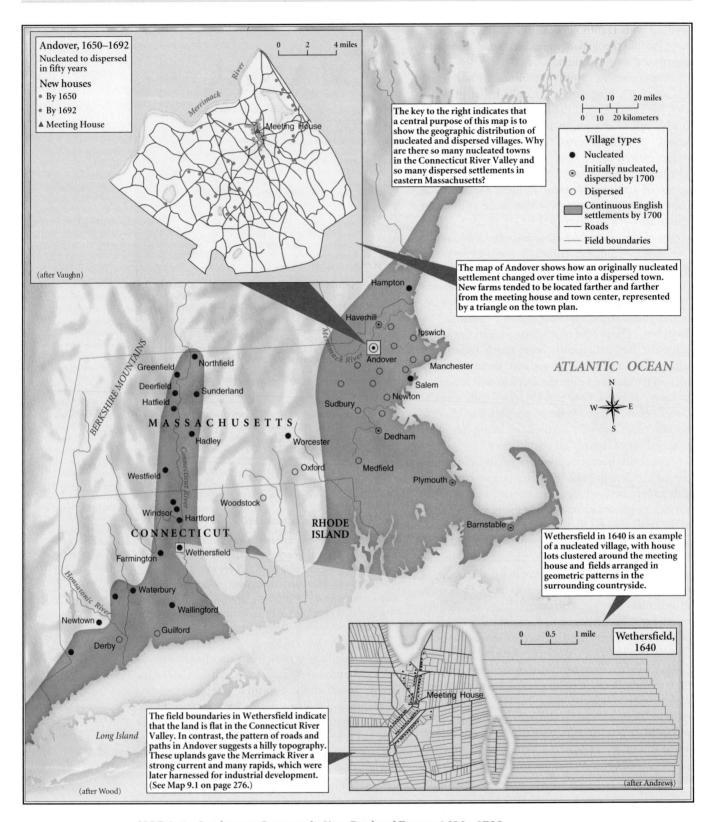

The key to the right indicates that a central purpose of this map is to show the geographic distribution of nucleated and dispersed villages. Why are there so many nucleated towns in the Connecticut River Valley and so many dispersed settlements in eastern Massachusetts?

The map of Andover shows how an originally nucleated settlement changed over time into a dispersed town. New farms tended to be located farther and farther from the meeting house and town center, represented by a triangle on the town plan.

Wethersfield in 1640 is an example of a nucleated village, with house lots clustered around the meeting house and fields arranged in geometric patterns in the surrounding countryside.

The field boundaries in Wethersfield indicate that the land is flat in the Connecticut River Valley. In contrast, the pattern of roads and paths in Andover suggests a hilly topography. These uplands gave the Merrimack River a strong current and many rapids, which were later harnessed for industrial development. (See Map 9.1 on page 276.)

Andover, 1650–1692
Nucleated to dispersed in fifty years
New houses
● By 1650
● By 1692
▲ Meeting House

(after Vaughn)

Village types
● Nucleated
◉ Initially nucleated, dispersed by 1700
○ Dispersed
▢ Continuous English settlements by 1700
— Roads
— Field boundaries

Wethersfield, 1640

(after Andrews)

(after Wood)

MAP 2.6   Settlement Patterns in New England Towns, 1630–1700

Initially, most Puritan towns were compact: Regardless of the local topography — hills or plains — families lived close to one another in the village center and traveled daily to work in the surrounding fields. This pattern is clearly apparent in the 1640 map of Wethersfield, which is situated on the broad plains of the Connecticut River Valley. The first settlers in Andover, Massachusetts, also chose to live in the village center. However, the rugged topography of eastern Massachusetts encouraged the townspeople to disperse; and by 1692, many Andover residents were living on their own farms.

An Affluent Puritan Woman
This well-known painting (c. 1671) of Elizabeth Freake and her daughter, Mary, is perhaps the finest portrait we have of a seventeenth-century American. The skill of the artist, probably a visiting English portraitist, and the finery of Mrs. Freake's dress and bonnet suggest the growing cosmopolitanism and prosperity of Boston's merchant community. Worcester Art Museum.

settlers of Watertown in Massachusetts Bay, and vowed "to sit down . . . close togither." They refused to live as tenants of wealthy aristocrats or submit to oppressive taxation by a distant government. Instead, the General Courts of Massachusetts Bay and Connecticut bestowed the title to each township on a group of settlers, or **proprietors**, who then distributed the land among the male heads of families.

Widespread ownership of land did not mean equality of wealth or status. "G.od had Ordained different degrees and orders of men," proclaimed Boston merchant John Saffin, "some to be Masters and Commanders, others to be Subjects, and to be commanded." Town proprietors normally awarded the largest plots to men of high social status, who often became selectmen and justices of the peace. However, all families received some land, and most adult men had a vote in the **town meeting**, the main institution of local government (Map 2.6).

In this society of independent households and self-governing communities, ordinary farmers had much more political power than Chesapeake yeomen and European peasants did. Although Nathaniel Fish was one of the poorest men in the town of Barnstable—he owned just a two-room cottage, eight acres of land, an ox, and a cow—he was a voting member of the town meeting. Each year, Fish and other Barnstable farmers levied taxes, enacted ordinances governing fencing and road building, regulated the use of common fields for grazing livestock, and chose the selectmen who managed town affairs. Moreover, they selected the town's representatives to the General Court, which gradually displaced the governor as the center of political authority. For Fish and thousands of other ordinary settlers, New England had proved to be the promised land, a new world of opportunity.

➤ What problems did the Puritans have with the Church of England? What beliefs made the Puritans different?

➤ The Puritans of Massachusetts Bay had fled an established church and religious persecution in England. Why, then, did they promptly establish their own church and persecute dissenters?

➤ Describe the political structure that developed in the New England colonies. What was the relationship between local government and the Puritan churches?

The Eastern Indians' New World

Native Americans along the Atlantic coast of North America also lived in a new world, but for them it was a bleak and dangerous place. Europeans had invaded their lands, introduced deadly diseases, and erected hundreds of permanent settlements. Some Indian peoples, among them the Pequots in New England and the Susquehannocks in Virginia, resisted the invaders by force. Others, most prominently the Iroquois, used European guns and manufactures to dominate other tribes. Still other native peoples retreated into the mountains or moved west to preserve their traditional cultures.

Puritans and Pequots

As the Puritans embarked for New England, they pondered the morality of intruding on Native American lands. "By what right or warrant can we enter into the land of the Savages?" they asked themselves. Responding to such concerns, John Winthrop detected God's hand in these events and pointed to a recent smallpox epidemic that devastated the local Indian peoples. "If God were not pleased with our inheriting these parts," he asked, "why doth he still make roome for us by diminishing them as we increase?" Citing the Book of Genesis, the magistrates of Massachusetts Bay declared that the Indians had not "subdued" their land and therefore had no "just right" to it.

Believing they were God's chosen people, the Puritans often treated Native Americans with a brutality equal to that of the Spanish conquistadors and Nathaniel Bacon's frontiersmen. When Pequot warriors attacked English farmers who had intruded onto their lands in the Connecticut River Valley in 1636, a Puritan militia attacked a Pequot village and massacred some five hundred men, women, and children. "God laughed at the Enemies of his People," one soldier boasted, "filling the Place with Dead Bodies."

Like most Europeans, English Puritans saw the Indians as "savages" and culturally inferior peoples. But the Puritans were not *racists* as the term is understood today. They did not believe that Native Americans were genetically inferior to them; in fact, they believed they were white people with sun-darkened skin. "Sin," not race, accounted for the Indians' degeneracy. "Probably the devil" delivered these "miserable savages" to America, Cotton Mather suggested, "in hopes that the gospel of the Lord Jesus Christ would never come here to destroy or disturb his absolute empire over them."

This interpretation of the Indians' history inspired another Puritan minister, John Eliot, to convert them to Christianity. Eliot translated the Bible into Algonquian and undertook numerous missions to Indian villages in the Massachusetts Bay Colony. Because the Puritans demanded that Indians understand the complexities of Protestant theology, only a few Native Americans became full members of Puritan congregations. The Puritans created **praying towns** that were similar to the Franciscan missions in New Mexico. By 1670, more than 1,000 Indians lived in fourteen special towns like Natick (Massachusetts) and Maanexit (Connecticut). Even the coastal Indians who remained in their ancestral villages had lost much of their independence and traditional culture.

Metacom's Rebellion

By the 1670s, there were three times as many whites as Indians in New England. The English population now totaled some 55,000, while the number of Native peoples had plummeted—from an estimated 120,000 in 1570 to 70,000 in 1620, to barely 16,000. To Metacom, leader of the Wampanoags, the future looked grim. When his people copied English ways by raising hogs and selling pork in Boston, Puritan officials accused them of selling at "an under rate" and placed restrictions on their trade. When they killed wandering livestock that damaged their cornfields, authorities denounced them for violating English property rights.

Metacom (King Philip), Chief of the Wampanoags

The Indian uprising of 1675–1676 left an indelible mark on the history of New England. This painting from the 1850s, done on semitransparent cloth and lit from behind for effect, was used by traveling performers to tell the story of King Philip's War. Notice that Metacom is not pictured as a savage but is depicted with dignity. No longer in danger of Indian attack, nineteenth-century whites in New England could adopt a romanticized version of their region's often brutal history. Shelburne Museum.

Like Opechancanough in Virginia and Popé in New Mexico, Metacom concluded that only military resistance could save Indian lands and culture. So in 1675, the Wampanoags' leader, whom the English called King Philip, forged a military alliance with the Narragansetts and Nipmucks and began attacking white settlements throughout New England. Almost every day, settler William Harris fearfully reported, he heard new reports of the Indians' "burneing houses, takeing cattell, killing men & women & Children: & carrying others captive." Bitter fighting continued into 1676, ending only when the Indian warriors ran short of guns and powder and when the Massachusetts Bay government hired Mohegan and Mohawk warriors, who ambushed and killed Metacom (see Comparing American Voices, "The Causes of the War of 1675–1676," pp. 64–65).

The rebellion was a deadly affair. The Indians went to war, a party of Narragansetts told Roger

Williams, because the English "had forced them to it." The fighting was long and hard. Indians destroyed 20 percent of the English towns in Massachusetts and Rhode Island and killed 1,000 settlers, nearly 5 percent of the adult population. The very future of the Puritan experiment hung in the balance. Had "the Indeans not been divided," remarked one settler, "they might have forced us [to evacuate] to Som Islands: & there to have planted a little Corne, & fished for our liveings." But the Natives' own losses—from famine and disease, death in battle, and sale into slavery—were much larger: About 4,500 Indians died, a quarter of an already-diminished population. Many of the surviving Wampanoag, Narragansett, and Nipmuck peoples migrated farther into the New England backcountry, where they intermarried with Algonquin tribes allied to the French. Over the next century, these displaced Indian peoples would take their revenge, joining with French Catholics to attack their Puritan enemies.

The Human and Environmental Impact of the Fur Trade

As English towns slowly filled the river valleys along the Atlantic coast, the Indians who lived in the great forested areas beyond the Appalachian Mountains remained independent. Yet the distant Indian peoples—the Iroquois, Ottawas, Crees, Illinois, and many more—also felt the European presence through the fur trade. As they bargained for woolen blankets, iron cooking ware, knives, and guns, Indians learned to avoid the French at Montreal, who demanded two beaver skins for a woolen blanket. Instead, they dealt with the Dutch and English merchants at Albany, who asked for only one pelt and who could be played off against one another. "They are marvailous subtle in their bargains to save a penny," an English trader complained. "They will beate all markets and try all places . . . to save six pence." Still, because the Indians had no way of knowing the value of their pelts in Europe, they rarely secured the highest possible price.

Nor could they control the impact of European traders and settlers on their societies. All Indian peoples were diminished in number and vitality as they encountered European diseases, European guns, and European rum. "Strong spirits . . . Causes our men to get very sick," a Catawba leader in Carolina protested, "and many of our people has Lately Died by the Effects of that Strong Drink." Most Native societies also lost their economic independence. As they exchanged furs for European-made iron utensils and woolen blankets, Indians neglected their traditional artisan skills, making fewer flint hoes, clay pots, and skin garments. A Cherokee chief complained in the 1750s, "Every necessity of life we must have from the white

Étatis suæ 21. A. 1616.

An English View of Pocahontas

By depicting the Indian princess Pocahontas as a well-dressed European woman, the artist casts her as a symbol of peaceful assimilation to English culture. In actuality, marriages between white men (often fur traders) and Indian women usually resulted in bilingual families that absorbed elements from both cultures. National Portrait Gallery, Smithsonian Institution/Art Resource, New York.

people." Religious autonomy vanished as well. When French missionaries won converts among the Hurons, Iroquois, and Illinois, they divided Indian communities into hostile religious factions.

Likewise, constant warfare for furs altered the dynamics of tribal politics by shifting power from cautious elders to headstrong young warriors. The sachems (chiefs), a group of young Seneca warriors said scornfully, "were a parcell of Old People who say much but who Mean or Act very little." The position and status of Indian women changed in especially complex ways. Traditionally, eastern woodland women had asserted authority as the chief providers of food and handcrafted goods. As a French Jesuit noted of the Iroquois, "The women are always the first to deliberate . . . on private or community matters. They hold their councils apart and . . . advise the chiefs . . . , so that the latter may deliberate on them in their turn." The disruption of farming by warfare and the influx of European goods undermined the economic basis of women's power. Paradoxically, though, among the Iroquois and other victorious tribes, the influence of women may have increased because they assumed responsibility for the cultural assimilation of hundreds of captives.

The Causes of the War of 1675–1676

The causes of—and responsibility for—every American war have been much debated, and the war of 1675–1676 between Puritans and Native Americans is no exception. The English settlers called it King Philip's War, as if the Wampanoag chief instigated it. Is that the case? What were the underlying causes of the uprising? When did it actually begin? We have no firsthand Indian accounts of its origins, but three English accounts tell the story from different perspectives. Given the differences among these accounts and their fragmentary character, how can historians reconstruct what "really happened"? Moreover, from whose point of view, the Indians' or the Europeans', should the story be told?

JOHN EASTON
A Relacion of the Indyan Warre

John Easton was the deputy governor of Rhode Island and a Quaker. Like many other Quakers, he was a pacifist and did what he could to prevent the war. He wrote this "Relacion" shortly after the conflict ended.

In [January 1675], an Indian was found dead; and by a coroner inquest of Plymouth colony judged murdered.... The dead Indian was called Sassamon, and a Christian that could read and write....

The report came that the three Indians had confessed and accused Philip [of employing them to do so, and that consequently] . . . the English would hang Philip. So the Indians were afraid, and reported that the English had . . . by threats [led] Philip [to believe] that they might kill him to have his land.... So Philip kept his men in arms.

Plymouth governor [Josias Winslow] required him to disband his men, and informed him his jealousy was false. Philip answered he would do no harm, and thanked the governor for his information. The three Indians were hung [on June 8, 1675].... And it was reported [that] Sassamon, before his death, had informed [the English] of the Indian plot, and that if the Indians knew it they would kill him, and that the heathen might destroy the English for their wickedness as God had permitted the heathen to destroy the Israelites of old.

So the English were afraid and Philip was afraid and both increased in arms; but for forty years' time reports and jealousies of war had been very frequent, that we did not think that now a war was breaking forth. But about a week before it did we had cause to think it would; then to endeavor to prevent it, we sent a man to Philip....

He called his council and agreed to come to us; [Philip] came himself, unarmed, and about forty of his men, armed.

Then five of us went over. Three were magistrates. We sat very friendly together [June 14–18]. We told him our business was to endeavor that they might not . . . do wrong. They said that that was well; they had done no wrong; the English had wronged them. We said we knew the English said that the Indians wronged them, and the Indians said the English wronged them, but our desire was the quarrel might rightly be decided in the best way, and not as dogs decide their quarrels.

The Indians owned that fighting was the worst way; then they propounded how right might take place; we said by arbitration. They said all English agreed against them; and so by arbitration they had had much wrong, many square miles of land so taken from them, for the English would have English arbitrators....

Another grievance: the English cattle and horses still increased that when [the Indians] removed thirty miles from where English had anything to do, they could not keep their corn from being spoiled [by the English livestock]....

So we departed without any discourtesies; and suddenly [circa June 25] had [a] letter from [the] Plymouth governor, [that] they intended in arms to [subjugate] Philip . . . and in a week's time after we had been with the Indians the war thus begun.

SOURCE: John Easton, "A Relacion of the Indyan Warre, by Mr. Easton, of Roade Isld., 1675," in *Narratives of the Indian Wars, 1675–1699,* ed. Charles H. Lincoln (New York: Charles Scribner's Sons, 1913), 7–17.

EDWARD RANDOLPH
Short Narrative of My Proceedings

Edward Randolph was an English customs official who denounced the independent policies of the Puritan colonies and tried to subject them to English control. His "Short Narrative," written in 1675, was a report on the war and other matters to his superiors in London.

Various are the reports and conjectures of the causes of the present Indian warre. Some impute it to an impudent zeal in the magistrates of Boston to Christianize those heathen before they were civilized and enjoining them the strict observation of their laws, which, to a people so rude and licentious, hath proved even intolerable....While the magistrates, for their profit, put the laws severely in execution against the Indians, the people, on the other side, for lucre and gain, entice and provoke the Indians to the breach thereof, especially to drunkenness, to which those people are so generally addicted that they will strip themselves to their skin to have their fill of rum and brandy....

Some believe there have been vagrant and jesuitical [French] priests, who have made it their business, for some years past, to go from Sachem to Sachem, to exasperate the Indians against the English and to bring them into a confederacy, and that they were promised supplies from France and other parts to extirpate the English nation out of the continent of America....

Others impute the cause to some injuries offered to the Sachem Philip; for he being possessed of a tract of land called Mount Hope ... some English had a mind to dispossess him thereof, who never wanting one pretence or other to attain their end, complained of injuries done by Philip and his Indians to their stock and cattle, whereupon Philip was often summoned before the magistrate, sometimes imprisoned, and never released but upon parting with a considerable part of his land.

But the government of the Massachusetts ... do declare [the following acts] are the great evils for which God hath given the heathen commission to rise against them....For men wearing long hair and periwigs made of women's hair; for women ... cutting, curling and laying out the hair.... For profaneness in the people not frequenting their [church] meetings.

SOURCE: Albert B. Hart, ed., *American History Told by Contemporaries* (New York: Macmillan, 1897), 1: 458–460.

BENJAMIN CHURCH
Entertaining Passages

Captain Benjamin Church fought in the war and helped end it by capturing King Philip's wife and son and leading the expedition that killed the Indian leader. Forty years later, in 1716, Church's son Thomas wrote an account of the war based on his father's notes and recollections.

While Mr. Church was diligently settling his new farm ... Behold! The rumor of a war between the English and the natives gave a check to his projects....Philip, according to his promise to his people, permitted them to march out of the neck [of the Mount Hope peninsula, where they lived].... They plundered the nearest houses that the inhabitants had deserted [on the rumor of a war], but as yet offered no violence to the people, at least none were killed....However, the alarm was given by their numbers, and hostile equipage, and by the prey they made of what they could find in the forsaken houses.

An express came the same day to the governor [circa June 25], who immediately gave orders to the captains of the towns to march the greatest part of their companies [of militia], and to rendezvous at Taunton....

The enemy, who began their hostilities with plundering and destroying cattle, did not long content themselves with that game. They thirsted for English blood, and they soon broached it; killing two men in the way not far from Mr. Miles's garrison. And soon after, eight more at Mattapoisett, upon whose bodies they exercised more than brutish barbarities....

These provocations drew out the resentments of some of Capt. Prentice's troop, who desired they might have liberty to go out and seek the enemy in their own quarters [circa June 26].

SOURCE: Benjamin Church, *Entertaining Passages Relating to Philip's War Which Began in the Year, 1675*, ed. Thomas Church (Boston: B. Green, 1716).

ANALYZING THE EVIDENCE

➤ Where do the documents agree and disagree about the causes of the war? Given what you know from the discussion in the text, how might the war have been prevented?

➤ In specific terms, what did the magistrates of Massachusetts Bay believe to be the prime cause of the war? Could historians verify or disprove their explanation? How? What additional sources of evidence might be useful?

➤ Make an argument for when the war began. Which documents provide the most compelling evidence? Why?

There is no doubt that the sheer extent of the fur industry—the slaughter of hundreds of thousands of beaver, deer, otter, and other animals—profoundly altered the environment. As early as the 1630s, a French Jesuit worried that the Montagnais people, who lived north of the St. Lawrence, were killing so many beaver that they would "exterminate the species in this Region, as has happened among the Hurons." As the animal populations died off, streams ran faster (there were fewer beaver dams) and the underbrush grew denser (there were fewer deer to trim the vegetation). The native environment, as well as its animals and peoples, were now part of a new American world.

➤ Compare the causes of the uprisings led by Popé in New Mexico and Metacom in New England. Which was more successful? Why?

➤ What were the major social and environmental developments that made America a new world for both Europeans and Indians?

SUMMARY

We have seen that Spain created a permanent settlement in North America in 1565; a half-century later, France, the Dutch Republic, and England did the same. These invasions of Native American lands had much in common. All spread devastating European diseases. All reduced the Indians to subject peoples. All sparked wars or revolts. And, except for the Dutch, all involved efforts to convert the Native peoples to Christianity. There were important differences as well. The French and the Dutch established fur-trading colonies; the Spanish and the English came in large numbers and formed settler colonies—although the Spanish intermarried with the Indians while the English did not.

There were also significant similarities and differences between the English settlements in the Chesapeake region, in which bound laborers raised tobacco for export to Europe, and those in New England, where pious Puritans lived in farming towns and fishing communities. Although the social structure of the Chesapeake colonies was less equal than that of the New England settlements, both regions boasted representative political institutions. Both regions also experienced Indian revolts and wars in the first decades of settlement (in Virginia in 1622 and in New England in 1636) and again in 1675–1676. Indeed, the simultaneous eruption of the Indian conflict that ignited Bacon's Rebellion and Metacom's War is evidence that the histories of the two regions of English settlement were beginning to converge.

Connections: Religion

In the part opener (p. 3), we state:

> The American experience profoundly changed religious institutions and values. Many migrants left Europe because of conflicts among rival Christian churches; in America, they hoped to practice their religion without interference.

In Chapter 2, we began our analysis of religion in English America by discussing the migration of Anglicans to Virginia, Catholics to Maryland, and Puritans to New England. We saw how the conditions of American life, especially religious diversity and weak state institutions, thwarted attempts by religious traditionalists to create strong established churches in the Chesapeake colonies and to enforce spiritual conformity in New England. We will revisit issues of religious uniformity and tolerance in Chapter 3, with a discussion of the Quaker settlement of Pennsylvania and West New Jersey in the 1680s, and in Chapter 4, with an analysis of the migration to British North America between 1720 and 1760 of tens of thousands of Scots-Irish Presbyterians, German Lutherans, and other European Protestants.

The forced migration of hundreds of thousands of Africans, one of the central themes of Chapter 3, will add complexity to our story of religion in colonial America. Some African slaves were Muslims; many more relied for spiritual substance and moral guidance on African gods and the powers they saw in nature. As we will see in Chapter 4, the Great Awakening, a far-reaching religious revival during the 1740s and 1750s, brought only a few Africans into the Christian fold; instead, it increased religious diversity among peoples of European ancestry. As the timeline for Part One (p. 2) suggests, religious liberty, pluralism, and tolerance are key themes of the American religious experience.

CHAPTER REVIEW QUESTIONS

➤ Outline the goals of the directors of the Virginia Company and the leaders of the Massachusetts Bay Company. Where did they succeed? In what ways did they fall short?

➤ Explain why there were no major witchcraft scares in the Chesapeake colonies and no uprising like Bacon's Rebellion in New England. Consider the possible social, economic, and religious causes of both phenomena.

TIMELINE

1539–1543	Coronado and de Soto lead gold-seeking expeditions
1565	Spain establishes a fort at St. Augustine
1598	Acomas rebel in New Mexico
1603–1625	Reign of James I, king of England
1607	English traders settle Jamestown (Virginia)
1608	Samuel de Champlain founds Quebec
1613	Dutch set up fur-trading post on Manhattan Island
1619	First Africans arrive in the Chesapeake region
	House of Burgesses convenes in Virginia
1620	Pilgrims found Plymouth Colony
1620–1660	Chesapeake colonies experience tobacco boom
1621	Dutch West India Company granted charter
1622	Opechancanough's uprising
1624	Virginia becomes a royal colony
1625–1649	Reign of Charles I, king of England
1630	Puritans found Massachusetts Bay Colony
1634	Maryland is settled
1636	Puritan-Pequot War
1636	Roger Williams founds Providence
1637	Anne Hutchinson banished from Massachusetts Bay
1640s	Iroquois initiate wars over fur trade
1642–1659	Puritan Revolution in England
1651	First Navigation Act
1660	Restoration of English monarchy
	Tobacco prices fall and remain low
1664	English conquer New Netherland
1675	Bacon's Rebellion
1675–1676	Metacom's uprising
1680	Popé's rebellion in New Mexico
1692	Salem witchcraft trials
1705	Virginia enacts law defining slavery

FOR FURTHER EXPLORATION

For a comprehensive and insightful narrative of the Spanish exploration and settlement of the lands to the north of the Rio Grande, consult David Weber, *The Spanish Frontier in North America* (1992). Bernard Bailyn, *The Peopling of British North America: An Introduction* (1986), presents a brief, vivid history of English migration and settlement. In *American Slavery, American Freedom* (1975), Edmund Morgan offers a compelling portrait of white servitude and black slavery in early Virginia. John Demos, *The Unredeemed Captive: A Family Story from Early America* (1994), relates the gripping tale of Eunice Williams, the daughter of a Puritan minister who was captured by and lived her life among the Mohawks. Two other fine studies of Native American life are James Merrell, *The Indians' New World: Catawbas and Their Neighbors from European Contact Through the Era of Removal* (1989), and Colin Calloway, *New Worlds for All: Indians, Europeans, and the Remaking of Early America* (1997). Arthur Quinn, *A New World: An Epic of Colonial America from the Founding of Jamestown to the Fall of Quebec* (1994), is a lively narrative filled with portraits of important political figures, macabre events, and high hopes that end disastrously. A recent biography is Francis J. Bremer, *John Winthrop: America's Forgotten Founding Father* (2003).

Two fine Web sites explore the history of the Pilgrims at Plymouth: "Caleb Johnson's Mayflower History" (**www.mayflowerhistory.com/**) and "The Plymouth Colony Archive Project" (**etext.lib.virginia.edu/users/deetz/**). For insight into life in colonial New England in 1628, see the excellent PBS series *Colonial House* (in eight parts) and the accompanying Web site (**www.pbs.org/wnet/colonialhouse/about.html**). Extensive materials on the witchcraft trials can be viewed at "Salem Witchcraft Trials" (**etext.lib.virginia.edu/salem/witchcraft/**). "Colonial Williamsburg" (**www.colonialwilliamsburg.org/history/**) offers an extensive collection of documents, illustrations, and secondary texts about colonial life, as well as information about the archaeological excavations at Williamsburg. "Historic Jamestowne" (**www.historicjamestowne.org/index.php**) offers documentation on recent archaeological finds and gives visitors the opportunity to participate in a virtual dig.

APBS video, *Surviving Columbus* (2 hours), traces the experiences of the Pueblo Indians over 450 years. "First Nations Histories" (**www.tolatsga.org/Compacts.html**) presents histories of many North American Indian peoples and information on their politics, language, culture, and demography.

TEST YOUR KNOWLEDGE

To assess your command of the material in this chapter, see the Online Study Guide at **bedfordstmartins.com/henretta**.

For Web sites, images, and documents related to topics and places in this chapter, visit **bedfordstmartins.com/makehistory**.

3
The British Empire in America
1660–1750

W HEN CHARLES II CAME TO THE throne in 1660, England was a second-class trading country, its merchants picking up the crumbs left by the much more efficient Dutch. "What we want is more of the trade the Dutch now have," declared the Duke of Albemarle, a trusted minister of the king and a proprietor of Carolina. To get it, the English government passed a series of Navigation Acts, which excluded Dutch ships from its colonies, and went to war to enforce the new legislation. By the 1720s, the recently unified kingdom of Great Britain (comprising England and Scotland) had taken control of commerce in the Atlantic. Trade in West Indian sugar and African slaves "is our chief support," Secretary of State Lord Carteret told the House of Lords in 1739. As ardent imperialist Malachy Postlethwayt explained, the British empire "was a magnificent superstructure of American commerce and naval power on an African foundation."

To protect the empire's valuable West Indian sugar colonies from European rivals — the Dutch in New Netherland, the Spanish in Mesoamerica and Florida, and especially the Catholic French in Quebec and the West Indies — British ministers repeatedly went to war and with considerable success. Boasted one English pamphleteer, "We are, of any nation, the best situated for trade, . . . capable of giving

◀ **Power and Race in the Chesapeake**

In this 1670 painting by Gerard Soest, Lord Baltimore holds a map of his proprietary colony, Maryland. The colony will soon belong to his grandson Cecil Calvert, who is pointing to his magnificent inheritance. The presence of a young African servant foretells the importance of slave labor in the post-1700 economy of the Chesapeake colonies.
Enoch Pratt Free Library of Baltimore.

maritime laws to the world." So when Edward Randolph, an imperial official in New England, reported in the early 1670s that "there is no notice taken [here] of the act of navigation," the home government set out to impose its political will on the American settlements.

Although that coercion was only partially successful, the mainland colonies became increasingly important to the prosperity of the British empire. "We have within ourselves and in our colonies in America an inexhaustible fund to supply ourselves" with a vast array of goods, another English pamphleteer proudly announced. The cost of creating this increasingly prosperous transatlantic commercial system was borne primarily by hundreds of thousands of enslaved Africans, who endured brutal, often deadly conditions on the plantations of the West Indies.

The Politics of Empire, 1660–1713

Before 1660, England governed its New England and Chesapeake colonies haphazardly. Taking advantage of that laxness and the English civil war, local oligarchies of Puritan magistrates and tobacco planter-merchants ran their societies as they wanted. After the monarchy was restored in 1660, royal bureaucrats tried to impose order on the unruly settlements and, with the help of Indian allies, went to war against rival European powers to further their imperial ambitions.

The Great Aristocratic Land Grab

When Charles II (r. 1660–1685) ascended the English throne, he quickly established a string of new settlements — the Restoration Colonies, as historians call them (Table 3.1). In 1663, Charles, a generous man who was always in debt, rewarded eight noblemen with the gift of Carolina, an area long claimed by Spain and populated by thousands of Indians. The following year, he bestowed an equally huge grant on his brother James, the Duke of York. James took possession of New Jersey and the just-conquered Dutch colony of New Netherland, which he renamed New York. Then James conveyed the ownership of New Jersey to two of the Carolina proprietors.

In one of the great land grabs in history, a handful of English nobles had taken title to vast provinces. Like Lord Baltimore's Maryland, their new colonies were proprietorships: The aristocrats owned all the land and could rule as they wished as long as their laws conformed broadly to those of England. Most proprietors envisioned a traditional European society presided over by the gentry and the Church of England. The Fundamental Constitutions of Carolina (1669), for example, prescribed a **manorial system**, a society in which a mass of serfs would be governed by a small number of powerful nobles.

The Carolinas. The manorial system proved to be a fantasy. The first settlers in North Carolina were primarily poor families and runaway servants from

TABLE 3.1	English Colonies Established in North America, 1660–1750				
Colony	**Date**	**Type**	**Religion**	**Status in 1775**	**Chief Export/ Economic Activity**
Carolina	1663	Proprietary	Church of England	Royal	
North	1691				Farming, naval stores
South	1691				Rice, indigo
New Jersey	1664	Proprietary	Church of England	Royal	Wheat
New York	1664	Proprietary	Church of England	Royal	Wheat
Pennsylvania	1681	Proprietary	Quaker	Proprietary	Wheat
Georgia	1732	Trustees	Church of England	Royal	Rice
New Hampshire (separated from Massachusetts)	1741	Royal	Congregationalist	Royal	Mixed farming, lumber, naval stores
Nova Scotia	1749	Royal	Church of England	Royal	Fishing, mixed farming, naval stores

Virginia, and equality-minded English Quakers, a radical Protestant sect also known as the Society of Friends. They "think there is no difference between a Gentleman and a labourer," complained one Anglican clergyman. Refusing to work on large manors, the settlers raised corn, hogs, and tobacco on modest family farms. And in 1677, inspired by Bacon's Rebellion in Virginia, the residents of Albemarle County staged their own uprising. Angered by taxes on tobacco exports and other levies imposed to support the Anglican church, they rebelled again in 1708. By deposing a series of governors, the "stubborn and disobedient" residents—the description was a wealthy Anglican landowner's—forced the proprietors to abandon their dreams of a feudal society.

In what would become South Carolina, the colonists also refused to accept the Fundamental Constitutions. Many of the white settlers there were migrants from the overcrowded sugar-producing island of Barbados, and they had their own vision of a hierarchical society. They used slaves—both Africans and Native Americans—to raise cattle and food crops for export to the West Indies. Carolina merchants also opened a lucrative trade with neighboring Indian peoples by exchanging English manufactures for deerskins. The Carolinians' reliance on slave labor encouraged their Indian trading partners to take captives from other Native American peoples and exchange them for alcohol and guns. By 1708, white Carolinians were working their coastal plantations with 1,400 Indian and 2,900 African slaves, and brutal Indian warfare continued in the backcountry. South Carolina would remain a violent frontier settlement until the 1720s.

William Penn and the Quakers. In dramatic contrast to the Carolinians, settlers in Pennsylvania

William Penn's Treaty with the Indians, 1683

In 1771, Benjamin West executed this famous picture of William Penn's meeting with the Lenni-Lanapes (or Delawares), who called themselves "the Common People." A Quaker, Penn refused to seize Indian lands by force; instead he negotiated purchases from the Indians. Penn was favorably impressed by the Lenni-Lanapes: "For their persons they are generally tall, straight, well built, and of singular proportion," he wrote in 1683. "They tread strong and clever, and mostly walk with a lofty chin." Pennsylvania Academy of the Fine Arts, Philadelphia.

pursued a pacifistic policy toward Native Americans and quickly became prosperous. In 1681, Charles II bestowed Pennsylvania (which included present-day Delaware) on William Penn in payment for a large debt owed to Penn's father. The younger Penn was born to wealth, owned substantial estates in Ireland and England, and lived in lavish style — with a country mansion, fine clothes, and eight servants. Seemingly destined for courtly pursuits, Penn instead joined the Society of Friends, a religious sect that condemned war and extravagance. Penn designed Pennsylvania as a refuge for his fellow Quakers, who were persecuted in England because they refused to serve in the military or pay taxes to support the Church of England. Penn himself spent more than two years in jail for preaching his beliefs.

Like the Puritans, the Quakers wanted to restore Christianity to its early simplicity and spirituality. But they rejected the Puritans' pessimistic religious doctrine of Calvinism, which restricted salvation to a small elect. Instead, they followed the teachings of two English visionaries, George Fox and Margaret Fell, who argued that God had imbued all men and women with an "inner light" of grace or understanding.

Penn's Frame of Government (1681) applied the Quakers' radical beliefs to the political structure of his colony. It ensured religious freedom by prohibiting a legally established church, and it promoted political equality by allowing all property-owning men to vote and hold office. These enlightened provisions prompted thousands of Quakers, mostly yeoman farm families from northwestern England, to come to Pennsylvania. Initially, they settled along the Delaware River near the city of Philadelphia, which Penn himself laid out in an grid with wide main streets and many parks. To attract European Protestants, Penn published pamphlets in Dutch and German that promised cheap land and freedom from religious persecution. In 1683, migrants from the German region of Saxony founded Germantown (just outside Philadelphia), and thousands of other Germans soon followed. Ethnic diversity, pacifism, and freedom of conscience made Pennsylvania the most open and democratic of the Restoration Colonies.

From Mercantilism to Imperial Dominion

As Charles II gave away his American lands, his ministers were devising policies to keep colonial trade in English hands. Since the 1560s, the English crown had used government subsidies and charters to stimulate English manufacturing and foreign trade. Now the English government extended these mercantilist policies to the American settlements through a series of Navigation Acts (Table 3.2).

Mercantilism: Theory and Practice. According to mercantilist theory, the colonies would produce agricultural goods and raw materials, which Eng-

TABLE 3.2	Navigation Acts, 1651–1751		
	Date	**Purpose**	**Result**
Act of 1651	1651	Cut Dutch trade	Mostly ignored
Act of 1660	1660	Ban foreign shipping; enumerated goods only to England	Partially obeyed
Act of 1663	1663	European imports only through England	Partially obeyed
Staple Act	1673	Ensure enumerated goods go only to England	Mostly obeyed
Act of 1696	1696	Prevent frauds; Create Vice-Admiralty Courts	Mostly obeyed
Woolen Act	1699	Prevent export or intercolonial sale of textiles	Partially obeyed
Hat Act	1732	Prevent export or intercolonial sale of hats	Partially obeyed
Molasses Act	1733	Cut American imports of molasses from French West Indies	Extensively violated
Iron Act	1750	Prevent manufacture of finished iron products	Extensively violated
Currency Act 1751	1751	End use of paper currency as legal tender in New England	Mostly obeyed

lish merchants would carry to England. Certain goods and materials then would be traded immediately in the European market; others would be manufactured into finished products and then exported to Europe (see Chapter 1). The Navigation Act of 1651 excluded Dutch merchants from the English colonies and required that goods imported into England or its American settlements be carried on ships owned by English or colonial merchants. New parliamentary acts in 1660 and 1663 strengthened the ban on foreign traders and stipulated that the colonists had to ship their sugar and tobacco only to England. To provide even more business for English merchants, the acts required that European exports to America pass through England. To pay the customs officials who enforced the mercantilist laws, the Revenue Act of 1673 imposed a "plantation duty" on American exports of sugar and tobacco.

The English government backed its mercantilist policy with the force of arms. In three commercial wars between 1652 and 1674, the English navy drove the Dutch from New Netherland; and by attacking Dutch forts and ships along the Gold Coast of Africa, the English encroached on Holland's dominance of the Atlantic slave trade. Meanwhile, English merchants expanded their fleets, which grew from 150,000 tons of shipping in 1640 to 340,000 tons in 1690, and seized control of commerce in the North Atlantic.

Many colonists refused to comply with the mercantilist laws, continuing to welcome Dutch merchants and to import sugar and molasses from the French West Indies. The Massachusetts Bay assembly boldly declared: "The laws of England are bounded within the [four] seas and do not reach America." Outraged by this insolence, an English official in the colony called for troops to "reduce Massachusetts to obedience." Instead, the Lords of Trade — the administrative body charged with colonial affairs — opted for a punitive legal strategy. In 1679, it denied the claim of Massachusetts Bay to New Hampshire and eventually established a completely separate colony there with a royal governor. Then, in 1684, the Lords of Trade persuaded the English Court of Chancery to annul the charter of Massachusetts Bay on the grounds that the Puritan government had violated the Navigation Acts and virtually outlawed the Church of England.

The Absolutism of James II. The Puritans' troubles had only begun. The accession to the throne of James II (r. 1685–1688) prompted more imperial regulations. The new king was an aggres-

The Target of the Glorious Revolution: James II

In Godfrey Kneller's portrait of James II (r. 1685–1688), the king's stance and facial expression suggest his forceful, arrogant personality. James's arbitrary measures and Catholic sympathies prompted rebellions in England and America, and cost him the throne. National Portrait Gallery, London.

sive and inflexible ruler. During the reign of Oliver Cromwell, James had grown up in exile in France, and he admired its authoritarian king, Louis XIV. Believing that monarchs had a "divine-right" to rule, James instructed the Lords of Trade to subject the American colonies to strict royal control. In 1686, the Lords revoked the corporate charters of Connecticut and Rhode Island and merged them with the Massachusetts Bay and Plymouth colonies to form a new royal province, the Dominion of New England. As governor of the Dominion, James II appointed Sir Edmund Andros, a former governor of New York. Two years later, James II added New York and New Jersey to the Dominion, creating a vast colony that stretched from Maine to the Delaware River (Map 3.1).

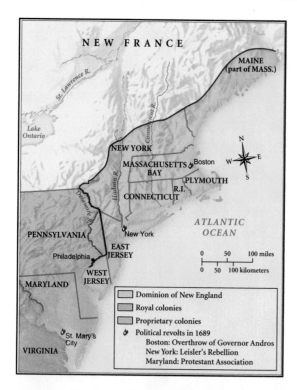

MAP 3.1   The Dominion of New England, 1686–1689

In the Dominion, James II created a vast royal colony that stretched nearly 500 miles along the Atlantic coast. During the Glorious Revolution in England, politicians and ministers in Boston and New York City led revolts that ousted Dominion officials and repudiated their authority. King William and Queen Mary replaced the Dominion with governments that balanced the power held by imperial authorities and local political institutions.

The king's administrative innovations in the Dominion went far beyond mercantilism, which primarily regulated trade. The Dominion extended to America the oppressive model of colonial rule the English government had imposed on Catholic Ireland. When England had retaken control of New York from the Dutch in 1674, James II refused to allow an elective assembly and ruled by decree. Now he imposed absolutist rule on the entire Dominion by ordering Governor Andros to abolish the existing legislative assemblies. In Massachusetts, Andros immediately banned town meetings, angering villagers who prized local self-rule. He also advocated public worship in the Church of England, offending Puritan Congregationalists. Even worse from the colonists' perspective, the governor challenged all land titles granted under the original Massachusetts Bay charter. Andros offered

to provide new deeds, but only if the colonists would agree to pay an annual fee.

The Glorious Revolution in England and America

Fortunately for the colonists, James II angered English political leaders as much as Andros alienated the American settlers. The king revoked the charters of many English towns, rejected the advice of Parliament, and aroused popular opposition by openly practicing Roman Catholicism. Then, in 1688, James's Spanish Catholic wife gave birth to a son, raising the prospect of a Catholic heir to the throne. To forestall that outcome, Protestant bishops and parliamentary leaders in the Whig Party led a quick and bloodless coup known as the Glorious Revolution. Buoyed by strong popular sentiment and the support of military leaders, they forced James into exile and in 1689 enthroned Mary, his Protestant daughter by his first wife, and her Dutch Protestant husband, William of Orange. The Whigs did not advocate democracy: They wanted political power, especially the power to levy taxes, in the hands of the gentry, merchants, and other substantial property owners. By forcing King William and Queen Mary to accept the Declaration of Rights in 1689, Whig politicians created a constitutional monarchy that enhanced the powers of the House of Commons at the expense of the crown.

To justify their coup, the members of Parliament relied on political philosopher John Locke. In his *Two Treatises on Government* (1690), Locke rejected the divine-right theory of monarchical rule advocated by James II; instead, he argued that the legitimacy of government rests on the consent of the governed, and that individuals have inalienable natural rights to life, liberty, and property. Locke's celebration of individual rights and representative government had a lasting influence in America, where many political leaders wanted to expand the powers of the colonial assemblies.

Uprisings in Massachusetts and Maryland. More immediately, the Glorious Revolution sparked rebellions by Protestant colonists in Massachusetts, Maryland, and New York. When the news of the coup reached Boston in April 1689, Puritan leaders, supported by two thousand militiamen, seized Governor Andros, accused him of Catholic sympathies, and shipped him back to England. Heeding American complaints of authoritarian rule, the new monarchs broke up the Dominion of New England. However, they refused to restore the old Puritan-dominated government of Massachusetts Bay; instead, in 1692, they created a new royal colony (which included Plymouth and Maine). The new colony's charter empowered the king to appoint the governor and customs officials; it also gave the vote to all male property owners, not just Puritan church members; and it eliminated Puritan restrictions on the Church of England.

The uprising in Maryland had economic as well as religious causes. Since 1660, falling tobacco prices had hurt smallholders, tenant farmers, and former indentured servants. These economically vulnerable people were overwhelmingly Protestants, and they resented the rising taxes and the high fees imposed by wealthy proprietary officials, who were primarily Catholics. When Parliament ousted James II, a Protestant association mustered seven hundred men and forcibly removed the Catholic governor. The Lords of Trade supported

this Protestant initiative: It suspended Lord Baltimore's proprietorship, imposed royal government, and made the Church of England the legal religion in the colony. This arrangement lasted until 1715, when Benedict Calvert, the fourth Lord Baltimore, converted to the Anglican faith, and the king restored the proprietorship to the Calvert family.

Jacob Leisler's Rebellion. In New York, Jacob Leisler led the rebellion against the Dominion of New England. Leisler was a German soldier who had worked for the Dutch West India Company, become a merchant, and married into a prominent Dutch family in New York. He was also a militant Calvinist, rigid and hot tempered. When New England settlers on Long Island, angered by James's prohibition of representative institutions, learned of the king's ouster, they repudiated the Dominion. The rebels quickly won the support of Dutch Protestant artisans in New York City, who welcomed

A Prosperous Dutch Farmstead

Dutch farmers in the Hudson River Valley prospered because of their easy access to market and their exploitation of black slaves, which they owned in much greater numbers than did their English neighbors. To record his good fortune, Martin Van Bergen of Leeds, New York, had this mural painted over his mantelpiece. New York State Historical Association, Cooperstown.

the succession of Queen Mary and her Dutch husband. Led by Leisler, the Dutch militia ousted Lieutenant Governor Nicholson, an Andros appointee and an alleged Catholic sympathizer.

Initially, all classes and ethnic groups rallied behind Leisler, who headed the new government. However, Leisler's denunciations of political rivals as "popish dogs" and "Roages, Rascalls, and Devills" soon alienated many English-speaking New Yorkers. When Leisler imprisoned forty of his political opponents, imposed new taxes, and championed the artisans' cause, the prominent Dutch merchants who had traditionally controlled the city's government condemned his rule. In 1691, the merchants found an ally in Colonel Henry Sloughter, the new English governor, who had Leisler indicted for treason. Convicted by an English jury, Leisler was hanged and then decapitated, an act of ethnic vengeance that offended Dutch residents and corrupted New York politics for a generation.

The Glorious Revolution of 1688–1689 led to a new political era in both England and America. In England, William and Mary ruled as constitutional monarchs and promoted an empire based on commerce. Equally important, because the new monarchs wanted colonial support for a war against Catholic France, they accepted the overthrow of the authoritarian Dominion of New England and allowed the restoration of self-government in Massachusetts and New York. Parliament created the Board of Trade in 1696 to supervise the American settlements, but it had limited success. Settlers and proprietors resisted the board's attempt to install royal governments in every colony, as did many English political leaders, who feared an increase in monarchical power. The result was another period of lax administration. The home government cut the high duties on West Indian sugar instituted by James II and imposed only a few laws and taxes on the mainland settlements. It allowed local merchants and landowners to run the American colonies and encouraged enterprising English merchants and financiers to develop them as sources of trade.

Imperial Wars and Native Peoples

In a world of nations competing for commerce, the growth of wealth in Britain depended on both mercantile skills and military power. Between 1689 and 1815, Britain fought a series of increasingly intense wars with France (Table 3.3). To win a dominant position in Western Europe and the Caribbean, government leaders in Britain created a powerful central state that spent three-quarters of its revenue on military and naval expenses. As the wars spread to the North American mainland, they involved growing numbers of colonists and Native American warriors, now armed with European guns. Indeed, many Indian peoples understood European goals and diplomacy well enough to turn the fighting to their own advantage.

Mayhem in Florida and the Carolinas. The first significant battles in North America occurred during the War of the Spanish Succession (1702–1713), which pitted Britain against France and Spain. To secure their foothold in the Carolinas, English settlers attacked Spanish Florida. The Carolinians armed the Creeks, whose fifteen thousand members

TABLE 3.3	English Wars, 1650–1750		
War	**Date**	**Purpose**	**Result**
Anglo-Dutch	1652–1654	Commercial markets	Stalemate
Anglo-Dutch	1664	Markets-Conquest	England takes New Amsterdam
Anglo-Dutch	1673	Commercial markets	England makes maritime gains
King William's	1689–1697	Maintain European balance of power	Stalemate in North America
Queen Anne's	1702–1713	Maintain European balance of power	British get Hudson Bay and Nova Scotia
Jenkins's Ear	1739–1741	Expand markets in Spanish America	English merchants expand influence
King George's	1740–1748	Maintain European balance of power	Capture and return of Louisbourg

farmed the fertile lands along the present-day border of Georgia and Alabama. A joint English-Creek expedition burned the Spanish town of St. Augustine but failed to capture the nearby fort. Fearing that future Carolinian-backed Indian raids would endanger Florida and pose a threat to Havana in nearby Cuba, the Spanish reinforced St. Augustine and unsuccessfully attacked Charleston (South Carolina).

The Creeks had their own agenda: They wanted to be the dominant tribe in the region. That meant defeating their longtime enemies, the pro-French Choctaws to the west and the Spanish-allied Apalachees to the south. Beginning in 1704, a force of Creek and Yamasee warriors destroyed the remaining Franciscan missions in northern Florida, attacked the Spanish settlement at Pensacola, and captured 1,000 Apalachees, whom they sold to South Carolinian slave traders for sale in the West Indies. Simultaneously, a Carolina-supplied Creek expedition attacked the Iroquois-speaking Tuscarora people of North Carolina, killing hundreds, executing 160 male captives, and sending 400 women and children into slavery. The surviving Tuscaroras migrated to the north and joined the Iroquois in New York (now the Six Iroquois Nations). The Carolinians, having used Indian guns against the Spaniards and their native allies, now died by them. When English traders demanded the payment of trade debts in 1715, the Creeks and Yamasees revolted. They killed 400 colonists before being overwhelmed by the Carolinians and their new allies, the Cherokees.

Native Americans also figured significantly in the warfare between French Catholics in Canada and English Protestants in New England. With French aid, Catholic Mohawk and Abenaki warriors took revenge on their Puritan enemies. They destroyed English settlements in Maine, and in 1704 attacked the western Massachusetts town of Deerfield, where they killed 48 residents and carried 112 into captivity. In response, New England militia attacked French settlements and, in 1710, joined with British naval forces to seize Port Royal in French Acadia (Nova Scotia). However, a major British-New England expedition against the French stronghold at Quebec failed miserably.

The Iroquois' Policy of Peace. The New York frontier remained quiet. French and English merchants did not want to disrupt the lucrative fur trade, and the Iroquois, tired of war, had adopted a policy of "aggressive neutrality." In 1701, the Iroquois concluded a peace treaty with France and its Indian allies. Simultaneously, they renewed the Covenant Chain, a series of military alliances with the English government in New York and various Indian peoples (see Chapter 2). For the next half-century, the Iroquois exploited their strategic location between the English and the French colonies by trading with both but refusing to fight for either one. The Delaware leader Teedyuscung urged an alliance with the Iroquois by showing his people a pictorial message: "You see a Square in the Middle, meaning the Lands of the Indians; and at one End, the Figure of a Man, indicating the English; and at the other End, another, meaning the French. Let us join together to defend our land against both."

Despite the military stalemate in the colonies, Britain won major territorial and commercial concessions through its victories in Europe. In the Treaty of Utrecht (1713), Britain obtained Newfoundland, Acadia, and the Hudson Bay region of northern Canada from France, as well as access through Albany to the western Indian trade. From Spain, Britain acquired the strategic fortress of Gibraltar at the entrance to the Mediterranean and a thirty-year contract to supply slaves to Spanish America. These gains solidified Britain's commercial supremacy, preserved the Protestant monarchy instituted in 1689, and brought peace to eastern North America for a generation (Map 3.2).

➤ What was the role of the colonies in the British mercantilist system?

➤ Explain the causes and the results of the Glorious Revolutions in England and America.

➤ How did Native Americans attempt to turn European rivalries to their advantage? How successful were they?

The Imperial Slave Economy

Britain's increasing interest in American affairs reflected the growth of a new agricultural and commercial order — the South Atlantic System — which produced sugar, tobacco, rice, and other subtropical products for a growing international market. At the center of this economy stood plantation societies ruled by powerful European planter-merchants and worked by hundreds of thousands of enslaved Africans. Indeed, by 1650, Africans

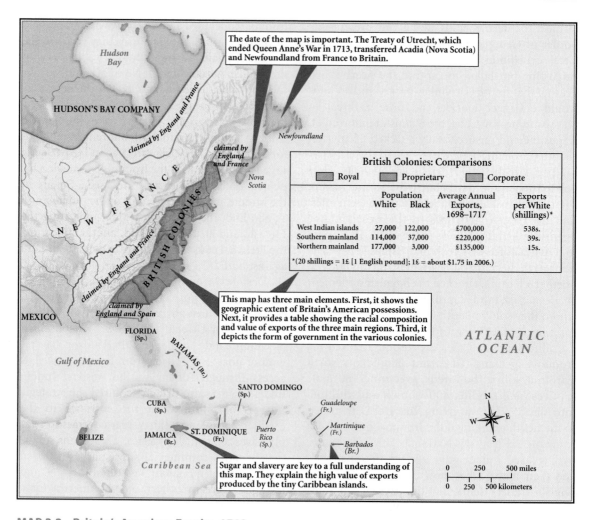

The date of the map is important. The Treaty of Utrecht, which ended Queen Anne's War in 1713, transferred Acadia (Nova Scotia) and Newfoundland from France to Britain.

British Colonies: Comparisons

| | Royal | Proprietary | Corporate |

	Population		Average Annual Exports, 1698–1717	Exports per White (shillings)*
	White	Black		
West Indian islands	27,000	122,000	£700,000	538s.
Southern mainland	114,000	37,000	£220,000	39s.
Northern mainland	177,000	3,000	£135,000	15s.

*(20 shillings = 1£ [1 English pound]; 1£ = about $1.75 in 2006.)

This map has three main elements. First, it shows the geographic extent of Britain's American possessions. Next, it provides a table showing the racial composition and value of exports of the three main regions. Third, it depicts the form of government in the various colonies.

Sugar and slavery are key to a full understanding of this map. They explain the high value of exports produced by the tiny Caribbean islands.

MAP 3.2 Britain's American Empire, 1713

Many of Britain's possessions in the West Indies were tiny islands, mere dots on the Caribbean Sea. However, in 1713, these small pieces of land were by far the most valuable parts of the empire. Their sugar crops brought wealth to English merchants, commerce to the northern colonies, and a brutal life and early death to hundreds of thousands of African workers.

formed the majority of transatlantic migrants to the Western Hemisphere (Table 3.4).

The South Atlantic System

The South Atlantic System had its center in Brazil and the West Indies, and sugar was its primary product. Before 1500, people in most lands had few sweeteners — mostly honey and fruit juices. Then Portuguese planters developed sugar plantations in the Atlantic islands off the African coast and, after 1550, in Brazil. As the cultivation of sugarcane spread, first Europeans and then other peoples developed a craving for the potent new sweetener. By 1900, sugar would account for an astonishing 20 percent of the calories consumed by the world's people.

European merchants, investors, and planters ran the South Atlantic System. Following mercantilist principles, they provided the organizational skill, ships, and money needed to grow and process sugarcane, carry the partially refined sugar to Europe, and supply the plantations with tools and equipment. To provide labor for the sugar plantations, the merchants imported slaves from Africa. Between 1520 and 1650, Portuguese traders transported 95 percent of the 820,000 Africans carried across the Atlantic — about 4,000 slaves a year before 1600 and 10,000 annually thereafter. Over the next half century, the Dutch dominated the Atlantic slave trade; between 1700 and 1800, the British became the prime carriers, transporting about half of the 6.1 million Africans

TABLE 3.4	African Slaves Imported to the Americas, 1520–1810

Destination	Number of Africans Arriving
South America	
Brazil	3,650,000
Dutch America	500,000
West Indies	
British	1,660,000
French	1,660,000
Central America (Spanish)	1,500,000
North America (British)	500,000
Europe	175,000
Total	**9,645,000**

sent to the Americas. To secure this vast number of workers, European merchants relied on African-run slave-catching systems. These systems extended far into the interior and funneled captives to the slave ports of Elmina on the Gold Coast, Whydah in the Bight (bay) of Benin, Bonny and Calabar in the Bight of Biafra, and, farther south, the ports of Loango, Cabinda, and Luanda (see Map 3.3).

The West Indies Turn to Sugar. The cultivation of sugar—and, after 1750, coffee—drove the slave trade. In the 1620s, the English colonized a number of small West Indian islands: St. Christopher, Nevis, Montserrat, and especially Barbados, which had an extensive amount of arable land. Until the 1650s, the colonists were primarily English, smallholders along with a few planters and their indentured servants, who exported tobacco and livestock hides. Actually, there were more English residents in the West Indies (some 44,000) than in the Chesapeake (12,000) and New England (23,000) colonies combined.

It was sugar that dramatically transformed these islands into slave-based plantation societies. Eager for a source of raw sugar for refineries in Amsterdam, Dutch merchants provided ambitious English planters with money to buy land, with sugar-processing equipment, and with slaves. By 1680, enslaved Africans made up a majority of the population of Barbados, and the majority of them were owned by the 175 planters who now dominated the island's economy. Unwilling to work as

tenants or overseers for wealthy planters, hundreds of English farmers looked elsewhere for cheap land. Many migrated to the new mainland colony of Carolina; many others to the large island of Jamaica, which England had seized from Spain in 1655. English sugar merchants and landowners invested heavily in Jamaica, which by 1750 would become the wealthiest British colony. That year, Jamaica had seven hundred large sugar plantations worked by more than 105,000 slaves.

Sugar was a rich man's crop because it could be produced most efficiently on large plantations. Scores of workers planted and cut the sugarcane, which was then processed by expensive equipment—crushing mills, boiling houses, distilling equipment—into raw sugar, molasses, and rum. Affluent planter-merchants controlled the sugar industry and drew annual profits of more than 10 percent on their investment. As Scottish economist Adam Smith noted in his famous treatise *The Wealth of Nations* (1776), sugar was the most profitable crop in Europe and America.

The Impact of Sugar on Europe. In fact, the South Atlantic System brought wealth to the entire British—and European—economy. Most of the owners of British West Indian plantations were absentee landlords: They lived in England, where they spent their profits and formed a powerful "sugar lobby." Moreover, the Navigation Acts required that sugar from the British islands be sold to British consumers or exported by British merchants to foreign markets. By 1750, British reshipments of American sugar and tobacco to Europe accounted for half of all the nation's exports. Substantial profits also flowed into Britain from the slave trade. The Royal African Company and other English traders sold slaves in the West Indies for three to five times what they paid for them in Africa. In addition, the value of the guns, iron, rum, cloth, and other European products exchanged for slaves amounted only to about one-tenth (in the 1680s) to one-third (by the 1780s) of the value of the goods those slaves subsequently produced in America.

These massive profits drove the expansion of the slave trade. At the height of the trade, in the 1790s, Britain was exporting 300,000 guns annually to Africa, to exchange for captives and equip slave raiders, and a British ship carrying 300 to 350 slaves left an African port every other day. The trade to Africa and America stimulated British shipbuilding and manufacturing. English shipyards built hundreds of vessels, and thousands of English and Scottish men and women worked in trade-related industries: building port facilities and warehouses,

A Sugar Mill in the French West Indies, 1655

Making sugar required hard labor and considerable expertise. Field slaves did the hard work, cutting the sugarcane and carrying or carting it to the oxen- (or wind-) powered mill, where it was pressed to yield the juice. Then skilled slave artisans took over. They carefully heated the juice and, at the proper moment, added ingredients that granulated the sugar and separated it from the molasses, which was later distilled into rum. The Granger Collection, New York.

refining sugar and tobacco, distilling rum from molasses (a by-product of sugar), and manufacturing textiles and iron products for the growing markets in Africa and America. Moreover, commercial expansion provided Britain with a supply of experienced sailors and helped the Royal Navy become the most powerful fleet in Europe.

Africa, Africans, and the Slave Trade

The South Atlantic system increased prosperity in Europe, but it did so at enormous economic, political, and human cost to West and West-Central Africa. Between 1550 and 1870, the Atlantic slave trade uprooted almost 11 million Africans, draining the lands south of the Sahara Desert of people and wealth. Equally important, the slave trade

changed the nature of West African society. By directing commerce away from the savannas and diminishing cultural contact with the Islamic world across the Sahara, the Atlantic slave trade diminished the vitality of many interior states and peoples. Simultaneously, it prompted the growth of militaristic centralized states in the coastal areas, and the use of imported European goods throughout the continent (Map 3.3).

Slavery in Africa. Warfare and slaving had been an integral part of African life for centuries, in part because of conflicts among numerous states and ethnic groups. As the demand for sugar increased the demand for slaves (and the price Europeans would pay for them), slaving wars increased dramatically in scale. Indeed, they became a favorite

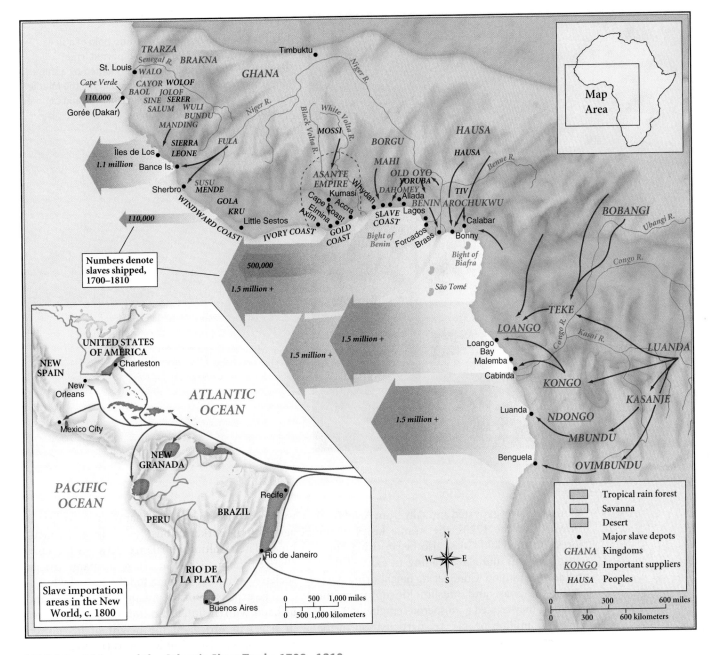

MAP 3.3   Africa and the Atlantic Slave Trade, 1700–1810

The tropical rain forest of West Africa was home to scores of peoples and dozens of kingdoms. Some kingdoms became aggressive slavers. Dahomey's army, for example, seized tens of thousands of captives in wars with neighboring peoples and sold them to European traders. About 15 percent of the captives died during the grueling Middle Passage, the transatlantic voyage between Africa and the Americas. Most of the survivors labored on sugar plantations in Brazil and the British and French West Indies (see Table 3.4).

tactic of ambitious kings and plundering warlords. "Whenever the King of Barsally wants Goods or Brandy," an observer noted, "the King goes and ransacks some of his enemies' towns, seizing the people and selling them." Supplying the Atlantic trade became a way of life in Dahomey, where the royal house made the sale of slaves a state monopoly and used European guns to establish a military despotism. Dahomey's army, which included a contingent of five thousand women, systematically raided the interior for captives; between 1680 and 1730, these raids accounted for many of the twenty

A View of the Middle Passage

This 1846 watercolor shows the cargo hold of a slave ship on a voyage to Brazil, which imported large numbers of Africans until the 1860s. Painted by a ship's officer, the picture minimizes the brutality of the Middle Passage — none of the slaves are in chains — and captures the Africans' humanity and dignity. Bridgeman Art Library.

thousand slaves exported annually from Allada and Whydah. In the 1720s, the Asante kings in the forests of the Gold Coast also began using European firearms and slave trading to expand their political dominion. Conquering neighboring states along the coast and Muslim kingdoms in the savanna, they created a prosperous empire of 3 million to 5 million people. Yet participation in the European slave trade remained a choice for Africans, not a necessity. For over a century, the powerful kingdom of Benin, famous for its cast bronzes and carved ivory, kept its many male slaves for labor at home and, for a time, prohibited the export of all slaves, male and female.

The trade in humans produced untold misery. Hundreds of thousands of young Africans died, and millions more were condemned to the brutal life of slaves in the Americas. In many African societies, class divisions hardened as people of noble birth enslaved and sold those of lesser status. Gender relations shifted as well. Men constituted two-thirds of the slaves sent across the Atlantic because European planters paid more for "men and stout men boys," and because African slave traders sold women captives in local or Saharan slave markets as agricultural workers, house servants, and concubines. The resulting imbalance between the sexes changed the nature of marriage in many African societies, encouraging men to take several wives.

The expansion of the Atlantic trade went hand in hand with an intensification of the commerce in slaves in Africa. At the height of his power, Sultan Mawlay Ismail of Morocco (r. 1672 – 1727) owned 150,000 black slaves, obtained by trade in Timbuktu and by force in Senegal. In Africa, as in the Americas, slavery was eroding the dignity of human life.

From Captive to Worker. Those Africans sold into the South Atlantic system had the bleakest fate. Torn from their villages, they were marched in chains to Elmina and other coastal ports. From there they made the perilous **Middle Passage** to the New World in hideously overcrowded ships. The captives had little to eat and drink, and some would die from dehydration. The feces, urine, and vomit prompted dangerous outbreaks of dysentery, which took more lives. "I was so overcome by the heat, stench, and foul air that I nearly fainted," reported a European doctor who ventured below deck. Some slaves jumped overboard, choosing to drown rather than endure more suffering (see Voices from Abroad, "Olaudah Equiano: The Brutal 'Middle Passage,'" p. 84). Believing that "they would be made into oil and eaten," many Africans staged violent revolts. Slaves attacked their captors on no fewer than two thousand voyages, roughly one of every ten Atlantic passages. Nearly 100,000 slaves died in these uprisings, and more than a million others — about 15 percent of those transported — died of sickness on the monthlong journey. Most died of dysentery or scurvy; others died of measles, yellow fever, and smallpox, which survivors often carried to American port cities and plantations.

For those who lived through the Middle Passage, things only got worse. Life on the sugar plantations of northwestern Brazil and the West Indies was a lesson in systematic violence and relentless exploitation. The slaves worked ten hours a day under the hot semitropical sun; slept in flimsy huts; and lived on a starchy diet of corn, yams, and dried fish. And they were subject to brutal discipline: "The fear of punishment is the principle [we use] . . . to keep them in awe and order," one planter declared. With sugar prices high and the cost of slaves low, many planters simply worked their slaves to death and then bought more. Between 1708 and 1735, British planters imported about 85,000 Africans into Barbados, but the island's black population increased by only 4,000 (from 42,000 to 46,000) during that period. The constant influx of new slaves kept the black population thoroughly "African" in its languages, religions, and culture. "Here," wrote a Jamaican observer, "each different nation of Africa meet and dance after the manner of their own country . . . [and] retain most of their native customs."

Slavery in the Chesapeake and South Carolina

Following Bacon's Rebellion, planters in Virginia and Maryland took advantage of the increased British trade in African slaves (see Chapter 2). In a "tobacco revolution," they created a new plantation regime based on African slavery rather than English indentured servitude. By 1720, Africans made up nearly 20 percent of the Chesapeake population, and slavery had become a central feature of the society, not just one of several forms of unfree labor. Equally important, slavery was now defined in racial terms. Virginia passed a law in 1692 that

Olaudah Equiano

This 1780 portrait by an unknown artist in England shows the freed slave and author Olaudah Equiano. Equiano was among the first individuals of African descent to develop a consciousness of African identity that transcended traditional ethnic and national boundaries. Royal Albert Memorial Museum, Exeter, England.

prohibited sexual intercourse between English and Africans; and a 1705 statute defined virtually all resident Africans as slaves: "All servants imported or brought into this country by sea or land who were not Christians in their native country shall be accounted and be slaves."

Conditions for slaves in Virginia and Maryland were much less severe than they were in the West Indies, and slaves lived relatively long lives. Sugar required strenuous labor during the planting and harvesting seasons, whereas tobacco cultivation required steady but undemanding labor. Slaves planted the young tobacco seedlings in the spring, hoed and weeded the crop during the summer, and in the fall picked and hung the leaves to cure over the winter. Moreover, diseases did not spread easily among slaves in the Chesapeake colonies, where plantation quarters were smaller and less crowded than those in the West Indies. In addition, because tobacco profits were low, planters could not always afford to buy new slaves and so treated those they had less harshly than West Indian planters did.

Olaudah Equiano

The Brutal "Middle Passage"

Olaudah Equiano, known also as Gustavus Vassa, claimed to have been born in Igboland (in present-day southern Nigeria). But two scholars, one African and one Euro-American, writing independently, have recently argued that Equiano was not born in Africa. One of them has discovered strong evidence that he was born into slavery in South Carolina and suggests that he drew on conversations with African-born slaves to create a fictitious history of an idyllic childhood in West Africa, his kidnapping and enslavement at the age of eleven, and a traumatic passage across the Atlantic. It now appears that Equiano worked as a plantation slave as a young boy and was then was purchased by an English sea captain. Equiano bought his freedom in 1766, settled in London, became an antislavery activist, and, in 1789, published the memoir containing these selections.

My father, besides many slaves, had a numerous family of which seven lived to grow up, including myself and a sister who was the only daughter. . . . I was trained up from my earliest years in the art of war, my daily exercise was shooting and throwing javelins, and my mother adorned me with emblems after the manner of our greatest warriors. One day, when all our people were gone out to their works as usual and only I and my dear sister were left to mind the house, two men and a woman got over our walls, and in a moment seized us both, and without giving us time to cry out or make resistance they stopped our mouths and ran off with us into the nearest wood. . . .

At length, after many days' travelling, during which I had often changed masters, I got into the hands of a chieftain in a very pleasant country. This man had two wives and some children, and they all used me extremely well and did all they could to comfort me, particularly the first wife, who was something like my mother. Although I was a great many days' journey from my father's house, yet these people spoke exactly the same language with us. This first master of mine, as I may call him, was a [blacksmith], and my principal employment was working his bellows.

I was again sold and carried through a number of places till . . . at the end of six or seven months after I had been kidnapped I arrived at the sea coast.

The first object which saluted my eyes when I arrived on the coast was the sea, and a slave ship which was then riding at anchor and waiting for its cargo. I now saw myself deprived of all chance of returning to my native country . . . ; and I even wished for my former slavery in preference to my present situation, which was filled with horrors of every kind. . . . I was soon put down under the decks, and there I received such a salutation in my nostrils as I had never experienced in my life; so that with the loathsomeness of the stench and crying together, I became so sick and low that I was not able to eat, nor had I the least desire to taste any thing. I now wished for the last friend, death, to relieve me; but soon, to my grief, two of the white men offered me eatables, and on my refusing to eat, one of them held me fast by the hands and laid me across I think the windlass, and tied my feet while the other flogged me severely. I had never experienced anything of this kind before, and although, not being used to the water, I naturally feared that element the first time I saw it, yet nevertheless could I have got over the nettings, I would have jumped over the side, but I could not. . . . One day, when we had a smooth sea and moderate wind, two of my wearied countrymen who were chained together (I was near them at the time), preferring death to such a life of misery, somehow made it through the nettings and jumped into the sea.

At last we came in sight of the island of Barbados; the white people got some old slaves from the land to pacify us. They told us we were not to be eaten but to work, and were soon to go on land where we should see many of our country people. This report eased us much; and sure enough soon after we were landed there came to us Africans of all languages.

SOURCE: *The Interesting Narrative of the Life of Olaudah Equiano, or Gustavus Vassa, the African, Written by Himself* (London, 1789), 15, 22–23, 28–29.

ANALYZING THE EVIDENCE

➤ In what ways is Equiano's description of slavery in Africa consistent with the analysis in the text?

➤ What evidence does Equiano offer in his description of the Middle Passage that explains the average slave mortality rate of about 15 percent during the Atlantic crossing?

➤ Assuming that the scholars are correct, that Equiano was not born in Africa, why do you think he wrote this fictitious narrative of his childhood instead of describing the facts of his own life in slavery?

In fact, some tobacco planters consciously increased their workforce by buying female slaves and encouraging them to have children. In 1720, women made up one-third of Africans in Maryland, and the black population had begun to increase naturally. One absentee owner instructed his plantation agent "to be kind and indulgent to the breeding wenches, and not to force them when with child upon any service or hardship that will be injurious to them." Moreover, he added, "the children are to be well looked after." By midcentury, slaves made up almost a third of the Chesapeake population, and more than three-quarters of them were American born.

Slaves in South Carolina labored under much more oppressive conditions. The colony grew slowly until 1700, when Africans from rice-growing societies, who knew how to plant and process the nutritious grain, turned it into a profitable export. To expand production, white planters imported thousands of slaves and changed the face of the colony (Figure 3.1). By 1705, there were more Africans in South Carolina than there were whites, and slaves made up 80 percent of the population in rice-growing areas.

Those areas were inland swamps, and the work was dangerous and exhausting. Slaves planted, weeded, and harvested the rice in ankle-deep mud. Pools of putrid water bred mosquitoes, which transmitted disease among the workers, taking hundreds of African lives. Other slaves, forced to move tons of dirt to build irrigation works, died from exhaustion. "The labour required [for growing rice] is only fit for slaves," a Scottish traveler remarked, "and I think the hardest work I have seen them engaged in." In South Carolina, as in the West Indies and Brazil, there were many deaths and few births, and the importation of new slaves constantly "re-Africanized" the black population.

The Emergence of an African American Community

Slaves came from many different states and peoples in West Africa and the West-Central African regions of Kongo and Angola (Table 3.5). Plantation owners in South Carolina preferred laborers from the Gold Coast and Gambia, who had a reputation as hardworking farmers. But as African sources of slaves shifted southward after 1730, more than 30 percent of the colony's workforce came from Kongo and Angola. Some white planters welcomed ethnic diversity as a deterrent to slave revolts. "The safety of the Plantations," declared a widely read English pamphlet, "depends upon having Negroes from all parts of Guiny, who do not understand each other's languages and Customs and cannot agree to Rebel." However, planters often had to take the workers offered by slave traders, whatever their region of origin. Of the slaves imported into the Upper James River region of Virginia after 1730, 41 percent embarked from ports in the Bight of Biafra (present-day Nigeria), where Kwa dialects were spoken. Another 25 percent came from West-Central Africa and were probably Kikongo- and Kimbundu-speakers. The rest hailed from the Windward and Gold coasts, Senegambia, and Sierra Leone, and spoke Mande and other regional languages.

Initially, the slaves did not think of themselves as Africans or blacks but as members of a specific family, clan, or people — Wolof, Hausa, Ibo, Yoruba, Teke, Ngola — and they associated with those who shared their language and customs. In the Upper James River region, where Ibo men and women arrived in equal numbers, they probably married other Ibos and so retained their African culture. Discoveries of spoons with incised handles, like those used by Ibo diviners, point to the persistence of traditional ways.

Over time, the slaves made friendships and married across ethnic lines, thereby transcending the cultural groups of their homeland. In the West Indies and the Carolina lowlands, the largely

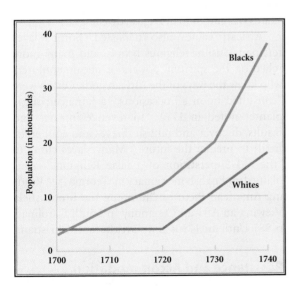

FIGURE 3.1 The Growth of Slavery in South Carolina, 1700–1740

To grow more rice, white planters in South Carolina imported thousands of enslaved Africans. By 1705, South Carolina had a black majority, which allowed the development among slaves of a strong Afro-centric language and culture.

TABLE 3.5	African Slaves Imported into North America by Region of Departure and Ethnicity, 1700–1775		
Region of Departure	**Ethnicity**	**Number**	**Percentage**
Senegambia	Mandinka, Fulbe, Serer, Jola, Wolof, Bambara	47,300	17
Sierra Leone	Vai, Mende, Kpelle, Kru	33,400	12
Gold Coast	Ashanti, Fanit	19,500	7
Bight of Benin, Bight of Biafra	Ibo, Ibibio	47,300	17
West-Central Africa	Kongo, Tio, Matamba	44,600	16
Southeast Africa	Unknown	2,800	1
Other or unknown		83,500	30
Total		**278,400**	**100**

The numbers are estimated from known voyages involving 195,000 Africans. The ethnic origins of the slaves are tentative because peoples from different regions often left from the same port and because the regions of departure of 83,500 slaves (30 percent) are not known.

SOURCE: Aaron S. Fogleman, "From Slaves, Convicts, and Servants to Free Passengers: The Transformation of Immigration in the Era of the American Revolution," *Journal of American History* 85 (June 1998), table A.4.

African-born population created new languages. One was the Gullah dialect, which combined English and African words in an African grammatical structure. "They have a language peculiar to themselves," a missionary reported, "a wild confused medley of Negro and corrupt English, which makes them very unintelligible except to those who have conversed with them for many years." In the Chesapeake region, where there were more American-born slaves, most people of African descent gradually gave up their native tongues. In the 1760s, a European visitor to Virginia reported with surprise that "all the blacks spoke very good English."

A common language—Gullah or English or French (in Louisiana and the French West Indies)—was key to the development of an African American community. A nearly equal number of men and women, which encouraged marriage, stable families, and continuity between generations, was another. In South Carolina, the high death rate among slaves undermined ties of family and kinship; but after 1725, Chesapeake-area blacks created strong nuclear families and extended kin relationships. For example, all but 30 of the 128 slaves on one of Charles Carroll's estates in Maryland were members of two extended families. These African Americans gradually developed a culture of their own, passing on family names, traditions, and knowledge to the next generation. As one observer suggested, blacks had created their own cultural world, "a Nation within a Nation."

As the slaves forged a new identity, they carried on certain African practices but let others go. Many Africans arrived in the colonies with ritualistic scars that white planters called "country markings"; this sign of ethnic identity fell into disuse on the culturally diverse plantations. But the slaves' African heritage took many other tangible forms: in their hairstyles; in the traditional motifs they used in wood carvings and pottery; in the large wooden mortars and pestles with which they hulled rice; and in the design of their houses, in which rooms often were arranged from front to back in a distinctive "I" pattern, not side by side as was common in English dwellings.

African values also persisted. Some slaves retained Muslim religious beliefs, and many more relied on the spiritual powers of obeah, conjurers who knew the ways of the African gods. Obeah were "consulted upon all occasions," a Jamaican sugar planter noted in 1774, "to revenge injuries and insults, discover and punish thieves and adulterers; [and] to predict the future." Many slaves clung to "the old Superstition of a false Religion," complained an English missionary in Georgia (see Reading American Pictures, "Jumping the Broomstick: Viewing an African Ceremony in South Carolina," p. 88). Until the 1790s, few slaves became Christians.

Resistance and Accommodation

There were drastic limits on African American creativity. Most slaves were denied education. They accumulated few material goods and had little opportunity to weave cloth or decorate pottery with traditional African designs. A well-traveled European who visited a slave hut in Virginia in the late eighteenth century found it "more miserable than

Hulling Rice in West Africa and Georgia

An eighteenth-century engraving depicts West African women using huge wooden mortars and pestles to strip the tough outer hull from rice kernels. A century and a half later, African American women in Georgia used the same tools to prepare rice for their families.

Library of Congress/Georgia Department of Archives and History, Atlanta.

the most miserable of the cottages of our peasants. The husband and wife sleep on a mean pallet, the children on the ground; a very bad fireplace, some utensils for cooking. . . . They work all week, not having a single day for themselves except for holidays."

Slaves who resisted did so at their peril. Planters resorted to the lash to punish slaves who refused to work; and some would amputate slaves' fingers, toes, or ears. Declaring the chronic runaway Ballazore an "incorrigeble rogue," a Virginia planter ordered all his toes cut off: "Nothing less than dismembering will reclaim him." Thomas Jefferson, who witnessed this cruelty on his father's Virginia plantation, noted that each generation of whites was "nursed, educated, and daily exercised in tyranny": The relationship "between master and slave is a perpetual exercise of the most unremitting despotism on the one part, and degrading submission on the other." A fellow Virginian, planter George Mason, agreed: "Every Master is born a petty tyrant."

The extent of white violence depended on the size and density of the slave population. As Virginia planter William Byrd II complained in 1736, "Numbers make them insolent." In the rural areas of the northern colonies, where there were few slaves, physical violence was sporadic. But assertive black slaves on the sugar and rice plantations in the West Indies and South Carolina were routinely whipped. Because Africans outnumbered Europeans eight to one in these plantation areas, planters prohibited slaves from leaving the plantation without special passes. They also forced their poor white neighbors to patrol the countryside at night, a duty that (authorities regularly reported) was "almost totally neglected."

Slaves dealt with their plight in several ways. Some newly arrived Africans fled to the frontier, where they established traditional villages or married into Indian tribes. Blacks who were fluent in English fled to towns, where they tried to pass as free men and women. Most African Americans remained enslaved and bargained continually with their masters over the terms of their bondage. Some blacks bartered extra work for better food and clothes; others seized a small privilege and dared the master to revoke it. That is how Sundays gradually became a day of rest — and a right rather than a privilege. When bargaining failed, slaves would protest silently, working slowly or stealing. Others, provoked beyond endurance, killed their owners or overseers: In the

Jumping the Broomstick: Viewing an African Ceremony

African Culture in South Carolina, c. 1800. Abby Aldrich Rockefeller Folk Art Center, Colonial Williamsburg.

African slaves carried their customs to British North America, where they created a new culture that combined the traditions of many African and European peoples. How can we better understand this cultural synthesis? Slaves left few written records; but we do have visual evidence, like this painting of a dance — possibly at a wedding ceremony — by an unknown artist.

ANALYZING THE EVIDENCE

➤ The painting is set on a rice plantation in the low country of South Carolina. What clues can you see in the image that confirm the location?

➤ Does the evidence in the picture suggest that these people are recent arrivals from Africa? What artifacts in the picture might be African in origin? What have you learned from the text about the conditions on rice plantations that would contribute to a steady stream of African-born workers on those plantations?

➤ Many African peoples mingled with one another on large plantations. Do you see any evidence in the painting that suggests tribal differences? What suggests that the two dancers in the center — perhaps a bride and groom — come from different African peoples?

➤ Around 1860, a Virginia slave recounted the story of her parents' marriage: "Ant Lucky read sumpin from de Bible, an' den she put de broomstick down an' dey locked dey arms together an' jumped over it. Den dey was married." In the scene depicted in this painting, the man in the red breeches is holding a long stick. If this is a wedding, is there any evidence of Christianity in the ceremony? Look carefully at the men's and women's clothes. Do they reveal signs of European cultural influence?

1760s, in Amherst County, Virginia, a slave killed four whites; in Elizabeth City County, eight slaves strangled their master in bed. A few blacks even plotted rebellion, despite white superiority in guns and, in most regions, in numbers as well.

Predictably, South Carolina witnessed the largest slave uprising, the Stono Rebellion of 1739. The governor of the Spanish colony of Florida instigated the revolt by promising freedom to fugitive slaves. By February 1739, at least sixty-nine slaves had escaped to St. Augustine, and rumors circulated "that a Conspiracy was formed by Negroes in Carolina to rise and make their way out of the province." When war between England and Spain broke out in September (see p. 95), seventy-five Africans rose in revolt and killed a number of whites near the Stono River. According to one account, some of the rebels were Portuguese-speaking Catholics from the Kingdom of Kongo attracted by the prospect of life in a Catholic colony. Displaying their skills as soldiers — decades of brutal slave raiding in Kongo had militarized the society there — the rebels marched toward Florida "with Colours displayed and two Drums beating." White militia killed many of the Stono rebels, preventing a general uprising; and frightened whites imported fewer new slaves and tightened discipline on the plantations.

William Byrd and the Rise of the Southern Gentry

As the southern colonies became full-fledged slave societies, life changed not only for blacks but also for whites. Consider the career of William Byrd II (1674–1744). Byrd's father was a London goldsmith who became a successful planter-merchant in Virginia. Like many first-generation planters, the elder Byrd hoped to return to England and marry his children into landed-gentry families. To smooth his son's entry into gentry society, Byrd sent him to be educated in England when the boy was just seven. But his status-conscious classmates at the Felsted School shunned the child, calling him a "colonial." This was the young Byrd's first taste of the gradations of rank that permeated English society.

Other rejections followed. Lacking aristocratic connections, Byrd was denied a post with the Board of Trade, was passed over three times for the royal governorship of Virginia, and — the most crushing psychological blow — failed utterly in his almost desperate efforts to marry a rich Englishwoman. His Virginia estate of 43,000 acres and 200 African slaves failed to impress the father of his intended bride. In 1726, at age 52, Byrd finally gave up his father's dream and moved back to Virginia, a "lonely . . . silent country" where he sometimes felt he was "being buried alive." Accepting his lesser destiny as a member of the colony's gentry, Byrd built an elegant brick mansion on the family's estate at Westover, sat in "the best pew in the church," and won the king's appointment to the governor's council.

William Byrd II's experience mirrored that of many planter-merchants, trapped in Virginia and South Carolina by the curse of their inferior colonial status. They used their economic muscle to control white yeomen families and tenant farmers,

"Virginian Luxuries"

This painting by an unknown artist (c. 1810) depicts the physical and sexual exploitation inherent in a slave society. On the right, an owner chastises a male slave by beating him with a cane; on the left, ignoring the cultural and legal rules prohibiting sexual intercourse between whites and blacks, a white master prepares to bed his black mistress. Abby Aldrich Rockefeller Folk Art Collection, Colonial Williamsburg Foundation.

and resorted to brute strength to exploit enslaved blacks, the American equivalent of the oppressed peasants and serfs of Europe. The planters used Africans to grow food as well as tobacco; build houses, wagons, and tobacco casks; and make shoes and clothes. By making their plantations self-sufficient, the Chesapeake elite survived the depressed tobacco market between 1670 and 1720. Small-scale planters who needed to buy cloth and other goods fared less well and fell into debt.

To prevent another uprising like Bacon's Rebellion, the Chesapeake gentry addressed the concerns of middling and poor whites (see Chapter 2). They began by gradually lowering taxes on smallholders: In Virginia, the annual poll tax fell from forty-five pounds of tobacco in 1675 to just five pounds in 1750. In addition, the gentry encouraged smallholders to improve their economic lot by investing in slaves. By 1770, 60 percent of the English families in the Chesapeake colonies owned at least one slave. There was change, too, on the political front, as planters allowed poor yeomen and some tenants to vote. The strategy of the leading families—the Carters, Lees, Randolphs, and Robinsons—was to curry favor with these voters by bribing them with rum, money, and the promise of minor offices in county governments. In return, they expected the yeomen and tenants to elect them to office and defer to them. This horse trading solidified the social position of the planter elite, which used its control of the House of Burgesses to limit the power of the royal governor. Hundreds of yeomen farmers benefited as well, tasting political power and garnering substantial fees and salaries as deputy sheriffs, road surveyors, estate appraisers, and grand jurymen.

Even as wealthy Chesapeake gentlemen were allying themselves with smallholders, they were consciously setting themselves apart from their less affluent neighbors. As late as the 1720s some leading planters were boisterous, aggressive men who enjoyed the amusements of common folk—from hunting, hard drinking, and gambling on horse races to demonstrating their manly prowess by seducing female servants and slaves. As time passed, they began, like William Byrd II to model themselves on the English aristocracy. Consciously cultivating **gentility**—a refined but elaborate lifestyle—wealthy planters replaced their modest wooden houses with mansions of brick and mortar. Robert "King" Carter, for example, built a house that was seventy-five feet long, forty-four feet wide, and forty feet high; and then he filled it with fine furniture and rugs. The planters acknowledged the source of their acquired gentility, sending their sons to London to be educated as lawyers and gentlemen. But, unlike Byrd's father, they intended them to return to America, marry local heiresses, and assume their fathers' roles, managing plantations, socializing with fellow gentry, and running the political system.

Wealthy Chesapeake and South Carolina women also emulated the English elite. They read English newspapers and fashionable magazines, wore the finest English clothes, and dined in the English fashion, with an elaborate afternoon tea. To improve their daughters' marriage prospects, they hired English tutors to teach young women etiquette. Once married, gentry women deferred to their husbands, reared pious children, and maintained elaborate social networks, in time creating a new ideal—the southern gentlewoman. Using the profits generated by enslaved Africans in the South Atlantic system of commerce, wealthy planters formed an increasingly well educated, refined, and stable ruling class.

The Northern Maritime Economy

The South Atlantic system had broad geographical reach. As early as the 1640s, New England farmers supplied the sugar islands with bread, lumber, fish, and meat. As a West Indian explained, planters in the islands "had rather buy foode at very deare rates than produce it by labour, soe infinite is the profitt of sugar works." By 1700, the economies of the West Indies and New England were closely interwoven. Soon farmers and merchants in New York, New Jersey, and Pennsylvania were also shipping wheat, corn, and bread to the Caribbean sugar islands. By the 1750s, about two-thirds of New England's exports and half of those from the Middle Colonies were going to places like Jamaica and Barbados.

In fact, the South Atlantic system linked the entire British empire. In return for the sugar they sent to England, West Indian planters received credit—in the form of **bills of exchange**—from London merchants. The planters used the bills to buy slaves from Africa and to pay North American farmers and merchants for their provisions and shipping services. The American farmers and merchants then exchanged the bills for British manufactures, primarily textiles and iron goods.

The West Indian trade created the first American merchant fortunes and the first urban industries (Map 3.4). Merchants in Boston, Newport, Providence, Philadelphia, and New York invested their profits in new ships and in factories that refined raw sugar into finished loaves. They also distilled West Indian molasses into rum—more than half a million gallons in Boston alone by the 1740s.

Preserving Fish, Eighteenth-Century Style

Without refrigeration, how can fish be kept from spoiling? Salt and sun were the answers. As fish were caught, sailors quickly gutted and cleaned them. Once on shore, they cut the fish into fillets (or "flakes"), added a liberal dose of salt, and placed them on wooden racks to dry in the sun. Properly preserved and packed, the fish remained edible for months, and merchant ships carried them to consumers in the West Indies and Europe.
© Bettmann/Corbis.

Merchants in Salem, Marblehead, and other small New England ports built a major fishing industry by selling salted mackerel and cod to the sugar islands and to southern Europe. Baltimore merchants transformed their town into a major port by developing a bustling export business in wheat, while traders in Charleston shipped deerskins, indigo, and rice to European markets.

As transatlantic commerce expanded — from five hundred voyages annually in the 1680s to fifteen hundred annually in the 1730s — American port cities grew in size and complexity. Seeking jobs and excitement, British and German migrants and young people from the countryside (servant girls, male laborers, and apprentice artisans) flocked to urban areas. By 1750, the populations of Newport and Charleston were nearly 10,000; Boston had 15,000 residents; and New York had almost 18,000. The largest port was Philadelphia, whose population by 1776 had reached 30,000, the size of a large provincial city in Europe. Smaller coastal towns emerged as centers of the lumber and shipbuilding industries. Seventy sawmills dotted the Piscataqua River in New Hampshire, providing low-cost wood for homes, warehouses, and especially shipbuilding. Taking advantage of the Navigation Acts, which allowed colonists to build and own trading vessels, hundreds of shipwrights turned out ocean-going vessels, while other artisans made ropes, sails, and metal fittings for the new fleet. By the 1770s, colonial-built ships made up one-third of the British merchant fleet.

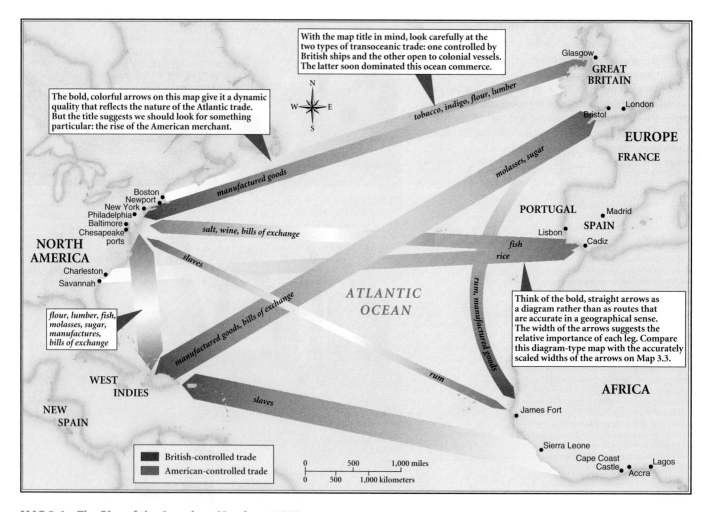

With the map title in mind, look carefully at the two types of transoceanic trade: one controlled by British ships and the other open to colonial vessels. The latter soon dominated this ocean commerce.

The bold, colorful arrows on this map give it a dynamic quality that reflects the nature of the Atlantic trade. But the title suggests we should look for something particular: the rise of the American merchant.

Think of the bold, straight arrows as a diagram rather than as routes that are accurate in a geographical sense. The width of the arrows suggests the relative importance of each leg. Compare this diagram-type map with the accurately scaled widths of the arrows on Map 3.3.

MAP 3.4 The Rise of the American Merchant, 1750

Throughout the colonial era, British merchant houses dominated the transatlantic trade in manufactures, sugar, tobacco, and slaves. However, by 1750, American-born merchants in Boston, New York, and Philadelphia had seized control of the commerce between the mainland and the West Indies. In addition, Newport traders played a small role in the slave trade from Africa, and Boston and Charleston merchants grew rich carrying fish and rice to southern Europe.

The South Atlantic System extended far into the interior. A fleet of small vessels sailed back and forth on the Hudson and Delaware rivers, delivering cargoes of European manufactures and picking up barrels of flour and wheat to carry to New York and Philadelphia for export to the West Indies and Europe. By the 1750s, hundreds of professional teamsters in Maryland were transporting 370,000 bushels of wheat and corn and 16,000 barrels of flour to urban markets each year—more than ten thousand wagon trips. To service this traffic, entrepreneurs and artisans set up taverns, horse stables, and barrel-making shops in towns along the wagon roads. Lancaster, a prosperous wheat-producing town in Pennsylvania, for example, boasted more than two hundred German and English artisans and a dozen merchants.

Prosperous merchants dominated seaport cities. In 1750, about forty merchants controlled over 50 percent of Philadelphia's trade; they had taxable assets averaging £10,000, a huge sum at the time. Like the Chesapeake gentry, these urban merchants modeled themselves after the British upper classes, importing design books from England and building Georgian-style mansions to display their wealth. Their wives created a genteel culture by decorating their houses with fine furniture and entertaining guests at elegant dinners.

Artisan and shopkeeper families, the middle ranks of seaport society, made up nearly half the population. Innkeepers, butchers, seamstresses, shoemakers, weavers, bakers, carpenters, masons, and dozens of other skilled workers formed mutual self-help societies and toiled to gain a competency — an income sufficient to maintain their families in modest comfort and dignity. Wives and husbands often worked as a team, teaching the "mysteries of the craft" to their children. Some artisans aspired to wealth and status, an entrepreneurial ethic that prompted them to hire apprentices and expand production. However, most were not well-to-do, and many were quite poor. During his working life, a tailor was lucky to accumulate £30 worth of property, far less than the £2,000 owned at death by an ordinary merchant or the £300 listed in the **probate inventory** of a successful blacksmith.

Laboring men and women formed the lowest ranks of urban society. Merchants needed hundreds of dockworkers to unload manufactured goods and molasses from inbound ships and reload them with barrels of wheat, fish, and rice. Often they filled these demanding jobs with black slaves, who constituted 10 percent of the workforce in Philadelphia and New York City; otherwise, they hired unskilled wageworkers. Poor white and black women — single, married, or widowed — eked out a living by washing clothes, spinning wool, or working as servants or prostitutes. To make ends meet, most laboring families sent their children out to work at an early age. Indispensable to the economy, yet virtually propertyless, urban laborers rented rooms in crowded tenements in back alleys. In good times, their jobs bought security for their families or as much cheap New England rum as they could drink.

Periods of stagnant commerce threatened the financial security of merchants and artisans. For laborers, seamen, and seamstresses, whose household budgets left no margin for sickness or unemployment, depressed trade meant hunger or dependence on charity from the Overseers of the Poor, and — for the most desperate — petty thievery or prostitution. The sugar- and slave-based South Atlantic system brought economic uncertainty as well as jobs and opportunities to farmers and workers in the northern colonies.

> ➤ Describe the major elements of the South Atlantic system. How did the system work? How did it shape the development of the various colonies?

> ➤ What role did Africans play in the expansion of the Atlantic slave trade? What role did Europeans play?

> ➤ In what colonies were enslaved Africans most successful in creating African American communities? Where were they least successful? How do you explain the differences?

The New Politics of Empire, 1713–1750

The South Atlantic system changed the politics of empire. British ministers, pleased with the commercial success of staple crops, ruled the colonies with a gentle hand. The colonists took advantage of that leniency to strengthen their political institutions and, eventually, would challenge the rules of the mercantilist system.

The Rise of Colonial Assemblies

After the Glorious Revolution of 1688–1689, representative assemblies in America followed the example of the English Whigs, limiting the powers of crown officials. In Massachusetts during the 1720s, the assembly repeatedly ignored the king's instructions to provide the royal governor with a permanent salary. Legislatures in North Carolina, New Jersey, and Pennsylvania likewise refused for several years to pay their governors a salary. Using this and other tactics, the colonial legislatures gradually took control of taxation and local appointments, which angered imperial bureaucrats and absentee proprietors. "The people in power in America," complained William Penn during a struggle with the Pennsylvania assembly, "think nothing taller than themselves but the Trees."

Leading the increasingly powerful assemblies were members of the colonial elite. Although most property-owning white men had the right to vote, only men of wealth and status stood for election. In New Jersey in 1750, 90 percent of assemblymen came from political families (Figure 3.2). In Virginia in the 1750s, seven members of the influential Lee family sat in the House of Burgesses and, along with other powerful families, dominated its major committees. In New England, affluent descendants of the original Puritans intermarried and formed a core of political leaders. "Go into every village in New England," John Adams wrote in 1765, "and you will find that the office of justice of the peace, and even the place of representative, have generally descended from generation to generation, in three or four families at most."

However, neither elitist assemblies nor wealthy property owners could impose unpopular edicts on

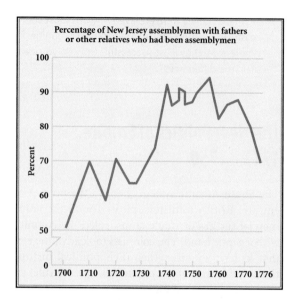

Percentage of New Jersey assemblymen with fathers or other relatives who had been assemblymen

FIGURE 3.2   Family Connections and Political Power, New Jersey, 1700–1776

By the 1750s, nearly every member of the New Jersey assembly came from a family with a history of political leadership, clear testimony to the emergence of an experienced governing elite in the mainland colonies.

the people. Purposeful crowd actions were a fact of colonial life. It was the uprising of ordinary citizens that overthrew the Dominion of New England in 1689. In New York, mobs closed houses of prostitution; in Salem (Massachusetts), they ran people with infectious diseases out of town. In Boston in 1710, angry crowds prevented merchants from exporting scarce grain; and in New Jersey in the 1730s and 1740s, mobs of farmers battled with proprietors who were forcing tenants off disputed lands. When officials in Boston restricted the sale of farm produce to a single public market, a crowd destroyed the building and its members defied the authorities to arrest them. "If you touch One you shall touch All," an anonymous letter warned the sheriff, "and we will show you a Hundred Men where you can show one." These expressions of popular power, combined with the growing authority of the assemblies, created a new political system. By the 1750s, colonial legislatures were broadly responsive to popular pressure and increasingly unresponsive to British control.

Salutary Neglect

British colonial policy during the reigns of George I (r. 1714–1727) and George II (r. 1727–1760) allowed the rise of American self-government. Royal bureaucrats, flush with growing tax receipts,

relaxed their supervision of internal colonial affairs and focused instead on defense and trade. In 1775, British political philosopher Edmund Burke would praise this strategy as **salutary neglect**.

Salutary neglect was a by-product of the political system developed by Sir Robert Walpole, the Whig leader in the House of Commons from 1720 to 1742. By providing supporters with appointments and pensions, Walpole won parliamentary approval for his policies. However, his use of patronage weakened the imperial system by filling the Board of Trade with political hacks. When Governor Gabriel Johnson arrived in North Carolina in the 1730s, he vowed to curb the powers of the assembly and "make a mighty change in the face of affairs." Receiving little support from the Board of Trade, Johnson renounced reform and decided "to do nothing which can be reasonably blamed, and leave the rest to time, and a new set of inhabitants."

Sir Robert Walpole, the King's Minister

All eyes are on Sir Robert Walpole (left) as he offers advice to the Speaker of the House of Commons. A brilliant politician, the treasury secretary used patronage to command a majority in the Commons and won the confidence of George I and George II, the German-speaking monarchs from the duchy of Hanover. Walpole's personal motto, "Let sleeping dogs lie," helps explain his colonial policy of salutary neglect.
© National Trust Photographic Library/John Hammond.

Walpole's tactics also weakened the empire by undermining the integrity of the political system. **Radical Whigs** protested that Walpole had betrayed the Glorious Revolution by using patronage and bribery to create the strong Court (or Kingly) Party. The Country Party—its members were landed gentlemen—likewise warned that Walpole's policies of high taxes and a bloated royal bureaucracy threatened British liberties. Heeding these arguments, colonial legislators complained that royal governors abused their patronage powers. To preserve American liberty, the colonists strengthened the powers of the representative assemblies, unintentionally laying the foundation for the American independence movement (see Comparing American Voices, "The Rise of Representative Assemblies," pp. 96–97).

Protecting the Mercantile System

Apart from patronage, Walpole's American policy had as its primary goal the protection of British commercial interests. Initially, Walpole pursued a cautious foreign policy to allow Britain to recover from a generation of war (1689–1713) against Louis XIV of France. But in 1732, he provided a parliamentary subsidy for the new colony of Georgia, which was intended by its reform-minded trustees as a refuge for Britain's poor. Envisioning a society of independent family farmers, the trustees limited most land grants to five hundred acres and initially outlawed slavery.

Walpole had little interest in social reform; he wanted Georgia subsidized to protect the valuable rice-growing colony of South Carolina. Britain's expansion into Georgia, a region long claimed by Spain, outraged Spanish officials, who were already angry because British merchants were illegally selling slaves and manufactured goods in Spain's American colonies. In fact, to counter Britain's commercial expansion, Spanish naval forces had stepped up their seizure of illegal traders—and sexually mutilated an English sea captain, Robert Jenkins.

Yielding to Parliamentary pressure, Walpole declared war on Spain in 1739. The War of Jenkins's Ear (1739–1741) was a largely unsuccessful attack on Spain's empire in North America. In 1740, British regulars failed to capture St. Augustine because South Carolina whites—still shaken by the Stono Rebellion—refused to commit militia units to the expedition. A year later, a major British and American assault on the prosperous Spanish seaport of Cartagena (in present-day Colombia) failed. Instead of enriching themselves with Spanish booty, hundreds of troops from the mainland colonies died in the attack, mostly from tropical diseases.

The War of Jenkins's Ear quickly became part of a general European conflict, the War of the Austrian Succession (1740–1748). Massive French armies battled British-subsidized German forces in Europe, and French naval forces roamed the West Indies, vainly trying to conquer a British sugar island. There was little fighting in North America until 1745, when three thousand New England militiamen, supported by a British naval squadron, captured Louisbourg, a French fortress at the entrance to the St. Lawrence River. To the dismay of New England Puritans, who feared invasion from Catholic Quebec, the Treaty of Aix-la-Chapelle (1748) returned Louisbourg to France. The treaty ensured British control over Georgia and reaffirmed its military superiority over Spain; more important, it made clear to colonial leaders that England would act in its own interests, not theirs.

The American Economic Challenge

The Walpole ministry had similar intentions about American economic activities. According to the Navigation Acts, the colonies were to produce staple crops and to consume British manufactured goods. To enforce the British monopoly on manufacturing, Parliament passed a series of additional Navigation Acts prohibiting Americans from selling colonial-made textiles (Woolen Act, 1699), hats (Hat Act, 1732), and iron products such as plows, axes, and skillets (Iron Act, 1750). As exports of tobacco, rice, and wheat grew by 400 percent between 1700 and 1750, colonists on the American mainland purchased more British textiles and iron goods.

However, the Navigation Acts had a major loophole: They allowed Americans to own ships and transport goods. Colonial merchants exploited those provisions to control 95 percent of the commerce between the mainland and the West Indies, and 75 percent of the transatlantic trade in manufactures. Quite unintentionally, the mercantilist system had created a dynamic community of colonial merchants, from which many of the early advocates for American independence would come.

Moreover, by the 1720s, the British sugar islands could not absorb all the flour, fish, and meat produced by mainland settlers. So, ignoring Britain's intense rivalry with France, colonial merchants sold their produce in the French West Indies. These supplies helped French planters produce

The Rise of Representative Assemblies

During the first six decades of the eighteenth century, the representative assemblies in British North America gradually expanded their authority and power. This development reflected greater popular respect for the assemblies, and, in turn, meant increased resistance to imperial policies. The shift in power from imperial authorities to colonial legislatures was piecemeal, the result of a series of small, seemingly inconsequential struggles. As you read this correspondence sent by two royal governors to officials back in England, look closely at the character of the disputes and think about how they were resolved.

ALEXANDER SPOTSWOOD
Confronting the House of Burgesses

As a reward for his military service in the wars against Louis XIV of France, Alexander Spotswood was made governor of Virginia in 1710. An often imperious and contentious man, Spotswood, though an effective governor, was a controversial one. He told the House of Burgesses to its face that the voters had mistakenly chosen "a set of representatives whom heaven has not generally endowed with the ordinary qualifications requisite to legislators." As the following selections show, Spotswood set out to reform the voting system that, in his judgment, produced such mediocre representatives. His efforts to oust popular members of the gentry from the House of Burgesses made him few friends; and in 1722, his enemies in Virginia used their influence in London to have him removed from office.

To ye Council of Trade, Virginia, October 15, 1712
MY LORDS:
. . . The Indians continue their Incursions in North Carolina, and the Death of Colo. Hyde, their Gov'r, which happened the beginning of last Month, increases the misery of that province, so much weakened already by their own divisions, that no measures projected by those in the Governm't for curbing the Heathen can be prosecuted.

This Unhappy State of her Maj't's Subjects in my Neighbourhood is ye more Affecting to me because I have very little hopes of being enabled to relieve them by our Assembly, which I have called to meet next Week; for the Mob of this Country, having tried their Strength in the late Election and finding themselves able to carry whom they please, have generally chosen representatives of their own Class, who as their principal Recommendation have declared their resolution to raise no Tax on the people, let the occasion be what it will. This is owing to a defect in the Constitution, which

allows to every one, tho' but just out of the Condition of a Servant, and that can but purchase half an acre of Land, an equal Vote with the Man of the best Estate in the Country.

The Militia of this Colony is perfectly useless without Arms or ammunition, and by an unaccountable infatuation, no arguments I have used can prevail on these people to make their Militia more Serviceable, or to fall into any other measures for the Defence of their Country. . . .

December the 17th 1714
The Governor this day laying before the Council a letter from the Right Honorable the Lords Commissioners for Trade dated the 23d of April 1713 directing him to advise with the Council & to recommend to the Generall Assembly to pass a law for qualifying the Electors & the persons Elected Burgesses to serve in the Generall Assembly of this Colony in a more just & equal manner than the Laws now in force do direct. . . . The Council declare that they cannot advise the Governor to move for any alteration in the present method of Electing of Burgesses, some being of opinion that this is not a proper time, & others that the present manner of electing of Burgesses & the qualifications of the elected is sufficiently provided for by the Laws now in force. . . .

To Mr. Secretary James Stanhope, July 15, 1715
I cannot forbear regretting yt I must always have to do with ye Representatives of ye Vulgar People, and mostly with such members as are of their Stamp and Understanding, for so long as half an Acre of Land, (which is of small value in this Country,) qualifys a man to be an Elector, the meaner sort of People will ever carry ye Elections, and the humour generally runs to choose such men as are their most familiar Companions, who very eagerly seek to be Burgesses merely for the lucre of the Salary, and who, for fear of not being

chosen again, dare in Assembly do nothing that may be disrelished out of the House by ye Common People. Hence it often happens yt what appears prudent and feasible to his Maj's Governors and Council here will not pass with the House of Burgesses, upon whom they must depend for the means of putting their designs in Execution. . . .

To the Lords Commissioners of Trade, May 23, 1716

. . . The behaviour of this Gentleman [Philip Ludwell Jr., the colony's auditor] in constantly opposing whatever I have offered for ye due collecting the Quitt rents and regulating the Acc'ts; his stirring up ye humours of the people before the last election of Burgesses; tampering with the most mutinous of that house, and betraying to them the measures resolved on in Council for his Maj't's Service, would have made me likewise suspend him from ye Council, but I find by the late Instructions I have received from his Maj'tie that Power is taken from ye Govern'r and transferred upon the majority of that Board, and while there are no less than seven of his Relations there, it is impossible to get a Majority to consent to the Suspension of him. . . .

GEORGE CLINTON
A Plea for Help

George Clinton served as governor of New York from 1744 to 1752. Like many governors appointed during the era of salutary neglect, Clinton owed his appointment to his social status and political connections. As the second son of the seventh Earl of Lincoln, he would not inherit the family's estate or his father's position in the House of Lords; to provide an income for Clinton, his family traded its votes in Parliament for patronage appointments to various naval and political positions. Once installed as governor of New York, Clinton found himself dependent on the assembly for the payment of his salary and the salaries of all the members of his government. Here, he explains his problems to the Board of Trade; by the end of Clinton's governorship, the Board was advocating increased imperial control over colonial life and politics.

My Lords,

I have in my former letters inform'd Your Lordships what Incroachments the Assemblys of this province have from time to time made on His Majesty's Prerogative & Authority in this Province in drawing an absolute dependence of all the Officers upon them for their Saleries & Reward of their services, & by their taking in effect the Nomination to all Officers . . . .

1stly, That the Assembly refuse to admit of any amendment to any money bill, in any part of the Bill; so that the Bill must pass as it comes from the Assembly, or all the Supplies granted for the support of Government, & the most urgent services must be lost.

2ndly, It appears that they take the Payment of the [military forces], passing of Muster Rolls into their own hands by naming the Commissaries for those purposes in the Act.

3rdly, They by granting the Saleries to the Officers personally by name & not to the Officer for the time being, intimate that if any person be appointed to any Office his Salary must depend upon their approbation of the Appointment. . . .

I must now refer it to Your Lordships' consideration whether it be not high time to put a stop to these usurpations of the Assembly on His Majesty's Authority in this Province and for that purpose may it not be proper that His Majesty signify his Disallowance of the Act at least for the payment of Saleries.

SOURCES: R. A. Brock, ed., *The Official Letters of Alexander Spotswood* (Richmond: Virginia Historical Society, 1885), 2: 1–2, 124, 154–155; H. R. MacIwaine, ed., *Executive Journals of the Council of Colonial Virginia* (Richmond: Virginia State Library, 1928), 3: 392; and E. B. O'Callaghan, ed., *Documents Relative to the Colonial History of the State of New York* (Albany, 1860), 2: 211.

ANALYZING THE EVIDENCE

➤ What policies did Spotswood want to pursue? Why couldn't he persuade the House of Burgesses to implement them? According to Spotswood, what was wrong with Virginia's political system? How did he propose to reform it?

➤ Unlike the House of Burgesses, whose members were elected by qualified voters, the members of the governor's council in Virginia were appointed by the crown, usually on the recommendation of the governor. What was the council's response to Spotswood's plan to reform the political system? Based on the Ludwell incident, where did the political sympathies of the council lie?

➤ What were Clinton's complaints about the actions of the New York assembly? Did those actions represent a more or less serious threat to imperial power than the activities of the Virginia Burgesses? Based on the material here, which governor was a stronger representative of the crown's interests?

Bristol Docks and Quay

Bristol, in southwest England, served as a hub for the trade with Africa, the West Indies, and the American mainland. This detail from an eighteenth-century painting of the bustling seaport shows horses drawing large hogsheads of West Indian sugar to local factories and workers readying smaller barrels of rum and other goods for export to Africa.
City of Bristol Museum and Art Gallery.

low-cost sugar and outsell Britain in the European sugar market. When American rum distillers began to buy cheap molasses from the French islands, the West Indian "sugar lobby" persuaded Parliament to enact the Molasses Act of 1733. The act allowed the mainland colonies to export fish and farm products to the French islands but—to give a price advantage to British sugar planters—placed a high tariff on French molasses. American merchants and legislators protested that the Molasses Act would cut farm exports, cripple the distilling industry, and, by slashing colonial income, reduce the colonists' purchases of British goods. When Parliament ignored their petitions, American merchants smuggled in French molasses by bribing customs officials. Luckily for the Americans, sugar prices rose sharply in the late 1730s and enriched planters in the British West Indies, so the act was not rigorously enforced.

The lack of adequate currency in the colonies prompted another conflict with British officials.

New England Sea Captains in Surinam

Flouting the Navigation Acts, New England traders developed a flourishing trade with plantation owners and merchant houses in the Dutch colony of Surinam on the east coast of South America (between Venezuela and Brazil). The traders carried fish and other footstuffs to the Dutch settlement and returned with cargoes of Surinamese molasses and Asian goods cotton cloth, ceramics, and tea provided by Dutch merchants. This tavern scene, painted by Boston artist John Greenwood in the 1750s, pokes fun at the hard-drinking New England sea captains. The Saint Louis Art Museum.

To pay for manufactured goods, American merchants sent to Britain the bills of exchange and the gold and silver coins they earned in the West Indian trade. These payments drained the colonial economy of money, which made it difficult for Americans to borrow funds or to buy and sell goods among themselves. To remedy the problem, ten colonial assemblies established **land banks** that lent paper money to farmers, who used their land as collateral for the loans. Farmers used the currency to buy tools or livestock or to pay their creditors, thereby stimulating trade. However, some assemblies, like the legislature in Rhode Island, issued large amounts of paper money (which consequently fell in value) and required merchants to accept it as legal tender. English merchants and other creditors rightly complained that they were being forced to accept worthless money. So in 1751, Parliament passed the Currency Act, which barred the New England colonies from establishing new land banks and prohibited the use of paper money to pay private debts.

These conflicts over trade and paper money angered a new generation of political leaders in England. In 1749, Charles Townshend of the Board of Trade charged that the American assemblies had assumed many of the "ancient and established prerogatives wisely preserved in the Crown"; he vowed to replace salutary neglect with more-rigorous imperial control.

The wheel of empire had come full circle. In the 1650s, England had set out to build a centrally managed colonial empire and, over the course of a century, achieved the economic part of that goal. Mercantilist legislation, commercial warfare against European rivals, and the forced labor of a million African slaves brought prosperity to Britain. However, internal unrest (the Glorious Revolution) and a policy of salutary neglect had weakened Britain's authority over its American colonies. Recognizing the threat self-government posed to the empire, British officials in the late 1740s vowed to reassert their authority in America, an initiative that would have disastrous results.

➤ How did the ideas and policies of the Whigs in England affect British and colonial political systems between 1700 and 1760?

➤ What was the British policy of salutary neglect? Why did the British follow this policy? What consequences did it have for the British colonies in North America?

SUMMARY

In this chapter we have examined two long-term processes of change, one in politics and one in society and economy. The political story began in the 1660s and 1670s, with Britain's attempt to centralize control over its American possessions. Parliament passed the Acts of Trade and Navigation to give Britain a monopoly over colonial products and trade. Then, King James II abolished representative institutions in the northern colonies and created the authoritarian Dominion of New England. The Glorious Revolution of 1688–1689 partially reversed these policies by restoring American self-government and by allowing colonists, during the subsequent era of salutary neglect, to avoid rigid compliance with mercantilist policies.

The core of the social and economic story centers on the development of the South Atlantic system of production and trade. It involved an enormous expansion of African slave raiding, the Atlantic slave trade, and the cultivation of sugar, rice, and tobacco in America. This complex story also includes the creation of exploited African American labor forces in the West Indies and the southern mainland, and of prosperous communities of European American farmers, merchants, and artisans in the northern mainland colonies. How would the stories develop? In 1750, slavery and the South Atlantic system seemed firmly in place; however, the days of salutary neglect appeared to be numbered.

Connections: Economy and Government

In the part opener (p. 3), we noted,

many European settlements became places of oppressive captivity for Africans, with pro-

found consequences for America's social development. . . . planters in the Chesapeake region imported enslaved African workers. Wealthy British and French planters in the West Indies, . . . bought hundreds of thousands of slaves from many African regions and forced them to labor on sugar, tobacco, and rice plantations.

As we can see in retrospect, the enormous expansion of the South Atlantic system of slavery and staple-crop production effected a dramatic change in the British colonies. In 1675, the three major English settlements—in the Chesapeake, New England, and Barbados—were small in numbers and reeling from Indian attacks, social revolts, and overpopulation. By 1750, all this had changed. British settlements in North America and the Caribbean had more than 2 million residents; produced vast amounts of sugar, rice, and tobacco; and were no longer in danger of being wiped off the map by Indian attacks. The South Atlantic system had brought wealth and opportunity to the white inhabitants not only of the sugar islands, the Chesapeake, and the Carolinas but also to the merchants and farm families of the New England and Middle Atlantic colonies.

If expansion solved some problems, it created others. As we have seen in Chapter 3, imperial officials imposed mercantilist laws regulating the increasingly valuable colonies and repeatedly went to war to safeguard them. This story of expanding imperial authority and warfare continues in Chapter 4, in the description of Britain's "Great War for Empire," a vast military conflict intended to expand British commercial power throughout the world and to establish Britain as the dominant nation in Europe.

CHAPTER REVIEW QUESTIONS

➤ Describe the dramatic expansion of the British empire in North America in the late seventeenth and early eighteenth centuries. What role did the South Atlantic System play?

➤ In what ways did politics in the British empire change in the decades following the Glorious Revolution? How do you explain those changes?

TIMELINE

1651	First Navigation Act
1660–1685	Reign of King Charles II
1663	Charles II grants Carolina proprietorship
1664	English capture New Netherland; rename it New York
1681	William Penn founds Pennsylvania
1685–1688	Reign of King James II
1686–1689	Dominion of New England
1688–1689	Glorious Revolution in England
1689	William and Mary ascend the throne in England
	Revolts in Massachusetts, Maryland, and New York
1689–1713	England, France, and Spain at war
1696	Parliament creates Board of Trade
1705	Virginia enacts slavery legislation
1714–1750	Britain follows policy of salutary neglect, allowing American assemblies to gain power
1720–1742	Sir Robert Walpole leads Parliament
1720–1750	African American community forms
	Rice exports from South Carolina soar
	Planter aristocracy emerges
	Seaport cities expand
1732	Parliament charters Georgia, challenging Spain
	Hat Act
1733	Molasses Act
1739	Stono Rebellion in South Carolina
1739–1748	War with Spain in the Caribbean and France in Canada
1750	Iron Act restricts colonial iron manufactures
1751	Currency Act prohibits land banks and use of paper money as legal tender

FOR FURTHER EXPLORATION

The best concise overview of America's place in England's empire is Michael Kammen, *Empire and Interest: The American Colonies and the Politics of Mercantilism* (1970). Linda Colley, *Britons: Forging the Nation, 1707–1837* (1992), explores the impact of empire on Britain. A clearly written study of multicultural tensions in early New York is Joyce Goodfriend, *Before the Melting Pot: Society and Culture in Colonial New York City, 1664–1730* (1992). Two fine portrayals of imperial military and political affairs in the eighteenth century are Fred Anderson, *A People's Army: Massachusetts Soldiers and Society in the Seven Years' War* (1984), a compelling picture of army life, and Richard Bushman, *King and People in Provincial Massachusetts* (1985), a nicely crafted story of the decline of British authority in New England.

Betty Wood, *Origins of American Slavery* (1998), and David Eltis, *The Rise of African Slavery in the Americas* (2000), offer fine surveys of this important topic. For compelling discussions of the diversity and evolving character of African bondage, see Ira Berlin, *Many Thousands Gone: The First Two Centuries of Slavery in North America* (1999), and Philip D. Morgan, *Slave Counterpoint: Black Culture in the Eighteenth-Century Chesapeake and Low Country* (1998). Olaudah Equiano, *The Interesting Narrative of the Life of Olaudah Equiano* (1789, 1995), provides a powerful account of slavery and the emergence of an African sense of identity. On Africa, consult Paul Bohannan and Philip Curtin, *Africa and the Africans* (3rd ed., 1988).

The PBS video *Africans in America, Part 1: Terrible Transformation, 1450–1750* (1.5 hours) covers the African American experience in the colonial period; the Web site (**www.pbs.org/wgbh/aia/part1/title.html**) contains a wide variety of pictures, historical documents, and scholarly commentary. The writings of enslaved and free African Americans are available at "Digital History" (**www.digitalhistory.uh.edu/black_voices/black_voices.cfm**). Jerome S. Handler and Michael L. Tuite Jr. present a comprehensive "Visual Record" of "The Atlantic Slave Trade and Slave Life in the Americas" (**hitchcock.itc.virginia.edu/Slavery/**). Also see the Library of Congress exhibit "African-American Odyssey" (**lcweb2.loc.gov/ammem/aaohtml/**), which provides digital access to court records, pamphlets, and slave narratives covering the period from 1740 to the present.

TEST YOUR KNOWLEDGE

To assess your command of the material in this chapter, see the Online Study Guide at **bedfordstmartins.com/henretta**.

For Web sites, images, and documents related to topics and places in this chapter, visit **bedfordstmartins.com/makehistory**.

4

Growth and Crisis in Colonial Society

1720–1765

IN 1736, ALEXANDER MACALLISTER LEFT the Highlands of Scotland for the backcountry of North Carolina, where his wife and three sisters soon joined him. Over the years, MacAllister prospered as a landowner and mill proprietor and had only praise for his new home. Carolina was "the best poor man's country I have heard in this age," he wrote to his brother Hector, urging him to "advise all poor people . . . to take courage and come." In North Carolina, there were no landlords to keep "the face of the poor . . . to the grinding stone," and so many Highlanders were arriving that "it will soon be a new Scotland." Here, on the far margins of the British empire, MacAllister wrote, people could "breathe the air of liberty, and not want the necessarys of life." Tens of thousands of European migrants — primarily Highland Scots, Scots-Irish, and Germans — heeded that advice, and they swelled the population of Britain's North American settlements from 400,000 in 1720 to almost 2 million by 1765.

The rapid increase in the number of white settlers — and enslaved Africans — transformed the character of life in every region of British America. Long-settled towns in New England became densely settled and then overcrowded; antagonistic ethnic and religious communities jostled uneasily with one another in the Middle Atlantic colonies; and the influx of the MacAllisters and thousands of other Celtic and German migrants altered the social and political landscape in the backcountry of

◄ **George Whitefield, Evangelist**

No painting could capture Whitefield's magical appeal, although this image conveys his open demeanor and religious intensity. When Whitefield spoke to a crowd near Philadelphia, an observer noted, his words were "sharper than a two-edged sword. . . . Some of the people were pale as death; others were wringing their hands . . . and most lifting their eyes to heaven and crying to God for mercy." *George Whitefield Preaching*, by John Collet (c. 1725–80). © Private Collection/The Bridgeman Art Library.

the South. Moreover, in every colony, two European cultural movements—the Enlightenment and Pietism—changed the tone of intellectual and spiritual life. Finally, and perhaps most important, as the migrants and the landless children of long-settled families moved inland, they sparked wars with the Native peoples and with France and Spain, the other European powers vying for empire in North America. A generation of dynamic growth produced a decade of deadly warfare that would set the stage for a new era in American history.

Freehold Society in New England

In the 1630s, the Puritans left a country where a handful of nobles and gentry owned 75 percent of the arable land and relied on servants, leaseholding tenants, and wageworkers to farm it. In New England, the Puritans set out to create a yeoman society, consisting primarily of freeholders, or landowning farm families. They succeeded all too well. By 1750, the region's rapidly growing yeoman population had settled on most of the best farmland, threatening the future of the freehold ideal.

Farm Families: Women and the Rural Household Economy

The Puritans' commitment to independence did not extend to women. Puritan ideology placed the husband at the head of the household and accorded him almost complete control over his dependents. As Reverend Benjamin Wadsworth of Boston advised women in *The Well-Ordered Family* (1712), being richer, more intelligent, or of higher social status than their husbands mattered little: "Since he is thy Husband, God has made him the head and set him above thee." Therefore, Wadsworth concluded, it was a wife's duty "to love and reverence" her husband.

Their subordinate role was made clear to women throughout their lives. Small girls watched their mothers defer to their fathers. As young women, they saw the courts prosecute many women and very few men for the crime of fornication (having sexual intercourse outside of marriage). And they learned that their marriage portions would be inferior in kind and size to those of their brothers: Instead of land, which was highly prized, daughters usually received livestock or household goods. Ebenezer Chittendon of Guilford (Connecticut), for example, left all his land to his sons, decreeing that "Each Daughter [shall] have half so much as Each Son, one half in money and the other half in Cattle." Because English law had eliminated many customary restrictions on the disposition of wealth, fathers generally were free to divide their property as they pleased.

In rural New England—in fact, throughout the colonies—women assumed the role of dutiful helpmeets (helpmates) to their husbands. Farmwives tended the garden that provided the family with fresh vegetables and herbs. They spun thread and yarn from flax or wool, and wove it into cloth for shirts and gowns. They knitted sweaters and stockings, made candles and soap, churned milk into butter and pressed curds into cheese, fermented malt for beer, preserved meats, and mastered dozens of other household tasks. And the most "notable," the most accomplished practitioners of these domestic arts, won praise from the community because their labor and skills were crucial to the rural household economy.

Bearing and rearing children were equally important tasks. Most women in New England married in their early twenties and by their early forties had given birth to six or seven children, usually delivered with the help of a neighbor or a midwife. Large families sapped the physical and emotional strength of most mothers for twenty or more of their most active years. One Massachusetts woman confessed that she had little time for religious activities because "the care of my Babes takes up so large a portion of my time and attention." Yet, more women than men became full members of Puritan congregations: "In a Church of between *Three* and *Four* Hundred *Communicants*," the eminent minister Cotton Mather noted, "there are but few more than *One* Hundred *Men*; all the Rest are Women." According to revivalist Jonathan Edwards, many women became full members both because they feared the dangers of childbirth and because that status meant that "their children may be baptized."

As the size of farms shrank in long-settled communities, many couples chose to have fewer children. After 1750, women in Andover, a typical farm village in Massachusetts, bore an average of only four children and had time and energy to pursue other tasks. Farm women now made extra yarn, cloth, or cheese to exchange with neighbors or sell to shopkeepers, which raised their families' standard of living. Or, like Susan Huntington of Boston, the wife of a prosperous merchant, they spent more time in "the care & culture of children, and the perusal of necessary books, including the scriptures."

Still, women's lives remained tightly bound by a web of legal and cultural restrictions. Ministers praised women's piety but excluded them from an equal role in the church. When Hannah Heaton, a farmwife in Connecticut, grew dissatisfied with her

Reflections on Mortality, 1775
This powerful image reveals both the artistic skills of colonial women working in the traditional mediums of quilting, embroidering, and weaving and the continuing concern of Puritan culture with the inevitability of death. Has the child of Prudence Punderson, a Rhode Island woman, already died and is soon to be placed in the coffin to the left? Or is Punderson picturing the progression of the child's life — from cradle, to marriage (note the image on the wall to the far right), to motherhood, and finally to death and burial? Connecticut Historical Society.

Congregationalist minister, thinking him unconverted and a "blind guide," she sought out Quaker and Baptist churches that welcomed questioning women and allowed them to become spiritual leaders. However, by the 1760s, many evangelical congregations were advocating traditional gender roles. "The government of Church and State must be . . . family government" controlled by its "king," declared the Danbury (Connecticut) Baptist Association. Willingly or not, most New England women abided by the custom that, as essayist Timothy Dwight put it, they should be "employed only in and about the house and in the proper business of the sex." This would not be the last time that men and women would clash over their proper social roles.

Farm Property: Inheritance

By contrast, European men who migrated to the colonies escaped many traditional constraints, including the curse of landlessness. "The hope of having land of their own & becoming independent of Landlords is what chiefly induces people into America," an official noted in the 1730s. For men who had been peasants and dependent on powerful lords in Europe, owning property gave them a new social identity.

Actually, property ownership and family authority were closely related. Most migrating Europeans wanted large farms that would provide sustenance for themselves and ample land for their children. Parents with small farms could not provide their offspring with land, so they placed them as indentured servants in more-prosperous households. When the indentures ended at age eighteen or twenty-one, their propertyless sons faced a decades-long climb up the agricultural ladder, from laborer to tenant and finally to freeholder.

Sons and daughters in well-to-do farm families were luckier: They received a marriage portion when they reached the age of twenty-three to twenty-five. The marriage portion — land, livestock, or farm equipment — repaid children for their past labor and allowed parents to choose their children's partners, which they did not hesitate to do. Parents' security during old age depended on a wise choice of son- or daughter-in-law. Although children could refuse an unacceptable match, they did not have the luxury of simply falling in love with whomever they pleased.

Marriage under eighteenth-century English common law was not a contract between equals. A bride relinquished to her husband the legal ownership of her land and her personal property. After his death, she received a dower right — the right to use, but not sell, a third of the family's property. The widow's death or remarriage canceled this use right, and her portion was divided among the children. The widow's property rights were subordinate to those of the family line, which stretched across the generations.

It was a father's duty to provide inheritances for his children, and men who failed to do so lost status in the community. Some fathers willed the family farm to a single son, providing their other children with money, apprenticeship contracts, or uncleared frontier tracts, or requiring the inheriting son to do so. Other yeomen moved their families to the frontier, where life initially was hard, but land for their children was cheap and abundant. "The Squire's House stands on the Bank of the Susquehannah," traveler Philip Fithian reported from the Pennsylvania backcountry in the early 1760s. "He tells me that he will be able to settle all his sons and his fair Daughter Betsy on the Fat of the Earth."

These farmers' historic accomplishment was the creation of whole communities of independent property owners. A French visitor noted the sense of personal dignity in this rural world, which contrasted sharply with European peasant life. Throughout the northern colonies, he found "men and women whose features are not marked by poverty, by lifelong deprivation of the necessities of life, or by a feeling that they are insignificant subjects and subservient members of society."

The Crisis of Freehold Society

How long would this happy circumstance last? Because of high rates of natural increase, New England's population doubled with each generation. The Puritan colonies had about 100,000 people in 1700, nearly 200,000 in 1725, and almost 400,000 in 1750. In long-settled areas, many farms had been divided and then subdivided; now they were so small—fifty acres or less—that many parents could not provide their children with an adequate inheritance. In the 1740s, Reverend Samuel Chandler of Andover was "much distressed for land for his children," seven of whom were male. A decade later, in nearby Concord, about 60 percent of the farmers owned less land than their fathers had.

Because parents had less to give their sons and daughters, they had less control over their children's lives. The system of arranged marriages broke down as young people engaged in premarital sex and used the urgency of pregnancy to win their fathers' permission to marry. Throughout New England, the number of premarital conceptions rose dramatically, from about 10 percent of first-born children in the 1710s to more than 30 percent in the 1740s. Given another chance, young people "would do the same again," an Anglican minister observed, "because otherwise they could not obtain their parents' consent to marry."

New England families met the threat to the freeholder ideal through a variety of strategies. Some parents chose to have smaller families by using various methods of birth control—abstention, coitus interruptus, or primitive condoms. Other families petitioned the provincial government for frontier land grants and hacked new farms out of the forests

of central Massachusetts, western Connecticut, and, eventually, New Hampshire and Vermont. Still others used their small plots more productively, replacing the traditional English crops of wheat and barley with high-yielding potatoes and Indian corn. Corn was an especially wise choice: It offered a hearty food for people, and its leaves furnished feed for cattle and pigs, which in turn provided farm families with milk and meat. Gradually, New England changed from a grain to a livestock economy, becoming the major supplier of salted and pickled meat to the plantations of the West Indies.

Finally, New England farmers survived on their smaller plots by developing the full potential of what one historian has called the "household mode of production." In this system, families exchanged labor and goods with one another. Women and children worked in groups to spin yarn, sew quilts, and shuck corn. Men lent one another tools, draft animals, and grazing land. Farmers plowed fields owned by artisans and shopkeepers, who repaid them with shoes, furniture, or store credit. In part because money was in short supply, no currency changed hands. Instead, farmers, artisans, and shopkeepers recorded their debits and credits in personal account books and every few years "balanced" the books by transferring small amounts of cash to one another. This system of community exchange allowed households—and the region's economy—to maximize their output and so preserve the freehold ideal.

➤ In what ways were the lives of women and men in New England similar? Different?

➤ By midcentury, the traditional strategies New England's farming families had relied on to provide marriage portions for children and security in old age for parents had become problematic. Why? How did farming households respond?

The Middle Atlantic: Toward a New Society, 1720–1765

The Middle Atlantic colonies—New York, New Jersey, and Pennsylvania—became home to peoples of differing origins, languages, and religions. Scots-Irish Presbyterians, English and Welsh Quakers, German Lutherans and Moravians, Dutch Reformed Protestants, and others formed ethnic and religious communities that coexisted uneasily with one another.

Economic Growth and Social Inequality

Ample fertile land and a longer growing season than New England attracted migrants to the Middle Atlantic colonies, and grain exports to Europe and the West Indies financed their rapid settlement. Between 1720 and 1770, growing demand doubled the price of wheat. By increasing their exports of wheat, corn, flour, and bread, Middle Atlantic farmers brought prosperity to the region, which, in turn, attracted more settlers. The population of the area surged from 120,000 in 1720 to 450,000 in 1765 (Figure 4.1).

Tenancy in New York. Despite the demand for land, many migrants refused to settle in New York's fertile Hudson River Valley. There, the Van Rensselaers and other Dutch landlords presided over manors created by the Dutch West India Company; and wealthy British families, such as the Clarkes and the Livingstons, dominated vast tracts granted by English governors (Map 4.1). Like the Chesapeake planters, the New York landlords aspired to live as European gentry, but few migrants wanted to labor as poor, dependent peasants. To attract tenants, the manorial lords had to grant them long leases and the right to sell their improvements—

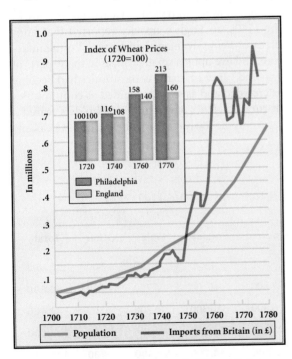

Figure 4.1 Population Growth, Wheat Prices, and British Imports in the Middle Colonies

Wheat prices doubled in Philadelphia between 1720 and 1770 as demand in the West Indies and Europe swelled. Exports of grain and flour paid for English manufactures, which the colonists imported in large quantities after 1750.

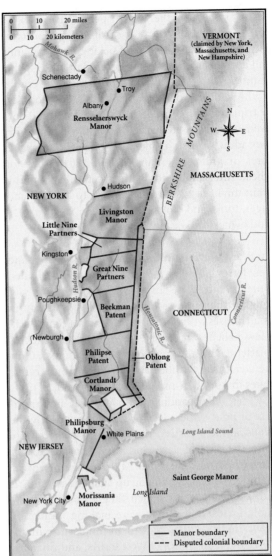

MAP 4.1 The Hudson River Manors

Dutch and English manorial lords owned much of the fertile eastern shore of the Hudson River, where they leased farms, on perpetual contracts, to German tenants and refused to sell land to freehold-seeking migrants from overcrowded New England. This powerful landed elite produced Patriot leaders, such as Gouverneur Morris and Robert Livingston, and prominent American families, such as the Roosevelts.

their houses and barns, for example—to the next tenant. The number of tenant families on the vast Van Rensselaer estate rose slowly at first, from 82 to 345 between 1714 and 1752, but then jumped to 700 by 1765.

Most tenant families hoped that with hard work and luck, they could sell enough wheat to buy their own farmsteads. But preindustrial technology limited their output, especially during the crucial harvest season. As the wheat ripened, it had to be harvested quickly, before it sprouted and became useless. A worker with a hand sickle could reap only half an acre of wheat, rye, or oats a day, limiting the number of acres a family could harvest. The cradle scythe, a tool introduced during the 1750s, doubled or tripled the amount of grain a worker could cut. Even so, during the harvest season, a family with two adult workers could reap only about twelve acres of grain—perhaps 150 to 180 bushels of wheat. After family needs were met, the remaining grain might be worth £15, enough to buy salt and sugar, tools, and cloth, but little else. The road to land ownership was not an easy one.

Quaker Pennsylvania. In rural Pennsylvania and New Jersey, at least initially, wealth was distributed more evenly. The first Quakers arrived with roughly the same resources and lived simply in small houses with one or two rooms, a sleeping loft, a few benches or stools, some wooden trenchers (platters), and a few wooden noggins (cups). Only the wealthiest families ate off pewter or ceramic plates imported from England or Holland. In time, however, the expanding trade in wheat and an influx of poor settlers led to social divisions. By the 1760s, affluent eastern Pennsylvania farmers were using the labor of slaves and immigrant workers to grow wheat on large farms. At the same time, other ambitious men were buying up land and dividing it into small tenancies, which they let out on profitable leases. Still others were making money by providing new settlers with farming equipment, sugar and rum from the West Indies, and financial services. These large-scale farmers, rural landlords,

speculators, storekeepers, and gristmill operators formed a distinct class of agricultural capitalists. They displayed their wealth by building large stone houses and furnishing them with expensive mahogany tables and four-poster beds, and laying their tables with elegant linen and handsomely decorated Dutch dinnerware.

At the other end of the social scale, one-half of the white population of the Middle Atlantic colonies owned no land and little personal property. Some propertyless men were the sons of farmers and would eventually inherit at least part of the family estate. But many were Scots-Irish "inmates"—single men or families, explained a tax assessor, "such as live in small cottages and have no taxable property, except a cow." In the predominantly German settlement of Lancaster, Pennsylvania, a merchant noted an "abundance of Poor people" who "maintain their Families with great difficulty by day Labour." Although these Scots-Irish and German migrants hoped to become tenants and eventually landowners, sharply rising land prices prevented many of them from realizing their dreams.

Merchants and artisans took advantage of the ample supply of labor to organize an outwork system. They bought wool or flax from farmers and paid propertyless workers and land-poor farm families to spin it into yarn or weave it into cloth. In the 1760s, an English traveler reported that hundreds of Pennsylvanians had turned "to manufacture, and live upon a small farm, as in many parts of England." Indeed, many communities had become as crowded and as socially divided as communities in rural England, and many smallholders feared a return to the lowly status of the European peasant.

TABLE 4.1 Estimated European Migration to the British Mainland Colonies, 1700–1780

Period	Germany	Northern Ireland	Southern Ireland	Scotland	England	Wales	Other	Total
1700–1719	4,000	2,000	2,500	700	1,700	1,200	300	**12,400**
1720–1739	17,900	6,900	10,400	2,800	7,100	4,700	1,000	**50,800**
1740–1759	52,700	25,400	18,200	6,800	16,300	10,700	2,300	**132,400**
1760–1779	23,700	36,200	13,400	25,000	19,000	12,400	2,300	**132,000**
Total	**98,300**	**70,500**	**44,500**	**35,300**	**44,100**	**29,000**	**5,900**	**327,600**

After 1720, European migration to British America increased dramatically, peaking between 1740 and 1780, when more than 264,000 settlers arrived in the mainland colonies. Immigration from Germany was at its highest in the mid-1750s, while that from Ireland, Scotland, England, and Wales continued to increase during the 1760s and early 1770s. Most migrants, including those from Southern Ireland, were Protestants.
SOURCE: Adapted from Aaron Fogelman, "Migrations to the Thirteen British North American Colonies, 1700–1775: New Estimates," *Journal of Interdisciplinary History* 22 (1992).

Cultural Diversity

The middle colonies were not a melting pot: European migrants held tightly to their traditions, creating a patchwork of ethnically and religiously diverse communities (Table 4.1). In 1748, a traveler counted no fewer than twelve religious denominations in Philadelphia, including Anglicans, Baptists, Quakers, Swedish and German Lutherans, Mennonites, Scots-Irish Presbyterians, and Roman Catholics.

Migrants preserved their cultural identity by marrying within their own ethnic group and maintaining the customs of their native land (see Comparing American Voices, "Ethnic Customs and Conflict," pp. 110–111). A major exception were the Huguenots, Calvinists who were expelled from Catholic France in the 1680s and moved to Holland, England, and the British colonies. Those Huguenots who settled in American port cities — Boston, New York, and Charleston — soon lost their French identity by intermarrying with other Protestants. More typical were the Welsh Quakers. Seventy percent of the children of the original Welsh migrants to Chester County, Pennsylvania, married other Welsh Quakers, as did 60 percent of the third generation.

In Pennsylvania and western New Jersey, Quakers were the dominant social group, at first because of their numbers and later because of their wealth and social cohesion. Because Quakers were pacifists, Pennsylvania officials dealt with Native Americans by negotiating treaties and buying land rather than seizing it. However, in 1737, Governor

A Quaker Meeting for Worship

Quakers dressed plainly and met in unadorned buildings, sitting in silence until inspired by an "inner light." Women spoke with near-equality to men, a tradition that prepared Quaker women to take a leading part in the nineteenth-century women's rights movement. In this English work, titled *Quaker Meeting*, an elder (his hat on a peg above his head) conveys his thoughts to the congregation. Museum of Fine Arts, Boston.

Ethnic Customs and Conflict

As we note in the text, people from many European regions migrated to British North America during the eighteenth century, bringing with them their languages, religions, and customs. What happened next? Did the migrants continue their old ways in the new land? Or did the new environment change them? Did they remain distinct groups? Or did they gradually create a composite Euro-American race and culture? The two accounts here, the first a contemporary essay and the second a memoir, offer insights on these cultural issues.

J. HECTOR ST. JEAN DE CRÈVECOEUR
"What, Then, Is the American, This New Man?"

A Frenchman by birth, Crèvecoeur (1735–1813) came to America during the French and Indian War, married a merchant's daughter, and settled in Orange County, New York, where he lived as a "gentleman farmer." In 1782, he published Letters from an American Farmer, *a justly famous book of essays that explored the character of his new land and its people.*

The next wish of this traveler will be to know whence came all these people. They are a mixture of English, Scotch, Irish, French, Dutch, Germans, and Swedes. From this promiscuous breed, that race now called Americans have arisen. The eastern provinces [New England] must indeed be excepted as being the unmixed descendants of Englishmen. I have heard many wish that they had been more intermixed also; I for my part, I am no wisher and think it much better as it has happened. I respect them for what they have done; for the accuracy and wisdom with which they have settled their territory; for the decency of their manners; for their early love of letters; their ancient college [Harvard], . . . for their industry. . . . There never was a people, situated as they are, who with so ungrateful a soil have done more in so short a time. . . .

In this great American asylum, the poor of Europe have by some means met together, . . . and here they are become men: in Europe they were as so many useless plants, wanting vegetative mould and refreshing showers; they withered, and were mowed down by want, hunger, and war; but now, by the power of transplantation, like all other plants they have taken root and flourished! Formerly they were not numbered in any civil lists of their country, except in those of the poor; here they rank as citizens. . . .

What, then, is the American, this new man? He is either an European or the descendant of an European; hence that strange mixture of blood, which you will find in no other country. I could point out to you a family whose grandfather was an Englishman, whose wife was Dutch, whose son married a French woman, and whose present four sons have now four wives of different nations. *He* is an American, who, leaving behind him all his ancient prejudices and manners, receives new ones from the new mode of life he has embraced, the new government he obeys, and the new rank he holds. . . . From involuntary idleness, servile dependence, penury, and useless labour, he has passed to toils of a very different nature, rewarded by ample subsistence. This is an American.

How much wiser, in general, the honest Germans than almost all other Europeans; . . . and [by] the most persevering industry, they commonly succeed. . . . The Scotch and the Irish [are different]. . . . The effects of their new situation do not strike them so forcibly, nor has it so lasting an effect. Whence the difference arises I know not, but out of twelve families of emigrants of each country, generally seven Scotch will succeed, nine German, and four Irish. The Scotch are frugal and laborious, but their wives cannot work so hard as German women, who on the contrary vie with their husbands, and often share with them the most severe toils of the field, which they understand better. . . . The Irish do not . . . prosper so well; they love to drink and to quarrel; they are litigious and soon take to the gun, which is the ruin of everything; they seem beside to labour under a greater degree of ignorance in husbandry than the others; . . . perhaps it is that their industry had less scope and was less exercised at home. . . . [In Ireland,] their potatoes, which are easily raised, are perhaps an inducement to laziness: their wages are too low and their whisky too cheap.

SOURCE: J. Hector St. Jean de Crèvecoeur, *Letters from an American Farmer*, ed. Albert E. Stone (New York: Penguin, 1981) 68–71, 85.

JOSEPH PLUMB MARTIN
A Narrative of a Revolutionary Soldier

Born in western Massachusetts, Joseph Plumb Martin (1760–1850) enlisted in the army in 1776 and served through the War of Independence. He then settled in Maine, where he worked as a town official and laborer, barely providing for his family. In 1830, he published his Narrative, *which was based on his wartime diary.*

I, with some of my comrades who were in the battle of the White plains in the year 76, one day took a ramble on the ground. . . . We saw a number of the graves of those who fell in that battle; some of the bodies had been so slightly buried that the dogs or hogs, or both, had dug them out of the ground. . . . Here were Hessian sculls as thick as a bomb shell — poor fellows! They were left unburied in a foreign land, . . . they should have kept at home. . . . But, the reader will say, they were forced to come and be killed here; forced by their rulers who have absolute power of life and death over their subjects. Well then, reader, bless a kind Providence that has made such a distinction between your condition and theirs. And be careful too that you do not allow yourself ever to be brought to such an abject, servile and debased condition. . . .

There were three regiments of Light Infantry, composed of men from the whole main army, — it was a motly group, — Yankees, Irishmen, Buckskins and what not. The regiment that I belonged to, was made up of about one half New-Englanders and the remainder were chiefly Pennsylvanians, two setts of people as opposite in manners and customs as Light and darkness, consequently there was not much cordialty subsisting between us; for, to tell the sober truth, I had in those days, as [soon] have been incorporated with a tribe of western Indians, as with any of the southern troops; especially of those which consisted mostly (as the Pennsylvanians did) of foreigners. But I was among them and in the same regiment too, . . . and had to do duty with them; to make a bad matter worse, I was often, when on duty, the only Yankee that happened to be on the same tour for several days together. "The bloody Yankee," or "the d—d Yankee," was the mildest epithets that they would bestow upon me at such times. It often made me think of home, or at *least* of my regiment of fellow-Yankees. . . .

After . . . being constantly interrogated by the passing officers, who we were, and how we came to be behind our troops, I concluded, that as most or all the troops had passed us, to stay where I then was, and wait the coming up of the baggage of our troops, thinking that the guard or drivers might have directions where to find them. . . . While we were waiting we had an opportunity to see the baggage of the army pass. When that of the middle States passed us,

it was truly amusing to see the number and habiliments of those attending it; of all specimens of human beings, this group capped the whole; a caravan of wild beasts could bear no comparison with it. There was "Tag, Rag and Bobtail;" "some in rags and some in jags," but none "in velvet gowns." Some with two eyes, some with one, and some, I believe, with none at all. They "beggared all description; their dialect, too, was as confused as their bodily appearance was odd and disgusting; there was the Irish and Scotch brogue, murdered English, that insipid Dutch and some lingos which would puzzle a philosopher to tell whether they belonged to this world or some "undiscovered country."

SOURCE: Joseph Plumb Martin, *A Narrative of a Revolutionary Soldier*, with an introduction by Thomas Fleming (New York: Signet, (2001), 116–117, 170.

ANALYZING THE EVIDENCE

▶ Crèvecoeur is known for suggesting that their environment forged a common character in the American people. Is this what he actually says? Consider his comments about the people of New England and about the relative success of Germans, Scots, and Irish.

▶ What do Martin's remarks suggest about the political consciousness of New Englanders? About the extent of geographical and ethnic consciousness in early America?

▶ How are the accounts of ethnicity by Crèvecoeur and Martin consistent with one another? In what ways do they conflict? How would you explain the similarities and differences?

Thomas Penn used dubious tactics to oust the Lenni-Lanape (or Delaware) Indians (see the painting on p. 71) from a vast area of land, creating bitterness that would lead to war in the 1750s. By this time, Quakers had begun to extend their religious values of equality and justice to African Americans. Many Quaker meetings (congregations) condemned the institution of slavery, and some expelled members who continued to keep slaves.

German Migration. The Quaker vision of a "peaceable kingdom" attracted 100,000 German migrants who were fleeing their homelands because of war and military conscription, religious persecution, and high taxes. First to arrive, in 1683, were the Mennonites, a group of religious dissenters drawn by the promise of religious freedom. In the 1720s, overcrowding and religious upheaval in southwestern Germany and German-speaking cantons in Switzerland brought a larger wave of migrants. "Wages were far better" in Pennsylvania, Heinrich

Schneebeli reported to his friends in Zurich, and "one also enjoyed there a free unhindered exercise of religion." A third wave of Germans and Swiss — nearly 40,000 strong — landed in Philadelphia between 1749 and 1756. Some of these newcomers were redemptioners, indentured servants who migrated as a family; but many more were propertied farmers and artisans in search of ample land for their children (see Voices from Abroad, "Gottlieb Mittelberger: The Perils of Migration," p. 113).

Germans soon dominated many districts of eastern Pennsylvania, and thousands more moved down the Shenandoah Valley into the western parts of Maryland, Virginia, and the Carolinas (Map 4.2). The migrants carefully guarded their language and cultural heritage. A minister in North Carolina admonished young people "not to contract any marriages with the English or Irish," explaining "we owe it to our native country to do our part that German blood and the German language be preserved in America." Well beyond 1800, these settlers spoke

MAP 4.2 Ethnic and Racial Diversity in the British Colonies, 1775

In 1700, most colonists in British North America were of English origin; by 1775, settlers of English descent constituted only about 50 percent of the total population. African Americans now accounted for one-third of the residents of the South, while thousands of German and Scots-Irish migrants contributed to ethnic and religious diversity in the middle colonies and southern backcountry (see Table 4.1).

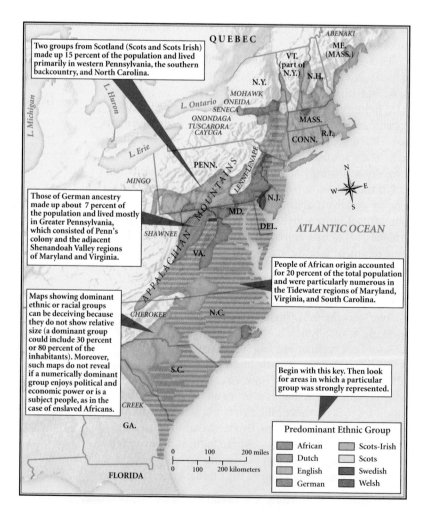

Gottlieb Mittelberger

The Perils of Migration

Gottlieb Mittelberger was a Lutheran minister who migrated to Pennsylvania with thousands of other Germans in the 1740s. Dismayed by the lack of piety among the colonists and the lack of state support for religious authority, he returned to his homeland after a few years. In Journey to America, *a book published in Germany in 1750, Mittelberger examined America with a critical eye, warning his readers of the difficulties of migration, the dangers of indentured servitude, and the hazards of life in a competitive society.*

[The journey from Germany to Pennsylvania via Holland and England] lasts from the beginning of May to the end of October, fully half a year, amid such hardships as no one is able to describe adequately with their misery. Both in Rotterdam and in Amsterdam the people are packed densely, like herrings so to say, in the large sea-vessels. One person receives a place of scarcely 2 feet width and 6 feet length in the bedstead, while many a ship carries four to six hundred souls. . . .

During the journey the ship is full of pitiful signs of distress—smells, fumes, horrors, vomiting, various kinds of sea sickness, fever, dysentery, headaches, heat, constipation, boils, scurvy, cancer, mouth-rot, and similar afflictions, all of them caused by the age and the highly-salted state of the food, especially of the meat, as well as by the very bad and filthy water, which brings about the miserable destruction and death of many. . . .

Children between the ages of one and seven seldom survive the sea voyage; and parents must often watch their offspring suffer miserably, die, and be thrown into the ocean, from want, hunger, thirst, and the like. I myself, alas, saw such a pitiful fate overtake thirty-two children on board our vessel, all of whom were finally thrown into the sea. Their parents grieve all the more, since their children do not find repose in the earth, but are devoured by the predatory fish of the ocean. . . .

When the ships finally arrive in Philadelphia after the long voyage only those are let off who can pay their sea freight or can give good security. The others, who lack the money to pay, have to remain on board until they are purchased and until their purchasers can thus pry them loose from the ship. In this whole process the sick are the worst off, for the healthy are naturally preferred and purchased first; and so the sick and wretched must often remain on board in front of the city for 2 or 3 weeks, and frequently die.

The sale of human beings in the market on board the ship is carried on thus: Every day Englishmen, Dutchmen and High-German people select among the healthy persons such as they deem suitable for their business, and bargain with them how long they will serve for their passage-money, which most of them are still in debt for. When they have come to an agreement, it happens that adult persons bind themselves in writing to serve 3, 4, 5 or 6 years for the amount due by them, according to their age and strength. But very young people, from 10 to 15 years, must serve till they are 21 years old.

Many parents must sell and trade away their children like so many head of cattle; for if their children take the debt upon themselves, the parents can leave the ship free and unrestrained. . . . It often happens that whole families, husband, wife, and children, are separated by being sold to different purchasers, especially when they have not paid any part of their passage money. . . .

When a serf has an opportunity to marry in this country, he or she must pay for each year which he or she would have yet to serve, 5 to 6 pounds. Thus let him who wants to earn his piece of bread honestly and in a Christian manner and who can only do this by manual labor in his native country stay there rather than come to America.

SOURCE: Gottlieb Mittelberger, *Journey to Pennsylvania*, ed. and trans. Oscar Handlin and John Clive (Cambridge, Mass.: Harvard University Press, 1960), 11–21.

ANALYZING THE EVIDENCE

➤ Most historians accept Mittelberger's account as generally accurate. How, then, do you explain the extent of German migration to the British colonies in North America?

➤ Why do you think most German migrants took passage to Philadelphia and not another colonial seaport?

➤ Compare Mittelberger's account of his Atlantic crossing with that of Olaudah Equiano (see Chapter 3, p. 84). How are they similar? How are they different?

German Farm in Western Maryland

Beginning in the 1730s, wheat became a major export crop in Maryland and Virginia. This engraving probably depicts a German farm: The harvesters are using oxen, not horses, and women are working in the field alongside the men. Using "a new method of reaping" that is possibly of German origin, the harvesters cut only the grain-bearing tip of the plants, leaving the wheat stalks in the fields to be eaten by livestock. Library of Congress.

German, read German-language newspapers, conducted church services in German, and preserved German farming practices, which sent women into the fields to plow and reap. Most German migrants were Protestants and lived easily as subjects of Britain's German-born and German-speaking monarchs, George I and George II. They engaged in local politics primarily to protect their churches and cultural practices, insisting, for example, that married women should have the right to hold property and write wills, as they did in Germany.

The Scots-Irish Influx. Migrants from Ireland accounted for the largest group of incoming Europeans, about 115,000 in number. Although some were Irish and Catholic, most were Scots and Presbyterians, the descendants of the Calvinist Protestants sent to Ireland by the English government during the seventeenth century to solidify its rule. Once in Ireland, the Scots faced hostility from both Irish Catholics and English officials and landlords. The Irish Test Act of 1704 restricted voting and office holding to Anglicans. English mercantilist regulations placed heavy import duties on the linens made by Scots-Irish weavers, and Scots-Irish farmers paid heavy taxes. "Read this letter, Rev. Baptist Boyd," a migrant to New York wrote back to his minister, "and tell all the poor folk of ye place that God has opened a door for their deliverance . . .

all that a man works for is his own; there are no revenue hounds to take it from us here."

Lured by reports like this one, thousands of Scots-Irish sailed for the colonies. The first migrants landed in Boston in the 1710s and settled primarily in New Hampshire. By 1720, though, most were sailing to Philadelphia, attracted by the religious tolerance there. In search of cheap land, they moved inland to central Pennsylvania and the fertile Shenandoah Valley, which stretched from Maryland to North Carolina. Governor William Gooch of Virginia welcomed their presence, which helped to secure "the Country against the Indians"; but an Anglican planter worried that the Scots-Irish "swarm like the Goths and Vandals of old, & will over-spread our continent soon." Like the Germans, the Scots-Irish retained their culture, living in ethnic communities and holding firm to the Presbyterian Church.

Religious Identity and Political Conflict

In Western Europe, the leaders of church and state condemned religious diversity. "To tolerate all [religions] without controul is the way to have none at all," an Anglican clergyman declared. Both English and German ministers carried these sentiments to Pennsylvania. "The preachers do not have the power to punish anyone, or to force anyone to go to church," complained Gottlieb Mittelberger, an influential minister. As a result, "Sunday is very badly kept. Many people plough, reap, thresh, hew or split wood and the like." He concluded: "Liberty in Pennsylvania does more harm than good to many people, both in soul and body."

Mittleberger was mistaken. Although ministers in Pennsylvania could not invoke government authority to uphold religious values, the result was not social anarchy. Instead, religious sects enforced moral behavior through communal self-discipline. Quaker families attended a weekly worship meeting and a monthly discipline meeting. Every three months, a committee from the monthly meeting reminded each mother and father to provide their children with proper religious instruction. Parents took the committee's words to heart. "If thou refuse to be obedient to God's teachings," Walter Faucit of Chester County admonished his son, "thou will be a fool and a vagabond." The committee also supervised adult behavior: A Chester County meeting, for example, disciplined one of its members "to reclaim him from drinking to excess and keeping vain company." Significantly, Quaker meetings granted permission to marry only to couples with land and livestock sufficient to support a family. As a result, the children of well-to-do Friends usually married within the sect, while poor Quakers remained unmarried, wed later in life, or married without permission — in which case they were often barred from Quaker meetings. These marriage rules helped build a self-contained and prosperous Quaker community.

In the 1740s, Quaker dominance in Pennsylvania came under attack. As German and Scots-Irish migration increased, Quakers became a minority, just 30 percent of the population. Simultaneously, Scots-Irish settlers in central Pennsylvania challenged the pacifism of the Quaker-dominated assembly by demanding an aggressive Indian policy. To maintain their influence, Quaker politicians looked for allies among the German migrants, many of whom embraced the Quakers' policies of pacifism and no compulsory militia service. In return, German leaders demanded fair representation of their communities in the provincial assembly and legislation that respected their inheritance customs. These ethnic-based conflicts over Indian policy and representation threw politics in Pennsylvania into turmoil. One European visitor noted that the attempts of Scots-Irish Presbyterians, German Baptists, and German Lutherans to form "a general confederacy" against the Quakers were likely to fail because of "a mutual jealousy, for religious zeal is secretly burning" (Map 4.3).

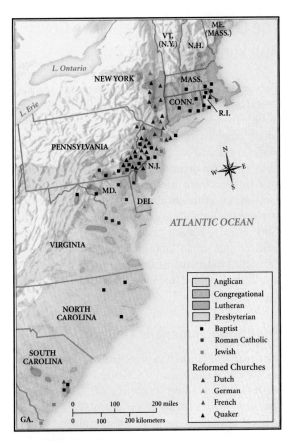

MAP 4.3 Religious Diversity in 1750

By 1750, religious diversity was on the rise, not only in the multiethnic middle colonies, but in all of British North America. Baptists had increased their numbers in New England, long the stronghold of Congregationalists, and would soon become important in Virginia. Already there were good-sized pockets of Presbyterians, Lutherans, and German Reformed in the South, where Anglicanism was the established religion.

By the 1750s, ethnic and religious passions flared in the Middle Atlantic colonies. In Pennsylvania, Benjamin Franklin disparaged the "boorish" character and "swarthy complexion" of German migrants; while in New York, a Dutchman declared that he "Valued English Law no more than a Turd." The region's experiment in cultural and religious diversity prefigured the bitter ethnic and social conflicts that would characterize much of American society in the centuries to come.

➤ What issues divided the various ethnic and religious groups of the middle colonies?

➤ How did Quakers maintain their economic and political primacy as Europeans from other cultures and traditions flooded into Pennsylvania during the eighteenth century?

The Enlightenment and the Great Awakening, 1720–1765

Two great European cultural movements reached America between the 1720s and the 1760s: the Enlightenment and Pietism. The Enlightenment, which emphasized the power of human reason to understand and shape the world, appealed especially to urban artisans and to well-educated men and women from merchant or planter families. Pietism, an evangelical Christian movement that stressed the individual's personal relationship with God, attracted many more adherents, primarily farmers and urban laborers. The two movements promoted independent thinking in different ways; together, they transformed American intellectual and cultural life.

The Enlightenment in America

Many early settlers in America turned to folk wisdom to explain the workings of the natural world. Swedish settlers in the lower counties of Pennsylvania (present-day Delaware), for example, attributed magical powers to the great white mullein, a common wildflower, and treated fevers by tying the plant's leaves around their feet and arms. Others relied on religion. Most Christians believed the earth stood at the center of the universe and that God (and Satan, by witchcraft and other means) intervened directly and continuously in human affairs. When a measles epidemic struck Boston in the 1710s, the Puritan minister Cotton Mather thought that only God could end it.

The European Enlightenment. Colonists held to their beliefs despite the scientific revolution of the sixteenth and seventeenth centuries, which challenged both folk and traditional Christian worldviews. In the 1530s, the astronomer Copernicus observed that the earth traveled around the sun, not vice versa. That discovery suggested that humans occupied a more modest place in the universe than Christian theology assumed. Eventually, Sir Isaac Newton, in his *Principia Mathematica* (1687), used the sciences of mathematics and physics to explain the movement of the planets around the sun. Newton's laws of motion and gravity described how the universe could operate by means of natural forces. This explanation, which did not require the constant intervention of a supernatural being, undermined the traditional Christian understanding of the cosmos.

In the century between the publication of *Principia Mathematica* and the outbreak of the French Revolution in 1789, the philosophers of the European Enlightenment used empirical research and scientific reasoning to study all aspects of life, including social institutions and human behavior. Enlightenment thinkers advanced four fundamental principles: the lawlike order of the natural world, the power of human reason, the "natural rights" of individuals (including the right to self-government), and the progressive improvement of society.

English philosopher John Locke was a major contributor to the Enlightenment. In his *Essay Concerning Human Understanding* (1690), Locke focused on the impact of environment and experience on human behavior. He argued that the character of individuals and societies was not fixed, that it could be changed through education, rational thought, and purposeful action. Locke's *Two Treatises on Government* (1690) advanced the revolutionary theory that political authority was not given by God to monarchs, as James II and other kings had insisted (see Chapter 3). Instead, it derived from social compacts that people made to preserve their "natural rights" to life, liberty, and property. In Locke's view, a people should have the right to change government policies — or even the form of government — through the decision of a majority.

Locke's ideas and those of other Enlightenment thinkers came to America by way of books, travelers, and educated migrants. Some clergymen responded to these ideas by devising a rational form of Christianity. Rejecting the supernatural and the early Puritans' arbitrary and vengeful God, Congregationalist minister Andrew Eliot maintained that "there is nothing in Christianity that is contrary to reason." Reverend John Wise of Ipswich, Massachusetts, used Locke's political principles to defend the Puritans' practice of vesting power in ordinary church members. Just as the social compact formed the basis of political society, Wise argued, so the religious covenant among the lay members of the congregation made them — not the bishops of the Church of England or even ministers like himself — the proper interpreters of religious truth. The Enlightenment influenced Cotton Mather as well. When a smallpox epidemic threatened Boston in the 1720s, this time Mather turned to a scientific rather than a religious remedy, joining with physician Nicholas Boyleston to publicize the new technique of inoculation.

Benjamin Franklin and the American Enlightenment. Benjamin Franklin was the exemplar of the American Enlightenment. Born in Boston

Benjamin Franklin's Influence

Benjamin Franklin's work as a scientist and inventor captivated subsequent generations of Americans. This painted panel (c. 1830) from a fire engine of the Franklin Volunteer Fire Company of Philadelphia depicts Franklin's experiment in 1752 in which he demonstrated the presence of electricity in lightning. Cigna Museum and Art Collection, Philadelphia/Photo by Joseph Painter.

in 1706 to a devout Calvinist family and, as a youth, apprenticed to his half-brother, a printer, Franklin was a self-taught man. While working as a printer and journalist in Philadelphia, he formed "a club of mutual improvement" that met weekly to discuss "Morals, Politics, or Natural Philosophy." These discussions and Enlightenment literature, rather than the Bible, shaped Franklin's mind. As Franklin explained in his *Autobiography* (1771), "From the different books I read, I began to doubt of Revelation [God-revealed truth] itself."

Like many urban artisans, wealthy Virginia planters, and affluent seaport merchants, Franklin became a **deist**. Influenced by Enlightenment science, deists believed that God had created the world but allowed it to operate through the laws of nature. The deists' god was a divine "watchmaker" who did not intervene directly in history or in people's lives. Rejecting the authority of the Bible, deists relied on people's "natural reason," their innate moral sense, to define right and wrong. A one-time slave owner, Franklin came to question the moral legitimacy of racial bondage and repudiated it as he began to contest the colonists' political bondage to the British.

Franklin popularized the practical outlook of the Enlightenment in *Poor Richard's Almanack* (1732–1757), an annual publication read by thousands. In 1743, he helped found the American Philosophical Society, an institution devoted to "the promotion of useful knowledge." Taking this message to heart, Franklin invented bifocal lenses for eyeglasses, the Franklin stove, and the lightning rod. His book on electricity, published in England in 1751, won praise as the greatest contribution to science since Newton's discoveries. Inspired by Franklin, ambitious printers in America's seaport cities published newspapers and gentlemen's magazines, the first significant nonreligious publications to appear in the colonies. The European Enlightenment, then, added a secular dimension to colonial intellectual life, preparing the way for the great American contributions to republican political theory by a new generation of intellectuals led by John Adams, James Madison, and Thomas Jefferson.

American Pietism and the Great Awakening

As many educated Americans turned to deism, thousands of colonists embraced Pietism, a Christian movement that emphasized "pious" behavior (hence the name) and had its origins in Germany around 1700. In its belief that individuals could form a mystical union with God and in its emotional services, Pietism appealed to the heart rather than the mind (see Reading American Pictures, "Almanacs and Meetinghouses: Exploring Popular Culture," p. 119). In the 1720s, German migrants carried Pietism to America, quickly sparking a religious **revival.** In Pennsylvania and New Jersey, Dutch minister Theodore Jacob Frelinghuysen moved from church to church, preaching rousing emotional sermons to German settlers. In private prayer meetings, he encouraged church members to spread the message of spiritual urgency. A decade later, William Tennent and his son Gilbert copied Frelinghuysen's approach and led revivals among Scots-Irish Presbyterians throughout the Middle Atlantic region.

Jonathan Edwards: Preacher and Philosopher.

Simultaneously, an American-born Pietist movement appeared in Puritan New England. The original Puritan settlers were intensely pious Christians, but over the decades their spiritual zeal had faded. In the 1730s, Jonathan Edwards restored that zeal to Congregational churches in the Connecticut River Valley. Edwards was born in 1703, the fifth child and only son among the eleven children of Timothy and Esther Stoddard Edwards. His father was a poorly paid rural minister, but his mother was the daughter of Solomon Stoddard, a famous preacher who taught that God was compassionate and that Sainthood was not limited to a select few.

As a young man, Edwards rejected Stoddard's thinking. Taking inspiration from the harsh theology of John Calvin, he preached that men and women were helpless, that they were completely dependent on God. In his most famous sermon, "Sinners in the Hands of an Angry God" (1741), Edwards declared: "There is Hell's wide gaping mouth open; and you have nothing to stand upon, nor any thing to take hold of: there is nothing between you and Hell but the air; 'tis only the power and mere pleasure of God that holds you up." According to one observer, the response was electric: "There was a great moaning and crying through the whole house, What shall I do to be saved — oh, I am going to Hell."

Surprisingly, Edwards's writings contributed to Enlightenment thought. The New England minister accepted Locke's argument in the *Essay Concerning Human Understanding* (1690), that ideas are the product of experience as conveyed by the senses; however, Edwards went on to claim that people's ideas depended on their passions. Edwards used his theory of knowledge to justify his preaching,

Almanacs and Meetinghouses: Exploring Popular Culture

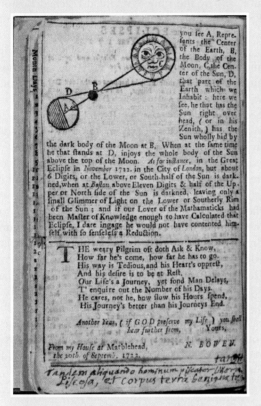

(above) **Mauck Meeting House, Mill Creek, Virginia.** H. Wickliffe Rose Papers, Yale University Library.

(left) **Explaining the Great Eclipse of 1722.** American Antiquarian Society, Worcester, Massachusetts.

From the writings of educated people and learned ministers, we know that the Enlightenment and Pietism changed the way they looked at the world. But what was the impact of these movements on ordinary people who had less education and lived predominantly as farmers or common folk? From almanacs, which enjoyed a wide readership, and churches, which were designed, built, and used by congregants, we can find clues to the impact of these transatlantic cultural and religious movements on colonial Americans.

ANALYZING THE EVIDENCE

➤ Almanacs provided information about a wide variety of subjects. Consider the page from Nathaniel Bowen's *Almanac*. How does Bowen explain why London was "wholly hid" by the "Great Eclipfe" in November 1722, while Boston was only partially darkened?

➤ Is Bowen's explanation based on a scientific or a religious view of the solar system? Would people who read and understood Bowen's account begin to see the world as Enlightenment thinkers did, to accept that it was governed by predictable "laws of nature"?

➤ What does the photograph of the interior of Mauck Meeting House tell us about the experience of Pietism in eighteenth-century Virginia? What is missing that you would expect to find in a church?

Who do you think sat on the raised bench? How would this relatively small and intimate space encourage communal worship? What can you conclude about Pietistic religious culture from this image?

➤ A building is concrete evidence of history: You can see it and touch it and experience it to learn more about the people who built and used it. Can you think of other types of concrete evidence that might provide insight into how ordinary people lived their lives in the eighteenth century? What do these sources reveal that print sources cannot? Think about your life and the meaning you attach to everyday objects.

Jonathan Edwards, c. 1750

In this portrait by Joseph Badger, Edwards looks directly at the viewer, as he looked directly at his congregation in Northampton, Massachusetts, and urged them to be "born again and made new creatures." At the time, Edwards was in his mid-forties and at the height of his powers as a scholar — but not as a pastor. When Edwards restricted full church membership to those who were Saints — the Calvinist "elect"—his congregation voted 200 to 20 to dismiss the great preacher and philosopher. Impoverished, Edwards moved to the frontier town of Stockbridge, where he ministered, without great success, to the Housatonic Indians. Yale University Art Gallery, Bequest of Eugene Philips Edwards.

arguing that vivid words would "fright persons away from Hell" and promote conversions. News of Edwards's success stimulated religious fervor up and down the Connecticut River Valley.

George Whitefield and the Great Awakening. George Whitefield transformed the local revivals inspired by Edwards and the Tennants into a Great Awakening that spanned the British colonies in North America. Whitefield had his own awakening after reading German Pietist tracts, and he became a follower of John Wesley, the founder of English Methodism. In 1739, Whitefield carried Wesley's fervent message to America. Over the next two years, he attracted huge crowds of "enthusiasts" as he preached at settlements from Georgia to Massachusetts (see the painting on p. 102). "Religion is become the Subject of most Conversations," the *Pennsylvania Gazette* reported. "No books are in Request but those of Piety and Devotion." The usu-

ally skeptical Benjamin Franklin was so impressed by Whitefield's preaching that when the revivalist asked for contributions, Franklin emptied the coins in his pockets "wholly into the collector's dish, gold and all." By the time Whitefield reached Boston, Reverend Benjamin Colman reported, the people were "ready to receive him as an angel of God."

Whitefield owed his appeal to skillful publicity and to his compelling presence. "He looked almost angelical; a young, slim, slender youth . . . cloathed with authority from the Great God," wrote a Connecticut farmer. Like most evangelical preachers, Whitefield did not read his sermons (which he sold in large numbers) but spoke from memory. He gestured eloquently, raised his voice for dramatic effect, and even assumed a female persona — a woman in labor struggling to deliver the word of God. When the young preacher told his spellbound listeners that they had all sinned and must seek salvation, hundreds of men and women suddenly felt a "new light" within them. As "the power of god come down," Hannah Heaton recalled, "my knees smote together . . . it seemed to me I was a sinking down into hell . . . but then I resigned my distress and was perfectly easy quiet and calm . . . it seemed as if I had a new soul & body both." Strengthened and self-confident, these "New Lights" were eager to spread Whitefield's message throughout their communities.

Religious Upheaval in the North

Like all cultural explosions, the Great Awakening was controversial. Conservative ministers — "Old Lights" — condemned the "cryings out, faintings and convulsions" that had become a part of revivalist meetings. Charles Chauncy, a minister in Boston, also attacked the New Lights' practice of allowing women to speak in public: It was, he stated, "a plain breach of that commandment of the LORD, where it is said, Let your WOMEN keep silence in the churches." In Connecticut, Old Lights persuaded the legislature to prohibit evangelists from speaking to established congregations without the ministers' permission. When Whitefield returned to Connecticut in 1744, he found many pulpits closed to him. But the New Lights refused to be silenced. Dozens of farmers, women, and artisans roamed the countryside, condemning the Old Lights as "unconverted" sinners and willingly accepting imprisonment: "I shall bring glory to God in my bonds," a dissident preacher wrote from jail.

As the Awakening proceeded, it undermined the allegiance to legally established churches and their tax-supported ministers. In New England, New Lights left the Congregational Church and founded

Figure 4.2 Church Growth by Denomination, 1700–1780

Some churches — such as the Dutch Reformed, Anglican, and Congregational — grew at a steady pace, primarily from the natural increase of their members. After 1740, the fastest-growing denominations were immigrant churches — German Reformed, Lutheran, and Presbyterian — and those, like the Baptists, with an evangelical message.

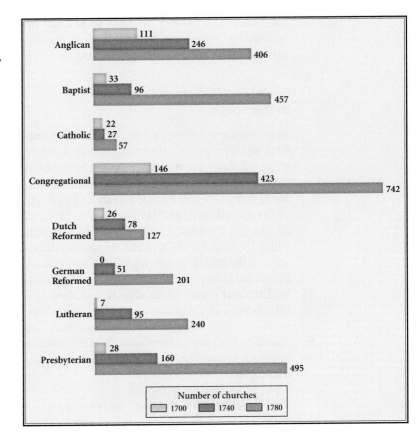

125 "separatist" churches that supported their ministers through voluntary contributions (Figure 4.2). Other religious dissidents joined Baptist congregations, which also condemned government support of churches. "God never allowed any civil state upon earth to impose religious taxes," declared Baptist preacher Isaac Backus. In New York and New Jersey, the Dutch Reformed Church split in two because New Lights refused to accept the doctrines and practices handed down by conservative church authorities in Holland.

In a sense, the Awakening challenged the authority of all ministers, an authority that rested in large part on respect for their education and knowledge of the Bible. In an influential pamphlet, *The Dangers of an Unconverted Ministry* (1740), Gilbert Tennent asserted that ministers' authority should come not from theological training but from the conversion experience. Reaffirming Martin Luther's belief in the priesthood of all Christians, Tennent suggested that anyone who had experienced the redeeming grace of God could speak with ministerial authority. Isaac Backus also celebrated a spiritual democracy, noting that "the common people now claim as good a right to judge and act in matters of religion as civil rulers or the learned

clergy." When challenged by her minister, Sarah Harrah Osborne, a New Light "exhorter" in Rhode Island, refused "to shut up my mouth and doors and creep into obscurity."

In many rural villages, revivalism reinforced the communal values of farm families by questioning the moneygrubbing practices of merchants and land speculators. Jonathan Edwards spoke for many rural colonists when he charged that a miserly spirit was more suitable "for wolves and other beasts of prey, than for human beings." Said Gilbert Tennent: "In any truly Christian society mutual love is the Band and Cement."

As religious enthusiasm spread, churches founded new colleges to educate their young men and train ministers. New Light Presbyterians established the College of New Jersey (Princeton) in 1746, and New York Anglicans founded King's College (Columbia) in 1754. Baptists set up the College of Rhode Island (Brown) in 1764; and the Dutch Reformed Church subsidized Queen's College (Rutgers) in New Jersey two years later. The intellectual legacy of the Awakening, however, was not education for the privileged few but a new sense of authority among the many. A European visitor to Philadelphia remarked in surprise, "The poorest day-laborer . . . holds it his right to advance his opinion, in religious as well as political matters, with as much freedom as the gentleman."

Social and Religious Conflict in the South

In the southern colonies, where the Church of England was legally established, religious enthusiasm triggered sharp social conflict. Anglican ministers were few in number and generally ignored the spiritual needs of African Americans (about 40 percent of the population), and landless whites (another 20 percent) attended church irregularly. Middling white freeholders (35 percent of the residents) formed the core of most Anglican congregations. Prominent planters and their families (just 5 percent) held the real power in the church, and they used their control of parish finances to discipline their ministers. One clergyman complained that dismissal awaited any minister who "had the courage to preach against any Vices taken into favor by the leading Men of his Parish."

The Presbyterian Revival. In the southern colonies, the Great Awakening challenged the dominance of both the Church of England and the planter elite. In 1743, bricklayer Samuel Morris, inspired by reading George Whitefield's sermons led a group of Virginia Anglicans out of the church. Seeking a more vital religious experience, Morris and his followers invited New Light Presbyterian ministers to lead their prayer meetings. Soon Presbyterian revivals spread not only to the Scots-Irish in the backcountry but also to English residents in the Tidewater region, where they threatened the social authority of the Virginia gentry. Traditionally, planters and their well-dressed families arrived at Anglican services in elaborate carriages drawn by well-bred horses, and the men flaunted their power by marching in a body to their front-pew seats. Those ritual reminders of the gentry's social superiority would be meaningless if all the freeholders were attending Presbyterian churches. Moreover, religious pluralism threatened the tax-supported status of the Anglican Church.

To halt the spread of New Light ideas, Virginia's governor William Gooch denounced them as "false teachings," and Anglican justices of the peace closed down Presbyterian meetinghouses. This harassment kept most white yeomen families and poor tenants in the Church of England; so did the fact that most Presbyterian ministers were well-educated men who refused to preach in

the "enthusiastic" style that appealed to ordinary folk.

The Baptist Insurgency. New Light Baptist ministers had no problem reaching out to ordinary folk, and they won large numbers of converts in Virginia during the 1760s. The Baptists were radical Protestants whose central ritual was adult (rather than infant) baptism. Once men and women had experienced the infusion of grace — had been "born again" — they were baptized in an emotional public ceremony, often involving complete immersion in water. The vigorous preaching and democratic message of the Baptist preachers drew thousands of yeomen and tenant farm families into their congregations.

Even slaves were welcome at Baptist revivals. During the 1740s, George Whitefield had urged Carolina slave owners to bring blacks into the Christian fold, but white hostility and the commitment of Africans to their ancestral religions kept the number of converts low. The first significant conversion of slaves to Christianity came in Virginia in the 1760s, as second- and third-generation African Americans responded to the Baptists' message that all people were equal in God's eyes. Sensing a threat to the system of racial slavery, the House of Burgesses imposed heavy fines on Baptists who preached to slaves without their owners' permission.

The Baptists posed a direct threat to the traditional authority of the gentry. Their preachers repudiated the social hierarchy, urging followers to call one another "brother" and "sister"; and they condemned the customary pleasures of Chesapeake planters. As planter Landon Carter complained, the Baptists were "destroying pleasure in the Country; for they encourage ardent Prayer; strong & constant faith, & an intire Banishment of *Gaming, Dancing,* & Sabbath-Day Diversions." Stung by such criticisms, the gentry responded with violence. Hearing Baptist Dutton Lane condemn "the vileness and danger" of drunkenness and whoring, planter John Giles took the charge personally: "I know who you mean! and by God I'll demolish you." In Caroline County, an Anglican posse attacked a prayer meeting led by Brother John Waller. A Baptist described the attack: "[He] was violently jerked off the stage; they caught him by the back part of his neck, beat his head against the ground, and a gentleman gave him twenty lashes with his horsewhip."

Despite these attacks, Baptist congregations continued to multiply. By 1775, about 15 percent of Virginia's whites and hundreds of black slaves had joined Baptist churches. To signify their state of grace, some Baptist men "cut off their hair, like Cromwell's round-headed chaplains." Many others refused to attend "a horse race or other unnecessary, unprofitable, sinful assemblies." Still others forged a new evangelical masculinity—"crying, weeping, lifting up the eyes, groaning" when touched by the Holy Spirit, but defending themselves with vigor. "Not able to bear the insults" of a heckler, a group of Baptists "took [him] by the neck and heels and threw him out of doors," setting off a bloody brawl.

The Baptist revival in the Chesapeake may have changed the form of worship, but it did not change the social order to a significant extent. Rejecting the requests of evangelical women, Baptist men kept church authority in the hands of "free born male members"; and Anglican slaveholders retained their power over the political system. Still, the Baptist insurgency infused the lives of poor tenant families with spiritual meaning and empowered yeomen to defend their economic interests. Moreover, as Baptist ministers spread Christianity among slaves, the cultural gulf between blacks and whites shrank, undermining one justification for slavery and giving blacks a new religious identity. Within a generation, African Americans would develop distinctive versions of Protestant Christianity.

➤ What was the significance of the Enlightenment in America?

➤ In what ways did the Enlightenment and the Great Awakening prompt Americans to challenge traditional sources of authority?

➤ How did the Baptist insurgency in Virginia challenge conventional assumptions about race, gender, and class in the colony?

The Midcentury Challenge: War, Trade, and Social Conflict, 1750–1765

Between 1750 and 1765, a series of events transformed colonial life. First, Britain embarked on a war against the French in America, which became a worldwide conflict—the Great War for Empire. Second, a surge in trade boosted colonial consumption but placed some Americans deeply in debt to British creditors. Third, a great westward migration of colonists sparked new conflicts with Indian

peoples, armed disputes between settlers and speculators, and backcountry rebellions against eastern-controlled governments.

The French and Indian War Becomes a War for Empire

By 1754, both France and Britain had laid claim to much of the land west of the Appalachians (Map 4.4). Still, only a few Europeans had moved into that vast area. One factor in limiting access from the British colonies was topography: There were few natural routes running east and west. More important, the Iroquois and other Indian peoples controlled the great valleys of the Ohio and Mississippi rivers, and they firmly opposed—through diplomacy and violent raids—extensive white settlement.

The End of the Play-off System. For decades, the Native peoples had used their control of the fur trade to bargain for guns and subsidies from French and British officials. By the 1740s, however, the Iroquois' strategy of playing off the French against the British was breaking down. The Europeans resented the rising cost of "gifts" of arms and money; equally important, alliances between the Indians and the British crumbled as Anglo-American demands for land escalated. In the late 1740s, the Mohawks rebuffed attempts by Sir William Johnson, an Indian agent and land speculator, to settle Scottish migrants west of Albany. The Iroquois also responded angrily when Governor Robert Dinwiddie of Virginia, along with Virginia land speculators and London merchants, formed the Ohio Company in 1749. The company's royal grant of 200,000 acres lay in the upper Ohio River Valley, an area the Iroquois controlled through alliances with the Delaware and Shawnee peoples. "We don't know what you Christians, English and French intend," the outraged Iroquois complained, "we are so hemmed in by both, that we have hardly a hunting place left."

To repair the British relationship with the Iroquois, the Board of Trade called a meeting at Albany in June 1754. At the Albany Congress, delegates from many of Britain's mainland colonies denied any designs on Iroquois lands; and they asked the Indians for their help against New France. Although still small in numbers, the French colony had a broad reach. In the 1750s, the 15,000 French farm families who lived along the St. Lawrence River provided food and supplies not only to the fur-trading settlements of Montreal and Quebec but also to the hundreds of fur traders, missionaries, and soldiers who lived among the

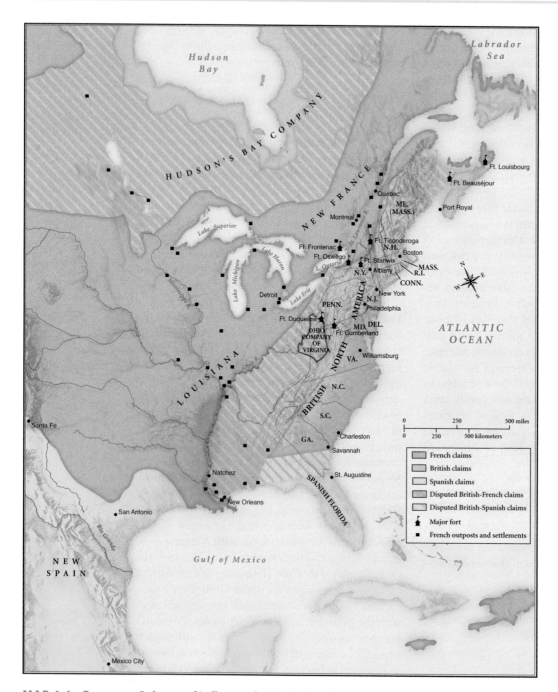

MAP 4.4 European Spheres of Influence in North America, 1754

France and Spain laid claim to vast areas of North America and relied on their Indian allies to combat the numerical superiority of British settlers. For their part, Native Americans played off one European power against another. As a British official observed: "To preserve the Ballance between us and the French is the great ruling Principle of Modern Indian Politics." By expelling the French from North America, the Great War for Empire disrupted this balance and left the Indian peoples on their own to resist encroaching Anglo-American settlers.

western Indian peoples. To counter the French, Benjamin Franklin proposed a Plan of Union to the delegates at Albany. Franklin's plan included a continental assembly that would manage trade, Indian policy, and defense in the West, and so increase British influence there. But neither Franklin's plan nor a proposal by the Board of Trade for a political "union between ye Royal, Proprietary, & Charter Governments" was in the cards. British ministers worried that a union would spark demands for American independence, and colonial leaders feared that a consolidated government would undermine the authority of the assemblies.

Meanwhile, the Ohio Company's land grant alarmed French authorities. For decades, they had given their Indian allies guns and other gifts to stop British settlers from pouring into the Ohio River Valley. Now they built a series of military forts, including Fort Duquesne at the point where the Monongahela and Allegheny rivers join to form the Ohio River (present-day Pittsburgh). Confrontation came when Dinwiddie dispatched a military expedition led by Colonel George Washington, a young Virginia planter and Ohio Company stockholder. In July 1754, French troops seized Washington and his men and sent them back to Virginia, prompting American and British expansionists to demand war. Henry Pelham, the British prime minister, urged calm: "There is such a load of debt, and such heavy taxes already laid upon the people, that nothing but an absolute necessity can justify our engaging in a new War."

Expansionism Triumphant. Pelham could not control the march of events. In Parliament, William Pitt, a rising British statesman, and Lord Halifax, the new head of the Board of Trade, were strong advocates for colonial expansion. They persuaded Pelham to dispatch military forces to America to join with colonial militias in attacking French forts. In June 1755, British and New England troops captured Fort Beauséjour in Nova Scotia (Acadia). Subsequently, troops from Puritan Massachusetts seized nearly 10,000 Acadians and deported them to France, the West Indies, and Louisiana (where they became known as Cajuns). English and Scottish Protestants took over the farms the French Catholics left behind.

These Anglo-American successes were quickly offset by a stunning defeat. In July 1755, 2,000 British regulars and Virginia militiamen advancing on Fort Duquesne without benefit of Indian scouts marched into a deadly ambush. A much smaller force of French soldiers and Delaware and Shawnee warriors rained fire on the British force, taking the life of the British commander, General Edward Braddock, and killing or wounding half of his troops. "We have been beaten, most shamefully beaten, by a handfull of Men," Washington complained bitterly as he led the militiamen back to Virginia.

The Great War for Empire

By 1756, the conflict in America had spread to Europe, where it was known as the Seven Years' War and arrayed France, Spain, and Austria against Britain and Prussia. When Britain mounted major offensives in India and West Africa as well as in North America, the conflict became a Great War for Empire. Since 1700, Britain had reaped unprecedented profits from its overseas trading empire; it was determined to crush France, the main obstacle to further expansion.

William Pitt emerged as the architect of the British war effort. Pitt was the grandson of the East Indies merchant "Diamond" Pitt, a committed expansionist and an arrogant man. "I know that I can save this country and that I alone can," he declared. In fact, Pitt was a master of strategy, both commercial and military, and planned to cripple France by seizing its colonies. In designing the critical campaign against New France, Pitt exploited a demographic advantage: On the North American mainland, King George II's 2 million subjects outnumbered the French by 14 to 1. To mobilize the colonists, Pitt paid half the cost of their troops and supplied them with arms and equipment, an expenditure of nearly £1 million a year. He also committed a fleet of British ships and 30,000 British regulars to the American conflict.

The Conquest of Canada. Beginning in 1758, the powerful Anglo-American forces moved from one triumph to the next. They forced the French to abandon Fort Duquesne (which they renamed Fort Pitt) and then captured Fort Louisbourg, a French stronghold at the mouth of the St. Lawrence. In 1759, a force led by General James Wolfe sailed down the St. Lawrence and took Quebec, the heart of France's American empire. The Royal Navy prevented French reinforcements from crossing the Atlantic; and in 1760, British forces captured Montreal, completing the conquest of Canada (Map 4.5).

Elsewhere the British also went from success to success. Fulfilling Pitt's dream, the East India Company ousted French traders from India; and British forces seized French Senegal in West Africa and the sugar islands Martinique and Guadeloupe in the French West Indies. From Spain, the British won

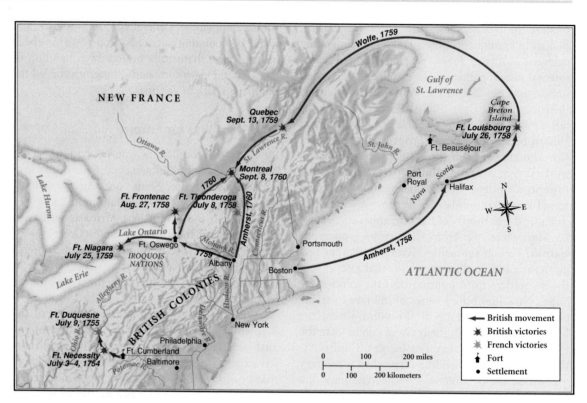

MAP 4.5   The Anglo-American Conquest of New France

After full-scale war with France broke out in 1756, it took almost three years for the British ministry to equip colonial forces and dispatch an army to America. Then British and colonial troops attacked the heartland of New France, capturing Quebec in 1759 and Montreal in 1760. The conquest both united and divided the allies. Colonists celebrated the great victory — "The Illuminations and Fireworks exceeded any that had been exhibited before," reported the *South Carolina Gazette.* However, British officers held the colonial soldiers in disdain. Said one: "[They are] the dirtiest, most contemptible, cowardly dogs you can conceive."

Cuba and the Philippine Islands. The Treaty of Paris of 1763 confirmed Britain's triumph. It granted the British sovereignty over half the continent of North America, including French Canada, all French territory east of the Mississippi River, and Spanish Florida. The French empire in North America was reduced to a handful of sugar islands in the West Indies and two rocky islands off the coast of Newfoundland.

Pontiac's Rebellion. Britain's territorial acquisitions alarmed Indian peoples from New York to Michigan, who rightly feared an influx of Anglo-American settlers. Hoping that the French would return as a counterweight to British power, the Ottawa chief Pontiac declared, "I am French, and I want to die French." Neolin, a Delaware prophet, went further; he taught that the suffering of the Indian peoples stemmed from their dependence on

Europeans' goods, guns, and rum, and called for their expulsion: "If you suffer the English among you, you are dead men. Sickness, smallpox, and their poison [rum] will destroy you entirely." In 1763, inspired by Neolin's vision and his growing anti-British sentiments, Pontiac led a group of loosely confederated tribes (stretching geographically from the New York Senecas to the Minnesota Chippewas) in a major uprising known as Pontiac's Rebellion. The Indian force seized nearly every British garrison west of Fort Niagara, besieged the fort at Detroit, and killed or captured more than 2,000 settlers. But the Indian alliance gradually weakened, and British military expeditions defeated the Delawares near Fort Pitt and broke the siege of Detroit. In the peace settlement, Pontiac and his allies accepted the British as their new political "fathers." In return, the British issued the Proclamation of 1763, which expressly prohibited

Pipe of Peace

In 1760, the Ottawa chief Pontiac welcomed British troops to his territory. Here he is shown offering a pipe of peace to their commander, Major Robert Rogers. Three years later, as British troops built forts in Indian lands and Anglo-American settlers moved west, Pontiac led a coordinated Indian uprising against the new European intruders. Library of Congress.

white settlements west of the Appalachians. It was an edict the colonists would ignore.

British Industrial Growth and the Consumer Revolution

Britain owed its military and diplomatic success to its unprecedented economic resources. Since 1700, when it had wrested control of many oceanic trade routes from the Dutch, Britain had been the dominant commercial power in the Atlantic and Indian oceans. By 1750, it had also become the first country to use new manufacturing technology and work discipline to expand output. This combination of commerce and industry would soon make Britain the most powerful nation in the world.

Mechanical power was a key ingredient of Britain's Industrial Revolution. British artisans designed and built water mills and steam engines that efficiently powered a wide array of machines: lathes for shaping wood, jennies and looms for spinning and weaving textiles, and hammers for forging iron. The new power-driven machinery produced woolen and linen textiles, iron tools, furniture, and chinaware in greater quantities than traditional manufacturing methods — and at lower cost. Moreover, the entrepreneurs who ran the new workshops drove their employees hard, forcing them to keep pace with the machines and to work long hours. To market the abundant products produced in the factories, English and Scottish merchants extended a full year's credit to colonial shopkeepers instead of the traditional six months'. Americans soon were purchasing 30 percent of all British exports.

To pay for British manufactured goods, the colonists increased their exports of tobacco, rice, indigo, and wheat. In Virginia, farmers moved into the Piedmont, a region of plains and rolling hills just inland from the Tidewater counties. Using credit advanced by Scottish tobacco merchants, planters bought land, slaves, and equipment. The merchants took their payment in tobacco and exported it to expanding markets in France and central Europe. In South Carolina, rice planters increased their wealth and luxurious lifestyles by using British government subsidies to develop indigo plantations. By the 1760s, they were exporting large quantities of the deep blue dye to English textile factories; at the same time, they were selling 65 million pounds of rice a year to Holland and southern Europe. Simultaneously, New York, Pennsylvania, Maryland, and Virginia became the breadbasket of the Atlantic world, supplying Europe's exploding population with wheat at ever-increasing prices. In Philadelphia, export prices for wheat jumped almost 50 percent between 1740 and 1765.

Americans used their profits from trade to buy English manufactures in a "consumer revolution" that raised their standard of living (Figure 4.3). However, this first American spending binge, like most subsequent splurges, landed many consumers in debt. Even during the booming wartime economy

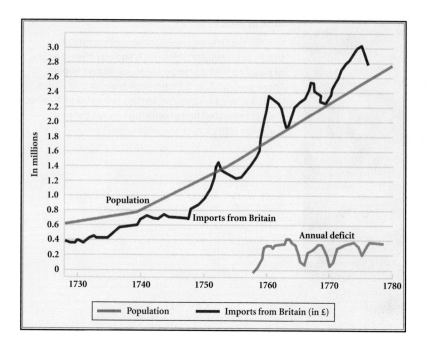

Figure 4.3 Mainland Population, British Imports, and the American Trade Deficit

Around 1750, British imports were growing at a faster rate than the American population, indicating that the colonists were consuming more per capita. But Americans went into debt to pay for these goods, running an annual trade deficit with their British suppliers that by 1772 meant a cumulative debt of £2 million.

of the 1750s, exports paid for only 80 percent of imported British goods. The remaining 20 percent—the Americans' trade deficit—was financed by Britain through the extension of credit and through Pitt's military expenditures. When the military subsidies ended in 1763, the colonies found themselves in an economic recession. Colonial merchants looked anxiously at their overstocked warehouses and feared bankruptcy. "I think we have a gloomy prospect before us," a Philadelphia trader noted in 1765, "as there are of late some Persons failed, who were in no way suspected." The increase in transatlantic trade had raised living standards; but it also had made Americans more dependent on overseas credit and markets.

The Struggle for Land in the East

In good times and bad, the colonial population continued to grow, intensifying the demand for arable land. The families who founded the town of Kent, Connecticut, in 1738 were descended from the original settlers of the colony. Like earlier generations, they had moved inland to establish new farms, but they had now reached the colony's western boundary. To provide for the next generation, many Kent families joined the Susquehanna Company. Started in 1749, the company undertook to settle lands in the Wyoming Valley and other areas along the upper Susquehanna River (in what is today the northeastern corner of Pennsylvania). As Connecticut settlers took up farm-

steads there, the company urged the Connecticut legislature to claim the region based on Connecticut's "sea-to-sea" royal charter of 1662. However, Charles II had also granted the Wyoming Valley region to William Penn, and the Penn family had sold farms there to Pennsylvania residents. By the late 1750s, settlers from Connecticut and Pennsylvania were at war, burning down their rivals' houses and barns.

Simultaneously, three distinct but related land disputes broke out in the Hudson River Valley (Map 4.6). Dutch tenant farmers, Wappinger Indians, and migrants from Massachusetts asserted ownership rights to lands long claimed by the Van Rensselaer, Livingston, and other manorial families. When the manorial lords turned to the legal system to uphold their claims, Dutch and English farmers in Westchester, Dutchess, and Albany counties rioted to close the courts. At the request of New York's royal governor, General Thomas Gage and two British regiments joined with local sheriffs and manorial bailiffs to put down the mob. They suppressed the tenant farmers, intimidated the Wappingers, and evicted the Massachusetts squatters.

Other land disputes erupted in New Jersey and the southern colonies, where resident landlords and English aristocrats successfully asserted legal claims based on long-dormant seventeenth-century charters. One court decision upheld the right of Lord Granville, an heir of an original Carolina proprietor, to collect an annual tax on

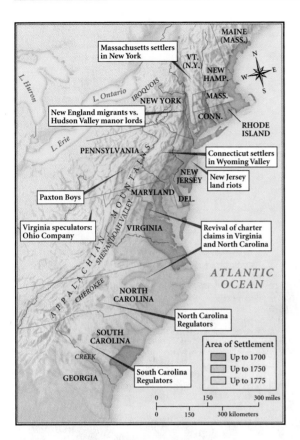

MAP 4.6 Westward Expansion and Land Conflicts, 1750–1775

Between 1750 and 1775, the mainland population more than doubled — from 1.2 million to 2.5 million — triggering both migration westward and legal battles over land, which had become increasingly valuable. Violence broke out in eastern areas, where tenant farmers and smallholders contested landlords' titles, and in the backcountry, where migrating settlers fought with Indians, rival claimants, and the officials of eastern-dominated governments.

land in North Carolina; another decision awarded ownership of the entire northern neck of Virginia (along the Potomac River) to Lord Fairfax.

This revival of proprietary claims by manorial lords and English nobles reflected the rising price of land on the Atlantic coastal plain. It also reflected the maturity of the colonial courts, which now had enough authority to uphold property rights. And both developments underscored the increasing resemblance between rural societies in Europe and America. Long-settled tenants and yeomen, fearing they would soon be reduced to the status of European peasants, joined with new migrants from Europe to look for cheap land near the Appalachian Mountains.

Western Uprisings and Regulator Movements

As would-be landowners moved westward, they sparked new disputes over Indian policy, political representation, and debts. During the war with France, Delaware and Shawnee warriors had extracted revenge for Thomas Penn's land swindle of 1737 by attacking frontier farms throughout central and western Pennsylvania, destroying property and killing and capturing hundreds of residents. Scots-Irish settlers demanded military action to expel all Indians, but Quaker leaders refused. In 1763, the Scots-Irish Paxton Boys took matters into their own hands and massacred twenty members of the peaceful Conestoga tribe. When Governor John Penn tried to bring the murderers to justice, about 250 armed Scots-Irish advanced on Philadelphia. Benjamin Franklin intercepted the angry mob at Lancaster and arranged a truce, narrowly averting a pitched battle with the militia. Prosecution of the Paxton Boys failed for lack of witnesses, and the Scots-Irish dropped their demands that the Indians be expelled; but the episode left a legacy of racial hatred and political resentment.

The South Carolina Regulators. Violence also broke out in the backcountry of South Carolina, where land-hungry Scottish and Anglo-American settlers clashed repeatedly with Cherokees during the war with France. When the war ended in 1763, a group of landowning vigilantes, the Regulators, tried to suppress outlaw bands of whites that were stealing cattle and other property. The Regulators also had political goals: They demanded that the eastern-controlled government provide the western districts with more courts and greater representation in the assembly, and distribute the tax burden fairly across the colony. Fearing slave revolts, the lowland rice planters who ran the South Carolina assembly chose to compromise with the Regulators rather than fight them. In 1767, the assembly created local courts in the western counties and reduced the fees for legal documents; but it refused to reapportion seats or to lower taxes in the backcountry. Like the Paxton Boys in Pennsylvania, the South Carolina Regulators attracted attention to western needs but ultimately failed to wrest power from the eastern elite.

Civil Strife in North Carolina. In 1766, a more radical Regulator movement arose in the backcountry of North Carolina. The economic recession

A Hudson River Manor

Philipse Manor encompassed 90,000 acres, and included mills and warehouses as well as a grand house. In this unattributed painting, the artist has dressed the women in the foreground in classical costumes, thereby linking the Philipses to the noble families of the Roman republic. To preserve their aristocratic lifestyle and the quasi-feudal leasehold system of agriculture, the Philipses joined with other Hudson River manorial lords to suppress tenant uprisings in the 1760s. Historic Hudson Valley, Tarrytown, New York.

of the early 1760s caused a sharp fall in tobacco prices, and many farmers could not pay their debts. When creditors sued for what they were owed, judges directed sheriffs to seize the debtors' property and sell it to pay debts and court costs. Backcountry farmers—including many German and Scots-Irish migrants—denounced the merchants' lawsuits, both because they generated high fees for lawyers and court officials and because they violated the rural custom of community exchange, which allowed loans to remain unpaid for years.

To save their farms from grasping creditors and tax-hungry officials, North Carolina's debtors defied the government's authority. Disciplined mobs of farmers intimidated judges, closed courts, and freed their comrades from jail. Significantly, the Regulators proposed a coherent set of reforms. They demanded legislation to lower legal fees and allow payment of taxes in the "produce of the country" rather than in cash. They also insisted on greater representation in the assembly and a fair tax system, proposing that each person be taxed "in proportion to the profits arising from his estate." To no avail. In May 1771, Royal Governor William Tryon decided to suppress the Regulators. Mobilizing British troops and the eastern militia, Tryon defeated a large Regulator

Governor Tryon and the Regulators Meet at Hillsborough, 1768

Orange County, North Carolina, was home to the Sandy Creek Association, a group of Quakers led by Herman Husband, a powerful advocate of social justice. Early in 1768 its members joined with other Piedmont farmers to create the Regulator movement. When the legislature ignored their petitions protesting corruption by government officials, the Regulators refused to pay taxes and shut down the courts. In September 1768, Royal Governor William Tryon and the low country militia confronted a group of Regulators near Hillsborough. As this engraving suggests, the possibility of violence was high and only narrowly averted. Three years later, Tryon and the Regulators engaged in a pitched battle near the Alamance River, twenty miles west of Hillsborough.

Picture Research Consultants and Archives.

force at the Alamance River. When the fighting ended, thirty men lay dead, and Tryon summarily executed seven insurgent leaders. Not since Bacon's Rebellion in Virginia in 1675 (see Chapter 2) had a domestic political conflict caused so much bloodshed.

In 1771, as in 1675, colonial conflicts became entwined with imperial politics. In Connecticut, Reverend Ezra Stiles defended the North Carolina Regulators. "What shall an injured & oppressed people do," he asked, when faced with "Oppression and tyranny?" His remarks reflected growing resistance to measures the British began introducing in 1765 to enhance their control of the colonies. As they had in 1686, when James II imposed the Dominion of New England, the American colonies still depended on Britain for their trade and mili-

tary defense. However, by the 1760s, the mainland settlements had developed an increasingly complex society with the potential to exist independently. British policies would determine the direction the maturing colonies would take.

➤ What were the major consequences of the Great War for Empire on the imperial balance of power, British-colonial relations, Indian peoples, and Anglo-American settlers?

➤ What impact did the Industrial Revolution in England have on the American colonies?

➤ What were the causes of unrest in the American backcountry in the mid-eighteenth century?

SUMMARY

In this chapter we explored the dramatic social and cultural changes between 1720 and 1765 in the British mainland colonies. Looking at the colonies as a whole, we noted an astonishing increase in population — from 400,000 to almost 2 million — the result of natural growth, immigration, and the forced transport of large numbers of slaves from Africa. At the same time, American settlers were introduced to and became well acquainted with two major cultural movements: the Enlightenment and Pietism. They also had access to a steady supply of new consumer goods churned out by English factories.

On the regional level, we noted that the colonists confronted three major challenges. First, by 1750, overpopulation had become a problem in many older settlements in New England, where farms could no longer be subdivided by inheritance and still support a family. To preserve the yeoman ideal of independent farming, some families migrated to new regions while others developed an "exchange" economy to maximize their resources. Second, in the middle colonies, where fertile land was more plentiful, English Quaker, German, and Scots-Irish residents struggled to maintain their religious and cultural identities while avoiding bruising ethnic conflicts. Finally, the pressures of westward migration disrupted life throughout the backcountry — the frontier regions from New England to the Carolinas. In 1754, Anglo-American expansion into the Ohio River Valley led to conflicts with Indian peoples, civil and political unrest among white settlers, and, ultimately, the Great War for Empire.

By 1765, Britain stood triumphant in Europe and America. But social and cultural developments in the colonies in combination with new British policies would soon revolutionize the character of life there.

Connections: Culture

In the part opener (p. 3), we provided a broad outline of cultural changes in America between 1600 and 1765:

> The new American society witnessed the appearance of new forms of family and community life. . . . [It was also] increasingly pluralistic, made up of migrants from many European ethnic groups — English, Scots, Scots-Irish, Dutch, and Germans — as well as West African slaves and Native Americans. Distinct regional cultures developed in New England, the Middle Atlantic colonies, the Chesapeake, and the Carolinas.

Now that we have tracked the trajectory of Britain's North American colonies, we can see a crucial turning point around 1700. Until that time, most settlers came from England, bringing with them traditional English social and political structures: Fathers ruled families, and authoritarian leaders dominated politics. Then came a massive wave of migrants — enslaved Africans, Germans, Scots-Irish, and Scots. By 1765, these migrants and their descendants constituted a majority of the population. As the people in British North America became more diverse, life there became less repressive and more open to innovation.

A second phase of cultural change began around 1740. An increasingly complex economy encouraged farmers to join the market economy; a responsive system of government prompted more men to seek office; a decline in parental power allowed young women greater choice in their marriage partners; and an outburst of religious enthusiasm shook established churches and advanced religious liberty. Taken together, these developments provided the colonists in British North America (as we put it in concluding the Part Opener) "unprecedented opportunities for economic security, political freedom, and spiritual fulfillment."

CHAPTER REVIEW QUESTIONS

➤ How did the three mainland regions in British North America — New England, the middle colonies, and, as discussed in Chapter 3, the South — become more like one another between 1720 and 1750? In what ways did they become increasingly different? From these comparisons, what conclusions can you draw about the character of American society in the mid-eighteenth century?

➤ Compare and contrast the ethnic complexity of the middle colonies with the racial (and, in the backcountry, the ethnic) diversity of the southern colonies. What conflicts did this diversity cause?

TIMELINE

1710s–1730s	Enlightenment ideas spread from Europe to America
	Germans and Scots-Irish settle in the Middle Atlantic colonies
	Theodore Jacob Frelinghuysen preaches Pietism to German migrants
1730s	William and Gilbert Tennent lead Presbyterian revivals among Scots-Irish
	Jonathan Edwards preaches in New England
1739	George Whitefield sparks the Great Awakening
1740s–1760s	Conflict between Old Lights and New Lights
	Shortage of farmland in New England threatens freehold ideal
	Growing ethnic and religious pluralism in Middle Atlantic colonies
	Religious denominations establish colleges
1743	Benjamin Franklin founds American Philosophical Society
	Samuel Morris starts Presbyterian revivals in Virginia
1749	Virginia speculators create Ohio Company, and Connecticut farmers form Susquehanna Company
1750s	Industrial Revolution in England
	Consumer revolution increases American imports and debt
1754	French and Indian War begins
	Iroquois and colonists meet at Albany Congress; Franklin's Plan of Union
1756	Britain begins Great War for Empire
1759–1760	Britain completes conquest of Canada
1760s	Land conflict along New York and New England
	Baptist revivals win converts in Virginia
1763	Pontiac's Rebellion leads to Proclamation of 1763
	Treaty of Paris ends Great War for Empire
	Scots-Irish Paxton Boys massacre Indians in Pennsylvania
1771	Royal governor puts down Regulator revolt in North Carolina

FOR FURTHER EXPLORATION

The social history of eighteenth-century America comes to life in the stories of individuals. In *Good Wives: Image and Reality in the Lives of Women in Northern New England, 1650–1750* (1982), Laurel Thatcher Ulrich paints a vivid picture of women's experiences. For further insight into the day-to-day lives of women, see the PBS video *A Midwife's Tale*, which tells the story of Martha Ballard; for additional materials on Ballard, see **www.pbs.org/amex/midwife** and **www.DoHistory.org.** Benjamin Franklin's *Autobiography* (1771; available in many editions) demonstrates Franklin's Enlightenment sensibilities, describes his pursuit of wealth and influence, and provides an entertaining look at the bustling city of Philadelphia. Also see the Library of Congress exhibit and Web page, "Benjamin Franklin . . . in His Own Words" (**www.loc.gov/exhibits/treasures/franklin-home.html**). For more on Franklin's life and times, see "The Electric Franklin" (**www.ushistory.org/franklin/index.htm**).

A less-successful quest for self-betterment is the subject of another autobiography, *The Infortunate: The Voyage and Adventures of William Moraley, an Indentured Servant* (1992), edited by Susan E. Klepp and Billy G. Smith. Harry S. Stout's *The Divine Dramatist: George Whitefield and the Rise of Modern Evangelicalism* (1991) shows how the charismatic preacher's flair for theatrics and self-promotion enabled him to preach effectively. "Jonathan Edwards On-Line" (**www.JonathanEdwards.com/**) presents the writings of the great philosopher and preacher; but note that the site uses Edwards's arguments to advance one side of a present-day theological debate.

On day-to-day economic life, see "Colonial Currency and Colonial Coin" (**www.coins.nd.edu/ColCurrency/index.html**), which contains detailed essays as well as pictures of colonial money. For a rich collection of documents and visual materials on the lives of migrant German sectarians, see "Bethlehem Digital History Project" (**bdhp.moravian.edu/**).

For an examination of the relationships between settlers and Indians, see Jane T. Merritt, *At the Crossroads: Indians and Empires on a Mid-Atlantic Frontier, 1700–1763* (2003), and three regional studies: Matthew C. Ward, *Breaking the Backcountry: The Seven Years' War in Virginia and Pennsylvania, 1754–1765* (2003); John Oliphant, *Peace and War on the Anglo-Cherokee Frontier, 1756–63* (2001); and Gregory Evans Dowd, *War Under Heaven: Pontiac, the Indian Nations, and the British Empire* (2002). Also see "The War That Made America," a PBS series about the French and Indian War, and the accompanying Web site (**www.thewarthatmadeamerica.com/**).

TEST YOUR KNOWLEDGE

To assess your command of the material in this chapter, see the Online Study Guide at **bedfordstmartins.com/henretta**.

For Web sites, images, and documents related to topics and places in this chapter, visit **bedfordstmartins.com/makehistory**.

PART TWO

The New Republic
1763–1820

	GOVERNMENT	DIPLOMACY	ECONOMY	SOCIETY	CULTURE
	Creating republican institutions	**European entanglements**	**Expanding commerce and manufacturing**	**Defining liberty and equality**	**Pluralism and national identity**
1763	▸ Stamp Act Congress (1765) ▸ Committees of correspondence ▸ First Continental Congress (1774)	▸ Treaty of Paris (1763) gives Britain control of Canada and Florida	▸ Merchants defy Sugar and Stamp Acts ▸ Boycotts spur domestic manufacturing	▸ Artisans seek influence ▸ Quebec Act (1774) allows Catholicism	▸ Patriots call for American unity ▸ Concept of popular sovereignty takes hold
1775	▸ Second Continental Congress (1775) ▸ States devise and implement constitutions	▸ Independence declared (1776) ▸ Treaty of Alliance with France (1778)	▸ Manufacturing expands during war ▸ Severe inflation threatens economy	▸ Judith Sargent Murray writes *On the Equality of the Sexes* (1779) ▸ Emancipation begins in the North	▸ Thomas Paine's *Common Sense* (1776) calls for a republic
1780	▸ Articles of Confederation ratified (1781) ▸ Legislatures assert supremacy in states ▸ Philadelphia convention drafts U.S. Constitution (1787)	▸ Treaty of Paris (1783) ▸ Britain restricts U.S. trade with West Indies ▸ U.S. government signs treaties with Indian peoples	▸ Bank of North America founded (1781) ▸ Commercial recession (1783–1789) ▸ Land speculation continues in West	▸ Virginia enacts religious freedom legislation (1786) ▸ Politicians and ministers endorse republican motherhood	▸ Noah Webster defines American English ▸ State cessions and land ordinances create national domain in West ▸ German settlers keep own language
1790	▸ Conflict over Alexander Hamilton's economic policies ▸ First national parties: Federalists and Republicans	▸ Wars between France and Britain ▸ Jay's Treaty and Pinkney's Treaty (1795) ▸ Undeclared war with France (1798)	▸ First Bank of the United States (1792–1811) ▸ States charter business corporations ▸ Outwork system grows	▸ Bill of Rights ratified (1791) ▸ Creation of French Republic (1793) sparks ideological debate ▸ Sedition Act limits freedom of press (1798)	▸ Indians form Western Confederacy (1790) ▸ Second Great Awakening (1790–1860) ▸ Divisions emerge between South and North
1800	▸ Jefferson's "Revolution of 1800" reduces activism of national government ▸ Chief Justice Marshall asserts judicial powers	▸ Napoleonic Wars (1802–1815) ▸ Louisiana Purchase (1803) ▸ Embargo Act (1807)	▸ Cotton farming expands ▸ Farm productivity improves ▸ Embargo encourages U.S. manufacturing	▸ New Jersey denies suffrage to propertied women (1807) ▸ Atlantic slave trade legally ends (1808)	▸ Tenskwatawa and Tecumseh revive Western Confederacy
1810	▸ Triumph of Republican Party and end of Federalist Party ▸ State constitutions democratized	▸ War of 1812 (1812–1815) ▸ Monroe Doctrine (1823)	▸ Second Bank of the United States chartered (1816–1836) ▸ Supreme Court rules for business ▸ Emergence of a national economy	▸ Suffrage for white men expands ▸ American Colonization Society (1817) ▸ Missouri Compromise (1819–1821)	▸ War of 1812 tests national unity ▸ Religious benevolence produces social reform

"The American war is over," Philadelphia Patriot Benjamin Rush declared in 1787, "but this is far from being the case with the American Revolution. On the contrary, nothing but the first act of the great drama is closed. It remains yet to establish and perfect our new forms of government." As we will suggest in Part Two, the job was even greater than Rush imagined. The republican revolution that began with the Patriot resistance movement of 1765 and took shape with the Declaration of Independence in 1776 reached far beyond politics. It challenged almost all the values and institutions of the colonial social order and forced Americans to consider fundamental changes in their economic, religious, and cultural practices. Here, in summary, are the main themes of our discussion of America's new political and social order.

GOVERNMENT   Once Americans had repudiated their allegiance to Britain and the monarchy, they faced the task of creating a new system of government. In 1776, no one knew how the states should go about setting up republican institutions. Nor did Patriot leaders know if there should be a permanent central authority along the lines of the Continental Congresses that led the resistance movement and the war. It would take time and experience to find out. It would take even longer to assimilate a new institution — the political party — into the workings of government. However, by 1820, years of difficult political compromise and constitutional revision had resulted in republican national and state governments that commanded the allegiance of their citizens.

DIPLOMACY   To create and preserve their new republic, Americans of European descent had to fight two wars against Great Britain, an undeclared war against France, and many battles with Indian peoples. The wars against Britain divided the country into bitter factions — Patriots against Loyalists in the War of Independence, and prowar Republicans against antiwar Federalists in the War of 1812 — and expended much blood and treasure. The extension of American sovereignty and settlements into the trans-Appalachian west was a cultural disaster for many Indian peoples, who were brutally driven from their lands by white farmers. Despite these external and internal wars, by 1820, the United States had emerged as a strong independent state. Freed from a half-century of entanglement in the wars and diplomacy of Europe, its people began to exploit the riches of the continent.

ECONOMY   By the 1760s, the expansion of markets and commerce had established the foundations for a vigorous national economy. Beginning in the 1780s, northern merchants financed a banking system and organized a rural outwork system. Simultaneously, state governments used charters and special privileges to help businesses and to improve roads, bridges, and waterways. African American slaves remained vital to the southern economy as planters began to export a new staple crop — cotton — to markets in the North and Europe. Many yeomen farm families migrated westward to grow grain; while those in the East turned to the production of raw materials — leather and wool, for example — for burgeoning manufacturing enterprises, and augmented their income with sales of shoes, textiles, tinware, and other handicrafts. By 1820, the young American republic was on the verge of achieving economic as well as political independence.

SOCIETY   As Americans undertook to create a republican society, they divided along lines of gender, race, religion, and class. In particular, they disagreed over fundamental issues like legal equality for women, the status of slavery, the meaning of free speech and religious liberty, and the extent of public responsibility for social inequality. As we shall see, political leaders managed to resolve some of these disputes. Legislatures abolished slavery in the North, broadened religious liberty by allowing freedom of conscience, and, except in New England, ended the system of established churches. However, Americans continued to argue over social equality, in part because their republican creed placed authority in the family and in society into the hands of men of property. This arrangement denied power not only to slaves but also to free blacks, women, and poor white men.

CULTURE   The diversity of peoples and regions that characterized the British colonies in North America complicated efforts after the Revolution to define a distinct American culture and identity. Native Americans still lived in their own clans and nations; and black Americans, one-fifth of the enumerated population, were developing a new, African American culture. Although white Americans were bound by vigorous regional cultures and their ancestral heritage — English, Scottish, Scots-Irish, German, or Dutch — in time, their political institutions began to unite them, as did their increasing participation in the market economy and in Evangelical Protestant churches. By 1820, to be an American meant, for many members of the dominant white population, to be a republican, a Protestant, and an enterprising individual in a capitalist-run market system.

5

Toward Independence: Years of Decision

1763–1776

A S THE GREAT WAR FOR empire ended in 1763, Seth Metcalf joined other American colonists in celebrating the triumph of British arms. A Massachusetts soldier during the conflict, Metcalf thanked "the Great Goodness of God" for the "General Peace" that was so "perculary Advantageous to the English Nation." Just two years later, Metcalf was less certain of God's favor. "God is angry with us of this land," the pious Calvinist wrote in his journal, "and is now Smiting [us] with his Rod Especially by the hands of our Rulers."

The rapid disintegration of the bonds uniting Britain and America — an event that Metcalf could explain only in terms of Divine Providence — mystified many Americans. How had it happened, the president of King's College in New York asked in 1775, that such a "happily situated" people were ready to "hazard their Fortunes, their Lives, and their Souls, in a Rebellion"? Unlike other colonial peoples of the time, white Americans lived in a prosperous society with a strong tradition of self-government. They had little to gain and much to lose by rebelling.

Or so it seemed in 1763, before the British government began to re-form the imperial system. "This year Came an act from England Called the Stamp Act . . . which is thought will be very oppressive to the Inhabitants of North America," Metcalf reflected, "But Mobbs keep it back."

◀ **British Troops Occupy Concord, 1775**

In April 1775, hundreds of British troops stationed in Boston marched to Lexington and Concord, Massachusetts, in search of Patriot arms and munitions. The raid led to a violent and deadly confrontation with the Patriot militia, an outcome prefigured by the unknown artist's depiction of a graveyard in the foreground of this painting. Courtesy, Concord Museum.

The British reforms quickly prompted violent resistance and a downward spiral of ideological debate and political conflict that ended in a war for American independence. Was this outcome inevitable? Could careful statecraft and political compromise have saved the empire? The likely answer is yes. But neither statecraft nor compromise was in evidence; instead, the inflexibility of British ministers and the passionate determination of Patriot leaders would destroy the British empire in North America.

Imperial Reform, 1763–1765

The Great War for Empire left a mixed legacy. Britain had driven the French out of Canada and the lands to the west of the Appalachian Mountains, and the Spanish out of Florida; and it now dominated all of eastern North America (Map 5.1). But the cost of the war had been high. To cope with the nation's enormous debt, the British ministry imposed new taxes on the American possessions. More fundamentally, the war spurred Parliament to redefine the character of the empire: Salutary Neglect, with its emphasis on trade and colonial self-government, gave way to imperial authority and the direct rule of Parliament.

The Legacy of War

The war changed the relationship between Britain and its North American colonies. During the fighting, British generals and American leaders disagreed sharply on military strategy. Moreover, the presence of 25,000 British troops revealed sharp cultural differences. The arrogance of British officers and their demands for deference shocked many Americans: British soldiers "are but little better than slaves to their officers," declared a Massachusetts militiaman. The hostility was mutual. British general James Wolfe complained that colonial troops were drawn from the dregs of society and that "there was no depending on them in action."

Disputes over Trade and Troops. The war also exposed the weakness of the royal governors. In theory, the governors had extensive political powers, including command of the provincial militia; in reality, they had to share power with the colonial assemblies, which outraged British officials. In Massachusetts, complained the Board of Trade, "almost every act of executive and legislative power is ordered and directed by votes and resolves

of the General Court." To strengthen imperial authority, Parliament passed the Revenue Act of 1762. The act tightened up the collection of trade duties, which colonial merchants had evaded for decades by bribing customs officials. The ministry also instructed the Royal Navy to seize American vessels carrying supplies from the mainland to the French West Indies. It was absurd, declared an outraged British politician, that French armies that were attempting "to Destroy one English province . . . are actually supported by Bread raised in another."

Britain's victory over France provoked a fundamental shift in military policy: the peacetime deployment of an army of ten thousand men in North America. Underlying that decision were several factors. King George III (r. 1760–1820) wanted military commands for his friends. The king's ministers feared a possible rebellion by the 60,000 French residents of Canada, Britain's new province to the north. The Native Americans were also a concern: Pontiac's Rebellion had nearly overwhelmed Britain's frontier forts; only a substantial military force could restrain the Indian peoples and deter land-hungry whites from settling west of the Appalachian Mountains in defiance of the Proclamation of 1763 (see Chapter 4). Finally, British politicians worried about the colonists' loyalty now that the French no longer controlled Canada. "The main purpose of Stationing a large Body of Troops in America," declared treasury official William Knox, "is to secure the Dependence of the Colonys on Great Britain." By deploying an army in America, the British ministry signaled its willingness to use military force to subdue conquered Frenchmen, unruly Indians, or rebellious colonists.

The National Debt. Troops cost money, which was in short supply because Britain's national debt had soared from £75 million in 1756 to £133 million in 1763. Indeed, the interest on the war debt was consuming 60 percent of the national budget, forcing cutbacks in other government expenditures. To restore fiscal stability, the prime minister, Lord Bute, needed to raise taxes. He began in England. The Treasury Department opposed increasing the land tax, which was already high and was paid primarily by the gentry and aristocracy, who had great influence in Parliament. So instead, Bute taxed those with little or no political power—the poor and middling classes—imposing higher import duties on tobacco and sugar, which raised their cost to consumers. The ministry also increased excise

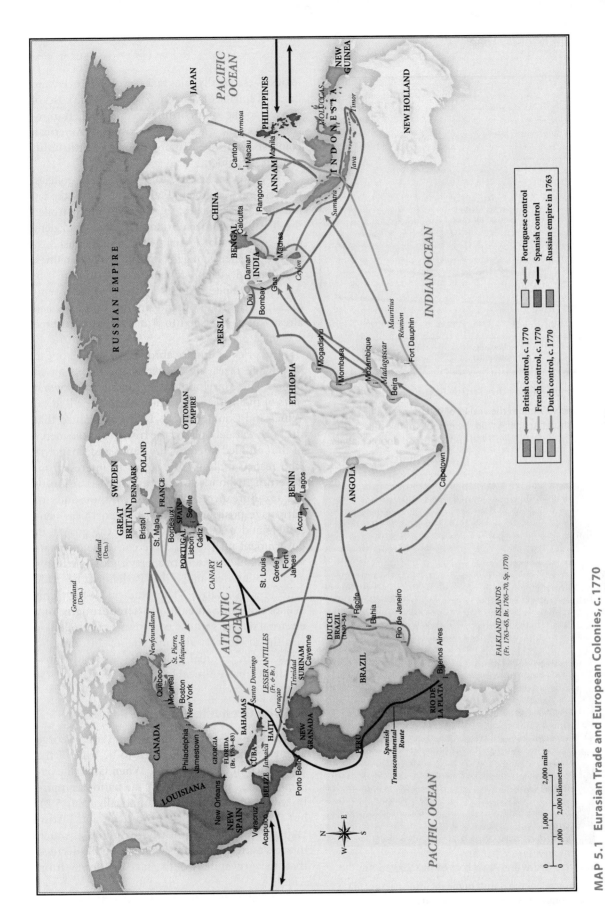

MAP 5.1 Eurasian Trade and European Colonies, c. 1770

By 1770, the Western European nations that had long dominated maritime trade had created vast colonial empires. Spain controlled the western halves of North and South America, Portugal owned Brazil, and Holland ruled Indonesia. Britain, a newer imperial power, boasted settler societies in North America, rich sugar islands in the West Indies, slave ports in West Africa, and a growing presence on the Indian subcontinent. Only France had failed to acquire and hold on to a significant colonial empire. (To trace changes in empire and trade routes, see Map 1.3 on p. 18 and Map 2.2 on p. 44.)

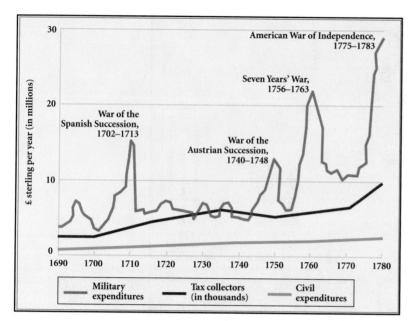

FIGURE 5.1 The Growing Power of the British State, 1690–1780

As Britain built a great navy and subsidized the armies of its European allies, the government's military expenditures soared, as did the number of tax collectors. The tax bureaucracy doubled in size between 1700 and 1735, and doubled again between 1750 and 1780.

George Grenville, Architect of the Stamp Act

This portrait of the British prime minister, painted in 1763, suggests Grenville's energy and ambition. As events were to show, he was determined to reform the imperial system and to ensure that the colonists shared the cost of the empire. The Earl of Halifax, Garrowby, Yorkshire.

levies — essentially sales taxes — on salt, beer, and distilled spirits, once again passing on the costs of the war to the king's ordinary subjects. Left unresolved was the question of taxing the American colonists, who, like Britain's poor, had little influence in Parliament.

To ensure adherence to its new fiscal policies, the British government doubled the size of the tax bureaucracy (Figure 5.1). Customs agents patrolled the coasts of southern Britain, arrested smugglers, and seized tons of French wines and Flemish textiles. Convicted smugglers faced heavy penalties, including death or forced "transportation" to America. Despite protests by the colonial assemblies, nearly fifty thousand English criminals had already been banished to America as indentured servants.

The price of empire abroad had turned out to be higher taxes and government intrusion at home. This development confirmed the worst fears of the British opposition parties, the Radical Whigs and Country Party. They complained that the huge war debt placed the treasury at the mercy of the "monied interest," the banks and financiers who reaped millions of pounds in interest from government bonds. Moreover, the expansion of the tax bureaucracy had created thousands of patronage positions filled with "worthless pensioners and placemen." To reverse the growth of government power — and the consequent threats to personal liberty and property rights — reformers in Britain demanded that Parliament be made more representative. The Radical Whig John Wilkes called for an end to **rotten boroughs**, tiny electoral districts whose voters were controlled by wealthy aristocrats and merchants. In domestic affairs as in colonial policy, the war had transformed British political life.

George Grenville: Imperial Reformer

A member of Parliament since 1741, George Grenville was widely conceded to be "one of the ablest men in Great Britain." When Grenville became prime minister in 1763, the nation's empire in America had expanded dramatically (Map 5.2); but the war had left Britain in debt, and British taxpayers were paying nearly five times as much in taxes as free Americans were. Grenville decided that new revenue would have to come from America.

Grenville carefully set out to reform the imperial system and began with a two-part plan. One part consisted of the Currency Act of 1764, which extended the ban on paper money as legal tender

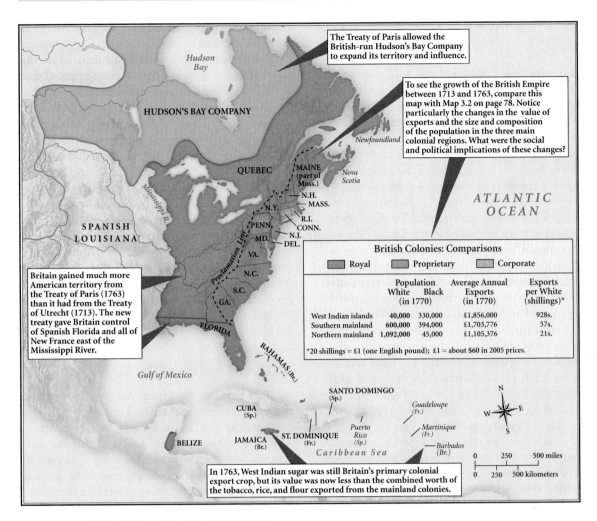

The Treaty of Paris allowed the British-run Hudson's Bay Company to expand its territory and influence.

To see the growth of the British Empire between 1713 and 1763, compare this map with Map 3.2 on page 78. Notice particularly the changes in the value of exports and the size and composition of the population in the three main colonial regions. What were the social and political implications of these changes?

Britain gained much more American territory from the Treaty of Paris (1763) than it had from the Treaty of Utrecht (1713). The new treaty gave Britain control of Spanish Florida and all of New France east of the Mississippi River.

British Colonies: Comparisons

Royal   Proprietary   Corporate

	Population White (in 1770)	Black	Average Annual Exports (in 1770)	Exports per White (shillings)*
West Indian islands	40,000	330,000	£1,856,000	928s.
Southern mainland	600,000	394,000	£1,703,776	57s.
Northern mainland	1,092,000	45,000	£1,105,376	21s.

*20 shillings = £1 (one English pound); £1 = about $60 in 2005 prices.

In 1763, West Indian sugar was still Britain's primary colonial export crop, but its value was now less than the combined worth of the tobacco, rice, and flour exported from the mainland colonies.

MAP 5.2   Britain's American Empire in 1763

The Treaty of Paris gave Britain control of the eastern half of North America and a dominant position in the West Indies. To protect the empire's new territories, British ministers dispatched troops to Florida and Quebec; they also sent troops to uphold the terms of the Proclamation of 1763, which prohibited Anglo-American settlement west of the Appalachian Mountains.

from New England to all the American colonies. Now American shopkeepers, planters, and farmers would have to pay their debts to British merchants in gold or silver coin, which was always in short supply.

The Sugar Act and Colonial Rights. Grenville also won parliamentary approval of the Sugar Act of 1764 to replace the widely ignored Molasses Act of 1733 (see Chapter 3). The prime minister and his subordinates who wrote the law understood the pattern of colonial trade: They knew that mainland settlers had to sell at least some of their wheat, fish, and lumber in the French sugar islands to accumulate funds to buy British manu-

factures. Grenville consequently resisted demands from British sugar planters, who wanted to retain a duty of 6 pence per gallon on French molasses, and instead settled on a duty of 3 pence per gallon.

This carefully crafted policy garnered little support in America. New England merchants—among them John Hancock of Boston—had made their fortunes smuggling French molasses, and they knew their profits would be reduced if the new regulations were enforced. These merchants and New England distillers, who relied on cheap French molasses to make rum, feared a rise in the price of molasses. They claimed publicly that the Sugar Act would wipe out trade with the French islands;

privately, they vowed to evade the duty by smuggling or by bribing officials.

Constitutional Objections. More important, the merchants' political allies raised constitutional objections to the Sugar Act. The Speaker of the Massachusetts House of Representatives argued that the new legislation was "contrary to a fundamental Principall of our Constitution: That all Taxes ought to originate with the people." "They who are taxed at pleasure by others cannot possibly have any property, and they who have no property, can have no freedom," warned Stephen Hopkins, the governor of Rhode Island. The Sugar Act raised other constitutional issues as well. Merchants prosecuted under the act would be tried without a jury by a **vice-admiralty court**, a maritime tribunal presided over by a British-appointed judge. American assemblies had long opposed the vice-admiralty courts, and they had found ways to have merchants accused of violating the Navigation Acts be tried by local common-law courts, where they often were acquitted by a jury. The Sugar Act closed this legal loophole by extending the jurisdiction of the vice-admiralty courts to all customs offenses.

The new taxes and trials imposed by the Sugar Act revived old American fears of British control. The influential Virginia planter Richard Bland admitted that the colonies had long been subject to the Navigation Acts, which restricted their manufactures and commerce. But, he protested, the American settlers "were not sent out to be the Slaves but to be the Equals of those that remained behind." John Adams, a young Massachusetts lawyer who was defending John Hancock on a charge of smuggling, phrased his concern in terms of the vice-admiralty courts: Those courts, he said, "degrade every American . . . below the rank of an Englishman."

While the logic of American arguments appeared compelling, some of the facts were wrong. The Navigation Acts certainly favored British merchants and manufacturers. However, trying accused smugglers in vice-admiralty courts was not discriminatory; similar rules had long been in force in Britain. The real issue was the growing administrative power of the British state. Having lived for decades under a policy of salutary neglect, a policy that allowed them to ignore certain provisions of the Navigation Acts, Americans understood the potential impact of the new policies: As a committee of the Massachusetts House of Representatives put it, they would "deprive the colonies of some of their most essential Rights as British subjects."

For their part, British officials insisted on the supremacy of parliamentary laws and denied that colonists should enjoy the traditional legal rights of Englishmen. When the royal governor of Massachusetts, Francis Bernard, heard that the Massachusetts House had objected to the Sugar Act, claiming there should be no taxation without representation, he asserted that Americans did not have that constitutional right: "The rule that a British subject shall not be bound by laws or liable to taxes, but what he has consented to by his representatives must be confined to the inhabitants of Great Britain only." In the eyes of George Grenville and other imperial reformers, the Americans were second-class subjects of the king, their rights limited by the Navigation Acts and the interests of the British state as determined by Parliament.

An Open Challenge: The Stamp Act

Another new tax, the Stamp Act of 1765, sparked the first great imperial crisis. The new levy would cover part of the cost of keeping British troops in America—some £200,000 a year (about $50 million today). The tax would require stamps on all court documents, land titles, contracts, playing cards, newspapers, and other printed items. A similar stamp tax in England was yielding £290,000 a year; Grenville hoped the American levy would raise £60,000. The prime minister knew that some Americans would object to the tax on constitutional grounds, and so raised the issue explicitly in the House of Commons: Did any member doubt "the power and sovereignty of Parliament over every part of the British dominions, for the purpose of raising or collecting any tax?" No one rose to object.

Confident of Parliament's support, Grenville threatened to impose a stamp tax unless the colonists paid for their own defense. The London merchants who served as agents for the colonial legislatures immediately protested that Americans did not have a continent-wide body that could impose taxes. Representatives from the various colonies had met together officially only once, at the Albany Congress of 1754, and not a single assembly had accepted that body's proposals for a colonial union (see Chapter 4). Benjamin Franklin, who was in Britain as the agent of the Pennsylvania assembly, proposed another solution to Grenville's challenge: American representation in Parliament.

"If you chuse to tax us," he suggested, "give us Members in your Legislature, and let us be one People."

With the exception of William Pitt, British politicians rejected Franklin's idea as too radical. They maintained that the colonists already had **virtual representation** in Parliament, that they were represented by members who were transatlantic merchants and West Indian sugar planters. Colonial leaders were equally skeptical of Franklin's plan. Americans were "situate at a great Distance from their Mother Country," the Connecticut assembly declared, and therefore "cannot participate in the general Legislature of the Nation."

When Grenville moved forward with the Stamp Act, his goal was not only to raise revenue but also to assert a constitutional principle: "the Right of Parliament to lay an internal Tax upon the Colonies." The House of Commons ignored American petitions opposing the act and passed the new legislation by an overwhelming vote of 205 to 49. At the request of General Thomas Gage, the British military commander in America, Parliament also passed the Quartering Act, which required colonial governments to provide barracks and food for British troops stationed within their borders. Finally, Parliament approved Grenville's proposal that violations of the Stamp Act be tried in vice-admiralty courts.

The design for reform was complete. Using the doctrine of parliamentary supremacy, Grenville had begun to fashion a centralized imperial system in America. He intended that system to function much like the system in Ireland: British officials would run the colonies with little regard for the local assemblies. Grenville's plan would provoke a constitutional confrontation not only on the specific issues of taxation, jury trials, and military quartering, but also on the general question of representative self-government.

➤ How did the Great War for Empire change the relationship between England and its American colonies?

➤ What were the goals of British imperial reformers?

➤ Why did the colonists object to the new taxes in 1764 and again in 1765? What arguments did they use?

➤ Why did these conflicts over specific policies turn into a constitutional crisis?

The Dynamics of Rebellion, 1765–1770

In the name of reform, Grenville had thrown down the gauntlet to the Americans. The colonists had often resisted unpopular laws and arbitrary governors, but they had faced an all-out attack on their institutions only once — in 1686, when James II had unilaterally imposed the Dominion of New England. The danger now was even greater: The new reforms were backed by both the king and Parliament. But the Patriots, as the defenders of American rights came to be called, met the challenge posed by Grenville and then by Charles Townshend. They organized protests, encouraged riots, and articulated a compelling ideology of resistance.

Politicians Protest, and the Crowd Rebels

In May 1765, Patrick Henry, a young headstrong member of the Virginia House of Burgesses, condemned Grenville's new legislation and attacked

The Intensity of Patrick Henry

This portrait, painted in 1795, when Henry was in his sixties, captures the Patriot's seriousness and intensity. As an orator, Henry drew on Evangelical Protestantism to create a new mode of political oratory. "His figures of speech ... were often borrowed from the Scriptures," a contemporary noted, and the content of his speeches mirrored "the earnestness depicted in his own features."
Mead Art Museum, Amherst College.

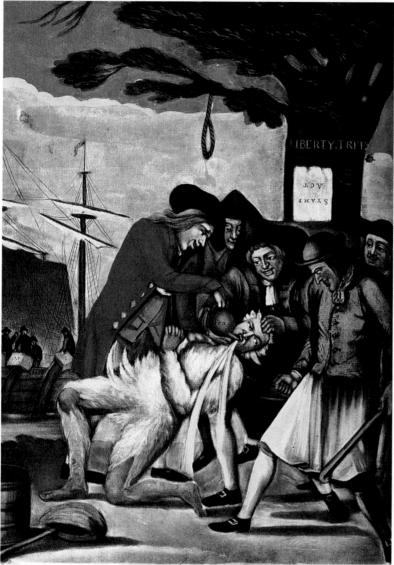

The BOSTONIAN'S Paying the EXCISE-MAN, or TARRING & FEATHERING

London Printed for Rob.ͭ Sayer & J.Bennett, Map & Printseller, N.º53, Fleet Street as the Act directs 31.Oct.ͬ1774.

A British View of American Mobs

This satiric etching of the Sons of Liberty, published in a British magazine, depicts their brutal treatment of John Malcolm, a commissioner of customs in Boston. The mob threatened to kill Malcolm — notice the noose hanging from the "liberty tree" — and then tarred and feathered him and forced him to drink huge quantities of tea. The men in the background are repudiating property rights by pouring tea into Boston Harbor. By labeling the tree, the artist seems to be asking "Does liberty mean anarchy?" Courtesy John Carter Brown Library at Brown University.

George III for supporting it. By comparing the king to Charles I, whose tyranny had led to religious and political conflict in the 1640s, Henry seemed to be calling for a new republican revolution. Although the assembly members were shaken by Henry's remarks, which bordered on treason, they condemned the Stamp Act as "a manifest Tendency to Destroy American freedom." In Massachusetts, James Otis, another republican-minded firebrand, persuaded the House of Representatives to call an all-colony congress "to implore Relief" from the act.

The Stamp Act Congress. Nine colonial assemblies sent delegates to the Stamp Act Congress, which met in New York City in October 1765. The congress issued a set of resolutions protesting the loss of American "rights and liberties," especially the right to trial by jury. The Stamp Act Resolves also challenged the constitutionality of the Stamp and Sugar acts by declaring that only the colonists' elected representatives could tax them. Still, the delegates were moderate men who wanted compromise, not confrontation. They assured Parliament that Americans "glory in being subjects of the best of Kings" and humbly petitioned for repeal of the Stamp Act. Other influential Americans, however, were advocating resistance, and they began to organize a boycott of British goods.

Popular opposition to the Stamp Act took more violent forms. When the act went into effect on

November 1, 1765, disciplined mobs demanded the resignation of stamp-tax collectors, most of whom had been born in the colonies. In Boston, the **Sons of Liberty** beheaded and burned an effigy of collector Andrew Oliver and then destroyed Oliver's new brick warehouse. Two weeks later, Bostonians attacked the house of Lieutenant Governor Thomas Hutchinson, long known as a defender of social privilege and imperial authority, breaking his furniture, looting his wine cellar, and setting fire to his library.

The men who inspired the mobs were wealthy merchants, like John Hancock, and Patriot lawyers, like John Adams; leading the crowds were middling artisans and minor merchants. "Spent the evening with the Sons of Liberty," Adams wrote in his diary, "John Smith, the brazier [metalworker], Thomas Crafts, the painter, Edes, the printer, Stephen Cleverly, the brazier; Chase, the distiller; [and] Joseph Field, Master of a vessel." Many of these men knew one another through their work; others were drinking buddies at the taverns that became centers of Patriot agitation.

In New York City, nearly three thousand shopkeepers, artisans, laborers, and seamen marched through the streets breaking streetlamps and windows and crying "Liberty!" And resistance to the Stamp Act spread far beyond the port cities. In nearly every colony, crowds of angry people — the "rabble," their detractors called them — intimidated royal officials. Near Wethersfield, Connecticut, five hundred farmers seized a tax collector, Jared Ingersoll, and forced him to resign his office in "the Cause of the People."

The Motives of the Crowd. Crowd protests were common in both Britain and America. Every November 5, Protestant mobs on both sides of the Atlantic burned effigies of the pope to celebrate the failure in 1605 of a Catholic plot, led by Guy Fawkes, to blow up the Houses of Parliament. Colonial mobs regularly destroyed brothels and rioted against the impressment (forced service) of merchant seamen by the Royal Navy. Governments tolerated the mobs because they usually did little damage and because, short of calling out the militia, they had no means of stopping them.

If rioting was traditional, its political goals were new. In New York City, for example, the leaders of the Sons of Liberty were two minor merchants, Isaac Sears and Alexander McDougall. Both Radical Whigs, Sears and McDougall were afraid that imperial reform would undermine political liberty. Other members of the mob had other agendas. Many artisans and their journeymen joined the protests because imports of low-priced British shoes and other manufactures threatened their livelihood. Some rioters also feared the financial burden of new taxes. Unlike "the Common people of England," a well-traveled colonist observed, "the people of America . . . never would submitt to be taxed that a few may be loaded with palaces and Pensions . . . while they themselves cannot support themselves and their needy offspring with Bread."

Religion motivated other protesters. Roused by the Great Awakening, evangelical Protestants resented the arrogance of British military officers and the corruption of royal bureaucrats. In New England, where many people lived into their sixties, and memories lived even longer, rioters looked back to the antimonarchy sentiments of their great-grandparents. A letter to a Boston newspaper signed "Oliver Cromwell," the name of the English republican revolutionary, promised to save "all the Free-born Sons of America." Finally, the mobs included apprentices, day laborers, and unemployed sailors — young men looking for excitement, who, when fortified by drink, were eager to resort to violence.

Throughout the colonies, popular resistance nullified the Stamp Act. Fearing a massive assault on Fort George on Guy Fawkes Day, New York lieutenant governor Cadwallader Colden called on General Gage to use his small military force to protect the stamps. Gage refused. "Fire from the Fort might disperse the Mob, but it would not quell them," he told Colden, and the result would be "an Insurrection, the Commencement of Civil War." Frightened collectors gave up their stamps, and angry Americans forced officials to accept legal documents without them. Popular insurrection gave a democratic cast to the emerging American Patriot movement. "Nothing is wanting but your own Resolution," declared a New York rioter, "for great is the Authority and Power of the People."

Because communication across the Atlantic was slow, the British response to the Stamp Act Congress and the Sons of Liberty mobs would not be known until the spring of 1766. However, royal officials in America already knew that they had lost the popular support that had sustained the empire for three generations. Lamented a customs collector in Philadelphia: "What can a Governor do without the assistance of the Governed?"

The Ideological Roots of Resistance

The American resistance movement emerged first in the seaports because British policies directly affected their residents. The Sugar Act raised the cost of molasses to urban distillers; the Stamp Act taxed the newspapers sold by printers and the contracts and other legal documents prepared by lawyers for merchants; and the flood of British manufactures threatened the livelihood of seaport artisans. The first protests, then, focused on economic grievances. According to one pamphleteer, Americans were being compelled to give the British "our money, as oft and in what quantity they please to demand it." Other writers alleged that the British had violated specific "liberties and privileges" embodied in colonial charters.

Initially, the resistance movement had no acknowledged leaders, no organization, and no clear goals. In time, however, lawyers took the lead, in part because merchants hired them to protect their goods from seizure by customs officials. Lawyers had another professional interest as well: As practitioners of English common law, they understood the importance to their clients of trial by jury and so opposed the extension of judge-run vice-admiralty courts. Composing pamphlets of remarkable political sophistication, Patriot lawyers gave the resistance movement its rationale, its political agenda, and its leaders.

Patriot writers drew on three intellectual traditions. The first was English common law, the centuries-old body of legal rules and procedures that protected the lives and property of the monarch's subjects. In the famous *Writs of Assistance* case of 1761, Boston lawyer James Otis invoked English legal precedents to dispute the legitimacy of a general search warrant that allowed customs officials to conduct wide-ranging inspections. And in demanding a jury trial for John Hancock, John Adams appealed to the jury-trial provision in the "29th Chap. of Magna Charta," an ancient document (1215) that "has for many Centuries been esteemed by Englishmen, as one of the . . . firmest Bulwarks of their Liberties." Other lawyers protested when the ministry declared that colonial judges served "at the pleasure" of the royal governors, claiming that would undermine the independence of the judiciary.

A second major intellectual resource was rationalist thought of the Enlightenment. Virginia planter Thomas Jefferson invoked David Hume and Francis Hutcheson, Enlightenment philosophers who applied reason in their critiques of traditional political practices and in their proposals to correct social ills. Jefferson and other Patriot writers also drew on John Locke, who argued that all individuals possessed certain "natural rights"—among them life, liberty, and property—and that governments must protect those rights (see Chapter 4). And they turned to French philosopher Montesquieu, who argued that a separation of powers among government departments prevented arbitrary rule.

The republican and Whig strands of the English political tradition provided a third ideological source for American Patriots. Puritan New England had long venerated the Commonwealth era, the brief period between 1649 and 1660 when England was a republic (see Chapter 2). After the Glorious Revolution of 1688–1689, the colonists praised the ban on royally imposed taxes and the other constitutional restrictions placed on the monarchy by English Whigs. And, Bostonian Samuel Adams and other Patriot leaders applauded Britain's Radical Whigs for denouncing political corruption among royal officials. Joseph Warren, a physician and a Patriot, reported that many Bostonians believed the Stamp Act was part of a plot "to force the colonies into rebellion," after which the ministry would use "military power to reduce them to servitude."

These diverse intellectual traditions and arguments—publicized in newspapers and pamphlets—helped to turn a series of impromptu riots and tax protests into a coherent Patriot-led political movement. The Patriots organized a highly successful boycott of British manufactures to force a repeal of the new imperial measures.

Sam Adams, Boston Agitator

This painting by John Singleton Copley (c. 1772) shows the radical Patriot pointing to the Massachusetts Charter of 1692, suggesting that Adams's determination to protect "charter rights" explained his opposition to British policies. However, Adams also was influenced by the natural-rights tradition. Deposited by the City of Boston. Courtesy Museum of Fine Arts, Boston.

TABLE 5.1	Ministerial Instability in Britain, 1760–1782	
Leading Minister	**Dates of Ministry**	**American Policy**
Lord Bute	1760–1763	Mildly reformist
George Grenville	1763–1765	Ardently reformist
Lord Rockingham	1765–1766	Accommodationist
William Pitt/Charles Townshend	1766–1770	Ardently reformist
Lord North	1770–1782	Coercive

Parliament Compromises, 1766

When news of the Stamp Act riots and the boycott reached Britain, Parliament was already in turmoil. Disputes over domestic policy had led George III to dismiss Grenville as the prime minister (Table 5.1). It was left to his successor, Lord Rockingham, to address the growing resistance in the colonies. The members of Parliament were divided. Grenville's followers demanded that imperial reform continue, if necessary at the point of a gun. The issue for them was the constitutional supremacy of Parliament: They were determined to maintain its status as one of the few powerful representative bodies in eighteenth-century Europe. "The British legislature," declared Chief Justice Sir James Mansfield, "has authority to bind every part and every subject, whether such subjects have a right to vote or not."

Three other factions were advocating for repeal of the Stamp Act. The Old Whigs, now led by Lord Rockingham, had long maintained that America was more important for its "flourishing and increasing trade" than for its tax revenues. A second group, representing the interests of British merchants and manufacturers, pointed out that the American trade boycott was cutting deeply into British exports. A committee of "London Merchants trading to America" joined with traders in the ports of Liverpool, Bristol, and Glasgow to petition Parliament for repeal. "The Avenues of Trade are all shut up," complained a Bristol merchant. "We have no Remittances and are at our Witts End for want of Money to fulfill our Engagements with our Tradesmen." Finally, former prime minister William Pitt and his allies in Parliament argued that the Stamp Act was a mistake and demanded it "be repealed absolutely, totally, and immediately." Pitt tried to draw a subtle distinction between taxation and legislation: Parliament lacked the authority to tax the colonies, he said, but its power over America was "sovereign and supreme, in every circumstance of government and legislation whatsoever." As Pitt's ambiguous formula suggested, the Stamp Act raised the difficult constitutional question of the extent of Parliament's sovereign powers.

Rockingham was a young and inexperienced minister facing complex issues. In the end, he decided on compromise. To mollify the colonists and help British merchants, he repealed the Stamp Act and reduced the duty imposed by the Sugar Act on French molasses to a penny a gallon. Then he pacified imperial reformers and hardliners with the Declaratory Act of 1766, which explicitly reaffirmed Parliament's "full power and authority to make laws and statutes . . . to bind the colonies and people of America . . . in all cases whatsoever." By ending the Stamp Act crisis swiftly, Rockingham hoped it would be forgotten just as quickly.

Charles Townshend Steps In

Often the course of history is changed by a small event—an illness, a personal grudge, a chance remark. So it was in 1767, when Rockingham's ministry collapsed over domestic issues and George III named William Pitt to head a new government. Pitt was chronically ill with gout, a painful disease of the joints, and often missed parliamentary debates, leaving the chancellor of the exchequer, Charles Townshend, in command. Pitt was sympathetic toward America; Townshend was not. As a member of the Board of Trade in the 1750s, Townshend had strongly supported restrictions on the colonial assemblies, and he was an outspoken advocate for the Stamp Act. So in 1767, when Grenville, now a member of Parliament, demanded that the colonists pay for the British troops in America, Townshend made an unplanned and fateful decision. Convinced of the necessity of imperial reform and eager to reduce the English land tax, he promised to find a new source of revenue in America.

The Townshend Act. The new tax legislation, the Townshend Act of 1767, had both fiscal and political goals. The statute imposed duties on colonial imports of paper, paint, glass, and tea, and would raise about £40,000 a year. To pacify Grenville, Townshend allocated some of this revenue for American military expenses. However, most of the money would fund a colonial civil list — paying the salaries of royal governors, judges, and other imperial officials. By freeing royal officials from financial dependence on the American assemblies, the ministry made it easier for them to enforce parliamentary laws and the king's instructions. And to strengthen imperial power further, Townshend devised the Revenue Act of 1767. This legislation created a board of customs commissioners in Boston and vice-admiralty courts in Halifax, Boston, Philadelphia, and Charleston. By using Parliament-imposed taxes to finance imperial administration, Townshend intended to undermine the autonomy and authority of American political institutions.

The Restraining Act. The full implications of Townshend's policies became clear in New York, where the assembly refused to comply with the Quartering Act of 1765. Fearing an unlimited drain on its treasury, the New York legislature first denied General Gage's requests for barracks and supplies for his troops and then offered limited assistance. In response, Townshend demanded full compliance, and Parliament threatened to impose a special duty on New York's imports and exports. The Earl of Shelburne, the new secretary of state, went even further: He proposed the appointment of a military governor with the authority to seize funds from New York's treasury and "to act with Force or Gentleness as circumstances might make necessary." Townshend decided on a less provocative but equally coercive measure, the Restraining Act of 1767, which suspended the New York assembly. Faced with the loss of self-government, New Yorkers reluctantly appropriated the funds to quarter the troops.

The Restraining Act raised the stakes for the colonists. Previously, the British Privy Council had invalidated a small proportion — about 5 percent — of colonial laws, like those establishing land banks. Townshend's Restraining Act went much further, declaring that American representative assemblies were completely dependent on the will of Parliament.

America Debates and Resists Again

The Townshend duties revived the constitutional debate over taxation. During the Stamp Act crisis, some Americans, including Benjamin Franklin, made a distinction between external and internal taxes. They suggested that external duties on trade, which Britain had long imposed through the Navigation Acts, were acceptable to Americans, but that direct, or internal, taxes, which had not previously been levied in the colonies, were not. Townshend thought this distinction was "perfect nonsense," but he indulged the Americans and laid duties only on trade.

The Second Boycott. Even so, most colonial leaders refused to accept the legitimacy of Townshend's measures. They agreed with lawyer John Dickinson, author of *Letters from a Farmer in Pennsylvania* (1768), that the real issue was not whether a tax was external or internal but the intention of the legislation. Because the Townshend duties were designed to raise revenue, they were taxes imposed without consent. In February 1768, the Massachusetts House of Representatives sent a letter condemning the Townshend Act to the other assemblies, and Boston and New York merchants began a new boycott of British goods. Public support for nonimportation quickly emerged in the smaller port cities of Salem, Newport, and Baltimore. Throughout Puritan New England, ministers and public officials discouraged the purchase of "foreign superfluities" and promoted the domestic manufacture of cloth and other necessities.

The Daughters of Liberty. American women, ordinarily excluded from public affairs, became crucial to the nonimportation movement through their production of **homespuns**. During the Stamp Act boycott in 1765, the wives and daughters of Patriot leaders had increased their output of yarn and cloth. Resistance to the Townshend duties mobilized many more women, including pious farmwives who spun yarn at the homes of their ministers. Some gatherings were openly patriotic. At one in Berwick, Maine, "true Daughters of Liberty" celebrated American products by "drinking rye coffee and dining on bear venison." Other women's groups combined support for the boycott with charitable work, spinning flax and wool to donate to the needy. Just as Patriot men followed tradition by joining crowd actions, so women's protests reflected their customary attention to the well-being of the community.

Newspapers celebrated the Daughters of Liberty. One Massachusetts town proudly claimed an annual output of thirty thousand yards of cloth; East Hartford, Connecticut, reported seventeen thousand yards. Although this surge in domestic production did not compensate for the loss of

British imports, which had averaged about 10 million yards of cloth each year, it brought thousands of women into the public arena.

Actually, the boycott mobilized many Americans to take political action. In the seaport cities, the Sons of Liberty published the names of merchants who imported British goods; they also broke the merchants' store windows and harassed their employees. By March 1769, tactics like these had convinced merchants and sailors in Philadelphia to join the nonimportation movement. Two months later, the members of the Virginia House of Burgesses vowed not to buy dutied articles, luxury goods, or slaves imported by British merchants. "The whole continent from New England to Georgia seems firmly fixed," the *Massachusetts Gazette* proudly announced. "Like a strong, well-constructed arch, the more weight there is laid upon it, the firmer it stands; and thus with America, the more we are loaded, the more we are united." Reflecting colonial self-confidence, Benjamin Franklin called for a return to the pre-1763 mercantilist system and proposed a "plan of conciliation" that was really a demand for British capitulation: "Repeal the laws, renounce the right, recall the troops, refund the money, and return to the old method of requisition."

Britain Responds. American resistance only increased British determination. When the Massachusetts House's letter opposing the Townshend duties reached London, Lord Hillsborough, the secretary of state for American affairs, branded it "unjustifiable opposition to the constitutional authority of Parliament." To strengthen the "Hand of Government" in Massachusetts and help the customs commissioners there, Hillsborough dispatched General Thomas Gage and four thousand British troops to Boston. Gage accused Massachusetts leaders of "Treasonable and desperate Resolves" and advised the ministry to "Quash this Spirit at a Blow." Parliament threatened to appoint a special commission to hear evidence of treason, and Hillsborough proposed to isolate Massachusetts from the other colonies and then use the army to bring the rebellious New Englanders to their knees (Map 5.3). In 1765, American resistance to taxation had provoked a parliamentary debate; in 1768, it produced a plan for military coercion.

Lord North Compromises, 1770

At this critical moment, the British ministry's resolve faltered. A series of harsh winters and dry summers cut grain output and raised food prices in Great Britain. In Scotland and northern England, thousands of tenants deserted their farms and boarded ships bound for America; and food riots spread across the English countryside. There were riots, too, in Ireland over the growing military budget there.

Adding to the ministry's difficulties was Radical Whig John Wilkes. Supported by associations of merchants, tradesmen, and artisans, Wilkes stepped up his attacks on government corruption and won election to Parliament. Overjoyed, American Patriots drank toasts to Wilkes and bought thousands of teapots and mugs emblazoned with his picture. When Wilkes was imprisoned for libel against parliament, an angry crowd protested his arrest. Troops killed seven protesters in the highly publicized

John Wilkes, British Radical

Wilkes won fame on both sides of the Atlantic as the author of *North Briton, Number 45* (depicted on the left), which called for major reforms in the British political system. At a dinner in Boston, Radical Whigs raised their wineglasses to Wilkes, toasting him forty-five times! But Wilkes had many enemies in Britain, including the artist who created this image. Wilkes is depicted as a cunning demagogue, brandishing the cap of Liberty to curry favor with the mob. Miriam and Ira D. Wallach Division of Art, Prints and Photographs, The New York Public Library. Astor, Lenox and Tilden Foundations.

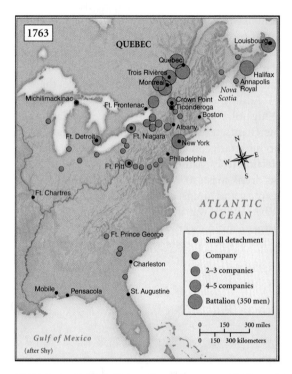
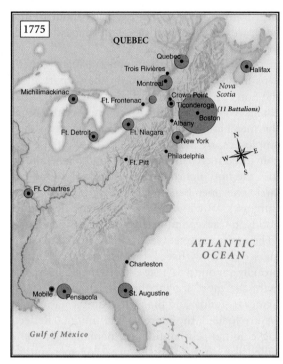

MAP 5.3   British Troop Deployments, 1763 and 1775

As the imperial crisis deepened, British military priorities changed. In 1763, most British battalions were stationed in Canada to deter Indian uprisings and French Canadian revolts. After the Stamp Act riots of 1765, the British established large garrisons in New York and Philadelphia. By 1775, eleven battalions of British regulars occupied Boston, the center of the Patriot movement.

Massacre of Saint George's Field, sparking more disturbances.

Nonimportation Succeeds. The American trade boycott also had a major impact on the British economy. The colonies usually had an annual trade deficit of £500,000; but in 1768, they imported less from Britain, cutting the deficit to £230,000. By 1769, the boycott of British goods, coupled with the colonies' staple exports and shipping services to overseas markets, had yielded a balance-of-payments surplus of £816,000. To revive their flagging sales to America, British merchants and manufacturers petitioned Parliament for repeal of the Townshend duties. British government revenues, which were heavily dependent on excise taxes and duties on imported goods, also had suffered from the boycott. By late 1769, some ministers felt that the Townshend duties were a mistake, and the king no longer supported Hillsborough's plan to use military force against Massachusetts.

Early in 1770, Lord North became prime minister. A witty man and a skillful politician, North set out to save the empire by designing a new compromise. Arguing that it was foolish to tax British exports to America (thereby raising their price and decreasing consumption), North persuaded Parliament to repeal most of the Townshend duties. However, he retained the tax on tea as a symbol of Parliament's supremacy. Gratified by North's initiative, colonial merchants called off the boycott (Figure 5.2).

Even an outbreak of violence did not rupture the compromise. During the boycott, New York artisans and workers had taunted British troops, mostly with words but occasionally with stones and their fists. In retaliation, the soldiers tore down a Liberty Pole (a Patriot flagpole), setting off a week of street fighting. In Boston, friction between residents and British soldiers over constitutional principles and everyday issues, like competition for part-time jobs, triggered a violent conflict. In March 1770, a group of soldiers fired into a crowd of rowdy demonstrators, killing five men, including one of the leaders, Crispus Attucks, an escaped slave who was working as a seaman. Convinced of a ministerial conspiracy against liberty, Radical Whigs labeled the

FIGURE 5.2   Trade as a Political Weapon, 1763–1776

Political upheaval did not affect the mainland colonies' exports to Britain, which rose slightly over the period, but imports fluctuated greatly. The American boycott of 1768–1769 led to a sharp fall in imports of British manufactures; but those imports soared after the Townshend duties were repealed.

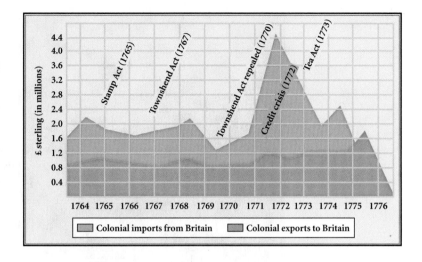

incident a "massacre" and filled the popular press with accusations that the British had planned the killings.

Sovereignty Debated. Although most Americans ignored the Radical Whigs' charges and remained loyal to the empire, five years of conflict over taxes and constitutional principles had taken their toll. In 1765, American leaders had accepted Parliament's authority; the Stamp Act Resolves had opposed only certain "unconstitutional" legislation. By 1770, the most outspoken Patriots — Benjamin Franklin in Pennsylvania, Patrick Henry in Virginia, and Samuel Adams in Massachusetts — had repudiated parliamentary supremacy and claimed equality for the American assemblies within the empire. Perhaps thinking of various European "composite monarchies," in which kings ruled far-distant provinces acquired by inheritance or conquest, Franklin suggested that the colonies were now "distinct and separate states" with "the same Head, or Sovereign, the King."

Franklin's suggestion outraged Thomas Hutchinson, the American-born royal governor of Massachusetts, whose house had been destroyed by a Stamp Act mob. A strong supporter of imperial rule, Hutchinson emphatically rejected the idea of "two independent legislatures in one and the same state"; in his mind, the British empire was a whole, its sovereignty indivisible. "I know of no line," he told the Massachusetts assembly, "that can be drawn between the supreme authority of Parliament and the total independence of the colonies."

There the matter rested. The British had twice imposed taxes on the colonies, and American Patri-ots had twice forced a retreat. If Parliament insisted on exercising Britain's claim to sovereign power a third time, some Americans were prepared to resist by force. Nor did they flinch when reminded that George III condemned their agitation. As the Massachusetts House told Hutchinson, "There is more reason to dread the consequences of absolute uncontrolled supreme power, whether of a nation or a monarch, than those of total independence." Fearful of civil war, Lord North's ministry hesitated to force the issue.

➤ What were the core constitutional principles over which the colonists and the ministers in Parliament disagreed?

➤ If Grenville's and Townshend's initiatives had been successful, how would the character of the British imperial system have changed?

➤ Weigh the importance of economic and ideological motives in creating and sustaining the colonial resistance movement. Which was more important? Why?

The Road to Independence, 1771–1776

The repeal of the Townshend duties in 1770 seemed to restore harmony to the British empire; but below the surface lay strong passions and mutual distrust. In 1773, those emotions erupted, destroying any hope of compromise. Within two years, the Americans and the British

Patriot Propaganda

Silversmith Paul Revere issued this engraving of the confrontation between British redcoats and snowball-throwing Bostonians. To whip up opposition to the military occupation of their town, Revere and other Patriots called the incident "The Boston Massacre." The shooting confirmed their Radical Whig belief that "standing armies" were instruments of tyranny. Library of Congress.

clashed in armed conflict, and Patriot legislators were forming provisional governments and building military forces, the two essentials for independence.

A Compromise Ignored

Once aroused, political passions are not easily quieted. In Boston, radical Patriots continued to warn Americans of the dangers of imperial domination. In November 1772, Samuel Adams persuaded the Boston town meeting to establish a committee of correspondence to urge Patriots "to state the Rights of the Colonists of this Province." Soon, eighty Massachusetts towns had similar committees. Then smugglers in Rhode Island burned the *Gaspée*, a customs vessel, and the British government set up a royal commission to investigate the incident. The commission's broad powers, particularly its authority to send Americans to Britain for trial, prompted the Virginia House of Burgesses to set up its own committee of correspondence "to communicate with the other colonies" about the situation in Rhode Island. By mid-1773, similar committees

The Boston Tea Party

Led by radical Patriots disguised as Mohawk Indians, Bostonians dump taxed tea owned by the East India Company into the harbor. The rioters made clear their "pure" political motives by punishing those who sought personal gain: A Son of Liberty who stole some of the tea was "stripped of his booty and his clothes together, and sent home naked." Library of Congress.

had appeared in Connecticut, New Hampshire, and South Carolina.

The Tea Act. These committees sprang into action when, at Lord North's behest, Parliament enacted the Tea Act in May 1773. The act provided financial relief for the British East India Company, which was deeply in debt because of military expeditions to extend Britain's influence in India. The Tea Act gave the company a government loan and canceled the import duty on its tea. But the act offended many Americans. Since 1768, when the Townshend Act had placed a duty of 3 pence a pound on tea, most colonists had bought tea smuggled in by Dutch traders. By relieving the East India Company of import duties, the Tea Act made its tea cheaper than that sold by Dutch merchants. So the act encouraged Americans to drink East India tea — and pay the Townshend duty.

Radical Patriots accused the ministry of bribing Americans to give up their principled opposition to British taxation. As an anonymous woman wrote in the *Massachusetts Spy,* "The use of [British] tea is considered not as a private but as a public evil . . . a handle to introduce a variety of . . . oppressions

amongst us." American merchants joined the protest because the East India Company planned to distribute its tea directly to shopkeepers, thereby excluding them from the profits of the trade. "The fear of an Introduction of a Monopoly in this Country," British general Frederick Haldimand reported from New York, "has induced the mercantile part of the Inhabitants to be very industrious in opposing this Step and added Strength to a Spirit of Independence already too prevalent."

The committees of correspondence organized resistance to the Tea Act. Committee members held public bonfires at which they persuaded their fellow townspeople — sometimes gently, sometimes not — to consign British tea to the flames. The Sons of Liberty patrolled the wharves and prevented East India Company ships from landing new supplies. In response, Royal Governor Hutchinson of Massachusetts hatched a scheme to land the tea and collect the tax. When a shipment of tea arrived in Boston Harbor on the *Dartmouth,* Hutchinson immediately passed the ship through customs so that it could enter the harbor. If the Sons of Liberty blocked the tea from coming ashore, Hutchinson intended to order British troops to unload the tea and supervise its sale by auction. But the Patriots foiled the governor's plan: After nightfall on December 16, 1773, a group of artisans and laborers disguised as Indians boarded the *Dartmouth*, broke open 342 chests of tea (valued at about £10,000, or roughly $800,000 today), and threw them into the harbor. "This destruction of the Tea is so bold and it must have so important Consequences," John Adams wrote in his diary, "that I cannot but consider it as an Epoch in History."

The Coercive Acts. The British Privy Council was outraged, as was the king. "Concessions have made matters worse," George III declared. "The time has come for compulsion." Early in 1774, Parliament decisively rejected a proposal to repeal the duty on American tea; instead, it enacted four Coercive Acts to force Massachusetts to pay for the tea and to submit to imperial authority. The Port Bill closed Boston Harbor; the Government Act annulled the Massachusetts charter and prohibited most local town meetings; the Quartering Act — a new one — required the colony to build barracks for British troops; and the Justice Act allowed trials for capital crimes to be transferred to other colonies or to Britain (see Reading American Pictures, "How Did the British View the Crisis in the Colonies?," p. 155).

Patriot leaders throughout the mainland branded the measures "intolerable" and rallied support for Massachusetts. In far-off Georgia, a Patriot warned the "Freemen of the Province" that "every privilege you at present claim as a birthright, may be wrested from you by the same authority that blockades the town of Boston." "The cause of Boston," George Washington declared in Virginia, "now is and ever will be considered as the cause of America." The committees of correspondence had created a firm sense of unity among Patriots.

In 1774, Parliament also passed the Quebec Act, recognizing Roman Catholicism in Quebec. This humane concession to Quebec's predominantly Catholic population reignited religious passions in New England, where Protestants associated Catholicism with arbitrary royal government and popish superstition. Because the act extended the boundaries of Quebec into the Ohio River Valley, it also angered influential land speculators and politicians in Virginia and other colonies (Map 5.4). Although the ministry did not intend the Quebec Act to be a coercive measure, many colonial leaders saw it as proof of Parliament's intention to intervene in American domestic affairs.

The Continental Congress Responds

In response to the Coercive Acts, Patriot leaders invited all colonial assemblies to send delegates to a new continent-wide body, the Continental Congress. Twelve did. The recently acquired mainland colonies — Florida, Quebec, Nova Scotia, and New-foundland — refused to attend, as did Georgia, where the royal governor controlled the legislature. And the assemblies of Barbados, Jamaica, and the other British sugar islands, fearful of revolts by their predominately African populations, reaffirmed their allegiance to the crown.

The delegates who met in Philadelphia in September 1774 had specific concerns. Southern representatives, fearing a British plot "to overturn the constitution and introduce a system of arbitrary government," advocated a new economic boycott. Independence-minded representatives from New England demanded political union and defensive military preparations. However, many delegates from the Middle Atlantic colonies favored a political compromise.

Led by Joseph Galloway of Pennsylvania, these men of "loyal principles" proposed a compromise that was much like the plan Franklin had proposed in Albany two decades earlier: Each colony would retain its assembly, which would legislate on local matters, and a new continent-wide body would handle general American affairs. The king would appoint a president-general, who would preside over a legislative council selected by the colonial assemblies. Although Galloway's plan gave the council veto power over parliamentary legislation that affected America, the delegates refused to endorse it. With British troops occupying Boston, most thought it was too conciliatory (see Comparing American Voices, "The Debate over Representation and Sovereignty," pp. 158–159).

Instead, a majority of the delegates passed a Declaration of Rights and Grievances, which demanded the repeal of the Coercive Acts. They also repudiated the Declaratory Act of 1766, which had proclaimed Parliament's supremacy over the colonies, and stipulated that British control be limited to matters of trade. Finally, the Congress approved a program of economic retaliation. It ordered a new non-importation pact that would take effect in December 1774. If Parliament did not repeal the Intolerable Acts by September 1775, the Congress vowed to cut off virtually all colonial exports to Britain, Ireland, and the British West Indies. Ten years of constitutional conflict had culminated in the threat of all-out commercial warfare.

Even at this late date, a few British leaders hoped for compromise. In January 1775, William Pitt, now sitting in the House of Lords as the Earl of Chatham, asked Parliament to renounce its power to tax the

How Did the British View the Crisis in the Colonies?

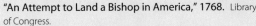

"An Attempt to Land a Bishop in America," 1768. Library of Congress.

"The Bostonians in Distress," 1774. Library of Congress.

Britain's colonial policy between 1763 and 1775 created controversy in Britain as well as in America. Grenville's ministry enacted the Stamp Act in 1765; the next year, Rockingham's government repealed it. The conflict over policy split Tory hard-liners, who believed the Patriots should be coerced into paying taxes and quartering troops, from Old Whigs, who preferred compromise. Their debates roiled the Halls of Parliament and spilled onto the pages of London's newspapers, where they took the form of controversial essays and political cartoons, like the two here. People of the time immediately understood the meaning—and the political bias—of these cartoons; more than two centuries later, we have to work a bit harder to understand what they are "saying."

ANALYZING THE EVIDENCE

➤ "An Attempt to Land a Bishop in America" addressed the dispute over a proposal to dispatch a bishop of the Church of England to America to supervise the clergy there. What is the cartoonist's position on the proposal?

➤ Look carefully at the signs and banners in "An Attempt to Land a Bishop in America." They celebrate John Locke, the advocate of self-government, and call for "Liberty and Freedom of Conscience." To interpret the words in the balloon, "No Lords Spiritual or Temporal in New England," think back to the Puritans and what they thought of bishops (see Chapter 2). What other aspects of the cartoon point to the artist's stance on the proposal to send a bishop to America?

➤ At first glance, "The Bostonians in Distress" seems sympathetic toward the colonists, caged as a consequence of the Coercive Acts (1774). What does a closer look suggest? How does the artist depict the colonists? What aspects of the picture suggest that the men in the cage do not deserve respect?

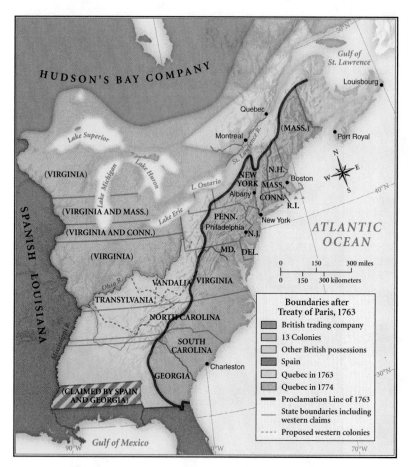

MAP 5.4   British Western Policy, 1763–1774

Despite the Proclamation of 1763, which restricted white settlement west of the Appalachian Mountains, Anglo-Americans settlers and land speculators proposed two new colonies in the West, Vandalia and Transylvania. But the Quebec Act of 1774 designated most western lands as Indian reserves and, by vastly enlarging the boundaries of Quebec, eliminated the sea-to-sea land claims of many seaboard colonies. The act also angered New England Protestants, who condemned its provisions allowing French residents to practice Catholicism, and colonial political leaders, who condemned its failure to provide a representative assembly there.

colonies and to recognize the Continental Congress as a lawful body. In return for these concessions, he suggested, the Congress should acknowledge parliamentary supremacy and grant a continuing revenue to help defray the British national debt.

The British ministry rejected Chatham's plan. Twice it had backed down in the face of colonial resistance; a third retreat was impossible. The honor of the nation was at stake. Branding the Continental Congress an illegal assembly, the ministry also ruled out Lord Dartmouth's proposal to send commissioners to America to negotiate a settlement. Instead, Lord North set stringent terms: Americans must pay for their own defense and administration, and must acknowledge Parliament's authority to tax them. To put teeth in these demands, North imposed a naval blockade on American trade with foreign nations and ordered General Gage to suppress dissent in Massachusetts. "Now the case seemed desperate," the prime minister told Thomas Hutchinson, whom the Patriots had forced into exile in London. "Parliament would not—could not—concede. For aught he could see it must come to violence."

The Countryside Rises Up

Ultimately, the success of the urban-led Patriot movement would depend on the large rural population. Most farmers had little interest in imperial affairs. Their lives were deeply rooted in the soil, and their prime allegiance was to family and community. But imperial policies increasingly intruded into the isolated world of farm families taking their sons for military duty and raising their taxes. Before the outbreak of the French and Indian War in 1754, farmers on Long Island had paid an average of 10 shillings a year in taxes; by 1756, their taxes had jumped to 30 shillings. Peace brought little relief: The British-imposed Quartering Act kept taxes high, an average of 20 shillings a year. These levies, though much less than the taxes most Britons paid, angered American farmers.

The Patriot Movement Expands. The urban-led boycotts of 1765 and 1768 raised the political consciousness of rural Americans. When the First Continental Congress placed a new ban on British goods in 1774, it easily established a rural network of committees of safety and inspection to enforce it. Appealing to rural thriftiness, the Congress discouraged the wearing of expensive imported clothes to funerals, suggesting instead "a black crape or ribbon on the arm or hat for gentlemen, and a black ribbon and necklace for ladies." In Concord, Massachusetts, 80 percent of the male heads of families and a number of single women signed a "Solemn League and Covenant" supporting nonimportation. In other towns, men blacked their faces, disguised themselves in blankets "like Indians," and threatened violence against shopkeepers who traded "in rum, molasses, & Sugar, &c." in violation of the boycott.

Patriots also appealed to the yeoman tradition of landownership, which was everywhere under threat. In long-settled communities, arable land was now scarce and expensive; and in new communities, merchants were seizing farmsteads as payment for delinquent debts. Money was always in short supply in rural households, and, complained the town meeting of Petersham, Massachusetts, new British taxes would further drain "this People of the Fruits of their Toil." "The duty on tea," warned a Patriot pamphlet, "was only a prelude to a window-tax, hearth-tax, land-tax, and poll-tax, and these were only paving the way for reducing the country to lordships." By the 1770s, many northern yeomen felt personally threatened by British imperial policy (Table 5.2).

Despite their higher standard of living, southern slave owners had similar fears. Many Virginia Patriots—including Patrick Henry, George Washington, and Thomas Jefferson—speculated in western lands, and they reacted angrily when first the Proclamation of 1763 and then the Quebec Act of 1774 invalidated their claims. Moreover, many Chesapeake planters lived extravagantly and were indebted to British merchants. A debt of £1,000 had once been considered excessive, a planter observed in 1766, but "ten times that sum is now spoke of with indifference and thought no great burthen on Some Estates." Although many planters faced financial disaster, George Washington noted, they were determined to live "genteely and hospitably" and were "ashamed" to adopt frugal ways. Accustomed to being absolute masters on their slave-labor plantations, they resented their financial dependence and dreaded the prospect of political subservience. After Parliament used the Coercive Acts to subdue Massachusetts, the planters feared Virginia would be next. The ministry might dissolve Virginia's representative assembly and judicial institutions, and allow British merchants to seize their debt-burdened property. That is why the Patriot gentry supported demands by yeomen farmers to close the law courts. Now, farmers and planters

alike could bargain with merchants over debts without the threat of legal action. "The spark of liberty is not yet extinct among our people," declared one planter, "and if properly fanned by the Gentlemen of influence will, I make no doubt, burst out again into a flame."

Loyal Americans

Although many wealthy planters and affluent merchants joined the Patriot cause, other prominent Americans worried that resistance to Britain would destroy respect for all political institutions and end in mob rule. Their fears increased when the Sons of Liberty upheld the boycotts by intimidation and force. One well-to-do New Yorker complained, "No man can be in a more abject state of bondage than he whose Reputation, Property and Life are exposed to the discretionary violence . . . of the community." As the crisis continued, these men rallied to the support of the royal governors.

Other social groups also refused to endorse the Patriot movement. In Pennsylvania and New Jersey, many Quakers and Germans tried to remain neutral because they held pacifist beliefs and because they feared political change. In regions where many wealthy landowners became Patriots—the Hudson River Valley of New York, for example—tenant farmers supported the king because they hated their landlords. Similar social divisions prompted some Regulators in the North Carolina backcountry and many farmers in eastern Maryland to oppose the Patriots there. And enslaved blacks had even less reason to support the cause of their Patriot masters. In November 1774, James Madison reported that some Virginia slaves planned to escape from their Patriot owners "when the English troops should arrive."

To mobilize support for the king, prominent American Loyalists—mostly royal officials, merchants with military contracts, clergy of the Church of England, and well-established lawyers—denounced the Patriot leaders and accused them of working toward independence. These Loyalists formed an articulate pro-British party, but one that remained small and ineffective. A Tory association started by Governor Benning Wentworth of New Hampshire enrolled just fifty-nine members, fourteen of whom were his relatives. At this crucial juncture, Americans who supported resistance to British rule commanded the allegiance—or at least the acquiescence—of the majority of white Americans.

Compromise Fails

When the Continental Congress met in September 1774, Massachusetts was already in open defiance of

The Debate over Representation and Sovereignty

Before 1763, Benjamin Franklin told the House of Commons, Americans had paid little attention to the question of Parliament's "right to lay taxes and duties" in the colonies. The reason was simple, Franklin said: "A right to lay internal taxes was never supposed to be in Parliament, as we are not represented there." Franklin recognized that representation was central to the imperial debate. As the following selections show, the failure to solve this problem—and the closely related issue of parliamentary sovereignty—led to the American rebellion.

JARED INGERSOLL
Report on the Debates in Parliament (1765)

Jared Ingersoll was a Connecticut lawyer who served as that colony's agent, or lobbyist, in Britain. In this letter written to the governor of Connecticut in 1765, Ingersoll summarizes the debate in Parliament over the Stamp Act. When the act passed, he accepted a commission as the stamp distributor in Connecticut. A mob forced him to resign that post. Ingersoll later served as a Vice Admiralty judge in Philadelphia and, during the revolution, remained loyal to Britain.

The principal Attention has been to the Stamp bill that has been preparing to Lay before Parliament for taxing America. The Point of the Authority of Parliament to impose such Tax I found on my Arrival here was so fully and Universally yielded, that there was not the least hopes of making any impressions that way.

I beg leave to give you a Summary of the Arguments which are made use of in favour of such Authority. The House of Commons, say they, is a branch of the supreme legislature of the Nation, and which in its Nature is supposed to represent, or rather to stand in the place of, the Commons, that is, of the great body of the people, who are below the dignity of peers....

That this house of Commons, therefore, is now fixt and ascertained and is a part of the Supreme unlimited power of the Nation, as in every State there must be some unlimited Power and Authority....

They say a Power to tax is a necessary part of every Supreme Legislative Authority, and that if they have not that Power over America, they have none, and then America is at once a Kingdom of itself.

On the other hand those who oppose the bill say, it is true the Parliament have a supreme unlimited Authority over every Part and Branch of the Kings dominions and as well over Ireland as any other place.

Yet [they say] we believe a British parliament will never think it prudent to tax Ireland [or America]. Tis true they say, that the Commons of England and of the British Empire are all represented in and by the house of Commons, but this representation is confessedly on all hands by Construction and Virtual [because most British subjects] ... have no hand in choosing the representatives....

[They say further] that the Effects of this implied Representation here and in America must be infinitely different in the Article of Taxation.... By any Mistake an act of Parliament is made that prove injurious and hard the Member of Parliament here sees with his own Eyes and is moreover very accessible to the people.... [Also,] the taxes are laid equally by one Rule and fall as well on the Member himself as on the people. But as to America, from the great distance in point of Situation [they are not represented in the same way]....

[Finally, they say] we already by the Regulations upon their trade draw from the Americans all that they can spare, at least they say this Step [of taxation] should not take place until or unless the Americans are allowed to send Members to Parliament.

Thus I have given you, I think, the Substance of the Arguments on both sides of that great and important Question of the right and also of the Expediency of taxing America by Authority of Parliament.... However, ... upon a Division of the house upon the Question, there was about 250 to about 50 in favour of the Bill....

SOURCE: New Haven Colonial Historical Society, *Papers* (1918), 9: 306–315.

JOSEPH GALLOWAY
Plan of Union (1775)

Joseph Galloway, a lawyer, was Speaker of the Pennsylvania assembly and a delegate to the First Continental Congress.

At the Congress, he proposed a plan that addressed the issue of representation. The colonies would remain British territories, but would operate under a continental government with the power to veto parliamentary laws that affected America adversely. Radical Patriots in the Congress, who favored independence, prevented a vote on Galloway's plan and suppressed mention of it in the records. Galloway remained loyal to Britain, fought on the British side in the war, and moved to England in 1778.

If we sincerely mean to accommodate the difference between the two countries, . . . we must take into consideration a number of facts which led the Parliament to pass the acts complained of . . . .[You will recall] the dangerous situation of the Colonies from the intrigues of France, and the incursions of the Canadians and their Indian allies, at the commencement of the last war. . . . Great-Britain sent over her fleets and armies for their protection. . . .

In this state of the Colonies, it was not unreasonable to expect that Parliament would have levied a tax on them proportionate to their wealth, . . . Parliament was naturally led to exercise the power which had been, by its predecessors, so often exercised over the Colonies, and to pass the Stamp Act. Against this act, the Colonies petitioned Parliament, and denied its authority. . . . The petitions rested in a declaration that the Colonies could not be represented in that body. This justly alarmed the British Senate. It was thought and called by the ablest men and Britain, a clear and explicit declaration of the American Independence, and compelled the Parliament to pass the Declaratory Act, in order to save its ancient and incontrovertible right of supremacy over all the parts of the empire. . . .

Having thus briefly stated the arguments in favour of parliamentary authority, and considered the state of the Colonies, I am free to confess that the exercise of that authority is not perfectly constitutional in respect to the Colonies. We know that the whole landed interest of Britain is represented in that body, while neither the land nor the people of America hold the least participation in the legislative authority of the State. Representation, or a participation in the supreme councils of the State, is the great principle upon which the freedom of the British Government is established and secured.

I wish to see . . . the right to participate in the supreme councils of the State extended, in some form . . . to America . . . [and therefore] have prepared the draught of a plan for uniting America more intimately, in constitutional policy, with Great-Britain. . . . I am certain when dispassionately considered, it will be found to be the most perfect union in power and liberty with the Parent State, next to a representation in Parliament, and I trust it will be approved of by both countries.

The Plan
That the several [colonial] assemblies shall [form an American union and] choose members for the grand council. . . .

That the Grand Council . . . shall hold and exercise all the like rights, liberties and privileges, as are held and exercised by and in the House of Commons of Great-Britain. . . .

That the President-General shall hold his office during the pleasure of the King, and his assent shall be requisite to all acts of the Grand Council, and it shall be his office and duty to cause them to be carried into execution. . . .

That the President-General, by and with the advice and consent of the Grand-Council, hold and exercise all the legislative rights, powers, and authorities, necessary for regulating and administering all the general police and affairs of the colonies. . . .

That the said President-General and the Grand Council, be an inferior and distinct branch of the British legislature, united and incorporated with it, . . . and that the assent of both [Parliament and the Grand Council] shall be requisite to the validity of all such general acts or statutes [that affect the colonies].

SOURCE: Joseph Galloway, *Historical and Political Reflections on the Rise and Progress of the American Rebellion* (1780), 70.

ANALYZING THE EVIDENCE

➤ According to Ingersoll, what were the main arguments of those in Parliament who opposed the Stamp Act? Did they agree with the act's supporters that Parliament had the right to tax the colonies?

➤ How did Galloway's plan solve the problem of colonial representation in Parliament? How do you think ministers who advocated parliamentary supremacy would have reacted to the plan?

➤ The framers of the U.S. Constitution addressed the problem of dividing authority between state governments and the national government by allowing the state governments to retain legal authority over most matters and delegating only limited powers to the national government (see Chapter 6). Do you think this type of solution could have been implemented in the British empire? Why or why not?

TABLE 5.2	Patriot Resistance, 1762–1776	
Date	**British Action**	**Patriot Response**
1762	Revenue Act	Merchants complain privately
1763	Proclamation Line	Land speculators voice discontent
1764	Sugar Act	Merchants and Massachusetts legislature protest
1765	Stamp Act	Sons of Liberty riot; Stamp Act Congress; first boycott of British goods
1765	Quartering Act	New York assembly refuses to fund until 1767
1767–1768	Townshend Act; military occupation of Boston	Second boycott of British goods; harassment of pro-British merchants
1772	Royal commission to investigate *Gaspée* affair	Committees of correspondence form
1773	Tea Act	Widespread resistance; Boston Tea Party
1774	Coercive Acts; Quebec Act	First Continental Congress; third boycott of British goods
1775	British raids near Boston; king's Proclamation for Suppressing Rebellion and Sedition	Armed resistance; Second Continental Congress; invasion of Canada; cut off of colonial exports
1776	Military attacks by royal governors in South	Paine's *Common Sense;* Declaration of Independence

British authority. In August, 150 delegates to an extralegal Middlesex County Congress advised Patriots to close the royal courts of justice and to transfer their political allegiance to the popularly elected House of Representatives. Following the Middlesex congress, armed crowds harassed Loyalists and ensured Patriot rule in most of New England.

General Thomas Gage, now the military governor of Massachusetts, tried desperately to maintain imperial power. In September, he ordered British troops in Boston to seize Patriot armories and storehouses in nearby Charlestown and Cambridge. In response, twenty thousand colonial militiamen mobilized to safeguard other military supply depots. The Concord town meeting raised a defensive force, the famous **Minutemen**, to "Stand at a minutes warning in Case of alarm." Increasingly, Gage's authority was limited to Boston, where it rested primarily on the bayonets of his 3,500 troops. Meanwhile, the Patriot-controlled Massachusetts House met in defiance of Parliament, collected taxes, bolstered the militia, and assumed the responsibilities of government.

In London, the colonial secretary, Lord Dartmouth, proclaimed Massachusetts to be in "open rebellion" and ordered Gage to march quickly against the "rude rabble." On the night of April 18, 1775, Gage dispatched seven hundred soldiers to capture colonial leaders and supplies at Concord.

Paul Revere and two other Bostonians warned the Patriots; and at dawn, local militiamen met the British troops first at Lexington and then at Concord. A handful of men lost their lives in the skirmishes. But as the British retreated to Boston, militiamen from neighboring towns repeatedly ambushed them. By the end of the day, 73 British soldiers were dead, 174 wounded, and 26 missing. British fire had killed 49 Americans and wounded 39. Too much blood had been spilled to allow another compromise. Twelve years of economic conflict and constitutional debate had ended in civil war.

The Second Continental Congress Organizes for War

In May 1775, Patriot leaders gathered in Philadelphia for the Second Continental Congress. Soon after the Congress opened, three thousand British troops attacked American fortifications on Breed's Hill and Bunker Hill overlooking Boston. After three assaults and one thousand casualties, they finally dislodged the Patriot militia. Inspired by his countrymen's valor, John Adams exhorted the Congress to rise to the "defense of American liberty" by creating a continental army and nominated George Washington to lead it. After bitter debate, the Congress approved the proposals, but, Adams lamented, only "by bare majorities."

Political Propaganda: The Empire Strikes Back

A British cartoon satirizes the women of Edenton, North Carolina, for supporting the boycott of British trade by hinting at their sexual lasciviousness and — by showing an enslaved black woman holding an inkstand for these supposed advocates of liberty — their moral hypocrisy. Library of Congress.

A SOCIETY of PATRIOTIC LADIES,
AT
EDENTON in NORTH CAROLINA.

Plate V.

Congress Versus the King. Despite the bloodshed in Massachusetts, a majority in the Congress still hoped for reconciliation. Led by John Dickinson of Pennsylvania, these moderates won approval of a petition expressing loyalty to George III and asking for repeal of oppressive parliamentary legislation. But Samuel Adams, Patrick Henry, and other zealous Patriots drummed up support for a much stronger statement, the Declaration of the Causes and Necessities of Taking Up Arms. Americans dreaded the "calamities of civil war," the declaration asserted, but were "resolved to die Freemen rather than to live [as] slaves." George III failed to exploit the divisions among the Patriots; instead, in August 1775, he issued the Proclamation for Suppressing Rebellion and Sedition.

Even before the king's proclamation reached America, the radicals in the Congress had won support for an invasion of Canada. They hoped to unleash an uprising among the French inhabitants and add a fourteenth colony to the rebellion. Patriot forces easily defeated the British forces at Montreal; but in December 1775, they failed to capture Quebec City. Meanwhile, American merchants waged financial warfare by carrying out the promise of the First Continental Congress to cut off all exports to Britain and its West Indian sugar islands. Parliament retaliated with the Prohibitory Act, which outlawed all trade with the rebellious colonies.

Rebellion in the South. Skirmishes between Patriot and Loyalist forces broke out in many areas. In Virginia, the Patriot-dominated House of Burgesses forced the royal governor, Lord Dunmore, to take refuge on a British warship in Chesapeake Bay. Branding the Patriots "traitors," the governor organized two military forces—one white, the Queen's Own Loyal Virginians, and one black, the

Drawn by Earl & engraved by A. Doolittle in 1775   Re-Engraved by A. Doolittle and J.W. Barber in 1832

BATTLE OF LEXINGTON.

The Confrontation on Lexington Green

Amos Doolittle's engraving accurately depicts the events of April 19, 1775. When British troops arrived in Lexington, a British officer recalled, they "found on a green close to the road a body of the country people drawn up in military order, with arms and accoutrements." When someone fired a shot, the British soldiers let loose a volley. The provincial militiamen scattered, finding cover behind nearby stone walls, and then returned fire. Library of Congress.

Ethiopian Regiment, which enlisted some one thousand slaves who had fled their Patriot owners. In November 1775, Dunmore issued a controversial proclamation promising freedom to slaves and indentured servants who joined the Loyalist cause. White planters denounced this "Diabolical scheme," claiming it "point[ed] a dagger to their Throats." Faced with black unrest and pressed by yeoman and tenant farmers demanding independence, Patriot planters called for a final break with Britain.

In North Carolina, too, military clashes prompted demands for independence. Early in 1776, Josiah Martin, the colony's royal governor, journeyed to the backcountry, where he raised a Loyalist force of 1,500 Scottish Highlanders. In response, Patriots mobilized the low-country militia and, in February, defeated Martin's army at the Battle of Moore's Creek Bridge, capturing more than 800 Highlanders. Following this victory, radical Patriots turned the North Carolina assembly into an independent provincial congress, which instructed its representatives in

Philadelphia "to concur with the Delegates of other Colonies in declaring Independence, and forming foreign alliances." In May, Virginia Patriots followed suit: Led by James Madison, Edmund Pendleton, and Patrick Henry, they met in convention and resolved unanimously to support independence.

Thomas Paine's *Common Sense*

As Patriots edged toward independence, many colonists retained a deep loyalty to the crown. Joyous crowds had toasted the health of George III when he ascended the throne in 1760 and again in 1766, when his ministers repealed the Stamp Act. Their loyalty to the king stemmed in part from the character of social authority in the patriarchal family. As the Stonington (Connecticut) Baptist Association put it, every father was "a king, and governor in his family." Just as the settlers obeyed elders in town meetings and ministers in churches, so they should obey the king, their imperial "father."

George III, 1771

King George III (b. 1738) was a young man when the American troubles began in 1765. Six years later, as this portrait by Johann Zoffany suggests, the king had aged. Initially, George was headstrong, trying to impose his will on Parliament, but he succeeded only in generating political confusion and inept policy. He did strongly support Parliament's attempts to tax the colonies, and continued the war with the colonies long after most of his ministers agreed that it had been lost. The Royal Collection. © Her Majesty Queen Elizabeth II.

Denial of the king's legitimacy might disrupt the social order.

But by 1775, many Americans had turned against the monarch. As military conflicts escalated, they accused George III of supporting oppressive legislation and ordering armed retaliation against them. Surprisingly, agitation became especially intense in Quaker-dominated Philadelphia, the largest — but hardly the most radical — seaport city. Many Philadelphia merchants harbored Loyalist sympathies and had been slow to join the boycott against the Townshend duties. However, artisans, who made up about half of Philadelphia's workers, had become a powerful force in the Patriot movement. Worried that British imports threatened their small-scale manufacturing enterprises, they organized a Mechanics Association to protect America's "just Rights and Privileges." By February 1776, forty artisans sat with forty-seven merchants on the Philadelphia Committee of Resistance, the extralegal body that enforced the trade boycott in the city.

Scots-Irish artisans and laborers became Patriots for cultural and religious reasons. They came from Presbyterian families that had fled British-controlled Ireland to escape economic and religious discrimination, and many of them had embraced the egalitarian message preached by Gilbert Tennent and other New Light ministers (see Chapter 4). As pastor of Philadelphia's Second Presbyterian Church, Tennent had told his congregation that all men and women were equal before God. Applying that idea to politics, New Light Presbyterians shouted in street demonstrations that they had "no king but King Jesus." Republican ideas derived from the European Enlightenment also circulated freely in Pennsylvania among artisans and political leaders. Patriot leaders Benjamin Franklin and Dr. Benjamin Rush questioned not only the wisdom of George III but the very idea of monarchy.

With popular sentiment in flux, a single pamphlet tipped the balance toward the Patriots. In January 1776, Thomas Paine published *Common Sense,* a rousing call for independence and a republican form of government. Paine had served as a minor bureaucrat in the customs service in England and was fired for protesting low wages. He found his way to London, where he wangled a meeting with Benjamin Franklin. In 1774, Paine migrated to Philadelphia, where he met Rush and other Patriots who shared his republican sentiments.

In *Common Sense,* Paine launched an assault on the traditional political order in language that stirred popular emotions. "Monarchy and hereditary succession have laid the world in blood and ashes," Paine proclaimed, leveling a personal attack at George III, "the hard hearted sullen Pharaoh of England." Mixing insults with biblical quotations, Paine blasted the British system of "mixed government" among the three estates of king, lords, and commoners. "That it was noble for the dark and slavish times in which it was created," Paine granted, but now it yielded only "monarchical tyranny in the person of the king" and "aristocratical tyranny in the persons of the peers."

Paine also made a compelling case for American independence. Turning the traditional metaphor of patriarchal authority on its head, he asked, "Is it the interest of a man to be a boy all his life?" Within six months, *Common Sense* had gone through twenty-five editions and reached hundreds of thousands of people throughout the colonies. "There is great talk of independence," a worried New York Loyalist noted, "and the unthinking multitude are mad for it. . . . A pamphlet called Common Sense has carried off . . . thousands." Paine called on Americans to reject the king and Parliament and create independent republican states. "A government of our own is our natural right, 'TIS TIME TO PART" (see Voices from Abroad, "Thomas Paine: *Common Sense,*" p. 164).

Thomas Paine

Common Sense

Thomas Paine was a sharp critic and an acute observer. Before arriving in Philadelphia from his native England in mid-1774, Paine had rejected the legitimacy of monarchy. He quickly came to understand that American politics was republican in spirit and could easily be adapted to create independent governments that might change the course of history. In his widely read political pamphlet, Common Sense (1776), he showed the colonists that American independence was "natural" and simply "common sense."

In the following pages I offer nothing more than simple facts, plain arguments, and common sense.... The sun never shined on a cause of greater worth. 'Tis not the affair of a city, a country, a province, or a kingdom, but of a continent—of at least one eighth part of the habitable globe. 'Tis not the concern of a day, a year, or an age; posterity are virtually involved in the contest, and will be more or less affected, even to the end of time....

We have boasted the protection of Great-Britain, without considering, that her motive was *interest* not *attachment;* that she did not protect us from *our enemies* on *our account,* but from *her enemies* on *her own account....* Our plan is commerce, and that, well attended to, will secure us the peace and friendship of all Europe; because, it is the interest of all Europe to have America a *free port.* Her trade will always be a protection, and her barrenness of gold and silver secure her from invaders. I challenge the warmest advocate for reconciliation, to shew, a single advantage that this continent can reap, by being connected with Great Britain.... Our corn will fetch its price in any market in Europe, and our imported goods must be paid for buy them where we will.

Every thing that is right or natural pleads for separation. The blood of the slain, the weeping voice of nature cries, 'TIS TIME TO PART. Even the distance at which the Almighty hath placed England and America, is a strong and natural proof, that the authority of the one, over the other, was never the design of Heaven.... There is something very absurd, in supposing a continent to be perpetually governed by an island. In no instance hath nature made the satellite larger than its primary planet, and as England and America, with respect to each other, reverses the common order of nature, it is evident they belong to different systems: England to Europe, America to itself.

But the most powerful of all arguments, is, that nothing but independence, i.e. a continental form of government, can keep the peace of the continent and preserve it inviolate from civil wars.... If there is any true cause of fear respecting independence, it is because no plan is yet laid down. Men do not see their way out—Wherefore, ... I offer the following hints....

Let the assemblies [of the former colonies] be annual, with a President only ... their business wholly domestic, and subject to the authority of a Continental Congress.

Let each colony be divided into six, eight, or ten convenient districts, each district to send a proper number of delegates to Congress, so that each colony send at least thirty. The whole number in Congress will be at least 390....

But where, say some, is the King of America? I'll tell you. Friend, he reigns above, and doth not make havoc of mankind like the Royal Brute of Britain. Yet that we may not appear to be defective even in earthly honors, let a day be solemnly set apart for proclaiming the charter [of the new Continental republic]; let it be brought forth placed on the divine law, the word of God; let a crown be placed thereon, by which the world may know ... that in America the LAW IS KING. For as in absolute governments the King is law, so in free countries the law ought to be King; and there ought to be no other.... Let the crown at the conclusion of the ceremony, be demolished, and scattered among the people whose right it is. A government of our own is our natural right....

O ye that love mankind! Ye that dare oppose, not only the tyranny, but the tyrant, stand forth! Every spot of the old world is overrun with oppression. Freedom hath been hunted round the globe. Asia, and Africa, have long expelled her. — Europe regards her like a stranger, and England hath given her warning to depart. O! receive the fugitive, and prepare in time an asylum for mankind.

SOURCE: Thomas Paine, *Common Sense* (Philadelphia, 1776).

ANALYZING THE EVIDENCE

➤ On what grounds does Paine argue for American independence? Where do you see the influence of Enlightenment thinking in his argument?

➤ Given that all European nations pursued mercantilist policies, was Paine correct in thinking they would welcome America as "a free port"? How were Europe's monarchies likely to respond to American independence?

➤ How could Paine celebrate America as a land of freedom and "an asylum for mankind" given the importance of slavery and indentured servitude to the economy there? What sort of liberty was Paine championing?

➤ Why do you think *Common Sense* struck such a chord with Americans throughout the colonies?

Independence Declared

Inspired by Paine's arguments and beset by armed Loyalists, Patriot conventions throughout the colonies urged a break from Britain. In June 1776, Richard Henry Lee presented the Virginia convention's resolution to the Continental Congress: "That these United Colonies are, and of right ought to be, free and independent states . . . absolved from all allegiance to the British Crown." Faced with certain defeat, staunch Loyalists and anti-independence moderates withdrew from the Congress, leaving committed Patriots to take the fateful step. On July 4, 1776, the Congress approved the Declaration of Independence (see Documents, p. D-1).

The main author of the Declaration was Thomas Jefferson, a young planter from Virginia. As a member of the Virginia legislature, Jefferson had mobilized resistance to the Coercive Acts with the pamphlet *A Summary View of the Rights of British America* (1774). To persuade Americans and foreign observers to support independence and a republican form of government, Jefferson vilified George III: "He has plundered our seas, ravaged our coasts, burned our towns, and destroyed the lives of our people. . . . A prince, whose character is thus marked by every act which may define a tyrant," Jefferson concluded, conveniently ignoring his own actions as a slave owner, "is unfit to be the ruler of a free people."

Independence Declared

In this painting by John Trumbull, Thomas Jefferson and the other drafters (John Adams of Massachusetts, Roger Sherman of Connecticut, Robert Livingston of New York, and Benjamin Franklin of Pennsylvania) present the Declaration of Independence to John Hancock, the president of the Second Continental Congress. When the Declaration was read at a public meeting in New York City on July 10, one Patriot reported, a massive statue of George III was "pulled down by the Populace" and its four thousand pounds of lead melted down to make "Musquet balls" for use against the British troops massed on Staten Island.

Yale University Art Gallery, Mabel Brady Garven Collection.

Employing the ideas of the European Enlightenment, Jefferson proclaimed a series of "self-evident" truths: "that all men are created equal"; that they possess the "unalienable rights" of "Life, Liberty, and the pursuit of Happiness"; that government derives its "just powers from the consent of the governed" and can rightly be overthrown if it "becomes destructive of these ends." By linking these doctrines of individual liberty, **popular sovereignty**, and republican government with American independence, Jefferson established them as the defining values of the new nation.

For Jefferson, as for Paine, the pen proved mightier than the sword. In rural hamlets and seaport cities, crowds celebrated the Declaration by burning effigies of George III and toppling statues of the king. These acts of destruction broke the Patriots' psychological ties to the father-monarch and established the legitimacy of republican state governments. On July 8, 1776, in Easton, Pennsylvania, a "great number of spectators" heard a reading of the Declaration, "gave their hearty assent with three loud huzzahs, and cried out, 'May God long preserve and unite the Free and Independent States of America.'"

➤ Why did the Patriot movement wane in the early 1770s? Why did the Tea Act reignite colonial resistance?

➤ Why did the leaders of the mainland colonies and of Britain fail to reach a political compromise to save the empire?

SUMMARY

In this chapter we have focused on a short span of time—a mere decade and a half—and laid out the plot of a political drama in three acts. In Act I, British political leaders begin to implement a program of imperial reform and taxation. Act II is full of dramatic action, as colonial mobs riot, Patriot writers articulate ideologies of resistance, and British ministers search for compromise between claims of parliamentary sovereignty and claims of colonial autonomy. Act III takes the form of tragedy: The once-proud British empire dissolves into civil war, an imminent nightmare of death and destruction.

Why did this happen? More than two centuries later, the answers still are not clear. Certainly, the lack of astute leadership in Britain was a major factor. But British leaders had to contend with circumstances that constrained their freedom to act: a huge national debt and a deeply held belief in the absolute authority of Parliament. Moreover, in America, decades of salutary neglect strengthened Patriots' demands for political autonomy, as did the fears and aspirations of artisans and farmers. The trajectory of their histories placed Britain and its American possessions on course for a disastrous—and fatal—collision.

Connections: Government

It is impossible to understand the Patriot resistance movement without understanding political developments during the colonial era. As we noted in the part opener (p. 135), after 1689,

> local governments and representative assemblies became more important and created a tradition of self-rule that would spark demands for political independence from Britain.

As we have seen in Chapter 5, and will see again in Chapter 6, the tradition of local self-rule retained its vitality. During the War of Independence, local communities equipped and supplied militia units. State legislatures not only raised money and men for the Continental army but also devised new republican constitutions. The states assumed the status of sovereign entities, subject only to the will of their voting citizens. Local, state-based political power was now a matter of constitutional law.

In fact, the tradition of local rule was so strong that it was only with great difficulty that nationalist-minded politicians were able to secure ratification of the Constitution of 1787, which restored a measure of political centralization to America. Even then, most Americans looked first to their local and state governments. Having resisted and fought a distant British regime, they were not eager to place control of their lives in the hands of a remote national government.

CHAPTER REVIEW QUESTIONS

➤ Trace the key events in both Britain and America from 1763 to 1776 that forged the Patriot movement. Why did those in Parliament believe that the arguments of the rebellious colonists were not justified? How did the Patriots gain the widespread support of the colonists?

➤ The narrative suggests that the war for American independence was not inevitable, that the British empire could have been saved. Do you agree? Was there a point during the imperial crisis at which peaceful compromise was possible?

TIMELINE

1756–1763	Great War for Empire
	British national debt almost doubles
1760	George III becomes king
1762	Revenue Act reforms customs service
	Royal Navy arrests smugglers
1763	Treaty of Paris ends Great War for Empire
	Proclamation Line restricts white settlement west of Appalachians
	George Grenville becomes Britain's prime minister
1764	Parliament passes Sugar Act and Currency Act
	Colonists oppose vice-admiralty courts
1765	Stamp Act imposes direct tax on colonists
	Quartering Act provides barracks for British troops
	Sons of Liberty riot throughout colonies
	Stamp Act Congress meets in New York City
	First American boycott of British goods begins
1766	First compromise: Parliament repeals Stamp Act but passes Declaratory Act
1767	Townshend duties on certain colonial imports
	Restraining Act suspends New York assembly
1768	Second American boycott of British goods begins
	Daughters of Liberty make "homespun" cloth
	British army occupies Boston
1770	Second compromise: Parliament repeals Townshend Act but retains tax on tea
	Boston Massacre
1772	Committees of correspondence form
1773	Tea Act assists British East India Company
	Boston Tea Party
1774	Coercive Acts punish Massachusetts
	Quebec Act angers Patriots
	First Continental Congress meets in Philadelphia
	Third American boycott of British goods begins
	Loyalists organize
1775	General Thomas Gage marches to Lexington and Concord
	Second Continental Congress meets in Philadelphia and creates Continental army
	Lord Dunmore promises freedom to slaves who join Loyalists
	American invasion of Canada
	Patriots and Loyalists skirmish in South
1776	Thomas Paine publishes *Common Sense*
	Declaration of Independence

FOR FURTHER EXPLORATION

Jack P. Greene and J. R. Pole, eds., *The Blackwell Encyclopedia of the American Revolution* (1991), illuminate many aspects of the Revolutionary era, as do the personal testimonies in Barbara DeWolfe, *Discoveries of America: Personal Accounts of British Emigrants to North America During the Revolutionary Era* (1997). A suspenseful journalistic account that focuses on leading men, A. J. Langguth's *Patriots: The Men Who Started the American Revolution* (1988), should be read in conjunction with Gary B. Nash's *The Unknown American Revolution: The Unruly Birth of Democracy* (2005).

Edmund Morgan and Helen Morgan tell the story of *The Stamp Act Crisis* (1953), and Philip Lawson's *George Grenville* (1984) offers a sympathetic portrait of a reform-minded prime minister. Benjamin Labaree's *The Boston Tea Party* (1979) shows how one "small" event altered the course of history; and David Hackett Fischer explains the rise of the radical Patriots in *Paul Revere's Ride* (1994). For events in Virginia, see the probing study by Woody Holton, *Forced Founders: Indians, Debtors, Slaves, & the Making of the American Revolution in Virginia* (1999).

Liberty! The American Revolution (6 hours), a PBS video, describes the main events of the era and has a fine Web site (**www.pbs.org/ktca/liberty/**). For a British perspective, see "The Sceptered Isle: Empire" (**www.bbc.co.uk/radio4/history/empire/regions/americas.shtml**).

Two fine collections of pamphlets and images of the revolutionary era are available at **odur.let.rug.nl/~usa/D/index.htm** and **www.research.umbc.edu/~bouton/Revolution.links.htm**. On its Web site (**www.nga.gov**), the National Gallery of Art shows American paintings of the colonial and Revolutionary periods. In *Angel in the Whirlwind: The Triumph of the American Revolution* (1997), Benson Bobrick narrates a grand epic that stretches from the French and Indian War to Washington's inauguration. For a more complex narrative, see John Ferling, *A Leap in the Dark: The Struggle to Create the American Republic* (2003). A compelling fictional account of Thomas Paine's life is Howard Fast, *Citizen Tom Paine* (1943). Pauline Maier, *American Scripture: Making the Declaration of Independence* (1997), explains the background of the Declaration and how it has been redefined over the past two-plus centuries. The Continental Congress Broadside Collection at the Library of Congress (**memory.loc.gov/ammem/collections/continental/**) contains early versions of the Declaration and many other documents.

TEST YOUR KNOWLEDGE

To assess your command of the material in this chapter, see the Online Study Guide at **bedfordstmartins.com/henretta**.

For Web sites, images, and documents related to topics and places in this chapter, visit **bedfordstmartins.com/makehistory**.

6

Making War and Republican Governments

1776–1789

W HEN THE PATRIOTS OF FREDERICK COUNTY, Maryland, demanded allegiance to the American cause in 1776, Robert Gassaway would have none of it. "It was better for the poor people to lay down their arms and pay the duties and taxes laid upon them by King and Parliament," he told the local committee of safety, "than to be brought into slavery and commanded and ordered about [by you]." The story was much the same in Farmington, Connecticut, where Patriot officials imprisoned Nathaniel Jones and seventeen other men for "remaining neutral." Throughout the colonies, the events of 1776 forced families to choose the Loyalist or the Patriot side.

Because Patriots controlled most local governments, they had an edge in the battle for the hearts and minds of ordinary men and women. Patriot leaders organized their neighbors into militia units and recruited volunteers for the Continental army, a ragtag force that held its own on the battlefield. "I admire the American troops tremendously!" exclaimed a French officer. "It is incredible that soldiers composed of every age, even children of fifteen, of whites and blacks, almost naked, unpaid, and rather poorly fed, can march so well and withstand fire so steadfastly."

Military mobilization created political commitment. To encourage Americans to support the war—as soldiers, taxpayers, and republican

◀ **The Battle of Bunker Hill**

As British warships and artillery lob cannon balls at Patriot positions, British redcoats advance up the steep slope of Bunker Hill (to the right). It took three assaults and one thousand casualties before they finally dislodged the Patriot militia. The British bombardment ignited fires in nearby Charlestown, which burns in the background. *Attack on Bunker's Hill, with the Burning of Charles Town*, American 18th Century, Gift of Edgar William and Bernice Chrysler Garbisch, Image © 2005 Board of Trustees, National Gallery of Art, Washington, D.C.

citizens — Patriot leaders encouraged them to take an active role in government. And as the common people exerted their influence, the character of politics changed. "From subjects to citizens the difference is immense," remarked South Carolina Patriot David Ramsay. "Each citizen of a free state contains . . . as much of the common sovereignty as another." By raising a democratic army and repudiating aristocratic and monarchical rule, the Patriots launched the age of republican revolution that would soon sweep the Americas and throw Europe into turmoil.

The Trials of War, 1776 – 1778

The Declaration of Independence coincided with a full-scale British military assault. For two years, British forces manhandled the Continental army. A few inspiring American victories kept the rebellion alive, but during the winters of 1776 and 1777, the Patriot cause hung in the balance.

War in the North

Once the British resorted to military force, few European observers gave the rebels a chance. Great Britain had a great demographic advantage: 11 million people compared to the colonies' 2.5 million, 20 percent of whom were enslaved Africans. Britain also had access to the immense wealth generated by the South Atlantic System and the emerging Industrial Revolution. Its financial resources paid for the most powerful navy in the world, a standing army of 48,000 Britons, and thousands of German (Hessian) soldiers. In addition, Britain had an experienced officer corps and the support of thousands of American Loyalists and many Indian tribes (Map 6.1). The Cherokees in the Carolinas were firmly committed to the British, as were four of the six Iroquois Nations of New York — the Mohawks, Senecas, Cayugas, and Onondagas — who were led by the pro-British Mohawk chief Joseph Brant.

By contrast, the Americans were economically and militarily weak. They had no strong central government to raise revenues, and the new Continental army, commanded by General George Washington, consisted of about 18,000 poorly trained recruits hastily assembled in Virginia and New England. The Patriots could field thousands more militiamen but only near their own farms. Although many American officers had served in the military during the Great War for Empire, they had never commanded a large force or faced a disciplined European army.

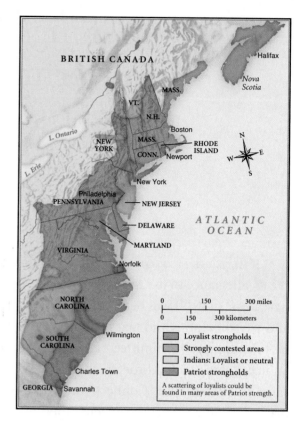

MAP 6.1 Patriot and Loyalist Strongholds

Patriots were in the majority in most of the thirteen mainland colonies and used their control of local governments to funnel men, money, and supplies to the rebel cause. Although Loyalists could be found in every colony, their strongholds were limited to Nova Scotia, eastern New York, New Jersey, and certain areas in the South. However, most Native American peoples favored the British cause and bolstered the power of Loyalist militias in central New York (see Map 6.3) and in the Carolina backcountry.

To exploit this military advantage, Britain's prime minister, Lord North, assembled a large invasion force under the command of General William Howe. North ordered Howe to capture New York City and seize control of the Hudson River, which would isolate the radical Patriots in New England from the colonies to the south. As the Second Continental Congress was declaring independence in Philadelphia in July 1776, Howe landed 32,000 troops — British regulars and German mercenaries — outside New York City, about 100 miles to the north.

British military superiority was immediately apparent. In August 1776, Howe defeated the Americans in the Battle of Long Island and forced their retreat to Manhattan Island. There, Howe outflanked Washington's troops and nearly trapped them. Outgunned and outmaneuvered, the

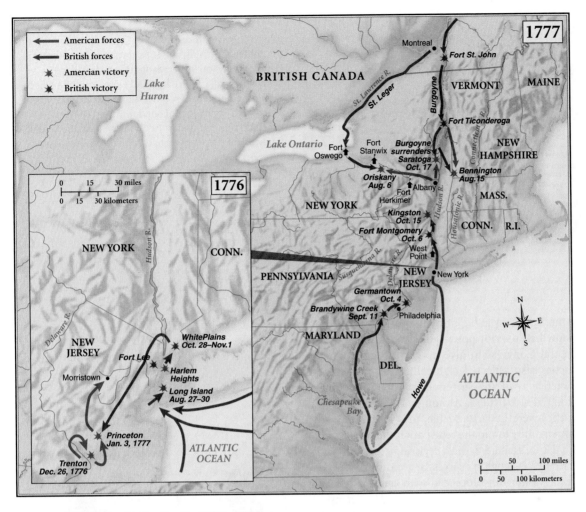

MAP 6.2   The War in the North, 1776–1777

In 1776, the British army drove Washington's forces across New Jersey into Pennsylvania. The Americans counterattacked successfully at Trenton and Princeton and then set up winter headquarters in Morristown. In 1777, British forces stayed on the offensive. General Howe attacked the Patriot capital, Philadelphia, from the south and captured it in early October. Meanwhile, General Burgoyne and Colonel St. Leger launched simultaneous invasions from Canada. With the help of thousands of New England militiamen, American troops commanded by General Horatio Gates defeated Burgoyne in August at Bennington, Vermont, and, in October 1777, at Saratoga, New York, the military turning point in the war.

Continental army again retreated, eventually crossing the Hudson River to New Jersey. By December, the British army had pushed the rebels across New Jersey and over the Delaware River into Pennsylvania.

From the Patriots' perspective, winter came just in time. Following eighteenth-century military custom, the British halted their campaign for the cold months, allowing the Americans to catch them off guard. On Christmas night 1776, Washington led his troops back across the Delaware River and staged a surprise attack on Trenton, New Jersey, where he forced the surrender of one thousand German soldiers. And in early January 1777, the

Continental army won a small victory at nearby Princeton (Map 6.2). Bright stars in a dark sky, these minor triumphs could not mask British military superiority. These are the times, wrote Tom Paine, that "try men's souls."

Armies and Strategies

Thanks in part to General Howe's tactical decisions, the Continental army remained intact and the rebellion survived. Howe had opposed the Coercive Acts of 1774, and he still hoped for a political compromise. He did not want to pursue the retreating

A British Camp, c. 1778

While American troops at Valley Forge took shelter from the cold in tents, British troops stationed just outside New York City (on upper Manhattan Island) lived in simple but well-constructed and warm log cabins. Each hut housed either a few officers or eight to ten soldiers of the 17th Regiment of Foot. John Ward Dunsmore executed this painting in 1915, basing it on the careful fieldwork of a team of archaeologists. New-York Historical Society.

American army and destroy it; he simply wanted to show his superior power and convince the Continental Congress to give up the struggle. Howe's tactics also reflected eighteenth-century military practice: Win the surrender of opposing forces, don't destroy them. Although Howe's restrained tactics were understandable, they cost Britain the opportunity to nip the rebellion in the bud.

Howe's failure to win a decisive victory was paralleled by Washington's success at avoiding a major defeat. Washington proceeded with caution, advising Congress, "On our Side the War should be defensive." His strategy was to draw the British away from the seacoast, extend their lines of supply, and sap their morale while keeping the Continental army intact.

Congress had promised Washington a regular force of 75,000 men, but the Continental army never reached a third of that number. Yeomen farmers wanted to plant and harvest their crops and so chose to serve in their local militia; consequently, most Continental army recruits were propertyless farmers and laborers. The Continental soldiers drawn from the state of Maryland and commanded by General William Smallwood were either poor American-born youths or older foreign-born men — often British ex-convicts and former indentured servants. They enlisted primarily for the bonus of $20 in cash (about $2,000 today) and the promise of 100 acres of land. Molding these recruits into a fighting force took time. Many men panicked in the face of a British artillery bombardment or flank attack; hundreds deserted, unwilling to submit to the discipline of military life. The soldiers who stayed resented the contempt their officers had for the "camp followers," the women who fed and cared for the troops.

Actually, the camp followers were crucial to the cause. The Continental army was poorly supplied and faintly praised. Radical Whig Patriots believed

American Militiamen

Beset by continuing shortages of cloth, the Patriot army dressed in a variety of uniforms and fabrics. This German engraving, based on a drawing by a Hessian officer, shows two barefoot American militiamen wearing hunting shirts and trousers made of ticking, a strong linen fabric that often was used to cover mattresses and pillows. Anne S. K. Brown Military Collection, Brown University.

a standing army was a threat to liberty; even in wartime, they preferred militias to a professional force. General Philip Schuyler of New York complained that his troops were "weak in numbers, dispirited, naked, destitute of provisions, without camp equipage, with little ammunition, and not a single piece of cannon." Given these handicaps, Washington was fortunate to have escaped sudden and overwhelming defeat.

Victory at Saratoga

Howe's failure to achieve a quick and total victory dismayed Lord North and his colonial secretary, Lord George Germain. But accepting the challenge of a long-term military commitment, the ministry increased the British land tax and used the funds to mount a major military campaign in 1777.

The isolation of New England remained Britain's primary goal. To achieve it, Germain planned a three-pronged attack converging on Albany, New York. General John Burgoyne would lead a large contingent of British regulars south from Quebec to Albany. Colonel Barry St. Leger and a force of Iroquois warriors would attack from the west, and General Howe would dispatch a force northward from New York City (see Map 6.2, p. 171).

Howe had a different plan, and it led to a disastrous result. He wanted to attack Philadelphia, the home of the Continental Congress, and end the rebellion with a single victory over Washington's army. Apparently with Germain's approval, Howe set his plan in motion — but very slowly. Instead of marching quickly through New Jersey, British troops sailed south from New York and then up the Chesapeake Bay to attack Philadelphia from the south. The strategy worked brilliantly. Howe's troops easily outflanked the American positions along Brandywine Creek in Delaware and, in late September, marched triumphantly into Philadelphia. Howe expected the capture of the rebels' capital would end the uprising, but the members of the Continental Congress, determined to continue the struggle, fled into the interior.

Howe's slow attack against Philadelphia contributed directly to the defeat of Burgoyne's army. Burgoyne's troops had advanced quickly from Quebec, crossing Lake Champlain, overwhelming the American defenses at Fort Ticonderoga in early July, and driving toward the upper reaches of the Hudson River. Then they stalled. Burgoyne fought with style — he was called "Gentleman Johnny" — stopping early each day to pitch comfortable tents and consume ample stocks of food and wine. The American troops led by General

Joseph Brant

Mohawk chief Thayendanegea, known to whites as Joseph Brant, was a devout member of the Church of England; later he helped translate the Bible into the Iroquois language. An influential man, Brant persuaded four of the six Iroquois Nations to support Britain in the war. In 1778 and 1779, he led Iroquois warriors and Tory rangers in devastating attacks on American settlements in the Wyoming Valley of Pennsylvania and Cherry Valley in New York. In this painting from 1797, Charles Willson Peale portrayed Brant with European features. *Independence National Historic Park, Philadelphia.*

Horatio Gates further slowed Burgoyne's progress by felling huge trees and raiding his long supply lines to Canada.

By summer's end, Burgoyne's army of six thousand British and German troops and six hundred Loyalists and Indians was bogged down near Saratoga, New York. Desperate for food and horses, the British raided nearby Bennington, Vermont, but were beaten back by two thousand American militiamen. Patriot forces in the Mohawk Valley also forced St. Leger and the Iroquois to retreat. To make matters worse, the British commander in New York City recalled four thousand troops he had sent toward Albany and dispatched them to Philadelphia to bolster Howe's force. While Burgoyne waited in vain for help, thousands of Patriot militiamen from Massachusetts, New Hampshire, and New York joined Gates's forces. They "swarmed around the army like birds of prey," reported an alarmed English sergeant, and in October 1777 they forced Burgoyne to surrender

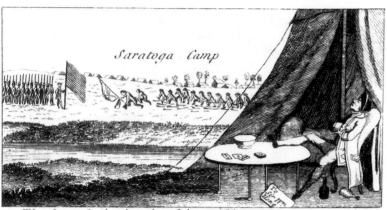

Saratoga Camp

The Generals in America doing nothing, or worse than nothing.

Losing the War of Public Opinion

The American victory at Saratoga shocked the British public. Opposition politicians heaped blame on the generals, many of whom had close ties to the ruling ministry. This political cartoon shows General Burgoyne abjectly surrendering to the Americans at Saratoga while General Howe, who failed to dispatch a supporting army from Philadelphia, sleeps outside his tent, oblivious to the situation. Library of Congress.

(see Voices from Abroad, "Baroness Von Riedesel: The Surrender of Burgoyne, 1777," p. 175).

The battle at Saratoga proved to be the turning point of the war. The Patriots captured more than five thousand British troops and their equipment. Equally important, the victory ensured the success of American diplomats, who were in Paris seeking a military alliance with France.

Social and Financial Perils

The Patriots' celebration of the triumph at Saratoga was tempered by wartime difficulties. A British naval blockade had cut supplies of European manufactures and disrupted the New England fishing industry; and the British occupation of Boston, New York, and Philadelphia had reduced domestic trade and manufacturing. As unemployed shipwrights, dock laborers, masons, coopers, and bakers moved to the countryside, New York City's population declined from 21,000 in 1774 to fewer than 10,000 three years later. In the Chesapeake, the British blockade cut tobacco exports and forced planters to grow grain that could be sold to the contending armies. All across the land, farmers and artisans adapted to a war economy.

With goods in short supply, government officials requisitioned military supplies directly from the people. In 1776, Connecticut officials asked the citizens of Hartford to provide 1,000 coats and 1,600 shirts, and they assessed smaller towns proportionately. The following year, they again pressed the citizenry to provide shirts, stockings, and shoes for the state's Continental units. Soldiers added personal pleas. After losing "all the shirts except the one on my back" during the Battle of Long Island, Captain Edward Rogers told his wife that "the making of cloath . . . must go on. . . . I must have shirts and stockings & a jacket sent me as soon as possible & a blankit."

Women and Household Production. Patriot women responded by increasing their output of homespun cloth. One Massachusetts town produced 30,000 yards of homespun, while women in Elizabeth, New Jersey, promised "upwards of 100,000 yards of linnen and woolen cloth." Other women assumed the burdens of farmwork while their men were away at war. Some went into the fields, plowing, harvesting, and loading grain, while others supervised laborers and acquired a taste for decision making. "We have sow'd our oats as you desired," Sarah Cobb Paine wrote to her absent husband. "Had I been master I should have planted it to Corn." Their self-esteem boosted by their wartime activities, some women expected greater legal rights in the new republican society.

Despite the women's efforts, goods remained scarce and prices rose sharply. Hard-pressed consumers decried merchants and traders as "enemies, extortioners, and monopolizers" and called for government regulation. But when a convention of New England states imposed price ceilings in 1777, many farmers and artisans refused to lower their prices. In the end, a government official admitted, consumers had to pay the higher market prices "or submit to starving."

Even more frightening, the fighting exposed tens of thousands of civilians to deprivation, displacement, and death. "An army, even a friendly one, are a dreadful scourge to any people," a Connecticut soldier wrote from Pennsylvania. "You cannot imagine what devastation and distress mark their steps." British and American armies marched back and forth across New Jersey, forcing Patriot and Loyalist families to flee their homes to escape arrest—or worse. Soldiers and partisans looted farms for food, and disorderly troops harassed and raped women and girls. When British warships sailed up the Potomac River, women and children

Baroness Von Riedesel

The Surrender of Burgoyne, 1777

Frederika Charlotte Louise, Baroness Von Riedesel, was the wife of General Friedrich Von Riedesel, commander of the Hessian soldiers in Burgoyne's army. An intrepid woman, the baroness was an eyewitness to the Saratoga campaign and a forthright critic of "Gentleman Johnny" Burgoyne. After Burgoyne's surrender, she, her husband, and their three children (ages six, three, and one) were held as prisoners of war, first in Massachusetts and then in Virginia.

We were halted at six o'clock in the morning [of October 9, 1777], to our general amazement. General Burgoyne ordered the artillery to be drawn up in a line, and to have it counted. This gave much dissatisfaction, as a few marches more would have ensured our safety. . . . At length we recommenced our march; but scarcely an hour had elapsed, before the army was again halted, because the enemy was in sight. They were but two hundred in number, who came to reconnoitre, and who might easily have been taken, had not general Burgoyne lost all his presence of mind. The rain fell in torrents. . . . On the 9th, it rained terribly the whole day; nevertheless we kept ourselves ready to march. The savages [Native Americans in Burgoyne's force] had lost their courage, and they walked off in all directions. The least untoward event made them dispirited, especially when there was no opportunity for plunder. . . .

We reached Saratoga about dark, which was but half an hour's march

from the place where we had spent the day. I was quite wet, and was obliged to remain in that condition, for want of a place to change my apparel. I seated myself near the fire, and undressed the children, and we then laid ourselves upon some straw. — I asked general Phillips, who came to see how I was, why we did not continue our retreat, my husband having pledged himself to cover the movement, and to bring off the army in safety. "My poor lady," said he, "you astonish me. Though quite wet, you have so much courage as to wish to go farther in this weather. What a pity it is that you are not our commanding general! He complains of fatigue, and has determined upon spending the night here, and giving us a supper."

It is very true, that General Burgoyne liked to make himself easy, and that he spent half his nights in singing and drinking, and diverting himself. . . . I refreshed myself at 7 o'clock, the next morning, (the 10th of October,) with a cup of tea, and we all expected that we should soon continue our march. About 2 o'clock [the next day] we heard again a report of muskets and cannon, and there was much alarm and bustle among our troops. My husband sent me word, that I should immediately retire into a house which was not far off. Soon after our arrival, a terrible cannonade began, and the fire was principally directed against the house, where we had hoped to find a refuge, probably because the enemy inferred, from the great number of people who went towards it, that this was the headquarters of the generals, while, in reality, none were there except women and crippled soldiers. We were at last obliged to descend into the cellar, where I laid myself in a corner near the door. My children put their heads upon my knees. An abominable smell,

the cries of the children, and my own anguish of mind, did not permit me to close my eyes, during the whole night.

On the next morning, the cannonade begun anew, but in a different direction. . . . Eleven cannonballs passed through the house, and made a tremendous noise. A poor soldier, who was about to have a leg amputated, lost the other by one of these balls. All his comrades ran away at that moment, and when they returned, they found him in one corner of the room, in the agonies of death. . . .

The want of water continuing to distress us, we could not but be extremely glad to find a soldier's wife so spirited as to fetch some from the river, an occupation from which the boldest might have shrunk, as the Americans shot every one who approached it. They told us afterwards that they spared her on account of her sex. . . .

On the 17th of October, the capitulation was carried into effect. The generals waited upon the American general Gates, and the troops surrendered themselves prisoners of war and laid down their arms.

SOURCE: Madame de Riedesel, *Letters and Memoirs Relating to the War of American Independence, and the Capture of the German Troops at Saratoga* (New York, 1827), 173–183.

ANALYZING THE EVIDENCE

➤ What light, if any, does Von Riedesel's account shed on the Battle of Saratoga? How reliable a witness was she?

➤ What does the presence of the baroness, her children, and the wives of several British officers suggest about the nature of eighteenth-century warfare?

fled from Alexandria, Virginia, and "stowed themselves into every Hut they can get, out of the reach of the Enemys canon" and troops.

The war divided many communities. Patriots formed committees of safety that collected taxes to support the Continental army, and imposed fines or jail sentences on those who refused to pay. In New England, mobs of Patriot farmers beat suspected Tories and destroyed their property. "Every Body submitted to our Sovereign Lord the Mob," a Loyalist preacher lamented. In some areas of Maryland, the number of "nonassociators"—those who refused to join either side—was so large that they successfully defied Patriot organizers. "Stand off you dammed rebel sons of bitches," Robert Davis of Anne Arundel County shouted, "I will shoot you if you come any nearer."

Financial Crisis. Such defiance exposed the weakness of the new state governments. Most governments were afraid to raise taxes, forcing Patriot officials to pay war expenses by borrowing gold or silver currency from wealthy individuals. When those funds ran out, individual states printed paper money: Eventually, they issued $260 million in currency. Because the new currency was printed in huge quantities and was not backed by gold, tax revenues, or mortgages on land, many Americans refused to accept it at face value. North Carolina's paper money came to be worth so little that even the state's tax collectors refused it.

The finances of the Continental Congress collapsed too, despite the efforts of Philadelphia merchant Robert Morris, the government's chief treasury official. Because Congress lacked the authority to impose taxes, Morris relied on funds requisitioned from the states, but they paid late or not at all. So the treasury looked to France and Holland for loans, and encouraged wealthy Americans to purchase Continental bonds. Eventually, Congress followed the lead of the states and printed $191 million in currency and bills of credit, which also fell quickly in value. In 1778, a family needed $7 in Continental bills to buy goods worth $1 in gold or silver. As the rate of exchange between paper currency and specie rose—to 42 to 1 in 1779, 100 to 1 in 1780, and 146 to 1 in 1781—it sparked social upheaval. In Boston, a mob of women accosted merchant Thomas Boyleston, "seazd him by his Neck," and forced him to sell his wares at traditional prices. In rural Ulster County, New York, women demanded that the local committee of safety lower food prices; otherwise, they said, "their husbands and sons shall fight no more." Civilian and military morale crumbled, and some Patriot leaders doubted the rebellion could succeed.

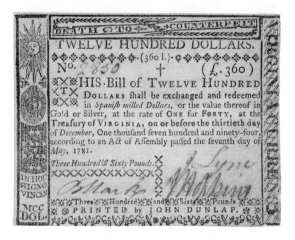

Paper Currency

To symbolize their independent status, the new state governments printed their own currency. Rejecting the English system of pounds and shillings, Virginia used the Spanish gold dollar as its basic unit of currency, although the currency also showed the equivalent in English pounds. Initially, $1,200 was equal to £360 — a ratio of 3.3 to 1. By 1781, Virginia had printed so much paper money to pay its soldiers and wartime expenses that the value of its currency had depreciated. It now took $40 in Virginia currency to buy the same amount of goods as £1 sterling. American Numismatic Society, New York City.

Valley Forge. Fears reached their peak during the winter of 1777. While Howe's army partook of warm lodgings and ample food in Philadelphia, Washington's army retreated 20 miles to the west to Valley Forge, where 12,000 soldiers and hundreds of camp followers suffered horribly. "The army . . . now begins to grow sickly," a surgeon confided to his diary. "Poor food—hard lodging—cold weather—fatigue—nasty clothes—nasty cookery. . . . Why are we sent here to starve and freeze?" Nearby farmers refused to help. Some were pacifists, Quakers and German sectarians unwilling to support either side. Others looked out for their families by refusing to sell grain for worthless Continental currency, accepting only the gold and silver offered by British quartermasters. "Such a dearth of public spirit, and want of public virtue," Washington lamented. By spring, one thousand hungry soldiers had vanished into the countryside, and another three thousand had died from malnutrition and disease. One winter at Valley Forge took as many American lives as had two years of fighting.

In this dark hour, Baron von Steuben raised the self-respect and readiness of the American army. A former Prussian military officer, von Steuben was one of a handful of republican-minded foreign aristocrats who helped the American cause. To counter falling morale, he instituted a strict system of drill and encouraged officers to become more professional. Thanks to von Steuben, the smaller Continental army that emerged from Valley Forge in the spring of 1778 was a much tougher and better-disciplined force.

➤ Why were British forces militarily superior to American forces in the first years of the war? How did the Americans sustain the Revolution between 1776 and 1778?

➤ Who was most to blame for Britain's failure to win a quick victory over the American rebels — General Howe, General Burgoyne, or the ministers in London? Explain your answer.

➤ What were the most important economic and fiscal problems facing the Patriots at the outset of the war? How successful were they in addressing them?

The Path to Victory, 1778–1783

Wars are often won by astute diplomacy, and that was the case with the War of Independence. The Patriots' prospects improved dramatically in 1778, when the Continental Congress concluded a military alliance with France, the most powerful nation in Europe. The alliance gave the Americans a source of desperately needed money, supplies, and, eventually, troops. Equally important, it confronted Britain with an international war that challenged its domination of the Atlantic world.

The French Alliance

France and America were unlikely partners. France was Catholic and a monarchy; the United States was Protestant and a federation of republics. From 1689 to 1763, the two peoples had been enemies: New Englanders had brutally expelled the French population from Acadia (Nova Scotia); and the French, with the help of Indian allies, had organized raids of British settlements. But the Comte de Vergennes, the French foreign minister, was determined to avenge the loss of Canada to Britain in the Great War for Empire. He persuaded King Louis XVI to provide the rebellious colonies with a secret loan and much-needed gunpowder, and he opened contact with American diplomats. When news of the rebel victory at Saratoga reached Paris in December 1777, Vergennes sought a formal alliance.

Negotiating the Treaty. Benjamin Franklin and other American diplomats craftily exploited France's rivalry with Britain to win an explicit commitment to American independence. The Treaty of Alliance of February 1778 specified that once France entered the war, neither partner would sign a separate peace without the "liberty, sovereignty, and independence" of the United States. In return, the Continental Congress agreed to recognize any French conquests in the West Indies.

The alliance gave new life to the Patriots' cause. "There has been a great change in this state since the news from France," a Patriot soldier reported from Pennsylvania. Farmers — "mercenary wretches," he called them — "were as eager for Continental Money now as they were a few weeks ago for British gold." Its confidence bolstered by the alliance, the Continental Congress addressed the financial demands of the officer corps. Most officers came from the upper ranks of society, equipped themselves, and often served without pay; in return, they insisted on lifetime military pensions at half pay. John Adams condemned the officers for "scrambling for rank and pay like apes for nuts," but General Washington urged Congress to grant the pensions and warned the lawmakers that "the salvation of the cause depends upon it." Congress reluctantly granted the officers half pay, but only for seven years.

The British Response. Meanwhile, the war was becoming increasingly unpopular in Britain. Radical Whig politicians and republican-minded artisans supported American demands for autonomy and campaigned for domestic political reforms, among them greater representation for cities in Parliament and the elimination of the rotten boroughs. The gentry protested increases in the land tax, and merchants condemned new levies on carriages, wine, and imported goods. "It seemed we were to be taxed and stamped ourselves instead of inflicting taxes and stamps on others," a British politician complained.

At first, George III remained committed to crushing the rebellion. If America won independence, he warned Lord North, "the West Indies must follow them. Ireland would soon follow the same plan and be a separate state, then this island would be reduced to itself, and soon would be a poor island indeed." Stunned by the British defeat at

Saratoga, the king changed his mind. To prevent an American alliance with France, he authorized North to seek a negotiated settlement. In February 1778, North persuaded Parliament to repeal the Tea and Prohibitory acts and, in an amazing concession, to renounce its power to tax the colonies. Opening discussions with the Continental Congress, the prime minister proposed a return to the constitutional "condition of 1763," before the Sugar and Stamp acts. But the Patriots, now allied with France and committed to independence, rejected North's overture.

War in the South

The French alliance did not bring a rapid end to the war. When French forces entered the conflict in June 1778, they were sent to capture Barbados or Jamaica or another rich sugar island. Spain, which joined the war against Britain in 1779, wanted to regain Florida and the fortress of Gibraltar at the entrance to the Mediterranean Sea. As the agendas of France and Spain turned the war into a worldwide conflict, the British ministry revised its military strategy in America and shifted the main theater of war to the South.

Britain's Southern Strategy. Rather than using their army to isolate New England, British ministers turned their attention to the rich tobacco- and rice-growing colonies—Virginia, the Carolinas, and Georgia. They planned to win these areas and then rely on local Loyalists to hold them. In the Carolinas, the British counted on the allegiance of Scottish Highlanders. They hoped to recruit other Loyalists from the ranks of the Regulators, the enemies of the low-country Patriot planters (see Chapter 4), and to mobilize the Cherokees and other Indian peoples against the land-hungry Americans (Map 6.3). The ministry also planned to exploit racial divisions in the South. In 1776, more than one thousand slaves had fought for Lord Dunmore under the banner "Liberty to Slaves!"; a British invasion might prompt thousands more to flee their Patriot owners. South Carolina whites knew that slavery was a double-edged sword, a source of wealth in peacetime but a danger in war. The state could not raise an army, its representative told the Continental Congress, "by reason of the great proportion of citizens necessary to remain at home to prevent insurrection among the Negroes."

Implementing Britain's southern military strategy became the responsibility of Sir Henry Clinton. Moving the main British army to secure quarters in New York City, Clinton ordered a seaborne attack on Savannah, Georgia; troops under the command of Colonel Archibald Campbell captured the town in December 1778. Mobilizing hundreds of blacks to unload and transport supplies, Campbell moved inland and captured Augusta early in 1779. By year's end, Clinton's forces and local Loyalists controlled coastal Georgia, and 10,000 troops were poised for an assault on South Carolina.

During most of 1780, British forces in the South marched from victory to victory (Map 6.4). In May, Clinton laid siege to Charleston, South Carolina, and forced the surrender of General Benjamin Lincoln and his garrison of 5,000 troops. Then Lord Cornwallis assumed control of the British forces and marched into the countryside. In August, at the Battle of Camden, Cornwallis defeated an American force commanded by General Horatio Gates, the hero of Saratoga. Only 1,200 Patriot militiamen joined Gates at Camden—a fifth of the number at Saratoga—and many of them panicked. As Cornwallis took control of South Carolina, hundreds of African Americans fled to freedom in British-controlled Florida, while hundreds more found refuge with the British army.

Then the tide of battle turned. The Dutch declared war against Britain, and France finally dispatched troops to the American mainland. The French decision was in part the work of the Marquis de Lafayette, a republican-minded aristocrat who had long supported the American cause. In 1780, Lafayette persuaded Louis XVI to send General Comte de Rochambeau and 5,500 men to Newport, Rhode Island, where they threatened British forces in New York City.

Partisan Warfare in the Carolinas. Meanwhile, Washington dispatched General Nathanael Greene to recapture the Carolinas. Greene faced a difficult task. His troops, he reported, "were almost naked and we subsist by daily collections and in a country that has been ravaged and plundered by both friends and enemies." To make use of local militiamen, who were "without discipline and addicted to plundering," Greene placed them under strong leaders and unleashed them on less-mobile British forces. In October 1780, a militia of Patriot farmers defeated a regiment of Loyalists at King's Mountain, South Carolina, taking about one thousand prisoners. Led by the "Swamp Fox," General Francis Marion, American guerrillas won a series of small but fierce battles in South Carolina. Then, in January 1781, General Daniel Morgan led another American force to a bloody victory at Cowpens, South Carolina. But Loyalist garrisons and militia

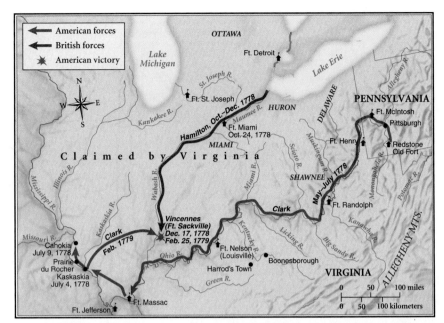

MAP 6.3 Native Americans and the War in the West, 1778–1779

Many Indian peoples remained neutral, but some, fearing land-hungry Patriot farmers, used British-supplied guns to raid American settlements. To thwart attacks by militant Shawnees, Cherokees, and Delawares, a Patriot militia led by George Rogers Clark captured the British fort and supply depot at Vincennes on the Wabash River in February 1779. To the north, Patriot generals John Sullivan and James Clinton defeated pro-British Indian forces near Tioga (on the New York–Pennsylvania border) in August 1779 and then systematically destroyed villages and crops throughout the Iroquois' lands.

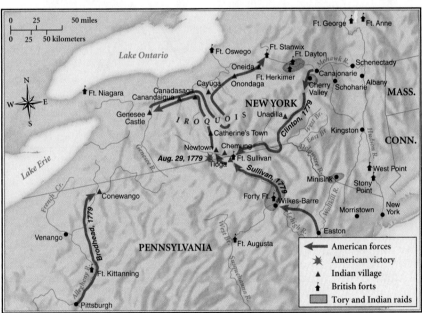

units remained powerful, helped by the well-organized Cherokees, who were determined to protect their lands from American settlers and troops. "We fight, get beaten, and fight again," General Greene declared doggedly. In March 1781, Greene's soldiers fought Cornwallis's seasoned army to a draw at North Carolina's Guilford Court House. Weakened by this **war of attrition**, the British general decided to concede the Carolinas to Greene and seek a decisive victory in Virginia.

Benedict Arnold and Conflicting Loyalties.

In the summer of 1781, Cornwallis invaded the Tidewater region of Virginia. He was joined there by British reinforcements from New York under the command of General Benedict Arnold. Arnold was born in Connecticut and had joined the War of Independence on the American side. Troops under his command captured Fort Ticonderoga for the Patriots in 1775 and then launched an unsuccessful assault on Quebec City. In that battle, Arnold stormed over a barricade and took a musket ball through his leg. At Saratoga, he led an attack against the center of the British line and was again wounded in the leg. Admiring Arnold's boldness and courage, General Washington appointed him to various commands, including the important Hudson River fort at West Point. There, Arnold turned against his country.

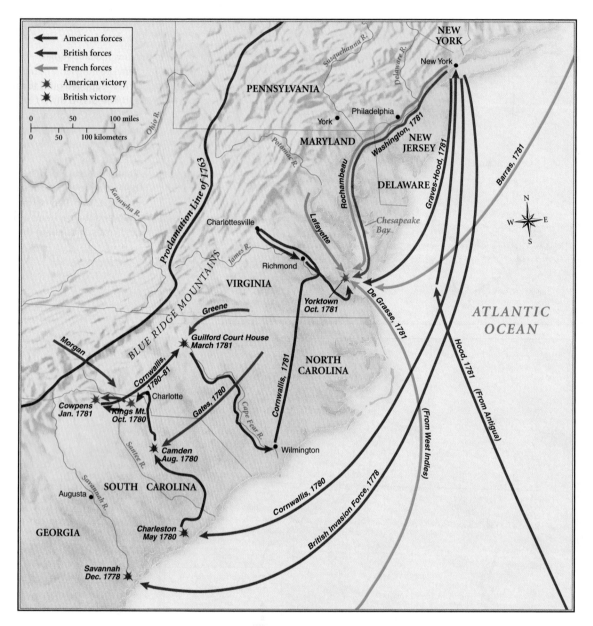

MAP 6.4 The War in the South, 1778–1781

Britain's southern strategy started well. British forces captured Savannah in December 1778, took control of Georgia during 1779, and vanquished Charleston in May 1780. Over the next eighteen months, brutal warfare between British and Loyalist units and the American army and militia raged in the interior of the Carolinas and ended in a stalemate. Hoping to break the deadlock, British general Charles Cornwallis carried the battle into Virginia in 1781. A Franco-American army led by Washington and Lafayette, with the help of the French fleet under Admiral de Grasse, surrounded Cornwallis's forces on the Yorktown Peninsula and forced their surrender.

Facing ruin because of shady financial dealings, uncertain of future promotion because of his reputation for arrogance and avarice, and disgusted with congressional politics, Arnold promised to deliver West Point and its three thousand defenders to the British for £20,000 sterling (about $1 million today). When his plan was exposed, Arnold became a British brigadier general and served George III with the same skill and enthusiasm he had shown in the Patriot cause. Supporting Cornwallis, he led raiding parties along the James River and, in a daring attack on Richmond, destroyed large stocks of munitions and grain.

Britain Defeated. While troops led by Arnold and Cornwallis sparred near the York Peninsula with an American force commanded by Lafayette, France ordered its fleet from the West Indies to North America. Emboldened by the French naval forces, Washington launched a well-coordinated attack. Feinting an assault on New York City, he secretly marched General Rochambeau's army from Rhode Island to Virginia, where it joined his Continental forces. Simultaneously, the French fleet massed off the coast, taking control of Chesapeake Bay. By the time the British discovered Washington's audacious plan, Cornwallis was surrounded — his 9,500-man army outnumbered 2 to 1 on land and cut off from reinforcement or retreat by sea. In a hopeless position, Cornwallis surrendered at Yorktown in October 1781.

The Franco-American victory at Yorktown broke the resolve of the British government. "Oh God! It is all over!" Lord North exclaimed when he heard the news. Isolated diplomatically in Europe, stymied militarily in America, and lacking public support at home, the British ministry gave up active prosecution of the war.

The Patriot Advantage

Angry members of Parliament demanded an explanation. How could mighty Britain, victorious in the Great War for Empire, be defeated by a motley rebel army? The ministry blamed the military leadership, pointing with some justification to a series of blunders. Why had Howe not ruthlessly pursued Washington's army in 1776? Why had Howe and Burgoyne failed to coordinate the movement of their armies in 1777? Why had Cornwallis marched deep into the Patriot-dominated state of Virginia in 1781?

Although historians acknowledge British blunders, most agree that the decisive factor in the rebels' victory was the broad support in America for their cause. At least a third of the white colonists were zealous Patriots, and another third supported the war effort by paying taxes and joining the militia. Moreover, the Patriots were led by experienced politicians who commanded public support. And then there was George Washington. Washington emerged as an inspired military leader and an astute politician. By deferring to the civil authorities, he won the support of the Continental Congress and the state governments. Confident of his military leadership, he acted decisively. When unruly troops stationed at Morristown, New Jersey, mutinied because of low pay and sparse rations, Washington ordered the execution of several soldiers. At

Benedict Arnold, 1776

Arnold first captured British attention because of his daring assault on Quebec City, which is pictured in the background of this painting. But the portrait is imaginary, the creation of a London bookseller eager to capitalize on British interest in the American revolt. After Arnold defected to the crown in 1780, British engravers usually portrayed him in profile, a pose traditionally reserved for those of noble character. Anne S. K. Brown Military Collection, Brown University.

the same time, he urged Congress to pacify the troops with back pay and new clothing. Later in the war, the American general thwarted a dangerous challenge to Congress's authority by discontented officers at Newburgh, New York. Finally, Washington had a greater margin for error than the British generals did because the Patriots controlled local governments. At crucial moments, he was able to get those governments to mobilize rural militias to reinforce the Continental army. Alone, Patriot militias lacked the weapons and tactical knowledge needed to defeat the British army. However, in combination with Continental forces, they provided the margin of victory at Saratoga in 1777 and forced Cornwallis from the Carolinas in 1781. Once the rebels had French support, they could reasonably hope for a decisive triumph, as happened at Yorktown.

In the end, it was the American people who decided the outcome of the war. Preferring Patriot rule, they refused to support the British army or accept occupation by Loyalist forces. Most

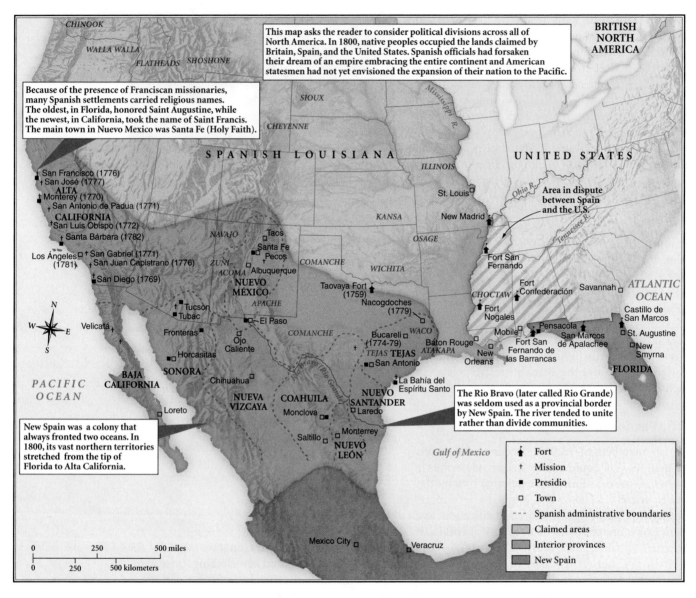

MAP 6.5 New Spain's Northern Empire, 1763–1800

After it acquired Louisiana from France in 1763, Spain tried to create a great northern empire. It established missions and forts (presidos) in California (such as that at Monterey), expanded its settlements in New Mexico, and, by allying with France during the War of Independence, won the return of Florida from Britain. By the early nineteenth century, however, Spain's dream of a northern empire had been shattered by Indian uprisings in California and Texas, Napoleon's seizure of Louisiana, and the Americans' imminent takeover of Florida.

important, they endured the inflation that placed most of the costs of the war on their shoulders. Tens of thousands of farmers and artisans accepted Continental bills in payment for supplies, and thousands of soldiers took them as pay—even as the currency literally depreciated in their pockets. Every paper dollar held for a week lost value, imposing a hidden "currency tax" on those who accepted payment in the paper currency. Each individual tax was small—a few pennies on each

dollar. But as millions of dollars changed hands multiple times, these currency taxes paid the huge cost of the American military victory.

Diplomatic Triumph

After Yorktown, diplomats took two years to end the war. Peace talks began in Paris in April 1782, but the French and Spanish stalled because they still hoped for a major naval victory or territorial conquest. Their delaying tactics infuriated the American diplomats—Benjamin Franklin, John Adams, and John Jay. Fearing that France might sacrifice American interests, the Patriot diplomats negotiated secretly with the British, prepared if necessary to ignore the Treaty of Alliance and sign a separate peace. British ministers were eager for a quick settlement because Parliament no longer supported the war and because they feared the loss of a rich West Indian sugar island.

Exploiting this situation, the American diplomats secured peace on very favorable terms. In the Treaty of Paris, signed in September 1783, Great Britain formally recognized the independence of the rebel colonies. While retaining Canada, Britain relinquished its claims to lands south of the Great Lakes and east of the Mississippi River, and promised to withdraw British garrisons from this trans-Appalachian region "with all convenient speed." Leaving its native allies to their fate, the British negotiators did not insist on a separate Indian territory. "In endeavouring to assist you," a Wea Indian complained to a British general, "it seems we have wrought our own ruin."

Other provisions of the treaty were equally favorable to the Americans. The treaty granted Americans fishing rights off Newfoundland and Nova Scotia, prohibited the British from "carrying away any negroes or other property," and guaranteed freedom of navigation on the Mississippi to American citizens "forever." In return, the American government allowed British merchants to pursue legal claims for prewar debts and agreed to encourage the state legislatures to return confiscated property to Loyalists and grant them citizenship.

In the Treaty of Versailles, signed simultaneously, Britain made peace with France and Spain. Neither American ally gained very much. Spain reclaimed Florida from Britain (Map 6.5), but failed to win back the strategic fortress at Gibraltar. France gained control of the Caribbean island of Tobago, small consolation for a war that sharply raised taxes and quadrupled the national debt. Just six years later, cries for tax relief and political liberty would spark the French Revolution. Only the Americans profited handsomely from the treaties, which gave them independence from Britain and opened the trans-Appalachian west for settlement.

> ➤ Why did Britain switch to a southern military strategy? Why did that strategy ultimately fail?

> ➤ How did the French alliance ensure the success of the American rebellion?

> ➤ The text argues that "it was the American people who decided the outcome of the war." Based on the evidence presented in the chapter, do you agree? Why or why not?

Creating Republican Institutions, 1776–1787

When the Patriot leaders declared independence at the beginning of the war, they had to decide how to allocate political power among themselves. "Which of us shall be the rulers?" asked a Philadelphia newspaper. The question was multifaceted: Where would power reside, in the national government or the states? Who would control the new republican institutions, traditional elites or average citizens? Would women have greater political and legal rights? And what about the slaves? What would their status be in the new republic? Many of the answers to these questions began to emerge from Americans' wartime experience.

The State Constitutions: How Much Democracy?

In May 1776, the Second Continental Congress urged Americans to reject royal authority and establish republican governments. Most states quickly complied. Within six months, Virginia, Maryland, North Carolina, New Jersey, Delaware, and Pennsylvania had written new constitutions, and Connecticut and Rhode Island had revised their colonial charters by deleting references to the king. "Constitutions employ every pen," an observer noted.

Americans Define Popular Sovereignty. Re-publicanism meant more than ousting the king. The Declaration of Independence had stated the principle of popular sovereignty: that governments derive "their just powers from the consent of the governed." In the heat of revolution, many Patriots gave this clause a democratic twist. In North Carolina, the backcountry farmers of Mecklenburg County instructed their delegates to the state's constitutional convention to "oppose everything that leans to aristocracy or power in the hands of the rich and chief men exercised to the oppression of the poor." In Virginia, voters elected a new

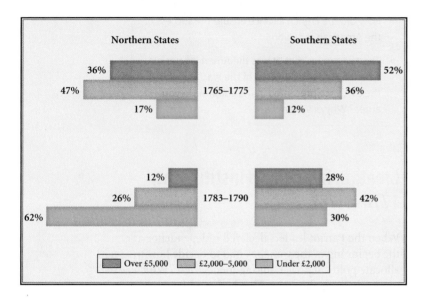

Northern States   Southern States

36%
47%   1765–1775   52%
17%   36%
                                    12%

12%   28%
26%   1783–1790   42%
62%   30%

Over £5,000   £2,000–5,000   Under £2,000

FIGURE 6.1 Middling Men Enter the Halls of Government, 1765–1790

Before the Revolution, wealthy men dominated most colonial assemblies, particularly in the southern colonies. In the new American republic, the proportion of middling legislators (yeoman farmers and others of little wealth, as measured by tax lists and probate records) increased dramatically, especially in the northern states. SOURCE: Adapted from Jackson T. Main, "Government by the People: The American Revolution and the Democratization of the Legislatures," *William and Mary Quarterly*, 3d ser., vol. 23 (1966).

assembly that, an eyewitness remarked, "was composed of men not quite so well dressed, nor so politely educated, nor so highly born" as colonial-era legislatures (Figure 6.1).

This democratic impulse achieved its fullest expression in Pennsylvania, thanks to a coalition of Scots-Irish farmers, Philadelphia artisans, and Enlightenment-influenced intellectuals. The Pennsylvania Constitution of 1776 abolished property ownership as a test of citizenship and granted taxpaying men the right to vote and hold office. It also created a unicameral (one-house) legislature with complete power. There was no upper house, and no governor who exercised veto power. Other provisions mandated an extensive system of elementary education and protected citizens from imprisonment for debt.

John Adams and Conservative Republicanism.

Pennsylvania's democratic constitution alarmed many leading Patriots. From Boston, John Adams denounced the unicameral legislature as "so democratical that it must produce confusion and every evil work." "Remember," Adams continued, invoking history as his guide, "democracy never lasts long. It soon wastes, exhausts, and murders itself." Along with other conservative Patriots, Adams believed office holding should be restricted to "men of learning, leisure and easy circumstances" and feared that ordinary citizens would use their larger numbers to tax the rich: "If you give [democrats] the command or preponderance in the . . . legislature, they will vote all property out of the hands of you aristocrats."

To counter the appeal of the Pennsylvania Constitution, Adams published *Thoughts on Government* (1776). In this treatise, he adapted the British Whig

theory of mixed government (in which power is shared by the monarch and Houses of Lords and Commons) to a republican society. To disperse authority and preserve liberty, he assigned the different functions of government—lawmaking, administering, and judging—to separate institutions. Legislatures would make the laws, the executive would administer them, and the judiciary would enforce them. Adams also called for a bicameral (two-house) legislature with an upper house, its members substantial property owners, that would check the power of popular majorities in the lower house. As a further curb on democracy, he proposed an elected governor with the power to veto laws and an appointed—not elected—judiciary to review them.

Conservative Patriots endorsed Adams's scheme for a bicameral legislature because it preserved representative government while restricting popular power. But they hesitated to give the veto power to governors because they recalled the arbitrary conduct of royal governors and feared executive authority. Most states did follow Adams's suggestion about retaining traditional property qualifications for voting. Under the terms of the New York Constitution of 1777, for example, 80 percent of white men had enough property to vote in elections for the assembly, but only 40 percent could vote for the governor and the upper house. The most flagrant use of property to retain power for the wealthy was in South Carolina, where the 1778 constitution required candidates for governor to have a debt-free estate of £10,000 (about $700,000 today), senators to be worth £2,000, and assemblymen to own property valued at £1,000. These provisions ruled out office holding for about 90 percent of white men.

John and Abigail Adams

Both Adamses had strong personalities and often disagreed in private about political and social issues. In 1794, John playfully accused his wife of being a "Disciple of Wollstonecraft," but Abigail's commitment to legal equality for women long predated Mary Wollstonecraft's treatise, *A Vindication of the Rights of Woman* (1792). Boston Athenaeum; New York State Historical Association, Cooperstown.

The political legacy of the Revolution was complex. Only in Pennsylvania and Vermont were radical Patriots able to take power and create truly democratic institutions. Yet everywhere, representative legislatures had acquired more power, and the day-to-day politics of electioneering and interest-group bargaining had become much more responsive to average citizens.

Women Seek a Public Voice

The extraordinary excitement of the Revolutionary era tested the dictum that only men could engage in politics. Although men controlled all public institutions — legislatures, juries, government offices — upper-class women entered political debate and, defying male opposition, filled their letters, diaries, and conversations with opinions on public issues. "The men say we have no business [with politics]," Eliza Wilkinson of South Carolina complained in 1783. "They won't even allow us liberty of thought, and that is all I want."

These American women did not insist on civic equality with men; but they did insist on ending various restrictive customs and laws. Abigail Adams, for example, demanded equal legal rights for married women, who under common law could not own property, enter into contracts, or initiate lawsuits. "Men would be tyrants" if they continued to hold such power over women, Adams declared to her husband, criticizing him and other Patriots for "emancipating all nations" from monarchical despotism while "retaining absolute power over Wives."

Most men ignored women's requests, and most husbands remained patriarchs who dominated their household. Even young men who embraced the republican ideal of "companionate marriage" (see Chapter 8) did not support legal equality or a public role for their wives and daughters. With the exception of New Jersey, which until 1807 allowed unmarried and widowed female property holders to vote, women remained disenfranchised.

The republican belief in an educated citizenry created opportunities for at least some American women. In her 1779 essay "On the Equality of the Sexes," Judith Sargent Murray argued that men and women had an equal capacity for memory and that women had a superior imagination. She conceded that most women were inferior to men in judgment and reasoning, but insisted that was only because they had not been trained: "We can only reason from what we know," she argued, and most women had

Judith Sargent (Murray), Age Nineteen

The well-educated daughter of a wealthy Massachusetts merchant, Judith Sargent enjoyed a privileged childhood. As an adult, however, she endured a difficult seventeen-year marriage to John Stevens, who ultimately went bankrupt, fled from his creditors, and died in the West Indies. In 1788, she married John Murray, a minister who became a leading American Universalist. Her portrait, painted around 1771 by John Singleton Copley, captures the young woman's skepticism, which enabled her to question customary gender roles. Terra Museum of American Art, Chicago, Illinois. Daniel J. Terra Collection.

suffered severe financial losses. John Tabor Kempe, the last royal attorney general of New York, wanted £65,000 sterling (about $4.5 million today) from the British government to compensate for Patriot land seizures; he received £5,000. Refugees often suffered psychologically too. Prominent Loyalists who fled to England found little happiness there; many complained of "their uneasy abode in this country of aliens." Among the great mass of Loyalist evacuees who moved to Canada or the West Indies, many lamented the loss of their old lives. Watching "sails disappear in the distance," wrote an exiled woman in Nova Scotia, "[I had] such a feeling of loneliness . . . I sat down on the damp moss with my baby on my lap and cried bitterly."

Some Patriots demanded that the state governments seize all Loyalist property and distribute it to needy Americans; but most Patriot leaders argued that confiscation would violate republican principles. In Massachusetts, officials cited the state's constitution of 1780, which declared that every citizen should be protected "in the enjoyment of his life, liberty, and property, according to the standing laws." So the new republican governments confiscated only a small amount of Loyalist property and usually sold it to the highest bidder, more likely a wealthy Patriot than a yeoman farmer or a propertyless foot soldier. In a few cases, confiscation did produce a democratic result: In North Carolina, about half the new owners of Loyalist lands were small-scale farmers; in New

been denied "the opportunity of acquiring knowledge." That began to change in the 1790s, when the attorney general of Massachusetts declared that girls had an equal right to schooling under the state constitution. With greater access to public elementary schools and the rapid growth of girls' academies (private high schools), many young women became literate and knowledgeable. By 1850, the literacy rates of women and men in the northeastern states would be much the same, and educated women would again challenge their subordinate legal and political status (see Reading American Pictures, "Did the Revolution Promote Women's Rights?" p. 187).

The Loyalist Exodus

The creation of republican institutions was greatly helped by the voluntary exodus of 100,000 supporters of the monarchy. Departing Loyalists usually

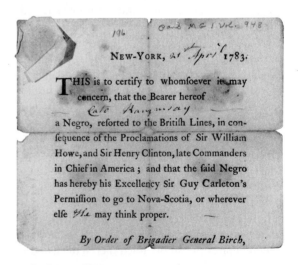

A Black Loyalist Pass, 1783

White Patriots claimed their freedom by fighting *against* the British; thousands of black slaves won liberty by fighting *for* them. This pass certifies that Cato Rammsay, "a Negro," supported the Loyalist cause in New York and is now free "to go to Nova-Scotia, or wherever else He may think proper." Nova Scotia Archives and Record Management, Halifax.

Did the Revolution Promote Women's Rights?

Frontispiece from *Lady's Magazine,* 1792. The Library Company of Philadelphia.

"Keep Within Compass," c. 1785. Henry Francis du Pont Winterthur Museum, Winterthur, Delaware.

According to the text, the republican revolution forced Americans to examine the meaning of equality. One question centered on women's rights: Did the doctrine of popular sovereignty apply to women as well as to men? These two engravings, both published in American magazines, are evidence that the question was the subject of public debate. Pictures like these pose a twofold challenge to historians — to see them as contemporaries did, and, with the power of hindsight, to understand them in their historical context. How do these pictures help us understand the status of women in the young republic?

ANALYZING THE EVIDENCE

➤ The illustration on the left appeared at the front of *The Lady's Magazine and Repository of Entertaining,* which was published in Philadelphia in 1792. The magazine contained excerpts from Mary Wollstonecraft's *A Vindication of the Rights of Woman* (1792), which explicitly linked the republican ideology of the American and French revolutions with women's rights. What sort of clothing are the women wearing? Whom do they represent? Do you think this imagery was empowering to women at the time? Why or why not?

➤ The engraving on the right urges women to "Keep Within Compass." What does the phrase mean? What does it mean in the context of the picture? Look at the smaller pictures on the lower left and lower right corners. What do they suggest might happen to women who challenge their place in society?

York, the state government seized the Philipse manor (see p. 107) and sold its farmsteads to the tenants. When Frederick Philipse III tried to reclaim his estate, former tenants replied that they had "purchased it with the price of their best blood" and "will never become your vassals again." In general, though, the Revolution did not drastically alter the structure of rural society.

Social turmoil was greater in the cities, where Patriot merchants replaced Tories at the top of the economic ladder. In Massachusetts, the Lowell, Higginson, Jackson, and Cabot families moved their trading enterprises to Boston to fill the vacuum created by the departure of the Loyalist Hutchinson and Apthorp clans. In Philadelphia, small-scale Patriot traders stepped into the vacancies created by the collapse of Anglican and Quaker mercantile firms. The War of Independence replaced a traditional economic elite — one that invested its profits from trade in real estate and became landlords — with a group of republican entrepreneurs who promoted new trading ventures and domestic manufacturing. This shift helped ensure America's rapid economic development in the years to come.

The Articles of Confederation

As the Patriots moved toward independence in 1776, they envisioned a central government with limited powers. Carter Braxton of Virginia thought the Continental Congress should have the power to "regulate the affairs of trade, war, peace, alliances, &c." but "should by no means have authority to interfere with the internal police [governance] or domestic concerns of any Colony."

That thinking — that the powers of the central government should be limited — informed the Articles of Confederation, which were passed by the Continental Congress in November 1777. The first national constitution, the Articles provided for a loose confederation — "The United States of America" — in which "each state retains its sovereignty, freedom, and independence." Still, the Articles gave the Confederation government considerable authority: It could declare war and peace, make treaties with foreign nations, adjudicate disputes between the states, borrow and print money, and requisition funds from the states "for the common defense or general welfare." These powers would be exercised by a central legislature, the Congress, in which each state had one vote regardless of its population or wealth. Important laws needed the approval of at least nine of the thirteen states, and changes in the Articles required the consent of all states. In the Confederation government, there was neither a separate executive nor a judiciary.

Disputes over western lands delayed ratification of the Articles until 1781. Many states — including Virginia, Massachusetts, and Connecticut — claimed that their royal charters gave them boundaries that stretched to the Pacific Ocean. States without western claims — Maryland and Pennsylvania — refused to accept the Articles until the land-rich states relinquished their claims. Threatened by Cornwallis's army in 1781, Virginia agreed to give up its land claims, and Maryland, the last holdout, finally ratified the Articles (Map 6.6).

Ongoing Fiscal Crisis. Formal ratification of the Articles was anticlimactic. Over the previous four years, Congress had exercised de facto constitutional authority — raising the Continental army, negotiating foreign treaties, and financing the war through loans and requisitions. The Confederation did have a major weakness though: It lacked the authority to tax either the states or the people. Indeed, by 1780, the central government was nearly bankrupt, and General Washington was calling urgently for a national system of taxation, warning Patriot leaders that otherwise "our cause is lost."

In response, nationalist-minded members of Congress tried to expand the Confederation's authority. Robert Morris, who became superintendent of finance in 1781, persuaded Congress to charter the Bank of North America, a private institution in Philadelphia, arguing that its notes would stabilize the inflated Continental currency. Morris also set up a comprehensive financial system to handle army expenditures, apportion war expenses among the states, and centralize the foreign debt. He hoped that the existence of a "national" debt would underline the Confederation's need for an import duty to pay it off. However, Rhode Island and New York rejected Morris's proposal for a tax of 5 percent on imports. New York's representative told Morris that his state had opposed British-imposed duties and would not accept them from Congress.

The Organization of the Southwest. To raise revenue, Congress looked to the sale of western lands, which were coveted by farmers and speculators. In 1783, it opened negotiations with Native American peoples, arguing that the recently signed Treaty of Paris had extinguished the Indians' land rights. Congress also sought payment from squatters — "white savages," John Jay called them — who had illegally settled on frontier tracts. In 1784, settlers in what is now eastern Tennessee organized a new state, gave it the name Franklin, and sought admission to the Confederation. To preserve its authority over the West, Congress refused to recognize Franklin and gave Virginia control over the region. Subsequently,

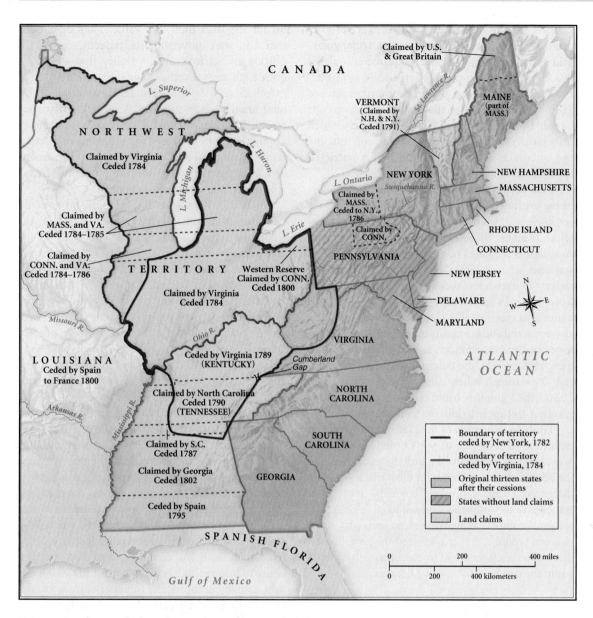

MAP 6.6 The Confederation and Western Land Claims, 1781–1802

The Congress of the Confederation inherited the conflicting claims of the states to western lands. For example, notice the huge — and overlapping — territories claimed by New York and Virginia on the basis of their royal charters. Between 1781 and 1802, the Confederation Congress and, after 1789, the U.S. Congress persuaded all of the states to cede their claims, creating a "national domain" open to all citizens. In the Northwest Ordinances, the Congress divided the domain north of the Ohio River into territories and set up democratic procedures by which they could join the Union. South of the Ohio River, the Congress allowed the existing southern states to play a substantial role in the settling of the ceded lands.

Congress created the Southwest Territory, the future states of Alabama and Mississippi, on lands ceded by North Carolina and Georgia. Because these cessions carried the stipulation that "no regulation . . . shall tend to emancipate slaves," the states that eventually formed in the Southwest Territory (and the entire region south of the Ohio River) allowed slavery.

The Northwest Territory. The Confederation Congress did ban slavery north of the Ohio River. Between 1784 and 1787, it issued three important ordinances organizing the "Old Northwest." The Ordinance of 1784, written by Thomas Jefferson, divided the region into territories that would become states when their population equaled that of the smallest existing state. The Land Ordinance of 1785 promoted settlement by mandating a rectangular-grid system of surveying that could be completed quickly, and by encouraging large-scale land purchases. The ordinance specified a minimum price of $1 an acre and required that half of the townships be sold in single blocks of 23,040 acres each, which only large-scale speculators could afford, and the rest in parcels of 640 acres each, which restricted their sale to well-to-do farmers (Map 6.7).

The Northwest Ordinance of 1787 put the finishing touches on the settlement plans. It created the territories that would eventually become the states of Ohio, Indiana, Illinois, Michigan, and Wisconsin. And, in line with the Enlightenment beliefs of Jefferson and other Patriots, the ordinance prohibited slavery in those territories and earmarked funds from land sales for the support of schools. The ordinance also specified that Congress would appoint a governor and judges to administer each new territory until the population reached 5,000 free adult men; at that point, the citizens could elect a territorial legislature. When the population reached 60,000, the legislature could ratify a republican constitution and apply to join the Confederation.

The land ordinances of the 1780s were a great and enduring achievement of the Confederation Congress. They provided for the orderly settlement and the admission of new states on the basis of equality; there would be no dependent "colonies" in the West. But even as the ordinances helped to transform thirteen governments along the eastern seaboard into a national republic, they perpetuated the geographical division between slave and free territories that would haunt the nation in the coming decades.

Shays's Rebellion

However bright the future of the West, postwar conditions in the East were grim. Peace brought economic recession, not a return to prosperity. The war had destroyed many American merchant ships and disrupted the export of tobacco, rice, and wheat. The British Navigation Acts, which had nurtured colonial commerce, now barred Americans from legal trade with the British West Indies. Moreover, low-priced British manufactures were flooding American markets, driving urban artisans and wartime textile firms out of business.

The economic condition of the state governments was equally fragile, a function of political conflicts over large war debts. On one side were speculators—mostly wealthy merchants and landowners—who had purchased huge quantities of state debt certificates from farmers and soldiers for far less than their face value. They demanded that the state governments redeem the bonds quickly and at full value, a policy that would require high taxes. On the other side were the elected members of the state legislatures, now the dominant branch of government. Because the new state constitutions apportioned seats on the basis of population, they increased the number of representatives from rural and western communities, many of whom were men of "middling circumstances" who knew "the wants of the poor."

Indeed, by the mid-1780s, middling farmers and urban artisans controlled the lower houses of the legislature in most northern states and formed a sizable minority in southern assemblies (see Figure 6.1 on p. 184). Their representatives opposed the collection of back taxes and other measures that tended "toward the oppression of the people." Pressure from western farmers prompted some legislatures to move the state capital from merchant-dominated seaports like New York City, Philadelphia, and Charleston, to inland cities like Albany, Harrisburg, and Columbia. And when yeomen farmers and artisans demanded tax relief, most state legislatures reduced levies and refused to redeem the war bonds held by speculators. State legislatures also printed paper currency and enacted laws allowing debtors to pay their private creditors in installments. Although wealthy men deplored these measures, claiming they destroyed "the just rights of creditors," the measures probably prevented a major social upheaval.

A case in point was Massachusetts, where lawmakers did not enact debtor-relief legislation. Instead, merchants and creditors persuaded the legislature to impose high taxes to pay off the state's war debt, and to cut the supply of paper currency to deter inflation. When cash-strapped farmers could not pay their debts, creditors threatened them with lawsuits. Debtor Ephraim Wetmore heard that merchant Stephan Salisbury "would have my Body Dead or Alive in case I did not pay." To protect their farms, residents of inland counties called extralegal conventions. The conventions protested the tax increases and property seizures and demanded the abolition of debtors' prisons, property qualifications for office holding, and the elitist upper house of the state legislature. Then mobs of angry farmers—including men of status and substance—closed the courts by force. "[I] had no Intensions to Destroy the Publick Government," declared Captain Adam Wheeler, a former town selectman; he had joined the mob to prevent "Valuable and Industrious members of Society [being] dragged from their families to prison [because of their debts], to the great damage . . . of the Community

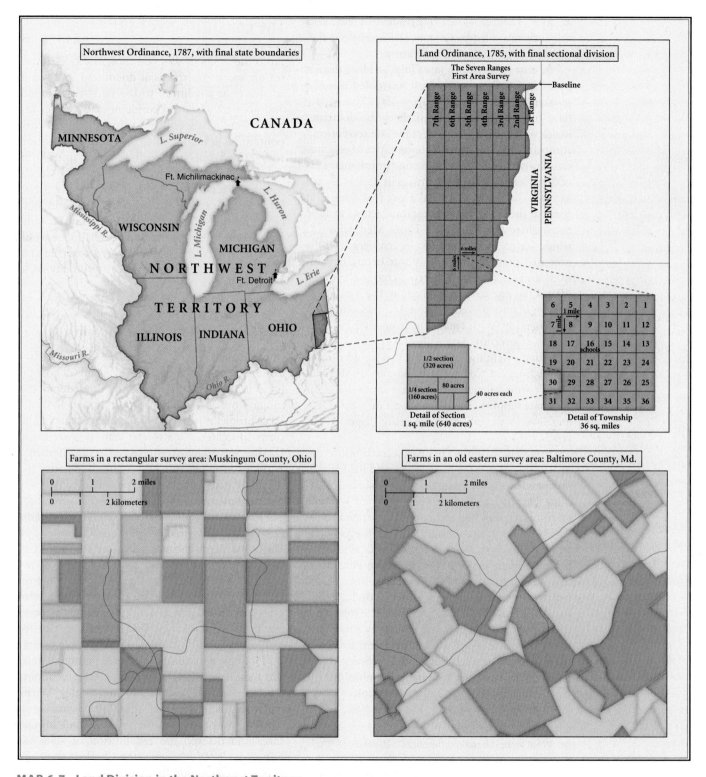

MAP 6.7 Land Division in the Northwest Territory

Throughout the Northwest Territory, government surveyors imposed a rectangular grid on the landscape, regardless of the local topography, so that farmers bought neatly defined tracts of land. The right-angled property lines in Muskingum County, Ohio (lower left), contrasted sharply with those in Baltimore County, Maryland (lower right), where — as in most of the eastern and southern states — boundaries followed the contours of the land.

at large." These crowd actions gradually grew into a full-scale revolt led by Captain Daniel Shays, a former officer in the Continental army.

As a struggle against taxes imposed by a distant government, Shays's Rebellion resembled colonial resistance to the British Stamp Act. "The people have turned against their teachers the doctrines which were inculcated to effect the late revolution," complained Fisher Ames, a conservative Massachusetts lawmaker. To drive home that point, members of Shays's army placed pine twigs in their hats, just as troops in the Continental army had done. But some of the men who were radical Patriots in 1776 condemned the Shaysites: "Those Men, who . . . would lessen the Weight of Government lawfully exercised must be Enemies to our happy Revolution and Common Liberty," charged Samuel Adams. To put down the rebellion, the Massachusetts legislature passed the Riot Act, outlawing illegal assembly. With financing from eastern merchants, Governor James Bowdoin equipped a formidable fighting force and called for additional troops from the Continental Congress. In the end, Shays's army fell victim to freezing weather and inadequate supplies during the winter of 1786–1787, and Bowdoin's military force easily dispersed the rebels.

Shays's Rebellion did not succeed; but it did provide proof that the costs of war and the fruits of independence were not being evenly shared. Middling Patriot families who had endured wartime sacrifices felt they had exchanged British tyrants for American oppressors. Angry Massachusetts voters turned Governor Bowdoin out of office, and debt-ridden farmers in New York, northern Pennsylvania, Connecticut, and New Hampshire closed courthouses and demanded economic relief. British officials in Canada predicted the imminent demise of the United States, and many Americans feared for their republican experiment. Events in Massachusetts, declared nationalist Henry Knox, formed "the strongest arguments possible" for the creation of "a strong general government."

▶ What were the main differences between conservative state constitutions, like that of Massachusetts, and more-democratic constitutions, like Pennsylvania's?

▶ Was there a consensus among different social groups about the meaning of America's republican revolution? What evidence does the chapter provide?

▶ What were the causes of Shays's Rebellion?

The Constitution of 1787

From the moment of its creation, the U.S. Constitution was a controversial document, praised by advocates as a solution to the nation's economic and political woes and condemned by critics as a perversion of republican principles. The main point at issue was whether republican institutions were suited only to small political units—the states—or could govern a vast nation? The Constitution addressed this question by creating a two-level republican government, national and state, both elected by the people. In this composite political system, the new national government would exercise limited, delegated powers, and the state governments would retain legal authority in all other matters.

The Rise of a Nationalist Faction

Money questions—debts, taxes, and tariffs—dominated the postwar political agenda. Those political leaders who had served the Confederation as military officers, officials, and diplomats looked at these problems from a national perspective and became advocates of a stronger central government. George Washington, Robert Morris, Benjamin Franklin, John Jay, and John Adams demanded that the states give Congress the power to control foreign commerce and impose tariffs. However, most state legislators wanted to manage their own affairs. For example, lawmakers in Massachusetts, New York, and Pennsylvania, states with strong commercial traditions, insisted on controlling their own tariffs so that they could protect artisans from low-cost imports while limiting the burden on their merchants. Most southern planters opposed any tariffs because they wanted to import British textiles and ironware at the lowest possible prices.

Nonetheless, some southern planters joined the nationalist faction because of the economic policies of the legislatures in their states. During the economic recession of the 1780s, lawmakers in Virginia and other southern states had lowered taxes and delayed the redemption of state war bonds. Such actions, lamented Charles Lee of Virginia, a wealthy bondholder, led taxpayers to believe that they would "never be compelled to pay" the public debt. Creditors had similar complaints about state laws that "stayed" (delayed) the payment of mortgages and other private debts. "While men are madly accumulating enormous debts, their legislators are making provisions for their non-payment," complained a South Carolina merchant. To these procreditor nationalists, the democratic majorities in the state legislatures constituted a grave threat to republican government.

In 1786, James Madison and other nationalists persuaded the Virginia legislature to invite all the states to a convention to discuss tariff and taxation policies. Only five state governments sent delegates to the meeting, which took place in Annapolis, Maryland. Ignoring their small number, the delegates called for another meeting in Philadelphia to undertake a broad review of the Confederation. Spurred on by Shays's Rebellion, nationalists in Congress secured a resolution calling for a revision of the Articles of Confederation and endorsing the Philadelphia convention. "Nothing but the adoption of some efficient plan from the Convention," a fellow nationalist wrote to James Madison, "can prevent anarchy first & civil convulsions afterwards."

The Philadelphia Convention

In May 1787, fifty-five delegates arrived in Philadelphia. They came from every state except Rhode Island, where the legislature opposed any increase in central authority. Most of the delegates were men of property: merchants, slaveholding planters, or "monied men." There were no artisans, backcountry settlers, or tenants, and there was only a single yeoman farmer.

Some delegates, among them Benjamin Franklin, had been early advocates of independence. Others, including George Washington and Robert Morris, had risen to prominence during the war. A number of longtime Patriots missed the convention. John Adams and Thomas Jefferson were abroad, serving as American ministers to Britain and France, respectively. The Massachusetts General Court did not send Samuel Adams because he favored a strictly limited national government, and his fellow firebrand from Virginia, Patrick Henry, refused to attend because he "smelt a rat."

The absence of these experienced leaders allowed capable young nationalists to set the agenda. Arguing that the convention would "decide for ever the fate of Republican Government," James Madison insisted on an increase in national authority. Alexander Hamilton of New York also demanded a strong central government that would protect the republic from "the imprudence of democracy."

James Madison and the Virginia Plan. The delegates elected Washington as their presiding officer and, to prevent popular interference with their deliberations, met in secret. They ignored their mandate to revise the Articles of Confederation and instead considered the Virginia Plan, a scheme for a powerful national government devised by James Madison.

Just thirty-six years old, Madison had arrived in Philadelphia determined to fashion new political institutions and to populate the government with men of high character. A graduate of Princeton, he had read classical and modern political theory and served in both the Confederation Congress and the Virginia assembly. Once an optimistic Patriot, Madison had become discouraged by the "narrow ambition" and outlook of many state officials.

Madison's Virginia Plan differed from the Articles of Confederation in three crucial respects. First, the plan rejected state sovereignty in favor of the "supremacy of national authority." The central government would have the power not only to "legislate in all cases to which the separate States are incompetent" but also to overturn state laws. Second, the plan called for a national government to be established by the people as a whole and to have direct authority over them. As Madison explained, national laws would bypass the state governments and operate directly "on the individuals composing them." Third, the plan created a three-tier election

James Madison, Statesman

Throughout his long public life, Madison kept the details of his private life to himself. His biography, he believed, should be a record of his public accomplishments. Future generations celebrated him not as a great man (like Hamilton or Jefferson) or as a great president (like Washington), but as an original and incisive political thinker. The chief architect of the U.S. Constitution and the Bill of Rights, Madison was the preeminent republican political theorist of his generation. Library of Congress.

system that would reduce popular power. Citizen voters would elect only the lower house of the national legislature. The lower house would name the members of the upper house, and then both houses would choose the executive and judiciary.

From a political perspective, Madison's plan had two fatal flaws. First, the provision allowing the national government to veto state laws was unacceptable to most state politicians and to many ordinary citizens. Second, the power accorded to the lower house of the legislature, in which states were represented on the basis of their population, would enhance the influence of the large states. Small-state delegates immediately rejected this provision. According to a Delaware delegate, Madison's scheme would allow the populous states to "crush the small ones whenever they stand in the way of their ambitious or interested views."

The Challenge of the New Jersey Plan. Small-state delegates rallied behind a plan devised by William Paterson of New Jersey. The New Jersey Plan gave the Confederation the power to raise revenue, control commerce, and make binding requisitions on the states. But it preserved the states' control of their own laws and guaranteed their equality: Each state would have one vote in a unicameral legislature, the form in use in the Confederation. Delegates from the populous states vigorously opposed this provision. Finally, after a month of debate, a bare majority of the states agreed to take Madison's Virginia Plan as the basis of discussion.

This decision raised the prospect of a dramatically different constitutional system, so different that two New York representatives accused the delegates of exceeding their mandate and left the convention. During the hot humid summer of 1787, the remaining delegates met six days a week, debating high principles and discussing practical details. Experienced politicians, they knew that their plan had to be acceptable to existing political interests and powerful social groups. Pierce Butler of South Carolina invoked a classical Greek precedent: "We must follow the example of Solon, who gave the Athenians not the best government he could devise but the best they would receive."

Compromise over Representation. Representation of large and small states remained the central problem. To satisfy both large and small states, the Connecticut delegates suggested that the upper chamber, the Senate, have two members from each state, while seats in the lower chamber, the House of Representatives, be apportioned by population (determined every ten years by a national census). After bitter debate, this "Great Compromise" was ac-

cepted, but only reluctantly; to at least some delegates from populous states, it seemed less a compromise than a victory for the small states.

Other state-related issues were quickly settled by restricting (or leaving ambiguous) the extent of central authority. A number of delegates opposed a national system of courts, warning "the states will revolt at such encroachments" on their judicial authority. So the convention defined the judicial power of the United States in broad terms, vesting it "in one supreme Court" and leaving the new national legislature to decide whether to establish lower courts within the states. The convention also refused to require that voters in national elections be landowners. "Eight or nine states have extended the right of suffrage beyond the freeholders," George Mason of Virginia pointed out. "What will people there say if they should be disfranchised?" Finally, the convention placed the selection of the president in an electoral college chosen on a state-by-state basis, and specified that state legislatures would elect members of the U.S. Senate. By giving states and their legislatures important roles in the new constitutional system, the delegates hoped their citizens would accept a reduction in state sovereignty.

Gouverneur Morris and the Debate over Slavery. Slavery hovered in the background of the debates, and Gouverneur Morris of New York brought it to the fore. Born into the comfortable world of the New York aristocracy, Morris initially opposed independence out of fear it would result in the "domination of a riotous mob." Becoming a Patriot and a nationalist, he came to the Philadelphia convention convinced that the protection of "property was the sole or primary object of Government & Society." To safeguard property rights, Morris demanded life terms for senators, a property qualification for voting in national elections, and a strong president with veto power. Still, despite his conservative politics, Morris rejected the legitimacy of two traditional types of property—the feudal dues claimed by aristocratic landowners and the ownership of slaves. An advocate of **free markets** and personal liberty, he condemned slavery as "a nefarious institution" and called for its end "so that in future ages, every human being who breathes the air . . . shall enjoy the privileges of a freeman."

Southern delegates joined together to defend slavery, citing its long history and continuing economic importance; but they disagreed on the issue of the Atlantic slave trade. George Mason called for an end to that trade. He was representing planters in the Chesapeake region, who already owned ample numbers of slaves. Rice planters from South Carolina and Georgia, however, argued that slave

Gouverneur Morris, Federalist Statesman

When the war with Britain broke out, Morris had debated joining the Loyalist cause: He was a snob who liked privilege and feared the common people. ("The mob begins to think and reason," he once noted with disdain.) He became a Federalist for much the same reasons. He helped write the Philadelphia constitution and, after 1793, strongly supported the Federalist Party. National Portrait Gallery, Smithsonian Institution/Art Resource, New York.

imports must continue; otherwise, their states "shall not be parties to the Union." At their insistence, the delegates denied Congress the power to regulate immigration — and so the slave trade — until 1808 (see Comparing American Voices, "The First National Debate over Slavery," pp. 196–197).

To preserve national unity, the delegates also treated other slavery-related issues as political rather than moral questions. To satisfy southern slave owners, they agreed to a "fugitive" clause that allowed masters to reclaim enslaved blacks (or white indentured servants) who fled to other states. Acknowledging the antislavery sentiments of Morris and other northerners, the delegates refused to mention slavery explicitly in the Constitution, which spoke instead of citizens and "all other Persons." They also compromised on the issue of counting slaves in determining a state's representation in Congress. Because slaves could not vote, antislavery delegates did not want to count them in apportioning the national legislature; southerners, on the other hand, demanded they be counted as full citizens. Ultimately, the delegates agreed to count each slave as three-fifths of a free person for purposes of representation and taxation, a compromise that helped the South dominate the national government until 1860.

National Power. Having allayed the concerns of small states and slave states, the delegates created a powerful procreditor national government. The finished document made the Constitution and all national legislation the "supreme" law of the land. It gave the national government broad powers over taxation, military defense, and external commerce, as well as the authority to make all laws "necessary and proper" to implement those and other provisions. To protect creditors and establish the fiscal integrity of the new government, the Constitution mandated that the United States honor the existing national debt. Moreover, it restricted the ability of state governments to help debtors by forbidding the states to issue money or enact "any Law impairing the Obligation of Contracts."

The proposed constitution was not a "perfect production," Benjamin Franklin admitted on September 17, 1787, as he urged the forty-one delegates still present to sign it. But the great statesman confessed his astonishment at finding "this system approaching so near to perfection as it does." His colleagues apparently agreed; all but three signed the document.

The People Debate Ratification

The procedures for ratifying the new constitution were as controversial as its contents. The delegates refused to submit the Constitution to the state legislatures for their unanimous consent, as required by the Articles of Confederation, because they knew that Rhode Island (and perhaps a few other states) would reject it. So they arbitrarily specified that the Constitution would go into effect when ratified by special conventions in nine states. Because of its nationalist sympathies, the Confederation Congress winked at this extralegal procedure; surprisingly, so, too, did most state legislatures, which promptly called ratification conventions.

Federalists Versus Antifederalists. As the great constitutional debate began, the nationalists seized the initiative with two bold moves. First, they called themselves **Federalists**, suggesting that they supported a federal union — a loose, decentralized system — obscuring their commitment to a strong national authority. Second, they launched a coordinated campaign in pamphlets and newspapers touting the proposed constitution.

The opponents of the Constitution, the Antifederalists, had diverse backgrounds and motives. Some, like Governor George Clinton of New York,

The First National Debate over Slavery

In Part Two of the text, "The New Republic," we trace the impact of republican ideology on American politics and society. What happened when republicanism collided head-on with the well-established practice of slavery? After the Revolution, the Massachusetts courts abolished slavery (see Chapter 8). But in 1787, in the rest of the Union, slavery was legal; and in the southern states, it was the bedrock of both the social order and agricultural production. A look at the debates on the issue of the African slave trade at the Philadelphia convention and in a state ratifying convention tells us how divisive an issue slavery already was at the birth of the nation, a dark cloud threatening the bright future of the young republic.

The Constitutional Convention

Slavery was not a major topic of discussion in Philadelphia, but it surfaced a number of times, notably in the important debate over representation (which produced the three-fifths clause). The discussion of the Atlantic slave trade began when Luther Martin, a delegate from Maryland, proposed changing a clause to allow Congress to impose a tax on or prohibit the importation of slaves.

Mr. Martin proposed to vary article 7, sect. 4 so as to allow a prohibition or tax on the importation of slaves.... [He believed] it was inconsistent with the principles of the Revolution, and dishonorable to the American character, to have such a feature [promoting the slave trade] in the Constitution.

Mr. [John] Rutledge [of South Carolina] did not see how the importation could be encouraged by this section.... [Moreover,] religion and humanity had nothing to do with this question. Interest alone is the governing principle with nations. The true question at present is whether the Southern states shall or shall not be parties to the Union....

Mr. [Oliver] Ellsworth [of Connecticut] was for leaving the clause as it stands. Let every state import what it pleases. The morality or wisdom of slavery are considerations belonging to the states themselves.... The old Confederation had not meddled with this point, and he did not see any greater necessity for bringing it within the policy of the new one.

Mr. [Charles C.] Pinckney [said] South Carolina can never receive the plan if it prohibits the slave trade. In every proposed extension of the powers of Congress, that state has expressly and watchfully excepted that of meddling with the importation of Negroes....

Mr. [Roger] Sherman [of Connecticut] was for leaving the clause as it stands. He disapproved of the slave trade; yet, as the states were now possessed of the right to import slaves, ... and as it was expedient to have as few objections as possible to the proposed scheme of government, he thought it best to leave the matter as we find it.

Col. [George] Mason [of Virginia stated that] this infernal trade originated in the avarice of British merchants. The British government constantly checked the attempts of Virginia to put a stop to it. The present question concerns not the importing states alone, but the whole Union.... Maryland and Virginia, he said, had already prohibited the importation of slaves expressly. North Carolina had done the same in substance. All this would be in vain if South Carolina and Georgia be at liberty to import. The Western people are already calling out for slaves for their new lands, and will fill that country with slaves, if they can be got through South Carolina and Georgia. Slavery discourages arts and manufactures. The poor despise labor when performed by slaves. They prevent the immigration of whites, who really enrich and strengthen a country....

Every master of slaves is born a petty tyrant. They bring the judgment of Heaven on a country. As nations cannot be rewarded or punished in the next world, they must be in this. By an inevitable chain of causes and effects, Providence punishes national sins by national calamities.... He held it essential, in every point of view, that the general government should have power to prevent the increase of slavery.

Mr. Ellsworth, as he had never owned a slave, could not judge of the effects of slavery on character. He said, however, that if it was to be considered in a moral light, we ought to go further, and free those already in the country.... Let us not intermeddle. As population increases, poor laborers will be so plenty as to render slaves useless. Slavery, in time, will not be a speck in our country. . . .

Gen. [Charles C.] Pinckney [argued that] South Carolina and Georgia cannot do without slaves. As to Virginia, she will gain by stopping the importations. Her slaves will rise in value, and she has more than she wants. It would be unequal to require South Carolina and Georgia to confederate on such unequal terms. . . . He contended that the importation of slaves would be for the interest of the whole Union. The more slaves, the more produce to employ the carrying trade; the more consumption also; and the more of this, the more revenue for the common treasury. . . . [He] should consider a rejection of the [present] clause as an exclusion of South Carolina from the Union.

SOURCE: Max Farrand, ed., *The Records of the Federal Convention of 1787* (New Haven: Yale University Press, 1911), 2: 364–365, 369–372.

The Massachusetts Ratifying Convention

In Philadelphia, the delegates agreed on a compromise: They gave Congress the power to tax or prohibit slave imports, as Luther Martin had proposed, but withheld that power for twenty years. In the Massachusetts convention, the delegates split on this issue and on many others. They eventually did ratify the Constitution but by a narrow margin, 187 to 168.

Mr. Neal (from Kittery) [an Antifederalist] went over the ground of objection to . . . the idea that slave trade was allowed to be continued for 20 years. His profession, he said, obliged him to bear witness against any thing that should favor the making merchandize of the bodies of men, and unless his objection was removed, he could not put his hand to the constitution. Other gentlemen said, in addition to this idea, that there was not even a proposition that the negroes ever shall be free: and Gen. Thompson exclaimed — "Mr. President, shall it be said, that after we have established our own independence and freedom, we make slaves of others? Oh! Washington . . . he has immortalized himself! but he holds those in slavery who have a good right to be free as he is. . . ."

On the other side, gentlemen said, that the step taken in this article, towards the abolition of slavery, was one of the beauties of the constitution. They observed, that in the confederation there was no provision whatever for its ever being abolished; but this constitution provides, that Congress may after twenty years, totally annihilate the slave trade. . . .

Mr. Heath (Federalist): . . . I apprehend that it is not in our power to do any thing for or against those who are in slavery in the southern states. No gentleman within these walls detests every idea of slavery more than I do: it is generally detested by the people of this commonwealth, and I ardently hope that the time will soon come, when our brethren in the southern states will view it as we do, and put a stop to it; but to this we have no right to compel them.

Two questions naturally arise: if we ratify the Constitution, shall we do any thing by our act to hold the blacks in slavery or shall we become the partakers of other men's sins? I think neither of them: each state is sovereign and independent to a certain degree, and they have a right, and will regulate their own internal affairs, as to themselves appears proper. . . . We are not in this case partakers of other men's sins, for nothing do we voluntarily encourage the slavery of our fellow men. . . .

The federal convention went as far as they could; the migration or immigration &c. is confined to the states, now existing only, new states cannot claim it. Congress, by their ordnance for erecting new states, some time since, declared that there shall be no slavery in them. But whether those in slavery in the southern states, will be emancipated after the year 1808, I do not pretend to determine: I rather doubt it.

SOURCE: Jonathan Elliot, ed., *The Debates . . . on the Adoption of the Federal Constitution* (Philadelphia: J. B. Lippincott, 1863), 1: 103–105, 107, 112, 117.

ANALYZING THE EVIDENCE

➤ At the Constitutional Convention in Philadelphia, what were the main arguments for and against federal restrictions on the Atlantic slave trade? How do you explain the position taken by the Connecticut delegates in Philadelphia and Mr. Heath in the Massachusetts debate?

➤ Why did George Mason, a Virginia slave owner, demand a prohibition of the Atlantic slave trade?

➤ What evidence of regional tensions do you see in the documents? Several men from different states — Mason from Virginia, Ellsworth from Connecticut, and Heath from Massachusetts — offered predictions about the future of slavery. How accurate were they?

feared that state governments would lose power. Rural democrats protested that the proposed constitution, unlike most state constitutions, lacked a declaration of individual rights. These smallholding farmers were concerned that the central government would be run by wealthy men. "Lawyers and men of learning and monied men expect to be managers of this Constitution," worried a Massachusetts farmer, "and get all the power and all the money into their own hands and then they will swallow up all of us little folks . . . just as the whale swallowed up Jonah." Giving political substance to these fears, Melancton Smith of New York argued that the large electoral districts prescribed by the Constitution would bring wealthy upper-class men into office, whereas the smaller districts used in state elections usually produced legislatures "composed principally of respectable yeomanry."

Well-educated Americans with a traditional republican outlook also opposed the new system. To keep government "close to the people," they wanted the nation to remain a collection of small sovereign republics tied together only for trade and defense — not the "United States" but the "States United." Citing French political philosopher Montesquieu, the Antifederalists argued that republican institutions were best suited to cities or small states, a localist perspective that shaped American political thinking well into the twentieth century. "No extensive empire can be governed on republican principles," declared James Winthrop of Massachusetts. Patrick Henry predicted the Constitution would recreate the worst features of British rule: high taxes, an oppressive bureaucracy, a standing army, and a "great and mighty President . . . supported in extravagant munificence."

The Federalist Papers. In New York, where ratification was hotly contested, James Madison, John Jay, and Alexander Hamilton countered the arguments against a strong national government in a series of eighty-five essays collectively called *The Federalist*. Although the essays were not widely read outside New York City — only a few were reprinted in newspapers elsewhere — *The Federalist* came to be recognized as an important statement of republican political doctrine. Its authors stressed the need for a strong national government to conduct foreign affairs, and they denied that a centralized government would foster domestic tyranny. Drawing on Montesquieu's theory of mixed government and John Adams's *Thoughts on Government*, Madison, Jay, and Hamilton pointed out that authority would be divided among an executive (the president), a bicameral legislature, and a judiciary. Each branch of government would "check and balance" the others and so preserve liberty.

In "Federalist No. 10," Madison made a significant contribution to political thought by challenging the traditional belief that republican governments were suited only to cities or small states. Rather, large states would better protect republican liberty. It was "sown in the nature of man," Madison wrote, that individuals would seek power and form factions to advance their interests. Indeed, "a landed interest, a manufacturing interest, a mercantile interest, a moneyed interest, with many lesser interests, grow up of necessity in civilized nations." He argued that a free society should not suppress those groups but rather prevent any one of them from becoming dominant — an end best achieved in a large republic. "Extend the sphere," Madison concluded, "and you take in a greater variety of parties and interests; you make it less probable that a majority of the whole will have a common motive to invade the rights of other citizens."

The Ratification Conventions. The delegates who debated these issues in the state ratification conventions were a diverse group. They included untutored farmers and middling artisans as well as educated gentlemen. Generally, backcountry delegates were Antifederalists, while those from the coast were Federalists. In Pennsylvania, Philadelphia merchants and artisans combined with commercial farmers to ratify the Constitution. Other early Federalist successes came in four less-populous states — Delaware, New Jersey, Georgia, and Connecticut — where delegates hoped a strong national government would offset the power of large neighboring states (Map 6.8).

The Constitution's first real test came in January 1788 in Massachusetts, a populous state filled with Antifederalists. Influential Patriots, including Samuel Adams and Governor John Hancock, opposed the new constitution, as did many admirers of Daniel Shays. But Boston artisans, who wanted tariff protection from British imports, supported ratification. To win the votes needed for ratification, Federalist leaders assured the convention that they would enact a national bill of rights to protect individuals from possible oppression by the new government. That promise swayed some delegates. By a close vote of 187 to 168, the Federalists carried the day.

Spring brought Federalist victories in Maryland and South Carolina. When New Hampshire narrowly ratified the Constitution in June, the required nine states had approved it. Still, the essential states of Virginia and New York had not yet acted. It took the powerful arguments advanced in *The Federalist* and the promise of a bill of rights to secure the Constitution's adoption. It won ratification in Virginia by 10 votes, 89 to 79; and that success carried the Federalists to victory — by just 3 votes, 30 to 27 — in

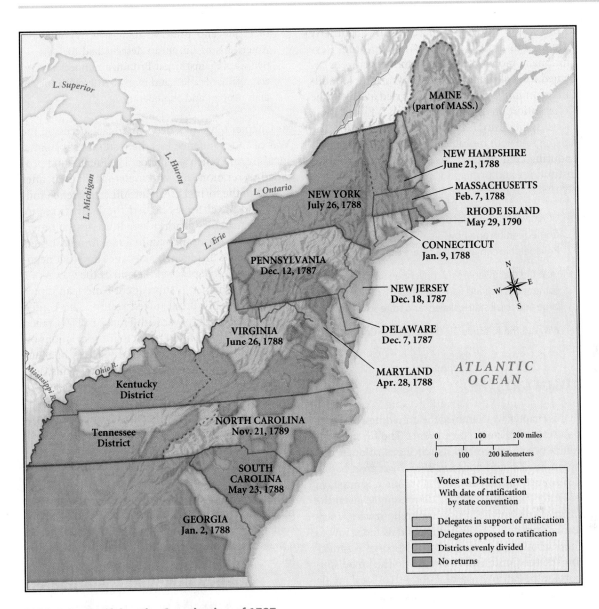

MAP 6.8 Ratifying the Constitution of 1787

In 1907, geographer Owen Libby mapped the votes of members of the state conventions that ratified the Constitution. His map showed that most delegates from seaboard or commercial farming districts, which sent many delegates to the conventions, supported the Constitution, while those from sparsely represented backcountry areas opposed it. Subsequent research has confirmed Libby's socioeconomic interpretation of the voting patterns in North and South Carolina and in Massachusetts. However, other factors influenced delegates in other states. For example, in Georgia, delegates from all regions voted for ratification.

New York. Suspicious of centralized power, voters in North Carolina did not ratify the Constitution until 1789; and voters in Rhode Island held out until 1790.

Testifying to their respect for popular sovereignty and majority rule, most Americans accepted the verdict of the ratifying conventions. The Antifederalist movement withered away, and state legislatures and politicians accepted the Constitution. "A decided majority" of the New Hampshire as-sembly had opposed the "new system," reported Joshua Atherton, but now they said, "It is adopted, let us try it." In Virginia, Patrick Henry vowed to "submit as a quiet citizen" and fight for amendments "in a constitutional way."

Working against great odds, the Federalists had created a national republic and partly restored an elitist system of political authority. Federalists cele-brated their triumph by organizing great processions in the seaport cities. By marching in an orderly fashion — in conscious contrast to the riotous Revolutionary mobs — Federalist-minded citizens affirmed their allegiance to a self-governing republican community. The marchers carried a copy of the Constitution on an "altar of liberty." By invoking sacred symbolism, Federalists hoped to endow the new regime with moral legitimacy and to create an enduring **civil religion** based on national political institutions and principles.

➤ What were the central problems of the Articles of Confederation and how did the delegates to the Philadelphia convention address them?

➤ How did the Philadelphia convention resolve three contentious political issues: the representation of large and small states, slavery, and state sovereignty?

➤ Why did the Antifederalists oppose the Constitution?

SUMMARY

In this chapter, we examined the unfolding of two important and related sets of events. The first was the war between Britain and its rebellious colonies that began in 1776 and ended in 1783. Two great battles determined the outcome of that conflict, Saratoga in 1777 and Yorktown in 1781. Surprisingly, given the military might of the British empire, both were American victories. These triumphs stand as testimony to the determination and resilience of George Washington and the Continental army and to the broad support for the Patriot cause of thousands of local militia units and tens of thousands of taxpaying citizens.

This popular support reflected the Patriots' success in building effective institutions of republican government. These institutions had their origins in the colonial period, in the town meetings and assemblies that were responsive to popular pressure and increasingly independent of imperial control. They took on new meaning between 1776 and 1781 in the state constitutions that made British subjects into American citizens, and in the first national constitution, the Articles of Confederation. Despite the challenges of the postwar economy, these fledgling political institutions laid the foundation for the Constitution of 1787, the national charter that endures today.

Connections: Diplomacy

In the essay that introduces Part Two (p. 135), we pointed out that

to create and preserve their new republic, Americans of European descent had to fight two wars against Great Britain, an undeclared war against France, and many battles with Indian peoples and confederations.

As Chapter 6 has revealed, American success in the War of Independence was the result, in substantial measure, of French assistance. The French first provided secret monetary and material aid; then, after 1778 and the formal Treaty of Alliance, French military and naval forces helped the Patriots secure their great victory at Yorktown. It was astute American diplomacy by Benjamin Franklin and others that obtained this French assistance and that negotiated a favorable peace at the end of the war. As we will see in Chapter 7, subsequent American diplomatic efforts produced mixed results: The United States nearly went to war with France in 1798, failed to force the British and French to lift restrictions on American merchant vessels in 1807, and maneuvered itself into a second, nearly disastrous, war with Great Britain in 1812. Only the purchase of Louisiana from France in 1803 stands out as an unblemished American diplomatic triumph.

Still, the number and form of these diplomatic initiatives point out the crucial importance of relationships with foreign nations and, to a lesser extent, Indian peoples during the era of the early American republic. European entanglements — diplomatic, military, commercial, and ideological — stood at the center of American history during these years and are a major focus of our discussion in the chapters that follow.

CHAPTER REVIEW QUESTIONS

➤ The text states that Saratoga was the turning point of the War of Independence. Do you agree? Explain your answer.

➤ How revolutionary was the American Revolution? What political, social, and economic changes did it produce? What stayed the same?

➤ Why was the Constitution a controversial document even as it was being written?

➤ Both the Federalists and the Antifederalists claimed to represent the true spirit of the Revolution. Which group do you think was right? Why?

TIMELINE

1776	Second Continental Congress declares independence
	Howe forces Washington to retreat from New York and New Jersey
	Pennsylvania approves a democratic state constitution
	John Adams publishes *Thoughts on Government*
1777	Articles of Confederation
	Patriot women become important in war economy
	Howe occupies Philadelphia (September)
	Gates defeats Burgoyne at Saratoga (October)
	Severe inflation of paper currency begins
1778	Franco-American alliance (February)
	Lord North seeks political settlement; Congress rejects negotiations
	British adopt southern strategy; capture Savannah (December)
1779	British and American forces battle in Georgia
1780	Sir Henry Clinton seizes Charleston (May)
	French troops land in Rhode Island
1781	Lord Cornwallis invades Virginia (April); surrenders at Yorktown (October)
	States finally ratify Articles of Confederation
	Large-scale Loyalist emigration
1783	Treaty of Paris (September 3) officially ends war
1784–1785	Congress enacts political and land ordinances for new states
1786	Nationalists hold convention in Annapolis, Maryland
	Shays's Rebellion roils Massachusetts
1787	Congress passes Northwest Ordinance
	Constitutional Convention in Philadelphia
1787–1788	Jay, Madison, and Hamilton write *The Federalist*
	Eleven states ratify U.S. Constitution

FOR FURTHER EXPLORATION

For vivid accounts of the war, see John C. Dann, ed., *The Revolution Remembered: Eyewitness Accounts of the War for Independence* (1980). "The Virtual Marching Tour" at **www.ushistory .org/brandywine/index.html** offers an interesting multimedia view of Howe's attack on Philadelphia. For a fascinating analysis of espionage during the Revolution, prepared by the Central Intelligence Agency, see **www.odci.gov/cia/publications/ warindep/frames.html.**

Colin G. Calloway, *The American Revolution in Indian Country* (1995), traces the Revolution's impact on Native peoples, while Robin Blackburn, *The Overthrow of Colonial Slavery, 1776–1848* (1988), studies its impact on racial bondage in the Western Hemisphere. Sylvia R. Frey, *Water from the Rock* (1991), shows how African Americans absorbed and used republican ideology and Christian beliefs. A data-rich source on the black experience is "Africans in America: Revolution" (**www.pbs.org/wgbh/ aia/part2/title.html**). Two Canadian Web sites, "Black Loyalists: Our History, Our People" (**collections.ic.gc.ca/blackloyalists/ wireframe.htm**) and "Remembering Black Loyalists, Black Communities in Nova Scotia" (**museum.gov.ns.ca/blackloyalists/**), provide vivid accounts of African American refugees.

Two important studies of women are Mary Beth Norton, *Liberty's Daughters: The Revolutionary Experience of American Women, 1750–1800* (1980), and Carol Berkin, *Revolutionary Mothers: Women in the Struggle for America's Independence* (2005). Also see Cynthia Kierner, *Southern Women in Revolution, 1776–1800: Personal and Political Narratives* (1998), and the analysis of women's political activism during the Revolution at the Women and Social Movements Web site (**womhist. binghamton.edu/amrev/abstract.htm**).

For a dramatic retelling of the Constitutional Convention, see Catherine Drinker Bowen's *Miracle at Philadelphia* (1966). Jack Rakove's *Original Meanings: Politics and Ideas in the Making of the Constitution* (1996) offers a more complex analysis of the Framers. Saul Cornell, *The Other Founders: The Antifederalists and the American Dissenting Tradition* (1999), addresses opposition to the Constitution; and Michael Kammen, *A Machine That Would Go by Itself* (1986), explains its changing reputation. David Waldstreicher's *In the Midst of Perpetual Fetes: The Making of American Nationalism, 1776–1820* (1997) is a fascinating analysis of public celebrations. Also see the Library of Congress site, "Religion and the Founding of the American Republic" (**www.loc.gov/exhibits/religion/rel03.html**). For music of the period, see "Folk Music of the American Revolution" (**members.aol.com/bobbyj164/mrev.htm**).

TEST YOUR KNOWLEDGE

To assess your command of the material in this chapter, see the Online Study Guide at **bedfordstmartins.com/henretta.**

For Web sites, images, and documents related to topics and places in this chapter, visit **bedfordstmartins.com/makehistory.**

7 Politics and Society in the New Republic

1787–1820

LIKE AN EARTHQUAKE, THE AMERICAN Revolution shook the foundations of the European monarchical order, and its aftershocks reverberated far into the nineteenth century. By "creating a new republic based on the rights of the individual, the North Americans introduced a new force into the world," eminent German historian Leopold von Ranke explained to the king of Bavaria in 1854. In the end, Ranke warned, American republicanism might cost the monarch his throne. Before the Revolution, "a king who ruled by the grace of God had been the center around which everything turned. Now the idea emerged that power should come from below [from the people]."

Other republican revolutions — England's Puritan Commonwealth of the 1640s and 1650s and the French Revolution of 1789 — had ended in political chaos and military rule. A similar fate would befall many of the republics in Latin America that would achieve independence from Spain in the early nineteenth century. But somehow the American states escaped a military dictatorship. When the War of Independence ended and General George Washington left public life in 1783 to return to his plantation, Europeans were astonished. "Tis a Conduct so novel," American painter John Trumbull reported from London, that it is "inconceivable to People [here]." Washington's voluntary retirement both preserved

◄ **American Commerce, c. 1800**

In 1800, when Thomas Birch painted this view of shipping along the Delaware River, Philadelphia was still the nation's largest and wealthiest seaport. The city's merchants were especially active in the Caribbean sugar and coffee trade and in the importation of mahogany and other valuable woods from Central America. Notice the presence of several black longshoremen, members of the city's substantial African American population. Rare Book Department, The Free Library of Philadelphia.

and bolstered the authority of the elected Patriot leaders, who were fashioning representative republican governments.

This great task absorbed the energy and intellect of an entire generation. As Americans wrote new state and federal constitutions, some political leaders worried that the new constitutions—state and national—were too democratic. When a bill was introduced into a state legislature, grumbled Connecticut conservative Ezra Stiles, every elected official "instantly thinks how it will affect his constituents" rather than its impact on the public as whole. What Stiles criticized as the irresponsible pursuit of self-interest, most Americans welcomed. The interests of ordinary citizens had taken center stage in the halls of government, and the monarchs of Europe trembled.

The Political Crisis of the 1790s

The final decade of the eighteenth century brought fresh political challenges. The Federalists divided into two irreconcilable factions, first over financial policy and then over the French Revolution. During these struggles, Alexander Hamilton and Thomas Jefferson offered contrasting visions of the future. Would the United States remain, as Jefferson hoped, an agricultural nation governed by local and state officials? Or would Hamilton's vision of a strong national government and an economy based on manufacturing become reality?

The Federalists Implement the Constitution

The Constitution expanded the dimensions of American political life. Previously voters had elected local and state officials; now, they chose national leaders as well. The Federalists swept the election of 1788, winning forty-four seats in the first House of Representatives; only eight Antifederalists won election. As expected, members of the Electoral College chose George Washington as president. John Adams received the second highest number of electoral votes, and he became vice president.

Once the military savior of his country, Washington now became its political father. At fifty-seven, the first president was a man with great personal dignity. Recognizing that he would be setting precedents for his successors, Washington proceeded cautiously (see Reading American Pictures, "Creating a National Political Tradition" p. 205). He adopted many of the administrative practices of the Confederation and asked Congress to reestablish the existing

executive departments: Foreign Affairs (State), Finance (Treasury), and War. He did introduce one important innovation: The Constitution specified that the president needed the consent of the Senate to appoint major officials, but Washington insisted that only he—not the Senate—could remove them, ensuring the president's control over the executive bureaucracy. To head the Department of State, Washington chose Thomas Jefferson, a fellow Virginian and an experienced diplomat. For secretary of the treasury, he turned to Alexander Hamilton, a lawyer and his military aide during the war. Then the new president designated Jefferson, Hamilton, and Secretary of War Henry Knox as his cabinet, or advisory body.

The Constitution had created a supreme court but left to Congress the task of establishing the rest of the national court system. Because the Federalists wanted strong national institutions, they enacted the far-reaching Judiciary Act in 1789. The act established a federal district court in each state and provided three circuit courts to hear appeals from the districts, with the Supreme Court having the final say. The Judiciary Act also allowed appeals to the Supreme Court of federal legal issues that arose in the courts of the various states. This provision ensured that national judges would have the final say on the meaning of the Constitution.

The Federalists kept their promise to add a declaration of rights to the Constitution. James Madison, now a member of the House of Representatives, submitted a list of nineteen amendments to the First Congress; ten were approved by Congress and ratified by the states in 1791. These ten amendments, known as the Bill of Rights, safeguard fundamental personal rights, including freedom of speech and religion, and mandate trial by jury and other legal procedures that protect individual citizens (see Documents, p. D-x). By easing Antifederalists' concerns about an oppressive national government, the amendments secured the legitimacy of the Constitution. However, they did not resolve the core issue of federalism—the proper balance between national and state power. That issue would divide the nation until the Civil War, and it remains important today.

Hamilton's Financial Program

George Washington's most important decision was his choice of Alexander Hamilton as secretary of the treasury. An ambitious self-made man of great charm and intelligence, Hamilton married into the Schuyler family, rich and influential Hudson River Valley landowners, and became a prominent lawyer in New York City. As a delegate to the Philadelphia convention, Hamilton took a strongly conservative

Creating a National Political Tradition

Washington's Journey from Mount Vernon.
The City of New York, The Harry T. Peters Collection (56.300.847).

"Independence Declared 1776. The Union Must Be Preserved." Library of Congress.

"Four score and seven years ago our fathers brought forth, upon this continent, a new nation. . . ." So Abraham Lincoln began his famous address at Gettysburg in 1863. Although a new republic was founded in 1776, it became a *nation*, with a sense of national consciousness, only in subsequent decades. How did America's nationhood develop? Graphic evidence like these engravings played an important role in the process of reaching a national consensus on the meaning of being an American. By carefully interpreting the symbols in pictures like these, historians broaden our understanding of the past.

ANALYZING THE EVIDENCE

➤ George Washington had a lot to do with creating America's sense of nationhood. How is Washington portrayed in the image on the left, a depiction of his journey from Virginia to New York in 1789 to assume the presidency? What symbols does the artist use? What do these symbols suggest about Washington? About the presidency? How might those interpretations conflict with America's republican self-image?

➤ In the Gettysburg Address, Lincoln speaks reverently of "our fathers." The banner in the engraving of Washington, which was created in 1845, reads: "THE DEFENDER OF THE MOTHERS WILL BE THE PROTECTOR OF THE DAUGHTERS." What is the significance of the use of family imagery by Lincoln and the engraver? How does this imagery "make personal" the abstract concept of the nation?

➤ The engraving on the right, from 1839, supports the incumbent president, Martin Van Buren (see Chapter 10). He firmly clasps the hand of Andrew Jackson, his predecessor, political ally, and the author of the famous toast "The Union Must Be Preserved." What use does the engraver make of Washington and the presidents who followed him? How do you think this imagery might have helped create a national political tradition?

stance. He condemned the "amazing violence and turbulence of the democratic spirit" and called for an authoritarian government headed by a president with near-monarchical powers.

As treasury secretary, Hamilton devised bold policies to enhance national authority and to favor wealthy financiers and merchants. He outlined his plans in three groundbreaking reports to Congress: on public credit (January 1790), on a national bank (December 1790), and on manufactures (December 1791). These reports laid out a program of national mercantilism, a system of state-assisted economic development.

"Report on the Public Credit." The financial and social implications of Hamilton's "Report on the Public Credit" made it instantly controversial. Hamilton called on Congress to redeem at face value the millions of dollars in securities issued by the Confederation (Figure 7.1). He reasoned that, as an underdeveloped nation, the United States was heavily dependent on Dutch and British loans and needed good credit to survive. However, the redemption plan would also ensure enormous profits to speculators and that offended a majority of Americans, who had yet to accept the inequalities inherent in a full-fledged capitalist economy. For example, a Massachusetts merchant firm, Burrell & Burrell, had paid $600 for Confederation notes with a face value of $2,500; it stood to reap a profit of $1,900 (about $38,000 today). Equally controversial, Hamilton proposed to pay the Burrells and other Confederation noteholders with new government-issued, interest-bearing securities, thereby creating a permanent **national debt** owned mostly by wealthy families.

Hamilton's plan for a national debt reawakened the fears of Radical Whigs and "Old Republicans." Speaking for the Virginia House of Burgesses, Patrick Henry condemned this plan "to erect, and concentrate, and perpetuate a large monied interest" and warned that it would prove "fatal to the existence of American liberty." James Madison challenged the morality of Hamilton's redemption proposal. Madison demanded that Congress help the original owners of Confederation securities—the thousands of shopkeepers, farmers, and soldiers who had been paid with the securities during the dark days of the war and later sold them to speculators. However, it would have been difficult to find the original owners; moreover, nearly half the members of the House of Representatives owned Confederation securities and would profit personally from Hamilton's plan. Melding practicality with self-interest, the House rejected Madison's suggestion.

Hamilton then proposed that the national government enhance the public credit by assuming the war debts of the states. This plan also would favor wealthy creditors. In fact, it unleashed a flurry of speculation and government corruption. Knowing Hamilton's intentions, Assistant Secretary of the Treasury William Duer and his associates bought

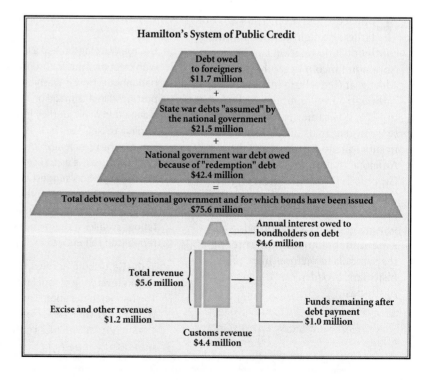

FIGURE 7.1 Hamilton's Fiscal Structure, 1792

As treasury secretary, Alexander Hamilton established a national debt by redeeming Confederation securities and assuming the states' war debts. He then used the revenue from excise taxes and customs duties to defray the annual interest on the national debt. Hamilton deliberately did not pay off the debt because he wanted to tie wealthy American bondholders to the new national government.

Hamilton's System of Public Credit

Debt owed to foreigners $11.7 million

+

State war debts "assumed" by the national government $21.5 million

+

National government war debt owed because of "redemption" debt $42.4 million

=

Total debt owed by national government and for which bonds have been issued $75.6 million

Annual interest owed to bondholders on debt $4.6 million

Total revenue $5.6 million

Excise and other revenues $1.2 million

Customs revenue $4.4 million

Funds remaining after debt payment $1.0 million

up the war bonds of southern states at cheap rates. Members of Congress condemned that speculation. They also pointed out that some states had already paid off their war debts, an argument Hamilton countered by modifying his plan to include reimbursement of the states. Representatives from Virginia and Maryland worried that assumption would enhance the already excessive financial sway of the national government. To quiet their fears, the treasury chief agreed to locate the permanent national capital along the banks of the Potomac, where suspicious southerners could easily watch its operations. This kind of astute political bargaining gave Hamilton the votes he needed to enact both his redemption and assumption plans.

A National Bank. In December 1790, Hamilton issued a second report, which asked Congress to charter the Bank of the United States. The bank would be jointly owned by private stockholders and the national government. Hamilton argued that the bank, by making loans to merchants, handling government funds, and issuing bills of credit, would provide financial stability and a respected currency for the specie-starved American economy. These potential benefits persuaded Congress to charter Hamilton's bank — for a period of twenty years — and send the legislation to the president for approval.

At this critical juncture, Secretary of State Thomas Jefferson joined ranks with James Madison against Hamilton's financial initiatives. Jefferson had condemned the "corrupt squadron of paper dealers" who speculated in southern war bonds. Now he charged that Hamilton's scheme for a national bank was unconstitutional. "The incorporation of a Bank," Jefferson told President Washington, was not a power expressly "delegated to the United States by the Constitution." Jefferson's argument rested on a strict interpretation of the national charter. In response, Hamilton devised a loose interpretation of the Constitution, stating that Article 1, Section 8, empowered Congress to make "all Laws which shall be necessary and proper" to carry out the provisions of the Constitution. Agreeing with his treasury secretary, Washington signed the legislation.

Revenue and Tariffs. Hamilton turned now to the final element of his financial system: revenue to pay the annual interest on the national debt. At Hamilton's insistence, Congress imposed a number of domestic excise taxes, including a duty on whiskey distilled in the United States. These taxes would yield $1 million a year. To raise another $4 million to $5 million, the treasury secretary proposed higher tariffs on foreign imports (see Figure 7.1).

Although Hamilton's "Report on Manufactures" (1791) urged the nation to become self-sufficient in manufacturing, he did not support high **protective tariffs** that would exclude competing foreign products. Instead, he advocated **revenue tariffs** that would pay the interest on the debt and defray the expenses of the national government.

Hamilton's scheme worked brilliantly. As American trade increased, customs revenue rose steadily and allowed the treasury to implement the redemption and assumption programs. Tariffs also had the unexpected effect of encouraging rapid settlement of the West, an outcome opposed by Hamilton and favored by his political opponents. Because import duties brought in 90 percent of the U.S. government's income from 1790 to 1820, the government was able to sell lands in the national domain at ever-lower prices. All in all, Hamilton had devised a strikingly modern fiscal system that provided the new national government with financial flexibility.

Jefferson's Agrarian Vision

Hamilton paid a high political price for his success. Even before Washington began his second four-year term in 1793, Hamilton's financial measures had split the Federalists into two irreconcilable factions. Most northern Federalists adhered to the political alliance led by Hamilton, while most southern Federalists joined a rival group headed by Madison and Jefferson. By the elections of 1794, the two factions had acquired names. Hamilton's supporters retained the original name: Federalists. Madison and Jefferson's allies called themselves Democratic Republicans or simply Republicans.

Thomas Jefferson spoke for the southern planters and western farmers who rejected Hamilton's economic and social policies. Well-read in architecture, natural history, agricultural science, and political theory, Jefferson embraced the optimistic spirit of the Enlightenment. He firmly believed in the "improvability of the human race" and so deplored the corrupt financial practices and emerging social divisions that threatened its achievement. Having seen the poverty of factory laborers in the manufacturing regions of Britain, Jefferson doubted that wageworkers had the economic and political independence necessary to sustain a republic.

Jefferson's democratic vision of America, then, was of an agricultural society based on free labor. Although he had grown up (and remained) a slave owner, Jefferson pictured the West settled by productive farm families. "Those who labor in the earth are the chosen people of God," he wrote in *Notes on the State of Virginia* (1785). The grain and

Two Visions of America

Thomas Jefferson (left) and Alexander Hamilton confront each other in these portraits, as they did in political battles during the 1790s. Jefferson was pro-French, Hamilton pro-British. Jefferson favored farmers and artisans; Hamilton supported merchants and financiers. Jefferson believed in democracy and rule by legislative majorities; Hamilton argued for strong executives and judges. Still, in the contested presidential election of 1800, Hamilton threw his support to Jefferson (he detested Aaron Burr) and secured the presidency for his longtime political foe. Jefferson, by Rembrandt Peale, © White House Historical Association/Photo by National Geographic Society; Yale University Art Gallery, Mabel Brady Garven Collection.

meat from their farms would feed European nations, which "would manufacture and send us in exchange our clothes and other comforts." Jefferson's notion of an international division of labor was similar to that proposed by Scottish economist Adam Smith in *The Wealth of Nations* (1776).

Turmoil in Europe brought Jefferson's vision closer to reality by creating new opportunities for American farmers. The French Revolution began in 1789; four years later, France's republican government went to war against a British-led coalition of monarchies. As warfare disrupted European farming, wheat prices leaped from 5 to 8 shillings a bushel and remained high for twenty years, bringing substantial profits to Chesapeake and Middle Atlantic farmers. Simultaneously, a boom in the export of raw cotton, fueled by the invention of the cotton gin and the mechanization of cloth production in Britain (see Chapter 9), boosted the economies of Georgia and South Carolina. As Jefferson had hoped, European markets brought prosperity to American farmers and planters.

The French Revolution Divides Americans

American merchants profited even more handsomely from the European war. In 1793, President Washington issued a Proclamation of Neutrality, which allowed U.S. citizens to trade with both sides. As neutral carriers, American merchants were initially able to pass their ships through the British naval blockade of French ports; soon they dominated the lucrative sugar trade between France and its West Indian islands. Commercial earnings rose spectacularly, averaging $20 million annually in the 1790s — twice the value of cotton and tobacco exports. As the American merchant fleet increased

dramatically, from 355,000 tons in 1790 to more than 1.1 million tons in 1808, northern shipowners provided work for thousands of shipwrights, sailmakers, laborers, and seamen. Hundreds of carpenters, masons, and cabinetmakers in the major seaports of Boston, New York, and Philadelphia found work building warehouses and fashionable "Federal-style" town houses for newly affluent merchants. In Philadelphia, a European visitor reported, "a great number of private houses have marble steps to the street door, and in other respects are finished in a style of elegance."

Ideological Conflicts. Even as they profited from the European struggle, Americans argued passionately over its ideologies. Most Americans had welcomed the French Revolution of 1789 because it abolished feudalism and established a constitutional monarchy. There was much less consensus, however, in 1792, when the French formed a democratic republic. Many Americans applauded the downfall of the French monarchy. Urban artisans were particularly taken with the egalitarianism of the Jacobins, a radical French group, and followed their example — addressing one another as "citizen" and starting democratic political clubs. Conversely, American with strong religious beliefs condemned the new French government because it rejected Christianity and closed many churches, instead promoting a "rational" religion based on "natural morality." Wealthy Americans also condemned Robespierre and his radical republican followers for executing King Louis XVI, three thousand of the king's aristocratic supporters, and fourteen thousand other citizens (see Voices from Abroad, "William Cobbett: Peter Porcupine Attacks Pro-French Americans," p. 210).

These ideological conflicts sharpened the debate over Hamilton's economic policies and helped to foment a domestic insurrection. In 1794, farmers in western Pennsylvania mounted the Whiskey Rebellion to protest Hamilton's excise tax on spirits, which had raised the price — and cut the demand — for the corn whiskey they bartered for eastern manufactures. Like the Sons of Liberty in 1765 and the Shaysites in 1786, the Whiskey Rebels attacked both local tax collectors and the authority of a distant government. They also waved banners proclaiming the French revolutionary slogan "Liberty, Equality, and Fraternity!" To uphold national authority and deter secessionist movements along the frontier, President Washington raised an army of twelve thousand troops and dispersed the Whiskey rebels.

Jay's Treaty. Britain's maritime strategy widened the political divisions in America. In November 1793, the Royal Navy began to stop American ships carrying French sugar, eventually seizing more than 250 vessels. Hoping to protect American property rights though diplomacy, President Washington dispatched John Jay to Britain. Jay returned with a controversial treaty that acknowledged Britain's right to remove French property from neutral ships, rejecting American merchants' claim that "free ships make free goods." The treaty also required the U.S. government to make "full and complete compensation" to British merchants for pre–Revolutionary War debts owed by American citizens who refused to pay them. In return, the agreement allowed American merchants to submit claims of illegal seizure to arbitration and, more important, required the British to remove their military garrisons from the Northwest Territory and to end their alliance with the Indians there. Jefferson and other Republicans attacked the treaty for being too conciliatory, but the Senate ratified it in 1795, albeit by the bare two-thirds majority required by the Constitution. As long as Hamilton and his Federalist allies were in power, the United States would have a pro-British foreign policy.

The Rise of Political Parties

The appearance of Federalists and Republicans marked a new stage in American politics, the rise of what historians call the First Party System. Although colonial legislatures had often divided temporarily into factions based on family, ethnicity, or region, they did not form organized political parties. The new state and national constitutions made no provision for political societies. In fact, most Americans thought parties were unnecessary and even dangerous to the government; they had little notion of a "loyal opposition." Following classical republican principles, American leaders maintained that voters and legislators should act independently in the interest of the public as a whole. Senator Pierce Butler of South Carolina criticized his congressional colleagues as "men scrambling for partial advantage, State interests, and in short, a train of narrow, impolitic measures."

Federalist Gentry

A prominent New England Federalist, Oliver Ellsworth served as chief justice of the United States from 1796 to 1800. His wife, Abigail Wolcott Ellsworth, was the daughter of a Connecticut governor. In 1792, portraitist Ralph Earl captured the aspirations of the Ellsworths by painting them as aristocrats and prominently displaying their mansion (in the window). Like other Federalists who tried to reconcile their wealth and social authority with republican values, Ellsworth dressed with restraint and his manners, remarked Timothy Dwight, were "wholly destitute of haughtiness and arrogance."
Wadsworth Atheneum, Hartford.

William Cobbett

Peter Porcupine Attacks Pro-French Americans

The Democratic Republican followers of Thomas Jefferson declared that "he who is an enemy to the French Revolution, cannot be a firm republican." William Cobbett, a British journalist who settled in Philadelphia and wrote under the pen name "Peter Porcupine," contested this definition of republicanism. A strong supporter of the Federalist Party, Cobbett regularly attacked its opponents in caustic and widely read pamphlets and newspaper articles like this one, which was published in 1796.

France is a republic, and the decrees of the Legislators were necessary to maintain it a republic. This word outweighs, in the estimation of some persons (I wish I could say they were few in number), all the horrors that have been and that can be committed in that country. One of these modern republicans will tell you that he does not deny that hundreds of thousands of innocent persons have been murdered in France; that the people have neither religion nor morals; that all the ties of nature are rent asunder; . . . that its riches, along with millions of the best of the people, are gone to enrich and aggrandize its enemies; that its commerce, its manufactures, its sciences, its arts, and its honour, are no more; but at the end of all this, he will tell you that it must be happy, because it is a republic. I have heard more than one of these republican zealots declare, that he would sooner see the last of the French exterminated, than see them adopt any other form of government. Such a sentiment is characteristic of a mind locked up in a savage ignorance.

Shall we say that these things never can take place among us? . . . We are not what we were before the French revolution. Political projectors from every corner of Europe, troublers of society of every description, from the whining philosophical hypocrite to the daring rebel, and more daring blasphemer, have taken shelter in these States.

We have seen the guillotine toasted to three times three cheers. . . . And what would the reader say, were I to tell him of a Member of Congress, who wished to see one of these murderous machines employed for lopping off the heads of the French, permanent in the State-house yard of the city of Philadelphia?

If these men of blood had succeeded in plunging us into a war; if they had once got the sword into their hands, they would have mowed us down like stubble. The word Aristocrat would have been employed to as good account here, as ever it had been in France. We might, ere this, have seen our places of worship turned into stables; we might have seen the banks of the Delaware, like those of the Loire, covered with human carcasses, and its waters tinged with blood: ere this we might have seen our parents butchered, and even the head of our admired and beloved President rolling on a scaffold.

I know the reader will start back with horror. His heart will tell him that it is impossible. But, once more, let him look at the example before us. The attacks on the character and conduct of the aged Washington, have been as bold, if not bolder, than those which led to the downfall of the unfortunate French Monarch [Louis XVI, executed in 1793]. Can it then be imagined, that, had they possessed the power, they wanted the will to dip their hands in his blood?

SOURCE: William Cobbett, *Peter Porcupine in America*, ed. David A. Wilson (Ithaca: Cornell University Press, 1994), 150–154.

ANALYZING THE EVIDENCE

➤ What horrors does Cobbett describe? Why does he believe a similar fate could befall the United States?

➤ By 1796, Americans had a long tradition of popular protests. Which of those protests gave credence to Cobbett's warning that a bloodbath might "take place among us"?

➤ Why do you think Americans generally were able to resolve their political disputes peacefully, while the French took up arms to do so?

Still, the conflict in the 1790s over fiscal policies divided America's legislators, and popular sovereignty, which drew average citizens into politics, accentuated the division. Most merchants, creditors, and urban artisans supported Federalist policies, as did wheat-exporting slaveholders in the Tidewater districts of the Chesapeake. The emerging Republican coalition was more diverse. It included not only southern tobacco and rice planters and debt-conscious western farmers but also Germans and Scots-Irish in the southern backcountry and subsistence farmers in the Northeast.

Party identity crystallized in 1796. To prepare for the presidential election, Federalist and Republican leaders called caucuses in Congress and conventions in the states to discuss policies and nominate candidates. The parties organized the citizenry through public festivals and processions: The Federalists celebrated Washington's birthday in February, and the Republicans honored the Declaration of Independence on July Fourth.

Federalist candidates triumphed in the national elections of 1796, winning a majority in Congress and electing John Adams to the presidency. Adams continued Hamilton's pro-British foreign policy and reacted sharply to seizures of American merchant ships by the French navy. When the French foreign minister Talleyrand solicited a loan and a bribe from American diplomats to stop the seizures, Adams charged that Talleyrand's agents, whom he dubbed X, Y, and Z, had insulted America's honor. Responding to the XYZ Affair, the Federalist-controlled Congress cut off trade with France in 1798 and authorized American privateers to seize French ships. The party conflict that had begun over Hamilton's financial policies now extended to foreign affairs.

Constitutional Crisis, 1798–1800

Ominously, the controversial foreign policy of the Federalists prompted domestic protest and governmental repression. As the United States fought an undeclared maritime war against France, immigrants from Ireland vehemently attacked Adams's pro-British foreign policy. A Federalist pamphleteer in Philadelphia responded in kind: "Were I president, I would hang them for otherwise they would murder me." To silence their critics, the Federalist-controlled Congress enacted three coercive laws that threatened individual rights and the fledgling party system. The Naturalization Act lengthened the residency requirement for American citizenship — and so the right to vote — from five to fourteen years; the Alien Act authorized the deportation of foreigners; and the Sedi-

tion Act prohibited the publication of insults or malicious attacks on the president or members of Congress. "He that is not for us is against us," thundered the Federalist *Gazette of the United States*. It was the Sedition Act that generated the most controversy. Prosecutors arrested more than twenty Republican newspaper editors and politicians, accused them of sedition, and convicted and jailed a number of them.

What ensued was a constitutional crisis. With justification, Republicans charged that the Sedition Act violated the First Amendment's prohibition against "abridging the freedom of speech, or of the press." They did not appeal to the Supreme Court because the Court's power to review congressional legislation was uncertain and because most of the justices were Federalists. Instead, Madison and Jefferson looked to the state legislatures for a remedy. At their urging, the Kentucky and Virginia legislatures issued resolutions in 1798 declaring the Alien and Sedition Acts to be "unauthoritative, void, and of no force." The resolutions set forth a **states' rights** interpretation of the Constitution, asserting that the states had a "right to judge" the legitimacy of national laws.

The debate over the Sedition Act set the stage for the presidential election of 1800. Jefferson, once opposed in principle to political parties, now saw them as a valuable way "to watch and relate to the people" the activities of an oppressive government. With Republicans strongly supporting Jefferson's bid for the presidency, President Adams reevaluated his foreign policy. Adams was a complicated man: He was easily offended but had great personal strength and determination. Rejecting Hamilton's advice to declare war against France (and so benefit from an upsurge in patriotism), Adams put country ahead of party and entered into diplomatic negotiations that ended the fighting.

Despite Adams's statesmanship, the campaign of 1800 degenerated into name-calling. The Federalists attacked Jefferson's values, branding him an irresponsible pro-French radical and, because he opposed state support of religion in Virginia, "the arch-apostle of irreligion and free thought." And both parties changed state election laws to favor their candidates. In fact, tensions ran so high that there were rumors the Federalists were planning a military coup and civil war.

The election did not end these worries. Thanks to a low Federalist turnout in Virginia and Pennsylvania and the three-fifths rule (which boosted electoral votes in the southern states), Jefferson won a narrow 73 to 65 victory over Adams in the Electoral College. However, the Republican electors also gave 73 votes to Aaron Burr of New York, who was Jefferson's vice presidential running mate (Map 7.1).

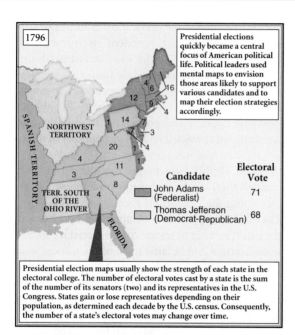

Presidential elections quickly became a central focus of American political life. Political leaders used mental maps to envision those areas likely to support various candidates and to map their election strategies accordingly.

Candidate	Electoral Vote
John Adams (Federalist)	71
Thomas Jefferson (Democrat-Republican)	68

Presidential election maps usually show the strength of each state in the electoral college. The number of electoral votes cast by a state is the sum of the number of its senators (two) and its representatives in the U.S. Congress. States gain or lose representatives depending on their population, as determined each decade by the U.S. census. Consequently, the number of a state's electoral votes may change over time.

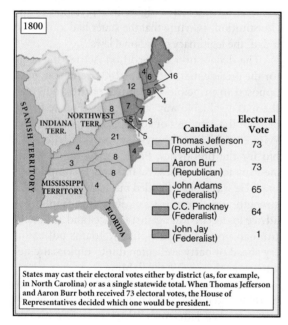

Candidate	Electoral Vote
Thomas Jefferson (Republican)	73
Aaron Burr (Republican)	73
John Adams (Federalist)	65
C.C. Pinckney (Federalist)	64
John Jay (Federalist)	1

States may cast their electoral votes either by district (as, for example, in North Carolina) or as a single statewide total. When Thomas Jefferson and Aaron Burr both received 73 electoral votes, the House of Representatives decided which one would be president.

MAP 7.1 The Presidential Elections of 1796 and 1800

Both elections pitted Federalist John Adams of Massachusetts against Republican Thomas Jefferson of Virginia, and both saw voters split along regional lines. Adams carried every New England state and, reflecting Federalist strength in maritime and commercial areas, the eastern districts of the Middle Atlantic states; Jefferson won most of the agricultural-based states of the South and West (Kentucky and Tennessee). New York was the pivotal swing state. It gave its twelve electoral votes to Adams in 1796 and, thanks to the presence of Aaron Burr on the Republican ticket, to Jefferson in 1800.

The Constitution specified that in the case of a tie vote, the House of Representatives would choose the president. For thirty-five ballots, Federalists in the House blocked Jefferson's election, prompting a new rumor that Virginia was raising a military force to put Jefferson into office.

Ironically, it was arch-Federalist Alexander Hamilton who ushered in a more democratic era by supporting Jefferson. Calling Burr an "embryo Caesar" and the "most unfit man in the United States for the office of president," he persuaded key Federalists to allow Jefferson's election. The Federalists' concern for political stability also played a role. As Senator James Bayard of Delaware explained, "It was admitted on all hands that we must risk the Constitution and a Civil War or take Mr. Jefferson."

Jefferson called the election the "Revolution of 1800," and so it was. The bloodless transfer of power demonstrated that governments elected by the people could be changed in an orderly way, even in times of bitter partisan conflict. In his inaugural address in 1801, Jefferson praised this achievement, declaring, "We are all Republicans, we are all Federalists." Defying the predictions of European conservatives, the republican experiment of 1776 had survived a quarter-century of economic and political turmoil.

➤ What was Hamilton's vision of the future? What policies did he advocate to achieve it? How was Jefferson's vision different?

➤ What were the consequences of the French Revolution in America? How did it affect the development of American politics?

➤ Do you agree with Jefferson that the election of 1800 was a revolution? Explain your answer.

The Westward Movement and the Jeffersonian Revolution

"It is a country in flux," a French aristocrat observed of the United States in 1799, and "that which is true today as regards its population, its establishments, its prices, its commerce will not be true six months from now." Indeed, the American republic was poised to begin a period of dynamic westward expansion. Beginning in the 1780s, thousands of extraordinarily self-confident farm families began to trek into the interior. George Washington, himself a western land speculator, noted that the Sons of

Liberty had become "the lords and proprietors of a vast tract of continent." Unfortunately for Washington's Federalist Party, most western farmers supported Thomas Jefferson's Republicans.

The Expanding Republic and Native American Resistance

In the Treaty of Paris of 1783, Great Britain relinquished its claims to the trans-Appalachian region and, as one British diplomat put it, left the Indian nations "to the care of their [American] neighbours." *Care* was hardly the right term: Many white Americans, including a number of influential men, wanted to destroy native communities and even the native peoples themselves. "Cut up every Indian Cornfield and burn every Indian town," proclaimed William Henry Drayton, a congressman from South Carolina, so that their "nation be extirpated and the lands become the property of the public." Other leaders, including Henry Knox, Washington's first secretary of war, favored assimilating the Indians into Euro-American society. Knox proposed the division of commonly held tribal lands among individual Indian families, who would become citizens of the various states. This debate among whites over the fate of Native Americans would hold an important place on the nation's agenda until 1900, and continues even today.

Conflict over Land Rights. Not surprisingly, the major struggle between Indians and whites centered on land. Invoking the Treaty of Paris and classifying Britain's Indian allies as conquered peoples, the U.S. government asserted its ownership of the trans-Appalachian west. Native Americans rejected that claim, insisting that they had not signed the Paris treaty and had not been conquered. Brushing aside those arguments, U.S. commissioners used the threat of military action to force the pro-British Iroquois peoples — the Mohawks, Onondagas, Cayugas, and Senecas — to relinquish much of their land in New York and Pennsylvania in the Treaty of Fort Stanwix (1784). New York officials and land speculators used liquor and bribes to take title to millions of additional acres, confining the once powerful Iroquois to relatively small tribal reservations.

American negotiators used similar tactics to grab western lands. In 1785, they persuaded the Chippewas, Delawares, Ottawas, and Wyandots to sign away most of the future state of Ohio. The tribes quickly repudiated the agreements, justifiably claiming they were made under duress. To defend their lands, they joined with the Shawnee, Miami, and Potawatomi peoples in the Western Confeder-acy. Led by Miami chief Little Turtle, confederacy warriors crushed American expeditionary forces sent by President Washington in 1790 and 1791.

Fearing an alliance between the Western Confederacy and the British in Canada, Washington doubled the size of the U.S. Army and ordered General "Mad Anthony" Wayne to lead a new expedition. In August 1794, Wayne defeated the Indians in the Battle of Fallen Timbers (near present-day Toledo, Ohio), but the resistance continued. In the Treaty of Greenville (1795), American negotiators acknowledged Indian ownership of the land; in return, the Indian peoples ceded most of Ohio and various strategic areas along the Great Lakes, including Detroit and the future site of Chicago (Map 7.2). The members of the Western Confederacy also agreed to place themselves "under the protection of the United States, and no other Power whatever." These American advances prompted Britain to change its policies in North America: It reduced its trade with the Indian peoples and, following Jay's Treaty (1795), began to remove its military garrisons from the region.

The Greenville Treaty sparked a wave of white migration. By 1805, Ohio, a state for just two years, had more than 100,000 residents. Thousands more farm families moved into the future states of Indiana and Illinois, sparking new conflicts with native peoples over land and hunting rights. Declared one Delaware Indian: "The Elks are our horses, the buffaloes are our cows, the deer are our sheep, & the whites shan't have them."

Assimilation Proposed and Rejected. To alleviate these tensions, the U.S. government encouraged Native Americans to assimilate into white society. The goal, as one Kentucky Protestant minister put it, was to make the Indian "a farmer, a citizen of the United States, and a Christian." But most Indians rejected assimilation. Even those who embraced Christian teachings held to many of their ancestral values. To think of themselves as individuals or even as members of a nuclear family, as white Americans were demanding, meant repudiating the clan, the very essence of Indian life. To preserve their traditional cultures, many Indian communities expelled white missionaries and forced Christianized Indians to participate in tribal rites. As a Munsee prophet put it, "There are two ways to God, one for the whites and one for the Indians."

A few Indian leaders tried to find a middle path. Among the Senecas, the prophet Handsome Lake encouraged traditional animistic ceremonies that gave thanks to the sun, the earth, water, plants, and animals. But he also included some Christian ele-

Treaty Negotiations at Greenville, 1795

In 1785, a number of Indian tribes formed the Western Confederacy to prevent white settlement north of the Ohio River. The American victory at the Battle of Fallen Timbers (1794) opened up the region for white farmers. Peace came the following year with the Treaty of Greenville. That treaty recognized many Indian rights because it was negotiated between relative equals. The artist suggests this equality: Notice the height and stately bearing of the Indian leaders and their placement slightly in front of the American officers.
Unknown, *Treaty of Greenville*, n.d., Chicago Historical Society.

ments in his teachings — the concepts of heaven and hell, for example — to deter his followers from alcohol, gambling, and witchcraft. Handsome Lake's doctrines divided the tribe into hostile factions. More conservative Senecas, led by Chief Red Jacket, condemned Indians who accepted white ways and demanded a return to ancestral customs.

Most Indians also rejected the efforts of American missionaries to turn warriors into farmers and women into domestic helpmates. Among eastern woodland peoples, women were primarily responsible for growing staple foods; as a result, women controlled cultivation rights — they passed through the female line — and exercised considerable political power, which they were eager to retain. Nor were Indian men interested in becoming farmers. When war raiding and hunting were no longer possible, they turned to grazing cattle and sheep.

Migration and the Changing Farm Economy

Native American resistance slowed the advance of white farmers and planters but did not stop it. Between 1790 and 1820, settlers continued to pour across the Appalachian Mountains and to move southward along the Atlantic coastal plain (Map 7.3). This migratory surge transformed America's farm economy.

Movement out of the South. Between 1790 and 1820, two great streams of migrants moved out of the southern states. One stream, composed primarily of white tenant farmers and struggling yeomen families, flocked through the Cumberland Gap into Kentucky and Tennessee. "Boundless settlements open a door for our citizens to run off and leave us," a worried

MAP 7.2 Indian Cessions and State Formation, 1776–1840

By virtue of the Treaty of Paris (1783) with Britain, the United States claimed sovereignty over the entire trans-Appalachian west. The Western Confederacy contested this claim, but the U.S. government upheld it with military force. By 1840, armed diplomacy had forced most Native American peoples to move west of the Mississippi River. White settlers occupied their lands, formed territorial governments, and eventually entered the Union as members of separate — and equal —states. Gradually, the trans-Appalachian region emerged as an important economic and political force.

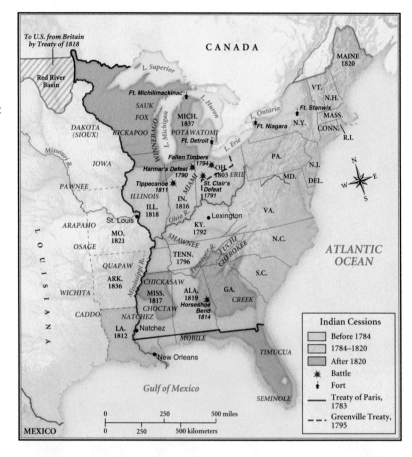

eastern landlord lamented in the *Maryland Gazette,* "depreciating all our landed property and disabling us from paying taxes." In fact, many migrants were fleeing from this planter-controlled society: They wanted more freedom and hoped to prosper by growing cotton and hemp, which were in great demand.

But many of the settlers in Kentucky and Tennessee lacked ready cash to buy land. These settlers invoked the principle articulated in the 1770s by the North Carolina Regulators, that poor settlers had a customary right to occupy "back waste vacant Lands" sufficient "to provide a subsistence for themselves and their posterity." Virginia, which administered the Kentucky Territory, had a more elitist vision. Although it allowed poor settlers to purchase up to 1,400 acres of land at reduced prices, it also sold or granted estates of 20,000 to 200,000 acres to scores of wealthy slave owners and land speculators. When Kentucky became a state in 1792, a handful of speculators owned one-fourth of the state, while half the white men there owned no land and lived as squatters or tenant farmers.

Widespread landlessness — and opposition to slavery — prompted a new migration across the Ohio River into the future states of Ohio, Indiana, and Illinois. In a free community, thought Peter Cartwright, a Methodist lay preacher from southwestern Kentucky who moved to Illinois, "I would be entirely clear of the evil of slavery ... [and] could raise my children to work where work was not thought a degradation."

Meanwhile, a second stream of southern migrants from the Carolinas, dominated by slave-owning planters and their enslaved African Americans, moved along the coastal plain toward the Gulf of Mexico. The planters set up new cotton plantations in the interior of Georgia and South Carolina. Then they moved into the Old Southwest, the future states of Alabama, Mississippi, and Louisiana. "The Alabama Feaver rages here with great violence," a North Carolina planter remarked, "and has carried off vast numbers of our Citizens." To cultivate their cotton crop, the planters bought more slaves: They imported about 115,000 Africans between 1776 and 1808, when Congress cut off the Atlantic slave trade. The black population in

Chief Red Jacket, or Sagoyewatha, c. 1828
Like most Senecas, Sagoyewatha fought for the British during the American War of Independence. In fact, he was called Red Jacket for the red coat a British officer had given him. In 1792, Red Jacket journeyed to Philadelphia as a member of a delegation that ceded Iroquois lands to the United States. There he met with President Washington, who presented him with a silver peace medal. Later Red Jacket would strongly oppose Christian missionary efforts and would call for a return to the traditional Indian way of life. This painting by an unknown artist is based on a portrait by Robert W. Weir painted around 1828. Fenimore Art Museum/© New York State Historical Association, Cooperstown.

America grew even more through reproduction, increasing from 500,000 in 1775 to 1.8 million in 1820.

Beginning around 1750, water-powered spinning jennies, weaving mules, and other technological innovations boosted textile production in Europe, greatly increasing the demand for raw wool and cotton. Responding to that demand, South Carolina and Georgia planters began growing cotton, and American inventors — including Connecticut-born Eli Whitney — built machines (called gins) that efficiently extracted seeds from strands of cotton. The cotton boom financed the rapid settlement of Mississippi and Alabama — in a single year, a government land office in Huntsville, Alabama, sold $7 million of uncleared land — and the two states entered the Union in 1817 and 1819, respectively.

Exodus from New England. As southern whites and blacks moved across the Appalachians and along the Gulf Coast, a third stream of migrants flowed out of the overcrowded communities of New England. Previous generations of farm families from Massachusetts and Connecticut had moved north and east, settling New Hampshire, Vermont, and Maine. Now farmers throughout New England were on the move, this time to the west. Seeking land for their children, thousands of parents packed their wagons with tools and household goods and migrated to New York. By 1820, almost 800,000 New England migrants lived in a string of settlements that stretched from Albany to Buffalo, and many others had moved on to Ohio and Indiana.

This vast migration was organized by the settlers themselves, who often moved in large family or religious groups. One traveler reported from central New York: "The town of Herkimer is entirely populated by families come from Connecticut. We stayed at Mr. Snow's who came from New London with about ten male and female cousins." When 176 residents of Granville, Massachusetts, relocated to Ohio,

MAP 7.3 Regional Cultures Move West, 1790–1820

By 1790, four core cultures had developed in the long-settled states along the Atlantic seaboard. Between 1790 and 1820, residents of these four regions migrated into the trans-Appalachian west, carrying their cultures with them. New England customs and institutions were a dominant influence in upstate New York and along the Great Lakes, while the Lower South's hierarchical system of slavery and heavy concentration of African Americans shaped the culture of the new states along the Gulf of Mexico. The pattern of cultural diffusion was more complex in the Ohio and Tennessee river valleys, which were settled by migrants from various core regions.

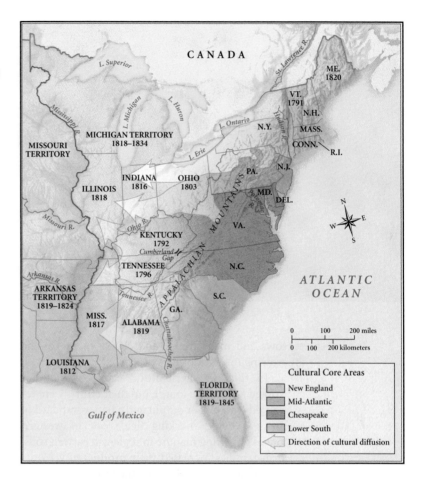

they were led by the minister and elders of their Congregational church. Throughout the Northwest Territory, many new communities were actually old New England communities that had moved inland.

In New York, as in Kentucky, well-connected speculators snapped up much of the best land. In the 1780s, financier Robert Morris acquired 1.3 million acres in the Genesee region of central New York. The Wadsworth family also bought thousands of acres and tried to set up a manorial system like the one in the Hudson River Valley. To attract tenants, the Wadsworths leased farms rent-free for the first seven years, after which they charged rents. Many New England farm families chose instead to sign agreements with the Holland Land Company, a Dutch-owned syndicate of speculators, which allowed settlers to buy the land as they worked it. But high interest rates and, at least initially, a lack of markets for their crops mired thousands of these aspiring freeholders in debt.

Agricultural Change in the East. To pay their debts, farmers in central New York exported wheat to the east, forcing major changes in agriculture there. Unable to compete with low-priced New York grains, farmers in New England switched to potatoes, which were high yielding and nutritious. To compensate for the labor of sons and daughters who had moved inland, Middle Atlantic farmers bought more efficient farm equipment. For example, they replaced metal-tipped wooden plows with cast-iron models that dug deeper and required a single yoke of oxen instead of two or three. This advance in technology kept production high even with fewer workers.

Easterners also took advantage of the progressive farming methods touted by British agricultural reformers. "Improvers" in Pennsylvania doubled their average yield per acre by rotating their crops and planting nitrogen-rich clover to offset nutrient-hungry wheat and corn. Yeomen farmers diversified production by raising sheep and selling the wool to textile manufacturers. Many farmers adopted a year-round planting cycle, sowing wheat in early winter for market and corn in the spring for animal fodder. Women and girls milked the family

Hop Picking, 1801

Farm labor was nothing new for rural women and children, who had always worked about the farm. What was different after 1800 was the growing number of outworkers, landless or poor families who labored for wages paid by shopkeepers and manufacturers. In this somewhat romanticized watercolor by Lucy Sheldon, a Connecticut schoolgirl at the Litchfield Female Academy, a young couple and their children pick hops, which they will deliver to a storekeeper or local brewer to be made into beer. Litchfield Historical Society.

cows and made butter and cheese to sell in the growing towns and cities nearby.

In this new agricultural economy, families worked harder and longer, but their efforts were rewarded with higher output and a better standard of living. Whether hacking fields out of western forests or carting manure to replenish eastern soils, farm families increased their productivity. Westward migration had boosted the farming economy throughout the country.

The Jeffersonian Presidency

From 1801 to 1825, three Republicans from Virginia — Thomas Jefferson, James Madison, and James Monroe — served two terms each as president. Supported by farmers in the South and West and strong Republican majorities in Congress, this "Virginia Dynasty" completed what Jefferson had called the Revolution of 1800. It reversed many Federalist policies and actively supported westward expansion.

When Jefferson took office in 1801, he became the first chief executive to live in the White House in the District of Columbia, the new national capital. His administration began with an international crisis inherited from the Federalists. During the 1790s, the Barbary States of North Africa had systematically raided merchant ships in the Mediterranean and, like many European states, the United States had paid an annual bribe to protect its vessels. Jefferson refused to pay this "tribute"; and when the Barbary pirates renewed their raids, he ordered the U.S. Navy to retaliate. The president did not want all-out war, which would have

increased taxes and the national debt, so he negotiated a settlement that restored the tribute but at a lower rate.

At home, Jefferson inherited a national judiciary filled with Federalist appointees, including the formidable John Marshall of Virginia, the new chief justice of the Supreme Court. Marshall had been appointed by President Adams at the end of his term and quickly confirmed by the Federalist-controlled Senate. To add more Federalists to the court system, the outgoing Congress had also passed the Judiciary Act of 1801. The act created sixteen new judgeships and six additional circuit courts, which Adams filled with "midnight appointees" just before he left office. The Federalists "have retired into the judiciary as a stronghold," Jefferson complained, "and from that battery all the works of Republicanism are to be beaten down and destroyed."

Jefferson's fears were soon realized. When Republican legislatures in Kentucky and Virginia repudiated the Alien and Sedition Acts and claimed the authority to determine the constitutionality of national laws, the Federalist judiciary responded quickly. The Constitution stated that "the judicial Power shall extend to all Cases . . . arising under this Constitution [and] the Laws of the United States," which implied that the Supreme Court held the power of constitutional review. This important issue came to the fore when James Madison, the new secretary of state, refused to deliver the commission of William Marbury, one of Adams's midnight appointees. Marbury petitioned the Supreme Court to compel delivery under the terms of the Judiciary Act of 1789. In *Marbury v. Madison* (1803),

BOMBARDMENT OF TRIPOLI.

America in the Middle East, 1804

To protect American merchants from capture and captivity in the Barbary States, President Thomas Jefferson sent in the U.S. Navy. This 1846 lithograph, created by the famous firm of Currier & Ives, depicts the attack on the North African port of Tripoli by Commodore Edward Preble in August 1804 and his intentional destruction of the *USS Philadelphia,* which had been captured by the Tripolians. The Granger Collection, New York..

Marshall wrote that although Marbury had the right to the appointment, the Court did not have the power under the Constitution to enforce it. In defining the authority of the Court, Marshall had voided a section of the Judiciary Act of 1789, in effect asserting the Court's power to review congressional legislation and decide the meaning of the constitution. "It is emphatically the province and duty of the judicial department to say what the law is," the chief justice declared, directly challenging the Republican view, outlined in the Virginia and Kentucky resolutions of 1798, that the state legislatures had authority to interpret the constitution.

Implementing the Revolution of 1800. Ignoring this setback, Jefferson and the Republicans turned their attention to reversing Federalist policies. When the Alien Act and the Sedition Act expired in 1801, Congress branded them political and unconstitutional, and refused to reenact them. It also amended the Naturalization Act to allow resident aliens to become citizens after five years, the original waiting period. Charging the Federalists with grossly expanding the national government's size and power, Jefferson mobilized the Republican Congress to shrink it. He abolished all internal taxes, including the excise tax that had sparked the Whiskey Rebellion of 1794. Addressing "Old Republican" fears of a military coup, Jefferson reduced the size of the permanent army. He also secured repeal of the Judiciary Act of 1801, thereby ousting forty of Adams's midnight appointees.

But Jefferson governed tactfully. He allowed competent Federalist bureaucrats to retain their jobs. Apart from the midnight appointees, he removed only 69 of 433 Federalist officeholders during his eight years as president. He also tolerated the economically important Bank of the United States, which he had condemned as unconstitutional in 1791. He chose as his secretary of the treasury Albert Gallatin, a fiscal conservative who believed that the national debt was "an evil of the first magnitude." By carefully controlling expenditures and using customs revenues to redeem government bonds, Gallatin reduced the debt from $83 million in 1801 to $45 million in 1808. With Jefferson and Gallatin at the helm, the nation was no longer run in the interests of northeastern creditors and merchants.

Jefferson and the West

Long before he became president, Jefferson championed settlement of the West. He celebrated the yeoman farmer in *Notes on the State of Virginia*, wrote one of the Confederation's western land ordinances, and strongly supported Thomas Pinckney's treaty (1795), which allowed settlers in the Mississippi River Valley to export crops by way of the river and Spanish-held New Orleans.

As president, Jefferson pursued similar policies. In 1796, the Federalist-dominated Congress had doubled the minimum price of land in the national domain to $2 per acre. In response, Republican congresses passed a series of laws that made it easier for farm families to acquire land. By 1820, a farmer needed only $100 in cash to buy eighty acres. Inspired by Jeffersonian policies, subsequent congresses reduced the price still further and eventually, in the Homestead Act of 1862, gave farmsteads to settlers at no cost.

The Louisiana Purchase. International events challenged Jefferson's vision of westward expansion. In 1799, Napoleon Bonaparte seized power in France and began an ambitious campaign to establish a French empire in Europe and in America. In 1801, he coerced Spain into signing a secret treaty that returned Louisiana to France. A year later, he directed Spanish officials in Louisiana to restrict American access to New Orleans, violating the terms of Pinckney's Treaty. Meanwhile, Napoleon planned an invasion to restore French rule in Haiti (then called Saint-Domingue), a rich sugar island seized in 1793 by rebellious black slaves led by Toussaint L'Ouverture.

Napoleon's aggression prompted Jefferson to question his party's pro-French foreign policy. "The day that France takes possession of New

Toussaint L'Ouverture, Haitian Revolutionary and Statesman

The American Revolution represented a victory for republicanism; the Haitian revolt represented a triumph of liberty and a demand for racial equality. After leading the black army that ousted French planters and British invaders from Haiti, Toussaint formed a constitutional government in 1801 that gave him great authority. A year later, he negotiated a treaty with the French, who had invaded the island; the treaty halted Haitian resistance in exchange for a promise that the French would not reinstate slavery. Subsequently, the French seized Toussaint and sent him to France, where he died in a prison in 1803. Snark/Art Resource, New York.

Orleans," the president warned, "we must marry ourselves to the British fleet and nation." Jefferson feared that the French might close the Mississippi River to western farmers, threatening his vision of an expanding yeoman republic. He instructed Robert Livingston, the American minister in Paris, to negotiate the purchase of New Orleans. Simultaneously, Jefferson sent James Monroe to Britain to negotiate an alliance in case of war with France.

Jefferson's diplomacy yielded a magnificent prize: the entire territory of Louisiana. By 1802, the French invasion of Haiti was faltering in the face of disease and determined black resistance, a new war threatened in Europe, and Napoleon feared an American invasion of Louisiana. Acting with characteristic decisiveness, the French ruler offered to sell not only New Orleans but the entire territory of Louisiana for $15 million (about $500 million today). "We have lived long," Livingston remarked to Monroe as they concluded the Louisiana Purchase in 1803, "but this is the noblest work of our lives."

The Louisiana Purchase forced the president to reconsider his strict interpretation of the Constitution. Jefferson had always maintained that the national government possessed only the powers "expressly" delegated to it in the Constitution, but there was no constitutional provision for adding new territory. In this instance, a pragmatic Jefferson accepted a loose interpretation of the Constitution, using the treaty-making powers authorized there to complete the deal with France.

A scientist as well as a statesman, Jefferson wanted detailed information about the physical features of the new territory, its plant and animal life, and its Native peoples. In 1804, he sent his personal secretary, Meriwether Lewis, to explore the region with William Clark, an army officer. With the help of Indian guides, Lewis and Clark and their party of American soldiers and frontiersmen traveled up the Missouri River, across the Rocky Mountains, and, venturing beyond the bounds of the Louisiana Purchase, down the Columbia River to the Pacific Ocean. After two years, they returned with the first maps of the immense wilderness and vivid accounts of its natural resources and inhabitants (Map 7.4).

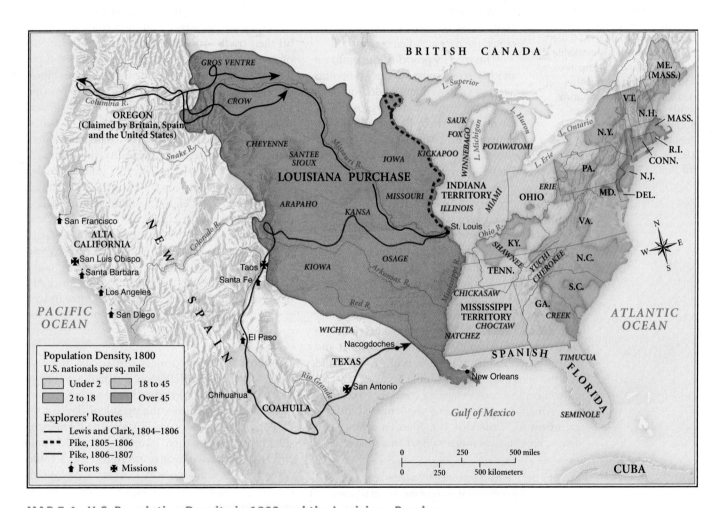

MAP 7.4   U.S. Population Density in 1803 and the Louisiana Purchase

When the United States purchased Louisiana from France in 1803, much of the land between the Appalachian Mountains and the Mississippi River remained in Indian hands: Only a few residents were of European or African descent. The vast lands beyond the Mississippi were virtually unknown, even after the epic explorations of Meriwether Lewis and William Clark, and Zebulon Pike. Still, President Jefferson predicted quite accurately that the vast Mississippi River Valley "from its fertility . . . will ere long yield half of our whole produce, and contain half of our whole population."

Aaron Burr, Man of Ambition
Burr came from distinguished stock. His maternal grandfather was the great revivalist Jonathan Edwards; his father, the president of Princeton. In this portrait of Burr as young man, artist Gilbert Stuart captures his remarkable hazel eyes, handsome features, and compelling charm. After dedicated service in the army during the revolution, Burr became a lawyer, a leading Republican politician, and, from 1801 to 1805, vice president of the United States. From the Collections of the New Jersey Historical Society, Newark, New Jersey.

Threats to the Union: Aaron Burr. Although the Louisiana Purchase was a stunning accomplishment that doubled the size of the nation, it created a new threat. New England Federalists, fearing that western expansion would diminish the power of their states and their party, were talking openly of leaving the Union. Alexander Hamilton refused to support their plan for a northern confederacy, so the secessionists turned to Aaron Burr, the ambitious vice president. When Hamilton accused Burr of participating in a conspiracy to destroy the Union, Burr challenged him to a pistol duel, which was illegal in most northern states. To uphold his aristocratic sense of "honor," Hamilton accepted the dare and died by gunshot.

This tragedy propelled Burr into yet another secessionist scheme. When his term as vice president ended in 1805, Burr moved west to avoid prosecution for dueling. There he conspired with General James Wilkinson, the military governor of the Louisiana Territory. Their plan remains a mystery, but it probably involved either the capture of territory in New Spain or a rebellion to establish Louisiana as a separate nation headed by Burr. But Wilkinson betrayed Burr: He arrested the former vice president as he led an armed force down the Ohio River. In a highly politicized trial presided over by Chief Justice John Marshall, the jury acquitted Burr of treason. Ultimately, the verdict was less important than the dangers to national unity that the trial revealed. The Republicans' policy of western expansion had increased party conflict and generated secessionist schemes in both New England and the Southwest. In the coming decades, regional differences and conflicts would continue to complicate American politics and challenge Madison's argument in "Federalist No. 10" that a large and diverse republic was more stable than a small one.

➤ Why did the Western Indian Confederacy fail to limit white settlement west of the Appalachians?

➤ How did Jeffersonian policy encourage expansion westward? Why did Jefferson and other expansionists believe the West was crucial to the well-being of the republic?

➤ Why did easterners leave their communities and move to the trans-Appalachian west?

The War of 1812 and the Transformation of Politics

Trouble was also brewing in Europe, where war had broken out again in 1802. For the next decade, American politicians tried to safeguard national interests while avoiding war. When this effort finally failed, it set in motion a series of dramatic political changes that destroyed the Federalist Party and split the Republicans into National and Jeffersonian factions.

Conflict in the Atlantic and the West

The Napoleonic Wars that ravaged Europe between 1802 and 1815 endangered American commerce. As Napoleon conquered European countries, he cut off their trade with Britain and ordered the seizure of neutral merchant ships that had stopped there. The British ministry responded with a naval blockade that stopped ships carrying goods to Europe, including American vessels filled with sugar and molasses from the French West Indies. The British navy also searched American merchant ships ostensibly for British deserters; in reality, the navy used these raids to replenish its forces, a practice known as impressment. Between 1802 and 1811, British officers seized nearly eight thousand sailors, including many American citizens. In 1807, American anger over these seizures turned to outrage when a British warship attacked the U.S. Navy vessel *Chesapeake*, killing three, wounding eighteen, and seizing four alleged deserters. "Never since the battle of Lexington have I seen this country in such a state of exasperation as at present," Jefferson declared.

The Embargo. To protect American interests while avoiding war, Jefferson pursued a policy of peaceful coercion. Working closely with Secretary of State James Madison, the president devised the Embargo Act of 1807, which prohibited American ships from leaving their home ports until Britain and France repealed their restrictions on U.S. trade. Although the embargo was a creative diplomatic measure — an economic weapon inspired by the successful boycotts of the 1760s and 1770s — it overestimated the dependence of Britain and France on American shipping, and it underestimated the resistance of New England merchants, who feared it would ruin them.

In fact, the embargo was a disaster for the American economy. Exports plunged from $108 million in 1806 to $22 million in 1808, which hurt farmers as well as merchants and prompted widespread demands for repeal. "Would to God," exclaimed one Federalist, "that the Embargo had done as little evil to ourselves as it has done to foreign nations."

Despite discontent over the embargo, voters elected Republican James Madison to the presidency in 1808. A powerful advocate for the Constitution, the architect of the Bill of Rights, and a prominent congressman and party leader, Madison had served the nation well. However, John Beckley, a loyal Republican, worried that Madison was "too timid and indecisive as a statesman." Events would prove Beckley right. Acknowledging the embargo's failure, Madison replaced it with a series of new economic restrictions, none of which persuaded Britain or France to respect American interests. "The Devil himself could not tell which government, England or France, is the most wicked," an exasperated congressman declared.

Tenskwatawa and Tippecanoe. Republican congressmen from the West had no doubts: For them, Britain was the primary offender. In particular, they pointed to its continued assistance to the Indians in the Ohio River Valley, a violation of the Treaty of Paris. In 1809, bolstered by British guns and supplies, the Shawnee war chief Tecumseh [*ta-KUM-sa*] and his brother, the prophet Tenskwatawa [*tens-QUA-ta-wa*], revived the Western Confederacy. As a young man, Tenskwatawa was known as Lalawethika ("Rattle" or "Noisemaker") because of his boastful ways and blatant alcoholism. In 1805, at age thirty, he had a profound emotional experience: He lapsed into unconsciousness; and when he awoke, he claimed to have visited the Master of Life, the main Shawnee god. Taking the name Tenskwatawa ("The One Who Opens the Door"), he preached a nativist message, urging his followers to shun Americans, "the children of the Evil Spirit . . . who have taken away your lands"; renounce alcohol; and return to

Tenskwatawa, "The Prophet," 1836

Tenskwatawa added a spiritual dimension to Native American resistance by urging a holy war against the invading whites and by calling for a return to sacred ancestral ways. His dress reflects his teachings: Note the animal skin shirt and the heavily ornamented ears. Tenskwatawa's religious message transcended the cultural differences among Indian peoples and helped his brother, Tecumseh, create a formidable political and military alliance. Smithsonian American Art Museum, Washington, D.C./Art Resource.

traditional ways. When Tenskwatawa founded a holy village, Prophetstown, near the juncture of the Tippecanoe and Wabash rivers in the Indiana Territory, he attracted warriors and wise men from many peoples — Kickapoo, Potawatomi, Winnebago, Ottawa, and Chippewa.

Inspired by the prophet's teachings, Tecumseh mobilized the western Indian peoples for war. Realizing the threat to American settlers, William Henry Harrison, the governor of the territory, decided on a preemptive strike. Taking advantage of Tecumseh's absence in the South (where he was seeking the support of the Chickasaws, Choctaws, and Creeks), Harrison mobilized one thousand troops and militiamen. Fending off the confederacy's warriors at the Battle of Tippecanoe, he burned Prophetstown to the ground In November 1811.

Republican War Hawks. With Britain helping the Indians in the West and seizing American ships and sailors in the Atlantic, Henry Clay of Kentucky, the new Speaker of the House of Representatives, and John C. Calhoun, a rising young congressman from South Carolina, pushed Madison toward war. Like other Republican war hawks from the West and South, they supported the acquisition of territory in British Canada and Spanish Florida. With national elections approaching, Madison demanded British respect for American sovereignty in the West and neutral rights on the Atlantic. When the British were slow to respond, Madison asked Congress for a declaration of war. In June 1812, a sharply divided Senate voted 19 to 13 for war, and the House of Representatives concurred, 79 to 49.

The underlying causes of the War of 1812 have been much debated. Officially, the United States went to war because of violations of its neutral rights: the seizure of merchant ships and the impressment of American sailors. But the Federalists who represented merchants' and seamen's interests in Congress voted against the war; and in the election of 1812, voters in New England and the Middle Atlantic states cast their ballots (and 89 electoral votes) for the Federalist candidate for president, De Witt Clinton of New York. Madison amassed most of his 128 electoral votes in the South and West, where voters strongly supported the war. Because of this regional split, many historians argue that the conflict was actually "a western war with eastern labels" (see Comparing American Voices, "Factional Politics and the War of 1812," pp. 226–227).

The War of 1812

The War of 1812 was a near disaster for the United States, both militarily and politically. Predictions of an easy advance into British Canada quickly proved wrong when an American invasion force had to retreat to Detroit. But Americans stayed on the offensive in the West: In April 1813, an American expedition burned York (present-day Toronto) before withdrawing. In September 1813, Commodore Oliver Hazard Perry defeated a small British flotilla on Lake Erie. And the next month, General William Henry Harrison led an expedition into Canada and triumphed over a British and Indian force at the Battle of the Thames. In that battle, Harrison's forces killed Tecumseh, who had become a general in the British army.

Political divisions prevented a major invasion of Canada in the East. New England Federalists opposed the war and prohibited their states' militias from attacking Canada. Boston merchants and banks refused to lend money to the federal government, making the war difficult to finance. In Congress, Daniel Webster, a dynamic young representative from New Hampshire, led Federalist opposition to higher taxes and tariffs and to the national conscription of state militiamen.

These domestic political conflicts contributed to the tide of battle gradually turning in Britain's favor. When the war began, American privateers had quickly captured scores of British merchant vessels but the Royal Navy soon seized the initiative. By 1813, a flotilla of British warships was harassing American ships and threatening seaports along the Atlantic coast. In 1814, a British fleet sailed up Chesapeake Bay. In August, British troops stormed ashore to attack Washington City and burn U.S. government buildings, including the Capitol. After two years of warfare, the United States was stalemated along the Canadian frontier and on the defensive in the Atlantic, and its new capital city was in ruins. The only positive news came from the Southwest. There a rugged slave-owning planter named Andrew Jackson led a force of militiamen from Tennessee to victory over the British-supported Creek Indians in the Battle of Horseshoe Bend (1814) and forced the Indians to cede 23 million acres of land (Map 7.5).

American military setbacks strengthened opposition to the war in New England. In 1814, Massachusetts Federalists called for a convention "to lay the foundation for a radical reform in the National Compact," and New England Federalists met in Hartford, Connecticut, to discuss strategy.

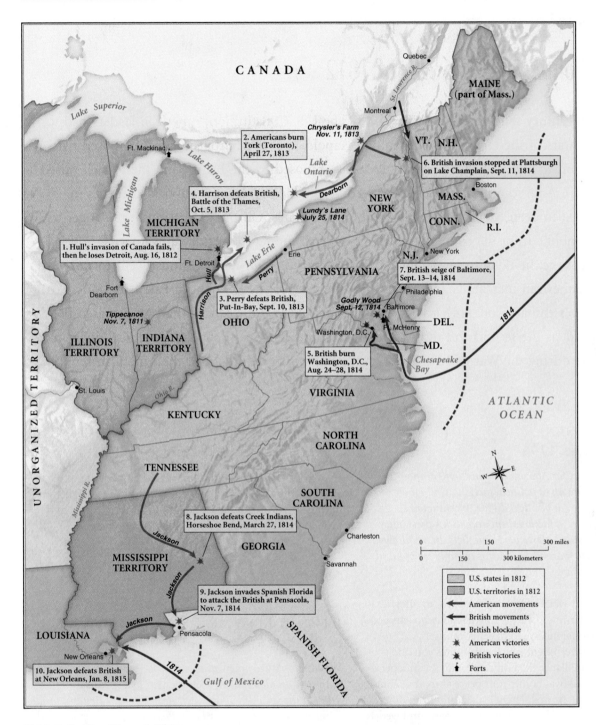

MAP 7.5 The War of 1812

Unlike the War of Independence, the War of 1812 had few large-scale military campaigns. In 1812 and 1813, most of the fighting took place along the Canadian border, as American armies and naval forces attacked British targets with mixed success (#1–4). The British took the offensive in 1814, launching a successful raid on Washington, but their attack on Baltimore failed; and they suffered heavy losses when they invaded the United States along Lake Champlain (#5–7). Near the Gulf of Mexico, American forces moved from one success to another: General Andrew Jackson defeated the pro-British Creek Indians at the Battle of Horseshoe Bend, won a victory in Pensacola, and, in the single major battle of the war, routed an invading British army at New Orleans (#8–10).

Factional Politics and the War of 1812

In the quarter-century following the ratification of the U.S. Constitution, American leaders had to deal with the wars of the French Revolution and Napoleon. These European conflicts posed two dangers to the United States. First, the naval blockades imposed by the British and the French raised the prospect of an American military response. Second, the ideological and political struggles in Europe threatened to deepen party conflicts in the United States. On three occasions, the danger to the American republic from the combination of an external military adversary and internal political turmoil loomed large. In 1798, the Federalist administration of John Adams almost went to war with France to help American merchants and undermine support for the Republican Party. In 1807, Thomas Jefferson's embargo on American commerce shocked Federalists and sharply increased political tensions. And, as the second and third of the following selections show, these political divisions became so acute during the War of 1812 that they threatened the existence of the American republic.

GEORGE WASHINGTON
Farewell Address, 1796

Washington's support for Alexander Hamilton's economic policies promoted the growth of political factionalism. Ignoring his own role in creating that political divide, Washington spoke out about the dangers of factionalism and, as his presidency proceeded, tried to stand above party conflicts. In his farewell address, Washington warned Americans to stand united and avoid the "Spirit of Party."

A solicitude for your welfare [prompts me] . . . to offer . . . the disinterested warnings of a parting friend, who can possibly have no personal motive to bias his counsels. . . .

The Unity of Government which constitutes you one people . . . is a main Pillar in the Edifice of your real independence . . . your tranquility at home; your peace abroad. . . . But it is easy to foresee, that, from different causes, and from different quarters, much pains will be taken, many artifices employed, to weaken in your minds the conviction of this truth. . . .

I have already intimated to you the danger of parties in the State, with particular reference to founding them on geographical discriminations. Let me now take a more comprehensive view, and warn you, in the most solemn manner, against the baneful effects of the Spirit of Party, generally.

This spirit, unfortunately, is inseparable from our nature, having its root in the strongest passions of the human mind. It exists under different shapes, in all governments, more or less stifled, controlled or repressed; but in those of the popular form, it is seen in its greatest rankness, and is truly their worst enemy.

The alternate dominion of one faction over another, sharpened by the spirit of revenge. . . , is itself a frightful despotism; but this leads at length to a more formal and permanent despotism.

SOURCE: James D. Richardson, ed., *A Compilation of the Messages and Papers of the Presidents, 1789–1896* (Washington, D.C.: U.S. Government Printing Office, 1896), 1: 213–215.

JOSIAH QUINCY ET AL.
Federalists Protest "Mr. Madison's War"

Washington's warning was to no avail. The parties — and the nation — divided sharply over the War of 1812. As Congress debated the issue of going to war against Great Britain, Josiah Quincy and other antiwar Federalist congressmen published a manifesto that asked a series of probing questions about the justifications for the war offered by President Madison and the military strategy proposed by Republican war hawks.

How will war upon the land [an invasion of British Canada] protect commerce upon the ocean? What balm has Canada for wounded honor? How are our mariners benefited by a war which exposes those who are free, without promising release to those who are impressed?

But it is said that war is demanded by honor. Is national honor a principle which thirsts after vengeance, and is appeased only by blood? . . . If honor demands a war with England, what opiate lulls that honor to sleep over the wrongs done us by France? On land, robberies, seizures, imprisonments, by French authority; at sea, pillage, sinkings, burnings, under French orders. These are notorious. Are they unfelt because they are French? . . .

There is . . . a headlong rushing into difficulties, with little calculation about the means, and little concern about the consequences. With a navy comparatively [small], we are about to enter into the lists against the greatest marine [power] on the globe. With a commerce unprotected and spread over every ocean, we propose to make a profit by privateering, and for this endanger the wealth of which we are honest proprietors. An invasion is threatened of the colonies [in Canada] of a power which, without putting a new ship into commission, or taking another soldier into pay, can spread alarm or desolation along the extensive range of our seaboard. . . .

What are the United States to gain by this war? Will the gratification of some privateersmen compensate the nation for that sweep of our legitimate commerce by the extended marine of our enemy which this desperate act invites? Will Canada compensate the Middle states for [the loss of] New York; or the Western states for [the loss of] New Orleans?

Let us not be deceived. A war of invasion may invite a retort of invasion. When we visit the peaceable, and as to us innocent, colonies of Great Britain with the horrors of war, can we be assured that our own coast will not be visited with like horrors?

SOURCE: *Annals of Congress*, 12th Cong., 1st sess., vol. 2, cols. 2219–2221.

HEZEKIAH NILES
A Republican Defends the War

During 1814, what the Federalists feared had come to pass: British ships blockaded American ports, and British troops invaded American territory. In January 1815, Republican editor Hezekiah Niles used the pages of his Baltimore newspaper, Niles's Weekly Register, *to explain current Republican policies and blame the Federalists for American reverses.*

It is universally known that the causes for which we declared war are no obstruction to peace. The practice of blockade and impressment having ceased by the general pacification of Europe, our government is content to leave the principle as it was. . . .

We have no further business in hostility, than such as is purely defensive; while that of Great Britain is to humble or subdue us. The war, on our part, has become a contest for

life, liberty and property — on the part of our enemy, of revenge or ambition. . . .

What then are we to do? Are we to encourage him by divisions among ourselves — to hold out the hope of a separation of the states and a civil war — to refuse to bring forth the resources of the country against him? . . . I did think that in a defensive war — a struggle for all that is valuable — that all parties would have united. But it is not so — every measure calculated to replenish the treasury or raise men is opposed as though it were determined to strike the "star spangled banner" and exalt the bloody cross. Look at the votes and proceedings of congress — and mark the late spirit [to secede from the Union] . . . that existed in Massachusetts, and see with what unity of action every thing has been done [by New England Federalists] to harass and embarrass the government. Our loans have failed; and our soldiers have wanted their pay, because those [New England merchants] who had the greater part of the monied capital covenanted with each other to refuse its aid to the country. They had a right, legally; to do this; and perhaps, also, by all the artifices of trade or power that money gave them, to oppress others not of their "stamp" and depress the national credit — but history will shock posterity by detailing the length to which they went to bankrupt the republic. . . .

To conclude — why does the war continue? It is not the fault of the government — we demand no extravagant thing. I answer the question, and say — *it lasts because Great Britain depends on the exertions of her "party" in this country to destroy our resources, and compel "unconditional submission."*

Thus the war began, and is continued, by our divisions.

SOURCE: *Niles Weekly Register*, January 28, 1815.

ANALYZING THE EVIDENCE

➤ According to Washington, what is the ultimate cause of political factionalism? Why might he believe that factionalism is most dangerous in "popular" — that is, republican — governments?

➤ What specific dangers did Josiah Quincy and the Federalists foresee with regard to Republican war policies? Read the section on the War of 1812 in the text, and then discuss the accuracy of their predictions. Why might New England Federalists oppose an imperialistic war that would add western states to the Union?

➤ According to Hezekiah Niles, by 1815, what were the war goals of the Republican administration? How had those goals changed since the start of the war? Niles charged the Federalists and their supporters with impeding the American war effort. What were his specific charges? Did they have any merit?

Some delegates to the Hartford convention proposed secession, but most wanted to revise the Constitution instead. To end Virginia's domination of the presidency, the delegates proposed a constitutional amendment that would limit the office to a single four-year term and rotate it among citizens from different states. They also suggested amendments restricting commercial embargoes to sixty days and requiring a two-thirds majority in Congress to declare war, prohibit trade, or admit a new state to the Union.

As a minority party in Congress and the nation, the Federalists could prevail only if the war was going badly—a very real prospect. Britain's triumph over Napoleon in Europe, Albert Gallatin warned Henry Clay in May, meant that a "well organized and large army is [now] ... ready together with a super abundant naval force, to act immediately against us." As the British took the offensive late in the summer of 1814, only an American naval victory on Lake Champlain averted an invasion of the Hudson River Valley. A few months later, thousands of seasoned British troops landed outside New Orleans, threatening American control of the Mississippi River. The United States was under military pressure from both north and south. Given the "hostile attitude" of New England, Gallatin feared that "a continuance of the war might prove vitally fatal to the United States."

Fortunately for the young American republic, Britain wanted peace. The twenty-year war with France in Europe had sapped its wealth and energy, and so it entered into negotiations with the United States in Ghent, Belgium. At first the American commissioners—John Quincy Adams, Gallatin, and Clay—demanded territory in Canada and Florida, and British diplomats insisted on an Indian buffer state between the United States and Canada. Ultimately, both sides realized that these objectives were not worth the costs of prolonged warfare. The Treaty of Ghent, signed on Christmas Eve 1814, retained the prewar borders of the United States.

The result hardly justified three years of fighting, but a final military victory lifted Americans' morale. Before news of the Treaty of Ghent reached the United States, newspaper headlines proclaimed an "ALMOST INCREDIBLE VICTORY!! GLORIOUS NEWS": On January 8, 1815, General Jackson's troops (including a contingent of French-speaking black Americans, the Corps d'Afrique) crushed the British forces attacking New Orleans. The Americans fought from carefully constructed breastworks and rained "grapeshot and cannister bombs" on the massed British formations. The British lost seven hundred men, and two thousand more were wounded or taken prisoner. By contrast, just thirteen Americans died, and only fifty-eight were wounded. The victory made Jackson a national hero and redeemed the nation's battered pride. The war had increased regional tensions, but the peace undercut the Hartford convention's demands for a significant revision of the Constitution.

The Federalist Legacy

The War of 1812 ushered in a new phase of the Republican political revolution. Before the conflict, Federalists had strongly supported Alexander Hamilton's program of national mercantilism—a funded debt, a central bank, and tariffs—while Jeffersonian Republicans opposed Hamilton's program. After the war, the Republicans split into two factions. Henry Clay led the National Republicans. In 1816, he pushed through legislation creating the Second Bank of the United States and, in part because of the difficulties in financing the War of 1812, President Madison signed it. The following year, Clay won passage of the Bonus Bill, sponsored by Representative Calhoun of South Carolina, which established a national fund for roads and other internal improvements. Madison vetoed it: Along with many other Jeffersonian Republicans, he believed that funding internal improvements by the national government was contrary to the Constitution.

Meanwhile, the Federalist Party was in severe decline. Nationalist Republicans had won the allegiance of many Federalist voters in the East, and the profarmer policies of Jeffersonian Republicans maintained their party's dominance in the South and West. "No Federal character can run with success," Gouverneur Morris of New York lamented. The election of 1818 bore out his pessimism: Following the election Republicans outnumbered Federalists 37 to 7 in the Senate and 156 to 27 in the House. Westward expansion and the success of Jefferson's Revolution of 1800 had ended both the Federalists and the First Party System.

John Marshall's Jurisprudence. Although the Federalists were no more, their policies remained very much in evidence because of John Marshall's long tenure on the Supreme Court. Appointed chief justice by President John Adams in January 1801, Marshall, a committed Federalist, dominated the Court until 1822 and strongly influenced its deliberations until his death in 1835. Marshall's success reflected the power of his logic and the

***Battle of New Orleans,* by Jean Hyacinthe de Laclotte (detail)**
As their artillery (right center) bombarded the American lines, British troops attacked the center of General Andrew Jackson's troops. At the same time, a column of redcoats (foreground) tried to turn the right flank of the American fortifications. Secure behind their battlements, Jackson's forces repelled the assaults, leaving the ground littered with British casualties and taking thousands of prisoners. New Orleans Museum of Art, gift of Edgar William and Bernice Chrysler Garbisch.

force of his personality. By winning the support of Joseph Story and other Nationalist Republican justices on the Court, Marshall shaped the evolution of the Constitution.

Three principles informed Marshall's jurisprudence: He was committed to judicial authority, the supremacy of national laws, and traditional property rights (Table 7.1). After Marshall claimed the right of judicial review for the Court in 1803, in *Marbury v. Madison,* the doctrine evolved slowly. The Supreme Court did

not void another congressional law until the *Dred Scott* decision in 1857 (see Chapter 13). But the Marshall Court frequently overturned state laws that infringed on the U.S. Constitution, as it did in the important case of *McCulloch v. Maryland* (1819). When Congress created the Second Bank of the United States in 1816, it allowed the bank to set up branches in the states. To preserve the competitive position of its state-chartered banks, the Maryland legislature imposed an annual tax of $15,000 on notes issued by the Baltimore

John Marshall, **by Chester Harding, c. 1830**
Even at the age of seventy-five, John Marshall (1755–1835) had a commanding personal presence. After he became chief justice of the U.S. Supreme Court in 1801, Marshall elevated the Court from a minor department of the national government to a major institution in American legal and political life. His decisions on judicial review, contract rights, the regulation of commerce, and national banking permanently shaped the character of American constitutional law. Boston Athenaeum.

branch of the Second Bank. The Second Bank immediately protested that the Maryland law infringed on the powers of the national government and was therefore unconstitutional. In response, lawyers for the state of Maryland invoked Jefferson's argument that Congress lacked the constitutional authority to charter a national bank. Even if a national bank was legitimate, the lawyers argued, Maryland had a right to tax its activities within the state.

Marshall and the Nationalist Republicans on the Court firmly rejected both arguments. The

Second Bank was constitutional, said the chief justice, because it was "necessary and proper" given the national government's responsibility to control currency and credit. Like Alexander Hamilton, Marshall adopted a loose construction of the Constitution. If the goal of a law is "legitimate [and] ... within the scope of the Constitution," he wrote, then "all means which are appropriate" to secure that goal are also constitutional. The chief justice also argued that "the power to tax involves the power to destroy" and suggested that Maryland's bank tax would render the national government

TABLE 7.1	Major Decisions of the Marshall Court	
Date	**Case**	**Significance of Decision**
1803	*Marbury v. Madison*	Asserts principle of judicial review
1810	*Fletcher v. Peck*	Protects property rights through broad reading of Constitution's contract clause
1819	*Dartmouth College v. Woodward*	Safeguards property rights, especially of chartered corporations
1819	*McCulloch v. Maryland*	Interprets Constitution to give broad powers to national government
1824	*Gibbons v. Ogden*	Gives national government jurisdiction over interstate commerce

"dependent on the states," an outcome that "was not intended by the American people" who ratified the Constitution.

The Marshall Court again asserted the dominance of national statutes over state legislation in *Gibbons v. Ogden* (1824). The decision struck down a monopoly that the New York legislature had granted Aaron Ogden for steamboat passenger service across the Hudson River to New Jersey. Asserting that the Constitution gave the federal government the authority to regulate interstate commerce, the chief justice sided with Thomas Gibbons, who held a federal license to transport people and goods between the two states.

Property Rights. Marshall also used the Constitution to uphold Federalist notions of property rights. During the 1790s, Thomas Jefferson and other Republicans had celebrated the primacy of statutes enacted by "the will of THE PEOPLE." In response, Federalist politicians warned that popular sovereignty would lead to "tyranny of the majority" if state legislatures enacted statutes that infringed on the property rights of wealthy citizens, and Federalist judges vowed to void those laws.

Marshall was no exception. He was determined to protect individuals' property from laws passed by the state legislatures, and he invoked the contract clause of the Constitution to do it. The contract clause (in Article 1, Section 10) prohibits the states from passing any law "impairing the obligation of contracts." The delegates at the Philadelphia convention included the clause to prevent state legislation that kept creditors from seizing the lands and goods of debtors. In *Fletcher v. Peck* (1810), Marshall expanded the clause by

broadly defining *contract* to include the grants and charters made by state governments. The case involved a large grant of land made by the Georgia legislature to the Yazoo Land Company. When a new legislature canceled the grant, alleging fraud and bribery, speculators who had already purchased Yazoo lands appealed to the Supreme Court to uphold their titles. Marshall ruled that the legislative grant was a contract that could not subsequently be changed. This far-reaching decision safeguarded vested property rights and, by protecting out-of-state investors, promoted the development of a national capitalist economy.

The Court extended its defense of vested property rights in *Dartmouth College v. Woodward* (1819). Dartmouth College was a private institution established by a charter granted by King George III. In 1816, New Hampshire's Republican legislature enacted a statute that converted the school into a public university. The Dartmouth trustees opposed the legislation and hired Daniel Webster to plead their case. A renowned constitutional lawyer, as well as a leading Federalist, Webster cited the Court's decision in *Fletcher v. Peck* and argued that the royal charter constituted a contract that could not be altered by the state legislature. The Supreme Court agreed and upheld the rights of the college.

The Rise of John Quincy Adams. Even as Marshall incorporated the important Federalist principles of judicial review, the primacy of national law, and corporate property rights into the American legal system, the political elite and the voting citizenry embraced the outlook of the Republican party. The career of John Quincy Adams was a case in point. Although he was the son of President John Adams, a Federalist, John Quincy had joined the Republican Party before the War of 1812. He came to national attention for his role in negotiating the Treaty of Ghent, which ended the war.

Adams then served brilliantly as secretary of state for two terms under President James Monroe (1817–1825). Ignoring traditional Republican antagonism toward Great Britain, in 1817 Adams negotiated the Rush-Bagot Treaty, which limited American and British naval forces on the Great Lakes. The following year, he concluded another agreement with Britain that set the forty-ninth parallel as the border between Canada and the lands of the Louisiana Purchase. In the Adams-Onís Treaty of 1819, the secretary persuaded Spain to cede Florida to the United States (Map 7.6). In return, the American government took responsibility for its citizens' financial claims against Spain, renounced Jefferson's earlier claim that Spanish

Texas was part of the Louisiana Purchase, and agreed on a compromise boundary between New Spain and the state of Louisiana, which had entered the Union in 1812.

Finally, Adams persuaded President Monroe to articulate American national policy with respect to the Western Hemisphere. At Adams's behest, Monroe warned Spain and other European powers in 1823 to keep their hands off the Spanish colonies in Latin America that had fought for and established independent republics. The American continents were not "subject for further colonization," the president declared—a policy that thirty years later became known as the Monroe Doctrine. In return, Monroe pledged that the United States would not "interfere in the internal concerns" of European nations. Thanks to Adams, the United States had asserted diplomatic leadership of the Western Hemisphere and gained international acceptance of its claims to nearly all the lands

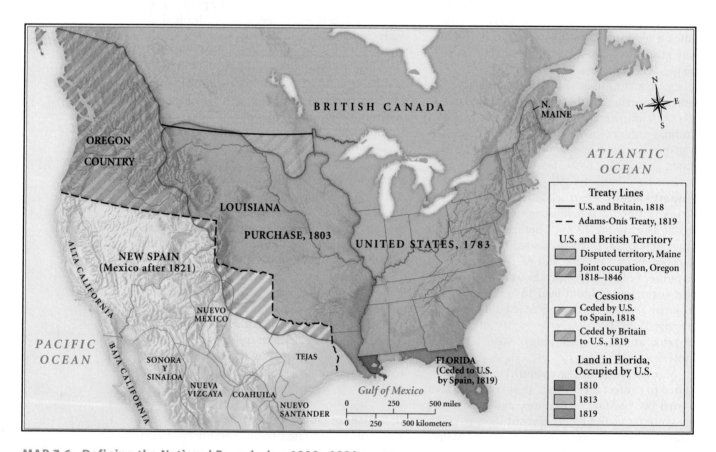

MAP 7.6   Defining the National Boundaries, 1800–1820

After the War of 1812, American diplomats negotiated treaties with Great Britain and Spain that defined the boundaries of the Louisiana Purchase, with British Canada to the north and New Spain (which in 1821 became the independent nation of Mexico) to the south and west. These treaties eliminated the threat of border wars with neighboring states for a generation, giving the United States a much-needed period of peace and security.

The American Eagle Over New Orleans

Jefferson's purchase of Louisiana made New Orleans part of the United States, but many districts in the city retained their French look (note the steeply pitched roofs on the right) and culture for decades. A traveler noted that "the great enmity existing between the Creoles [the French settlers] . . . and the Americans results in fights and Challenges — there are some of both sides in jail. This *View of New Orleans Taken from the Plantation of Marigny* was painted by John L. Boqueto de Woiserie in 1803. Chicago Historical Society.

south of the forty-ninth parallel and east of the Rocky Mountains.

The appearance of a national consensus after two decades of bitter party politics prompted observers to dub James Monroe's presidency the "Era of Good Feeling." The political harmony was real; but it was also transitory. The Republican Party was increasingly divided between the National faction, led by Clay and Adams, and the Jeffersonian faction, soon to be led by Martin Van Buren and Andrew Jackson. The two groups differed sharply over many issues, including federal support for internal improvements like roads and canals. As the aging Jefferson himself complained about the National Republicans, "You see so many of these new republicans main-taining in Congress the rankest doctrines of the old federalists." This division in the ranks of the Republican Party and the disappearance of the Federalists would soon produce a Second Party System, in which new parties — national-minded Whigs and state-focused Democrats — faced off against each other (see Chapter 10). By the early 1820s, one cycle of American politics and economic debate had ended, and another was about to begin.

➤ What were the causes of the War of 1812? Where did Republicans and Federalists stand on declaring and then fighting the war? What regional tensions did the war expose?

➤ How did the decisions of the Supreme Court between 1801 and 1820 affect the nation's understanding of the Constitution? How did they change American society?

SUMMARY

In this chapter, we have traced three interrelated themes: public policy, westward expansion, and party politics. We began by examining the contrasting public policies advocated by Alexander Hamilton and Thomas Jefferson. A Federalist, Hamilton supported a strong national government and created a fiscal infrastructure (the national debt, tariffs, and a national bank) to spur economic development in trade and manufacturing. By contrast, Jefferson wanted to preserve the authority of state governments; and he envisioned an America enriched by farming rather than industry.

The westward movement promoted by Jefferson and his Republican Party changed many aspects of American life. As hundreds of thousands of yeomen farmers, southern planters, and enslaved Africans moved west, they sparked new conflicts with the Indian peoples and transformed the agricultural economy by dramatically increasing the market sale of farm produce. Expansion westward also shaped American diplomacy: The Louisiana Purchase, the War of 1812, and many of the treaties negotiated by John Quincy Adams were a response, at least in part, to the American drive west.

Finally, there was the unexpected rise of the First Party System and its equally unexpected decline. As Hamilton's policies split the political elite, the French Revolution divided Americans into hostile ideological groups. The result was two decades of bitterness over controversial measures — the Federalists' Sedition Act, the Republicans' Embargo Act, and Madison's decision to go to war with Britain. Although the Federalist Party faded away, it left as its enduring legacy Hamilton's financial innovations and John Marshall's constitutional jurisprudence. Tempered by war and political factions, a new generation of Republican leaders would face the task of devising their own vision of America's future. As Chapter 8 will show, mounting regional tensions over a number of issues — most important, the future of slavery — would cloud this vision.

Connections: Economy and Society

Before the American Revolution, both northern and southern colonies had different types of farming economies: one characterized by yeoman families' raising grain; the other, by large planters, who relied on enslaved laborers to grow tobacco and rice for export. After the Revolution, the two economies began to diverge in other ways. As we pointed out in the essay that began Part Two (p. 135):

> Beginning in the 1780s, northern merchants financed a banking system and organized a rural system of manufacturing. . . . Meanwhile, southern planters continued their dependence on enslaved African Americans and began to export a new staple crop — cotton — to markets in the North and in Europe.

In Chapter 8, we will explore the creation of a capitalist commonwealth — an increasingly urban, commercial society — in the North. And we will show how life in this society fostered a democratic republican culture that encouraged social mobility for men and new marriage rules and child-rearing practices. In Chapter 8, we also will probe the nature of the aristocratic republican culture that continued to characterize the slave-based society of the South, and we will examine the Missouri crisis of 1819–1821, the first major conflict between these two increasingly distinct societies.

In the part opening, we also noted that "many yeomen farm families migrated to the West to grow grain." As we will see in Chapter 8, these families were particularly affected by the Second Great Awakening, the religious revival that fundamentally changed American culture.

CHAPTER REVIEW QUESTIONS

➤ Explain the rise and fall of the First Party System. How did the policies pursued by Republican presidents between 1801 and 1825 differ from those implemented by Hamilton and the Federalists during the 1790s? Why did the Federalist agenda fall out of favor? What legacy did the Federalists leave?

➤ What impact did the two great developments of this period — the French Revolution and war in Europe, and westward expansion in the United States — have on each other?

TIMELINE

1783	Treaty of Paris opens access to the west
1784	Iroquois peoples cede lands in New York
1787	Northwest Ordinance
1789	Judiciary Act establishes federal court system Outbreak of French Revolution
1790	Hamilton wins public credit system
1790–1791	Western Confederacy defeats American armies
1791	Bill of Rights ratified Bank of the United States is chartered
1792	Kentucky joins Union; Tennessee follows (1796) French Republic formed
1793	King Louis XVI executed Madison and Jefferson found Republican Party War between Britain and France; Washington's Proclamation of Neutrality
1794	Whiskey Rebellion in western Pennsylvania Battle of Fallen Timbers
1795	Jay's Treaty with Great Britain Pinckney's Treaty with Spain Treaty of Greenville recognizes Indian land rights
1798	XYZ Affair cuts off trade with France Alien, Sedition, and Naturalization Acts Kentucky and Virginia resolutions
1800	Jefferson elected in "Revolution of 1800"
1801	John Marshall heads Supreme Court
1801–1807	Gallatin reduces national debt
1802–1807	France and Britain seize American ships
1803	Louisiana Purchase *Marbury v. Madison* asserts judicial review
1804–1806	Lewis and Clark explore West
1807	Embargo Act cripples American shipping
1808	Madison elected president
1811	Battle of Tippecanoe
1812–1815	War of 1812
1817–1825	Era of Good Feeling
1819	Adams-Onís Treaty *McCulloch v. Maryland* *Dartmouth College v. Woodward*

FOR FURTHER EXPLORATION

In *American Politics in the Early Republic* (1993), James Roger Sharp describes the near disintegration of the new nation. One cause was the Whiskey Rebellion, the subject of a probing study by Thomas P. Slaughter (1986). For the impact of the French Revolution on the Atlantic world, see "Liberty, Equality, Fraternity: Exploring the French Revolution" (**chnm.gmu.edu/revolution/**). Women are the subject of Rosemarie Zagarri, *A Woman's Dilemma: Mercy Otis Warren and the American Revolution* (1995), and Linda Kerber, *No Constitutional Right to Be Ladies: Women and the Obligations of Citizenship* (1999).

Washington's strong leadership is a central theme of William Martin's fictionalized biography, *Citizen Washington* (1999). For a sense of Washington's personality, read his correspondence, available at **www.virginia.edu/gwpapers/**. Abundant material on Thomas Jefferson's life can be accessed online at **www.pbs.org/jefferson**; Jefferson's ideas "On Politics & Government" are available at **etext.virginia.edu/jefferson/quotations**. David McCullough's highly readable biography, *John Adams* (2001), draws material from **www.masshist.org/digitaladams/aea**. For Alexander Hamilton, see Ron Chernow, *Alexander Hamilton* (2004), and **www.alexanderhamilton exhibition.org/**. On the tumultuous election of 1800, see John Ferling, *Adams vs. Jefferson* (2004).

For the explorations of the West, visit **www.pbs.org/lewisandclark** and **www.americanjourneys.org/**. Gregory Evans Dowd, *A Spirited Resistance: The North American Indian Struggle for Unity, 1745–1815* (1992), describes the Indian Resistance, as does the "Chickasaw Historical Research Page" (**home.flash.net/~kma/**). Two fine studies of cultural interactions between native peoples and white Americans are Theda Perdue, *Cherokee Women: Gender and Culture Change, 1700–1835* (1998), and William G. McLoughlin, *Cherokee Renascence in the New Republic* (1986).

Ralph Louis Ketcham's *Presidents Above Party: The First American Presidency, 1789–1829* (1984) probes the political ideology of the early republic; Gore Vidal's *Burr: A Novel* (1973) offers an entertaining narrative of the life of Aaron Burr. See "A Century of Lawmaking for a New Nation" (**memory.loc.gov/ammem/amlaw/lawhome.html**) for the text of congressional documents and debates. The site also contains information about and maps of Indian land cessions between 1784 and 1894. Donald R. Hickey, *The War of 1812: A Forgotten Conflict* (1989), places that struggle in its economic and diplomatic context. Also see "The War of 1812" (**members.tripod.com/~war1812/**).

TEST YOUR KNOWLEDGE

To assess your command of the material in this chapter, see the Online Study Guide at **bedfordstmartins.com/henretta**.

For Web sites, images, and documents related to topics and places in this chapter, visit **bedfordstmartins.com/makehistory**.

8

Creating a Republican Culture

1790–1820

B Y THE 1820S, A SENSE of optimism pervaded white American society. "The temperate zone of North America already exhibits many signs that it is the promised land of civil liberty, and of institutions designed to liberate and exalt the human race," declared a Kentucky judge in a Fourth of July speech. White Americans had good reason to feel fortunate. They lived under a representative republican government, free from arbitrary taxation and the oppression of an established church.

Inspired by their political freedom, these Americans sought to extend republican principles throughout their society. However, they did not agree on what those principles were. For entrepreneurial-minded merchants, farmers, and political leaders, republicanism meant **capitalism**: They wanted to use the power of republican government to solidify capitalist cultural values and create a dynamic market economy. Invoking the assistance of state governments, they advocated mercantilist policies that would assist private businesses to enhance the "common-wealth." Other citizens celebrated republican social values. In the North, they championed a democratic republicanism, an equality in family and social relationships. In the South, where class and race sharply divided society, politicians and political writers devised an aristocratic republicanism that stressed liberty for whites rather than equality for all. Yet

◀ *The Fourth of July in Philadelphia,* **c. 1811**

By the early nineteenth century, the Fourth of July had become a popular holiday celebrating America's republican government. This detail from a painting by John Lewis Krimmel links the new nation to the Greek and Roman republics through architecture (the building and the statue), notes its social diversity (by including blacks as well as whites), and hints at the tenor of its social life. The young man buying an alcoholic drink and flirting with the young mother may well engage in some rowdy behavior before Independence Day is over. Pennsylvania Academy of the Fine Arts, Philadelphia. Pennsylvania Academy Purchase (from the estate of Paul Beck, Jr.).

another vision of American republicanism that attracted adherents in all regions emerged during the Second Great Awakening, the massive religious revival that swept the nation during the first half of the nineteenth century. For the many Americans who embraced this religious vision, the United States was both a great experiment in republican government and the seedbed of a new Christian civilization that would redeem the world — a moral mission that, for better or worse, would inform American diplomacy in the centuries to come.

The Capitalist Commonwealth

"If movement and the quick succession of sensations and ideas constitute life," observed a French visitor to the United States, "here one lives a hundred fold more than elsewhere; here, all is circulation, motion, and boiling agitation." Circulation and motion were especially evident in the Northeast, where republican state legislatures actively promoted banking and commerce. "Experiment follows experiment; enterprise follows enterprise," a European traveler noted, and "riches and poverty follow." Of the two, riches were the more apparent. Beginning around 1800, the per capita income of Americans increased by more than 1 percent a year, more than 30 percent in a single generation.

Banks, Manufacturing, and Markets

America was "a Nation of Merchants," a British visitor reported from Philadelphia in 1798, "keen in the pursuit of wealth in all the various modes of acquiring it." And acquire it they did, exploiting the opportunities to make spectacular profits from the wars (1793-1815) triggered by the French Revolution. Fur trader John Jacob Astor and merchant Robert Oliver became the nation's first millionaires. Oliver began his career working for an Irish linen firm in Baltimore and then started trading on his own in West Indian coffee and sugar. Astor, who migrated from Germany to New York in 1784, became wealthy carrying furs from the Pacific Northwest to markets in China.

Banking and Credit. To finance mercantile enterprises, Americans needed a banking system. Before the Revolution, farmers relied on government-sponsored land banks for loans, while merchants arranged partnerships or obtained credit from

A Cloth Merchant, 1789

Elijah Boardman (1760–1832) was a prosperous storekeeper in New Milford, Connecticut, who eventually became a U.S. senator. Like other American traders, he imported huge quantities of cloth from Britain. When the wars of the 1790s cut off trade, some merchants financed the domestic production of textiles. Others, including Boardman, turned to land speculation. In 1795, he joined the Connecticut Land Company and bought huge tracts in Connecticut's Western Reserve, including the present towns of Medina, Palmyra, and Boardman, Ohio. Ralph Earl painted this portrait in 1789. Elijah Boardman, the Metropolitan Museum of Art, New York, Bequest of Susan W. Tyler, 1979.

British suppliers. To facilitate commercial transactions, Philadelphia merchants persuaded the Confederation Congress to charter the Bank of North America in 1781, and traders in Boston and New York soon founded similar lending institutions. "Our monied capital has so much increased from the Introduction of Banks, & the Circulation of the Funds," Philadelphia merchant William Bingham boasted in 1791, "that the Necessity of Soliciting Credits from England will no longer exist."

That same year, Federalists in Congress chartered the First Bank of the United States. The Bank

The China Trade

Following the Revolution, New England merchants took an active role in the long-standing European trade with China. In this painting by George Chinnery (1774–1852), the American flag flies prominently in front of the warehouse district in Canton. There, merchants exchanged bundles of American furs for cargoes of Chinese silks and porcelain plates, cups, and serving dishes. Bridgeman Art Library Ltd.

issued notes and made commercial loans. Its profits averaged a handsome 8 percent annually; and by 1805, the bank had branches in eight major cities. However, Jeffersonian Republicans opposed the Bank: They claimed it was unconstitutional and potentially oppressive, and that it encouraged "a consolidated, energetic government supported by public creditors, speculators, and other insidious men lacking in public spirit of any kind." When the bank's twenty-year charter expired in 1811, it was not renewed. To fill the gap, merchants, artisans, and farmers petitioned their state legislatures to charter banks. By 1816, when Congress chartered the Second Bank of the United States, there were 246 state-chartered banks with $68 million in banknotes in circulation. But many of these state banks were shady operations that issued notes without adequate specie reserves and made ill-advised loans to insiders.

State banking policies and those of the Second Bank were a factor in the Panic of 1819. But the primary cause of the financial crisis was an abrupt 30 percent drop in world agricultural prices. As their income plummeted, many planters and farmers could not pay their debts to storekeepers, wholesale merchants, and banks, sending those businesses into bankruptcy. By 1821, the state banks that were still solvent had just $45 million in circulation. The panic gave Americans their first taste of a **business cycle,** the periodic expansion and contraction of production and employment that are inherent to a market economy. And it left a legacy of popular hostility to banks that would prove a political force in the coming decades.

Rural Manufacturing. The Panic of 1819 also revealed that artisans and yeomen as well as

The Yankee Peddler, c. 1830

Even in 1830, most Americans lived too far from a market town to go there regularly to buy goods. Instead, they purchased their tinware, clocks, textiles, and other manufactures from peddlers, often from New England, who traveled far and wide in small horse-drawn vans like the one pictured in the doorway. Courtesy IBM Corporation, Armonk, New York.

merchants now depended for their prosperity on the market economy. Before 1800, most artisans in New England worked part-time and sold their handicrafts locally. In central Massachusetts, a French traveler found many houses "inhabited by men who are both cultivators and artisans; one is a tanner, another a shoemaker, another sells goods, but all are farmers." In the Middle Atlantic region, artisans bartered products with neighbors. Clock-maker John Hoff of Lancaster, Pennsylvania, exchanged his fine, wooden-cased instruments for a dining table, a bedstead, and labor on his small farm. By 1820, many artisans — shipbuilders in seacoast towns, ironworkers in Pennsylvania and Maryland, and shoemakers in Massachusetts — had expanded their reach and were selling their products in regional and national markets.

By 1800, American entrepreneurs had developed a rural manufacturing network similar to the European outwork system (see Chapter 1). Enterprising merchants bought raw materials, hired workers

in farm families to process them, and sold the finished manufactures in regional or national markets. "Straw hats and Bonnets are manufactured by many families," an official in Maine noted in the 1810s, while another observer estimated that "probably 8,000 females" in the vicinity of Foxborough, Massachusetts, braided rye straw into hats for market sale. Merchants shipped these products — shoes, brooms, palm-leaf hats, and cups, baking pans, and other tin utensils — to seaport cities, and New England peddlers, equipped "with a horse and a cart covered with a box or with a wagon," carried them to the rural South, where they earned the dubious reputation of being crafty, hard-bargaining Yankees.

This expansion of household production and the market economy reflected innovations in the organization of production and in marketing rather than in technology. American manufacturers only gradually adopted water-powered machines, the technology that triggered the Industrial Revolution in Britain. As early as the 1780s, merchants in New England and the Middle Atlantic states built small mills with water-powered machines that carded and combed wool — and later cotton — into long strands. But until the 1820s, they used the household-based outwork system for the next steps in the textile manufacturing process: They paid women and children on farms to spin the strands into thread and yarn on foot-driven spinning wheels, and men in other households to use foot-powered looms to weave the yarn into cloth. In his "Letter on Manufactures" (1810), Secretary of the Treasury Albert Gallatin estimated that there were 2,500 outwork weavers in New England. A decade later, more than 12,000 household workers were weaving woolen cloth, which was then pounded flat and given a smooth finish in water-powered fulling mills. Even before production was centralized in factories, then, America had a profitable and expanding system of textile manufacturing in the Northeast (see Chapter 9).

The penetration of the market economy into rural areas offered new opportunities — and new risks — to farmers. Ambitious farm families switched from growing crops for subsistence to raising livestock for sale. They sold meat, butter, and cheese to city markets and cattle hides to the booming shoe industry. "Along the whole road from Boston, we saw women engaged in making cheese," a Polish traveler reported from central Massachusetts. Other farm families raised sheep and sold raw wool to textile manufacturers. Processing these raw materials brought new businesses to many farming towns. In 1792, Concord, Massachusetts, had one slaughterhouse and five small tanneries; a decade later, the town boasted eleven slaughterhouses and six large tanneries.

The Environmental Impact of Early Industry. As the rural economy churned out more goods, it significantly altered the environment. Foul odors from stockyards and tanning pits wafted over Concord and many other leather-producing towns. In addition, tanners, who used hemlock bark to process hides into leather, cut down thousands of acres of trees each year. The multiplication of livestock — dairy cows, cattle, and especially sheep — brought the destruction of even more trees, felled to create vast pastures and meadows. By the mid-nineteenth century, most of the forests in southern New England and eastern New York were gone: "The hills had been stripped of their timber," New York's *Catskill Messenger* noted, "so as to present their huge, rocky projections." Scores of textile milldams dotted New England's rivers, altering

their flow and making it difficult for fish to reach their upriver spawning grounds. Even as the income of many farmers rose, the quality of their natural environment deteriorated.

The new capitalist-run market economy had other drawbacks, too. Rural parents and their children worked longer and harder, making yarn, hats, and brooms during the winter and then doing their regular farming chores during the warmer seasons. More important, these farm families lost a measure of their economic independence as they toiled as part-time wage earners and bought the textiles, shoes, and hats they had once made for themselves. At the same time the new market economy was making families and communities more productive and prosperous, it was reducing their self-sufficiency.

Transportation Bottlenecks and Government Initiatives

America's very size threatened to stifle its economic growth. Water transport was the quickest and cheapest way to get goods to market, but most new settlements were not near navigable streams. Consequently, improved overland trade became a high priority for the new state governments. Between 1793 and 1812, the Massachusetts legislature granted charters to more than one hundred private turnpike companies. These charters gave the companies special legal status and often included monopoly rights to a transportation route. Pennsylvania issued fifty-five charters, including one to the Lancaster Turnpike Company. The company quickly built a graded gravel road between Lancaster and Philadelphia, a distance of 65 miles. The venture was expensive — investors saw only modest profits — but it gave an enormous boost to the regional economy. "The turnpike is finished," a farm woman noted, "and we can now go to town at all times and in all weather." A boom in turnpike construction soon connected dozens of inland market centers to seaport cities.

Meanwhile, state governments and private entrepreneurs improved water transport by dredging rivers to make them navigable and by constructing canals to bypass waterfalls or rapids. But there was no water route through the Appalachian Mountains until the 1820s, when New York built the Erie Canal to connect the state's central and western counties to the Hudson River (see Chapter 9). Until then, settlers in Kentucky, Tennessee, and the southern regions of Ohio, Indiana, and Illinois paid premium prices for land near the tributaries of the great Ohio and Mississippi

View of Cincinnati, **by John Casper Wild, c. 1835**
Thanks to its location on the Ohio River, Cincinnati quickly became one of the major processing centers for grain and hogs in the trans-Appalachian west. By the 1820s, passenger steamboats and freight barges connected the city with Pittsburgh to the north and the ocean port of New Orleans far to the south. Museum of Fine Arts, Boston.

rivers, and speculators bought up property in the cities along their banks: Cincinnati, Louisville, Chattanooga, and St. Louis. Farmers and merchants built barges to carry cotton, surplus grain, and meat downstream to New Orleans, which by 1815 was handling about $5 million in agricultural products yearly.

Public Policy: The Commonwealth System

Legislative support for road and canal companies was part of a broad system of state mercantilism known as the Commonwealth system. Just as the British Parliament had enacted the Navigation Acts to spur trade and manufacturing, so the American state legislatures passed measures they

thought would be "of great public utility" and increase the "common wealth." These laws generally took the form of special charters to corporate enterprises, and often included grants of limited liability, which made it easier to attract investors: If a business failed, the shareholders' personal assets could not be seized to pay the corporation's debts. And most transportation charters included the valuable power of eminent domain, which allowed turnpike, bridge, and canal corporations to force the sale of privately owned land along their routes. State legislatures also aided capitalist flour millers and textile manufacturers, who often had to flood adjacent farmland when they constructed dams to power their water-driven machinery. In Massachusetts, the Mill Dam Act of 1795 deprived farmers of their traditional right under common law to stop the flooding and forced them to accept "fair compensation" for their lost acreage.

Critics condemned these grants of special rights to private enterprises as violations of republican principles. The award of "peculiar privileges" to corporations, they argued, not only violated the "equal rights" of all citizens but also restricted the sovereignty of the people. As a Pennsylvanian put it, "Whatever power is given to a corporation, is just so much power taken from the State" and its citizens. Nonetheless, judges in state courts, following the lead of John Marshall's Supreme Court (see Chapter 7), consistently upheld corporate charters and routinely approved grants of eminent domain to private transportation corporations. "The opening of good and easy internal communications is one of the highest duties of government," declared a New Jersey judge.

State mercantilism soon encompassed much more than transportation. Following Jefferson's embargo of 1807, which cut off goods and credit from Europe, the New England states awarded charters to two hundred iron-mining, textile-manufacturing, and banking companies, and Pennsylvania granted more than eleven hundred. By 1820, innovative state governments had created a republican political economy: a Commonwealth system that funneled state aid to private businesses whose projects would improve the general welfare.

➤ How did the development of a market economy change the lives of artisans and farm families?

➤ What challenges did the promoters of the Commonwealth system face? How did they use government at state and national levels to promote economic growth and the market economy?

➤ Why did many Americans believe that the grant of special privileges and charters to private businesses was in conflict with republican principles?

Toward a Democratic Republican Culture

After independence, many Americans in the northern states embraced a democratic republicanism that celebrated political equality and social mobility, at least for white males. These citizens, primarily members of the emerging **middle class**, also redefined the nature of the family and of education by seeking more egalitarian marriages and more affectionate ways of rearing and educating their children.

Social and Political Equality for White Men

Between 1780 and 1820, hundreds of well-educated Europeans visited the United States and agreed, almost unanimously, that the American republic embodied a genuinely new social order. In his famous *Letters from an American Farmer* (1782), French-born essayist J. Hector St. Jean de Crèvecoeur wrote that European society was composed "of great lords who possess everything, and of a herd of people who have nothing." America, by contrast, had "no aristocratical families, no courts, no kings, no bishops."

The absence of a hereditary aristocracy encouraged Americans to condemn inherited social privilege and to extol the republican principle of legal equality for all free men. "The law is the same for everyone both as it protects and as it punishes," noted one European traveler. Yet Americans willingly accepted social divisions that reflected personal achievement. As individuals used their "talents, integrity, and virtue" to amass wealth, their social standing rose—a phenomenon that astounded some Europeans. "In Europe to say of someone that he rose from nothing is a disgrace and a reproach," remarked an aristocratic Polish visitor. "It is the opposite here. To be the architect of your own fortune is honorable. It is the highest recommendation."

Some Americans from long-distinguished families questioned the morality of a system of status based on financial success. "The aristocracy of Kingston [New York] is more one of money than any village I have ever seen," complained Nathaniel Booth, whose family had once ruled the small port town along the Hudson River. "Man is estimated by dollars," he lamented; "what he is worth determines his character and his position." However, for most white men, such a merit-based system meant the opportunity to better themselves.

Cultural rules—and new laws—continued to deny that opportunity to most women and African American men. As the republican doctrine of equality gained acceptance, it raised the prospect of voting rights for all citizens (see Map 8.1). To limit those rights to white men, legislators explicitly wrote race or gender restrictions into the law. In 1802, Ohio disfranchised African Americans, and the New York constitution of 1821 required blacks (but not whites) to meet a property-holding requirement to vote. The most striking case of explicit racial and sexual discrimination occurred in

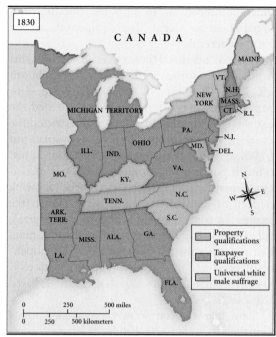

MAP 8.1 The Expansion of Voting Rights for White Men, 1800 and 1830

Between 1800 and 1830, the United States moved steadily toward political equality for white men. Many existing states revised their constitutions and replaced a property qualification for voting with a less-restrictive criterion (the voter must pay taxes or have served in the militia). Some new states in the West extended the suffrage for all adult white men. As parties sought votes from a broader electorate, the tone of politics became more open and competitive — swayed by the interests and values of ordinary people.

New Jersey, where the state constitution of 1776 had granted **suffrage** to all property holders. After 1800, as Federalists and Republicans competed for votes, they challenged political custom by encouraging voting by property-owning single women and widows. Sensing a threat to the male-centered political world, in 1807 the New Jersey legislature limited voting rights to white men only. To justify the exclusion of women, legislators invoked both biology and custom. As one letter to a newspaper put it, "Women, generally, are neither by nature, nor habit, nor education, nor by their necessary condition in society fitted to perform this duty with credit to themselves or advantage to the public."

Toward a Republican System of Marriage

The controversy over women's political rights mirrored a debate over authority within the household. British and American husbands had long dominated their wives and controlled their family's property. But as John Adams lamented in 1776, the republican doctrine of political equality had "spread where it was not intended," encouraging some white women to speak out on public matters and to demand control of their finances. These women insisted that their subordinate social position was at odds with the republican ideology of equal natural rights. Patriarchy was not a "natural" rule but a social contrivance, argued Patriot author and historian Mercy Otis Warren; placing men at the head of households was justified only "for the sake of order in families."

Economic and cultural changes also eroded customary paternal authority over children and their marriages. In colonial America, most property-owning parents had arranged their children's marriages. To ensure the welfare of the entire family, they tended to place the highest priority on the personal character and financial resources of a prospective son- or daughter-in-law; the physical attraction between the young people and their emotional compatibility were secondary considerations. However, as land holdings shrank in long-settled rural communities, many yeomen fathers could no longer leave substantial farms to their children and so could no longer select their spouses. Young men and women began to choose their own partners, influenced by a new cultural attitude, **sentimentalism**.

The Wedding, **1805**

Bride and groom stare intently into each other's eyes as they exchange vows, suggesting that their union was a love match, not a marriage based on economic calculation. Given the plain costumes of the guests and the sparse furnishings of the room, the unknown artist may have provided us with a picture of a rural Quaker wedding. Philadelphia Museum of the Fine Arts.

The Effects of Sentimentalism. Sentimentalism originated in Europe as part of the Romantic movement of the late eighteenth century; it came to America in the early nineteenth century and spread quickly through all classes of society. Rejecting the Enlightenment's emphasis on rational thought, sentimentalism celebrated the importance of "feeling" — a physical, sensuous appreciation of God, nature, and other human beings. This new sensibility dripped from the pages of German and English literary works, fell from the lips of actors in popular melodramas, and infused the emotional rhetoric of revivalist preachers.

As the hot sentimental passions of the heart overwhelmed the cool rational logic of the mind, a new marriage system appeared. Around 1800, magazines began to encourage marriages "contracted from motives of affection, rather than of interest," and many young people looked for a spouse who was, as Eliza Southgate of Maine put it, "calculated to promote my happiness." As young people fell in love and married, many fathers saw their roles change

from authoritarian patriarchs to watchful paternalists, from dictating their children's behavior to protecting them from the consequences of their behavior. To guard against a free-spending son-in-law, for example, a wealthy father might place his daughter's inheritance in a legal trust, where her husband could not get at it. Wrote one Virginia planter to his lawyer: "I rely on you to see the property settlement properly drawn before the marriage, for I by no means consent that Polly shall be left to the Vicissitudes of Life."

As voluntary agreements between individuals, love-marriages conformed more closely to republican principles than did arranged matches. And, in theory, **companionate marriages** gave wives "true equality, both of rank and fortune" with their husbands, as one Boston man suggested. In practice, though, husbands continued to dominate most marriages, both because male authority was deeply ingrained in cultural mores and because husbands controlled the family's property under English and American common law. Moreover, the new love-based marriage system discouraged parents

The Trials of Married Life

As the text explains, the ideal American marriage of the early nineteenth century was republican (a contract between equals) and romantic (a match in which mutual love was foremost). Were these ideals attainable, given the social authority of men and the volatility of human passions? These selections from a variety of American women offer insights into the new system of marriage. Letters, memoirs, and diaries are excellent sources for understanding historical change at the personal level. They provide a window through which we can see changes in cultural values intersecting with individual lives.

EMMA HART WILLARD
The Danger of High Expectations

Born in Connecticut in 1787, Emma Hart married John Willard in 1809. An early proponent of advanced education for women, she founded Female Seminaries in Middlebury, Vermont, in 1814 and in Troy, New York, in 1821. She wrote this letter to her sister, Almira Hart, in 1815.

You think it strange that I should consider a period of happiness as more likely than any other to produce future misery. I know I did not sufficiently explain myself. Those tender and delicious sensations which accompany successful love, while they soothe and soften the mind, diminish its strength to bear or to conquer difficulties. It is the luxury of the soul; and luxury always enervates. . . . This life is a life of vicissitude. . . .

[Suppose] you are secured to each other for life. It will be natural that, at first, he should be much devoted to you; but, after a while, his business must occupy his attention. While absorbed in that he will perhaps neglect some of those little tokens of affection which have become necessary to your happiness. His affairs will sometimes go wrong, . . . and he may sometimes hastily give you a harsh word or a frown.

But where is the use, say you, of diminishing my present enjoyment by such gloomy apprehensions? Its use is this, that, if you enter the marriage state believing such things to be absolutely impossible, if you should meet them, they would come upon you with double force.

CAROLINE HOWARD GILMAN
Female Submission in Marriage

Caroline Howard was born in Boston in 1794 and moved to Charleston, South Carolina, with her husband, Samuel Gilman, a Unitarian minister. A novelist, she published Recollections of a Housekeeper *(1835), a portrait of domestic life in New England, and* Recollections of a Southern Matron *(1838), from which this selection is taken.*

The planter's bride, who leaves a numerous and cheerful family in her paternal home, little imagines the change which awaits her in her own retired residence. She dreams of an independent sway over her household, devoted love and unbroken intercourse with her husband, and indeed longs to be released from the eyes of others, that she may dwell only beneath the sunbeam of his. And so it was with me. . . .

There we were together, asking for nothing but each other's presence and love. At length it was necessary for him to tear himself away to superintend his interests. . . . But the period of absence was gradually protracted; then a friend sometimes came home with him, and their talk was of crops and politics, draining the fields and draining the revenue. . . . A growing discomfort began to work upon my mind. I had undefined forebodings; I mused about past days; my views of life became slowly disorganized; my physical powers enfeebled; a nervous excitement followed: I nursed a moody discontent. . . .

If the reign of romance was really waning, I resolved not to chill his noble confidence, but to make a steadier light rise on his affections. . . . This task of self-government was not easy. To repress a harsh answer, to confess a fault . . . in gentle submission, sometimes requires a struggle like life and death; but these . . . efforts are the golden threads with which domestic happiness is woven. . . . How clear is it, then, that woman loses by petulance and recrimination! Her first study must be self-control, almost to hypocrisy. A good wife must smile amid a thousand perplexities.

MARTHA HUNTER HITCHCOCK

Isolation, Unmentionable Sorrows, and Suffering

Martha Hunter Hitchcock married a doctor in the U.S. Army. These letters to her cousins Martha and Sarah Hunter describe her emotional dependence on her husband and her unhappy life. The letters are in the collection of the Virginia Historical Society.

To Martha Hunter, 1840:

If I had never married how much of pain, and dissatisfaction, should I have escaped — at all events I should never have known what jealousy is. You must not betray me, dear cousin, for despite all my good resolutions, I find it impossible always to struggle against my nature — the school of indulgence, in which I was educated, was little calculated to teach me, those lessons of forbearance, which I have had to practice so frequently, since my marriage — it is ungrateful in me to murmur, if perchance a little bitter is mingled in my cup of life.

To Sarah Hunter, 1841:

I have lived so long among strangers since my marriage, that when I contrast it with the old warm affection, in which I was nurtured, the contrast is so tremble, that I cannot refrain from weeping at the thought of it — I hope my dear cousin, that yours, will be a happier destiny than mine, in that respect — only think of it! Nearly a year and a half have passed away, since I have seen, a single relation!

To Martha Hunter, 1845:

Uneasiness about [my daughter] Lillie, and very great sorrows of my own, which I cannot commit to paper, have almost weighed me down to the grave; and indeed, without any affectation, I look forward to that, as the only real rest, I shall ever know.

To Martha Hunter, 1846:

Lillie had the scarlet fever, during our visit to Alabama, and she has never recovered from the effects of it — My life is a constant vigil — and there is nothing which wearies mind, and body, so much, as watching a sickly child. . . . All this I have to endure, and may have to suffer more for I know not, what Fate may have in store for me.

ELIZABETH SCOTT NEBLETT

"My Seasons of Gloom and Despondency"

Elizabeth Scott Neblett lived with her husband and children in Navarro County, Texas. In 1860, she reflected on eight years of marriage in her diary.

It has now been almost eight years since I became a married woman. Eight years of checkered good and ill, and yet thro' all it seems the most of the ill has fallen to my lot, until now my poor weak cowardly heart sighs only for its final resting place, where sorrow grief nor pain can never reach it more.

I feel that I have faithfully discharged my duty towards you and my children, but for this I know that I deserve no credit nor aspire to none; my affection has been my prompter, and the task has proven a labor of love. You have not rightly understood me at all times, and being naturally very hopeful you could in no measure sympathize with me during my seasons of gloom and despondency. . . . But marriage is a lottery and that your draw proved an unfortunate one on your part is not less a subject of regret with me than you. . . .

It is useless to say that during these eight years I have suffered ten times more than you have and ten times more than I can begin to make you conceive of, but of course you can not help the past, nor by knowing my suffering relieve it, but it might induce you to look with more kindness upon [my] faults. . . . The 17th of this month I was 27 years old and I think my face looks older than that, perhaps I'll never see an other birth day and I don't grieve at the idea.

SOURCE: All of the selections are abridged versions of materials in Anya Jabour, ed., *Major Problems in the History of American Families and Children* (Boston: Houghton Mifflin, 2005), 108–113.

ANALYZING THE EVIDENCE

➤ What problems do these women share? How might their problems be related to larger social and economic changes in the nineteenth century?

➤ Was Emma Willard correct? Did the emotional problems experienced by these women stem, at least in part, from their overly optimistic expectations of love-based marriage? Or was something else the cause of their unhappiness?

➤ What was Caroline Gilman's advice to wives? Did the other women follow her advice?

➤ Do these selections prove that most American women had unfulfilled marriages? Or were these isolated cases? Would you expect to find more records of unhappy marriages than happy ones?

from protecting the interests of young wives, and governments refused to prevent domestic tyranny. Women who would rather "starve than submit" to the orders of their husbands, a lawyer noted, were left to their fate. The marriage contract "is so much more important in its consequences to females than to males," a young man at the Litchfield Law School in Connecticut astutely observed in 1820, "for besides leaving everything else to unite themselves to one man, they subject themselves to his authority. He is their all—their only relative—their only hope" (see Comparing American Voices, "The Trials of Married Life," pp. 246–247).

Young adults who chose partners unwisely were severely disappointed when their spouses failed as providers or faithful companions. Divorces were very difficult to obtain and, before 1800, were only granted in cases of neglect, abandonment, or adultery—serious offenses against the moral order of society. After 1800, most divorce petitions cited emotional grounds. One woman complained that her husband had "ceased to cherish her," while a man grieved that his wife had "almost broke his heart." In response to changes in cultural values, several states expanded the legal grounds for divorce to include drunkenness and personal cruelty.

Republican Motherhood

Traditionally, most American women spent their time on family duties: working in the home or on the farm and bearing and nurturing children. But by the 1790s, the birthrate in the northern seaboard states was dropping dramatically. In the farming village of Sturbridge in central Massachusetts, women who had married before 1750 gave birth, on average, to eight or nine children; in contrast, women who married around 1810 had an average of six children. In the growing seaport cities, native-born white women bore an average of only four children.

The United States was one of the first countries in the world to experience a sharp decline in birthrate—what historians call a demographic transition. There were several causes. Beginning in the 1790s, thousands of young men migrated to the trans-Appalachian west; their departure left some women without partners for life and delayed marriage for many more. Women who married later in life had fewer children. In addition, thousands of white couples in the increasingly urban middling classes deliberately limited the size of their families. Fathers favored smaller families so that they could provide their children with an adequate inheritance;

and mothers, influenced by new ideas of individualism and self-achievement, refused to spend all of their active years bearing and rearing children. After having four or five children, these couples used birth control or abstained from sexual intercourse.

Women's lives changed as well because of new currents in Christian social thought. Traditionally, most religious writers had argued that women were morally inferior to men, that they were dangerous sexual temptresses or witches. By 1800, Protestant ministers were blaming men for sexual and social misconduct and claiming that modesty and purity were inherent in women's nature. Soon political leaders were echoing that thinking, calling on women to become dedicated "republican wives" and "republican mothers" to shape the character of American men. In his *Thoughts on Female Education* (1787), Philadelphia physician Benjamin Rush argued that a young woman should receive intellectual training so that she would be "an agreeable companion for a sensible man" and ensure "his perseverance in the paths of rectitude." Rush also called for loyal "republican mothers" who would instruct "their sons in the principles of liberty and government."

Christian ministers readily embraced the idea of **republican motherhood.** "Preserving virtue and instructing the young are not the fancied, but the real 'Rights of Women,'" Reverend Thomas Bernard told the Female Charitable Society of Salem, Massachusetts. He urged his audience to dismiss the public roles for women—for example, voting and holding office—that English feminist Mary Wollstonecraft had advocated in *A Vindication of the Rights of Woman* (1792). Instead, women should care for their children, a responsibility that gave them "an extensive power over the fortunes of man in every generation." A few religious leaders expanded Bernard's argument and suggested a different public role for women as purveyors of republican ethics. "Give me a host of educated pious mothers and sisters and I will revolutionize a country, in moral and religious taste," declared South Carolina minister Thomas Grimké.

Raising and Educating Republican Children

Republican values also altered assumptions about inheritance and child rearing. Under English common law, property owned by a father who died without a will passed to his eldest son, a practice known as primogeniture (see Chapter 1).

After the Revolution, most state legislatures enacted statutes that required that such estates be divided equally among all the offspring. Most American parents applauded these statutes because they had already begun to treat their children equally.

Encouraging Independence. Many European visitors believed that republican parents gave their children too much freedom. Because of the "general ideas of Liberty and Equality engraved on their hearts," suggested a Polish aristocrat who traveled around the United States in 1800, American children had "scant respect" for their parents. Several decades later, a British traveler stood dumbfounded as an American father excused his son's "resolute disobedience" with a smile and the remark "A sturdy republican, sir." The traveler guessed that American parents encouraged their children to be independent to help the young people "go their own way" in the world.

Permissive child rearing was not universal. Foreign visitors interacted primarily with well-to-do Americans, who were mostly members of Episcopal or Presbyterian churches. These parents often followed the teachings of rationalist religious writers influenced by John Locke and other Enlightenment thinkers. According to these authors, children were "rational creatures" who should be encouraged to act appropriately by means of advice and praise. The parents' role was to develop their child's conscience and self-discipline so that the child would be able to control his or her own behavior and act responsibly. This rationalist method of child rearing was widely adopted by families in the rapidly expanding middle class.

By contrast, many yeomen and tenant farmers, influenced by the Second Great Awakening, raised their children with authoritarian methods. Evangelical Baptist and Methodist writers insisted that children were "full of the stains and pollution of sin" and needed strict rules and harsh discipline. Fear was a "useful and necessary principle in family government," John Abbott, a minister, advised parents; a child "should submit to your authority, not to your arguments or persuasions." Abbott told parents to instill humility in children and to teach them to subordinate their personal desires to God's will (see Reading American Pictures, "Changing Middle-Class Families: Assessing the Visual Record," p. 250).

Expanding Education. The values transmitted within families were crucial because most education still took place within the household. In New England, locally funded public schools provided most boys and some girls with basic instruction in reading and writing. However, there were few publicly funded schools in other regions: About 25 percent of the boys and perhaps 10 percent of the girls attended private institutions or had personal tutors. Even in New England, only a small percentage of young men and almost no young women went on to grammar school (high school today). And only 1 percent of men attended college.

In the 1790s, Bostonian Caleb Bingham, an influential textbook author, called for "an equal distribution of knowledge to make us emphatically a 'republic of letters.'" Both Thomas Jefferson and Benjamin Rush proposed an ambitious scheme for a comprehensive system of primary and secondary schooling, followed by college for bright young men. They also advocated the establishment of a

The Battle over Education

The artist is poking fun at a tyrannical schoolmaster and, indirectly, at the evangelicals' strict approach to child rearing. The students' faces reflect the artist's own rationalist outlook. One minister who had been influenced by the Enlightenment suggested that we see in young children's eyes "the first dawn of reason, beaming forth its immortal rays." Copyright The Frick Collection, New York City.

Changing Middle-Class Families: Assessing the Visual Record

Throughout the text, we have discussed and analyzed American families—yeoman families, black slave families, and now republican families. These images allow us to compare two families of similar status—a middle-class eighteenth-century family typical of the colonial era, the Cheneys (top), with a nineteenth-century family, the Caverlys (bottom). Because families are the basic social unit in all societies, comparing paintings of family scenes helps us see change over time and understand how change in daily lives and relationships alters the nature of society.

The Cheneys, c. 1795. National Gallery of Art, Washington, Gift of Edgar William and Bernice Chrysler Garbisch.

ANALYZING THE EVIDENCE

➤ Count the number of children in each painting and look closely at their mothers. Given the decline in birthrates discussed in the text, how many more children is Mrs. Caverly likely to bear? Why?

➤ How are the children posed in each painting? What do their poses reveal about how adults thought of children? In the paintings, is there evidence of change in that thinking from the colonial era to the nineteenth century?

➤ Mrs. Caverly is depicted with a Bible, and her husband is reading a newspaper. What do these clues suggest about the roles of women and men in the 1830s? From your reading of the text, how does this symbolism reflect important social and cultural changes at the time?

➤ Whom do you see first when you look at the painting of the Cheneys? Is there a similar visual center in the image of the Caverlys? Notice the differences in the physical settings and in the placement of the family members. Compare the two backgrounds: Why is one plain and gray, and the other decorated and filled with objects? What do the differences tell you about the changing values of the American middle class?

The Caverlys, 1836. New York State Historical Society, Cooperstown.

Women's Education

Even in education-conscious New England, few girls attended free public primary schools for more than a few years. After 1800, as this scene from *A Seminary for Young Ladies* (c. 1810–1820) indicates, some girls stayed in school into their teenage years and studied a wide variety of subjects, including geography. Many graduates of these female academies became teachers, a new field of employment for women. St. Louis Art Museum.

university in which distinguished scholars would lecture on law, medicine, theology, and political economy.

To ordinary citizens, talk of secondary and college education smacked of elitism. Farmers, artisans, and laborers wanted elementary schools that would instruct their children in the "three Rs": reading, 'riting, and 'rithmetic. Because their teenage children had to work, they generally refused to fund secondary schools or colleges. "Let anybody show what advantage the poor man receives from colleges," an anonymous "Old Soldier" wrote to the *Maryland Gazette*. "Why should they support them, unless it is to serve those who are in affluent circumstances, whose children can be spared from labor, and receive the benefits?"

Although many state constitutions encouraged legislatures to support education, few legislatures acted until the 1820s, when a new generation of reformers, primarily merchants and manufacturers, successfully campaigned to raise educational standards by certifying qualified teachers and appointing statewide superintendents of schools. To encourage self-discipline and individual enterprise in students, the reformers chose textbooks like *The Life of George Washington* (c. 1800) — an account embellished by the author, Parson Mason Weems, to praise honesty and hard work and to condemn gambling, drinking, and laziness. Believing that patriotic instruction would foster shared cultural ideals, they also required the study of American history. Thomas Low recalled his days as a New Hampshire schoolboy: "We were taught every day and in every way that ours was the freest, the happiest, and soon to be the greatest and most powerful country of the world."

Promoting Cultural Independence. Writer Noah Webster believed education should develop the American intellect. Asserting that "America must be as independent in *literature* as she is in politics," he called on his fellow citizens to detach themselves "from the dependence on foreign opinions and manners, which is fatal to the efforts of genius in this country." Webster's *Dissertation on the English Language* (1789) helpfully defined words according to American usage. It less successfully proposed that words be spelled as they were pronounced, that *labour* (British spelling), for example, be spelled *labur*. Still, Webster's famous "blueback speller," a compact textbook first published in 1783, sold 60 million copies over the next half-century and helped give Americans of all backgrounds a common vocabulary and grammar. "None of us was 'lowed to see a book," an enslaved African American recalled, "but we gits hold of that Webster's old blue-back speller and we . . . studies [it]."

Despite Webster's efforts, a republican literary culture was slow to develop. Ironically, the most accomplished and successful writer in the new republic was Washington Irving, an elitist-minded Federalist. His essays and histories, including *Salmagundi* (1807) and *Dietrich Knickerbocker's History of New York* (1809), which told the tales of "Rip Van Winkle" and "The Legend of Sleepy Hollow," sold well in America and won praise abroad. Impatient with the slow pace of American literary development, Irving lived for seventeen years in Europe, where he reveled in its aristocratic culture and intense intellectual life.

Apart from Irving, no American author was well known in Europe or, indeed, in the United States. "Literature is not yet a distinct profession with us," Thomas Jefferson told an English friend. "Now and then a strong mind arises, and at its intervals from business emits a flash of light. But the first object of young societies is bread and covering." Not until the 1830s and 1840s would American authors achieve a professional identity and, in the works of Ralph Waldo Emerson and novelists of the **American Renaissance,** make a significant contribution to the great literature of Western society (see Chapter 11).

➤ In what ways did American culture become more democratic in the early nineteenth century? How did the social and political status of women and African Americans change in relation to the status of white males?

➤ How did republican ideas shape marital relations and expectations?

➤ How did the nature of fathering change in the period? Why did it change?

Aristocratic Republicanism and Slavery

Republicanism in the South differed significantly from that in the North. Enslaved Africans constituted one-third of the South's population and exposed an enormous contradiction in white Americans' ideology of freedom and equality. "How is it that we hear the loudest yelps for liberty among the drivers of Negroes?" British author Samuel Johnson had chided the American rebels in 1775, a point some Patriots took to heart. "I wish most sincerely there was not a Slave in the province," Abigail Adams confessed to her husband, John. "It always appeared a most iniquitous Scheme to me — to fight ourselves for what we are daily robbing and plundering from those who have as good a right to freedom as we have."

The Revolution and Slavery, 1776–1800

In fact, the whites' struggle for independence raised the prospect of freedom for blacks. As the war began, a black preacher in Georgia told his fellow slaves that King George III "came up with the Book [the Bible], and was about to alter the World, and set the Negroes free." Similar rumors, probably prompted by Governor Dunmore's proclamation of 1775 (see Chapter 5), circulated among slaves in Virginia and the Carolinas and prompted thousands of African Americans to flee behind British lines. Two neighbors of Richard Henry Lee, the

Symbols of Slavery — and Freedom

The scar on the forehead of this black woman, who was widely known as "Mumbet," underlined the cruelty of slavery. Winning emancipation through a legal suit in Massachusetts, she chose a name befitting her new status: Elizabeth Freeman. This watercolor, by Susan Sedgwick, was painted in 1811. Massachusetts Historical Society, Boston.

Virginia Patriot, lost "every slave they had in the world," as did many other planters. In 1781, when the British army evacuated Charleston, more than six thousand former slaves went with them; another four thousand left from Savannah. All told, thirty thousand blacks may have fled their owners. Hundreds of freed black Loyalists settled permanently in Canada. More than a thousand others, poorly treated by British officials in Nova Scotia, sought a better life in Sierra Leone, West Africa, a settlement established by English antislavery organizations.

Yet thousands of African Americans supported the Patriot cause. Eager to raise their social status, free blacks in New England volunteered for military service in the First Rhode Island Company and the Massachusetts "Bucks." In Maryland, a significant number of slaves took up arms for the rebels in return for the promise of freedom. Slaves in Virginia struck informal bargains with their Patriot masters, trading loyalty in wartime for the promise of liberty. In 1782, the Virginia assembly passed a **manumission** act, which allowed individual owners to free their slaves; and within a decade, planters had released ten thousand slaves.

Quakers took the lead in condemning slavery. Beginning in the 1750s, Quaker evangelist John

Woolman urged Friends to free their slaves, and, during the war, many did so. Rapidly growing evangelical Christian churches, notably the Methodists and the Baptists, also advocated emancipation and admitted both enslaved and free blacks to their congregations. In 1784, a conference of Virginia Methodists declared that slavery was "contrary to the Golden Law of God on which hang all the Law and Prophets."

Enlightenment philosophy also undermined the widespread belief among whites that Africans were inherently inferior to Europeans. John Locke had argued that ideas were not innate, that they stemmed from a person's experiences in the world. Accordingly, Enlightenment thinkers suggested that the oppressive conditions of captivity accounted for the debased situation of blacks: "A state of slavery has a mighty tendency to shrink and contract the minds of men." Anthony Benezet, a Quaker philanthropist who funded a school for blacks in Philadelphia, defied popular opinion when he declared that African Americans were "as capable of improvement as White People."

These new religious and intellectual currents sparked legal change. In 1784, judicial rulings abolished slavery in Massachusetts; and, over the next twenty years, every state north of Delaware enacted legislation to end slavery (Map 8.2). Emancipation itself was gradual: The laws compensated white owners by requiring years — even decades — of continuing servitude. For example, the New York Emancipation Act of 1799 granted freedom to slave children only when they reached the age of twenty-five. As late as 1810, almost thirty thousand blacks in the northern states — nearly a fourth of the African Americans living there — were still enslaved. Two other factors contributed to the slow pace of emancipation in the North: competition for jobs and the fear of racial melding. Massachusetts addressed the racial issue in 1786 by reenacting an old law that prohibited whites from marrying blacks, mulattos, or Indians.

The tension in American republican ideology between respect for liberty and respect for property rights was greatest in the South, where slaves represented a huge financial investment. Some Chesapeake tobacco planters, moved by religious principles or an oversupply of workers, allowed blacks to buy their freedom through paid work as artisans or laborers. Manumission and self-purchase gradually brought freedom to one-third of the African American residents of Maryland. However, in 1792, the Virginia legislature made manumission more difficult. Following the lead of Thomas Jefferson, who owned more than one

Captain Absalom Boston

Absalom Boston was born in 1785 on the island of Nantucket, Massachusetts, the heart of America's whaling industry. A member of a community of free African American whalers manumitted from slavery by their Quaker owners, Boston went to sea at age fifteen. By the age of thirty, he had used his earnings to become the proprietor of a public inn. In 1822, Boston became the first black master with an all-black crew to undertake a whaling voyage from Nantucket. Later he served as a trustee of the island's African School. Nantucket Historical Association.

hundred slaves, the Virginia legislators argued that slavery was a "necessary evil" required to maintain white supremacy and the luxurious planter lifestyle. Resistance to black freedom was even greater in North Carolina, where the legislature condemned Quaker manumissions as "highly criminal and reprehensible." The slave-hungry rice-growing states of South Carolina and Georgia rejected emancipation out of hand. In fact, between 1776 and 1809, merchants and planters in the Lower South imported about 115,000 Africans — nearly half the number introduced into Britain's mainland settlements during the entire colonial period (Table 8.1).

The debate over emancipation among southern whites ended in 1800, when Virginia authorities thwarted an uprising planned by Gabriel Prosser,

TABLE 8.1	African Slaves Imported into the United States, by Ethnicity, 1776–1809		
African Region of Departure	**Ethnicity**	**Number**	**Percentage of Imported Slaves**
Senegambia	Mandinka, Fulbe, Serer, Jola, Wolof, and Bambara	8,000	7
Sierra Leone	Via, Mende, Kpelle, and Kru	18,300	16
Gold Coast	Ashanti and Fanit	15,000	13
Bight of Benin; Bight of Biafra	Ibo and Ibibio	5,700	5
West Central Africa	Kongo, Tio, and Matamba	37,800	33
Southeast Africa	Unknown	1,100	1
Other or unknown		28,700	25
Total		**114,600**	**100**

NOTE: Recent research suggests that 433,000 enslaved Africans arrived in British North America and the United States between 1607 and 1820: 33,200 before 1700; 278,400 from 1700 to 1775; 114,600 from 1776 to 1809; and 7,000 from 1810 to 1819. The numbers in this table are based on known voyages of 65,000 Africans.

SOURCE: Aaron S. Fogleman, "From Slaves, Convicts, and Servants to Free Passengers: The Transformation of Immigration in the Era of the American Revolution," *Journal of American History,* June 1998, table 1 and table A.6.

an enslaved artisan, and hanged him and thirty of his followers. "Liberty and equality have brought the evil upon us," a letter to the *Virginia Herald* proclaimed; such doctrines are "dangerous and extremely wicked in this country, where every white man is a master, and every black man is a slave." To preserve their privileged social position, southern whites redefined republicanism so that its principles of individual liberty and legal equality applied only to members of the "master race"—creating what historians call a *herrenvolk* (master people) republic.

The North and South Grow Apart

European visitors to the United States agreed that the South formed a distinct society, and many cast doubts on its character. New England was home to religious "fanaticism," according to a British observer, but "the lower orders of citizens" there had "a better education, are more intelligent, and better informed" than those he met in the South. "The state of poverty in which a great number of white people live in Virginia" surprised the Marquis de Chastellux, and other visitors to the South commented on the rude manners, heavy drinking, and weak work ethic of its residents. White tenant farmers and small freeholders seemed only to have a "passion for gaming at the billiard table, a cock-fight

or cards," and many planters squandered their wealth on extravagant lifestyles while their slaves suffered in bitter poverty.

Some southerners admitted that human bondage corrupted their society and induced ignorance and poverty among whites as well as blacks. A South Carolina merchant observed, "Where there are Negroes a White Man despises to work, saying what, will you have me a Slave and work like a Negroe?" For their part, wealthy planters wanted a compliant labor force that was content with the drudgery of agricultural work. Consequently, they trained most of their slaves as field hands (allowing only a few to learn the arts of the blacksmith, carpenter, or bricklayer), and did little to provide ordinary whites with elementary instruction in reading or arithmetic. In 1800, the political leaders of Essex County, Virginia, spent about 25 cents per person for local government, including schooling, while their counterparts in Acton, Massachusetts, expended about $1 per person. This difference in support for education mattered: By the 1820s, nearly all native-born men and women in New England could read and write; more than one-third of white southerners lacked these basic intellectual skills.

Slavery and National Politics. As the northern states ended human bondage, the South's continuing

MAP 8.2 The Status of Slavery, 1800

In 1775, racial slavery was legal in all of the British colonies in North America. By the time the states achieved their independence in 1783, most African Americans in New England had also been freed. By 1800, all of the states north of Maryland had provided for the gradual abolition of slavery, but the process was not completed until the 1830s. Some slave owners in the Chesapeake region also manumitted their slaves, leaving only the whites of the Lower South firmly committed to racial bondage.

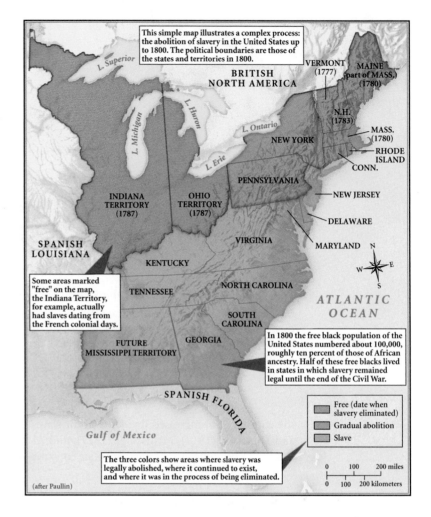

This simple map illustrates a complex process: the abolition of slavery in the United States up to 1800. The political boundaries are those of the states and territories in 1800.

Some areas marked "free" on the map, the Indiana Territory, for example, actually had slaves dating from the French colonial days.

In 1800 the free black population of the United States numbered about 100,000, roughly ten percent of those of African ancestry. Half of these free blacks lived in states in which slavery remained legal until the end of the Civil War.

Free (date when slavery eliminated)
Gradual abolition
Slave

The three colors show areas where slavery was legally abolished, where it continued to exist, and where it was in the process of being eliminated.

(after Paullin)

---

commitment to slavery became a political issue. At the Philadelphia convention in 1787, northern and southern delegates had compromised. Northerners accepted clauses guaranteeing the return of fugitive slaves and allowing slave imports from Africa to continue for twenty years; in return, southerners agreed that Congress could end the Atlantic slave trade after 1807 (see Chapter 6). Seeking a protection for their "peculiar institution," southerners in the new national legislature won approval of James Madison's resolution that "Congress have no authority to interfere in the emancipation of slaves, or in the treatment of them within any of the States."

Nonetheless, slavery remained a contested issue. The successful slave revolt in Haiti in the 1790s brought a flood of white refugees to the United States and prompted congressional debates about diplomatic relations with the island's new black government. Simultaneously, northern politicians assailed the British impressment of American sailors as just "as oppressive and tyrannical as the slave trade" and demanded the end of both. When

Congress outlawed American participation in the Atlantic slave trade in 1808, some northern representatives called for a similar prohibition on the interstate trade in black labor. In response, southern leaders mounted a defense of their slave society. "A large majority of people in the Southern states do not consider slavery as even an evil," declared one congressman. The South's political clout—especially its domination of the presidency and the Senate—ensured that the national government would continue to protect slavery. During the War of 1812, American diplomats vigorously, and successfully, demanded compensation for slaves freed by the British; subsequently, Congress enacted legislation upholding the property rights of slave owners in the District of Columbia.

Political conflict over slavery increased as the South expanded its slave-based agricultural economy into the lower Mississippi Valley. Antislavery advocates had hoped that African bondage would "die a natural death" following the end of the Atlantic slave trade and with the decline of the tobacco economy. Their hopes quickly faded as

The Reverend Richard Allen and the African Methodist Episcopal Church

One of the best known African Americans in the early republic, Allen founded a separate congregation for Philadelphia's black Methodists, the Bethel Church. Working with other ministers in 1816, Allen created the first independent black religious denomination in the United States — the African Methodist Episcopal (AME) Church — and became its first bishop. Library of Congress; Bethel AME Church, Philadelphia.

the cotton boom increased the demand for slaves, and Louisiana (1812), Mississippi (1817), and Alabama (1819) joined the Union with state constitutions permitting slavery.

Richard Allen Responds to Colonization Proposals. In 1817, influential Americans who were worried about the impact of slavery and race on society founded the American Colonization Society. According to Henry Clay, the Speaker of the House of Representatives and a slave owner, racial bondage had placed his state, Kentucky, "in the rear of our neighbors . . . in the state of agriculture, the progress of manufactures, the advance of improvement, and the general prosperity of society." Slavery had to end, and, members of the society argued, freed blacks had to be sent back to Africa. Emancipation without removal, Clay predicted, "would be followed by instantaneous collisions between the two races, which would break out into a civil war that would end in the extermination or subjugation of the one race or the other." To prevent racial chaos, the society planned to encourage planters to emancipate their slaves, who now numbered almost 1.5 million people; then, it would resettle them in Africa.

The society's plan was a dismal failure. Few planters freed their slaves, and the organization raised only enough money to purchase freedom for

a few hundred slaves. Equally important, most free blacks rejected colonization. They agreed with Bishop Richard Allen of the African Methodist Episcopal Church that "this land which we have watered with our tears and our blood is now our mother country." Allen knew of what he spoke. Born into slavery in Philadelphia in 1760 and sold to a farmer in Delaware, Allen had lived in bondage. In 1777, Freeborn Garretson, an itinerant preacher, converted Allen to Methodism and convinced his owner that on Judgment Day slaveholders would be "weighted in the balance, and . . . found wanting." Allowed to buy his freedom, Allen raised the money by working for years sawing cordwood and loading wagons. He then enlisted in the Methodist cause, becoming a "licensed exhorter" and then a regular minister in Philadelphia. In 1795, he formed a separate black congregation, the Bethel Church; and in 1816, he became the first bishop of a new denomination, the African Methodist Episcopal Church. Two years later, three thousand African Americans met in Allen's church to condemn colonization and to claim citizenship. Echoing the principles of democratic republicanism, they vowed to defy racial prejudice and advance in American society using "those opportunities . . . which the Constitution and the laws allow to all."

Lacking significant support from white slave owners and from free blacks like Richard Allen, the

American Colonization Society transported only six thousand African Americans to Liberia, a colony it established on the west coast of Africa.

The Missouri Crisis, 1819–1821

The failure of colonization set the stage for a new political conflict over slavery. In 1818, Congressman Nathaniel Macon of North Carolina warned slave owners that radical members of the "colonizing bible and peace societies" hoped to use the national government "to try the question of emancipation." In fact, a major national struggle erupted even more quickly than Macon had anticipated. When Missouri applied for admission to the Union in 1819 with a constitution that allowed slavery, Congressman James Tallmadge of New York proposed a ban on the importation of slaves into Missouri and the gradual emancipation of its black residents. Missouri whites rejected Tallmadge's proposals, and the northern majority in the House of Representatives responded by blocking the territory's admission to the Union.

White southerners were horrified. "It is believed by some, & feared by others," Alabama senator John Walker reported from Washington, that Tallmadge's amendment was "merely the entering wedge and that it points already to a total emancipation of the blacks." "You conduct us to an awful precipice, and hold us over it," Mississippi congressman Christopher Rankin warned his northern colleagues. To underline their commitment to slavery, southerners used their power in the Senate — where they held half the seats — to withhold statehood from Maine, which was seeking to separate itself from Massachusetts.

In the ensuing debate over slavery, southerners advanced three constitutional arguments. First, raising the principle of "equal rights," they argued that Congress could not impose conditions on Missouri that it had not imposed on other territories seeking statehood. Second, they maintained that slavery fell under the sovereignty of the state governments: Under the Constitution, states exercised control over their internal affairs and domestic institutions, including slavery and marriage. Finally, they insisted that Congress had no authority to infringe on the property rights of individual slaveholders. Going beyond these constitutional issues, southern leaders reaffirmed their commitment to a slave society. Abandoning their Revolutionary-era argument that slavery was a "necessary evil," they now relied on religion to champion it as a "positive good." "Christ himself gave a sanction to slavery," declared Senator William Smith of South Carolina. "If it be offensive and sinful to own slaves," a prominent Mississippi Methodist added, "I wish someone would just put his finger on the place in Holy Writ."

Controversy raged in Congress and newspapers for two years before Henry Clay put together a series of political agreements known collectively as the Missouri Compromise. Faced with unwavering southern opposition to Tallmadge's plan, a group of northern congressmen deserted the antislavery coalition. They accepted a deal that allowed Maine to enter the Union as a free state in 1820 and Missouri to follow as a slave state in 1821. By admitting both states, the agreement preserved a balance in the Senate between North and South and set a precedent for future additions to the Union. For their part, southern senators accepted the prohibition of slavery in the vast northern section of the Louisiana Purchase, the lands north of latitude 36°30' (the southern boundary of Missouri) (Map 8.3).

As they had in the Constitutional Convention of 1787 (see Chapter 6), white politicians once again preserved the Union by compromising over slavery. But the task had become more difficult. The delegates in Philadelphia had resolved their sectional differences in two months; it took Congress two years to work out the Missouri Compromise, and even then the agreement did not command universal support. "If we yield now, beware," the *Richmond Enquirer* warned as southern congressmen agreed to exclude slavery from most of the Louisiana Purchase. "What is a *territorial* restriction today becomes a *state* restriction tomorrow." The fate of the western lands, the black race, and the Union itself were now inextricably entwined — an ominous conjuncture that raised the specter of civil strife, the dissolution of the Union, and the end of the American experiment in republican government. As the aging Thomas Jefferson exclaimed in the midst of the Missouri crisis, "This momentous question, like a fire-bell in the night, awakened and filled me with terror."

➤ How did the aristocratic republicanism of the South differ from the democratic republicanism of the North? How did slavery affect the culture and values of the white population of the South?

➤ What compromises over slavery did the members of Congress make to settle the Missouri crisis? How did the compromises over slavery in 1820–1821 compare with those made by the delegates to the Constitutional Convention in 1787?

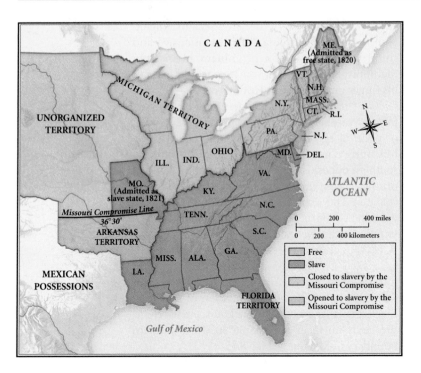

MAP 8.3 The Missouri Compromise, 1820–1821

The Missouri Compromise resolved for a generation the issue of slavery in the lands of the Louisiana Purchase. The agreement prohibited slavery north of the Missouri Compromise line (36°30′ north latitude), with the exception of the state of Missouri. To maintain an equal number of senators from free and slave states in the U.S. Congress, the compromise provided for the nearly simultaneous admission to the Union of Maine and Missouri.

Protestant Christianity as a Social Force

Throughout the colonial era, religion played a significant role in American life. Beginning in 1790, a series of religious revivals planted the values of Protestant Christianity deep in the national character, giving a spiritual definition to American republicanism. These revivals especially changed the lives of blacks and of women. Thousands of African Americans absorbed the faith of white Baptists and Methodists and created a distinctive and powerful institution—the black Christian church. Evangelical Christianity also created new public roles for women, especially in the North, and set in motion a long-lasting movement for social reform.

A Republican Religious Order

The demand for greater liberty unleashed by the republican revolution of 1776 forced American lawmakers to devise new relationships between church and state. Previously, only the Quaker- and Baptist-controlled governments of Pennsylvania and Rhode Island had repudiated the idea of an **established church**. Then, in 1776, James Madison and George Mason used Enlightenment principles to undermine the legal status of the Anglican Church in Virginia. They persuaded the state's constitutional convention to issue a declaration guaranteeing all Christians the "free exercise of religion." To win Presbyterian and Baptist support for the War of Independence, Virginia's Anglican elite accepted the legitimacy of the churches they had previously persecuted. In fact, in 1778, Virginia Anglicans launched their own revolution by severing ties with the hierarchy of the Church of England and founding the Protestant Episcopal Church of America.

Following independence, an established church and compulsory religious taxes were no longer the norm in the United States. Baptists, in particular, opposed the use of taxes to support religion. In Virginia, the Baptists' political influence prompted lawmakers to reject a bill, supported by George Washington and Patrick Henry, that would have imposed a general tax to fund all Christian churches. Instead, in 1786, the Virginia legislature enacted Thomas Jefferson's Bill for Establishing Religious Freedom, which made all churches equal before the law and granted direct financial support to none.

In New York and New Jersey, the sheer number of churches—Episcopalian, Presbyterian, Dutch Reformed, Lutheran, and Quaker, among others—prevented lawmakers from agreeing on an established church or compulsory religious taxes. Congregationalism remained the official state church in New England until the 1830s, but members of other denominations could pay taxes to their own churches.

TABLE 8.2	Number of Church Congregations by Denomination, 1780 and 1860		
Denomination	Number of Congregations		Increased roughly by a factor of:
	1780	1860	
Anglican/Episcopalian	406	2,100	5
Baptist	457	12,150	26
Catholic	50	2,500	50*
Congregational	742	2,200	3
Lutheran	240	2,100	9
Methodist	50	20,000	400
Presbyterian	495	6,400	13

NOTE: The increase in Catholic congregations occurred mostly after 1840, as the result of immigration from Ireland and Germany. See Chapter 9.

Even in Jefferson's Virginia, the separation of church and state was not complete. Many influential Americans believed that such ties promoted morality and respect for authority. "Pure religion and civil liberty are inseparable companions," a group of North Carolinians advised their minister. "It is your particular duty to enlighten mankind with the unerring principles of truth and justice, the main props of all civil government." Accepting this premise, most state governments provided churches with indirect aid by exempting their property and ministers from taxation.

Freedom of conscience proved equally difficult to achieve. In Virginia, Jefferson's Bill for Establishing Religious Freedom prohibited religious requirements for holding public office, but other states discriminated against those who dissented from the doctrines of Protestant Christianity. The North Carolina Constitution of 1776 disqualified from public employment any citizen "who shall deny the being of God, or the Truth of the Protestant Religion, or the Divine Authority of the Old or New Testament." New Hampshire's constitution contained a similar provision until 1868.

Americans influenced by Enlightenment deism and by Evangelical Protestantism condemned these religious restrictions. Leading American intellectuals, including Jefferson and Benjamin Franklin, argued that God had given humans the power of reason so that they could determine moral truths for themselves. To protect society from "ecclesiastical tyranny," they demanded complete freedom of conscience. Many evangelical Protestants also demanded religious liberty; their goal was to protect their churches from an oppressive

government. Isaac Backus, a New England minister, warned Baptists not to incorporate their churches or accept public funds because that might lead to state control. In Connecticut, a devout Congregationalist welcomed voluntarism, the voluntary funding of churches by their members, because it allowed the laity to control the clergy, thereby furthering self-government and "the principles of republicanism."

The Second Great Awakening

Overshadowing this debate was a decades-long series of religious revivals — the Second Great Awakening — that made the United States a Christian society. The churches that prospered during the revivals were those that preached spiritual equality and governed themselves democratically. Because bishops and priests dominated the Roman Catholic Church, it attracted few Protestants, who preferred Luther's doctrine of the priesthood of all believers. The unchurched — the great number of Americans who ignored religion — likewise shunned Catholicism because they feared its clergy's power. Few Americans joined the Episcopal Church (the successor to the Church of England) because it also had a hierarchical structure and was dominated by its wealthiest members (Table 8.2). The Presbyterian Church attracted more members, in part because its members elected laymen to the synods, the church congresses that determined doctrine and practice. Evangelical Methodist and Baptist churches were by far the most popular. The Baptists boasted a republican church organization, with self-governing congregations. In common with

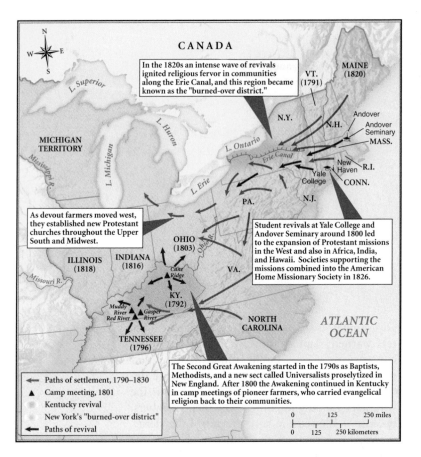

CANADA

In the 1820s an intense wave of revivals ignited religious fervor in communities along the Erie Canal, and this region became known as the "burned-over district."

MICHIGAN TERRITORY

As devout farmers moved west, they established new Protestant churches throughout the Upper South and Midwest.

OHIO (1803)

ILLINOIS (1818)   INDIANA (1816)   VA.   Cane Ridge

Student revivals at Yale College and Andover Seminary around 1800 led to the expansion of Protestant missions in the West and also in Africa, India, and Hawaii. Societies supporting the missions combined into the American Home Missionary Society in 1826.

KY. (1792)

Muddy River Gasper River   NORTH CAROLINA   ATLANTIC OCEAN
Red River

TENNESSEE (1796)

VT. (1791)   MAINE (1820)

N.Y.   N.H.   Andover   Andover Seminary   MASS.

L. Ontario   Erie Canal   New Haven   R.I.   Yale College   CONN.

PA.   N.J.

The Second Great Awakening started in the 1790s as Baptists, Methodists, and a new sect called Universalists proselytized in New England. After 1800 the Awakening continued in Kentucky in camp meetings of pioneer farmers, who carried evangelical religion back to their communities.

← Paths of settlement, 1790–1830
▲ Camp meeting, 1801
■ Kentucky revival
■ New York's "burned-over district"
← Paths of revival

0   125   250 miles
0   125   250 kilometers

MAP 8.4   The Second Great Awakening, 1790–1860

The awakening lasted for decades and invigorated churches in every part of the nation. The revivals in Kentucky and New York State, though, were particularly influential. As thousands of farm families migrated to the west, they carried with them the fervor generated by the Cane Ridge revival in Kentucky in 1801. And, between 1825 and 1835, the area along the Erie Canal in New York witnessed so many revivals that it came to be known as the Burned-over District.

Methodists, they developed an egalitarian religious culture marked by communal singing and emotional services.

The Revivalist Impulse. The revivalist movement that began in the 1790s was much broader than the First Great Awakening of the 1740s. Baptists and Methodists evangelized in the cities and the backcountry of New England. A new sect of Universalists, who repudiated the Calvinist doctrine of predestination and preached universal salvation, gained thousands of converts, especially in Massachusetts and northern New England. After 1800, enthusiastic camp meetings swept the frontier regions of South Carolina, Tennessee, Ohio, and Kentucky. The largest gathering, at Cane Ridge in Kentucky in 1801, lasted for nine electrifying days and nights, and attracted almost 20,000 people (Map 8.4).

Through these revivals, Baptist and Methodist preachers reshaped the spiritual landscape of the South and the Old Southwest. Offering a powerful emotional message and the promise of religious fellowship, revivalists attracted both unchurched individuals and pious families searching for social ties

in their new frontier communities (see Voices from Abroad, "Frances Trollope: A Camp Meeting in Indiana," p. 262).

The Second Great Awakening changed the denominational makeup of American religion. The most important churches of the colonial period — the Congregationalists, Episcopalians, and Quakers — grew slowly from the natural increase of their members. The Methodist and Baptist churches expanded in spectacular fashion by winning converts, and soon were the largest denominations. In the urbanized Northeast, pious Methodist and Baptist women aided their ministers by holding prayer meetings and providing material aid to members in need. In the rural South and West, Methodist preachers followed a circuit, "riding a hardy pony or horse . . . with . . . Bible, hymnbook, and Discipline," and visiting existing congregations on a regular schedule. They established new churches by searching out devout families, bringing them together for worship, and then appointing lay elders to lead the congregation and enforce moral discipline.

Evangelical ministers copied the "practical preaching" techniques of George Whitefield and

Women in the Awakening

The Second Great Awakening was a pivotal moment in the history of American women. In this detail from *Religious Camp Meeting,* painted by J. Maze Burbank in 1839, all the preachers are men, but women fill the audience and form the majority of those visibly "awakened." By transforming millions of women into devout Christians, the Awakening provided Protestant churches with dedicated workers, teachers, and morality-minded mothers. When tens of thousands of these women also joined movements for temperance, abolition, and women's rights, they spurred a great wave of social reform. Old Dartmouth Historical Society/New Bedford Whaling Museum, New Bedford, Massachusetts.

other eighteenth-century revivalists (see Chapter 4). To attract converts, preachers spoke from memory in plain language but with theatrical gestures and flamboyance. "Preach without papers" and emphasize piety rather than theology, advised one minister, "seem earnest & serious; & you will be listened to with Patience, & Wonder."

Black Protestantism. In the South, evangelical religion was initially a disruptive force because it spoke of spiritual equality and criticized slavery.

Husbands and planters grew angry when their wives became more assertive and when blacks were welcomed into their congregations. To retain white men in their churches, Methodist and Baptist preachers gradually adapted their religious message to justify the authority of yeomen patriarchs and slave-owning planters. A Baptist minister declared that a man was naturally at "the head of the woman," while a Methodist conference proclaimed, "We hold that a Christian slave must be submissive, faithful, and obedient."

Frances Trollope

A Camp Meeting in Indiana

Frances Trollope, a successful English author and the mother of novelist Anthony Trollope, lived for a time in Cincinnati, where she owned a bazaar that sold imported goods from Europe. Unsuccessful as a storekeeper, she won great acclaim as a social commentator. Her critical and at times acerbic Domestic Manners of the Americans *(1832) was a best-seller in both Europe and the United States. Here she provides her readers with a vivid description of a revivalist meeting in Indiana around 1830.*

The prospect of passing a night in the back-woods of Indiana was by no means agreeable, but I screwed my courage to the proper pitch, determined to see with my own eyes, and hear with my own ears, what a camp meeting really was. . . . We reached the ground about an hour before midnight, and the approach to it was highly picturesque. The spot chosen was the verge of an unbroken forest, where a space of about twenty acres appeared to have been partially cleared for the purpose. Tents of different sizes were pitched very near together in a circle round the cleared space. . . .

Four high frames, constructed in the form of altars, were placed at the four corners of the inclosure; on these were supported layers of earth and sod, on which burned immense fires of blazing pine-wood. On one side a rude platform was erected to accommodate the preachers, fifteen of whom attended this meeting, and with very short intervals for necessary refreshment and private devo-

tion, preached in rotation, day and night, from Tuesday to Saturday.

When we arrived, the preachers were silent; but we heard issuing from nearly every tent mingled sounds of praying, preaching, singing, and lamentation. . . . The floor [of one of the tents] was covered with straw, which round the sides was heaped in masses, that might serve as seats, but which at that moment were used to support the heads and arms of the close-packed circle of men and women who knelt on the floor.

Out of about thirty persons thus placed, perhaps half a dozen were men. One of these [was] a handsome-looking youth of eighteen or twenty. . . . His arm was encircling the neck of a young girl who knelt beside him, with her hair hanging dishevelled upon her shoulders, and her features working with the most violent agitation; soon after they both fell forward on the straw, as if unable to endure in any other attitude the burning eloquence of a tall grim figure in black, who, standing erect in the center, was uttering with incredible vehemence an oration that seemed to hover between praying and preaching; his arms hung stiff and immoveable by his side, and he looked like an ill-constructed machine, set in action by a movement so violent as to threaten its own destruction, so jerkingly, painfully, yet rapidly, did his words tumble out; the kneeling circle ceasing not to call, in every variety of tone, on the name of Jesus. . . .

One tent was occupied exclusively by Negroes. They were all full-dressed, and looked exactly as if they were performing a scene on a stage. One woman wore a dress of pink gauze trimmed with silver lace; another was dressed in pale yellow silk; one or two had splendid turbans; and all wore a profusion of ornaments. The men were in snow white pantaloons, with gay colored linen jackets. One of these, a youth of coal-black

comeliness, was preaching with the most violent gesticulations. . . .

At midnight, a horn sounded through the camp, which, we were told, was to call the people from private to public worship; and we presently saw them flocking from all sides to the front of the preacher's stand. . . . There were about two thousand persons assembled.

One of the preachers began in a low nasal tone, and, like all other Methodist preachers, assured us of the enormous depravity of man. . . . Above a hundred persons, nearly all females, came forward, uttering howlings and groans so terrible that I shall never cease to shudder when I recall them. They appeared to drag each other forward, and on the word being given, "let us pray," they fell on their knees . . . and they were soon all lying on the ground in an indescribable confusion of heads and legs.

SOURCE: Frances Trollope, *Domestic Manners of the Americans* (London: Whittaker, Treacher, 1832), 139–142.

ANALYZING THE EVIDENCE

➤ What is Trollope's opinion about what she witnessed "in the back-woods of Indiana"? Did she see what she expected to see? What clues does the narrative provide?

➤ Who attended the camp meeting? How would you explain the different dress and deportment of the African American believers?

➤ How did the worship at this nineteenth-century camp meeting differ from that in, say, a New England Congregational church in the eighteenth century? How do you explain the difference?

➤ How does Trollope describe the words of the Methodist preacher? How did the Methodists' theology differ from that of earlier Calvinists?

Other evangelists ignored the objections of slave owners and carried the teachings of Protestant Christianity to enslaved African Americans. For much of the eighteenth century, most blacks had maintained the religious practices of their African homelands, giving homage to African gods and spirits or practicing Islam. "At the time I first went to Carolina," remembered Charles Ball, an escaped slave, "there were a great many African slaves in the country. . . . Many of them believed there were several gods [and] I knew several . . . Mohamedans [Muslims]." Then, in the mid-1780s, Protestant evangelists converted hundreds of African Americans along the James River in Virginia and throughout the Chesapeake region.

Subsequently, black preachers adapted the teachings of the white Protestant churches to their own needs. Black Christians generally ignored the doctrines of original sin and Calvinist predestination as well as biblical passages that encouraged unthinking obedience to authority. Some African American converts envisioned the Christian God as a warrior who had liberated the Jews. Their "cause was similar to the Israelites," Martin Prosser, Gabriel's brother and a preacher, told his fellow slaves as they plotted rebellion in Virginia in 1800. "I have read in my Bible where God says, if we worship him, . . . five of you shall conquer a hundred and a hundred of you a hundred thousand of our enemies." Confident of a special relationship with God, Christian slaves prepared themselves spiritually for emancipation, the first step in their journey to the Promised Land.

New Religious Thought and Institutions. Influenced by republican ideology, whites also rejected the Calvinist preoccupation with human depravity and weakness, embracing instead Christian doctrines that focused on human ability and free will. In New England, many educated and affluent Congregationalists placed increasing emphasis on the power of human reason. Discarding the concept of the Trinity—Father, Son, and Holy Spirit—they worshiped an indivisible and "united" God; hence they took the name Unitarians. "The ultimate reliance of a human being is, and must be, on his own mind," argued William Ellery Channing, the famous Unitarian minister, "for the idea of God is the idea of our own spiritual nature, purified and enlarged to infinity."

Other New England Congregationalists reinterpreted Calvinist doctrines. Lyman Beecher, the preeminent Congregationalist clergyman of the early nineteenth century, retained the traditional Christian belief that people had a natural tendency to sin; but, rejecting predestination, he affirmed the capacity of all men and women to choose God. In accepting the doctrines of free will and universal salvation, Beecher testified to the growing belief that people could shape their destiny.

Reflecting this optimism, Reverend Samuel Hopkins linked individual salvation to religious benevolence—the practice of disinterested virtue. As the Presbyterian minister John Rodgers explained, fortunate individuals who had received God's grace had a duty "to dole out charity to their poorer brothers and sisters." Heeding this message, pious merchants in New York founded the Humane Society and other charitable organizations. By the 1820s, so many devout Protestant men and women had embraced benevolent reform that conservative church leaders warned them not to neglect spiritual matters. Still, improving society was a key element of the new religious thought. Said Lydia Maria Child, a devout Christian social reformer: "The only true church organization [is] when heads and hearts unite in working for the welfare of the human-race."

By the 1820s, Protestant Christians were well positioned to undertake that task. Unlike the First Great Awakening, which split churches into warring factions, the Second Great Awakening fostered cooperation among denominations. Religious leaders founded five interdenominational societies: the American Education Society (1815), the Bible Society (1816), the Sunday School Union (1824), the Tract Society (1825), and the Home Missionary Society (1826). Although based in eastern cities—New York, Boston, and Philadelphia—the societies ministered to a national congregation, dispatching hundreds of missionaries to western regions and distributing tens of thousands of religious pamphlets.

Increasingly, Protestant ministers and laypeople saw themselves as part of a united religious movement that could change the course of history. "I want to see our state evangelized," declared a pious churchgoer near the Erie Canal (where the fires of revivalism were so hot that it was known as the "Burned-over District"): "Suppose the great State of New York in all its physical, political, moral, commercial, and pecuniary resources should come over to the Lord's side. Why it would turn the scale and could convert the world. I shall have no rest until it is done."

Because the Second Great Awakening aroused such enthusiasm, religion became an important force in political life. On July 4, 1827, Reverend Ezra

Republican Motherhood

Art often revels much of the cultural values of the time. In this 1795 painting, the artist James Peale, brother of the famous portraitist Charles Willson Peale, depicts himself with his wife and children. The mother stands in the foreground, offering advice to her eldest daughter, while her husband stands to the rear, pointing to the other children. The father, previously the center of attention in family protraits during the colonial era, now gives pride of place to his wife and offspring (see also Reading American Pictures, "Changing Middle-Class Families," p. 250). Pennsylvania Academy of the Fine Arts, Philadelphia.

Stiles Ely called on the members of the Seventh Presbyterian Church in Philadelphia to begin a "Christian party in politics." Ely's sermon, "The Duty of Christian Freemen to Elect Christian Rulers," proclaimed a religious goal for the American republic — an objective that Thomas Jefferson and John Adams would have found strange and troubling. The two founders had died the same day, July 4, 1826, on the fiftieth anniversary of the Declaration of Independence, and had gone to their graves believing that America's mission was to spread political republicanism. In contrast, Ely urged the United States to become an evangelical Christian nation dedicated to religious conversion at home and abroad: "All our rulers ought in their official capacity to serve the Lord Jesus Christ." Similar calls for a union of church and state would arise again during the Third (1880–1900) and Fourth (1970–present) Great Awakenings among American Christians.

Women's New Religious Roles

The upsurge in religious enthusiasm allowed women to demonstrate their piety and even to found new sects. Mother Ann Lee organized the Shakers in Britain and then, in 1774, migrated to America, where she attracted numerous recruits; by the 1820s, Shaker communities dotted the American countryside from New Hampshire to Indiana

(see Chapter 11). Jemima Wilkinson, a young Quaker woman in Rhode Island, founded a more controversial sect. Stirred by reading George Whitefield's sermons, Wilkinson had a vision that she had died and been reincarnated as Christ. Repudiating her birth name, Wilkinson declared herself the "Publick Universal Friend," dressed in masculine attire, and preached a new gospel. Her teachings blended the Calvinist warning of "a lost and guilty, gossiping, dying World" with Quaker-inspired plain dress, pacifism, and abolitionism. Wilkinson's charisma initially won scores of converts, but her radical lifestyle and the challenge she presented to traditional gender roles aroused hostility, and her sect dwindled away.

Increasing Public Activities. These female-led religious experiments were less significant than the activities of thousands of women in mainstream churches. To give but a few examples: Women in New Hampshire managed more than fifty local "cent" societies that raised funds for the Society for Promoting Christian Knowledge; New York City women founded the Society for the Relief of Poor Widows; and young Quaker women in Philadelphia ran the Society for the Free Instruction of African Females.

Women took charge of religious and charitable enterprises both because they were excluded from other public roles and because ministers relied increasingly on them to do the work of the church. After 1800, more than 70 percent of the members of New England Congregational churches were female, which prompted ministers to end long-standing practices like gender-segregated prayer meetings. In fact, evangelical Methodist and Baptist preachers encouraged mixed praying. "Our prayer meetings have been one of the greatest means of the conversion of souls," a minister in central New York reported in the 1820s, "especially those in which brothers and sisters have prayed together."

Far from leading to promiscuity, as critics feared, mixing the sexes promoted greater self-discipline. Believing in female virtue, many young women and the men who courted them now postponed sexual intercourse until after marriage — previously a rare form of self-restraint. In Hingham, Massachusetts, and many other New England towns, more than 30 percent of the women who married between 1750 and 1800 bore a child within eight months of their wedding day; by the 1820s, the rate had dropped to 15 percent.

As women claimed new spiritual authority, men tried to curb their power. Evangelical Baptist churches that had once advocated spiritual equality now denied women the right to vote on church matters or to offer testimonies of faith before the congregation. Those activities, declared one layman, were "directly opposite to the apostolic command in Cor[inthians] XIV, 34, 35, 'Let your women learn to keep silence in the churches.'" "Women have a different *calling*," claimed another. "That they *be chaste, keepers at home* is the Apostle's direction." Combining that injunction with the concept of republican motherhood, mothers throughout the United States founded maternal associations to encourage Christian child rearing. By the 1820s, *Mother's Magazine* and other newsletters, widely read in hundreds of small towns and villages, were giving women a sense of shared purpose and identity.

Women's Education. Religious activism advanced female education. Churches established scores of seminaries and academies where girls from the middling classes received sound intellectual and moral instruction. Emma Willard, the first American advocate of higher education for women, opened the Middlebury Female Seminary in Vermont in 1814 and later founded girls' schools in Waterford and Troy, New York. Beginning in the 1820s, women educated in these seminaries and academies displaced men as public-school teachers.

Because educated women had few other opportunities for paid employment, they accepted lower pay than men would. Female schoolteachers earned from $12 to $14 a month with room and board — less than a farm laborer. But as schoolteachers, women had an acknowledged place in public life, a goal that had been beyond their reach in colonial and Revolutionary times.

Just as the ideology of democratic republicanism had expanded voting rights and the political influence of ordinary men in the North, so the values of Christian republicanism had bolstered the public authority of middling women. The Second Great Awakening made Americans a fervently Protestant people. Along with the values of republicanism and capitalism, this religious impulse formed the core of an emerging national identity. This identity would be tested in the decades to come, when fundamental economic changes and the growing sectional conflict over slavery would divide the nation along economic and sectional lines.

➤ How did republicanism affect the organization, values, and popularity of American churches?

➤ Why did Protestant Christianity and Protestant women emerge as forces for social change? In what areas did women become active?

SUMMARY

Like all important ideologies, republicanism has many facets, and we have explored three of them in this chapter. We saw how state legislatures created a capitalist commonwealth, a political economy that encouraged government support of private business. This republican-inspired policy of state mercantilism remained dominant until the 1840s, when it was replaced by classical liberal doctrines (see Chapter 10).

We also saw how republicanism gradually changed social and family values. The principle of legal equality encouraged social mobility among white men and prompted both men and women to seek companionate marriages. Republicanism likewise encouraged parents to provide their children with equal inheritances and to allow them to choose their marriage partners. In the South, republican doctrines of liberty and equality coexisted uneasily with slavery, and ultimately were restricted to the white population.

Finally, we observed the complex interaction of republicanism and religion. Stirred by republican principles, many citizens joined denominations with democratic forms of governance and egalitarian religious cultures, like the Methodist and Baptist churches. Inspired by "benevolent" ideas and the enthusiastic preachers of the Second Great Awakening, many churchgoers joined reformist organizations and infused the emergent republican society with religious values. The result of all these initiatives—in economic policy, social relations, and religious institutions—was the creation of a distinctive American republican culture.

Connections: Culture

In 1763, the year in which Part Two begins, the residents of British North America had little in common. Over the next six decades, they began to create a common culture, an emerging sense of American nationality that would flower in the nineteenth century. As we suggested in the essay that opened Part Two (p. 135),

> by 1820, to be an American meant, for many members of the dominant white population, to be a republican, a Protestant, and an enterprising individual in a capitalist-run market system.

This process of creating a national culture took place in stages. As we saw in Chapter 5, the Patriot movement generated a sense of American identity—as opposed to a Virginian or New York identity—and the republican revolution of 1776 gave it ideological content. And as we noted in Chapter 6, the creation of a national government, first in the Articles of Confederation and then in the Constitution of 1787, greatly augmented that political identity.

As people began to think of themselves as American citizens, they acted purposefully to create a dynamic market-based economy. As we pointed out in Chapter 7 both the state and the national governments took an active role in the development of a capitalist economy. Simultaneously, the intense focus on financial gain by tens of thousands of entrepreneurial farmers, planters, artisans, and merchants shaped a culture that placed high value on hard work and economic achievement. Those characteristics emerged as markers of American identity.

Finally, as we noted in this chapter, the Revolution dramatically increased the commitment to religious liberty on the part of people and government, and set in motion the revivalism that added a Christian component to the emergent American identity.

In 1820, many Americans—blacks, women, laborers, native peoples, the unchurched—either refused to embrace some or all of these values or were denied full membership in republican governments, religious institutions, and business organizations. However, in subsequent decades, these American values—republicanism, capitalism, and Protestantism—would become more widely shared. At the same time, as we will see in Part Three, "Economic Revolution and Sectional Strife, 1820–1876," they become more complex and a source of deep conflict.

CHAPTER REVIEW QUESTIONS

➤ Explain how the republican ideas of the Revolutionary era shaped American society and culture in the late eighteenth and early nineteenth centuries. What regional differences in the social development of republicanism emerged? How can we account for these differences?

➤ Trace the relationship between America's republican culture and the surge of evangelism called the Second Great Awakening. In what ways are the goals of the two movements similar? How are they different?

➤ The text argues that by 1820, a distinct American identity had begun to emerge. How would you describe this identity? What were the forces for unity? And what were the points of contention?

TIMELINE

1782	St. Jean de Crèvecoeur publishes *Letters from an American Farmer* Virginia passes law allowing manumission (reversed in 1792)
1783	Noah Webster publishes his "blue-back" speller
1784	Slavery abolished in Massachusetts; other northern states legislate gradual emancipation
1787	Benjamin Rush writes *Thoughts on Female Education*
1790s	States grant corporations charters and special privileges Private companies build roads and canals to facilitate trade Merchants develop rural outwork system Chesapeake blacks adopt Protestant beliefs Parents limit family size as farms shrink Second Great Awakening expands church membership
1791	Congress charters First Bank of the United States
1792	Mary Wollstonecraft, *A Vindication of the Rights of Woman*
1795	Massachusetts Mill Dam Act promotes textile industry
1800	Gabriel Prosser plots slave rebellion in Virginia
1800s	Rise of sentimentalism and of companionate marriages Women's religious activism; founding of female academies Religious benevolence sparks social reform
1801	Cane Ridge revival in Kentucky
1807	New Jersey excludes propertied women from suffrage
1816	Congress charters Second Bank of the United States
1817	American Colonization Society is founded
1819	Plummeting agricultural prices set off panic
1819–1821	Missouri Compromise
1820s	States begin reforming public education Women become schoolteachers in increasing numbers

FOR FURTHER EXPLORATION

R. Kent Newmyer, *The Supreme Court Under Marshall and Taney* (1968), concisely analyzes constitutional development; Jeffrey L. Pasley, Andrew W. Robertson, and David Waldstreicher, eds. *Beyond the Founders: New Approaches to the Political History of the Early American Republic* (2004), show how ordinary citizens promoted a democratic polity. Jack Larkin, *The Reshaping of Everyday Life, 1790–1840* (1997), explores changes in material culture, as do two excellent Web sites: **memorialhall.mass.edu/collection/index.html** and **memorialhall.mass.edu/activities/turns_activities/index.html**.

Nancy Cott analyzes changing marriage rules in *Public Vows: A History of Marriage and the Nation* (2000); an interview with the author can be heard at **www.npr.org/templates/story/story.php?storyId=1054009**. For an intimate portrayal of family life on the Maine frontier, see Laurel Thatcher Ulrich, *A Midwife's Tale: The Life of Martha Ballard* (1990), the subject of a PBS documentary. Additional materials on Ballard's experiences are available on the Web at **www.pbs.org/amex/midwife** and **www.DoHistory.org**.

Jan Lewis's *The Pursuit of Happiness: Family and Values in Jefferson's Virginia* (1983) explores the lives of the paternalistic slave-owning gentry of the Upper South; James David Miller, *South by Southwest: Planter Emigration and Identity in the Slave South* (2002), discusses their subsequent migration to the Mississippi Valley. For analyses of slavery and the slave trade, see Ira Berlin, *Generations of Captivity: A History of African-American Slaves* (2003); Douglas R. Egerton, *Gabriel's Rebellion: The Virginia Slave Conspiracies of 1800 and 1802* (1995); and the rich Web site at **dpls.dacc.wisc.edu/slavedata/index.html**.

In *The Democratization of American Christianity* (1987), Nathan Hatch traces the impact of evangelical Protestantism. Other fine overviews of American religion are Mark A. Noll, *America's God: From Jonathan Edwards to Abraham Lincoln* (2003), and Bernard Weisberger, *They Gathered at the River* (1958).

TEST YOUR KNOWLEDGE

To assess your command of the material in this chapter, see the Online Study Guide at **bedfordstmartins.com/henretta**.

For Web sites, images, and documents related to topics and places in this chapter, visit **bedfordstmartins.com/makehistory**.

PART THREE | Economic Revolution and Sectional Strife

1820–1877

	ECONOMY	SOCIETY	GOVERNMENT	CULTURE	SECTIONALISM
	The economic revolution begins	A new class structure emerges	Creating a democratic polity	Reforming people and institutions	From compromise to Civil War and Reconstruction
1820	▸ Waltham textile factory opens (1814) ▸ Erie Canal completed (1825) ▸ Market economy expands nationwide ▸ Cotton belt emerges in South ▸ Protective tariffs passed (1824, 1828)	▸ Business class emerges ▸ Rural women and girls recruited as factory workers ▸ Mechanics form craft unions	▸ Spread of universal white male suffrage ▸ Rise of Andrew Jackson and Democratic Party ▸ Anti-Masonic Party rises and declines	▸ American Colonization Society (1817) ▸ Benevolent reform movements ▸ Revivalist Charles Finney	▸ Missouri Crisis and Compromise (1819–1821) ▸ David Walker's *Appeal... to the Colored Citizens of the World* (1829) ▸ Domestic slave trade moves African Americans west
1830	▸ Protective tariff (1832) triggers nullification crisis ▸ Panic of 1837 ▸ U.S. textile makers outcompete British	▸ Depression (1839–1843) shatters labor movement ▸ New urban popular culture appears	▸ Whig Party forms (1834) ▸ Second Party System emerges	▸ Joseph Smith founds Mormonism ▸ Female Moral Reform Society (1834) ▸ Temperance crusade expands	▸ Ordinance of Nullification (1832) and Force Bill (1833) ▸ W. L. Garrison forms American Anti-Slavery Society (1833)
1840	▸ Irish immigrants join labor force ▸ *Commonwealth v. Hunt* (1842) legalizes unions in Massachusetts	▸ Working-class districts emerge in cities ▸ Irish and German immigration accelerates	▸ Log cabin campaign (1840) mobilizes voters ▸ Antislavery parties: Liberty (1840) and Free-Soil (1848)	▸ Fourierist and other communal settlements founded ▸ Seneca Falls Women's Rights convention (1848)	▸ Texas annexation (1845), Mexican War (1846–1848), and Wilmot Proviso (1846) increase sectional conflict
1850	▸ Surge of cotton output in South and of railroads in North and Midwest ▸ Manufacturing expands ▸ Panic of 1857	▸ Expansion of farm society into Midwest and Far West ▸ Free-labor ideology justifies inequality	▸ Whig Party disintegrates ▸ Republican Party founded (1854) ▸ Third Party System begins	▸ Harriet Beecher Stowe's *Uncle Tom's Cabin* (1852) ▸ Anti-immigrant nativist movement and Know-Nothing Party	▸ Compromise of 1850 ▸ Kansas-Nebraska Act (1854) and "Bleeding Kansas" ▸ *Dred Scott* decision (1857)
1860	▸ Republicans enact policy agenda: Homestead Act (1862), railroad aid, high tariffs, and national banking	▸ Emancipation Proclamation (1863) ▸ Free blacks in the South struggle for control of land	▸ Thirteenth Amendment (1865) ends slavery ▸ Fourteenth Amendment (1868) extends legal and political rights	▸ U.S. Sanitary Commission founded (1861)	▸ South Carolina leads secession movement (1860) ▸ Confederate States of America (1861–1865)
1870	▸ Panic of 1873	▸ Rise of sharecropping in the South	▸ Fifteenth Amendment (1870) extends vote to black men	▸ Freed African Americans create schools and churches	▸ Compromise of 1877 ends Reconstruction

In America, a French visitor remarked in 1839, "all is circulation, motion, and boiling agitation. Enterprise follows enterprise [and] riches and poverty follow." Indeed, as we shall see in Part Three, American society was rapidly changing in basic ways. In 1820, the United States was predominately an agricultural nation; by 1877, it boasted one of the world's most powerful industrial economies. Two other sets of dramatic events marked this era. The first was the creation of a genuinely modern polity: a democratic political system with competitive political parties. Second, many Americans developed a complex social identity that was both staunchly nationalistic and resolutely sectional. These profound transformations affected every aspect of life in the northern and midwestern states and brought important changes in the South as well. Here, in brief, is an outline of that story.

ECONOMY An economic revolution, powered by advances in industrial production and a vast expansion in the market system, transformed the nation's economy. Factory owners used high-speed machines and a new system of labor discipline to boost the output of goods dramatically. Simultaneously, enterprising merchants made use of a new network of canals and railroads to create a vast national market. Manufacturers produced 5 percent of the country's wealth in 1820 but more than 30 percent in 1877, and now sold their products throughout the nation.

SOCIETY The new economy created a class-based society in the North and Midwest. A wealthy elite of merchants, manufacturers, bankers, and entrepreneurs struggled to the top of the social order. Once in charge, they tried to maintain social stability through a paternalistic program of benevolent reform. However, a rapidly growing urban middle class created a distinct material and religious culture and spearheaded movements for radical

social reform. Moreover, a mass of propertyless workers, many of them impoverished immigrants from Germany and Ireland, joined labor unions to win better wages and working conditions. Thanks to the interstate slave trade, Southern planters extended the plantation society of the Chesapeake and Carolinas as far south and west as Texas.

GOVERNMENT The rapid growth of political parties sparked the creation of a democratic polity open to many social groups. Between 1790 and 1830, farmers, workers, and entrepreneurs persuaded governments to improve transportation, shorten workdays, and award valuable corporate charters. Catholic immigrants from Ireland and Germany entered the political arena to protect their religion and cultures from restrictive legislation advocated by Protestant nativists and reformers.

With Andrew Jackson at its head, the Democratic Party advanced the interests of southern planters, farmers, and urban workers. In the 1830s and 1840s, the Jacksonians led a political and constitutional revolution that cut government aid to financiers, merchants, and corporations. To contend with the Democrats, the Whig Party (and, in the 1850s, the Republican Party) devised a competing program that stressed economic development, moral reform, and individual social mobility. This party competition engaged the energies of the electorate and helped unify a fragmented social order.

CULTURE Between 1820 and 1860, a series of reform movements, many with religious roots and goals, swept across America. Dedicated men and women preached the gospel of temperance, Sunday observance, prison reform, and dozens of other causes. Some Americans pursued their social dreams in isolated utopian communities, but most reformers worked within society. Two interrelated groups—abolitionists and women's rights activists—demanded

radical changes: the immediate end of slavery and the overthrow of the patriarchal legal and political order. As southern planters increasingly defended slavery as a "positive good," antislavery advocates turned to political action. During the 1840s and 1850s, they demanded free soil in the western territories and charged that a "slave power conspiracy" threatened free labor and republican values throughout the nation.

SECTIONALISM The economic revolution and social reform sharpened sectional divisions: The North developed into an urban industrial society based on free labor, whereas the South remained a rural agricultural society dependent on slavery. Following the Mexican War (1846–1848), northern and southern politicians struggled bitterly over the expansion of slavery into the vast territories seized from Mexico and the lands of the Louisiana Purchase. The election of Republican Abraham Lincoln in 1860 prompted the secession of the South from the Union and the onset of sectional warfare. The conflict became a total war, a struggle between two societies as well as two armies. And because of new technology and the mobilization of huge armies, the two sides endured unprecedented casualties and costs.

The fruits of victory for the North were substantial. During Reconstruction, the Republican Party ended slavery, imposed its economic policies and constitutional doctrines, and extended full democratic rights to former slaves. In the face of massive resistance from white Southerners, northern leaders gradually abandoned the effort to secure African Americans the full benefits of freedom. These decades, which began with great optimism and impressive achievements, thus ended on the bitter notes of a costly war, an acrimonious peace, and a half-won freedom.

ART IS THE HANDMAID OF HUMAN GOOD. · LOWELL. ·

9

Economic Transformation

1820–1860

IN 1804, LIFE TURNED GRIM FOR eleven-year-old Chauncey Jerome of Connecticut. His father died suddenly, and Jerome faced indentured servitude on a nearby farm. Knowing that few farmers "would treat a poor boy like a human being," Jerome bought out his indenture by making dials for clocks and eventually ended up a journeyman clockmaker for Eli Terry. A manufacturing wizard, Terry had designed an enormously popular desk clock with brass parts; his business turned Litchfield, Connecticut, into the clock-making center of the United States. Jerome followed in Terry's footsteps and in 1816 set up his own clock factory. By organizing work more efficiently and using new machines that made interchangeable metal parts, Jerome drove down the price of a simple clock from $20 to $5 and then to less than $2. By the 1840s, he was selling his clocks in England, the hub of the Industrial Revolution; two decades later, his workers were turning out 200,000 clocks a year, clear testimony to American enterprise and the American economic transformation. By 1860, the United States was not only the world's leading exporter of cotton and wheat but also the third-ranked manufacturing nation behind Britain and France.

"Business is the very soul of an American: the fountain of all human felicity," Francis Grund, a European immigrant, observed shortly after

◄ **Technology Celebrated**

Artists joined with manufacturers in praising the new industrial age. In this 1836 image, a cornucopia (horn of plenty) spreads its bounty over the city of Lowell, Massachusetts. The bales of raw cotton in the foreground will be transformed in the water-powered textile factories into smooth cloth, for shipment to far-flung markets via the new railroad system. The image of prosperity was deceptive. Two years earlier, two thousand women textile workers had gone on strike in Lowell, claiming that their wages failed to provide a decent standard of living. Private Collection.

his arrival. "It is as if all America were but one gigantic workshop, over the entrance of which there is the blazing inscription, 'No admission here, except on business.'" As the editor of *Niles' Weekly Register* in Baltimore put it, there was an "almost universal ambition to get forward." Stimulated by the entrepreneurial culture of early-nineteenth-century America, thousands of artisan-inventors like Eli Terry and Chauncey Jerome and thousands of merchants and traders propelled the country into a new economic era. Two great changes defined that era: the growth and mechanization of industry, the Industrial Revolution, and the expansion and integration of markets, the **Market Revolution**.

Not all Americans embraced the new ethic of enterprise, and many of the most ambitious failed to share in the new prosperity. The spread of industry and commerce created a class-divided society that challenged the founders' vision of an agricultural republic with few distinctions of wealth. As the philosopher Ralph Waldo Emerson warned in 1839: "The invasion of Nature by Trade with its Money, its Credit, its Steam, [and] its Railroad threatens to . . . establish a new, universal Monarchy."

The American Industrial Revolution

Industrialization came to the United States between 1790 and 1820, as merchants and manufacturers reorganized work routines and built factories. The rapid construction of turnpikes, canals, and railroads by state governments and private entrepreneurs, working together in the Commonwealth system (see Chapter 8) allowed manufactures to be sold throughout the land, and goods that once had been luxury items became part of everyday life (Table 9.1).

The Division of Labor and the Factory

Rising living standards stemmed initially from changes in the organization of work. Consider the shoe industry. Traditionally, New England shoemakers worked in small wooden shacks called "ten-footers," where they controlled the pace of work as they turned leather hides into finished shoes and boots. During the 1820s and 1830s, the merchants and manufacturers of Lynn, Massachusetts, gradually took over the shoe industry by increasing efficiency through an outwork system and a **division of labor**. The employers hired semiskilled journeymen and set them to work in large shops cutting leather into soles and uppers. They sent out the upper sections to dozens of rural Massachusetts towns, where women binders sewed in fabric linings. The manufacturers then had other journeymen attach the uppers to the soles and return the shoes to the central shop for inspection, packing, and sale. The new system turned employers into powerful "shoe bosses" and eroded workers' control of their labor. Whatever the cost to workers, the division of labor dramatically increased the output of shoes and cut their price.

TABLE 9.1 Leading Branches of Manufacture, 1860				
Item	Number of Workers	Value of Product (millions)	Value Added by Manufacture (millions)	Rank by Value Added
Cotton textiles	115,000	$107.3	$54.7	1
Lumber	75,600	$104.9	$53.8	2
Boots and shoes	123,000	$91.9	$49.2	3
Flour and meal	27,700	$248.6	$40.1	4
Men's clothing	114,800	$80.8	$36.7	5
Iron (cast, forged, etc.)	49,000	$73.1	$35.7	6
Machinery	41,200	$52.0	$32.5	7
Woolen goods	40,600	$60.7	$25.0	8
Leather	22,700	$67.3	$22.8	9
Liquors	12,700	$56.6	$22.5	10

SOURCE: Adapted from Douglass C. North, *Growth and Welfare in the American Past*, 2nd ed. (Paramus, NJ: Prentice Hall, 1974), table 6.1.

Pork Packing in Cincinnati

The only modern technology in this Cincinnati pork-packing plant was the overhead pulley that carried hog carcasses past the workers. The plant's efficiency came from its organization, a division of labor in which each worker performed a specific task. Plants like this pioneered the design of the moving assembly line, which would reach a high level of sophistication in the early twentieth century, in Henry Ford's automobile factories. Cincinnati Historical Society.

For products that were not suited to the outwork system, manufacturers created the modern **factory**, which concentrated production under one roof. For example, in the 1830s, Cincinnati merchants built large slaughterhouses that processed thousands of hogs every month. A simple system of overhead rails moved the hog carcasses past workers who performed specific tasks. One worker split the animals, another removed various organs, and still others trimmed the carcasses into pieces. Packers then stuffed the cuts of pork into barrels and pickled them to prevent spoilage. The Cincinnati system was so efficient and quick — processing 60 hogs an hour — that by the 1840s, the city was known as "Porkopolis." By 1850, factories in the city were slaughtering hogs in even greater volume — 334,000 a year. Reported Frederick Law Olmsted:

We entered an immense low-ceiling room and followed a vista of dead swine, upon their backs, their paws stretching mutely toward heaven. Walking down to the vanishing point, we found there a sort of human chopping-machine where the hogs were converted into commercial pork.... Plump falls the hog upon the table, chop, chop; chop, chop; chop, chop, fall the cleavers.... We took out our watches and counted thirty-five seconds, from the moment when one hog touched the table until the next occupied its place.

Some factories boasted impressive new technology. As early as the 1780s Oliver Evans, a prolific Delaware inventor, built a highly automated flour mill driven by waterpower. His machinery lifted the wheat to the top of the mill, cleaned the grain as it fell into hoppers, ground it into flour, conveyed the flour back to the top of the mill, and then cooled the flour as it was poured into barrels. Evans's factory, remarked one observer, "was as full of machinery as the case of a watch." It needed only six men to mill 100,000 bushels of wheat a year—perhaps ten times as much as they could grind in a traditional flour mill.

By the 1830s, factory owners were using newly improved stationary steam engines to power their mills, which now manufactured a wide array of products. Previously, most factories processed agricultural goods: pork, leather, wool, and cotton; by the 1830s and 1840s, they were fabricating metal goods. Cyrus McCormick of Chicago used power-driven machines to make parts for reaping machines, which workers assembled on a power-driven conveyor belt (see Reading American Pictures, "How Did Americans Dramatically Increase Farm Productivity?" p. 275). In Hartford, Connecticut, Samuel Colt built an assembly line to produce his invention—the six-shooter revolver, as it became known. These technological advances alarmed a team of British observers: "The contriving and making of machinery has become so common in this country, and so many heads and hands are at work with extraordinary energy, that . . . it is to be feared that American manufacturers will become exporters not only to foreign countries, but even to England."

The Textile Industry and British Competition

British textile manufacturers were particularly worried about American competition. To protect its industrial leadership, the British government prohibited the export of textile machinery and the emigration of **mechanics** who knew how to build it. Lured by high wages or offers of partnerships, though, thousands of British mechanics disguised themselves as ordinary laborers and set sail for the United States. By 1812, there were at least three hundred British mechanics at work in the Philadelphia area alone.

Samuel Slater was the most important of them. Slater came to America in 1789 after working for Richard Arkwright, who invented the most advanced British machinery for spinning cotton. Slater reproduced Arkwright's innovations in merchant Moses Brown's cotton mill in Providence, Rhode Island; its opening in 1790 marks the start of the Industrial Revolution in America.

American and British Advantages. In competing with British mills, American manufacturers had the advantage of an abundance of natural resources. The nation's farmers produced a wealth of cotton and wool, and its fast-flowing rivers provided a cheap source of energy. As rivers cascaded down from the Appalachian foothills to the Atlantic coastal plain, they were easily harnessed to power machinery. From Massachusetts to Delaware, these waterways became dotted with industrial villages and towns dominated by massive textile mills, some as large as 150 feet long, 40 feet wide, and four stories high (Map 9.1).

Still, British textile producers easily undersold their American competitors. Thanks to cheap transatlantic shipping and low interest rates in Britain, they could import raw cotton from the United States, manufacture it into cloth, ship the cloth to America, and sell it there at a bargain price. Moreover, well-established British companies could engage in cutthroat competition, slashing prices to drive fledgling American firms out of business. The most important British advantage was cheap labor: Britain had a larger population—about 12.6 million in 1810 compared to 7.3 million Americans—and thousands of landless laborers who were willing to take low-paying factory jobs.

To offset these British advantages, American entrepreneurs won help from the federal government. In 1816 Congress passed a tariff that protected textile manufacturers from low-cost imports of cotton cloth. In 1824 a new tariff levied a tax of 35 percent on higher-grade woolen and cotton textiles, imported iron goods, and various agricultural products; in 1828 the textile duty rose to 50 percent. But in 1833, under pressure from southern planters, western farmers, and urban consumers—who wanted inexpensive imports—Congress began to reduce the tariffs (see Chapter 10), a decision that led to hard times and even bankruptcy for some American textile companies.

Improved Technology and Women Workers. American producers used two other strategies to compete with their British rivals. First, they improved on British technology. In 1811, Francis Cabot Lowell, a wealthy Boston merchant, toured British textile mills. A charming young man, he flattered his hosts by asking many questions; he also duped them, secretly making detailed drawings of their power machinery. Paul Moody, an experienced American mechanic, then copied the machines and refined them. In 1814, Lowell joined with merchants Nathan Appleton and Patrick Tracy Jackson to form the Boston Manufacturing Company. Raising the staggering sum of $400,000, they built a textile plant on the Charles River in Waltham, Massachusetts. The Waltham factory was

How Did Americans Dramatically Increase Farm Productivity?

A central aspect of the economic transformation during the mid-nineteenth century was the increased productivity brought about by harnessing machinery to human power. It is easy to understand how the use of water to power spinning and weaving machines increased output in factories. But what impact did machines have on farming, the dominant occupation in the United States at the time? Did farmers' productivity improve?

Wheat Farming at Bishop Hill, Illinois. Bishop Hill Historic Site/Illinois Historic Preservation Agency.

ANALYZING THE EVIDENCE

➤ The picture on the top shows the wheat harvest at Bishop Hill, a commune founded in Illinois in 1848 by Swedish Pietists (see Chapter 11 for a discussion of rural communes). What tools are the men using to cut the wheat? What are the women's tasks? Do you think these communalists harvested wheat significantly more efficiently than individual farm families had done for a hundred years?

➤ Now look at the picture of McCormick's reaper, taken from an advertisement. Using this machine, the farmer and his son could harvest as much in a day as the nineteen workers at Bishop Hill. How did it achieve such a dramatic increase in productivity?

➤ Look closely at the reaper in the advertisement. What is the purpose of the letters inscribed on each part of the machine? What does

Diagram of McCormick's Reaper from *The Cultivator,* **May 1846.** Wisconsin Historical Society.

this tell you about the standardization of parts that was crucial to the Industrial Revolution?

Why do you think the manufacturer provided this information to potential buyers?

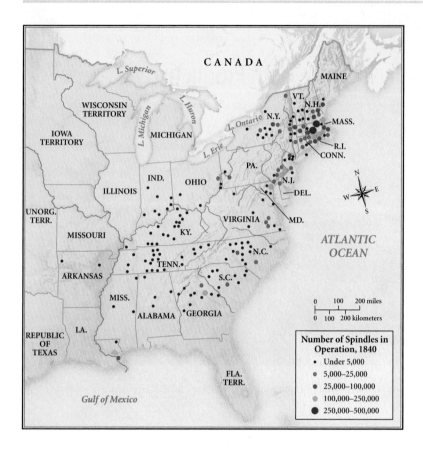

MAP 9.1 New England's Dominance in Cotton Spinning, 1840

Although the South grew the nation's cotton, it did not process it. Entrepreneurs in Massachusetts and Rhode Island built most of the factories that spun and wove raw cotton into cloth. The new factories made use of the abundant waterpower available in New England and the area's surplus labor force. Initially, factory managers hired young farm women to work the machines; later, they would rely on immigrants from Ireland and French-speaking regions of Canada.

the first in America to perform all the operations of cloth making under one roof. Thanks to Moody's improvements, Waltham's power looms operated at higher speeds than British looms and needed fewer workers.

The second American strategy was to tap a new, and cheaper, source of labor. In the 1820s, the Boston Manufacturing Company pioneered a labor system that became known as the Waltham plan. The company recruited thousands of young women from farm families to work in its textile factories. To lure the women, it provided them with rooms in boardinghouses and with evening lectures and other cultural activities. To reassure their parents about their daughters' moral welfare, the mill owners enforced strict curfews, prohibited alcoholic beverages, and required regular church attendance. At Lowell (1822), Chicopee (1823), and other sites in Massachusetts and New Hampshire, the company built new cotton factories modeled on the Waltham plan; other Boston-based companies quickly followed suit.

By the early 1830s, more than 40,000 New England women were working in textile mills. As an observer noted, the wages were "more than could be obtained by the hitherto ordinary occupation of housework," and the living conditions were often better than those in crowded farmhouses. Lucy

Larcom became a textile operative at age eleven so that she could support herself and not be "a trouble or burden or expense" to her widowed mother. Other women operatives used their wages to pay off their father's farm mortgages, send their brothers to school, or accumulate a dowry for themselves.

A few operatives just had a good time. Susan Brown, a Lowell weaver, spent half of her earnings on food and lodging and the rest on plays, concerts, lectures, and a two-day excursion to Boston. Like most textile workers, Brown soon tired of the monotony and rigor of factory work and the never-ceasing clatter of the machinery, which ran twelve hours a day, six days a week. After eight months, she quit, lived at home for a spell, and then moved to another mill. Whatever the hardships, waged work gave young women a new sense of freedom and autonomy. "Don't I feel independent!" a woman mill worker wrote to her sister. "The thought that I am living on no one is a happy one indeed to me."

The owners of the Boston Manufacturing Company were even happier. By combining tariff protection with improved technology and female labor, they could undersell their British rivals. Their textiles were also cheaper than those manufactured in New York and Pennsylvania, where farmworkers were better paid than in New England and textile wages consequently were higher. Manufacturers in

Mill Girl, c. 1850

This fine daguerreotype (an early photograph) shows a neatly dressed textile worker of about twelve. The harsh working conditions in the mill have taken a toll on her spirit and body: The girl's eyes and mouth show little joy or life, and her hands are rough and swollen. She probably worked either as a knotter, tying broken threads on spinning jennies, or a warper, straightening out the strands of cotton or wool as they entered the loom. Jack Naylor Collection.

those states remained in business by using advanced technology to produce higher-quality cloth. Even Thomas Jefferson, the great champion of yeoman farming, was impressed. "Our manufacturers are now very nearly on a footing with those of England," he boasted in 1825.

American Mechanics and Technological Innovation

By the 1820s, American-born artisans had replaced British immigrants at the cutting edge of technological innovation. Although few of these mechanics had a formal education, they now claimed respect as "men professing an ingenious art." In the Philadelphia region, the most important inventors came from the remarkable Sellars family. Samuel Sellars Jr. invented a machine for twisting worsted woolen yarn to give it an especially smooth surface. His son John devised more efficient ways of using waterpower to run the family's sawmills and built a machine to weave wire sieves. John's sons and

grandsons built machine shops that turned out riveted leather fire hoses, papermaking equipment, and eventually locomotives. In 1824, the Sellars family joined with other mechanics to found the Franklin Institute in Philadelphia. Named after Benjamin Franklin, whom the mechanics admired for his scientific accomplishments and idealization of hard work, the Franklin Institute published a journal; provided high-school-level instruction in mechanics, chemistry, mathematics, and mechanical drawing; and organized annual fairs to exhibit new products. Craftsmen in Ohio and many other states established their own mechanics' institutes, which disseminated technical knowledge and encouraged innovation. Around 1820, the U.S. Patent Office was issuing about two hundred patents for new inventions each year, mostly to gentlemen and merchants. By 1860, the office was awarding four thousand patents annually, mostly to mechanics from modest backgrounds.

Eli Whitney and Machine Tools. American craftsmen facilitated the rapid spread of the Industrial Revolution by pioneering the development of

Eli Whitney

Eli Whitney posed for this portrait in the 1820s, when he had achieved both prosperity and social standing as the inventor of the cotton gin and other machines. Whitney's success prompted the artist, his young New Haven, Connecticut, neighbor Samuel F. B. Morse, to turn his creative energies from painting to industrial technology. By the 1840s, Morse had devised the first successful commercial telegraph. Yale University Art Gallery, Gift of George Hoadley, BA 1801.

An Early Cotton Gin

This picture shows the bottom part of a cotton gin, which contained the moving parts. The worker fed the bolls of cotton into the bottom compartment in the front of the machine (to your right) and turned the crank. The toothed cylinder caught the fibers and pulled them from the seeds; the revolving brushes then removed the fibers from the cylinder and pushed them out of the gin, either through the rear or the top. The gin processed cotton quickly and cheaply, and thereby facilitated the dramatic expansion of the cotton textile industry. Over the years, inventors devised much larger gins, powered by water and steam, to process huge bales of raw cotton. Smithsonian Institution, Washington, D.C.

machine tools—machines that made parts for other machines. The key innovator was Eli Whitney (1765–1825), the son of a middling New England farm family. At the age of fourteen, Whitney began manufacturing nails and knife blades and, later, women's hatpins and men's walking sticks. Aspiring to wealth and high social status, Whitney won admission to Yale College and subsequently became a tutor on a Georgia cotton plantation. Using his expertise in making hatpins, he built a simple machine that separated the seeds from the delicate cotton fibers. Although Whitney patented his cotton "engine" (or "gin," as it became known), other manufacturers improved on his design and captured the market.

To restore his finances, Whitney decided in 1798 to manufacture military weapons, a product with a guaranteed government market. With the help of Secretary of the Treasury Oliver Wolcott, he won a U.S. government contract to manufacture 10,000 muskets within twenty-eight months.

Although Whitney failed to meet the deadline, he eventually designed and built machine tools that could rapidly produce interchangeable musket parts. This success won him new contracts for weapons during the War of 1812, and the wealth, social position, and fame as an inventor that he had long craved. After Whitney's death, his partner John H. Hall, an engineer at the federal armory in Harpers Ferry, Virginia (now West Virginia), built lathes to fashion gun stocks and an array of machine tools to work metal: turret lathes, milling machines, and precision grinders.

Entrepreneurial Energy Unleashed. Technological innovation now swept through the rest of American manufacturing. Mechanics in the textile industry invented lathes, planers, and boring machines that turned out standardized parts for new spinning jennies and weaving looms. Although produced in large numbers, these jennies and looms were precise enough in design and construction to operate at higher speeds than British equipment. In 1837, Richard Garsed fashioned improvements that nearly doubled the speed of the power looms in his father's factory in Delaware. Garsed also patented a cam and harness device that allowed machines to weave damask and other fabrics with elaborate designs. Meanwhile, the mechanics employed by Samuel W. Collins in his Connecticut ax-making company built a vastly improved die-forging machine, a device that pressed and hammered hot metal into dies, or cutting forms. Using this machine, a worker could make three hundred ax heads a day—versus twelve using the traditional method. In Richmond, Virginia, Welsh- and American-born mechanics made similar technical advances at the Tredegar Iron Works. Soon, many manufacturers were using machine tools to produce complicated manufacturing equipment with great speed, at low cost, and in large quantities. As a team of British observers noted with admiration, many American products were made "with machinery applied to almost every process . . . all reduced to an almost perfect system of manufacture."

With the expanded availability of machines, the American Industrial Revolution came of age. The sheer volume of output elevated some products—Remington rifles, Singer sewing machines, and Yale locks—into household names in the United States and abroad. After showing their machine-tooled goods at the Crystal Palace Exhibition in London in 1851, the first major international display of industrial goods, Remington, Singer, and other American businesses built factories in Great Britain and soon dominated many European markets.

Wageworkers and the Labor Movement

As the Industrial Revolution gathered momentum, it changed the nature of work and of workers' lives. By the early nineteenth century, many American **craft workers** had developed an "artisan republican ethic" — a collective identity based on the principles of liberty and equality. They saw themselves as small-scale producers, equal to one another and free to work for themselves. The poet Walt Whitman summed up their outlook: "Men must be masters, under themselves."

However, as the outwork and factory systems spread, more and more workers took jobs as wage earners. They no longer labored "under themselves" but under the control and direction of their employers. Unlike women, who embraced factory work because it freed them from parental control and domestic service, men often bridled at their status as wageworkers. To maintain a sense of their personal independence, most male wageworkers repudiated the traditional terms *master* and *servant*; instead, they used the Dutch *boss* to refer to their employer. But as *hired hands*, they received meager wages and had little job security. The artisan-republican ideal, a by-product of the American Revolution, was giving way to the harsher reality of the waged workforce in an industrializing capitalist society.

The Emergence of Unions. Some wageworkers labored as journeymen carpenters, stonecutters, masons, and cabinetmakers, traditional crafts that required specialized skills and so generated a strong sense of identity. Both factors enabled these workers to form unions and bargain with their master-artisan employers. The journeymen's main concern was the increasing length of the workday, which kept them from their families and from educational opportunities. Before 1800, the workday in the building trades averaged about twelve hours, including breaks for meals. By the 1820s, masters were demanding a longer day during the summer, when it stayed light longer, while paying journeymen the old daily rate. In response, six hundred carpenters in Boston went on strike in 1825, demanding a ten-hour workday, 6 A.M. to 6 P.M., with an hour each for breakfast and lunch. Although the Boston protest failed, journeymen carpenters in Philadelphia won a similar strike in 1827. By the mid-1830s, building-trades workers had won a ten-hour workday from many employers and from the federal government at the Philadelphia navy yard.

Artisans whose occupations were threatened by industrialization were less successful in preserving

Woodworker, c. 1850

Skilled furniture makers took great pride in their work, which was often intricately designed and beautifully executed. To underline the dignity of his occupation, this woodworker poses in formal dress and proudly displays the tools of his craft. A belief in the value of labor was an important ingredient of the artisan-republican ideology held by many workers. Library of Congress.

their living standards. As aggressive entrepreneurs and machine technology changed the nature of production, shoemakers, hatters, printers, furniture makers, and weavers faced falling income, unemployment, and loss of status. To avoid the regimentation of factory work, some artisans in these trades moved to small towns or set up specialized shops. In New York City, 800 highly skilled cabinetmakers owned small shops that made fashionable or custom-made furniture. In status and income, they outranked a much larger group of 3,200 semi-trained workers — derogatively called "botches" — who labored for wages in factories making cheap mass-produced tables and chairs. The new industrial system had divided the traditional artisan class into two groups: self-employed craftsmen and wage-earning workers.

In many industries, wage earners banded together to form unions and bargain for better pay and working conditions. However, under English and American common law, unions were illegal. As a Philadelphia judge put it, unions were "a government unto themselves," and unlawfully interfered with an employer's authority over his "servant" and with workers who wanted to bargain for their own wages and working conditions. Despite the legal obstacles, unions sprang up. In 1830, journeymen shoemakers founded a mutual benefit society in Lynn, Massachusetts, and similar organizations soon appeared in other shoemaking centers. "The division of society into the producing and non-producing classes," the journeymen explained, had made workers like themselves into a mere "commodity" whose labor could be bought and sold without regard for their welfare. As another group of workers put it, "The capitalist has no other interest in us, than to get as much labor out of us as possible. We are hired men, and hired men, like hired horses, have no souls." Indeed, we are "slaves in the strictest sense of the word," declared various groups of Lynn shoemakers and Lowell textile workers. But one Lowell worker pointed out, "We are not a quarter as bad off as the slaves of the south. . . . They can't vote nor complain and we can." To exert more pressure on their capitalist employers, in 1834, local unions from Boston to Philadelphia formed the National Trades' Union, the first regional union of different trades.

Labor Ideology and Strikes. Union leaders criticized the new industrial order by endorsing and expanding **artisan republicanism** to include waged laborers. Pointing out that wage earners were becoming "slaves to a monied aristocracy," they condemned the new outwork and factory systems in which "capital and labor stand opposed." To restore a just society in which artisans and waged workers could "live as comfortably as others," they advanced a **labor theory of value**. This theory, or standard, proposed that the price of a good should reflect the labor required to make it and that most of the money from its sale should go to the individual or individuals who produced it — not to factory owners, middlemen, or storekeepers. Appealing to the spirit of the American Revolution, which had destroyed the aristocracy of birth, union publicists called for a new revolution to destroy the aristocracy of capital. In 1836, armed with this artisan-republican ideology, unionized men organized nearly fifty strikes for higher wages.

Women textile operatives were equally active. Competition in the woolen and cotton textile industries was fierce because the output of textiles was growing faster than demand, causing prices to fall. As their profits declined, employers reduced workers' wages and imposed more-stringent work rules. In 1828, women mill workers in Dover, New Hampshire, struck against new rules and won some

relief; six years later, more than eight hundred Dover women walked out to protest wage cuts. In Lowell, two thousand women operatives backed a strike by withdrawing their savings from an employer-owned bank. "One of the leaders mounted a pump," the *Boston Transcript* reported, "and made a flaming . . . speech on the rights of women and the iniquities of the 'monied aristocracy.'" When conditions did not improve, young women in New England refused to enter the mills, and impoverished Irish (and later French Canadian) immigrants took their places.

By the 1850s, many industrial workers were facing the threat of unemployment. As machines produced more goods, the supply of manufactures exceeded the demand for them and prompted employers to lay off workers. In 1857, overproduction coincided with a financial panic that was sparked by speculative investments in railroads that went bankrupt. The result was a major economic recession. Unemployment rose to 10 percent, reminding Americans of the social costs of the new — and otherwise very successful — system of industrial production.

➤ How did American textile manufacturers compete with British manufacturers? How successful were they?

➤ In what ways did the emerging industrial economy conflict with artisan republicanism?

➤ How did wage laborers respond to the new economy?

The Market Revolution

As American factories and farms turned out more goods, businessmen and legislators created faster and cheaper ways to get those products to consumers. Beginning in the late 1810s, they constructed a massive system of canals and roads that linked the states along the Atlantic coast with one another and with the new states in the trans-Appalachian west. This transportation system set in motion both a market revolution and a great migration of people. By 1860, nearly one-third of the nation's citizens lived in the Midwest (the five states carved out of the Northwest Territory — Ohio, Indiana, Illinois, Michigan, and Wisconsin — along with Missouri, Iowa, and Minnesota), where they created a complex society and economy that increasingly resembled the Northeast.

The Transportation Revolution Forges Regional Ties

With the Indian peoples in retreat, slave-owning planters from the Lower South settled in Missouri (admitted to the Union in 1821), and pushed on to Arkansas (1836). Simultaneously, yeomen farm families from the Upper South joined migrants from New England and New York in taking control of the fertile farmlands of the Great Lakes basin. Once Indiana and Illinois were settled, land-hungry farmers poured into Michigan (1837), Iowa (1846), and Wisconsin (1848) (see Voices from Abroad, "Ernst Stille: German Immigrants in the Midwest," p. 282). In 1820, to meet the demand for cheap farmsteads, Congress reduced the price of federal land from $2.00 an acre to $1.25 — just enough to cover the cost of the survey and sale. For $100, a farmer could buy eighty acres, the minimum required under federal law. By 1840, this generous land-distribution policy had lured about 5 million people to states and territories west of the Appalachians (Map 9.2).

To link these settlers to one another, state governments chartered private companies to build toll roads, or turnpikes. In 1806, Congress approved funds for the construction of the National Road, which would tie the Midwest to the seaboard states. The project began in Cumberland in western Maryland in 1811; reached Wheeling, Virginia (now West Virginia), in 1818; crossed the Ohio River in 1833; and ended in Vandalia, Illinois, in 1839. The National Road and other interregional highways carried migrants and their heavily loaded wagons westward; along the way, they passed herds of livestock destined for eastern markets.

Canals. Long-distance travel overland was slow and expensive. To carry people, crops, and manufactures to and from the Midwest, public and private sectors developed a water-borne transportation system of unprecedented size, complexity, and cost. The key event was the decision of the New York legislature in 1817 to build the Erie Canal, a 364-mile waterway from Lake Erie to the Hudson River. It was

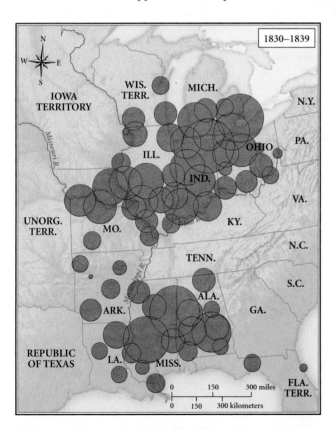
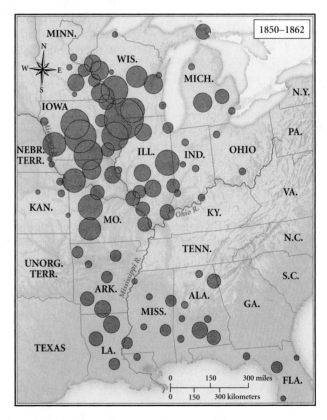

MAP 9.2 Western Land Sales, 1830–1839 and 1850–1862

The federal government set up land offices to sell farmsteads to settlers. During the 1830s, the offices sold huge amounts of land in the corn and wheat belt of the Old Northwest (Ohio, Indiana, Illinois, and Michigan) and the cotton belt of the Old Southwest (especially Alabama and Mississippi). By the 1850s, most sales of government land were in the upper Mississippi River Valley (particularly Iowa and Wisconsin). Each circle centers on a government land office and indicates the relative amount of land sold at that office.

Ernst Stille

German Immigrants in the Midwest

Between 1830 and 1860, Germans flooded into the midwestern states. Among them were twenty-three members of the interrelated Stille and Krumme families from the Prussian province of Westphalia in northwestern Germany. Most of the migrating Stilles and Krummes were younger sons and daughters, who could not hope to inherit farms or make good marriages if they stayed in Westphalia. The letters of Ernst Stille reveal the economic opportunities—and the hardships—of working life in America during the Market Revolution.

Cincinäti, May 20th 1847

Dearest friends and relatives,

I can't neglect sending a short letter from a foreign country to you in the Fatherland. . . . We went from Bremen to Neu Orleans in 2 months. . . . The trip from Neu Orleans to Cincinäti took 12 days. When I got here there was little work and wage in the city since it was the worst time of the whole year that there is, but I was lucky enough to get a job with Fr. Lutterbeck from Ladbergen [a village near his home in Prussia]. . . . In April all the brickmakers started to work again, many Germans work this trade and earn a good wage and I set to work at this too and earn a dollar a day, of that I have to pay 7 dollars a month for board and washing. . . . We make 8,500 bricks a day and it's hard work but when we start at 4 o'clock in the morning we can be finished by 3 o'clock, if I can stay healthy I will keep working here since if you're healthy and can stand the work, it pays the best.

The only people who are really happy here are those who were used to work in Germany and with toil and great pains could hardly earn their daily bread. When people like that come here, even if they don't have any money, they can manage, they rent a room and the husband goes to work, earns his dollar a day and so he can live well and happily, with a wife and children. But a lot of people come over here who were well off in Germany but were enticed to leave their fatherland by boastful and imprudent letters from their friends or children and thought they could become rich in America, this deceives a lot of people, since what can they do here, if they stay in the city they can only earn their bread at hard and unaccustomed labor? If they want to live in the country and don't have enough money to buy a piece of land that is cleared and has a house then they have to settle in the wild bush and have to work very hard to clear the trees out of the way so they can sow and plant, but people who are healthy, strong and hard-working do pretty well. Here in Cincinati I know a lot of people who have made it by working hard, like Ernst Lots for example he does very well he also owns a brickyard and earns good money. . . .

Cincinäti, July 10th 1848

At the beginning of April, I started working for Ernst Lots in the brickyard. . . . In the winter no one can work at this trade because of the snow and ice, then there's a huge number of idle people. The main work in the winter is with fat livestock, brought in from the country in large herds, on the outer edge of the city there are large buildings where about 1000 a day are slaughtered and cleaned, then they're brought into the city where they are cut up and salted and put in barrels that's how they're sent from here to other countries. This is a pretty hard and dirty job, that's why most people would rather do nothing for ¼ year than do this, but if you want to put up with this you can earn 1 to 1½ dollars a day.

I also want to let you know that I got married on the 4th of May of this year, to Heinriette Dickmans, the daughter of one of Dieckman's tenants in Leeden [another village near his Prussian home]. She is 20 years old, left on the same day from Bremerhafen as we went on board but she went via Baltimore. I didn't know her before, neither in Germany nor here, but I got to know her this spring through her uncle Rudolph Expel from Lienen, a good friend of mine who also works for Ernst Lots, who is his son-in-law.

My plan is if I stay in good health for the next couple of years to buy a piece of land and live there, since from my childhood I've been used to farming, I'd rather do that than stay in the city all my life, you can't start very well unless you have 300 dollars.

SOURCE: Walter D. Kamphoefner, Wolfgang Helbid, and Ulrike Sommer, eds., *News from the Land of Freedom: German Immigrants Write Home,* trans. Susan Carter Vogel (Ithaca, NY: Cornell University Press, 1991), 83–87.

ANALYZING THE EVIDENCE

➤ What does it suggest about the immigrant experience that so many people from a cluster of villages in Prussia ended up in contact with one another in Cincinnati, Ohio?

➤ What is Ernst Stille's opinion about what it takes to be successful in America? What will be the key factors in determining whether he achieves his dream of owning a farm?

Building the Erie Canal

By 1860, the success of the Erie Canal had prompted the construction of a vast system of canals, an infrastructure that was as important to the nation as the railroad network of the late nineteenth century, and the interstate highway and airport transportation systems of the late twentieth century. Tens of thousands of workers — many of them Irish immigrants and free blacks — dug out thousands of miles of canals by hand and, with the aid of the simple hoists shown here, built hundreds of stone locks. The unknown artist who sketched this scene focused on the scale of the project, leaving faceless the laborers who undertook this dangerous work. In the marshes near Syracuse, New York, one thousand workers fell ill with fever, and many died. Miriam and Ira D. Wallach Division of Art, Prints and Photographs. The New York Public Library. Astor, Lenox and Tilden Foundations.

an ambitious undertaking. At the time, the longest artificial waterway in the United States was just 28 miles long — a reflection of the huge capital cost of canals and the lack of American engineering expertise. The New York project did have three things in its favor: the vigorous support of New York City's merchants, who wanted access to western markets; the backing of New York's governor, De Witt Clinton, who persuaded the legislature to finance the waterway from tax revenues, tolls, and bond sales to foreign investors; and the relative gentleness of the terrain west of Albany. Even so, the task was enormous. Workers — many of them Irish immigrants — had to dig out millions of cubic yards of soil, quarry thousands of tons of rock to build the huge locks that raised and lowered the boats, and construct vast reservoirs to ensure a steady supply of water.

The first great engineering project in American history, the Erie Canal altered the ecology and the economy of an entire region. As farming communities and market towns sprang up along the waterway, settlers cut down millions of trees to provide wood for building and heating, and land for growing crops and grazing animals. Cows and sheep foraged on pastures recently occupied by deer and bears, and spring rains caused massive erosion of the denuded landscape.

Whatever its ecological consequences, the Erie Canal was an instant economic success. The first section, a stretch of 75 miles, opened in 1819 and immediately generated enough revenue to repay its cost. When the canal was completed in 1825, a 40-foot-wide ribbon of water stretched 364 miles from Buffalo, on the eastern shore of Lake Erie, to

Albany, where it joined the Hudson River for a 150-mile trip to New York City. After an excursion on the canal, novelist Nathaniel Hawthorne suggested that its water "must be the most fertilizing of all fluids, for it causes towns with their masses of brick and stone, their churches and theaters, their business and hubbub, their luxury and refinement, their gay dames and polished citizens, to spring up."

The Erie Canal brought prosperity to the farmers of central and western New York by carrying wheat, flour, and meat to eastern cities and from there to foreign markets. One-hundred-ton freight barges, each pulled by two horses, moved along the canal at a steady 30 miles a day, cutting transportation costs and greatly accelerating the flow of goods. In 1818, the mills in Rochester had processed 26,000 barrels of flour; ten years later, their output had soared to 200,000 barrels; and by 1840, it was at 500,000 barrels. Northeastern manufacturers used the canal to ship clothing, boots, and agricultural equipment to farm families throughout the Great Lakes basin and the Ohio River Valley. In payment, the farmers sent grain, cattle, and hogs as well as raw materials (leather, wool, and hemp, for example) to the East.

The spectacular benefits of the Erie Canal prompted a national canal boom. Civic and business leaders in Philadelphia and Baltimore proposed waterways to link their cities to the West. Implementing New York's fiscal innovations, they persuaded their state governments to invest directly in canal companies or to force state-chartered banks to do so. They also won state guarantees for

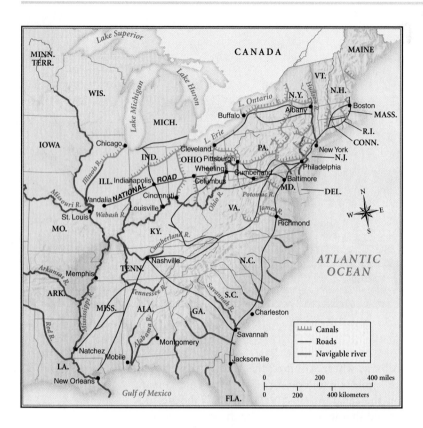

MAP 9.3 The Transportation Revolution: Roads and Canals, 1820–1850

By 1850, the United States had an efficient transportation system with three distinct parts. One system, composed of short canals and navigable rivers, carried cotton, tobacco, and other products from the countryside of the southern seaboard states into the Atlantic commercial system. A second system, centered on the Erie, Chesapeake and Ohio, and Pennsylvania Mainline canals, linked the major seaport cities of the Northeast to the vast trans-Appalachian region. Finally, a set of regional canals in the Old Northwest connected most of the Great Lakes region to the Ohio and Mississippi rivers and the port of New Orleans.

canal bonds to encourage British and Dutch investors to buy them. In fact, foreign investors provided almost three-quarters of the $400 million invested in canals by 1840. Waterways connected the farms and cities of the Great Lakes region with the great port cities of New York, Philadelphia, and Baltimore (via the Erie, Pennsylvania, and Chesapeake and Ohio canals) and with New Orleans (via the Ohio and Mississippi Rivers). In 1848, the completion of the Michigan and Illinois Canal, which linked Chicago to the Mississippi River, completed an inland all-water route from New York City to New Orleans (Map 9.3).

Steamboats Improve Interregional Transportation. The steamboat, another product of the industrial age, ensured the economic success of the river-borne transportation system of the Midwest. Engineer-inventor Robert Fulton had built the first American steamboat, the *Clermont*, which he navigated up the Hudson River in 1807. However, the first steamboats could not navigate shallow western rivers. During the 1820s, engineers broadened the hulls of the steamboats to reduce their draft and enlarge their cargo capacity. The improved steamboats halved the cost of upstream river transport and, along with the canals, dramatically increased the flow of goods, people, and news to the Midwest.

In 1830, a traveler or a letter from New York could go by water to Buffalo or Pittsburgh in less than a week, and to Detroit or St. Louis in two weeks. Thirty years earlier, the same journeys had taken twice as long.

The states and the national government played key roles in the development of this interregional system of transportation and communication. Working through the Commonwealth system, state governments subsidized the canals. For its part, the national government created a vast postal system, the first network for the exchange of information. Following passage of the Post Office Act of 1792, the mail system grew rapidly—to eight hundred post offices by 1800 and to more than eight thousand by 1830—and safely carried thousands of letters and millions of dollars of banknotes from one end of the country to the other. The U.S. Supreme Court, headed by John Marshall, likewise encouraged interstate trade by striking down state restrictions on commerce. In *Gibbons v. Ogden* (1824), the Court voided a New York law that created a monopoly on steamboat travel into New York City, establishing the authority of the federal government over interstate commerce (see Chapter 7). That decision meant that no local or state monopolies—or tariffs—would impede the flow of goods, services, and news across the nation.

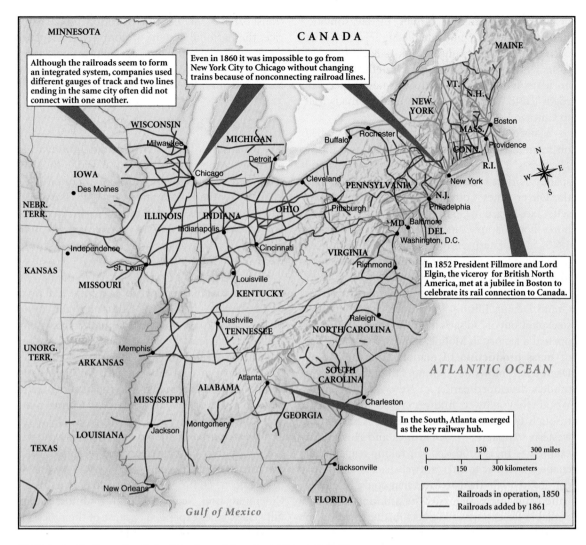

Although the railroads seem to form an integrated system, companies used different gauges of track and two lines ending in the same city often did not connect with one another.

Even in 1860 it was impossible to go from New York City to Chicago without changing trains because of nonconnecting railroad lines.

In 1852 President Fillmore and Lord Elgin, the viceroy for British North America, met at a jubilee in Boston to celebrate its rail connection to Canada.

In the South, Atlanta emerged as the key railway hub.

	Railroads in operation, 1850
	Railroads added by 1861

MAP 9.4 Railroads of the North and South, 1850 and 1861

In the decade before the Civil War, entrepreneurs in the Northeast and the Midwest laid thousands of miles of new railroad lines, creating an extensive and dense transportation system that stimulated economic development. The South built a more limited system of railroads. In all regions, railroad companies used different track gauges, which hindered the efficient flow of traffic.

Railroads and Regional Ties. By the 1850s, another product of industrial technology — the railroad — linked the Northeast and the Midwest and soon replaced the canals as the center of the national transportation system (Map 9.4). To capture the market in midwestern grain, capitalists in Boston and New York invested heavily in transportation routes on or near the Great Lakes. In 1852, the canals of the region carried twice the tonnage transported by railroads; within a decade, railroads became the main carriers of wheat and freight. Serviced by a vast network of locomotive and freight-car repair shops, the Erie Railroad, the Pennsylvania Railroad, the New York Central

Railroad, and the Baltimore and Ohio Railroad connected the Atlantic ports — New York, Philadelphia, and Baltimore — with the rapidly expanding Great Lakes cities of Cleveland and Chicago.

Moreover, the railroad boom of the 1850s opened up the vast territory south and west of Chicago. Trains carried large quantities of lumber from Michigan to the treeless prairies of Indiana, Illinois, Iowa, and Missouri, where settlers built 250,000 new farms (covering 19 million acres) and hundreds of small towns. The rail lines moved millions of bushels of wheat to Chicago, for transport by boat or rail to eastern markets. Increasingly, they also carried hogs and cattle to Chicago's growing stockyards. A farmer in Jacksonville, Illinois, reported that he intended to feed his entire corn crop of 1,500 bushels "to hogs & cattle, as we think it is more profitable than to sell the corn." "In ancient times," boasted a Chicago newspaper, "all roads led to Rome; in modern times all roads lead to Chicago."

Many of the first migrants to the Midwest relied on manufactured goods made in Britain or in the Northeast. They bought high-quality shovels and spades fabricated at the Delaware Iron Works and the Oliver Ames Company in Easton, Massachusetts; axes forged in Connecticut factories; and steel horseshoes manufactured in Troy, New York. By the 1840s, midwestern entrepreneurs were beginning to produce these and other manufactures: machine tools, hardware, furniture, and especially agricultural implements. Working as a blacksmith in Grand Detour, Illinois, John Deere made his first steel plow out of old saws in 1837; ten years later, he opened a factory in Moline, Illinois, that made use of **mass production** to manufacture the plows. Deere's steel plows were stronger than the cast-iron models developed earlier in New York by Jethro Wood; they allowed midwestern farmers to cut through the thick sod of the prairies. Other midwestern companies — McCormick and Hussey, for example — mass-produced self-raking reapers that enabled a farmer to harvest twelve acres of grain a day (rather than the two acres that could be cut by hand) and vastly increased the amount of wheat available for export to markets in the East and in Europe.

Extraregional trade also linked southern planters to northeastern textile plants and foreign markets. This commerce bolstered the wealth of the South but did not transform the economic and social order there as it did in the Midwest. Southern investors continued to commit their capital to land and slaves, which yielded high profits and provided impressive increases in output (see Chapter 12). By the 1840s, the South produced more than two-thirds of the world's cotton and accounted for almost two-thirds of American exports. With the exception of Richmond, Virginia, and a few other places, though, planters did not invest their cotton profits in manufacturing. Lacking cities, factories, and highly trained workers, the South remained an agricultural economy that provided high living standards only to the 25 percent of the white population that owned plantations and slaves. By 1860, the southern economy generated an average annual per capita income of $103, while the more productive economic system of the Northeast yielded an average income of $141. By facilitating the transport of the staple crops of cotton, tobacco, and rice, the national system of commerce deepened the South's commitment to agriculture and slavery, even as it promoted diversified economies in the Northeast and Midwest.

The Growth of Cities and Towns

The expansion of industry and trade dramatically increased America's urban population. In 1820, there were only 58 towns with more than 2,500 inhabitants in the United States; by 1840, there were 126 urban centers, located mostly in the Northeast and Midwest. During those two decades, the total number of city dwellers grew more than fourfold, from 443,000 to 1,844,000.

The most rapid growth occurred in the new industrial towns that sprang up along the "fall line," where rivers began their rapid descent to the coastal plain. In 1822, the Boston Manufacturing Company expanded north from its base in Waltham and built a complex of mills in the sleepy Merrimack River village of East Chelmsford, Massachusetts, and quickly transformed it into the bustling textile factory town of Lowell. Hartford, Connecticut; Trenton, New Jersey; and Wilmington, Delaware, also became urban centers as mill owners exploited the waterpower of their rivers and recruited workers from the countryside.

Western commercial cities like Pittsburgh, Cincinnati, and New Orleans grew almost as rapidly. These cities expanded because of their location at points where goods were transferred from one mode of transport to another — canal boats or farmers' wagons, for example, to steamboats or sailing vessels. As the midwestern population grew during the 1830s and 1840s, St. Louis, Detroit, and especially Buffalo and Chicago emerged as dynamic centers of commerce. "There can be no two places in the world," journalist and author Margaret Fuller wrote from Chicago in 1843, "more completely thoroughfares than this place and Buffalo. They are the correspondent valves that open and shut all the time, as the life-blood rushes from east to west, and back again from west to east." To a German visitor, the city seemed "for the most part to consist of shops . . . [as if] people came here merely to trade, to make money, and not to live" (see Chapter 18). Chicago's merchants and bankers developed the marketing, provisioning, and financial services that were essential to farmers and small-town merchants in the surrounding countryside. "There can be no better [market] anywhere in the Union," declared a farmer in Paw Paw, Illinois.

MAP 9.5 The Nation's Major Cities, 1840

By 1840, the United States boasted three major conglomerations of cities. The oldest ports on the Atlantic — from Boston to Baltimore — served as centers for import merchants, banks, insurance companies, and manufacturers of ready-made clothing, and their reach extended far into the interior — nationwide in the case of New York City. A second group of cities stretched along Lake Erie and included the wholesale distribution hubs of Buffalo, Detroit, and Chicago, as well as the manufacturing center of Cleveland. A third urban system extended along the Ohio River, comprising the industrial cities of Pittsburgh and Cincinnati and the wholesale centers of Louisville and St. Louis.

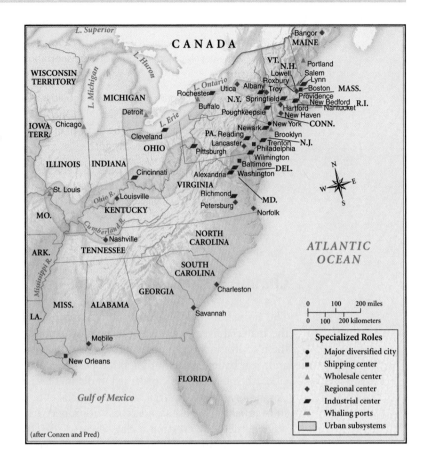

The midwestern commercial hubs quickly became manufacturing centers as well. Maximizing the cities' locations as key junctions for railroad lines and steamboats, entrepreneurs built docks, warehouses, flour mills, and packing plants, creating work for hundreds of artisans and factory laborers. In 1846, Cyrus McCormick moved his reaper factory from western Virginia to Chicago to be closer to his midwestern customers. By 1860, St. Louis and Chicago had become the nation's third and fourth largest cities, respectively, after New York and Philadelphia (Map 9.5).

The old Atlantic seaports — Boston, Philadelphia, Baltimore, Charleston, and especially New York City — remained important for their foreign commerce and, increasingly, as centers of finance and manufacturing. New York City and nearby Brooklyn grew at a phenomenal rate: Between 1820 and 1860, its population quadrupled to nearly one million as tens of thousands of German and Irish immigrants poured into the city. Drawing on the abundant supply of labor, New York became a center of small-scale manufacturing and the ready-made clothing industry, which relied on the labor of thousands of low-paid seamstresses. "The

wholesale clothing establishments are . . . absorbing the business of the country," a "Country Tailor" complained to the *New York Tribune,* "casting many an honest and hardworking man out of employment [and allowing] . . . the large cities to swallow up the small towns."

New York's growth stemmed primarily from its dominant position in foreign and domestic trade. It had the best harbor in the United States and, thanks to the Erie Canal, was the best gateway to the West for immigrants and manufactures and the best outlet for shipments of western grain. Exploiting the city's prime location, in 1818, four Quaker merchants founded the Black Ball Line, which carried cargo, people, and mail on a regular schedule between New York and the European ports of Liverpool, London, and Le Havre. New York merchants likewise dominated trade with the newly independent South American nations of Brazil, Peru, and Venezuela. New York–based traders took over the cotton trade by offering finance, insurance, and shipping to export merchants in southern ports. By 1840, the port of New York handled almost two-thirds of foreign imports into the United States, almost half of all foreign trade, and much of the immigrant traffic.

➤ What roles did government — state and national — play in the development of America's transportation networks?

➤ From the evidence provided in the text, could it be argued that the construction of the Erie Canal was the central economic event of the first half of the nineteenth century? Why or why not?

➤ Describe the different types of cities that emerged in the United States in the first half of the nineteenth century. How do you explain the differences in their development?

Changes in the Social Structure

The Industrial and Market revolutions improved the material lives of many Americans by enabling them to live in larger houses, cook on iron stoves, and wear better-made clothes. But especially in the cities, the new economic order led to distinct social classes: a wealthy industrial and commercial elite, a substantial middle class, and a mass of propertyless wage earners. By creating a class-divided society, industrialization posed a momentous challenge to America's republican ideals.

The Business Elite

Before industrialization, white Americans thought of their society in terms of rank: That is, "notable" families had higher status than families of the "lower orders." Yet in most rural areas, people in the different ranks shared a common culture: Gentlemen farmers talked easily with yeomen about crop yields, while their wives conversed about the art of quilting. In the South, humble tenants and aristocratic slave owners shared the same amusements: gambling, cockfighting, and horse racing. Rich and poor attended the same Quaker meetinghouse or Presbyterian church. "Almost everyone eats, drinks, and dresses in the same way," a European visitor to Hartford, Connecticut, reported in 1798, "and one can see the most obvious inequality only in the dwellings."

The Industrial Revolution shattered this agrarian social order and created a fragmented society composed of distinct regions, classes, and cultures. The new economic system pulled many Americans into large cities, thereby accentuating the differences between rural and urban life. Moreover, it made a few city residents — the merchants, manufacturers, bankers, and landlords who comprised the business elite — very rich. In 1800, the top 10 percent of the nation's families owned about 40 percent of the wealth; by 1860, the richest 10 percent owned nearly 70 percent of the wealth. In large cities like New York, Chicago, Baltimore, and New Orleans, the superrich — the top 1 percent — owned more than 40 percent of all tangible property (land and buildings, for example) and an even higher share of intangible property (stocks and bonds).

Government tax policies facilitated the accumulation of wealth. In an era before federal taxes on individual and corporate income, the U.S. Treasury raised most of its revenue from tariffs — taxes on textiles and other imported goods that were purchased mostly by ordinary citizens. State and local governments also favored the wealthier classes. They usually taxed real estate (farms, city lots, and buildings) and tangible personal property (furniture, tools, and machinery) but almost never taxed the stocks and bonds owned by the rich or the inheritances they passed on to their children.

Cities that were once relatively homogenous took on an increasingly fragmented character. Over time, the wealthiest families consciously set themselves apart. They dressed in well-tailored clothes, rode in fancy carriages, and lived in expensively furnished houses tended by butlers, cooks, and other servants. The women no longer socialized with those of lesser wealth, and the men no longer labored side by side with their journeymen. Instead, they became managers and directors and relied on trusted subordinates to issue orders to hundreds of factory operatives. Increasingly, merchants, manufacturers, and bankers, searching for privacy, chose to live in separate neighborhoods, often at the edge of the city. The reclusiveness of privileged families and the massive flow of immigrants into other districts divided cities geographically along lines of class, race, and ethnicity.

The Middle Class

Standing between wealthy owners at one end of the urban social spectrum and propertyless wage earners at the other was a growing middle class — the social product of the economic revolution. As a Boston printer explained, the bulk of the "middling class" was made up of "the farmers, the mechanics, the manufacturers, the traders, who carry on professionally the ordinary operations of buying, selling, and exchanging merchandize." Other members of the middle class came from various professional groups — building contractors, lawyers, and surveyors — who suddenly found their services in great demand and financially profitable. Middle-class business owners, employees, and professionals were most numerous in the Northeast, where in the 1840s they numbered about 30 percent of the population. But they also could be found in the agrarian South: In 1854, Oglethorpe, Georgia (population 2,500), a cotton boomtown, had eighty "business houses" and eight hotels.

The growing size, wealth, and cultural influence of the middle class reflected a dramatic rise in urban prosperity. Between 1830 and 1857, the per capita income of Americans increased by about 2.5 percent a year, a remarkable rate never since matched. This surge in income, along with the availability of inexpensive mass-produced goods, facilitated the emergence of a distinct middle-class urban culture. Middle-class husbands earned enough to support their families and to save about 15 percent of their income, which they used to buy a well-built house in a "respectable part of town." They purchased handsome clothes and drove about town in smart carriages. Relieved from the burden of labor, their wives became purveyors of genteel culture, buying books, pianos, lithographs, and commodious furniture for their front parlors. Instead of hiring Irish or African Americans to perform menial tasks, some middle-class families relied on the new industrial technology. They outfitted their residences with furnaces that heated water for bathing and for radiators that warmed entire rooms; they bought cooking stoves with ovens and treadle-operated sewing machines. Well-to-do urban families now kept their perishable food in iceboxes, which ice-company wagons filled periodically, and bought many varieties of packaged goods. As early as 1825, the Underwood Company of Boston was marketing well-preserved Atlantic salmon in jars.

If material comfort was one distinguishing mark of the middle class, moral and mental discipline was another. Middle-class writers denounced the black-led festivals of Election Day and Pinkster as a "chaos of sin and folly, of misery and fun," and, by the 1830s, had secured their suppression. Ambitious parents were equally concerned with their children's moral character and stressed discipline, integrity, and hard work. To ensure their success, middle-class parents usually provided their offspring with a high school education (in an era when most white children received only five years of schooling). Many American Protestants had long believed that diligent work in an earthly "calling" was a duty owed to God. Now the business elite and the middle class gave this idea a secular twist. They celebrated work as the key to a higher standard of living for the nation and to social mobility for the individual.

Benjamin Franklin gave classical expression to the secular work ethic in his *Autobiography*, which was published in full in 1818 (almost thirty years after Franklin died) and immediately found a huge audience. Heeding Franklin's suggestion that an industrious man would become a rich one, tens of thousands of young American men worked hard, saved their money, adopted temperate habits, and practiced honesty in their business dealings. Countless magazines, children's books, self-help manuals, and novels taught the same lessons. The **self-made man** became a central theme of American popular culture. Knowing that many affluent families had risen from modest beginnings, middle-class men and women took them as models. Just as the rural-producer ethic had united the social ranks in pre-1800 America, personal achievement linked the upper and middle classes of the new industrializing society.

Urban Workers and the Poor

As thoughtful business leaders surveyed their industrializing society, they concluded that the yeoman and artisan-republican's ideal—a society of independent producers—was no longer possible. "Entire independence ought not to be wished for," Ithamar A. Beard, the paymaster of the Hamilton Manufacturing Company, told a mechanics' association in 1827. "In large manufacturing towns, many more must fill subordinate stations and must be under the immediate direction and control of a master or superintendent, than in the farming towns."

Wageworkers Increase. Beard had a point. In 1840, all of the nation's slaves and about half of its native-born free workers were laboring for others. The bottom 10 percent of white wage earners consisted of casual workers—those hired on a short-term basis for the most arduous jobs. Poor women washed clothes, while their husbands and sons carried lumber and bricks for construction projects, loaded ships, and dug out dirt and stones to build canals. When they could find work, these men earned "their dollar *per diem*," an "Old Inhabitant" wrote to the *Baltimore American*, but he cautioned that those workers could never save enough "to pay rent, buy fire wood and eatables" when the harbor froze up. During business depressions, they bore the brunt of unemployment; and even in the best of times, their jobs were temporary and dangerous.

Other laborers had greater security of employment, but few were prospering. In Massachusetts in 1825, the daily wage of an unskilled worker was about two-thirds that of a mechanic; two decades later it was less than half as much. The 18,000 native-born and immigrant women who made men's clothing in New York City in the 1850s earned a few pennies a day, less than $80 a year. Those meager wages barely paid for food and rent, which meant that many wage earners were unable to take advantage of the rapidly falling prices of manufactured goods. Only the most fortunate working-class families could afford to educate their children, buy an apprenticeship for their sons, or accumulate small dowries so that their daughters could marry men with better prospects. Most families sent their ten-year-old children out to work, and the death of a parent often threw the survivors into dire poverty. As a charity worker noted, "What can a bereaved widow do, with 5 or 6 little children, destitute of every means of support but what her own hands can furnish (which in a general way does not amount to more than 25 cents a day)."

The Lives of the Poor. Over time, their poverty forced these urban workers to move into dilapidated housing or bad neighborhoods. Single men and women lived in crowded boardinghouses, while families jammed themselves into tiny apartments in the basements and attics of small houses. As immigrants poured into the nation after 1840, urban populations soared, and developers squeezed more and more dwellings and foul-smelling outhouses onto a single lot. Venturing into the slums of New York City in the 1850s, shocked state legislators found gaunt shivering people with "wild ghastly faces" living amid "hideous squalor and deadly effluvia, the dim, undrained courts oozing with pollution, the dark, narrow stairways, decayed with age, reeking with filth, overrun with vermin."

Many wage earners sought solace in alcohol. Beer and rum had long been standard fare in many American rituals: patriotic ceremonies, work breaks, barn raisings, and games. But during the 1820s and 1830s, the consumption of intoxicating beverages and alcoholism throughout the population reached new heights. Heavy drinking killed Daniel Tomkins, vice president under James Monroe, and undermined Henry Clay's bid for the presidency. It had a devastating impact on urban wage earners. Although Methodist artisans and ambitious craft workers "swore off" liquor to protect their work skills, health, and finances, other workers began to drink heavily on the job — not just during the traditional 11 A.M. and 4 P.M. "refreshers." A baker recalled how "one man was stationed at the window to watch, while the rest drank." Long before the arrival of spirit-drinking Irish and beer-drinking German immigrants, there were grogshops on almost every block in working-class districts. These saloons became focal points of disorder. Unrestrained drinking by young men led to fistfights, brawls, and robberies; and the urban police, mostly low-paid watchmen and untrained constables, were unable to contain the lawlessness.

The Benevolent Empire

The disorder among native-born urban wage earners alarmed the rising middle class, who profited from their labors but feared their potential power. Many upwardly mobile men and women embraced the principle of religious benevolence and now used it to spearhead a movement of conservative social reform. In the 1820s, they joined with their Congregational and Presbyterian ministers and launched programs of social reforms that historians refer to collectively as the **Benevolent Empire**. The purpose of the reforms, announced Lyman Beecher, a minister who spoke out loudly against intemperance and poverty, was to restore "the moral government of God." The reformers introduced new forms of moral discipline into their own lives and tried to infuse them into the lives of working people as well. They would regulate popular behavior — by persuasion if possible, by law if necessary.

Although the Benevolent Empire targeted age-old evils like drunkenness, adultery, prostitution, and crime, its methods were new. Instead of relying on church sermons and the suasion of community leaders, the reformers set out to institutionalize charity and systematically combat evil. They established large-scale organizations — the Prison Discipline Society and the American Society for the Promotion of Temperance, among many others. Each organization had a managing staff, a network of hundreds of chapters, thousands of volunteer members, and a newspaper.

Often working in concert, these benevolent groups wanted to improve society. First, they encouraged people to lead well-disciplined lives by campaigning for temperance (moderation or even abstention from alcohol) and "regular habits." They persuaded local governments to ban the carnivals of drink and dancing, such as Negro Election Day (mock festivities in which African Americans symbolically took over the government), which had been enjoyed by whites as well as blacks. Second, they devised new institutions to help those in need and to control those they considered threats to society. Reformers provided homes of refuge for abandoned children and asylums for insane individuals, who previously had been confined by their families in

Five Points, New York City, 1827

To upper-class New Yorkers, like the top-hatted gentleman at the center of the picture, Five Points was a frightening slum. Indeed, the neighborhood of overcrowded tenement buildings filled with impoverished Irish immigrants and African Americans had all too much physical violence and early death. Still, it was home to thousands of working-class New Yorkers, who created a rich social life in local taverns and markets. *Valentine's Manual*, 1855.

attics and cellars. They campaigned to end corporal punishment and to rehabilitate criminals in new penitentiaries designed to modify criminal behavior.

Women were a crucial part of the Benevolent Empire. Since the 1790s, upper-class women had sponsored charitable organizations like the Society for the Relief of Poor Widows with Small Children, which was founded in New York by Isabella Graham, a devout Presbyterian widow. Her daughter Joanna Bethune set up other charitable institutions, including the Orphan Asylum Society and the Society for the Promotion of Industry, which found jobs for hundreds of poor women as spinners and seamstresses.

Some reformers believed that the greatest threat to the "moral government of God" was the decline of the traditional Sabbath. As commerce increased, merchants and storekeepers conducted business on Sundays, and urban saloons provided drink and entertainment. To halt these activities, in 1828, Lyman Beecher and other ministers formed the General Union for Promoting the Observance of the Christian Sabbath. General Union chapters — replete with women's auxiliaries — sprang up from Maine to the Ohio River Valley. To rally Christians to its cause, the General Union demanded repeal of a law Congress had enacted in 1810 allowing mail to be transported — though not delivered — on

An Inside View of the Benevolent Empire

Early-nineteenth-century reformers condemned corporal punishment for criminals. So they built prisons designed to rehabilitate offenders and turn them into responsible citizens. As this folk painting by a prisoner at a Massachusetts penitentiary suggests, prison officials imposed tight discipline on inmates. The inmates marched in silence: In line with the latest penal theories, prisoners were not allowed to speak with one another, the silence key to their reflection on their crimes and ultimate penitence. David A. Schorsch.

Sunday. Its members also boycotted shipping companies that did business on the Sabbath and campaigned for municipal laws forbidding games and festivals on the Lord's day.

The Benevolent Empire's efforts to enforce the Sabbath aroused controversy. Many men who labored twelve or fourteen hours a day for six days a week refused to spend their one day of leisure in meditation and prayer. Shipping company managers demanded that the Erie Canal provide lockkeepers on Sundays and joined those Americans who argued that using laws to enforce a particular set of moral beliefs was "contrary to the free spirit of our institutions." When some evangelical reformers proposed to teach Christianity to slaves, many white southerners were outraged. This kind of popular resistance limited the success of the Benevolent Empire.

Charles Grandison Finney: Revivalism and Reform

Presbyterian minister Charles Grandison Finney found a new way to propagate religious values among Americans. Finney was not part of the traditional religious elite. Born into a poor farming family in Connecticut, he planned to become a lawyer and rise into the middle class. But in 1823, Finney underwent an intense conversion experience and chose the ministry as his career. Beginning in towns along the Erie Canal, the young minister conducted emotional revival meetings that stressed conversion rather than instruction and discipline. Repudiating traditional Calvinist beliefs, he maintained that God would welcome any sinner who submitted to the Holy Spirit. Finney's ministry drew on—and greatly accelerated—the Second Great Awakening, the wave of Protestant revivalism that had begun after the Revolution (see Chapter 8).

Evangelical Ideology. Finney's central message was that "God has made man a moral free agent" who could choose salvation. This doctrine of free will was particularly attractive to members of the new middle class, who had already chosen to improve their material lives. But Finney also had great

Charles Grandison Finney, Evangelist (1792–1875)

When an unknown artist painted this flattering portrait in 1834, Finney was forty-two years old and at the height of his career as an evangelist. Handsome and charismatic, Finney had just led a series of enormously successful revivals in Rochester, New York, and other cities along the Erie Canal. In 1835, he established a theology department at newly founded Oberlin College in Ohio, where he trained a generation of ministers and served as president from 1851 to 1866. Oberlin College Archives.

success in converting those at the ends of the social spectrum: the haughty rich, who had placed themselves above God, and the abject poor, who seemed lost to drink and sloth. Finney celebrated their common fellowship in Christ and identified them spiritually with pious middle-class respectability.

Finney's most spectacular triumph came in 1830, when he moved his revivals from small towns to Rochester, New York, now a major milling and commercial city on the Erie Canal. Preaching every day for six months and promoting group prayer meetings in family homes, he won over the influential merchants and manufacturers of Rochester, who pledged to reform their lives and those of their workers. They promised to attend church, give up intoxicating beverages, and work hard. To encourage their employees to follow suit, wealthy businessmen founded a Free Presbyterian church — "free" because members did not have to pay for pew space. Other evangelical Protestants founded similar churches to serve transient canal laborers,

and pious businessmen set up a savings bank to encourage thrift among the working classes. Meanwhile, Finney's wife, Lydia, and other pious middle-class women carried the Christian message to the wives of the unconverted, set up Sunday schools for poor children, and formed the Female Charitable Society to assist the unemployed.

Finney's efforts to create a harmonious community of morally disciplined Christians were not completely successful. Skilled workers who belonged to strong craft organizations — boot makers, carpenters, stonemasons, and boatbuilders — argued that they needed higher wages and schools more urgently than sermons and prayers. Poor people ignored Finney's revival, as did the Irish Catholic immigrants who had recently begun arriving in Rochester and other northeastern cities, bringing with them a hatred of Protestants as both religious heretics and political oppressors.

Ignoring this resistance, revivalists from New England to the Midwest copied Finney's evangelical message and techniques. In New York City, wealthy silk merchants Arthur and Lewis Tappan founded a magazine, *The Christian Evangelist*, which promoted Finney's ideas. The revivals swept through Pennsylvania, North Carolina, Tennessee, and Indiana, where, a convert reported, "you could not go upon the street and hear any conversation, except upon religion." The success of the revivals "has been so general and thorough," concluded a Presbyterian general assembly, "that the whole customs of society have changed."

The Temperance Crusade. The **temperance movement** proved to be the most effective arena for evangelical social reform. In 1832, evangelicals gained control of the American Temperance Society; soon the society boasted two thousand chapters and more than 200,000 members. The society employed the methods that had worked so well in the revivals — group confession and prayer, a focus on the family and the spiritual role of women, and sudden emotional conversion — and took them to every northern town and southern village. On one day in New York City in 1841, more than 4,000 people took the temperance "pledge." Throughout America, the consumption of spirits fell dramatically, from an average of five gallons per person in 1830 to two gallons in 1845.

Evangelical reformers celebrated religion as the moral center of the temperance movement and the foundation of the American work ethic. Laziness and drinking could not be cured by Benjamin Franklin's method of self-discipline, they argued; instead, people had to experience a profound

The Drunkard's Progress: From the First Glass to the Grave

This 1846 lithograph, published by N. Currier, depicts the inevitable fate of those who drink. The drunkard's descent into "Poverty and Disease" ends with "Death by suicide," leaving a grieving and destitute wife and child. Temperance reformers urged Americans to take "The Cold Water Cure," to drink water instead of liquor. To promote abstinence among the young, Reverend Thomas Hunt founded the Cold Water Army, an organization that grew to embrace several hundred thousand children, all of whom pledged "perpetual hate to all that can Intoxicate." Library of Congress.

change of heart through religious conversion. This evangelical message fostered individual enterprise and moral discipline not only among middle-class Americans but also among many wage earners. Thus, religion and the ideology of social mobility served as powerful cement that held society together in the face of the divisions created by industrialization, the market economy, and increasing cultural diversity.

Immigration and Cultural Conflict

Cultural diversity stemmed in part from a vast wave of immigrants. Between 1840 and 1860, about 2 million Irish, 1.5 million Germans, and 750,000 Britons poured into the United States. They were a diverse lot. The British migrants were primarily Protestant and relatively prosperous; their ranks included many trained professionals, propertied farmers, and skilled workers. Many

German immigrants also came from property-owning farming and artisan families and had the resources to move to the midwestern states of Wisconsin, Iowa, and Missouri. Other Germans and most of the Irish settled in the Northeast, where by 1860 they accounted for nearly one-third of white adults. Most immigrants avoided the South because they opposed slavery or feared competition from enslaved workers.

Irish Immigration. The poorest migrants were Irish peasants and laborers, who were fleeing a famine caused by severe overpopulation and a devastating blight on the potato crop. Arriving in dire poverty, the Irish settled mostly in the cities of New England and New York; the men took low-paying jobs as factory hands, construction workers, and canal diggers, while the women took positions as domestic servants in middle- and upper-class homes. Irish families crowded into cheap tenement buildings with primitive sanitation systems and were the first to die when disease struck. In the summer of 1849, a cholera epidemic took the lives of thousands of poor immigrants in St. Louis and New York City.

In times of hardship and sorrow, immigrants turned to their churches. Many Germans and virtually all the Irish were Catholics, and they fueled the growth of the Catholic Church. In 1840, there were sixteen Catholic dioceses and seven hundred churches in the United States; by 1860, there were forty-five dioceses and twenty-five hundred churches. Under the guidance of their priests and bishops, Catholics built an impressive network of institutions — charitable societies, orphanages, militia companies, parochial schools, and political organizations — that helped them maintain both their religion and their German or Irish identity.

Anti-Catholic Riots

When riots against Irish Catholics broke out in Philadelphia in 1844, the governor of Pennsylvania called out the militia to protect Catholic churches and residential neighborhoods. In the foreground, two Protestant rioters, depicted by the artist as well-dressed gentlemen, attack an Irish family with sticks; in the background, militiamen fire on other members of the mob. *Library Company of Philadelphia.*

Nativism and Anti-Catholicism. The Protestant fervor stirred up by the Second Great Awakening meant that a rash of anti-Catholic publications greeted the immigrants (see Comparing American Voices, "A Debate over Catholic Immigration," pp. 296–297). One of the most militant critics of Catholicism was artist and inventor Samuel F. B. Morse. In 1834, Morse published *Foreign Conspiracy Against the Liberties of the United States*, which warned of a Catholic threat to American republican institutions. Morse believed that Catholic immigrants would obey the dictates of Pope Gregory XVI, who in an encyclical in 1832 had condemned liberty of conscience, freedom of publication, and the separation of church and state, and had urged Catholics to repudiate republicanism and acknowledge the "submission due to princes." Republican-minded Protestants of many denominations shared Morse's fears, and *Foreign Conspiracy* became their textbook.

The social tensions stemming from industrialization also intensified anti-Catholic sentiment. During business recessions, unemployed Protestant mechanics and factory workers joined mobs that attacked Catholics, accusing them of taking jobs and driving down wages. These cultural conflicts inhibited the creation of a unified labor movement. Many Protestant wage earners felt they had more in common with their Protestant employers than with their Catholic coworkers. Other Protestants organized nativist clubs, which called for limits on immigration, the restriction of public office to native-born citizens, and the exclusive use of the Protestant version of the Bible in public schools. Benevolent-minded Protestant reformers supported the anti-Catholic movement for reasons of public

policy. As crusaders for public education, they opposed the diversion of tax resources to Catholic schools; as advocates of a civilized society, they condemned the rowdyism of drunken Irish men.

In many northeastern cities, religious and cultural conflicts led to violence. In 1834, in Charlestown, Massachusetts, a quarrel between Catholic laborers repairing a convent owned by the Ursuline order of nuns and Protestant workers in a neighboring brickyard turned into a full-scale riot and led to the destruction of the convent. In Philadelphia, violence erupted in 1844, when the Catholic bishop persuaded public-school officials to use both Catholic and Protestant versions of the Bible. Anti-Irish rioting incited by the city's nativist clubs lasted for two months and escalated into open warfare between Protestants and the Pennsylvania militia. Even as economic revolution brought prosperity to many Americans and attracted millions of immigrants, it divided the society along the lines of class, ethnicity, and religion.

➤ Identify the social classes created by the economic revolution, and describe their defining characteristics.

➤ What were the main goals of the Benevolent Empire? To what extent were they achieved?

A Debate over Catholic Immigration

Between 1776 and 1830, relatively few Europeans immigrated to the United States. Then, as the text explains, population growth and poverty sparked the migration of increasing numbers of Germans (mostly Protestants) and Irish Catholics. The arrival of hundreds of thousands of foreign Catholics in the midst of the Second Great Awakening led to riots, the formation of the American Party, and debates in the public press. By using contemporary newspapers and other writings as a source, historians come to understand the public rhetoric (and often the private passions) of the time.

LYMAN BEECHER
Catholicism Is Incompatible with Republicanism

Lyman Beecher (1775–1863) was one of the leading Protestant ministers of his generation and the father of a family of Christian social reformers and well-known authors: minister Henry Ward Beecher, Harriet Beecher Stowe (Uncle Tom's Cabin), and Catharine Beecher (A Treatise on Domestic Economy). In A Plea for the West (1835), Beecher alerted his fellow Protestants to the centralized power of the Roman Catholic Church and its opposition to republican institutions. That opposition was formalized in papal encyclicals issued by Pope Gregory XVI (Mirari Vos, 1832) and Pope Pius IX (Quanta Cura, 1864), both of which condemned republicanism and freedom of conscience as false political ideologies.

Since the irruption of the northern barbarians, the world has never witnessed such a rush of dark-minded population from one country to another, as is now leaving Europe, and dashing upon our shores. . . .

They come, also, not undirected. There is evidently a supervision abroad — and one here — by which they come, and set down together, in city or country, as a Catholic body, and are led or followed quickly by a Catholic priesthood, who maintain over them in the land of strangers and unknown tongues an [absolute] ascendancy. . . .

The ministers of no Protestant sect could or would dare to attempt to regulate the votes of their people as the Catholic priests can do, who at the confessional learn all the private concerns of their people, and have almost unlimited power over the conscience as it respects the performance of every civil or social duty.

There is another point of dissimilarity of still greater importance. The opinions of the Protestant clergy are congenial with liberty — they are chosen by the people who have been educated as freemen, and they are dependent on them for patronage and support. The Catholic system is adverse to liberty, and the clergy to a great extent are dependent on foreigners [the Pope and church authorities in Rome] opposed to the principles of our government.

Nor is this all — the secular patronage at the disposal of an associated body of men, who under the influence of their priesthood may be induced to act as one . . . would enable them to touch far and wide the spring of action through our cities and through the nation. . . . How many mechanics, merchants, lawyers, physicians, in any political crisis, might they reach and render timid . . . ? How will [the priesthood's] power extend and become omnipresent and resistless as emigration shall quadruple their numbers and action on the political and business men of the nation?

A tenth part of the suffrage of the nation, thus condensed and wielded by the Catholic powers of Europe, might decide our elections, perplex our policy, inflame and divide the nation, break the bond of our union, and throw down our free institutions. . . .

[Catholicism is] a religion which *never prospered but in alliance with despotic governments, has always been and still is the inflexible enemy of Liberty of conscience and free inquiry, and at this moment is the main stay of the battle against republican institutions.*

SOURCE: Lyman Beecher, *A Plea for the West* (Cincinnati: Truman & Smith, 1835), 72–73, 126, 59–63, 85–86, 59.

ORESTES BROWNSON

Catholicism as a Necessity for Popular Government

Like Lyman Beecher, Orestes Brownson was born into the Presbyterian Church, but he quickly grew dissatisfied with its doctrines. After experimenting with Unitarianism, communalism, socialism, and transcendentalism (see Chapter 11), Brownson converted to Catholicism in 1844. A zealous convert, Brownson defended Catholicism with rigorous, logical, and provocative arguments in this article, "Catholicity Necessary to Sustain Popular Liberty" (1845).

Without the Roman Catholic religion it is impossible to preserve a democratic government, and secure its free, orderly, and wholesome action. . . . The theory of democracy is, Construct your government and commit it to the people to be taken care of . . . as they shall think proper.

It is a beautiful theory, and would work admirably, if it were not for one little difficulty, namely, the people are fallible, both individually and collectively, and governed by their passions and interests, which not unfrequently lead them far astray, and produce much mischief.

We know of but one solution of the difficulty, and that is in RELIGION. There is no foundation for virtue but in religion, and it is only religion that can command the degree of popular virtue and intelligence requisite to insure to popular government the right direction. . . . But what religion? It must be a religion which is above the people and controls them, or it will not answer the purpose. It cannot be Protestantism, . . . for Protestantism assumes as its point of departure that Almighty God has indeed given us a religion, but has given it to us not to take care of us, but to be taken care of by us.

[However,] Protestant faith and worship tremble as readily before the slightest breath of public sentiment, as the aspen leaf before the zephyr. The faith and discipline of a sect take any and every direction the public opinion of that sect demands. All is loose, floating, — is here to-day, is there tomorrow, and, next day, may be nowhere. The holding of slaves is compatible with Christian character south of the geographical line, and incompatible north; and Christian morals change according to the prejudices, interests, or habits of the people. . . .

Here, then, is the reason why Protestantism, though it may institute, cannot sustain popular liberty. It is itself subject to popular control, and must follow in all things the popular will, passion, interest, ignorance, prejudice, or caprice.

If Protestantism will not answer the purpose, what religion will? The Roman Catholic, or none. The Roman Catholic religion assumes, as its point of departure, that it is instituted not to be taken care of by the people, but to take care of the people; not to be governed by them, but to govern them. The word is harsh in democratic ears, we admit; but it is not the office of religion to say soft or pleasing words. . . . The people need governing, and must be governed, or nothing but anarchy and destruction await them. They must have a master. . . .

Quote our expression, THE PEOPLE MUST HAVE A MASTER, as you doubtless will; hold it up in glaring capitals, to excite the unthinking and unreasoning multitude, and to doubly fortify their prejudices against Catholicity; be mortally scandalized at the assertion that religion ought to govern the people, and then go to work and seek to bring the people into subjection to your banks or moneyed corporations. . . .

The Roman Catholic religion, then, is necessary to sustain popular liberty, because popular liberty can be sustained only by a religion free from popular control, above the people, speaking from above and able to command them, and such a religion is the Roman Catholic.

SOURCE: Orestes A. Brownson, *Essays and Reviews, Chiefly on Theology, Politics, and Socialism* (New York: D. & J. Sadlier, 1852), 368–370, 372–373, 376, 379–381.

ANALYZING THE EVIDENCE

➤ According to Beecher, what specific dangers does Catholicism pose to American republican institutions? Why would he argue that Protestant churches do not pose the same dangers?

➤ Does Brownson disagree with Beecher's criticism of the social and political impact of Catholicism? Or does he simply think it is good and necessary, while Beecher believes it is dangerous? Explain your answer.

➤ Given Brownson's statement that "the people must have a master," what would be his view of democracy and popular government?

➤ Do you think the leaders of the Benevolent Empire would agree with any parts of Brownson's social and political philosophy? Why or why not?

SUMMARY

In this chapter, we examined the causes and consequences of the economic transformation that marked the first half of the nineteenth century. That transformation had two facets: the increase in production known as the Industrial Revolution, and the expansion of commerce known as the Market Revolution. Water and steam were crucial ingredients in both revolutions — driving factory machinery, carrying goods to market in canals and rivers, and propelling steamboats and railroad engines.

We also explored the many important results of the economic transformation: the rise of an urban society, the regional similarity of the East and Midwest and their difference from the South, and the creation of a class-divided society. Responding to these changes, benevolent reformers and evangelical revivalists worked to instill middle-class and Christian values in the entire population. However, other social groups — artisan republicans, unionized workers, Irish and German immigrants — accepted only those beliefs that were compatible with their own economic or cultural goals. The result was a fragmented society. Differences of class and culture now split the North just as race and class had long divided the South. As we will see in the next chapter, to address these divisions, Americans looked to the political system, which was becoming increasingly democratic. The resulting tension between social inequality and political democracy would become a troubling, and enduring, part of American life.

Connections: Economy and Society

In 1820, most Americans lived in a rural, agricultural society that was similar to the world of their parents and grandparents. Then, as we noted in the opening essay for Part Three (p. 269), came dramatic changes that "affected every aspect of life in the northern and midwestern states and brought important changes in the South as well." In this chapter, we have described the industrial and market factors that played a major role in creating a new economy and a new society in the Northeast and the Midwest. Our analysis of this economic and social transformation in the South will continue in Chapter 12, where we assess the causes and consequences of the enormous expansion in plantation agriculture and cotton production between 1820 and 1860 and the devastating impact of the domestic slave trade on the lives of millions of African Americans.

In the opening essay, we also observed that the new economy created a class-based society in the North and Midwest. A wealthy elite of merchants, manufacturers, bankers, and entrepreneurs struggled to the top of the social order. Once in charge, they tried to maintain social stability through a paternalistic program of benevolent reform.

This discussion of social reform continues in Chapter 11, which describes how advocates of temperance, religious utopianism, abolitionism, and women's rights took the reform movement in new directions. Their radical outlooks and activities were the result, in part, of the overthrow of the traditional political system and the rise of Jacksonian democracy, the subjects of Chapter 10.

CHAPTER REVIEW QUESTIONS

➤ Weigh the relative importance of the Industrial and Market revolutions in changing the American economy. In what ways was the economy different in 1860 from what it had been in 1800? How would you explain those differences?

➤ What was the impact of the economic revolution on the lives of women in various social groups and classes?

➤ Did the Industrial and Market revolutions make America a more or less republican society? How so?

TIMELINE

1782	Oliver Evans develops automated flour mill
1790	Samuel Slater opens spinning mill in Providence, Rhode Island
1792	Congress passes the Post Office Act
1793	Eli Whitney manufactures cotton gins
1800–1830	Entrepreneurs take over shoe industry, introduce division of labor
1807	Robert Fulton launches the *Clermont*, the first American steamboat
1814	Boston Manufacturing Company opens cotton mill in Waltham, Massachusetts
1816–1828	Congress passes series of protective tariffs on textiles and other imports
1817	Erie Canal begun (completed in 1825)
1820	Minimum federal land price reduced to $1.25 per acre
1820–1840	Urban population in Northeast and Midwest increases more than fourfold
1820s	New England women begin working in textile factories Rise of Benevolent Empire leads to conservative social reform
1824	*Gibbons v. Ogden* promotes interstate trade
1830s	Emergence of western commercial cities Labor movement gains strength Cities begin to segregate by class Middle-class culture emerges Growth of temperance movement
1830	Charles Grandison Finney begins Rochester revivals
1834	Local unions form National Trades' Union John Deere invents steel plow
1840s	Irish and German immigration sparks ethnic riots Rise of machine-tool industry
1848	Michigan and Illinois Canal completes inland water route from New York City to New Orleans
1850s	Expansion of railroads in Northeast and Midwest
1857	Overproduction and speculation trigger a financial panic

FOR FURTHER EXPLORATION

Stuart Bruchey, *Enterprise: The Dynamic Economy of a Free People* (1990), offers a panoramic history; Charles G. Sellers, *The Market Revolution: Jacksonian America, 1815–1846* (1991), focuses on the social and cultural aspects of economic change. Scott A. Sandage, *Born Losers: A History of Failure in America* (2005), explores the fate of unsuccessful entrepreneurs. David Freeman Hawke, *Nuts and Bolts of the Past: A History of American Technology, 1776–1860* (1988), offers an entertaining account of eccentric inventors and technical progress. A Web site that explores the impact of technology is "The Eli Whitney Museum & Workshop" (**www.eliwhitney.org/**).

Stephen Aron, *How the West Was Lost: The Transformation of Kentucky from Daniel Boone to Henry Clay* (1996), explores economic and political conflict in the trans-Appalachian west; Peter Way, *Common Labor: Workers and the Digging of North American Canals, 1780–1860* (1993), describes the hard lives of the men who dug the canals. For New York's Erie Canal, go to **www.canals.state.ny.us/cculture/index.html**. First-person accounts, biographies, and promotional literature about the settlement of Michigan, Minnesota, and Wisconsin (1820–1910) are online at "Pioneering the Upper Midwest" (**memory.loc. gov/ammem/umhtml/umhome.html**).

Stuart M. Blumin's *The Emergence of the Middle Class: Social Experience in the American City, 1760–1900* (1989), discusses urban class formation; Stephen P. Rice, *Minding the Machine: Languages of Class in Early Industrial America* (2004), traces the middle-class triumph in the culture wars of the early nineteenth century. A fine study of urban disorder is David Grimsted, *American Mobbing* (1998). In *Home and Work* (1990), Jeanne Boydston takes a critical look at the impact of the market and the city on women's lives. For a woman textile operative's first-hand account of mill life, see **www.fordham. edu/halsall/mod/robinson-lowell.html**.

In *The Democratization of American Christianity* (1987), Nathan Hatch traces the impact of Evangelical Protestantism; for dramatic portraits of revivals and revivalists, consult Mark A. Noll, *America's God: From Jonathan Edwards to Abraham Lincoln* (2003), and Bernard Weisberger's classic study, *They Gathered at the River* (1958). The Library of Congress offers a fine collection on "Religion and the Founding of the American Republic" at **www.loc.gov/exhibits/religion/**. An important recent study is William R. Hutchison, *Religious Pluralism in America: The Contentious History of a Founding Ideal* (2003).

TEST YOUR KNOWLEDGE

To assess your command of the material in this chapter, see the Online Study Guide at **bedfordstmartins.com/henretta**.

For Web sites, images, and documents related to topics and places in this chapter, visit **bedfordstmartins.com/makehistory**.

10

A Democratic Revolution

1820–1844

EUROPEAN VISITORS TO THE UNITED STATES during the 1820s and 1830s generally praised America's republican society, but they found little to celebrate in its political parties and politicians. "The gentlemen spit, talk of elections and the price of produce, and spit again," Frances Trollope reported in *Domestic Manners of the Americans* (1832). In her view, American politics was the sport of party hacks who reeked of "whiskey and onions." Other Europeans lamented the low intellectual level of political debates and their bombastic character. The "clap-trap of praise and pathos" uttered by a leading Massachusetts politician "deeply disgusted" Harriet Martineau, while Basil Hall could only shake his head in astonishment at the shallow arguments, the "conclusions in which nothing was concluded," that were advanced by the inept "farmers, shopkeepers, and country lawyers" who sat in the New York assembly.

The verdict was unanimous and negative. "The most able men in the United States are very rarely placed at the head of affairs," French aristocrat Alexis de Tocqueville observed in *Democracy in America* (1835). Tocqueville ascribed this unhappy result to the character of democracy itself. Ordinary citizens ignored important issues of policy, refused to elect their intellectual superiors to office, and willingly assented to "the

◄ **The Inauguration of President William Henry Harrison, March 4, 1841**

After being sworn into office, President Harrison stands on the steps of the U.S. Capitol (in the box on the left) reviewing a parade of military units. The short balding man to Harrison's right is Martin Van Buren, the departing president. Although they could not vote, many women attended the ceremony, both to enjoy the festivities and to indicate their support for the Whig Party's policies of social and moral reform. Anne S. K. Brown Military Collection, Brown University.

clamor of a mountebank [a charismatic fraud] who knows the secret of stimulating their tastes."

The European visitors were witnesses to the unfolding of the American Democratic Revolution. In the early decades of the American republic, men of great ability had sat in the seats of government, and the prevailing ideology had been republicanism, rule by property-owning "men of TALENTS and VIRTUE." By the 1820s and 1830s, the watchword was *democracy*, which in practice meant rule by popularly elected party politicians. "That the majority should govern was a fundamental maxim in all free governments," declared Martin Van Buren, the most talented of the new breed of middle-class professional politicians who had taken over the halls of government and who would soon build America's Second Party System. The new party politicians often pursued selfish goals; but by uniting ordinary Americans in "election fever" and party organizations, they held together a social order increasingly fragmented by economic change and cultural diversity.

The Rise of Popular Politics, 1820–1829

Expansion of the **franchise** was the most dramatic symbol of the Democratic Revolution. As early as the 1810s, some states had extended the right to vote to almost all white men, bringing many farmers and wage earners into the political arena by ending traditional property qualifications for voting. Nowhere else in the world did ordinary men have so much power. In England, for example, the Reform Bill of 1832 extended the vote to only 600,000 out of 6 million English men—a mere 10 percent.

The Decline of the Notables and the Rise of Parties

The American Revolution weakened the deferential society of the colonial era, but it did not overthrow it. Only two state constitutions—those of Pennsylvania and Vermont—allowed all male taxpayers to vote; and even in those states, families in the low and middle ranks continued to accept the leadership of their social "betters." Consequently, wealthy notable men—northern landlords, slave-owning planters, and seaport merchants—continued to dominate the political system in the first decades of the republic. And rightly so, thought the first chief justice of the Supreme Court, John Jay. As he put it in 1810, "Those who own the country are the most fit persons to participate in the government of it." Local notables managed elections by building up an "interest": lending money to small farmers, giving business to storekeepers, and treating their tenants to rum at election time. An outlay of $20 for refreshments, remarked one poll watcher, "may produce about 100 votes." This gentry-dominated system excluded men without wealth and powerful family connections from running for office.

The Advance of Democracy. The struggle to expand the suffrage began in the 1810s. Reformers in Maryland challenged local notables in the language of Revolutionary-era republicans, condemning property qualifications as a "tyranny" that endowed "one class of men with privileges which are denied to another." To defuse this criticism and deter migration to the West, notables in Maryland and other seaboard state legislatures grudgingly accepted a broader franchise. The new voters changed the tone of politics. They refused to support politicians who flaunted their high social status by wearing "top boots, breeches, and shoe buckles," their hair in "powder and queues." Instead, they elected men who dressed simply and endorsed democracy, even if those politicians favored policies that benefited those with substantial wealth.

Smallholding farmers and ambitious laborers in the Midwest and Southwest pushed forward this challenge to the traditional hierarchical social and political order. In Ohio, a traveler reported, "no white man or woman will bear being called a servant." The constitutions of the new states of Indiana (1816), Illinois (1818), and Alabama (1819) prescribed a broad male franchise, and voters usually elected middling men to local and state offices. A well-to-do migrant in Illinois noted with surprise that the man who plowed his fields "was a colonel of militia, and a member of the legislature." Once in public office, men from modest backgrounds enacted laws that restricted imprisonment for debt, kept taxes low, and allowed farmers to claim squatters' rights to unoccupied land.

By the mid-1820s, only a few states—North Carolina, Virginia, and Rhode Island—required the ownership of freehold property for voting. Many states had instituted universal white male suffrage, and others—Ohio and Louisiana, for example—excluded only the relatively few men who did not pay taxes or serve in the militia. Moreover, between 1818 and 1821, Connecticut, Massachusetts, and

New York wrote new constitutions that reapportioned legislative districts on the basis of population and made local governments more democratic by mandating the election, rather than the appointment, of judges and justices of the peace.

Democratic politics was contentious and, because it was run by men on the make, often corrupt as well. Powerful entrepreneurs and speculators—both notables and self-made men—demanded government assistance for their business enterprises and paid bribes to get it. To secure charters or increase interest rates, bankers distributed shares of stock to key legislators, while speculators won land grants by paying off the members of key committees. And legislators soon found ways to help themselves directly. When the Seventh Ward Bank of New York City received a charter in 1833, the supervising commissioners appointed by the legislature set aside one-third of the bank's 3,700 shares of stock for themselves and their friends, and almost two-thirds for their political allies holding state offices, leaving just 40 shares for public sale.

Other Americans turned to politics to advance the religious and cultural agenda advocated by the benevolent reformers (see Chapter 9). The result of this crusade was political controversy. When evangelical Presbyterians in Utica, New York, called for a town ordinance in 1828 to restrict Sunday entertainment, a member of the local Universalist church—Universalism is a freethinking Protestant denomination—denounced the coercive reforms and called for "Religious Liberty."

Martin Van Buren and the Rise of Parties. The appearance of political parties encouraged debate on issues of government policy. Revolutionary-era Americans had condemned political "factions" and "parties" as antirepublican; consequently, neither the national nor the state constitutions gave parties a role in the governing process. But as the power of notables waned, political parties became more prominent. By the 1820s, parties in a number of states were highly disciplined organizations managed by professional politicians, often middle-class lawyers and journalists. One observer noted that the parties were like a well-designed textile loom, "machines" that wove the diverse interests of various social and economic groups into the elaborate tapestry of a coherent legislative program.

Martin Van Buren of New York was the chief architect of the emerging system of party government, first at the state and then at national level. The son of a tavernkeeper, Van Buren grew up in the landlord-dominated society of the Hudson River Valley. He relied on the powerful Van Ness clan to get his training as a lawyer; then, to avoid becoming the dependent "Tool" of this notable family, he repudiated their tutelage and set out to create a new political order. Van Buren rejected the traditional republican belief that political parties were dangerous and argued that the opposite was true: "All men of sense know that political parties are inseparable from free government" because they check the government's "disposition to abuse power . . . [and curb] the passions, the ambition, and the usurpations" of potential tyrants.

Having defended the legitimacy of political parties, Van Buren undertook to create one of his own. Between 1817 and 1821, he turned his "Bucktail" supporters (so called because they wore a deer's tail on their hats) into the first statewide **political machine**, the Albany Regency. Purchasing a newspaper, the *Albany Argus*, Van Buren used its pages to promote a platform and get out the vote. **Patronage** was an even more important tool. When Van Buren and the Regency won control of the New York legislature in 1821, they acquired a political "interest" much greater than that of the notables—the power to appoint some six thousand of their followers to positions in New York's legal bureaucracy of judges, justices of the peace, sheriffs, deed commissioners, and coroners. This **spoils system** was fair, Van Buren suggested, for it "would operate sometimes in favour of one party, and sometimes of another." And it was thoroughly republican because it was based on rule by the majority. To ensure the passage of important legislation, Van Buren insisted on party discipline and required elected officials to follow the dictates of the **party caucus**. On one crucial occasion, the "Little Magician"—a nickname that acknowledged both Van Buren's height (or lack of it) and his political dexterity—persuaded seventeen New York legislators "magnanimously [to] sacrifice individual preferences for the general good" and lauded them at a banquet with "something approaching divine honors."

The Election of 1824

The advance of political democracy and party government in the states undermined the old consensus system of national politics and the power of the notables who ran it. After the War of 1812, the aristocratic Federalist Party virtually disappeared, and the Republican Party broke up into competing factions (see Chapter 7). As the election of 1824 approached, no fewer than five candidates, all calling themselves Republicans, campaigned for the presidency. Three were veterans of President James Monroe's cabinet: Secretary of State John Quincy Adams, the son of former president John Adams; Secretary of War John C. Calhoun; and Secretary of the Treasury William H. Crawford. The fourth candidate was Henry Clay of Kentucky, the dynamic Speaker of the House of Representatives; and the fifth was General Andrew Jackson, now a senator from Tennessee.

When a caucus of Republicans in Congress selected Crawford as the party's official nominee, the other candidates refused to withdraw. Instead, they introduced competition to national politics by seeking popular support. Democratic reforms in eighteen of the twenty-four states required popular elections (rather than a vote of the state legislature) to choose members of the Electoral College from their states. The battle was closely fought. Thanks to his diplomatic successes as secretary of state (see Chapter 7), John Quincy Adams enjoyed national recognition; and his Massachusetts origins gave him the electoral votes of New England. Henry Clay framed his candidacy around domestic issues. As a congressman, Clay promoted the **American System**, an integrated program of national economic development similar to the Commonwealth policies pursued by state governments. Clay wanted the Second Bank of the United States to regulate state banks and advocated the use of tariff revenues to build roads and canals. His nationalistic program was popular in the West, which needed transportation improvements, but was sharply criticized in the South, which relied on rivers to carry its cotton to market and did not have manufacturing industries to protect. William Crawford of Georgia, an ideological heir of Thomas Jefferson, spoke for the South. Fearing the "consolidation" of political power in Washington, Crawford and other Old Republicans denounced the American System. Recognizing Crawford's appeal in the South, John C. Calhoun of South Carolina withdrew from the presidential race and endorsed Andrew Jackson.

As the hero of the Battle of New Orleans, Jackson benefited from the wave of patriotism that flowed from the War of 1812. Born in the Carolina backcountry, Jackson had settled in Nashville, Tennessee, where he formed ties to influential families through marriage and his career as an attorney and slave-owning cotton planter. His rise from common origins fit the tenor of the new democratic age, and his reputation as a "plain solid republican" attracted voters in all regions.

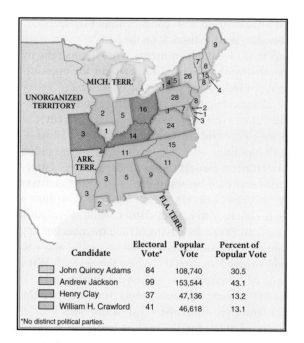

Candidate	Electoral Vote*	Popular Vote	Percent of Popular Vote
John Quincy Adams	84	108,740	30.5
Andrew Jackson	99	153,544	43.1
Henry Clay	37	47,136	13.2
William H. Crawford	41	46,618	13.1

*No distinct political parties.

MAP 10.1 The Presidential Election of 1824

Regional voting was the dominant factor in 1824. John Quincy Adams captured every electoral vote in New England and most of those in New York. Henry Clay carried Ohio and Kentucky, the most populous trans-Appalachian states; and William Crawford took the southern states of Virginia and Georgia. Only Andrew Jackson claimed a national constituency, winning Pennsylvania and New Jersey in the East, Indiana and most of Illinois in the Midwest, and much of the South. Only 356,000 Americans voted, about 27 percent of the eligible electorate.

Still, Jackson's strong showing in the election surprised most political leaders. The Tennessee senator received 99 votes in the Electoral College; Adams garnered 84 votes; Crawford, who suffered a stroke during the campaign, won 41; and Clay finished with 37 (Map 10.1). Because no candidate received an absolute majority, the decision fell to the House of Representatives, as it had in the election of 1800. The Twelfth Amendment to the Constitution (ratified in 1804) specified that the House would choose the president from among the three leading contenders. This procedure hurt Jackson because many congressmen did not want a rough-hewn "military chieftain" in the White House, worried he might become a tyrant. Personally out of the race, Henry Clay used his influence as Speaker to thwart Jackson's election. When the House met in February 1825, Clay assembled a coalition of congressmen from New England and the Ohio River Valley that voted Adams into the presidency.

Adams showed his gratitude by appointing Clay his secretary of state, then the traditional stepping-stone to the presidency.

Clay's appointment was a politically fatal mistake for both men. John C. Calhoun accused Adams of abusing the power of the presidency to thwart the popular will. Along with other Jackson supporters, Calhoun suspected that Clay had made a deal with Adams to become secretary of state. Condemning this "corrupt bargain," they vowed that Clay would never become president.

The Last Notable President: John Quincy Adams

As president, Adams called for bold national leadership. "The moral purpose of the Creator," he told Congress, was to use the president and every other public official to "improve the conditions of himself and his fellow men." Adams called for the establishment of a national university in Washington, extensive scientific explorations in the Far West, and a uniform standard of weights and measures. Most important, he endorsed Henry Clay's American System of national economic development and its three key elements: protective tariffs to stimulate manufacturing, federally subsidized roads and canals to facilitate commerce, and a national bank to control credit and provide a uniform currency.

Resistance to the American System. Manufacturers, entrepreneurs, and growers in the Northeast and Midwest welcomed Adams's policies. But those policies won little support in the South, where planters opposed protective tariffs because they raised the price of manufactures, and smallholders feared powerful banks that could force them into bankruptcy. From his deathbed, Thomas Jefferson condemned Adams for promoting "a single and splendid government of [a monied] aristocracy . . . riding and ruling over the plundered ploughman and beggared yeomanry."

Other politicians objected to the American System on constitutional grounds. In 1817, President Madison had vetoed the Bonus Bill, which would have used the national government's income from the Second Bank of the United States to fund improvement projects in the states. These kinds of projects, Madison had argued, were the sole responsibility of the states, a sentiment that was widely shared among Old Republicans. After a trip to Monticello to meet Thomas Jefferson, his long-time hero, Martin Van Buren declared his allegiance to the constitutional "doctrines of the Jefferson School." Now a member of the U.S.

John Quincy Adams
This famous daguerreotype of the former president, taken about 1843 by Philip Haas, conveys his rigid personality and high moral standards. Although these personal attributes contributed to Adams's success as an antislavery congressman from Massachusetts in the 1830s and 1840s, they hindered his effectiveness as the nation's chief executive. Metropolitan Museum of Art, New York. Gift of I. N. Phelps Stokes, Edward S. Hawes, Alice Mary Hawes, Marion Augusta Hawes.

Senate, Van Buren joined the Old Republicans in defeating most national subsidies for roads and canals. Congress approved only a few of Adams's proposals for internal improvements, among them the short extension of the National Road from Wheeling, Virginia, into Ohio.

The Tariff Battle. The most far-reaching battle of the Adams administration came over tariffs. The Tariff of 1816 placed relatively high duties on imports of cheap English cotton cloth, allowing New England textile producers to dominate that market. In 1824, Adams and Clay secured a new tariff that protected manufacturers in New England and Pennsylvania against imports of iron goods and more-expensive woolen and cotton textiles. When Van Buren and his Jacksonian allies won control of Congress in the election of 1826, they proposed higher tariffs on wool, hemp, and other imported

A CARTOON COMPARING CONDITIONS UNDER FREE TRADE AND
PROTECTIVE TARIFF

From "The United States Weekly Telegram," November 5, 1832.

The "Tariff of Abominations"

Political cartoons enjoyed wide use in eighteenth-century England and became popular in the United States during the political battles of the First Party system (1794–1815). By the 1820s, American newspapers, most of which were subsidized by political parties, published cartoons on a daily basis. This political cartoon attacks the tariffs of 1828 and 1832 as hostile to the interests and prosperity of the South. The gaunt figure on the left represents a southern planter, starved by exactions of the tariff, while the northern textile manufacturer has grown stout feasting on the bounty of protectionism. Corbis-Bettmann.

raw materials. Their goal was to win the support of wool- and hemp-producing farmers in New York, Ohio, and Kentucky for Jackson's presidential candidacy in 1828. The tariff had become a prisoner of politics. "I fear this tariff thing," remarked Thomas Cooper, the president of the College of South Carolina and an advocate of free trade, "by some strange mechanical contrivance . . . it will be changed into a machine for manufacturing Presidents, instead of broadcloths, and bed blankets." Disregarding southern protests, northern Jacksonians joined with Adams and Clay's supporters to enact the Tariff of 1828, which significantly raised duties on raw materials, textiles, and iron goods.

The new tariff enraged the South. As the world's cheapest producer of raw cotton, the South did not need a tariff to protect its main industry. Moreover, by raising the price of manufactures, the tariff cost southern planters about $100 million a year. Planters had the unpleasant choice of buying either higher-cost American textiles and iron goods, thus enriching northeastern businesses and workers, or highly duties British imports, thus paying the cost of the national government. The new tariff was "little less than legalized pillage," an Alabama legislator declared, calling it a "Tariff of Abominations."

Ignoring the Jacksonians' support for the Tariff of 1828, most southerners blamed President Adams for the new act. They also criticized Adams's Indian policy. A deeply moral man, the president had supported the land rights of Native Americans against expansionist whites in the South. In 1825, U.S. commissioners had secured a treaty from one Creek faction that would have ceded the tribe's lands in Georgia to the United States, for eventual sale to the citizens of that state. When the Creek National Council repudiated the treaty, claiming it was fraudulent, Adams called for new negotiations. Eager to acquire the Creeks' land, Georgia governor George M. Troup attacked the president as a "public enemy . . . the unblushing ally of the savages." Joining forces with Georgia's representatives in Congress, Troup persuaded the national legislature to enact a measure that extinguished the Creeks' land titles and forced most Creeks to leave the state.

Elsewhere in the nation, Adams's primary weakness was his increasingly out-of-date political style. The last notable to serve in the White House, he acted the part: aloof, moralistic, and paternalistic. When Congress rejected his activist economic policies, Adams questioned the wisdom of the people and advised elected officials not to be "palsied by the will of our constituents." Ignoring his waning popularity, the president did not use patronage to reward his supporters and allowed hostile federal officials to remain in office. Rather than "run" for reelection in 1828, Adams "stood" for it, telling supporters, "If my country wants my services, she must ask for them."

"The Democracy" and the Election of 1828

Martin Van Buren and the professional politicians handling Andrew Jackson's campaign had no reservations about running for the presidency or any other elected office. To recreate the national political coalition first formed by Thomas Jefferson, Van Buren championed policies that appealed both to northern farmers and artisans (whom he called the "plain Republicans of the North") and to southern slave owners and smallholders who had voted for the Virginia Dynasty. John C. Calhoun, Jackson's vice presidential running mate, brought his South Carolina allies into Van Buren's party, and Jackson's close friends in Tennessee rallied voters there and throughout the states of the Old Southwest. By creating a national political party, Jackson's friends hoped to overcome the diversity of economic and social "interests" that, as James Madison had noted in "Federalist No. 10," would inevitability arise in a large republic.

At Van Buren's direction, his Jacksonian allies orchestrated a massive publicity campaign. In New York, fifty newspapers declared their support for Jackson on the same day. Elsewhere, Jacksonians organized mass meetings, torchlight parades, and barbecues to celebrate their candidate's frontier origin and his rise to fame. They praised "Old Hickory" — the name they gave Jackson saying he was as hard as hickory wood — as a "natural" aristocrat, a self-made man. "Jackson for ever!" was their cry.

Initially, the Jacksonians called themselves Democratic Republicans; but as the campaign wore on, they became Democrats or "the Democracy," names that conveyed their egalitarian message. As Jacksonian Thomas Morris told the Ohio legislature, he and his party believed that the republic had been corrupted by legislative gifts of corporate charters that gave "a few individuals rights and privileges not enjoyed by the citizens at large." Morris promised that the Democracy would destroy such "artificial distinction in society." And Jackson himself declared that "equality among the people in the rights conferred by government" was the "great radical principle of freedom."

Jackson's message of equal rights and popular rule appealed to many social groups. His hostility to business corporations and to Clay's American System won support among northeastern artisans and workers who felt threatened by industrialization. Jackson also won the votes of Pennsylvania ironworkers and New York farmers who had been enriched by the controversial Tariff of Abominations. Yet, by astutely declaring his personal preference for a "judicious"

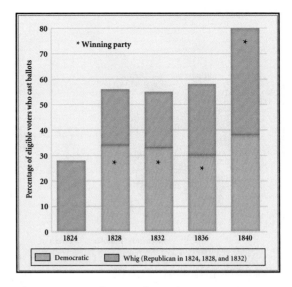

Figure 10.1 Changes in Voting Patterns, 1824–1840

Voter participation soared in 1828 and again in 1840 as competition heated up between Democrats and Whigs, who advocated different policies and philosophies of government.

tariff that would balance regional interests, Jackson remained popular in the South as well. In the Southeast and the Midwest, Old Hickory garnered votes because his well-known hostility toward Native Americans reassured white farmers who wanted the Indians removed from their ancestral lands.

The Democrats' celebration of popular rule carried Jackson into office. In 1824, little more than a quarter of the eligible electorate had voted; in 1828, more than half of all potential voters went to the polls, and 56 percent cast their ballots for the senator from Tennessee (Figure 10.1). Jackson received 178 of 261 electoral votes and became the first president from a trans-Appalachian state (Map 10.2). As the president-elect traveled to Washington, he cut a dignified figure. According to an English observer, he "wore his hair carelessly but not ungracefully arranged, and in spite of his harsh, gaunt features looked like a gentleman and a soldier." However, the outpouring of popular enthusiasm for Jackson frightened men of wealth. As Senator Daniel Webster of Massachusetts, a former Federalist Congressman from New Hampshire and now a corporate lawyer in Boston, warned his clients, the new president would "bring a breeze with him. Which way it will blow, I cannot tell [but] . . . my fear is stronger than my hope." Supreme Court Justice Joseph Story and other influential observers shared Webster's apprehensions. Watching an unruly crowd clamber over the elegant

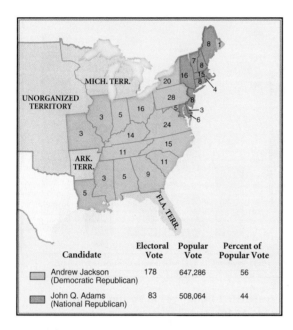

MAP 10.2   The Election of 1828

As he did in 1824, John Quincy Adams carried all of New England and some of the Mid-Atlantic states. However, Andrew Jackson swept the rest of the nation and won a resounding victory in the Electoral College. More than 1.1 million American men cast ballots in 1828, more than three times the number who voted in 1824.

furniture in the White House to shake the hand of the newly inaugurated president, Story lamented that "the reign of King 'Mob' seemed triumphant."

➤ Was there necessarily a connection between the growth of democracy and the emergence of disciplined political parties? Or did they just happen at the same time? Explain your answer.

➤ How do you explain John Quincy Adams's great success as secretary of state (see Chapter 7) and his relative lack of success as president?

The Jacksonian Presidency, 1829–1837

American-style political democracy—a broad franchise, a disciplined political party, and policies that addressed the interests of specific social groups—ushered Andrew Jackson into office. Subsequently, Jackson used his popular mandate to transform the presidency and the policies of the national government. During his two terms in office, he enhanced the authority of the president over that of Congress, destroyed the nationalistic American System, and ordained a new ideology for the Democracy. An Ohio supporter summarized Jackson's vision this way: "the Sovereignty of the People, the Rights of the States, and a Light and Simple Government."

Jackson's Agenda: Rotation and Decentralization

Although Jackson had a formal cabinet, for policy-making he relied primarily on an informal group of advisors that came to be known as the Kitchen Cabinet. Its most influential members were Francis Preston Blair of Kentucky, who edited the Democracy's main newspaper, the *Washington Globe*; Amos Kendall, also from Kentucky, who helped Jackson write his speeches; Roger B. Taney of Maryland, who became attorney general, treasury secretary, and then chief justice of the United States; and, most important, Secretary of State Martin Van Buren.

Following Van Buren's example in New York, Jackson used patronage to create a loyal and disciplined national party. He insisted on rotation in office: When an administration was voted out of office, the officials it had appointed would have to leave government service. Dismissing the argument that rotation would lessen expertise, Jackson suggested that most public duties were "so plain and simple that men of intelligence may readily qualify themselves for their performance." William L. Marcy, a New York Jacksonian, put it more bluntly: Government jobs were like the spoils of war, and "to the victor belong the spoils of the enemy." Using the spoils system, Jackson dispensed government jobs to help his friends and to win support for his legislative program.

Jackson's priority was to destroy the centralized plan of economic development known as the American System. As Henry Clay noted apprehensively, the new president wanted "to cry down old constructions of the Constitution . . . to make all Jefferson's opinions the articles of faith of the new Church." Declaring that the "voice of the people" called for "economy in the expenditures of the Government," Jackson rejected national support for transportation projects, which he also opposed on constitutional grounds. In 1830, he vetoed four internal improvement bills, including an extension of the National Road, because they amounted to "an infringement of the reserved powers of states."

President Andrew Jackson, 1830

The new president came to Washington with a well-deserved reputation as an aggressive Indian fighter and dangerous military leader. But in this official portrait, he looks "presidential"—his dress and posture, and the artist's composition, created the image of a calm deliberate statesman. Subsequent events would show that Jackson had not lost his hard-edged authoritarian personality. Library of Congress.

Then Jackson turned his attention to two complex and equally controversial parts of the American System: protective tariffs and the national bank.

The Tariff and Nullification

The Tariff of 1828 had helped Jackson win the presidency, but it saddled him with a major political crisis. Fierce opposition to high protective tariffs arose in South Carolina, where white planters suffered from chronic insecurity. South Carolina was the only state with an African American majority — 56 percent of the population in 1830 — and its slave owners, like the white sugar planters in the West Indies, lived in fear of a black rebellion. They also worried about the legal abolition of slavery. The British Parliament had promised to end slavery in the West Indies and did so in

August 1833; remembering the northern effort to prohibit bondage in Missouri (see Chapter 8), South Carolina planters worried that the U.S. government might do the same. To limit the powers of the central government, South Carolina politicians launched an attack against protective tariffs.

The crisis began in 1832, when high-tariff congressmen ignored southern warnings that they were "endangering the Union" and passed new legislation that retained the high rates of the Tariff of Abominations. In response, leading South Carolinians called a state convention in November, which boldly adopted the Ordinance of Nullification. The ordinance declared the tariffs of 1828 and 1832 to be null and void, prohibited the collection of those duties in South Carolina after February 1, 1833, and threatened secession if federal officials tried to collect them.

South Carolina's act of **nullification** rested on the constitutional arguments developed in *The South Carolina Exposition and Protest* (1828). Written anonymously by Vice President John C. Calhoun, the *Exposition* gave a localist interpretation to the federal union. Because each region had distinct interests, localists argued, protective tariffs and other national legislation that operated unequally on the various states lacked both fairness and legitimacy — in fact, they were unconstitutional. Obsessively determined to protect the economic interests of the white South, Calhoun exaggerated the frequency and extent of such legislation, declaring: "Constitutional government and the government of a majority are utterly incompatible."

To develop an alternative interpretation of the Constitution, Calhoun turned to the arguments first advanced by Jefferson and Madison in the Kentucky and Virginia resolutions of 1798. Because the U.S. Constitution had been ratified by conventions in the various states, the resolutions suggested, sovereignty lay in the states, not in the people. From this dubious proposition, Calhoun developed a states' rights interpretation of the Constitution. He also advanced the even more dubious claim that a state convention could decide if a congressional law was unconstitutional and declare it null and void within the state's borders. Replying to this argument, which had no basis in the text of the Constitution, Daniel Webster articulated a nationalist construction that endorsed popular sovereignty and celebrated the frequent success of Congress in securing the "general welfare."

Jackson hoped to find a middle path. Although he wanted to limit the reach and power of the

Fashion and Fear in South Carolina, 1831

This painting, executed by South Carolina artist S. Bernard around the time of the nullification crisis, shows fashionably dressed whites strolling along the East Battery of Charleston. To the left, two black boys are fighting, while other African Americans sit and watch. Although the scene is tranquil, many whites feared an uprising by enslaved blacks, who formed a majority of the state's population. Yale University Art Gallery.

national government, he denounced Calhoun's radical doctrine of localist federalism. The Constitution clearly gave the federal government the authority to establish tariffs, and, whatever the costs, Jackson would enforce that power. The president's response to South Carolina's Ordinance of Nullification was direct: Jackson declared that nullification violated the Constitution and was "unauthorized by its spirit . . . and destructive of the great object for which it was formed." "Disunion by armed force is treason," he warned. At Jackson's request, Congress passed the Force Bill early in 1833, which authorized the president to use military force to compel South Carolina to obey national laws. Simultaneously, Jackson addressed the South's objections to high import duties by winning passage of an act that gradually reduced tariff rates. By 1842, tariffs would revert to the modest levels of 1816,

thereby eliminating another part of Clay's American System.

The compromise worked. Having won a gradual reduction in duties, the South Carolina convention rescinded its nullification of the tariff (although it defiantly nullified the Force Bill). Jackson was satisfied. He had addressed the economic demands of the South while upholding the constitutional principle that no state could nullify a law of the United States — a principle that Abraham Lincoln would embrace in defense of the Union during the secession crisis of 1861.

The Bank War

In the middle of the tariff crisis, Jackson faced another major challenge, this time from the political supporters of the Second Bank of the United States.

The Great Webster-Hayne Debate, 1830

The Tariff of Abominations sparked one of the greatest debates in American history. When Senator Robert Y. Hayne of South Carolina (seated in the middle of the picture, with his legs crossed) opposed the federal levies by invoking the doctrines of states' rights and nullification, Daniel Webster rose to the defense of the Union. Speaking for two days to a spellbound Senate, Webster delivered an impassioned oration that celebrated the unity of the American people as the key to their freedom. His parting words—"Liberty *and* Union, now and forever, one and inseparable!"—quickly became part of the national memory.

Webster's Reply to Hayne, by G. P. A. Healy. City of Boston Art Commission.

Founded in Philadelphia in 1816 (see Chapter 7), the bank was a privately managed institution that held a twenty-year charter from the federal government, which owned 20 percent of its stock. The bank's most important role was to stabilize the nation's money supply. Most American money consisted of notes and bills of credit — in effect, paper money — issued by state-chartered banks. The banks promised to redeem the notes on demand with "hard" money — that is, gold or silver coins (also known as specie). By collecting those notes and regularly demanding specie, the Second Bank kept the state banks from issuing too much paper money.

During the prosperous 1820s, the Second Bank maintained monetary stability by closing reckless state banks and restraining expansion-minded bankers in the western states. This tight-money

policy pleased bankers and entrepreneurs in Boston, New York, and Philadelphia, whose capital investments were underwriting economic development. However, most ordinary Americans did not understand the regulatory role the Second Bank played; they were simply worried about the national bank's ability to force bank closures, which left them holding worthless paper notes. Some politicians opposed the Second Bank because of the financial clout wielded by its arrogant president, Nicholas Biddle. "As to mere power," Biddle boasted, "I have been for years in the daily exercise of more personal authority than any President habitually enjoys." Fearing Biddle's influence, bankers in New York and other states wanted the specie owned by the federal government to be deposited in their institutions rather than in the

Second Bank. Other bankers, including friends of Jackson's in Nashville, wanted to escape supervision by any central bank.

Jackson Vetoes the Rechartering Bill. Although the Bank had many enemies, it was a political miscalculation by its friends that brought its downfall. In 1832, Jackson's opponents in Congress, led by Henry Clay and Daniel Webster, persuaded Biddle to seek an early extension of the bank's charter. They commanded enough votes in Congress to enact the required legislation and hoped to lure Jackson into a veto that would split the Democrats just before the 1832 elections.

Jackson turned the tables on Clay and Webster. He did veto the bill that rechartered the bank, and he did so with a masterful veto message that blended constitutional arguments with class rhetoric and patriotic fervor. Adopting Jefferson's position, Jackson declared that Congress had no constitutional authority to charter a national bank, which was "subversive of the rights of the States." Using the populist republican rhetoric of the American Revolution, he then attacked the Second Bank as "dangerous to the liberties of the people." He called it a nest of special privilege and monopoly power that promoted "the advancement of the few at the expense of . . . farmers, mechanics, and laborers." Finally, the president evoked nationalism and patriotism by pointing out that British aristocrats owned much of the bank's stock; any such powerful institution should be "purely American," he declared.

Jackson's attack on the bank carried him to victory in the election of 1832. Prior to the election Calhoun had resigned as vice president in order to advance Southern interests as a senator from South Carolina. As his new running mate, Jackson chose his longtime political ally Martin Van Buren. Together Old Hickory and "Little Van" overwhelmed Henry Clay, who headed the National Republican ticket, by 219 to 49 electoral votes. Jackson's most fervent supporters were eastern workers and western farmers, whose lives had been disrupted by falling wages or price fluctuations, and who blamed their fate on the Second Bank. "All the flourishing cities of the West are mortgaged to this money power," charged Senator Thomas Hart Benton, a Jacksonian from Missouri. "They may be devoured by it at any moment." But many Jackson supporters had prospered during a decade of strong economic growth. Along with thousands of middle-class Americans—lawyers, clerks, shopkeepers, artisans—they wanted equal opportunity to rise in the world and cheered Jackson's attacks on privileged corporations.

The Bank Destroyed. Early in 1833, Jackson called on Roger B. Taney to launch an assault on the Second Bank, which still had four years left on its original charter. A strong opponent of corporate privilege, Taney assumed control of the Treasury Department and promptly withdrew the government's gold and silver from the Second Bank. He deposited the specie in various state banks, which critics called Jackson's "pet banks." To justify this abrupt (and probably illegal) transfer, Jackson claimed that his reelection represented "the decision of the people against the bank" and gave him a mandate to destroy it. This occasion was the first in which a president claimed that victory at the polls allowed him to pursue a controversial policy or to act independently of Congress.

The "bank war" escalated into an all-out political battle. In March 1834, Jackson's opponents in the Senate passed a resolution written by Henry Clay that censured the president and warned of executive tyranny: "We are in the midst of a revolution, hitherto bloodless, but rapidly descending towards a total change of the pure republican character of the Government, and the concentration of all power in the hands of one man." Jackson was not deterred by these charges or the widespread opposition in Congress to his policies. "The Bank is trying to kill me but I will kill it," he vowed to Van Buren. And so he did. When the Second Bank's national charter expired in 1836, Jackson prevented its renewal.

Jackson had destroyed both national banking—the creation of Alexander Hamilton—and the American System of protective tariffs and internal improvements instituted by Henry Clay and John Quincy Adams. The result was a profound reduction in the economic activities and the creative energy of the national government. "All is gone," observed a Washington newspaper correspondent. "All is gone, which the General Government was instituted to create and preserve."

Indian Removal

The status of Native American peoples posed an equally complex political problem. By the late 1820s, white voices throughout the states and territories of the South and Midwest were calling for the Indian peoples to be moved and resettled west of the Mississippi River. Many easterners who were sympathetic to Native Americans also favored resettlement. Removal to the West seemed the only way to protect Indian societies from alcohol, financial exploitation, and the loss of their culture.

Most Indians, however, did not want to leave their ancestral lands. The Old Southwest was home to the so-called Five Civilized Tribes: the Cherokees and Creeks in Georgia, Tennessee, and Alabama; the Chickasaws and Choctaws in Mississippi and Alabama; and the Seminoles in Florida. During the War of 1812, Andrew Jackson had forced the Creeks to relinquish millions of acres of land, but Indian peoples still controlled vast tracts. Moreover, the mixed-blood offspring of white traders and Indian women had now assumed the leadership of many tribes. Growing up in a bicultural world, mixed-bloods knew the political ways of whites; most of them strongly resisted removal, and some favored assimilation into white society.

Actually, a number of prominent Indians had adopted the institutions and the lifestyle of southern planters. James Vann, a Georgia Cherokee, owned more than twenty black slaves, two trading posts, and a gristmill. Forty other mixed-blood Cherokee families owned twenty or more African American slaves. To protect their property and the lands of their people, the mixed-bloods promoted a strong Indian identity. For example, Sequoyah, a mixed-blood, spent years developing a system of writing for the Cherokee language that he perfected in 1821; and in 1827, mixed-blood Cherokees introduced a new charter of government modeled directly on the U.S. Constitution. Full-blood Cherokees, who made up 90 percent of the population, resisted many of the mixed-bloods' cultural and political innovations but were equally determined to retain their ancestral lands. "We would not receive money for land in which our fathers and friends are buried," one full-blood chief declared. "We love our land; it is our mother" (see Comparing American Voices, "The Cherokees Debate Removal to the Indian Territory," pp. 314–315).

What the Cherokees wanted carried no weight with the Georgia legislature. In 1802, Georgia had given up its western land claims in return for a federal promise to extinguish Indian landholdings in the state. Now it demanded fulfillment of that pledge. Having spent his military career fighting Indians and seizing their lands, Andrew Jackson gave his full support to Georgia. On assuming the presidency, he withdrew the federal troops that had protected Indian enclaves there and in Alabama and Mississippi. The states, he declared, were sovereign within their borders.

Jackson then pushed the Indian Removal Act of 1830 through Congress. The act granted money and land in present-day Oklahoma and Kansas to Native American peoples who would give up their ancestral holdings. To persuade Indians to move, government officials promised that they could live on the new lands, "they and all their children, as long as grass grows and water runs." When Chief Black Hawk and his Sauk and Fox followers refused to move from rich farmland in western Illinois in 1832, Jackson sent troops to expel them. Rejecting Black Hawk's offer to surrender, the American army pursued him into the Wisconsin Territory and, in the brutal eight-hour Bad Axe Massacre, killed 850 of Black Hawk's 1,000 warriors. Over the next five years, American diplomatic

Black Hawk

This portrait of Black Hawk (1767–1838), by Charles Bird King, shows the Indian leader as a young warrior, wearing a medal commemorating an early-nineteenth-century agreement with the U.S. government. Later, in 1830, when Congress approved Andrew Jackson's Indian Removal Act, Black Hawk mobilized Sauk and Fox warriors to protect their ancestral lands in Illinois. "It was here, that I was born—and here lie the bones of many friends and relatives," the aging chief declared. "I ... never could consent to leave it." Newberry Library, Chicago.

The Cherokees Debate Removal to the Indian Territory

President Jackson's policy of Indian removal divided many native peoples. Because some influential Cherokee leaders were literate in English, historians know the most about their debate over removal. The selections here focus on the Treaty of New Echota (1835), which traded the Cherokees' land east of the Mississippi for new land in the Indian Territory (in present-day Oklahoma and Kansas). Most full-blood Cherokees never accepted the legitimacy of the treaty, and some sought revenge. When Elias Boudinot, one of the Cherokees who signed the treaty, settled in the Indian Territory in 1839, members of the antitreaty faction labeled him a traitor and stabbed him to death.

JOHN ROSS

"A Fraud upon the Cherokee People," July 2, 1836

John Ross was the public voice of the antitreaty faction, writing petitions to Congress and publishing various letters, such as the one below, to marshal support for his position. Ross had fought as an officer under General Andrew Jackson against the Creeks in 1813. Now he vigorously opposed Jackson's removal policy, in part because he owned a three-hundred-acre cotton plantation in Georgia, which was worked by twenty African American slaves. Following the death of his Cherokee wife, Quatie, during the Trail of Tears (the forced march westward), Ross set up a new cotton plantation in the Indian Territory, which was worked by slaves he brought from Georgia. He continued to lead his people until his death in 1866.

I believe, the document [the Treaty of New Echota] signed by unauthorized individuals at Washington, will never be regarded by the Cherokee nation as a Treaty. The delegation appointed by the people to make a Treaty, have protested against that instrument "as deceptive to the world and a fraud upon the Cherokee people." . . .

Suppose we are to be removed through it from a home, by circumstances rendered disagreeable and even untenable, to be secured in a better home, where nothing can disturb or dispossess us. *Here is the great mystification.* We are not secured in the new home promised to us. We are exposed to precisely the same miseries, from which, if this measure is enforced, the United States' power professes to relieve us, but does so entirely by the exercise of that power, against our will.

One impression concerning us, is, that though we object to removal, as we are equally averse to becoming citizens of the United States, we ought to be forced to remove; to be tied hand and foot and conveyed to the extreme western frontier, and then turned loose among the wild beasts of the wilderness. Now, the fact is, we never have objected to become citizens of the United States and to conform to her laws; but in the event of conforming to her laws, we have required the protection and privileges of her laws to accompany that conformity on our part. We have asked this repeatedly and repeatedly has it been denied. . . .

In conclusion I would observe, that I still strongly hope we shall find ultimate justice from the good sense of the administration and of the people of the United States. . . . I am persuaded they have erred only in ignorance, and an ignorance forced upon them by the misrepresentation and artifices of the interested.

ELIAS BOUDINOT

Removal as "the Only Practicable Remedy," 1837

Elias Boudinot was born Gallegina ("Buck") Watie to Cherokee parents in Georgia in 1804. His father sent him to a local Moravian missionary school. In 1817, Gallegina transferred to a religious academy in Connecticut and took the name of one of its patrons, New Jersey lawyer and congressman Elias Boudinot (1740–1821). Returning to Georgia, Boudinot became the editor of the bilingual Cherokee Phoenix, *the first Native American newspaper, in 1828. His belief that removal was "the only practicable remedy" was at odds with the Cherokee government and led to his resignation from the newspaper in 1832. The selection here was a response to John Ross's writings on the Treaty of New Echota.*

What is to be done?" was a natural inquiry, after we found that all our efforts to obtain redress from the General Government, on the land of our fathers, had been of no avail. The first rupture among ourselves was the moment we presumed to answer that question. To a portion of the Cherokee people it early became evident that the interest of their countrymen and the happiness of their posterity depended upon an entire change of policy. Instead of contending uselessly against superior power, the only course left, was, to yield to circumstances over which they had no control.

In all difficulties of this kind, between the United States and the Cherokees the only mode of settling them has been by treaties; consequently, when a portion of our people became convinced that no other measures would avail, they became the *advocates of a treaty*, as the only means to extricate the Cherokees from their perplexities; hence they were called *the treaty party*. Those who maintained the old policy were known as the *anti-treaty party*. At the head of the latter has been Mr. John Ross. . . . To advocate a treaty was to declare war against the established habits of thinking peculiar to the aborigines. It was to come in contact with settled prejudices with the deep rooted attachment for the soil of our forefathers. Aside from these natural obstacles, the influence of the chiefs, who were ready to take advantage of the well known feelings of the Cherokees in reference to their lands was put in active requisition against us. . . .

It is with sincere regret that I notice you [here, Boudinot is addressing John Ross directly] say little or nothing about the moral condition of this people, as affected by present circumstances. . . . Look at the mass, look at the entire population as it now is, and say, can you see any indication of a progressing improvement, anything that can encourage a philanthropist? You know that it is almost a dreary waste. I care not if I am accounted a slanderer of my country's reputation; every observing man in this nation knows that I speak the words of truth and soberness. . . . I say their condition is wretched. Look, my dear sir, around you, and see the progress that vice and immorality have already made! See the spread of intemperance and the wretchedness and misery it has already occasioned! I need not reason with a man of your sense and discernment, and of your observation, to show the debasing character of that vice to our people; you will find an argument in every tippling shop in the country; you will find its cruel effects in the bloody tragedies that are frequently occurring in the frequent convictions and executions for murders, and in the tears and groans of the widows and fatherless, rendered homeless, naked, and hungry, by this vile curse of our race. And has it stopped its cruel ravages with the lower or poorer classes of our people? Are the higher orders, if I may so speak, left untainted? . . . It is not to be denied that, as a people, we are making a rapid tendency to a general immorality and debasement. . . .

If the dark picture which I have here drawn is a true one, and no candid person will say it is an exaggerated one, can we see a brighter prospect ahead? In another country, and under other circumstances, there is a *better* prospect. Removal, then, is the only remedy, the only *practicable* remedy. By it there *may be* finally a renovation; our people *may* rise from their very ashes, to become prosperous and happy, and a credit to our race. . . . My language has been; "fly for your lives"; it is now the same. I would say to my countrymen, you among the rest, fly from the moral pestilence that will finally destroy our nation.

What is the prospect in reference to your plan of relief, if you are understood at all to have any plan? It is dark and gloomy beyond description. Subject the Cherokees to the laws of the States in their present condition? . . . Instead of remedying the evil you would only rivet the chains and fasten the manacles of their servitude and degradation. . . . May God preserve us from such a destiny.

SOURCE: Both selections are taken from Theda Perdue and Michael D. Green, eds., *The Cherokee Removal: A Brief History with Documents,* 2d ed. (Boston: Bedford/St. Martin's, 2005), 147–151, 153–159.

ANALYZING THE EVIDENCE

➤ What are John Ross's main arguments against removal? What alternative does he implicitly propose?

➤ Why does Elias Boudinot believe that removal is the best alternative? In what ways is he hopeful that it will improve the lives of the Cherokees?

➤ Suppose that Boudinot and his associates had not signed the Echota Treaty. Would anything have turned out differently for the Cherokees?

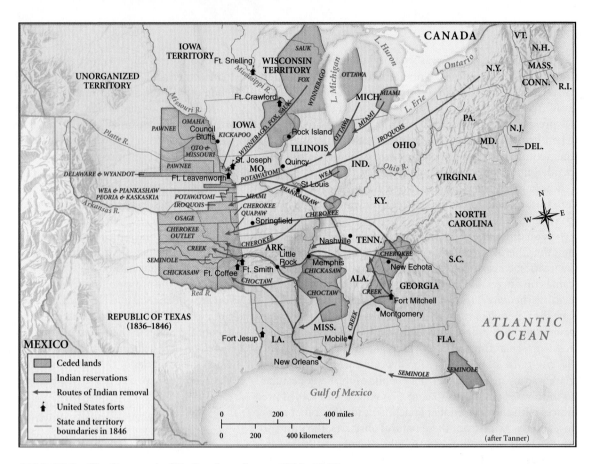

MAP 10.3   The Removal of Native Americans, 1820–1846

Beginning in the 1820s, the U.S. government forced scores of native American peoples to sign treaties that exchanged Indian lands in the East for money and designated reservations west of the Mississippi River. Then, in the 1830s, the government used military force to expel the Cherokees, Chickasaws, Choctaws, Creeks, and many Seminoles from their ancestral homes in the Old Southeast and to resettle them in the Indian Territory, land in the present-day states of Oklahoma and Kansas.

pressure and military power forced seventy Indian peoples to sign treaties and move west of the Mississippi (Map 10.3).

In the meantime, the Cherokees had carried their case to the Supreme Court, where they claimed the status of a "foreign nation." In *Cherokee Nation v. Georgia* (1831), Chief Justice John Marshall, writing for the majority, denied the Cherokees' claim of independence, declaring that Indian peoples were "domestic dependent nations." However, in *Worcester v. Georgia* (1832), Marshall and the court sided with the Cherokees against Georgia. Voiding Georgia's extension of state law over the Cherokees, they held that Indian nations were "distinct political communities, having territorial boundaries, within which their authority is exclusive [and this is] guaranteed by the United States."

Instead of guaranteeing the Cherokees' territory, the U.S. government took it from them. After

negotiating a removal treaty with a minority Cherokee faction in 1835 — the Treaty of New Echota — American officials insisted that all Cherokees abide by it. When only two thousand of seventeen thousand Cherokees had moved west by the deadline, May 1838, President Martin Van Buren ordered General Winfield Scott to enforce the treaty. Scott's army rounded up some fourteen thousand Cherokees and forcibly marched them 1,200 miles to the Indian Territory, an arduous journey they described as the Trail of Tears. Along the way, three thousand Indians died of starvation and exposure.

After the Creeks, Chickasaws, and Choctaws moved west of the Mississippi, the Seminoles were the only numerically significant Indian people remaining in the Old Southwest. With the aid of runaway slaves who had married into the tribe, the Seminoles fought a successful guerrilla war against the U.S. Army during the 1840s and retained their

Raising Public Opinion Against the Seminoles

During the eighteenth century, hundreds of black slaves fled South Carolina and Georgia, and found refuge in Spanish Florida, where they lived among and intermarried with the Seminole people. This color engraving from the 1830s — showing red and black Seminoles butchering respectable white families — was intended to bolster political support for the forced removal of the Seminoles to the Indian Territory. By the mid-1840s, after a decade of warfare, the U.S. army had forced 2,500 Seminoles to migrate to Oklahoma. However, another 2,500 Seminoles continued their armed resistance and eventually won a new treaty allowing them to live in Florida. Granger Collection.

lands in Florida, which was still a sparsely settled frontier region. The Seminoles were an exception. The national government had forced the removal of most eastern Indian peoples.

The Jacksonian Impact

Jackson's legacy, like that of every great president, is complex and rich. On the institutional level, he permanently expanded the potential authority of the nation's chief executive by identifying it with the voice of the people. As Jackson put it, "The President is the direct representative of the American people." Assuming that role during the nullification crisis, he upheld national authority by threatening the use of military force, laying the foundation for Lincoln's defense of the Union a generation later. At the same time (and somewhat contradictorily), Jackson purposefully curbed the reach of the national government. By undermining Henry Clay's American System of national banking, protective tariffs, and internal improvements, he reinvigorated the Jeffersonian tradition of a limited and frugal central government.

Roger B. Taney and the Court. Jackson also undermined the constitutional jurisprudence of John Marshall by appointing Roger B. Taney as Marshall's successor. During his long tenure as chief justice from 1835 to 1864, Taney partially reversed the na-

tionalist and property-rights decisions of the Marshall Court and gave constitutional legitimacy to Jackson's policies endorsing states' rights and free enterprise. In the landmark case *Charles River Bridge Co. v. Warren Bridge Co.* (1837), Taney declared that a legislative charter — in this case, to build and operate a toll bridge — did not necessarily bestow a monopoly, and that a legislature could charter a competing bridge to promote the general welfare: "While the rights of private property are sacredly guarded, we must not forget that the community also has rights." This decision directly challenged Marshall's interpretation of the contract clause of the Constitution in *Dartmouth College v. Woodward* (1819), which had stressed the binding nature of public charters (see Chapter 7). By limiting the property claims of existing canal and turnpike companies, the decision opened the way for legislatures to charter railroads that would provide cheaper and more-efficient transportation.

Other decisions by the Taney Court placed limits on Marshall's nationalistic interpretation of the commerce clause by enhancing the regulatory role of state governments. For example, in *Mayor of New York v. Miln* (1837), the Taney Court ruled that New York State could use its "police power" to inspect the health of arriving immigrants. The Court also restored to the states some of the economic powers they had exercised before 1787. In *Briscoe v. Bank of Kentucky* (1837), for example, the justices found that when it issued currency, a bank owned by the state of Kentucky did not violate the provision of the U.S. Constitution (Article 1, Section 10) that prohibits states from issuing "bills of credit."

States Embrace Classical Liberal Doctrines. Inspired by Jackson and Taney's example, Democrats in the various states mounted their own constitutional revolutions. Between 1830 and 1860, twenty states called conventions to write new constitutions that would extend democracy. The revised constitutions were more democratic because they usually gave the vote to all white men and reapportioned state legislatures on the basis of population. They also brought government "near to the people" by mandating the election, rather than the appointment, of most public officials, including sheriffs, justices of the peace, and judges.

Most of the new constitutions also introduced the principles of **classical liberalism**, or **laissez-faire** — that the government's role in the economy should be limited. (Twentieth-century social-welfare liberalism endorses the opposite principle, that government should intervene in economic and social life. See Chapter 24.) As president, Jackson had destroyed the American system and its program of national government subsidies; now his disciples in the states set out to undermine the Commonwealth philosophy, the use of chartered corporations and state funds to promote economic development. Most Jackson-era constitutions prohibited states from granting exclusive charters to corporations or extending loans and credit guarantees to private businesses. "If there is any danger to be feared in . . . government," declared a New Jersey Democrat, "it is the danger of associated wealth, with special privileges." The revised state constitutions also protected taxpayers by setting strict limits on state debt and encouraging judges to enforce them. Said one New York reformer: "We will not trust the legislature with the power of creating indefinite mortgages on the people's property."

"The world is governed too much," the Jacksonians proclaimed as they condemned government-granted special privileges and embraced a small-government, laissez-faire outlook. The first American populists, they celebrated the power of ordinary people to make decisions in the marketplace and the voting booth.

> ➤ What were Andrew Jackson's policies on banking and tariffs? How did they evolve? Do you think those policies helped or hurt the American economy? Why?

> ➤ Why did Jackson support Indian removal? Did removal help to preserve, or to destroy, Native American culture? Explain your answer.

> ➤ How did the constitutional interpretations of the Taney Court differ from those of the Marshall Court? What changed as a result of the Taney Court's decisions?

Class, Culture, and the Second Party System

The rise of the Democracy and Jackson's tumultuous presidency sparked the creation in the mid-1830s of a second national party — the **Whigs** — and a new party system. For the next two decades, Whigs and Democrats competed fiercely for votes. Each party appealed to different cultural groups: Many evangelical Protestants became Whigs, while most Catholic immigrants and traditional Protestants joined the Democrats. By debating issues of economic policy, class power, and moral reform, party politicians offered Americans a clear choice between competing programs and political leaders. "Of the two great parties," remarked philosopher and essayist Ralph Waldo Emerson, the Democracy "has the best cause . . . for free trade, for wide suffrage." The Whig party, he said, "has the best men."

The Whig Worldview

The Whig Party began in 1834, when a group of congressmen banded together to oppose Andrew Jackson's policies and his high-handed, "kinglike" conduct. They took the name *Whigs* to identify themselves with the pre-Revolutionary American and British parties — also called Whigs — that had opposed the arbitrary actions of British monarchs. The Whigs accused "King Andrew I" of violating the Constitution by creating a "spoils system" and increasing presidential authority. Jackson's "executive usurpation," they charged, undermined government by elected legislators, who were the true representatives of the sovereign people (see Reading American Pictures, "Politics and the Press: Cartoonists Take Aim at Andrew Jackson," p. 319).

Whig Ideology. Initially, the Whigs were a diverse group, a "heterogeneous mass" drawn from various political factions and outlooks. However, under the leadership of Senators Webster of Massachusetts, Clay of Kentucky, and Calhoun of South Carolina, the Whigs gradually articulated a distinct vision.

Politics and the Press: Cartoonists Take Aim at Andrew Jackson

The Rats Leaving a Falling House, 1831. Library of Congress.

King Andrew the First, 1832. New-York Historical Society.

The 1830s witnessed the rise of the Second Party System, in which Whigs and Democrats competed fiercely for power and patronage. They also witnessed an expansion of the franchise. These two factors—party conflict and democratic suffrage—produced an outpouring of political literature, especially in party-subsidized newspapers. Cartoons quickly became a staple of democratic politics because their use of simple terms and caricature appealed to ordinary voters. Cartoons like these—and thousands more—give us insight into the partisan political culture of the era.

ANALYZING THE EVIDENCE

➤ The cartoon on the left was inspired by Edward Williams Clay (no relation to Henry Clay), a Philadelphia portrait painter and engraver who was also a great cartoonist. In 1831, President Jackson's critics printed 10,000 copies of "The Rats Leaving a Falling House." Why was this cartoon so popular? What does the use of rats suggest about the tone of politics in the 1830s? What other visual clues reveal the artist's political grievances?

➤ In the image to the right, how does the cartoonist depict the threat Jackson poses to the republic? Based on the material in this chapter, do you think there was any justification for the artist's point of view?

➤ Do these cartoons suggest why Andrew Jackson became a prime target of cartoonists? What was there about his personality, appearance, or political style that made him especially vulnerable to caricature?

➤ Why were cartoons like the two here particularly effective as political weapons in the early nineteenth century? How do they work as propaganda? In what ways do they try to persuade their audience?

Their goal, like that of the Federalists of the 1790s, was a political world dominated by men of ability and wealth; unlike the Federalists, though, the Whig elite would be chosen by talent, not birth.

The Whigs celebrated the entrepreneur and the enterprising individual: "This is a country of self-made men," they boasted, pointing to the relative absence of permanent distinctions of class and status among the white citizens of the United States. Embracing the Industrial Revolution, northern Whigs welcomed the investments of "moneyed capitalists," which provided workers with jobs and so "bread, clothing and homes." Whig congressman Edward Everett told a Fourth of July crowd in Lowell, Massachusetts, that there should be a "holy alliance" among laborers, owners, and governments. Many workers agreed, especially those who held jobs in the New England textile factories and Pennsylvania iron mills that benefited from government subsidies and protective tariffs. To ensure continued economic progress, Everett and other northern Whigs called for a return to the American System.

Support for the Whigs in the South rested on the appeal of specific policies and politicians rather than agreement with the Whigs' social vision. Some southern Whigs were wealthy planters who invested in railroads and banks or sold their cotton to New York merchants. Most were yeomen whites who wanted to break the grip over state politics held by low-country planters, most of whom were Democrats. In addition, some states' rights Democrats in Virginia and South Carolina became Whigs because, like John C. Calhoun, they condemned Andrew Jackson's crusade against nullification.

Like Calhoun, most southern Whigs did not share the Whig Party's enthusiasm for high tariffs for industry and social mobility for individual Americans. Calhoun was extremely conscious of class divisions in society. He maintained that the northern Whig ideal of equal opportunity was contradicted not only by slavery, which he considered a fundamental American institution, but also by the wage-labor system of industrial capitalism. "There is and always has been in an advanced state of wealth and civilization a conflict between labor and capital," Calhoun declared in 1837. He urged slave owners and factory owners to unite against their common foe: a working class comprised of enslaved blacks and propertyless whites.

Most northern Whigs rejected Calhoun's class-conscious social ideology. "A clear and well-defined line between capital and labor" might fit the slave South or class-ridden European societies, Daniel Webster conceded, but in the North "this distinction grows less and less definite as commerce ad-

vances." Ignoring the ever-increasing mass of propertyless immigrants, Webster focused on the growing size and affluence of the northern middle class, whose members became strong supporters of Whig candidates. In fact, in the election of 1834, the Whigs won a majority in the House of Representatives by appealing to evangelical Protestants and the upwardly mobile — prosperous farmers, small-town merchants, and skilled industrial workers in New England, New York, and the new communities along the Great Lakes.

Anti-Masonic Influence. Many of these Whig voters had previously supported the Anti-Masons, a powerful but short-lived political party that formed in the late 1820s. As their name implies, Anti-Masons opposed the Order of Freemasonry, a republican organization that began in eighteenth-century Europe. The order was a secret society of men, its rituals closely guarded. New members had to be vouched for by a Mason and profess a belief in a supreme being. Freemasonry spread rapidly in America and attracted political leaders — including George Washington, Henry Clay, and Andrew Jackson — and ambitious businessmen. By the mid-1820s, there were twenty thousand Masons in New York State, organized into 450 local lodges. Following the kidnapping and murder in 1826 of William Morgan, a New York Mason who had threatened to reveal the order's secrets, the Freemasons fell into disrepute. Thurlow Weed, a Rochester newspaper editor, spearheaded the Anti-Masonic Party, which attacked the order for being a secret aristocratic fraternity and ousted its members from local and state offices.

The Whigs recruited Anti-Masons to their party by endorsing the Anti-Masons' support for temperance, equality of opportunity, and evangelical moralism. Throughout the Northeast and Midwest, Whig politicians advocated legal curbs on the sale of alcohol and supported local bylaws to preserve Sunday as a day of worship. The Whigs also won congressional seats in the Ohio and Mississippi valleys, where farmers, bankers, and shopkeepers favored Henry Clay's advocacy of government subsidies for roads, canals, and bridges. For these citizens of the growing Midwest, the Whigs' program of nationally subsidized transportation projects was as important as their moral agenda.

The Election of 1836. In the election of 1836, the Whig Party faced Martin Van Buren, the architect of the Democratic Party and Jackson's handpicked successor. Van Buren denounced the American System

Celebrating a Political Triumph, 1836

To commemorate Martin Van Buren's election in 1836 and to reward friends for their support, the Democratic Party distributed thousands of snuff boxes inscribed with the new president's portrait. By using gifts and other innovative measures to enlist the loyalty of voters, Van Buren and his allies transformed American politics from an upper-class avocation to a democratic contest for votes and power. Collection of Janice L. and David J. Frent.

and warned that its revival would undermine the rights of the states and create an oppressive system of "consolidated government." Positioning himself as a defender of individual rights, Van Buren also opposed the efforts of Whigs and moral reformers to use state laws to impose temperance and national laws to restrict or abolish slavery. "The government is best which governs least" became his motto in economic, cultural, and racial matters.

To oppose Van Buren, the Whigs ran four candidates, each of whom had a strong regional reputation. Their plan was to garner enough electoral votes to throw the contest into the House of Representatives. However, the Whig tally — 73 electoral votes collected by William Henry Harrison of Ohio, 26 by Hugh L. White of Tennessee, 14 by Daniel Webster of Massachusetts, and 11 by W. P. Magnum of Georgia — fell far short of Van Buren's 170 votes. Still, the size of the popular vote for the four Whig candidates — 49 percent of the total — showed that the party's message of economic and moral improvement appealed not only to middle-class Americans but also to farmers and workers with little or no property (see Voices from Abroad, "Alexis de Tocqueville: Parties in the United States," p. 323).

Labor Politics and the Depression of 1837–1843

As the Democrats struggled to maintain their national political supremacy, they faced a challenge on the local level from a new political party made up primarily of artisans and laborers. Market expansion and urban growth had swelled the number of nonfarm workers, and these workers were demanding attention to their economic and political needs (see Chapter 9).

Working Men's Parties and Unions. In 1827, artisans and workers in Philadelphia organized the Mechanics' Union of Trade Associations, a group of fifty unions with ten thousand members. The following year, they founded a Working Men's Party to secure "a just balance of power . . . between all the various classes." The new party campaigned for the abolition of banks, fair taxation, and universal public education. Equally important, it blazed the trail for similar organizations: By 1833, laborers had established Working Men's Parties in fifteen states.

The new parties had a clear agenda. The economic transformation had brought prosperity to bankers and entrepreneurs, but rising prices and stagnant wages had lowered the standard of living of many urban artisans and wage earners. These contradictory trends exposed what workers called "the glaring inequality of society" and prompted them to organize for political action. "Past experience teaches us that we have nothing to hope from the aristocratic orders of society," declared the New York Working Men's Party. It vowed "to send men of our own description, if we can, to the Legislature at Albany" and to win the passage of laws that would put an end to private banks, chartered monopolies, and debtors' prisons. In Philadelphia, the Working Men's Party demanded higher taxes on the wealthy and, in 1834, persuaded the Pennsylvania legislature to authorize tax-supported schools to educate workers' children.

Artisan republicanism — workers' independence — was the core ideology of the working men's parties. According to radical thinker Orestes Brownson, their goal was a society without dependent wage earners: "All men will be independent proprietors, working on their own capitals, on their own farms, or in their own shops." This ideal prompted many artisan republicans to join Jacksonian Democrats in demanding equal rights and attacking chartered corporations. "The only safeguard against oppression," argued William Leggett, a leading member of the New York Loco-Foco (Equal Rights) Party, "is a system of legislation

Frances Wright: Radical Reformer

Wright (1795–1852) grew up in a wealthy, republican-minded merchant family in Scotland. After a sojourn in the United States, she published *Views of Society and Manners in America* (1821), which won her the friendship of Lafayette and Jefferson. In 1825, she founded a utopian community of whites and freed slaves at Nashoba in western Tennessee. Three years later, Wright took New York by storm, lecturing to large audiences that a "monied aristocracy" of bankers and a "professional aristocracy" of ministers and lawyers were oppressing the "laboring class." She set up a reading room and medical dispensary and won a following among artisans and journeymen, some of whom turned to politics and energized the Working Men's Party. This portrait, painted at Nashoba in 1826, relays a subversive message. Wright is wearing pantaloons covered by a tunic. Compounding that masculine imagery, she is standing next to a horse, a traditional symbol of virility. Miriam and Ira D. Wallach Division of Art, Prints and Photographs. The New York Public Library. Astor, Lenox and Tilden Foundations.

which leaves to all the free exercise of their talents and industry." Working Men's candidates initially won office in many cities, but divisions over policy and the parties' weakness in statewide contests soon took a toll. By the mid-1830s, most politically active workers had joined the Democratic Party, which already had a strong base in the dominant farm population, and urged that party to enact legislation to eliminate protective tariffs and to tax the stocks and bonds of wealthy capitalists.

As they campaigned for a more egalitarian society, workers formed unions to bargain for higher wages for themselves. Employers responded by attacking the union movement. In 1836, clothing manufacturers in New York City agreed to dismiss workers who belonged to the Society of Journeymen Tailors and circulated a list—a so-called **blacklist**—of the society's members. The employers also brought lawsuits to overturn **closed-shop agreements** that required them to hire only union members. They argued that these contracts violated both the common law and legislative statutes that prohibited "conspiracies" in restraint of trade.

Judges usually sided with the employers. In 1835, the New York Supreme Court found that a shoemakers' union in Geneva had illegally caused "an industrious man" to be "driven out of employment" because he would not join the union. "It is important to the best interests of society that the price of labor be left to regulate itself," the court declared. When a court in New York City upheld a conspiracy verdict against a tailors' union, a crowd of 27,000 people denounced the decision in a mass meeting, and tailors circulated handbills proclaiming that the "Freemen of the North are now on a level with the slaves of the South." Juries were more

Alexis de Tocqueville

Parties in the United States

In Democracy in America (1835), Alexis de Tocqueville presented both a philosophical analysis of the society of the United States and an astute description of its political institutions. Here the republican-minded French aristocrat explains the role of lawyers in American politics, why "great political parties" are not to be found in the United States, and how regional interests and political ambition threaten the stability of the political system.

In visiting the Americans and studying their laws, we perceive that the authority they have entrusted to the members of the legal profession, and the influence that these individuals exercise in the government, are the most powerful existing security against the excesses of democracy.... Men who have made a special study of the laws derive from [that] occupation certain habits of order, a taste for formalities, and a kind of instinctive regard for the regular connection of ideas, which naturally render them very hostile to the revolutionary spirit and the unreflecting passions of the multitude.... Lawyers belong to the people by birth and interest, and to the aristocracy by habit and taste; they may be looked upon as the connecting link between the two great classes of society....

The political parties that I style great are those which cling to principles rather than to their consequences; to general and not to special cases; to ideas and not to men.... In them private interest, which always plays the chief part in political passions, is more studiously veiled under the pretext of the public good....

Great political parties ... are not to be met with in the United States at the present time. Parties, indeed, may be found which threaten the future of the Union; but there is none which seems to contest the present form of government or the present course of society. The parties by which the Union is menaced do not rest upon principles, but upon material interests. These interests constitute, in the different provinces of so vast an empire, rival nations rather than parties. Thus, upon a recent occasion [the Tariff of 1832 and the nullification crisis in South Carolina] the North contended for the system of commercial prohibition, and the South took up arms in favor of free trade, simply because the North is a manufacturing and the South an agricultural community; and the restrictive system that was profitable to the one was prejudicial to the other.

In the absence of great parties the United States swarms with lesser controversies.... The pains that are taken to create parties are inconceivable, and at the present day it is no easy task. In the United States there is no religious animosity, ... no jealousy of rank, ... no public misery.... Nevertheless, ambitious men will succeed in creating parties.... A political aspirant in the United States begins by discerning his own interest [and] then contrives to find out some doctrine or principle that may suit the purposes of this new organization, which he adopts in order to bring forward his party and secure its popularity....

The deeper we penetrate into the inmost thought of these parties, the more we perceive that the object of the one [the Whigs] is to limit and that of the other [the Democrats] to extend the authority of the people. I do not assert that the ostensible purpose or even that the secret aim of American parties is to promote the rule of aristocracy or democracy in the country; but I affirm that aristocratic or democratic passions may easily be detected at the bottom of all parties....

To quote a recent example, when President Jackson attacked the Bank of the United States, the country was excited, and parties were formed; the well-informed classes rallied round the bank, the common people round the President. But it must not be imagined that the people had formed a rational opinion upon a question which offers so many difficulties to the most experienced statesmen. By no means. The bank is a great establishment, which has an independent existence; and the people ... are startled to meet with this obstacle to their authority [and are] led to attack it, in order to see whether it can be shaken, like everything else.

SOURCE: Alexis de Tocqueville, *Democracy in America* (1835; New York: Random House, 1981), 1: 94–99.

ANALYZING THE EVIDENCE

➤ Based on your understanding of the Second Party System, was Tocqueville correct in arguing that American parties were the creation of "ambitious" men? How does Tocqueville characterize the Whigs and Democrats? Do you think he is accurate?

➤ Tocqueville claims that there was "no religious animosity" in American society and politics. Do you agree? What was the position of the parties with respect to the legal enforcement of morality?

likely to reflect public opinion, which opposed conspiracy prosecutions. In 1836, local juries acquitted shoemakers in Hudson, New York, carpet makers in Thompsonville, Connecticut, and plasterers in Philadelphia of similar conspiracy charges.

The Panic of 1837 and the Depression. At this juncture, the Panic of 1837 threw the American economy—and the union movement—into disarray. The panic began when the Bank of England, hoping to boost the faltering British economy, sharply curtailed the flow of money and credit to the United States. Over the previous decade and a half, British manufacturers and investors had extended credit to southern planters to expand cotton production and had purchased millions of dollars of the canal bonds issued by northern states. Suddenly deprived of British funds, American planters, merchants, and canal corporations had to withdraw specie from domestic banks to pay their commercial debts and interest on their foreign loans. Moreover, because the Bank of England refused credit to British cotton brokers, the price of raw cotton in the South collapsed, plummeting from 20 cents a pound to 10 cents or less.

The drain of gold and silver to Britain and falling cotton prices set off a financial panic. On May 8, the Dry Dock Bank of New York City closed its doors. Worried depositors quickly withdrew more than $2 million in gold and silver coins from other New York banks, forcing them to suspend all specie payments. Within two weeks, every bank in the United States stopped trading specie and curtailed credit. These measures turned a financial panic into an economic crisis because many businesses had to curtail production. "This sudden overthrow of the commercial credit and honor of the nation" had a "stunning effect," observed Henry Fox, the British minister in Washington. "The conquest of the land by a foreign power could hardly have produced a more general sense of humiliation and grief."

A second, longer-lasting downturn began in 1839. To revive the economy after the Panic of 1837, state governments increased their investments in canals and other transportation ventures. As they issued more and more bonds to finance these ventures, bond prices fell sharply in Europe, sparking a four-year-long international financial crisis. The crisis engulfed state governments in America, which were unable to meet the substantial interest payments on their bonds. Nine states defaulted on their obligations to foreign creditors, which, in turn, undermined the confidence of European investors and cut the flow of capital to the United States. Bumper crops drove down cotton prices even further, bringing more bankruptcies.

The American economy fell into a deep depression. By 1843, canal construction had dropped by 90 percent, and prices by nearly 50 percent. Unemployment reached almost 20 percent of the workforce in seaports and industrial centers. Minister Henry Ward Beecher described a land "filled with lamentation . . . its inhabitants wandering like bereaved citizens among the ruins of an earthquake, mourning for children, for houses crushed, and property buried forever."

The Fate of the Labor Movement. By creating a surplus of unemployed workers, the depression devastated the labor movement. In 1837, six thousand masons, carpenters, and other building-trades workers lost their jobs in New York City, depleting unions' rosters and destroying their bargaining power. By 1843, most local unions and all the national labor organizations had disappeared, along with their newspapers.

However, two events in this dismal period improved the long-term prospects of the labor movement. The first was a major legal victory. In *Commonwealth v. Hunt* (1842), the Massachusetts Supreme Judicial Court upheld the rights of workers to form unions. Chief Justice Lemuel Shaw, one of the great jurists of the nineteenth century, overturned common-law precedents, ruling that a union was not an inherently illegal organization and could strike to enforce a closed-shop agreement. Courts in many states accepted Shaw's opinion, but Whigs on the bench—and there were many of them—found other ways to deter unions. For example, some courts issued injunctions, orders that prohibited workers from picketing or striking. Labor's second success was political. Continuing Jackson's effort to recruit workers to the Democratic Party, President Van Buren signed an executive order in 1840 setting a ten-hour day for federal employees. This victory showed that the outcome of workers' struggles—like conflicts over tariffs, banks, and internal improvements—depended not only on economic factors but also on political decisions.

"Tippecanoe and Tyler Too!"

The depression had a major impact on politics because many Americans blamed the Democrats for their economic woes. In particular, they derided Jackson for destroying the Second Bank and for issuing the Specie Circular of 1836, which had

Hard Times

The Panic of 1837 struck Americans hard. As this anti-Democratic political cartoon suggests, unemployed workers turned to drink; women and children begged in the streets; and fearful depositors tried to withdraw funds before banks collapsed. As the plummeting hot-air balloon in the background symbolized, the rising "Glory" of America had come crashing to earth. Library of Congress.

required western settlers to use gold and silver coins to pay for land purchases from the federal government. Not realizing that specie shipments to Britain were the main cause of the financial panic, the Whigs—and many voters—blamed Jackson's policies.

The public turned its anger on Van Buren, who took office just as the panic struck. Ignoring the pleas of influential bankers, the new president refused to revoke the Specie Circular or take other actions that might have reversed the downturn. Holding to his philosophy of limited government, Van Buren advised Congress that "the less government interferes with private pursuits the better for the general prosperity." As the depression deepened in 1839, this laissez-faire policy commanded less and less political support. Worse, Van Buren's major piece of economic legislation, the Independent Treasury Act of 1840, actually delayed recovery. The act pulled federal specie out of Jackson's pet banks (which had used it to back loans) and placed it in government vaults, where it did no economic good at all.

The Election of 1840. Determined to exploit Van Buren's weakness, the Whigs organized their first national convention in 1840 and nominated William Henry Harrison of Ohio for president and John Tyler of Virginia for vice president. A military hero of the Battle of Tippecanoe and the War of 1812, Harrison was well advanced in age (sixty-eight) and had little political experience. But the Whig leaders in Congress, Clay and Webster, simply wanted a president who would rubber-stamp their program for protective tariffs and a national bank. An unpretentious, amiable man, Harrison told

The Log Cabin Campaign, 1840
During the Second Party system, politics became more responsive to the popular will as ordinary people voted for candidates who shared their values and lifestyles. The barrels of hard cider framing this homemade campaign banner evoke the drink of the common man, while the central image falsely portrays William Henry Harrison as a poor and simple frontier farmer. New-York Historical Society, New York City.

voters that Whig policies were "the only means, under Heaven, by which a poor industrious man may become a rich man without bowing to colossal wealth."

Panic and depression stacked the political cards against Van Buren, although the contest turned as much on style as on substance. It became the great "log cabin campaign" — the first time two well-organized parties competed for the loyalties of a mass electorate through a new style of campaigning. Whig songfests, parades, and well-orchestrated mass meetings drew new voters into the political arena. Whig speakers assailed "Martin Van Ruin" as a manipulative politician with aristocratic tastes — a devotee of fancy wines and elegant clothes, as indeed he was. Less truthfully, they portrayed Harrison as a self-made man who would have been happy living in a log cabin and drinking hard cider, a drink of the common people. In fact, Harrison's father was a wealthy Virginia planter who had signed the Declaration of Independence.

The Whigs boosted their electoral hopes by welcoming women to campaign festivities. Previously,

President John Tyler (1790–1862)

Both as an "accidental" president and as a man, Tyler left his mark upon the world. His initiative to annex Texas made the election of 1844 a crucial contest and helped to trigger war with Mexico in 1846. His first wife, Letitia, gave birth to eight children before dying in the White House in 1842. Two years later, Tyler married 24-year-old Julia Gardiner, who bore him seven more children. White House Historical Association (White House Collection).

women had been excluded not only from voting and jury duty but also from marching in political parades. Jacksonian Democrats, in particular, thought of politics as a "manly" affair. They denounced women who ventured into the political arena, likening them to "public" women, the prostitutes who plied their trade in theaters and other public places. The Whigs recognized that women from Yankee families, a key Whig constituency, had already entered American public life through religious revivalism, the temperance movement, and other benevolent activities. In October 1840, Daniel Webster addressed a meeting of twelve hundred Whig women, praised their support for moral reform, and urged them to back Whig candidates. "This way of making politicians of their women is something new under the sun," noted one Democrat, worried that it would bring more Whig men to the polls. And it did: More than 80 percent of the eligible male voters cast ballots in 1840 (up from less than 60 percent in 1832 and 1836; see Figure 10.1, p. 307). Heeding the Whig slogan "Tippecanoe and Tyler Too," they voted Harrison into the White House — he won 53 percent of the popular vote and 80 percent of the electoral vote — and gave the Whigs a majority in Congress.

John Tyler versus the Whigs. Led by Clay and Webster, the Whigs in Congress were poised to reverse Jacksonian policies. Their anticipation was short-lived, though; barely a month after his inauguration, Harrison died of pneumonia, and the nation got "Tyler Too." But in what capacity, as acting president or as president? The Constitution was silent on the issue. Ignoring his Whig associates in Congress, who feared a strong president like Jackson, Tyler not only took the presidential oath of office but also declared his intention to govern as he pleased.

And that would not be like a Whig. Tyler had served in the House and the Senate as a Jeffersonian Democrat, firmly committed to slavery and states' rights. He had joined the Whigs only to protest Jackson's stance against nullification. On economic issues, Tyler shared Jackson's hostility to the Second Bank and the American System. And so the new president vetoed Whig bills that would have raised tariffs and created a new national bank. Disgusted, most of the members of Tyler's cabinet resigned in 1842, and the Whigs expelled him from their party. "His Accidency," as he was called by his critics, was now a president without a party.

The split between Tyler and the Whigs allowed the Democrats to regroup. The party vigorously recruited supporters among subsistence farmers in the North, smallholders in the South, and former members of the Working Men's parties in the cities. It also won success among Irish and German Catholic immigrants — whose numbers had increased during the 1830s — by supporting their demands for religious and cultural freedom. In time, this pattern of **ethnocultural politics**, as historians refer to the practice of voting along ethnic and religious lines, became a prominent feature of American life. Thanks to these urban and rural recruits, the Democrats remained the majority party in most parts of the nation. Their program of equal rights, states' rights, and cultural liberty was more attractive than the Whig platform of economic nationalism, moral reform, and individual mobility.

➤ How did the ideology of the Whigs differ from that of the Working Men's Party? From that of the Jacksonian Democrats?

➤ Why did the Democrats win the election of 1836 but lose the election of 1840?

SUMMARY

In this chapter, we have examined the causes and the consequences of the democratic political revolution that went hand in hand with the economic transformation of the early nineteenth century. We saw that the expansion of the franchise weakened the political system run by notables of high status. In its place emerged a system managed by professional politicians, men like Martin Van Buren, who were mostly of middle-class origin.

We also witnessed a revolution in government policy, as Andrew Jackson and his Democratic party dismantled the political foundation of the mercantilist system. On the national level, Jackson destroyed Henry Clay's American System; on the state level, Democrats wrote new constitutions that ended the Commonwealth system of government charters and subsidies to private businesses.

Finally, we watched the emergence of the Second Party System. In the aftermath of the fragmentation of the Republican Party during the election of 1824, two new parties — the Democrats and the Whigs — appeared on the national level and eventually absorbed the members of two other political movements, the Anti-Masonic and Working Men's parties. The new party system continued to deny women, Native Americans, and most African Americans a voice in public life, but it established universal suffrage for white men and a mode of representative government that was responsive to ordinary citizens. In their scope and significance, these political innovations matched the economic advances of the Industrial and Market revolutions.

Connections: Government

In this chapter, we witnessed the process that transformed the republican polity and culture described in Chapters 7 and 8 into a new, democratic political culture and the Second Party System of Whigs and Democrats. As we observed in the essay that opened Part Three (p. 269):

> The rapid growth of political parties sparked the creation of a democratic polity open to many social groups. . . . Party competition engaged the energies of the electorate and provided unity to a fragmented social order.

We continue the story of America's political development in Chapter 13, which covers the years between 1844 and 1860. There we will watch the disintegration of the Second Party System over the issue of slavery. The political problems posed by the westward expansion of plantation slavery were not new; as the discussion in Chapter 8 showed, the North and the South quarreled bitterly between 1819 and 1821 over the extension of slavery into Missouri. At that time, notable politicians raised in the old republican culture resolved the issue through compromise. Would democratic politicians be equally adept at fashioning a compromise over slavery in the territories seized from Mexico in 1848? Even more important, would their constituents accept that compromise? These questions are difficult to answer because, by 1848, the United States had become a more complex and contentious society, a change that at least in part stemmed from the appearance of new cultural movements and radical reform organizations, which are the subject of Chapter 11.

CHAPTER REVIEW QUESTIONS

➤ In what respects did the Jackson era fundamentally change the American economy, public policy, and society?

➤ Explain the rise of the Second Party System. How would you characterize American politics in the early 1840s?

➤ The chapter argues that a democratic revolution swept America in the decades after 1820. What evidence does the text present to support this argument? How persuasive is the evidence?

TIMELINE

1810s	State constitutions begin expanding voting rights for white men Martin Van Buren creates a disciplined party in New York
1825	John Quincy Adams is elected president by House and adopts Henry Clay's American System
1828	Artisans and laborers in Philadelphia organize Working Men's Party Tariff of Abominations raises duties on imported goods and manufactures Andrew Jackson is elected to first term as president *The South Carolina Exposition and Protest* challenges national legislation and majority rule
1830	Jackson vetoes extension of National Road Congress enacts Jackson's Indian Removal Act
1831	*Cherokee Nation v. Georgia* denies Indians' claim of national independence
1832	American troops kill 850 Sauk and Fox warriors in Bad Axe Massacre President Jackson vetoes renewal of the Second Bank's charter South Carolina adopts Ordinance of Nullification *Worcester v. Georgia* upholds political autonomy of Indian peoples
1833	Congress passes Force Bill and compromise tariff
1834	Whig Party formed by Henry Clay, John C. Calhoun, and Daniel Webster
1835	Roger Taney named Supreme Court chief justice
1836	Martin Van Buren elected president
1837	*Charles River Bridge Co. v. Warren Bridge Co.* weakens legal position of chartered monopolies Panic of 1837 ends long period of economic expansion and derails labor movement
1838	Thousands of Cherokees die on forced march (Trail of Tears) to Indian Territory
1839–1843	American loans spark international financial crisis and four-year economic depression
1840	Whigs win victory in log cabin campaign
1841	John Tyler succeeds William Henry Harrison as president
1842	*Commonwealth v. Hunt* legitimizes trade unions

FOR FURTHER EXPLORATION

George Dangerfield, *The Era of Good Feelings* (1952), remains the classic study of American politics between 1815 and 1828. For a new synthesis, see Sean Wilentz, *The Rise of American Democracy: Jefferson to Lincoln* (2005). Two concise surveys of the Jackson era are Harry L. Watson, *Liberty and Power: The Politics of Jacksonian America* (1990), which emphasizes republican ideology and the Market Revolution, and Daniel Feller, *The Jacksonian Promise: America, 1815–1840* (1995), which underlines the tremendous optimism of the time. In *The Idea of a Party System* (1969), Richard Hofstadter lucidly explains the triumphant entry of parties into America politics. The Internet Public Library (**www.ipl.org/div/potus/jqadams.html**) covers the election of 1824 and the administration of John Quincy Adams. For an audio account of the election of 1824, go to **www.albany.edu/talkinghistory/arch2000july–december.html**, and listen to the interview with Professor Paul Finkelman.

Robert V. Remini, *The Life of Andrew Jackson* (1988), highlights Jackson's triumphs without neglecting his shortcomings. For a brief treatment of Jackson's life and some of his important state papers, log on to **odur.let.rug.nl/~usa/P/aj7/aj7.htm**. The brutal impact of Jackson's Indian policy is brought to life in Robert J. Conley, *Mountain Windsong: A Novel of the Trail of Tears* (1992), and in two studies by historians: Sean Michael O'Brien, *In Bitterness and in Tears: Andrew Jackson's Destruction of the Creeks and Seminoles* (2003), and John Buchanan, *Jackson's Way: Andrew Jackson and the People of the Western Waters* (2001). For material on the Cherokees, see the Web site maintained by Ken Martin, a member of the Cherokee Nation of Oklahoma, **cherokeehistory.com/**. Also see **www.rosecity.net/tears/**, which has links to articles, primary sources, and other Web sites.

Major L. Wilson, *The Presidency of Martin Van Buren* (1984), provides a shrewd assessment of the man and his policies. The best treatment of leading Whigs is Merrill D. Peterson's *The Great Triumvirate: Webster, Clay, and Calhoun* (1987). For the ideology and politics of artisans and laborers, see Sean Wilentz, *Chants Democratic: New York City and the Rise of the American Working Class, 1788–1850* (1986).

Alexis de Tocqueville's classic, *Democracy in America* (1835), has wonderful insights into the character of American society and political institutions in the early nineteenth century. It is available online, along with an excellent exhibit and collection of essays at **xroads.virginia.edu/~hyper/detoc/home.html**. For ordinary and outrageous political cartoons, go to "American Political Prints, 1766–1876" at **loc.harpweek.com/**.

TEST YOUR KNOWLEDGE

To assess your command of the material in this chapter, see the Online Study Guide at **bedfordstmartins.com/henretta**.

For Web sites, images, and documents related to topics and places in this chapter, visit **bedfordstmartins.com/makehistory**.

Little acts of kindness
Little words of love

Make our earthly eden
like our Heaven above

Is our
Home a
Heaven

Heaven
is our
Home

Peace
be still

Kind
words
Never
Die

Forgive
as you
hope to be
Forgiven

Earth has
no sorrow
Heaven
cannot
heal

Be still
and know
that I am
God

No Cross
No Crown

Thy will
be done

Oh sacred
Patience
with my
soul abide

There is a
magic in
kindness
that springs
from above

Maria
Cadman
Hubbard
aged 79

If you can
not be a
Golden pipp
and don't turn
crab apple

Bear it
with a

Love one
another

1848

11 Religion and Reform
1820–1860

"THE SPIRIT OF REFORM IS in every place," the children of legal reformer David Dudley Field wrote in their handwritten monthly *Gazette* in 1842:

> The labourer with a family says "reform the common schools"; the merchant and the planter say, "reform the tariff"; the lawyer "reform the laws," the politician "reform the government," the abolitionist "reform the slave laws," the moralist "reform intemperance," . . . the ladies wish their legal privileges extended, and in short, the whole country is wanting reform.

Like many Americans, the young Fields sensed that the political whirlwind of the 1830s had transformed the way people thought about themselves as individuals and as a society. Suddenly, thousands of men and women, inspired by the economic progress and democratic spirit of the age and the religious optimism of the Second Great Awakening believed they could improve not just their personal lives but society as a whole. Some dedicated themselves to the cause of reform. William Lloyd Garrison started out as an antislavery advocate, and then went on to embrace women's rights, pacifism, and the abolition of prisons. Such obsessive individuals, warned the Unitarian minister Henry W. Bellows, were pursuing "an object, which in its very nature is unattainable — the perpetual improvement of the outward condition."

◄ **"Pieties Quilt," by Maria Cadman Hubbard, 1848**

Maria Hubbard may have been a Quaker: "No Cross, No Crown" (a pious saying stitched on the far right) was the title of a pamphlet William Penn wrote in the 1670s attacking the Church of England. Whatever Hubbard's affiliation, she used her skills as a quilt maker to express deeply held religious beliefs. By stitching her name and age on the quilt, she created a cultural artifact that would perpetuate both her memory and the religious spirit of her era. Unlike most women (and men), she would not vanish from the record of the past. Museum of American Folk Art. Gift of Cyril Irwin Nelson in loving memory of his parents, Cyril Arthur and Elise Mary Nelson.

Reform was complex and contradictory. Some reformers vowed to improve society by preventing people from behaving in ways the reformers considered dangerous or simply wrong. Indeed, the first wave of American reformers, the benevolent religious improvers of the 1820s, advocated the extension of discipline to all phases of life. To solve the nation's ills, they championed regular church attendance, temperance, and the strict moral codes of the evangelical churches. Their righteousness prompted one critic to protest, "A peaceable man can hardly venture to eat or drink, . . . to correct his child or kiss his wife, without obtaining the permission . . . of some moral or other reform society."

A second wave of reformers, which emerged during the 1830s and 1840s, was more intent on liberating people from archaic customs and encouraging them to devise new lifestyles. These new reformers were mostly middle-class northerners and midwesterners. They propounded a bewildering assortment of radical ideals—extreme individualism, common ownership of property, the immediate emancipation of slaves, and sexual equality—and demanded prompt action to satisfy their visions. Although their numbers were small, these reformers launched an intellectual and cultural debate that won the attention, and often the horrified opposition, of the majority of Americans. As one fearful southerner saw it, the goal of these reformers was a chaotic world in which there would be "No-Marriage, No-Religion, No-Private Property, No-Law and No-Government."

The Founder of Transcendentalism

As this painting of Ralph Waldo Emerson by an unknown artist indicates, the young philosopher was an attractive man, his face brimming with confidence and optimism. With his radiant personality and incisive intellect, Emerson deeply influenced dozens of influential writers, artists, and scholars, and enjoyed great success as a lecturer to the emerging middle class. The Metropolitan Museum of Art, bequest of Chester Dale, 1962 [64.97.4].

Individualism

Those fears were not exaggerated. Rapid economic development and geographical expansion had weakened many traditional institutions and social rules, forcing individuals to fend for themselves. In 1835, Alexis de Tocqueville coined a new word, *individualism,* to describe the social world of native-born white Americans. Americans were "no longer attached to each other by any tie of caste, class, association, or family," and so lived more solitary lives than most Europeans did. Unlike Tocqueville, an aristocrat who feared the disintegration of society, the New England transcendentalist Ralph Waldo Emerson (1803–1882) celebrated the liberation of the individual from traditional constraints. Emerson's vision of individual freedom influenced thousands of ordinary Americans and a generation of important artists.

Ralph Waldo Emerson and Transcendentalism

Emerson was the leading voice of **transcendentalism,** an intellectual movement rooted in the religious soil of New England. Its first advocates were spiritual young men, often Unitarian ministers from well-to-do New England families, who questioned the constraints of their Puritan heritage (see Chapter 8). For inspiration, they turned to Europe and a new conception of self and society known as romanticism. Romantic thinkers, like German philosopher Immanuel Kant and English poet Samuel Taylor Coleridge, rejected the ordered, rational world of the eighteenth-century Enlightenment. They wanted to capture the passionate aspects of the human spirit and so gain deeper insight into the mysteries of existence. By tapping their intuitive powers, the young Unitarians believed, people could transcend the limits of ordinary existence and come to know the infinite and the eternal.

As a Unitarian minister, Emerson already stood outside the mainstream of American Protestantism. Unlike most Christians, Unitarians believed that God was a single being, not a trinity of Father, Son, and Holy Spirit. In 1832, Emerson took a more radical step by resigning his Boston pulpit and rejecting all organized religion. He moved to Concord, Massachusetts, and gradually articulated the philosophy of transcendentalism. In a series of influential essays, Emerson focused on what he called "the infinitude of the private man," the idea of the radically free individual.

The young philosopher argued that people were trapped by inherited customs and institutions. They wore the ideas of earlier times — the tenets of New England Calvinism, for example — as a kind of "faded masquerade"; and they needed to shed those values and practices. "What is a man born for but to be a Reformer, a Remaker of what man has made?" he asked. For Emerson, an individual could be remade only by discovering his or her own "original relation with Nature," an insight that would produce a mystical union with the "currents of Universal Being." The ideal setting for this kind of transcendent discovery: under an open sky, in solitary communion with nature.

Emerson's genius lay in his capacity to translate his abstract ideas into examples that made sense to middle-class Americans. His essays and lectures suggested that all nature was saturated with the presence of God, a pantheistic spiritual outlook that departed from traditional Christian doctrine. Emerson also warned his readers that the new market society was diverting the nation's spiritual energy, that the preoccupation with work, profits, and the consumption of factory-made goods would hurt Americans spiritually and physically (Figure 11.1). "Things are in the saddle," he wrote, "and ride mankind."

The transcendentalist message of self-realization reached hundreds of thousands of people, primarily through Emerson's writings and lectures. Public lectures had become a spectacularly successful way of spreading information and fostering discussion among the middle classes. Beginning in 1826, the Lyceum movement promoted "the general diffusion of knowledge," organizing lecture tours by hundreds of poets, preachers, scientists, and reformers. (A *lyceum* is a public hall; the word derives from the name of the place where the ancient Greek philosopher Aristotle taught.) The lyceum became an important cultural institution in the North and Midwest — but not in the South, where popular education was a lower priority and apologists for slavery discouraged the open discussion of controversial ideas. In 1839, nearly 150 local lyceums in Massachusetts invited lecturers to speak to more than 33,000 subscribers. The most popular speaker on the circuit was Emerson, who gave fifteen hundred lectures in more than three hundred towns in twenty states.

Emerson celebrated individuals who rejected traditional social restraints but retained both self-discipline and civic responsibility. In fact, his words

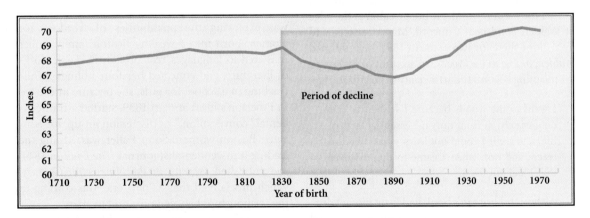

FIGURE 11.1 Environment and Health: Average Height of Native-born Men, by Year of Birth, 1710–1970

The transcendentalists sensed that the new urban and industrial society would damage people's health and welfare, and modern research suggests they were right. The average height of men born in America from the 1830s to the 1890s (as recorded in military records and other sources) was significantly lower than that of men born between 1710 and 1830. Researchers attribute the phenomenon to the men's childhood experiences: less-adequate nutrition and greater exposure to infectious diseases, especially in urban areas. SOURCE: Richard Steckel, "Health and Nutrition in the Preindustrial Era" (Working Paper 8452, National Bureau of Economic Research, Cambridge, Mass., 2001), fig. 3.

spoke directly to the personal experience of many mid-nineteenth-century middle-class Americans, who had left family farms and made their own way in the urban world. The great revivalist Charles Grandison Finney published an account of his religious conversion that underscored the influence of Emerson's ideas and values. Finney pictured his conversion as the mystical union of an individual, alone in the woods, with God. Like Emerson, Finney stressed the need to transcend the constraints and doctrines of the past. He taught that "God has made man a moral free agent," endowing individuals with the ability — and the responsibility — to determine their spiritual fate.

Emerson's Literary Influence

Emerson took as one of his tasks the remaking of American literature. In an address entitled "The American Scholar" (1837), the philosopher issued a literary declaration of independence from the "courtly muse" of Old Europe. He urged American writers to celebrate democracy and individual freedom and to find inspiration in ordinary human experiences: "the ballad in the street; the news of the boat; the glance of the eye; the form and gait of the body."

Henry David Thoreau and Margaret Fuller. One young New England intellectual, Henry David Thoreau (1817–1862), heeded Emerson's call by turning to the American environment for inspiration. In 1845, depressed by his beloved brother's death, Thoreau turned away from society and embraced the natural world. He built a cabin at the edge of Walden Pond near Concord, Massachusetts, and lived alone there for two years. In 1854, he published *Walden, or Life in the Woods,* an account of his search for meaning beyond the artificiality of "civilized" life:

> I went to the woods because I wished to live deliberately, to front only the essential facts of life, and see if I could not learn what it had to teach, and not, when I came to die, discover that I had not lived.

Although Thoreau's book had little impact during his lifetime, *Walden* has become an essential text of American literature and an inspiration to those who reject the dictates of society. Its most famous metaphor provides an enduring justification for independent thinking: "If a man does not keep pace with his companions, perhaps it is because he hears a different drummer." Beginning from this premise, Thoreau advocated social nonconformity and civil disobedience against unjust laws.

As Thoreau was seeking independence and self-realization for men, Margaret Fuller (1810–1850)

Margaret Fuller, 1848

At thirty-eight, Fuller moved to Italy, where she worked as a correspondent for a New York newspaper and reported on the Revolution of 1848. There, too, she fell in love with Thomas Hicks (1823–1890), a much younger American artist. Hicks rebuffed Fuller's advances but painted this flattering portrait, softening her features and giving her a pensive look. Fuller married a Roman nobleman, Giovanni Angelo, Marchese d'Ossoli, and gave birth to a son in September 1848. Two years later, the entire family died in shipwreck. Constance Fuller Threinen.

was exploring the possibilities of freedom for women. Born into a wealthy Boston family, Fuller mastered six languages, read broadly in classic works of literature, and educated her four siblings. While teaching in a school for girls, she became interested in Emerson's ideas and, in 1839, started a transcendental "conversation," or discussion group, for educated Boston women. Soon Fuller was editing the leading transcendentalist journal, *The Dial*. In 1844, she published *Woman in the Nineteenth Century,* which proclaimed that a "new era" was coming in the relationships between men and women.

Fuller's philosophy began with the transcendental belief that women, like men, had a mystical relationship with God that gave them identity and dignity. Every woman, therefore, deserved psychological and social independence — the ability "to grow, as an intellect to discern, as a soul to live freely and unimpeded." "We would have every arbitrary barrier thrown down," she wrote, and "every path laid open to Woman as freely as to Man." Embracing that vision, Fuller became the literary critic of the *New York Tribune* and traveled to Italy to report on the Revolution of 1848. Her adventurous life led to an early death; in 1850 she drowned in a shipwreck while returning to the United States. Fuller's life and writings inspired a rising generation of women writers and reformers.

Walt Whitman. Another writer who responded to Emerson's call was the poet Walt Whitman (1819–1892). When Whitman first met Emerson, he had been "simmering, simmering"; then Emerson "brought me to a boil." Whitman worked as a teacher, a journalist, an editor of the *Brooklyn Eagle,* and an influential publicist for the Democratic Party. But poetry was the "direction of his dreams." In *Leaves of Grass,* a wild, exuberant poem first published in 1855 and constantly revised and expanded, Whitman recorded in verse his efforts to pass a number of "invisible boundaries": between solitude and community, between prose and poetry, even between the living and the dead. At the center of *Leaves of Grass* is the individual — the figure of the poet, "I, Walt." He begins alone: "I celebrate myself, and sing myself." But because he has an Emersonian "original relation" with nature, Whitman claims perfect communion with others: "For every atom belonging to me as good belongs to you." Whitman celebrates democracy as well as himself by seeking a profoundly intimate, mystical relationship with a mass audience. For Emerson, Thoreau, and Fuller, the individual had a divine spark; for Whitman, the individual had expanded to become divine, and democracy assumed a sacred character.

The transcendentalists were optimistic but not naive. Whitman wrote about human suffering with passion, and Emerson laced his accounts of transcendence with twinges of anxiety. "I am glad," he once said, "to the brink of fear." Thoreau was gloomy about everyday life: "The mass of men lead lives of quiet desperation." Still, dark murmurings remain muted in their work, overshadowed by assertions that nothing was impossible for the individual who could break free from tradition, law, and other social restraints.

Darker Visions: Nathaniel Hawthorne and Herman Melville. Emerson's writings also influenced two great novelists, Nathaniel Hawthorne and Herman Melville, who had more pessimistic worldviews. Both sounded powerful warnings that unfettered egoism could destroy individuals and those around them. Hawthorne brilliantly explored the theme of excessive individualism in his novel *The Scarlet Letter* (1850). The two main characters, Hester Prynne and Arthur Dimmesdale, challenge their seventeenth-century New England community in the most blatant way — by committing adultery

and producing a child. Their choice to ignore social restraints is not liberation but degradation; it earns them a profound sense of guilt and the condemnation of the community.

Herman Melville explored the limits of individualism in even more extreme and tragic terms and emerged as a scathing critic of transcendentalism. He made his most powerful statement in *Moby Dick* (1851), the story of Captain Ahab's obsessive hunt for a mysterious white whale that ends in death for Ahab and all but one member of his crew. Here the quest for spiritual meaning in nature brings death, not transcendence, because Ahab, the liberated individual, lacks inner discipline and self-restraint.

Moby Dick was a commercial failure. The middle-class audience that was the primary target of American publishers refused to follow Melville into the dark, dangerous realm of individualism gone mad. Readers also lacked enthusiasm for Thoreau's advocacy of civil disobedience during the U.S. war with Mexico (see Chapter 13) and Whitman's boundless claims of a mystical union between the man of genius and the democratic masses. What middle-class readers emphatically preferred were the more modest examples of individualism offered by Emerson and Finney — personal improvement through spiritual awareness and self-discipline.

Brook Farm

To escape the constraints of America's emerging market society, transcendentalists and other radical reformers created ideal communities, or utopias. They hoped that these planned societies, which organized life in new ways, would allow their members to realize their spiritual and moral potential. The most important transcendentalist communal experiment was Brook Farm, founded just outside Boston in 1841. The intellectual life at Brook Farm was electric. Hawthorne lived there for a time and later used the setting for his novel *The Blithedale Romance* (1852). All the major transcendentalists, including Emerson, Thoreau, and Fuller, were residents or frequent visitors. A former member recalled that they "inspired the young with a passion for study, and the middle-aged with deference and admiration, while we all breathed the intellectual grace that pervaded the atmosphere."

Whatever its spiritual rewards, Brook Farm was an economic failure. The residents hoped to escape the ups and downs of the market economy by becoming self-sufficient in food and exchanging their surplus milk, vegetables, and hay for nonagricultural goods. However, most members were ministers, teachers, writers, and students who had few farming skills; only the cash contributions of affluent residents kept the enterprise afloat. And after a devastating fire in 1846, the organizers disbanded the community and sold the farm.

With Brook Farm a failure, the Emersonians abandoned their quest for a new system of social organization. They accepted the brute reality of the emergent industrial order and tried to reform it, especially through the education of workers. The passion of the transcendentalists for individual freedom and social progress lived on, though, in the movement to abolish slavery, which many of them actively supported.

> ➤ What were the main beliefs of transcendentalism? How was transcendentalism an expression of the social changes sweeping nineteenth-century society?

> ➤ How does transcendentalism embody American individualism? What was the relationship between transcendentalism and social reform?

Rural Communalism and Urban Popular Culture

Even as Brook Farm collapsed, thousands of Americans were joining communal settlements in rural areas of the Northeast and Midwest (Map 11.1).

Many communalists were farmers and artisans seeking refuge and security during the seven-year economic depression that began with the Panic of 1837. However, these rural utopias were also symbols of social protest and experimentation. By prescribing the common ownership of property and unconventional forms of marriage and family life, communalist leaders and their followers challenged the legitimacy of capitalist values and traditional gender roles.

Simultaneously, tens of thousands of rural Americans and immigrants poured into the larger cities of the United States. There they created a popular culture that repudiated customary sexual norms, reinforced traditional racist feelings, and encouraged new styles of dress and behavior.

Mother Ann Lee and the Shakers

The Shakers were the first successful American communal movement. In 1770, Ann Lee Stanley (Mother Ann), a young cook in Manchester, England, had a vision that she was an incarnation of Christ and that Adam and Eve had been banished from the Garden of Eden because of their sexual lust. Four years later, she led a band of eight followers to America, where they established a church near Albany, New York. Because of the ecstatic dances that were part of their worship, the sect became known as the Shakers (see Voices from Abroad, "The Mystical World of the Shakers," p. 337).

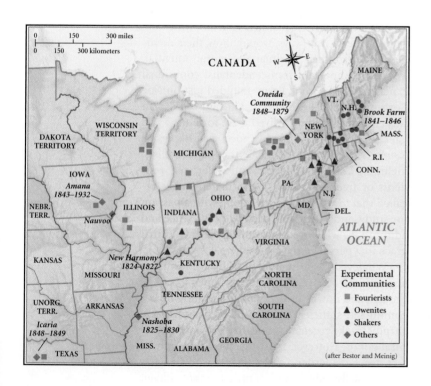

MAP 11.1 Major Communal Experiments Before 1860

Some experimental communities settled along the frontier, but the vast majority chose relatively secluded areas in well-settled regions of the North and Midwest. Because of their opposition to slavery, communalists usually avoided the South. Most secular experiments failed within a few decades, as the founders lost their reformist enthusiasm or died off; religious communities — like those of the Shakers and the Mormons (see Map 11.2 on p. 342) — were longer-lived.

The Mystical World of the Shakers

Foreigners were both attracted to, and distressed by, the strange religious practices they observed in the United States. In either case, they made certain to include reports of revivals and communal settlements in their letters and journals. In a book recounting his travels in America in the 1830s, an anonymous British visitor describes a Shaker dance and the sect's intimate contact with spiritual worlds inaccessible to those without faith.

At half past seven P.M. on the dancing days, all the members retired to their separate rooms, where they sat in solemn silence, just gazing at the stove, until the silver tones of the small tea-bell gave the signal for them to assemble in the large hall. Thither they proceeded in perfect order and solemn silence. Each had on dancing shoes; and on entering the door of the hall they walked on tip-toe, and took up their positions as follows: the brothers formed a rank on the right, and the sisters on the left, facing each other, about five feet apart. After all were in their proper places the chief Elder stepped into the center of the space, and gave an exhortation for about five minutes, concluding with an invitation to them all to "go forth, old men, young men and maidens, and worship God with all [your] might in the dance." . . .

First they formed a procession and marched around the room in double-quick time, while four brothers and sisters stood in the center singing for them. . . . They commenced dancing, and continued it until they were pretty well tired.

During the dance the sisters kept on one side, and the brothers on the other, and not a word was spoken by any one of them. . . . [Then] each one took his or her place in an oblong circle formed around the room, and all waited to see if anyone had received a "gift," that is, an inspiration to do something odd. Then two of the sisters would commence whirling round like a top, with their eyes shut; and continued this motion for about fifteen minutes. . . .

On some occasions when a sister had stopped whirling, she would say, "I have a communication to make"; . . . The first message I heard was as follows. "Mother Ann has sent two angels to inform us that a tribe of Indians has been round here two days, and want the brothers and sisters to take them in. They are outside the building there, looking in at the windows." I shall never forget how I looked round at the windows, expecting to see the yellow faces, when this announcement was made; but I believe some of the old folks who eyed me, bit their lips and smiled. It caused no alarm to the rest, but the first Elder exhorted the brothers "to take in the poor spirits and assist them to get salvation." He afterward repeated more of what the angels had said, viz., "that Indians were a savage tribe who had all died before Columbus discovered America, and had been wandering about ever since. Mother Ann wanted them to be received into the meeting tomorrow night."

The next dancing night we again assembled in the same manner as before. . . . The elder then urged upon the members the duty of "taking them in." Whereupon eight or nine sisters became possessed of the spirits of Indian squaws, and about six of the brethren became Indians. Then ensued a regular pow-wow, with whooping and yelling and strange antics, such as would require a Dickens to describe. . . . These performances continued till about ten o'clock: then the chief Elder requested the Indians to go away, telling them they would find someone waiting to conduct them to the Shakers in the heavenly world. . . .

At one of the meetings . . . two or three sisters commenced whirling . . . and revealed to us that Mother Ann was present at the meeting, and that she had brought a dozen baskets of spiritual fruit for her children; upon which the Elder invited all to go forth to the baskets in the center of the floor, and help themselves. Accordingly they all stepped forth and went through the various motions of taking fruit and eating it. You will wonder if I helped myself to the fruit, like the rest. No; I had not faith enough to see the baskets or the fruit.

SOURCE: Noel Rae, ed., *Witnessing America* (New York: Penguin Press, 1966), 372–373.

ANALYZING THE EVIDENCE

➤ Why do you think the author — a visitor from England — was fascinated with the Shakers and their ceremonies?

➤ How might the episode with the Indians be explained? What was the policy of state and federal governments toward the Indians in the 1830s? Do you think that policy had any bearing on the Shakers' worship? Explain your answer.

➤ How would you characterize the roles ascribed to men and women? Were the Shakers' ideas about gender typical of communal movements? Were their ideas more radical or more conservative than those of the society at large?

After Mother Ann's death in 1784, the Shakers honored her as the Second Coming of Christ, withdrew from the profane world, and formed disciplined religious communities. Members embraced the common ownership of property, accepted the strict oversight of church leaders, and pledged to abstain from alcohol, tobacco, politics, and war. Shakers also repudiated marriage and sexual pleasure. Their commitment to celibacy followed Mother Ann's testimony against "the lustful gratifications of the flesh as the source and foundation of human corruption."

The Shakers' theology was as radical as their social thought. They held that God was "a dual person, male and female," and that Mother Ann represented God's female component. These doctrines underpinned their efforts to eliminate arbitrary distinctions of authority between the sexes. They placed community governance in the hands of both women and men — the Eldresses and the Elders — but maintained a traditional division of labor between the sexes.

Beginning in 1787, Shakers founded twenty communities, mostly in New England, New York, and Ohio. Their agriculture and crafts, especially furniture making, acquired a reputation for quality that made most Shaker communities self-sustaining and even comfortable. Because the Shakers did not engage in sexual intercourse and had no children of their own, they relied on conversions and the adoption of thousands of young orphans to increase their numbers. During the 1830s, three thousand adult converts joined the Shakers, attracted by the sect's economic success and ideology of sexual equality. Women converts outnumbered men more than two to one, and included blacks as well as whites. To Rebecca Cox Jackson, an African American seamstress from Philadelphia, the Shakers seemed to be "loving to live forever." As the supply of orphans dried up during the 1840s and 1850s (with the increase in publicly and privately funded orphanages), Shaker communities stopped growing and eventually began to decline. By 1900, the Shakers had virtually disappeared, leaving as their material legacy a distinctive plain-but-elegant style of wood furniture.

Arthur Brisbane and Fourierism

As the number of Shakers leveled off during the 1840s, the American Fourierist movement was rapidly expanding. Charles Fourier (1777–1837) was a French reformer who devised an eight-stage theory of social evolution that predicted the imminent decline of individualism and capitalism. According to Arthur Brisbane, Fourier's leading disciple in America, Fourierism would free workers from the "menial and slavish system of Hired Labor or Labor for Wages," just as republicanism ("our great political movement of 1776") had freed Americans from the slavish monarchical system of government. The new order replaced capitalism with **socialism**. Instead of working for themselves or for employers, men and women would work for the community, in cooperative groups called phalanxes. The members of a phalanx would be its shareholders; they would own all its property in common, including stores and a bank, a school, and a library.

Fourier and Brisbane saw the phalanx as a humane system that would liberate women as well as men. "In society as it is now constituted," Brisbane wrote, individual freedom was possible only for men, while "woman is subjected to unremitting and slavish domestic duties." In the "new Social Order . . . based upon Associated households," men would share women's domestic labor and thereby increase sexual equality.

Brisbane skillfully promoted Fourier's ideas in his influential book *The Social Destiny of Man* (1840), a regular column in Horace Greeley's *New York Tribune,* and hundreds of lectures, many of them in towns along the Erie Canal. Fourierist ideas found a receptive audience among educated farmers and craftsmen, who yearned for economic stability and communal solidarity in the wake of the Panic of 1837. During the 1840s, Brisbane and his followers started nearly one hundred cooperative communities, mostly in western New York and in the Midwest (see Map 11.1). However, most of the communities collapsed within a decade or two because of disputes over work responsibilities and social policies. If the rise of Fourierism testified to the social impact of the depression, then its decline showed the difficulty of establishing a utopian community in the absence of a charismatic leader or a compelling religious vision.

John Humphrey Noyes and the Oneida Community

John Humphrey Noyes (1811–1886) was both charismatic and deeply religious. He ascribed the failure of the Fourierists to their secular outlook and took as his model the pious Shakers, the true "pioneers of modern Socialism." The Shakers' marriageless society also appealed to Noyes, and inspired him to create a community that defined sexuality and gender roles in radically new ways.

Shakers at Prayer

Most Americans viewed the Shakers with a mixture of fascination and distaste. They feared the sect's commitment to celibacy and communal property and considered the Shakers' dancing more an invitation to debauchery than a form of prayer. Those apprehensions surfaced in this engraving, which expresses both the powerful intensity and the menacing character of the Shaker ritual. © Bettman.

Noyes was a well-to-do graduate of Dartmouth College who became a minister after hearing Charles Grandison Finney preach. Dismissed as the pastor of a Congregational church for holding unorthodox beliefs, Noyes turned to perfectionism. Perfectionism was an evangelical Protestant movement of the 1830s that attracted thousands of religious New Englanders who had moved to New York and Ohio. Perfectionists believed that Christ had returned to earth (the Second Coming) and that people could therefore aspire to sinless perfection in their earthly lives. Unlike most perfectionists, who lived conventional personal lives, Noyes believed that the major barrier to achieving this ideal

state was marriage, which did not exist in heaven and should not exist on earth. "Exclusiveness, jealousy, quarreling have no place at the marriage supper of the Lamb," Noyes wrote. Like the Shakers, Noyes wanted to liberate individuals from sin by reforming relationships between men and women. But instead of the Shakers' celibacy, Noyes and his followers embraced "complex marriage"—all the members of the community were married to one another.

Noyes's marriage system reflected the growing debate over the legal and cultural constraints on women's lives. He rejected monogamy in order to free women from being regarded as the property of their husbands, as they were by custom and by

"Bloomerism — An American Custom"

The hippies of the 1960s weren't the first to draw attention to themselves with their dress (sloppy) and smoking (marijuana). Independent women of the 1850s took to wearing bloomers and puffing on cigars, behaviors that elicited disapproving stares from matrons and verbal and physical assaults from street urchins. Both movements questioned existing cultural norms and sought to expand the boundaries of personal freedom. This cartoon appeared in 1851 in *Harper's New Monthly Magazine,* a major periodical of the time. *Harper's New Monthly Magazine* (August 1851)/Picture Research Consultants & Archives.

common law. To give women the time and energy to become full participants in the community, Noyes urged them to avoid multiple pregnancies. He asked men to assist in this effort by avoiding orgasm during intercourse. To raise the children of his followers, Noyes set up communal nurseries run by both men and women. To symbolize sexual equality, Noyes's women followers cut their hair short and wore pantaloons under calf-length skirts.

In 1839, Noyes established a Perfectionist community near his hometown, Putney, Vermont, and introduced the practice of complex marriage in the mid-1840s. When the community's unorthodox sexual practices aroused opposition, Noyes moved his followers to an isolated area near Oneida, New York. By the mid-1850s, the Oneida settlement had two hundred residents; it became financially self-sustaining when the inventor of a highly successful steel animal trap joined the community. With the profits acquired by making traps, the Oneidians

diversified into the production of silverware. When Noyes fled to Canada in 1879 to avoid prosecution for adultery, the community abandoned complex marriage but retained its cooperative spirit. Its members founded Oneida Community, Ltd., a jointly owned, silverware-manufacturing company that remained an independent and prosperous enterprise until the end of the twentieth century.

The historical significance of the Oneidians, Shakers, and Fourierists does not lie in their numbers, which were small, or in their fine crafts. These groups were important because their members, in a dramatically more radical fashion than Emerson and the transcendentalists, repudiated both traditional sexual norms and the principles and class divisions of the emergent capitalist society. Their utopian communities stood as countercultural blueprints of a more egalitarian social and economic order.

A Mormon Man and His Wives

The practice of polygamy split the Mormon community and, because it deviated from traditional religious principles, enraged other Christian denominations. This Mormon household, pictured in the late 1840s, was unusually prosperous, partly because of the labor of the husband's multiple wives. Although the cabin provides cramped quarters for such a large family, it boasts a brick chimney and — a luxury for any pioneer home — a glass window.

Library of Congress.

Joseph Smith and the Mormon Experience

The Shakers and the Oneidians were radical utopians because they challenged marriage and family life, two deeply rooted institutions. However, their communities remained small and consequently aroused relatively little hostility. The Mormons, members of the Church of Jesus Christ of Latter-day Saints, were utopians with a much more conservative social agenda — perpetuating the traditional patriarchal family. But because of their cohesive organization and substantial numbers, the Mormons provoked more animosity than the radical utopians did.

Joseph Smith. Like many social movements of the era, Mormonism emerged from the religious ferment among families of Puritan descent who lived along the Erie Canal. The founder of the Mormon Church was Joseph Smith Jr. (1805–1844). Smith was born in Vermont to a poor farming and shop-keeping family, which then migrated to Palmyra in central New York. In a series of religious experiences that began in 1820, Smith came to believe that God had singled him out to receive a special revelation of divine truth. In 1830, he published *The Book of Mormon,* which he claimed to have translated from ancient hieroglyphics on gold plates shown to him by an angel named Moroni. *The Book of Mormon* told the story of ancient civilizations from the Middle East that had migrated to the Western Hemisphere and of the visit of Jesus Christ, soon after the Resurrection, to one of them. Smith's account provided an explanation of the presence of native peoples in the Americas and integrated them into the Judeo-Christian tradition.

Smith proceeded to organize the Church of Jesus Christ of Latter-day Saints. Seeing himself as a prophet in a sinful, excessively individualistic society, Smith revived traditional social doctrines, among them patriarchal authority within the family. Like many Protestant ministers, he encouraged practices that were central to individual success in the age of capitalist markets and factories — frugality, hard work, and enterprise. But Smith also placed great emphasis on communal discipline that would safeguard the Mormon "New Jerusalem" from individualism and rival religious doctrines. His goal was a church-directed society that would inspire moral perfection.

Smith struggled for years to establish a secure home for his new religion. Constantly harassed by hostile anti-Mormons, Smith and his growing congregation trekked west and eventually settled in Nauvoo, Illinois, a town they founded on the Mississippi River (Map 11.2). By the early 1840s, Nauvoo had become the largest utopian community in the United States, with 30,000 inhabitants. The rigid discipline and secret rituals of the Mormons — along with their prosperity, hostility toward other sects, and bloc voting in Illinois elections — fueled resentment among their neighbors. This resentment turned to overt hostility when Smith refused to abide by any Illinois law of which he disapproved, asked Congress to turn Nauvoo into a separate federal territory, and declared himself a candidate for president of the United States.

Moreover, Smith claimed to have received a new revelation that justified polygamy, the practice of a man's having more than one wife at one time. When leading Mormon men took several wives, they sparked a contentious debate within the Mormon community and enraged Christians in neighboring

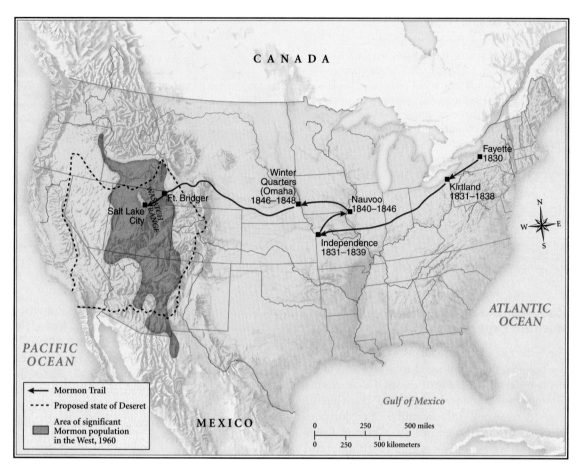

MAP 11.2   The Mormon Trek, 1830–1848

Because of their unorthodox religious views and communal solidarity, Mormons faced hostility first in New York and then in Missouri and Illinois. After founder Joseph Smith Jr. was murdered, Brigham Young led the polygamist faction of Mormons into lands thinly populated by Native American peoples. From Omaha, the migrants followed the path of the Oregon Trail to Fort Bridger and then struck off to the southwest. In 1847, they settled along the Wasatch Mountains in the basin of the Great Salt Lake, in Indian lands that were part of Mexico and are now in Utah.

towns and villages. In 1844, Illinois officials arrested Smith and charged him with treason for allegedly conspiring with foreign powers to create a Mormon colony in Mexican territory. An anti-Mormon mob stormed the jail in Carthage, Illinois, where Smith and his brother were being held, and murdered them.

Brigham Young and Utah. Led by Brigham Young, Smith's leading disciple and an energetic missionary, a large contingent of Mormons fled the United States. Beginning in 1847, approximately 10,000 people crossed the Great Plains into Mexican territory, where they settled in the Great Salt Lake Valley in present-day Utah. Using cooperative labor and an elaborate irrigation system based on com-

munal water rights, the Mormon pioneers transformed the region. They quickly spread planned agricultural communities along the base of the Wasatch mountain range. Many Mormons who rejected polygamy remained in the United States. Under the leadership of Smith's son, Joseph Smith III, they formed the Reorganized Church of Jesus Christ of Latter-day Saints and settled throughout the Midwest.

When the United States acquired title to Mexico's northern territories in 1848 (see Chapter 13), the Salt Lake Mormons petitioned Congress to create a vast new state, Deseret, which would stretch from present-day Utah to the Pacific coast. Instead, Congress set up the much smaller Utah Territory in 1850 and named Brigham Young its governor. In

1858, President James Buchanan responded to pressure from Protestants to eliminate polygamy by removing Young from the governorship and sending a small army to Salt Lake City. However, the "Mormon War" proved bloodless. Fearing that the forced abolition of polygamy would serve as a precedent for ending slavery, the pro-South Buchanan withdrew the troops. (To win support for Utah's bid to join the Union in 1896, its citizens ratified a constitution that "forever" banned the practice of polygamy, but the state government has never strictly enforced that ban.)

Mormons had succeeded even as other social experiments and utopian communities had failed. By endorsing the private ownership of property and encouraging individual enterprise, they became prosperous contributors to the new market society. However, Mormon leaders resolutely used strict religious controls to create patriarchal families and disciplined communities, reaffirming traditional eighteenth-century values. This blend of economic innovation, social conservatism, hierarchical leadership, in combination with a strong missionary impulse, created a wealthy and expansive church, which now claims a worldwide membership of about 12 million people.

Urban Popular Culture

As utopian reformers organized new communities on the land, rural migrants and foreign immigrants created a new culture in the cities. In 1800, American cities were overgrown towns: New York had only 60,000 residents, and Philadelphia 41,000. Then urban growth accelerated. By 1840, New York's population had ballooned to 312,000; Philadelphia and its suburbs had 150,000 residents; and three other cities — New Orleans, Boston, and Baltimore — each had about 100,000. By 1860, New York had become a metropolis with more than 1 million residents: 813,000 in Manhattan and another 266,000 in the adjacent community of Brooklyn.

These new cities, particularly New York, generated a new urban culture. At its center were thousands of young men and women from rural areas, who flocked to the city in search of fortune and adventure. Many found only hard work and a hard life. Young men labored for meager wages on the construction crews that erected thousands of new buildings each year. Or they worked as low-paid operatives or clerks in hundreds of mercantile and manufacturing firms. The young women were even worse off. Thousands toiled as live-in domestic servants, ordered about by the mistress of the household and often sexually abused by their well-to-do masters (see Reading American Pictures, "Looking for Clues in Art About Women's Lives," p. 344). Thousands more scraped out a bare living as needlewomen in New York's booming clothes manufacturing industry. Unable to abide the humiliations of domestic service or the subsistence wages of the needlewoman, thousands of young girls turned to prostitution. In the 1850s, Dr. William Sanger's careful survey in New York City found six thousand women engaged in commercial sex. Three-fifths of them were native-born Americans, and most were young — between fifteen and twenty years old. Half were or had been domestic servants, half had children, and half were infected with syphilis.

Sex and Dress. Commercialized sex — and sex in general — formed one facet of the new urban culture. "Sporting men" engaged freely in sexual conquests; respectable married men kept mistresses in handy apartments; and working men frequented bawdy houses in the city. In New York City there were some two hundred brothels in the 1820s and five hundred in the 1850s. Prostitutes openly advertised their wares on Broadway, the city's fashionable thoroughfare, and welcomed clients on the infamous "Third Tier" of the theaters. This illicit sexuality was widely considered by men as their right. "Man is endowed by nature with passions that must be gratified," declared the *Sporting Whip*, a working-class magazine. Reverend William Berrian, pastor of the ultrarespectable Trinity Episcopal Church, did not disagree; he remarked from the pulpit that he had resorted to "a house of ill-fame" a mere ten times.

Prostitution formed only the tip of the urban sexual mountain. Freed from family oversight, the young men and women in the city pursued romantic adventure and sexual pleasure. Many moved from partner to partner until they chanced on an ideal mate. To enhance their attractiveness, they dressed in the latest fashions: elaborate bonnets and silk dresses for young women; flowing capes, leather boots, and silver-plated walking sticks for young men. Rivaling the elegant style on Broadway was the colorful style visible on the Bowery, the broad avenue that ran up the east side of lower Manhattan. By day, the "Bowery Boy" worked as an apprentice or journeyman; by night, he prowled the streets a "consummate dandy," his hair cropped at the back of his head "as close as scissors could cut," with long front locks "matted by a lavish application of *bear's grease,* the ends tucked under so as to form a roll and brushed until they shone like glass bottles." The "B'hoy," as he was called, cut a dashing figure, as he

Looking for Clues in Art About Women's Lives

A Nineteenth-Century Job Interview. © Collection of the New-York Historical Society.

This rather somber painting, *The Intelligence Office*, by William Henry Burr (1849), depicts a scene at an urban employment agency. The woman sitting to the right, dressed formally in green satin, is deciding whether to hire the two standing women as domestic servants. What does this picture tell us about social relations in nineteenth-century America? Burr's work refers to various hallmarks of the new age: contractual labor relations, then-current forms of communication, and the intensification of class identity. Look closely. Do you see them?

ANALYZING THE EVIDENCE

➤ Study the applicants' clothing. How does their garb differ from that of the employer? Look carefully at their faces and posture. Does the expression on the face of the seated woman in the dark outfit suggest her anxiety about finding a position? And how do you interpret the attitude of the standing girl, facing outward, looking down?

➤ Suppose Burr had been painting in 1749, a century earlier. How would

a wealthy village squire or a prosperous merchant go about hiring domestic help? What had changed over the decades? Why did an employer in 1849 need the services of a professional agent? What clues in the painting point to those changes?

➤ How did the women applicants come to use the agent's services? What clues has the artist placed in the picture that suggest an answer?

Night Life in Philadelphia

This watercolor by Russian painter Pavel Svinin (1787–1839) captures the diversity and allure of urban America. A respectable gentleman relishes the delicacies sold by a black oysterman. Meanwhile, a young woman — probably a prostitute — engages the attention of two well-dressed young "swells" outside the Chestnut Street Theatre. The Metropolitan Museum of Art, Rogers Fund, 1942 (42.95.18). Photograph © 1989 The Metropolitan Museum of Art.

walked along, often with a "Bowery Gal" in a striking dress and shawl: "a light pink contrasting with a deep blue" or "a bright yellow with a brighter red."

Racism and Nativism. Popular entertainment was a third facet of the new urban culture in New York. Workingmen could partake of traditional rural blood sports — rat and terrier fights — at Sportsmen Hall, or they could crowd into the pit of the Bowery Theatre to see the "Mad Tragedian," Junius Brutus Booth, deliver a stirring performance of Shakespeare's *Richard III*. Middle-class couples could venture out to the huge Broadway Tabernacle to listen to an abolitionist lecture and see the renowned Hutchinson Family Singers of New Hampshire lead the audience in a spirited, roof-raising rendition of their antislavery anthem, "Get Off the Track." Or they could visit the museum of oddities (and hoaxes) created by P. T. Barnum, the great cultural entrepreneur and founder of the Barnum & Bailey Circus.

But the most popular and most original theatrical entertainments were the minstrel shows. Performed by white actors in blackface, minstrel shows were a complex blend of racist caricature and social criticism. Minstrelsy began around 1830, when a few individual actors put on blackface and performed comic song-and-dance routines. The most famous was John Dartmouth Rice, whose "Jim Crow" blended a weird shuffle-dance-and-jump with unintelligible lyrics delivered in "Negro dialect." By the 1840s, there were hundreds of minstrel troupes, whose members sang rambling improvisational songs. The actor-singers poked racist fun at the African Americans they depicted, portraying them as lazy, sensual, and irresponsible, while using them as a vehicle for social criticism. The minstrels also ridiculed the drinking habits of Irish immigrants, parodied the speech of recent German arrivals, denounced women's demands for political rights, and mocked the arrogance of upper-class men.

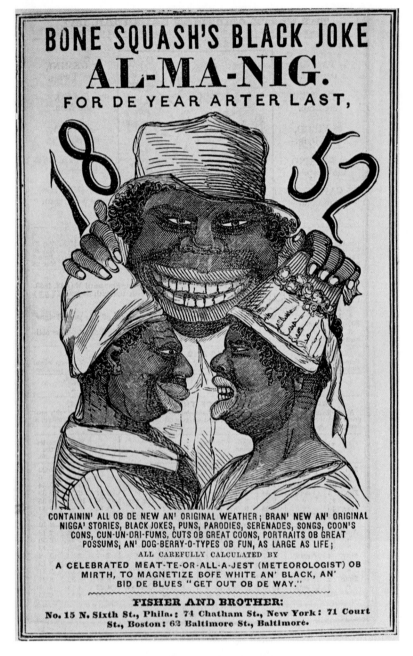

Still, by performing in blackface, the minstrels declared the importance of being white. The shows' racism allowed Irish and German immigrants to identify with the dominant native-born white culture and eased their entry into New York society. By the 1830s, most new residents in New York City were foreign-born; by 1855, 200,000 Irish men and women lived in the city, along with 110,000 Germans (Figure 11.2). German-language shop signs dominated entire sections of the city, and German foodways (sausages, hamburgers, sauerkraut, and beer) became part of the city's culture. The mass of impoverished Irish migrants, fleeing the potato famine, found allies in the American Catholic Church, which soon became an Irish-dominated institution, and the Democratic Party, which gave them a foothold in the political process.

Many native-born New Yorkers denounced this ethnic diversity, creating a nativist movement that was the final aspect of the new urban culture. Beginning in the mid-1830s, nativists opposed further immigration and mounted a cultural and political assault on foreign-born residents (see Chapter 9). Gangs of B'hoys assaulted Irish youth in the streets, employers hired Irish workers for only the most menial jobs, and temperance reformers denounced the German fondness for beer.

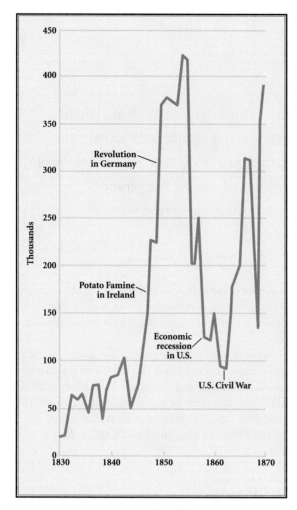

FIGURE 11.2 The Surge in Immigration, 1842–1855

The failure of the potato crop prompted the wholesale migration of peasants from the overcrowded farms of western Ireland. Population pressure likewise spurred the migration of tens of thousands of German peasants, while the failure of the liberal republican political revolution of 1848 prompted hundreds of prominent German politicians and intellectuals to settle in the United States.

In 1844, the American Republican Party, with the endorsement of the Whigs, swept to victory in the city elections by focusing on the emotional issues of temperance and anti-Catholic nativism (see Comparing American Voices, "Saving the Nation from Drink," pp. 348–349).

In the city, as in the countryside, a struggle to define a new society and culture was under way. The sexual freedom advocated by Noyes at Oneida had its counterpart in the commercialized sex and male promiscuity in New York City. Similarly, the disciplined rejection of tobacco and alcohol by the Shakers and the Mormons found a parallel in the Washington

Temperance Society and other urban reform organizations. American society was in ferment, and the outcome was far from clear.

➤ How do you explain the proliferation of rural utopian communities in the nineteenth century? What made some more successful than others? Why were gender relationships so prominent in their beliefs?

➤ In what respects were the new cultures of the mid-nineteenth century — those of utopian communalists and of urban residents — different from the mainstream culture described in Chapters 8 and 9? How were they alike?

Abolitionism

Like other reform movements, abolitionism drew on the religious energy and ideas generated by the Second Great Awakening. Early-nineteenth-century reformers had argued that human bondage was contrary to republicanism and liberty. Abolitionists condemned slavery as a sin, and took it as their moral duty to end this violation of God's law. Their demands for the immediate end to slavery led to fierce political debates, urban riots, and sectional conflicts.

Black Social Thought: Uplift, Race Equality, Rebellion

Beginning in the 1790s, leading African Americans in the North advocated a strategy of social uplift. They encouraged free blacks to "elevate" themselves through education, temperance, moral discipline, and hard work. By securing "respectability," they argued, blacks could assume a position of equality with whites. To promote that goal, black leaders — men like James Forten, a Philadelphia sailmaker; Prince Hall, a Boston barber; and ministers Hosea Easton and Richard Allen (see Chapter 8) — founded an array of churches, schools, and self-help associations. Capping off this effort in 1827, John Russwurm and Samuel D. Cornish of New York published the first African American newspaper, *Freedom's Journal*.

The black quest for respectability elicited a violent response from whites in Boston, Pittsburgh, and many other northern cities, who refused to accept African Americans as their social equals. "I am Mr. ____'s *help*," a white maid informed a British

Saving the Nation from Drink

The temperance crusade was the first and greatest antebellum reform movement. It mobilized more than a million supporters from all sections of the country and significantly lowered the consumption of alcoholic beverages. Like other reform efforts, the crusade divided over questions of strategy and tactics. The following passages, taken from the writings of leading temperance advocates, show that some reformers favored legal regulation while others preferred voluntary restraint.

LYMAN BEECHER
"Intemperance Is the Sin of Our Land"

A leading Protestant minister and spokesman for the Benevolent Empire, Lyman Beecher conceived of drunkenness as a sin. His Six Sermons on . . . Intemperance *(1829) had one message for temperate members of the middle class and a very different one for working-class drunkards.*

Intemperance is the sin of our land, and, with our boundless prosperity, is coming in upon us like a flood; and if anything shall defeat the hopes of the world, which hang upon our experiment of civil liberty, it is that river of fire. . . .

In every city and town the poor-tax, created chiefly by intemperance, is augmenting. . . . The frequency of going upon the town [relying on public welfare] has taken away the reluctance of pride, and destroyed the motives to providence which the fear of poverty and suffering once supplied. The prospect of a destitute old age, or of a suffering family, no longer troubles the vicious portion of our community. They drink up their daily earnings, and bless God for the poorhouse, and begin to look upon it as, of right, the drunkard's home. . . . Every intemperate and idle man, whom you behold tottering about the streets and steeping himself at the stores, regards your houses and lands as pledged to take care of him, puts his hands deep, annually, into your pockets. . . .

What then is this universal, natural, and national remedy for intemperance? IT IS THE BANISHMENT OF ARDENT SPIRITS FROM THE LIST OF LAWFUL ARTICLES OF COMMERCE, BY A CORRECT AND EFFICIENT PUBLIC SENTIMENT; SUCH AS HAS TURNED SLAVERY OUT OF HALF OUR LAND, AND WILL YET EXPEL IT FROM THE WORLD.

We are not therefore to come down in wrath upon the distillers, and importers, and venders of ardent spirits. None of us are enough without sin to cast the first stone. . . . It is the buyers who have created the demand for ardent spirits, and made distillation and importation a gainful traffic. . . .

Let the temperate cease to buy — and the demand for ardent spirits will fall in the market three fourths, and ultimately will fail wholly, as the generation of drunkards shall hasten out of time. . . .

This however cannot be done effectually so long as the traffic in ardent spirits is regarded as lawful, and is patronized by men of reputation and moral worth in every part of the land. Like slavery, it must be regarded as sinful, impolitic, and dishonorable. That no measures will avail short of rendering ardent spirits a contraband of trade, is nearly self-evident.

ABRAHAM LINCOLN
"A New Class of Champions"

In Baltimore in 1840, a group of reformed drunkards formed the Washington Temperance Society, which turned the movement in a new direction. By relating their personal experience of alcoholic decline and spiritual recovery, they inspired thousands of men to "sign the pledge" of total abstinence. In 1842, Lincoln, a teetotaler, and an ambitious lawyer and member of the Illinois legislature at the time, spoke to the Washingtonian Society of Springfield, Illinois.

Although the temperance cause has been in progress for near twenty years, it is apparent to all that it is just now being crowned with a degree of success hitherto unparalleled. The list of its friends is daily swelled by the additions of fifties, of hundreds, and of thousands.

The warfare heretofore waged against the demon intemperance has somehow or other been erroneous. . . . [Its] champions for the most part have been preachers, lawyers, and hired agents. Between these and the mass of mankind there is a want of approachability. . . .

But when one who has long been known as a victim of intemperance bursts the fetters that have bound him, and appears before his neighbors "clothed and in his right mind," . . . to tell of the miseries once endured, now to be endured no more . . . there is a logic and an eloquence in it that few with human feelings can resist. . . .

In my judgment, it is to the battles of this new class of champions that our late success is greatly, perhaps chiefly, owing. . . . [Previously,] too much denunciation against dram-sellers and dram-drinkers was indulged in. This I think was both impolitic and unjust. . . . When the dram-seller and drinker were incessantly told . . . . in the thundering tones of anathema and denunciation . . . that their persons should be shunned by all the good and virtuous, as moral pestilences . . . they were slow, very slow, to . . . join the ranks of their denouncers in a hue and cry against themselves.

By the Washingtonians this system of consigning the habitual drunkard to hopeless ruin is repudiated. They adopt a more enlarged philanthropy. . . . They teach hope to all—despair to none. As applying to their cause, they deny the doctrine of unpardonable sin. . . .

If the relative grandeur of revolutions shall be estimated by the great amount of human misery they alleviate, and the small amount they inflict, then indeed will this be the grandest the world shall ever have seen. Of our political revolution of '76 we are all justly proud. It has given us a degree of political freedom far exceeding that of any other nation of the earth. . . . But, with all these glorious results, past, present, and to come, it had its evils too. It breathed forth famine, swam in blood, and rode in fire; and long, long after, the orphan's cry and the widow's wail continued to break the sad silence that ensued. These were the price, the inevitable price, paid for the blessings it brought.

Turn now to the temperance revolution. In it we shall find a stronger bondage broken, a viler slavery manumitted, a greater tyrant deposed; in it, more of want supplied, more disease healed, more sorrow assuaged. By it no orphans starving, no widows weeping.

Glorious consummation! Hail, fall of fury! Reign of reason, all hail!

AMERICAN TEMPERANCE MAGAZINE
"You Shall Not Sell"

In 1851, the Maine legislature enacted a statute prohibiting the sale of alcoholic beverages in the state. The Maine Supreme Court upheld the statute declaring the legislature's "right to regulate by law the sale of any article, the use of which would be detrimental of the morals of the people." As this article from 1852 shows, American Temperance Magazine *became a strong advocate of legal prohibition and, within four years, had won passage of "Maine Laws" in twelve other states (see Chapter 9).*

This is a utilitarian age. The speculative has in all things yielded to the practical. Words are mere noise unless they are things.

In this sense, moral suasion is moral balderdash. "Words, my lord, words" . . . are a delusion. . . . The drunkard's mental and physical condition pronounces them an absurdity. He is ever in one or other extreme—under the excitement of drink, or in a state of morbid collapse. . . . Reason with a man when all reason has fled, and it is doubtful whether he or you is the greater fool. . . . Moral suasion! Bah!

Place this man we have been describing out of the reach of temptation. He will have time to ponder. His mind and frame recover their native vigor. The publichouse does not beset his path. . . . Thus, and thus only, will reformation and temperance be secured. And how is this accomplished? Never except through the instrumentality of the law. If it were possible to reason the drunkard into sobriety, it would not be possible to make the rumseller forego his filthy gains. Try your moral suasion on him. . . . The only logic he will comprehend, is some such ordinance as this, coming to him in the shape and with the voice of law—you shall not sell.

SOURCE: All three selections are from David Brion Davis, *Antebellum American Culture: An Interpretative Anthology* (University Park: Pennsylvania State University Press, 1997), 395–398, 403–409.

ANALYZING THE EVIDENCE

➤ What does Lincoln's address to the Washingtonians tell us about his general political philosophy?

➤ Compare Lincoln's position to Beecher's. In what ways are they similar? How are they different?

➤ Where in these selections do you see the influence of the Second Great Awakening, especially the evangelical message of Charles Grandison Finney? Where do you see the influence of the Market Revolution and the middle-class values of the market economy? Do all of the selections take the same position concerning the role of government in regulating morality?

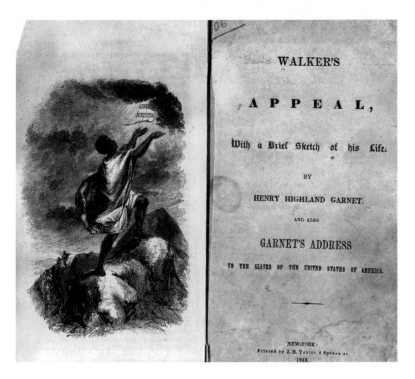

A Call for Revolution

David Walker (1785–1830), who ran a used clothing shop in Boston, used his hard-earned savings to publish *An Appeal . . . to the Colored Citizens of the World*, a learned and passionate attack on racial slavery. In the pamphlet, Walker depicted Christ as an avenging "God of justice and of armies" and raised the banner of slave rebellion. A year later, he was found in his shop, dead from unknown causes. Library of Congress.

visitor, "I am no *sarvant*; none but *negers* are *sarvants*." This racial contempt led white mobs to terrorize black communities. The attacks in Cincinnati were so violent and destructive that several hundred African Americans fled to Canada for safety.

Responding to the attacks, David Walker published a stirring pamphlet: *An Appeal . . . to the Colored Citizens of the World* (1829). Walker was a free black from North Carolina who had moved to Boston, where he sold secondhand clothes and *Freedom's Journal*. A self-educated critic of racial slavery, Walker devoured volumes of history as well as the writings and speeches of Thomas Jefferson. His *Appeal* ridiculed the religious pretensions of slaveholders, justified slave rebellion, and in biblical language warned white Americans that slaves would revolt if justice were delayed. "We must and shall be free," he told white Americans. "And woe, woe, will be it to you if we have to obtain our freedom by fighting. . . . Your DESTRUCTION is at hand, and will be speedily consummated unless you REPENT." Within a year, Walker's pamphlet had gone through three printings and, carried by black merchant seamen, had begun to reach free African Americans in the South.

In 1830, Walker and other African American activists called a national convention in Philadelphia. The delegates refused to endorse Walker's radical call for a slave revolt; they also refused to restrict their focus to the welfare and uplift of free blacks.

Instead, this new generation of African American leaders demanded freedom and equality for all members of their race. To attain what they called "race-equality," they urged free blacks to use every legal means, including petitions and other forms of political protest, to break "the shackles of slavery."

As Walker threatened violence in Boston, Nat Turner, a slave in Southampton County, Virginia, staged a bloody revolt — a coincidence that had far-reaching consequences. As a child, Turner had taught himself to read and had hoped for emancipation, but a new owner forced him to work in the fields, and another new owner separated him from his wife. Turner became deeply spiritual and, in a religious vision, "the Spirit" told him that "Christ had laid down the yoke he had borne for the sins of men, and that I should take it on and fight against the Serpent, for the time was fast approaching when the first should be last and the last should be first." Taking an eclipse of the sun as an omen, Turner and a handful of relatives and friends decided to meet the masters' terror with their own. In August 1831, Turner and his followers rose in rebellion and killed at least fifty-five white men, women, and children. Turner hoped that a vast army of slaves would rally to his cause, but he mustered only sixty men. The white militia quickly dispersed his poorly armed force and then took their revenge. One company of cavalry killed forty blacks in two days, and put the heads of fifteen on poles to warn "all those who should undertake a similar plot."

Captured after two months in hiding, Turner died by hanging, still identifying his mission with that of his Savior. "Was not Christ crucified?" he asked.

Deeply shaken by Turner's Rebellion, the Virginia assembly debated a bill providing for gradual emancipation and colonization. When the representatives rejected the bill by a vote of 73 to 58, the possibility that southern planters would legislate an end to slavery was gone. Instead, the southern states toughened their slave codes, limited the movement of blacks, and prohibited anyone from teaching slaves to read. They would meet Walker's radical *Appeal* with radical measures of their own.

Evangelical Abolitionism

Concurrently, a cadre of evangelical Christians in the North and Midwest launched a moral crusade to abolish slavery. Many Quakers—and some pious Methodists and Baptists—had already freed their slaves; they advocated the gradual emancipation of all blacks. But in 1831, radical Christian abolitionists demanded that southerners free their slaves immediately. The issue was absolute: If the slave owners did not allow slaves their God-given status as free moral agents, they faced revolution in this world and damnation in the next.

William Lloyd Garrison and the American Anti-Slavery Society. The most uncompromising abolitionist was William Lloyd Garrison (1805–1879). A Massachusetts-born printer, Garrison had worked in Baltimore during the 1820s with Quaker Benjamin Lundy, the publisher of the *Genius of Universal Emancipation*. In 1830, Garrison went to jail, convicted of libeling a New England merchant engaged in the domestic slave trade. The following year, Garrison moved to Boston, started his own antislavery weekly, *The Liberator,* and founded the New England Anti-Slavery Society.

From the outset, *The Liberator* demanded the immediate abolition of slavery without compensation to slaveholders. In pursuing this goal, Garrison declared, "I will not retreat a single inch — AND I WILL BE HEARD." Indeed, Garrison was heard, accusing the American Colonization Society (see Chapter 8) of perpetuating slavery because of its voluntary and gradual approach, and assailing the U.S. Constitution as "a covenant with death and an agreement with Hell" because of its implicit acceptance of racial bondage.

In 1833, Garrison met with Theodore Dwight Weld and sixty other abolitionists, black and white, and established the American Anti-Slavery Society. The society received financial support from Arthur

William Lloyd Garrison, c. 1835

As this portrait suggests, William Lloyd Garrison was an intense and righteous man. In 1831, his hatred of slavery prompted Garrison to demand an immediate end to it, which marked the beginning of the abolitionist movement. Believing that the U.S. Constitution upheld slavery, Garrison publicly burned a copy of the document, declaring, "So perish all compromises with tyranny." From slavery, Garrison moved on to attack other institutions and cultural practices that prevented individuals — whites as well as blacks, women as well as men — from achieving their full potential and enjoying civic equality. Trustees of the Boston Public Library.

and Lewis Tappan, wealthy silk merchants in New York City. Women abolitionists established separate organizations, including the Philadelphia Female Anti-Slavery Society, founded by Lucretia Mott in 1833, and the Anti-Slavery Conventions of American Women, formed by a network of local societies in the late 1830s. The women's societies raised money for *The Liberator* and carried the movement to the farm villages of the Midwest, where they distributed abolitionist literature and collected tens of thousands of signatures on antislavery petitions.

Abolitionist leaders developed a three-pronged plan of attack. One prong consisted of an appeal to religious Americans. In 1837, Weld published *The Bible Against Slavery,* which used passages from Christianity's holiest book to discredit slavery. Two

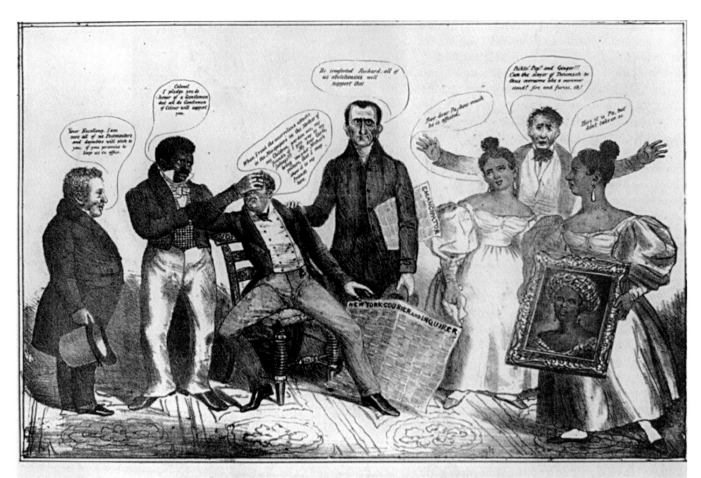

AN AFFECTING SCENE IN KENTUCKY.

The Complexities of Race

This cartoon takes aim at Richard Mentor Johnson of Kentucky, pictured here as a distraught man being comforted by a black and an abolitionist. Surprisingly, Johnson was the Democrats' vice presidential candidate in 1836. Although the party stood for the South and slavery — and condemned mixed-race unions — Johnson lived openly with an enslaved woman, Julia Chinn, whose portrait is held by his mixed-race daughters. Future Supreme Court justice John Catron noted with disgust that Johnson "endeavored often to force his daughters into society," and that they and their mother "rode in carriages, and claimed equality." Racial prejudice cost Johnson some votes; but, he won a plurality in the electoral college, and, on a party-line vote, Democrats in the Senate elected him Martin Van Buren's vice president. Library of Congress.

years later, Weld teamed up with the Grimké sisters — Angelina, whom he married, and Sarah. The Grimkés had left their father's plantation in South Carolina, converted to Quakerism, and taken up the abolitionist cause in Philadelphia. In *American Slavery as It Is: Testimony of a Thousand Witnesses* (1839), Weld and the Grimkés addressed a simple question: "What is the actual condition of the slaves in the United States?" Using reports from southern newspapers and firsthand testimony, they presented a mass of incriminating evidence. In her testimonial, Angelina Grimké told of a treadmill that South Carolina slave owners used for punishment:

> One poor girl, [who was] sent there to be flogged, and who was accordingly stripped naked and whipped, showed me the deep gashes on her back — I might have laid my whole finger in them — large pieces of flesh had actually been cut out by the torturing lash.

The book sold more than 100,000 copies the year it was published.

To distribute their message, the abolitionists used the latest techniques of mass communication. With the help of new steam-powered printing presses, the American Anti-Slavery Society distributed thousands of pieces of literature in 1834. In 1835, the society launched its "great postal campaign," which flooded the nation, including the South, with a million pamphlets.

The abolitionists' second tactic was to help African Americans who had fled from slavery. Blacks who lived near a free state had the greatest chance of success, but fugitives from plantations deeper in the South received aid from the Underground Railroad, an informal network of whites and free blacks in Richmond, Charleston, and other southern cities (Map 11.3). In Baltimore, a free African American sailor lent his identification papers to future abolitionist Frederick Douglass, who

used them to escape to New York. Some runaway slaves, among them Harriet Tubman, risked reenslavement or death by returning repeatedly to the South to help others escape. "I should fight for … liberty as long as my strength lasted," Tubman explained, "and when the time came for me to go, the Lord would let them take me." Thanks to the Railroad, each year about a thousand African Americans reached freedom in the North.

There they faced an uncertain future because most whites did not favor civic equality for African Americans. In fact, voters in six northern and midwestern states adopted constitutional amendments that denied or limited the franchise for free blacks. "We want no masters," declared a New York artisan, "and least of all no negro masters." Moreover, the Fugitive Slave Law (1793) allowed owners and their hired slave catchers to

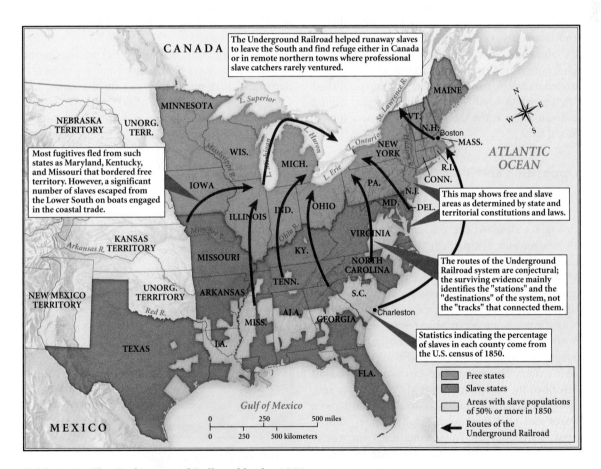

MAP 11.3   The Underground Railroad in the 1850s

Before 1840, most blacks who fled slavery did so on their own or with the help of family and friends. Thereafter, they could count on support from members of the Underground Railroad. Provided with food, directions, and free black guides in the South, fugitive slaves crossed into free states. There, they received protection and shelter from sympathetic men and women who arranged for their transportation to Canada or to "safe" American cities and towns.

seize suspected runaways and carry them back to bondage. To thwart these efforts, white abolitionists and free blacks in northern cities formed mobs that seized recaptured slaves and drove slave catchers out of town.

The third element of the abolitionists' program was an appeal to state and national legislators. In 1835, members of the American Anti-Slavery Society bombarded Congress with petitions demanding the abolition of slavery in the District of Columbia, an end to the interstate slave trade, and a ban on admission to the Union of new slave states. By 1838, petitions with close to 500,000 signatures had arrived in Washington.

This protest activity drew thousands of deeply religious farmers and small-town proprietors to abolitionism. The number of local abolitionist societies grew from two hundred in 1835 to two thousand by 1840, with nearly 200,000 members, including many leading transcendentalists. Emerson condemned American society for tolerating slavery, and Thoreau was even more assertive. Claiming that the Mexican War was an attempt to extend slavery, Thoreau refused to pay his taxes in 1846 and submitted to arrest. Two years later, Thoreau published "Resistance to Civil Government," an essay urging individuals to resist the state and follow a higher moral law.

Opposition and Internal Conflict

Still, abolitionists remained a small minority. Perhaps 10 percent of northerners and midwesterners strongly supported the movement, and another 20 percent were sympathetic to its goals. Its opponents were more numerous and equally aggressive. Men of wealth feared that the attack on slave property might become a general assault on all property rights; conservative clergymen condemned the public roles assumed by abolitionist women; and northern merchants and textile manufacturers supported the southern planters who supplied them with cotton. Northern wage earners, who already described themselves as "white slaves" to their employers, feared that freed blacks would work for lower wages and take their jobs. Finally, whites almost universally opposed "amalgamation," the racial mixing and intermarriage that Garrison seemed to support by encouraging meetings of black and white abolitionists of both sexes.

Antiabolitionist Mobs. Motivated by racial fears, white workers in the North periodically took part in violent mob actions. They attacked places of dubious reputation where blacks and whites mixed,

including taverns and brothels; they also attacked "respectable" African American institutions: churches, temperance halls, and orphanages. In 1833, a mob of fifteen hundred New Yorkers stormed a church in search of Garrison and Arthur Tappan. Another white mob swept through Philadelphia's African American neighborhoods, clubbing and stoning residents and destroying homes and churches. "Gentlemen of property and standing" led some of these riots. In 1835, a group of lawyers, merchants, and bankers broke up an abolitionist convention in Utica, New York, and beat several delegates. Two years later, in Alton, Illinois, a mob shot and killed Elijah P. Lovejoy, editor of the abolitionist *Alton Observer*. By pressing the issues of emancipation and equality, the abolitionists revealed the extent of racial prejudice in the North and the near impossibility of creating a biracial middle class of respectable whites and blacks. In fact, the abolitionist crusade had heightened race consciousness and encouraged whites—and blacks—to identify across class lines with those of their own race.

Racial solidarity was especially strong in the South, where whites banned abolitionist groups and demanded that northern states do the same. The Georgia legislature offered a $5,000 reward to anyone who would kidnap Garrison and bring him south to be tried for inciting rebellion. In Nashville, vigilantes whipped a northern college student for distributing abolitionist pamphlets; in Charleston, a mob attacked

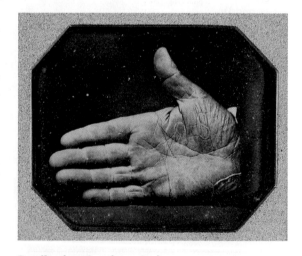

Retribution, Southern Style

Jonathan Walker, a Massachusetts shipwright, paid for his abolitionist activities by being branded, as this daguerreotype shows. Captured off the coast of Florida in 1844 while trying to smuggle seven slaves to freedom in the Bahama islands, Walker had the initials *SS* (for "slave stealer") burned into his hand. Massachusetts Historical Society.

the post office and destroyed sacks of abolitionist mail. After 1835, southern postmasters simply refused to deliver mail suspected to be of abolitionist origin.

Politicians also joined the fray. President Andrew Jackson, a longtime slave owner, asked Congress in 1835 to restrict the use of the mails by abolitionist groups. Congress did not comply; but in 1836, the House of Representatives adopted the so-called gag rule. Under this informal rule, which remained in force until 1844, antislavery petitions were automatically tabled so that they could not become the subject of debate in the House, thus keeping the explosive issue of slavery off the national stage.

The Fight over Gender Splits the Abolitionist Movement. Assailed by racists from the outside, abolitionists fought among themselves over gender issues. Many antislavery clergymen opposed an activist role for women and condemned the Grimké sisters for lecturing to mixed-sex audiences. But Garrison had broadened his reform agenda to include pacifism, the abolition of prisons, and women's rights. Arguing that "our object is universal emancipation, to redeem women as well as men from a servile to an equal condition," he demanded that the American Anti-Slavery Society support women's rights. In 1840, that demand split the abolitionist movement. Abby Kelley, Lucretia Mott, Elizabeth Cady Stanton, and other women's rights advocates remained with Garrison in the American Anti-Slavery Society and proclaimed the common interests of enslaved blacks and free white women.

Garrison's opponents founded a new organization, the American and Foreign Anti-Slavery Society, which focused its energies on ending slavery. Some of its members mobilized their churches to oppose racial bondage; others established the Liberty Party, the first antislavery political party. In 1840, the new party nominated James G. Birney, a former Alabama slave owner, for president. Birney and the Liberty Party argued that the Constitution did not recognize slavery and, consequently, that slaves automatically became free when they entered areas of federal authority, including the District of Columbia and the national territories. However, Birney won few votes in the election, and the future of political abolitionism appeared dim.

Coming hard on the heels of popular violence in the North and government suppression in the South, schisms and electoral failure stunned the abolitionist movement. By melding the energies and ideas of evangelical Protestants, moral reformers, and transcendentalists, it had raised the banner of antislavery to new heights. Indeed, it was the growing visibility of the abolitionist movement that had sparked a hostile backlash. "When we first unfurled the banner of *The Liberator*," Garrison admitted, "it did not occur to us that nearly every religious sect and every political party would side with the oppressor."

➤ What were the origins of the abolitionist movement?

➤ How did black social thought change over the first half of the nineteenth century? What role did black activists play in the abolitionist movement?

➤ How did the abolitionists' proposals and methods differ from those of earlier antislavery movements (see Chapter 8)? Why did those proposals and methods arouse such hostility in the South and in the North?

The Women's Rights Movement

The prominence of women among the abolitionists reflected a broad shift in American culture. By joining religious revivals and reform movements like the temperance crusade and the abolitionist movement, women had entered public life. Their activism caused issues of gender — sexual behavior, marriage, family authority — to become subjects of debate. In 1848, the debate entered a new phase, when some reformers turned their advocacy toward women's rights and demanded complete equality with men.

Origins of the Women's Movement

"Don't be afraid, not afraid, fight Satan; stand up for Christ; don't be afraid." So spoke Mary Walker Ostram on her deathbed in 1859. Her religious convictions were as firm at the age of fifty-eight as they had been in 1816, when she helped found the first sabbath school in Utica. Married to a lawyer-politician but childless, Ostram had devoted her life to evangelical Presbyterianism and its program of benevolent social reform. Her minister, Philemon Fowler, celebrated Ostram in his eulogy of her as a "living fountain" of faith, an exemplar of "Women's Sphere of Influence" in the world.

Transcending the "Separate Sphere." A public presence for women was hard won and still contested. Even as Reverend Fowler heaped praise on Ostram, he reiterated the Revolutionary-era precept that women should limit their political role to that of "republican mother," instructing "their sons in the principles of liberty and government." According to Fowler, women inhabited a "**separate sphere**" and had no place in "the markets of trade, the scenes of politics and popular agitation, the courts of justice and the halls of legislation. Home is her peculiar sphere and members of her family her peculiar care."

Ostram and many other middle-class women had transcended these rigid boundaries by joining in the Second Great Awakening. Their spiritual activities bolstered their authority within the household and allowed them to influence many areas of family life, including the timing of pregnancies. Publications like *Godey's Lady's Book* and Catharine Beecher's *Treatise on Domestic Economy* (1841) taught women how to make their homes examples of middle-class efficiency and domesticity. Women in propertied farm families were equally vigilant. To protect their homes and husbands from alcoholic excess, they joined the Independent Order of Good Templars, a family-oriented temperance organization that granted them full membership.

Some women used their religious activities to enhance the position of their gender. In 1834, a group of middle-class women in New York City founded the Female Moral Reform Society and elected Lydia Finney, the wife of revivalist Charles Grandison Finney, as its president. The society's goals were to end the prostitution that was so prevalent in New York City and to protect the city's single women from moral corruption. Rejecting the sexual double standard, its members demanded chastity for men as well as for women. By 1840, the Female Moral Reform Society had grown into a national association, with 555 chapters and 40,000 members throughout the North and Midwest. Employing only women as agents, the society provided moral guidance for young women working in factories, as seamstresses, or as servants and living away from their families. Society members visited brothels, where they sang hymns, offered prayers, searched for runaway girls, and noted the names of clients. They also founded homes of refuge for prostitutes, and won the passage of laws in Massachusetts and New York regulating men's sexual behavior by making seduction a crime.

Dorothea Dix and Institutional Reform. Other women turned their energies to the improvement of public institutions, and Dorothea Dix (1801–1887) was their model. Dix's paternal grandparents were prominent Bostonians, but her father, a Methodist minister, ended up an impoverished alcoholic. Poor and emotionally abused as a child, Dix grew up to become a compassionate young woman with a strong sense of moral purpose. She used her grand-

Dorothea Dix

This daguerreotype captures Dix's firm character, which helped her endure emotional abuse as a child and achieve great success as a social reformer. Her call for government action to address social problems anticipated twentieth-century reform and social-welfare measures. Boston Athenaeum.

parents' resources to set up charity schools to "rescue some of America's miserable children from vice." While teaching, Dix became a successful author and a public figure. By 1832, she had published seven books, including *Conversations on Common Things* (1824), an enormously successful treatise on natural science and moral improvement.

In 1841, Dix took up a new cause. Discovering that insane women were jailed alongside male criminals, she persuaded Massachusetts lawmakers to enlarge the state hospital to accommodate indigent mental patients. Exhilarated by that success, Dix began a national movement to establish separate, well-funded state hospitals for those with mental illness. By 1854, she had traveled more than 30,000 miles and visited eighteen state penitentiaries, three hundred county jails and houses of correction, and more than five hundred almshouses in addition to innumerable hospitals. Issuing dozens of reports, she aroused public support and prompted many states to expand their state hospitals and improve their prisons.

Both as reformers and as teachers, other northern women transformed public education. From Maine

MAP 11.4   Women and Antislavery, 1837–1838

Beginning in the 1830s, abolitionists and antislavery advocates dispatched dozens of petitions to Congress demanding an end to slavery. Women accounted for two-thirds of the 67,000 signatures on the petitions submitted in 1837–1838, a fact that suggests not only the influence of women in the antislavery movement but also the extent of female organizations and social networks. Lawmakers, eager to avoid sectional conflict, had an informal agreement to table the petitions without discussion.

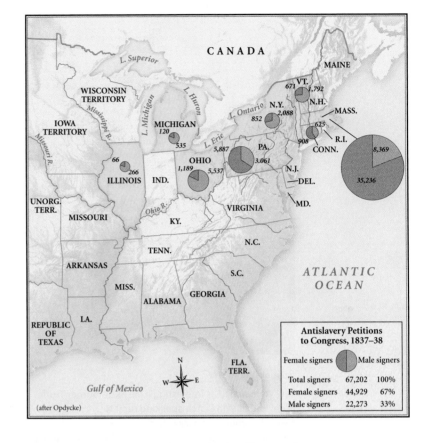

Antislavery Petitions to Congress, 1837–38		
Female signers	Male signers	
Total signers	67,202	100%
Female signers	44,929	67%
Male signers	22,273	33%

(after Opdycke)

to Wisconsin, women vigorously supported the movement led by Horace Mann to increase the number of elementary schools and improve their quality. As secretary of the Massachusetts Board of Education from 1837 to 1848, Mann lengthened the school year; established teaching standards in reading, writing, and arithmetic; and improved instruction by recruiting well-educated women as teachers. The intellectual leader of the new corps of women educators was Catharine Beecher, who founded academies for young women in Hartford and Cincinnati. In widely read publications, Beecher argued that "energetic and benevolent women" were better qualified than men were to impart moral and intellectual instruction to the young. By the 1850s, most teachers were women both because local school boards heeded Beecher's arguments and because women could be paid less than men.

Abolitionist Women

Women had long been active in the antislavery movement. During the Revolutionary era, Quaker women in Philadelphia established schools for freed slaves, and Baptist and Methodist women in the Upper South endorsed religious arguments against slavery. One of the first abolitionists recruited by William Lloyd Garrison was Maria W. Stewart, an

African American, who spoke to mixed audiences of men and women in Boston in the early 1830s. As the abolitionist movement mushroomed, scores of white women delivered lectures condemning slavery, and thousands more made home "visitations" to win converts to their cause (Map 11.4).

Women abolitionists were particularly aware of the special horrors of slavery for their sex. In her autobiography, *Incidents in the Life of a Slave Girl,* black abolitionist Harriet Jacobs described being forced to have sexual relations with her white owner: "I cannot tell how much I suffered in the presence of these wrongs." According to Jacobs and the other female slaves who testified, the sexual assaults were compounded by the cruel treatment they suffered at the hands of their owners' wives, who were enraged by their husbands' promiscuity. In her best-selling novel, *Uncle Tom's Cabin* (1852), Harriet Beecher Stowe charged that among the greatest moral failings of slavery was the degradation of slave women.

As abolitionist women attacked slavery and sexual oppression, many men challenged their right to participate in public debate. In response, women activists rejected the subordinate status of their sex. The most famous advocates were Angelina and Sarah Grimké, who had become antislavery lecturers. When some Congregationalist clergymen demanded in 1836 that they stop lecturing to mixed

Sojourner Truth

Few women had as interesting a life as Sojourner Truth. Born "Isabella" in Dutch-speaking rural New York about 1797, she labored as a slave until 1827. Following a religious vision, Isabella moved to New York City, learned English, and worked for deeply religious — and ultimately fanatical — Christian merchants. In 1843, in search of further spiritual enlightenment, she took the name "Sojourner Truth" and left New York. After briefly joining the Millerites (who believed the world would end in 1844), Truth became famous as a forceful speaker on behalf of abolitionism and women's rights. This illustration, showing Truth addressing an antislavery meeting, suggests her powerful personal presence. Miriam and Ira D. Wallach Division of Art, Prints and Photographs. The New York Public Library.

male and female audiences, Sarah Grimké turned to the Bible for justification: "The Lord Jesus defines the duties of his followers in his Sermon on the Mount . . . without any reference to sex or condition," she wrote. "Men and women are CREATED EQUAL! They are both moral and accountable beings and whatever is right for man to do is right for woman." In a debate with Catharine Beecher (who believed that women should exercise power primarily as wives, mothers, and schoolteachers), Angelina Grimké pushed the argument beyond religion, invoking Enlightenment principles to claim equal civic rights for women:

It is a woman's right to have a voice in all the laws and regulations by which she is governed,

whether in Church or State. . . . The present arrangements of society, on these points are a violation of human rights, a rank usurpation of power, a violent seizure and confiscation of what is sacredly and inalienably hers.

By 1840, female abolitionists were asserting that traditional gender roles amounted to the "domestic slavery" of women. "How can we endure our present marriage relations," asked Elizabeth Cady Stanton, relations that gave a woman "no charter of rights, no individuality of her own?" Said another female reformer: "The radical difficulty . . . is that women are considered as *belonging* to men." Drawn into public life by abolitionism, thousands of northern women now advocated greater rights not only for enslaved African Americans but also for themselves.

The Program of Seneca Falls and Beyond

During the 1840s, women's rights activists devised a pragmatic program of reform. They did not challenge the institution of marriage or even the conventional division of labor within the family. Instead, they tried to strengthen the legal rights of married women, especially with respect to property. This initiative won crucial support from affluent men, who wanted to protect their wives' assets in case their own businesses went into bankruptcy in the volatile new market economy. By ensuring that their married daughters had property rights, fathers also hoped to protect them (and their inheritances) from spendthrift sons-in-law. These considerations prompted legislatures in three states — Mississippi, Maine, and Massachusetts — to enact married women's property acts between 1839 and 1845. In New York, women activists won a more comprehensive statute (1848), which gave women full legal control over the property they brought to a marriage and became the model for similar laws in fourteen other states.

To advance the nascent women's movement, Elizabeth Cady Stanton and Lucretia Mott organized a gathering in the small town of Seneca Falls in central New York in 1848. Seventy women and thirty men attended the meeting, which issued a rousing manifesto for women's equality. Taking the Declaration of Independence as a model, the attendees explicitly extended its republican ideology to women. "All men and women are created equal," the Declaration of Sentiments declared. Yet, "the history of mankind is a history of repeated injuries and usurpations on the part of man toward woman, having in direct object the establishment

Crusading Women Reformers

Elizabeth Cady Stanton (1815–1902) and Susan B. Anthony (1820–1906) were a dynamic duo of social reformers. Stanton was the well-educated daughter of a prominet New York judge and an early supporter of the abolitionist movement. In 1840 she married abolitionist lawyer Henry Stanton, by whom she had seven children. Anthony was raised as a Quaker, worked for ten years as a teacher, and then became a temperance activist. After meeting in 1851, Stanton and Anthony became intimate friends and successful reformers and organizers. From 1854 to 1860, they led a successful struggle to expand the New York's Married Women's Property Law of 1848. During the Civil War, they set up the Women's Loyal National League, which supported the Union war effort and helped to win passage of the Thirteenth Amendment. In 1866, they helped to found the American Equal Rights Association, which demanded the vote for all women as well as African American men. Corbis/Bettman.

of an absolute tyranny over her." To persuade Americans to right this long-standing wrong, the activists resolved to "use every instrumentality within our power . . . [to] employ agents, circulate tracts, petition the State and National legislatures, and endeavor to enlist the pulpit and the press on our behalf." By staking out claims for equality for women in public life, the Seneca Falls reformers repudiated the idea that the natural order of society demanded separate spheres for men and women.

Most men dismissed the Seneca Falls declaration as nonsense, and many women repudiated the activists and their message. Writing in her diary, one small-town mother and housewife lashed out at the female reformer who "aping mannish manners . . . wears absurd and barbarous attire, who talks of her wrongs in harsh tone, who struts and strides, and thinks that she proves herself superior to the rest of her sex."

Still, the women's rights movement attracted a growing number of supporters. In 1850, delegates to the first national women's rights convention in Worcester, Massachusetts, hammered out a program of action. The women called on churches to revise concepts of female inferiority in their theology. Addressing state legislatures, they proposed laws to guarantee the custody rights of mothers in the event of divorce or a husband's death, and to allow married women to institute lawsuits and testify in court. Finally, and above all else, they began a concerted campaign to win the vote for women. The national women's rights convention of 1851 declared that suffrage was "the corner-stone of this enterprise, since we do not seek to protect woman, but rather to place her in a position to protect herself."

The activists' legislative campaign required leaders who had talents as organizers and lobbyists. The most prominent political operative was Susan B. Anthony (1820–1906). Anthony came from a Quaker family and as a young woman participated in the temperance and antislavery movements. That experience, Anthony explained, had taught her "the great evil of woman's utter dependence on man" and led her to the women's rights movement. Working closely with Stanton, Anthony created a network of political "captains," all women, who relentlessly lobbied the legislature in New York and other states. In 1860, her efforts culminated in a New York law granting women the right to collect and spend their own wages (which fathers or husbands had previously controlled), own property acquired by "trade, business, labors, or services," and, if widowed, to assume sole guardianship of their children. These successes laid the foundation for more-aggressive attempts at reform after the Civil War.

➤ Why did religious women like Mary Walker Ostram and the Grimké sisters become social reformers?

➤ What were the principles and the goals of the women's rights movement? Why did they arouse intense opposition?

SUMMARY

In this chapter, we have examined four major intellectual and cultural movements of the mid-nineteenth century and explored the character of the new popular culture in New York City. One focus of our discussion of the transcendentalists was the influence of Ralph Waldo Emerson on the great literary figures of the era; we also linked transcendentalism to the rise of individualism and the character of middle-class culture.

Our analysis of communal movements had a different thrust. It probed the efforts of communalists to devise new rules for sexual behavior, gender relationships, and property ownership. We saw that successful communal experiments — Mormonism, for example — began with a charismatic leader and a religious foundation, and endured through the development of strong, authoritarian institutions.

We also traced the extremely close connections between the abolitionist and women's rights movements. Personal and ideological factors linked the two causes. Lucretia Mott, Elizabeth Cady Stanton, and the Grimké sisters began as antislavery advocates; but, denied access to lecture platforms by male abolitionists, they gradually became staunch defenders of women's rights. This transition was a logical one: Both enslaved blacks and married women were "owned" by men, either as property or as their legal dependents. In fact, the efforts of women's rights advocates to abolish the legal prerogatives of husbands were as controversial as the abolitionists' efforts to end the legal ownership of human property. As reformers took aim at these deeply rooted institutions and customs, many Americans feared that their activism would not perfect society but destroy it.

Connections: Culture

Before 1800, the United States contained a variety of regional cultures in New England, the Middle Atlantic region, and the Chesapeake Bay area. Mixed in with these English cultures, were a variety of eighteenth-century immigrant cultures, primarily African, German, and Scots-Irish. As we saw in Chapter 8, between 1790 and 1820, the immigrant societies slowly became more American in character, while the regional cultures acquired distinct republican outlooks and a strong religious impulse.

Then, as we observed in the essay opening Part Three, (p. 269), beginning in the 1820s,

> a series of reform movements, many with religious roots and goals, swept across America. Dedicated men and women preached the gospel of temperance, Sunday observance, prison reform, and dozens of other causes.

The reform movements sparked a series of culture wars, as temperance advocates won laws regulating drink, Sabbatarians tried to curtail work and entertainment on Sundays, white mobs rioted against abolitionists, and community hostility forced Mormons westward. The sudden appearance of millions of new Catholic migrants from Germany and Ireland sparked more cultural conflicts. These confrontations caused some observers to worry that American society, particularly in the Northeast and Midwest, was coming apart at the seams. Meanwhile, in the South, a vast movement of peoples — white and black — into the lower Mississippi Valley disrupted the traditional English- and African-based cultures of the Chesapeake states and the Carolinas. The creation of a new "cotton states" culture is the subject of the next chapter.

CHAPTER REVIEW QUESTIONS

➤ Did the era of reform increase or decrease the belief in and practice of liberty in American society?

➤ Explain the relationship between individualism and communalism as presented in the chapter. How were these movements related to the social and economic changes in America in the decades after 1820?

➤ Explain the relationship between religion and reform in the decades from 1820 to 1860. Why did many religious people feel compelled to remake society? What was their motivation? How successful were they? Do you see any parallels with social movements today?

➤ What was the relationship between the abolitionist and women's rights movements?

➤ Why did women's issues suddenly become so prominent in American culture?

TIMELINE

1826	Lyceum movement begins
1829	David Walker's *Appeal . . . to the Colored Citizens of the World*
1830	Joseph Smith publishes *The Book of Mormon*
1830s	Emergence of minstrelsy shows Nativist movement mounts assault on immigrants and immigration
1831	William Lloyd Garrison founds *The Liberator* Nat Turner's uprising in Virginia
1832	Ralph Waldo Emerson rejects organized religion and begins defining transcendentalism
1833	Garrison organizes American Anti-Slavery Society
1834	New York activists create Female Moral Reform Society
1835	Abolitionists launch mail campaign; antiabolitionists riot against them
1836	House of Representatives adopts gag rule on antislavery petitions Grimké sisters defend public roles for women
1840	Liberty Party runs James G. Birney for president
1840s	Fourierist communities arise in Midwest Commercialized sex flourishes in New York City
1841	Transcendentalists found Brook Farm Dorothea Dix promotes hospitals for the insane
1844	Margaret Fuller publishes *Woman in the Nineteenth Century*
1845	Henry David Thoreau withdraws to Walden Pond
1846	Mormon followers of Brigham Young reach Salt Lake
1848	John Humphrey Noyes founds Oneida Community Seneca Falls convention proposes women's equality
1850	Nathaniel Hawthorne publishes *The Scarlet Letter*
1851	Herman Melville issues *Moby Dick*
1852	Harriet Beecher Stowe writes *Uncle Tom's Cabin*
1855	Walt Whitman issues first edition of *Leaves of Grass*
1858	"Mormon War" over polygamy

FOR FURTHER EXPLORATION

Ronald Walters, *American Reformers, 1815–1860* (1978), offers a succinct discussion of the major antebellum reform movements, while Robert H. Abzug, *Cosmos Crumbling: American Reform and the Religious Imagination* (1994), demonstrates their religious roots. David S. Reynolds, *Walt Whitman's America: A Cultural Biography* (1995), is a fine study of the poet and his society. Charles Capper, *Margaret Fuller: An American Romantic Life* (1992), illuminates her intellectual milieu. Fuller inspired the character of Zenobia in Nathaniel Hawthorne's *The Blithedale Romance* (1852), which reflects his life at Brook Farm. Peter S. Field, in *Ralph Waldo Emerson: The Making of a Democratic Individual* (2003), offers a convincing profile. For fine Web sites on transcendentalism and other American religious sects, go to **www.vcu.edu/engweb/transcendentalism/** and **religiousmovements.lib.virginia.edu/**. For religious utopianism gone mad, read Paul E. Johnson and Sean Wilentz, *The Kingdom of Matthias: A Story of Sex and Salvation in Nineteenth-Century America* (1995).

James B. Stewart, *Holy Warriors: The Abolitionists and American Slavery* (1976), places Garrison's movement in a broad social context. Also see Mark Perry, *Lift Up Thy Voice: The Grimké Family's Journey* (2001). Stephen B. Oates, *The Fires of Jubilee: Nat Turner's Fierce Rebellion* (1975), explores the life of the insurrectionist; the text of *The Confessions of Nat Turner* (1831) is available at **docsouth.unc.edu/turner/menu.html**. *The Narrative of the Life of Frederick Douglass, an American Slave, Written by Himself* (1845), is a literary masterpiece. John Stauffer, *The Black Hearts of Men* (2001), is a fine collective biography of Douglass and other abolitionists. Important new biographies of Harriet Tubman are Kate Clifford Larson, *Bound for the Promised Land* (2004), and Catherine Clinton, *Harriet Tubman: The Road to Freedom* (2004). For antiabolitionism, see Leonard L. Richards, *"Gentlemen of Property and Standing": Anti-Abolition Mobs in Jacksonian America* (1970), and David Roediger, *The Wages of Whiteness* (1995). For many resources on slavery and abolition, consult the PBS "Africans in America" site (**www.pbs.org/wgbh/aia/ part4/**).

Anne M. Boylan, *The Origins of Women's Activism . . . 1797–1840* (1992), and Mary Ryan, *Women in Public . . . 1825–1880* (1990), explore women's civic activities. Also see Eleanor Flexner, *Century of Struggle* (1959); the PBS video directed by Ken Burns, "Not for Ourselves Alone: The Story of Elizabeth Cady Stanton and Susan B. Anthony" (3 hours); and the National Park Service Web site for Seneca Falls (**www.nps.gov/wori/home.htm**).

TEST YOUR KNOWLEDGE

To assess your command of the material in this chapter, see the Online Study Guide at **bedfordstmartins.com/henretta**.

For Web sites, images, and documents related to topics and places in this chapter, visit **bedfordstmartins.com/makehistory**.

12

The South Expands: Slavery and Society

1820–1860

Life in South Carolina had been good to James Lide. A slave-owning planter who lived near the Pee Dee River, Lide and his wife had raised twelve children and lived in relative comfort. Content with his lot, Lide had long resisted the "Alabama Fever" that had prompted thousands of Carolina families to move west. Finally, at age sixty-five, probably seeking land for his many offspring, he moved his slaves and family—including six children and six grandchildren—to a plantation near Montgomery, Alabama. There, the family took up residence in a squalid double log cabin with airholes but no windows; still, Lide's daughter Maria remarked, "Our house is considered quite a comfortable one for this country." Even as their living conditions improved, the Lides' family life remained unsettled. "Pa is quite in the notion of moving somewhere," Maria reported a few years later, "his having such a good crop seems to make him more anxious to move." Although James Lide lived out his years in Alabama, many of his children did not. In 1854, at the age of fifty-eight, Eli Lide moved to Texas, telling his father, "Something within me whispers onward and onward."

The story of the Lide family was the story of American society. Between 1800 and 1860, white planters from the South and yeomen farmers from the North were moving west. As historian James Oakes

◄ **Generations in Slavery**

In 1862, a traveling photographer, Timothy O'Sullivan, took this picture at the Beaufort, South Carolina, plantation of J. J. Smith. It shows four—perhaps five—generations of a slave family, all of whom were born on the plantation. As you read this chapter, consider whether the experience of this African American family was the exception or the rule. Who might be missing from this family photograph? For example, what happened to the brothers and sisters of the man standing in the back? Library of Congress.

has suggested, the South's "master class was one of the most mobile in history." The southerners' goal was to make the West into a "slave society" similar to the one their fathers and grandfathers had built in Virginia and South Carolina. Using their own muscles and those of thousands of enslaved African Americans, the planters rapidly cultivated millions of acres of land. By 1840, the South was at the cutting edge of the American Market Revolution. It annually produced and exported 1.5 million bales of raw cotton—over two-thirds of the world's supply—and its economy was larger and richer than that of most nations. "Cotton is King," boasted the *Southern Cultivator,* the leading Georgia farm journal, "and wields an astonishing influence over the world's commerce."

No matter how rich they were, few cotton planters in the southwestern states of Alabama, Mississippi, and Texas lived in elegant houses or led cultured lives. The slave owners of the Cotton South largely abandoned the aristocratic gentility characteristic of the Chesapeake region and the Carolinas. The goal of these agricultural capitalists was to make money. "To sell cotton in order to buy negroes—to make more cotton to buy more negroes, 'ad infinitum,' is the aim . . . of the thorough-going cotton planter," a New England traveler reported from Mississippi in 1835. "His whole soul is wrapped up in the pursuit." A generation later, Frederick Law Olmsted found that little had changed: "The plantations are all large" in Mississippi, but their owners do not live well, he observed; "the greater number have but small and mean residences." Plantation women were especially aware of the loss of genteel surroundings and polite society. Raised in North Carolina, where she was "blest with every comfort, & even luxury," a "discontented" Mary Drake found Mississippi and Alabama "a dreary waste."

Tens of thousands of enslaved African Americans in the Lower Mississippi River Valley knew what "dreary waste" really was: unremitting toil, poverty, and profound sadness. Sold south from Maryland, where his family had lived for generations, Charles Ball's father became "gloomy and morose" and, when threatened again with sale, ran off and disappeared. With good reason. On cotton plantations, slaves labored from "sunup to sundown" and from one end of the year to the other. As one field hand put it, there was "no time off [between] de change of de seasons. . . . Dey was allus clearin' mo' lan' or sump'." Day by day, the forced labor of unwilling migrants extracted the great wealth of the Cotton South from its bountiful lands. And wanting more, southern planters and politicians plotted to extend the sway of slave property rights across the continent.

Creating the Cotton South

American slavery began on the tobacco plantations of the Chesapeake and in the rice fields of the Carolina Low Country. It grew to maturity on the sugar fields of Louisiana, the hemp farms of Kentucky and Tennessee, and especially on the cotton plantations of the states bordering the Gulf of Mexico: Alabama, Mississippi, and Texas (Figure 12.1). The transplantation of slavery to these new lands brought vast changes to the lives of enslaved blacks, slave-owning planters, and white farmers. Beyond that, it led planters to believe that American slavery could and should continue to expand—across the continent or to the Caribbean. "We want land, and have a right to it," declared a Georgia planter on the eve of the Civil War.

The Domestic Slave Trade

By 1817, when the American Colonization Society announced its plan to return freed blacks to Africa (see Chapter 8), the southern plantation system was rapidly expanding, as was the demand for slave labor. In 1790, the western boundary of the plantation system ran through the middle of Georgia; by 1830, it stretched through western Louisiana; by 1860, the slave frontier extended far into Texas. (Map 12.1).

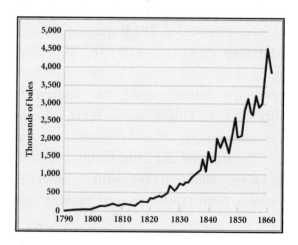

FIGURE 12.1 The Surge in Cotton Production, 1835–1860

Between 1835 and the mid-1840s, southern planters doubled their output of 500-pound bales of cotton from 1 million per year to 2 million. Another dramatic rise came in the 1850s, as production doubled again — reaching 4 million bales per year by the end of the decade. Because the price of raw cotton rose slightly (from about 11 cents a pound in the 1830s to 13 cents in the 1850s), planters reaped substantial profits, an economic incentive that reinforced their commitment to the slave system. SOURCE: Robert William Fogel and Stanley L. Engerman, *Time on the Cross* (Boston: Little, Brown, 1974), fig. 25.

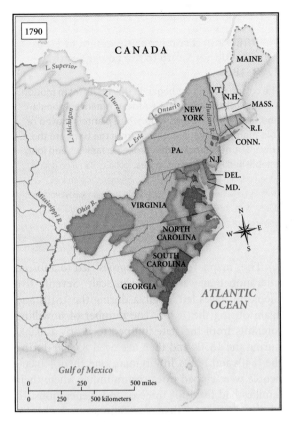

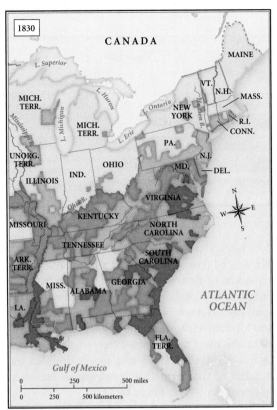

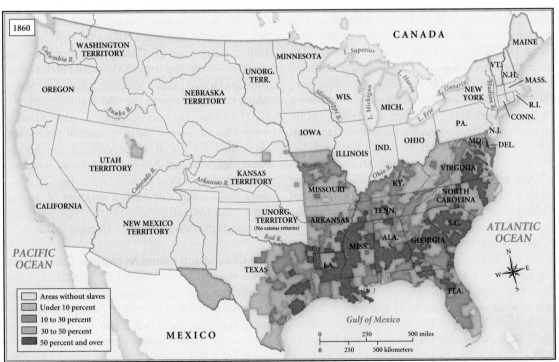

MAP 12.1   Distribution of the Slave Population in 1790, 1830, and 1860

The cotton boom shifted many African Americans to the Old Southwest. In 1790, most slaves lived and worked on the tobacco plantations of the Chesapeake and in the rice and indigo areas of South Carolina. By 1830, hundreds of thousands of enslaved blacks were laboring on the cotton and sugar lands of the Lower Mississippi Valley and on cotton plantations in Georgia and Florida. Three decades later, the centers of slavery lay along the Mississippi River and in an arc of fertile cotton land — the "black belt" — sweeping from Mississippi through Georgia.

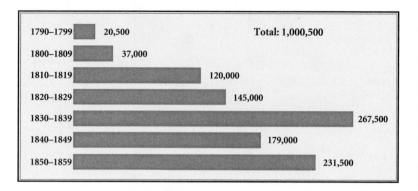

1790–1799	20,500
1800–1809	37,000
1810–1819	120,000
1820–1829	145,000
1830–1839	267,500
1840–1849	179,000
1850–1859	231,500

Total: 1,000,500

FIGURE 12.2 Estimated Movement of Slaves from the Upper South to the Lower South, 1790–1860

The cotton boom that began in the 1810s set in motion a great redistribution of the African American population. Between 1790 and 1860, white planters moved or sold more than a million slaves from the Upper to the Lower South, a process that broke up families and long-established black communities. SOURCE: Based on data in Robert William Fogel and Stanley L. Engerman, *Time on the Cross* (Boston: Little, Brown, 1974); and Michael Tadman, *Speculators and Slaves: Masters, Traders, and Slaves in the Old South* (Madison: University of Wisconsin Press, 1996).

The federal government played a major role in this expansion of slavery by securing Louisiana from the French in 1803, removing Native Americans from the southeastern states in the 1830s, and annexing Texas and Mexican territories in the 1840s. That advance of 900 miles more than doubled the geographical area cultivated by slave labor and nearly doubled the number of southern slave states, which increased from eight in 1800 to fifteen by 1850.

To cultivate this vast area, white planters turned first to Africa for slaves and then to the Chesapeake region. Between 1776 and 1809, when Congress outlawed the Atlantic slave trade, planters imported about 115,000 Africans (see Table 8.1, p. 254). "The Negro business is a great object with us," one slave trader declared, "the Planter will . . . sacrifice every thing to attain Negroes." Despite the influx of Africans, the demand for labor on the new cotton plantations in the Gulf region far exceeded the supply. Consequently, planters in the Cotton South began importing thousands of new African workers illegally, through the Spanish colony of Florida until 1819 and then through the Mexican province of Texas. Yet these Africans were too few to satisfy the demand for labor.

So planters looked to the Chesapeake region, home in 1800 to nearly half of the country's black population. Throughout the Old South, the African American population was growing rapidly from natural increase—an average of 27 percent a decade—and creating a surplus of enslaved laborers. Before the War of 1812, "Georgia traders" had begun to exploit this surplus by buying slaves to work their plantations. After the war, the internal trade in slaves expanded vastly in scope and size. Each decade, planters and slave traders moved to the rich soils of the Cotton South about 10 percent of the African Americans who lived in the main exporting states of the Upper South—Maryland and Virginia before 1820, plus the Carolinas by 1830, plus Kentucky by 1840.

The "mania for buying negroes" led to a forced migration that was massive in scale. Seventy-five thousand slaves left Virginia during the 1810s and again during the 1820s. The number of unwilling migrants from the state jumped to nearly 120,000 during the 1830s and then averaged 85,000 during the 1840s and 1850s. In Virginia alone, then, 440,000 people were ripped from communities where their families had lived for three or four generations. In all, by 1860, more than 1 million slaves had been forced to leave the Upper South (Figure 12.2).

This movement of African Americans took two forms: transfer and sale. Looking for new opportunities, thousands of Chesapeake and Carolina planters—men like James Lide—sold their plantations and moved to the Southwest with their slaves. Many other planters in the Old South signed over slaves to their sons and daughters, who migrated west. This transfer of entire or partial plantations accounted for about 40 percent of the African Americans migrants. The rest—about 60 percent of the total migration of more than 1 million slaves—were "sold south." By 1860 a majority of African Americans lived and worked in the New South, the vast lands that stretched from Georgia to Texas.

The Coastal and Inland Networks. Just as the Atlantic slave trade was a major industry in the eighteenth century, so the domestic slave trade was a great commercial enterprise in the nineteenth century. The trade took two forms: a coastal system through the Atlantic seaports and inland commerce using river and roads. Beginning in the late eighteenth century, French settlers in the hot lowlands of Louisiana set up sugar plantations; and even before Louisiana became a state in 1812, hundreds of American planters had joined them. Sugar was a "killer" crop, and Louisiana (like the West Indies) soon had a reputation among African Americans "as a place of slaughter," where hundreds of field workers died each year. Moreover, the ratio of men

The Internal Slave Trade

Mounted whites escort a convoy of slaves from Virginia to Tennessee in Lewis Miller's *Slave Trader, Sold to Tennessee* (1853). For white planters, the interstate trade in slaves was lucrative; it pumped money into the declining Chesapeake economy and provided young workers for the expanding plantations of the cotton belt. For blacks it was a traumatic journey, a new Middle Passage that broke up their families and communities. Abby Aldrich Rockefeller Folk Art Center, Williamsburg, VA. Gift of Dr. and Mrs. Richard M. Kain in memory of George Hay Kain.

to women was severely skewed—with 130 men for every 100 women—and slave fertility remained low. Planters constantly needed new workers.

To meet the insatiable demand for male labor in the sugar fields, slave traders developed a coastal network. They scoured the countryside near the port cities of the Chesapeake and the Carolinas—Baltimore, Alexandria, Richmond, Charleston—searching, as one of them put it, for "likely young men such as I think would suit the New Orleans market." Each year, hundreds of young muscular slaves passed through the auction houses of the port cities bound for the massive trade mart in New Orleans. Because this traffic in laborers was highly visible, it elicited widespread condemnation by northern abolitionists.

The inland trade in slaves for the Cotton South was less visible but much more extensive. To some extent, it also relied on professional slave traders, who went from one rural village to another buying "young and likely Negroes." The traders then marched their purchases in coffles—columns of slaves bound to one another—to Alabama, Mississippi, and Missouri in the 1830s and to Arkansas and Texas in the 1850s. One slave described the arduous journey: "Dem Speculators would put the chilluns in a wagon usually pulled by oxens and de older folks was chained or tied together sos dey could not run off." Once a coffle reached its destination, the trader would offer slaves for sale "at every village in the county."

Established Chesapeake and Carolina planters provided the inland slave trade with its human cargo. Some planters sold slaves when poor management or their "own extravagances" threw them into debt. "Trouble gathers thicker and thicker

around me," Thomas B. Chaplin of South Carolina lamented in his diary, "I will be compelled to send about ten prime Negroes to Town on next Monday, to be sold." Many more planters speculated in slaves: They earned substantial profits by traveling south to sell some of their slaves and those of their neighbors. As prices soared during the cotton boom of the 1850s, one owner noted, a slave that "wouldn't bring over $300, seven years ago, will fetch $1000, cash, quick, this year." Exploiting this demand for laborers, Thomas Weatherly of South Carolina drove his surplus slaves to Hayneville, Alabama, where he lived "in his tents" and "sold ten negroes last week at fair prices." Colonel E. S. Irvine, a member of the South Carolina legislature and "a highly respected gentleman" in white circles, likewise traveled frequently "to the west to sell a drove of Negroes."

The domestic slave trade was crucial to the prosperity of the southern economy. Obviously, it provided tens of thousands of workers to carve new cotton plantations out of the forests of the Gulf states. But equally important, the trade bolstered the economy of the Upper South. By selling their surplus workers, tobacco, rice, and grain planters in the Chesapeake and Carolinas added about 20 percent to their income from the sale of agricultural goods. The domestic trade in slaves, remarked a Maryland newspaper, served as "an almost universal resource to raise money."

The Impact on Slave Families. For African American families, the domestic slave trade was a disaster that accentuated their status—and vulnerability—as property. On this issue, black and white commentators were in full agreement As W. C. Pennington,

The Business of Slavery

In the 1850s, Virginia slaves were still being "sold South." The painting above, *Slave Auction in Richmond, Virginia* (1852), captures the pensive and apprehensive emotions of the enslaved women and the discontent of the man, none of whom can control their fate. Whites — plantation overseer, slave trader, top-hatted aristocratic planter — lurk in the background, where they are completing the commercial transaction. The illustration to the right, a public notice for a slave auction to be held in Iberville, Louisiana, advertises "24 Head of Slaves" as if they were cattle — a striking statement on the business of slavery. The Granger Collection, New York / Library of Congress.

a former slave, reflected, "The being of slavery, its soul and its body, lives and moves in the chattel principle, the property principle, the bill of sale principle." The slave's earnings "belong to *me*," a South Carolina master boasted, "because I bought him." There was an "immense amount of capital which is invested in slave property," declared Henry Clay in 1839. "It is owned by widows and orphans, by the aged and infirm, as well as the sound and vigorous. It is the subject of mortgages, deeds of trust, and family settlements." The Whig politician concluded: "I know that there is a visionary dogma, which holds that negro slaves cannot be the subject of property. I shall not dwell long on this speculative abstraction. That is property which the law declares to be property."

As a slave owner, Clay knew that property rights were key to slave discipline. As one master put it, "I govern them . . . without the whip by stating . . . that I should sell them if they do not conduct themselves as I wish." The threat was effective. "The Negroes here dread nothing on earth so much as this," an observer in Maryland noted. "They regard the south with perfect horror, and to be sent there is considered as the worst punishment that could be inflicted on them."

The sheer size of the domestic trade meant that it touched thousands of families and destroyed about one in every four slave marriages. "I am Sold to a man by the name of Peterson a trader," lamented a Georgia slave. "My Dear wife for you and my Children my pen cannot Express the griffe I feel to be parted from you all." And the

BY HEWLETT & RASPILLER,

On Saturday, 14th April, inst.

At 1-2 12 o'clock, at Hewlett's Exchange,

WILL BE SOLD,

24 HEAD OF SLAVES,

Lately belonging to the Estate of Jno. Erwin, of the parish of Iberville. These Slaves have been for more than 10 years in the country, and are all well acclimated, and accustomed to all kinds of work on a Sugar Plantation. There are among them a first rate cooper, a first rate brick maker, and an excellent hostler and coachman. They will be sold chiefly in families.

TERMS-----One year's credit, payable in notes endorsed to the satisfaction of the vendor, and bearing mortgage until final payment. Sales to be passed before Carlisle Pollock, Esq. at the expense of the purchasers.

Fielding, aged 27 years, field hand,
Sally, aged 24 do. field hand and cook,
Levi, aged 26 years, cooper and field hand,
Aggy, do. 24 do. house servant and field hand.
James, do. 6 do.
Emeline, do. 3 do.
Stephen, do. 3 do.
Priscilly, 1 do.

Bill, aged 24 years, field hand,
Leah, do. 22 do. field hand,
Rosette, do. 3 do.
Infant child.

Alfred, aged 22 years, brick maker, servant and field hand,
Charlotte, do. 20 years, house servant and field hand,
Infant.

Forrester, aged 41 years, hostler, house servant and field hand,
Mary, aged 22 years, field hand and cook.
Infant.

Harry, aged 24 years, field hand,
Charity, aged 24 years, field hand,
Polly, aged 22 years, house servant and seamstress,
Sam, aged 2 years.
Bedford, aged 14 years, field hand,
Mahaly, aged 12 years, field hand,

trade was not limited to adults: Planters sold many slaves as they reached maturity, separating them forever from their families. "Dey sole my sister Kate," Anna Harris remembered decades later, "and I ain't seed or heard of her since." The trade also separated almost a third of all slave children under the age of fourteen from one or both of their parents. Sarah Grant remembered, "Mamma used to cry when she had to go back to work because she was always scared some of us kids would be sold while she was away." Well she might worry, for slave traders worked quietly and fast. "One night I lay down on de straw mattress wid my mammy," Vinny Baker recalled, "an' de nex' mo'nin I woke up an' she wuz gone." When their owner sold seven-year-old Laura Clark and ten other children from their plantation in North Carolina, Clark sensed that she would see her mother "no mo' in dis life."

Despite these sales, 80 percent of slave marriages remained unbroken, and the majority of children lived with one or both parents until puberty. Consequently, the sense of family among African Americans remained strong. Sold from Virginia to Texas in 1843, Hawkins Wilson carried with him a detailed mental picture of his family and kin. Twenty-five years later and now a freedman, Wilson set out to find his "dearest relatives" in Virginia. "My sister belonged to Peter Coleman in Caroline County and her name was Jane. . . . She had three children, Robert Charles and Julia, when I left — Sister Martha belonged to Dr. Jefferson. . . . Sister Matilda belonged to Mrs. Botts."

During the intervening quarter century, Laura Clark, Hawkins Wilson, and thousands of other African Americans constructed new lives for themselves in the Mississippi River Valley. Undoubtedly, many of these forced migrants did so with a sense of foreboding: They knew from experience that at any moment, their lives could be shaken to the core. Like Charles Ball, some "longed to die, and escape from the bonds of my tormentors." Even moments of joy were shadowed by the darkness of slavery. When enslaved men and women married in a Christian ceremony, the rites rarely ended with the customary phrase "until death do you part." Knowing that sales often ended slave marriages, a white minister blessed one couple "for so long as God keeps them together."

That a substantial majority of African American marriages endured allowed slave owners to see themselves as benevolent masters, committed to the welfare of "my family, black and white." Some masters gave substance to this paternalist ideal by treating with kindness various "loyal and worthy" slaves — the drivers, the mammy who raised their children, and trusted house servants. By safeguarding the families of these slaves from sale, many planters convinced themselves that they "sold south" only "coarse" troublemakers and uncivilized slaves who had "little sense of family." Other owners were more honest about the impact of their pursuit of economic gain. "Tomorrow the negroes are to get off" to Kentucky, a slave-owning woman in Virginia wrote to a friend, "and I expect there will be great crying and mourning, with children Leaving there mothers, mothers there children, and women there husbands."

Whether or not they acknowledged the slaves' pain, few southern whites questioned the morality of the domestic trade in slaves. As a committee of the Charleston City Council declared in response to abolitionist criticism, slavery was completely consistent "with moral principle and with the highest order of civilization," as was "the removal of slaves from place to place, and their transfer from master to master, by gift, purchase, or otherwise."

The Dual Cultures of the Planter Elite

Westward movement had a profound impact on the small elite of extraordinarily wealthy planter families who stood at the top of southern society. These families — about three thousand in number — each owned more than one hundred slaves and huge tracts of the most fertile lands. Their ranks included many of the richest families in the entire United States. On the eve of the Civil War, nearly two-thirds of all American men with wealth of $100,000 or more were southern plantation owners.

The plantation elite consisted of two distinct groups: the traditional aristocrats in the Old South, who had grown rich planting tobacco and rice and who lived in large and impressive mansions; and the market-driven entrepreneurs in the New South, whose wealth came from the booming cotton industry and who usually lived in relatively modest houses.

Slave-owning Aristocrats. With the increase in tobacco and rice production that occurred around 1700, a wealthy planter elite came to dominate the social and political life of the Tidewater region of the Chesapeake and the low country of South Carolina and Georgia. During the eighteenth century, these planters adopted the manners and values of the English landed gentry (see Chapter 3), and their aristocratic culture survived the republican revolution of 1776. Classical republican theorists had long identified political tyranny as a major threat to liberty, and southern aristocrats, who feared government interference with their property in slaves, embraced this ideological outlook. To prevent despotic rule by democratic demagogues or radical legislatures, planters demanded that authority rest in the hands of incorruptible men of "virtue."

Indeed, affluent planters cast themselves as the embodiment of this ideal — a republican aristocracy (see Chapter 8). "The planters here are essentially what the nobility are in other countries," declared James Henry Hammond of South Carolina. "They stand at the head of society & politics . . . [and form] an aristocracy of talents, of virtue, of generosity and courage." Most of these planters criticized the increasingly democratic polity and egalitarian society, especially as they were developing in the Northeast and Midwest. "Inequality is the fundamental law of the universe," declared one would-be aristocrat. Others condemned professional politicians as "a set of demagogues" and questioned the legitimacy of universal suffrage. "Times are sadly different now to what they were when I was a boy," lamented South Carolinian David Gavin. Then, the "Sovereign people, alias mob" had little power; now they vied for power with the elite. How can "I rejoice for a freedom," Gavin demanded to know, "which allows every bankrupt, swindler, thief, and scoundrel, traitor and seller of his vote to be placed on an equality with myself?"

To maintain their exclusivity, their very identity, aristocratic planters married their sons and daughters to one another and taught them to follow in their footsteps — the men working as planters, merchants, lawyers, newspaper editors, and ministers, and the women hosting plantation balls and church bazaars. To confirm their social preeminence, they lived extravagantly and entertained graciously. James Henry Hammond built a Greek Revival mansion with a center hall 53 feet by 20 feet, its floor embellished with stylish Belgian tiles and expensive Brussels carpets. "Once a year, like a great feudal landlord," a guest recounted, Hammond "gave a fete or grand dinner to all the country people."

As the nineteenth century progressed, rice planters remained at the apex of the plantation aristocracy. In 1860, the fifteen proprietors of the vast plantations in All Saints Parish in the Georgetown District of South Carolina owned 4,383 slaves, who annually grew and processed 14 million pounds of rice. As cheaper rice from Asia entered the world market and cut the profit margins of Carolina planters, they sold some slaves and worked the others harder — two strategies that allowed them to sustain their luxurious lifestyle. The "hospitality and elegance" of Charleston and Savannah greatly impressed savvy English traveler John Silk Buckingham. Buckingham likewise found "polished" families among long-established French Catholic planters in New Orleans and along the Mississippi River. There, "the sugar and cotton planters live in splendid edifices, and enjoy all the luxury that wealth can impart" (see Voices from Abroad, "Bernhard, Duke of Saxe-Weimar-Eisenach: The Racial Complexities of Southern Society," p. 372).

In tobacco-growing regions, the lives of the planter aristocracy followed a different course, in part because of the widespread diffusion of slave ownership. In the 1770s, about 60 percent of white families in the Chesapeake region owned at least one African American slave. The subsequent westward migration of thousands of wealthy planters and their slaves created a tobacco-growing economy in which families that owned between five and twenty slaves played an increasingly important role. The descendants of the old planter aristocracy remained influential in the Chesapeake, but increasingly as slave-owning grain farmers, lawyers,

A Louisiana Plantation, 1861

This view of a southern Louisiana plantation by Marie Adrien Persac, a French-born artist, presents an exquisitely detailed but romanticized vision of the planter lifestyle. Well-dressed slaves stand amid neatly spaced rows of cotton as the women of the household prance by on well-groomed horses. Off to the right, smoke rises from the chimneys of a small mill, probably used to process the sugarcane grown elsewhere on the plantation. Louisiana State University Museum of Art.

merchants, industrialists, and politicians. Those slaves they didn't need for their own businesses, they hired out, sold, or allowed to purchase their freedom.

Although this genteel planter aristocracy flourished primarily around the periphery of the South — in Virginia, South Carolina, and Louisiana, its members took the lead in defending slavery as a benevolent social system. Ignoring the old Jeffersonian defense of slavery as a "necessary evil" (see Chapter 8), southern apologists now maintained that slavery was a "positive good" that allowed a civilized lifestyle for whites and provided tutelage for genetically inferior Africans. "As a race, the African is inferior to the white man," declared Alexander Stephens, the future vice president of the

Confederacy. "Subordination to the white man, is his normal condition." Stephens and other apologists depicted planters and their wives as aristocratic models of "disinterested benevolence," who provided food and housing for their workers and cared for them in old age. Declared one wealthy Georgian: "Plantation government should be eminently patriarchal"; the planter, as "the *pater-familias*, or head of the family, should, in one sense, be the father of the whole concern, negroes and all."

Taking this ideology to heart, many planters intervened increasingly in the lives of their slaves. Some built cabins for their workers and insisted they be whitewashed regularly. Many others supervised the religious activities of their laborers. They welcomed evangelical preachers, built churches on

Bernhard, Duke of Saxe-Weimar-Eisenach

The Racial Complexities of Southern Society

In 1825 and 1826, Bernhard, Duke of the German principality of Saxe-Weimar-Eisenach, traveled throughout the United States; and in 1828, he published an account of his adventures. Subsequently, Bernhard compiled a distinguished military record in the service of the king of the Netherlands and then ruled his principality from 1853 until his death in 1862. In this selection from his Travels, *Bernhard notes the migration to the cotton belt and describes the racial intricacies of New Orleans society.*

[On our way to New Orleans] we met several parties of emigrants from the eastern sections of Georgia on their way to Butler County in Alabama. They proposed to settle on lands that they had acquired very cheaply from the federal government. The number of their Negroes, horses, wagons, and cattle showed that these wanderers were well off.

In New Orleans we were invited to a subscription ball. These affairs are held twice a week, on Tuesdays and Fridays, in the same hall, the French theater. Only good society is invited to these balls. The first to which we came was not very well attended; but most of the ladies were very nice looking and well turned out in the French manner. Their clothing was elegant after the latest Paris fashions. They danced very well and did credit to their French dancing masters. Dancing and some music are the main branches of the education of a Creole woman. . . .

The native men are far from matching the women in elegance. And they stayed only a short time, preferring to escape to a so-called "Quarterons Ball" which they find more amusing and where they do not have to stand on ceremony. There were, as a result, soon many more women than men.

A "quarteron" (octoroon) is the offspring of a mestizo mother and a white father, just as the mestizo is the child of a mulatto and a white man. The "quarterons" are almost completely white. There would be no way of recognizing them by their complexion, for they are often fairer than the Creoles. Black hair and eyes are generally the signs of their status, although some are quite blond. The ball is attended by the free "quarterons." Yet the deepest prejudice reigns against them on account of their colored origin; the white women particularly feel or affect to feel a strong repugnance to them.

Marriage between colored and white people is forbidden by the laws of the state. Yet the "quarterons," for their part, look upon the Negroes and mulattoes as inferiors and are unwilling to mix with them. The girls therefore have no other recourse than to become the mistresses of white men. The "quarterons" regard such attachment as the equivalent of marriage. They would not think of entering upon it other than with a formal contract in which the man engages to pay a stipulated sum to the mother or father of the girl. The latter even assumes the name of her lover and regards the affair with more faithfulness than many a woman whose marriage was sealed in a church.

Some of these women have inherited from their fathers and lovers, and possess considerable fortunes. Their status is nevertheless always very depressed. They must not ride in the street in coaches, and their lovers can bring them to the balls in their own conveyances only after nightfall. They must never sit opposite a white lady, nor may they enter a room without express permission. . . . But many of these girls are much more carefully educated than the whites, behave with more polish and more politeness, and make their lovers happier than white wives their husbands. And yet the white ladies speak of these unfortunate depressed creatures with great disdain, even bitterness. Because of the depth of these prejudices, many fathers send their daughters, conceived after this manner, to France where good education and wealth are no impediments to the attainment of a respectable place.

SOURCE: C. J. Jeronimus, ed., *Travels by His Highness Duke Bernhard of Saxe-Weimar-Eisenach Through North America in the Years 1825 and 1826,* trans. William Jeronimus (Lanham, Md.: University Press of America, 2001), 296–297, 343, 346–347.

ANALYZING THE EVIDENCE

➤ What does this passage suggest about the effect of racial slavery on white marriages?

➤ Why were France and French fashions so important in the lives of the white and "quarteron" population of New Orleans?

➤ How does Bernhard's account help explain the values and outlook of the free black population in the Slave South?

their plantations, and often required their slaves to attend services. A few encouraged African Americans with spiritual "gifts" to serve as exhorters and deacons. The motives of the planters were mixed. Some acted from sincere Christian belief, while others wanted to counter abolitionist criticism or to use religious teachings to control their workers.

Southern apologists also sought religious justification for human bondage. Protestant ministers pointed out that the Hebrews, God's chosen people, had owned slaves and that Jesus Christ had never condemned slavery. As Hammond told a British abolitionist in 1845: "What God ordains and Christ sanctifies should surely command the respect and toleration of man." Many apologists and wealthy planters lived in towns or were absentee landlords, and rarely glimpsed the day-to-day brutality of the slave regime. "I was at the plantation last Saturday and the crop was in fine order," an absentee's son wrote to his father, "but the negroes are most brutally scarred & several have run off."

Slave-owning Entrepreneurs. There was much less hypocrisy and far less elegance among the entrepreneurial slave owners of the Cotton South. "The glare of expensive luxury vanishes" in the black soil regions of Alabama and Mississippi, John Silk Buckingham noted as his travels took him to inland areas, and so, too, did aristocratic paternalism. A Mississippi planter put it plainly: "Everything has to give way to large crops of cotton, land has to be cultivated wet or dry, negroes [must] work, hot or cold." Angry at being separated from their kinfolk and pressed to hard labor, many slaves grew "mean" and stubborn. Those who would not labor were subject to the lash. "Whiped all the hoe hands," Alabama planter James Torbert wrote matter-of-factly in his journal. Overseers pushed their workers equally hard because their salaries usually depended on the quantity of cotton they were able "to make for the market." "When I wuz so tired I cu'dnt hardly stan'," a Mississippi slave recalled, "I had to spin my cut of cotton befor' I cu'd go to sleep. We had to card, spin, an' reel at nite."

Cotton was a demanding crop because of its long growing season. Slaves plowed the land in March, dropped seeds into the ground in early April, and, once the plants began to grow, continually chopped away the surrounding grasses. In between these tasks, they planted the corn and peas that would provide food for them and the plantation's hogs and chickens. When the cotton bolls ripened in late August, the long four-month picking season began. Slaves in the Cotton South, concluded traveler Frederick Law Olmsted, worked

The Inherent Brutality of Slavery
Like all systems of forced labor, American racial slavery relied on physical coercion. Slave owners and overseers routinely whipped slaves who worked slowly or defied their orders. On occasion, they applied the whip with such ferocity that the slave died or was permanently injured. This photograph of a slave named Gordon stands as graphic testimony to the inherent brutality of the system. National Archives.

"much harder and more unremittingly" than those in other regions. Moreover, their labor demanded fewer skills: No coopers were needed to make casks for tobacco or sugar; no engineers to build the irrigation systems for the rice fields.

To increase the output of their enslaved workers, profit-conscious cotton planters began during the 1820s to use a rigorous **gang-labor system.** Previously, many planters had either supervised their workers sporadically, or assigned them random jobs and let them work at their own pace. Now masters with twenty or more slaves organized disciplined teams, or "gangs," supervised by black drivers and white overseers. They instructed drivers and overseers to use the lash to work the gangs at a steady pace, clearing and plowing land or hoeing and picking cotton. A traveler in Mississippi described two gangs returning from work:

> First came, led by an old driver carrying a whip, forty of the largest and strongest women I ever saw together; they were all in a simple uniform dress of a bluish check stuff, the skirts reaching little below the knee; . . . they carried themselves loftily, each having a hoe over the shoulder, and walking with a free, powerful swing.

Next marched the plow hands with their mules, "the cavalry, thirty strong, mostly men, but a few of them women." Finally, "a lean and vigilant white overseer, on a brisk pony, brought up the rear."

The cotton planters' quest for profits and their use of gang labor to expand cotton production had mixed results. Cotton monoculture and the failure to rotate crops quickly depleted the nutrients in the soil and gradually reduced the output per acre. Still, because slaves working in gangs finished as much work in thirty-five minutes as yeomen farmers or enslaved blacks did in an hour when working in the traditional way, the new system produced impressive profits and became ever more prevalent. In one Georgia county, the percentage of slaves working on gang-labor plantations doubled between 1830 and 1850. Their increased productivity brought great wealth to the planter class as the demand for, and the price of, raw cotton surged after 1846. During the 1850s, the number of planters using gang labor increased by 70 percent and their wealth soared. And no wonder: Nearly 2 million enslaved African Americans now labored on the plantations of the Cotton South which annually produced 4 million bales of the valuable fiber.

Planters, Smallholding Yeomen, and Tenants

Despite the fact that the South was a "slave society"—that is, the institution of slavery affected all aspects of life there—most white southerners did not own slaves. The absolute number of slave owners increased constantly between 1800 and 1860; however, the white population of the South rose even faster. Consequently, the percentage of white families who held blacks in bondage continually went down—from 36 percent in 1830, to 31 percent in 1850, to about 25 percent a decade later. There were significant variations among the regions in most states. In some cotton-rich counties, 40 percent or more of the white families owned slaves; in the hill country near the Appalachian Mountains, the proportion dropped to 10 percent.

Among the privileged minority of 395,000 families who owned slaves in 1860, there was a strict hierarchy. The top one-fifth of these families—a planter elite that constituted just 5 percent of the South's white population—owned twenty or more slaves; together, they owned over 50 percent of the entire slave population of 4 million, and their plantations grew 50 percent of the South's cotton crop. These planters had an average wealth of $56,000; by contrast, the average southern yeoman or northern farmer owned property worth $3,200.

A group of substantial proprietors, another fifth of the slave-owning population, held title to six to twenty bondsmen and -women. These "middle-class" planters played a substantial role in the slave society: They owned almost 40 percent of the slave population and produced more than 30 percent of the cotton. Many of these planters pursued dual careers as skilled artisans or professional men. Thus, many of the fifteen slaves owned by Samuel L. Moore worked in his brick factory; the others labored on his Georgia farm. In Macon County, Alabama, James Tolbert owned a plantation that yielded 50 bales of cotton a year; but Tolbert also ran a sawmill, "which pays as well as making Cotton." Dr. Thomas Gale used the income from his medical practice to buy a Mississippi plantation that annually produced 150 bales of cotton. In Alabama, a young lawyer named Benjamin Fitzpatrick invested the profits from his law office to buy ten slaves.

Many other lawyers joined Fitzpatrick as slave-owning planters, and some became influential politicians. Scattered widely among the small towns of the Cotton South, lawyers became wealthy by handling the legal affairs of elite planters, representing merchants and storekeepers in suits for debt, and settling disputes over property. They also became well known by helping smallholders and tenants register their deeds and contracts. Standing at the legal crossroads of their small towns and personally known by many of the residents, lawyers regularly won election to public office. Less than 1 percent of the male population, lawyers made up 16 percent of the Alabama legislature in 1828 and an astounding 26 percent in 1849.

Less visible than the wealthy grandees and the prominent middle-class lawyer-planters were the smallholders who made up the majority of slave owners. Because they worked the land themselves, they were similar in many respects to the yeomen in the North. These slave owners held from one to five black laborers in bondage and claimed title to a few hundred acres of land. Some smallholders were well-connected young men, who would rise to wealth when the death of a father or another benefactor blessed them with more land and slaves. Others were poor men trying to pull themselves up by their bootstraps, often with the encouragement of elite planters and proslavery advocates. "Ours is a pro-slavery form of Government, and the pro-slavery element should be increased," declared a Georgia newspaper. "We would like to see every white man at the South the owner of a family of negroes."

Taking this advice to heart, ambitious men saved or borrowed enough to acquire more land and more laborers. Many achieved modest prosperity. One German settler in Alabama reported in 1855 that "nearly all his countrymen" who emigrated with him were now slaveholders. "They were poor on their arrival in the country; but no sooner did they realize a little money than they invested it in slaves" and grew rich from their labors.

Influenced by the patriarchal ideology of the planter class, these yeomen farmers ruled their smallholdings with a firm hand. According to a South Carolina judge, the male head of the household had authority over all the dependents — wives, children, and slaves — and the legal right on his property "to be as churlish as he pleases." The wives of southern yeomen had very little power. Like women in the North, they lost their legal identity when they married and had many fewer legal rights than male citizens did. Looking for ways to express their concerns and interests, southern women turned to religion in huge numbers, and regularly outnumbered male church members by a margin of two to one. Many welcomed the message of spiritual equality preached in evangelical Baptist and Methodist churches; they hoped that the church communities would hold their husbands to the same standards of Christian faith and action to which they themselves were held. Still, most churches supported patriarchal rule and encouraged their female members to continue in "wifely obedience," whatever the behavior of their husbands. Thus, the Gum Branch Baptist Church refused to aid a member who "wished to attend church but . . . was prevented . . . by her husband."

Whatever the extent of their authority within the household, most yeomen lived and died hardscrabble farmers. They worked alongside their slaves in the fields, struggled to make ends meet as their families grew, and moved regularly in search of opportunity. Thus, in 1847, James Buckner Barry left North Carolina with his new wife and two slaves to settle in Bosque County, Texas. There he worked part-time as an Indian fighter while his slaves toiled on his drought-ridden farm and barely kept the family in food. In South Carolina, W. J. Simpson struggled for years planting cotton on his small farm before he gave up. He hired out one of his two slaves and went to work as an overseer on his father's farm.

Other smallholders fell from the privileged ranks of the slave-owning classes. Selling their land and slaves to pay off debts, they joined the large group of propertyless tenants who farmed the estates of wealthy landlords. In 1860, in Hancock County, Georgia, there were fifty-six slave-owning planters and three hundred propertyless white farm laborers and factory workers; in Hart County, 25 percent of the white farmers were tenants. Across the South, about 40 percent of the white population worked as tenants or farm laborers; as the *Southern Cultivator* noted, they had "no legal right nor interest in the soil [and] no homes of their own."

Propertyless whites enjoyed few of the benefits of slavery and suffered many of its ill consequences. Because hard labor was deemed fit only for enslaved blacks, white workers received little respect. Nor could they hope for a better life for their children because planters refused to pay taxes to fund public schools. Moreover, wealthy slave owners bid up the price of slaves, depriving white laborers and tenants of easy access to the slave labor required to accumulate wealth. Finally, planter-dominated legislatures forced all white men — whether they owned slaves or not — to serve in the patrols and militias that deterred black uprisings. For their sacrifices, poor whites gained only the psychological satisfaction that they ranked above blacks. In the words of Alfred Iverson, a U.S. senator from Georgia, a white man "walks erect in the dignity of his color and race, and feels that he is a superior being, with the more exalted powers and privileges than others." Hoping to reinforce this sense of racial and social superiority, planter James Henry Hammond told his poor white neighbors, "In a slave country every freeman is an aristocrat."

Rejecting that half-truth, many southern whites fled planter-dominated counties and sought farms in the Appalachian hill country and beyond — in western Virginia, Kentucky, Tennessee, Missouri, and the southern regions of Illinois and Indiana. There they took up lives as yeomen farmers, using family labor to grow foodstuffs for sustenance. To obtain cash or store credit to buy agricultural implements, cloth, shoes, salt, and other necessities, yeomen families sold their surplus crops, raised hogs for market sale, and — when the price of cotton rose sharply in the 1850s — a few bales of cotton. Their goals were modest: On the family level, they wanted to preserve their holdings and secure enough new land to set up all of

Starting Out in Texas

Thousands of white farmers, some owning a few slaves, moved onto small farms in Texas and Arkansas during the 1840s and 1850s. They lived in crudely built log huts; owned a few cows, horses, and oxen; and eked out a meager living by growing a few acres of cotton in addition to their corn crops. Their aspirations were simple: to achieve modest prosperity during their lives and to leave their property to their children. Daughters of the Republic of Texas Library.

their children as small-scale farmers. As citizens, these smallholders wanted to control local governments by electing men of their own kind to public office. Thoughtful yeomen knew, and others sensed, that the cotton revolution of the nineteenth century had undercut the democratic potential of the Revolutionary era and sentenced independent family farmers of the South to a subordinate place in the social and political order. They could hope for a life of independence and dignity only by moving north or farther west, where labor was "free" and hard work was considered respectable.

The Politics of Democracy

Despite their economic and social prominence, the slave-owning elite did not dominate the political life of the Cotton South. Unlike the planter-aristocrats of the eighteenth century, they lived in a republican society with democratic institutions. The Alabama Constitution of 1819 granted suffrage to all white men; it also provided for a **secret ballot**, apportionment based on population, and the election of county supervisors, sheriffs, and clerks of court. Given this democratic ethos, political factions in Alabama had to compete with one another for popular favor. When a Whig newspaper sarcastically asked whether the state's policies should "be governed and controlled by the whim and caprice of the majority of the people," Democrats immediately stood forth as champions of the common folk. They called on "Farmers, Mechanics, laboring men" to repudiate Whig "aristocrats . . . the soft handed and soft headed gentry."

Cultivating Popular Support. To curry favor among voters, Alabama Democrats nominated candidates and endorsed low taxes and other policies that would command popular support. The Whigs, their opponents in the Second Party System, continued to advocate government support for banks, canals, roads, and other internal improvements; but they also turned to candidates who appealed to the common people. Most candidates from both parties were men of wealth and high status. In the early 1840s, nearly 90 percent of Alabama's legislators owned slaves, testimony to the power of the slave-owning minority. Still, relatively few lawmakers — only about 10 percent — were rich planters, a group voters by and large distrusted. "A rich man cannot sympathize with the poor," declared one candidate. Consequently, the majority of elected state officials, like most county officials in the Cotton South, came from the ranks of middle-class planters and planter-lawyers.

Whatever their social rank, Alabama's legislators usually enacted policies that reflected the interests of the slave-owning population. Still, they were careful not to alienate the mass of yeomen farmers and propertyless whites by proposing too many of the expensive public works projects favored by the Whig Party. "Voting against appropriations is the safe and popular side," one senator declared, and his colleagues agreed; until the 1850s, they rejected most of the bills that would have granted subsidies to railroads, canals, and banks. They also took care not to lay "oppressive" taxes on the people, particularly the poor white majority, those who owned no slaves. Between 1830 and 1860, the Alabama legislature extracted about 70 percent of the state's revenue from taxes on slaves and on land. Another 10 to 15 percent came from levies on carriages, gold watches, and other luxury goods, and on the capital invested in banks, transportation companies, and manufacturing enterprises.

Taxes in Alabama had a democratic thrust and placed the burden on those best able to pay; but the policies pursued by other southern states divided the white population along lines of class and geography. In some states, wealthy planters used their political influence to exempt slave property from taxation. They shifted the tax burden to backcountry yeomen farmers by taxing land on the basis of acreage rather than value. Planter-legislators also spared themselves the cost of building fences around their fields by enacting laws that forced yeomen to fence in their livestock. Moreover, by the 1850s, wealthy legislators throughout the South began to encourage economic development by subsidizing canals and railroads and increasing allocations for public education.

Seen from one perspective, these measures were desperately needed. Even as the top 10 percent of the white population grew rich from the cotton, rice, tobacco, and sugar produced by their slaves, the economic well-being of ordinary southerners — white and black — did not improve significantly. In fact, the South's standard of living fell behind that of the North. Both in 1840 and in 1860, the per capita wealth of the South was only 80 percent of the national average, while that in the industrializing Northeast was 139 percent of the average.

Yet this comparison with the Northeast is a bit misleading. If the South had been a separate nation, its economy would have been the fourth most prosperous in the world, with a per capita income higher than that of France and Germany. It ranked second in the world in the construction of railroads, sixth in cotton textiles, and eighth in the smelting of pig iron. As a contributor to a Georgia newspaper argued in the 1850s, it was beside the point to protest "tariffs, and merchants, and manufacturers" because "the most highly prosperous people now on earth, are to be found in these very [slave] States."

The paradox of the southern economy is that he was both right and wrong. Many white southerners lived better than other peoples of the world did, but most African Americans — 30 percent of the population — did not. Perceptive southerners recognized that their farm-based economy failed to raise the living standards of the entire population. Pointing to South Carolina's fixation on an "exclusive and exhausting" system of agriculture, textile entrepreneur William Gregg asked, "Who can look forward to the future destiny of our State . . . without dark forebodings?" Other leaders acknowledged the South's predicament but blamed it on outsiders: "Purely agricultural people," intoned planter-politician James Henry Hammond, "have been in all ages the victims of rapacious tyrants grinding them down."

Attempts at Economic Diversification. Thinking like Hammond's discouraged purposeful private or government action to create a more diversified economy; so did the booming market in cotton. Wealthy southerners continued to invest in land and slaves, a strategy that brought substantial short-run profits but diverted capital resources and entrepreneurial energies from more-productive forms of economic activity. In particular, southerners failed to take advantage of the many opportunities created during the early nineteenth century by a series of technological innovations — water- and steam-powered factories, machine tools, steel plows, and macadamized roads, for example—that would have raised the region's productivity. Urban growth took place mostly in the commercial cities around the periphery of the South: New Orleans, St. Louis, and Baltimore. Factories—often staffed by slave labor—likewise appeared primarily in the Chesapeake, which had already diversified its economy and had a surplus of bound workers. Within the Cotton South, a few wealthy planters invested in railroads but only to open up new lands for commercial farming; when the Western & Atlantic Railroad reached the Georgia upcountry, the cotton crop quickly doubled. Cotton—and agriculture—remained "King."

Slavery worked in yet another way to deter industrialization. Fearing competition from slave labor, poor European immigrants refused to settle in the South, depriving the region of the laborers needed to drain swamps, dig canals, smelt iron, and work on railroads. Nor were there enough enslaved African Americans to undertake these tasks because slave owners often refused to rent their slaves to entrepreneurs. The work was dangerous, they said, and "a negro's life is too valuable to be risked at it." Other slave owners feared the work would make their slaves too independent. As one of them explained to Frederick Law Olmsted, rented-out workers "had too much liberty . . . and got a habit of roaming about and taking care of themselves."

Thus, despite the South's expansion in territory and exports, in 1860, it remained an economic colony of Great Britain and the North, which bought its staple crops and provided its manufactures, financial services, and shipping facilities. Most southerners—some 84 percent—still worked in agriculture, more than double the percentage in the northern states; and southern factories turned out only 10 percent of the nation's manufactured goods. Textile entrepreneur William Gregg lamented that the combination of cotton and slave labor had been to the South

> what the mines of Mexico were to Spain. It has produced us such an abundant supply of all the luxuries and elegances of life, with so little exertion on our part, that we have become enervated, unfitted for other and more laborious pursuits.

➤ How would you explain the large and expanding domestic trade in slaves between 1800 and 1860? What combination of factors produced this result?

➤ By 1860, what different groups made up the South's increasingly complex society? How did these groups interact in the political arena?

➤ Why in 1860 did the South remain committed to the institution of slavery and its expansion?

The African American World

By the 1820s, the cultural life of most slaves was a complex blend of African and American influences. It was shaped in part by the values and customs of their West African ancestors and in part by the language, laws, and religious beliefs of the dominant white society. Because blacks were denied access to the way of life in that society, they relied heavily on forms of cultural expression that reflected their African heritage and their condition as an enslaved people.

Evangelical Black Protestantism

The emergence of a black form of evangelical Christianity exemplified the synthesis of African and American cultures. Evangelical Protestantism came to the South in the late eighteenth century with the Second Great Awakening and the conversion by Baptist and Methodist preachers of thousands of white families and hundreds of enslaved blacks (see Chapter 8). Until that time, African-born blacks, often identifiable by their ritual scars, had maintained the religious practices of their homelands: Some practiced Islam, and the majority gave homage to African gods and spirits. As late as 1842, Charles C. Jones, a Presbyterian minister, noted that many of the blacks on his family's plantation in Georgia believed "in second-sight, in apparitions, charms, witchcraft . . . [and other] superstitions brought from Africa." Fearing "the consequences" for their own souls if they withheld "the means of salvation from them," Jones and other zealous white Protestant preachers and planters set out to save African American souls for Christ.

Other Protestant crusaders came from the ranks of pious black men and women. Converted in the Chesapeake and then swept off to the Cotton South by the domestic slave trade, they carried the evangelical message of emotional conversion, ritual baptism, and communal spirituality with them. Equally important, they adapted Protestant doctrines to black needs. Enslaved Christians pointed out that masters and slaves were all "children of God" and should be dealt with according to the Golden Rule—treat others as you would be treated by them. Moreover, black preachers generally ignored the doctrines of original sin and predestination as well as biblical passages that encouraged unthinking obedience to authority. A white minister in Liberty County, Georgia, reported that when he urged slaves to obey their masters, "one half of my audience deliberately rose up and walked off" (see Reading American Pictures, "How Did Slaves Live on Cotton Plantations?" p. 381).

Indeed, many African American converts saw themselves as "de people dat is born of God" and envisioned the deity as the Old Testament warrior who had liberated the Jews. Charles Davenport, a Mississippi slave, recalled black preachers' "exhort[ing] us dat us was the chillum o' Israel in de wilderness an' de Lawd done sont us to take dis lan' o' milk an' honey." And it was a vision of Christ

that impelled Nat Turner to lead a bloody rebellion against slavery in Virginia (see Chapter 11).

Although they now worshipped a European Christian god, slaves expressed their religiosity in distinctively African ways. The thousands of African Americans who joined the Methodist Church respected its ban on secular dancing but praised the Lord in the African-derived "ring shout." Minister Henry George Spaulding explained the "religious dance of the Negroes" this way:

> Three or four, standing still, clapping their hands and beating time with their feet, commence singing in unison one of the peculiar shout melodies, while the others walk around in a ring, in single file, joining also in the song.

Plantation Burial, **1860**

This painting by John Antrobus, who came to America from England in 1850, records the religious service following the death of an enslaved African American. A black preacher intones a prayer as the coffin is lowered into the ground. The burial comes at twilight, when the day's work is done, and friends and kin from neighboring plantations can attend. The Historic New Orleans Collection.

The songs themselves were usually collective creations, devised impromptu from bits of old hymns and tunes. Recalled an ex-slave:

> We'd all be at the "prayer house" de Lord's day, and de white preacher he'd splain de word and read whar Esekial done say — *Dry bones gwine ter lib ergin.* And, honey, de Lord would come a-shinin' thoo dem pages and revive dis ole nigger's heart, and I'd jump up dar and den and holler and shout and sing and pat, and dey would all cotch de words and I'd sing it to some ole shout song I'd heard 'em sing from Africa, and dey'd all take it up and keep at it, and keep a-addin' to it, and den it would be a spiritual.

By African-influenced means, black congregations devised a distinctive and joyous brand of Protestant worship to sustain them on the long journey to emancipation and the Promised Land. "O my Lord delivered Daniel," the slaves sang, "O why not deliver me too?"

Slave Society and Culture

Black Protestantism represented one facet of an increasingly homogeneous African American culture in the rural South. Even in South Carolina — a major point of entry for recently imported slaves — only 20 percent of the black residents in 1820 had been born in Africa. The rapid transfer of slaves from other regions into the Lower Mississippi Valley significantly reduced cultural differences. A prime example was the fate of the Gullah dialect (see Chapter 3). Long spoken by residents of the Carolina low country, Gullah did not take root on the cotton plantations of Alabama and Mississippi, where there were many more speakers of the black English spoken in the Chesapeake region. Black English, like Gullah, used double-negatives and other African grammatical forms but consisted primarily of English words rendered in an African manner (for example, with "th" spoken as "d" — "de preacher").

Although the black population was becoming more homogeneous, African cultural influences remained important. At least one-third of the slaves who entered the United States between 1776 and 1809 came from the Congo region of West-Central Africa, and they brought their culture with them. One traveler, Isaac Holmes, reported in 1821: "In Louisiana, and the state of Mississippi, the slaves . . . dance for several hours during Sunday afternoon. The general movement is in what they call the Congo dance." Similar descriptions of blacks who "danced the Congo and sang a purely African song to the accompaniment of . . . a drum" appeared as late as 1890.

Marriage and Kinship Relations. African Americans also continued to respect African incest taboos by shunning marriages between cousins. On the Good Hope Plantation on the Santee River in South Carolina, nearly half of the slave children born between 1800 and 1857 were related by blood to one another, yet only one marriage (out of forty-one) took place between cousins. This taboo was not learned from their white owners: Among the 440 South Carolina men and women who owned at least one hundred slaves in 1860, cousin marriages were frequent, in part because they kept wealth and political power within the extended family.

Unlike the marriages of whites, slave unions were not recognized by the law. Southern legislatures and courts prohibited legal marriages among slaves so that they could be sold without breaking a legal bond. Still, many young African Americans did have their marriage blessed by a Christian minister. Others marked their married state by following the African custom of jumping over a broomstick together in a public ceremony (see Reading American Pictures, "Jumping the Broomstick: Viewing an African Ceremony in South Carolina," p. 88). Once married, young couples in the Cotton South whose parents had remained behind in the Chesapeake often adopted elderly slaves in their new communities as their "aunts" and "uncles." The slave trade had destroyed their family but not their family values.

The creation of fictive kinship networks was part of a complex community-building process. Naming children was another. Recently imported slaves frequently gave their children African names. Males born on Friday, for example, were often called Cuffee — the name of that day in several West African languages. Many American-born parents chose names of British origin, but they usually named sons after fathers, uncles, or grandfathers, and daughters after grandmothers. Those transported to the Cotton South often named their children for relatives left behind. Like incest rules and marriage rituals, this intergenerational sharing of names solidified memories of a lost world and kinship ties in the present one.

By forming stable families and strong communities, African Americans gradually created a sense of order in the harsh and arbitrary world of slavery. Slaves in a few regions won substantial control over their lives. Blacks in the rice-growing lowlands of

How Did Slaves Live on Cotton Plantations?

What was it like to live as a slave on a large cotton plantation? Historians can consult a mass of evidence to answer this question: the testimonials of escaped slaves, the recollections of former slaves, masters diaries, travelers' accounts, and contemporary engravings and photographs. These two images tell a very small part of the story, and, like all historical sources, have to be carefully examined for bias and reliability.

ANALYZING THE EVIDENCE

➤ Who is harvesting the cotton in the photograph? Slaves of all ages, male and female, worked at picking cotton. Although the work was physically demanding, children had an advantage. Why? Notice the posture of the adult pickers. What were the physical effects of working like this all day?

➤ How would you describe the religious service pictured in the engraving *Family Worship in a Plantation in South Carolina*? How is the audience reacting to the minister's message? Is it significant that the minister is black? How do we know that he is literate?

➤ Whites are present in both images: an overseer in the photograph, and the master and mistress of the plantation and their children in the engraving. What is the effect of their presence on the African American workers and worshippers? What is the posture of the white onlookers? Is it significant? Why or why not?

Picking Cotton. National Archives.

Family Worship at a Plantation in South Carolina. *The Illustrated London News*/Picture Research Consultants & Archives.

➤ Would either of these images have been useful to abolitionists to support their demands for immediate emancipation? Would either image have furthered the cause of authors who extolled slavery? Imagine you are an advocate first of abolition and then of slavery. How would you fashion an argument using these pictures as evidence?

Antebellum Slave Quarters

During the colonial period, owners often housed their slaves in communal barracks by gender. In the nineteenth century, slaves usually lived in family units in separate cabins. The slave huts on this South Carolina plantation were sturdily built but had few windows. Inside, they were sparsely furnished. William Gladstone.

South Carolina successfully asserted the right to labor by the "task" rather than to work under constant supervision. Each day, task workers had to complete a precisely defined job — for example, turn over a quarter-acre of land, hoe half an acre, or pound seven mortars of rice. By working hard, many finished their tasks "by one or two o'clock in the afternoon," a Methodist preacher reported, and had "the rest of the day for themselves, which they spend in working their own private fields . . . planting rice, corn, potatoes, tobacco &c. for their own use and profit." Slaves on sugar and cotton plantations were less fortunate. The gang-labor system imposed a regimented work schedule, and many owners prohibited slaves from growing crops on their own. "It gives an excuse for trading," explained one slave owner, and that encouraged roaming.

Resistance. Planters worried constantly that enslaved African Americans — a majority of the population in the counties of the Cotton South — would rise in rebellion. They knew that in law, masters had virtually unlimited power over their slaves. Justice Thomas Ruffin of the North Carolina Supreme Court wrote in a decision in 1829: "The power of the master must be absolute to render the submission of the slave perfect." But absolute power required unremitting and brutal coercion, and only the most hardened or most sadistic master had the stomach for that, especially as slave prices rose.

Moreover, African American resistance seriously limited masters' power. Slaves slowed the pace of work by feigning illness and losing or breaking tools. Some blacks insisted that people be sold "in families." One Maryland slave, faced with transport to Mississippi and separation from his wife, "neither yields consent to accompany my people, or to be exchanged or sold," his owner reported. Because of the bonds of community among African Americans in the Chesapeake and Carolinas and the increasing black majorities in the Gulf states — masters ignored slaves' resistance at their peril. A slave (or his relatives) might retaliate by setting fire to the master's house and barns, poisoning his food, or destroying crops or equipment. Fear of resistance, as well as the increasingly critical scrutiny of abolitionists, prompted many masters to reduce their reliance on the lash. Instead, they tried to devise "a wholesome and well regulated system" of work discipline and to use positive incentives like food and special privileges to manage their laborers. Noted Frederick Law Olmsted: "Men of sense have discovered that it was better to offer them rewards than to whip them." Nonetheless, owners always had the option of resorting to

CLASS No. 1.

Comprises those prisoners who were found guilty and executed.

Prisoners Names.	Owners' Names.	Time of Commit.	How Disposed of.
Peter	James Poyas	June 18	
Ned	Gov. T. Bennett,	do.	Hanged on Tuesday
Rolla	do.	do	the 2d July, 1822,
Batteau	do.	do.	on Blake's lands,
Denmark Vesey	A free black man	22	near Charleston.
Jessy	Thos. Blackwood	23	
John	Elias Horry	July 5	Do on the Lines near
Gullah Jack	Paul Pritchard	do.	Ch.; Friday July 12.
Mingo	Wm. Harth	June 21	
Lot	Forrester	27	
Joe	P. L. Jore	July 6	
Julius	Thos. Forrest	8	
Tom	Mrs. Russell	10	
Smart	Robt. Anderson	do.	
John	John Robertson	11	
Robert	do.	do.	
Adam	do.	do.	
Polydore	Mrs. Faber	do.	Hanged on the Lines
Bacchus	Benj. Hammet	do.	near Charleston,
Dick	Wm. Sims	13	on Friday, 26th
Pharaoh	— Thompson	do.	July.
Jemmy	Mrs. Clement	18	
Mauidore	Mordecai Cohen	19	
Dean	— Mitchell	do.	
Jack	Mrs. Purcell	12	
Bellisle	Est. of Jos. Yates	18	
Naphur	do.	do.	
Adam	do.	do.	
Jacob	John S. Glen	16	
Charles	John Billings	18	
Jack	N. McNeill	22	
Cæsar	Miss Smith	do.	
Jacob Stagg	Jacob Lankester	23	Do. Tues. July 30.
Tom	Wm. M. Scott	24	
William	Mrs. Garner	Aug. 2	Do. Friday, Aug. 9.

"An Account of the Late Intended Insurrection, Charleston, South Carolina"

Charleston had a free black population of 1,500, which boasted an array of institutions, including a Brown Fellowship Society (for those of mixed racial ancestry) and an African Methodist Episcopal (AME) church. In 1822, Charleston authorities accused one of those free African Americans, Denmark Vesey, of organizing a rebellion to free the city's slaves, and historians have long accepted the validity of that charge. However, recent studies suggest that Vesey's only offense was antagonizing some whites by claiming his rights as a free man, and that the alleged insurrection was a figment of the imagination of fearful slave owners. In any event, South Carolina officials hanged Vesey and thirty-four alleged co-conspirators and tore down the AME church where they were said to have plotted the uprising. Rare Book, Manuscript & Special Collections, Duke University Library.

violence, and many masters continued to satisfy themselves sexually by raping their female slaves.

Slavery, then, remained an exploitative system grounded in fear and coercion. Over the decades, hundreds of individual slaves responded to this violence by attacking their masters and overseers. Blacks like Gabriel and Martin Prosser in Virginia (1800) plotted mass uprisings, but only a few — among them, Nat Turner (1831), — mounted revolts that took revenge on their white captors. Most slaves recognized that uprisings would be futile. In most states they were outnumbered by whites, and everywhere they lacked the strong institutions — the communes of free peasants or serfs in Europe, for example — needed to organize a successful rebellion. Moreover, whites were well armed, unified, and determined to maintain their position of racial superiority (see Comparing American Voices, "Slaves and Masters," pp. 384–385).

Escape was equally problematic. Blacks in the Upper South could flee to the North, but only by leaving their family and kin. Slaves in the Lower South could seek freedom in Spanish Florida until 1819, when the United States annexed that territory. Even then, hundreds of blacks continued to flee to Florida, where they intermarried with the Seminole Indians. Elsewhere in the South, small groups of escaped slaves eked out a meager existence in deserted marshy areas or in mountain valleys.

Given these limited options, most slaves built the best possible lives for themselves on the plantations where they lived. In doing so, they developed a positive mode of resistance by demanding and, in many cases, winning a greater share of the product of their labor — much like unionized workers in the North were trying to do. Slaves insisted on getting paid for "overwork" and on the right to cultivate a garden and sell its produce. "De menfolks tend to de gardens round dey own house," recalled a Louisiana slave. "Dey raise some cotton and sell it to massa and git li'l money dat way." They then bought what they wished with the proceeds. An Alabama slave remembered buying "Sunday clothes with dat money, sech as hats and pants and shoes and dresses." By the 1850s, thousands of African Americans were reaping the rewards of this underground economy. But even as their material circumstances improved, few slaves accepted the legitimacy of their fate. Although well fed and never whipped, a former slave explained, "I was cruelly treated because I was kept in slavery."

The Free Black Population

Some African Americans managed to escape slavery through flight or manumission. The proportion of free blacks rose from 8 percent of the African American population in 1790 to about 13 percent between 1820 and 1840, and then fell to 11 percent by 1860. Nearly half of all free blacks in 1840 (some 170,000) and again in 1860 (250,000) lived in the North. Many of those African Americans were refugees from the South, either runaway

Slaves and Masters

Looked at closely, slavery was a multitude of individual relationships between African Americans and their white owners. But it was also a system of chattel property, forced labor, sexual abuse, and racial domination. As you read these selections, two documents excerpted from interviews with former slaves and one diary entry written by a cotton planter, think about how the system of slavery shaped the possibilities open to individuals.

MOLLIE DAWSON
Memories of a Slave Childhood

Mollie Dawson was born into slavery in Texas, where her owner had migrated from Tennessee. At the time Dawson told her story to the Writers' Project of the Work Projects Administration in the 1930s, she was eighty-five years old.

Dat makes me bo'n in january sometime, of 1852. . . . Mah maw was de slave of Nath Newman and dat made me his slave. Mah maw's name was Sarah Benjamin. Mah father's name was Carrol Benjamin, and he belonged ter different white folks. . . .

De plantation dat he worked on was j'inin' our'n. I would go ovah ter see him once in a while when I was little, and de last time I goes ovah dar dey whips a man. . . . Dat was the only slave I ever seed gits a whippin', and I never did wants ter see dis white man anymo'. . . .

Mah mother and father was slavery time married darkies. Dat didn't mean nuthin' dem days, but jest raisin' mo' darkies, and every slave darkie woman had ter do dat whether she wanted to or not. Dey would let her pick out a man, or a man pick him out a woman, and dey was married, and if de woman wouldn't have de man dat picks her, dey would take her ter a big stout high husky nigger somewhere and leave her a few days, jest lak dey do stock now'days, and she bettah begin raisin' chilluns, too. . . .

Mah mother and father never did love each other lak dey ought to, so dey separated as soon as dey was free. Mah father married another woman by law. Mah mother married George Baldwin, and dey lives together fer about twelve years. Dey separated den, and she married Alfred Alliridge and dey lives together till she dies. . . .

I was too young ter do much work durin' slavery time, but I picks lots of cotton, and all de pay we got fer it was a place ter stay, water ter drink, wood ter burn, food ter eat, and clothes ter wear, and we made de food and clothes ourselves. We eats corn pones three times a day, 'ceptin' Sunday and Christmas mornings; Maser Newman lets us have flour fer biscuits, den.

In de summah we wore cotton clothes. All of dem was made on de plantation. Some of de women would spin and some would weave and some would make clothes. . . .

Maser Newman was a tall, slender man nearly six foot tall and was blue-eyed. He sho' was good ter all us slaves, but we all knew he means fer us ter work. He never whipped any of us slaves, but he hit one of de men wid a leather line 'bout two times once, 'cause dis slave kinda talked back ter him. . . .

Maser Newman was a slow easy-goin' sort of a man who took everything as it comes, takin' bad and good luck jest alak. . . . Maser Newman was lots older dan his wife. She was a real young woman, and they 'peared ter think quite a bit of each other. . . . Maser and Missus Newman jest had two chilluns and both of dem was little girls. . . . Dey sho' was pretty little gals and dey was smart, too. Dey played wid de little slave chilluns all de time, and course dey was de boss, same as deir mother and father.

Maser Newman was a poor man, compared wid some of de other slave owners. He only had about seven slaves big enough ter work all de year round in de fields. . . . He didn't have no drivah; he would jest start dem all out ter work, and dey kept at it all day. But he generally worked around pretty close ter dem.

SOURCE: James Mellon, ed., *Bullwhip Days* (New York: Weidenfeld & Nicolson, 1988), 421–428.

LOUISA PICQUET
Sexual Exploitation under Slavery

Louisa Picquet was born into slavery in Georgia in 1827; around 1840, she became the property of a John Williams of New Orleans. On his death in 1848, she was freed and moved to Ohio with her four children. In 1860, she related the story of her life in an interview with Hiram Mattison, a white abolitionist minister, who published it the following year in Boston.

Q: How did you say you come to be sold?

A: Well, you see, Mr. Cook [my master] made great parties, and go off to watering-places, and get in debt, and had to break up, and then he took us to Mobile, and hired the most of us out, so the men he owe could not find us, and sell us for the debt. Then, after a while, the sheriff came from Georgia after Mr. Cook's debts, and found us all, and took us to auction, and sold us. My mother and brother was sold to Texas, and I was sold to New Orleans.

Q: How old were you, then?

A: Well, I don't know exactly, but the auctioneer said I wasn't quite fourteen. . . .

Q: Were there others there white like you?

A: Oh yes, plenty of them. . . . You see Mr. Cook had my hair cut off. My hair grew fast, and look so much better than Mr. Cook's daughter, and he fancy I had better hair than his daughter, and so he had it cut off to make a difference. . . . Then I was sold. . . . Mr. Williams allowed that he did not care what they bid, he was going to have me anyhow. Then he bid fifteen hundred. Mr. Horton said 'twas no use to bid anymore, and I was sold to Mr. Williams. I went right to New Orleans then.

Q: Who was Mr. Williams?

A: I didn't know then, only he lived in New Orleans. Him and his wife had parted, some way he had three children, boys. When I was going away I heard someone cryin' and prayin' the Lord to go with her only daughter, and protect me.

Q: Have you never seen her [Piquet's mother] since?

A: No, never since that time. I went to New Orleans, and she went to Texas. So I understood.

A: Mr. Williams told me what he bought me for, soon as we started for New Orleans. He said he was getting old, and when he saw me he thought he'd buy me, and end his days with me. He said if I behave myself he'd treat me well; but, if not, he'd whip me almost to death.

Q: How old was he?

A: He was over forty; I guess pretty near fifty. He was grayheaded. That's the reason he was always so jealous. He never let me go out anywhere. . . .

Q: Had you any children while in New Orleans?

A: Yes, I had four.

Q: Who was their father?

A: Mr. Williams. . . .

Q: Were your children mulattoes?

A: No, sir! They were all white. They look just like him. The neighbors all see that.

SOURCE: H. Mattison, Louisa Picquet, *The Octoroon: Or Inside Views of Southern Life* (New York: Published by the Author, 1861), 17–19.

BENNETT BARROW
Enforcing Labor Discipline

Bennett Barrow (1811–1854) inherited a substantial cotton plantation in Louisiana from his father. From 1837 to 1845, he kept a diary that consisted of brief remarks on the day's events, primarily on his plantation.

January 1838

14   Appearance of rain—pressed 7 B.[bales of cotton] last Sunday—pressing to day at Gibsons—will ship on Tuesday next 66 B . . . to Gin—On selling from 5 to 11½ cts.—The times are seriously hard all most impossible to raise one dollar . . . great Excitement in Congress, Northern States medling with slavery—first they com'ced by petition—now by openly speaking of the sin of Slavery in the southern states . . . must eventually cause a separation of the Union.

October 1838

12   Clear verry cold morning—hands picked worse yesterday than they have done this year. . . . Whiped near half the hands to day for picking badly & trashy. . . .

26   Clear pleasant weather—Cotton picks very trashy—Whiped 8 or 10 for weight today. . . .

May 1839

21   Clear verry warm—Finished hilling Cotton—Darcas & Fanny are the greatest shirks of any negroes I have—laid up twicet a month—Went to Town—man tried for whipping a negro to Death. trial will continue till to morrow—deserves death—Cleared!

July 1841

18   . . . Received a note from Ruffin stating that several of my negroes were implicated in an intended insurrection on the 1st of August next. . . . mine are O Fill O Ben Jack Dennis & Demps will go to Robert J. B. to have them examined . . .

27   Cloudy. Verry warm, Negros all Cleared. But will be tried by the Planters themselves &c.

SOURCE: Edwin Davis Adams, *Plantation Life in the Florida Parishes of Louisiana, 1836–1845 as Reflected in the Diary of Bennet H. Barrow* (New York: AMS Press, 1967 [c1943]), 105–106, 133, 135, 148, 236, 237.

ANALYZING THE EVIDENCE

➤ How strong is this evidence? Is there any reason to question its accuracy? Mollie Dawson was eighty-five when she was interviewed. How reliable do you think her memory was? Louisa Picquet's account was published by an abolitionist as an indictment of slavery. Is his account trustworthy? Is Bennett Barrow's diary a more reliable source than the other two? Explain your answer.

➤ Were you surprised by any of these accounts? If so, why? What did they tell you about day-to-day life under slavery that you did not know?

➤ Why do you suppose Picquet was freed in 1848?

A Master Bridge Builder

Horace King (1807–1885) was a self-made man of color, a rare achievement in the South in the nineteenth century. Born a slave of mixed European, African, and Native American (Catawba) ancestry, King built major bridges in Georgia, Alabama, and Mississippi during the early 1840s. After winning his freedom in 1846, he built and ran a toll bridge across the Chattahoochee River in Alabama. During the Civil War, King worked as a contractor for the Confederacy; during Reconstruction, he served two terms as a Republican member of the Alabama House of Representatives. Collection of the Columbus Museum, Columbus, Georgia; Museum purchase.

slaves or, more often, free blacks who feared reenslavement.

Even in the North, few free blacks enjoyed unfettered freedom. Most whites regarded all African Americans as their social inferiors and did all they could to confine them to low economic and political status. In rural areas, free blacks worked as farm laborers or tenant farmers; in towns and cities, they toiled as domestic servants, laundresses, or day laborers. Only a small number of free African Americans owned land. "You do not see one out of a hundred . . . that can make a comfortable living, own a cow, or a horse," a traveler in New Jersey noted. In addition, blacks were usually forbidden to vote, attend public schools, or sit next to whites in churches. Only a few states extended the vote to free blacks, and they could testify against whites in court only in Massachusetts. The federal government did not allow free African Americans to work for the postal service, claim public lands, or hold a U.S. passport. Martin Delaney, a black activist, remarked in 1852: "We are slaves in the midst of freedom."

Of the few African Americans who were able to make full use of their talents, several achieved great distinction. Mathematician and surveyor Benjamin Banneker (1731–1806) published an almanac and helped lay out the new capital in the District of Columbia; Joshua Johnston (1765–1832) won praise for his portraiture; and merchant Paul Cuffee (1759–1817) acquired a small fortune from his business enterprises. More impressive and enduring were the community institutions created by the early generations of free African Americans. Throughout the North, they founded schools, mutual-benefit organizations, and fellowship groups, often called Free African Societies. Discriminated against by white Protestants, they formed their own congregations and a new religious denomination — the African Methodist Episcopal Church, headed by Bishop Richard Allen (see Chapter 8).

These institutions gave free African Americans a sense of cultural, if not political, autonomy. They also institutionalized sharp social divisions within the black community. "Respectable" blacks tried through their dress, conduct, and attitude to win the "esteem and patronage" of prominent whites, first Federalists and then Whigs and abolitionists, who were sympathetic to their cause. Those efforts separated them from impoverished blacks, who distrusted whites and those who "acted white."

The free black population in the slave states numbered approximately 94,000 in 1810 and 225,000 in 1860. Most of these men and women lived in coastal cities — Mobile, Memphis, New Orleans — and especially in the Upper South. In Maryland on the eve of the Civil War, half of the black population was free. But that freedom was fragile. Free blacks accused of crimes were often denied a jury trial, and those charged with vagrancy were sometimes forced back into slavery. To prove their free status, African Americans had to carry manumission documents, which did not necessarily protect them from being kidnapped and sold. However, because skilled as well as unskilled Europeans generally refused to migrate to the South, blacks became the backbone of the region's urban artisan workforce. African American carpenters, blacksmiths, barbers, butchers, and shopkeepers played prominent roles in the economies of Baltimore, Richmond, Charleston, and New Orleans.

A privileged group among African Americans, free blacks had divided loyalties. To advance the welfare of their families, they had to distance themselves from plantation slaves and assimilate white culture

An African American Clergyman

This flattering portrait is one of two paintings of African Americans by black artist Joshua Johnston (who also went by the name Johnson). Born into slavery in 1765, Johnston somehow became a free man and a successful artist. In an advertisement in the *Baltimore Intelligence* in 1798, he described himself as a "Portrait Painter . . . a self-taught genius deriving from nature and industry his knowledge of the Art." Merchant families in Maryland and Virginia held Johnston's work in high regard and commissioned most of his thirty or so extant works.

Bowdoin College Museum of Art, Brunswick, Maine. Museum purchase, George Otis Hamlin Fund.

and values. In fact, some privileged blacks adopted the perspective of the planter class. David Barland, one of twelve children born to a white Mississippi planter and his black slave Elizabeth, owned no fewer than eighteen slaves. In neighboring Louisiana, some free blacks supported secession because they "own slaves and are dearly attached to their native land."

But these men were exceptions. Most free African Americans acknowledged their unity with the great mass of impoverished slaves, which usually included some of their relatives. "We's different [from whites] in color, in talk and in 'ligion and beliefs," said one. White planters reinforced unity among blacks by justifying slavery as a "positive good" and, by the 1840s and 1850s, calling for the reenslavement of free African Americans. Knowing their own liberty was not secure so long as slavery existed, these blacks sought freedom for all those of African ancestry. As a delegate to the National Convention of Colored People in 1848 noted, "Our souls are yet dark under the pall of slavery." Free African Americans in the South — often the offspring of white planters — helped fugitive slaves, while northern blacks supported the antislavery movement. In the rigid caste system of American race relations, free blacks stood as symbols of hope to enslaved African Americans and as symbols of danger to most whites.

➤ Compare the religion and culture of enslaved African Americans with those of the other groups in southern society. What similarities do you find? How were they different?

➤ How do you explain the persistence in America of certain African practices (the ring shout and incest taboos, for example) and the gradual disappearance of others (among them ritual scarring)?

➤ Describe the place of free blacks in America. Where in the South in the mid-nineteenth century would free blacks most likely be found? What kind of work would they have been doing?

SUMMARY

In this chapter, we have seen how the theme of an expanding South ties together two important historical developments. First, there was the rapid expansion of the plantation system from its traditional home in the Upper South to the Mississippi Valley and beyond. Powered by cotton, this movement westward divided the planter elite into aristocratic paternalists and entrepreneurial capitalists, and involved the forced migration or sale of more than 1 million enslaved African Americans.

We also examined in detail the character of white and black societies in the Cotton South. We noted that after 1820, less than a third of white families owned slaves and that another third were yeoman farmers; propertyless tenant farmers and laborers made up the rest. Many of these whites joined evangelical Protestant churches, as did blacks, who infused them with African modes of expression. Indeed, church and family became the core institutions of African American society, providing strength and solace amid the tribulations of slavery.

Connections: Society and Culture

Following the Tobacco and Rice Revolutions around 1700 and the subsequent importation of tens of thousands of enslaved Africans, the South became a dual society. Those of English and African birth shared geographical space but little else. As we discovered in Chapter 3, they spoke different languages, worshipped different gods, and had different legal status. Coercion — forced work and forced sex — was a major factor in most interactions between the two peoples.

This dual society began to break down during the Revolutionary era (see Chapter 8). By 1780, most slaves had been born in America, and most spoke English; some had become Christians; and thousands would soon become free, the result of gradual emancipation in the North and individual manumissions in the Chesapeake region. Coercion remained a potent force in the slave system; but as masters and slaves negotiated work rules, the use of physical force became a measure of last resort for many planters. Thus, as we noted in the essay that opened Part Three (p. 269), it was not surprising that "southern planters increasingly defended slavery as a 'positive good'" and considered slaves to be a part of their extended family.

Of course, as we saw in this chapter, the behavior of most planters contradicted their words. They callously "sold south" hundreds of thousands of African Americans and treated the remaining black members of their "families" far differently than they did their white kin. Still, the social and cultural differences between the two peoples continued to diminish. By the 1840s, slaves spoke black English, practiced black Protestantism, and were on their way to becoming a black peasantry — a dependent agricultural people similar to the oppressed peasant peoples of Ireland and Central Europe. Indeed, as we shall see in Chapter 15, the abolition of slavery following the Civil War and the events of Reconstruction (1865–1877) would leave most African Americans poor sharecroppers, a peasantry in fact if not in name.

CHAPTER REVIEW QUESTIONS

➤ How did plantation crops and the slavery system change between 1800 and 1860? Why did these changes occur?

➤ Based on what you've learned so far in Part Three, compare and contrast society in the American South with that of the North. Is it fair to say that by 1860, America was, in fact, two distinct societies?

TIMELINE

1810s	Africans from Congo region influence black culture
	Natural increase produces surplus of slaves in Old South
	Domestic slave trade expands, disrupting black family life
1812	Louisiana becomes a state, and its sugar production increases
1817	Mississippi becomes a state; Alabama follows (1819)
1820s	Substantial growth in free black population in North and South
	Slave-owning aristocrats in Old South adopt paternalistic ideology
	Entrepreneurial planters in Cotton South turn to gang labor
	Southern Methodists and Baptists become socially conservative
	African Americans adopt Christian beliefs
1830s	Advocates of slavery argue it is a "positive good"
	Boom in cotton production
	Percentage of slave-owning families falls
	Yeomen farm families retreat to hill country
	Lawyers become influential in southern politics
1840s	Southern Whigs advocate economic diversification
	Gradual emancipation completed in North
1850s	Price of slaves and cotton rises, and production expands
	Southern states subsidize railroads, but industrialization remains limited

FOR FURTHER EXPLORATION

Charlene M. Boyer Lewis explores the lives of the planter class in *Ladies and Gentlemen on Display: Planter Society at the Virginia Springs, 1790–1860* (2001). Three other recent studies of slave owners are: William Kauffman Scarborough, *Masters of the Big House: Elite Slaveholders of the Mid-Nineteenth-Century South* (2003); Jeffrey Robert Young, *Domesticating Slavery: The Master Class in Georgia and South Carolina, 1670–1837* (1999); and James David Miller, *South by Southwest: Planter Emigration and Identity in the Slave South* (2002). For a look into the intellectual life of planters, see Michael O'Brien, *Conjectures of Order: Intellectual Life and the American South, 1810–1860* (2004). The story of Edward Ball's attempt to come to terms with his slaveholding ancestors appears in his *Slaves in the Family* (1998), winner of a National Book Award. For an audio interview recounting Ball's search for the slaves' descendants go to **www.albany.edu/talkinghistory/arch2000july-december .html**. Stephanie McCurry's *Masters of Small Worlds: Yeomen Households, Gender Relations, and the Political Culture of the Antebellum South Carolina Low Country* (1995) offers a brilliant analysis of yeomen families. For plantation discipline, see Sally E. Hadden, *Slave Patrols: Law and Violence in Virginia and the Carolinas* (2001), and John Hope Franklin and Loren Sweninger, *Runaway Slaves, Rebels on the Plantation* (1999).

Ira Berlin's *Generations of Captivity: A History of African-American Slaves* (2003) offers a stimulating analysis of the changing character of slavery and African American society. See also the Web site to the PBS video on "Slavery and the Making of America" at **www.pbs.org/wnet/slavery/about/ index.html**. For primary documents that illustrate the ways in which African Americans acquired and transformed Protestant Christianity, log on to "Documenting the American South: The Church in the Southern Black Community" at **docsouth .unc.edu/church/index.html**. Marcus Wood, *Blind Memory: Visual Representations of Slavery in England and America, 1780–1865* (2000), offers many images of slave life, while Walter Johnson, *Soul by Soul: Life Inside the Antebellum Slave Market* (1999), closely examines the New Orleans slave mart. Two document-rich Web sites are "The African-American Mosaic" at **www.loc.gov/exhibits/african/intro.html** and "Slaves and the Courts, 1740–1860" at **lcweb2.loc.gov/ammem/aaohtml/**.

TEST YOUR KNOWLEDGE

To assess your command of the material in this chapter, see the Online Study Guide at **bedfordstmartins.com/henretta**.

For Web sites, images, and documents related to topics and places in this chapter, visit **bedfordstmartins.com/makehistory**.

13

The Crisis of the Union
1844–1860

Throughout the nation during the 1850s, crusaders for temperance and abolition faced off against defenders of personal liberties and property rights. The struggle in South Carolina was especially intense. When temperance activists demanded a "Maine law" to prohibit the sale of intoxicants, Randolph Turner, a candidate for the South Carolina assembly, was outraged: "Legislation upon Liquor would cast a shade on my character which as a Caucassian and a white man, I am not willing to bear." Indeed, Turner vowed to shoulder his musket and, along with "hundreds of men in this district, . . . fight for individual rights, as well as State Rights."

In Washington, South Carolina congressman Preston Brooks battled for "Southern Rights." In an inflammatory speech in 1856, Senator Charles Sumner of Massachusetts denounced the South and, mixing invective with metaphor, declared that Senator Andrew P. Butler of South Carolina had taken "the harlot slavery" as his mistress. Outraged by Sumner's verbal attack on his uncle, Brooks accosted the Massachusetts legislator at his desk in the Senate chamber and beat him unconscious with a walking cane. As the impact of Brooks's attack reverberated throughout Washington and the nation, Axalla Hoole of South Carolina and other proslavery migrants in the Kansas Territory leveled their guns

◄ *War News from Mexico,* **1848**

In this painting of a crowd gathered on the porch of the "American Hotel" in an unknown town, artist Richard Caton Woodville (1825–1855) captures the public's hunger for news of the Mexican War, the first military conflict with a foreign nation since the War of 1812. As a journalist in Baltimore, Woodville's hometown, noted, "People begin to collect every evening, about 5 o'clock at the telegraph and newspaper offices, waiting for extras and despatches, where they continue even to 12 or 1 o'clock at night, discussing the news that may be received." National Gallery of Art, Washington, D.C.

at an armed force of abolitionist settlers. Passion and violence had replaced political compromise as the hallmark of American public life.

The causes of the upsurge in political violence in the 1850s were complex. The immediate spark was the admission of Texas to the Union in 1845 and the acquisition of vast territories from Mexico in 1848. But at the root of the violence were the increasing differences between northern and southern states, and the resentment and alarm those differences raised in the South. White southerners feared the North's increasing wealth, political power, and moral righteousness, John C. Calhoun explained in 1850, especially its "long-continued agitation of the slavery question."

A massive surge of population in the West accentuated the importance of this sectional conflict. Emboldened by the nation's growing population and wealth, many Americans believed in **Manifest Destiny**—that it was their duty to extend republican institutions to the Pacific Ocean. But whose republican institutions: the aristocratic traditions and practices of the slaveholding South, or the more democratic customs and culture of the reform-minded North and Midwest? The answer to this question would determine the future of the nation. Beginning in 1844, Americans in the North, South, and West took up the challenge of answering it. In doing so, they would rip apart America's political and social institutions and, ultimately, the nation itself.

Manifest Destiny: South and North

The crisis over slavery in Missouri that began in 1819 (see Chapter 8) had frightened the nation's politicians. For the next two decades, the professional politicians who managed the Second Party System avoided policies that would spark another confrontation along regional lines. This strategy worked as long as the geographical boundaries of the United States remained unchanged. But during the 1840s, as the belief in Manifest Destiny led Americans toward the Pacific Ocean, the threat of confrontation loomed again.

The Independence of Texas

By the 1830s, settlers from the Ohio River Valley and the South had carried both yeoman farming and plantation slavery into Arkansas and Missouri. Between those states and the Rocky Mountains stretched the semiarid lands of the Great Plains. An army explorer, Major Stephen H. Long, labeled the

area the **Great American Desert** and noted that it was "almost wholly unfit for cultivation." Settlers looking for land, then, turned south, to the Mexican province of Texas.

Although Texas was occupied primarily by Indian peoples and claimed by Spain, it had long been a zone of conflict between European nations. In the eighteenth century, Spanish authorities in Mexico dispatched a few military garrisons to the region, and Texas became a buffer zone against French settlements along the Mississippi River. After the Louisiana Purchase (1803), the Spanish saw the province as a shield against the expansion-minded American republic. Although some adventurers from the United States settled in Texas, the Adams-Onís Treaty of 1819 guaranteed Spanish sovereignty over the region.

Austin Family: Texas Pioneers and Speculators. After winning independence from Spain in 1821, the Mexican government used lavish land grants to encourage both Mexicans and Americans to move to Texas. One early grantee was Moses Austin, an American land speculator who created a vast estate occupied by white tenants and smallholders. Adopting a paternalistic tone, Austin described the settlers as "one great family who are under my care." His son, Stephen F. Austin, acquired even more land from the Mexican government—some 180,000 acres—which he sold to incoming settlers. Most of these American residents did not assimilate Mexican culture. Equally important, in 1829, Austin and other grantees requested—and won—an exemption from a law ending slavery in Mexico. By 1835, about 27,000 white Americans and 3,000 African American slaves were raising cotton and cattle in eastern and central Texas. They far outnumbered the 3,000 Mexican residents, most of whom lived in the southwestern towns of Goliad and San Antonio (see Map 13.1).

As the Mexican government asserted greater political control over Texas in the 1830s, the American settlers split into two groups. Members of the "peace party," led by Stephen Austin and other longtime settlers, were content with Mexican rule but wanted greater political autonomy for the province; the "war party," headed mostly by recent migrants from Georgia, was demanding independence. Austin again won significant concessions from Mexican authorities. But in 1835, Mexico's president, General Antonio López de Santa Anna, began to strengthen national authority throughout Mexico, and he nullified those concessions. When Santa Anna appointed a military commandant for Texas, the war party provoked a rebellion that most

"The Father of Texas"

Stephen F. Austin (1793–1836) grew up in Missouri, where he worked as the manager of a lead mine and a banker and served in the territory's legislature. In 1822, he established an American colony on the lower Colorado and Brazos rivers in the Mexican province of Texas, where he proudly posed for the original of this engraving. A skilled negotiator, Austin persuaded the Mexican government to allow the unrestricted migration of American planters — and their slaves — into Texas.
Texas State Library and Archives Commission.

New York newspapers romanticized the heroism of the Texans and the deaths at the Alamo of folk heroes Davy Crockett and Jim Bowie. Drawing on anti-Catholic sentiment aroused by Irish immigrants in northern cities, American newspapers described the Mexicans as tyrannical butchers in the service of the pope. Hundreds of adventurers, lured by offers of land grants, flocked to Texas to join the rebel army. Led by General Sam Houston, the Texas rebels routed the Mexican army in the Battle of San Jacinto in April 1836, establishing de facto independence. The Mexican government refused to recognize the Texas Republic but abandoned efforts to reconquer it.

The Texans quickly voted by plebiscite for annexation by the United States, but President Martin Van Buren refused to bring the issue before Congress. As a Texas diplomat reported to his government, Van Buren and other American politicians feared that annexation would spark a war with Mexico and, beyond that, a "desperate death-struggle . . . between the North and the South; a struggle involving the probability of a dissolution of the Union."

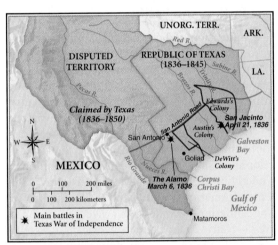

MAP 13.1 American Settlements and the Texas War of Independence

During the 1820s Mexican authorities granted huge tracts of land in Texas to Stephen F. Austin and other land speculators, who were expected to encourage Americans to migrate to Texas and grow cotton. By 1835, the nearly thirty thousand Americans in Texas far outnumbered Mexican settlers. To put down the American revolt, General Santa Anna led an army of six thousand men into Texas in early 1836. After overwhelming the Texans at the Alamo in March, Santa Anna set out to capture the Texas Provisional Government, which had fled to Galveston. But in April, his army was defeated and he was captured at the Battle of San Jacinto by a Texan force commanded by Sam Houston.

of the American settlers ultimately supported. On March 2, 1836, the American rebels proclaimed the independence of Texas and adopted a constitution that legalized slavery.

Rebellion and War. President Santa Anna vowed to put down the rebellion personally. On March 6, he led an army that wiped out the rebel garrison defending the Alamo in San Antonio and then took control of Goliad (Map 13.1). Santa Anna thought he had crushed the rebellion, but New Orleans and

SIEGE OF THE ALAMO.

Assault on the Alamo

After a thirteen-day siege, on March 6, 1836, a Mexican army of 4,000 stormed the wall of the small fort—it was originally a Spanish mission—in San Antonio. "The first to climb were thrown down by bayonets ... or by pistol fire," reported a Mexican officer. After a half-hour of continuous and costly assaults, the attackers won control of the wall. This contemporary woodcut shows the fierceness of the battle, which took the lives of all 250 American defenders; 1,500 Mexicans were killed or wounded in the fighting. Archives Division, Texas State Library.

The Push to the Pacific

The annexation of Texas became a more pressing issue in the 1840s, as expansionists in the South and the North developed continental ambitions. The term Manifest Destiny, coined in 1845 by John L. O'Sullivan, the editor of the *Democratic Review*, captured those dreams. As O'Sullivan put it, "Our manifest destiny is to overspread the continent allotted by Providence for the free development of our yearly multiplying millions." Underlying the rhetoric of Manifest Destiny was a sense of American cultural and racial superiority: The "inferior" peoples who lived in the Far West—Native Americans and Mexicans—were to be brought under American dominion, taught republicanism, and converted to Protestantism (see Reading American Pictures, "Marching from the Atlantic to the Pacific: Visualizing Manifest Destiny," p. 396).

Oregon. Residents of the Ohio River Valley were already casting their eyes westward to the fertile lands of the Oregon Country. This region stretched along the Pacific Coast between the Russian-dominated lands of Alaska and the Mexican province of California, and was claimed by both Britain and the United States. Since 1818, a British-American convention had allowed fur traders and settlers from both nations to live in

MAP 13.2 Territorial Conflict in Oregon, 1819–1846

As thousands of American settlers poured into the Oregon Country in the early 1840s, British authorities tried to keep them south of the Columbia River. However, the migrants—and fervent midwestern expansionists—asserted that Americans could settle anywhere in the territory, raising the prospect of armed conflict. In 1846, British and American diplomats resolved the dispute by dividing the region at the forty-ninth parallel.

the Oregon Country. The British-run Hudson's Bay Company developed a lucrative fur trade north of the Columbia River, while several hundred Americans settled to the south, mostly in the fertile lands of the Willamette Valley (see Chapter 16). Based on this settlement, the United States claimed ownership of the area between California and the Columbia River (Map 13.2).

In 1842, American interest in Oregon increased dramatically. The U.S. Navy published a glowing report of fine harbors in the Puget Sound, which was welcome news to New England merchants plying the China trade. In the same year, a party of one hundred farmers journeyed along the Oregon Trail, a route fur traders and explorers had blazed through the Great Plains and the Rocky Mountains (Map 13.3). Their reports from Oregon told of a mild climate and fertile soil.

"Oregon fever" suddenly raged. By May 1843, 1,000 men, women, and children—in more than one hundred wagons and with five thousand oxen and cattle—had gathered in Independence, Missouri, for the six-month trek to Oregon. The migrants were mostly yeomen farming families from the southern border states (Missouri, Kentucky, and Tennessee) who were looking for free land and a new life. They overcame flooding streams, dust storms, dying livestock, and a few armed encounters with Indians before they reached the Willamette Valley, a journey of 2,000 miles. Over the next two years, another 5,000 people reached Oregon, and the numbers continued to grow.

By 1860, about 350,000 Americans had braved the Oregon Trail. More than 34,000 of them died in the effort, mostly from disease and exposure; fewer than 500 deaths resulted from Indian attacks. The walking migrants wore three-foot-deep paths, and their wagons carved five-foot-deep ruts across sandstone formations in southern Wyoming—tracks that are visible today. Women found the trail especially difficult because it exaggerated the authority of their husbands, who directed the enterprise, and added the labor of driving wagons and animals to their usual chores. Hundreds of women endured pregnancy or gave birth during the long journey, and some did not survive the ordeal. "There was a woman died in this train yesterday," Jane Gould Tortillott noted in her diary. "She left six children, one of them only two day's old."

California. Some pioneers ended up in the Mexican province of California. They left the Oregon Trail along the Snake River, trudged down the California Trail, and settled in the interior along the Sacramento

MAP 13.3 Routes to the West, 1835–1860

By the 1840s, a variety of trails spanned the arid zone between the ninety-fifth meridian and the Pacific Coast. From the south, El Camino Real linked Mexico City to the California coast and to Santa Fe. From the east, the Mormon, Oregon, and Santa Fe trails carried tens of thousands of Americans from departure points on the Mississippi and Missouri rivers to new communities in Utah and along the Pacific Coast. By the 1860s, both the Pony Express and Butterfield Overland mail routes provided reliable communication between the eastern states and California.

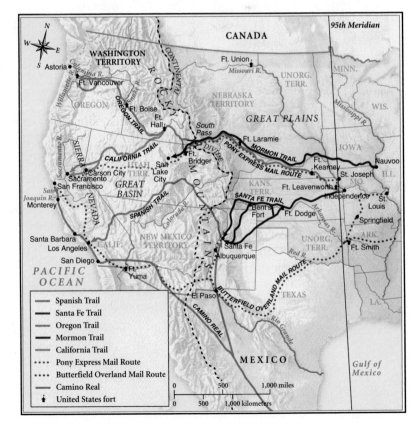

Visualizing Manifest Destiny

American Progress, John Gast. Library of Congress; Picture Research Consultants & Archives.

In 1845, John O'Sullivan, a newspaper and journal editor, coined the term *Manifest Destiny* to describe Americans' sudden — and urgent — longing to migrate westward and extend the boundaries of the nation to the Pacific Ocean. More than a quarter century later, John Gast's painting, *American Progress* (1872), gave visual form to that aspiration and was widely distributed in engravings and lithographs. What do the details of the painting tell us about the meaning of Manifest Destiny?

ANALYZING THE EVIDENCE

➤ The painting is an allegory: The artist uses symbols to depict America's expansion to the Pacific. The central symbol is the goddess Liberty; she floats westward, her forehead emblazoned with the "Star of Empire." Why do you think Gast chose Liberty to lead the republic to the West? What is the significance of the "School Book" in her right hand?

➤ The painting has three horizontal planes — foreground, middle ground, and background — and each tells a separate story. What stages of social evolution are pictured in each plane? What symbols of progress does Gast employ? How is technology depicted? What role does it play in the artist's depiction of progress?

➤ Gast also has divided the painting into two vertical planes. What do you think the transition from lightness to darkness symbolizes?

➤ In the background on the far right stands New York City, with the great Brooklyn Bridge (which was still being built in 1872) spanning the East River. Far off on the left, you can see the Pacific Ocean. Why did Gast include these elements in the painting?

River. The region was sparsely populated by native peoples or Mexicans. California had formed the remote northern corner of Spain's American empire, and Spanish authorities in Mexico established a significant foothold there only in the 1770s, when they built a chain of religious missions and forts (presidios) along the coast. New England merchants soon struck up trade with the Spanish settlers in California, buying sea otter pelts that the merchants then carried to China.

Commerce increased after Mexico won independence from Spain in 1821. To promote California's development, the Mexican government took over the Franciscan-run missions and liberated the twenty thousand Indians who had been induced to work on them. Some mission Indians rejoined their Native American tribes, but many intermarried with mestizos (Mexicans of mixed Spanish and Indian ancestry) and worked as laborers and cowboys on the large cattle ranches that the government in Mexico was promoting.

The rise of cattle ranching linked California to the American economy. New England merchants dispatched dozens of agents westward to buy leather and tallow for use in the booming Massachusetts boot and shoe industry. Many of those resident agents married into the families of the elite Mexican landowners and ranchers—the Californios—and adopted their dress, manners, outlook, and Catholic religion (see Chapter 16). A crucial exception was Thomas Oliver Larkin, the most successful merchant in the coastal town of Monterey. Larkin worked closely with Mexican ranchers, but he remained an American citizen and plotted for the peaceful annexation of California to the United States.

Like Larkin, the American migrants in the Sacramento River Valley did not want to assimilate into Mexican society. Many were squatters or held land grants of dubious legality. Some of them hoped to emulate the Americans in Texas by colonizing the country and then seeking annexation to the United States. However, these settlers numbered only about 700 in the early 1840s; by contrast, 7,000 Mexicans and 300 American traders lived along the coast.

The Fateful Election of 1844

The election of 1844 determined the American government's policy toward California, Oregon, and Texas. Since 1836, when Texas requested annexation, many southern leaders had advocated territorial expansion to extend slavery. Cautious party politicians and northern abolitionists resisted

A Californio Patriarch

The descendant of a Spanish family that had lived—and prospered—in Mexico since the Spanish conquest, Mariano Guadalupe Vallejo (1808–1890) served in Mexican California as a military officer. In the 1820s, he acquired title to 270,000 acres of land in the Sonoma Valley, north of San Francisco. Vallejo, the father of nine children, presents himself in this photograph as a proud patriarch, surrounded by two daughters and three granddaughters. During the American takeover in 1846, he was imprisoned for a short period and then, like many of the Californios, lost most of his vast land holdings to squatters and rival claimants. Bancroft Library, University of California, Berkeley.

their efforts. Now there were rumors that Britain wanted the Mexican government to cede California in payment for large debts owed to British investors. Southern leaders also believed that Britain was encouraging Texas to remain independent and had designs on Spanish Cuba, which some southerners wanted to annex. To thwart possible British schemes, southern expansionists demanded the immediate annexation of Texas.

At this crucial juncture, Oregon fever and Manifest Destiny opened up the possibility of annexing Texas by altering the political and diplomatic landscape in the North. In 1843, Americans in the Ohio River Valley and the Great Lakes states organized "Oregon conventions" that called on the federal government to end joint occupation of the region with Britain. In July, Democratic and Whig politicians met in a bipartisan national convention and demanded that the United States seize Oregon all the way to 54°40′ north latitude, the southern border of Russian Alaska.

With northern Democrats demanding expansion in Oregon, southern Democrats seized the opportunity to champion the annexation of Texas without threatening party unity. Moreover, they had the support of President John Tyler. Disowned by the Whigs because of his opposition to Henry Clay's nationalist economic program, Tyler hoped to win reelection in 1844 as a Democrat. To curry favor among expansionists, Tyler proposed to annex Texas and seize all of Oregon. In April 1844, Tyler and John C. Calhoun, an expansionist and the new secretary of state, sent the Senate a treaty to annex Texas. Two rival presidential candidates, Democrat Martin Van Buren and Whig Henry Clay, quickly declared their opposition. Knowing that annexation would raise the issue of the expansion of slavery and divide the nation, these cautious party politicians persuaded the Senate to defeat the treaty.

Expansion into Texas and Oregon became the central issue in the election of 1844. The Democrats passed over Tyler, whom they did not trust, and Van Buren, whom southerners despised for his opposition to the acquisition of Texas. They selected as their candidate Governor James K. Polk of Tennessee, a slave owner who favored annexation. Widely known as "Young Hickory," Polk was a protégé of Andrew Jackson and, like his mentor, was a man of iron will and boundless ambition for the nation. Accepting the claim of the Democratic Party platform that both areas already belonged to the United States, Polk campaigned for the "Re-occupation of Oregon and the Re-annexation of Texas—the whole of the territory of Oregon" to the Alaskan border. "Fifty-four forty or fight!" became the jingoistic cry of his expansionist campaign.

The Whigs nominated Henry Clay, who again championed his American System of internal improvements, high tariffs, and national banking. Clay initially dodged the issue of Texas but ultimately indicated support for annexation. His evasive position disappointed thousands of northern Whigs and Democrats, who opposed any expansion of slavery. Rather than vote for Clay, they cast their ballots for James G. Birney of the Liberty Party (see Chapter 11). Birney garnered less than 3 percent of the national vote but won enough support among Whigs in New York to cost Clay the state and the national election. By narrowly taking New York's thirty-six electoral votes, Polk won the presidency; without them, he would have lost by a margin of seven votes.

Following Polk's victory, Democrats in Congress called for the immediate annexation of Texas. When Whig opposition denied them the needed two-thirds majority in the Senate to ratify a treaty of annexation with the Republic of Texas, the Democrats approved the deal in February by a joint resolution of Congress, which required just a majority vote in each house. In a matter of months, a convention in Austin drafted a constitution and the people of Texas voted for statehood. On December 29, 1845, Texas joined the Union as the twenty-eighth state. Polk's strategy of linking Texas and Oregon had put him in the White House and Texas in the Union. Shortly, it would make the expansion of the South—and its system of slavery—the central topic of American politics.

➤ Both elected officials and private individuals shaped America's western policy. Which group was more important? Why?

➤ How did western expansion become linked with the sectional conflict between the North and the South? Why, after two decades of hesitation, did politicians support territorial expansion in the 1840s?

War, Expansion, and Slavery, 1846–1850

The acquisition of Texas whetted Polk's appetite. The president now saw an opportunity to assert American control over all Mexican territory between Texas and the Pacific Ocean. Moreover, he was prepared to go to war to get it. What he and the majority of the Democratic Party consciously ignored was the crisis over slavery they would unleash by pursuing this expansionist dream.

The War with Mexico, 1846–1848

Since gaining independence in 1821, Mexico had not prospered. Its stagnant economy yielded few surpluses and modest tax revenues, which were quickly devoured by interest payments on foreign debts and a bloated bureaucracy. The vast and distant northern provinces of California and New Mexico contributed little to the national economy and remained sparsely settled, with a Spanish-speaking population of only 75,000 in 1840. Still, Mexican officials vowed to preserve their nation's historical territories; and when the Texas constitutional convention voted to enter the American

Street Fighting in the Calle de Iturbide, 1846

The American conquest of Monterrey, which Spanish troops had been unable to capture during Mexico's war for independence (1820–1821), came after bloody house-to-house fighting. Protected by thick walls and shuttered windows, Mexican defenders poured a withering fire on the dark-uniformed American troops and buckskin-clad frontier fighters. A large Catholic cathedral looms in the background, its foundations obscured by the smoke from the Mexicans' cannons. West Point Museum, United States Military Academy, West Point, NY. From *The Old West: The Mexican War*, photographed by Paulus Lesser. © 1978 Time-Life Books.

Union on July 4, 1845, Mexico broke off diplomatic relations with the United States.

Polk's Expansionist Program. Taking advantage of this diplomatic rupture, President Polk set into motion his plans to acquire Mexico's far northern provinces. To intimidate the Mexican government, he ordered General Zachary Taylor and an American army of two thousand soldiers to occupy disputed lands between the Nueces River (the historical southern boundary of Texas) and the Rio Grande, which

the Republic of Texas had claimed as its border with Mexico (see Map 13.1, p. 393). Simultaneously, Polk launched a secret diplomatic initiative. He appointed John Slidell, a congressman from Louisiana, as minister to Mexico with instructions to win acceptance of the Rio Grande boundary and to buy the Mexican provinces of California and New Mexico, allotting up to $30 million for the purchase. When Slidell arrived in Mexico City in December 1845, Mexican officials refused to see him, reiterating their position that America's annexation of Texas was illegal. Purchasing

The Bear Flag Republic

When news of the war between the United States and Mexico reached California in June 1846, a group of American settlers captured the Mexican garrison at Sonoma and, raising a crude handmade flag, proclaimed California an independent republic. The star on the flag imitated the lone star of the Texas Republic, and the grizzly bear represented California. The Bear Flag Republic was short-lived; within a few months, American naval and ground forces had taken control of most of California. Society of California Pioneers.

New Mexico and California was now definitely out of the question.

Anticipating the failure of Slidell's mission, Polk had already embarked on an alternative plan. He hoped to foment a revolution in California that, like the rebellion in Texas, would lead to an independent republic and a request for annexation. In October 1845, Secretary of State James Buchanan told merchant Thomas Oliver Larkin, now the U.S. consul in the port of Monterey, to encourage influential Mexican residents to declare independence and support peaceful annexation. To add military muscle to the initiative, Polk ordered American naval commanders to seize San Francisco Bay and California's coastal towns in case of war with Mexico. The president also had the War Department dispatch Captain John C. Frémont and an "exploring" party of heavily armed soldiers into Mexican territory. By December 1845, Frémont had reached California's Sacramento River Valley.

Events now moved quickly toward war. Polk ordered General Taylor toward the Rio Grande to incite an armed response by Mexico. "We were sent to provoke a fight," recalled Ulysses S. Grant, then a young officer serving with Taylor, "but it was essential that Mexico should commence it." When the armies clashed near the Rio Grande in May 1846, Polk delivered the war message he had drafted long before. Taking liberties with the truth, the president declared that Mexico "has passed the boundary of the United States, has invaded our territory, and shed American blood upon the American soil." Ignoring Whig pleas for a negotiated settlement, the Democratic majority in Congress voted for war, a decision that was greeted with great popular acclaim. To avoid a simultaneous conflict with Britain, Polk retreated from "fifty-four forty or fight" and accepted a British proposal to divide the Oregon Country at the forty-ninth parallel.

American Military Successes. American forces in Texas quickly established their military superiority. Zachary Taylor's army crossed the Rio Grande, occupied Matamoros, and, after a fierce six-day battle in September 1846, took the interior Mexican town of Monterrey. Two months later, a U.S. naval squadron in the Gulf of Mexico seized Tampico, Mexico's second most important port. By the end of 1846, the United States controlled much of northeastern Mexico (Map 13.4).

Fighting had also broken out in California. In June 1846, naval commander John Sloat landed 250 marines in Monterey and declared that California "henceforward will be a portion of the United States." Almost simultaneously, American settlers in the Sacramento River Valley staged a revolt and, supported by Frémont's forces, captured the town of Sonoma and proclaimed an independent California—the "Bear Flag Republic." To cement these victories by American marines and settlers, Polk ordered army units to capture Santa Fe in New Mexico and then march to California. Despite stiff Mexican resistance, American forces secured control of California early in 1847.

Polk expected these American victories would end the war, but he had underestimated the Mexicans' national pride and the determination of President Santa Anna. Santa Anna went on the offensive and attacked Taylor's depleted units at Buena Vista in February 1847. Only superior artillery enabled Taylor to hold the American line in northeastern Mexico.

MAP 13.4 The Mexican War, 1846–1848

Departing from Fort Leavenworth in present-day Kansas, American forces commanded by Captain John C. Frémont and General Stephen Kearney defeated Mexican armies in California in 1846 and early 1847. Simultaneously, U.S. troops under General Zachary Taylor and Colonel Alfred A. Doniphan won victories over General Santa Anna's forces far to the south of the Rio Grande. In mid-1847, General Winfield Scott mounted a successful attack on Mexico City, ending the war.

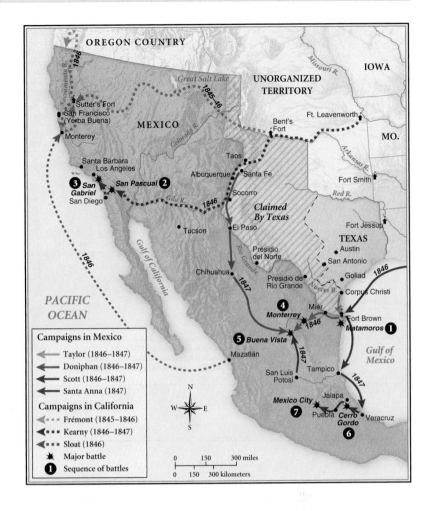

To bring Santa Anna to terms, Polk accepted General Winfield Scott's plan to strike deep into the heart of Mexico. In March 1847, Scott captured the port of Veracruz and began the 260-mile march to Mexico City. Leading Scott's 14,000 troops was a cadre of talented West Point officers who would become famous in the Civil War: Robert E. Lee, George Meade, and P. G. T. Beauregard. Scott's troops crushed Santa Anna's forces at Cerro Gordo and at Churubusco, just outside Mexico City, and seized the Mexican capital in September 1847. Those defeats cost Santa Anna his power, and a new Mexican government agreed to make peace with the United States.

A Divisive Victory

Initially, the war with Mexico sparked an explosion of patriotic support. Politicians and newspaper editors hailed the war as a noble struggle to extend American republican institutions. However, the conflict soon divided the nation. A few Whigs—among them Charles Francis Adams of Massachusetts (the son of President John Quincy Adams) and Joshua Giddings of Ohio—opposed the war from the beginning on moral grounds. Known as **conscience Whigs**, they warned of a southern conspiracy to add new slave states in the West. The expansion of slavery, they argued, would undermine the Jeffersonian ideal of a freeholder society and ensure permanent control of the federal government by slaveholding Democrats. These antislavery Whigs grew bolder after the elections of 1846 repudiated Polk's war policy and gave their party control of Congress.

The Wilmot Proviso. Polk's expansionist agenda split the Democrats into sectional factions. As early as 1839, Democratic senator Thomas Morris of Ohio had warned that "the power of slavery is aiming to govern the country, its Constitutions and laws." In August 1846, David Wilmot, a Democratic congressman from Pennsylvania, took up that refrain. To limit the spread of slavery, Wilmot proposed to prohibit slavery in any territories acquired from Mexico. His proposal rallied antislavery northerners. In the House of Representatives, northern Democratic allies of Martin Van Buren

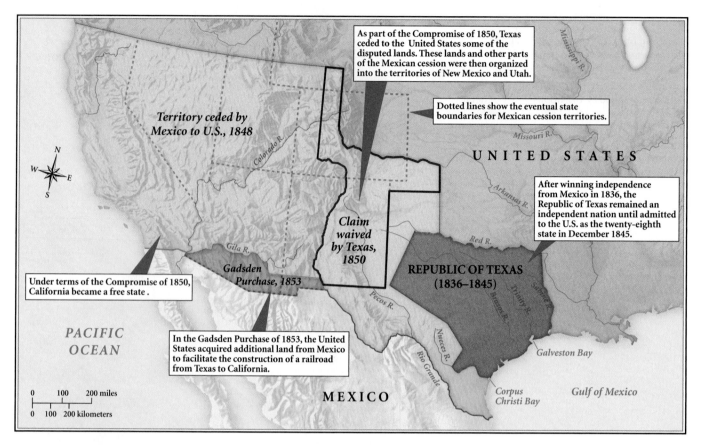

MAP 13.5 The Mexican Cession, 1848

In the Treaty of Guadalupe Hidalgo (1848), Mexico ceded to the United States its vast northern territories — the present-day states of California, Nevada, Utah, Arizona, New Mexico, half of Colorado and Texas. These new territories, President Polk boasted to Congress, "constitute of themselves a country large enough for a great empire, and the acquisition is second in importance only to that of Louisiana in 1803."

joined forces with antislavery Whigs to pass the Wilmot Proviso. "The madmen of the North . . . ," declared the *Richmond Enquirer*, "have, we fear, cast the die and numbered the days of this glorious Union." Fearing just such an outcome, the Senate, dominated by southerners and proslavery northern Democrats, killed the proviso.

Fervent Democratic expansionists became even more aggressive. Polk, Secretary of State Buchanan, and Senators Stephen A. Douglas of Illinois and Jefferson Davis of Mississippi called for the United States to take Mexican territory south of the Rio Grande. However, to avoid a longer war and the assimilation of a huge number of Mexicans, John C. Calhoun and other southern leaders insisted that the United States should annex only California and New Mexico, Mexico's most sparsely populated provinces. "Ours is a government of the white man," Calhoun proclaimed, arguing that the United

States had never "incorporated into the Union any but the Caucasian race."

To reunify the Democratic Party before the next election, Polk and Buchanan abandoned their dreams to expand deep into Mexico and accepted Calhoun's policy. In February 1848, Polk signed the Treaty of Guadalupe Hidalgo, in which the United States agreed to pay Mexico $15 million in return for more than one-third of its territory: Texas, New Mexico, and California. The Senate ratified the treaty in March 1848 (Map 13.5).

Free Soil. The passions aroused by the war dominated the election of 1848. The Senate's rejection of the Wilmot Proviso prompted antislavery advocates to revive Thomas Morris's charge of a massive "Slave Power" conspiracy. To thwart any such plan, thousands of ordinary northerners joined a new movement, the **free-soil movement.** To Abijah

Beckwith of Herkimer County, New York, and other yeomen farmers, slavery was an institution of "aristocratic men" and a threat to the liberties of "the great mass of the people." "The curse of slavery," Beckwith told his grandson, "threatens the general and equal distribution of our lands into convenient family farms."

The free-soilers quickly organized as a political party. They abandoned the Liberty Party's emphasis on the sinfulness of slavery and the natural rights of African Americans. Instead, like Beckwith, they depicted slavery as a threat to republican liberties and white yeoman farming. The Wilmot Proviso's call for free soil was the first antislavery proposal to attract broad popular support. Hundreds of women in the Great Lakes states joined the female free-soil organizations formed by the American and Foreign Anti-Slavery Society. The Free-Soilers' shift in emphasis—from freeing slaves toward preserving the West for freehold farms—led abolitionist William Lloyd Garrison to denounce free-soil doctrine as racist "whitemanism."

Frederick Douglass: Political Abolitionist. But Frederick Douglass, the foremost black abolitionist, endorsed the Free-Soil movement. Born to a slave mother on a Maryland plantation in 1818, Douglass grew up as Frederick Bailey. He never knew the identity of his father, though it was undoubtedly his owner, Thomas Auld. Auld had Frederick raised by his brother in Baltimore, where he learned to read and mingled with the free blacks of the city. Later, when Frederick faced deportation to the Deep South for attempting to escape from plantation labor, Auld again intervened. In 1835, he returned Frederick to Baltimore, allowed him to hire himself out as caulker, and promised him freedom in eight years, at the age of twenty-five.

Frederick plunged enthusiastically into the life of Baltimore's free African American community. He courted a free black woman, Anna Murray; joined the East Baltimore Mental Improvement Society; and hatched a plan of escape. In 1838, he borrowed the identification papers of a free African American sailor and sailed to New York City. He took the last name Douglass, married Murray, and settled in New Bedford, Massachusetts. Inspired by Garrison, Douglass began to speak publicly on the issue of slavery and, in 1841, became a lecturer for Garrison's American Anti-Slavery Society. Soon, he became a celebrity. His partly African ancestry drew crowds to his lectures, as did his commanding presence, dramatic rhetoric, and forceful intellect.

In his speeches, Douglass denounced slavery in the South and racial discrimination in the North. Gradually, his views diverged from those of Garrison. To rid America of the sin of slavery, Garrison would expel the southern states from the Union. To Douglass, that policy was madness because it would perpetuate slavery. Rejecting Garrison's moral radicalism, he founded an antislavery newspaper, the *North Star*, and became a political abolitionist—dedicated to using political means and government power to overthrow slavery. In 1848, Douglass attended the Buffalo convention that established the Free-Soil Party and endorsed its political strategy as the best means of confronting the South.

Frederick Douglass, c. 1848
This daguerreotype of Douglass was made when he was about thirty years old. Describing Douglass, an admirer wrote: "He was more than six feet in height, and his majestic form … straight as an arrow, muscular, yet lithe and graceful, his flashing eye, and more than all, his voice, that rivaled Webster's in its richness and in the depth … of its cadences, made up such an ideal of an orator as the listeners never forgot." Chester County Historical Society.

The Election of 1848. The conflict over slavery took a toll on Polk and the Democratic Party. Opposed by Whigs and Free-Soilers and exhausted by his rigorous dawn-to-midnight work regime, Polk refused to run for a second term; he would die just three months after leaving office. In his place, the Democrats nominated Senator Lewis Cass of Michigan, an avid expansionist who had advocated buying Cuba, annexing Mexico's Yucatán Peninsula, and taking all of Oregon. To maintain party unity, Cass took a deliberately vague position on the question of slavery in the West. He promoted a new idea—squatter sovereignty—that would allow settlers in each territory to determine its status as free or slave.

Cass's political ingenuity failed to hold the Democracy together. Demanding unambiguous opposition to the expansion of slavery, some northern Democrats joined the newly formed Free-Soil Party, which nominated Martin Van Buren for president. Van Buren genuinely supported free soil, but he also wanted to punish southern Democrats for denying him the presidential nomination in 1844. To attract Whig votes, the Free-Soilers chose conscience Whig Charles Francis Adams as their candidate for vice president.

To keep their party intact, the Whigs nominated General Zachary Taylor for president. Taylor was a Louisiana slave owner, but he had not taken a position on the charged issue of slavery in the territories. Equally important, the general's military exploits had made him a popular hero. Known as "Old Rough and Ready," Taylor had a common touch that won him the affection of his troops. "Our Commander on the Rio Grande," wrote Walt Whitman, "emulates the Great Commander of our revolution"—George Washington.

In 1848, as in 1840, running a military hero worked for the Whigs. Taylor took 47 percent of the popular vote to Cass's 42 percent. However, he won a majority in the Electoral College (163 to 127) only because the Free-Soil ticket of Van Buren and Adams deprived the Democrats of enough votes in New York to cost Cass that state and the presidency. The bitter debate over the Wilmot Proviso had fractured the Democratic Party in the North and changed the dynamics of national politics.

1850: Crisis and Compromise

Even before Taylor took office, events in California triggered a new political crisis over slavery. In January 1848, workmen building a mill for John A. Sutter in the Sierra Nevada foothills in northern California discovered flakes of gold. Sutter was a Swiss immigrant who arrived in California in 1839, became a Mexican citizen, and established an estate in the Sacramento River Valley. He tried to keep the discovery a secret; but by May, American settlers from Monterey and San Francisco were pouring into the foothills. When President Polk confirmed the discovery in December, the gold rush was on. By January 1849, sixty-one crowded ships had left from northeastern ports to sail around Cape Horn to San Francisco; by May, twelve thousand wagons had crossed the Missouri River bound for the gold-fields (Map 13.6). In 1849 alone, more than eighty thousand "forty-niners" had arrived in California (see Chapter 16).

Statehood for California. The rapid influx of settlers revived the national debate over free soil. The forty-niners, who lived in crowded, chaotic towns and mining camps, demanded the forma-tion of a territorial government to protect their lives and property. To avoid an extended debate over slavery, President Taylor advised the Californians to apply for statehood immediately; and in November 1849, they ratified a state constitution that prohibited slavery. Taylor had never believed that the defense of slavery in the South required its expansion into the territories. Now, urged on by William H. Seward, the former Whig governor of New York, Taylor tried to strengthen the Whig Party in the North by appealing to Free-Soilers and northern Democrats. As part of this political strategy, he urged Congress to admit California as a free state.

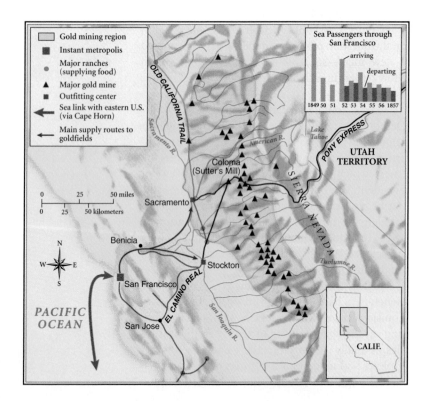

MAP 13.6 The California Gold Rush, 1849–1857

Traveling from all parts of the world—Europe, China, and Australia, as well as the eastern United States—hundreds of thousands of bonanza-seekers converged on the California goldfields. Miners traveling by sea landed at San Francisco, which quickly mushroomed into a substantial city; many other prospectors trekked overland to the goldfields on the Old California Trail. By the mid-1850s, the gold rush was over: Almost as many people were sailing from San Francisco each year as were arriving to seek their fortune.

A ROAD SCENE IN CALIFORNIA.

The Gold Rush Creates a Mix of Peoples

This well-composed drawing, sketched by German-born artist and California prospector Charles Nahl, captures the racial complexity of the gold rush. Displaced from their home by a horde of newcomers, a Native American family trudges away from the goldfields (left). Meanwhile, a contingent of Chinese miners marches toward the diggings (center), and a group of American men struggle to right their overturned wagon. University of California at Berkeley, Bancroft Library.

The swift triumph of antislavery forces in California alarmed southern politicians. Admitting California as a free state would prevent the expansion of slavery to the Pacific. More troubling, it would increase the number of free states in the Union to sixteen, giving the free states a one-state majority in the Senate. Fearing that the South would be placed at a permanent disadvantage in the national government, which they had long controlled, some southerners threatened secession. "[If] you seek to drive us from the territories of California and New Mexico," Representative Robert Toombs of Georgia warned northern congressmen, "*I am for disunion.*" However, the majority of southern politicians preferred a strategy of political resistance. They vowed to block California's admission unless the federal government guaranteed the future of slavery.

Constitutional Conflict. The resulting political impasse produced passionate debates in Congress and four distinct positions with respect to slavery in the territories. On the verge of death, John C. Calhoun took his usual extreme stance. Like Senator Albert Gallatin Brown of Mississippi, Calhoun had long resented the "social and sectional degradation" of the South by northern critics of slavery. To uphold southern honor, he now asserted the right of states to secede from the Union and proposed a constitutional amendment that would permanently balance the political power of the North and the South by creating a dual presidency. Calhoun also advanced the radical doctrine that Congress had no constitutional authority to regulate slavery in the territories. This argument ran counter to a half century of practice. In 1787, Congress had prohibited slavery in the Northwest Territory; and in the Missouri Compromise of 1820, it had extended that ban to most of the Louisiana Purchase.

Calhoun's assertion that the territories were open to slavery won support in the Deep South, but many southerners favored a second, more moderate, proposal to extend the Missouri Compromise line to the Pacific Ocean. This plan also won the support of Pennsylvanian James Buchanan, the former secretary of state, and other influential northern Democrats. Because an extension of the compromise line would guarantee slave owners access to at least some western territory, including a separate state in southern California, they championed it as a simple compromise that would resolve the crisis.

A third alternative for resolving the status of slavery in the territories was squatter sovereignty, the idea advanced by Lewis Cass in 1848 and now advocated by Democratic senator Stephen Douglas of Illinois. Douglas called his plan **popular sovereignty** to emphasize its roots in republican ideology, and it had considerable appeal. Politicians liked the fact that it would remove the explosive issue of slavery from national politics; and local settlers welcomed the power it would put in their hands. However, popular sovereignty was a vague and slippery concept. Could residents accept or ban slavery when a territory was first organized? Or must they delay that decision until a territory had enough people to frame a constitution and apply for statehood?

For their part, antislavery advocates were unwilling to accept any plan for California that might allow the expansion of slavery in the territories. Senator Salmon P. Chase of Ohio, elected by a Democratic–Free-Soil coalition, and Senator William H. Seward, a New York Whig, urged a fourth position—that federal authorities restrict slavery within its existing boundaries and then extinguish it completely. Condemning slavery as "morally unjust, politically unwise, and socially pernicious" and invoking "a higher law than the Constitution," Seward demanded bold action to protect freedom, "the common heritage of mankind."

A Complex Compromise. Standing on the brink of disaster, senior Whig and Democratic politicians desperately sought a compromise that would preserve the Union. With the help of Millard Fillmore, who became president in 1850, after Zachary Taylor died suddenly, Whig leaders Henry Clay and Daniel Webster and Democrat Stephen A. Douglas secured the passage of five separate laws known collectively as the Compromise of 1850. To mollify the South, the Compromise included a new Fugitive Slave Act that enlisted federal magistrates in the task of returning runaway slaves. To satisfy the North, the legislation admitted California as a free state, resolved a boundary dispute between New Mexico and Texas in favor of New Mexico, and abolished the slave trade (but not slavery) in the District of Columbia. Finally, the Compromise organized the rest of the lands acquired from Mexico into the territories of New Mexico and Utah and left the decision to allow or prohibit slavery in those vast areas to popular sovereignty (Map 13.7).

The Compromise averted a secession crisis in 1850, but only barely. In the middle of the political struggle, the governor of South Carolina declared that there was not "the slightest doubt" that his state would secede from the Union. He and other militant secessionists (known as "fire-eaters") in Georgia,

Mississippi, and Alabama organized special conventions to safeguard "Southern Rights" through secession. In Georgia, U.S. Congressman Alexander H. Stephens called on the delegates to make "the necessary preparations of men and money, arms and munitions, etc. to meet the emergency." However, most delegates to these conventions remained committed to the Union—though now only conditionally. Accepting the principle of secession, they agreed to leave the Union if Congress abolished slavery anywhere or refused to grant statehood to a territory with a proslavery constitution. Political wizardry had solved the immediate constitutional crisis, but the underlying issue of slavery remained unresolved.

➤ Why did President Polk go to war with Mexico? Why did the war become so divisive in Congress?

➤ What issues were resolved by the Compromise of 1850? Who benefited more from its terms, the North or the South? Why?

The End of the Second Party System, 1850–1858

The architects of the Compromise of 1850 expected it to last for at least a generation, as the Missouri Compromise had. Their hopes were quickly dashed. Demanding freedom for fugitive slaves and free soil in the West, antislavery northerners refused to accept the Compromise. For their part, proslavery southerners were plotting to extend slavery into the West, the Caribbean, and Central America. The resulting disputes destroyed the Second Party System and deepened the crisis of the Union.

Resistance to the Fugitive Slave Act

The Fugitive Slave Act proved the most controversial element of the Compromise. Under its terms, federal magistrates in the northern states determined the status of blacks who were alleged to be runaway slaves. The law denied a jury trial to the accused blacks and even their right to testify. Under its provisions, southern owners reenslaved about two hundred fugitives (as well as some free northern blacks).

The plight of runaways and the appearance of slave catchers in the North and Midwest aroused popular hostility. Free blacks and abolitionists openly resisted the new law, despite its provision of substantial fines and prison sentences for those who aided fugitive slaves or interfered with their capture. In October 1850, Boston abolitionists

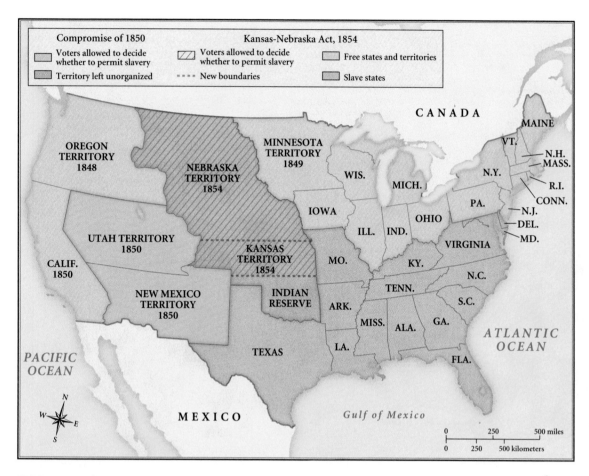

MAP 13.7 The Compromise of 1850 and the Kansas-Nebraska Act of 1854

Vast territories were at stake in the contest over the expansion of slavery. The Compromise of 1850 resolved the status of lands in the Far West: California would be a free state, and the settlers of the Utah and New Mexico territories would vote for or against slavery (the doctrine of popular sovereignty). The decision in 1854 to void the Missouri Compromise (1820) and use popular sovereignty to decide the fate of slavery in the Kansas and Nebraska territories sparked a bitter local war and revealed a fatal flaw in the doctrine.

helped two slaves escape and drove a Georgia slave catcher out of town. The following year, rioters in Syracuse, New York, broke into a courthouse to free a fugitive slave. Abandoning his commitment to nonviolence, Frederick Douglass declared, "The only way to make a Fugitive Slave Law a dead letter is to make half a dozen or more dead kidnappers." As if in response, in September 1851, a deadly confrontation took place in the Quaker village of Christiana, Pennsylvania. About twenty African Americans exchanged gunfire with a party of slave catchers from Maryland, killing two of them. Federal authorities indicted thirty-six blacks and four whites for treason. But a Pennsylvania jury acquitted one defendant, and public opinion in the North forced the government to drop the charges against the rest.

Upping the ante was Harriet Beecher Stowe's abolitionist novel, *Uncle Tom's Cabin* (1852), which

magnified northern opposition to the Fugitive Slave Act. By translating the moral principles of abolitionism into heartrending personal situations, Stowe's melodramatic book evoked empathy and outrage throughout the North. Members of northern state legislatures were equally incensed that the act allowed the federal government to intervene in the internal affairs of their states. In response, they enacted **personal-liberty laws** that increased the legal rights of their residents, including accused fugitives. In 1857, the Wisconsin Supreme Court went even further. In *Ableman v. Booth,* it ruled that the Fugitive Slave Act was void in Wisconsin because it was contrary to state law and the constitutional rights of its citizens. Taking a states' rights stance—a position usually associated with the South—the Wisconsin court challenged the authority of federal courts to review its decision. When the case reached the U.S. Supreme Court in 1859,

Presidential Election of 1852

In this cartoon, Franklin Pierce races toward the White House on a fleet Democratic horse, while General Winfield Scott futilely beats his stubborn Whig mule, which is being pulled by members of the Know-Nothing Party ("Native Americans") and prodded by a group of African Americans. By identifying Scott and the Whigs as anti-foreigner and pro-black, the cartoonist hoped to garner votes for Pierce and the Democrats from New York's large population of Irish and German immigrants. Collection of Janice L. and David J. Frent.

Chief Justice Roger B. Taney led a unanimous Court in affirming the supremacy of federal courts over state courts—a position that has stood the test of time—and upheld the constitutionality of the Fugitive Slave Act. But by that time, popular opposition in the North had made it nearly impossible to catch fugitive blacks. As Frederick Douglass had hoped, the act had become a "dead letter."

The Political System in Decline

The conflict over slavery split both major political parties along sectional lines and stymied their leaders. The Whigs, weakened by the death of Henry Clay, chose General Winfield Scott, another hero of the war with Mexico, as their presidential candidate in 1852. However, many southern Whigs refused to support Scott because northern Whigs refused to support slavery. The Democrats were equally divided: Southerners wanted a candidate who would support Calhoun's constitutional argument that all territories should be open to slavery; but northern and midwestern Democrats advocated popular sovereignty, as did the three leading candidates—Lewis Cass of Michigan, Stephen Douglas of Illinois, and James Buchanan of Pennsylvania. Ultimately, the party settled on a compromise nominee, Franklin Pierce of New Hampshire, a congenial man reputed to be sympathetic to the South.

The Democrats' cautious strategy paid off, and they swept the election. Pleased by the admission of California as a free state, Martin Van Buren and many other Free-Soilers voted for Pierce, reuniting the Democratic Party. Conversely, disagreements over slavery fragmented the Whig Party into sectional wings; it would never again wage a national campaign.

As president, Pierce pursued an expansionist foreign policy. To assist northern merchants, he sent a mission to Japan to negotiate a commercial treaty. To mollify southern expansionists, he revived Polk's plan to annex extensive Mexican territories south of the Rio Grande. When Mexico rejected this initiative, Pierce settled for the purchase of a narrow slice of land that would enable his negotiator, James Gadsden, to build a transcontinental rail line from New Orleans to California (see Map 13.5, p. 402).

Pierce's most dramatic, and most controversial, foreign policy initiative came in the Caribbean and Central America. Southern expansionists had previously funded three clandestine military expeditions to Cuba, where they hoped to prod sugar-producing slave owners to declare independence from Spain and join the United States. Beginning in 1853, Pierce covertly supported new expeditions to Nicaragua and Cuba and, to further the venture in Cuba, threatened war with Spain over the seizure of an American ship. When northern Democrats in Congress refused to support this aggressive diplomacy, Pierce and Secretary of State William L. Marcy had to back down. Marcy then tried to buy the island from Spain. When that scheme also failed, Marcy arranged for American diplomats in Europe to inform Pierce, in the so-called Ostend Manifesto of 1854, that the United States would be justified "by every law, human and Divine" in seizing Cuba. Leaked to the press by antiexpansionists, the Ostend Manifesto revived fears of a "Slave Power" conspiracy; and determined northern resistance scuttled the planters' dreams of carving out an empire for slavery in the Caribbean.

The Kansas-Nebraska Act and the Rise of New Parties

In 1854, a new struggle over westward expansion deepened sectional divisions. Because the Missouri Compromise prohibited new slave states in the Louisiana Purchase north of 36°30′, southern senators had for two decades delayed the political organization of the area. Now residents of the Ohio River Valley and the Upper South were demanding

its settlement. Senator Stephen A. Douglas of Illinois became their spokesman, partly because he supported the construction of a transcontinental railroad linking Chicago to California. In 1854, Douglas introduced a bill to extinguish Native American rights on the central Great Plains and organize a large free territory to be called Nebraska.

Douglas's bill conflicted with the plans of southern politicians who wanted to extend slavery throughout the Louisiana Purchase and wanted a southern city — New Orleans, Memphis, or St. Louis — to serve as the eastern terminus of a transcontinental railroad. To win southern support for the organization of Nebraska, Douglas made two major concessions. First, he amended his bill so that it explicitly repealed the Missouri Compromise and organized the region on the basis of popular sovereignty. Second, Douglas agreed to the formation of two territories, Nebraska and Kansas. This provision would give southern planters the opportunity to settle Kansas and, through popular sovereignty, eventually make it a slave state (see Map 13.7, p. 407). Douglas knew that his bill would "raise a hell of a storm." To win the support of northern congressmen, he argued that Kansas was not suited to plantation agriculture and would become a free state. After weeks of bitter debate, the Senate enacted the Kansas-Nebraska Act. When sixty-six northern Democrats in the House of Representatives defied party policy to vote against the act, President Pierce used patronage and persuasion to get twenty-two members to change their votes, and the measure squeaked through.

The Republican and American Parties. The Kansas-Nebraska Act had disastrous consequences for the American political system. It completed the destruction of the Whig Party and nearly wrecked the Democratic Party. Denouncing the act as "part of a great scheme for extending and perpetuating supremacy of the slave power," northern Whigs and "anti-Nebraska" Democrats abandoned their respective parties. They joined with Free-Soilers and abolitionists in a new Republican Party. Although the new party was a coalition of "strange, discordant and even hostile elements," as one Republican put it, its founders shared a determination to ban slavery from the territories and a common economic philosophy. They condemned slavery because it degraded the dignity of manual labor and drove down the wages and working conditions of free white workers. Like Thomas Jefferson, they celebrated the moral virtues of a society based on "the middling classes who own the soil and work it with their own hands." Abraham Lincoln, an Illinois Whig who became a Republican, articulated the party's vision of social mobility. "There is no permanent class of hired laborers among us," he declared, which meant that every free man had a chance to become a property owner. In the face of increasing class divisions in the industrializing North and Midwest, Lincoln and his fellow Republicans asserted the values of republican liberty and individual enterprise.

The Republicans faced strong competition from the American, or Know-Nothing, Party. The party had its origins in the anti-immigrant and anti-Catholic organizations of the 1840s (see Chapter 9). In 1850, these secret nativist societies banded together as the Order of the Star-Spangled Banner; and the following year, they entered politics, forming the American Party. The secrecy-conscious members of the party often replied "I know nothing" to outsiders' questions, thus giving the party its nickname. But the party's program was far from secret: It wanted to unite all native-born Protestants against the "alien menace" of Irish and German Catholics, prohibit further immigration, and institute literacy tests for voting. In 1854, voters angered by the Kansas-Nebraska Act elected dozens of Know-Nothing candidates to the House of Representatives and gave the party control of the state governments of Massachusetts and Pennsylvania. The emergence of a major party led by nativists suddenly became a real possibility.

"Bleeding Kansas." The Kansas-Nebraska Act created yet another national political crisis. As soon as the act was passed, thousands of settlers rushed into the Kansas Territory, putting Douglas's theory of popular sovereignty to the test. On the side of slavery, Senator David R. Atchison of Missouri organized residents of his state to cross temporarily into Kansas and vote in crucial elections there. Opposing Atchison was the abolitionist New England Emigrant Aid Society, which dispatched hundreds of free-soilers to Kansas. In March 1855, the Pierce administration stepped into the fray by accepting the legitimacy of the territorial legislature sitting in Lecompton, Kansas, which had been elected primarily by border-crossing Missourians and had adopted proslavery legislation. However, the majority of Kansas residents favored free soil and refused allegiance to the Lecompton government.

In May 1856, both sides turned to violence and soon the territory was known as "Bleeding Kansas," a term coined by Horace Greeley of the *New York Tribune*. A proslavery gang, seven hundred strong, sacked the free-soil town of Lawrence; the gang wrecked two newspaper offices, looted stores, and burned down buildings. The attack enraged John Brown, a fifty-six-year-old abolitionist from New York and Ohio, whose free-state militia arrived too late to save the town. Brown was a complex man with a checkered financial past. Despite a long record of failed businesses, he had an intellectual and a moral intensity that won the trust of influential people. Taking vengeance for the sack of Lawrence, Brown and a few followers murdered and mutilated five proslavery settlers at Pottawatomie. We must "fight fire with fire" and "strike terror in the hearts of the proslavery people," Brown declared. The southerners' attack on Lawrence and the Pottawatomie killings started a guerrilla war in Kansas that took almost two hundred lives (see Comparing American Voices, "Civil Warfare in Kansas" pp. 412–413).

Armed Abolitionists in Kansas, 1859

The confrontation between North and South in Kansas took many forms. In the spring of 1859, Dr. John Doy (seated) slipped across the border into Missouri and tried to lead thirteen escaped slaves to freedom in Kansas, only to be captured and jailed in St. Joseph, Missouri. The serious-looking men standing behind Doy, well armed with guns and Bowie knives, attacked the jail and carried Doy back to Kansas. The photograph celebrated — and memorialized — their successful exploit. Kansas State Historical Society.

Buchanan's Failed Presidency

The violence in Kansas dominated the presidential election of 1856. The two-year-old Republican Party counted on anger over Bleeding Kansas to boost its fortunes. The party's platform denounced the Kansas-Nebraska Act and, alleging a Slave Power conspiracy, insisted that the federal government prohibit slavery in all the territories. Its platform also called for federal subsidies for transcontinental railroads, reviving an element of the Whig's economic program that was popular among midwestern Democrats. For president the Republicans nominated Colonel John C. Frémont, a free-soiler famous for his role in the conquest of Mexican California.

The Election of 1856. The American Party also entered the election with high hopes, but it quickly split along sectional lines over the conflict in Kansas. The southern faction of the party nominated former Whig president Millard Fillmore, while the northern contingent endorsed Frémont—thanks to clever maneuvering by Republican political operatives. During the campaign, Republicans won the votes of Know-Nothing workingmen in the North by demanding a ban on foreign immigrants and high tariffs on foreign manufactures. As

a Pennsylvania Republican put it, "Let our motto be, protection to everything American, against everything foreign." In New York, Republicans likewise shaped their policies "to cement into a harmonious mass . . . all of the Anti-Slavery, Anti-Popery and Anti-Whiskey" voters.

The Democrats reaffirmed their support for popular sovereignty and the Kansas-Nebraska Act, and nominated James Buchanan of Pennsylvania. A tall, dignified man, Buchanan was an experienced but unimaginative politician who was known for his support of the South. Drawing on that support and his party's organizational strength in the North, Buchanan won the three-way race with 1.8 million votes (45 percent) and 174 electoral votes. Frémont polled 1.3 million votes (33 percent) and 114 electoral votes Buchanan took only five free states; the Republican candidate took eleven. A small shift of the popular vote to Frémont in Illinois and Pennsylvania would have given him the presidency.

The dramatic restructuring of parties was now apparent (Map 13.8). With the splintering of the American Party, the Republicans had replaced the Whigs as the second major party. Moreover, because the Republicans had no support in the South, they would have to tread carefully; a Republican

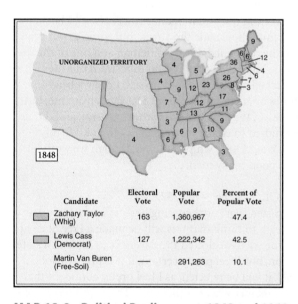

Candidate	Electoral Vote	Popular Vote	Percent of Popular Vote
Zachary Taylor (Whig)	163	1,360,967	47.4
Lewis Cass (Democrat)	127	1,222,342	42.5
Martin Van Buren (Free-Soil)	—	291,263	10.1

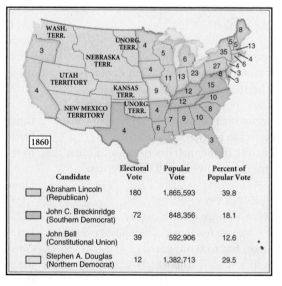

Candidate	Electoral Vote	Popular Vote	Percent of Popular Vote
Abraham Lincoln (Republican)	180	1,865,593	39.8
John C. Breckinridge (Southern Democrat)	72	848,356	18.1
John Bell (Constitutional Union)	39	592,906	12.6
Stephen A. Douglas (Northern Democrat)	12	1,382,713	29.5

MAP 13.8 Political Realignment, 1848 and 1860

In the presidential election of 1848, both the Whig and the Democratic candidates won electoral votes in most parts of the nation. Subsequently, the political conflict over slavery and the Compromise of 1850 destroyed the Whig Party in the South. As the only nationwide party, the Democrats won easily over the Whigs in 1852 and, because of the split between Republicans and Know-Nothings, in 1856 as well. However, by 1860, a new regional party system had taken shape—and would persist for the next seventy years—with Democrats dominant in the South and Republicans dominant in the Northeast, Midwest, and Far West.

Civil Warfare in Kansas

The Kansas-Nebraska Act of 1854 and its doctrine of popular sovereignty set off a mad scramble. The New England Emigrant Aid Society provided support to antislavery northerners who wanted to settle in Kansas, while southern politicians mobilized supporters in Missouri and elsewhere to save the new territory for slavery. The no-holds-barred struggle for control of the territorial legislature led to fraud, intimidation, and, by 1856, the guerrilla warfare described in these letters.

Letters are valuable sources. Because they are written as private communications, they tend to depict the writers' values and passions frankly and realistically. What writers say in letters, they often mean. Still, letters—like all sources—have to be read carefully to probe the psychology and the motives of their authors.

AXALLA JOHN HOOLE
"Coming Here Will Do No Good at Last"

Early in 1856, Axalla John Hoole and his bride left South Carolina to build a new life in the Kansas Territory (K.T.). These letters from Hoole to his family show that things did not go well from the start and gradually got worse; after eighteen months, the Hooles returned to South Carolina. A Confederate militia captain during the Civil War, Axalla Hoole died in the Battle of Chickamauga in September 1863.

Kansas City, Missouri, Apl. 3d., 1856.

The Missourians . . . are very sanguine about Kansas being a slave state & I have heard some of them say it shall be. . . . But generally speaking, I have not met with the reception which I expected. Everyone seems bent on the Almighty Dollar, and as a general thing that seems to be their only thought. . . .

Well, dear brother, the supper bell has rung and I must close. Give my love to [the family] and all the Negroes. . . .

Lecompton, K.T., Sept. 12, 1856.

I have been unwell ever since the 9th of July. . . . I thought of going to work in a few days, when the Abolitionists broke out and I have had to stand guard of nights when I ought to have been in bed, took cold which . . . caused diarrhea, but . . . I feel quite well [now]. Betsie is well—

You perceive from the heading of this that I am now in Lecompton, almost all of the Proslavery party between this place and Lawrence are here. We brought our families here, as we thought that we would be better able to defend ourselves when altogether than if we scattered over the country. . . .

Lane [and a free-state army] came against us last Friday (a week ago to-day). As it happened we had about 400 men with two cannon—we marched out to meet him, though we were under the impression at the time that he had 1,000 men. We came in gunshot of each other, but the regular [U.S. Army] soldiers came and interferred, but not before our party had shot some dozen guns, by which it is reported that five of the Abolitionists had been killed or wounded. We had strict orders from our commanding officer (Gen'l Marshall) not to fire until they made the attack, but some of our boys would not be restrained. I was a rifleman and one of the skirmishers, but did all that I could to restrain our men though I itched all over to shoot myself. I drew a bead a dozen times on a big Yankee about 150 yards from me, but did not fire. . . . We were acting on the defensive, and did not think it prudent to commence the engagement. I firmly believe we would have whipped them, though we would have lost a good many men. . . .

Douglas, K.T., July the 5th., 1857.

I fear, Sister, that [our] coming here will do no good at last, as I begin to think that this will be made a Free State at last. 'Tis true we have elected Proslavery men to draft a state constitution, but I feel pretty certain, if it is put to a vote of the people, it will be rejected, as I feel pretty confident that they have a majority here at this time. The South has ceased all efforts, while the North is redoubling her exertions. We nominated a candidate for Congress last Friday—Ex-Gov. Ransom of Michigan. I must confess I have not much faith in him, tho he professes to hate the abolitionists bitterly, and I have heard him say that Negroes were a great deal better off with Masters. Still, I fear him, but it was the best we could do. If we had nominated a Southern man, he would have been sure to have been beaten and I doubt whether we can even elect a Northerner who favors our side. . . .

Give my love to Mother. . . . Tell all the Negroes howdie, and my best regards to enquiring friends.

SOURCE: William Stanley Hoole, ed., "A Southerner's Viewpoint of the Kansas Situation, 1856–1857," *Kansas Historical Quarterly* 3 (1934): 43–65, 149–171, passim.

JOHN LAWRIE
"A Few Goddamned White-livered Lawyers"

Unlike Axalla Hoole and his wife, Indiana farmer John Lawrie initially had no intention of settling in Kansas. However, after fighting there for ten months in 1856 and 1857, he seems to have warmed to the idea. When the Civil War broke out, Lawrie would join the Union army and serve for nearly four years.

Wolf Mound Farm, White Co., Indiana
Apl. 16th, 1857
Dear [brother] Art,

When I left home on the Fifteenth of last June I had no intention of making a home in Kansas. I intended in case I could find any organization ready to take the field against the Missourians, to use my utmost endeavors to change the attitude of the Free-State settlers from a defensive to an offensive warfare. When I reached Leavenworth, I was unable to find any organization of Free-State men, and could only tell one when I met him by his hanging head and subdued tone of voice. . . .

Hearing that people held up their heads and spoke what they thought in Lawrence, I started for that point and soon found myself at home as far as a hatred of tyranny and a thirst for vengeance for the insult [the sack of Lawrence] of the 21st of May was concerned. The people had concluded to try whether there was truth in the Border Ruffian assertion *The Damned Yankees won't fight!* There was quite a stir among the young men in the way of target firing and drilling in order to prepare themselves for any emergency that might arise requiring them *to contend with superior numbers*, the only thing that thus far had held them back. I found that arms were really scarce. I expected to find plenty of improved firearms, and it was with the greatest difficulty I succeeded in getting an old condemned musket.

I went up to Topeka [and] found the people discussing the propriety of defending the legislature against all who might attempt to disperse it. A few goddamned white-livered lawyers succeeded in getting through a resolution that it was the determination of the Free State men *not to molest or hinder the U.S. troops* [sent by authorities in Washington to preserve order]. On the fourth of July at an hour before noon the troops charged into town and dispersed the legislature and retired again unmolested.

I went back to the place where I worked near Lawrence, and did nothing but damn and curse lawyers and professional politicans until the sixth of August, when it was decided by some of the boys in town to go down to a block house erected by a company of Georgian robbers in the lower part of the territory and whip the robbers. . . .

We were all rather anxious to see how the boys would behave under fire, many of them never having as yet heard singing lead. The night was rather dark, and the enemy showed no light and made no noise. Our captain (who by the way was an old man of wars man) reconnoitered the ground and concluded to lead us right on to the place and take it by assault. . . . We went up as well as old veterans ever dared to go. . . . The sound of our steady *tramp! tramp!* was too much for the garrison and they incontinently fled. . . .

I shall remain here until the middle of June when I intend returning to Kansas.

SOURCE: V. E. Gibbens, ed., "Letters on the War in Kansas in 1856," *Kansas Historical Quarterly* 10 (1941): 370–373.

ANALYZING THE EVIDENCE

➤ What do these letters suggest about the character of the armed conflict in Kansas? Just how bloody was it?

➤ Why do you think Axalla Hoole and John Lawrie took up arms? Is it significant that both of them would go on to fight in the Civil War?

➤ Like most political or ideological doctrines, popular sovereignty only works well in certain circumstances. What were the conditions in Kansas between 1854 and 1860 that made it virtually unworkable? Can you see any parallels with the experiment of popular sovereignty in Iraq since 2004? Explain your answer.

triumph in the next presidential election might prompt the southern states to withdraw from the Union. A North Carolina newspaper threatened as much in 1856: "If the Republicans should succeed, the result will be a separation of the states. No human power can prevent it." The fate of the republic hinged on the ability of President Buchanan to defuse the passions of the past decade and devise a way of protecting free soil in the West and slavery in the South.

Dred Scott: Petitioner for Freedom. Events — and his own values and weaknesses — conspired against Buchanan. In 1856, the Supreme Court had considered the case of *Dred Scott v. Sandford*, which raised the controversial issue of Congress's constitutional authority to regulate slavery in the territories. Dred Scott was an enslaved African American who had lived for a time with his owner, an army surgeon, in the free state of Illinois and at Fort Snelling, then in the Wisconsin Territory, where the Northwest Ordinance (1787) prohibited slavery. Seeking freedom for himself and his family, Scott claimed in his suit that residence in a free state and a free territory had made him free. Hoping naively that a strong proslavery decision would settle the issue of slavery in the territories, Buchanan pressured several northern justices to vote in tandem with their southern colleagues. In the Court's decision, handed down in 1857, seven of the nine members of the Court agreed that Scott was still a slave; but the members of the majority were unable to agree on the legal issues, and each justice wrote a separate opinion.

Chief Justice Roger B. Taney of Maryland, a slave owner himself, composed the most influential opinion. He declared that Negroes, whether enslaved or free, could not be citizens of the United States, and that Scott therefore had no right to sue in federal court. That argument was controversial: Free blacks were citizens in many states, which presumably gave them access to the federal courts. But then Taney proceeded to make two even more controversial points. First, he endorsed John C. Calhoun's argument: Because the Fifth Amendment prohibited "takings" of property without due process of law, Taney ruled that Congress could not deny southern citizens the right to take their slave property into the territories and own it there. Consequently, the chief justice concluded, the provisions of the Northwest Ordinance and the Missouri Compromise that prohibited slavery had never been constitutional. Second, Taney declared that Congress could not give to territorial governments any powers that

Congress itself did not possess. Because Congress had no authority to prohibit slavery in a territory, neither did a territorial government. Taney thereby endorsed Calhoun's interpretation of popular sovereignty: Only when settlers wrote a constitution and requested statehood could they prohibit slavery.

In a single stroke, Taney and the Democrat-dominated Supreme Court had declared the Republicans' antislavery platform to be unconstitutional. The Republicans could never accept the legitimacy of that decision. Led by Senator Seward of New York, they accused the Supreme Court and President Buchanan of participating in the Slave Power conspiracy.

Buchanan then added fuel to the raging constitutional fire. In early 1858, he recommended the admission of Kansas as a slave state under a constitution written by the proslavery Lecompton legislature, although the legitimacy of the constitution was widely questioned. Angered that Buchanan would not permit a popular referendum on the Lecompton constitution, Stephen Douglas, the most influential Democratic senator, broke with the president and persuaded Congress to deny statehood to Kansas. (Kansas would enter the Union as a free state in 1861.) By pursuing a proslavery agenda — first in the *Dred Scott* decision and then in Kansas — Buchanan had widened the split in his party and the nation.

➤ Why did the Compromise of 1850 fail?

➤ What did Stephen Douglas try to accomplish with the Kansas-Nebraska Act of 1854?

➤ Was that act any more successful than the Compromise of 1850? Explain your answer.

➤ What were the main constitutional arguments advanced during the debate over slavery in the territories? Which of those arguments influenced Chief Justice Taney's opinion in *Dred Scott*?

Abraham Lincoln and the Republican Triumph, 1858–1860

The crisis of the Union intensified as the Democratic Party fragmented along sectional lines and the Republicans gained support in the North and Midwest. Abraham Lincoln emerged as the pivotal figure in American politics, the only Republican leader whose policies and temperament might have saved the Union. But few southerners trusted Lincoln, and the prospect of his election to the presidency renewed the commitment of the southern secessionists who had been threatening to leave the Union since 1850.

Lincoln's Political Career

The middle-class world of storekeepers, lawyers, and entrepreneurs in the small towns of the Ohio River Valley shaped Lincoln's early career. He came from an impoverished yeoman farm family that had moved from Kentucky, where Lincoln was born in 1809, to Indiana and then to Illinois. In 1831, Lincoln rejected his father's life as a subsistence farmer and became a store clerk in New Salem. Socially ambitious, Lincoln sought entry into the middle class by mastering its literary and professional culture; he joined the New Salem Debating Society, read the works of Shakespeare, and studied law.

Admitted to the bar in 1837, Lincoln moved to Springfield, the new state capital. There he met Mary Todd, the cultured daughter of a Kentucky banker; they married in 1842. The couple was a picture in contrasts: Her tastes were aristocratic; his were humble. She was volatile; he was easygoing but suffered bouts of depression that tried her patience and tested his character.

Abraham Lincoln, 1859

Lincoln was not a handsome man, and he photographed poorly. In fact, his campaign photographs were often retouched to hide his prominent cheekbones and nose. More important, no photograph ever captured Lincoln's complex personality and wit or the intensity of his spirit and intellect. To grasp Lincoln, it is necessary to read his words. Chicago Historical Society.

Abraham Lincoln: Ambitious Politician. Lincoln's ambition was "a little engine that knew no rest," his closest associate remarked, and it prompted him to seek fame and fortune in politics. An admirer of Henry Clay, Lincoln joined the Whig Party and won election to four terms in the Illinois legislature, where he promoted education, state banking, and canals and railroads. He became a dexterous party politician, adept in the distribution of patronage and the passage of legislation.

In 1846, the rising lawyer-politician won election to a Congress that was bitterly divided over the Wilmot Proviso. Lincoln had long felt that human bondage was unjust but did not believe that the federal government had the constitutional authority to tamper with slavery in the South. With respect to the war with Mexico, he took the middle ground. He supported bills for military appropriations but, determined to exclude the institution of slavery from the territories, voted for Wilmot's proposal. He himself proposed that Congress enact legislation for the gradual (and compensated) emancipation of slaves in the District of Columbia. He argued that a series of measures—firm opposition to the

expansion of slavery, gradual emancipation, and the colonization of freed slaves in Africa—was the only practical way to address the issues of slavery and racial diversity. However, both abolitionists and proslavery activists rejected Lincoln's pragmatic policies, and he lost his bid for reelection. Dismayed at the rancor of ideological politics, he withdrew from the political arena and developed a lucrative legal practice representing railroads and manufacturers.

Lincoln returned to the political fray after passage of Stephen Douglas's Kansas-Nebraska Act. Shocked by the act's repeal of the Missouri Compromise, Lincoln warned the citizens of Illinois that the American "republican robe is soiled and trailed in the dust" and called on them to "repurify it and wash it white in the spirit, if not the blood of the Revolution." Rejecting Douglas's scheme to let residents decide the fate of slavery in the territories, Lincoln reaffirmed his position that slavery be allowed to continue in the states where it existed but that national authority should be used to exclude it from the territories. Confronting the moral issue of slavery, Lincoln declared that if the nation was going to uphold its republican ideals, it must eventually cut out slavery like a "cancer."

The Lincoln-Douglas Debates. Abandoning the Whig Party in favor of the Republicans, Lincoln quickly emerged as their leader in Illinois. Campaigning for the U.S. Senate against Douglas in 1858, Lincoln alerted his audiences to the dangers of the Slave Power. He warned that the proslavery Supreme Court might soon declare that the Constitution "does not permit a state to exclude slavery from its limits," just as it had decided in *Dred Scott* that "neither Congress nor the territorial legislature can do it." In that event, he continued, "we shall awake to the reality ... that the Supreme Court has made Illinois a slave state." The prospect of slavery spreading into the North informed Lincoln's famous "House Divided" speech. Quoting from the Bible, "A house divided against itself cannot stand," he predicted a crisis: "I believe this government cannot endure permanently half slave and half free. . . . It will become all one thing, or all the other."

The contest in Illinois attracted national interest because of Douglas's prominence in the Democratic Party and Lincoln's reputation as a formidable speaker. During a series of seven debates, Douglas declared his support for white supremacy: "This government was made by our fathers, by white men for the benefit of white men and their posterity forever," he asserted, and he attacked Lincoln for supporting "negro equality." Put on the defensive by Douglas's racial rhetoric, Lincoln advocated economic opportunity for free blacks but not equal political rights. He asked how Douglas could accept the decision in *Dred Scott* (which protected slave owners' property in the territories) and yet advocate popular sovereignty (which asserted settlers' power to exclude slavery). Douglas responded with the so-called Freeport Doctrine, which suggested that a territory's residents could exclude slavery simply by not adopting a law to protect it. Although that doctrine pleased neither proslavery advocates nor abolitionists, the Democrats won a narrow victory over the Republicans in Illinois, and the state legislature reelected Douglas to the U.S. Senate.

The Union Under Siege

The debates with Douglas gave Lincoln a national reputation, and the election of 1858 established the Republican Party as a formidable political force.

Republicans won control of the House of Representatives and various state legislatures.

The Rise of Radicalism. Shaken by the Republican advance, southern Democrats divided into two groups: moderates and fire-eaters. The moderates, among them Senator Jefferson Davis of Mississippi, were known as Southern Rights Democrats; their goal was to win ironclad political commitments to protect slavery. The fire-eaters—men like Robert Barnwell Rhett of South Carolina and William Lowndes Yancey of Alabama—rejected that strategy; they repudiated the Union and actively promoted the secession of the southern states. Radical antislavery northerners played into their hands. Senator Seward of New York declared that freedom and slavery were locked in "an irrepressible conflict," and militant abolitionist John Brown demonstrated what that might mean. In October 1859, Brown led eighteen heavily armed black and white men in a raid on the federal arsenal at Harpers Ferry, Virginia. Brown hoped to secure hundreds of weapons, spark a slave rebellion, and establish a separate African American state in the South.

Republican leaders disavowed Brown's unsuccessful raid, but Democrats called his plot "a natural, logical, inevitable result of the doctrines and teachings of the Republican party." The state of Virginia charged Brown with treason, tried him in court, and sentenced him to be hanged. Virginians—and all white southerners—were horrified when reformer Henry David Thoreau called Brown "an angel of light" and other northerners leaped to Brown's defense. The slaveholding states looked to the future with fear. "The aim of the present black republican organization is the destruction of the social system of the Southern States, without regard to consequences," warned one newspaper. Once in power, another southern paper warned, the Republicans "would create insurrection and servile war in the South—they would put the torch to our dwellings and the knife to our throats." Brown had predicted as much. As he faced the gallows, Brown apocalyptically (and correctly) predicted "that the crimes of this guilty land will never be purged away but with blood."

Nor could the South count on the Democratic Party to protect its interests. At the party's convention in April 1860, northern Democrats rejected Jefferson Davis's proposal to protect slavery in the territories. In response, the delegates from eight southern states quit the meeting. At a second Democratic convention in Baltimore, northern and midwestern delegates

Harper's Ferry, Virginia

On Sunday evening, October 19,1859, abolitionist John Brown and his band of nineteen men seized the federal armory and arsenal (the large buildings along the river) in the small industrial town of Harper's Ferry. The town lies at the junction of the Shenandoah (hidden behind the hill and house at right) and Potomac rivers in the Blue Mountains of northwestern Virginia. The Baltimore and Ohio Railroad crossed the Potomac on the bridge in the middle of the picture, and Hall's Rifle Works, where sixty gunsmiths produced firearms for the U.S. Army, occupied a nearby island in the Shenandoah. National Archives.

nominated Stephen Douglas for president; meeting separately, southern Democrats nominated the sitting Vice President, John C. Breckinridge of Kentucky.

The Election of 1860. With the Democrats divided, the Republicans sensed victory in the election of 1860. They courted white voters with a free-soil platform that opposed both slavery and racial equality: "Missouri for white men and white men for Missouri," declared that state's Republican platform. The national Republican convention chose Lincoln as its presidential candidate because his position on slavery was more moderate than that of the best-known Republicans, Senators Seward

of New York and Chase of Ohio, who were demanding abolition. Lincoln also conveyed a compelling egalitarian image that appealed to small-holding farmers and wage earners. And Lincoln's home territory—the rapidly growing Midwest—was crucial in the competition between Democrats and Republicans.

The Republican strategy worked. Although Lincoln received only 40 percent of the popular vote, he won a majority in the Electoral College by carrying every northern and western state except New Jersey. Douglas took 30 percent of the total vote, but won electoral votes only in Missouri and New Jersey. Breckinridge captured every state in the Deep South as well as Delaware, Maryland, and

Salomon de Rothschild

A French Banker Analyzes the Election of 1860 and the Threat of Secession

Salomon de Rothschild, the son of Baron James de Rothschild of Paris, traveled around the United States from 1859 to 1861. In a series of detailed letters to his cousin Nathaniel in London, Rothschild offered an astute (and often cynical) analysis of the sectional crisis. Although his comments are generally evenhanded, Rothschild feared social revolution and so favored the South; following secession, he supported diplomatic recognition of the Confederacy.

You know that the . . . United States was made up of two great parties, the Democrats and the Republicans. These two parties were subdivided into groups, only a few, but extremely violent ones. The abolitionists were the extremist Republicans; the "fire-eaters" or secessionists, the extremist Democrats. Fanaticism and the extremist parties always win out, and, exactly as I expressed my forebodings to you a very long time ago, abolitionism on one side and secession on the other dragged along the moderate neutrals despite themselves.

The point of departure was, as you know, the slavery question. Naturally, this institution, on which the wealth of the South was based, was defended to the limit by those who profited from it. Two reasons pushed the people of the North to seek to destroy slavery by any means. The first . . . was a simple humanitarian reason. In a free country like America, there must be no slaves, and complete equality must reign in all ranks of society. . . . But the real sentiment that guided them . . . was the spirit of leveling; everyone must be equal in abjection. They cannot tolerate someone in the South having 200 arms for his use while they have only their own two. This sentiment was the first seed of the social revolution which is at this very moment taking giant strides behind the political revolution.

You doubtless have read in the newspapers about the first effects of Lincoln's election; . . . several Southern states—Florida, Georgia, Alabama, and Mississippi, with South Carolina as their guide—have for all practical purposes seceded from the United States and are going to form a new confederation. . . . If this state of affairs should continue, the City of New York, whose interests are closely tied to those of the South, will secede from the State of New York, declare itself a free port, and form a new independent state. . . .

There may be two means of restoring the situation. The first (which seems impracticable to me) would be for Lincoln and [vice-President-elect] Hamlin, frightened by the political and financial crisis that their election has created, to submit their resignation. . . . The second expedient would be for those *slave* states which do not want to secede . . . to urge the two parties to make mutual concessions.

[However, Rothschild writes in another letter, compromise is unlikely because] the South is simply a producer and consumer; the West and the North, and especially the East, are almost entirely manufacturers, but they need strong protection. The South could supply itself with all necessary items in Europe, at prices from twenty-five to forty percent lower than what they have been paying up to now. It contends that these duties do it no good and that the money goes back into the pockets of the Northern manufacturers. Therefore it wants to escape from this tax. The suppression of, or even a strong reduction in, these duties would completely ruin the eastern states of New Jersey and Pennsylvania, which could not compete with the cheap prices attained by England and even by France. Thousands of men would find themselves unemployed and would therefore threaten the well-being and the very existence not only of their employers, but even of the merchants and the producers in those areas, leading to an imminent danger of social revolution, which the North must avoid at all costs. . . .

The future is as black as it can be. . . . For some months I have been predicting to you what is now happening. I was all alone in my opinion then, and the Americans, always optimistic in things that concern their country and themselves, laughed at my fears and my doubts. Now it is too late to change; half of America is ruined. . . .

SOURCE: Sigmund Diamond, ed., *A Casual View of America, 1859–1861: The Home Letters of Salomon de Rothschild* (Stanford, Calif.: Stanford University Press, 1961), 82–83, 118–119.

ANALYZING THE EVIDENCE

➤ Do you agree with Salomon de Rothschild's analysis of the motives of antislavery northern whites?

➤ Is Rothschild correct about the role of tariffs in the secession crisis? What happened to tariffs after the nullification crisis of the 1830s (see Chapter 10)?

➤ From what you have read in the text, is Rothschild's speculation that New York City will secede along with the South a realistic one? What argument does he make? Why was he wrong?

THE NATIONAL GAME. THREE "OUTS" AND ONE "RUN".
ABRAHAM WINNING THE BALL.

Lincoln on Home Base

As early as 1860, the language and imagery of sports had penetrated politics. Sporting a long raillike bat labeled "EQUAL RIGHTS AND FREE TERRITORY," Lincoln has scored a victory in the election. His three opponents—from left to right, Bell, Douglas, and Breckinridge—are "out." Indeed, they had been "skunk'd" and, as Douglas laments, their attempt to put a "short stop" to Lincoln's career had failed. Museum of American Political Life.

North Carolina; while John Bell, a former Tennessee Whig who was the nominee of the compromise-seeking Constitutional Union Party, carried the Upper South states where the Whigs had been strongest: Kentucky, Tennessee, and Virginia (see Voices from Abroad, "Salomon de Rothschild: A French Banker Analyzes the Election of 1860 and the Threat of Secession," p. 418.)

The Republicans had united voters in the Northeast, the Midwest, and California and Oregon behind free soil, and had gained national power. A revolution was in the making. Slavery had permeated the American federal republic for so long and so thoroughly that southerners had come to see it as part of the constitutional order—an order now under siege. A Republican administration in Washington, warned John Townsend of South Carolina, might suppress "the inter-State slave trade" and thereby "*cripple this vital Southern institution* of slavery." To many southerners, it seemed time to think carefully about the meaning of Lincoln's words in 1858 that the Union must "become all one thing, or all the other."

➤ How did Lincoln's position on slavery differ from that of Stephen Douglas?

➤ Did the Republicans win the election of 1860, or did the Democrats lose it? Explain your answer.

SUMMARY

In this chapter, we have examined three important and related themes: the movement of Americans into Texas and Oregon in the 1830s and early 1840s, the causes and consequences of the war with Mexico in the late 1840s, and the gradual decline and destruction of the Second Party System during the 1850s. We saw that the coming of the Mexican War was a result of the political agendas of Presidents John Tyler and James Polk. Their determination to add territory, and slave states, to the Union pushed the United States into the war. As we have noted, the consequences of the war were immense because the acquisition of vast new territories raised the explosive and long-postponed question of the expansion of slavery.

To address this dangerous issue, Henry Clay and Daniel Webster devised the Compromise of 1850. As we have seen, their efforts were in vain. Antislavery northerners defied the Fugitive Slave Act, and expansionist-minded southerners sought to acquire new slave states in the Caribbean. Ideology—the pursuit of absolutes—replaced politics—the art of compromise—as the ruling principle of American political life.

The Second Party System rapidly disintegrated. The Whig Party crumbled and then vanished; two issue-oriented parties, the nativist American Party and the antislavery Republican Party, competed for its members. As the Republicans gained strength, the Democratic Party splintered into sectional factions over Bleeding Kansas and other slavery-related issues. The stage was set for Lincoln's victory in the climactic election of 1860.

Connections: Sectionalism

Sectionalism has been a constant factor in American history. In the seventeenth century, different groups of English settlers migrated to the Chesapeake and New England regions; and during the eighteenth century, their economies and societies developed along different lines. Then, as we pointed out in the essay that began Part Three, (p. 269), in the early nineteenth century,

the economic revolution and social reform sharpened sectional divisions: The North developed into an urban industrial society based on free labor, whereas the South remained a rural agricultural society dependent on slavery.

As we saw in Chapter 8, the first major conflict between North and South came in 1819 over the admission of Missouri to the Union as a slave state. A decade later, as we learned in Chapter 10, the Tariff of Abominations renewed the sectional struggle and sparked the nullification movement in South Carolina. Both the Missouri crisis of 1819–1821 and the tariff-nullification crisis of 1829–1832 ended with political compromises. And as we have just seen in this chapter, political leaders crafted the Compromise of 1850 to resolve yet another sectional conflict. However, as we will observe in the next chapter, the crisis sparked by the election of Abraham Lincoln, the presidential candidate of the northern- and midwestern-based Republican Party, could not be resolved through compromise. Nor did the Union's triumph in the Civil War end sectional strife. As Chapter 15 will demonstrate, Reconstruction created new sectional antagonisms and ended only with the Compromise of 1877—yet another political settlement of divisive social differences. Only in the mid-twentieth century, with the migration out of the South of millions of African Americans and the movement into the South of northern business corporations and millions of northern-born whites, would the sectional struggle begin to abate.

CHAPTER REVIEW QUESTIONS

➤ What were the links between the Mexican War of 1846–1848 and Abraham Lincoln's election as president in 1860?

➤ When and why did the Second Party System of Whigs and Democrats collapse?

➤ Some historians claim that the mistakes of a "Blundering Generation" of political leaders led, by 1860, to the imminent breakup of the Union. Do you agree with their assessment? Why or why not?

TIMELINE

1844	James Polk is elected president
1845	John Slidell's diplomatic mission to Mexico fails
	Texas admitted into the Union
1846	United States declares war on Mexico
	Treaty with Britain divides Oregon Country at forty-ninth parallel
	Wilmot Proviso is approved by House but not by Senate
1847	American troops under General Winfield Scott capture Mexico City
1848	Gold is discovered in California
	In Treaty of Guadalupe Hidalgo, Mexico cedes its provinces of California, New Mexico, and Texas to United States
	Free-Soil Party forms
	Zachary Taylor is elected president
1850	President Taylor dies, and Millard Fillmore assumes presidency
	Compromise of 1850 seeks to preserve the Union
	Northern abolitionists reject Fugitive Slave Act
	South seeks to expand slavery by acquiring Spanish Cuba
1851	American (Know-Nothing) Party forms
1852	Harriet Beecher Stowe publishes *Uncle Tom's Cabin*
	Franklin Pierce is elected president
1854	Ostend Manifesto promotes seizure of Cuba
	Kansas-Nebraska Act tests policy of popular sovereignty
	Republican Party forms
1856	Turmoil in Kansas undermines popular sovereignty
	James Buchanan is elected president
1857	Supreme Court's decision in *Dred Scott v. Sandford* allows slavery in U.S. territories
1858	President Buchanan backs Lecompton constitution
	Abraham Lincoln and Stephen Douglas debate in U.S. Senate race
1859	John Brown leads armed raid on federal arsenal at Harpers Ferry
1860	Abraham Lincoln is elected president in four-way contest

FOR FURTHER EXPLORATION

Patricia Nelson Limerick, *The Legacy of Conquest: The Unbroken Past of the American West* (1989), provides a sharply written interpretation of the struggle among individuals, groups, and nations for control of the West. "First-Person Narratives of California's Early Years, 1849–1900" is available through the Library of Congress (**lcweb2.loc.gov/ammem/cbhtml/cbhome.html**). *The West* (6 hours), a fine documentary by Ken Burns and Stephen Ives, has a useful Web site at **www.pbs.org/thewest**. For the early history of Texas, see **www.tsl.state.tx.us/treasures/**. The PBS documentary *U.S.-Mexican War: 1846–1848* (4 hours) and the companion Web site (**www.pbs.org/usmexicanwar**) view the war from both American and Mexican perspectives and draw on the expertise of historians from both countries.

David Potter, *The Impending Crisis, 1848–1861* (1976), presents a lucid account of the political history of the pre–Civil War years. For the role of slavery in sparking the Civil War, see episode 4 of the PBS documentary *Africans in America* and the related Web site (**www.pbs.org/wgbh/aia/home.html**). An audio discussion of the election of 1860 is available at **www.albany.edu/talkinghistory/arch2000july-december.html**. Two recent works—John Patrick Daly, *When Slavery Was Called Freedom: Evangelicalism, Proslavery, and the Causes of the Civil War* (2002), and Leonard L. Richards, *The Slave Power: The Free North and Southern Domination, 1780–1860* (2000)—offer a broad cultural analysis of the sectional conflict. For one state's struggle, see William A. Link, *Roots of Secession: Slavery and Politics in Antebellum Virginia* (2003). For proslavery ideology, consult Manisha Sinha, *The Counterrevolution of Slavery: Politics and Ideology in Antebellum South Carolina* (2000).

Eric Foner, *Free Soil, Free Labor, Free Men* (1970), provides an eloquent analysis of the ideology and politics of the Republican Party. Michael Holt's *The Political Crisis of the 1850s* (1978) shows how the collapse of the Second Party System allowed sectional rivalries to engulf the nation in war. For an evocative treatment of Lincoln, read Stephen Oates, *With Malice Toward None: A Life of Abraham Lincoln* (1977). The justices' opinions in the *Dred Scott* case are at **odur.let.rug.nl/~usa/D/1851-1875/dredscott/dredxx.htm**; for Lincoln's response, see **www.usconstitution.com/AbrahamLincolnonDredScottDecision.htm**. "*Uncle Tom's Cabin* and American Culture: A Multi-Media Archive" (**jefferson.village.virginia.edu/utc/**) is an extremely rich Web site that places the novel in its literary and cultural context.

TEST YOUR KNOWLEDGE

To assess your command of the material in this chapter, see the Online Study Guide at **bedfordstmartins.com/henretta**.

For Web sites, images, and documents related to topics and places in this chapter, visit **bedfordstmartins.com/makehistory**.

14

Two Societies at War

1861–1865

"**WHAT A SCENE IT WAS**," Union soldier Elisha Hunt Rhodes wrote in his diary as the Battle of Gettysburg ended. "Oh the dead and the dying on this bloody field." By July 1862, thousands of men had died in battle, and the slaughter would continue for two more years. "What is this all about?" asked Confederate lieutenant R. M. Collins at the end of another gruesome battle. "Why is it that 200,000 men of one blood and tongue . . . [are] seeking one another's lives? We could settle our differences by compromising and all be at home in ten days." But there was no compromise and no peace, a tragic outcome that President Lincoln found beyond human comprehension. "The Almighty has His own purposes," he reflected in 1862 and again in 1864. "God wills this contest, and wills that it shall not yet end."

To explain why Southerners seceded and then fought to the bitter end is not simple, but racial slavery is an important part of the answer. For southern political leaders, the Republican victory in 1860 presented a clear and immediate danger to the slave-owning republic that had existed since 1776. Lincoln was elected without a single electoral vote from the South, and Southerners knew that his Republican Party would prevent the extension of slavery into the territories.

◀ **Fields of Death**

Fought with mass armies and new weapons, the Civil War took a huge toll in human lives, as evidenced by this grisly photograph of a small section of the battlefield at Antietam, Maryland. At Shiloh, Tennessee, General Ulysses Grant surveyed a field "so covered with dead that it would have been possible to walk . . . in any direction, stepping on dead bodies, without a foot touching the ground." Library of Congress.

Moreover, they did not believe Lincoln when he promised not "directly or indirectly, to interfere with the institution of slavery in the States where it exists." "The mission of the Republican party," a southern newspaper declared, was "to meddle with everything—to meddle with the domestic institutions of other States, and to meddle with family arrangements in their own states—to overthrow Democracy, Catholicism and Slavery." Soon, a southern senator warned, "cohorts of Federal office-holders, Abolitionists, may be sent into [our] midst" to mobilize the African American population. The result would be bloody slave revolts and racial intermixture—by which was meant sexual relations between black men and white women, because white owners had already fathered untold numbers of children by their black women slaves. "Better, far better! endure all horrors of civil war," insisted a Confederate recruit from Virginia, "than to see the dusky sons of Ham leading the fair daughters of the South to the altar." To preserve black slavery and the supremacy of white men, radical southern leaders embarked on the dangerous journey of secession.

Lincoln and the North would not let them go in peace. Living in a world still ruled by kings and princes, northern leaders believed that the collapse of the American Union might destroy for all time the prospect of a republican government based on constitutional procedures, majority rule, and democratic elections. "We cannot escape history," the new president eloquently declared. "We shall nobly save, or meanly lose, the last best hope of earth." A young Union army recruit from Ohio put the issue simply: "If our institutions prove a failure . . . of what value will be house, family, or friends?"

And so came the Civil War. Called the War Between the States by Southerners and the War of the Rebellion by Northerners, the struggle continued until the great issues of the Union and slavery had finally been resolved. The cost was incredibly high: more lives lost than in all the nation's subsequent wars and a century-long legacy of bitterness between the triumphant North and the vanquished South.

Secession and Military Stalemate, 1861–1862

After Lincoln's election in November 1860, secessionist fervor swept through the Deep South and the future of the Union appeared dim. Still, the professional politicians in Washington—veteran party leaders who had run the country for a generation—did not give up. In the four months between Lincoln's election and his inauguration on March 4, 1861, they struggled to forge a new compromise that would preserve the Union.

The Secession Crisis

The movement toward secession was most rapid in South Carolina, the home of John C. Calhoun, nullification, and southern rights. Robert Barnwell Rhett and other fire-eaters had been calling for secession since the crisis of 1850; and with Lincoln's election, their goal was within reach. On December 20, a special state convention voted unanimously to dissolve "the union now subsisting between South Carolina and other States."

The Lower South Secedes. Moving quickly, fire-eaters elsewhere in the Lower South called similar conventions and mobilized vigilante groups and militia units to suppress local Unionists and prepare for war. In early January, in an atmosphere of public celebration, Mississippi enacted a secession ordinance. Within a month, Florida, Alabama, Georgia, Louisiana, and Texas had also left the Union (Map 14.1). In early February, the jubilant secessionists met in Montgomery, Alabama, to proclaim a new nation—the Confederate States of America. Adopting a provisional constitution, the delegates named Jefferson Davis of Mississippi, a former U.S. senator and secretary of war, as the Confederacy's president and Alexander Stephens, a congressman from Georgia, as vice president.

Secessionist fervor was less intense in the four states of the Middle South (Virginia, North Carolina, Tennessee, and Arkansas), where there were fewer slaves. Moreover, white opinion was sharply divided in the four border slave states (Maryland, Delaware, Kentucky, and Missouri), where yeomen farmers had greater political power. Yeomen had long resented the authority claimed by the slave-owning gentry, and some actively opposed it. In the 1850s, journalist Hinton Helper of North Carolina roused the "Non-slaveowners of the South! farmers, mechanics and workingmen," warning, "the slaveholders, the arrogant demagogues whom you have elected to offices of honor and profit, have hoodwinked you." Influenced partly by these sentiments, the legislatures of Virginia and Tennessee refused to join the secessionist movement in January 1861. Seeking a compromise, Upper South leaders proposed federal guarantees for slavery in the states where it existed.

Meanwhile, the Union government floundered. In his final message to Congress in December 1860, President Buchanan declared secession illegal but,

Agitating for Secession

Lincoln's election triggered a vigorous response from South Carolina's fire-eaters, who called a secession rally in Charleston. On December 1, 1860, hundreds of well-dressed planters and merchants met at the Mills Hotel to hear prominent secessionists demand withdrawal from the Union. Three weeks later, in a unanimous vote, a special state convention did just that. Library of Congress.

timid and indecisive, denied that the federal government had the authority to restore the Union by force. South Carolina viewed Buchanan's message as implicit recognition of its independence and demanded the surrender of Fort Sumter, a federal garrison in Charleston Harbor. To test the secessionists' resolve, Buchanan ordered that the fort be supplied by an unarmed merchant ship. When South Carolinians fired on the ship, Buchanan

showed his own lack of resolve by refusing to order the navy to escort it into the harbor.

The Crittenden Compromise. Instead, Buchanan urged Congress to find a compromise. The scheme proposed by Senator John J. Crittenden of Kentucky, an aging follower of Henry Clay, received the most support. Crittenden's plan had two parts. The first, which won congressional approval, called for a

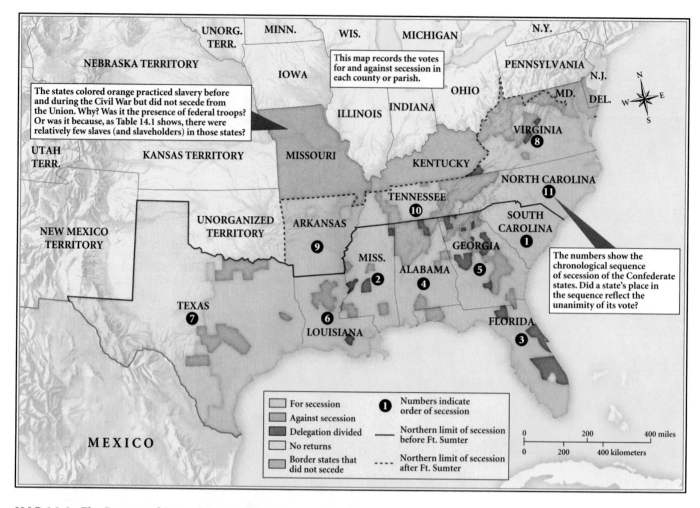

MAP 14.1 The Process of Secession, 1860–1861

The states of the Lower South had the highest concentration of slaves, and they led the secessionist movement. After the attack on Fort Sumter in April 1861, the states of the Upper South joined the Confederacy. Yeomen farmers in Tennessee and the backcountry of Alabama, Georgia, and Virginia opposed secession but, except in the future state of West Virginia, initially rallied to the Confederate cause. Consequently, the South entered the Civil War with its white population relatively united.

constitutional amendment to protect slavery from federal interference in any state where it already existed. Crittenden's second provision called for the westward extension of the Missouri Compromise line (36°30′ north latitude) to the California border. Slavery would be barred north of the line and protected to the south, including any territories "hereafter acquired," thus holding out the prospect of future private military expeditions to acquire Cuba or Nicaragua.

On strict instructions from President-elect Lincoln, congressional Republicans rejected this part of Crittenden's plan. Lincoln was firmly committed to the doctrine of free soil and feared this compromise would encourage the South to

embark on new imperialist adventures in the Caribbean and Latin America. Crittenden's plan, Lincoln charged, would be "a perpetual covenant of war against every people, tribe, and State owning a foot of land between here and Tierra del Fuego [the southern tip of South America]." In 1787, 1820, and 1850, the political leaders of the North and South had found ways to resolve their differences over slavery. In 1861, there would be no compromise.

In his inaugural address in March 1861, Lincoln carefully articulated his position on slavery and the Union. He promised to safeguard slavery where it existed; however, there must be free soil in the territories. Most important, Lincoln stated that the

Union was "perpetual"; consequently, the secession of the Confederate states was illegal, and acts of violence in support of their action constituted insurrection. The new president clearly declared his intention to enforce federal law throughout the Union and—of particular relevance to Fort Sumter—to continue to "hold, occupy, and possess" federal property in the seceded states and "to collect duties and imposts" there. If force was necessary to preserve the Union, Lincoln—like Andrew Jackson during the nullification crisis—would use it. The choice was the South's: Return to the Union or face war.

The Upper South Chooses Sides

The South's decision came quickly. The garrison at Fort Sumter urgently needed food and medi-cine. Upholding his promise to defend federal property, Lincoln dispatched a relief expedition and assured the Confederate government of its peaceful mission. However, Jefferson Davis and his associates wanted a military confrontation to win the support of the states of the Middle and Border South; so Davis demanded the surrender of the fort. When Major Robert Anderson refused, the Confederate forces opened fire—ardent fire-eater Edmund Ruffin supposedly fired the first cannon on April 12. Isolated and under heavy bombardment, the Union forces capitulated on April 14. The next day, Lincoln called 75,000 state militiamen into federal service for ninety days to put down an insurrection "too powerful to be suppressed by the ordinary course of judicial proceedings." All talk of compromise was past.

The Bombardment of Fort Sumter, 1861
Currier & Ives, a New York publishing house, brought colorful art into thousands of middle-class homes by printing inexpensive lithographs of pastoral scenes and dramatic historical events. This fairly realistic depiction of the Confederate bombardment of Fort Sumter in Charleston Harbor in April 1861 was especially popular in the South. Library of Congress.

Northerners responded to Lincoln's call to arms with wild enthusiasm. Asked to provide thirteen regiments of volunteers, Republican governor William Dennison of Ohio sent twenty. Many northern Democrats declared their support for the Union cause, even as they prepared their party to function as the "loyal opposition," to oppose various initiatives of Lincoln's Republican administration. "Every man must be for the United States or against it," Stephen Douglas declared. "There can be no neutrals in this war, only patriots—or traitors."

The white residents of the Middle and Border South now had to choose between the Union and the Confederacy, and their decision was crucial. Those eight states accounted for two-thirds of the South's white population, more than three-fourths of its industrial production, and well over half of its food and fuel. They were home to many of the nation's best military leaders, including Colonel Robert E. Lee of Virginia, a career officer whom veteran General Winfield Scott recommended to Lincoln to lead the new Union army. And they were geographically strategic. Kentucky, with its 500-mile border on the Ohio River, was essential to the movement of troops and supplies. Maryland was vital to the Union's security because it bordered the nation's capital on the north.

The weight of history decided the outcome in Virginia, the original home of American slavery. Three days after the fall of Fort Sumter, a Virginia convention approved secession by a vote of 88 to 55, with the dissenters drawn mainly from the yeomen-dominated northwestern counties. Elsewhere, Virginia whites rallied to the Confederate cause. "The North was the aggressor," declared Richmond lawyer William Poague as he enlisted. "The South resisted her invaders." Refusing Scott's offer of the Union command, Robert E. Lee resigned from the U.S. Army. "Save in defense of my native state," Lee told Scott, "I never desire again to draw my sword." Arkansas, Tennessee, and North Carolina quickly joined Virginia in the Confederacy.

Lincoln moved aggressively to hold the states of the Border South, where relatively few families owned slaves (see Table 14.1). In May 1861, he ordered General George B. McClellan to take control of northwestern Virginia to secure the railway line between Washington and the Ohio River Valley. In October, voters in that yeoman region overwhelmingly approved the formation of a breakaway territory, West Virginia, which was admitted to the Union as a state in 1863. Unionists easily carried the day in Delaware but not in Maryland, where slavery was well entrenched. A pro-Confederate mob attacked Massachusetts troops marching between railroad stations in Baltimore, causing the war's first combat deaths: four soldiers and twelve civilians. When Maryland secessionists destroyed railroad bridges and telegraph lines, Lincoln ordered the military occupation of the state and the arrest of Confederate sympathizers, including legislators. He released them only in November 1861, after Unionists gained control of Maryland's government.

Lincoln was equally energetic and resourceful in the Southwest. To win Missouri (and control of the Missouri and upper Mississippi rivers), Lincoln mobilized the German American militia, which strongly opposed slavery; in July, it defeated a force of Confederate sympathizers commanded by the governor. Despite continuing raids by Confederate guerrilla bands, the Union retained control of Missouri (see Voices from Abroad, "Ernest Duvergier de Hauranne: German Immigrants and the Civil War Within Missouri," p. 429). In Kentucky, secessionist and Unionist sentiment was evenly balanced, so Lincoln moved cautiously. When Unionists took control of the state government in August, Lincoln ordered federal troops to halt Kentucky's thriving trade with the Confederacy. In September, Illinois volunteers under the command of a relatively unknown brigadier general named Ulysses S. Grant crossed the Ohio River into Kentucky and drove out an invading Confederate force. Lincoln had kept the four border states (Delaware, Maryland, Missouri, and Kentucky) and the northwestern portion of Virginia in the Union.

TABLE 14.1 Slavery and Secession

Group	Percentage of Whites in Slave-owning Families	Percentage of Slaves in Population
Original Confederate states	38	47
Border states that later joined the Confederacy	24	32
Border states that remained in the Union	14	15

Ernest Duvergier
de Hauranne

German Immigrants and the Civil War Within Missouri

Tens of thousands of German immigrants settled in Missouri and other midwestern states in the two decades before the Civil War; and as this letter written by Ernest Duvergier de Hauranne indicates, most of them supported the Union cause. Duvergier de Hauranne (1843–1877), a Frenchman, traveled widely, and his letters home offer intelligent commentary on American politics and society during the Civil War.

St. Louis, September 12, 1864

Missouri is to all intents and purposes a rebel state, an occupied territory where the Federal forces are really nothing but a garrison under siege; even today it is not certain what would happen if the troops were withdrawn. Party quarrels here are poisoned by class hatreds. Not only are questions of peace and war, of national honor and humiliation, hotly debated, but so is the much more explosive question of slavery versus abolition. . . . It is a war over private interests between two irreconcilable classes. The old Anglo-French families, attached to Southern institutions, harbor a primitive, superstitious prejudice in favor of slavery. Conquered now, but full of repressed rage, they exhibit the implacable anger peculiar to the defenders of lost causes. They no longer have any hope of reviving slavery or their own past fortunes; . . . they seem to be lying low while hoping for an opportunity to take their revenge.

The more recent German population is strongly abolitionist. They have brought to the New World the instincts of European democracy, together with its radical attitudes and all-or-nothing doctrines. Ancient precedents and worn-out laws matter little to them. They have not studied history and have no respect for hallowed injustices; but they do have, to the highest degree, that sense of moral principle which is more or less lacking in American democracy. They aren't afraid of revolution: to destroy a barbarous institution they would, if necessary, take an axe to the foundations of society. Furthermore, their interests coincide with their principles. . . . Even if their democratic beliefs and innate sense of justice did not cause them to rise up against slavery, they would still detest it as an obstacle to their prosperity and as a source of unfair competition with their labor.

The immigrant arrives poor and lives by his work. A newcomer, having nothing to lose and caring little for the interests of established property owners, sees that the subjection of free labor to the ruinous competition of slave labor must be ended. At the same time, his pride rebels against the prejudice attached to work in a land of slavery; he wants to reestablish its value. . . .

There is no mistaking the hatred the two parties, not to say the two peoples, have for each other. . . . As passions were coming to a boil, the Federal government sent General [John C.] Frémont here as army commander and dictator. . . . An abolitionist and a self-made man, he put himself firmly at the head of the German party, determined to crush the friends of slavery. He formed an army of Germans who are completely devoted to their chief. . . . He left the abolitionist party in the West organized, disciplined, stronger and more resolute, but he also left the pro-Southern party more exasperated than ever, and society divided, without intermediaries, into two hostile camps. . . .

Everyone is an extremist; between the radical abolitionists and the friends of the South there is no moderate Unionist middle ground. Bands of guerrillas hold the countryside, where they raid as much as they please; politics serves as a fine pretext for looting. Their leaders are officers from the army of the South who receive their orders from the Confederate government. . . . These "bushwackers," who ordinarily rob indiscriminately, maintain their standing as political raiders by occasionally killing some poor, inoffensive person. Finally, people bent on personal vengeance take advantage of the state of civil war: sometimes one hears of villages divided against themselves so bitterly that massacres are carried on from door to door with incredible ferocity. . . . You can see what emotions are still boiling in this region that is supposed to be pacified.

SOURCE: Ernest Duvergier de Hauranne, *A Frenchman in Lincoln's America* (Chicago: Lakeside Press, 1974), 1: 305–309.

ANALYZING THE EVIDENCE

➤ According to Duvergier de Hauranne, why did German immigrants oppose slavery? How does his explanation help us understand the free-soil movement?

➤ Why, as late as 1864, did the federal government lack control over Missouri, a border state that remained in the Union? What clues does Duvergier de Hauranne provide?

➤ Ethnic rivalries loomed large in the civil warfare in Missouri. As you read the chapter, look for other ethnic conflicts that exploded during the war. Why did they do so?

Setting War Objectives and Devising Strategies

At his inauguration in February 1861, Jefferson Davis identified the Confederates' cause with that of the American revolutionaries: Like their grandfathers, white Southerners were fighting against tyranny and for the "sacred right of self-government." As Davis put it, the Confederacy sought "no conquest, no aggrandizement . . . ; all we ask is to be let alone." The South's decision to renounce expansion was ironic: It was the region's quest for western lands that had sparked the conflict. However, the decision simplified the Confederacy's military strategy; it needed only a stalemate to achieve the goal of independence. Ignoring the strong opposition to slavery among potential European allies, the Confederate constitution explicitly stated that "no . . . law denying or impairing the right of property in negro slaves shall be passed," and Vice President Alexander Stephens ruled out gradual emancipation. In Stephens's view, the Confederacy's "cornerstone rests upon the great truth that the Negro is not equal to the white man, that slavery—subordination to the superior race—is his natural or normal condition."

Lincoln outlined the Union's military goals in a speech to Congress on July 4, 1861. He portrayed secession as an attack on popular government, which was America's great contribution to world history; it tested "whether a constitutional republic . . . [can] maintain its territorial integrity against a domestic foe." Convinced that the Union had to crush the rebellion, Lincoln rejected General Winfield Scott's plan to use economic sanctions and a naval blockade to persuade the Confederates to return to the Union. Instead, the president insisted on an aggressive military strategy and a policy of unconditional surrender.

Union Thrusts Toward Richmond. The president hoped that a quick strike against the Confederate capital of Richmond, Virginia, would end the rebellion. So he dispatched General Irvin McDowell and an army of 30,000 men to attack General P. G. T. Beauregard's force of 20,000 troops at Manassas, a rail junction in Virginia 30 miles southwest of Washington. In July 1861, McDowell launched a strong assault near Manassas Creek (also called Bull Run), but panic swept his troops when the Confederate soldiers counterattacked. For the first time, Union soldiers heard the hair-raising rebel yell. "The peculiar corkscrew sensation that it sends down your backbone under these circumstances can never be told," one Union veteran wrote. "You

have to feel it." McDowell's troops—along with the many civilians who had come to observe the battle—retreated in disarray to Washington.

The rout of the Union army at Bull Run made it clear that the rebellion would not be easily crushed. Lincoln replaced McDowell with General McClellan and enlisted an additional million men who would serve for three years in the newly created Army of the Potomac. A cautious military engineer, McClellan spent the winter of 1861 training the recruits; then, early in 1862, he launched a major offensive. With great logistical skill, the Union general transported 100,000 troops by boat down the Potomac River and put them ashore on the peninsula between the York and James rivers (Map 14.2). Ignoring Lincoln's advice to "strike a blow" quickly, McClellan advanced slowly toward the South's capital, giving the Confederates time to mount a counterstroke. To relieve the pressure on Richmond, a Confederate army under Thomas J. "Stonewall" Jackson marched rapidly north up the Shenandoah Valley in western Virginia and threatened Washington. Lincoln recalled 30,000 troops from McClellan's army to protect the Union's capital, but Jackson, a brilliant general, tied down the larger Union forces. Then Jackson returned quickly to Richmond to bolster the main Confederate army commanded by General Robert E. Lee. Lee launched a ferocious attack that lasted for days (June 25–July 1), suffering 20,000 casualties to the Union's 10,000. When McClellan failed to exploit the Confederates' weakness, Lincoln ordered the withdrawal of the Army of the Potomac, and Richmond remained secure.

Lee Moves North: Antietam. Hoping for victories that would humiliate Lincoln's government, Lee went on the offensive. Joining with Jackson in northern Virginia, he routed Union troops in the Second Battle of Bull Run (August 1862) and then struck north through western Maryland. There, he nearly met with disaster. When Lee divided his force—sending Jackson to capture Harpers Ferry in West Virginia—a copy of his orders fell into McClellan's hands. The Union general again failed to exploit his advantage. He delayed his attack, thereby allowing Lee's depleted army to occupy a strong defensive position behind Antietam Creek, near Sharpsburg, Maryland. Outnumbered 87,000 to 50,000, Lee desperately fought off McClellan's attacks. Just as Union regiments were about to overwhelm Lee's right flank, Jackson's troops arrived and saved the Confederates from a major defeat. Appalled by the number of Union casualties, McClellan let Lee retreat to Virginia.

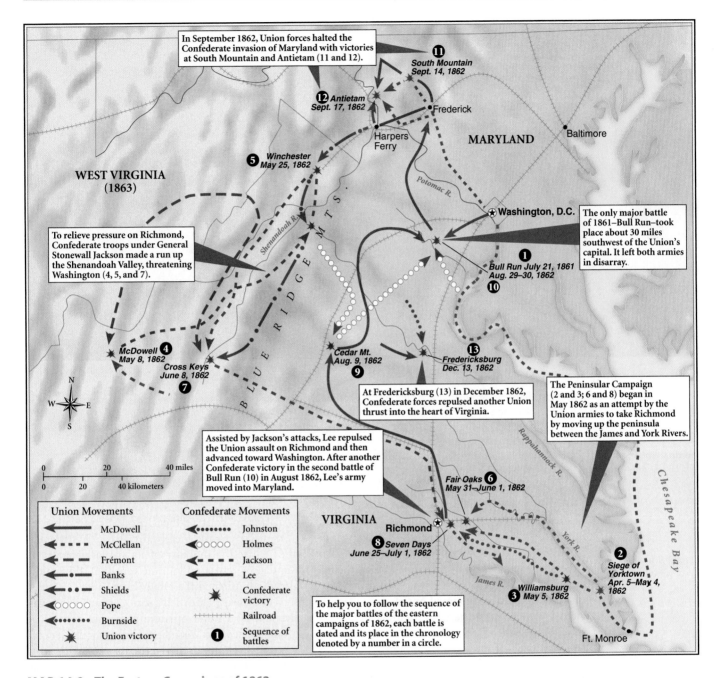

In September 1862, Union forces halted the Confederate invasion of Maryland with victories at South Mountain and Antietam (11 and 12).

South Mountain Sept. 14, 1862

⑫ **Antietam** Sept. 17, 1862

Frederick

Harpers Ferry

MARYLAND

Baltimore

⑤ **Winchester** May 25, 1862

WEST VIRGINIA (1863)

Potomac R.

Shenandoah R.

Washington, D.C.

The only major battle of 1861–Bull Run–took place about 30 miles southwest of the Union's capital. It left both armies in disarray.

To relieve pressure on Richmond, Confederate troops under General Stonewall Jackson made a run up the Shenandoah Valley, threatening Washington (4, 5, and 7).

① **Bull Run** July 21, 1861 Aug. 29–30, 1862 ⑩

McDowell May 8, 1862 ④

Cross Keys June 8, 1862 ⑦

B L U E · R I D G E · M T S.

Cedar Mt. Aug. 9, 1862 ⑨

Fredericksburg Dec. 13, 1862 ⑬

At Fredericksburg (13) in December 1862, Confederate forces repulsed another Union thrust into the heart of Virginia.

The Peninsular Campaign (2 and 3; 6 and 8) began in May 1862 as an attempt by the Union armies to take Richmond by moving up the peninsula between the James and York Rivers.

N
W   E
S

| 0 | 20 | 40 miles |
| 0 | 20 | 40 kilometers |

Assisted by Jackson's attacks, Lee repulsed the Union assault on Richmond and then advanced toward Washington. After another Confederate victory in the second battle of Bull Run (10) in August 1862, Lee's army moved into Maryland.

Rappahannock R.

Chesapeake Bay

Fair Oaks ⑥ May 31–June 1, 1862

York R.

VIRGINIA   **Richmond**

⑧ **Seven Days** June 25–July 1, 1862

② **Siege of Yorktown** Apr. 5–May 4, 1862

James R.

Williamsburg ③ May 5, 1862

Ft. Monroe

Union Movements

	McDowell
	McClellan
	Frémont
	Banks
	Shields
	Pope
	Burnside
	Union victory

Confederate Movements

	Johnston
	Holmes
	Jackson
	Lee
	Confederate victory
	Railroad
①	Sequence of battles

To help you to follow the sequence of the major battles of the eastern campaigns of 1862, each battle is dated and its place in the chronology denoted by a number in a circle.

MAP 14.2   The Eastern Campaigns of 1862

Many of the great battles of the Civil War took place in the 125 miles separating the Union capital, Washington, D.C., and the Confederate capital, Richmond, Virginia. During 1862, Confederate generals Robert J. "Stonewall" Jackson and Robert E. Lee won defensive victories that protected the Confederate capital (3, 6, 8, and 13) and launched offensive strikes against Union forces guarding Washington (1, 4, 5, 7, 9, and 10). They also suffered a defeat—at Antietam (12), in Maryland—that was almost fatal. As was often the case in the Civil War, the victors in these battles were either too bloodied or too timid to exploit their advantage.

The fighting at Antietam was savage. A Wisconsin officer described his men "loading and firing with demoniacal fury and shouting and laughing hysterically." At a critical point in the battle, a sunken road—nicknamed Bloody Lane—was filled with Confederate bodies two and three deep, and the attacking Union troops knelt on "this ghastly flooring" to shoot at the retreating Confederates. The battle at Antietam on September 17, 1862, remains the bloodiest single day in U.S. military

The Battle of Antietam: The Fight for Burnside's Bridge

Nearly eight thousand soldiers lost their lives at Antietam on September 17, 1862, many of them in the struggle for the Rohrback Bridge that crossed Antietam Creek. One of those who survived the battle, Captain James Hope of the Second Vermont Volunteers, recorded the event in this painting. In his description of the work, Hope gave the bridge the name of the Union general who sacrificed many of his troops trying to capture it. Antietam National Battlefield, National Park Service, Sharpsburg, Maryland.

history. Together, the Confederate and Union dead numbered 4,800 and the wounded 18,500, of whom 3,000 soon died. (By comparison, there were 6,000 American casualties on D-Day, which began the invasion of Nazi-occupied France in World War II.)

In public, Lincoln claimed Antietam as a Union victory; but privately he declared that McClellan should have fought Lee to the bitter end. A masterful organizer of men and supplies, McClellan lacked the stomach for an all-out attack. Dismissing McClellan as his chief commander, Lincoln began a long search for an effective replacement. His first choice was Ambrose E. Burnside, who proved to be more daring but less competent than his predecessor. In December, after heavy losses in futile attacks against well-entrenched Confederate forces at Fredericksburg, Virginia, Burnside resigned his command, and Lincoln replaced him with Joseph "Fighting Joe" Hooker. As 1862 ended, the Confederates were optimistic: The war in the East was stalemated.

The War in the West. In the West, Union commanders were more successful (Map 14.3). Their goal was to control the Ohio, Mississippi, and Missouri rivers, and thereby divide the Confederacy and reduce the mobility of its armies. Thanks to Kentucky's refusal to join the rebellion, the Union already dominated the Ohio River Valley. In 1862, the Union army launched a series of highly innovative land and water operations to gain control of the Tennessee and Mississippi rivers as well. General Ulysses S. Grant used riverboats clad with iron plates to take Fort Henry on the Tennessee River and Fort Donelson on the Cumberland River. Grant then moved south to seize critical railroad lines. On April 6, a Confederate army led by Albert Sidney Johnston and P. G. T. Beauregard caught Grant by surprise near a small log church named Shiloh. In the ensuing battle, Grant relentlessly committed troops until he forced a Confederate withdrawal. As the fighting ended on April 7, Grant looked out over a large field "so covered with dead that it would have been possible to walk over the clearing in any direction, stepping on dead bodies, without a foot touching the ground." The cost in lives was high, but Lincoln was pleased: "What I want . . . is generals who will fight battles and win victories."

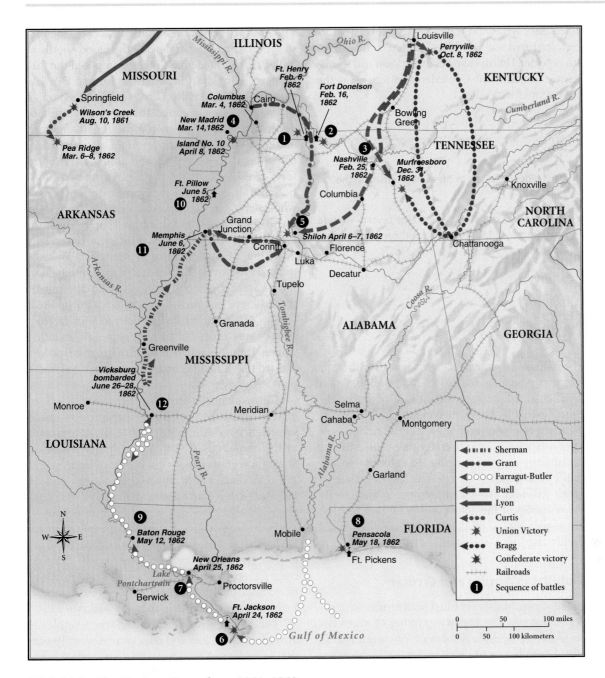

MAP 14.3   The Western Campaigns, 1861–1862

As the Civil War intensified in 1862, Union and Confederate military and naval forces fought to control the great valleys of the Ohio, Tennessee, and Mississippi rivers. From February through April 1862, Union armies moved south through western Tennessee (1–3 and 5). By the end of June, Union naval forces controlled the Mississippi River north of Memphis (4, 10, and 11) and from the Gulf of Mexico to Vicksburg (6, 7, 9, and 12). These military and naval victories gave the Union control of crucial transportation routes, kept Missouri in the Union, and carried the war to the borders of the states of the Deep South.

Less than three weeks later, Union naval forces commanded by David G. Farragut struck the Confederacy from the Gulf of Mexico. They captured New Orleans and took control of fifteen hundred plantations and fifty thousand slaves in the sur-

rounding region. The Union now held the South's financial center and largest city, and were in a strong position to conduct future naval operations. Equally important, slaves on many plantations looted their owner's mansion and refused to work unless they were paid wages. Slavery there "is forever destroyed and worthless," declared one Northern reporter. Union victories in the West had significantly undermined Confederate strength in the Mississippi River Valley.

> ➤ Why was there no new compromise over slavery in 1861?
>
> ➤ Why did most of the border states remain in the Union?
>
> ➤ Why did the Confederacy—and the Union—decide to go to war in 1861? What were the military goals of each side?

Toward Total War

The military carnage in 1862 made it clear that the war would be long and costly. After Shiloh, Grant later remarked, he "gave up all idea of saving the Union except by complete conquest." The conflict became a **total war**, arraying the entire resources of the two societies against each other. Aided by the Republican Party and a talented cabinet, Lincoln skillfully organized an effective central government. Jefferson Davis had less success harnessing the resources of the South, a difficult task because the eleven states of the Confederacy remained deeply suspicious of centralized rule.

Mobilizing Armies and Civilians

Initially, patriotic fervor filled both armies with eager volunteers. The widowed mother of nineteen-year-old Elisha Hunt Rhodes of Pawtuxet, Rhode Island, sent her son to war, saying, "My son, other mothers must make sacrifices and why should not I?" The call for soldiers was especially successful in the South, which had a strong military tradition, an ample supply of trained officers, and a culture that stressed duty and honor. "Would you, My Darling, . . . be willing to leave your Children under such a [despotic Union] government?" James B. Griffin of Edgefield, South Carolina, asked his wife. "No—I know you would sacrifice every comfort on earth, rather than submit to it." However, enlistments fell off as potential recruits learned the realities of mass warfare: heavy losses to epidemic diseases in the camps and wholesale death on the battlefields. Both governments soon faced the necessity of conscription.

The Military Draft. The Confederacy was the first to act. In April 1862, following the bloody battle at Shiloh, the Confederate Congress imposed the first legally binding draft in American history. One law extended existing enlistments for the duration of the war; another required three years of military service from all men between the ages of eighteen and thirty-five. In September 1862, after the heavy casualties at Antietam, the age limit was raised to forty-five. The Confederate draft had two loopholes, both controversial. First, it exempted one white man—the planter, a son, or an overseer—for each twenty slaves, and so allowed some whites on large plantations to avoid military service. This provision, Mississippi senator James Phelan wrote to Jefferson Davis, "has aroused a sprit of rebellion in some places." Second, draftees could hire substitutes. Before this provision was repealed in 1864, the price for a substitute had risen to $300 in gold, about three times the annual wages of a skilled worker. Laborers and yeomen farmers angrily complained that it had become "a rich man's war and a poor man's fight."

Consequently, some Southerners refused to serve. Because the Confederate constitution vested sovereignty in the individual states, the government in Richmond could not compel military service. Strong governors like Joseph Brown of Georgia and Zebulon Vance of North Carolina simply ignored President Davis's first draft call in early 1862. Elsewhere, state judges issued writs of **habeas corpus**—a legal instrument used to protect people from arbitrary arrest—and ordered the Confederate army to release reluctant draftees. However, the Confederate Congress overrode the judges' authority to free conscripted men, enabling the government to keep substantial armies in the field well into 1864.

The Union government acted more ruthlessly toward potential foes and reluctant citizens. To prevent sabotage and resistance by Confederate sympathizers, Lincoln suspended habeas corpus and over the course of the war imprisoned about fifteen thousand people without trial. The president also extended martial law to civilians who discouraged enlistments or resisted the draft, putting them under the jurisdiction of military courts rather than local juries. These firm policies had the wanted effect. When the Militia Act of 1862 set local recruitment quotas, states and towns enticed volunteers with cash bounties and eventually signed up nearly a million men. In the North, as in the South, wealthy men could avoid military service by providing a substitute or paying a $300 commutation fee.

The Enrollment Act of 1863 initiated conscription in the North and was strongly opposed by recent

Draft Riots and Antiblack Violence in New York City

The Enrollment Act of 1863 enraged many workers in New York City, especially recent Irish and German immigrants who did not want to go to war. In July, they took out their anger on free blacks in a weeklong series of riots. This engraving depicts a mob burning the Colored Orphan Asylum on Fifth Avenue, home to two hundred African American children. All of the children escaped safely, but the fire spread to adjoining structures, forcing residents to flee with whatever possessions they could carry. Library of Congress.

immigrants from Germany and Ireland, who protested that it was not their war. Northern Democrats, who became increasingly critical of Lincoln's policies as the war progressed, used the furor over conscription to bolster political support for their party. They accused Lincoln of drafting poor whites to win freedom for blacks, who would flood into the cities and take the whites' jobs. "Slavery is dead," declared a Democratic newspaper in Cincinnati, "the negro is not, there is the misfortune." In July 1863, the immigrants' hostility to the draft and to African Americans brought violence to the streets of New York City. For five days, Irish and German workers ran rampant, burning draft offices, sacking the homes of influential Republicans, and attacking the police. The rioters also lynched and mutilated a dozen African Americans, drove hundreds of black families from their homes, and burned down the Colored Orphan Asylum. Lincoln

responded by rushing in Union troops who had just fought at Gettysburg; the soldiers killed more than one hundred rioters and suppressed the insurrection.

Women and the War Effort. The Union government's campaign of total war won greater support among native-born middle-class citizens. In 1861, prominent New Yorkers established the U.S. Sanitary Commission to provide medical services and prevent the spread of epidemic diseases. Through its network of seven thousand local auxiliaries, the commission collected clothing, food, and medicine, and recruited battlefield nurses and doctors for the Union Army Medical Bureau. Despite the commission's efforts, dysentery, typhoid, and malaria spread through the camps, as did mumps and measles, childhood viruses to which many rural men had not developed immunity. Diseases and infections killed about 250,000 Union soldiers, roughly twice the number who died in combat. Still, better sanitation and high-quality food kept the mortality rate among Union troops significantly below that of soldiers in nineteenth-century European wars. Confederate soldiers were less fortunate. Thousands of women volunteered as nurses,

Hospital Nursing

Working as nurses in battlefront hospitals, thousands of Union and Confederate women gained firsthand experience of the horrors of war. A sense of calm prevails in this behind-the-lines Union hospital in Nashville, Tennessee, as nurse Anne Belle tends to the needs of soldiers recovering from their wounds. Most Civil War nurses were volunteers; they spent time cooking and cleaning for their patients as well as tending their injuries. U.S. Army Military History Institute.

but the Confederate health system was poorly organized. Scurvy was a special problem for southern soldiers, who lacked vitamin C in their diets, and they died from camp diseases at higher rates than did Union soldiers.

War-relief measures had a significant impact on women's lives. More than 200,000 northern women worked as volunteers in the Sanitary Commission and the Freedman's Aid Society, which collected supplies for liberated slaves, and some women took leading roles in wartime agencies. Dorothea Dix (see Chapter 11) served as superintendent of female nurses, the first woman to receive a major federal appointment. Dix successfully combated the prejudice against women's providing medical treatment to men and thereby opened a new occupation to women. Thousands of educated Union women joined the war effort as clerks in the expanding government bureaucracy, while in the South women staffed the efficient Confederate postal service. Indeed, in both sections of the country, millions of women assumed new economic responsibilities. They took over many farm tasks previously done by men and filled jobs not only in schools and offices but also in textile, clothing, and shoe factories. A number of women even took on military duties as spies, scouts, and (disguising themselves as men) soldiers. As nurse Clara Barton, who later founded the American Red Cross, recalled, "At the war's end, woman was at least fifty years in advance of the normal position which continued peace would have assigned her."

Mobilizing Resources

Wars are usually won by the side with greater resources and better economic organization. In this regard, the Union entered the war with a distinct advantage. With nearly two-thirds of the nation's population, two-thirds of the railroad mileage, and almost 90 percent of the industrial output, the North's economy was far superior to the South's (Figure 14.1). The North had an especially great advantage in the manufacture of cannon and rifles because many of its arms factories were equipped for mass production.

But the Confederate position was far from weak. Virginia, North Carolina, and Tennessee had substantial industrial capacity. Richmond, with its Tredegar Iron Works, was an important manufacturing center; and in 1861, the Confederacy moved the gun-making machinery from the U.S. armory at Harpers Ferry to Richmond. The production at the Richmond armory, the purchase of Enfield rifles from Britain, and the capture of 100,000 Union

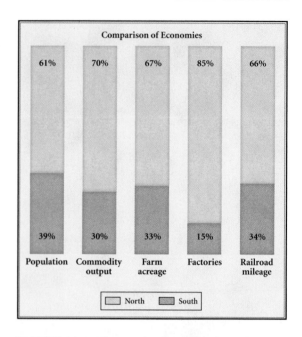

FIGURE 14.1   Economies, North and South, 1860
The military advantages of the North were even greater than this chart suggests because the population figures include slaves, whom the South feared to arm, and because its commodity output was primarily in farm goods rather than manufactures. Moreover, on average, southern factories were much smaller than those in the North. SOURCES: Stanley Engerman, "The Economic Impact of the Civil War," in *The Reinterpretation of American Economic History*, ed. Robert W. Fogel and Stanley L. Engerman (New York: Harper & Row, 1971); and U.S. census data.

guns enabled the Confederacy to provide every infantryman with a modern rifle-musket by 1863.

Moreover, with 9 million people, the Confederacy could mobilize enormous armies. Although more than one-third of that number were slaves, they contributed to the war effort by producing food for the army and cotton for export. Confederate leaders counted on **"King Cotton"** to provide the revenue to purchase clothes, boots, blankets, and weapons from abroad. They also counted on cotton as a diplomatic weapon that would persuade Britain and France, whose textile factories needed raw cotton, to grant the Confederacy diplomatic recognition. However, British manufacturers had stockpiled cotton; and when those stocks ran out, they found new sources in Egypt and India. Still, the South's hope was partially fulfilled. Although Britain never recognized the Confederacy as an independent nation, it granted the rebel government the status of a belligerent power—with the right under international law to borrow money and purchase weapons. The odds, then, did not necessarily favor the Union, despite its superior resources.

Richmond: Capital City and Industrial Center

The Confederacy chose Richmond as its capital because of the historic importance of Virginia as the home of Washington, Jefferson, Madison, and Monroe. However, Richmond was also a major industrial center. Exploiting the city's location at the falls of the James River, the city's entrepreneurs had developed a wide range of industries: flour mills, tobacco factories, railroad and port facilities, and, most important, a profitable and substantial iron industry. In 1861, the Tredegar Iron Works employed nearly one thousand workers and, as the only facility in the South that could manufacture large machinery and heavy weapons, made a major contribution to the Confederate war effort. Virginia State Library.

Forging New Economic Policies. To mobilize the resources of the North, the Republican-dominated Congress enacted a program of government-assisted national economic development that far surpassed Henry Clay's American System. First, the Republicans raised tariffs to win the political support of northeastern manufacturers and workers, who feared competition from cheaper foreign goods. Then Secretary of the Treasury Salmon P. Chase secured legislation that forced thousands of local banks to accept federal charters and regulations. This integrated national banking system was far more effective in raising capital and controlling inflation than the First and Second Banks of the United States had been. Finally, the Republican Congress implemented Clay's program for a nationally financed system of internal improvements. In 1862, it chartered the Union Pacific and Central

Pacific companies to build a transcontinental railroad line and assisted them with lavish subsidies. In addition, the Republicans provided northern and midwestern farmers with "free land." The Homestead Act of 1862 gave heads of families or individuals age twenty-one or older the title to 160 acres of public land after five years of residence. This economic program won the Republican Party the allegiance of many farmers, workers, and entrepreneurs, and bolstered the Union's ability to fight a long war.

New industries sprang up to meet the army's need for guns, clothes, and food. More than 1.5 million men served in the Union army, and they consumed more than half a billion pounds of pork and other packed meats. To supply this immense quantity, Chicago railroads built new lines to carry tens of thousands of hogs and cattle to the city's ever-larger stockyards and slaughtering houses. By 1862,

Chicago passed Cincinnati as the meatpacking capital of the nation, bringing prosperity to thousands of midwestern farmers and great wealth to Philip D. Armour and other entrepreneurs.

A similar concentration of capital took place in many industries. The war, an observer commented, gave a few men "the command of millions of money"; such massed financial power threatened not only the prewar society of small producers but also the future of democracy. Americans "are never again to see the republic in which we were born," lamented abolitionist and social reformer Wendell Phillips.

The Confederate government slowly developed a coherent economic policy. True to its states' rights philosophy, the Confederacy initially left most economic matters in the hands of the state governments. However, as the realities of total war became clear, the Davis administration took some extraordinary measures: It built and operated shipyards, armories, foundries, and textile mills; commandeered food and scarce raw materials like coal, iron, copper, and lead; requisitioned slaves to work on fortifications; and exercised direct control over foreign trade. Ordinary southern citizens increasingly resented and resisted these measures by the government in Richmond. To sustain the war effort, the Confederacy increasingly relied on white solidarity: Jefferson Davis warned that a Union victory would destroy slavery "and reduce the whites to the degraded position of the African race."

Raising Money in the North. For both sides, the cost of fighting a total war was enormous. The annual spending of the Union government shot up from $63 million in 1860 to more than $865 million in 1864 (Table 14.2). To meet that vast outlay, the Republicans established a powerful modern state that raised money in three ways. First, the government increased tariffs on consumer goods, placed high excise duties on alcohol and tobacco, and imposed direct taxes on business corporations, large inheritances, and incomes. These levies paid for about 20 percent of the cost of the war. The sale of treasury bonds financed another 65 percent. Led by Jay Cooke, a Philadelphia banker, the Treasury Department used newspaper advertisements and 2,500 subagents to persuade nearly a million northern families to buy war bonds. In addition, the National Banking Acts of 1863 and 1864 forced most banks to purchase treasury bonds.

The Union paid the remaining cost of the war by printing paper money. The Legal Tender Act of 1862 authorized the issue of $150 million in treasury notes—which soon became known as **greenbacks**—and required the public to accept them as legal tender. Like the Continental currency issued during the War of Independence, these treasury notes were not backed by specie; unlike the earlier currency, this paper money was printed in relatively limited amounts and so did not depreciate disastrously in value. By imposing broad-based taxes, borrowing from the middle classes, and creating a national monetary system, the Union government had created the financial foundations of a modern nation-state.

The South Resorts to Inflation. The financial demands on the South were just as great, but it lacked a powerful central government that could tax and borrow. The Confederate Congress fiercely opposed taxes on cotton exports and slaves, the most valuable property held by wealthy planters; and the urban middle class and yeomen farm families refused to bear the entire tax burden. Consequently, the Confederacy covered less than 5 percent of its expenditures through taxation. The government paid for another 35 percent by borrowing, although wealthy planters and foreign bankers became increasingly wary of investing in Confederate bonds that might never be redeemed.

TABLE 14.2	The Cost of War: Union Finances, 1860 and 1864	
	1860	**1864**
Income	$56.1 million	$264.6 million
Expenditures	$63.1 million	$865.3 million
General	32.0 million	35.1 million
Army and navy	27.9 million	776.5 million
Interest on debt	3.2 million	53.7 million
Public debt	$64.8 million	$1,815.8 million

In 1864, the Union government received almost five times as much revenue as it had in 1860, but it spent nearly fourteen times as much, mostly to pay soldiers and buy military supplies. In four years, the public debt had risen by a factor of twenty-eight, so that interest payments in 1864 nearly equaled the level of all federal government spending in 1860.

The War's Toll on Civilians

In the spring of 1862, fighting along the Mississippi River and the Union blockade in the Gulf of Mexico disrupted the commerce of New Orleans. By the time Union troops captured the city in May, the stock of food in the city was very low. In June, hungry citizens — men in top hats, fashionably dressed women, barefoot children, and white and black workers — stormed the stores and emptied them of their last supplies of food. This engraving, titled *Starving People of New Orleans*, appeared in *Harper's Weekly*, a prominent New York journal. Library of Congress.

This meant that the Confederacy had to finance about 60 percent of its expenses by printing paper money. The flood of currency created a spectacular inflation: By 1865, prices had risen to ninety-two times their 1861 level. As the vast supply of money (and a shortage of goods) caused food prices to soar, riots broke out in more than a dozen southern cities and towns. In Richmond, several hundred women broke into bakeries, crying, "Our children are starving while the rich roll in wealth." In Randolph County, Alabama, women confiscated grain from a government warehouse "to prevent starvation of themselves and their families." As inflation increased, Southerners refused to accept Confederate money, sometimes with serious consequences. When South Carolina storekeeper Jim Harris rejected the Confederate notes presented by a group of soldiers, they raided his storehouse and "robbed it of about five thousand dollars worth of goods." Army supply officers seized goods from storekeepers and merchants, and offered payment in worthless IOUs. Faced with a public that feared strong government and high taxation, the Confederacy could sustain the war effort only by seizing the property of its citizens.

➤ Which government — the Union or the Confederacy — imposed greater military and economic burdens on its citizens? How successful was that strategy?

➤ What were the main economic policies enacted by the Republican-controlled Congress?

The Turning Point: 1863

By 1863, the Lincoln administration had finally created an efficient war machine, a coherent financial system, and a set of strategic priorities. The perceptive young diplomat Henry Adams, the grandson of President John Quincy Adams and a future novelist and historian, noted the change from his post in London: "Little by little, one began to feel that, behind the chaos in Washington power was taking shape; that it was massed and guided as it had not been before." Slowly but surely, the tide of the struggle shifted toward the Union.

Emancipation

When the war began, antislavery Republicans demanded that their party make abolition — as well as restoration of the Union — a central goal. The fighting should continue, a Massachusetts abolitionist declared, "until the Slave power is completely subjugated, and *emancipation made certain*." Because slave-grown crops sustained the Confederacy, antislavery activists argued for black emancipation on military grounds. As Frederick Douglass put it, "Arrest that hoe in the hands of the Negro, and you smite the rebellion in the very seat of its life." Initially, Lincoln subordinated demands for black freedom to the survival of the Union. "If I could save the Union without freeing any slave, I would do it," he told Horace Greeley in a letter published in the *New York Tribune* in August 1862, "and if I could save it by freeing all the slaves, I would do it." By implicitly asserting his constitutional authority to end slavery, Lincoln was beginning to define the conflict as both a struggle to preserve the Union and to destroy slavery, the cornerstone of southern society.

"Contrabands." As Lincoln moved cautiously toward emancipation, enslaved African Americans forced the issue by seizing freedom for themselves. Exploiting the disorder of wartime, tens of thousands of slaves fled their plantations and sought refuge behind Union lines. In May 1861, when three slaves reached the camp of General Benjamin Butler in Virginia, he labeled them "contraband of war" and refused to return them. The term stuck, and within a few months a thousand "contrabands" were camping with Butler's army. In August 1861, to provide these fugitives with legal status, Congress passed the Confiscation Act, authorizing the seizure of all property—including slaves—used to support the rebellion.

Radical Republicans—Treasury Secretary Salmon Chase, Senator Charles Sumner of Massachusetts, and Representative Thaddeus Stevens of Pennsylvania—now saw a way to use wartime legislation to destroy slavery. A longtime member of Congress, Stevens was a masterful politician and adept at fashioning legislation that could win majority support. In April 1862, Stevens and his Radical allies persuaded Congress to end slavery in the District of Columbia by providing compensation for owners. In June, Congress outlawed slavery in the federal territories (finally enacting the Wilmot Proviso of 1846); and in July, it passed a second Confiscation Act. This act simply overrode the property rights of Confederate slave owners by declaring "forever free" all fugitive slaves and all slaves captured by the Union army. Emancipation had become an instrument of war.

The Emancipation Proclamation. Lincoln built on the Radical Republicans' initiative. In July 1862, he prepared a general proclamation of emancipation; considering the Battle of Antietam "an indication of the Divine Will," he issued the proclamation five days later, on September 22, 1862. The statement relied for its legal authority on the president's responsibility as commander in chief to suppress the rebellion. It declared that slavery would be legally abolished in all states that remained out of the Union on January 1, 1863. The rebel states had a hundred days in which to preserve slavery by renouncing secession. None chose to do so.

The proclamation was politically astute. Lincoln wanted to avoid opposition from slave owners in the Union-controlled border states, such as Maryland and Missouri, so the proclamation left slavery intact in those states. It also left slavery intact in areas occupied by Union armies—western and central Tennessee, western Virginia, and southern Louisiana, including New Orleans. Consequently, the Emancipation Proclamation did not actually free a single slave, at least not immediately. Yet, as abolitionist Wendell Phillips perceived, Lincoln's proclamation had moved the institution of slavery to "the edge of Niagara," from where it would soon be swept over the brink. Indeed, advancing Union troops became the agents of its destruction. "I became free in 1863, in the summer, when the yankees come by and said I could go work for myself," Jackson Daniel of Maysville, Alabama, recalled. "I was farming after that [and also] . . . making shoes." As Lincoln now saw it, the conflict had become a war of "subjugation" in which "the old South is to be destroyed and replaced by new propositions and ideas" (see Comparing American Voices, "Blacks and Whites Describe the End of Slavery," pp. 442–443).

As an objective of the war, emancipation was controversial. In the Confederacy, Jefferson Davis labeled it the "most execrable measure recorded in the history of guilty man"; in the North, it produced a racist backlash among white voters. During the congressional election of 1862, the Democrats denounced emancipation as unconstitutional, warned of slave uprisings, and claimed that a "black flood" would take white jobs. Democrat Horatio Seymour won the governorship of New York by declaring that if abolition was a goal of the war, the South should not be conquered. Other Democrats swept to victory in Pennsylvania, Ohio, and Illinois, and the party gained thirty-four seats in Congress. But the Republicans still held a twenty-five-seat majority in the House and had gained five seats in the Senate. Lincoln refused to retreat. On New Year's Day 1863, he signed the Emancipation Proclamation. To reassure Northerners, Lincoln urged slaves to "abstain from all violence" and justified emancipation as an "act of justice." "If my name ever goes into history," he said, "it was for this act."

Vicksburg and Gettysburg

The fate of the proclamation would depend on the political success of the Republican Party and the military victories of the Union armies. The outlook was not encouraging on either front. Democrats had registered significant gains in the election of 1862, and popular support was growing for a negotiated peace. Two brilliant victories in Virginia by Lee, whose army defeated Hooker's forces at Fredericksburg (December 1862) and Chancellorsville (May 1863), caused further erosion of northern support for the war.

The Crucial Battles of July 1863. At this critical juncture, General Grant mounted a major offensive in the West designed to split the Confederacy in two. Grant drove south along the west bank of the Mississippi and then moved his troops across the river near Vicksburg, Mississippi, where he defeated two Confederate armies and laid siege to the city. After repelling Union assaults for six weeks, the exhausted and starving Vicksburg garrison surrendered on July 4, 1863. Five days later, Union forces took Port Hudson, Louisiana (near Baton Rouge), and established complete control of the Mississippi River. Grant had taken 31,000 prisoners; cut off Louisiana, Arkansas, and Texas from the rest of the Confederacy; and prompted thousands of slaves to desert their plantations or demand wages.

As Grant advanced along the Mississippi in May, Confederate leaders were arguing over the best strategic response. President Davis and other politicians wanted to reinforce Vicksburg and send another army to Tennessee to draw Grant out of Mississippi. But General Robert E. Lee, buoyed by his recent victories over Hooker, favored a new invasion of the North. That strategy, Lee suggested, would either draw Union armies to the east, thereby relieving the pressure on Vicksburg, or give the Confederacy a major victory that would undermine northern support for the war.

Lee won out. In June 1863, he maneuvered his army north through Maryland into Pennsylvania. The Union's Army of the Potomac moved along with him, positioning itself between Lee and Washington, D.C., the federal capital. On July 1, the two great armies met by accident at Gettysburg, Pennsylvania, in what became a decisive confrontation (Map 14.4). On the first day of battle, Lee drove the Union's advance guard to the south of town. General George G. Meade, who had just

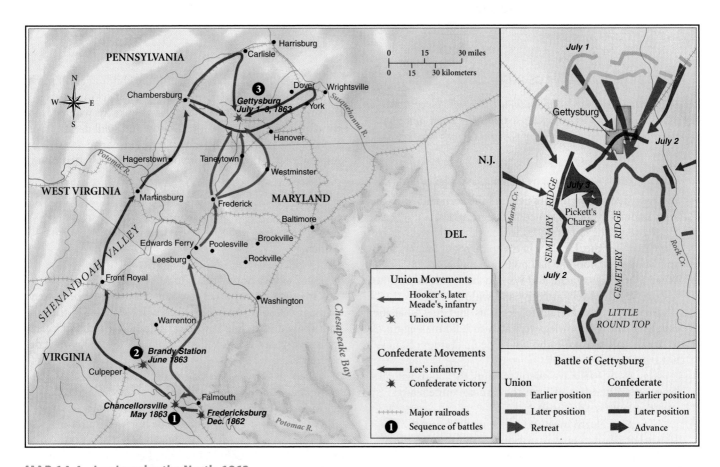

MAP 14.4 Lee Invades the North, 1863

After Lee's victories at Chancellorsville (1) in May and Brandy Station (2) in June, the Confederate forces moved northward, constantly shadowed by the Union army. On July 1, the two armies met accidentally near Gettysburg. In the ensuing battle (3), the Union army, commanded by General George Meade, emerged victorious, primarily because it was much larger than the Confederate force and held well-fortified positions along Cemetery Ridge, which gave its units a major tactical advantage.

Blacks and Whites Describe the End of Slavery

Ratification of the Thirteenth Amendment on December 6, 1865, legally ended chattel slavery—the ownership of people as property. In fact, slavery died a million deaths, each at a different time and under different circumstances. Some deaths happened years before 1865; others, long after. Because slavery was a personal as well as a property relationship, it ended in a psychological sense only when a slave claimed freedom. As you read these stories, consider the various ways in which slaves became free and the extent of their freedom.

These stories come from the journal of a slave-owning woman and from transcriptions of oral interviews of ex-slaves during the 1930s. Most of the interviewers, from the Federal Writers' Project, were white men and women. Most of the ex-slaves were in their eighties and nineties. Use this knowledge as you read these sources.

ELIZABETH MARY MEADE INGRAHAM

Elizabeth Mary Meade Ingraham was the mistress of Ashwood Plantation near Vicksburg, Mississippi. Her diary describes the impact on plantation life of General Grant's advance on Vicksburg in 1863.

May 4. [Union general] Osterhaus' Division, scum of St. Louis, camped in the big field. All the corn ruined in the field, and nearly all consumed in the granaries. . . .

May 8. The last thing Eddens [a slave] did was to save some meat for me. He slept in the spare room Sunday night, and Monday at noon he had quit our service. . . . Parker, Sol, Mordt, Jim Crow, Isaiah, and Wadloo, have quit us, but the rest are here, and very attentive and willing. . . .

May 13. Elsy still faithful, feeds us, and does what she can; Rita Jane too; Bowlegs very attentive. Emma beginning to tire of waiting on me, did not come up at noon; Nancy not true. . . .

May 18. [We] have reason to think the hands will all leave; only a question of time, they are not quite ready; Elsy still true; but Jack doubtful. . . .

May 27. Negro meetings are being held, and the few whites left begin to be very anxious. . . . Powers was burnt out by his own negroes. I fear the blacks more than I do the Yankees. Jack trying to persuade Elsy to leave. . . . She tells him to get her a home and a way of earning a living, and she is ready to go, but [I] told her, if he left here, to move up into the wash-house with her children. I would give her $12 a month and free her four children.

June 6–10. Martha with her three children and Emma, left at midnight Friday . . . and the rest are packing to-day. Hays resolved to go, and I dread lest he take his wife with him, for I can hardly get along as it is, and shall die if I have the cooking to do. . . . Those who have stayed are utterly demoralized; if they work for you, the job is only half done.

SARAH DEBRO

Sarah Debro grew up in slavery in Orange County, North Carolina.

I wuz to be a house maid [to Miss Polly]. The day she took me my mammy cried cauz she knew I never be 'lowed to live at de cabin wid her no more. . . . [Working in the big house] my dresses and apron was starched stiff. I had a clean apron every day. . . . I loved Mis' Polly an' loved stayin' at de big house. . . .

When de War was over, de Yankees was all roun' de place telling niggers what to do. Dey tole dem dey was free, dat dey didn' have to slave for de white folks no more.

One day my mammy come to de big house after me. I didn' want to go. I wanted to stay wid Mis' Polly. I 'gun to cry, an' Mammy caught hold of me. I grabbed Mis' Polly an' held so tight dat I tore her skirt bindin' loose, an' her skirt fell down 'bout her feets.

"Let her stay wid me," Mis' Polly said to Mammy. But Mammy shook her head. "You took her away from me an' didn' pay no mind to my cryin', so now I's takin' her back home. We's free now Mis' Polly. We ain' gwine be slaves no more to nobody." She dragged me away. I can see how Mis Polly looked, now. She didn' say nothin', but she looked hard at Mammy, an' her face was white.

ALLEN WILLIAMS

Allen Williams lived as a slave on a small farm in Texas.

You ought to been behind a tree the day young Master George told me I was free. You would have laughed fit to kill. I was down on farm plowing, and Master George rid up on a hoss and say, "Morning, Allen." I say, "Morning, Master George." "Laying by the crap [crop]?" he say. "Yes, Sah," I told him. Then, he say, "Allen, you is free." I say, "What you mean, 'free'?" "The damn Yankees is freed you," he say.

I got off the plow, and he grabbed me by the arm, and pushed my sleeve up, and p'inted to my skin, and say, "Allen, my daddy give a thousand dollars in gold for that, didn't he?" "He sho' did," I told him. Then, he say, "Didn't my daddy give you to me? And didn't I put them clothes on you?" "Sho' 'nuf, you did," I say to him. Then, Master George say, "Yes, and the damn Yankees took you away from me. But them is my clothes." Then, he made like he was gonna take my clothes away from me, and we scuffled all round the field.

Then, Master George begin to laugh, and say, "Allen, I ain't gonna take your clothes. I's gonna put some better ones on you. You is free, but I want you to stay right on and tend to your mistress, like you been doing." I lived with them till after I was grown. I was in and out five or six years, 'fore married. When I couldn't get work, I went back to them and et Old Mistress' meat and bread.

ANNIE RO

Annie Ro worked as a household servant on a plantation in Alabama.

One day, aftah de am fightin' fo' mo' dan two yeahs, de marster gits a letter f'om Marster Billy. Dat letter says de niggar sho' am gwine to be free, de Wah am 'bout over, dat him will be home soon, an' dat John am killed. . . . De marster says nothin', jus' sit and stares. Den, suddenly, him jumps up an' stahts cussin' de War, de nigger, Abe Lincoln, an' ever'body . . . an' says, "Free de nigger, will dey? Ise free dem." . . . Den, him takes his gun off de rack an' stahts fo' de field whar de niggers am a-wukkin'. . . .

De good Lawd took a han' in dat mess, den. De marster ain' gone far in de field, when he draps [dead], all of a sudden.

DELICIA PATTERSON

Delicia Patterson was ninety-two when she was interviewed in St. Louis, Missouri.

I was born in Boonville, Missouri, January 2, 1845. My mother's name was Maria and my father's was Jack Wiley. Mother had five children but raised only two of us. I was owned by Charles Mitchell until I was fifteen years old. They were fairly nice to all of their slaves and they had several of us. . . . When I was fifteen years old, I was brought to the courthouse, put up on the auction block to be sold. . . . I was sold to a Southern Englishman named Thomas Steele for fifteen hundred dollars. . . . I lived in that family until after the Civil War was over. . . .

When freedom was declared Mr. Steele told me that I was as free as he was. He said I could leave them if I please or could stay, that they wanted me [to stay] . . . and his wife said, "Course she is our nigger. She is as much our nigger now as she was the day you bought her two years ago and paid fifteen hundred dollars for her."

That made me mad so I left right then, since she was so smart. . . . I hired myself out to a family named Miller at three dollars a week, and lived on the place. . . .

I don't know what the ex-slaves expected, but I do know they didn't get anything. After the War we just wandered from place to place, working for food and a place to stay.

SOURCES: W. Maury Darst, "The Vicksburg Diary of Mrs. Alfred Ingraham," *Journal of Mississippi History* 44 (May 1982): 148–179; James Mellon, ed., *The Slaves Remember: An Oral History* (New York: Avon Books, 1988), 347 (Williams), and 352 (Debro); and Norman Yetman, ed., *Memoirs from the Slave Narrative Collection* (New York: Dover, 2002), 72 (Ro) and 101–103 (Patterson).

ANALYZING THE EVIDENCE

➤ How does Elizabeth Mary Meade Ingraham react to the end of slavery? How does her reaction compare with those of the other slave owners described in the interviews? What are the owners' strategies and goals with regard to their workers?

➤ Do you think the interviewers' race or outlook affected the content of the interviews here? Is it important that some transcriptions are in Standard English and that others are in black dialect?

➤ What impact do you think the age of the ex-slaves had on their stories? How might the passage of decades have affected their memory of events? Is it significant that most of those interviewed were either children or teenagers when slavery ended?

➤ What specific event or set of factors prompted each of these former slaves to claim his or her freedom? Can you detect any patterns in the stories? What are they?

replaced Hooker as the Union commander, placed his troops in well-defended hilltop positions and called up reinforcements. By the morning of July 2, Meade had 90,000 troops to Lee's 75,000. Aware that he was outnumbered but bent on victory, Lee ordered assaults on both of Meade's flanks but failed to turn them. General Richard B. Ewell, assigned to attack the right side of the Union line, refused to risk his men in an all-out assault, and General Longstreet, on the Union left, failed to dislodge Meade's forces from a hill known as Little Round Top.

On July 3, Lee decided on a frontal assault against the center of the Union line. He recognized the danger of this tactic, but he had enormous confidence in his troops. After the heaviest artillery barrage of the war, Lee ordered General George E. Pickett and his 14,000 men to take Cemetery Ridge. Anticipating this attack, Meade had reinforced his line with artillery and his best troops. When Pickett's men charged across a mile of open terrain, they were met by deadly fire from artillery and rifle-muskets; thousands were killed, wounded, or captured. When the three-day battle ended, Lee had suffered 28,000 casualties, one-third of the Army of Northern Virginia, while 23,000 of Meade's soldiers lay killed or wounded. Shocked by the bloodletting, Meade allowed the remaining Confederate units to escape. Lincoln was furious: "As it is," the president brooded, "the war will be prolonged indefinitely."

Still, Gettysburg was a great Union victory and, together with the triumph at Vicksburg, was the major turning point in the conflict. Southern armies would never again invade the North, and the people in the South were growing increasingly weary of the war. The Confederate elections of 1863 went sharply against the politicians who supported Jefferson Davis. Many ordinary citizens, and even a few members of the Confederate Congress, began to criticize the war effort.

Vicksburg and Gettysburg also transformed the political situation in the North and in Europe. In the fall of 1863, Republicans swept state and local elections in Pennsylvania, Ohio, and New York. Equally important, American diplomats were finally able to prevent the Confederacy from acquiring advanced weapons. In 1862, British shipbuilders had supplied the Confederacy with an ironclad cruiser, the *Alabama*, which had sunk or captured more than one hundred Union merchant ships, and the delivery of two more ironclad cruisers was imminent. News of the Union victories in early July changed everything. Charles Francis Adams, the American minister, persuaded the British government to impound the ships. Britain did not want to risk Canada or its merchant marine by provoking the military might of the United States. Moreover, the

country had become increasingly dependent for its food supply on imports of wheat from the American Midwest, and British workers and reformers were strongly opposed to slavery. "King Cotton" diplomacy had failed; "King Wheat" stood triumphant. "Rest not your hopes in foreign nations," President Jefferson Davis now advised his nation, "This war is ours; we must fight it ourselves."

➤ Antislavery Republican politicians and the thousands of "contrabands" played a role in President Lincoln's decision to declare and sign the Emancipation Proclamation. What role did each of them play?

➤ Why were the battles at Gettysburg and Vicksburg significant? How did they change the tide of war strategically? Diplomatically? Psychologically?

The Union Victorious, 1864–1865

The Union victories of 1863 meant that the South could not win its independence through a decisive military triumph. However, the Confederacy could still hope for a stalemate on the battlefield and a negotiated peace. Lincoln faced a daunting task as the bloody war entered its fourth year: He had to win an overwhelming victory, or he would lose the support of the northern voters.

Soldiers and Strategy

Two developments allowed the Union to prosecute the war with continued vigor: the enlistment of African American soldiers and the emergence of capable and determined generals.

The Impact of Black Troops. As early as 1861, free African Americans and fugitive slaves had volunteered for the Union army, and Frederick Douglass had embraced their cause: "Once let the black man get upon his person the brass letters, 'U.S.' . . . a musket on his shoulder and bullets in his pockets, and there is no power on earth which can deny that he has earned the right to citizenship in the United States." The prospect of citizenship for blacks frightened many northern whites, and most Union generals doubted that former slaves would make good soldiers. Consequently, the Lincoln administration initially refused to enlist African Americans. But by 1862, free and contraband blacks had formed regiments in New England, South Carolina, Louisiana, and Kansas, and were eager to join the fighting.

Black Soldiers in the Union Army

Determined to end racial slavery, tens of thousands of African Americans volunteered for service in the Union army in 1864 and 1865, boosting the northern war effort at a critical moment. These proud soldiers were members of the 107th Colored Infantry, stationed at Fort Corcoran near Washington, D.C. In January 1865, their regiment participated in the daring capture of Fort Fisher, which protected Wilmington, North Carolina, the last Confederate port open to blockade runners. Library of Congress.

The Emancipation Proclamation changed popular thinking and military policy with respect to black soldiers. The proclamation invited former slaves to serve in the Union army; northern whites, long suspicious of arming African Americans, now agreed that because blacks were to benefit from a Union victory, they should share in the fighting and dying. The valor exhibited by the first African American regiments to go into combat also influenced opinion in the North. In January 1863, Thomas Wentworth Higginson, the white abolitionist commander of the black First South Carolina Volunteers, wrote a glowing newspaper account of the regiment's military prowess: "No officer in this regiment now doubts that the key to the successful prosecution of the war lies in the unlimited employment of black troops." In July, a heroic and costly attack on Fort Wagner, South Carolina, by another black regiment, the Fifty-fourth Massachusetts Infantry, convinced many Union officers of the value of black soldiers. The War Department authorized black enlistment; and as white resistance to conscription increased, the Lincoln administration recruited as many African Americans as it could. Without black soldiers, the president suggested in the autumn of 1864, "we would be compelled to abandon the war in three weeks." By the spring of 1865, there were nearly 200,000 African American soldiers and sailors in the Union forces.

Military service did not end racial discrimination. Black soldiers served under white officers in segregated regiments and were used primarily to build fortifications, garrison forts, and guard supply lines. At first they were paid less than white soldiers ($10 a month versus $13) and won equal pay only by threatening to lay down their arms. Despite this treatment, African Americans volunteered for military service in disproportionate numbers and diligently served the Union cause. They were fighting for freedom and a new social order. "Hello, Massa," said one black soldier to his former master, who had been taken prisoner. "Bottom rail on top dis time." The worst fears of the secessionists had come true: Through the agency of the Union army, blacks had risen in a great rebellion against slavery.

Capable Generals Take Command. As African Americans joined the army's ranks, Lincoln finally found an efficient and ruthless commanding general. In March 1864, Lincoln placed General Ulysses S. Grant in charge of all the Union armies and created a unified structure of command. From then on, the president determined general strategy and Grant decided how to implement it. Lincoln directed Grant to advance simultaneously against all the major Confederate armies, a strategy Grant had long favored. Both the president and the general wanted a decisive victory before the election of 1864.

As the successful western campaign of 1863 showed, Grant knew how to fight a modern war, a war that relied on industrial technology and targeted an entire society. At Vicksburg, he had besieged the whole city and forced its surrender. Then, in November 1863, he had used railroad transport to charge to the rescue of a Union army near Chattanooga, Tennessee, and drive back an invading Confederate army. Moreover, Grant was willing to accept heavy casualties in assaults on strongly defended positions. The attempts of earlier Union commanders "to conserve life" through cautious tactics had prolonged the war, Grant argued. However, Grant's aggressiveness earned him a reputation as a butcher—of enemy armies and his own men.

In May 1864, Grant ordered major new offensives on two fronts. Personally taking charge of the

Grant Planning an Attack

On June 2, 1864, the day this photograph was taken, Grant moved his headquarters to Bethesda Church, moved its pews outside, under the shade of the surrounding trees, and planned the costly attack he would make at Cold Harbor, Virginia, the next day—a frontal assault that resulted in seven thousand Union casualties. While Grant (to the left) leaned over a pew, gesturing at a map, his officers smoked their pipes and read reports of the war in newspapers that had just arrived from New York City. Library of Congress.

115,000-man-strong Army of the Potomac, he set out to destroy Lee's force of 75,000 troops in Virginia. Simultaneously, he instructed General William Tecumseh Sherman, who shared his ruthless views on warfare, to invade Georgia and take Atlanta. As Sherman prepared for battle, he wrote that "all that has gone before is mere skirmish. The war now begins."

Grant advanced toward Richmond, hoping to force Lee to fight in open fields, where the Union's superior manpower and artillery would prevail. But remembering his tactical errors at Gettysburg, Lee remained in strong defensive positions and attacked only when he held an advantage. The Confederate general seized that opportunity twice: He won narrow victories in early May 1864 at the extraordinarily bloody battles of the Wilderness and Spotsylvania Court House. At Spotsylvania, the soldiers fought at point-blank range, often using their bayoneted rifles as spears. Despite heavy losses in these battles and at Cold Harbor, Grant drove on (Map 14.5). Although his attacks severely eroded Lee's forces, which suffered 31,000 casualties, Union losses were even higher: 55,000 men.

The fighting also took a heavy psychological toll. "Many a man has gone crazy since this campaign began from the terrible pressure on mind and body," observed a Union captain. As the morale and health of the soldiers on both sides weakened, many deserted. In June 1864, Grant laid siege to Petersburg, an important railroad center near Richmond. Protracted trench warfare—like that American troops would face in World War I—made the spade as important as the sword. Union and Confederate soldiers built complex networks of trenches, tunnels, and artillery emplacements for almost fifty miles around Richmond and Petersburg. Invoking the intense imagery of the Bible, an officer described the continuous artillery firing and sniping as "living night and day within the 'valley of the shadow of death.'" The stress was especially great for the outnumbered Confederate troops, who spent months in the muddy, sickening trenches without rotation to the rear.

As time passed, Lincoln and Grant felt pressures of their own. The enormous casualties and continued military stalemate threatened Lincoln with defeat in the November election. The outlook for the Republicans worsened in July 1864, when a raid near Washington by Jubal Early's cavalry forced Grant to divert his best troops from the Petersburg campaign. To punish farmers in the Shenandoah Valley, who had provided a base for Early and food for Lee's army, Grant ordered General Philip H. Sheridan to turn the region into "a barren waste." Sheridan's troops conducted a scorched-earth campaign, destroying grain supplies, barns, farming implements, and gristmills. These terrorist tactics went beyond the military norms of the day: Most

MAP 14.5 The Closing Virginia Campaign, 1864–1865

Beginning in May 1864, General Ulysses Grant launched an all-out campaign against Richmond. By threatening General Robert E. Lee's lines of supply from Richmond, Grant tried to lure him into open battle. Lee avoided a major test of strength. Instead, he retreated to defensive positions and inflicted heavy casualties on Union attackers at the Wilderness, Spotsylvania Court House, North Anna, and Cold Harbor (1–4). From June 1864 to April 1865, the two armies faced each other across defensive fortifications outside Richmond and Petersburg (5), a protracted siege finally broken by Grant's flanking maneuver at Five Forks (6). Lee's surrender followed shortly.

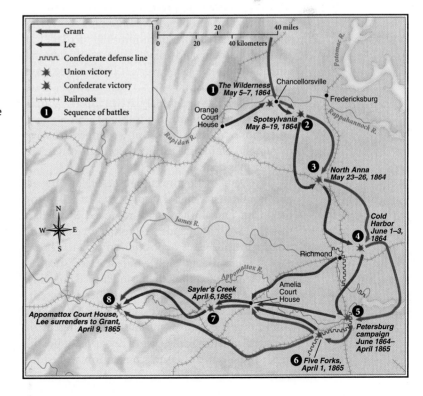

officers regarded civilians as noncombatants and feared that punishing them would erode military discipline. Grant's practice of carrying the war to Confederate civilians was changing the definition of conventional warfare.

The Election of 1864 and Sherman's March

As the siege at Petersburg dragged on, the president's hopes for reelection increasingly depended on General Sherman in Georgia. Sherman had gradually penetrated to within about thirty miles of Atlanta, a great railway hub at the heart of the Confederacy. Although his army outnumbered that of General Joseph E. Johnston—90,000 men to 60,000 men—Sherman avoided a direct attack and slowly pried the Confederates out of one defensive position after another. Finally, on June 27, at Kennesaw Mountain, Sherman engaged Johnston in a set battle, only to suffer 3,000 casualties, five times the losses he inflicted on Johnston's troops. By late July 1864, the Union general had laid siege to Atlanta on the north, but the next month brought little gain. Like Grant, Sherman seemed bogged down in a hopeless campaign.

The National Union Party Versus the Peace Democrats. Meanwhile, the presidential campaign of 1864 was well under way. In June, a Republican convention attended by both Republicans and Unionist Democrats resisted the attempt of some Republicans to prevent Lincoln's renomination. The convention endorsed the president's war strategy, demanded the unconditional surrender of the Confederacy, and called for a constitutional amendment to abolish slavery. It likewise accepted Lincoln's political strategy. To attract border-state voters and create a national party, Lincoln and his allies took a new name, the National Union Party, and chose Andrew Johnson, a Tennessee slave owner and Unionist Democrat, as their candidate for vice president.

The Democratic convention met in late August and nominated General George B. McClellan for president. Lincoln had twice removed McClellan from military commands: first for an excess of caution and then for his opposition to emancipation. Like their candidate, the Democratic delegates rejected freedom for blacks and condemned Lincoln's uncompromising repression of domestic dissent. However, they split into two camps over the issue of continuing the war. A substantial contingent of "Peace Democrats" called for "a cessation of hostilities" and a constitutional convention to restore peace. Although personally a "War Democrat," McClellan promised if elected to recommend to Congress an immediate armistice and a peace convention. Rejoicing in "the first ray of real light I have seen since the war began," Confederate vice president Alexander Stephens declared that if Atlanta and Richmond held out, Lincoln could be defeated. Then, McClellan and the northern Democrats could be persuaded to accept an independent Confederacy.

The Fall of Atlanta and Lincoln's Victory. Stephens's hopes collapsed on September 2, 1864, as Atlanta fell to Sherman's army. In a stunning move, the Union general pulled his troops from the trenches, swept around the city, and destroyed its rail links to the rest of the Confederacy. Fearing that Sherman would encircle and trap his army, Confederate general John B. Hood abandoned the city. "Atlanta is ours, and fairly won," Sherman telegraphed Lincoln, sparking hundred-gun salutes and wild Republican celebrations in northern cities. "The national resources . . . are unexhausted, and . . . unexhaustible," Lincoln warned Confederate leaders. "We are *gaining* strength, and may, if need be, maintain the contest indefinitely."

A deep pessimism settled over the Confederacy. Mary Chesnut, a plantation mistress, "felt as if all were dead within me, forever" and foresaw the end of the Confederacy: "We are going to be wiped off the earth," she wrote in her diary. Acknowledging the dramatically changed military situation, McClellan repudiated the Democratic peace platform, and dissident Republicans abandoned efforts to dump Lincoln. Instead, the National Union Party went on the offensive. Its newspapers charged that McClellan was still a peace candidate and that Peace Democrats were "copperheads" (poisonous snakes) who were hatching treasonous plots.

Sherman's success in Georgia gave Lincoln a clear-cut victory in November. The president received 55 percent of the popular vote and won 212 of 233 electoral votes. Republicans and National Unionists captured 145 of the 185 seats in the House of Representatives and increased their Senate majority to 42 of 52 seats. Many victories came from the votes of Union troops, who wanted the war to continue until the Confederacy met every Union demand, including emancipation.

Legal emancipation was already under way at the edges of the South. In 1864, Maryland and Missouri amended their constitutions to free their slaves, and the three occupied states—Tennessee, Arkansas, and Louisiana—followed suit. However, abolitionists were worried that the Emancipation

William Tecumseh Sherman

Sherman was a nervous man who smoked cigars and talked continuously. When he was seated, he crossed and uncrossed his legs incessantly, and a journalist described his fingers as constantly "twitching his red whiskers — his coat buttons — playing a tattoo on the table — or running through his hair." But Sherman was a decisive general who commanded the loyalty of his troops. This photograph was taken in 1865, after Sherman's devastating march through Georgia and the Carolinas. Library of Congress.

Proclamation, which was based on the president's wartime powers, would lose its force at the end of the war. Urged on by Lincoln and the black-organized National Equal Rights League, the Republican-dominated Congress took a major step to guarantee black freedom. On January 31, 1865, it approved the Thirteenth Amendment, which prohibited slavery throughout the United States, and sent it to the states for ratification. Slavery was nearly dead.

William Tecumseh Sherman: "Hard War" Warrior. Thanks to William Tecumseh Sherman, the Confederacy was nearly dead as well. The Civil War had rescued Sherman from life as an undistinguished military officer and a failed businessman. An 1840 graduate of West Point, Sherman had missed out on the military action during the Mexican War and so rose slowly in the ranks. In 1860, he had just taken charge of the brand-new Louisiana Military

Seminary. Although he was born and raised in Ohio, Sherman had served in the South and mixed easily with the planter class. Moreover, he believed that slavery was necessary to maintain the stability of the southern social order.

But Sherman was a staunch nationalist and a firm supporter of the Union. Secession meant "anarchy," he told his southern friends in early 1861, and had to be crushed. "If war comes, as I fear it surely will, I must fight your people whom I best love." He resigned his position in Louisiana and took command of the Union forces in Kentucky, his first wartime command. There he was unsuccessful in recruiting troops — and so darkly pessimistic about Union prospects that Lincoln relieved him of his command.

Then Sherman got lucky. Assigned to serve under Ulysses S. Grant, Sherman took his commander as a model. After distinguishing himself during Grant's victories at Shiloh and Vicksburg, Sherman was given command of a Union army in Tennessee. There, finally, he achieved success both as a commanding general and as an architect of modern warfare. As he fought, Sherman developed the philosophy and tactics of "hard war." "When one nation is at war with another, all the people of one are enemies of the other," Sherman declared, as he turned his troops loose against pro-Confederacy civilians suspected of helping anti-Union guerrillas. After guerrillas fired on a boat with Unionist passengers near Randolph, Tennessee, Sherman sent a regiment to level the town, asserting, "We are justified in treating all inhabitants as combatants."

After he captured Atlanta, Sherman decided on a bold strategy based on hard-war tactics. Instead of following the retreating Confederate army northward into Tennessee, he proposed to move south and "cut a swath through to the sea." To persuade Lincoln and Grant to approve his unconventional plan to live off the land, Sherman pointed out that his march would devastate Georgia and score a major psychological victory. It would be "a demonstration to the world, foreign and domestic, that we have a power Davis cannot resist."

Sherman set out to fight a campaign that would destroy the South's economic resources and will to resist. "We are not only fighting hostile armies," Sherman wrote, "but a hostile people, and must make old and young, rich and poor, feel the hard hand of war." He left Atlanta in flames and, during his 300-mile march to the sea (Map 14.6), consumed or demolished everything in his path. A Union veteran wrote, "[We] destroyed all we could not eat, stole their niggers, burned their cotton & gins, spilled their sorghum, burned & twisted their R.Roads and raised Hell generally." The havoc so

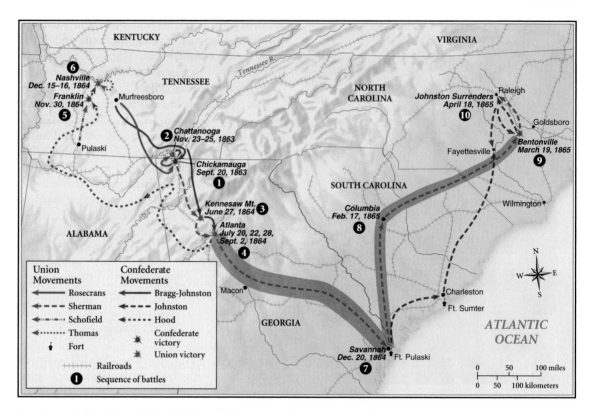

MAP 14.6 Sherman's March Through the Confederacy, 1864–1865

The Union victory in November 1863 at Chattanooga, Tennessee (2), was almost as critical as the victories in July at Gettysburg and Vicksburg, because it opened up a route of attack into the heart of the Confederacy. In mid-1864, General Sherman advanced on the railway hub of Atlanta (3 and 4). After finally taking the city in September 1864, Sherman relied on other Union armies to stem General Hood's invasion of Tennessee (5 and 6) while he began a devastating "March to the Sea." By December, he had reached Savannah (7); from there, he cut a swath through the Carolinas (8–10).

demoralized Confederate soldiers that many deserted their units and fled home to protect their farms and families. When Sherman reached Savannah in mid-December, the city's ten thousand defenders left without a fight.

Georgia's slaves treated Sherman as a savior. "They flock to me, old and young, they pray and shout and mix up my name with Moses . . . as well as 'Abram Linkom', the Great Messiah of 'Dis Jubilee.'" To provide for the hundreds of blacks now following his army, Sherman issued Special Field Order No. 15, which set aside 400,000 acres of prime rice-growing land for the exclusive use of freedmen. By June 1865, some 40,000 blacks were cultivating "Sherman lands," which many freedmen believed would be theirs forever, belated payment for generations of enslaved labor. "All the land belongs to the Yankees now and they gwine divide it out among de coloured people."

In February 1865, Sherman invaded South Carolina, both to link up with Grant at Petersburg and to punish the state where secession had begun. His troops ravaged the countryside as they cut a comparatively narrow swath across the state. After capturing South Carolina's capital, Columbia, they burned the business district, most churches, and the wealthiest residential neighborhoods. "This disappointment to me is extremely bitter," lamented Jefferson Davis. By March, Sherman had reached North Carolina and was on the verge of linking up with Grant and crushing Lee's army.

The Confederate Collapse. Grant's war of attrition had already exposed a weakness in the Confederacy: rising class resentment on the part of poor whites. Long angered by the "twenty-negro" exemption from military service given to slave owners and fearing that the Confederacy was doomed, ordinary southern farmers now repudiated the draft. "All they want is to git you . . . to fight for their infurnal negroes," grumbled an Alabama hill farmer. More and more soldiers fled their units. "I am now going to work instead of to the war," declared David Harris, a backcountry farmer. By 1865, at least 100,000 men had deserted from Confederate armies, and there were so few white recruits that southern leaders decided to take an extreme measure. Urged on by General Lee, the Confederate Congress voted to enlist black soldiers, and President Davis issued an executive order granting freedom to blacks who served in the Confederate army. But the war ended too soon to reveal whether any slaves would have fought for the Confederacy.

The symbolic end of the war took place in Virginia. In April 1865, Grant finally gained control of the crucial railroad junction at Petersburg and cut off Lee's supplies. Lee abandoned Richmond and retreated toward North Carolina, to join up with Confederate forces there. While Lincoln visited the ruins of the Confederate capital and was mobbed by joyful ex-slaves, Grant cut off Lee's escape route. On April 9, almost four years to the day after the attack on Fort Sumter, Lee surrendered at Appomattox Court House. By late May, all the Confederate generals had stopped fighting, and the Confederate army and government simply dissolved (Map 14.7).

The hard and bitter war was finally over. Union armies had destroyed the Confederate government; and the South's factories, warehouses, and railroads were in ruins, as were many of its farms and some of its most important cities. Almost 260,000 Confederate soldiers had paid for secession with their lives. The cost to the North was equally great in money, resources, and lives. More than 360,000 Union soldiers had died, and hundreds of thousands had been maimed (see Reading American Pictures, "What Do Photographs Tell Us About the Civil War?" p. 452). Delivering his second inaugural address as the fighting continued, Abraham Lincoln confessed his inability to justify the hideous carnage of the war in human terms:

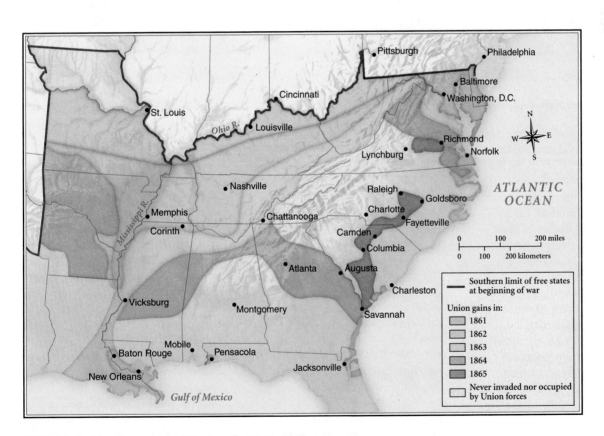

MAP 14.7   The Conquest of the South, 1861–1865

It took four years for the Union armies to defeat those of the Confederacy. Until the last year of the long conflict, most of the South remained in Confederate hands; even at the end of the war, Union armies had never entered many parts of the rebellious states. Most of the Union's territorial gains came on the vast western front, where its control of strategic lines of communication (the Mississippi River and major railroads) gave its forces a decisive advantage.

What Do Photographs Tell Us About the Civil War?

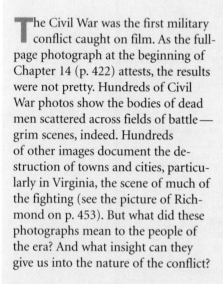

Captain George A. Custer and a Confederate Prisoner. Library of Congress.

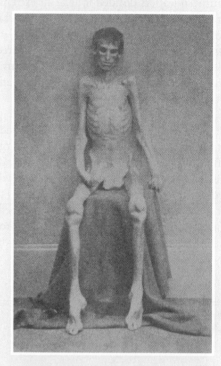

A Federal Prisoner. Library of Congress.

The Civil War was the first military conflict caught on film. As the full-page photograph at the beginning of Chapter 14 (p. 422) attests, the results were not pretty. Hundreds of Civil War photos show the bodies of dead men scattered across fields of battle—grim scenes, indeed. Hundreds of other images document the destruction of towns and cities, particularly in Virginia, the scene of much of the fighting (see the picture of Richmond on p. 453). But what did these photographs mean to the people of the era? And what insight can they give us into the nature of the conflict?

ANALYZING THE EVIDENCE

➤ Study the pictures on pages 422 and 453. Then look at the picture above of the emaciated body of a Massachusetts soldier who has just been freed from a Confederate military prison. Which image is more powerful intellectually? Emotionally? How do you think nineteenth-century Americans responded to the three photographs?

➤ The other image shows Captain (later General) George A. Custer (right) conversing quietly with a captured Confederate officer. These men had just tried to kill each other. Why are they now behaving with such civility? The rules of war? Respect between officers?

➤ Why did the photographer, the great Mathew Brady, take this picture of Custer? Brady chose his images carefully so that they conveyed meaning or a perspective on events. Is the black boy, the

Southerner's slave property, the clue to the meaning of this picture? Do you think Brady is suggesting that the struggle is really about the values and ideology of white men?

➤ Look carefully at the picture of the destroyed buildings in Richmond on page 453. What does the presence of the two women in the right foreground add to the image and to its effect on the viewer?

➤ Go to **memory.loc.gov/ammem/ cwphtml/cwphome.html** for additional Civil War photographs available at the Library of Congress.

The Devastation of War

From June 1864 to April 1865, Union troops commanded by General Grant besieged Richmond and the neighboring city of Petersburg, Virginia. As this photograph from the studio of Mathew Brady shows, Union artillery destroyed large sections of the Confederate capital, especially its flour mills, tobacco factories, and ironworks. Library of Congress.

If God wills that it continue until all the wealth piled by the bondsman's two hundred and fifty years of unrequited toil shall be sunk, and until every drop of blood drawn with the lash shall be paid by another drawn with the sword, as was said three thousand years ago, so still it must be said "the judgments of the Lord are true and righteous altogether."

As a reunited nation turned to the tasks of peace, it found that they were to be equally hard and bitter.

➤ What was the effect of emancipation on the politics and military affairs of the North?

➤ What were the strengths and weaknesses of Grant's military strategy and tactics? How was Grant's way of warfare different from traditional military practice?

➤ Describe Sherman's hard-war strategy. How did he pursue this strategy? With what results?

SUMMARY

In this chapter, we have surveyed the dramatic events of the Civil War. Looking at the South, we watched the fire-eaters attack Fort Sumter, which prompted the secession of the states of the Middle South and greatly strengthened the Confederacy. The potential of that new nation grew as its generals repulsed Union attacks against Richmond and went on the offensive. However, as the war continued, the inherent economic and social weaknesses of the Confederacy came to the fore. Enslaved workers fled or refused to work; yeomen farmers refused to fight for an institution that benefited wealthy planters; and European nations refused to recognize a nation created to preserve racial slavery.

Examining the North, we witnessed the initial failure of its leaders to exploit the Union's significant advantages in industrial output, financial resources, and military manpower. The generals—McClellan and Meade—moved slowly to attack and refused to pursue their weakened foes. But over time, the inherent strengths of the Union became manifest. Congress created efficient systems of banking and war finance; Lincoln found efficient and ruthless generals; and the emancipation and recruitment of enslaved African Americans provided an abundant supply of soldiers determined to fight for their freedom.

Looking at both sides, we explored the impact of total war on civilians: the imposition of conscription and high taxes; the increased workload of farm women and the employment of urban women as nurses and postal workers; and the constant food shortages and soaring prices. Above all else, there was the omnipresent fact of death—a tragedy that touched nearly every family, North and South.

Connections: Government

Since the beginning of the American republic, political leaders have argued over the scope and powers of the national government. As we learned in Chapter 7, during the 1790s, Alexander Hamilton, reading the Constitution expansively, devised a policy of national mercantilism. In response, Thomas Jefferson and James Madison created the Republican Party, which reduced the scope of the national government when it came to power in 1800, and which encouraged state governments to promote economic development. In the 1820s, as we discussed in Chapter 10, Henry Clay and John Quincy Adams revived Hamilton's nationalistic program through their calls for an American System. It would consist of a national bank to oversee the financial system, national tariff protection for American manufacturers, and national subsidies for roads, canals, and other internal improvements. As we noted in the essay that opened Part Three (p. 269), Jacksonian Democrats condemned Clay's scheme and

> in the 1830s and 1840s . . . led a political and constitutional revolution that cut government aid to financiers, merchants, and corporations.

As we saw in this chapter, during the Civil War, the Republican administration of Abraham Lincoln reversed the Jacksonian policies by enacting legislation that helped farmers, railroads, and corporations. Indeed, as we will see in Chapter 17, these Hamilton-Clay-Lincoln policies continued after the war. By enacting and upholding legislation favorable to banking enterprises and other businesses during the late nineteenth century, Congress and the federal judiciary actively promoted the development of a powerful industrial economy. Although the Jeffersonian-Jacksonian ideology of small government continued to command support in the South, it receded as a significant force in national life.

CHAPTER REVIEW QUESTIONS

➤ As the war began, politicians and ordinary citizens in both North and South were supremely confident of victory. Why did Southerners believe they would triumph? Why did the North ultimately win the Civil War?

➤ In 1860, the institution of slavery was firmly entrenched in the United States; by 1865, it was dead. How did this happen? How did Union policy toward slavery and enslaved people change over the course of the war? Why did it change?

TIMELINE

1860
Abraham Lincoln elected president (November 6)

South Carolina votes to secede from the Union (December 20)

1861
President Lincoln inaugurated (March 4)

Confederates fire on Fort Sumter (April 12)

Virginia leads Upper South out of the Union (April 17)

Union general Benjamin Butler declares runaway slaves "contraband of war" (May)

Confederates rout Union forces at first Battle of Bull Run (July 21)

First Confiscation Act authorizes seizure of all property, including slaves, used to support Confederacy's rebellion (August)

1862
Legal Tender Act authorizes issue of greenbacks (February)

Battle of Shiloh advances Union cause in West (April 6–7)

Confederacy introduces first draft (April)

Congress passes Homestead Act, which provides free land to settlers (May)

Congress gives federal subsidies to transcontinental railroads (July)

Second Confiscation Act declares all fugitive and contraband slaves to be "forever free" (July)

Union halts Confederate offensive at Antietam (September 17)

Lincoln issues preliminary Emancipation Proclamation (September 22)

1863
Lincoln signs Emancipation Proclamation (January 1)

Union wins battles at Gettysburg (July 1–3) and Vicksburg (July 4)

Enrollment Act initiates draft in North (March), and leads to riots in New York City (July)

1864
President Lincoln gives Ulysses S. Grant command of all Union armies (March)

Grant begins advance on Richmond (May)

William Tecumseh Sherman takes Atlanta (September 2)

President Lincoln is reelected (November 8)

Sherman marches through Georgia (November and December)

1865
Congress approves Thirteenth Amendment, outlawing slavery (January 31)

Robert E. Lee surrenders at Appomattox Court House (April 9)

Lincoln assassinated by John Wilkes Booth (April 14)

Thirteenth Amendment is ratified (December 6)

FOR FURTHER EXPLORATION

Charles P. Roland, *An American Iliad: The Story of the Civil War* (1991), is an excellent brief survey; James M. McPherson, *The Battle Cry of Freedom* (1988), offers a fine synthesis of the war. For the story of the complex mixture of policies, personalities, and accidents that precipitated the conflict, read Richard Current, *Lincoln and the First Shot* (1963). John Hope Franklin, *The Emancipation Proclamation* (1963), explains the background of Lincoln's edict and its impact.

Nancy Scott Anderson and Dwight Anderson, *The Generals: Ulysses S. Grant and Robert E. Lee* (1988), is a vivid popular account of the men's lives and exploits. For scholarly analyses of the war, consult Mark Grimsley, *The Hard Hand of War: Union Military Policy Toward Southern Civilians, 1861–1865* (1995), and Gary W. Gallagher, *The Confederate War* (1997). William W. Freehling in *The South vs. the South* (2001) explores the impact of anti-Confederate sentiment.

James M. McPherson, *For Cause and Comrades: Why Men Fought in the Civil War* (1997), allows ordinary soldiers to explain their commitment to the Union and Confederacy. For firsthand accounts of black soldiers, see Ira Berlin et al., eds., *Freedom's Soldiers: The Black Military Experience in the Civil War* (1998). Earl J. Hess, *The Union Soldier in Battle: Enduring the Ordeal of Combat* (1997), presents a vivid account of the smell, sound, and feel of combat, as does Michael Shaara's *Killer Angels* (1974), a masterful novel about the Battle of Gettysburg.

For an incisive portrait of southern society from the diary of a planter's wife, see *Mary Chesnut's Civil War*, edited by C. Vann Woodward (1981). Jane E. Schultz details the experiences of *Women at the Front: Hospital Workers in Civil War America* (2004); and Laura F. Edwards compellingly describes the war's impact on all southern women in *Scarlett Doesn't Live Here Anymore* (2000).

For Civil War photographs, log on to **memory.loc.gov/ ammem/ndlpcoop/nhihtml/cwnyhshome.html** and **memory .loc.gov/ammem/cwphtml/cwphome.html**. An award-winning Web site is "The Valley of the Shadow" (**jefferson.village .virginia.edu/vshadow2/**), which traces the parallel histories of a northern and a southern community using a multitude of hyperlinked sources; the companion book is Edward L. Ayers, *In the Presence of Mine Enemies: War in the Heart of America, 1859–1863* (2003). Another award-winning Web site that captures the drama of war and emancipation in the words of liberated slaves and defeated masters is "Freedmen and Southern Society Project" (**www.history.umd.edu/Freedmen/home.html**).

TEST YOUR KNOWLEDGE

To assess your command of the material in this chapter, see the Online Study Guide at **bedfordstmartins.com/henretta**.

For Web sites, images, and documents related to topics and places in this chapter, visit **bedfordstmartins.com/makehistory**.

15

Reconstruction
1865–1877

I N HIS SECOND INAUGURAL ADDRESS, President Lincoln spoke of the need to "bind up the nation's wounds." No one knew better than Lincoln how daunting a task that would be. Slavery was finished. That much was certain. But what system of labor should replace plantation slavery? What rights should the freedmen be accorded beyond emancipation? How far should the federal government go to settle these questions? And, most immediately pressing, on what terms should the rebellious states be restored to the Union?

The last speech Lincoln delivered, on April 11, 1865, demonstrated his grasp of these issues. Reconstruction, he said, had to be regarded as a practical, not a theoretical, problem. It could be solved only if Republicans remained united, even if that meant compromising on principled differences dividing them, and only if the defeated South gave its consent, even if that meant forgiveness of the South's transgressions. The speech revealed the middle ground, at once magnanimous and open-minded, on which Lincoln hoped to reunite a wounded nation.

What course Reconstruction might have taken had Lincoln lived is one of the unanswerable questions of American history. On April 14, 1865 — five days after Lee's surrender at Appomattox — Lincoln was shot in the head at Ford's Theatre in Washington by John Wilkes Booth, a

◄ **Chloe and Sam (1882)**

After the Civil War the country went through the wrenching peacemaking process known as Reconstruction. The struggle between the victorious North and the vanquished South was fought out on a political landscape, but Thomas Hovenden's heartwarming painting reminds us of the deeper meaning of Reconstruction: that Chloe and Sam, after lives spent in slavery, might end their days in the dignity of freedom. Thomas Colville Fine Art.

prominent Shakespearean actor and Confederate sympathizer who had been plotting to abduct Lincoln and rescue the South. After Lee's surrender, Booth became bent on revenge. Without regaining consciousness, Lincoln died on April 15, 1865.

With one stroke John Wilkes Booth sent Lincoln to martyrdom, hardened many Northerners against the South, and handed the presidency to a man utterly lacking in Lincoln's moral sense and political judgment, Vice President Andrew Johnson.

Presidential Reconstruction

The problem of Reconstruction—how to restore rebellious states to the Union—was not addressed by the Founding Fathers. The Constitution does not say which branch of government handles the readmission of rebellious states or, for that matter, even contemplates the possibility of secession. It was an open question whether, upon seceding, the Confederate states had legally left the Union. If so, their reentry surely required legislative action by Congress. If not, if even in defeat they retained their constitutional status, then the terms for restoring them to the Union might be treated as an administrative matter best left to the president. In a constitutional system based on the **separation of powers**, the absence of clarity on so fundamental a matter made for explosive politics. The ensuing battle between the White House and Capitol Hill over who was in charge became one of the fault lines in Reconstruction's stormy history.

Presidential Initiatives

Lincoln, as wartime president, had the elbow room to take the lead, offering in December 1863 a general amnesty to all but high-ranking Confederates willing to pledge loyalty to the Union. When 10 percent of a state's 1860 voters had taken this oath, the state would be restored to the Union, provided that it accepted the Thirteenth Amendment abolishing slavery (see Chapter 14). The Confederate states did not bite, however, and congressional Republicans proposed a harsher substitute for Lincoln's Ten Percent Plan. The Wade-Davis Bill, passed on July 2, 1864, laid down, as conditions on the rebellious states, an oath of allegiance to the Union by a majority of each state's adult white men; new governments formed only by those who had never borne arms against the North; and permanent disfranchisement of Confederate leaders. The Wade-Davis bill served notice that the con-

gressional Republicans were not about to hand over Reconstruction policy to the president.

Lincoln executed a **pocket veto** of the Wade-Davis bill by not signing it before Congress adjourned. At the same time he initiated informal talks with congressional leaders aimed at a compromise. It was this stalemate that Lincoln was addressing when he appealed for Republican flexibility in the last speech of his life. Lincoln's successor, however, had no such inclinations. Andrew Johnson believed that Reconstruction was the president's prerogative, and by an accident of timing, he was free to act on his convictions. Under leisurely rules that went back to the early republic, the 39th Congress elected in November 1864 was not scheduled to convene until December 1865.

Andrew Johnson and Reconstruction. Johnson was a self-made man from the hills of eastern Tennessee. Born in 1808, he was apprenticed as a boy to a tailor and set up shop in Greeneville. Despite his lack of formal schooling—his wife was his teacher—Johnson prospered. His tailor shop became a political meeting place, and, natural leader that he was, he soon entered local politics with the backing of Greeneville's small farmers and laborers. In 1857, after a relentless climb up the political ranks, he became a U.S. Senator. A Jacksonian

Andrew Johnson

The president was not an easy man. This photograph of Andrew Johnson (1808–1875) conveys some of the prickly qualities that contributed so centrally to his failure to reach an agreement with Republicans on a moderate Reconstruction program. Library of Congress.

Democrat, Johnson despised equally the "bloated, corrupt aristocracy" of the Northeast and the Tennessee planter elite that dominated Memphis and its environs. It was the poor whites that Johnson championed, however, not the enslaved blacks nor, for that matter, emancipation.

Loyal to the Union, Johnson refused to leave the Senate when his state seceded. In this, he was utterly alone; no southern colleague stayed with him. When federal forces captured Nashville in 1862, Lincoln appointed Johnson Tennessee's military governor. Tennessee, one of the war's bloodiest battlefields, was bitterly divided along geographical lines: Unionist in the east and Rebel in the west. Johnson's assignment was to hold the state together, and he did so, with an iron hand. He was rewarded by being named Lincoln's running mate in 1864. Choosing this war Democrat seemed a smart move, designed to promote wartime unity and court the support of southern Unionists.

In May 1865, just a month after Lincoln's death, Johnson advanced his version of Reconstruction. He offered amnesty to all Southerners who took an oath of allegiance to the Constitution, except for high-ranking Confederate officials and wealthy planters, the elite whom Johnson blamed for secession. Johnson appointed provisional governors for the southern states, requiring as conditions for their restoration only that they revoke their ordinances of secession, repudiate their Confederate debts, and ratify the Thirteenth Amendment. Within months all the former Confederate states had met Johnson's terms and enjoyed functioning, elected governments.

At first Republicans responded favorably. The moderates among them were sympathetic to Johnson's argument that it was up to the states, not the federal government, to define the civil and political rights of the freedmen. Even the Radicals—the Republicans bent on a hard line toward the South—held their fire. They liked the stern treatment of Confederate leaders, and hoped that the new southern governments would show good faith by generous treatment of the freed slaves.

Nothing of the sort happened. The South lay in ruins (see Voices from Abroad, "David Macrae: The Devastated South," p. 460). But Southerners held fast to the old order. The newly seated legislatures moved to restore slavery in all but name. They enacted laws—known as **Black Codes**—designed to drive the former slaves back to the plantations. The new governments had been formed mostly by southern Unionists, but when it came to racial attitudes, little distinguished these loyalists from the Confederates. Despite his hard words against them, more-

over, Johnson forgave ex-Confederate leaders easily, so long as he got the satisfaction of humbling them when they appealed for pardons. Soon the ex-Confederates, emboldened by Johnson's indulgence, were filtering back into the halls of power. Old comrades packed the delegations to the new Congress: nine members of the Confederate Congress, seven former officials of Confederate state governments, four generals and four colonels, and even the vice president of the Confederacy, Alexander Stephens. This was the last straw for the Republicans.

The Battle Joined. Under the Constitution, Congress is "the judge of the Elections, Returns and Qualifications of its own Members" (Article 1, Section 5). With this power the Republican majorities in both houses refused to admit the southern delegations when Congress convened in early December 1865, effectively blocking Johnson's Reconstruction program. In response the southern states backed away from the Black Codes, replacing them with regulatory ordinances silent on race yet, in practice, applying only to blacks, not to whites. On top of that, a wave of violence erupted across the South. In Tennessee a Nashville paper reported that white gangs "are riding about whipping, maiming and killing all negroes who do not obey the orders of their former masters, just as if slavery existed." Congressional Republicans concluded that the South had embarked on a concerted effort to circumvent the Thirteenth Amendment. They decided that the federal government had to intervene.

Back in March 1865, before adjourning, the 38th Congress had established the Freedmen's Bureau to aid ex-slaves during the transition from war to peace. Now in early 1866, under the leadership of the moderate Republican Senator Lyman Trumbull, Congress voted to extend the Freedmen's Bureau's life, gave it direct funding for the first time, and authorized its agents to investigate mistreatment of blacks.

More extraordinary was Trumbull's civil rights bill, declaring the ex-slaves to be citizens and granting them, along with every other citizen, equal rights of contract, access to the courts, and protection of person and property. Trumbull's bill nullified all state laws infringing on citizens' equal protection under the law, authorized U.S. attorneys to bring enforcement suits in the federal courts, and provided for fines and imprisonment for violators. Provoked by an unrepentant South, even the most moderate Republicans demanded that the federal government assume responsibility for the civil rights of the freedmen.

David Macrae

The Devastated South

In this excerpt from The Americans at Home *(1870), an account of his tour of the United States, the Scottish clergyman David Macrae describes the war-stricken South as he found it in 1867–1868, at a time when the crisis over Reconstruction was boiling over.*

I was struck with a remark made by a Southern gentleman in answer to the assertion that Jefferson Davis [the president of the Confederacy] had culpably continued the war for six months after all hope had been abandoned.

"Sir," he said, "Mr. Davis knew the temper of the South as well as any man in it. He knew if there was to be anything worth calling peace, the South must win; or, if she couldn't win, she wanted to be whipped — well whipped — thoroughly whipped."

The further south I went, the oftener these remarks came back upon me. Evidence was everywhere that the South had maintained the desperate conflict until she was utterly exhausted. . . . Almost every man I met at the South, especially in North Carolina, Georgia, and Virginia, seemed to have been in the army; and it was painful to find many who had returned were mutilated, maimed, or broken in health by exposure. When I remarked this to a young Confederate officer in North Carolina, and said I was glad to see that he had escaped unhurt, he said, "Wait till we get to the office, sir, and I will tell you more about that." When we got there, he pulled up one leg of his trousers, and showed me that he had an iron rod

there to strengthen his limb, and enable him to walk without limping, half of his foot being off. He showed me on the other leg a deep scar made by a fragment of a shell; and these were but two of seven wounds which had left their marks upon his body. When he heard me speak of relics, he said, "Try to find a North Carolina gentleman without a Yankee mark on him."

Nearly three years had passed when I traveled through the country, and yet we have seen what traces the war had left in such cities as Richmond, Petersburg, and Columbia. The same spectacle met me at Charleston. Churches and houses had been battered down by heavy shot and shell hurled into the city from Federal batteries at a distance of five miles. Even the valley of desolation made by a great fire in 1861, through the very heart of the city, remained unbuilt. There, after the lapse of seven years, stood the blackened ruins of streets and houses waiting for the coming of a better day. . . . Over the country districts the prostration was equally marked. Along the track of Sherman's army — especially, the devastation was fearful — farms laid waste, fences burned, bridges destroyed, houses left in ruins, plantations in many cases turned into wilderness again.

The people had shared in the general wreck, and looked poverty-stricken, careworn, and dejected. Ladies who before the war had lived in affluence, with black servants round them to attend to their every wish, were boarding together in half-furnished houses, cooking their own food and washing their own linen, some of them, I was told, so utterly destitute that they did not know when they finished one meal where they were to find the next. . . . Men who

had held commanding positions during the war had fallen out of sight and were filling humble situations — struggling, many of them, to earn a bare subsistence. . . . I remember dining with three cultured Southern gentlemen, one a general, the other, I think, a captain, and the third a lieutenant. They were all living together in a plain little wooden house, such as they would formerly have provided for their servants. Two of them were engaged in a railway office, the third was seeking a situation, frequently, in his vain search, passing the large blinded house where he had lived in luxurious ease before the war.

SOURCE: Allan Nevins, ed., *America through British Eyes* (Gloucester, MA: Peter Smith, 1968), 345–347.

ANALYZING THE EVIDENCE

➤ In general, we value accounts by foreigners for insights they provide into America that might not be visible to its own citizens. Do you find any such insights in the Reverend Macrae's account of the postwar South?

➤ The South proved remarkably resistant to northern efforts at reconstruction. Can we find explanations for that resistance in Macrae's account?

➤ The North quickly became disillusioned with radical Reconstruction (see p. 466). Is there anything in Macrae's sympathetic interviews with wounded southern gentlemen and destitute ladies that sheds light on the susceptibility of many Northerners to propaganda depicting a South in the grip of "a mass of black barbarism"?

Acting on Freedom

While Congress debated, emancipated slaves acted on their own ideas about freedom. News that their bondage was over left them exultant and hopeful (see Comparing American Voices, "Freedom," pp. 462–463). Freedom meant many things — the end of punishment by the lash; the ability to move around; the reuniting of families; and the opportunity to begin schools, to form churches and social clubs, and, not least, to engage in politics. Across the South blacks held mass meetings, paraded, and formed organizations. Topmost among their demands was the right to vote — "an essential and inseparable element of self-government." No less than their former masters, ex-slaves intended to be actors in the savage drama of Reconstruction.

Struggling for Economic Independence.
Ownership of land, emancipated blacks believed, was the basis for true freedom. In the chaotic final months of the war, freedmen seized control of plantations where they could. In Georgia and South Carolina, General William T. Sherman reserved large coastal tracts for liberated slaves and settled them on 40-acre plots. Sherman just didn't want to be bothered with the refugees as his army drove across the Lower South, but the freedmen assumed that Sherman's order meant that the land would be theirs. When the war ended, resettlement became the responsibility of the Freedmen's Bureau, which was charged with distributing confiscated land to "loyal refugees and freedmen" and regulating labor contracts between freedmen and planters. Many black families stayed on their old plantations, awaiting redistribution of the land to them. When the South Carolina planter Thomas Pinckney returned home, his freed slaves told him: "We ain't going nowhere. We are going to work right here on the land where we were born and what belongs to us."

Johnson's amnesty plan, entitling pardoned Confederates to recover property seized during the war, blasted these hopes. In October 1865 Johnson ordered General Oliver O. Howard, head of the Freedmen's Bureau, to restore the plantations on the Sea Islands off the South Carolina coast to their white owners. When Howard reluctantly obeyed, the dispossessed blacks protested: "Why do you take away our lands? You take them from us who have always been true, always true to the Government! You give them to our all-time enemies! That is not right!"

In the Sea Islands and elsewhere, former slaves resisted efforts to evict them. Led by black veterans of the Union army, they fought pitched battles with plantation owners and bands of ex-Confederate soldiers. Landowners struck back hard. One black veteran wrote from Maryland: "The returned colard Solgers are in Many cases beten, and their guns taken from them, we darcent walk out of an evening. . . . They beat us badly and Sumtime Shoot us." Often aided by federal troops, the local whites generally prevailed in this land war.

Resisting Wage Labor.
As planters prepared for a new growing season, a great battle took shape over the labor system that would replace slavery. Convinced that blacks needed supervision, planters wanted to retain the gang labor of the past, only now with wages replacing the food, clothing, and shelter their slaves had once received. The Freedmen's Bureau, although watchful against exploitative labor contracts, sided with the planters. The main thing, its reform founders believed, was not to encourage dependency under "the guise of guardianship." Rely on your "own efforts and exertions," an agent told a large crowd of freedmen in North Carolina, "make contracts with the planters" and "respect the rights of property."

This was advice given with little regard for the world in which those North Carolina freedmen lived. It was not only their unequal bargaining power they worried about or even that their ex-masters' real desire was to re-enslave them under the guise of "free" contracts. In their eyes the condition of wage labor was, by definition, debasing. The rural South was not like the North, where working for wages was by now the norm and qualified a man as independent. In the South, selling one's labor to another — and in particular, selling one's labor to work another's land — implied not freedom, but dependency. "I mean to own my own manhood," responded one South Carolina freedman to an offer of wage work. "I'm going to own my own land."

The wage issue cut to the very core of the former slaves' struggle for freedom. Nothing had been more horrifying than that as slaves their persons had been the property of others. When a master cast his eye on a slave woman, her husband had no recourse; nor, for that matter, was rape of a slave a crime. In a famous oration celebrating the anniversary of emancipation, the Reverend Henry M. Turner spoke bitterly of the time when his people had "no security for domestic happiness" and "our wives were sold and husbands bought, children were begotten and enslaved by their fathers." That was why formalizing marriage was so urgent a matter and why, when hard-pressed planters demanded that freedwomen go back into the fields, they resisted so resolutely. If the ex-slaves were to be free as white folk, then their wives could not, any

Freedom

In the annals of America, probably no human relationship was so conducive to mutual incomprehension as enslavement. Slavery meant one thing to the masters, something altogether different to the slaves. And when freedom came, there was no bridging this bottomless gulf. That, more than anything, explains the racial strife over land, over equal rights, and over political power that engulfed the Reconstruction South. The following documents offer vivid testimony to this bitter legacy of slavery.

EDWARD BARNELL HEYWARD

This letter is from the son of a (formerly) wealthy plantation owner, to his friend Jim, evidently a Northerner. Heyward has not quite gotten over the fact that he — and his northern friend — has survived the war, nor that he is now poor. And, in defeat, he feels deeply alienated from America; he is thinking of migrating to England. What is most telling about his letter, however, is his despair over the future of his ex-slaves. He is afraid, remarkably, that emancipation means "their best days are over."

E. B. Heyward
Gadsden P.O.
South Carolina
22 January 1866

My dear Jim

Your letter of date July 1865, has just reached me and you will be relieved by my answer, to find, that I am still alive, and extremely glad to hear from you. . . .

I have served in the Army, my brother died in the Army, and every family has lost members. No one can know how reduced we are, particularly the refined & educated. . . .

Our losses have been frightful, and we have now, scarcely a support. My Father had five plantations on the coast, and all the buildings were burnt, and the negroes, now left to themselves, are roaming in a starving condition . . . like lost sheep, with no one to care for them.

They find the Yankee only a speculator, and they have no confidence in anyone. They very naturally, poor things, think that freedom means doing nothing, and this they are determined to do. They look to the government, to take care of them, and it will be many years, before this once productive country will be able to support itself. The former kind and just treatment of the slaves, and their docile and generous temper, makes them now disposed to be [quiet] and obedient: but the determination of your Northern people to give them a place in the councils of the Country and make them the equal of the white man, will at last, bear its fruit, and we may *then* expect them, to rise against the whites, and in the end, be exterminated themselves.

I am now interested in a school for the negroes, who are around me, and will endeavor to do my duty, to them, as ever before, but I am afraid their best days are past.

As soon as able, I shall quit the Country, and leave others to stand the storm, which I now see making up, at the North, which must soon burst upon *the whole* country, and break up everything which we have so long boasted of.

I feel now that I have *no country*, I *obey* like a subject, but I cannot love such a government. Perhaps the next letter, you get from me, will be from England.

I have, thank God! A house over my head & something to eat & am as ever always

your friend,
E. B. Heyward

JOURDON ANDERSON

This is a letter by Jourdan Anderson, a Tennessee slave who escaped with his family during the war and settled in Dayton, Ohio, to his former master. Folklorists have recorded the sly ways that slaves found, even in bondage, for "puttin' down" their masters. But only in freedom — and beyond reach in a northern state at that — could Anderson's sarcasm be expressed so openly, with the jest that his family might consider returning if they first received the wages due them, calculated to the dollar, for all those years in slavery. Anderson's letter, although probably written or edited by a white friend in Dayton, surely is faithful to what the ex-slave wanted to say.

Dayton, Ohio
August 7, 1865.

To My Old Master, Colonel P. H. Anderson, Big Spring,
Tennessee.
Sir:

I got your letter, and was glad to find that you had not forgotten Jourdon.... I thought the Yankees would have hung you long before this, for harboring Rebs they found at your house. I suppose they never heard about your going to Colonel Martin's house to kill the union soldier that was left by his company in their stable. Although you shot at me twice before I left you, I did not want to hear of your being hurt, and am glad you are still living. It would do me good to go back to the dear old home again, and see Miss Mary and Miss Martha and Allen, Esther, Green, and Lee. Give my love to them all, and tell them I hope we will meet in the better world, if not in this....

I want to know particularly what the good chance is you propose to give me. I am doing tolerably well here. I get twenty-five dollars a month, with victuals and clothing; have a comfortable home for Mandy,—the folks call her Mrs. Anderson,—and the children—Milly, Jane, and Grundy—go to school and are learning well.... We are kindly treated. Sometimes we overhear others saying, "Them colored people were slaves" down in Tennessee. The children feel hurt when they hear such remarks; but I tell them it was no disgrace in Tennessee to belong to Colonel Anderson. Many darkeys would have been proud, as I used to be, to call you master....

Mandy says she would be afraid to go back without some proof that you were disposed to treat us justly and kindly; and we have concluded to test your sincerity by asking you to send us our wages for the time we served you. This will make us forget and forgive old scores, and rely on your justice and friendship in the future. I served you faithfully for thirty-two years, and Mandy twenty years. At twenty-five dollars a month for me and two dollars a week for Mandy, our earnings would amount to eleven thousand six hundred and eighty dollars. Add to this the interest for the time our wages have been kept back, and deduct what you paid for our clothing, and three doctor's visits to me, and pulling a tooth for Mandy, and the balance will show what we are in justice entitled to....

In answering this letter, please state if there would be any safety for my Milly and Jane, who are now grown up, and both good-looking girls.... I would rather stay here and starve—and die, if it come to that—than have my girls brought to shame by the violence and wickedness of their young masters. You will also please state if there has been any schools opened for the colored children in your neighborhood. The great desire of my life now is to give my children an education, and have them form virtuous habits.

Say howdy to George Carter, and thank him for taking the pistol from you when you were shooting at me.

From your old servant,
Jourdon Anderson

SOURCE: Stanley I. Kutler, ed., *Looking for America: The People's History*, 2nd ed., 2 vols. (New York: W. W. Norton, 1979), 2: 4–6, 24–27.

ANALYZING THE EVIDENCE

➤ The South proved fiercely resistant to accepting the ex-slaves as citizens with equal rights. In what ways does Heyward's letter provide insight into that resistance and (despite Heyward's professed sympathy) help explain why so many blacks were beaten and killed when they tried to exercise their rights?

➤ In what ways does Anderson's letter suggest that, despite Heyward's dire prediction, the best days of the freed slaves were not "behind them" and that, on the contrary, they were hungry for the benefits of freedom?

➤ Once emancipated, ex-slaves were free to go wherever they wanted. Yet they mostly stayed put and, despite the bitterness of their enslavement, often became sharecroppers for their former masters, as, for example, on the Barrow plantation (see Map 15.2, p. 473). Does Anderson's letter suggest why they might have made that choice? Does it matter that his former master is also named Anderson?

Wage Labor of Former Slaves

This photograph, taken in South Carolina shortly after the Civil War, shows former slaves leaving the cotton fields. Ex-slaves were organized into work crews probably not that different from earlier slave gangs, although they now labored for wages and their plug-hatted boss bore little resemblance to the slave drivers of the past. New-York Historical Society.

more than white wives, labor for others. "I seen on some plantations," one freedman recounted, "where the white men would . . . tell colored men that their wives and children could not live on their places unless they work in the fields. The colored men [answered that] whenever they wanted their wives to work they would tell them themselves; and if he could not rule his own domestic affairs on that place he would leave it and go someplace else."

The reader will see the irony in this definition of freedom: It assumed the wife's subordinate role and designated her labor the husband's property. But if that was the price of freedom, freedwomen were prepared to pay it. Far better to take a chance with their own men than with their ex-masters.

Many former slaves voted with their feet, abandoning their old plantations and seeking better lives in the towns and cities of the South. Those who remained in the countryside refused to work the cotton fields under the hated **gang-labor system** or negotiated tenaciously over the terms of their labor contracts. Whatever system of labor finally might emerge, it was clear that the freedmen would never settle for anything resembling the old plantation system.

The efforts of former slaves to control their own lives challenged deeply entrenched white attitudes. "The destiny of the black race," asserted one Texan, could be summarized "in one sentence — subordination to the white race." Southern whites, a Freedmen's Bureau official observed, could not

"conceive of the negro having any rights at all." And when freedmen resisted, white retribution was swift and often terrible. In Pine Bluff, Arkansas, "after some kind of dispute with some freedmen," whites set fire to their cabins and hanged twenty-four of the inhabitants — men, women, and children. The toll of murdered and beaten blacks mounted into untold thousands. The governments established under Johnson's plan only put the stamp of legality on the pervasive efforts to enforce white supremacy. Blacks "would be *just as well* off with no law at all or no Government," concluded a Freedmen's Bureau agent, as with the justice they got under the restored white rule.

In this unequal struggle, blacks turned to Washington. "We stood by the government when it wanted help," a black Mississippian wrote President Johnson. "Now . . . will it stand by us?"

Congress versus President

Andrew Johnson was not the man to ask. In February 1866 he vetoed the Freedmen's Bureau bill. The bureau, Johnson charged, was an "immense patronage," showering benefits on blacks never granted to "our own people." Republicans could not muster enough votes to override his veto. A month later, again rebuffing his critics, Johnson vetoed Trumbull's civil rights bill, arguing that federal protection of black rights constituted "a stride toward centralization." His racism, hitherto muted, now blazed forth: "This is a country for white men, and by God, as long as I am president, it shall be government for white men."

Galvanized by Johnson's attack on their legislation, the Republicans went into action. In early April they got the necessary two-thirds majorities in both houses and enacted the Civil Rights Act. Republican resolve was reinforced by news of mounting violence in the South, culminating in three days of rioting in Memphis. Forty-six blacks were left dead, and hundreds of homes, churches, and schools were burned. In July an angry Congress renewed the Freedmen's Bureau over a second Johnson veto.

The Fourteenth Amendment. Anxious to consolidate their gains, Republicans moved to enshrine black civil rights in an amendment to the Constitution. The heart of the Fourteenth Amendment was Section 1, which declared that "all persons born or naturalized in the United States" were citizens. No state could abridge "the privileges or immunities of citizens of the United States," deprive "any person of life, liberty, or property, without due process of law," or deny anyone "the equal protection of the laws." These phrases were vague, intentionally so, but they established the constitutionality of the Civil Rights Act and, at the least, laid the groundwork for a federally enforced standard of equality before the law in the states.

For the moment, however, the Fourteenth Amendment was most important as a factor in partisan politics. With the 1866 congressional elections approaching, Johnson somehow figured he could turn the Fourteenth Amendment to his advantage. He urged the states not to ratify it. Months earlier, Johnson had begun maneuvering against the Republicans. He aimed at building a coalition of white Southerners, northern Democrats, and conservative Republicans under the banner of a new party, National Union. Any hope of launching it, however, was shattered by Johnson's intemperate behavior and by escalating violence in the South. A dissension-ridden National Union convention in July ended inconclusively, and Johnson's campaign against the Fourteenth Amendment became, effectively, a campaign for the Democratic Party.

"The First Vote"

This lithograph appeared in *Harper's Weekly* in November 1867. The voters represent elements of African American political leadership: an artisan with tools, a well-dressed member of the middle class, and a Union soldier. Corbis-Bettmann.

Republicans responded furiously, unveiling a practice that would become known as "waving the bloody shirt." The Democrats were traitors, charged Indiana governor Oliver Morton. Their party was "a common sewer and loathsome receptacle, into which is emptied every element of treason North and South." In late August Johnson embarked on a disastrous "swing around the circle"—a railroad tour from Washington to Chicago and St. Louis and back—that violated the custom against personal campaigning by presidents. Johnson made matters worse by engaging in shouting matches with hecklers and insulting the hostile crowds.

The 1866 congressional elections inflicted a humiliating defeat on Johnson. The Republicans won a three-to-one majority in Congress. They considered themselves "masters of the situation" and free to proceed "entirely regardless of [Johnson's] opinions or wishes." As a referendum on the Fourteenth Amendment, moreover, the election was a striking victory, demonstrating vast popular support for the civil rights of the former slaves. The Republican Party emerged with a new sense of unity—a unity coalescing not at the center, but on the left, around the unbending program of the Radical minority.

Radical Republicans. The Radicals represented the abolitionist strain within the Republican Party. Most of them hailed from New England or from the upper Midwest, which was heavily settled by New Englanders. In the Senate they were led by Charles Sumner of Massachusetts and in the House by Thaddeus Stevens of Pennsylvania. For them Reconstruction was never primarily about restoring the Union but about remaking southern society. "The foundations of their institutions . . . must be broken up and relaid," declared Stevens, "or all our blood and treasure will have been spent in vain."

Only a handful went as far as Stevens in demanding that the plantations be treated as "forfeited estates of the enemy" and broken up into small farms for the former slaves. About securing the freedmen's civil and political rights, however, there was agreement. In this endeavor Radicals had no qualms about expanding the powers of the national government. "The power of the great landed aristocracy in those regions, if unrestrained by power from without, would inevitably reassert itself," warned Congressman George W. Julian of Indiana. Radicals were aggressively partisan. They regarded the Republican Party as God's instrument for regenerating the South.

At first, in the months after Appomattox, few but the Radicals themselves imagined that so extreme a program had any chance of enactment. Black **suffrage** especially seemed beyond reach, since the northern states themselves (except in New England) denied blacks the vote. And yet, as fury mounted against the intransigent South, Republicans became ever more radicalized until, in the wake of the smashing congressional victory of 1866, they embraced the Radicals' vision of a reconstructed South.

> ➤ Why can the enactment of southern Black Codes in 1865 be considered a turning point in the course of Reconstruction?

> ➤ Why was working for wages resisted by ex-slaves struggling for freedom after emancipation?

> ➤ To what extent was President Johnson responsible for the radicalization of the Republican Party in 1866?

Radical Reconstruction

Afterward, thoughtful Southerners admitted that the South had brought radical Reconstruction on itself. "We had, in 1865, a white man's government in Alabama," remarked the man who had been Johnson's provisional governor, "but we lost it." The state's "great blunder" was not to "have at once taken the negro right under the protection of the laws." Remarkably, the South remained defiant even after the 1866 elections. Every state legislature but Tennessee's rejected the Fourteenth Amendment. It was as if they could not imagine that governments installed under the presidential imprimatur and fully functioning might be swept away. But that, in fact, is just what the Republicans intended to do.

Congress Takes Command

The Reconstruction Act of 1867, enacted in March by the Republican Congress, organized the South as a conquered land, dividing it into five military districts, each under the command of a Union general (Map 15.1). The price for reentering the Union was granting the vote to the freedmen and disfranchising those of the South's prewar leadership class who had participated in the rebellion. Each military commander was ordered to register all eligible adult males (black as well as white), supervise the election of state conventions, and make certain that

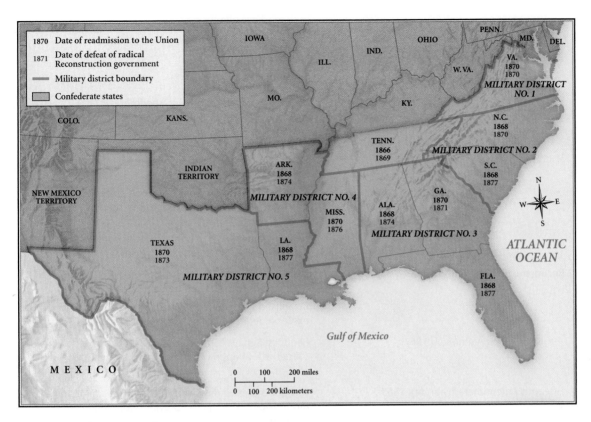

Map 15.1   Reconstruction

The federal government organized the Confederate states into five military districts during
radical Reconstruction. For each state the first date indicates when that state was readmitted
to the Union; the second date shows when Radical Republicans lost control of the state
government. All the ex-Confederate states rejoined the Union from 1868 to 1870, but the
periods of radical rule varied widely. Republicans lasted only a few months in Virginia; they
held on until the end of Reconstruction in Louisiana, Florida, and South Carolina.

the new constitutions contained guarantees of
black suffrage. Congress would readmit a state to
the Union if its voters ratified the constitution, if
that document proved acceptable to Congress, and
if the new state legislature approved the Fourteenth
Amendment (thus ensuring the needed ratification
by three-fourths of the states). Johnson vetoed the
Reconstruction Act, but Congress overrode the veto
(Table 15.1).

Impeachment. The Tenure of Office Act, a companion to the Reconstruction Act, required Senate
consent for the removal of any official whose
appointment had required Senate confirmation.
Congress chiefly wanted to protect Secretary of
War Edwin M. Stanton, a Lincoln holdover and the
only member of Johnson's cabinet who favored
radical Reconstruction. In his position Stanton
could do much to frustrate Johnson's anticipated
efforts to undermine Reconstruction. The law also
required the president to issue all orders to the

army through its commanding general, Ulysses
S. Grant. In effect, Congress was attempting to
reconstruct the presidency as well as the South.

Seemingly defeated, Johnson appointed generals recommended by Stanton and Grant to command the five military districts in the South. But he
was just biding his time. In August 1867, after Congress had adjourned, he "suspended" Stanton and
replaced him with Grant, believing that the general
would be a good soldier and follow orders. Next
Johnson replaced four of the commanding generals. Johnson, however, had misjudged Grant, who
publicly objected to the president's machinations.
When the Senate reconvened in the fall, it overruled
Stanton's suspension. Grant, now an open enemy
of Johnson's, resigned so that Stanton could resume
his office.

On February 21, 1868, Johnson formally dismissed Stanton. The feisty secretary of war, however,
barricaded the door of his office and refused to
admit Johnson's appointee. Three days later, for the

Table 15.1 Primary Reconstruction Laws and Constitutional Amendments

Law (Date of Congressional Passage)	Key Provisions
Thirteenth Amendment (December 1865*)	Prohibited slavery
Civil Rights Act of 1866 (April 1866)	Defined citizenship rights of freedmen
	Authorized federal authorities to bring suit against those who violated those rights
Fourteenth Amendment (June 1866†)	Established national citizenship for persons born or naturalized in the United States
	Prohibited the states from depriving citizens of their civil rights or equal protection under the law
	Reduced state representation in House of Representatives by the percentage of adult male citizens denied the vote
Reconstruction Act of 1867 (March 1867)	Divided the South into five military districts, each under the command of a Union general
	Established requirements for readmission of ex-Confederate states to the Union
Tenure of Office Act (March 1867)	Required Senate consent for removal of any federal official whose appointment had required Senate confirmation
Fifteenth Amendment (February 1869‡)	Forbade states to deny citizens the right to vote on the grounds of race, color, or "previous condition of servitude"
Ku Klux Klan Act (April 1871)	Authorized the president to use federal prosecutions and military force to suppress conspiracies to deprive citizens of the right to vote and enjoy the equal protection of the law

*Ratified by three-fourths of all states in December 1865.
†Ratified by three-fourths of all states in July 1868.
‡Ratified by three-fourths of all states in March 1870.

first time in U.S. history, House Republicans introduced articles of **impeachment** against a sitting president, employing the power granted the House of Representatives by the Constitution to charge high federal officials with "Treason, Bribery, or other high Crimes and Misdemeanors." The House serves in effect as the prosecutor in such cases. Eleven counts of presidential misconduct were brought, nine of them violations of the Tenure of Office Act.

The case went to the Senate, which acts as the court in impeachment cases, with Chief Justice Salmon P. Chase presiding. After an eleven-week trial, thirty-five senators on May 15 voted for conviction, one vote short of the two-thirds majority required. Seven moderate Republicans broke ranks, voting for acquittal along with twelve Democrats. The dissenting Republicans felt that the Tenure of Office Act was of dubious validity (in fact, the Supreme Court subsequently declared it unconstitutional) and that removing a president for defying Congress was too extreme, too damaging to the constitutional system of checks and balances, even for the sake of punishing

Johnson. And they were wary of the alternative, the Radical Republican Benjamin F. Wade, the president pro tem of the Senate, who, since there was no vice president, stood next in line for the presidency.

Despite his acquittal, however, Johnson had been defanged. For the remainder of his term he was powerless to alter the course of Reconstruction.

The Election of 1868. The impeachment controversy made Grant, already the North's war hero, a Republican hero as well, and he easily won the party's presidential nomination in 1868. In the fall campaign he supported radical Reconstruction, but he also urged reconciliation between the sections. His Democratic opponent, Horatio Seymour, a former governor of New York, almost declined the nomination because he doubted that the Democrats could overcome the stain of disloyalty.

As Seymour feared, the Republicans "waved the bloody shirt," stirring up old wartime emotions against the Democrats to great effect. Grant did about as well in the North (55 percent) as had

Lincoln in 1864. Overall, he won by a margin of 52.7 percent and received 214 of 294 electoral votes. The Republicans also retained two-thirds majorities in both houses of Congress.

The Fifteenth Amendment. In the wake of their victory, the Republicans quickly produced the last major piece of Reconstruction legislation—the Fifteenth Amendment, which forbade either the federal government or the states from denying citizens the right to vote on the basis of race, color, or "previous condition of servitude." The amendment left room for **poll taxes** and property requirements or literacy tests that might be used to discourage blacks from voting, a necessary concession to northern and western states that already relied on such provisions to keep immigrants and the "unworthy" poor from the polls. A California senator warned that in his state, with its rabidly anti-Chinese sentiment (see Chapter 16), any restriction on that power would "kill our party as dead as a stone."

Despite grumbling by Radical Republicans, the amendment passed without modification in February 1869. Congress required the states still under federal control—Virginia, Mississippi, Texas, and Georgia—to ratify it as a condition for being readmitted to the Union. A year later the Fifteenth Amendment became part of the Constitution.

Woman Suffrage Denied

If the Fifteenth Amendment troubled some proponents of black suffrage, this was nothing compared to the outrage felt by women's rights advocates. They had fought the good fight for the abolition of slavery for so many years, only to be abandoned when the chance finally came to get the vote for women. All it would have taken was one more word in the Fifteenth Amendment, so that the protected categories for voting would have read "race, color, *sex,* or previous condition." Leading suffragists such as Susan B. Anthony and Elizabeth Cady Stanton did not want to hear from Radical Republicans that this was "the Negro's hour" and that women should wait for another day. How could suffrage be granted to former slaves, Stanton demanded, but not to them?

In a decisive debate in May 1869 at the Equal Rights Association, the champion of universal suffrage, the black abolitionist Frederick Douglass, pleaded for understanding. "When women, because they are women, are hunted down . . . dragged from their homes and hung upon lamp posts . . . when their children are not allowed to enter schools; then they will have an urgency to obtain the ballot equal to our own." Not even all his black sisters agreed. "If colored men get their rights, and not colored women theirs," protested Sojourner Truth, "you see the colored men will be masters over the women, and it will be just as bad as it was before." As for white women in the audience, remarked Frances Harper in support of Douglass, they "all go for sex, letting race occupy a minor position," or worse. In her despair, Elizabeth Cady Stanton lashed out in ugly racist terms against "Patrick and Sambo and Hans and Ung Tung," aliens ignorant of the Declaration of Independence and yet entitled to vote while the most accomplished of American women remained voteless. Douglass's resolution in support of the Fifteenth Amendment failed, and the Equal Rights convention broke up in acrimony.

At this searing moment a rift opened in the ranks of the women's movement. The majority, led by Lucy Stone and Julia Ward Howe, reconciled themselves to disappointment and accepted the priority of black suffrage. Organized into the American Woman Suffrage Association, these moderates remained allied to the Republican Party, in hopes that once Reconstruction had been settled it would be time for the woman's vote. The Stanton-Anthony group, however, struck out in a new direction. The embittered Stanton declared that woman "must not put her trust in man." The new organization she headed, the New York–based National Woman Suffrage Association, accepted only women, focused exclusively on women's rights, and resolutely took up the battle for a federal woman suffrage amendment.

The fracturing of the women's movement obscured the common ground the two sides shared. Both appealed to constituencies beyond the narrow confines of abolitionism and evangelical reform. Both elevated suffrage into the preeminent women's issue. And both were energized for the battles that lay ahead. "If I were to give vent to all my pent-up wrath concerning the subordination of woman," Lydia Maria Child wrote the Republican warhorse Charles Sumner in 1872, "I might frighten *you*. . . . Suffice it, therefore, to say, either the theory of our government is *false,* or women have a right to vote." If radical Reconstruction seemed a barren time for women's rights, in fact it had planted the seeds of the modern feminist movement.

Republican Rule in the South

Between 1868 and 1871 all the southern states met the congressional stipulations and rejoined the Union. Protected by federal troops, state Republican organizations took hold across the South. The Reconstruction administrations they set up remained in power for periods ranging from a few months in Virginia to nine years in South Carolina, Louisiana, and Florida. Their core support came

Women's Rights, 1870s

This 1870s engraving reveals a distinguishing feature of the woman suffrage movement as it emerged after Reconstruction, which was that it became exclusively a movement of women (although there are a couple of men in the audience). Bettmann/Corbis.

from African Americans, who constituted a majority of registered voters in Alabama, Florida, South Carolina, and Mississippi.

Carpetbaggers and Scalawags. Ex-Confederates had a name for Southern whites who supported Reconstruction: **scalawags,** an ancient Scots-Irish term for runty, worthless animals. Whites who had come from the North they denounced as **carpetbaggers**—self-seeking interlopers who carried all their property in cheap suitcases called carpetbags. Such labels glossed over the actual diversity of these white Republicans.

Some carpetbaggers, while motivated by personal profit, also brought capital and skills. Others were Union army veterans taken with the South— its climate, people, and economic opportunities. And interspersed with the self-seekers were many idealists anxious to advance the cause of emancipation.

The scalawags were even more diverse. Some were former slave owners, ex-Whigs and even ex-Democrats, drawn to Republicanism as the best way to attract northern capital to southern railroads, mines, and factories. But most were yeomen farmers from the backcountry districts who wanted to rid the South of its slaveholding aristocracy. They had generally fought against, or at least refused to support, the Confederacy, believing that slavery had victimized whites as well as blacks. "Now is the time," a Georgia scalawag wrote, "for every man to come out and speak his principles publickly [*sic*] and vote for liberty as we have been in bondage long enough."

African American Leadership. The Democrats' scorn for black leaders as ignorant field hands was just as false as stereotypes about white Republicans. The first African American leaders in the South came from an elite of free blacks. They were joined by northern blacks who moved south heartened by the arrival of radical Reconstruction. Like their white allies, many were Union army veterans. Some had participated in the antislavery crusade; a number were employed by the Freedmen's Bureau or northern missionary societies. Others had escaped from slavery and were returning home. One of these was Blanche K. Bruce, who had been tutored on the Virginia plantation of his white father. During the war Bruce escaped and established a school for ex-slaves in Missouri. In 1869 he moved to Mississippi, became active in politics, and in 1874 became Mississippi's second black U.S. senator.

As the reconstructed Republican governments of 1867 began to function, this diverse group of ministers, artisans, shopkeepers, and former soldiers reached out to the freedmen. African American speakers, some financed by the Republican Party, fanned out into the old plantation districts and recruited ex-slaves for political roles. Still, few of the new leaders were field hands; most had been preachers or artisans. The literacy of one ex-slave, Thomas Allen, who was a Baptist minister and shoemaker, helped him win election to the Georgia legislature. "In my county," he recalled, "the colored people came to me for instructions, and I gave them the best instructions I could. I took the *New York Tribune* and other papers, and in that way I found out a great deal, and I told them whatever I thought was right."

Although never proportionate to their numbers in the population, black officeholders were prominent across the South. In South Carolina African Americans constituted a majority in the lower house of the legislature in 1868. Three were elected to Congress; another joined the state supreme court. Over the entire course of Reconstruction, twenty African Americans served in state administrations as governor, lieutenant governor, secretary of state, treasurer, or superintendent of education; more than six hundred served as state legislators; and sixteen were U.S. congressmen.

The Radical Program. The Republicans had ambitious plans for a reconstructed South. They wanted to end its dependence on cotton agriculture, build an entrepreneurial economy like the North's, and make a better life for all southerners. Although they fell short, they accomplished more than their critics gave them credit for.

The Republicans modernized state constitutions, eliminated property qualifications for the vote, and swept out the Black Codes restricting the lives of the freedmen. Women also benefited from the Republican defense of personal liberty. The new constitutions expanded the rights of married women, enabling them to hold property and earnings independent of their husbands — "a wonderful reform," a Georgia woman wrote, for "the cause of Women's Rights." Republican social programs called for the establishment of hospitals, more humane penitentiaries, and asylums for orphans and the mentally ill. Money poured into road-building projects and the region's shattered railroad network.

To pay for their ambitious programs the Republican governments copied taxes that Jacksonian reformers had earlier introduced in the North — in particular, property taxes on both real estate and personal wealth (see Chapter 10). The goal was to make planters pay their fair shares and to broaden the tax base. In many plantation counties, former slaves served as tax assessors and collectors, administering the taxation of their one-time owners.

Higher tax revenues never managed to overtake the huge obligations assumed by the Reconstruction governments. State debts mounted rapidly, and, as crushing interest on bonds fell due, public credit collapsed. On top of that, much spending was wasted or ended up in the pockets of public officials. Corruption was ingrained in American politics, rampant everywhere in this era, not least in the Grant administration itself. Still, in the free-spending atmosphere of the southern Republican regimes, corruption was especially luxuriant and damaging to the cause of radical Reconstruction.

Schools and Churches. Nothing, however, could dim the achievement in public education. Here the South had lagged woefully; only Tennessee had a system of public schooling before the Civil War. Republican state governments vowed to make up for lost time, viewing education as the foundation for a democratic order. African Americans of all ages rushed to the newly established schools, even when they had to pay tuition. An elderly man in Mississippi explained his hunger for education: "Ole missus used to read the good book [the Bible] to us . . . on Sunday evenin's, but she mostly read dem places where it says, 'Servants obey your masters.' . . . Now we is free, there's heaps of tings in that old book we is just suffering to learn."

Hiram R. Revels

In 1870 Hiram R. Revels (1822–1901) was elected to the U.S. Senate from Mississippi to fill Jefferson Davis's former seat. Revels was a free black from North Carolina who had migrated to the North and attended Knox College in Illinois. He recruited blacks for the Union army and, as an ordained Methodist minister, served as chaplain of a black regiment in Mississippi, where he settled after the war. Library of Congress.

Freedmen's School, c. 1870

This rare photograph shows the interior of one of the three thousand freedmen's schools established across the South after the Civil War. Although many of these schools were staffed by white missionaries, a main objective of northern educators was to prepare blacks to take over the classrooms. The teacher shown here is surely one of the first. Library of Congress.

The building of schools was part of a larger effort by African Americans to fortify the institutions that had sustained their spirits in the slave days, most especially, Christianity. Now, in freedom, the African Americans left the white-dominated congregations, where they had been relegated to segregated balconies and denied any voice in church governance, and built churches of their own. These churches joined together to form African American versions of the Southern Methodist and Baptist denominations, including, most prominently, the National Baptist Convention and the African Methodist Episcopal Church. Everywhere the black churches served not only as places of worship but also as schools, social centers, and political meeting halls.

Black clerics were community leaders and often political leaders as well. As Charles H. Pearce, a Methodist minister in Florida, declared, "A man in this State cannot do his whole duty as a minister except he looks out for the political interests of his people." Calling forth the special destiny of the ex-slaves as the new "Children of Israel," black ministers provided a powerful religious underpinning for the Republican politics of their congregations.

The Quest for Land

In the meantime the freedmen were locked in a great economic struggle with their former owners. In 1869 the Republican government of South Carolina had established a land commission empowered to buy property and resell it on easy terms to the landless. In this way about 14,000 black families acquired farms. South Carolina's land distribution plan showed what was possible, but it was the exception and not the rule. Despite a lot of rhetoric, Republican regimes elsewhere did little to help the freedmen fulfill their dreams of becoming independent farmers. Federal efforts proved equally feeble. The Southern Homestead Act of 1866 offered 80-acre grants to settlers, limited for the first year to freedmen and southern Unionists. The advantage was mostly symbolic, however, since only marginal land was made available, off the beaten track in swampy, infertile parts of the Lower South. Few of the homesteaders succeeded.

There was no reversing President Johnson's order restoring confiscated lands to ex-Confederates. Property rights, it seemed, trumped everything else, even for most Radical Republicans. The Freedman's Bureau, which had earlier championed the land claims of the ex-slaves, now devoted itself to teaching them how to be good agricultural laborers.

Sharecropping. While they yearned for farms of their own, most freedmen started out landless, with no option but to work for their former owners—but not, they vowed, under the conditions of slavery—no gang work, no supervision by overseers, no fines or punishments, no regulation of their private lives. In certain parts of the agricultural South wage work became the norm—for example, on the great sugar plantations of Louisiana financed by northern capital. The problem was that cotton planters lacked the money to pay wages, at least not until the crop came in, and sometimes, in lieu of a straight wage, they offered a share of the crop. As a wage, this was a bad deal for the freedmen, but if they could be paid in shares for their work, why could they not pay in shares to rent the land they worked?

This form of land tenancy was already familiar in parts of the white South, and the freedmen now seized on it for the independence it offered them. Planters resisted, believing, as one wrote, that "wages are the only successful system of controlling hands." But, in a battle of wills that broke out all across the cotton South, the planters yielded to "the inveterate prejudices of the freedmen, who desire to be masters of their own time."

Thus there sprang up the distinctive laboring system of cotton agriculture called **sharecropping**, in which the freedmen worked as renters, exchanging their labor for the use of land, house, implements, seed, and fertilizer, and typically turning over one-half to two-thirds of their crops to the landlord (Map 15.2). The sharecropping system joined laborers and the owners of land and capital in a common sharing of risks and returns. But it

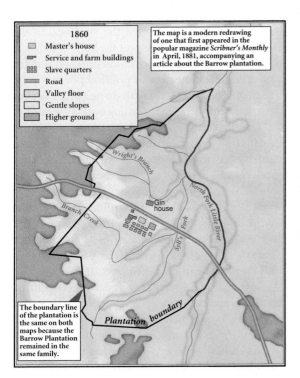

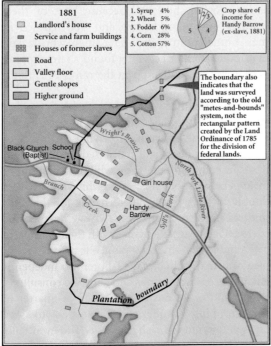

Map 15.2 The Barrow Plantation, 1860 and 1881

Comparing the 1860 map of this central Georgia plantation with the 1881 map reveals the impact of sharecropping on patterns of black residence. In 1860 the slave quarters were clustered near the planter's house. In contrast, by 1881 the sharecroppers scattered across the plantation's 2,000 acres, building cabins on the ridges between the low-lying streams. The name Barrow was common among the sharecropping families, which means almost certainly that they had been slaves on the Barrow plantation who, years after emancipation, still had not moved on. For all the croppers freedom surely meant not only their individual lots and cabins, but also the school and church shown on the map.

was a very unequal relationship, given the force of southern law and custom on the white landowner's side and the sharecroppers' dire economic circumstances. Starting out penniless, they had no way of making it through the first growing season without borrowing for food and supplies.

Country storekeepers stepped in. Bankrolled by their northern suppliers, they "furnished" the sharecropper and took as collateral a **lien** on the crop, effectively assuming ownership of the cropper's share and leaving him only the proceeds that remained after his debts had been paid. Once indebted at one store, sharecroppers were no longer free to shop around. They became an easy target for exorbitant prices, unfair interest rates, and crooked bookkeeping. As cotton prices declined during the 1870s, more and more sharecroppers failed to settle accounts and fell into permanent debt. And if the merchant was also the landowner, or conspired with the landowner, the debt became a pretext for forced labor, or **peonage,** although evidence now suggests that sharecroppers generally managed to pull up stakes and move on once things became hopeless. Sharecroppers always thought twice about moving, however, because part of their "capital" was being known and well reputed in their home communities. Freedmen who lacked that local standing generally found sharecropping hard going and ended up in the ranks of agricultural laborers.

In the face of so much adversity, black families struggled to better themselves. That it enabled family struggle was, in truth, the saving advantage of sharecropping because it mobilized husbands and wives in common enterprise while shielding both from personal subordination to whites. Wives were doubly blessed. Neither field hands for their ex-masters nor dependent housewives, they became partners laboring side by side with their husbands. The trouble with sharecropping, one planter grumbled, was that "it makes the laborer too independent; he becomes a partner, and has to be consulted." By the end of Reconstruction, about a quarter of sharecropping families had managed to save enough to rent with cash payments, and eventually black farmers owned about a third of the land they cultivated (see Reading American Pictures, "Why Sharecropping?," p. 475).

A Comparative Perspective. The battle between planters and freedmen over the land was by no means unique to the American South. Whenever slavery ended — in Haiti after the slave revolt of 1791, in the British Caribbean by abolition in 1833, in Cuba and Brazil by gradual emancipation during the 1880s — a fierce struggle ensued between planters bent on restoring a gang-labor system and ex-slaves bent on gaining economic autonomy. The outcome of this universal conflict depended on the ex-slaves' access to land. Where vacant land existed, as in British Guiana, or where plantations could be seized, as in Haiti, the ex-slaves became subsistence farmers, and insofar as the Caribbean plantation economy survived without the ex-slaves, it did so by the importation of indentured servants from India and China. Where land could not be had, as in British Barbados or Antigua, the ex-slaves returned to plantation labor as wage workers, although often in some combination with customary rights to housing and garden plots. The cotton South fit neither of these broad patterns. The freedmen did not get the land, but neither did the planters get field hands. What both got was sharecropping.

There are two ways of explaining this outcome. One is political. Outside the American South, emancipated slaves rarely got civil or political equality. Even in the British islands, where substantial self-government existed, high property qualifications effectively disfranchised the ex-slaves. In the United States, however, hard on the heels of emancipation came civil rights, manhood suffrage, and, for a brief era, a real measure of political power for the freedmen. Sharecropping took shape during Reconstruction, and there was no going back afterward.

That there was no going back suggests a second explanation for the triumph of sharecropping, namely, that it was a good fit for cotton agriculture. We can see this in the experience of other countries that became major producers in response to the global cotton famine set off by the Civil War. In all these places, in India, Egypt, Brazil and West Africa, some variant of the sharecropping system emerged. Most striking was the adoption everywhere of crop-lien laws, at the behest of the international merchants and bankers putting up the capital. Indian and Egyptian villagers got the advances they needed to shift from subsistence agriculture to cotton, but at the price of being placed, as in America, permanently under the thumb of the furnishing merchants. Implicit in advancing that money, of course, was the realization that cotton, unlike sugar cane, could be raised efficiently by small farmers (provided they had the lash of indebtedness always on their backs). American planters resisted sharecropping because they started at a different place: not traditional, subsistence economies that had to be converted to cotton but a proven plantation system over which they had been absolute masters.

Why Sharecropping?

Sharecroppers in Georgia. Brown Brothers.

The account of sharecropping on the neighboring pages describes the experience of hundreds of thousands of ex-slaves and plantation owners. How do we know that our generalizations are true? Or, more concretely, that a sharecropper reading our account would nod and say, "Yes, that's the way it was." One sliver of evidence is this photograph depicting a family of ex-slaves standing proudly by their new cabin and young cotton crop. In what ways does this contemporary photograph confirm or amplify our account of sharecropping?

ANALYZING THE EVIDENCE

➤ The cotton rows go right up to the house. Why would this family not have set aside land for a garden and for some livestock? And what does this suggest about the historians' claim that sharecropping doomed the South to a cash-crop monoculture?

➤ Note the gent in the background — most likely the landowner — with his handsome horse and carriage. The family is posing for the photograph, yet he pays no heed and breaks into the frame. And he seems to feel, although he has rented it out, that he still has the run of the place. What does this suggest about the limits of sharecropping as a means of achieving independence by the freedmen?

➤ In that struggle, of course, everything was relative. What elements in the photograph suggest that, compared to what they had known as slaves or, after emancipation, would have faced as day laborers, this family might have thought they had not fared so badly? (Students are urged to consult Map 15.2 on p. 473, bearing in mind of course that this family did not actually live on the Barrow plantation.)

For America's ex-slaves sharecropping was not the worst choice; it certainly beat laboring for their former owners. But for southern agriculture the costs were devastating. Sharecropping committed the South inflexibly to cotton because, as a market crop, it generated the cash required by landlords and furnishing merchants. Neither soil depletion nor low prices ever enabled sharecroppers to shift away from cotton. With farms leased year to year, neither tenant nor owner had much incentive to improve the property. And the crop-lien system lined merchants' pockets with unearned profits that might otherwise have gone into agricultural improvement. The result was a stagnant farm economy, blighting the South's future and condemning it to economic backwardness—a kind of retribution, in fact, for the fresh injustices visited on the people it had once enslaved.

➤ Do you think it was predictable in 1865 that five years later the ex-slaves would receive the constitutional right to vote? Or that, having gone that far, the nation would deny the vote to women?

➤ What do you regard as the principal achievements of radical Reconstruction in the South? Do you think the achievements outweigh the failures?

➤ Why did the ex-slaves' struggle for land end in the sharecropping system?

The Undoing of Reconstruction

Ex-Confederates were blind to the achievements of radical Reconstruction. Indeed, no amount of success could have persuaded them that it was anything but an abomination, undertaken without their consent and denying them their rightful place in southern society. Led by the planters, ex-Confederates staged a massive counterrevolution—one designed to "redeem" the South and restore them to political power under the banner of the Democratic Party. But the Redeemers could not have succeeded on their own. They needed the complicity of the North. The undoing of Reconstruction is as much about northern acquiescence as it is about southern resistance.

Counterrevolution

Insofar as they could win at the ballot box, southern Democrats took that route. They worked hard

to get ex-Confederates restored to the voting rolls, they appealed to southern patriotism, and they campaigned against black rule. But force was equally acceptable. Throughout the Deep South, especially where black voters were heavily concentrated, ex-Confederate planters and their supporters organized secretly and terrorized blacks and their white allies.

Nathan Bedford Forrest and the Politics of Terror. No one looms larger in this bloody story than Nathan Bedford Forrest, the Confederacy's most decorated cavalry general. Born in poverty in 1821, he scrambled up the booming cotton economy and became a big-time Memphis slaver trader and Mississippi plantation owner. A man of fiery temper, he championed secession. When the war broke out, Forrest immediately formed a Tennessee cavalry regiment, fought bravely (and was badly wounded) at the battle of Shiloh, and won fame as a daring cavalry raider. On April 12, 1864, his troopers perpetrated one of the war's worst atrocities, the slaughter of black troops at Fort Pillow, Tennessee, acting on rumors that they had harassed local whites. The Fort Pillow massacre foreshadowed the civil strife that would consume Tennessee during Reconstruction.

Nathan Bedford Forrest in Uniform, c. 1865

Before he became Grand Wizard of the Ku Klux Klan, Forrest had been a celebrated cavalry general in the Confederate army. This photograph shows him in uniform before he was mustered out. Library of Congress.

Although nominally in control since 1862, Union authorities never managed to subdue Tennessee's irreconcilable Confederate sympathizers. The Republican-elected governor in 1865, William G. Brownlow, was a tough man, a former Confederate prisoner not shy about calling his enemies to account. They struck back with a campaign of terror, targeting especially Brownlow's black supporters. It was amidst this general mayhem that the first den of the Ku Klux Klan emerged in Pulaski, Tennessee, in late 1865 or early 1866. As it proliferated across the state, the Klan turned to General Forrest, who had been trying, unsuccessfully, to rebuild his pre-war fortunes. Late in 1866, at a clandestine meeting in Nashville, Forrest donned the robes of Grand Wizard. His activities are mostly cloaked in mystery, but there is no mystery about why Forrest gravitated to the Klan. For him, the Klan was politics by other means, the instrument by which disfranchised former Confederates like himself might strike a blow against the despised Republicans who ran Tennessee.

In many towns the Klan became virtually identical to the Democratic clubs. In fact, Klan members—including Forrest—dominated Tennessee's delegation to the Democratic national convention of 1868. The Klan unleashed a murderous campaign of terror against Republican sympathizers. Governor Brownlow responded resolutely, threatening to mobilize the state militia and root out the Klan. If Brownlow tried, answered Forrest, "There will be war, and a bloodier one than we have ever witnessed." In the end, it was the Republicans, not the Klan, who cracked. In March 1869 Brownlow retreated to the U.S. Senate. The Democrats were on their way back to power, and the Klan, having served its purpose, was officially disbanded in Tennessee.

Elsewhere, the Klan raged on, murdering Republican politicians, burning black schools and churches, and attacking party gatherings, with more or less the same results as in Tennessee. By 1870, the Democrats had seized power in Georgia and North Carolina and were making headway across the South.

The Federal Reaction. Congress responded by passing legislation, including the Ku Klux Klan Act of 1871, designed to enforce the rights of ex-slaves under the Fourteenth and Fifteenth Amendments. These so-called enforcement laws authorized federal prosecutions, military intervention, and martial

"Worse than Slavery," 1874

This cartoon by Thomas Nast registers the despair felt by advocates of racial equality at the failure of Reconstruction. The Klan ruffians and White Leaguers have prevailed, Nast is saying, and white terrorism has reduced the oppressed black family to conditions worse than slavery. Granger Collection.

law to suppress terrorist activities that deprived citizens of their civil and political rights. In South Carolina, where the Klan became most deeply entrenched, federal troops occupied nine counties, made hundreds of arrests, and drove as many as two thousand Klansmen from the state.

The Grant administration's assault on the Klan raised the spirits of southern Republicans, but also revealed how dependent they were on the federal government. The potency of the Ku Klux Klan Act, a Mississippi Republican wrote, "derived alone from its source" in the federal government. "No such law could be enforced by state authority, the local power being too weak." If they were to prevail over antiblack terrorism, Republicans needed what one carpetbagger described as "steady, unswerving power from without."

But northern Republicans grew weary of Reconstruction and the endless bloodshed it seemed to produce. Prosecuting Klansmen was an uphill battle. U.S. attorneys usually faced all-white juries and unsympathetic federal judges, with scant resources for handling the cases. After 1872 prosecutions began to drop off; many Klansmen received hasty pardons. And then the constitutional underpinnings of the antiterrorist campaign came into question, culminating in the Supreme Court's decision in *United States v. Cruikshank* (1876) that the federal government had exceeded its authority under the Fourteenth Amendment. If the rights of the ex-slaves were being violated by individuals or private groups (like the KKK), that was a state responsibility and beyond the federal jurisdiction.

In a kind of self-fulfilling prophecy, the reluctance of the Grant administration to shore up Reconstruction guaranteed that it would fail. Republican governments that were denied federal help one by one fell victim to the massive resistance of their ex-Confederate enemies: Texas in 1873, Alabama and Arkansas in 1874, Mississippi in 1875.

The Mississippi campaign showed all too clearly what the Republicans were up against. As elections neared in 1875, paramilitary groups such as the Rifle Clubs and Red Shirts operated openly. Mississippi's Republican governor, Adelbert Ames, a Congressional Medal of Honor winner from Maine, appealed to President Grant for federal troops, but Grant refused. Brandishing their guns and stuffing the ballot boxes, the Redeemers swept the 1875 elections and took control of Mississippi. Facing impeachment, Governor Ames resigned his office and returned to the North.

By 1876 Republican governments, backed by token U.S. military units, remained in only three states—Louisiana, South Carolina, and Florida. Elsewhere, the former Confederates were back in power.

The Acquiescent North

The faltering of Reconstruction stemmed from more than discouragement about prosecuting the Klan, however. Sympathy for the freedman began to wane. The North was flooded with one-sided, often racist reports, such as James M. Pike's *The Prostrate State* (1873), describing South Carolina in the grip of "a mass of black barbarism." The impact of this propaganda could be seen in the fate of the Civil Rights bill, which Charles Sumner introduced in 1870 in an attempt to apply federal power against the discriminatory treatment of African Americans, guaranteeing them, among other things, equal access to public accommodation, schools, and jury service. By the time the bill passed in 1875, it had been stripped of its key provisions. The Supreme Court finished the demolition job when in 1883 it declared the remnant Civil Rights Act unconstitutional.

The political cynicism that overtook the Civil Rights Act signaled the Republican Party's reversion to the practical politics of earlier days. In many states a second generation took over the party—men like Roscoe Conkling of New York, who treated the Manhattan Customs House, with its regiment of political appointees, as an auxiliary of his organization. Conkling and similarly minded politicos had little enthusiasm for Reconstruction, except when it benefited the Republican Party. As the party lost headway in the South, Republicans lost interest in the battle for black rights. In Washington President Grant presided benignly over this transformation of his party, turning a blind eye on corruption even as its waters began to lap against the White House.

Not all Republicans embraced Grant's politics as usual. Yet even the high-minded, the heirs of antislavery Christian reform, turned against Reconstruction. The touchstone for them was "free labor," the idea of America as a land of self-reliant, industrious property owners. They had framed the Civil War as a battle between "free labor" and its antithesis, the plantation society of masters and slaves. And now, with the South defeated, the question became: Would the emancipated slaves embrace "free labor"? No, asserted Pike's *The Prostrate State* and similarly inflammatory reports. Instead of choosing self-reliance, the freedmen were running riot, demanding patronage, becoming dependents of the corrupt Reconstruction regimes they had voted into power. With this tragic misreading of the former slaves—and of their uphill struggle for land and self-rule—Republican allies drifted away and turned against radical Reconstruction.

More was at work, however, than disillusionment with the freedmen. In the aftermath of war, a broader loss of nerve gripped northern reformers. The meaning of "free labor" had not been uncontested. If middle-class Republicans juxtaposed it against black slavery, labor leaders juxtaposed it also against *wage* slavery, and suddenly, when peace arrived, there was a burst of trade-union activity, calls for sweeping labor reform, and a formidable new organization on the scene, the National Labor Union. Radical proposals came forth, most famously, Ira Steward's demand for the eight-hour day, which, by his cock-eyed theory, would close the gap between rich and poor "until the capitalist and laborer are one"—a true "free labor" society. The labor reform movement lacked staying power, however. The eight-hour drive failed, and so did campaigns for cooperative industry and currency reform. After an abortive effort at launching a labor party in 1872, the National Labor Union collapsed.

If the surge of labor agitation died, not so the fear it inspired among middle-class reformers. Intent on a "harmony of interests," they got instead a strong whiff of class conflict. These advocates of "free labor," once zealous for black freedom and equal rights, clambered to the safer ground of civil-service reform. Henceforth it was the evils of corrupt politics that would claim their attention. They repudiated the wartime expansion of federal power and refashioned themselves as **liberals**—believers in free trade, market competition, and limited government. And, with unabashed elitism, they denounced universal suffrage, which "can only mean in plain English the government of ignorance and vice." American reform had arrived at a dispiriting watershed. The grand impulse that had driven the antislavery struggle, insofar as it survived the trauma of Reconstruction, now took the form of pallid efforts at purifying American politics, with Grant as the first target.

The Liberal Republicans and the Election of 1872.
As Grant's administration lapsed into cronyism, a revolt took shape inside the Republican Party, led by an influential collection of intellectuals, journalists, and reform-minded businessmen. Unable to deny Grant renomination, the dissidents broke away and formed a new party under the name Liberal Republican. Their candidate was

Horace Greeley, longtime editor and publisher of the *New York Tribune* and veteran of American reform in all its variety, including antislavery. The Democrats, still in disarray, also nominated Greeley, notwithstanding his editorial diatribes against them. A poor campaigner, Greeley was assailed so bitterly that, as he said, "I hardly knew whether I was running for the Presidency or the penitentiary."

Grant won overwhelmingly, capturing 56 percent of the popular vote and every electoral vote. Yet the Liberal Republicans had managed to shift the terms of political debate in the country. The agenda they had established—civil service reform, limited government, reconciliation with the South—was adopted by the Democrats as they shed their disloyal reputation and reclaimed their place as a legitimate national party.

Scandal and Depression.
Charges of Republican corruption, mounting ever since Grant's reelection, came to a head in 1875. The scandal involved the Whiskey Ring, a network of liquor distillers and treasury agents who defrauded the government of millions of dollars of excise taxes on whiskey. The ringleader was a Grant appointee, and Grant's own private secretary, Orville Babcock, had a hand in the thievery. The others went to prison, but Grant stood by Babcock, possibly perjuring himself to save his secretary from jail. The stench of scandal, however, had engulfed the White House.

On top of this, a financial panic struck in 1873, triggered by the bankruptcy of the Northern Pacific Railroad and its main investor, Jay Cooke. Both Cooke's privileged role as financier of the Civil War and the generous federal subsidies to the Northern Pacific caused many economically pressed Americans to blame Republican financial mismanagement and thievery. Grant's administration responded ineffectually, rebuffing the pleas of debtors for relief by increasing the money supply (see Chapter 19).

Among the casualties of the bad economy was the Freedman's Savings and Trust Company, which held the small deposits of thousands of ex-slaves. When the bank failed in 1874, Congress refused to compensate the depositors, and many lost their life savings. In denying their pathetic pleas, Congress was signaling also that Reconstruction had lost its moral claim on the country. National politics had moved on; concerns about the economy and political fraud, not the plight of the ex-slaves, absorbed the northern voter as another presidential election approached in 1876.

The Political Crisis of 1877

Abandoning Grant, the Republicans nominated Rutherford B. Hayes, governor of Ohio, a colorless figure but untainted by corruption or by strong convictions—in a word, a safe man. His Democratic opponent was Samuel J. Tilden, governor of New York, a wealthy lawyer with ties to Wall Street and a reform reputation for his role in cleaning up New York City politics. The Democrat Tilden, of course, favored **home rule** for the South, but so, more discreetly, did the Republican Hayes. Reconstruction actually did not figure prominently in the campaign and was mostly subsumed under

broader Democratic charges of "corrupt centralism" and "incapacity, waste, and fraud." By now Republicans had essentially written off the South. Not a lot was said about the states still ruled by Reconstruction governments—Florida, South Carolina, and Louisiana.

Once the returns started coming in on election night, however, those three states began to loom very large indeed. Tilden led in the popular vote and, victorious in key northern states, he seemed headed for the White House until sleepless politicians at Republican headquarters realized that if they kept Florida, South Carolina, and Louisiana, Hayes would win by a single electoral vote. Republicans still controlled the state election machinery and, citing Democratic fraud and intimidation, they certified Republican victories. The audacious announcement came forth from Republican headquarters: Hayes had carried Florida, South Carolina, and Louisiana and won the election. Newly elected Democratic officials also sent in electoral votes for Tilden, and, when Congress met in early 1877, it faced two sets of electoral votes from those states.

The Constitution does not provide for this contingency. All it says is that the president of the Senate (in 1877, a Republican) opens the electoral certificates before the House (Democratic) and the Senate (Republican) and that "the Votes shall then be counted" (Article 2, Section 1). Suspense gripped the country. There was talk of inside deals, of a new election, even of a violent coup. Just in case, the commander of the army, General William T. Sherman, deployed four artillery companies in Washington. Finally, Congress appointed an electoral commission to settle the question. The commission included seven Republicans, seven Democrats, and, as the deciding member, David Davis, a Supreme Court justice not known to have fixed party loyalties. Davis, however, disqualified himself by accepting an Illinois seat in the Senate. He was replaced by Republican justice Joseph P. Bradley, and by 8 to 7 the commission awarded the disputed votes to Hayes.

Outraged Democrats had one more trick up their sleeves. They controlled the House, and they stalled a final count of the electoral votes so as to prevent Hayes's inauguration on March 4. But a week before, secret Washington talks had begun between southern Democrats and Ohio Republicans representing Hayes. Everything turned on South Carolina and Louisiana, where rival governments were encamped at the state capitols, with federal soldiers holding the Democrats at bay. Exactly what deal was struck or how involved Hayes himself was will probably never be known, but on March 1 the House Democrats suddenly ended their delaying tactics, the ceremonial counting of votes went forward, and Hayes was inaugurated on schedule. He soon ordered the Union troops back to their barracks, the Republican governors in South Carolina and Louisiana fled the unprotected statehouses, and Democratic claimants took control. Reconstruction had ended.

In 1877 political leaders on all sides seemed ready to say that what Lincoln had called "the work" was complete. But for the former slaves, the work had only begun. Reconstruction turned out to have been a magnificent aberration, a leap beyond what most white Americans actually felt was due their black fellow citizens. Still, something real

had been achieved—three rights-defining amendments to the Constitution, some elbow room to advance economically, and, not least, a stubborn confidence among blacks that, by their own efforts, they could lift themselves up. Things would get worse, in fact, before they got better, but the work of Reconstruction was imperishable and could never be erased.

➤ Why did the Redeemers resort to terror in their campaign to regain political control of the South?

➤ What changes in the North explain why the Republicans abandoned the battle for Reconstruction?

➤ Explain how the contested presidential election of 1876–1877 brought an end to Reconstruction.

SUMMARY

By any measure—in lives, treasure, or national amity—the Civil War was the most shattering event in American history. In this chapter we describe how the nation picked up the pieces. Reconstruction confronted two great tasks: first, restoring the rebellious states to the union, and second, incorporating the emancipated slaves into the national citizenry. Separable perhaps in theory, the two tasks were inseparably part of a single grand struggle.

Reconstruction went through three phases. In what has been called the presidential phase, Lincoln's successor Andrew Johnson unilaterally offered the South easy terms for reentering the Union. This might have succeeded had Southerners responded with restraint, but instead they adopted oppressive Black Codes and welcomed ex-Confederates back into power. Infuriated by southern arrogance, congressional Republicans closed ranks behind the Radicals, embraced the freedmen's demand for full equality, placed the South under military rule in 1867, and inaugurated radical Reconstruction.

In this second phase, the new Republican state governments tried to transform the South's decrepit economic and social structures, while on the plantations ex-slaves battled for economic independence. No amount of accomplishment, however, could reconcile the ex-Confederates to Republican rule, and they staged a violent counterrevolution in the name of white supremacy and "redemption."

Distracted by Republican scandals and economic problems, the Grant administration had little stomach for a protracted guerrilla war in the

South. Left on their own, the Reconstruction governments fell one by one to Redeemer intimidation and violence. In this third phase, as Reconstruction wound down, the concluding event was the contested election of 1876, which the Republicans resolved by trading their last remaining southern strongholds, South Carolina and Louisiana, for retention of the White House. On that unsavory note, Reconstruction ended.

Connections: Sectionalism

In many ways, Reconstruction marked the final stage in a titanic sectional struggle whose origins went back to the early nineteenth century. As we noted in the essay opening Part Three (p. 269):

> The North developed into an urbanizing and industrializing society based on free labor, whereas the South remained a rural, agricultural society dependent on slavery.

In Chapter 13 we described how the sectional crisis arising from these differences broke apart the Union in 1861. The Civil War (Chapter 14) tested the war-making capacities of the rival systems. At first the advantage lay with the military prowess of the agrarian South, but in the end the superior resources of the industrial North prevailed. Even in defeat, however, the South could not be forced into a national mold. That was the ultimate lesson of Reconstruction. In the aftermath, the South persisted on its own path, as we will see in Chapter 17, which discusses the emergence of its distinctive low-wage labor system, and Chapter 19, which describes the development of its one-party, whites-only politics. The gradual, if partial, dissolution of southern uniqueness in the twentieth century is a theme of later chapters of this book.

CHAPTER REVIEW QUESTIONS

➤ Why did the debate over restoring the South to the Union devolve into an institutional struggle between the presidency and the Congress?

➤ Do you believe that the failure of Reconstruction was primarily a failure of leadership? Or, to put it more concretely, that the outcome might have been different had Lincoln lived? Or chosen a different vice president?

➤ Was there any way of reconciling the Republican desire for equality for the ex-slaves with the ex-Confederate desire for self-rule in the South?

TIMELINE

1863	Lincoln announces his Ten Percent Plan
1864	Wade-Davis Bill passed by Congress
	Lincoln "pocket" vetoes Wade-Davis Bill
1865	Freedmen's Bureau established
	Lincoln assassinated; Andrew Johnson succeeds as president
	Johnson implements his restoration plan
1866	Civil Rights Act passes over Johnson's veto
	Johnson makes disastrous "swing around the circle"; defeated in congressional elections
1867	Reconstruction Act
	Tenure of Office Act
1868	Impeachment crisis
	Fourteenth Amendment ratified
	Ulysses S. Grant elected president
1870	Ku Klux Klan at peak of power
	Fifteenth Amendment ratified
1872	Grant's reelection
1873	Panic of 1873 ushers in depression of 1873–1877
1875	Whiskey Ring scandal undermines Grant administration
1877	Compromise of 1877; Rutherford B. Hayes becomes president
	Reconstruction ends

FOR FURTHER EXPLORATION

The best current book on Reconstruction is Eric Foner's major synthesis, *Reconstruction: America's Unfinished Revolution, 1863–1877* (1988), available also in a shorter version. *Black Reconstruction in America* (1935), by the African American activist and scholar W. E. B. Du Bois, deserves attention as the first book on Reconstruction that stressed the role of blacks in their own emancipation. For the presidential phase of Reconstruction, see Dan T. Carter, *When the War Was Over: The Failure of Self-Reconstruction in the South, 1865–1867* (1985). On the freedmen, Leon F. Litwack, *Been in the Storm So Long: The Aftermath of Slavery* (1979), provides a stirring account. More recent emancipation studies emphasize slavery as a labor system: Julie Saville, *The Work of Reconstruction: From Slave to Wage Laborer in South Carolina, 1860–1870* (1994), and Amy Dru Stanley, *From Bondage to Contract* (1999), which expands the discussion to show what the onset of wage labor meant for freedwomen. In *Gendered Strife & Confusion: The Political Culture of Reconstruction* (1997), Laura F. Edwards explores via a local study the impact of "peripheral" people—the ordinary folk of both races—on Reconstruction politics. Eric Foner, *Nothing But Freedom: Emancipation and Its Legacy* (1983), helpfully places emancipation in a comparative context. William S. McFeely, *Grant: A Biography* (1981), deftly explains the politics of Reconstruction. The emergence of the sharecropping system is explored in Gavin Wright, *Old South, New South* (1986), and Edward Royce, *The Origins of Southern Sharecropping* (1993). On the Compromise of 1877, see C. Vann Woodward's classic *Reunion and Reaction* (1956). A helpful Web site on Reconstruction, with documents and illustrations, can be found at **www. pbs.org/wgbh/amex/reconstruction/index.html**, which derives from the PBS documentary in the *American Experience* series.

TEST YOUR KNOWLEDGE

To assess your command of the material in this chapter, see the Online Study Guide at **bedfordstmartins.com/henretta**.

For Web sites, images, and documents related to topics and places in this chapter, visit **bedfordstmartins.com/makehistory**.

PART FOUR

A Maturing Industrial Society

1877–1914

	ECONOMY	SOCIETY	CULTURE	POLITICS	DIPLOMACY
	The Triumph of Industrialization	**The West**	**The Industrial City**	**From Inaction to Progressive Reform**	**An Emerging World Power**
1877	▸ Andrew Carnegie launches modern steel industry ▸ Knights of Labor becomes national movement (1878)	▸ Nomadic Indian life ends	▸ National League founded (1876) ▸ Dwight L. Moody pioneers urban revivalism	▸ Election of Rutherford B. Hayes ends Reconstruction	▸ United States becomes net exporter
1880	▸ Gustavus Swift pioneers vertically integrated firm ▸ American Federation of Labor (1886)	▸ Chinese Exclusion Act (1882) ▸ Dawes Act divides tribal lands (1887)	▸ Electrification brightens city life ▸ First Social Register defines high society (1888)	▸ Ethnocultural issues dominate state and local politics ▸ Civil service reform (1883)	▸ Diplomacy of inaction ▸ Naval buildup begins
1890	▸ United States surpasses Britain in iron and steel output ▸ Economic depression (1893–1897) ▸ Industrial merger movement begins	▸ U.S. Census declares westward movement over ▸ Wounded Knee Massacre; Indian resistance ends ▸ California national parks established	▸ Immigration from southeastern Europe rises sharply ▸ William Randolph Hearst's *New York Journal* pioneers yellow journalism	▸ Black disfranchisement in South ▸ Populist Party founded (1892) ▸ William McKinley wins presidency; defeats Bryan's freesilver crusade (1896)	▸ Social Darwinism and Anglo-Saxonism promote expansion ▸ Spanish-American War (1898–1899); conquest of the Philippines
1900	▸ Immigrants dominate factory work ▸ Industrial Workers of the World (1905)	▸ California farmers rely on Japanese labor ▸ "Gentlemen's Agreement" (1908) excludes Japanese workers	▸ Social progressivism comes to the city ▸ Movies begin to overtake vaudeville	▸ McKinley assassinated; Roosevelt inaugurates progressivism in national politics ▸ Hepburn Act regulates railroads (1906)	▸ Panama cedes Canal Zone to United States (1903) ▸ Roosevelt Corollary to Monroe Doctrine (1904)
1910	▸ Henry Ford builds first automobile assembly line	▸ Women vote in western states ▸ U.S. government approves Hetch Hetchy reservoir	▸ Urban liberalism ▸ World War I halts European immigration	▸ NAACP (1910) ▸ Woodrow Wilson elected (1912) ▸ New Freedom legislation creates Federal Reserve, FTC	▸ Taft's diplomacy promotes U.S. business ▸ Wilson proclaims U.S. neutrality in World War I

The year 1876 marked the hundredth anniversary of the Declaration of Independence. In celebration the nation mounted a Centennial Exposition where it all began, in Philadelphia. Observing the hectic preparations, the German journalist Ernst Otto Hopp anticipated the impact that this grand world's fair would have on his European compatriots. "Foreigners will be astounded at the vision of American production. . . . The pits of Nevada will display their enormous stores of silver, Michigan its copper, California its gold and quicksilver, Missouri its lead and tin, Pennsylvania its coal and iron. . . . And from a thousand factories will come the evidences of the wonders of American mechanical skill." Herr Hopp got it right. In 1876 the country Hopp described as a "young giant" was on the cusp of becoming, for better or worse, the economic powerhouse of the world. In Part Four we undertake to explain how it happened and what it meant for American life.

ECONOMY Equally as momentous as the final settlement of the West was the fact that for the first time, as the decade of the 1870s passed, farmers no longer constituted a majority of working Americans. Henceforth, America's future would be linked to its development as an industrializing society. In the manufacturing sector, production became increasingly mechanized and increasingly directed at making the capital goods that undergirded economic growth. As the railroad system was completed, the vertically integrated model began to dominate American enterprise. The labor movement became firmly established, and as immigration surged, the foreign-born and their children became America's workers. What had been partial and limited now became general and widespread; America turned into a land of factories, corporate enterprise, and industrial workers.

SOCIETY In his catalogue of achievements, Ernst Hopp emphasized the mining pits of Nevada and California's gold and quicksilver. He might also have mentioned the corn, wheat, and livestock flowing cityward from the Great Plains. For it was the eastern demand for new sources of food and mineral resources that drove the final surge of western settlement and integrated the Great Plains and Far West into the nation's industrializing economy. Defending their way of life, western Indians were ultimately defeated not so much by army rifles as by the encroachment of railroads, mines, ranches, and proliferating farms. These same forces disrupted the old established Hispanic communities of the Southwest but spurred Asian, Mexican, and European migrations that made for a multiethnic western society.

CULTURE Industrialization also transformed the nation's urban life. By 1900 one in five Americans lived in cities. That was where the jobs were—as workers in the factories; as clerks and salespeople; as members of a new, salaried middle class of managers, engineers, and professionals; and, at the apex, as a wealthy elite of investors and entrepreneurs. The city was more than just a place to make a living, however. It provided a setting for an urban lifestyle unlike anything seen before in America.

POLITICS The unfettered, booming economy of the Gilded Age at first marginalized political life, or rather, the role of government, which, for most Americans, was very nearly invisible. The major parties remained robust because they exploited a culture of popular participation and embraced the ethnic and religious identities of their constituencies. The depression of the 1890s triggered a major challenge to the political status quo, with the rise of the agrarian Populist Party and its radical demand for free silver. The election of 1896 turned back that challenge and established the Republicans as the dominant national party.

Still unresolved was the threat that corporate power posed to the marketplace and democratic politics. How to curb the trusts dominated national debate during the Progressive era. From different angles political reformers, women progressives, and urban liberals went about the business of cleaning up machine politics and making life better for America's urban masses. African Americans, victimized by disfranchisement and segregation, found allies among white progressives and launched a new drive for racial equality.

DIPLOMACY Finally, the dynamism of America's economic development altered the country's foreign relations. In the decades after the Civil War, America had been inward-looking, neglectful of its navy and inactive diplomatically. The business crisis of the 1890s brought home the need for a more aggressive foreign policy that would advance the nation's overseas economic interests. In short order, the United States went to war with Spain, acquired an overseas empire, and became actively engaged in Latin America and Asia. There was no mistaking America's standing as a Great Power and, as World War I approached, no evading the entanglements that came with that status.

16

The American West

IN THE WANING DECADES OF the nineteenth century, America seemed like two nations. One was an advanced industrial society—the America of factories and sprawling cities. But another America remained frontier country, with pioneers streaming onto the Great Plains, repeating the old dramas of "settlement" they had been performing ever since Europeans had first set foot on the continent. Not until 1890 did the U.S. census declare that a "frontier of settlement" no longer existed: The country's "unsettled area has been so broken into . . . that there can hardly be said to be a frontier line."

Eighteen-ninety also marked the year the country surpassed Great Britain in the production of iron and steel. Newspapers carried reports of Indian wars and industrial strikes in the same edition. The last tragic episode in the suppression of the Plains Indians, the massacre at Wounded Knee, South Dakota, occurred only eighteen months before the great Homestead steel strike of 1892. This alignment of events from the distant worlds of factory and frontier was not accidental. The final surge of settlement across the Great Plains and the Far West was powered primarily by the energy of American industrialism.

◄ **The Yo-Hamite Falls, 1855**

This is one of the earliest artistic renderings of Yosemite Valley, drawn, in fact, before the place came to be called Yosemite. The scale of the waterfall, which drops 2,300 feet to the valley below, is dramatized by artist Thomas A. Ayres's companions in the foreground. In this romantic lithograph one can already see the grandeur of the West that Yosemite came to represent for **Americans.** University of California at Berkeley, Bancroft Library, Honeyman Collection.

The Great Plains

During the 1860s agricultural settlement reached the western margins of the tall-grass prairie. Beyond, roughly at the ninety-eighth meridian (Map 16.1), stretched a vast, dry country, uninviting to farmers accustomed to woodlands and ample rainfall. They saw it much as did the New York publisher Horace Greeley on his way to California in 1859: "a land of starvation," "a treeless desert," baking in heat in the daytime and "chill and piercing" cold at night.

Greeley was describing the Great Plains. The geologic event creating the Great Plains occurred sixty million years ago when the Rocky Mountains arose out of the ocean covering western North America. With no outlet, the shallow inland sea to the east dried up, forming a hard pan on which sediment washing down from the mountains built up a loose, featureless surface. Because the moisture-laden winds from the Pacific spent themselves on the western slopes of the Sierras, the climate was dry, but variable, interspersing cycles of rainfall and drought. The prevailing notion of a **Great American Desert** was not fanciful: Much of the Great Plains had been drought-stricken and desert-like when American explorers first traversed it in the early nineteenth century. Only vegetation resistant to the harsh climate could take hold on the plains. Bunch grasses like blue grama, the linchpins of this

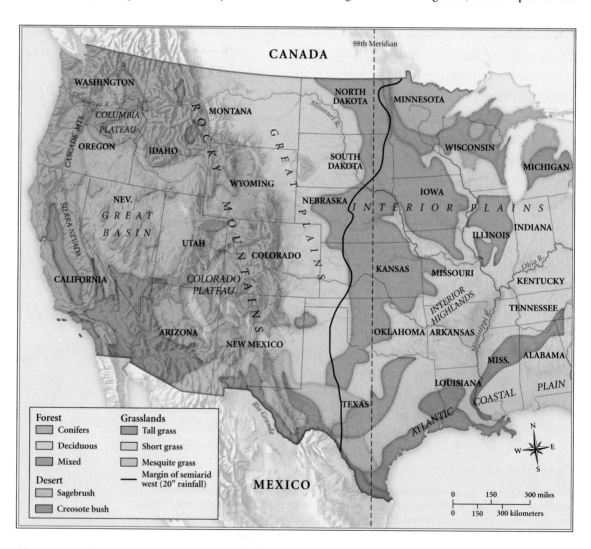

Map 16.1 The Natural Environment of the West, 1860s

As settlers pushed into the Great Plains and beyond the line of semiaridity, they sensed the overwhelming power of the natural environment. In a landscape without trees for fences and barns, and without adequate rainfall, ranchers and farmers had to relearn their business. The Native Americans peopling the plains and mountains had learned to live in this environment, but this knowledge counted for little against the ruthless pressure of the settlers to domesticate the West.

fragile ecosystem, matted the easily blown soil into place and sustained a rich wildlife dominated by grazing antelope and buffalo. What the dry short-grass country had not permanently sustained, until the past few centuries, was human settlement.

Indians of the Great Plains

Probably 100,000 Native Americans lived on the Great Plains at mid-nineteenth century. They were a diverse people, divided into six linguistic families and at least thirty tribal groupings. On the eastern margins and along the Missouri River, the Mandans, Arikaras, and Pawnees planted corn and beans and lived in permanent villages. Smallpox and measles introduced by Europeans ravaged these settled tribes. Less vulnerable to epidemics because they were dispersed were the hunting tribes that had first arrived on the Great Plains in the seventeenth century: Kiowas and Comanches in the southwest; Arapahos and Cheyennes on the central plains; and, to the north, Blackfeet, Crows, and the great Sioux nation.

The Sioux. Originally the Sioux had been eastern prairie people, occupying settlements in the lake country of northern Minnesota. With fish and game dwindling, some tribes drifted westward and around 1760 began to cross the Missouri River. These Sioux, or Lakota (meaning "allies"), became nomadic, living in portable skin tepees and hunting buffalo, or, more properly, bison. From tribes to the southwest, they acquired horses. Once mounted, the Sioux became splendid hunters and formidable fighters, claiming the entire Great Plains north of the Arkansas River as their hunting grounds and driving out or subjugating longer-settled tribes.

A society that celebrates the heroic virtues of hunting and war — men's work — is likely to define gender roles sharply. But before the Sioux had horses, buffalo hunting could not be an exclusively male enterprise. It took the efforts of both men and women to construct the "pounds" into which, beating the brush side by side, they endeavored to stampede the herds. Once on horseback, however, the men rode off to the hunt while the women stayed behind to prepare the mounting piles of buffalo skins. Subordination to the men was not how Sioux women understood their unrelenting labor; this was their allotted share in a partnership on which the proud, nomadic life of the Sioux depended.

Sioux Religion. Living so close to nature, depending on its bounty for survival, the Sioux endowed every manifestation of the natural world with sacred meaning. Unlike Europeans, they conceived of God not as a supreme being but, in the words of the pioneering ethnologist Clark Wissler, as a "series of powers pervading the universe" — Wi, the sun; Skan, the sky; Maka, the earth; Inyan, the rock. Below these came the moon, wind, and buffalo down through a hierarchy embodying the entire natural order.

By prayer and fasting Sioux prepared themselves to commune with these mysterious powers. Medicine men provided instruction, but the religious experience was personal and open to both sexes. The vision, when a supplicant achieved it, attached itself to some object — a feather, an animal skin, or a shell — that was tied into a sacred bundle and became the person's lifelong talisman. In the Sun Dance the entire tribe celebrated the rites of coming of age, fertility, the hunt, and combat, followed by fasting and dancing in supplication to Wi, the sun.

The world of the Lakota Sioux was not self-contained. From their earliest days as nomadic hunters, they had exchanged pelts and buffalo robes for the produce of agriculturalist Pawnees and Mandans. When white traders appeared on the upper Missouri River during the eighteenth century, the Sioux began to trade with them. Although the buffalo remained their staff of life, the Sioux came to rely as well on the traders' kettles, blankets, knives, and guns. The trade system they entered was linked to the Euro-American market economy, yet it was also integrated into the Sioux way of life. Everything depended on the survival of the Great Plains as the Sioux had found it — wild grassland on which the antelope and buffalo ranged free (see Reading American Pictures, "Uncovering the Culture of the Plains Indians," p. 490).

Wagon Trains, Railroads, and Ranchers

On first encountering the Great Plains, Euro-Americans thought these unforested lands best left to the Indians. After exploring a drought-stricken stretch in 1820, Major Stephen H. Long declared it "almost wholly unfit for cultivation, and of course uninhabitable by a people depending upon agriculture for their subsistence."

For years thereafter maps marked the plains as the Great American Desert. In 1834 Congress formally designated the Great Plains as permanent Indian country. The army wanted the border forts, stretching from Lake Superior to Fort Worth, Texas, constructed of stone because they would be there forever. Trade with the Indians would continue but now closely supervised and licensed by the federal government, with the Indian country otherwise off limits to whites.

Events swiftly overtook the nation's solemn commitment as Americans began to eye Oregon and California; Indian country became a bridge to the Pacific. The first wagon train headed west for

Uncovering the Culture of the Plains Indians

Tepee Liner. American Hurrah, New York City.

Preliterate peoples, by definition, do not leave written records, which are the staff of life for historians. For ancient civilizations, all historians have to go on are archeological ruins, surviving artifacts, and artwork. In the case of the Plains Indians, who also had no written language, historians are more fortunate because white contemporaries observed, interviewed, and even painted the Plains Indians. The drawback is that this evidence is secondhand, filtered through the preconceptions and prejudices of white Americans. So surviving artifacts that speak directly about the Indian way of life are highly prized. One such artifact is this artfully decorated dewcloth, which hung inside a tepee to shield the privacy of the occupants and keep out the cold.

ANALYZING THE EVIDENCE

➤ By looking at the dewcloth, can you explain why the Plains Indians developed a sharply divided sexual division of labor, with the women relegated to the laborious domestic tasks?

➤ Although the dewcloth celebrates fighting prowess, the Plains Indians were ultimately defeated by the U.S. Army. Do the images you see give you any clues about why they lost?

➤ The dewcloth depicts both battle scenes and buffalo hunting. Although visually they appear seamless, in reality, of course, fighting and hunting were entirely separate activities. By inspecting the images, can you see why the artist chose to depict them as a single phenomenon? Does your answer offer any insight into the culture of the Plains Indians?

Oregon from Missouri in 1842. Soon thousands of emigrants traveled the Oregon Trail to the Willamette Valley or cut south beyond Fort Hall into California. Approaching Fort Hall in 1859, Horace Greeley thought "the white coverings of the many emigrant and transport wagons dott[ing] the landscape" gave "the trail the appearance of a river running through great meadows, with many ships sailing on its bosom." Only these "ships" left behind not a trailing wake of foam but a rutted landscape littered with abandoned wagons and rotting garbage.

The Railroads. Talk about the need for a railroad to the Pacific soon surfaced in Washington. How else could the Pacific territories acquired from Mexico and Britain in 1848 (see Chapter 13) be linked to the Union or the ordeal of the overland journey by wagon train be alleviated? The project languished while North and South argued over the terminus for the route. Meanwhile, the Indian country was crisscrossed by overland freight lines, and Pony Express riders delivered mail between Missouri and California. In 1861 telegraph lines brought San Francisco into instant communication with the East. The next year, with the South in rebellion, the federal government finally moved forward with the transcontinental rail project.

No private company could be expected to foot the bill by itself. The construction costs were staggering, and in the short run not much traffic could be expected along the thinly populated route. So the federal government awarded generous land grants plus millions of dollars in loans to the two companies that undertook the transcontinental project (Map 16.2).

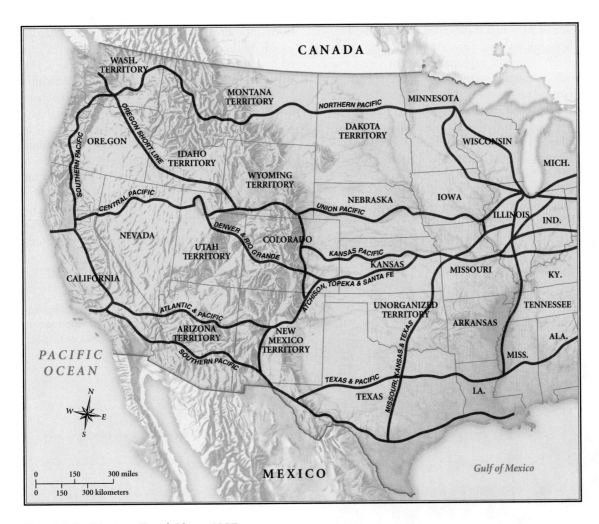

Map 16.2   Western Trunk Lines, 1887

In the 1850s the talk in Washington had been about the need for a transcontinental railroad to bind the West to the Union. This map shows vividly how fully that talk had turned into reality in a matter of three decades. By 1887 no portion of the Pacific Coast lacked a rail connection to the East.

The Union Pacific, building westward from Omaha, made little headway until the Civil War ended but then advanced rapidly across Indian country, reaching Cheyenne, Wyoming, in November 1867. It took the Central Pacific nearly that long moving eastward from Sacramento, California, to cross the crest of the Sierra Nevada. Both then worked furiously — since the government subsidy was based on miles of track laid — until, to great fanfare, the tracks met at Promontory, Utah, in 1869. None of the other railroads following other westward routes made it as far as the Rockies before Jay Cooke's Northern Pacific failed, triggering the Panic of 1873 and bringing work on all the western roads to an abrupt halt (see Chapter 17).

By then, however, railroad tycoons had changed their minds about the Great Plains. No longer did they see it through the eyes of the Oregon-bound settlers traveling on foot and in wagons — as a place to be gotten through en route to the Pacific. They realized that railroads were laying the basis for the economic exploitation of the Great Plains. With economic recovery in 1878, construction soared. During the 1880s, 40,000 miles of track were laid west of the Mississippi, including links from southern California, via the Southern Pacific to New Orleans and via the Santa Fe to Kansas City, and from the Northwest, via the Northern Pacific to St. Paul, Minnesota (see Map 17.1, p. 524).

The Cattle Kingdom. Of all the opportunities beckoning, the most obvious was cattle raising. Grazing buffalo made it easy to imagine the plains as cow country. But first the buffalo had to go. All that it would take was the right commercial incentives. A small market for buffalo robes had existed for years, and hunters made good livings provisioning army posts and leading sporting parties. Then in the early 1870s, as the arriving railroads lowered transportation costs and eastern tanneries learned how to cure the hides, the demand for buffalo skins skyrocketed. Parties of professional hunters with high-powered rifles began a systematic slaughter of the buffalo. Already diminished by disease and shrinking pasturage, the great herds almost vanished within ten years. Many people spoke out against this mass killing, but no way existed to stop people bent on making a quick dollar. Besides, as General Philip H. Sheridan pointed out, exterminating the buffalo would starve the Indians into submission.

In south Texas about five million head of longhorn cattle already grazed on Anglo ranches, hardly worth bothering about because they could not be profitably marketed. In 1865, however, the Missouri Pacific Railroad reached Sedalia, Missouri, far enough west to be accessible to Texas ranchers and their herds. At the Sedalia terminus, a longhorn worth $3 in Texas might command $40. With this incentive Texas ranchers inaugurated the famous Long Drive, hiring cowboys to herd the longhorn cattle hundreds of miles north to the railroads that were pushing west across Kansas.

At Abilene, Ellsworth, and Dodge City, ranchers sold their cattle, and trail-weary cowboys went on binges. These cattle towns captured the nation's

Killing the Buffalo

This woodcut shows passengers shooting buffalo from a Kansas Pacific Railroad train — a small thrill added to the modern convenience of traveling west by rail. North Wind Picture Archives.

Cowboys on the Open Range

In open-range ranching, cattle from different ranches grazed together. At the roundup, cowboys separated the cattle by owner and branded the calves. Cowboys, celebrated in dime novels, were really farmhands on horseback, with the skills to work on the range. An ethnically diverse group, including blacks and Hispanics, they earned $25 a month, plus meals and a bed in the bunkhouse, in return for long hours of grueling, lonesome work. Library of Congress.

imagination as symbols of the Wild West. The reality was much more ordinary. The cowboys, many of them African Americans and Hispanics, were in fact farmhands on horseback who worked long hours under harsh conditions for small pay. Colorful though it seemed, the Long Drive was actually a makeshift method of bridging a gap in the developing transportation system. As soon as railroads reached the Texas range country during the 1870s, ranchers abandoned the Long Drive.

The Texas ranchers owned or leased the land they used, sometimes in huge tracts. North of Texas, where the land was in the public domain, cattlemen simply helped themselves. Hopeful ranchers would spot a likely area along a creek and claim as much land as they could qualify for as settlers under federal homesteading laws, plus what might be added by the fraudulent claims taken out by one or two ranch hands. By a common usage that quickly became established, ranchers had a "range right" to all the adjacent land rising up to the divide—the point where the land sloped down to the next creek.

News of easy money traveled fast. Calves cost $5; steers sold for maybe $60 on the Chicago market. Rail connections were in place or coming in. The grass was free. The rush was on, drawing from as far away as Europe both hardheaded investors and romantics (like the recent Harvard graduate Teddy Roosevelt) eager for a taste of the Wild West. By the early 1880s the plains overflowed with cattle—as many as 7.5 million head ravaging the grass and trampling the water holes.

A cycle of good weather only postponed the inevitable disaster. When it came—a hard winter in 1885, a severe drought the following summer, then record blizzards and bitter cold—cattle died by the hundreds of thousands. An awful scene of rotting carcasses greeted the cowhands riding out onto the range the following spring. Beef prices plunged when hard-pressed ranchers dumped the surviving cattle on the market. The boom collapsed and investors fled, leaving behind a more enduring ecological catastrophe: the destruction of native grasses from the relentless overgrazing by the cattle herds.

Open-range ranching came to an end. Ranchers fenced their land and planted hay. Instead of merely exploiting the plains ecosystem, they now managed and shaped it to their own purposes. And with cattle no longer fending for themselves over the winters, it became feasible to cross-breed the hardy longhorns with white-faced Herefords and get a meatier and tastier animal. Ranching entered a more placid, domesticated era. In the meantime, Hispanic shepherds from New Mexico brought sheep in to feed on the mesquite and prickly pear that supplanted the native grasses. Sheep raising, previously scorned by ranchers as unmanly and resisted as a threat to cattle, became a major enterprise in the sparser high country. Some ranchers even sold out to the despised "nesters"—those who wanted to try farming the Great Plains.

Buffalo Bill and the Mythic West. As the romance faded on the ground, it flowered in the American imagination. The grand perpetrator of a mythic West, William F. Cody, was an unlikely candidate for that role, a barely educated, hard-drinking ex-guerrilla fighter (and occasional horse thief). At loose ends after the Civil War, Cody got a lucky break in 1867 when he was hired to provide buffalo meat for work crews laying railroad track through Indian country in Kansas. A crack shot

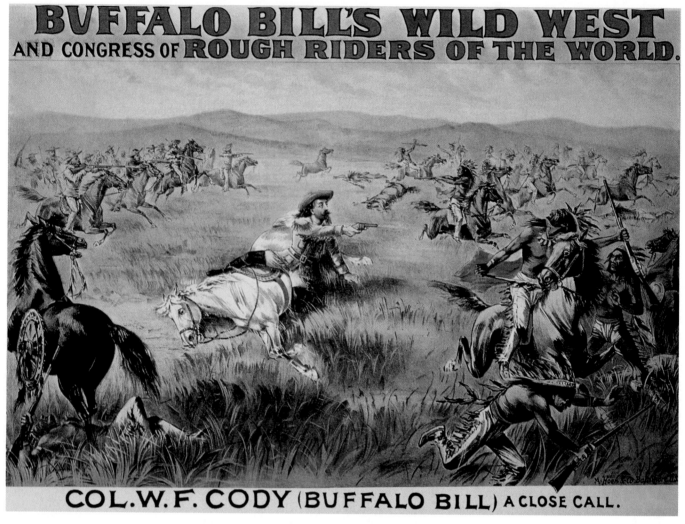

"A Close Call"

One of the charms of Buffalo Bill's Wild West Show was that it reenacted exploits of his that actually happened or, at any rate, that Buffalo Bill claimed to have happened. In this poster advertising the 1894 season, U.S. troopers are rescuing him in the nick of time from a scalping.

Granger Collection, New York.

and excellent horseman, Cody's skills as a buffalo hunter soon won him the name "Buffalo Bill." In 1868 Indian war broke out, and Cody got his second claim to fame as an intrepid army scout.

Out of these promising materials, a legendary figure emerged. In July 1869 the dime novelist Ned Buntline came through Kansas, met Cody, and immediately wrote *Buffalo Bill, the King of the Border Men* — the first of some 1,700 potboilers featuring Cody and his exploits. Then there were the buffalo-hunting parties for the rich and famous that Cody led, and his appearance in 1872 on the New York stage in a Buntline creation, playing himself. The line between reality and make-believe began to blur. In the Sioux wars of 1875–1876, serving again as an army scout, Cody rode into battle in his stage vaquero outfit — black velvet and scarlet with lace — so that when he reenacted the mayhem on stage he could wear the very clothes in which he had seen action.

Cody's mythic West became full blown in his Wild West Show, first staged in 1883, that offered displays of horsemanship, sharp-shooting by Little Annie Oakley, and real Indians (in one season Chief Sitting Bull toured with the company). Buffalo Bill traded on his talents as showman, but he also knew the authentic world that lay behind the make-believe. Long after that world was gone, his Wild West Show kept it alive in legend, where it still remains in the cowboys and Indians that populate our movies and television screens.

Homesteaders

No westerners had less in common with Buffalo Bill's world than the settlers who followed the cattlemen on to the Great Plains. Before coming, of course, they needed to be persuaded that crops would grow in that dry country. Powerful interests worked hard to overcome the popular notion that the plains were the Great American Desert. Foremost were the railroads, eager to sell off the public land they had been granted — 180 million acres of it — and to develop traffic for their routes. They aggressively advertised, offered cut-rate tickets, and sold off their land at bargain prices. Land speculators, transatlantic steamship lines, and the western states and territories did all they could to encourage settlers. And so did the federal government, which offered 160 acres of public land to all comers under the Homestead Act (1862).

"Why emigrate to Kansas?" asked a testimonial in *Western Trail*, the Rock Island Railroad's gazette. "Because it is the garden spot of the world. Because it will grow anything that any other country will grow, and with less work. Because it rains here more than any other place, and at just the right time."

As if to confirm the optimists, an exceptionally wet cycle occurred between 1878 and 1886. Some settlers attributed the increased rainfall to soil cultivation and tree planting. Others credited

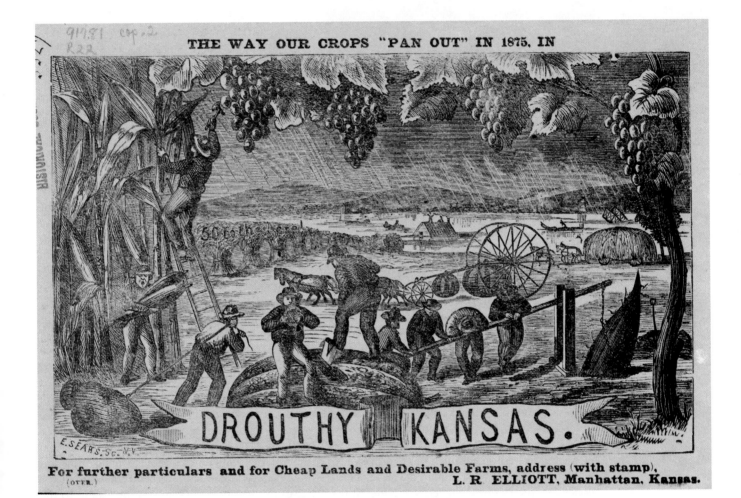

Drouthy Kansas

This tongue-in-cheek sketch, with its humongous pumpkins and melon-sized grapes, was drawn in 1868 by Henry Worrall, a local Topeka artist, as humorous reassurance to friends thinking about settling in Kansas but worried about its dry climate. The sketch then developed a life of its own. It was widely reproduced and used by the railroads and land agents to encourage people to come to Kansas. The illustration above, dated 1875, is one such reproduction, sent around by a Manhattan, Kansas, dealer offering land and farms for sale. By that time, "drouthy" weather — a sharp dry spell — had set in and hard-pressed farmers were cursing "that damn sketch of Henry Worrall's." Kansas State Historical Society.

The Shores Family, Custer County, Nebraska, 1887
Whether the Shores family came west as Exodusters, we do not know. But in 1887, when this photograph was taken, they were well settled on their Nebraska farm, although still living in sod houses. The patriarch of the family, Jerry Shores, an ex-slave, is second from the right. Nebraska State Historical Society.

God. As a settler on the southern plains remarked, "The Lord just knowed we needed more land an' He's gone and changed the climate."

No amount of optimism, however, could dispel the pain of migration. "That last separating word of *Farewell!* sinks deeply into the heart," one pioneer woman recorded in her diary, thinking of family and friends left behind. But then came the treeless plains. "Such an air of desolation," wrote a Nebraska-bound woman; from another woman in Texas, "such a lonely country."

Some women were liberated by this hard experience. Prescribed gender roles broke down as women shouldered men's work on new farms and became self-reliant in the face of danger and hardship. When husbands died or gave up, wives operated farms on their own. Under the Homestead Act, which accorded widows and single women the same rights as men, women filed 10 percent of the claims. Even with a man around, women contributed crucially to the farm enterprise. Farming might be thought of as a dual economy in which men's labor brought in the big wage at harvest time, while women provisioned the family day by day and produced a steady bit of money for groceries by selling eggs or butter. If the crop failed, it was women's labor that carried the family through. No wonder farming placed a high premium on marriage: a mere 2.4 percent of Nebraska women in 1900 had never married.

Male or female, the vision of new land beckoned people onto the plains. By the 1870s the older agricultural states had filled up, and farmers looked hungrily westward. "Hardly anything else was talked about," recalled the short-story writer Hamlin Garland about his Iowa neighbors. "Every man who could sell out had gone west or was going. . . . Farmer after farmer joined the march to Kansas, Nebraska, and Dakota. . . . The movement . . . had . . . become an exodus, a stampede."

The same excitement took hold in northern Europe, as Norwegians and Swedes for the first time joined the older German migration. At the peak of the "American fever" in 1882, over 105,000 Scandinavians emigrated to the United States. Swedish and Norwegian became the primary languages in parts of Minnesota and the Dakotas. Roughly a third of the farmers on the northern plains were foreign-born.

The motivation for most settlers, American or European, was to better themselves economically. But for some southern blacks, Kansas briefly represented something more precious—the Promised Land of racial freedom. In the spring of 1879, with Reconstruction over and federal protection withdrawn, black communities fearful of white vengeance were swept by enthusiasm for Kansas. Within a month or so, some 6,000 blacks left Mississippi and Louisiana, most of them with nothing more than the clothes on their backs and faith in the Lord. They called themselves Exodusters, participants in the exodus to the dry prairie. How many of them remained is hard to say, but the 1880 census reported 40,000 blacks in Kansas—by far the largest African American concentration in the West aside from Texas, whose expanding cotton frontier attracted hundreds of thousands of black migrants during the 1870s and 1880s.

Taming the Land. No matter where they came from, homesteaders found the plains an alien place. A cloud of grasshoppers might descend and destroy a crop in a day; a brush fire or hailstorm could do the job in an hour. What forested land had always provided — ample water, lumber for cabins and fencing, firewood — was absent. For shelter, settlers often cut dugouts into hillsides and after a season or two erected houses made of turf cut from the ground.

The absence of trees, on the other hand, meant an easier time clearing the land. New technology overcame obstacles once thought insurmountable. Steel plows enabled homesteaders to break the tightly matted ground, and barbed wire provided cheap, effective fencing against roaming cattle. Strains of hard-kernel wheat tolerant of the extreme temperatures of the plains came in from Europe. Homesteaders had good crops while the wet cycle held and began to anticipate the wood-frame house, deep well, and full coal bin that might make life tolerable on the plains.

In the mid-1880s the dry years came and wrecked those hopeful calculations. "From day to day," reported the budding novelist Stephen Crane from Nebraska, "a wind hot as an oven's fury . . . raged like a pestilence," destroying the crops and leaving farmers "helpless, with no weapon against this terrible and inscrutable wrath of nature." Land only recently settled emptied out as homesteaders fled in defeat. The Dakotas lost 50,000 settlers between 1885 and 1890, and comparable departures occurred up and down the drought-stricken plains.

Other settlers held on grimly. Stripped of the illusion that rain followed the plow, the survivors came to terms with the semiarid climate prevailing west of the ninety-eighth meridian. Mormons around the Great Salt Lake had demonstrated how irrigation could turn a wasteland into a garden.

But the Great Plains generally lacked the water reserves needed for irrigation. The answer lay in dry-farming methods, which involved deep planting to bring subsoil moisture to the roots and quick harrowing after rainfalls to turn over a dry mulch that slowed evaporation. Dry farming developed most fully on the huge corporate farms in the Red River Valley of North Dakota. But even family farms, the norm elsewhere, could not survive on less than 300 acres of grain crops, plus machinery for plowing, planting, and harvesting. Dry farming was not for unequipped homesteaders.

In this struggle there was little room for sentiment about nature's bounty. Indeed, settlers regarded themselves as nature's conquerors, striving, as one pioneer remarked, "to get the land subdued and the wilde [sic] nature out of it." Much about its "wilde nature" was of course unknown to these strangers to the semiarid West. They did not understand that plowing under the native bunch grasses rendered the soil vulnerable to erosion and sandstorms. Or that the attack on biodiversity, which was what farming the plains really meant, opened pathways for exotic, destructive pests and weeds. They knew that wheat crops depleted the soil, but not that the remedy that worked elsewhere — letting the land lie fallow periodically — raised salinity to destructive levels (because, without absorption by the native grasses, rainfall dissolved salts in the underlying shale).

Few counted the environmental costs when there was money to be made. By the turn of the century, about half the nation's cattle and sheep, a third of its cereal crops, and nearly three-fifths of its wheat came from the newly settled lands. But this was not a sustainable achievement. In the twentieth

Buffalo Chips

With no trees around for firewood, settlers on the plains had to make do with dried cow and buffalo droppings. Gathering the "buffalo chips" must have been a regular chore for Ada McColl and her daughter on her homestead near Lakin, Kansas, in 1893. Kansas State Historical Society.

century, this celebrated nation's bread basket was revealed to have been, in words of modern scientists, "the largest, longest-run agricultural and environmental miscalculation in American history."

Farmers' Woes. Taming the Great Plains had involved little of the "pioneering" that Americans associated with the westward movement. The railroads came before the settlers, eastern capital financed the ranching bonanza, dry farming depended on sophisticated technology, and western wheat was a commodity in the international economy. The nerve center of the Great Plains, indeed, was Chicago, from whence, at the hub of the nation's rail system, the wheat pit traded western grain and consigned it to world markets; the great packing houses turned livestock into the nation's beef; and building supplies, McCormick reapers, and Sears, Roebuck catalogues flowed backed to western ranches and homesteads.

American farmers embraced this commercial world. They had little of the passionate identification with the soil that tied European peasants to the land, regarding their acreage instead as a commodity. In frontier areas, where newly developed land appreciated rapidly, they anticipated as much profit, if not more, from the rising value of the land as from the crops it produced. Nor were American farmers averse to borrowing money. In boom times they rushed into debt to acquire more land and better farm equipment. All these enthusiasms—for cash crops, for land speculation, for borrowed money, for new technology—bore witness to the conviction that farming was, as one agricultural journal remarked, a business "like all other business."

Somehow, however, farmers went unrewarded for their faith in free enterprise. The basic problem was that they remained individual operators in an ever more complex and far-flung economic order. And they were, in certain ways, acutely aware of their predicament. They understood, for example, the disadvantages they faced in dealing with the big businesses that supplied them with machinery, arranged their credit, and marketed their products.

One answer was cooperation. In 1867 Oliver H. Kelley, a government clerk, founded the National Grange of the Patrons of Husbandry mainly in hopes of improving the social life of farm families. Local granges spread by the thousands across rural America, providing meeting places and a rich array of dances, picnics, and lectures. The Grange soon added cooperative programs, purchasing in bulk from suppliers and setting up its own banks, insurance companies, grain elevators, and, in Iowa, even a manufacturing plant for farm implements. Although most of these poorly managed, underfi-

nanced ventures eventually failed, the cooperative idea was highly resilient, and would be embraced by every successive farmers' movement. Rural hostility to middlemen also left as a legacy the great mail-order house of Montgomery Ward, which had been founded in 1872 to serve Grange members.

The power of government might also be enlisted on the farmers' side. In the early 1870s the Grange encouraged independent political parties that ran on antimonopoly platforms. In a number of prairie states these agrarian parties enacted so-called Granger laws regulating grain elevators, fixing maximum railroad rates, and prohibiting discriminatory treatment of small and short-haul shippers.

Farmers turned to cooperatives and state regulation out of a deep sense of organizational disadvantage. But what really put them at risk was beyond anyone's control. This was the movement of farm prices. Especially endangered were farmers exposed to the global commodity markets, most notably, wheat farmers. Also at risk in deflationary periods were farmers in debt since falling prices forced them to pay back in real terms more than they had borrowed. And who was most deeply in debt? The same group: wheat farmers.

In the 1870s the major wheat-growing states had been Illinois, Wisconsin, and Minnesota. These states had been at the center of the Granger agitation of that decade. By the 1880s wheat had moved onto the Great Plains. Among the indebted farmers of Kansas, Nebraska, and the Dakotas, the deflationary economy of the 1880s made for stubbornly hard times. All that was needed to bring on a real crisis was a sharp drop in world prices for wheat.

The Fate of the Indians

What of the Native Americans who inhabited the Great Plains? Basically, their history has been told in the foregoing account of western settlement. "The white children have surrounded me and have left me nothing but an island," lamented the great Sioux chief Red Cloud in 1870, the year after the completion of the transcontinental railroad. "When we first had all this land we were strong; now we are all melting like snow on a hillside, while you are grown like spring grass."

Settlement occurred despite the provisions for a permanent Indian country that had been written into federal law and ratified by treaties with various tribes. As incursions into their lands increased from the late 1850s onward, the Indians resisted as best they could, striking back all along the frontier: the Apaches in the Southwest, the Cheyennes and Arapahos in Colorado, and the Sioux in the Wyoming and Dakota Territories. The Indians

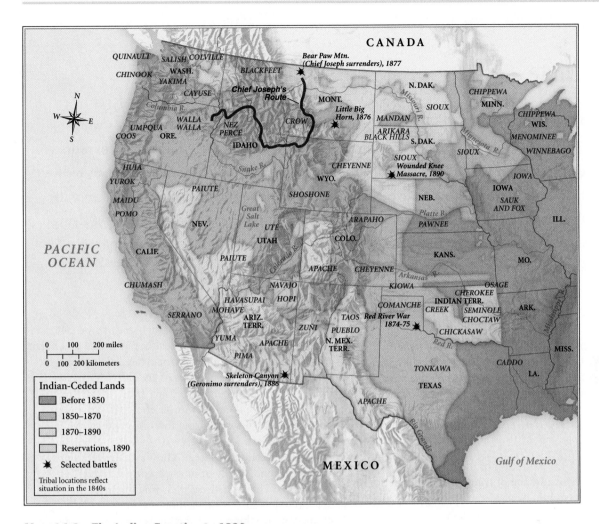

CANADA

QUINAULT SALISH COLVILLE
CHINOOK WASH. BLACKFEET
YAKIMA
CAYUSE Chief Joseph's
Route
Columbia R.
UMPQUA WALLA NEZ
WALLA PERCE CROW
COOS ORE.
IDAHO

Bear Paw Mtn.
(Chief Joseph surrenders), 1877

N. DAK.
CHIPPEWA
MONT. MINN.
Little Big SIOUX
Horn, 1876 MANDAN CHIPPEWA
ARIKARA WIS.
BLACK HILLS S. DAK. MENOMINEE
Missouri R. WINNEBAGO
SIOUX
Wounded Knee SIOUX
Massacre, 1890 IOWA
Minnesota R.

HUIA
YUROK
MAIDU
POMO
NEV. UTE
UTAH
CALIF.
PAIUTE
Snake R.
CHEYENNE
WYO.
SHOSHONE
Great
Salt
Lake
COLO.
APACHE CHEYENNE
Colorado R.
ARAPAHO
PAWNEE
Platte R.
NEB.
IOWA
SAUK
AND FOX
ILL.
KANS.
MO.
Arkansas

PACIFIC
OCEAN

CHUMASH

SERRANO
MOHAVE
HAVASUPAI
ARIZ.
TERR.
YUMA
PIMA
APACHE

NAVAJO
HOPI

ZUNI

TAOS Red River War
PUEBLO 1874-75
N. MEX.
TERR.

KIOWA OSAGE
CHEROKEE
COMANCHE INDIAN TERR.
CREEK SEMINOLE ARK.
CHOCTAW
CHICKASAW
Red R.

OSAGE

MISS.
CADDO
LA.
TONKAWA
TEXAS

Skeleton Canyon
(Geronimo surrenders), 1886

APACHE

Rio Grande

MEXICO Gulf of Mexico

0 100 200 miles
0 100 200 kilometers

Indian-Ceded Lands
Before 1850
1850–1870
1870–1890
Reservations, 1890
★ Selected battles

Tribal locations reflect
situation in the 1840s

Map 16.3 The Indian Frontier, to 1890

As settlement pushed onto the Great Plains after the Civil War, the Indians put up bitter
resistance but ultimately to no avail. Over a period of decades, they ceded most of their
lands to the federal government, and by 1890 they were confined to scattered reservations
where the most they could expect was an impoverished and alien way of life.

hoped that, if they resisted stubbornly enough, the
whites would tire of the struggle and leave them in
peace. This reasoning seemed not altogether fanciful given the country's exhaustion after the Civil
War. But the federal government did not give up;
instead it formulated a new policy for dealing with
the western Indians.

The Reservation Solution. Few whites questioned
the necessity of moving the Native Americans out of
the path of settlement and into reservations. That,
indeed, had been the fate of the eastern and southern tribes. Now, however, Indian removal included
something new: a strategy for undermining the
Indians' tribal way of life. The first step was a peace
commission appointed in 1867 to negotiate an end
to the fighting and sign treaties by which the western
Indians would cede their lands and move to reser-

vations. There, under the tutelage of the Office of
Indian Affairs and officials like Thomas J. Morgan
(see Comparing American Voices, "Becoming
White," pp. 500–501), they would be wards of
the government until they learned "to walk on the
white man's road."

The government set aside two extensive areas,
allocating the southwestern quarter of the Dakota
Territory—present-day South Dakota west of the
Missouri River—to the Lakota Sioux tribes and
assigned what is now Oklahoma to the southern
Plains Indians, along with the major southern
tribes—the Choctaw, Cherokee, Chickasaw, Creek,
and Seminole—and eastern Indians who had been
removed there thirty years before. Scattered reservations went to the Apaches, Navajos, and Utes in
the Southwest and to the mountain Indians in the
Rockies and beyond (Map 16.3).

Becoming White

What should be done about the Indians? That was a question that reverberated across white America during the course of the entire nineteenth century. Many were indifferent, or worse. For some a welcome solution would have been for the Indians just to die out, not an implausible thought given the rate of decline of the Native American population. The high-minded and morally sensitive, of course, deplored so inhumane an attitude, but in fact they also favored a kind of dying-out, by a process of assimilation. The Indians would simply disappear into the white population. To make that happen nothing was more important than the right kind of education.

THOMAS J. MORGAN

In the following document, the U.S. Commissioner of Indian Affairs, Thomas J. Morgan, lays out his views in a lengthy report entitled Indian Education *(1891). His words express the most advanced thinking of the age and indeed are written as if looking over his shoulder was Helen Hunt Jackson, whose book,* A Century of Dishonor *(1881), was the bible of friends of the Indian.*

When we speak of the education of the Indians, we mean that comprehensive system of training and instruction which will convert them into American citizens, put within their reach the blessings which the rest of us enjoy, and enable them to compete successfully with the white man on his own ground and with his own methods. . . . Education should seek the disintegration of the tribes, and not their segregation. They should be educated, not as Indians, but as Americans. In short, public schools should do for them what they are so successfully doing for all the other races of this country—assimilate them.

The work of education should begin with them while they are young and susceptible, and should continue until habits of industry and love of learning have taken the place of indolence and indifference. . . . Children should be taken as early as possible, before camp life has made an indelible stamp upon them. The earlier they can be brought under the beneficent influence of a home school, the more certain will the current of their young lives set in the right direction. . . . During the grammar school period of, say, five years, from ten to fifteen, much can be accomplished in giving to girls a fair knowledge of and practical experience in all the common household duties, such as cooking, sewing, laundry work, etc; and the boys may acquire an acquaintance with farming, gardening, care of stock, etc. . . . Personal cleanliness, care of the health, politeness, and spirit of mutual helpfulness should be inculcated. Schoolrooms should be supplied with pictures of civilized life. . . . Much can be done to fix the current of their thoughts in the right channels by having them memorize choice maxims and literary gems in which inspiring thoughts and noble sentiments are embodied. . . .

No pains should be spared to teach them that their future must depend chiefly upon their own characters and endeavors. . . . They must win their way in life just as other people do—by hard work, virtuous conduct, and thrift. Nothing can save them from the necessity of toil; and they should be inured to it as at the same time a stern condition of success in life's struggle and as one of life's privileges, that brings its own reward.

All this will be of little worth without a high order of moral training. The whole atmosphere of the school should be of the highest character. . . . The school itself should be an illustration of the superiority of our Christian civilization. . . .

It is of prime importance that a fervent patriotism should be awakened in their minds. . . . Everything should be done to awaken the feeling that they are Americans, having common rights and privileges with their fellows. It is more profitable to instruct them as to their duties and obligations than as to their wrongs. . . . If their unhappy history is alluded to, it should be to contrast it with the better future that is within their grasp. The new era that has come though the munificent scheme of education devised for and offered to them should be the means of awakening loyalty to the government, gratitude to the nation, and hopefulness for themselves.

SOURCE: Thomas J. Morgan, *Indian Education* (Washington, 1891).

ZITKALA-ŠA (GERTRUDE SIMMONS BONNIN)

How Commissioner Morgan's ideas about Indian education was actually experienced by one of its "beneficiaries" is vividly described by Zitkala-Ša, known later as the author Gertrude Simmons Bonnin, who recalled in 1900 her painful transformation from Sioux child to pupil at a Quaker missionary school in Indiana.

The first day . . . a paleface woman, with white hair, came up after us. We were placed in a line of girls who were marching into the dining room. These were Indian girls, in stiff shoes and closely clinging dresses. The small girls wore sleeved aprons and shingled hair. As I walked noiselessly in my soft mocassins, I felt like sinking into the floor, for my blanket had been stripped from my shoulders. . . . Late in the morning, my friend Judewin gave me a terrible warning. Judewin knew a few words of English; and she had overheard the paleface woman talk about cutting our long, heavy hair. Our mothers had taught us that only unskilled warriors who were captured had their hair shingled by the enemy. Among our people, short hair was worn by mourners, and shingled hair by cowards! . . . In spite of myself, I was carried downstairs and tied fast in a chair. I cried aloud, shaking my head all the while until I felt the cold blades of the scissors against my neck, and heard them gnaw off one of my thick black braids. Then I lost my spirit. . . .

Now, as I look back upon the recent past, I see it from a distance, as a whole. I remember how, from morning till evening, many specimens of civilized peoples visited the Indian school. The city folks with canes and eyeglass, the countrymen with sunburned cheeks and clumsy feet. . . . Both sorts of these Christian palefaces were alike astounded at seeing the children of savage warriors so docile and industrious.

As answers to their shallow inquiries they received the students' sample work to look upon. Examining the neatly figured pages, and gazing upon the Indian girls and boys bending over their books, the white visitors walked out of the schoolhouse well-satisfied: they were educating the children of the red man! . . .

In this fashion many have passed idly through the Indian schools during the last decade, afterward to boast of their charity to the North American Indian. But few there are who have paused to question whether real life or long lasting death lies beneath this semblance of civilization.

SOURCE: Linda K. Kerber and Jane De-Hart Mathews, eds., *Women's America: Refocusing the Past*, 2nd ed. (New York: Oxford University Press, 1987), 254–257.

ANALYZING THE EVIDENCE

➤ Why, in Commissioner Morgan's conception of Indian education, was it necessary to cut off Zitkala-Ša's beautiful black braids?

➤ Zitkala-Ša went on to become a well-known author and reformer; indeed, she took an Anglo-American name. Commissioner Morgan would surely have regarded her as a triumph of his system of Indian education. So why is she not more appreciative of his efforts on her behalf?

➤ Commissioner Morgan's report is concerned strictly with education. Can it also be read as a primer of American values? If so, in what ways?

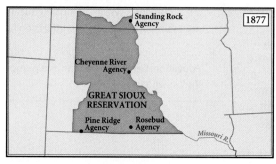

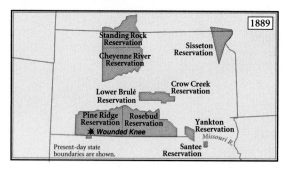

Map 16.4   The Sioux Reservations in South Dakota, 1868–1889

In 1868, when they bent to the demand that they move onto the reservation, the Sioux thought they had gained secure rights to a substantial part of their ancestral hunting grounds. But as they learned to their sorrow, fixed boundary lines only increased their vulnerability to the land hunger of the whites and sped up the process of expropriation.

That the Plains Indians would resist was inevitable. "You might as well expect the rivers to run backward as that any man who was born a free man should be contented when penned up and denied liberty to go where he pleases," said Chief Joseph of the Nez Percé, who led his people in 1877, including women and children, on an epic 1,500-mile march from eastern Oregon to escape confinement in a small reservation. In a series of heroic engagements, the Nez Percé fought off the pursuing U.S. Army until, after four months of extraordinary hardship, the remnants of the tribe were finally cornered and forced to surrender in Montana near the Canadian border.

The U.S. Army was thinly spread, having been cut back after the Civil War to a total force of 27,000.

But these were veteran troops, including 2,000 black cavalrymen of the Ninth and Tenth Regiments, whom Indians called, with grim respect, "buffalo soldiers." Technology also favored the army. Telegraph communications and railroads enabled the troops to be quickly concentrated; repeating rifles and Gatling machine guns increased their firepower. As fighting intensified in the mid-1870s, a reluctant Congress appropriated funds for more western troops. Because of tribal rivalries, the army could always find Indian allies. Worst of all, however, beyond the U.S. Army's advantages or the Indians' disunity, was the overwhelming impact of white settlement.

Resisting the reservation solution, the Indians fought on for years — in Kansas in 1868 and 1869, in the Red River Valley of Texas in 1874, and sporadically among the fierce Apaches, who made life miserable for white settlers in the Southwest until their wily chief Geronimo was finally captured in 1886. On the northern plains the crisis came in 1875, when the Office of Indian Affairs — despite an 1868 treaty — ordered the Sioux to vacate their Powder River hunting grounds and withdraw to the reservation.

Led by Sitting Bull, Sioux and Cheyenne warriors gathered on the Little Big Horn River west of the Powder River country. In a typical concentrating maneuver, army columns from widely separated forts converged on the Little Big Horn. The Seventh Cavalry, commanded by famous Civil War hero George A. Custer, came upon the Sioux encampment on June 25, 1876. Disregarding orders, the reckless Custer sought out battle on his own. He attacked from three sides, hoping to capitalize on the element of surprise. But his forces were spread too thin. The other two contingents fell back with heavy losses to defensive positions, but Custer's own force of 256 men was surrounded and annihilated by Crazy Horse's warriors. It was a great victory but not a decisive one. The day of reckoning was merely postponed.

Pursued by the military, physically exhausted Sioux bands one by one gave up and moved to the reservation. Last to come in were Sitting Bull's followers. They had retreated to Canada, but in 1881, after five hard years, they recrossed the border and surrendered at Fort Buford, Montana.

Not Indian resistance, but white greed wrecked the reservation solution. In the mid-1870s prospectors began to dig for gold in the Black Hills, land sacred to the Sioux and entirely inside their Dakota reservation. Unable to hold back the prospectors or to buy out the Sioux, the government opened up the Black Hills to gold seekers at their own risk. In 1877, after Sioux resistance had crumbled, federal agents forced the tribes to cede the western third of their Dakota reservation (Map 16.4).

Indian School

In this photograph taken at the Riverside Indian School in Anadarko, Oklahoma Territory, the pupils have been shorn of their braids and dressed in laced shoes, Mother Hubbard dresses, and shirts and trousers — one step on the journey into the mainstream of white American society. Children as young as five were separated from their families and sent to Indian schools like this one that taught them new skills while encouraging them to abandon traditional Indian ways.

University of Oklahoma, Western History Collections.

The Indian Territory of Oklahoma met a similar fate. Two million acres in the heart of the territory had not been assigned, and white homesteaders coveted that fertile land. The "boomer" movement, stirred up initially by railroads operating in the Indian Territory, agitated for an opening of this so-called Oklahoma District to settlers. In 1889 the government reluctantly placed the Oklahoma District under the Homestead Act. On April 22, 1889, a horde of claimants rushed in and staked out the entire district within a few hours. Two tent cities — Guthrie with 15,000 people and Oklahoma City with 10,000 — were in full swing by nightfall.

Undermining Tribal Culture. In the meantime the campaign to move the Indians onto "the white man's road" relentlessly went forward. During the 1870s the Office of Indian Affairs developed a program to train Indian children for farm work and prepare them for citizenship. Some attended reservation schools, while the less lucky were sent to distant boarding schools. Mother Hubbard dresses and shirts and trousers visibly demonstrated that these bewildered children were being inducted into white society (see Comparing American Voices, "Becoming White," pp. 500–501).

And not a moment too soon, believed many avowed friends of the Native Americans. The Indians had never lacked sympathizers — especially in the East, where reformers created the Indian Rights Association after the Civil War. The movement got a boost from Helen Hunt Jackson's influential book *A Century of Dishonor* (1881), which told the story of the unjust treatment of the Indians. What would save them, the reformers believed, was assimilation

into white society, starting with the children. The reformers also favored efforts by the Office of Indian Affairs to undermine tribal authority. Above all, they esteemed private property as a "civilizing force" and hence advocated **severalty,** land ownership by individuals.

The result was the Dawes Severalty Act (1887), authorizing the president to carve up tribal lands, with each family head receiving an allotment of 160 acres and individuals receiving smaller parcels. The land would be held in trust for twenty-five years, and the Indians would be granted U.S. citizenship. Remaining reservation lands would be sold off, with the proceeds placed in an Indian education fund.

The Last Battle: Wounded Knee. The Sioux were among the first to bear the brunt of the Dawes Act. The federal government, announcing it had gained tribal approval, opened their "surplus" land to white settlement on February 10, 1890. But no surveys had been made nor had any provision been made for land allotments for the Indians living in the ceded areas. On top of these signs of bad faith, drought wiped out the Indians' crops that summer. It seemed beyond endurance. They had lost their ancestral lands. They faced a future as farmers, which was alien to their traditions. And immediately confronting them was a winter of starvation.

But news of salvation had also come. An Indian messiah, a holy man who called himself Wovoka, was preaching a new religion on a Paiute reservation in Nevada. In a vision Wovoka had gone to heaven and received God's word that the world would be regenerated. The whites would disappear, all the Indians of past generations would return to Earth, and life on the Great Plains would be as it was before the white man appeared. All this would come to pass in the spring of 1891. Awaiting that great day the Indians should practice the Ghost Dance, a day-long ritual that sent the spirits of the dancers rising to heaven. As the frenzy of the Ghost Dance swept through some Sioux encampments in the fall of 1890, resident whites became alarmed and called for army intervention.

Wovoka had an especially fervent following among the Minneconjous, where the medicine man Yellow Bird held sway. But their chief, Big Foot, had fallen desperately ill with pneumonia, and the Minneconjous agreed to come in under military escort to an encampment at Wounded Knee Creek on December 28. The next morning, when the soldiers attempted to disarm the Indians, a battle exploded in the encampment. Among the U.S. troopers, 25 died; among the Indians, 146 men, women, and children perished, many of them shot down as they fled.

Wounded Knee was the final episode in the war against the Plains Indians but not the end of their story. The division of tribal lands now proceeded without hindrance. The Lakota Sioux fared relatively well, and many of the younger generation settled down as small farmers and stock grazers. Ironically,

the more fortunate tribes were probably those occupying infertile land that settlers did not want. The flood of whites into South Dakota and Oklahoma, on the other hand, left the Indians as small minorities in lands once wholly theirs — 20,000 Sioux in a South Dakotan population of 400,000 in 1900; 70,000 of various tribes in a population of a million when Oklahoma became a state in 1907.

Even so, tribal life survived until, with the restoration of the reservation policy in 1934, it once again rested on a communal territorial basis. All along, Native American cultures had been adaptive, changing in the face of adversity and even absorbing features of white society. This cultural resilience persisted — in religion, in tribal structure, in crafts — but the fostering pre-conquest world was gone, swept away, as an Oklahoma editor put it in the year of statehood, by "the onward march of empire."

➤ What was the role of the railroads in the settlement of the Great West?

➤ How would you characterize the agricultural settlers' relationship to the natural environment of the Great Plains?

➤ What was the new Indian reservation policy, and why was it a failure?

The Dead at Wounded Knee

In December 1890 U.S. soldiers massacred 146 Sioux men, women, and children in the Battle of Wounded Knee in South Dakota. It was the last big fight on the northern plains between the Indians and the whites. Black Elk, a Sioux holy man, related that "after the soldiers marched away from their dirty work, a heavy snow began to fall . . . and it grew very cold." The body of Yellow Bird lay frozen where it had fallen. National Anthropological Archives, Smithsonian Institution, Washington, DC.

The Far West

On the western edge of the Great Plains, the Rocky Mountains rise up to form a great barrier between the mostly flat eastern two-thirds of the country and the rugged Far West. Beyond the Rockies lie two vast highlands: in the north the Columbia plateau, extending into eastern Oregon and Washington, and, flanking the southern Rockies, the Colorado plateau. Where the plateaus break off, the desertlike Great Basin begins, covering western Utah and all of Nevada. Separating this arid interior from the Pacific Ocean are two great mountain ranges — the Sierra Nevada and, to the north, the Cascades — beyond which lies a coastal region that is cool and rainy in the north but increasingly dry southward, until in southern California rainfall becomes almost as sparse as in the interior.

Clearly the trans-mountain West could not be occupied in standard American fashion — that is, by a multitude of settlers moving along a broad front and, homestead by homestead, bringing it under cultivation. The wagon trains heading to Oregon's Willamette Valley adopted an entirely different strategy — the planting of an island of settlement in a vast, often barren landscape.

New Spain had pioneered this strategy when in 1598 it had sent the first wagon trains 700 miles northward from Mexico into the upper Rio Grande Valley and established Santa Fe. When the United States seized the Southwest 250 years later, major Hispanic settlements existed in New Mexico and California, with lesser settlements scattered along the borderlands into south Texas. At that time, aside from Oregon, the only significant Anglo settlement was around the Great Salt Lake in Utah, where persecuted Mormons had planted a New Zion. Fewer than 100,000 Euro-Americans — roughly 25,000 of them Anglo, the rest Hispanic — lived in the entire Far West when it became U.S. territory in 1848.

The Mining Frontier

More emigrants would be coming, certainly, but the Far West seemed unlikely to be much of a magnet. California was "hilly and mountainous," noted a U.S. naval officer in 1849, too dry for farming and surely not "susceptible of supporting a very large population." He had not taken account of the recent discovery of gold in the Sierra foothills. California would indeed support a very large population, drawn not by arable land but by dreams of gold.

Extraction of mineral wealth became the basis for the Far West's development (Map 16.5). By 1860, when the Great Plains was still Indian country, California was a booming state with 300,000 residents. In a burst of city building, San Francisco became a bustling metropolis — it had 57,000 residents in 1860 — and was the hub of a mining empire that stretched to the Rockies.

In its swift urbanization the Far West resembled southeastern Australia, whose gold rush began in 1851, much more than the American Midwest. Like San Francisco, Melbourne was a city incongruously grand amid the empty spaces and rough mining camps of the Australian "outback." The distinctive pattern of isolated settlement persisted in the Far West, driven now, however, by a proliferation of mining sites and by people moving not east to west but west to east, coming mainly from California.

By the mid-1850s, as easy pickings in the California gold country diminished, prospectors began to pull out and spread across the West in hopes of striking it rich elsewhere. Gold was discovered on the Nevada side of the Sierra Nevada, in the Colorado Rockies, and along the Fraser River in British Columbia. New strikes occurred in Montana and Wyoming during the 1860s, a decade later in the Black Hills of South Dakota, and in the Coeur d'Alene region of Idaho during the 1880s.

As the news of each gold strike spread, a wild, remote area turned almost overnight into a mob scene of prospectors, traders, gamblers, prostitutes, and saloon keepers (see Voices from Abroad, "Baron Joseph Alexander von Hübner: A Western Boom Town," p. 507). At least 100,000 fortune seekers flocked to the Pike's Peak area of Colorado in the spring of 1859. Trespassers on government or Indian land, the prospectors made their own law. The mining codes devised at community meetings limited the size of a mining claim to what a person could reasonably work. This kind of informal lawmaking also became an instrument for excluding or discriminating against Mexicans, Chinese, and African Americans in the gold fields. It turned into hangman's justice for the many outlaws who infested the mining camps.

The heyday of the prospectors was always brief. They were equipped only to skim gold from the surface outcroppings and stream beds. Extracting the metal locked in underground lodes required mine shafts and crushing mills — hence capital, technology, and business organization. The original claim holders quickly sold out when a generous

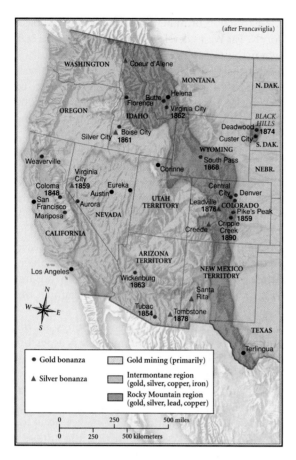

Map 16.5 The Mining Frontier, 1848–1890

The Far West was America's gold country because of its geological history. Veins of gold and silver form when molten material from the earth's core is forced up into fissures caused by the tectonic movements that create mountain ranges, such as the ones that dominate the far western landscape. It was these veins, the product of mountain-forming activity many thousands of years earlier, that prospectors began to discover after 1848 and furiously exploit. Although widely dispersed across the Far West, the lodes that they found followed the mountain ranges bisecting the region and bypassing the great plateaus not shaped by the ancient tectonic activity.

bidder came along. At every gold-rush site the prospector soon gave way to entrepreneurial development and large-scale mining. Rough mining camps turned into big towns.

Consider Nevada's Virginia City, which started out as a bawdy, ramshackle mining camp, but then, with the opening of the Comstock silver lode in 1859, acquired a stock exchange, fancy hotels, even Shakespearean theater. The rough edges were never quite smoothed out. In 1870 a hundred saloons operated day and night, brothels lined D Street, and men outnumbered women two to one. But in its booming heyday Virginia City seemed a

place that would last forever. In the 1880s, however, as the Comstock lode played out, Virginia City declined and, in a fate all too familiar in bonanza mining, became a ghost town. What remained, likewise entirely familiar, was a ravaged landscape, with mountains of debris, poisoned water sources, and woods denuded by the mines' insatiable need for timbering. Comstock, one critic remarked, was "the tomb of the forests of the Sierras."

In its final stage the mining frontier entered the industrial world. At some sites gold and silver proved less important than the more common metals — copper, lead, and zinc — for which there was a huge demand by eastern industry. Entrepreneurs raised capital, built rail connections, financed the technology for treating the lower-grade copper deposits, constructed smelting facilities, and recruited a labor force. Like other workers, western miners organized trade unions (see Chapter 17). As elsewhere in corporate America, the western mining industries went through a process of consolidation, culminating by the turn of the century in near-monopoly control of western copper and lead production.

The Pacific Slope. Without its mineral wealth, Far West history would have been very different. Oregon's Willamette Valley, not dry California, had mostly attracted westward-bound settlers before the gold strike at Sutter's Mill in 1848. And, but for that, California would likely have remained like the Willamette Valley — an agricultural backwater with no markets for its products and a slow-growing population. In 1860, although already a state, Oregon had scarcely 25,000 inhabitants, and its principal city, Portland, was little more than a village. Booming California and its tributary mining country pulled Oregon from the doldrums by creating a market for the state's produce and timber. During the 1880s Oregon and Washington (which became a state in 1889) grew prodigiously. Where scarcely 100,000 settlers had lived twenty years earlier, there were nearly 750,000 by 1890 (Map 16.6). Portland and Seattle blossomed into important commercial centers, both prospering from a mixed economy of farming, ranching, logging, and fishing.

At a certain point, especially as railroads gave access to eastern markets, this diversified growth became self-sustaining. But what had triggered it — what had provided the first markets and underwritten the economic infrastructure — was the bonanza mining economy, at the hub of which

Baron Joseph Alexander von Hübner

A Western Boom Town

During a leisurely trip around the world in 1871, Baron von Hübner, a distinguished Austrian diplomat, traveled across the United States, taking advantage of the newly completed transcontinental railroad to see the Wild West. After observing Mormon life in Salt Lake City, he went northward to Corinne, Utah, near the juncture where the Central Pacific and Union Pacific railroads met (see Map 16.2, p. 491). The baron might have arrived with romantic notions of the Wild West popular among Europeans of his class. That was not, however, how he departed.

Corinne has only existed for four years. Sprung out of the earth as if by enchantment, this town now contains upwards of 2,000 inhabitants, and every day increases in importance. It is a victualing center for the advanced posts of the [miners] in Idaho and Montana. A coach runs twice a week to Virginia City and to Helena, 350 and 500 miles to the north. Despite the serious dangers and the terrible fatigue of the journeys, these diligences are always full of passengers. Various articles of consumption and dry goods of all sorts are sent in wagons. The "high road" is but a rough track in the soil left by the wheels of the previous vehicles.

The streets of Corinne are full of white men armed to the teeth, miserable looking Indians dressed in the ragged shirts and trousers furnished by the federal government, and yellow Chinese with a business-like air and hard, intelligent faces. No town in the Far West gave me so good an idea as this little place of what is meant by "border life," the struggle between civilization and savage men and things. . . .

All commercial business centers in Main Street. The houses on both sides are nothing but boarded huts. I have seen some with only canvas partitions. . . . The lanes alongside of the huts, which are generally the resort of Chinese women of bad character, lead into the desert, which begins at the doors of the last houses. . . .

To have on your conscience a number of man-slaughters committed in full day, under the eyes of your fellow citizens; to have escaped the reach of justice by craft, audacity, or bribery; to have earned a reputation for being "sharp," that is, for knowing how to cheat all the world without being caught — those are the attributes of the true rowdy in the Far West. . . . Endowed as they often are with really fine qualities — courage, energy, and intellectual and physical strength — they might in another sphere and with the moral sense which they now lack, have become valuable members of society. But such as they are, these adventurers have a reason for being, a providential mission to fulfill. The qualities needed to struggle with and conquer savage nature have naturally their corresponding defects. Look back, and you will see the cradles of all civilization surrounded with giants of Herculean strength ready to run every risk and to shrink from neither danger nor crime to attain their ends. It is only by the peculiar temper of the time and place that we can distinguish them from the backwoodsman and rowdy of the United States.

SOURCE: Oscar Handlin, ed., *This Was America* (Cambridge, MA: Harvard University Press, 1949), 313–315.

ANALYZING THE EVIDENCE

➤ We read foreign impressions of America because we hope to find in them insights that Americans themselves might not have. In what ways, if any, do you find such insights in Baron von Hübner's account of Corrine?

➤ The baron describes Corrine as a booming supply center for the hard-rock mining industry of Montana and Idaho. Yet his explanation of Corrine is more romantic. He sees in its activities a "struggle between civilization and savage men and things." Is that a helpful insight for us? Would it have been shared or seen as helpful, say, by a Boston businessman looking to invest in real estate in Corrine?

➤ The baron is unsparing in his description of the prostitutes, "miserable looking" Indians, and other low-life inhabiting Corrine. But he makes an exception for the gunmen roaming the streets. Despite their "defects," they have "a providential mission to fulfill." What does he mean by that? Would his view have made sense to the hypothetical Boston businessman mentioned above? Or to other Americans who saw in the West the economic opportunity of a lifetime?

Hydraulic Mining

When surface veins of gold were played out, miners turned to hydraulic mining, which was invented in California in 1853. The technology was simple, using high-pressure streams of water to wash away hillsides of gold-bearing soil. Although building the reservoirs, piping systems, and sluices cost money, the profits from hydraulic mining helped transform western mining into big business. But, as this daguerreotype suggests, hydraulic mining wreaked havoc on the environment. Collection of Matthew Isenburg.

stood San Francisco, the metropolis for the entire Far West.

Hispanics, Chinese, Anglos

California was the anchor of two distinct far western regions. First, it joined with Oregon and Washington to form the Pacific slope. Second, by climate and Hispanic heritage, California was linked to the Southwest, which today includes Arizona, New Mexico, and Texas.

The Hispanic Southwest. The first Europeans to enter the Far West — two centuries before the earliest Anglos — were Hispanics moving northward out of Mexico. There, along a 1,500-mile borderland, outposts had been planted over many years by the viceroys of New Spain. Most populous were the settlements along New Mexico's upper Rio Grande Valley; the main town, Santa Fe, was over 200 years old and contained 4,635 residents in 1860. Farther down the Rio Grande was El Paso, nearly as old but much smaller, and, to the west in present-day

Map 16.6 The Settlement of the Pacific Slope, 1860–1890

In 1860 the settlement of the Pacific slope was remarkably uneven — fully underway in northern California and scarcely begun anywhere else. By 1890 a new pattern had begun to emerge, with the swift growth of southern California foreshadowed and the settlement of the Pacific Northwest well launched.

Arizona, Tucson, an old presidio, or garrison, town. At the western end of this Hispanic crescent, in California, a Spanish-speaking population was spread thinly in the old presidio towns along the coast and on a patchwork of great ranches.

The economy of this Hispanic crescent was pastoral, consisting primarily of cattle and sheep ranching. In south Texas there were family-run ranches. Everywhere else the social order was highly stratified. At the top stood an elite — the dons occupying royal land grants — who were proudly Spanish and devoted to the traditional life of a landed aristocracy. Below them, with little in between, was a laboring class of servants, artisans, vaqueros (cowboys), and farm hands. New Mexico also contained a large mestizo population — people of mixed Hispanic and Indian blood, a Spanish-speaking and Catholic peasantry, but still faithful to the village life and farming methods of their Pueblo heritage.

Pueblo Indians, although their dominance over the Rio Grande Valley had long passed, still occupied much of the region, living in the old ways in adobe villages, rendering the New Mexico countryside a patchwork of Hispanic and Pueblo settlements. To the north a vibrant new tribe, the Navajos, had taken shape, warriors like the Apaches from whom they descended but also skilled at crafts and sheep raising.

New Mexico was one place where European and Native American cultures managed a successful, if uneasy, coexistence and where the Indian inhabi-

tants were equipped to hold their own against the Anglo challenge. In California, by contrast, the Hispanic occupation had been harder on the indigenous hunter-gatherer peoples, undermining their tribal structure, reducing them to forced labor, and making them easy prey for the aggressive Anglo miners and settlers, who, in short order, nearly wiped out California's once numerous Indian population.

Anglo-Hispanic Conflict. The fate of the Hispanic Southwest after its incorporation into the United States in 1848 depended on the rate of Anglo immigration. In New Mexico, which remained off the beaten track even after the railroads arrived in the 1880s, the Santa Fe elite more than held its own, incorporating the Anglo newcomers into Hispanic society through intermarriage and business partnerships. In California, however, expropriation of the great ranches was relentless, even though the 1848 treaty with Mexico had recognized the property rights of the *Californios* and had made them U.S. citizens. Around San Francisco the great ranches disappeared almost in a puff of smoke. Farther south, where Anglos were slow to arrive, the dons held on longer, but by the 1880s just a handful of the original Hispanic families still retained their Mexican land grants.

The New Mexico peasants found themselves equally embattled. Crucial to their livelihood was the grazing of livestock on communal lands. But these were customary rights that could not withstand legal challenge when Anglo ranchers established title and began putting up fences. The peasants responded as best they could. Their subsistence economy relied on a division of labor that gave women a productive role in the village economy. Women tended the small gardens, engaged in village bartering, and maintained the households. With the loss of the communal lands, the men began migrating seasonally to the Colorado mines and sugar-beet fields, earning dollars while leaving the village economy in their wives' hands.

Elsewhere, hard-pressed Hispanics struck back for what they considered rightfully theirs. When Anglo ranchers began to fence in communal lands in San Miguel County, the New Mexicans long settled there, *los pobres* (the poor ones), organized themselves into masked night-riding raiders and in 1889 mounted an effective campaign of harassment against the interlopers. After 1900, when Anglo farmers swarmed into south Texas, the displaced Tejanos (Hispanic residents of Texas) responded with sporadic but persistent night-riding attacks. Much of the raiding by Mexican "bandits" from across the border in the years before World War I was really more in the nature of a civil war by embittered Hispanics who had lived north of the Rio Grande for generations (see Chapter 21).

But they, like the New Mexico villagers who became seasonal wage laborers, could not avoid being driven into the ranks of a Mexican American working class as the Anglo economy developed. This same development also began to attract increasing numbers of immigrants from Mexico itself.

Mexican Migrants. All along the Southwest borderlands, economic activity picked up in the late nineteenth century. Railroads were being built, copper mines opening in Arizona, cotton and vegetable agriculture spreading in south Texas, and orchards being planted in southern California. In Texas the Hispanic population increased from about 20,000 in 1850 to 165,000 in 1900. Some came as contract workers for railway gangs and harvest crews; virtually all were relegated to the lowest-paying and most back-breaking work; and everywhere they were discriminated against by Anglo employers and workers.

The galloping economic development that drew Mexican migrants also accounted for the exceptionally high rate of European immigration to the West. One-third of California's population was foreign-born, more than twice the level for the country as a whole. Most numerous were the Irish, followed by the Germans and British. But there was another group unique to the West — the Chinese.

The Chinese Migration. Attracted initially by the California gold rush, 200,000 Chinese came to the United States between 1850 and 1880. In those years they constituted a considerable minority of

Mexican Miners

When large-scale mining began to develop in Arizona and New Mexico in the late nineteenth century, Mexicans crossed the border to earn Yankee dollars. In this unidentified photograph from the 1890s, the men are wearing traditional clothing, indicating perhaps that they are recent arrivals at the mine. Division of Cultural Resource, Wyoming Department of Commerce.

California's population — around 9 percent — but because virtually all were actively employed, they represented probably a quarter of the state's labor force. Elsewhere in the West, at the crest of mining activity, their numbers could surge remarkably, to over 25 percent of Idaho's population in 1870, for example.

The arrival of the Chinese was part of a worldwide Asian migration that had begun in the mid-nineteenth century. Driven by poverty, the Chinese went to Australia, Hawaii, and Latin America; Indians to Fiji and South Africa; and Javanese to Dutch colonies in the Caribbean. Most of these Asians migrated as **indentured servants**, which in effect made them the property of others. In America, however, indentured servitude was no longer lawful — by the 1820s state courts were banning it as involuntary servitude — so the Chinese came as free workers, going into debt for their passage money but not surrendering their personal freedom or right to choose their employers.

Once in America, Chinese immigrants normally entered the orbit of the Six Companies, a powerful confederation of Chinese merchants in San Francisco's Chinatown. Most of the arrivals were young men eager to earn a stake and return to their native Cantonese villages. The few Chinese women — the male-female ratio was thirteen to one — worked mostly as servants and prostitutes, sad victims of the desperate poverty that drove the Chinese to America. Some were sold by impoverished parents; others were enticed or kidnapped by procurers and transported to America.

Until the early 1860s, when surface mining played out, Chinese men labored mainly in the California gold fields — as prospectors where white miners permitted it and as laborers and cooks where they did not. Then, when construction began on the transcontinental railroad, the Central Pacific hired Chinese workers. Eventually they constituted four-fifths of the railroad's labor force, doing most of the pick-and-shovel work laying the track across the Sierra Nevada. Many were recruited by labor agents and worked in labor gangs run by "China bosses," who not only supervised but fed, housed, paid, and often cheated them.

When the transcontinental railroad was completed in 1869, the Chinese scattered. Some stayed in railroad construction gangs, while others labored in California's Central Valley as agricultural workers or, if they were lucky, became small farmers and orchardists. The mining districts of Idaho, Montana, and Colorado also attracted large numbers of Chinese, but according to the 1880 census, nearly three-quarters remained in California. "Wherever we put them, we found them good," remarked Charles Crocker, one of the promoters of the Central Pacific. "Their orderly and industrious habits make them a very desirable class of immigrants."

Anti-Chinese Agitation. White workers did not share Crocker's enthusiasm. Elsewhere in the country, racism was directed against African Americans; in California, where there were few blacks, it found a target in the Chinese. "They practice all the unnameable vices of the East," wrote the young journalist Henry George. "They are utter heathens, treacherous, sensual, cowardly and cruel." Sadly, this vicious racism was intertwined with labor's republican ideals. The Chinese, argued George, would "make nabobs and princes of our capitalists, and crush our working classes into the dust . . . substitut[ing] . . . a population of serfs and their masters for that population of intelligent freemen who are our glory and our strength."

The anti-Chinese frenzy climaxed in San Francisco in the late 1870s when mobs ruled the streets, at one point threatening to burn the docks of the Pacific Mail Steamship Company where the Chinese immigrants debarked. The fiercest agitator, an Irish teamster named Denis Kearney, quickly became a dominant figure in the California labor movement. Under the slogan "The Chinese Must Go!" Kearney led a Workingmen's Party against the state's major parties. Democrats and Republicans jumped on the bandwagon, joining together in 1879 to write a new state constitution replete with anti-Chinese provisions and pressuring Washington to take up the issue. In 1882 Congress passed the Chinese Exclusion Act, which barred further entry of Chinese laborers into the country.

The injustice of this law — no other nationality was similarly targeted — rankled the Chinese. Why us, protested one woman to a federal agent, and not the Irish, "who were always drunk and fighting?" Merchants and American-born Chinese, who were free to come and go, routinely registered a newly born son after each trip, enabling many an unrelated "paper son" to enter the country. Even so, resourceful as the Chinese were at evading the exclusion law, the flow of immigrants slowed to a trickle.

But the job opportunities that had attracted the Chinese to America did not subside. If anything, the West's agricultural development intensified the demand for cheap labor, especially in California, which was shifting from wheat, the state's first great cash crop, to fruits and vegetables.

Building the Central Pacific

Chinese laborers in 1867 at work on the great trestle spanning the canyon at Secrettown in the Sierra Nevada. University of California at Berkeley, Bancroft Library.

Such intensive agriculture required lots of workers — stoop labor, meagerly paid, and mostly seasonal. This was not, as one San Francisco journalist put it, "white men's work." That ugly phrase serves as a touchstone for California agricultural labor as it would thereafter develop — a kind of caste labor system, always drawing some downtrodden, footloose whites, yet basically defined along color lines.

But if not the Chinese, then who? First, Japanese immigrants, who came in increasing numbers and by the early twentieth century constituted half of the state's agricultural labor force. Then, when anti-Japanese agitation closed off that population flow in 1908, Mexico became the next, essentially permanent, source of migratory workers for California's booming commercial agriculture.

The irony of the state's social evolution is painful to behold. Here was California, a land of limitless opportunity, boastful of its democratic egalitarianism, and yet simultaneously, and from its very birth, a racially torn society, at once exploiting and despising the Hispanic and Asian minorities whose hard labor helped make California the enviable land it was.

Golden California

Life in California contained all that the modern world of 1890 had to offer — cosmopolitan San Francisco, comfortable travel, colleges and universities, even resident painters and writers. Yet California was still remote from the rest of America, a long journey away and, of course, differently and spectacularly endowed by nature. Location, environment, and history all conspired to set California somewhat apart from the American nation. In certain ways so did the Californians.

Creating a California Culture. What Californians yearned for was a cultural tradition of their own. Closest to hand was the bonanza era of the forty-niners, captured on paper by Samuel Clemens. Clemens left his native Missouri for Nevada in 1861. He did a bit of prospecting, worked as a reporter, and adopted the pen name Mark Twain. In 1864 he arrived in San Francisco, where he became a newspaper columnist writing about what he pronounced "the livest, heartiest community on our continent."

Listening to the old miners in Angel's Camp in 1865, Twain jotted down one tale in his notebook, as follows:

Coleman with his jumping frog—bet stranger $50—stranger had no frog, and C. got him one:—in the meantime stranger filled C's frog full of shot and he couldn't jump. The stranger's frog won.

In Twain's hands, this fragment was transformed into a tall tale that caught the imagination of the country and made his reputation as a humorist. "The Celebrated Jumping Frog of Calaveras County" somehow encapsulated the entire world of make-or-break optimism in the mining camps.

In such short stories as "The Luck of Roaring Camp" and "The Outcasts of Poker Flat," Twain's fellow San Franciscan Bret Harte developed this theme in a more literary fashion and firmly implanted it in California's memory. But this past was too raw, too suggestive of the tattered beginnings of so many of the state's leading citizens—in short too disreputable—for an up-and-coming society.

Then in 1884 Helen Hunt Jackson published her novel *Ramona.* In this story of a half-Indian girl caught between two cultures, Jackson intended to advance the cause of the Native Americans, but she placed her tale in the evocative context of early California, and that rang a bell. By then the missions planted by the Catholic Church had been long abandoned. The padres were wholly forgotten, their Indian converts scattered and in dire poverty. Now that lost world of "sun, silence and adobe" became all the rage. Sentimental novels and histories appeared in abundance. There was a movement to restore the missions. Many communities began to stage Spanish fiestas, and the mission style of architecture enjoyed a great vogue among developers.

In its Spanish past California found the cultural traditions it needed. The same kind of discovery was taking place elsewhere in the Southwest, although in the case of Santa Fe and Taos there really were live Hispanic roots to celebrate.

Land of Sunshine. All this enthusiasm was strongly tinged with commercialism. And so was a second distinctive feature of California's development—the exploitation of its climate. While northern California boomed, the southern part of the state remained thinly populated, too dry for anything but grazing and some chancy wheat growing. What it did have, however, was an abundance of sunshine. At the beginning of the 1880s there burst upon the country amazing news of the charms of southern California. "There is not any malaria, hay fever, loss of appetite, or languor in the air; nor any thunder, lightning, mad dogs . . . or cold snaps." This publicity was mostly the work of the Southern Pacific Railroad, which had reached Los Angeles in 1876 and was eager for business.

When the Santa Fe Railroad arrived in 1885, a furious rate war broke out. One-way fares from Chicago or St. Louis to Los Angeles dropped to $25 or less. Thousands of people, mostly midwesterners, poured in. A dizzying real estate boom developed, along with the frantic building of such resort hotels as San Diego's opulent Hotel del Coronado. Los Angeles County, which had less than 3 percent of the state's population in 1870, had 12 percent by 1900. By then southern California had firmly established itself as the land of sunshine. It had found a way to translate climate into riches.

That was what California wheat farmers discovered when they began to convert to "specialty" crops. Some of these, like the peaches and pears grown in the Sierra foothills, competed with crops elsewhere in the country, but others—oranges, almonds, raisins—required California's Mediterranean climate. By 1910, the state had essentially abandoned wheat, its original money crop, and was shipping vast quantities of fruit across the country. Although heavily dependent on migrant labor—hence its reputation as an "industrial" form of agriculture—California fruit farming was actually carried on in mostly small-scale units because it required intensive, hands-on cultivation. Indeed, the vineyards around Fresno, from whence came virtually all the nation's raisins, began as a planned community, sold off in 20-acre units. What perhaps came closer to an industrial model were the big cooperatives set up by these modest-sized producers to market and brand

John Muir

John Muir spent a lifetime studying, glorying in, and defending the California wilderness. This arresting photograph (c. 1902) catches him as he would have wanted to be remembered — a man at home with nature. Library of Congress.

their crops. For most Americans, the taste of California came via Sunkist oranges, Sun Maid raisins, and Blue Diamond almonds. And, as an added dividend, it was this same clever marketing that persuaded Americans that fruit was an everyday food, not a luxury saved for birthdays and Christmas.

John Muir and the Great Outdoors. That California was specially favored by nature some Californians knew even as the great stands of redwoods were being hacked down, the streams polluted, and the hills torn apart by reckless hydraulic mining. Back in 1864 influential Americans who had visited it prevailed on Congress to grant to the state of California "the Cleft, or Gorge in the granite peak of the Sierra Nevada Mountain, known as Yosemite Valley," which would be reserved "for public pleasuring, resort, and recreation." When the young naturalist John Muir arrived in California four years later, he headed straight for Yosemite. Its "grandeur . . . comes as an endless revelation," he wrote.

Muir's environmentalism was at once scientific and romantic. An exacting researcher, he demonstrated for the first time that Yosemite was the product of glacial action (and went on to study glaciers around the world). California scientists who accepted Muir's thesis were persuaded also by his concept of wilderness as a laboratory and joined him against "despoiling gain-seekers . . . eagerly trying to make everything immediately and selfishly commercial." Married to Muir's scientific appeal, however, was a powerful dose of romanticism, sanctifying nature as sacred space and elevating its defense into a kind of religious crusade, a battle "between landscape righteousness and the devil." One result of Muir's zeal was the creation of California's national parks in 1890 — Yosemite, Sequoia, and General Grant (later part of King's Canyon). Another was a campaign launched immediately afterward to mandate a system of national forest reserves. And a third was the formation in 1892 of the Sierra Club, which became a powerful voice for the defenders of California's wilderness.

They won some and lost some. Advocates of water-resource development insisted that California's irrigated agriculture and thirsty cities could not grow without tapping the abundant snow pack of the Sierra Nevada. By the turn of the century, Los Angeles faced a water crisis that threatened its growth. The answer was a 238-mile aqueduct to the Owens River in the southern Sierra. A bitter controversy blew up over this immense project, driven by the resistance of local residents to the flooding of the beautiful Owens Valley. More painful for John Muir and his preservationist allies was their failure to save the Hetch Hetchy Valley — "one of nature's rarest and most precious mountain temples," in Muir's words — on the northern edge of Yosemite National Park. After years of controversy the federal government in 1913 approved the damming of Hetch Hetchy's Tuolumne River to serve the water needs of San Francisco.

When the stakes became high enough, nature preservationists like John Muir generally came out on the short end. Even so, something original and distinctive had been added to California's heritage — the linking of a society's well-being with the protection of its natural environment. This realization, in turn, said something important about the nation's relationship to the West. If the urge to conquer and exploit persisted, at least it was now tempered by a sense that nature's bounty was not limitless. And this, more than any announcement by the U.S. census that a "frontier line" no longer existed, registered the country's acceptance that the age of heedless westward expansion had ended.

➤ Why is mining the key to understanding the settlement of the Far West?

➤ In what ways are the experiences of Hispanics and Chinese in the Far West similar? In what ways are they different?

➤ Why can we speak of a distinctly California history in the late nineteenth century?

SUMMARY

In this chapter, we trace the final stages of the Euro-American occupation of the continental United States, now strongly driven by the nation's industrial development. Factories needed the West's mineral resources; urbanites depended on its agricultural products; and, from railroads to barbed wire, the implements of industrialism accelerated the pace of conquest. The patterns of settlement, however, differed in the two great ecological regions that make up the trans-Mississippi West.

East of the Rockies, the semiarid Great Plains remained in 1860 the ancestral home to nomadic Indian tribes, still living in a vibrant society based on the horse and the buffalo. With the U.S. military leading the way, cattle ranchers and homesteaders in short order displaced the Indians and domesticated the Great Plains. Despite fierce resistance, by 1890 the Indians had been crowded onto reservations and forced to abandon their tribal ways of life.

Beyond the Rockies, where the terrain was largely arid and uninhabitable, occupation took the form of islands of settlement rather than progressive occupation along a broad frontier that had prevailed on the Great Plains. And while arable land had been the lure for settlers up to that point, what drove settlement in the Far West was the discovery of mineral wealth.

Also distinctive of Far Western development was its dominance by a single state, California, which anchored both the crescent of Hispanic settlement across the Southwest and the Pacific slope region stretching to the Canadian border. The discovery of gold set off a huge migration that overwhelmed the thinly spread Hispanic population and transformed California into a populous state with a large urban sector centered in San Francisco. California developed a distinctive culture that capitalized on its rediscovered Hispanic heritage and its climate and natural environment. California also capitalized on the Chinese, Japanese, and Mexicans who provided the state's cheap labor, infusing a dark streak of racism into its otherwise sunny culture.

Connections: The American West

As readers of earlier chapters of this text know, there were many "Wests" in American history. Colonists considered the Appalachians the West; for Jeffersonians, it was the Ohio Valley; for Jacksonians, the Mississippi Valley. The land beyond the Mississippi Valley — the Great Plains, the Rockies, and the Pacific slope discussed in this chapter — constitutes the last American West, the region that remains, even to readers of this text, the country's West. What distinguishes the settlement of this last American West is that it coincided with, and was driven by, America's industrial revolution. As we observe in the part opener (p. 485):

It was eastern demand for new sources of food and mineral resources that drove the final surge of western settlement and integrated the Great Plains and Far West into the nation's industrializing economy.

Integration, of course, worked in both directions, so that students should bear in mind as they read Chapters 17 and 18 the West's role in fostering the nation's industrializing economy and urban growth. The West also had a distinctive impact on American politics, driving the Populist movement in the 1890s (Chapter 19) and strongly influencing progressivism after 1900 (Chapter 20). In the twentieth century the West becomes increasingly absorbed in the national narrative, but students should be watchful for where its distinctive role pops up, as, for example, Hollywood in the 1920s (Chapter 23) and as a site for the defense industry during World War II (Chapter 25).

CHAPTER REVIEW QUESTIONS

➤ Do you think this chapter successfully makes the case that the final phases of the frontier movement should be seen as an extension of American industrialization?

➤ Would it be possible to write an account of the settlement of the Great Plains and Far West without taking account of the natural environment?

➤ Although frontier history is generally treated as an Anglo-American story, in the Far West it is much more about ethnic diversity. Why is that?

TIMELINE

1849	California gold rush
	Chinese migration begins
1862	Homestead Act
1864	Yosemite Valley reserved as public park
1865	Long Drive of Texas longhorns begins
1867	Patrons of Husbandry (the Grange) founded
	U.S. government adopts reservation policy for Plains Indians
1868	Indian treaty confirms Sioux rights to Powder River hunting grounds
1869	Union Pacific–Central Pacific transcontinental railroad completed
1875	Sioux ordered to vacate Powder River hunting grounds; war breaks out
1876	Battle of Little Big Horn
1877	San Francisco anti-Chinese riots
1879	Exoduster migration to Kansas
1882	Chinese Exclusion Act
1884	Helen Hunt Jackson's novel *Ramona* published
1886	Dry cycle begins on the Great Plains
1887	Dawes Severalty Act
1889	Oklahoma opened to white settlement
1890	Indian massacre at Wounded Knee, South Dakota
	U.S. census declares end of the frontier

FOR FURTHER EXPLORATION

The starting point for western history is Frederick Jackson Turner's famous essay, "The Significance of the Frontier in American History" (1893), reprinted in Ray A. Billington, ed., *Frontier and Section: Selected Essays of Frederick Jackson Turner* (1961). In recent years there has been a reaction against Turnerian scholarship for being Eurocentric — for seeing western history only through the eyes of frontiersmen and settlers — and for masking the rapacious and environmentally destructive underside of western settlement. Patricia N. Limerick's skillfully argued *The Legacy of Conquest* (1987) opened the debate. Richard White's *"It's Your Misfortune and None of My Own": A New History of the American West* (1991) provides the fullest synthesis. For some of the most debated issues, see the essays in Clyde A. Milner, ed., *A New Significance: Re-envisioning the History of the American West* (1996). On women's experiences — another primary concern of the new scholarship — a useful introduction is Susan Armitage and Elizabeth Jameson, eds., *The Women's West* (1987). On the Plains Indians, a lively account is Robert M. Utley, *The Indian Frontier of the American West* (1984). The ecological impact of Plains settlement is subtly probed in Frieda Knobloch, *The Culture of Wilderness: Agriculture as Colonization in the American West* (1996). One facet of this subject is reconsidered in Andrew C. Isenberg, *The Destruction of the Bison: An Environmental History* (2000). On the integration of the Plains economy with the wider world, an especially rich book is William Cronon, *Nature's Metropolis: Chicago and the Great West* (1991). Sarah Deutsch, *No Separate Refuge* (1987), offers an imaginative treatment of the New Mexican peasantry. On the Asian migration to America, the best introduction is Ron Takaki, *Strangers from a Different Shore* (1989). David Vaught, *Cultivating California: Growers, Specialty Crops, and Labor, 1875–1920* (1999), offers a fresh interpretation of California's agricultural development, especially debunking the widely held view that California farms were "factories in the field." Kevin Starr, *California and the American Dream, 1850–1915* (1973), provides a full account of the emergence of a distinctive California culture. A comprehensive Web site with many links is **www.americanwest.com**.

TEST YOUR KNOWLEDGE

To assess your command of the material in this chapter, see the Online Study Guide at **bedfordstmartins.com/henretta**.

For Web sites, images, and documents related to topics and places in this chapter, visit **bedfordstmartins.com/makehistory**.

17 Capital and Labor in the Age of Enterprise

1877–1900

THE YEAR THAT RECONSTRUCTION ENDED, 1877, also marked the first great labor crisis of American industrial history. Much like the dot.com bust of our own time, the post–Civil War railroad boom collapsed after the Panic of 1873. Railroad building ground to a halt, workers lost their jobs, and wages fell. On July 16, 1877, railroad workers went on strike to protest a wage cut at the Baltimore and Ohio Railroad. In towns along the B&O tracks, crowds cheered as the strikers attacked company property and prevented trains from running. The strike rippled across the country, reaching as far as the Pacific Coast and provoking rioting in San Francisco. The Pennsylvania Railroad's roundhouse in Pittsburgh went up in flames on July 21, and at many rail centers rioters and looters roamed freely. Only the arrival of federal troops restored order. On August 15 President Rutherford B. Hayes wrote in his diary, "The strikers have been put down *by force*." The Great Strike of 1877 had been crushed, but only after raising the specter of social revolution.

And then recovery came. Within months railroad building resumed. The economy boomed. In the next fifteen years, the output of manufactured goods increased by over 150 percent. Confidence in the nation's industrial future rebounded. "Upon [material progress] is founded all other progress," asserted a railroad president in 1888. "Can there be any

◀ **Homestead at Twilight**

In this evocative painting Aaron Henry Gorson (1872–1933) looks across the Monongahela River at Andrew Carnegie's great steel mill, a symbol of America's industrial prowess but also, as the clouds of smoke lighting the sky suggest, a major source of the Pittsburgh district's polluted air. Westmorland Museum of Art.

doubt that cheapening the cost of necessaries and conveniences of life is the most powerful agent of civilization and progress?"

The rail magnate's boast represents the confident face of America's industrial revolution. President Hayes's anxious diary entries suggest a darker side. After 1877 armories appeared in cities across the country. They were fortresses designed to withstand assault by future strikers and rioters. It was a paradox of the nation's industrial history that an economy celebrated for its dynamism and inventiveness was also brutally indifferent to the many who fell by the wayside and hence an economy never secure, never free of social conflict.

Industrial Capitalism Triumphant

Economic historians speak of the late nineteenth century as the age of the Great Deflation, an era when worldwide prices fell steadily. Falling prices normally signal economic stagnation; there is not enough demand for available goods and services. In England, a mature industrial power, the Great Deflation did indeed signal economic decline. That was not the case in the United States. In fact, industrial expansion here went into high gear during the Great Deflation. Manufacturing efficiencies enabled American firms to cut prices and yet earn profits and afford still better equipment. Real income for Americans went up dramatically, increasing by nearly 50 percent (from $388 to $573 per year) between 1877 and 1900. The industrializing economy was a wealth-creating machine beyond anything the world had ever seen (Figure 17.1).

The Age of Steel

By the 1870s, factories were a familiar sight in America. But the goods they produced — textiles, shoes, paper, and furniture — mainly replaced articles made at home or by individual artisans. Early manufacturing was really an extension of the pre-industrial economy. Gradually, however, a different kind of demand developed as the country's economy surged. Railroads needed locomotives; new factories needed machinery; cities needed trolley lines, sanitation systems, and commercial buildings. Railroad equipment, machinery, and construction materials were *capital goods*, that is, goods that added to the nation's productive capacity.

Central to the capital-goods sector was a technological revolution in steel making. The country already had a large iron industry, turning out a product called wrought iron, a malleable metal easily worked by blacksmiths and farmers. But wrought iron was ill suited for industrial uses; in particular, it did not stand up under heavy use as railway track. Additionally, wrought iron was expensive because it could be produced only in small batches by skilled puddlers. In 1856 the British inventor Henry Bessemer designed a furnace — the Bessemer converter — that refined raw pig iron into an essentially new product: steel, a metal more durable than wrought iron and, on top of that, much cheaper to produce because the process required virtually no hands-on labor. Bessemer's invention attracted many users, but it was Andrew Carnegie who fully exploited its potential.

Andrew Carnegie and American Steel. Carnegie's was the great American success story. He arrived from Scotland in 1848 at the age of twelve with his

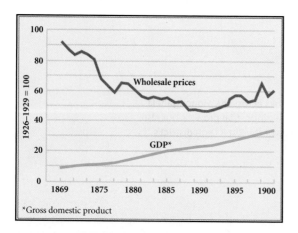

FIGURE 17.1 Business Activity and Wholesale Prices, 1869–1900

This graph shows the key feature of the performance of the late-nineteenth-century economy: While output was booming, the price of goods was falling.

Bessemer Converter, Bethlehem Works, Steelton, Pennsylvania, 1885

Workers for Bethlehem Steel in Steelton, Pennsylvania, posed for this 1885 photograph with a Bessemer converter. The late nineteenth century in America came to be known as "America's Age of Steel," thanks to the increased steel production that the Bessemer converter helped generate. Hagley Museum and Library.

poverty-stricken family. He became a telegraph operator, and then went to work for the Pennsylvania Railroad and rapidly scaled the managerial ladder. In 1865, having amassed a fortune in wartime speculation, Carnegie struck out on his own as an iron manufacturer. His main customers were his network of former associates in the railroad business.

In 1872 Carnegie erected a massive steel mill outside Pittsburgh, with the Bessemer converter as its centerpiece. Ferrous metallurgy involves three steps: blast furnaces smelt ore into pig iron; the pig iron is refined into useable metal, either wrought iron or steel; finally, the refined metal is stamped or rolled into desired shapes for purchasers. The Bessemer converter broke a bottleneck at the refining stage, enabling Carnegie's engineers to construct larger blast furnaces and faster rolling mills, and design an integrated plant that achieved continuous operation: Iron ore entered the blast furnaces at one end and came out the other end as finished steel rails. Carnegie's new plant became a model for the industry, setting in motion the replacement of the iron mills that had once dotted western Pennsylvania by giant steel mills.

The United States was blessed with rich mineral resources that enabled the steel industry to capitalize on Carnegie's technological breakthroughs. From the great Mesabi range in northern Minnesota, iron ore came down the Great Lakes by ship in vast quantities. The other key ingredient, coal, arrived from the great Appalachian field that stretched from Pennsylvania to Alabama. A minor enterprise before the Civil War, coal production doubled every decade after 1870, exceeding 400 million tons a year by 1910.

As steam engines became the nation's energy workhorses, prodigious amounts of coal began to

Andrew Carnegie

Carnegie was born in poverty in Scotland. He clawed his way up in America, via his Pittsburgh steel mills, to fabulous wealth. Once he got there, Carnegie liked to think of himself as a lord of the manor or, in his case, "laird" of a grand estate in Scotland. In this photograph, taken in his retirement, he is properly attired for that role and properly attended by a handsome collie.

Holton-Deutsch Collection/Corbis.

be consumed by railroads and factories. Industries previously dependent on waterpower rapidly converted to steam. The turbine, utilizing continuous rotation rather than the steam engine's back-and-forth piston motion, marked another major advance during the 1880s. With the coupling of the steam turbine to the electric generator, the nation's energy revolution was completed, and after 1900 America's factories began a massive conversion to electric power.

The Railroad Boom

Although water transportation was perfectly adequate for the country's needs before the Civil War, it was love at first sight when locomotives arrived from Britain in the early 1830s. Americans were impatient for the year-round, on-time service not achievable by canal barges and riverboats. By 1860, as a network of tracks crisscrossed the eastern half of the country, the railroad clearly was on the way to being industrial America's mode of transportation.

Constructing the Railroads. The question was, who would pay for it? Railroads could be state enterprises, like the canals, or they could be financed by private investors. Unlike most European countries, the United States chose free enterprise. Even so, government played a big role. Eager for the economic benefits, many states and localities lured railroads with offers of financial aid, mainly by buying railroad bonds. Land grants were the principal means by which the federal government encouraged interregional rail construction.

The most important boost, however, was not money or land but a legal form of organization—the corporation—that enabled private capital to be raised in prodigious amounts. Investors who bought stock in the railroads enjoyed *limited liability:* They risked only the money they had invested; they were not personally liable for the railroad's debts. A corporation could also borrow money by issuing interest-bearing bonds, which was how the railroads actually raised most of the money they needed.

Railroad building generally was handed over to construction companies, which, despite the name, were primarily financial structures. Hiring contractors and suppliers often involved persuading them to accept the railroad's bonds as payment and, when that failed, wheeling and dealing to raise cash by selling or borrowing on the bonds. The construction companies were notoriously corrupt. In the worst case, the Union Pacific's Credit Mobilier, probably half the construction funds was the pocketed by the promoters.

The railroad business was not for the faint of heart. Most successful were promoters with the best access to capital, such as John Murray Forbes, a great Boston merchant in the China trade who developed the Chicago, Burlington, and Quincy Railroad in the Midwest; or Cornelius Vanderbilt, who started with the fortune he had made in the steamboat business. Vanderbilt was primarily a consolidator, linking previously independent lines and ultimately, via his New York Central, providing unified railroad service between New York City and Chicago. James J. Hill, who without federal subsidy made the Great Northern into the best of the

Wall Street: Gould's Private Bowling Alley

This 1882 cartoon testifies vividly to Jay Gould's unsavory reputation as a financial manipulator, bowling over his adversaries with Trickery and False Reports and keeping score of his ill-gotten gains on the slate at lower right. Granger Collection.

transcontinental railroads, was certainly the nation's champion railroad builder. In contrast Jay Gould, who at various times controlled the Erie, Wabash, Union Pacific, and Missouri Pacific railroads, always remained a stock market speculator at heart. But even Gould, although he rigged stock prices and looted his properties, made a positive contribution. By throwing his weak railroads against better-established operators (in hopes of being bought out), he forced down rates and benefited shippers. A gifted strategist, Gould was an early promoter of integrated railroads, the catalyst prompting Vanderbilt's creation of the New York Central.

Railroad development in the United States was often sordid, fiercely competitive, and subject to boom and bust. Yet promoters raised vast sums of capital and built a network bigger than that of the rest of the world combined. By 1900 virtually no corner of the country lacked rail service.

The Railway System. Along with this prodigious growth came increasing efficiency. The early railroads, built by competing local companies, had been a jumble of discontinuous segments. Gauges of track — the width between the rails — varied widely, and at terminal points railroads were not connected. As late as 1880, goods could not be shipped through from Massachusetts to South Carolina. Eight times along the way, freight cars had to be emptied and their contents transferred to other cars across a river or at a different terminal.

In 1883 the railroads rebelled against the jumble of local times that made scheduling a nightmare and, acting on their own, divided the country into the standard time zones still in use (Map 17.1). By the end of the 1880s, a standard track gauge (4 feet, 8½ inches) had been adopted everywhere. Fast-freight firms and standard accounting procedures enabled shippers to move goods without breaks in transit, transfers between cars, or the other delays that had once bedeviled them.

At the same time railroad technology was advancing. Durable steel rails permitted heavier traffic. Locomotives became more powerful and capable of pulling more freight cars. To control the greater mass being hauled, the inventor George Westinghouse perfected the automatic coupler, the air brake, and the friction gear for starting and stopping a long line of cars. Costs per ton-mile fell by 50 percent between 1870 and 1890, resulting in a steady drop in freight rates for shippers.

The railroads fully met the transportation needs of the maturing industrial economy. For investors, however, the costs of freewheeling competition and unrestrained growth were painfully high. Many railroads were saddled with huge debts from the extravagant construction era; about a fifth of railroad bonds failed to pay interest even in a good year like 1889. When the economy turned bad, as it did in 1893, a third of the industry went into bankruptcy.

Out of the rubble came a massive railroad reorganization. This was primarily the handiwork of

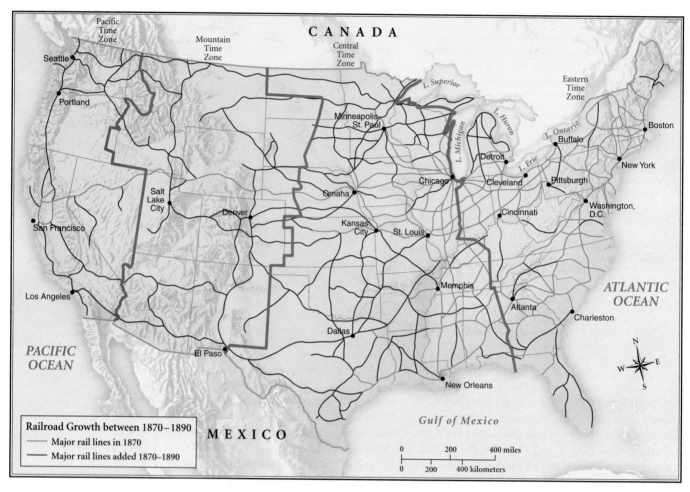

MAP 17.1   The Expansion of the Railroad System, 1870–1890

In 1870 the nation had 53,000 miles of rail track; in 1890 it had 167,000 miles. That burst of construction essentially completed the nation's rail network, although there would be additional expansion for the next two decades. The main areas of growth were in the South and west of the Mississippi. The time zones introduced in 1883 are marked by the gray lines.

Wall Street investment banks such as J. P. Morgan & Co. and Kuhn, Loeb & Co., whose main role had been to market railroad stocks and bonds. When railroads failed, the investment bankers stepped in to pick up the pieces. They persuaded investors to accept lower interest rates or put up more money. They eased competitive pressures by consolidating rivals. By the early twentieth century, half a dozen great regional systems had emerged, and the nerve center of American railroading had shifted to Wall Street.

Large-Scale Enterprise

Until well into the industrial age, all but a few manufacturers operated on a small scale, producing mostly for nearby markets. Then, after the Civil War, big business arrived. "Combinations of capital on a scale hitherto wholly unprecedented constitute one of the remarkable features of modern business methods," the economist David A. Wells wrote in 1889. He could see "no other way in which the work of production and distribution can be prosecuted." What was there about the nation's economy that led to Wells's sense that big business was inevitable?

Most of all, the American market. Unlike Europe, the United States was not carved up by national borders that impeded the flow of goods. The population, swelled by immigration and a high birthrate, jumped from 40 million in 1870 to over 60 million in 1890. People flocked to the cities, and the railroads brought these expanding markets within the reach of distant producers. Nowhere else did manufacturers have so vast and receptive a market for standardized products.

Gustavus Swift and Vertical Integration. How they seized that opportunity is perhaps best revealed in the meatpacking industry. With the opening of the Union Stock Yards in 1865, Chicago became the cattle market for the country. Livestock came in by rail from the Great Plains, was auctioned off at the Chicago stockyards, and then shipped to eastern cities, where, as in the past, the cattle were slaughtered in local "butchertowns". Such an arrangement — a national livestock market but localized processing — adequately met the needs of an exploding urban population and could have done so indefinitely, as was the case, in fact, in Europe.

Gustavus F. Swift, a shrewd Chicago cattle dealer from Massachusetts, saw the future differently. He recognized that livestock lost weight en route to the East and that local slaughterhouses lacked the scale to utilize waste by-products or cut labor costs. If he could keep it fresh in transit, how-

ever, dressed beef could be processed in bulk at the Chicago stockyards. Other packers, like Armour & Co., already did that for smoked and salted pork products that did not require refrigeration. Once his engineers figured out a cooling system, Swift invested in a fleet of refrigerator cars and constructed a central packing plant next to the Chicago stockyards. This was only the beginning of Swift's innovations. In the cities receiving his chilled meat, Swift built his own network of branch houses and a fleet of delivery wagons. He constructed facilities to process the fertilizer, chemicals, and other usable by-products (wasting, it was said, only the pig's squeal). As demand grew, Swift expanded to other stockyard centers, including Kansas City, Fort Worth, and Omaha (Map 17.2).

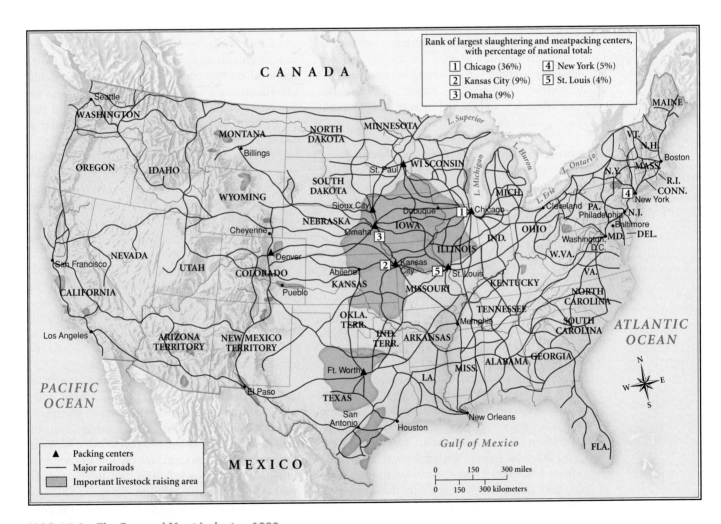

MAP 17.2 The Dressed Meat Industry, 1900

The meatpacking industry clearly shows how transportation, supply, and demand combined to foster the growth of the American industrial economy. The main centers of beef production in 1900 — Chicago, Omaha, Kansas City, and St. Louis — were rail hubs with connections westward to the cattle regions and eastward to cities hungry for cheap supplies of meat. Vertically integrated enterprises sprang from these elements, linked together by an efficient and comprehensive railroad network.

Step by step Swift created a new kind of enterprise—a *vertically integrated firm* capable of handling within its own structure all the functions of an industry. Swift's lead was followed by several big Chicago pork packers. By 1900 five firms, all of them nationally organized and vertically integrated, produced nearly 90 percent of the meat shipped in interstate commerce.

The term that describes this condition is *oligopoly*—market dominance by the few. In meatpacking, that was mostly the result of a radically new form of business. As the vertically integrated firms emerged, the livestock dealers and small slaughterhouses that populated the earlier industry were simply squeezed out or bypassed. But at the consuming end, where competition had to be met, Swift and fellow Chicago packers ruthlessly cut prices and drove independent distributors to the wall. And that brings into focus the second reason for large-scale enterprise—not greater efficiency, but market control. The impulse to drive out the competition, although universally felt, was strongest in bonanza industries, where (a) no player started with any particular advantage and (b) the market was especially chaotic, as, for example, petroleum.

John D. Rockefeller and Monopoly Power.

Rural Americans had long been aware of scattered pools of petroleum oozing up mysteriously from the bowels of the earth. Snake-oil salesmen sometimes added the black stuff to their concoctions. Farmers used it to grease their wagons. Mostly, it was just a nuisance. Then in the 1850s experimenters figured out how to extract kerosene, a clean-burning fuel excellent for domestic heating and lighting. The potential market was vast. All that was needed was the crude oil. One likely place was Titusville, Pennsylvania, where the air stunk from pools of petroleum. In 1859, Edwin L. Drake drilled down and at 69 feet struck oil. Overnight a forest of derricks and makeshift refineries sprung up around Titusville. Much of the refining, however, soon shifted to population centers with better transshipping facilities. Chief among these, once it got a rail connection to the Pennsylvania fields in 1863, was Cleveland, Ohio.

At that time, John D. Rockefeller was an up-and-coming Cleveland grain dealer, twenty-four years old, and doing nicely thanks to the Civil War (which he, like Carnegie and virtually all the budding tycoons of his time, sat out). Rockefeller liked to boast of his humble origins, but in fact he grew up comfortably, even if it was tainted money from his father's escapades as an itinerant quack doctor. Initially skeptical of the wild oil business, Rockefeller soon plunged in. He had a sharp eye for able partners, a genius for finance, and strong nerves. Betting on the industry's future, he borrowed heavily to expand capacity. Within a few years his firm—Standard Oil of Ohio—was Cleveland's leading refiner, and Rockefeller was casting his eyes on the entire industry.

His natural allies were the railroads, who, like him, hated the boom-and-bust of the oil business. What they wanted was predictable, high-volume traffic, and for a good customer like Rockefeller, they offered secret rebates that gave him a leg up on competitors. Then in 1870, hit by another oil bust, the railroads concocted a remarkable scheme. Operating under cloak of the innocent-sounding South Improvement Company, they invited key refiners, including Rockefeller, to join a conspiracy to take over the industry. The participants would cease competing and instead divide up traffic and production. And for the cooperating refiners there was this delicious bonus: rebates not only on their own shipments, but on those of their *rivals*. With this deal in his pocket, Rockefeller offered his Cleveland competitors a stark choice: sell out or die. News of the conspiracy leaked out, and the South Improvement Company collapsed under a hail of denunciations, but not before Rockefeller had taken over the Cleveland industry. With his power-play tactics perfected, he was on his way to national dominance. By the early 1880s Standard Oil controlled 95 percent of the nation's refining capacity. In Washington, outraged politicians began to consider legislation intended to rein in Rockefeller's monopoly.

If countless critics reviled him, Rockefeller didn't seem to mind. A church-going Baptist, Rockefeller was invincibly convinced of his own rectitude; he was doing the Lord's work by bringing order out of industrial chaos. The small fry his company swallowed, he once remarked, should regard Standard Oil as "an angel of mercy."

Rockefeller was not satisfied, in fact, merely to milk his monopoly advantage in refining. Obsessed from the outset with efficiency, he was quick to see the advantages of vertical integration. In this, Rockefeller was like Gustavus Swift, bent on designing a business structure capable of serving a national (and, in Rockefeller's case, international) market. Starting with refining, Standard Oil rapidly added a vast distribution network, oil pipe lines and tankers, and even, despite Rockefeller's distaste for speculative ventures, a big stake in the oil fields.

The Birth of Consumer Marketing.

In retailing, the lure of a mass market brought comparable

Kellogg's Toasted Corn Flakes

Like crackers, sugar, and other nonperishable products, cereal had been traditionally sold in bulk from barrels. In the 1880s the Quaker Oats Company hit on the idea of selling oatmeal in boxes of standard size and weight. A further wrinkle was to process the cereal so that it could be consumed right from the box (with milk) for breakfast. And lo and behold: Kellogg's Corn Flakes! This is one of Kellogg's earliest advertisements. Picture Research Consultants & Archives.

changes. For rural consumers, Montgomery Ward and Sears, Roebuck developed huge mail-order enterprises. From Vermont to California, farm families selected identical goods from catalogues and became part of a nationwide consumer market. In the cities, retailers followed different strategies. The department store, pioneered by John Wanamaker in Philadelphia in 1875, soon became a fixture in downtowns across the country. Alternatively, retailers could reach consumers efficiently by opening a chain of stores, which was the strategy of the Great Atlantic and Pacific Tea Company (A&P) and F. W. Woolworth.

Americans were ready consumers of standardized, mass-marketed goods. Their geographic mobility tended to erase the preference for local

products that shaped European tastes. Moreover, social class in America, though by no means absent, was blurred at the edges and did not call, for example, for class-specific ways of dressing. Foreign visitors often noted that ready-made clothing made it difficult to tell salesgirls from debutantes on city streets.

It was not, however, always smooth going for the innovative national marketers. Shop owners put up stiff resistance, appealing to local pride and sometimes agitating for ordinances to keep Swift and A&P at bay. Nor were standardized goods universally welcomed. Many people were leery, for example, of Swift's Chicago beef. How could it be wholesome weeks later in Boston or Philadelphia? Cheap prices helped, but advertising mattered more.

Modern advertising was born in the late nineteenth century, bringing brand names and a billboard-cluttered urban landscape. By 1900 companies were spending over $90 million a year for space in newspapers and magazines. Advertisements urged readers to bathe with Pears' soap, eat Uneeda biscuits, sew on a Singer machine, and snap pictures with a Kodak camera. The active molding of demand became a major challenge for the managers of America's national firms.

The Managerial Revolution. And so, even more urgently, did the task of controlling such far-flung enterprises. Nothing in the world of small business prepared Swift and other industrial pioneers for this challenge. Fortunately for them, railroaders had already paved the way. A managerial crisis had overtaken the trunk lines as they thrust westward before the Civil War. On a 50-mile road, remarked the Erie executive Daniel C. McCallum in a classic statement of the problem, the superintendent could personally attend to every detail, "and any system, however imperfect, may prove comparatively successful." But 500-mile trunk lines were too big for even the most energetic superintendent to oversee directly. It was in "the want of a system" that lay "the true secret of their failure." Acknowledging that he was working in the dark—"we have no precedent or experience upon which we can fully rely"—McCallum urged that the railroads begin devising the structures, the *system*, that would enable them to control their widespread activities. Step by step, always under the prod of necessity, the trunk lines separated overall management from day-to-day operations, departmentalized operations by function (maintenance of way, rolling stock, traffic), defined lines of communication, and perfected cost-accounting methods enabling managers to assess performance of operating units. By the end of the 1870s, the railroads' managerial crisis had been resolved.

Just in time for emerging industrial firms like Swift's, which, sometimes quite directly, drew on the railroad management model. With few exceptions, vertically integrated firms followed a centralized, functionally departmentalized plan, with a main office housing top executives and departments covering specific areas of activity—purchasing, auditing, production, transportation, or sales. These functionally defined departments provided "middle management," something not seen before in American industry. Although managers of operating units functioned much like earlier factory owners, middle managers undertook entirely new tasks, directing the flow of goods and information through the integrated enterprise. They were key innovators, equivalent in matters of business practice to engineers in improving technology.

By the turn of the century, the hundred largest companies controlled roughly a third of the nation's total productive capacity. The day of small manufacturers had not passed. They still flourished, or at least survived, in many fields. Indeed, places like Philadelphia were hubs of small-scale, diversified industry—textiles, leather goods, **machine tools**—that excelled in what economic historians have called "flexible specialization." But the dominant form of industrial organization had become, and would long remain, large-scale enterprise.

➤ What factors account for the rise of the American steel industry in the late nineteenth century?

➤ Why did the railroad network grow so rapidly after the Civil War? And with what consequences for the country's economic development?

➤ How do you account for the growth of large-scale enterprise in the late nineteenth century?

The World of Work

In a free-enterprise system, profit drives the entrepreneur and produces, at the apex, the multimillionaire Carnegies and Rockefellers. But the industrial order is not populated only by profit makers. It includes—in vastly larger numbers—wage earners. Economic change always affects working people, but rarely as drastically as it did in the late nineteenth century.

Labor Recruits

Industrialization invariably set people in motion. Farm folk migrated to cities. Artisans entered factories (Figure 17.2). An industrial labor force emerged. This happened in the United States as it did in Europe, but with a difference. In the late nineteenth century rural Americans, although

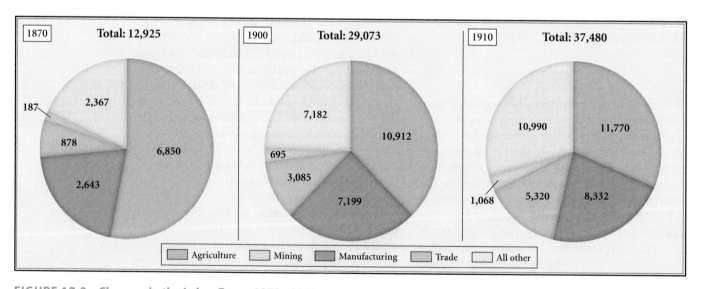

FIGURE 17.2 Changes in the Labor Force, 1870–1910

The numbers represent thousands of people (for example, 12,925 = 12,925,000 workers). They reveal both the enormous increase in the labor force between 1870 and 1910 and the dramatic shift from agriculture to industry and other nonagricultural jobs.

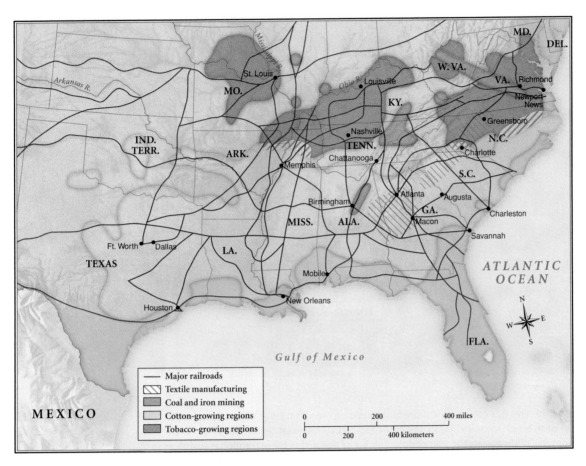

MAP 17.3   The New South, 1900

The economy of the Old South focused on raising staple crops, especially cotton and tobacco. In the New South staple agriculture continued to dominate, but there was marked industrial development as well. Industrial regions evolved, producing textiles, coal and iron, and wood products. By 1900 the South's industrial pattern was well defined.

highly mobile and frequently city-bound, mostly rejected factory work. They lacked the industrial skills for the higher-paid jobs as puddlers, rollers, molders, and machinists, but they did have skills — language, basic literacy, a cultural ease — that made them employable in the multiplying **white-collar** jobs in offices and retail stores.

Southern Labor. So the United States could not rely primarily on its own population for a supply of factory workers, except in the South. There a low-wage industrial sector emerged after Reconstruction as local boosters tried to build a "New South" and catch up with the North. The textile mills that sprang up in the Piedmont country of the Carolinas and Georgia recruited workers from the surrounding hill farms, where people struggled to make ends meet. To attract them mill wages had to exceed farm earnings, but not by much. Paying rock-bottom wages, the new mills had a competitive

advantage over the long-established New England industry — as much as 40 percent lower labor costs in 1897.

The labor system that evolved was based on hiring whole families. "Papa decided he would come because he didn't have nothing much but girls and they had to get out and work like men," recalled one woman. It was not Papa, in fact, but his girls whom the mills wanted to work as spinners and loom tenders. Only they could not be recruited individually: No right-thinking parent would have permitted that. Hiring by families, on the other hand, was already familiar; after all, everyone had been expected to work on the farm. So the family system of mill labor developed, with a labor force that was half female and very young. In the 1880s a quarter of all southern textile workers were under fifteen years of age. In the mill villages workers built close-knit, supportive communities, but for whites only. Although blacks sometimes worked as

Houston's Cotton Depot

After the Civil War cotton agriculture blossomed on the virgin lands of east Texas, and Houston simultaneously blossomed as the region's commercial center. This photograph from the 1890s reveals the tremendous volume of traffic that came through Houston as Texas cotton was unloaded and transshipped to be made into cloth in the mills of the Southeast and across the ocean in Britain. Houston Public Library, Houston Metropolitan Research Center.

day laborers and janitors, they hardly ever got jobs as operatives in the cotton mills. The same was true of James B. Duke's cigarette factories, where machine tending was restricted to white women.

In extractive natural-resource industries, the South's other growth sector, employers recruited with little regard for race. Logging in the vast pine forests, for example, was racially integrated, with a labor force evenly divided between blacks and whites. There was a similar influx of racially mixed rural southerners into Alabama's booming iron industry, which by 1890 was producing nearly a million tons of metal annually (Map 17.3).

What distinguished the southern labor market was that it was insulated from the rest of the country. Why so few southerners, black or white, left for the higher-wage North is puzzling. At its core the explanation is that the South was a place apart, with social and racial mores that discouraged all but the most resourceful from seeking opportunity elsewhere. For blacks, moreover, opportunity was scarce everywhere. Modest numbers did migrate out of the South—roughly 80,000 between 1870 and 1890 and another 200,000 between 1890 and 1910. Most

of them settled for day labor and service jobs. Industrial work was available, but not for them. Employers turned black applicants away from the factory gates—and away from their one best chance for a fair shake at American opportunity—because immigrant workers already supplied companies with as much cheap labor as they needed.

Immigrant Workers. The great migration from the Old World had started in the 1840s, when over a million Irish fled the potato famine. In the following years, as European agriculture became increasingly commercialized, the peasant economies began to fail, first in Germany and Scandinavia and then, later in the nineteenth century, across Austria-Hungary, Russia, Italy, and the Balkans. This upheaval set off a great migration of Europeans, some of them going to Europe's own mines and factories, others heading for South America and Australia, but most coming to the United States. Along with the peasantry came many seasoned workers, some of them—like hand-loom weavers—displaced by new technologies, others lured by higher American wages.

Ethnic origin largely determined the work the immigrants took in America. Seeking to use skills they already had, the Welsh labored as tin-plate workers, the English as miners, the Germans as machinists and traditional artisans (for example, bakers and carpenters), the Belgians as glass workers, and Scandinavians as seamen on Great Lakes boats. For common labor employers had long counted on the brawn of Irish rural immigrants, although all emigrating groups contributed to the pool of unskilled workers.

As mechanization advanced, the demand for ordinary labor skyrocketed. The sources of immigration began to shift, and by the early twentieth century arrivals from southern and eastern Europe far outstripped immigrants from western Europe (Figure 17.3). Heavy, low-paid labor became the domain of the recent immigrants (see Voices from Abroad, "Count Vay de Vaya und Luskod: Pittsburgh Inferno," p. 532). Blast-furnace jobs, a job-seeking investigator heard, were "Hunky work," not suitable for him or any other American. The derogatory term *Hunky,* although referring to Hungarian workers, was applied indiscriminately to Poles, Slovaks, and other ethnic Slavs arriving in America's industrial districts and, for all these groups, was tinged with racism. In the steel districts, it was commonly said that Hunky work was not for "white" men, that is, old-stock Americans.

Not only skill determined where immigrants ended up in American industry. The newcomers, although generally not traveling in groups, moved within well-defined networks, following relatives or fellow villagers already in America and relying on them to land a job. A high degree of ethnic clustering resulted, even within a single factory. At the Jones and Laughlin steel works in Pittsburgh, for example, the carpentry shop was German, the hammer shop Polish, and the blooming mill Serbian. Immigrants also had different job preferences. Men from Italy, for instance, favored outdoor work, often laboring in gangs under a *padrone* (boss), much as they had in Italy.

Immigrants entered a modern industrial order, but it was not a world they wanted. They were peasants, displaced by the breakdown of traditional rural economies. Many had lost their land and fallen into the class of dependent servants. They could reverse that bitter fate only by finding the money to buy property. In Europe job-seeking peasants commonly tried seasonal agricultural labor or temporary work in nearby cities. America represented merely a larger leap, made possible by cheap and speedy steamships across the Atlantic. The peasant immi-

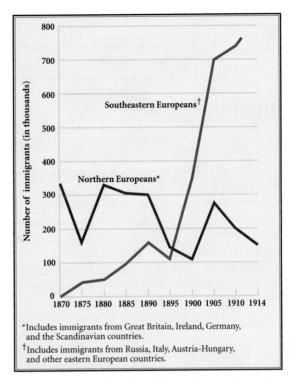

FIGURE 17.3 American Immigration, 1870–1914

This graph shows the surge of European immigration in the late nineteenth century. While northern Europe continued to send substantial numbers, it was overshadowed after 1895 by southern Europeans pouring into America to work in mines and factories. (See Map 18.2, Sources of European Immigration to the United States, 1871–1910, on p. 567.)

grants, most of them young and male, regarded their stay in America as temporary, although, once there, many changed their minds. About half did return, departing in great numbers during depression years. No one knows how many left because they had saved enough and how many left for lack of work. For their American employers it scarcely mattered. What did matter was that the immigrants took the worst jobs and were always available when they were wanted. For the new industrial order, they made an ideal labor supply.

Working Women and the Family Economy. Over four million women worked for wages in 1900. They made up a quarter of the nonfarm labor force and played a vital part in the industrial economy. The opportunities they found were shaped by gender—by the fact that they were women. Contemporary beliefs about womanhood largely determined which women took jobs and

Count Vay de Vaya und Luskod

Pittsburgh Inferno

Count Vay de Vaya und Luskod, a Hungarian nobleman and high functionary in the Catholic Church, crossed the United States several times between 1903 and 1906 en route to his post as the Vatican's representative to Asia. In a book about his travels, he expresses his distress at the plight of his countrymen laboring in the mills of the Pittsburgh steel district.

The bells are tolling for a funeral. The modest train of mourners is just setting out for the little churchyard on the hill. Everything is shrouded in gloom, even the coffin lying upon the bier and the people who stand on each side in threadbare clothes and with heads bent. Such is my sad reception at the Hungarian working-men's colony at McKeesport. Everyone who has been in the United States has heard of this famous town, and of Pittsburgh, its close neighbor. . . .

Fourteen-thousand tall chimneys are silhouetted against the sky . . . discharg[ing] their burning sparks and smok[ing] incessantly. The realms of Vulcan could not be more somber or filthy than this valley of the Monongahela. On every hand are burning fires and spurting flames. Nothing is visible save the forging of iron and the smelting of metal. . . .

And this fearful place affects us very closely, for thousands of immigrants wander here from year to year. Here they fondly seek the realization of their cherished hopes, and here they suffer till they are swallowed up by the inferno. He whom we are now burying is the latest victim. Yesterday he was in full vigor and at work at the foundry, toiling, struggling, hoping—a chain broke, and he was killed. . . .

This is scarcely work for mankind. Americans will hardly take anything of the sort; only [the immigrant] rendered desperate by circumstances . . . and thus he is at the mercy of the tyrannous Trust, which gathers him into its clutches and transforms him into a regular slave.

This is one of the saddest features of the Hungarian emigration. In making a tour of these prisons, wherever the heat is most insupportable, the flames most scorching, the smoke and soot most choking, there we are certain to find compatriots bent and wasted with toil. Their thin, wrinkled, wan faces seem to show that in America the newcomers are of no use except to help fill the moneybags of the insatiable millionaires. . . . In this realm of Mammon and Moloch everything has a value—except human life. . . . Why? Because human life is a commodity the supply of which exceeds the demand. There are always fresh recruits to supply the place of those who have fallen in battle; and the steamships are constantly arriving at the neighboring ports, discharging their living human cargo still further to swell the phalanx of the instruments of cupidity.

SOURCE: Oscar Handlin, ed., *This Was America* (Cambridge, MA: Harvard University Press, 1949), 407–410.

ANALYZING THE EVIDENCE

➤ The Count describes the Monongahela Valley as "this fearful place." What does he mean by this? What is he seeing that would not be apparent to an American observer?

➤ In the text (pp. 530–534) we offer an account of the industrial migration that the Count deplores in this document. In what ways do his comments amplify or make more understandable the text's discussion? Or, to reverse the question, in what ways does the text fill in gaps in the Count's understanding of what he is observing?

➤ Andrew Carnegie is the great American success story, a true rags-to-riches hero. How do you suppose Carnegie was regarded by Count Vay de Vaya und Luskod?

Switchboard Operators

Telephone work offers a prime historical example of sex-typing in American employment. When the first telephone exchange was set up in Boston in 1878, the lines were operated by teenage boys, following the practice set in the telegraph industry. During the 1880s, however, young women increasingly replaced the boys, and by 1900 switchboard operation was defined as women's work. In this photograph of a telephone exchange in Columbus, Ohio, in 1907, the older woman at left has risen to the position of supervisor, but it is the two men in the picture who are clearly in charge. The other major occupations in this new industry — telephone installation and line maintenance — were just as strictly male as switchboard operation was female but, of course, on a higher pay scale. Corbis-Bettmann.

how they were treated once they became wage earners (see Comparing American Voices, "Working Women," pp. 534–535).

Traditionally, wives were not supposed to work outside the home; in fact, fewer than 5 percent did so in 1890. Only among African Americans did many wives — above 30 percent — work for wages. Among whites, the typical working woman was under twenty-four and single; upon marrying, she quit her job and became a homemaker. When older women worked, remarked one observer, it "was usually a sign that something had gone wrong" — their husbands had died, deserted them, or lost their jobs.

Since women were held to be inherently different from men, it followed that they not be permitted to do "men's work." Nor, regardless of her skills, could a woman be paid a man's wage because, as one investigator reported, "it is expected that she has men to support her." The ideal at the time was not equal pay for equal work, but a "family wage" for men that would enable wives to stay home. The occupation that served as the baseline for women's jobs was domestic service, which was always poorly paid or, in a woman's own home, not paid at all.

At the turn of the century, women's work fell into three categories. A third worked as domestic servants. Another third held "female" white-collar jobs in teaching, nursing, sales, and office work. The remaining third worked in industry, mostly in the garment trades and textile mills, but also in many other industries as inspectors, packers, assemblers, and other "light" occupations. Few worked as supervisors, fewer in the skilled crafts, and nearly none as day laborers.

Although invariably defined as male or female, the allocation of jobs was anything but fixed. Telephone operators and store clerks, originally male occupations, became female over the course of the nineteenth century. Once women dominated an occupation, people attached feminine attributes to it, even though very similar or even identical work elsewhere was done by men. Jobs identified as women's work became unsuitable for men. There were no male telephone operators by 1900. And wherever they worked, women earned less than the lowest paid males. In industry, women's wages came to roughly $7 a week, $3 less than that of unskilled men.

Opposition to the employment of wives, although expressed in sentimental and moral terms, was based on solid necessity. Cooking, cleaning, and tending the children were not income producing or reckoned in terms of money. But everyone knew that the family household could not function without the wife's contribution. Therefore, her place was in the home.

Working-class families, however, found the going hard on a single income. Talk of a "family wage" was mostly just that — the talk of speech-makers. Only among highly skilled workers, wrote one investigator, "was it possible for the husband

Working Women

Shoe manufacturing was a pioneering American industry, one of the first to utilize a division of labor and move into factories. It was also, like textiles, an industry that relied heavily on female workers, who were generally girls or young married women without children. Mostly they worked as stitchers, using sewing machines to finish the shoe uppers. The lasting of the shoes—shaping the shoe on a wooden mold to conform to the foot—was handwork and the province of male shoe workers, who belonged to a strong trade union, the Knights of St. Crispin (St. Crispin was the saint of shoemakers). The sister organization was the Daughters of St. Crispin. During the 1870s, when the wages fell and work was short, married women entered the mills, and tensions rose between them and the women already in the labor force.

WIVES IN THE MILLS: A DEBATE

The documents that follow take the form of letters to the editor in the Lynn Record, *a weekly paper catering to the local factory workers. As was customary at the time, the authors adopted assumed names—in this case, A Stitcher, Americus, and Married Stitcher. Modern readers might be skeptical of the lady-like tone of the letters, but New England factory women, thanks to the region's excellent common schools, actually talked and wrote that way. These letters should be read on two levels. At first sight, they reveal sharp differences among working women over the employment of wives. But what of the larger employment system in which all of them are enmeshed? Do they question the role of gender in defining their place in the labor force?*

[February 1, 1879]
Mr. Editor,—In last week's *Record* . . . I notice this: "Working women, why don't you organize?" . . . I grew more and more indignant and resolved to write the *Record* a letter giving some of the reasons why the Daughters of St. Crispin's membership fails to increase. . . . Why my blood fairly boils and I get righteously angry when I think of some of the causes which have brought down the price of our labor! But let me tell you: In the first place, the shops are thronged with married women, the greater part of whom (and these are the ones I censure) have good, comfortable homes, and girls whose fathers are amply able to provide them with all the comforts and necessaries of life, but their inordinate love of dress, and a desire to vie in personal adornments with their more wealthy sisters, takes them into the workshops. . . . Ask *them* to join the order, and they are horrified at the thought! They don't want any better wages: they have a home, no board to pay, and so long as they can get enough for pin money, they are content. . . .

Our brother workmen can organize, and redress their wrongs; but for us there is no hope, and the bosses know it just as well as we; so they snap their fingers at us, and as each returning season comes round, they give us an extra cut in lieu of cutting down the men, knowing full well there are plenty of married women, with well-to-do husbands, and half-supported girls who stand ready to work the few short weeks in which work is given out, at any price they can get. . . .
A Stitcher

[February 8, 1879]
Mr. Editor,—. . . I cannot quite agree with "A Stitcher" in thinking that "married women" and "half-supported girls" are stumbling blocks in the way of organization. The great majority are not "half supported," neither are the majority of married women employed in our shops blessed with "comfortable homes" and "well-to-do husbands": if there are a few of this class, they are *very* few compared with the many who are obliged to work for their daily bread. . . . Married women have been well represented in the D.O.S.C. organization, and . . . they have always proved zealous and ardent supporters of that order. . . .
Americus

[February 15, 1879]
Mr. Editor,—. . . I am a married woman. I have worked in the shops some years, and never but one married woman have I

met but what claimed to work from necessity, not from choice. What sent many of the married women into the shops are the girls who [would] rather work with a crowd of men [as lasters] than in the stitching room with their own sex. They have been the cause of many men being cut down; many men with families to maintain. I for one, and I know many more situated in the same way, work to get bread for my children; my husband has been cut down [laid off] so that in the short time he has work he cannot support us. . . . I consider myself a Crispin in principle. But I will never join an order that takes in girl-lasters! Stitcher is altogether too hard on married women. I think some married woman of her acquaintance must have come out with a smarter silk [dress] or longer train than hers.
Married Stitcher

[February 15, 1879]
Mr. Editor, — I do not believe any woman, married or single, works for the fun of it in these times; neither do I believe most married women work in the shop because they are obliged to — that is, to provide themselves with the actual necessaries of life. To be sure, some of them may have shiftless husbands, but I think the men would make greater exertions if the women were not so eager and willing to take a man's place. If married women had to pay board bills, washing bills, and then had to be denied all the comforts of home, with no one to look to for aid or support, they would be less content to sit quietly down and submit to reduction after reduction, but would be ready to join any honorable scheme which would bring relief.

Were times good, work and money plenty, why, then, if married wanted to work out and neglect their homes, they could do so for all [I care]. But so long as there are a surplus of laborers, with scarcity of work, I shall protest against the married woman question, even though I stand alone. . . .
A Stitcher

[February 22, 1879]
Mr. Editor, — Ah! my dear Stitcher . . . when the husband and father cannot provide for his wife and children, it is perfectly natural that the wife and mother should desire to work for her husband and her little ones, and we have no right to deny her that privilege.

My dear child, don't blame married women if the land of the free has become a land of slavery and oppression. Women are not to blame. . . .
Americus

[March 1, 1879]
Mr. Editor, — For years I have been homeless, thrown here and there by circumstances, but have kept my eyes and ears open to all that has been going on around me; and many times I have been deeply pained at the utter selfishness manifested by a certain class of married women in the shops, till I have been thoroughly disgusted with them all. . . .

From statistical reports there is found to be sixty odd thousand more females than males in the state of Massachusetts, and it is safe to say three-fourths of them have to earn their own support. Now these can never have homes of their own unless they make them. No strong arm on which to lean can ever rightfully be theirs. In the face and eyes of this, can it be fair for them to have to compete with married women who have protectors, in the struggle for bread, besides all the other obstacles in their way?

It is no use, "Americus," since the days of Mother Eve women have been at the bottom of nearly every trouble: and . . . I think a foolish extravagance in dress and love of display on the part of women, has caused many a once honest man to turn thief, and has helped, if did not wholly, bring about this fearful crisis of distress and want. . . .
A Stitcher

SOURCE: Mary H. Blewett, ed., *We Will Rise in Our Might: Workingwomen's Voices from Nineteenth-Century New England* (Ithaca, NY: Cornell University Press, 1991), 140–144.

ANALYZING THE EVIDENCE

➤ How do you explain A Stitcher's objection to married women working in the shoe factories?

➤ Married Stitcher, like Americus, defends the employment of married women, but she also has a complaint, which, in her case, is against single women. Why does she claim they wrong married women? And what does this suggest about her attitude to the sex-typing that confined women in inferior gender-defined jobs?

➤ Is there any evidence in these documents that Married Stitcher's sister letter-writers share her conservative views about the segregation of women? Consider what they say about the trade unions in their industry.

➤ In our time — at the beginning of the twenty-first century — it is taken for granted that if a woman wants to work, that's her personal choice and her right. Do any of the letter-writers subscribe to that view?

Breaker Boys

In the anthracite districts of eastern Pennsylvania, giant machines called "breakers" processed the coal as it came out of the mines, crushing it and sorting it by size for sale as domestic fuel. The boys shown in this photograph had the job of picking out the stones as the processed coal came down the chutes, working long hours in a constant cloud of coal dust for less than a dollar a day. Breaker boy was the first job, often begun before the age of ten, in a lifetime in the mines. The photograph does not show any old men, but sick and disabled miners often ended their careers as breaker boys — hence the saying among coal diggers, "Twice a boy and once a man is the poor miner's life." Library of Congress.

unaided to support his family." The rockiest period came during the wife's childbearing years, when there were many mouths to feed and only the wages of the father to provide the food. Thereafter, as the children grew old enough to work, the family income began to increase. One of every five children under sixteen worked in 1900. "When the people own houses," remarked a printer from Fall River, Massachusetts, "you will generally find that it is a large family all working together."

Autonomous Labor

No one supervised the nineteenth-century coal miner. He was a tonnage worker, paid for the amount of coal he produced. He provided his own tools, worked at his own pace, and knocked off early when he chose. Such autonomous craft workers — almost all of them men — flourished in many branches of nineteenth-century industry. They were mule spinners in cotton mills; puddlers and rollers in iron works; molders in stove making; and machinists, glass blowers, and skilled workers in many other industries.

In the shop they abided by the *stint*, a self-imposed limit on how much they would produce each day. This informal system of restricting output infuriated efficiency-minded engineers. But to the worker it signified personal dignity and "unselfish brotherhood" with fellow employees. The male craft worker took pride in a "manly" bearing, toward both his fellows and the boss. One day a shop in Lowell, Massachusetts, posted regulations requiring all employees to be at their posts in work clothes at the opening bell and to remain, with the shop door locked, until the dismissal bell. A machinist promptly packed his tools, declaring that he had not "been brought up under such a system of slavery."

Underlying this ethical code was a keen sense of the craft, each with its own history and customs. Hat finishers — masters of the art of applying fur felting to top hats and bowlers — had a language of their own. When a hatter was hired, he was "shopped"; if fired, he was "bagged"; when he quit work, he "cried off"; and when he took an apprentice, the boy was "under teach." The hatters, most of whom worked in Danbury, Connecticut, or Orange, New Jersey, formed a distinctive, self-contained community.

Women workers found much the same kind of social meaning in their jobs. Department-store clerks, for example, developed a work culture and language just as robust as that of any male craft group. The most important fact about wage-earning women, however, was their youth. For many their first job was a chance to be independent, to form friendships with other young women, and to experience, however briefly, a fun-loving time of nice clothes, dancing, and other "cheap amusements." Young male workers, by contrast, underwent a process of job socialization presided over by seasoned, older workers. Being young mattered to male workers, certainly, but did not define work experience as it did for women.

To some degree their youthful preoccupations made it easier for working women to accept the miserable terms under which they labored. But this did not mean that they lacked a sense of solidarity or self-respect. A pretty dress might appear

Ironworkers — Noontime

The qualities of the nineteenth-century craft worker — dignity, "unselfish brotherhood," a "manly" bearing — shine through in this painting by Thomas P. Anschutz. *Ironworkers — Noontime* became a popular painting when it was reproduced as an engraving in *Harper's Weekly* in 1884. Fine Arts Museum of San Francisco.

frivolous to the casual observer but also conveyed the message that the working girl considered herself as good as anyone. Rebellious youth culture sometimes united with job grievances to produce astonishing strike movements, as demonstrated, for example, after the turn of the century by the Jewish garment workers of New York and the Irish American telephone operators of Boston.

Rarely, however, did women workers wield the kind of craft power that the skilled male worker commonly enjoyed. He hired his own helpers, supervised their work, and paid them from his earnings. In the late nineteenth century, when increasingly sophisticated production called for closer shop floor supervision, many factory managers deliberately shifted this responsibility to craft workers. In metal-fabricating firms that did precise machining and complex assembling, a system of inside contracting developed in which skilled employees bid for a production run, taking full responsibility for the operation, paying their crew and pocketing the profits.

Dispersal of authority was characteristic of nineteenth-century industry. The aristocracy of the workers — the craftsmen, inside contractors, and foremen — enjoyed a high degree of autonomy. But their subordinates often paid dearly for that independence. Any worker who paid his helpers from his own pocket might be tempted to exploit them. In Pittsburgh foremen were known as "pushers," notorious for driving their gangs mercilessly. On the other hand industrial labor in the nineteenth century remained on a human scale. People dealt with each other face to face, often developing cohesive ties within the shop. Striking craft workers commonly received the support of helpers and laborers, and labor gangs sometimes walked out on behalf of a popular foreman.

Systems of Control

As technology advanced, workers increasingly lost the proud independence characteristic of nineteenth-century craft work. One cause of this de-skilling process was a new system of manufacture—Henry Ford named it "**mass production**"—that lent itself to mechanization. Agricultural implements, typewriters, bicycles, and, after 1900, automobiles were assembled from standardized parts. The machine tools that cut, drilled, and ground these metal parts were originally operated by skilled machinists. But because they produced long runs of a single item, these machine tools became more specialized; they became *dedicated* machines—machines set up to do the same job over and over without the need for skilled operatives. In the manufacture of sewing machines, one machinist complained in 1883, "the trade is so subdivided that a man is not considered a machinist at all. One man may make just a particular part of a machine and may not know anything whatever about another part of the same machine." Such a worker, noted one observer, "cannot be master of a craft, but only master of a fragment."

Mechanization made it easier to control workers, but that was only an incidental benefit; employers favored automatic machinery because it increased output. Gradually, however, the idea took hold that focusing on workers—getting them to work harder or more efficiently—might itself be a way to reduce the cost of production (see Reading American Pictures, "The Killing Floor: Site of America's Mass-Production Revolution?", p. 539).

The pioneer in this field was Frederick W. Taylor. An expert on metal-cutting methods, Taylor believed that the engineer's approach might be applied to managing workers, hence the name for his method: **scientific management**. To get the maximum work from the individual worker, Taylor suggested two basic reforms. First, eliminate the brain work from manual labor. Managers would assume "the burden of gathering together all of the traditional knowledge which in the past has been possessed by the workmen and then of classifying, tabulating, and reducing this knowledge to rules, laws, and formulae." Second, withdraw the authority that workers had exercised on the shop floor. They would now "do what they are told promptly and without asking questions or making suggestions. . . . The duty of enforcing . . . rests with the management alone."

Once managers had the knowledge and the power, they would be able to put labor on a "scientific" basis. This meant subjecting each task to *time-and-motion study* by an engineer timing each job with a stopwatch. Workers would be paid at a differential rate—that is, a certain amount if they met the stopwatch standard and a higher rate

for additional output. Taylor's assumption was that only money mattered to workers and that they would respond automatically to the lure of higher earnings.

Scientific management was not, in practice, a great success. Implementing it proved to be very expensive, and workers stubbornly resisted the job-analysis method. "It looks to me like slavery to have a man stand over you with a stopwatch," complained one iron molder. A union leader insisted that "this system is wrong, because we want our heads left on us." Far from solving the labor problem, as Taylor claimed it would, scientific management embittered relations on the shop floor.

Yet Taylor achieved something of fundamental importance. He was a brilliant publicist, and his teachings spread throughout American industry. Taylor's disciples moved beyond his simplistic economic psychology, creating the new fields of personnel work and industrial psychology, whose practitioners purported to know how to extract more and better labor from workers. A threshold had been crossed into the modern era of labor management.

So the circle closed on American workers. With each advance the quest for efficiency eroded their cherished autonomy, diminishing them and cutting them down to fit the industrial system. The process occurred unevenly. For textile workers the loss had come early. Miners and ironworkers felt it much more slowly. Others, such as construction workers, escaped almost entirely. But increasing numbers of workers found themselves in an environment that crushed any sense of mastery or even understanding.

➤ Why were ethnicity and gender key determinants in how jobs were allocated in late-nineteenth-century industry?

➤ What accounts for the high degree of autonomy that many workers enjoyed in the early phases of industrialization?

➤ Why did that autonomy steadily erode as industrialization advanced?

The Labor Movement

Wherever it took hold, industrialization spurred workers to organize and form labor unions. The movements they built, however, varied from one

The Killing Floor: Site of America's Mass-Production Revolution?

Chicago Meatpacking Plant, 1882. Library of Congress.

The invention of the refrigerator car (p. 525) enabled Gustavus Swift to concentrate his meat processing operations at a giant packing plant next to the Chicago stockyards. But what did Swift have to gain by processing cattle in "bulk"? In this 1882 engraving of a Chicago packing plant we have visual evidence of the system of high-volume meat processing that Swift introduced. It was, in fact, a variant of the mass-production system discussed in this section and, like other examples of that system, yielded far higher output per worker and lower labor costs than had been possible under traditional methods. Swift's competitive advantage helped drive his locally-based competitors out of business and make him a multimillionaire.

ANALYZING THE EVIDENCE

► As you inspect this engraving, you will see many workers, but no machinery. All the work is done by hand. Can you explain, by looking at the tasks the workers are doing, why, even without machinery, they would be more efficient collectively than the same number of butchers working in the traditional way, each one handling his own cow? Can you think of a term that describes the system of labor depicted in the engraving?

► Although lacking any mechanized tools, Swift's mass-production system did benefit from one key technological advance. If you look at the ceiling, you will see an overhead pulley system. (This one appears to be manual; eventually it would be power-driven.) Can you explain, by inspecting the engraving, what this pulley system did and why it was important, crucially important, in fact for Swift's new system of production?

► Can you explain why Henry Ford, whose great innovation in car manufacture was the moving assembly line, claimed he got the idea after visiting a meatpacking plant, like the one in this engraving?

► In the text, we say that mass production was a de-skilling process. Is there any evidence of that effect in this engraving?

industrial society to another. In the United States workers were especially torn about how to proceed, and only in the 1880s did they settle on a labor movement that was distinctively American, like no other. While European movements embraced some variant of politically engaged socialism, American unionists rejected politics and emphasized **collective bargaining** with employers.

Reformers and Unionists

Thomas B. McGuire, a New York wagon driver, was ambitious. He had saved $300 from his wages "so that I might become something of a capitalist eventually." But his venture as a cab driver in the early 1880s soon failed:

> Corporations usually take that business themselves. They can manage to get men, at starvation wages, and put them on a hack, and put a livery on them with a gold band and brass buttons, to show that they are slaves — I beg pardon; I did not intend to use the word slaves; there are no slaves in this country now — to show that they are merely servants.

Slave or liveried servant, the symbolic meaning was the same to McGuire. He was speaking of the crushed aspirations of the independent American worker.

The Knights of Labor. What would satisfy the Thomas McGuires of the nineteenth century? Only the establishment of an egalitarian society in which every citizen might become economically independent. This republican goal resembled Jefferson's yeoman society, but labor reformers had no interest in returning to an agrarian past. They accepted industrialism, but not the accompanying unjust wage system that distinguished between capitalists and workers. In the future, all would be "producers," laboring together in what labor reformers commonly called the "cooperative commonwealth." This was the ideal that inspired the Noble and Holy Order of the Knights of Labor.

Founded in 1869 as a secret society of garment workers in Philadelphia, the Knights of Labor spread to other cities and, by 1878, emerged as a national movement. The Knights boasted an elaborate ritual that appealed to the fraternal spirit of nineteenth-century workers. The local assemblies of the Knights engendered a spirit of comradeship, very much like the Masons or Odd Fellows. For the Knights, however, fraternalism was harnessed to labor reform. The goal was to "give voice to that grand undercurrent of mighty thought, which is

today [1880] crystallizing in the hearts of men, and urging them on to perfect organization through which to gain the power to make labor emancipation possible."

But how was "emancipation" to be achieved? Through cooperation, the Knights argued. They intended to set up factories and shops that would be owned and run by the employees. As these cooperatives flourished, American society would be transformed into a cooperative commonwealth. But little was actually done. Instead the Knights devoted themselves to "education." Their leader, Grand Master Workman Terence V. Powderly, regarded the organization as a vast labor college open to all but lawyers and saloonkeepers. The cooperative commonwealth would arrive in some mysterious way as more and more "producers" became members and learned the group's message from lectures, discussions, and publications. Social evil would not end in a day but "must await the gradual development of educational enlightenment."

Trade Unionism. The labor reformers, exemplified by the Knights, expressed the grander aspirations of American workers. Another kind of organization — the trade union — tended to their everyday needs. Ever since they had first appeared early in the century, trade unions had been at the center of the lives of craft workers. Apprenticeship rules regulated entry into a trade, and the **closed shop** — reserving all jobs for union members — kept out lower-wage and incompetent workers. Union rules specified the terms of work, sometimes in minute detail. Above all, trade unionism defended the craft worker's traditional skills and rights.

The trade union also expressed the craft's social identity. Hatters took pride in their alcohol consumption, an on-the-job privilege that was jealously guarded. More often craft unions had an uplifting character. A Birmingham ironworker claimed that his union's "main object was to educate mechanics up to a standard of morality and temperance, and good workmanship." Some unions emphasized mutual aid. Because operating trains was a high-risk occupation, the railroad brotherhoods provided accident and death benefits and encouraged members to assist one another. On and off the job, the unions played a big part in the lives of craft workers.

The earliest unions were local craft organizations, sometimes limited to a single ethnic group, especially among German workers. As expanding markets intruded, breaking down their ability to control local conditions, unions formed national organizations, beginning with the International

The Knights of Labor

The caption on this union card — "By Industry We Thrive" — expresses the core principle of the Knights of Labor that everything of value is the product of honest labor. The two figures are ideal representations of that "producerist" belief — handsome workers, respectably attired, doing productive labor. A picture of the Grand Master Workman, Terence V. Powderly, hangs on the wall, benignly watching them. Picture Research Consultants & Archives.

"BY INDUSTRY WE THRIVE."

Typographical Union in 1852. By the 1870s molders, ironworkers, bricklayers, and about thirty other trades had done likewise. The national union, uniting local unions of the same trade, was becoming the dominant organizational form in America.

The practical job interests that trade unions espoused might have seemed a far cry from the idealism of the Knights of Labor. But both kinds of motives arose from a single worker's culture. Seeing no conflict, many workers carried membership cards in both the Knights and a trade union. And

because the Knights, once established in a town or city, tended to become politically active and to field independent slates of candidates, that too became a magnet attracting trade unionists interested in local politics.

Trade unions generally barred women, and so did the Knights until 1881, when women shoe workers in Philadelphia struck in support of their male coworkers and won the right to form their own local assembly. By 1886 probably 50,000 women belonged to the Knights of Labor. Their courage on the picket line prompted Powderly's rueful remark that women "are the best men in the Order." For a handful of women, such as the hosiery worker Leonora M. Barry, the Knights provided a rare chance to take up leadership roles as organizers and officials.

Similarly, the Knights of Labor grudgingly opened the door for black workers, out of the need for solidarity and, just as important, in deference to the Order's egalitarian principles. The Knights could rightly boast that their "great work has been to organize labor which was previously unorganized."

The Emergence of the AFL

In the early 1880s the Knights began to act more like trade unions, negotiating over wages and hours and going on strike to win their demands. They made especially effective the use of boycotts against "unfair" employers. And with the economy booming, the Knights began to win strikes, including a major victory against Jay Gould's Southwestern railway system in 1885. Workers flocked to the organization, and its membership jumped from 100,000 to perhaps 700,000.

The rapid growth of the Knights frightened the national trade unions. They began to insist on a clear separation of roles, with the Knights confined to labor reform activities. This was partly a battle over turf, but it also reflected a deepening divergence of labor philosophies.

Samuel Gompers and Pure-and-Simple Unionism. On the union side, the key figure was Samuel Gompers, a Dutch-Jewish cigar maker whose family had emigrated, via London, to New York in 1863. Gompers was a worker-intellectual, a familiar type in the craft trades, little educated, but widely read and engaged by ideas. Gompers always contended that what he missed at school (he had gone to work at ten) he more than made up for in the shop, where cigar makers commonly paid one of their number to read to them while they worked.

Worker-intellectuals like Gompers gravitated to New York's radical circles, where during the 1870s the right course for bringing about the revolution was being fiercely debated. Partly out of these debates, partly from his experience in the Cigar Makers Union, Gompers hammered out a doctrine that he called "pure-and-simple" unionism. "Pure" referred to membership: strictly limited to workers, organized by craft and occupation, with no participation by middle-class reformers. "Simple" referred to goals: only what immediately benefited

Samuel Gompers

This is a photograph of the labor leader in his forties taken when he was visiting striking miners in West Virginia, an area where mine operators resisted unions with special fierceness. The photograph was taken by a company detective. *George Meany Memorial Archives.*

workers—wages, hours, and working conditions. Pure-and-simple unionism focused on the workplace, where workers had some power, and was suspicious of politics. What it aimed at was collective bargaining with employers. For Gompers, the key-word was *power.* "No matter how just," he said, "unless the cause is backed up with power to enforce it, it is going to be crushed and annihilated." This was at the crux of the dispute with the Knights: that they were innocent, with their grand schemes, of American power realities, and, on top of that, by mucking around on union turf, harmful to power-building unions.

In December 1886, having failed to persuade the Knights of Labor to desist, the national trade unions formed the American Federation of Labor (AFL), with Gompers as president. The AFL in effect locked into place the trade-union structure as it had evolved by the 1880s. Underlying this structure was the conviction that workers had to take the world as it was, not as they dreamed it might be.

Haymarket. The issue that crystallized the rupture between the rival movements was the eight-hour workday. Nothing, the trade unions believed, would do more to improve the everyday lives of American workers. The Knights leaders, although sympathetic, regarded shorter hours as a secondary issue and a distraction from higher goals. They demurred when the trade unions set May 1, 1886, as the deadline for achieving the eight-hour workday. But many Knights, ignoring the leadership, responded enthusiastically, and as the deadline approached, a wave of strikes and demonstrations broke out across the country.

At one such eight-hour-day strike, at the Mc-Cormick reaper works in Chicago, a battle erupted on May 3, leaving four strikers dead. Chicago was a hotbed of **anarchism** — the revolutionary advocacy of a stateless society — and local anarchists, most of them German immigrants, called a protest meeting the next evening at Haymarket Square. When police began to disperse the crowd, someone threw a bomb that killed or wounded several of the police, who responded with wild gunfire. Most of the casualties, including some policemen, came from police bullets. Despite the lack of evidence, the anarchists were found guilty of murder and criminal conspiracy. Four were executed, one committed suicide, and the others received long prison sentences — victims of one of the great miscarriages of American justice.

Seizing on the antiunion hysteria set off by the Haymarket affair, employers took the offensive. They broke strikes violently, compiled blacklists of strikers, and forced workers to sign **yellow-dog contracts**, in which, as a condition of employment, workers pledged not to join labor organizations. If trade unionists needed any confirmation of the tough world in which they lived, they found it in Haymarket and its aftermath.

The Knights of Labor, hard-hit despite its official opposition to the eight-hour strikes, never recovered from Haymarket. In the meantime the more resilient AFL took firm root, justifying Gompers's confidence that he had found the correct formula for the American labor movement. What he overlooked was the generous inclusiveness of the Knights of Labor. The AFL was far less welcoming to women and blacks, confining them, where they were admitted, to separate, second-class organizations. It was a flaw that would come back to haunt the labor movement.

Industrial War

Radical as were its intellectual origins, pure-and-simple unionism was conservative in effect. American trade unions did not challenge the economic order. All they wanted was a larger share for working people. But it was precisely that claim against company profits that made American employers so opposed to collective bargaining. In the 1890s they unleashed a fierce counterattack on the trade-union movement.

The Homestead Strike. The skilled workers of Homestead, Pennsylvania, the site of one of Carnegie's steel mills, imagined themselves safe from that threat. They earned good wages, lived comfortably, and generally owned their own homes. The mayor of the town was one of their own. And they had faith in Andrew Carnegie — for had not Good Old Andy said in a famous magazine article that workers had as sacred a right to combine as did capitalists?

Espousing high-toned principles made Carnegie feel good, but a healthy profit made him feel even better. He decided that collective bargaining had become too expensive, and he was confident that his skilled workers could be replaced by the advanced machinery he was installing. Lacking the stomach for the hard battle, Carnegie fled to a remote estate in Scotland, leaving behind a second-in-command well qualified to do the dirty work. This was Henry Clay Frick, a former coal baron and a veteran of labor wars in the coal fields.

After a brief pretense at bargaining, Frick announced that effective July 1, 1892, the company would no longer deal with the Amalgamated Association of Iron and Steel Workers. If the employees wanted to work, they would have to come back on an individual basis. The mill had already been fortified so that strikebreakers could be brought in to resume operations. At stake for Carnegie's employees now were not just wage cuts but the defense of a way of life. The town mayor, a union man, turned away the county sheriff when he tried to take possession of the plant. The entire community mobilized in defense of the union.

At dawn on July 6, barges were seen approaching Homestead up the Monongahela River. On board were armed guards hired by the Pinkerton Detective Agency to take possession of the steel works. Behind hastily erected barricades the strikers opened fire, and a bloody battle ensued. When the Pinkertons surrendered they were mercilessly pummeled by the enraged women of Homestead as they retreated to the railway station. Frick appealed to the governor of Pennsylvania, who called out the state militia and placed Homestead under martial law. The great steel works was taken over and opened to strikebreakers, while union leaders and town officials were arrested on charges of riot, murder, and treason.

The defeat at Homestead marked the beginning of the end for trade unions in the steel industry. Ended too were any lingering illusions about the sanctity of workers' communities like Homestead. "Men talk like anarchists or lunatics when they insist that the workmen of Homestead have done right," asserted one conservative journal. Nothing could be permitted to interfere with Carnegie's property rights or threaten law and order.

The Homestead strike ushered in a decade of strife, pitting working people against the formidable power of corporate industry and the even more formidable power of their own government. That hard reality was driven home to workers at a place that seemed an even less likely site for class warfare than Homestead.

The Great Pullman Boycott. Pullman, Illinois, was a model factory town, famous for its landscaping and city plan. The town's builder and sole employer was George M. Pullman, inventor of the sleeping car that brought comfort and luxury to railway travel. When business fell off during the economic depression in 1893, Pullman cut wages but not the rents for company housing. Confronted by a workers' committee in May 1894, Pullman denied any connection between his roles as employer and landlord. He then fired the workers' committee.

The strike that ensued would have warranted only a footnote in American history but for the fact that the Pullman workers belonged to the American Railway Union (ARU), a rapidly growing, new union of railroad workers. Its leader, Eugene V. Debs, directed ARU members not to handle Pullman sleeping cars, which, although operated by the railroads, were owned and serviced by the Pullman Company. This was a **secondary labor boycott**: force was applied on a second party (the railroads) to bring pressure on the primary target (Pullman). Since the railroads insisted on running the Pullman cars, a far-flung strike soon spread across the country, threatening the entire economy.

The railroads maneuvered quietly to bring the federal government into the dispute. Their hook was the U.S. mail cars, which they attached to every train hauling Pullman cars. When strikers stopped these trains, the railroads appealed to President Cleveland to protect the U.S. mail. Cleveland's Attorney General Richard Olney, a former railroad lawyer, unabashedly sided with his former employers. When federal troops failed to get the trains running again, Olney obtained court injunctions prohibiting the ARU leaders from conducting the strike. Debs and his associates refused, were charged with contempt of court, and jailed. Leaderless and uncoordinated, the strike quickly disintegrated.

No one could doubt why the great Pullman boycott had failed: It had been crushed by the naked use of government power on behalf of the railroad companies.

American Radicalism in the Making

Oppression does not radicalize every victim, but some it does radicalize. And when social injustice is most painfully felt, when the underlying power realities stand openly revealed, the process of radicalization speeds up. Such was the case during the depression of the 1890s. Out of the industrial strife of that decade emerged the main forces of twentieth-century American radicalism.

Eugene V. Debs and American Socialism. Very little in Eugene Debs's background would have suggested that he would one day become the nation's leading Socialist. A native of Terre Haute, Indiana, a prosperous railroad town, Debs grew up believing in the essential goodness of American society. A popular young man-about-town, Debs considered a career in politics or business but instead became involved in the local labor movement. In 1880, at the age of twenty-five, he was elected national secretary-treasurer of the Brotherhood of Locomotive Firemen, one of the craft unions that represented the skilled operating trades on the railroads. Troubled by his union's indifference to the low-paid track and yard laborers, Debs left his comfortable post to devote himself to the American Railway Union, an **industrial union**, that is, a union open to all railroad workers, regardless of skill. That was why the Pullman workers were eligible for ARU membership.

The Pullman strike visibly changed Debs. Sentenced to six months in a federal prison, he emerged an avowed radical, committed to a lifelong struggle against a system that enabled employers to enlist the powers of government to beat down working people. Initially, Debs identified himself as

The Pullman Strike

Chicago was the hub of the railway network and the strategic center of the battle between the Pullman boycotters and the trunk line railroads. For the strikers, the crucial thing was to prevent those trains with Pullman cars attached from running; for the railroads, it was to get the trains through at any cost. The arrival of federal troops meant that the trains would move and that the strikers would be defeated. *Harper's Weekly,* July 21, 1894.

a Populist (see Chapter 19), but he quickly gravitated to the Socialist camp.

German refugees had brought the ideas of Karl Marx, the radical German theorist, to America after the failed revolutions of 1848 in Europe. Marx postulated a class struggle between capitalists and workers, ending in a revolution that would abolish private ownership of the means of production and bring about a classless society. Little noticed by most Americans, Marxist socialism struck deep roots in the German American communities of Chicago and New York. With the formation of the Socialist Labor Party in 1877, Marxist socialism established itself as a permanent, if narrowly based, presence in American politics.

When Eugene Debs appeared in their midst in 1897, the Socialists were in disarray. American capitalism had just gone through its worst crisis, yet their party had failed to make much headway.

Many blamed the party head, Daniel De Leon, who considered ideological purity more important than winning elections. Debs joined in the revolt against the dogmatic De Leon and helped launch the rival Socialist Party of America in 1901.

A spellbinding campaigner, Debs talked socialism in an American idiom, making Marxism understandable and persuasive to many ordinary citizens. Under him the new party began to break out of its immigrant base and attract American-born voters. In Texas, Oklahoma, and Minnesota, socialism exerted a powerful appeal among distressed farmers. The party was also highly successful at attracting women activists. Inside of a decade, with a national network of branches and state organizations, the Socialist Party had become a force to be reckoned with in American politics.

KING DEBS.

King Debs

In this cartoon, *Harper's Weekly* depicts Eugene Debs as a tyrant, capable by his rule over the American Railway Union of halting all railway traffic and bringing the nation's economy to its knees. It was this conception of "King Debs" that, for many middle-class Americans, justified the extraordinary intervention by the federal government that crushed the Pullman boycott and landed Debs in prison. Library of Congress.

Western Radicalism. Farther west a different brand of American radicalism was taking shape. After many years of mostly friendly relations, the atmosphere in the western mining camps turned ugly during the 1890s. The powerful new corporations that were taking over wanted to be rid of the miners' union, the Western Federation of Miners (WFM). Moreover, silver and copper prices began to drop, bringing pressure to cut miners' wages. When strikes resulted, they took an especially violent turn.

In 1892 striking miners at Coeur d'Alene, a silver-mining district in northern Idaho, engaged in gun battles with company guards, sent a car of explosive powder careering into the Frisco mine, and threatened to blow up the smelters. Martial law was declared, the strikers were imprisoned in stockades, and the strike was broken. In subsequent miners' strikes, government intervention was equally naked

and unrestrained. By 1897 the WFM president, Ed Boyce, was calling on all union members to arm themselves, and his rhetoric—he called the wage system "slavery in its worst form"—developed a hard edge.

Led by the fiery Boyce and "Big Bill" Haywood, the WFM joined in 1905 with left-wing Socialists to create a new movement, the Industrial Workers of the World (IWW). The Wobblies, as IWW members were called, fervently supported the Marxist class struggle—but at the workplace rather than in politics. By resistance at the point of production and ultimately by means of a **general strike**, they believed that the workers would bring about a revolution. A new society would emerge, run directly by the workers through their industrial unions. The term **syndicalism** describes this brand of workers' radicalism.

Industrial Violence

Strikes in the western mining districts were generally bloody affairs. On management's side, the mayhem was often perpetrated by the forces of law and order. In this photograph, we see a line of mounted troopers during the 1894 strike at Cripple Creek, Colorado. Our view is from the rear. From the front, the sight would have been more fearsome because the formation of the troopers suggests they might be about to charge and begin breaking heads. Denver Public Library, Western History Division.

In both its major forms — politically-oriented Socialism and the syndicalist IWW — American radicalism flourished after the crisis of the 1890s, but only on a limited basis and never with the possibility of seizing national power. Nevertheless, Socialists and Wobblies served a real purpose. American radicalism, by its sheer vitality, bore witness to what was exploitative and unjust in the new industrial order.

➤ How would you distinguish between labor reform and trade unionism?

➤ Why did the AFL prevail over the Knights of Labor?

➤ Why are the 1890s the critical period in the rise of American radicalism?

SUMMARY

In this chapter, we trace the emergence of modern American industrialism during the late nineteenth century. We show how an unrivaled capacity for supplying the capital goods and energy fueled an expanding manufacturing economy. On the demand side, the key development was an efficient railway network that provided manufacturers with easy access to national markets. We show how entrepreneurs like Swift and Rockefeller, eager to exploit this opportunity, built vertically integrated firms and developed functions for shaping consumer demand and managing far-flung, complex business activities entirely new to American enterprise. Also new, and troubling, was the market power suddenly in the hands of great firms like Rockefeller's Standard Oil.

On the labor side, the biggest challenge was finding enough workers for America's burgeoning industries. The South recruited local populations, of both races, while the industrial North relied on immigrants from Europe; both regions drew on young and single women. Race, ethnicity, and gender became defining features of the American working class. Mass production — the high-volume output of standardized products — accelerated the productivity of industry but also de-skilled workers and mechanized their jobs, as did the systematizing methods of Frederick W. Taylor's scientific management.

In these years, after much trial and error, the American labor movement took shape. The Knights of Labor enjoyed one final surge in the mid-1880 and succumbed to the AFL. Although accepting of the economic order, the AFL's insistence on a larger share for workers evoked fierce opposition from employers. The resulting industrial warfare of the 1890s stirred new radical impulses, leading both to the political socialism of Eugene V. Debs and to the industrial radicalism of the IWW.

Connections: Economy

The economic developments described in this chapter originated far back in the nineteenth century, when the factory system first emerged in the Northeast and roads, canals, and the early railroads launched a market revolution (Chapter 9). The industrial power that resulted gave the North the upper hand in the Civil War, while in turn the war effort further stimulated the North's industrial development (Chapter 14). Only afterward, however, in the years covered by this chapter, was that development fully consolidated. As we observed in the part opener (p. 485):

What had been partial and limited now became general and widespread; America turned into a land of factories, corporate enterprise, and industrial workers.

Virtually every aspect of America's subsequent history is shaped by its consolidation as an industry power. That was the condition, as we shall see in Chapter 21, for the nation's foray into imperial politics in the 1890s. It was the condition for the dramatic rise in living standards in the 1920s (Chapter 23), when mass-produced automobiles and other consumer durables began to flow to the American masses, and by its failure after 1929, for the social upheaval that led to the New Deal (Chapter 24). In these and other ways, American industrialism is a central fact of our modern history. Because it is, in fact, so central a condition, students should be attentive to the impact of American industrialism as they read beyond Chapter 17.

CHAPTER REVIEW QUESTIONS

➤ Why is growth of capital goods important to the development of American industry after 1877?

➤ Why is it that the late nineteenth century became the age of big business?

➤ Does it matter that the United States had to rely on Europe to meet the nation's need for workers?

➤ Why did American workers find it hard to choose between labor reform and trade unionism? And why, when they did choose, did it take the form of the AFL's "pure-and-simple" unionism?

TIMELINE

1869	Knights of Labor founded in Philadelphia
1872	Andrew Carnegie starts construction of Edgar Thomson steelworks near Pittsburgh
1873	Panic of 1873 ends railroad boom
1875	John Wanamaker establishes first department store in Philadelphia
1877	Baltimore and Ohio workers initiate nationwide railroad strike
1878	Gustavus Swift introduces refrigerator car
1883	Railroads establish national time zones
1886	Haymarket Square bombing in Chicago
	American Federation of Labor (AFL) founded
1892	Homestead steel strike crushed
	Wave of western miners' strikes begins
1893	Panic of 1893 leads to national depression
	Surge of railroad bankruptcies; reorganization by investment bankers begins
1894	President Cleveland sends troops to break Pullman boycott
1895	Southeastern European immigration exceeds northern European immigration for first time
	Frederick W. Taylor formulates scientific management
1901	Eugene V. Debs helps found Socialist Party of America
1905	Industrial Workers of the World (IWW) launched

FOR FURTHER EXPLORATION

For students new to economic history, biography offers an accessible entry point into what can be a dauntingly technical subject. The biographical literature is especially rich in American history because of this country's fascination with its great magnates and because of a long-standing debate among historians over what contribution (if any) the business moguls made to America's industrializing economy. The initiating book was Matthew Josephson's classic *The Robber Barons* (1934), which, as the title implies, argued that America's great fortunes were built on the wealth that others had created. The contrary view was taken by the financial historian Julius Grodinsky, whose *Jay Gould: His Business Career, 1867–1892* (1957) explained masterfully how this railroad buccaneer helped shape the transportation system. Since then, there have been superb, mostly sympathetic, business biographies, including Joseph F. Wall, *Andrew Carnegie* (1970); Ron Chernow, *Titan: The Life of John D. Rockefeller* (1998); Jean Strouse, *Morgan: American Financier* (1999), and, for the man who revolutionized the newspaper business, David Nasaw, *The Chief: The Life of William Randolph Hearst* (2002). The founder of scientific management has also recently been the subject of a robust biography: Robert Kanigel, *The One Best Way: Frederick W. Taylor and the Enigma of Efficiency* (1997). On labor's side, the biographical literature is nearly as rich. The founder of the AFL is the subject of a lively brief biography by Harold Livesay, *Samuel Gompers and Organized Labor in America* (1978); Gompers's autobiography, *Seventy Years of Life and Labor* (2 vols., 1925), also makes rewarding reading. His main critic is treated with great insight in Nick Salvatore, *Eugene V. Debs: Citizen and Socialist* (1982). The IWW leader William D. Haywood left a colorful autobiography, *Bill Haywood's Book* (1929), and Haywood is also the subject of Peter Carlson's biography, *Roughneck* (1982). Biography, of course, tends to overlook the foot soldiers of history, but social historians have striven mightily in recent years to tell their stories. An excellent example is Paul Krause, *The Battle for Homestead, 1880–1892* (1992), which rescues from obscurity the working people who led that decisive steel strike. There is an excellent Web site on Andrew Carnegie at **http://andrewcarnegie.tripod.com/**.

TEST YOUR KNOWLEDGE

To assess your command of the material in this chapter, see the Online Study Guide at **bedfordstmartins.com/henretta**.

For Web sites, images, and documents related to topics and places in this chapter, visit **bedfordstmartins.com/makehistory**.

18

The Industrial City: Building It, Living in It

VISITING HIS FIANCÉE'S MISSOURI HOMESTEAD in 1894, Theodore Dreiser was struck by "the spirit of rural America, its idealism, its dreams." But this was an "American tradition in which I, alas, could not share," Dreiser wrote. "I had seen Pittsburgh. I had seen Lithuanians and Hungarians in their [alleys] and hovels. I had seen the girls of the city— walking the streets at night." Only twenty-three at the time, Dreiser would go on to write one of the great American urban novels, *Sister Carrie* (1900), about one young woman in the army of small-town Americans flocking to the Big City. But Dreiser, part of that army, already knew that between rural America and Pittsburgh an unbridgeable chasm had opened up.

In 1820, after two hundred years of settlement, fewer than one in twenty Americans lived in a city of 10,000 people or more. After that, decade by decade, the urban population swelled until, by 1900, one of every five Americans was a city dweller. Nearly 6.5 million inhabited just three great cities: New York, Chicago, and Philadelphia (Table 18.1).

The city was the arena of the nation's vibrant economic life. Here the factories went up, and here the new immigrants settled, constituting in 1900 a third of the residents of the major American cities. Here, too, lived the millionaires and a growing white-collar middle class. For all these

◄ **Mulberry Street, New York City, c. 1900**

The influx of southern and eastern Europeans created teeming ghettos in the heart of New York City and other major American cities. The view is of Mulberry Street, with its pushcarts, street peddlers, and bustling traffic. The inhabitants are mostly Italians, and some of them, noticing the photographer preparing his camera, have gathered to be in the picture. Library of Congress.

TABLE 18.1	Ten Largest Cities by Population, 1870 and 1900		
1870		**1900**	
City	**Population**	**City**	**Population**
1. New York	942,292	New York	3,437,202
2. Philadelphia	674,022	Chicago	1,698,575
3. Brooklyn*	419,921	Philadelphia	1,293,697
4. St. Louis	310,864	St. Louis	575,238
5. Chicago	298,977	Boston	560,892
6. Baltimore	267,354	Baltimore	508,957
7. Boston	250,526	Cleveland	381,768
8. Cincinnati	216,239	Buffalo	352,387
9. New Orleans	191,418	San Francisco	342,782
10. San Francisco	149,473	Cincinnati	325,902

*Brooklyn was consolidated with New York in 1898.
Source: U.S. Census data.

people the city was more than a place to make a living. It provided the setting for an urban culture unlike anything seen before in the United States. City people, although differing vastly among themselves, became distinctively and recognizably urban.

Urbanization

The march to the cities seemed irresistible to nineteenth-century Americans. "The greater part of our population must live in cities," declared the Congregational minister Josiah Strong. And from another writer: "There was no resisting the trend." Urbanization became inevitable because of another inevitability of American life—industrialism.

Until the Civil War, cities lived on commerce, not industry. They were the places where goods were bought and sold for distribution into the interior or out to world markets. Early industry, on the other hand, sprang up mostly in the countryside, where factories had access to water power from streams, nearby fuel and raw materials, and workers recruited from farms and villages.

As industrialization proceeded, city and factory began to merge. Once steam engines came along, mill operators no longer depended on water-driven power. Railroads enabled entrepreneurs to locate factories at places best situated in relation to suppliers and markets. Iron makers gravitated to Pittsburgh because of its superior access to coal and ore fields. Chicago, midway between western livestock

suppliers and eastern markets, became a great meatpacking center. Geographic concentration of industry meant urban growth. And so did the rising scale of production. A plant that employed thousands of workers instantly created a small city in its vicinity, sometimes in the form of a company town like Aliquippa, Pennsylvania, which became body and soul the property of the Jones and Laughlin Steel Company. Other firms built big plants at the edge of large cities so that they could draw on the available labor supply and transportation facilities. As the metropolis spread, the lines between industrial towns sometimes blurred and, as in northern New Jersey or along Lake Michigan south of Chicago, extended urban-industrial areas emerged.

Older commercial cities meanwhile became more industrial. Warehouse districts could readily be converted to small-scale manufacturing; a distribution network was right at hand. In addition, as gateways for immigrants, port cities offered abundant cheap labor. Boston, Philadelphia, Baltimore, and San Francisco became hives of small-scale, labor-intensive industrial activity. New York's enormous pool of immigrant workers made that city a magnet for the garment trades, cigar making, and diversified light industry. Preeminent as a city of trade and finance, New York also ranked as the nation's largest manufacturing center.

City Innovation

As cities expanded, so did the problems confronting them. How would so many people move around, communicate, have their physical needs met? The city demanded innovation no less than did industry itself and, in the end, compiled just as impressive a record of technological achievement.

The older commercial cities had been compact places, densely settled around harbors or riverfronts. As late as 1850, when it had 565,000 people, Philadelphia covered only ten square miles. From the foot of Chestnut Street on the Delaware River, a person could walk almost anywhere in the city within forty-five minutes. Thereafter, as it developed, Philadelphia spilled out and, like American cities everywhere, engulfed the surrounding countryside.

Nothing like this happened in continental Europe, where even rapidly growing cities remained physically compact, with built-up neighborhoods abruptly giving way to countryside. In America cities grew beyond their boundaries, forming what the federal census in 1910 began to designate as metropolitan areas. While highly congested at the center, American cities were actually thinly populated compared to German cities, which counted 158 people per acre as against 22 per acre in the United States.

"The only trouble about this town," wrote Mark Twain on arriving in New York in 1867, "is that it is too large. You cannot accomplish anything in the way of business, you cannot even pay a friendly call without devoting a whole day to it. . . . [The] distances are too great." Moving nearly a million New Yorkers around was not as hopeless as Twain thought, but it did challenge the ingenuity of city builders.

Mass Transit. The first innovation, dating back to the 1820s, was the omnibus, an elongated version of the horse-drawn carriage. More efficient was the horsecar, whose key advantage was that it ran on iron tracks so that the horses could pull more passengers at a faster clip through congested city streets. The chief objection to tracks was resolved by a modest but crucial refinement in 1852—a grooved rail that was flush with the pavement. Then came the electric trolley car, the brainchild primarily of Frank J. Sprague, an engineer once employed by the great inventor Thomas A. Edison. In 1887 Sprague designed an electric-driven system for Richmond, Virginia: A "trolley" carriage running along an overhead power line was attached by cable to streetcars equipped with an electric motor—hence the name "trolley car." After Sprague's success, the trolley swiftly displaced the horsecar and became the primary mode of transportation in most American cities.

In America's greatest metropolises, however, the streetcar itself was no solution. Congestion led to demands that transit lines be moved off the streets. In 1879 the first elevated railroads went into operation on Sixth and Ninth Avenues in New York City. Powered at first by steam engines, the "els" converted to electricity following Sprague's success with the trolley. Chicago developed elevated transit most fully (Map 18.1). Others looked below ground. Boston opened a short underground line in 1897, but it was the completion in 1904 of a subway running the length of Manhattan that demonstrated the full potential of the high-speed underground train. Mass transit had become *rapid* transit.

Skyscrapers. Equally remarkable was the architectural revolution sweeping metropolitan business districts. With steel girders, durable plate glass, and the passenger elevator available by the 1880s, a

The Chicago Elevated, 1900

This is Wabash Avenue, looking north from Adams Street. For Americans from farms and small towns, this photograph by William Henry Jackson captured something of the peculiarity of the urban scene. What could be stranger than a railroad suspended above the streets in the midst of people's lives? KEA Publishing Services, Ltd.

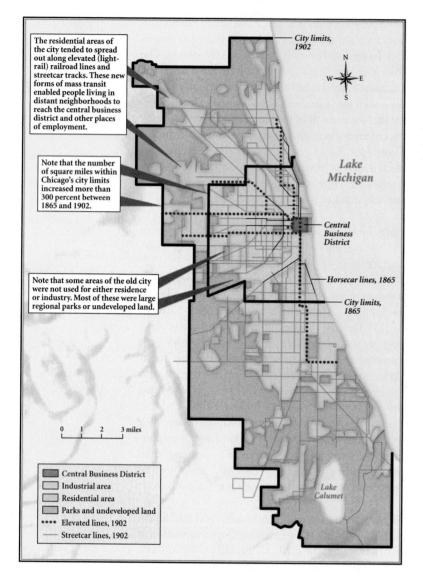

The residential areas of the city tended to spread out along elevated (light-rail) railroad lines and streetcar tracks. These new forms of mass transit enabled people living in distant neighborhoods to reach the central business district and other places of employment.

Note that the number of square miles within Chicago's city limits increased more than 300 percent between 1865 and 1902.

Note that some areas of the old city were not used for either residence or industry. Most of these were large regional parks or undeveloped land.

City limits, 1902

Lake Michigan

Central Business District

Horsecar lines, 1865

City limits, 1865

0 1 2 3 miles

■ Central Business District
□ Industrial area
□ Residential area
□ Parks and undeveloped land
•••• Elevated lines, 1902
— Streetcar lines, 1902

Lake Calumet

MAP 18.1   The Expansion of Chicago, 1865–1902

In 1865 Chicagoans depended on horsecar lines to get around town. By 1900 the city limits had expanded enormously and so had the streetcar service, which was by then electrified. Elevated trains eased the congestion on downtown streets. And the continuing extension of the streetcar lines, some beyond the city limits, assured that suburban development would be continuing as well.

wholly new way of construction opened up. A steel skeleton supported the building, while the walls, previously weight bearing, served as curtains enclosing the structure. The sky, so to speak, became the limit.

The first "skyscraper" to be built on this principle was William Le Baron Jenney's ten-story Home Insurance Building (1885) in Chicago. Although unremarkable in appearance—it looked just like the other downtown buildings—the steel-girder technology Jenney's building contained liberated the aesthetic perceptions of American architects. A Chicago school sprang up, dedicated to the design of buildings whose form expressed, rather than masked, their structure and function. The presiding genius was the architect Louis Sullivan, who developed a "vertical aesthetic" of set-back windows and strong columns that gave skyscrapers a "proud and soaring" presence. Chicago pioneered sky-

scraper construction, but New York, with its unrelenting demand for prime downtown space, took the lead after the mid-1890s. The fifty-five-story Woolworth Building, completed in 1913, marked the beginning of the modern Manhattan skyline.

The Electric City. For ordinary citizens the electric lights that dispelled the gloom at night offered the most dramatic evidence that times had changed. Gaslight—illuminating gas produced from coal—had been in use since the early nineteenth century but, at 12 candlepower, the lamps were too dim to brighten the city's downtown streets and public spaces. The first use of electricity, once generating technology made it commercially feasible in the 1870s, was for better city lighting. Charles F. Brush's electric arc lamps, installed in Wanamaker's department store in Philadelphia in 1878, threw a brilliant light and soon replaced

Lighting Up Minneapolis, 1883

Like other American cities, Minneapolis at night had been a dim place until the advent of Charles F. Brush's electric arc lamps. This photograph marks the opening day, February 28, 1883, of Minneapolis's new era, the installation of a 257-foot tower topped by a ring of electric arc lamps. The electric poles on the right, connecting the tower to a power station, would soon proliferate into a blizzard of poles and overhead wires, as Minneapolis, like every late nineteenth-century city, became an electric city. © Minnesota Historical Society/CORBIS.

gaslight on city streets across the country. Electric lighting then entered the American home, thanks to Thomas Edison's invention of a serviceable incandescent bulb in 1879. Edison's motto — "Let there be light!" — truly described the experience of the modern city.

Before it had any significant effect on industry, electricity gave the city its modern tempo, lifting elevators, powering streetcars and subway trains, turning night into day. Meanwhile, Alexander Graham Bell's telephone (1876) sped communica-

tion beyond anything imagined previously. Twain's complaint of 1867, that it was impossible to carry on business in New York, had been answered: All he needed to do was pick up the phone.

Private City, Public City

City building was mostly an exercise in private enterprise. The lure of profit spurred the great innovations — the trolley car, electric lighting, the skyscraper, the elevator, the telephone — and drove urban real estate development. The investment opportunities looked so tempting that new cities sprang up almost overnight from the ruins of the Chicago fire of 1871 and the San Francisco earthquake of 1906. Real estate interests, eager to develop subdivisions, often were instrumental in pushing streetcar lines outward from the central districts of cities. The subway, predicted the *New York Times*, would open the outer suburbs to "a population of ten millions . . . housed comfortably, healthfully and relatively cheaply" — a gold mine for developers.

America gave birth to what one urban historian has called the "private city" — shaped primarily by the actions of many individuals, all pursuing their own goals and bent on making money. The prevailing belief was that the sum of such private activity would far exceed what the community might accomplish through public effort.

Yet constitutionally it was up to city governments to draw the line between public and private. New York City was entirely within its rights to operate a municipally owned subway, the State Supreme Court ruled in 1897. Even the use of private land was subject to whatever regulations the city might impose. Moreover, city governance improved impressively in the late nineteenth century. Though by no means free of the corruption of earlier days, municipal agencies became far better organized and staffed and, above all, more expansive in the functions they undertook. Nowhere in the world, indeed, were there more massive public projects — aqueducts, sewage systems, bridges, and spacious parks.

The Urban Environment. In the space between public and private, however, was an environmental no-man's land. City streets were often filthy and poorly maintained. "Three or four days of warm spring weather," remarked a New York journalist, would turn Manhattan's garbage-strewn, snow-clogged streets into "veritable mud rivers." Air quality likewise suffered. A visitor to Pittsburgh noted "the heavy pall of smoke which constantly overhangs her . . . until the very sun looks coppery through the sooty haze." As for the lovely hills rising from the rivers, "They have been leveled down, cut into, sliced off, and ruthlessly marred and mutilated." Pittsburgh presented "all that is unsightly and forbidding in appearance, the original beauties of nature having been ruthlessly sacrificed to utility."

Hardest hit by urban growth were the poor. In earlier times they had mainly lived in makeshift wooden structures in alleys and back streets and then, as more prosperous families moved away, in the subdivided homes left behind. As land values climbed after the Civil War, speculators tore down these houses and began to erect buildings specifically designed for the urban masses. In New York City the dreadful result was five- or six-story tenements, structures housing twenty or more families in cramped, airless apartments (Figure 18.1). In New York's Eleventh Ward, an average of 986 persons occupied each acre, a density only to be exceeded in Bombay, India.

Reformers recognized the problem but seemed unable to solve it. Some favored model tenements financed by public-spirited citizens willing to accept a limited return on their investment. When private philanthropy failed to make much of a dent, cities turned to housing codes. The most advanced code was New York's Tenement House Law of 1901,

Figure 18.1   Floor Plan of a Dumbbell Tenement

In a contest for a design that met an 1879 requirement that every room have a window, the dumbbell tenement won. The interior indentation, which created an airshaft between adjoining buildings, gave the tenement its "dumbbell" shape. What was touted as a "model" tenement demonstrated instead the futility of trying to reconcile maximum land usage with decent housing. Each floor contained four apartments of three or four rooms, the largest only 10 by 11 feet. The two toilets in the hall became filthy or broke down under daily use by forty or more people. The narrow airshaft provided almost no light for the interior rooms and served mainly as a dumping ground for garbage. So deplorable were these tenements that they became the stimulus for the next wave of New York housing reform.

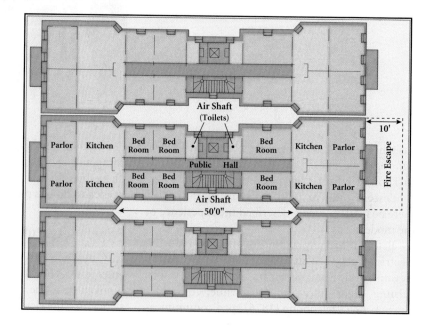

which required interior courts, indoor toilets, and fire safeguards for new structures, but did little for existing housing stock. Commercial development had pushed up land values in downtown areas. Only high-density, cheaply built housing could earn a sufficient profit for the landlords of the poor. This economic fact defied nineteenth-century solutions.

It was not that America lacked an urban vision. On the contrary, an abiding **rural ideal** had influenced American cities for many years. Frederick Law Olmsted, who designed New York City's Central Park, wanted cities that exposed people to the beauties of nature. One of Olmsted's projects, the Chicago Columbian Exposition of 1893, gave rise to the influential "City Beautiful" movement. The results included larger park systems, broad boulevards and parkways, and, after the turn of the century, zoning laws and planned suburbs.

Cities usually heeded urban planners too little and too late. "Fifteen or twenty years ago a plan might have been adopted that would have made this one of the most beautiful cities in the world," Kansas City's park commissioners reported in 1893.

City Garbage

"How to get rid of the garbage?" was a question that bedeviled every American city. The difficulties of keeping up are all too clear in this ground-level photograph by the great urban investigator, Jacob Riis, looking down Tammany Street in New York City circa 1890.

Museum of the City of New York.

At that time "such a policy could not be fully appreciated." Nor, even if Kansas City had foreseen its future, would it have shouldered the "heavy burden" of trying to shape its development. The American city had placed its faith in the dynamics of the marketplace, not the restraints of a planned future. The pluses and minuses are perhaps best revealed by the following comparison.

A Balance Sheet: Chicago and Berlin. Chicago, Illinois, and Berlin, Germany, had virtually equal populations in 1900. But they had very different histories. Seventy years earlier, when Chicago had been a muddy frontier outpost, Berlin was already a city of 250,000 and the royal seat of the Hohenzollerns of Prussia.

With German unification in 1871, the imperial authorities rebuilt Berlin on a grander scale. "A capital city is essential for the state, to act as a pivot for its culture," proclaimed the Prussian historian Heinrich von Treitschke. Berlin served that national purpose — "a center where Germany's political, intellectual, and material life is concentrated, and its people can feel united." Chicago had no such pretensions. It was strictly a place of business, made great by virtue of its strategic grip on the commerce of America's heartland. Nothing in Chicago approached the grandeur of Berlin's boulevards or its monumental palaces and public buildings, nor were Chicagoans witness to the pomp and ceremony of the imperial parades up broad, tree-lined Unter den Linden to the national cathedral.

Yet as a functioning city, Chicago was in many ways superior to Berlin. Chicago's waterworks pumped 500 million gallons of water a day, or 139 gallons of water per person, while Berliners had to make do with 18 gallons. Flush toilets, a rarity in Berlin in 1900, could be found in 60 percent of Chicago's homes. Chicago's streets were lit by electricity, while Berlin still relied mostly on gaslight. Chicago had a much bigger streetcar system, twice as much acreage devoted to parks, and a public library containing many more volumes. And Chicago had just completed an amazing sanitation project that reversed the course of the Chicago River so that its waters — and the city's sewage — would flow away from Lake Michigan and southward down into the Illinois and Mississippi rivers.

Giant sanitation projects were one thing; an inspiring urban environment was something else. For well-traveled Americans admiring of things European, the sense of inferiority was palpable. "We are enormously rich," admitted the journalist Edwin L. Godkin, "but . . . what have we got to show? Almost nothing. Ugliness from an artistic point of view is the mark of all our cities." Thus the urban balance sheet: a utilitarian infrastructure that was superb by nineteenth-century standards, but "no municipal splendors of any description, nothing but population and hotels."

➤ Why can we say that technological innovation was just as significant in building American cities as it was in driving American industrialization?

➤ Why was the American city not capable of doing a better job of protecting the environment and providing adequate housing for the poor?

➤ If we count the degraded environment and poor housing as failures, why does Chicago come off so well in comparison to Berlin?

Upper Class/Middle Class

In the compact city of the early republic, class distinctions had been embedded in the way men and women dressed and by the deference they demanded from or granted others. As the industrial city grew, these marks of class weakened. In the anonymity of a big city, recognition and deference no longer served as mechanisms for conferring status. Instead, people began to rely on conspicuous display of wealth, membership in exclusive clubs, and above all, residence in exclusive neighborhoods.

For the poor, place of residence depended, as always, on being close to their jobs. But for higher-income urbanites, where to live became a matter of personal means and social preference.

The Urban Elite

As early as the 1840s, Boston merchants had taken advantage of the new railway service to escape the congested city. Fine rural estates appeared in Milton, Newton, and other outlying towns. By 1848 roughly 20 percent of Boston's businessmen were making the trip by train to their downtown offices. Ferries that plied the harbor between Manhattan and Brooklyn or New Jersey served the same purpose for well-to-do New Yorkers.

Lifestyles of the Rich. As commercial development engulfed downtown residential areas, the exodus by the elite quickened. In Cincinnati, wealthy families settled on the scenic hills rimming the crowded, humid tableland that ran down to the

Ohio River. On those hillsides, a traveler noted in 1883, "The homes of Cincinnati's merchant princes and millionaires are found . . . elegant cottages, tasteful villas, and substantial mansions, surrounded by a paradise of grass, gardens, lawns, and tree-shaded roads." Residents of the area, called Hilltop, founded country clubs, downtown gentlemen's clubs, and a round of social activities for the pleasure of Cincinnati's elite.

Despite the attractions of country life, many of the very richest preferred the heart of the city. Chicago boasted its Gold Coast; San Francisco, Nob Hill; Denver, Quality Hill; and Manhattan, Fifth Avenue. New York novelist Edith Wharton recalled how the comfortable midcentury brownstones gave way to the "'new' millionaire houses," which spread northward on Fifth Avenue along Central Park. Great mansions, emulating the aristocratic houses of Europe, lined Fifth Avenue at the turn of the century.

But great wealth did not automatically confer social standing. An established elite dominated the social heights, even in such relatively raw cities as San Francisco and Denver. It had taken only a generation — sometimes less — for money made in commerce or real estate to shed its tarnish and become "old" and genteel. In long-settled Boston, wealth passed intact through several generations, creating a closely knit tribe of elite families that kept moneyed newcomers at bay. Elsewhere urban elites tended to be more open, but only to the socially ambitious who were prepared to make visible and energetic use of their money.

New York City became the home of a national elite as the most ambitious gravitated to this preeminent capital of American finance and culture. Manhattan's extraordinary vitality in turn kept the city's high society fluid and relatively open. In Theodore Dreiser's novel *The Titan* (1914), the tycoon Frank Cowperwood reassures his unhappy wife that if Chicago society will not accept them, "there are other cities. Money will arrange matters in New York — that I know. We can build a real place there, and go in on equal terms, if we have money enough." New York thus came to be a magnet for millionaires. The city attracted them not only as a business center but for the opportunities it offered for display and social recognition.

This infusion of wealth shattered the older elite society of New York. Seeking to be assimilated into the upper class, the flood of moneyed newcomers simply overwhelmed it. There followed a curious process of reconstruction, a deliberate effort to define the rules of conduct and identify those who properly "belonged" in New York society.

Ward McAllister and "High Society." The key figure was Ward McAllister, a southern-born lawyer who had made a quick fortune in gold-rush San Francisco and then took up a second career as the arbiter of New York society. In 1888 McAllister compiled the first *Social Register*, which announced that it would serve as a "record of society, comprising an accurate and careful list" of all those deemed eligible for New York society. McAllister instructed the socially ambitious on how to select guests, set a proper table, arrange a party, and launch a young lady into society. He presided over a round of assemblies, balls, and dinners that defined the boundaries of an elite society. At the apex stood "The Four Hundred" — the true cream of New York society. McAllister's list corresponded to those invited to Mrs. William Astor's gala ball of February 1, 1892.

From Manhattan an extravagant life of leisure radiated out to such favored resorts as Saratoga Springs, New York, and Palm Beach, Florida. In Rhode Island, Newport featured a grand array of summer "cottages," crowned by the Vanderbilts' Marble House and The Breakers. Visitors arrived via private railway car or aboard yachts and amused themselves at the races and gambling casinos. In the city, the rich dined extravagantly at Delmonico's, on one famous occasion while mounted on horseback. The underside to this excess — scandalous affairs, rowdy feasts that ended in police court, the notoriously opulent costume ball thrown at the Waldorf-Astoria by the Bradley Martins at the peak of economic depression in 1897 — was avidly followed in the press and awarded the celebrity we now accord to rock singers and Hollywood stars.

Americans were adept at making money, remarked the journalist Edwin L. Godkin in 1896, but they lacked the European aristocratic traditions for spending it. "Great wealth has not yet entered our manners," Godkin remarked. In their struggle to find the way and establish the manners, the moneyed elite made an indelible mark on urban life. If there was magnificence in the American city, that was mainly their handiwork. And if there was conspicuous waste and display, that too was their doing.

The Suburban World

The middle class left a smaller imprint on the public face of the city. Many of its members, unlike the rich, preferred privacy, retreating into a suburban world that insulated them from the hurly-burly of urban life.

Since colonial times, self-employed lawyers, doctors, merchants, and proprietors had been the backbone of a robust American middle class.

Going to the Opera, 1873

In this painting by Seymour J. Guy, William H. Vanderbilt, eldest son and successor of the railroad tycoon Cornelius Vanderbilt, has gathered with his family and friends preparatory to attending the opera. It was the sponsorship of New York's Metropolitan Opera that helped the Vanderbilts achieve social recognition among the older, more established moneyed families of New York City. Courtesy, Biltmore Estate, Asheville, NC.

While independent careers remained important, in the age of industrialism spawned a new middle class of salaried employees. Corporate organizations required managers, accountants, and clerks. Industrial technology called for engineers, chemists, and designers, while the distribution system needed salesmen, advertising executives, and store managers. These salaried ranks increased sevenfold between 1870 and 1910—much faster than any other occupational group. Nearly 9 million people held white-collar jobs in 1910, more than a fourth of all employed Americans.

Some members of this white-collar class lived in the row houses of Baltimore and Boston or the comfortable apartment buildings of New York City. More preferred to escape the clamor and congestion of the city. They were attracted by a persisting rural ideal, agreeing with the landscape architect Andrew Jackson Downing that "nature and domestic life are better than the society and manners of

town." As trolley service pushed out from the city center, middle-class Americans followed the wealthy into the countryside. All sought what one Chicago developer promised for his North Shore subdivision in 1875—"qualities of which the city is in a large degree bereft, namely, its pure air, peacefulness, quietude, and natural scenery."

No major American city escaped **suburbanization** during the late nineteenth century. City limits everywhere expanded rapidly, but even so, much of the suburban growth took place in outlying towns. By 1900 more than half of Boston's people lived in "streetcar suburbs" outside Boston proper; nationwide, according to the 1910 census, about 25 percent of the urban population lived in such autonomous suburbs.

The geography of the suburbs was truly a map of class structure; where a family lived told where it ranked socially. As one proceeded out from the city center, the houses became finer, the lots larger, the inhabitants wealthier. Affluent businessmen and professionals had the time and flexibility for a long commute into town. Closer in, people wanted transit lines that carried them quickly between home and office. Lower-income commuters generally had more than one wage earner in the family, less secure employment, and jobs requiring movement around the city. It was better for them to be closer to the city center because crosstown lines afforded the mobility they needed for their work.

Suburban boundaries shifted constantly, as working-class city residents who wanted to better their lives moved to the cheapest suburbs, prompting an exodus of older residents, who in turn pushed the next higher group farther out in search of space and greenery. Suburbanization was the sum of countless individual decisions. Each family's move represented an advance in living standards — not only more light, air, and quiet but better accommodation than the city afforded. Suburban houses were typically larger for the same money and came equipped with flush toilets, hot water, central heating, and, by the turn of the century, electricity.

The suburbs also restored an opportunity that Americans thought they had lost when they moved to the city. In the suburbs home ownership again became the norm. "A man is not really a true man until he owns his own home," propounded the Reverend Russell H. Conwell in his famous sermon on the virtues of moneymaking, "Acres of Diamonds."

The small towns of rural America had fostered community life. Not so the suburbs. The grid street pattern, while efficient for laying out lots, offered no natural focus for group life, nor did the shops and services that lay scattered along the trolley-car streets. Suburban development conformed to the economics of real estate and transportation, and so did the thinking of middle-class home seekers entering the suburbs. They wanted a house that gave them good value and convenience to the trolley line.

The need for community had lost some of its force for middle-class Americans. Two other attachments assumed greater importance: one was work; the other, family.

Middle-Class Families

In the pre-industrial economy, work and family life were intertwined. Farmers, merchants, and artisans generally worked at home. The household, as the unit of production, encompassed not only blood relatives, but everyone living and working there. As industrialism progressed, family life and economic activity parted company. The father departed every morning for the office, and children spent more years in school. Clothing was bought ready made; food came increasingly in cans and packages. Middle-class families became smaller, excluding all but nuclear members and consisting typically by 1900 of husband, wife, and three children.

Within this family circle relationships became intense and affectionate. "Home was the most expressive experience in life," recalled the literary critic Henry Seidel Canby of his growing up in the 1890s. "Though the family might quarrel and nag, the home held them all, protecting them against the outside world." The suburb provided a fit setting for such middle-class families. The quiet, tree-lined streets created a domestic space insulated from the harshness of commerce and enterprise.

The Wife's Role. The burdens of this domesticity fell heavily on the wife. It was nearly unheard of for her to seek an outside career — that was her husband's role. Her job was to manage the household. "The woman who could not make a home, like the man who could not support one, was condemned," Canby remembered. As the physical burdens of household work eased, higher-quality homemaking became the new ideal — a message propagated by Catharine Beecher's best-selling book *The American Woman's Home* (1869) and by such magazines as the *Ladies' Home Journal* and *Good Housekeeping*, which first appeared during the 1880s. This advice literature instructed wives that, in addition to their domestic duties, they had the responsibility for bringing sensibility, beauty, and love to the household. "We owe to women the charm and beauty of life," wrote one educator. "For the love that rests, strengthens and inspires, we look to women." In this idealized view the wife made the home a refuge for her husband and a place of nurture for their children.

Womanly virtue, even if much glorified, by no means put wives on equal terms with their husbands. Although the legal status of married women — their right to own property, control separate earnings, make contracts, and get a divorce — improved markedly during the nineteenth century, law and custom still dictated a wife's submission to her husband. She relied on his ability as the family breadwinner, and despite her superior virtues and graces she was thought to be below him in vigor and intellect. Her mind could be employed "but little and in trivial matters," wrote one prominent physician, and her proper place was as "the companion or ornamental appendage to man."

Not surprisingly, many bright, independent-minded women rebelled against marriage. The marriage rate fell to a low point during the last

Middle-Class Domesticity

For middle-class Americans the home was a place of nurture, a refuge from the world of competitive commerce. Perhaps that explains why their residences were so heavily draped and cluttered with bric-a-brac. All of it emphasized privacy and pride of possession. Culver Pictures.

forty years of the nineteenth century. More than 10 percent of women of marriageable age remained single, and the rate was much higher among college graduates and professionals. Only half the Mount Holyoke College class of 1902, for example, married. "I know that something perhaps, humanly speaking, supremely precious has passed me by," remarked the writer Vida Scudder. "But how much it would have excluded!" Married life "looks to me often as I watch it terribly impoverished, for women."

The Cult of Masculinity. If fewer women were marrying, of course, so were fewer men. We can, thanks to the census, trace the tardy progression into marriage of the male cohort born just after the Civil War: In 1890, when they were in their early thirties, two-fifths were unmarried; a decade later, in their early forties, a quarter still had not married; and ultimately, a hard-core, over 10 percent, never married. One historian has labeled the late nineteenth century the Age of the Bachelor, a time when being an unattached male lost its social

stigma and, especially in large cities, became a happy alternative for many men of marriageable age. A bachelor's counterpart to Vida Scudder's dim view of marriage was this ditty making the rounds in the early 1880s:

No wife to scold me
No children to squall
God bless the happy man
Who keeps bachelor's hall.

With its residential hotels, restaurants, and abundant personal services, the urban scene afforded bachelors all the comforts of home and, on top of that, a happy array of men's clubs, saloons, and sporting events.

The appeal of the manly life was not, however, confined to confirmed bachelors. American males inherited a pride in independence—achieved above all by being one's own boss—but the salaried jobs they increasingly held left them distinctly not their own bosses. Nor, once work and household had been severed, could they enjoy the patriarchal hold over family life that had empowered their fathers and grandfathers. A palpable anxiety arose that the American male was becoming, as one magazine editor warned, "weak, effeminate, decaying." There was a telling shift in language. While people had once spoken of *manhood*, which meant leaving *childhood* behind, they now spoke of *masculinity*, the opposite of *femininity*: Being a man meant surmounting the feminizing influences of modern life.

And how was this to be accomplished? By engaging in competitive sports like football, which became hugely popular in this era. By working out and becoming fit because, as the psychologist G. Stanley Hall put it, "you can't have a firm will without firm muscles." By resorting to the great outdoors—

preferably out west—and engaging in Theodore Roosevelt's "strenuous life." Or vicariously, by reading Owen Wister's best-selling cowboy novel, *The Virginian* (1902), or that celebration of primitive man, Edgar Rice Burroughs's *Tarzan of the Apes* (1912). The surging popularity of westerns and adventure novels was surely a marker of the fears by urban dwellers that theirs was not a life for real men.

Changing Views of Women's Sexuality. Women perhaps had an easier time of it because they were in the process of being liberated from a repressive past—from the medical judgment that, as one popular text put it, "the majority of women (happily for society) are not very much troubled by sexual feeling of any kind." Middle-class women had bought into

Manliness

A maxim of modern advertising states: Link your product to what the public admires. At the turn of the century, Americans admired real men, like the Graeco-Roman wrestlers in this 1911 advertisement. If you want to be like them, eat Grape-Nuts. An advertisement in *The All-Story*, December 1911.

MARBLE GROUP IN POSTUM OFFICES

In Olden Times

The Greek and Roman athletes trained on simple, wholesome foods, made largely from the field grains—*producing* and *maintaining* the old-world ideals of vigorous manhood.

These grains grow today as they did then.

Grape-Nuts
FOOD

—made of Wheat and Barley—contains the body- and brain-building elements stored in the grains by Nature, and is scientifically prepared for easy digestion.

One cannot find better food than Grape-Nuts!

"There's A Reason"

Postum Cereal Company, Ltd., Battle Creek, Michigan, U. S. A.

this dreary view of them because it eased a painful family dilemma. They wanted fewer children, but, other than abstinence, were often at a loss about what to do. Contraceptive devices, although heavily marketed, were either unreliable or, as in the case of condoms, stigmatized by association with the brothel.

On top of that, advocates of birth control had to contend with Anthony Comstock, an agent of the post office who was also secretary of the Society for the Suppression of Vice. In that capacity he campaigned relentlessly to uplift the nation's morals. The vehicle he chose was a federal law passed at his behest in 1873 prohibiting the sending of obscene materials through the U.S. mails. Comstock defined obscenity to include any information about birth control or, for that matter, any open discussion of sex. So powerful was Comstock's influence that the suppression of vice became a national obsession during the 1870s. Among the victims were women who wanted some release from the burden of unwanted pregnancies.

Many doctors disapproved of contraception, fearing that uncoupling sex from procreation would release the sexual appetites of men, to the detriment of their health and the moral fiber of society. It is this official writing (along with Comstock's anti-vice campaign) that has given us the notion of a Victorian age of sexual repression. Letters and diaries suggest that in the privacy of their homes husbands and wives acted otherwise. Yet they must have done so in constant fear of unwanted pregnancies. A fulfilling sexual relationship was not easily squared with desires to limit and space childbearing.

Around 1890 a change set in. Despite Comstock, contraception became more acceptable and reliable. Experts began to abandon the notion that women "are not very much troubled by sexual feelings of any kind." In succeeding editions of his book *Plain Home Talk on Love, Marriage, and Parentage*, for example, the physician Edward Bliss Foote began to favor a healthy sexuality that gave pleasure to women as well as men. It was the beginning of a sexual revolution.

During the 1890s the artist Charles Dana Gibson created the image of the "new woman." In his drawings the Gibson girl was tall, spirited, athletic, and chastely sexual. She rejected bustles, hoop skirts, and tightly laced corsets, preferring shirtwaists and other natural styles that did not disguise her female form (see Reading American Pictures, "Challenging Female Delicacy: The New Woman," p. 565). In the city, women's sphere began to take on a more public character. Among the new urban institutions catering to women, the most important was the department store, which became a temple for their emerging role as consumers.

Attitudes toward Children. The offspring of the middle class experienced their own revolution. In the past children had been regarded as an economic asset—added hands for the family farm, shop, or countinghouse. Especially for the urban middle class, this no longer held true. Parents stopped expecting their children to be working members of the family. In the old days Ralph Waldo Emerson remarked in 1880, "Children had been repressed and kept in the background; now they are considered, cosseted, and pampered." There was such a thing as "the juvenile mind," lectured Jacob Abbott in his book *Gentle Measures in the Management and Training of the Young* (1871). The family was responsible for providing a nurturing environment in which the young personality could grow and mature.

Preparation for adulthood became increasingly linked to formal education. School enrollment went up 150 percent between 1870 and 1900. As the years before adulthood began to stretch out, a new stage of life—adolescence—emerged. While rooted in longer years of family dependency, adolescence shifted much of the socializing role from parents to peer group. The impact was most marked on the daughters of the middle class, who, freed from the chores of housework, were now encouraged to devote themselves to self-development, including for many the chance to go to high school (Table 18.2). The liberating consequences surely went beyond their parents' expectations. In a revealing shift in terminology, "young lady" gave way to "school girl," and the daughterly submissiveness of earlier times gave way

TABLE 18.2 High School Graduates, 1870–1910

Year	Numbers	Percent 17-Year-Olds	Male	Female
1870	16,000	2.0	7,000	9,000
1890	44,000	3.0	19,000	25,000
1910	156,000	8.6	64,000	93,000

SOURCE: *Historical Statistics of the United States*, 2 vols. (Washington, DC: U.S. Bureau of the Census, 1975), 1:386.

Challenging Female Delicacy: The New Woman

Recalling her Baltimore girlhood, the president of Bryn Mawr College remembered "the awful doubt, felt by women themselves as well as by men, as to whether women as a sex were physically and mentally fit for" higher education. To male readers of this text, that might sound silly, what with the female classmates they see working out at the gym or that formidable woman professor they've encountered in a course (maybe this one). But it wasn't silly in the late nineteenth-century. On the neighboring page, we claim that the notion of female delicacy expired during the 1890s, but saying it is one thing, capturing so elusive a change is another, and for that we turn to an unexpected historical source—the fine art of the period. This wonderful painting (1897) is by John Singer Sargent, the greatest portraitist of the age, depicting a wealthy socialite couple, Mr. and Mrs. Isaac Newton Phelps Stokes.

Mr. and Mrs. Isaac Phelps Stokes, John Singer Sargent (1897). The Metropolitan Museum of Art, Bequest of Edith Minturn Phelps Stokes (Mrs. I.N.), 1938. Photo copyright 1992, The Metropolitan Museum of Art.

ANALYZING THE EVIDENCE

➤ Sargent presents Mrs. Phelps Stokes in a shirtwaist and long skirt, the uniform of the "New Woman." Does anything else about her appearance convey independence and strength? How do these qualities contrast with older views of women? Does she strike you as someone likely to suffer a nervous collapse?

➤ Implicit in the New Woman was a repudiation of the idea of wives as "the companion or ornamental appendage of man." Is there anything about the way Mr. and Mrs. Phelps Stokes are presented as a couple that suggests this marital revolution?

➤ Sargent was a high-society painter. His subjects were almost exclusively elite women, decked out in their finest. Wealthy patrons prized his portraits partly because they enjoyed having their women depicted as the objects of conspicuous consumption. But in this portrait, Sargent dispenses with the evening gown and jewels and shows Mrs. Phelps Stokes in everyday dress. Can the fact that she is not depicted as an object of conspicuous consumption be explained by her portrayal as a New Woman? Or throw any light on the changing relations between men and women in this period?

to self-expressive independence. On achieving adulthood, it was not so big a step for the daughters of the middle class to become Gibson's "new women."

> ➤ Why is Ward McAllister so significant a figure in the annals of the rich?

> ➤ Why did the suburbs become so prominent a feature of the late-nineteenth-century city?

> ➤ In the middle-class family of this era, how might the wife's position have been more stressful than that of her husband? Why was this so?

City Life

With its soaring skyscrapers, jostling traffic, and hum of business, the city symbolized energy and enterprise. When the budding writer Hamlin Garland and his brother arrived in Chicago from Iowa in 1881, they knew immediately that they had entered a new world: "Everything interested us. . . . Nothing was commonplace, nothing was ugly to us." In one way or another every city-bound migrant, whether fresh from the American countryside or from a foreign land, experienced something of this sense of wonder.

The city was utterly unlike the rural world. In the countryside every person had been known to his or her neighbors. Mark Twain found New York "a splendid desert, where a stranger is lonely in the midst of a million of his race. . . . Every man rushes, rushes, rushes, and never has time to be companionable [or] to fool away on matters which do not involve dollars and duty and business."

Migrants could never recreate in the city the communities they had left behind. But they found ways of belonging, they built new institutions, and they learned how to function in an impersonal, heterogeneous environment. An urban culture emerged, and through it there developed a new breed of American who was entirely at home in the modern city.

Newcomers

The explosive growth of America's big-city population—the numbers living in places of 100,000 people or more jumped from about 6 million to 14 million between 1880 and 1900—meant that cities were very much a world of newcomers (Map 18.2). Many came from the nation's countryside; half of rural families on the move in these years were city bound. But it was newcomers further marked off by skin color or ethnicity who found entry into city life most daunting. At the turn of the century, upwards of 30 percent of the residents of New York, Chicago, Boston, Cleveland, Minneapolis, and San Francisco were foreign-born. The biggest ethnic group in Boston was Irish; in Minneapolis, Swedish; in most other northern cities, German. But by 1910 the influx from southern and eastern Europe had changed the ethnic complexion of many of these cities. In Chicago, Poles took the lead; in New York, eastern European Jews; in San Francisco, Italians.

As the earlier "walking cities" disappeared, so did the opportunities for intermingling with older populations. The later arrivals from southern and eastern Europe had little choice about where they lived; they needed to find cheap housing near their jobs. Some gravitated to the outlying factory districts; others settled in the congested downtown **ghettos.** In New York Italians crowded into the Irish neighborhoods west of Broadway, and Russian and Polish Jews pushed the Germans out of the Lower East Side (Map 18.3). A colony of Hungarians lived around Houston Street, and Bohemians occupied the poorer stretches of the Upper East Side between Fiftieth and Seventy-sixth streets. Virtually every city with a large immigrant population experienced this kind of ethnic sorting-out, as, for example, San Francisco, with its Chinatown, Italian North Beach, and Jewish Hayes Valley.

Capitalizing on fellow feeling, immigrant institutions of many kinds sprang up. Newspapers appeared wherever substantial numbers lived. In 1911 the 20,000 Poles in Buffalo supported two Polish-language daily papers. Immigrants throughout the country avidly read *Il Progresso Italo-Americano* and the Yiddish-language *Jewish Daily Forward*, both published in New York City. Companionship could always be found on street corners, in barbershops and club rooms, and in saloons. Italians marched in saint's day parades, Bohemians gathered in singing societies, and New York Jews patronized a lively Yiddish theater. To provide help in times of sickness and death, the immigrants organized mutual-aid societies. The Italians of Chicago had sixty-six of these organizations in 1903, mostly composed of people from particular provinces or towns. Immigrants built a rich and functional institutional life in urban America to an extent unimagined in their native places (see Comparing American Voices, "Coming to America: The Downside," pp. 570–571).

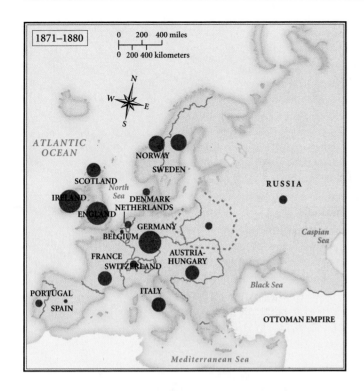

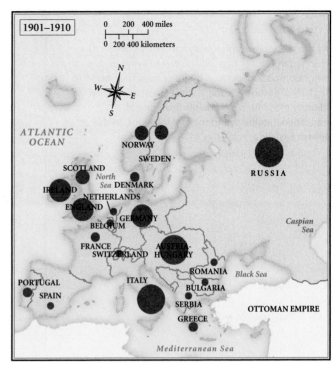

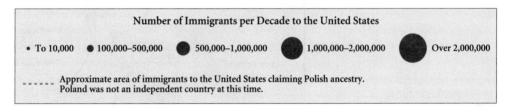

MAP 18.2   Sources of European Immigration to the United States, 1871–1910

Around 1900 Americans began to speak of the "new" immigration. They meant the large numbers of immigrants arriving from eastern and southern Europe — Poles, Slovaks and other Slavic groups, Yiddish-speaking Jews, Italians — and overwhelming the still substantial and more familiar immigrants from the British Isles and northern Europe (see also Figure 17.3, American Immigration, 1870–1914, on p. 531).

Urban Blacks. The African American migration from the rural South to northern cities was just beginning at the turn of the century. The black population of New York increased by 30,000 between 1900 and 1910, making New York second only to Washington, D.C., as a black urban center, but the 91,000 African Americans in New York in 1910 represented fewer than 2 percent of the population, and that was true of Chicago and Cleveland as well.

Urban blacks retreated from the scattered neighborhoods of older times into concentrated ghettos — Chicago's Black Belt on the South Side, for example, or the early outlines of New York's Harlem. Race prejudice cut down job opportunities. Twenty-six percent of Cleveland's blacks had been skilled workers in 1870; only 12 percent were skilled by 1890. Entire occupations such as barbering (except for a black clientele) became exclusively white. Cleveland's blacks in 1910 mainly worked as domestics and day laborers, with little hope of moving up the job ladder.

In the face of pervasive discrimination, urban blacks built their own communities. They created a flourishing press, fraternal orders, a vast array of women's organizations, and a middle class of doctors, lawyers, and small entrepreneurs. Above all, there were the black churches — twenty-five in Chicago in 1905, mainly Methodist and Baptist. More than any other institution, remarked one scholar in 1913, it was the church "which the

MAP 18.3   The Lower East Side, New York City, 1900

As this map shows, the Jewish immigrants dominating Manhattan's Lower East Side preferred living in neighborhoods populated by those from their home regions of eastern Europe. Their sense of a common identity made for a remarkable flowering of educational, cultural, and social institutions on the Jewish East Side.

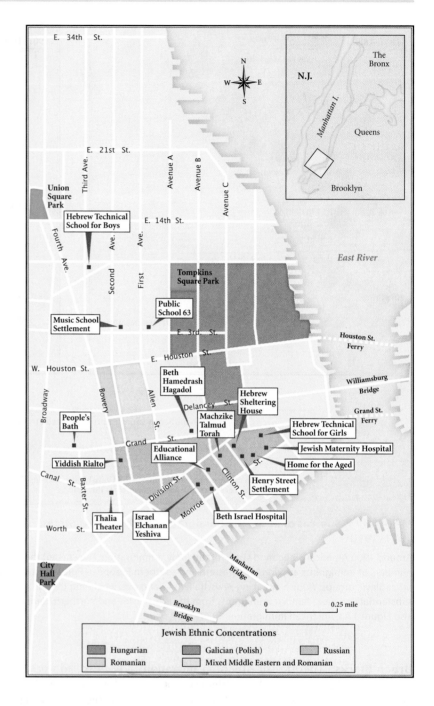

Negro may call his own. . . . A new church may be built . . . and . . . all the machinery set in motion without ever consulting any white person. . . . [Religion] more than anything else represents the real life of the race." As in the southern countryside, the church was the central institution for city blacks, and the preacher was the most important local citizen. Manhattan's Union Baptist Church, housed like many others in a storefront, attracted the "very recent residents of this new, disturbing city" and, ringing with spirituals and prayer, made Christianity come "alive Sunday mornings."

Ward Politics

Race and ethnicity divided newcomers. Politics, by contrast, integrated them into the wider urban society. Migrants to American cities automatically became ward residents and acquired a spokesman at city hall. Their alderman got streets paved, or water mains extended, or permits granted—so that, for example, in 1888 Vito Fortounescere could "place and keep a stand for the sale of fruit, inside the stoop-line, in front of the northeast corner of Twenty-eighth Street and Fourth Avenue" in Manhattan, or the

The Cherry Family Tree, 1906

Wiley and Fannie Cherry migrated in 1893 from North Carolina to Chicago, settling in the small African American community on the West Side. The Cherrys apparently prospered and by 1906, when this family portrait was taken, had entered the black middle class. When migration intensified after 1900, longer-settled urban blacks like the Cherrys became uncomfortable, and relations with the needy rural newcomers were often tense. Courtesy, Lorraine Heflin / Chicago Historical Society.

parishioners of Saint Maria of Mount Carmel could set off fireworks at their Fourth of July picnic.

These favors came via a system of boss control that, although present at every level of party politics, flourished most luxuriantly in the big cities. Urban **political machines** like Tammany Hall in New York depended on a grassroots constituency, so they recruited layers of functionaries—precinct captains, ward bosses, aldermen—whose main job was to be accessible and, as best they could, serve the needs of the party faithful.

The machine acted as a rough-and-ready social service agency, providing jobs for the jobless, a helping hand for a bereaved family, and intercession against an unfeeling city bureaucracy. The Tammany ward boss George Washington Plunkitt

had a "regular system" when fires broke out in his district. He arranged for housing for burned-out families, "fix[ing] them up till they get things runnin' again. It's philanthropy, but it's politics, too—mighty good politics."

The business community was similarly served. Contractors sought city business, gas companies and streetcar lines wanted licenses, manufacturers needed services and not-too-nosy inspectors, and the liquor trade and numbers rackets relied on a tolerant police force. All of them turned to the machine boss and his lieutenants.

Of course, the machine exacted a price for these services. The tenement dweller gave his vote. The businessman wrote a check. Naturally, some of the money that changed hands leaked into the pockets

Coming to America: The Downside

At the height of the eastern European immigration, sociologists became concerned about the problem of "anomie," the breakdown of codes of behavior under conditions of stress and social disorder. The classic study was William I. Thomas and Florian Znaniecki's *The Polish Peasant in Europe and America* (1918). Among the evidences of anomie, none were more heart-rending than the abandonment of families by their fathers. In Jewish communities of eastern Europe, desertion was nearly unheard of, although rabbis generally countenanced divorce in childless marriages. In America, however, desertion became a serious problem, so much so that the leading Yiddish-language newspaper in New York, the *Jewish Daily Forward*, ran a regular feature seeking information about wayward husbands.

DESERTED WIFE

The Daily Forward *also boasted a famous page entitled* Bintel Brief, *which in Yiddish means "bundle of letters." The letters from immigrant readers about their trials and tribulations in America are a unique documentary source, offering a window into the lives of obscure people who rarely left personal records for historians to study. Nothing, indeed, could have been more personal than the stories and pleas for advice from "Dear Editor." The document below, written in 1908 by a Deserted Wife, made use of Bintel Brief to appeal directly to her missing husband.*

Worthy Editor

Have pity on me and my two small children and print my letter in the *Forward.*

Max! The children and I now say farewell to you. You left us in such a terrible state. You had no compassion for us. For six years I loved you faithfully, took care of you like a loyal servant, never had a happy day with you. Yet I forgive you for everything.

Have you ever asked yourself why you left us? Max, where is your conscience: you used to have sympathy for the forsaken women and used to say their terrible plight was due to the men who left them in dire need. And how did you act? I was a young, educated, decent girl when you took me. You lived with me for six years, during which time I bore you four children. And then you left me.

Of the four children, only two remain, but you have made them living orphans. Who will bring them up? Who will support us? Have you no pity for your own flesh and blood? Consider what you are doing. My tears choke me and I cannot write any more.

Be advised that in several days I am leaving with my two living orphans for Russia. We say farewell to you and beg you to take pity on us and send us enough to live on.

Your Deserted Wife and Children

WAYWARD HUSBANDS

The letter below, written in 1910, offers the husbands' side of the story. Students should read both letters with this question in mind: What was there about the immigrant experience in America that might account for so profound a breakdown of traditional values and marital obligations?

Dear Editor:

This is the voice of thirty-seven miserable men who are buried but not covered over by earth, tied down but not in chains, silent but not mute, whose hearts beat like humans, yet are not like other human beings.

When we look at our striped clothes, at our dirty narrow cots, at our fellow companions in the cells, the beaten, lowest members of society, who long ago lost their human dignity, the blood freezes in our veins. We feel degraded and miserable here. And why are we confined here? For the horrible crime of being poor, not being able to satisfy the mad whims of our wives. That's why we pine away here, stamped with the name "convict." That's why we are despised, robbed of our freedom, and treated like dogs.

We ask you, worthy Editor, to publish our letter so your readers, especially the women, will know how we live here. This letter is written not with ink but with our hearts' blood. We are coughing from the polluted air that we breathe in the cells. Our bones ache from lying on the hard cots and we get stomach aches from the food they give us.

The non-support "plague" is the worst plague of all. For the merest nonsense, a man is caught and committed to the workhouse. He doesn't even get a chance to defend himself. Even during the worst times of the Russian reaction people didn't suffer as the men suffer here in America because of their wives. For a Jewish wife it's as easy here to condemn her husband to imprisonment as it is for her to try on a pair of gloves. In all the world there isn't such legal injustice as here in the alimony courts.

What do they think, these women! If they believe that the imprisoned husbands, after the six months, will become purified and come out good, sweet and loving, they're making a big mistake.

The worst offense is committed by the Jewish charity organizations. They sympathize with the wife when her husband is in jail. They forget, however, that they "manufacture" the grass widows and living orphans when they help the woman. As soon as the wife tastes an easy and a free dollar, as soon as she discovers that the "charities" won't let her starve, she doesn't care that her husband is condemned. She lives a gay life, enjoys herself, and doesn't think of her husband.

Therefore it is your duty as editor of the *Forward,* the news paper that is read mainly by the working class, the class that furnishes more than all others the candidates for the workhouse and for grass widowhood, to warn all the Jewish women not to take such revenge on their husbands. They do more harm to themselves than to their men. They drive away their husbands for life that way, and make themselves and their children miserable. The women must learn that sending their husbands to prison is a poor method of improving them. It is a double-edged sword that slashes one side as deeply as the other.

Finally, I appeal to all the women whose husbands are imprisoned for non-support in the workhouse on Blackwell's Island Prison, and I write to them as follows: Their husbands have sworn here that if they, the women, do not have them released in time for *Pesach* [Passover], they will never again return and the women will remain grass widows forever.

We ask you to publish this letter immediately.
Respectfully,
[The letter is signed by thirty-seven men]

SOURCE: Isaac Metzker, ed., *A Bintel Brief: Sixty Years of Letters from the Lower East Side* (Schocken: New York, 1971), 85–86, 110–112.

ANALYZING THE EVIDENCE

➤ In the first letter, the deserted wife seems bewildered by her situation. She has no idea why Max has abandoned her. How would you explain her incomprehension?

➤ In the second letter, the incarcerated husbands seem equally bewildered. They can't understand why refusing to support their wives would be regarded as a crime. Can you explain their irresponsibility? Or why they would resent the assistance given to their families by Jewish charity organizations? What part of their confusion would you ascribe to their traditional role as patriarchal heads of families? And what part to their American experience?

➤ In his response to their letter, the Editor acknowledged that among the thirty-seven "there must be some who weren't in a position to support their families, but it's nothing new to find innocent men suffering along with the guilty." Is that a distinction you would accept? And what does it suggest about the economic causes of family instability in the ghettoes?

➤ Deadbeat husbands, of course, are not a problem only of the past. They're still very much with us. Would you regard the sentence meted out to them a hundred years ago — six months in jail — an appropriate punishment today?

Italian Bread Peddlers, New York City
Because of crowded conditions in East Side tenements, immigrant life spilled out onto the streets, which offered a bit of fresh air, a chance to socialize with neighbors, and a place to shop for food, including bread. KEA Publishing Services Ltd.

of machine politicians. This "boodle" could be blatantly corrupt—kickbacks by contractors; protection money from gamblers, saloonkeepers, and prostitutes; payoffs from gas and trolley companies. In the 1860s boss William Marcy Tweed had made Tammany a byword for corruption, until he was brought down in 1871 by his extravagant graft in the building of a lavish city courthouse. Thereafter, machine corruption became less blatant. The turn-of-the-century Tammanyite George Plunkitt declared that he had no need for kickbacks and bribes. He favored what he called "honest graft," the easy profits that came to savvy insiders. Plunkitt made most of his money building wharves on Manhattan's waterfront. One way or another, legally or otherwise, machine politics rewarded its supporters.

Plunkitt was an Irishman, and so were most of the machine politicians controlling Tammany Hall. But by the 1890s Plunkitt's Fifteenth District was filling up with Italians and Russian Jews. In general, the Irish had no love for these newer immigrants, but Plunkitt played no favorites. On any given day (as recorded in a diary) he might attend an Italian funeral in the afternoon and a Jewish wedding in the evening, and at each he probably paid his respects with a few Italian words or a choice bit of Yiddish.

In an era when so many forces acted to isolate ghetto communities, politics served an *integrating* function, cutting across ethnic lines and giving immigrants and blacks a stake in the larger urban order.

Religion in the City

For urban blacks, as we have seen, the church was a mainstay of their lives. So it was for many other city dwellers. But cities were not easy ground for religious practice. All the great faiths—Judaism, Catholicism, and Protestantism—had to scramble to reconcile religious belief with the secular urban world.

Judaism: The Challenge to Orthodoxy. About 250,000 Jews, mostly of German origin, inhabited America when the eastern European Jews began arriving in the 1880s. Well established and prosperous, the German Jews embraced Reform Judaism, abandoning religious practices—from keeping a kosher kitchen to conducting services in Hebrew—"not adapted to the views and habits of modern civilization." This was not the way of the Yiddish-speaking Jews from eastern Europe. Eager to preserve their traditional piety, they founded their own Orthodox synagogues, often in vacant stores and ramshackle buildings, and practiced Judaism as they had at home.

In the villages of eastern Europe, however, Judaism had involved not only worship but an entire way of life. Insular though it might be, ghetto life in the American city could not recreate the communal environment on which strict religious observance depended. "The very clothes I wore and the very food I ate had a fatal effect on my religious habits," confessed the hero of Abraham Cahan's novel *The Rise of David Levinsky* (1917). "If you . . . attempt to bend your religion to the spirit of your surroundings, it breaks. It falls to pieces." Levinsky shaved off his beard and plunged into the Manhattan clothing business. Orthodox Judaism survived this shattering of faith but only by reducing its claims on the lives of the faithful.

"Americanism" and the Catholic Church. Catholics faced much the same problem, defined as "Americanism" by the church. To what degree should congregants adapt to American society? Should children attend parochial or public schools? Should they intermarry with non-Catholics? Should the traditional education for the clergy be changed? Bishop John Ireland of St. Paul, Minnesota, felt that "the principles of the Church are in harmony with the interests of the Republic." But traditionalists, led by Archbishop Michael A. Corrigan of New York, denied the possibility of such harmony and argued for insulating the church from the pluralistic American environment.

Immigrant Catholics, anxious to preserve what they had known in Europe, generally supported the church's conservative wing. But they also desired that church life express their ethnic identities. Newly arrived Catholics wanted their own parishes, where they could celebrate their customs, speak their languages, and establish their own parochial schools. When they became numerous enough, they also demanded their own bishops. The Catholic hierarchy, which was dominated by Irish Catholics, felt that the integrity of the church itself was at stake. The demand for ethnic parishes implied local control of church property. And if there were bishops for specific ethnic groups, this would mean disrupting the diocesan structure that unified the church.

With some strain, the Catholic Church managed to satisfy the immigrant faithful. It met the demand for representation by appointing immigrant priests as auxiliary bishops within existing dioceses. Ethnic parishes also flourished. By World War I, there were more than two thousand foreign-language churches and many others that were bilingual. Not without strain the Catholic Church accommodated itself to the demands of ethnic identity in urban America.

Protestantism: Regaining Lost Ground. For Protestant denominations the city posed different but not easier challenges. Every major city retained great downtown churches where wealthy Protestants worshiped. Some of these churches, richly endowed, took pride in nationally prominent pastors, such as Henry Ward Beecher of Plymouth Congregational Church in Brooklyn or Phillips Brooks of Trinity Episcopal Church in Boston. But the eminence of these churches, with their fashionable congregations and imposing edifices, could not disguise the growing remoteness of traditional Protestantism from much of its urban constituency. "Where is the city in which the Sabbath day is not losing ground?" lamented a minister in 1887. The families of businessmen, lawyers, and doctors could be seen in any church on Sunday morning, he noted, "but the workingmen and their families are not there."

To counter this decline the Protestant churches responded by evangelizing among the unchurched and indifferent. Starting in the 1880s they also began providing reading rooms, day nurseries, clubhouses, vocational classes, and other services. The Salvation Army, which arrived from Great Britain in 1879, spread the gospel of repentance among the urban poor and built an assistance program that ranged from soup kitchens to shelters for former prostitutes. When all else failed, the down-and-outers of American cities knew they could count on the Salvation Army.

For single people, there were the Young Men's and Women's Christian Associations, which had arrived from Britain before the Civil War. Housing for single women was an especially important mission of the YWCAs. The gymnasiums that made the YMCAs synonymous with "muscular Christianity" were equally important for young men. No other organizations so effectively combined activities for

Immaculate Heart of Mary Church, 1908

In crowded immigrant neighborhoods the church rose from undistinguished surroundings to assert the centrality of religious belief in the life of the community. This photograph is a view of Immaculate Heart of Mary Church, taken from Polish Hill in Pittsburgh in 1908. Pittsburgh City Photographer Collection, Archives Service Center, University of Pittsburgh.

young people with an evangelizing appeal through Bible classes, nondenominational worship, and a religious atmosphere.

The social meaning that people sought in religion explained the enormous popularity of a book called *In His Steps* (1896). The author, a Congregational minister named Charles M. Sheldon, told the story of a congregation that resolved to live by Christ's precepts for one year. "If the church members were all doing as Jesus would do," Sheldon asked, "could it remain true that armies of men would walk the streets for jobs, and hundreds of them curse the church, and thousands of them find in the saloon their best friend?"

The most potent form of urban evangelism — revivalism — said little about social uplift. From their origins in the eighteenth century, revival movements had steadfastly focused on individual redemption. The resolution of earthly problems, revivalists believed, would follow the conversion of the people to Christ. Beginning in the mid-1870s, revival meetings swept through the cities.

The pioneering figure was Dwight L. Moody, a former Chicago shoe salesman and YMCA official. After preaching in Britain for two years, Moody returned to America in 1875 and began staging revival meetings that drew thousands. He preached an optimistic, uncomplicated, nondenominational message. Eternal life could be had for the asking, Moody shouted as he held up his Bible. His listeners needed only "to come forward and take, TAKE!"

Many other preachers followed in Moody's path. The most colorful was Billy Sunday, a hard-drinking former outfielder for the Chicago White Stockings who mended his ways and found religion. Like Moody and other city revivalists, Sunday was a farm boy. His rip-snorting attacks on fash-ionable ministers and the "booze traffic" carried the ring of rustic America. By realizing that many people remained villagers at heart, revivalists found a key for bringing city dwellers back to the church.

City Amusements

City people compartmentalized life's activities, setting workplace apart from home and working time apart from free time. "Going out" became a necessity, demanded not only as solace for a hard day's work but proof that life was better in the New World than in the Old. "He who can enjoy and does not enjoy commits a sin," a Yiddish-language paper told its readers. And enjoyment now meant buying a ticket and being entertained (see Voices from Abroad, "José Martí: Coney Island, 1881," p. 575).

Music halls attracted huge audiences. Chicago had six **vaudeville** houses in 1896, twenty-two in 1910. Evolving from tawdry variety and minstrel shows, vaudeville cleaned up its routines, making them suitable for the entire family, and turned into professional entertainment handled by national booking agencies. With its standard program of nine singing, dancing, and comedy acts, vaudeville attained enormous popularity just as the movies arrived. The first primitive films, a minute or so of humor or glimpses of famous people, appeared in 1896 in penny arcades and as filler in vaudeville shows. Within a decade, millions of city people were watching films of increasing length and artistry at nickelodeons (named after the five-cent admission charge) across the country.

For young unmarried workers the cheap amusements of the city created a new social space. "I want a good time," a New York clothing operator told an investigator. "And there is no . . . way a

Amusement Park, Long Beach, California

The origins of the roller coaster go back to LaMarcus Thompson's Switchback Railway, installed at Coney Island in 1884 and featuring gentle dips and curves. By 1900, when Long Beach's Jack Rabbit Race was constructed, the goal was to create the biggest possible thrill. Angelenos journeyed out by trolley to Long Beach not only to take a dip in the ocean but also to ride the new roller coaster. The airplane ride in the foreground is a further wrinkle on the peculiarly modern notion that the way to have fun is to be scared to death. Curt Teich Postcard Archives.

José Martí

Coney Island, 1881

José Martí, a Cuban patriot and revolutionary (see p. 648), was a journalist by profession. In exile from 1880 to 1895, he spent most of his time in New York City, reporting to his Latin American readers on the customs of the Yankees. Martí took special — one might say perverse — pleasure in observing Americans at play. Bear in mind, as you read his account of Coney Island, that Martí is writing from a self-consciously different cultural perspective.

From all parts of the United States, legions of intrepid ladies and Sunday-best farmers arrive to admire the splendid sights, the unexampled wealth, the dizzying variety, the herculean surge, the striking appearance of Coney Island, the now famous island, four years ago an abandoned sand bank, that today is a spacious amusement area providing relaxation and recreation for hundreds of thousands of New Yorkers who throng to its pleasant beaches every day. . . .

Other nations — ourselves among them — live devoured by a sublime demon within that drives us to the tireless pursuit of an ideal of love or glory. . . . Not so with these tranquil souls, stimulated only by a desire for gain. One scans those shimmering beaches . . . one views the throngs seated in comfortable chairs along the seashore, filling their lungs with the fresh, invigorating air. But it is said that those from our lands who remain here long are overcome with melancholy . . . because this great nation is void of spirit.

But what coming and going! What torrents of money! What facilities for every pleasure! What absolute absence of any outward sadness or poverty! Everything in the open air: the animated groups, the immense dining rooms, the peculiar courtship of North Americans, which is virtually devoid of the elements that compose the shy, tender, elevated love in our lands, the theatre, the photographers' booth, the bathhouses! Some weigh themselves, for North Americans are greatly elated, or really concerned, if they find they have gained or lost a pound. . . .

This spending, this uproar, these crowds, the activity of this amazing ant hill never slackens from June to October, from morning 'til night. . . . Then, like a monster that vomits its contents into the hungry maw of another monster, that colossal crowd, that straining, crushing mass, forces its way onto the trains, which speed across wastes, groaning under their burden, until they surrender it to the tremendous steamers, enlivened by the sound of harps and violins, convey it to the piers, and debouch the weary merrymakers into the thousand trolleys that pursue the thousand tracks that spread through slumbering New York like veins of steel.

SOURCE: Juan de Onís, trans., *The America of José Martí: Selected Writings* (New York: Noonday Press, 1954), 103–10.

ANALYZING THE EVIDENCE

➤ When Martí says America is "devoid of spirit," what does he mean? Why would such a thought be prompted by his observation of people having fun at Coney Island?

➤ In the final paragraph, Martí describes what might be considered a technological marvel — the capacity of New York's transportation system to move many thousands of revelers from Coney Island back to their homes in a few hours. But consider how Martí characterizes this — "a monster that vomits its contents into the angry maw of another monster" — with this question in mind: Does Martí's distaste negate the value of his account as a historical source about city mass transit?

➤ Let's put the above question in a larger context. Suppose you hadn't read the text's treatment of urban leisure. Would you profit from reading Martí's account? Having read the text's discussion, do you find it amplified — are new insights added — by Martí's account?

girl can get it on $8 a week. I guess if anyone wants to take me to a dance he won't have to ask me twice." Hence the widespread ritual among the urban working class of "treating." The girls spent what money they had dressing up; their boyfriends were expected to pay for the fun. Parental control over courtship broke down, and amid the bright lights and lively music of the dance hall and amusement park, working-class youth forged a more easygoing culture of sexual interaction and pleasure seeking.

The geography of the big city carved out ample space for commercialized sex. Prostitution was not new to urban life, but in the late nineteenth century it became more open and more intermingled with other forms of public entertainment. Opium and cocaine were widely available and not yet illegal. In New York the red-light district was the Tenderloin, running northward from Twenty-third Street between Fifth and Eighth Avenues.

The Tenderloin and the Bowery farther downtown were also the sites of a robust gay subculture. The long-held notion that homosexual life was covert, in the closet, in late-nineteenth-century America appears not to be true, at least not in the country's premier city. In certain corners of the city, a gay world flourished, with a full array of saloons, meeting places, and drag balls, which were widely known and patronized by uptown "slummers."

Of all forms of (mostly) male diversion, none was more specific to the city, or so spectacularly successful, as professional baseball. The game's promoters decreed that baseball had been created in 1839 by Abner Doubleday in the village of Cooperstown, New York. Actually, baseball was neither of American origin — stick-and-ball games go far back into the European Middle Ages — nor particularly a product of rural life. Under a variety of names, team sports resembling baseball proliferated in early nineteenth-century America. In an effort to regularize the game, the New Yorker Alexander Cartwright codified the rules in 1845, only to see his Knickerbockers defeated the next year at Hoboken by the New York Baseball Club in what is regarded as the first modern baseball game. Over the next twenty years, clubs sprang up across the country, and intercity competition developed on a scheduled basis. In 1868 baseball became openly professional, following the lead of the Cincinnati Red Stockings in signing players to contracts for the season.

Big-time baseball came into its own with the launching of the National League in 1876. The team owners were profit-minded businessmen who shaped the sport to please the fans. Wooden grandstands gave way to the concrete and steel stadiums of the early twentieth century, such as Fenway Park in Boston, Forbes Field in Pittsburgh, and Shibe Park in Philadelphia. For the urban multitudes baseball grew into something more than an afternoon at the ballpark. By rooting for the home team, fans found a way of identifying with the city in which they lived. Amid the diversity and anonymity of urban life, the common experience and language of baseball acted as a bridge among strangers.

Most efficient at this task, however, was the newspaper. James Gordon Bennett, founder of the *New York Herald* in 1835, wanted "to record the facts . . . for the great masses of the community." The news was whatever interested city readers, starting with crime, scandal, and sensational

The Bowery at Night, 1895

The Bowery (a name dating back to the original Dutch settlement) is a major thoroughfare in lower Manhattan. This painting by W. Louis Sonntag, Jr., shows the street in all its glory, crowded with shoppers and pleasure seekers. It was during this time that the Bowery gained its raffish reputation. Museum of the City of New York.

The National Pastime

In 1897, as today, the end-of-season games filled the bleachers. Here the Boston Beaneaters are playing the Baltimore Orioles. Boston won. The Baltimore stadium would soon be replaced by a bigger concrete and steel structure, but what is happening on the field needs no updating. The scene is virtually identical to today's game. Library of Congress.

events. After the Civil War the *New York Sun* added the human-interest story, which made news of ordinary happenings. Newspapers also targeted specific audiences. A women's page offered recipes and fashion news, separate sections covered sports and high society, and the Sunday supplement helped fill the weekend hours. In the competition for readers, the champion newsman was Joseph Pulitzer, the owner of the *St. Louis Post-Dispatch* and, after 1883, the *New York World* (Table 18.3).

TABLE 18.3	Newspaper Circulation
Year	**Total Circulation**
1870	2,602,000
1880	3,566,000
1890	8,387,000
1900	15,102,000
1909	24,212,000

SOURCE: *Historical Statistics of the United States*, 2 vols. (Washington, DC: U.S. Bureau of the Census, 1975), 2:810.

William Randolph Hearst and Yellow Journalism. Pulitzer was in turn challenged by William Randolph Hearst. Hearst was an unlikely press magnate, the pampered son of a California silver king who, while at Harvard (on the way to being expelled) got interested in Pulitzer's newspaper game. He took over his father's dull *San Francisco Examiner* and rebuilt it into a highly profitable, sensationalist paper. For example: Were any grizzly bears left in California? Hearst dispatched a newsman to the Tehachapi Mountains, where after three months of arduous trapping he caught a grizzly. All this the *Examiner* reported in exhaustive detail, building suspense as the search progressed and ending triumphantly with the carnival display of the unfortunate beast. There was much more of the same—rescues, murders, scandals, sob stories, anything that might arouse in readers what Hearst's editor called "the gee-whiz emotion." Hearst's brand of sensationalism was was dubbed **yellow journalism,** after *The Yellow Kid* (1895), the first comic strip to appear in color.

"He who is without a newspaper," said the great showman P. T. Barnum, "is cut off from his species." Barnum was speaking of city people and their hunger for information. Hearst understood this. That's why he made barrels of money.

The Higher Culture

In the midst of this popular ferment, new institutions of higher culture were taking shape in America's cities. A desire for the cultivated life was not, of course, specifically urban. Before the Civil War the lyceum movement had sent lecturers to the remotest towns, bearing messages of culture and learning. Chautauqua, founded in upstate New York in 1874, carried on this work of cultural dissemination. However, great institutions such as museums, public libraries, opera companies, and symphony orchestras could flourish only in metropolitan centers.

Cultural Institutions. The nation's first major art museum, the Corcoran Gallery of Art, opened in Washington, D.C., in 1869. New York's Metropolitan Museum of Art started in rented quarters two years later, then moved in 1880 to its permanent site in Central Park and launched an ambitious program of art acquisition. When financier J. P. Morgan became chairman of the board in 1905, the Metropolitan's preeminence was assured. The Boston Museum of Fine Arts was founded in 1876 and Chicago's Art Institute in 1879.

Symphony orchestras also appeared, first in New York under the conductors Theodore Thomas and Leopold Damrosch in the 1870s and then in Boston and Chicago during the next decade. National tours by these leading orchestras planted the seeds for orchestral societies in many other cities. Public libraries grew from modest collections (in 1870 only seven had as many as fifty thousand books) into major urban institutions. The greatest library benefactor was Andrew Carnegie, who announced in 1881 that he would build a library in any town or city that was prepared to maintain it.

William Randolph Hearst

In this photograph, dated 1904, Hearst is forty-one and past his glory days as the child prodigy of American journalism. He had managed to get himself elected to Congress from New York City and at the time was maneuvering, unsuccessfully, for the Democratic nomination for president. Brown Brothers.

By 1907 Carnegie had spent more than $32.7 million to establish about a thousand libraries throughout the country.

The late nineteenth century was the great age not only of moneymaking, but also of money *giving*. Generous with their surplus wealth, new millionaires patronized the arts partly as a civic duty, partly to promote themselves socially, but also out of a sense of national pride.

"In America there is no culture," pronounced the English critic G. Lowes Dickinson in 1909. Science and the practical arts, yes — "every possible application of life to purposes and ends" — but "no life for life's sake." Such condescending remarks received a respectful American hearing out of a sense of cultural inferiority to the Old World. In 1873 Mark Twain and Charles Dudley Warner published a novel, *The Gilded Age*, satirizing America as a land of money grubbers and speculators. This enormously popular book touched a nerve in the American psyche. Its title has since been appropriated by historians to characterize the late nineteenth century — America's "Gilded Age" — as an era of materialism and cultural shallowness.

Some members of the upper class, such as the novelist Henry James, despaired of the country and moved to Europe. But the more common response was to try to raise the nation's cultural level. The newly rich had a hard time of it. They did not have much opportunity to cultivate a taste for art, and a great deal of what they collected was junk. On the other hand George W. Vanderbilt, grandson of the rough-hewn Cornelius Vanderbilt, championed French Impressionism, and the coal and steel baron Henry Clay Frick built a brilliant art collection that is still housed as a public museum in his mansion in New York City. The enthusiasm of moneyed Americans largely fueled the great cultural institutions that sprang up during the Gilded Age.

The Literary Scene. A deeply conservative idea of culture sustained this generous patronage. The aim was to embellish life, not to probe or reveal its meaning. "Art," says the hero of the Reverend Henry Ward Beecher's sentimental novel *Norwood* (1867), "attempts to work out its end solely by the use of the beautiful, and the artist is to select out only such things as are beautiful." The idea of culture also took on an elitist cast: Shakespeare, once a staple of popular entertainment (in various bowdlerized versions), was appropriated into the domain of "serious" theater. And simultaneously the world of culture became feminized. "Husbands or sons rarely share those interests," noted one observer. In American life, remarked the clergyman Horace Bushnell, men represented the "force principle," women the "beauty principle."

The depiction of life, the eminent editor and novelist William Dean Howells wrote, "must be tinged with sufficient idealism to make it all of a truly uplifting character. We cannot admit stories which deal with false or immoral relations. . . . The finer side of things — the idealistic — is the answer for us." The "genteel tradition," as this literary school came to be known, dominated the nation's purveyors of elite culture — its journals, publishers, and college professors — from the 1860s onward.

But the urban world could not finally be kept at bay. Howells himself resigned in 1881 from the *Atlantic Monthly,* a stronghold of the genteel tradition, and called for a literature that sought "to picture the daily life in the most exact terms possible." In a series of realistic novels — *A Modern Instance* (1882), *The Rise of Silas Lapham* (1885), and *A Hazard of New Fortunes* (1890) — Howells captured the urban middle class. Stephen Crane's *Maggie: Girl of the Streets* (1893), privately printed because no publisher would touch it, unflinchingly described the destruction of a slum girl.

The city had entered the American imagination and become, by the early 1900s, a main theme of American art and literature. And because it challenged so many assumptions of an older, republican America, the city also became an overriding concern of reformers and, after the run of the century, a main theater in the drama of the Progressive era.

➤ In both politics and religion, established institutions had to find ways of incorporating a flood of newcomers to the city. But the politicians seemed to have an easier time of it. Why was that?

➤ American cities housed a great many people struggling to get by. Yet they always seemed ready to dig into their pockets for a newspaper or a ticket to the ball game. Why was that?

➤ Why is it that we date the arrival of institutions of higher culture with the rise of the industrial city?

SUMMARY

In this chapter, we explore the emergence of a distinctively urban American society. The chapter is concerned, first of all, with how the great nineteenth-century cities came to be built. Urban growth was driven by industrialization — by the geographic concentration of industries, by the increasing scale of production, and by industry's need for city-based financial and administrative services. A burst of innovation brought forth mass transit, skyscrapers, electricity, and much else that made the big city livable. Although not constrained constitutionally, the public sector left city building as much as possible to private initiative and private capital. The result was dramatic growth, with an infrastructure superior to Europe's, but at the price of a degraded environment and nasty living conditions for the poor.

Our second concern is with an urban class structure defined most visibly by geography. The poor inhabited the inner cities and factory districts. The middle class spread out into the suburbs, while the rich lived insulated in fancy neighborhoods or beyond the suburbs. For the wealthy an elite society emerged, stressing an opulent lifestyle and exclusive social organizations. The middle class withdrew into the private world of the family. Intersecting with family were issues of gender identity, with white-collar husbands embracing a cult of masculinity, and wives emboldened by the liberating prospects of the "new woman."

Finally, this chapter describes the components of a distinctive urban culture. City life was strongly flavored by the ways that newcomers—European immigrants, southern blacks, small-town whites—adapted to an alien urban environment. In politics and religion, we see most vividly how American institutions adapted to the newcomers. City life was also distinguished by an explosion of leisure activities, ranging from vaudeville to the yellow press and, at a more elevated level, by the institutions of art, music, and literature that sustain a nation's higher culture.

Connections: Society

The first cities—Boston, New York, Philadelphia, New Orleans—go far back in American history, back indeed, in their origins to the earliest days of colonial settlement. Spurred by the market revolution, they and their counterparts in the interior grew prodigiously in the first half of the nineteenth century. As readers of earlier chapters will know, cities always played a disproportionate part in the nation's economic, political, and cultural life. But only in the late-nineteenth-century years, as the United States became an industrial power, did the rural/urban balance shift and the cities develop a distinctly urban culture. As we say in the part opener (p. 485), the city became

> more than just a place to make a living. . . . It provided a setting for an urban lifestyle unlike anything seen before in America.

The consequences of that development loom large in the nation's later history, for example, as the primary site for reform during the Progressive era (Chapter 20) and as the spark for cultural conflict in the 1920s (Chapter 23). In succeeding decades, we can still distinguish what is distinctively urban in American development, but in truth urban history and American history increasingly merge as the United States becomes in our own time ever more a nation of urban and suburban dwellers, and farmers the tiniest of fractions of the American labor force.

CHAPTER REVIEW QUESTIONS

➤ In what ways does the city growth we study in this chapter intersect with the industrial developments treated in the preceding chapter?

➤ Why did the rich and the middle class develop such different lifestyles in the late-nineteenth-century city?

➤ How did newcomers of deeply rooted, diverse rural backgrounds all become "city people"?

TIMELINE

1869	Corcoran Gallery of Art, nation's first major art museum, opens in Washington, D.C.
1871	Chicago fire
1873	Mark Twain and Charles Dudley Warner publish *The Gilded Age*
1875	Dwight L. Moody launches urban revivalist movement
1876	Alexander Graham Bell patents telephone National Baseball League founded
1879	Thomas Edison creates practical incandescent light bulb Salvation Army, originally formed in Britain, is established in the United States
1881	Andrew Carnegie offers to build a library for every American city
1883	New York City's Metropolitan Opera founded Joseph Pulitzer purchases *New York World*
1885	William Jenney builds first steel-framed structure, Chicago's Home Insurance Building
1887	First electric trolley line constructed in Richmond, Virginia
1893	Chicago Columbian Exposition "City Beautiful" movement
1895	William Randolph Hearst enters New York journalism
1897	Boston builds first American subway
1900	Theodore Dreiser publishes *Sister Carrie*
1901	New York Tenement House Law
1904	New York subway system opens
1906	San Francisco earthquake
1913	Fifty-five-story Woolworth Building opens in New York City

FOR FURTHER EXPLORATION

The starting point for modern urban historiography is Sam Bass Warner's pioneering book on Boston, *Streetcar Suburbs, 1870–1900* (1962). In a subsequent work, *The Private City: Philadelphia in Three Periods* (1968), Warner broadened his analysis to show how private decision making shaped the character of the American city. Innovations in urban construction are treated in Carl Condit, *Rise of the New York Skyscraper, 1865–1913* (1996); Harold L. Platt, *The Electric City: Energy and the Growth of the Chicago Area, 1880–1930* (1991); and Alan Trachtenberg, *The Brooklyn Bridge* (1965). On the social elite, see Frederic C. Jaher, *The Urban Establishment* (1982). Aspects of middle-class life are revealed in Howard B. Chudacoff, *The Age of the Bachelor* (1999); Michael A. Ebner, *Creating Chicago's North Shore: A Suburban History* (1988); Jane Hunter, *How Young Ladies Became Girls: The Victorian Origins of American Girlhood* (2003); John F. Kasson, *Rudeness and Civility: Manners in Nineteenth-Century America* (1990); Andrea Tone, *Devices and Desires: A History of Contraception in America* (2001). On urban life, see especially Gunther Barth, *City People: The Rise of Modern City Culture* (1982); David Block, *Baseball Before We Knew It* (2004); Timothy J. Gilfoyle, *City of Eros: New York City, Prostitution and the Commercialization of Sex, 1790–1920* (1991); John F. Kasson, *Amusing the Million: Coney Island at the Turn of the Century* (1978); and Kathy Peiss, *Cheap Amusements: Working Women and Leisure in Turn-of-the-Century New York* (1986). The best introduction to Gilded Age intellectual currents is Alan Trachtenberg, *The Incorporation of America: Culture and Society, 1865–1893* (1983). On the Columbian Exposition of 1893, an excellent Web site is "The World's Columbian Exposition: Idea, Experience, Aftermath" at **xroads.virginia.edu/~ma96/WCE/title.html**, including detailed guides to every site at the fair and analysis of its lasting impact.

TEST YOUR KNOWLEDGE

To assess your command of the material in this chapter, see the Online Study Guide at **bedfordstmartins.com/henretta**.

For Web sites, images, and documents related to topics and places in this chapter, visit **bedfordstmartins.com/makehistory**.

19 Politics in the Age of Enterprise, 1877–1896

EVER SINCE THE FOUNDING OF the republic, foreign visitors had been coming to America to observe the political goings-on of a democratic society. Most celebrated was the French aristocrat Alexis de Tocqueville, the author of *Democracy in America* (1832). When an equally brilliant visitor, the Englishman James Bryce, sat down to write his own account fifty years later, he decided that Tocqueville's great book could not be his model. For Tocqueville, Bryce noted, "America was primarily a democracy, the ideal democracy, fraught with lessons for Europe." In his own book, *The American Commonwealth* (1888), Bryce was much less rhapsodic. The robust democracy hailed by Tocqueville had descended into the barren politics of post–Civil War America.

Bryce was anxious, however, not to be misunderstood. Europeans would find in his book "much that is sordid, much that will provoke unfavorable comment." But they needed to be aware of "a reserve of force and patriotism more than sufficient to sweep away all the evils now tolerated, and to make a politics of the country worthy of its material grandeur and of the private virtues of its inhabitants." Bryce was ultimately an optimist: "A hundred times in writing this book have I been disheartened by the facts I was stating; a hundred times has the recollection of the abounding strength and vitality of the nation chased away these tremors."

◄ **Bandanna, 1888 Election**

During the late nineteenth century, politics was a vibrant part of America's culture. Party paraphernalia, such as this colorful bandanna depicting the Democratic presidential nominee Grover Cleveland and his running mate, A. G. Thurman, flooded the country. Collection of Janice L. and David J. Frent.

"Where Is He?"

This *Puck* cartoon, which appeared two weeks after Benjamin Harrison's defeat for reelection at Grover Cleveland's hands in 1892, is a commentary on Harrison's insignificance as president. The hat in Uncle Sam's hands belonged to Benjamin Harrison's grandfather, President William Henry Harrison. *Puck* started using the hat as a trademark for Benjamin Harrison after he had been elected in 1888. As his term progressed, the hat grew increasingly larger and the president successively smaller. By the time of his defeat, just the hat was left and Harrison had disappeared altogether. Bancroft Library, University of California at Berkeley. *Puck*, November 16, 1892.

What was it that Bryce found so disheartening in the practice of American politics? That is this chapter's first subject. The second is about the underlying vitality that Bryce sensed, and how it reemerged and reinvigorated the nation's politics by the century's end.

The Politics of the Status Quo, 1877–1893

In times of national ferment, as a rule, public life becomes magnified. Leaders emerge. Great issues are debated. The powers of government expand. All

this had been true of the Civil War era, when the nation's political structure had been severely tested, not least by the contested presidential election of 1876. In 1877, with Rutherford B. Hayes safely settled in the White House, the era of sectional strife finally ended.

Political life went on, but drained of its earlier drama. The 1880s heralded no Lincolns, no great national debates. While Republican defenders of the Union had envisioned a social and economic order reshaped by an activist state, now, in the 1880s, political leaders retreated to a more modest conception of national power. An irreducible core of public functions remained and even, as on the question of railroad regulation, grudging acceptance of new federal responsibilities. But the dominant rhetoric celebrated that government which governed least, and as compared to the Civil War era, American government did govern less.

The Washington Scene

There were five presidents from 1877 to 1893: Rutherford B. Hayes (Republican, 1877–1881), James A. Garfield (Republican, 1881), Chester A. Arthur (Republican, 1881–1885), Grover Cleveland (Democrat, 1885–1889), and Benjamin Harrison (Republican, 1889–1893). All were estimable men. Hayes had served effectively as governor of Ohio for three terms, and Garfield had done well as a congressional leader. Arthur, despite his reputation as a hack politician, had shown fine administrative skills as head of the New York Customs house. Cleveland enjoyed an enviable reputation as reform mayor of Buffalo and governor of New York. None was a charismatic leader, but circumstances, more than personal qualities, explain why these presidents did not make a larger mark on history.

The president's most demanding task was dispensing **patronage** to the faithful. Under the **spoils system**, government appointments were treated as rewards for those who had served the victorious party. Reform of this practice became urgent after President Garfield was shot and killed in 1881. The motives of his assassin, Charles Guiteau, were murky, but civil service reformers blamed the poisonous atmosphere of a spoils system that left many disappointed in the scramble for office. The resulting Pendleton Act (1883) established a nonpartisan Civil Service Commission authorized to fill federal jobs by examination. The original list covered only 10 percent of the jobs, however, and the White House still staggered (as Cleveland grumbled) under the "damned, everlasting clatter for office." Though standards of public administration did rise, there was no American counterpart to the professional civil services being trained in these years at France's *grand ecoles* and Germany's universities.

The duties of the executive branch were, in any event, modest. The White House staff consisted of a half dozen assistants plus a few clerks, doorkeepers, and messengers. Budgetary matters were not the president's province, but Congress's; federal agencies accordingly paid more heed to the key money-dispensing committees on Capitol Hill than to the White House. Of the 100,000 federal employees in 1880, 56 percent worked for the post office. Even the important cabinet offices—Treasury, State, War, Navy, Interior—were sleepy places carrying on largely routine duties. Virtually all federal funding came from customs duties and excise taxes on liquor and tobacco, which produced more money than the government spent. How to reduce the federal surplus ranked as one of the most nettlesome issues of the 1880s.

On matters of national policy, the presidents took a back seat to Capitol Hill. This was partly because—unlike in Lincoln's day—they took a modest view of their powers. "The office of President is essentially executive in nature," Cleveland conceded. On the congressional side, party leaders like Roscoe Conkling, Republican senator from New York, considered themselves coequal with the president. Conkling did not hesitate to take on Rutherford B. Hayes over the latter's lenient policy toward the South—hence the name of Conkling's faction, the Stalwarts. Even more incendiary was any tampering with the patronage prerogatives of congressional barons, as Hayes's successor James Garfield learned when he challenged Conkling over the New York Customs House. James G. Blaine, Conkling's rival and successor as Senate boss—Blaine's faction called itself the Half-Breeds—was equally imperious in dealing with Chester Arthur's administration.

This was the era, in Woodrow Wilson's scathing words, of "congressional government." But Congress was, in fact, not well set up to take command. It was regularly bogged down by arcane procedures and by unruly factions. Nor did either party have a strong agenda. Historically, the Democrats favored **states' rights**, while the Republicans were heirs to the Whig enthusiasm for federally assisted economic development. After Reconstruction, however, the Republicans backed away from state interventionism and, in truth, party differences became muddy. On most leading issues of the day—civil service reform, the currency, regulation of the railroads—divisions occurred within the parties and not between them.

Only the **tariff** remained a fighting issue. From Lincoln's administration onward, high duties had protected American industry from imported goods. It was an article of Republican faith, as President Harrison said in 1892, that "the protective system . . . has been a mighty instrument for the development of the national wealth." The Democrats, free traders by tradition, regularly attacked Republican protectionism. The tariff was a genuine issue, with real economic consequences. And on both sides, it stirred strong partisan feelings. Yet, in practice, the tariff was a negotiable issue like any other. Congressmen voted their constituents' interests regardless of party rhetoric. As a result, tariff bills were generally a patchwork of bargains among special interests.

Late in the decade, after a string of inconclusive revisions, the tariff debate suddenly heated up. An ardent free trader, Cleveland cast off his reluctance to lead the nation and campaigned in 1888 on a platform of thorough-going tariff reduction. His narrow defeat emboldened the Republicans, who in 1890 pushed through the McKinley tariff (after its author William McKinley), raising average rates to a record 49.5 percent, with even higher duties called for if other nations retaliated against American goods. The issue was by no means laid to rest, however. The McKinley tariff, coinciding with a surge of economic troubles in the country, proved unpopular and threw the Republicans very much on the defensive as the 1892 elections approached.

Campaign Politics. Taking a stand on big issues, like the tariff, was risky because the parties were so evenly balanced. By the end of Reconstruction, with the South solidly in their corner, the Democrats stood on equal terms with the Republicans. Every presidential election from 1876 to 1892 was decided by a thin margin (Map 19.1), and Congress regularly changed hands. Under these circumstances, when any false move might tip the scales, caution seemed the best policy.

That did not stop Republican orators from "waving the bloody shirt" against the Democrats. The tactic was not wholly cynical. In various ways, Civil War issues persisted. Pensions for disabled veterans and their widows was a perennial question, favored by Republicans as a matter of honor, resisted by Democrats as extravagant and fraud-ridden. In his first term, President Cleveland vetoed a record number of private pension bills, as well as general legislation for indigent veterans.

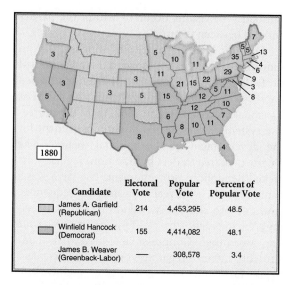

Candidate	Electoral Vote	Popular Vote	Percent of Popular Vote
James A. Garfield (Republican)	214	4,453,295	48.5
Winfield Hancock (Democrat)	155	4,414,082	48.1
James B. Weaver (Greenback-Labor)	—	308,578	3.4

MAP 19.1   Presidential Elections of 1880, 1884, and 1888

The anatomy of political stalemate is evident in this trio of electoral maps of the 1880s. First, note the equal division of the popular vote between Republicans and Democrats. Second, note the remarkable persistence in the pattern of electoral votes, in which overwhelmingly states went to the same party in all three elections. Finally, we can identify who determined the outcomes — the two "swing" states, New York and Indiana, whose vote shifted every four years and always in favor of the winning candidate.

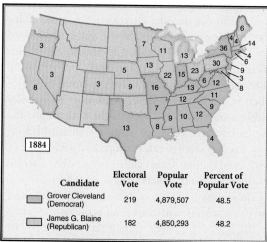

Candidate	Electoral Vote	Popular Vote	Percent of Popular Vote
Grover Cleveland (Democrat)	219	4,879,507	48.5
James G. Blaine (Republican)	182	4,850,293	48.2

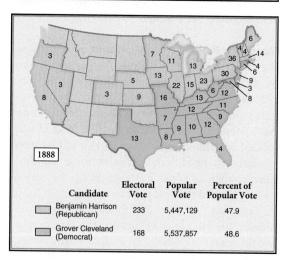

Candidate	Electoral Vote	Popular Vote	Percent of Popular Vote
Benjamin Harrison (Republican)	233	5,447,129	47.9
Grover Cleveland (Democrat)	168	5,537,857	48.6

Cleveland's electoral success—he was the first Democrat in the White House since the 1850s—only hardened Republican determination not to let go of the Civil War legacy. And so did anxiety about their own party's future. Keeping alive the sectional crisis that had given it birth was a form of party building, a way of cementing Republican solidarity. So "waving the bloody shirt" expressed concerns of real substance. Yet on Reconstruction's real unfinished business—the fate of ex-slaves—the Republicans backed away, never fulfilling their pledge to provide federal funding to combat illiteracy or effective protections for black voters. Nor was there denying the demagogic uses of "waiving the bloody shirt" during elections. Lord Bryce had grounds for criticizing the Republicans for "clinging too long to outworn issues and neglecting the problems . . . which now perplex the country."

Alternatively, campaigns could descend into comedy. In the hard-fought election of 1884, for example, the Democrat Cleveland burst on the scene as a reformer, fresh from his victories over corrupt machine politics in New York State. But years earlier Cleveland, a bachelor, had fathered an illegitimate child, and throughout the campaign he was dogged by the ditty, "Maw, Maw, where's my Paw?" (After his victory Cleveland's supporters gleefully responded, "He's in the White House, haw-haw-haw.") Cleveland's opponent, James G. Blaine, already on the defensive for taking favors from the railroads, was weakened by the unthinking charge of a too ardent Republican clergyman that the Democrats were the party of "Rum, Romanism and Rebellion." In a twinkling he had insulted Catholic voters and, so some believed, lost the election for Blaine. In the midst of all the mudslinging, the issues got lost.

The characteristics of public life in the 1880s—the passivity of the federal government, the evasiveness of the political parties, the absorption in politics for its own sake—derived ultimately from the underlying conviction that little was at stake in national affairs. In 1887 Cleveland vetoed a small appropriation for drought-stricken Texas farmers with the remark that "though the people support the Government, the Government should not support the people." Governmental activity was itself considered a bad thing. All the state could do, said Senator Conkling, was "to clear the way of impediments and dangers, and leave every class and every individual free and safe in the exertions and pursuits of life." Conkling was expressing the political corollary to the economic doctrine of **laissez-faire** — the belief, already well-rooted in the Jeffersonian-Jacksonian politics of the antebellum era — that the less government interfered, the better.

The Ideology of Individualism

At the peak of the labor strife of the 1880s, the cotton manufacturer Edward Atkinson gave a talk to the textile workers of Providence, Rhode Island. They had, he told them, no cause for discontent. "There is always plenty of room on the front seats in every profession, every trade. . . . There are men in this audience who will fill some of those seats, but they won't be boosted into them from behind." (There were certainly women in the audience — at least half the textile industry's labor force was female — but, as was the norm for the times, Atkinson assumed that economic advancement mattered only to men.) Atkinson's homely talk went to roots of conservative American thought: any man, however, humble, could rise as far as his talents would carry him; every person received his just reward, great or small; and the success of the individual, so encouraged, contributed to the progress of the whole. How persuasive the workers listening to Atkinson found his message we have no way of knowing. But the confidence with which he presented his case is evidence of the continuing appeal of the **ideology** of individualism in the age of enterprise.

A flood of popular writings trumpeted the creed of individualism, from the rags-to-riches tales of Horatio Alger to innumerable success manuals with such titles as *Thoughts for the Young Men of America, or a Few Practical Words of Advice to Those Born in Poverty and Destined to be Reared in Orphanages* (1871). Self-made men such as Andrew Carnegie became cultural heroes. A best seller was Carnegie's *Triumphant Democracy* (1886), which paid homage to a country that enabled a penniless Scottish child to rise from bobbin boy to steel magnate.

Facing the World

The cover of this Horatio Alger novel (1893) captures the American myth of opportunity. Our hero, Harry Vane, is a poor but earnest lad, ready to make his way in the world and, despite the many obstacles thrown in his path, sure to succeed. In some 135 books Horatio Alger repeated this story, with minor variations, for an eager reading public that numbered in the millions. Frank and Marie-Therese Wood Print Collections, Alexandria, VA.

From the pulpit came the assurances of the Episcopal bishop William Lawrence of Massachusetts that "godliness is in league with riches." Bishop Lawrence was voicing a familiar theme of American Protestantism: Success in one's earthly calling revealed the promise of eternal salvation. It was all too easy for a conservative ministry to bless the furious acquisitiveness of industrial America. "To secure wealth is an honorable ambition," intoned the Baptist minister Russell H. Conwell.

Social Darwinism. The celebration of individualism drew strong support from social theorizing drawn from biology. Evolution itself — the idea that the species are not fixed but change over time — was not new. It had been gathering scientific support ever since the early nineteenth century. But evolutionary science lacked an explanatory mechanism. This was what the British naturalist Charles Darwin provided in *On the Origin of Species* (1859), which advanced the concept of *natural selection*. In nature, Darwin wrote, all living things struggle to survive. Individual members of a species are born with genetic mutations that better fit them for their particular environment—camouflage coloring for a bird or butterfly, for example. These survival characteristics, since they are genetically transmissible, become dominant in future generations, and the species evolves.

Darwin himself disapproved of the term *evolution* (the word doesn't appear in his book) because it implied an upward progression. In his view, natural selection was blind—there was no intelligent design behind it. Since environments changed randomly, so did the adaptation of species. For Darwin, evolutionary progress was meaningless. But he had given evolution the stamp of scientific legitimacy and others, less scrupulous than he about drawing larger conclusions, moved confidently to apply evolution to social development.

Foremost was the British philosopher Herbert Spencer, who spun out an elaborate analysis of how human society had advanced through competition and "survival of the fittest." **Social Darwinism**, as Spencer's ideas became known, was championed in America by William Graham Sumner, a sociology professor at Yale. Competition, said Sumner, is a law of nature that "can no more be done away with than gravitation." And who are the fittest? "The millionaires. . . . They may fairly be regarded as the naturally selected agents of society. They get high wages and live in luxury, but the bargain is a good one for society."

Social Darwinists regarded with horror any interference with social processes. "The great stream of time and earthly things will sweep on just the same in spite of us," Sumner wrote in a famous essay, "The Absurd Attempt to Make the World Over" (1894). As for the government, it had "at bottom . . . two chief things . . . with which to deal. They are the property of men and the honor of women. These it has to defend against crime." And beyond that, it had to leave people alone.

The Supremacy of the Courts

Suspicion of government not only paralyzed political initiative; it also shifted power away from the executive and legislative branches. "The task of constitutional government," declared Sumner, "is to devise institutions which shall come into play at critical periods to prevent the abusive control of the powers of a state by the controlling classes in it." Sumner meant the judiciary. From the 1870s onward the courts increasingly accepted the role that he assigned to them, becoming the guardians of the rights of private property against the grasping tentacles of government.

The main target of the courts was not Washington, but the states. This was because, under the federal system as it was understood in the late nineteenth century, the **residual powers**—those not delegated by the Constitution to the federal government—left the states with primary authority over social welfare and economic regulation. The great question in American law was how to balance the states' police powers to defend the general welfare against the liberty of individuals to pursue their private interests. Most states, caught up in the conservative ethos of the day, were cutting back on expenditures and public services. Even so, there were more than enough state initiatives to alarm vigilant judges. Thus, in the landmark case *In re Jacobs* (1885), the New York State Court of Appeals struck down a law prohibiting cigar manufacturing in tenements on the grounds that such regulation exceeded the police powers of the state.

As the federal courts took up the battle against state activism, they found their strongest weapon in the Fourteenth Amendment (1868), the Reconstruction amendment that prohibited the states from depriving "any person of life, liberty, or property, without due process of law." The due process clause had been introduced to protect the civil rights of the former slaves. But due process protected the property rights and liberty of any "person," and legally, corporations counted as persons. So interpreted, the Fourteenth Amendment became by the turn of the century a powerful restraint on the power of the states to regulate private business.

The Supreme Court similarly hamstrung the federal government. In 1895 the Court ruled that the federal power to regulate interstate commerce did not cover manufacturing and struck down a federal income tax law. And in areas where federal power was undeniable—such as the regulation of railroads—the Supreme Court scrutinized every measure for undue interference with the rights of property.

The preeminent jurist of the day, Stephen J. Field, made no bones about the dangers he saw in the nation's headlong industrial development. "As the inequalities in the conditions of men become more and more marked and . . . angry menaces against order find vent in loud denunciations—it becomes more and more the imperative duty of the court to enforce with a firm hand every guarantee of the Constitution."

Power conferred status. The law, not politics, attracted the ablest people and held the public's esteem. A Wisconsin judge boasted, "The bench symbolizes on earth the throne of divine justice.... Law in its highest sense is the will of God." Judicial supremacy revealed how entrenched the ideology of individualism had become in industrial America and also how low American politicians had fallen in the esteem of their countrymen.

➤ A novel published in 1880 speaks derisively of American democracy as being "of the people, by the people, for the benefit of Senators." What was there about the political scene that would have prompted the author to say that?

➤ Why was Darwin's *Origin of Species,* which was strictly about biology, important in the development of the ideology of conservatism?

➤ How do you explain the reverence accorded to the judiciary in the late nineteenth century?

Politics and the People

The country may have felt, as Kansas editor William Allen White wrote, "sick with politics" and "nauseated at all politicians," but somehow this did not curb the popular appetite for politics. Proportionately more voters turned out in presidential elections from 1876 to 1892 than at any other time in American history. People voted Democratic or Republican loyally for a lifetime. National conventions attracted huge crowds. "The excitement, the mental and physical strains," remarked an Indiana Republican after the 1888 convention, "are surpassed only by prolonged battle in actual warfare, as I have been told by officers of the Civil War who latter engaged in convention struggles." The convention he described had nominated the colorless Benjamin Harrison on a routine platform. What was all the excitement about?

Cultural Politics: Party, Religion, and Ethnicity

In the late nineteenth century, politics was a vibrant part of the nation's culture. America "is a land of conventions and assemblies," a journalist noted,

The Presidential B.B. Club (1888)

On the left Grover Cleveland is the baseman; at center Benjamin Harrison is at bat; and on the right Cleveland tags Harrison out — not, alas, the right prediction, since Harrison won the 1888 election. Collection of Janice L. and David J. Frent.

"where it is the most natural thing in the world for people to get together in meetings, where almost every event is the occasion for speechmaking." During the election season the party faithful marched in torchlight parades. Party paraphernalia flooded the country—handkerchiefs, mugs, posters, and buttons emblazoned with the Democratic donkey or the Republican elephant, symbols that had been adopted in the 1870s. In the 1888 campaign the candidates were featured on cards, like baseball players, tucked into packets of Honest Long Cut tobacco. In an age before movies and radio, politics ranked as one of the great American forms of entertainment (see Reading American Pictures, "Parties and People," p. 591).

Party loyalty was a deadly serious matter, however. Long after the killing ended, Civil War emotions ran high. Among family friends in Cleveland, recalled the urban reformer Brand Whitlock, the Republican Party was "a synonym for patriotism, another name for the nation. It was inconceivable that any self-respecting person should be a Democrat"— or, among ex-Confederates in the South, that any self-respecting person could be a Republican.

Beyond these sectional differences the most important determinants of party loyalty were religion and ethnicity (Figure 19.1). Statistically, northern Democrats tended to be foreign-born and Catholic, while Republicans tended to be native-born and Protestant. Among Protestants, the more *pietistic* a person's faith—that is, the more personal and direct the believer's relationship to God—the more likely he or she was to be a Republican and to favor using the powers of the state to uphold moral values and regulate personal behavior.

During the 1880s, as ethnic tensions built up in many cities, education became an arena of bitter conflict. One issue was whether instruction in the public schools should be in English. Immigrant groups often wanted their children taught in their own languages. In St. Louis, a heavily German city, the long-standing policy of teaching German to all students was overturned after a heated campaign. Religion was an even more explosive educational issue. Catholics fought a losing battle over public aid for parochial schools, which by 1900 was prohibited by twenty-three states. In Boston a furious controversy broke out in 1888 over the use of an anti-Catholic history textbook. When the school board withdrew the offending book, angry Protestants elected a new board and returned the text to the curriculum.

Then there was the regulation of public morals. In many states, so-called *blue laws* restricted activity on Sundays. When Nebraska banned Sunday baseball, the state's courts approved the law as a blow struck in

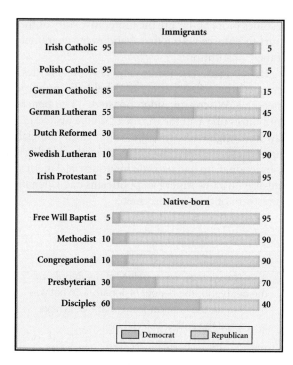

FIGURE 19.1 Ethnocultural Voting Patterns in the Midwest, 1870–1892

These figures demonstrate how voting patterns among midwesterners reflected ethnicity and religion in the late nineteenth century. Especially striking is the overwhelming preference by immigrant Catholics for the Democratic Party. Among Protestants there was an equally strong preference for the Republican Party by certain groups of immigrants (Swedish Lutherans and Irish Protestants) and native born (Free Will Baptists, Methodists, and Congregationalists), but other Protestant groups were more evenly divided in their party preferences.

"the contest between Christianity and wrong." But German and Irish Catholics, who saw nothing evil in a bit of fun on Sunday, considered blue laws a violation of their personal freedom. **Ethnocultural** conflict also flared over the liquor question. In many states, evangelical Christians pushed for strict licensing and local-option laws governing the sale of alcoholic beverages. Indiana permitted drinking but only joylessly in rooms containing "no devices for amusement or music . . . of any kind."

Because the hottest social issues of the day— education, the liquor question, and observance of the Sabbath—were also party issues, they lent deep significance to party affiliation (see Voices from Abroad, "Ernst Below: Beer and German American Politics," p. 593). And because these issues were fought out mostly at the state and local levels, they hit very close to home. Crusading Methodists thought of Republicans as the party of morality.

Parties and People: How Democratic Was American Politics?

In the text we say that the late nineteenth century was a great age of popular participation in politics. As indicators, we offer voter turnout, persisting voting patterns, and party participation. The photographs below provide an additional indicator, evidence of citizens as party activists. The upper photo shows the members of the local Republican Party organization of Newport, Rhode Island, named in honor of Levi P. Morton, vice president in the Benjamin Harrison administration (1889-1893). The lower photo shows farm families en route to a Populist rally in Dickinson County, Kansas, sometime in the 1890s.

The Levi P. Morton Association (1888). Newport Historical Society.

ANALYZING THE EVIDENCE

➤ Compare the people in the two photographs. Do the differences you see suggest anything about the class composition of American political parties in the late nineteenth century?

➤ Giving women the vote, as the text says, was a highly divisive and unresolved issue in the late nineteenth century. Do these photographs throw any light on that issue? Or on how Republicans and Populists aligned themselves on it?

➤ A hallmark of the nineteenth-century parties was their capacity to organize at the grassroots level. That is apparent in both photographs. But Populists regarded their brand of grassroots activism to be different — and far more democratic — from main-line parties. Do the photographs reveal any evidence that helps us understand why they might have felt that way?

En Route to a Populist Rally, Dickinson County, Kansas (1890s). Kansas State Historical Society.

For embattled Irish and German Catholics, who favored "the largest individual liberty consistent with public order," the Democratic Party was the defender of their freedoms.

It would have been easy enough to invoke these divisions in national politics as, for example, Senator Blaine did in 1875 when, angling for the Republican presidential nomination, he proposed a federal amendment banning public funding of parochial schools. But Republicans generally held back, and for good reason. They could never be sure, given the parity of the parties nationally, that more would be lost than gained by playing the values card. That was a lesson brought bitterly home to Republicans by the loose talk about "Rum, Romanism, and Rebellion" in the 1884 campaign. It is in this particular respect that the politics of morality has changed since the 1880s—not that it is any more potent today, but that it functions on a bigger stage. While battles over Demon Rum and the Sabbath played out locally, the equivalent battles over abortion and gay rights have become national issues and help define presidential politics.

Organizational Politics

Late nineteenth-century politics was robust also because of the organizational activity it generated. By the 1870s both major parties had evolved formal, well-organized structures. At the base lay the precinct or ward, where party meetings were open to all members. County, state, and national committees ran the ongoing business of the parties. Conventions determined party rules, adopted platforms, and selected the party's candidates. At election time the party's main job was to get out the vote. Wherever elections were close and hard fought, the parties mounted intensive efforts organized down to the individual voter. In Indiana, for example, the Republicans appointed ten thousand "district men," each responsible for turning out a designated group of voters.

Party governance seemed, on its face, highly democratic, since in theory all power derived from the party members. In practice, however, the parties were run by unofficial internal organizations—political machines—which consisted of insiders willing to do party work in exchange for public jobs or the sundry advantages of being connected. Although most evident in city politics (see Chapter 18), the machine system was integral to political life at every level, right up to the national parties. The machines tended toward one-man rule, although the "boss" ruled more by the consent of the secondary leaders than by his own absolute power. The high stakes of office, jobs, and influence made for intense intra-party factionalism. Absorbed in the tasks of power brokerage, machine bosses treated public issues as somewhat irrelevant. And the spoils system they managed unquestionably fouled the public realm with the stench of corruption.

Yet the record of machine politics was not wholly negative. In certain ways the standards of governance got better. Disciplined professionals, veterans of machine politics, proved effective as state legislators and congressmen because they were more experienced in the give-and-take of politics. More important, party machines filled a void in the nation's public life. They did informally much of what the governmental system left undone, especially in the cities.

The Mugwumps. Even so, machine politics never managed to become respectable. Many of the nation's social elite—intellectuals, well-to-do businessmen, and old-line families—resented a politics that excluded people like themselves, the "best men." There was, too, a genuine clash of values. Political reformers called for "disinterestedness" and "independence"—the opposite of the self-serving careerism fostered by the machine system. James Bryce, whose comments open this chapter, was wined and dined by this circle when he came to the United States. His writings were colored by the prejudices of the political reformers, and, like them, he discounted the cultural and organizational contributions of American party politics.

Many of them had earned their spurs as Liberal Republicans who dissented against President Grant's reelection in 1872. In 1884, led by Carl Schurz and Charles Francis Adams Jr., they again left the Republican Party because they could not stomach its tainted presidential candidate, James G. Blaine. Mainly from New York and Massachusetts, these reform Republicans became known as Mugwumps—a derisive bit of contemporary slang, supposedly of Indian origin, referring to pompous or self-important persons. The Mugwumps threw their support to Democrat Grover Cleveland and may have ensured his election by giving him the winning margin in New York State.

After the 1884 election the enthusiasm for reform spilled over into local politics, spawning good-government campaigns across the country. Although they won some municipal victories, the Mugwumps were more adept at molding public opinion than at running government. Controlling the newspapers and journals read by the educated middle class, the Mugwumps defined the terms of political debate, denying the machine system legitimacy and injecting an elitist bias into political opinion.

Mark Twain was not alone in proclaiming "an honest and saving loathing for universal suffrage."

Ernst Below

Beer and German American Politics

Ernst Below (1845–1910) toured the United States in the early 1890s, enjoying the hospitality of the prosperous German American communities he encountered along the way. Following is an excerpt from the book he published on his return to Germany, Bilder aus dem Westen (1894). The reader will note that the action takes place at a Turner festival. Turner is the German word for "gymnast." In the nineteenth century the gymnastic movement had an enormous vogue in Germany, helping to weld a spirit of German nationalism in that fragmented country before unification in 1871.

In Kansas City we sat on the veranda, taking coffee with Mr. Held, the attorney.... The men spoke of the chances of our host's election to Congress. Our friend, Karl, had the latest precise news from the battlefield and told of the stratagems used by one party or another in the attempt to make sure of victory. I showed my surprise that an educated, honest, thoughtful man, under such conditions, could bring himself to be concerned with politics....

The next night the great Turnverein [Gymnastic Association] hall was brightly lighted.... When I entered the hall the gymnastic exercises had already begun.... On the walls hung ... pictures of Washington, Lincoln and Grant; side by side with William I, Bismarck and Moltke.... At one end of the hall sat old Kumpf, the former mayor. Speaking to him from either side with great seriousness were two German Democrats, city officials. Kumpf was, like most of the old German turners, once a solid Republican.... Yet even he was displeased with the flirtation of his party with the

temperance and prohibition forces in recent times. Nevertheless, he could not bring himself publicly to go over to the Democrats, and he laughingly parried the attacks of the two city officials.... A little later one of them tried a different assault.... He pointed to the adjoining room, in which a great many men surrounded the refreshment table. In their midst stood Joe Davenport, the Republican candidate for mayor, who was ordering a round of drinks and cigars for everyone.

"Listen to what he says," went on the Democrat. "... I know for a fact that he wrote yesterday to the Young Men's Christian Association promising in return for their votes a complete closing of all saloons on Sundays. Either here or there he must break his word.... Go up to the scamp and expose his game!"

... Now the mayoralty candidate climbed onto a barrel and praised Germany and the Germans, the Rhine and the "Fatherland." ... After Davenport finished there was no end of *hochs* and *hurrays*. Only with difficulty did Old Kumpf succeed in getting the floor and drawing the attention of the crowd.... Pointing to Mr. Holmes the rival Democratic candidate who had, unnoticed, come into the hall during the concluding exercises [Kumpf said]: "Although I do not fight for exactly the same principles as this man, still I must acknowledge that he offers a true guarantee against the hypocritical attempts of the prohibitionists.... With this in mind, I say, 'long live our next mayor, Mister Holmes!'"

Loud applause arose from all sides; men, women, and children jostled about trying to shake the hand of the future mayor. The band struck up the "Star Spangled Banner" while the whole assemblage rose to its feet and loudly sang the words....

Soon a loud uproar reigned in the refreshment room. One group yelled ridicule against another, as the satellites of Davenport sought to ridicule the sudden change in sentiment. After

the beer had been poured out in streams on both sides for some time no one really knew what was going on; not a man could tell exactly who belonged to which party....

As I left the hall I was greeted by Rothmann, the director of the German school. He was indignant at the scenes which had so unworthily closed a meeting that had begun so well. "This time at least," he said, "the Germans should have held together to show that they could unitedly support Held, our [Republican] candidate for Congress. But when it comes to the most vital interest of the Germans in America, they are only concerned with their little appetites ...."

SOURCE: Oscar Handlin, ed., *This Was America* (Cambridge, MA: Harvard University Press, 1949), 383–89.

ANALYZING THE EVIDENCE

► In his speech, the Republican candidate Joe Davenport, himself no German, sings the praises of Germany, the "Fatherland." Why does he do that?

► In the Civil War era, German Americans were solidly Republican, loyal supporters of Lincoln. The former mayor, Old Kumpf, is of that generation. So why does he stand up and denounce the Republican candidate Davenport?

► The goings-on at the Turnverein hall are about the campaign for mayor. Yet when the school principal Rothman leaves, he is complaining about the injury done to Held, the Republican candidate for Congress. Does that call into question our claim in the text that national politics in the late nineteenth century was insulated — unlike in our own time — from ethnocultural politics?

This democratic triumph of the early republic—a beacon for other nations to follow—now went into reverse, as northern states began to impose **literacy tests** and limit the voting rights of immigrants. The **secret ballot**, an import from Australia widely adopted around 1890, abetted the Mugwump anti-democratic campaign. Traditionally, voters had submitted party-supplied tickets in public view at the polling place. With the Australian reform, citizens cast their ballots in voting booths, freed from party surveillance, but for the uneducated and foreign-speaking, navigating a lengthy official ballot could be intimidating. And so could new voter registration procedures that registrars commonly used to bar those considered unfit for the suffrage.

The Mugwumps were reformers, but not on behalf of social justice. The travails of working people meant little to them, while keeping the state out of the welfare business meant a great deal. As far as the Mugwumps were concerned, the government that was best was the government that governed least. Theirs was the brand of "reform" perfectly in keeping with the conservative ethos of the time. In this respect, they and their critics—conservative judges and party leaders who otherwise disdained Mugwumpery—were in agreement.

Women's Political Culture

The young Theodore Roosevelt, an up-and-coming Republican state politician in 1884, spoke contemptuously of the Mugwumps as "man-milliners" (makers of ladies' hats). The sexual slur was not accidental. In attacking organizational politics, the Mugwumps were challenging a bastion of male society. At party meetings and conventions, men carried on not only the business of politics but also the rituals of male sociability amid cigar smoke and whiskey. Politics was identified with manliness. It was competitive. It dealt in the commerce of power. It was frankly self-aggrandizing. Party politics, in short, was no place for a woman.

So, naturally, the woman suffrage movement met fierce opposition. Acknowledging the uphill battle that lay ahead, suffragists overcame the bitter divisions of the Reconstruction era (see Chapter 15), reuniting in 1890 in the National American Woman Suffrage Association. In that same spirit of realism, suffragists abandoned efforts to get a constitutional amendment and concentrated on state campaigns. Except out West—in Wyoming, Idaho, Colorado, and Utah—the most they could win was the right to vote for school boards or on tax issues. "Men are ordained to govern in all forceful and material things, because they are men," asserted an

anti-suffrage resolution, "while women, by the same decree of God and nature, are equally fitted to bear rule in a higher and more spiritual realm, where the strong frame and the weighty brain count for less"—that is to say, not in politics.

Yet this invocation of the doctrine of **"separate spheres"**—that men and women had different natures, and that women's nature fitted them for "a higher and more spiritual realm"—did open a channel for women into public life. "Women's place is Home," acknowledged the journalist Retha Childe Dorr. "But Home is not contained within the four walls of an individual house. Home is the community. The city full of people is the Family.... And badly do the Home and Family need their mother." Indeed, in antebellum times women had long engaged in uplifting activities—fighting prostitution, assisting the poor, agitating for prison reform, and demanding better educational and job opportunities (see Chapter 9). Since many of these goals required state action, women's organizations of necessity turned to politics, but they had to find a way in, and that meant first of all creating their own political sphere.

Just before Christmas in 1873 the women of Hillsboro, Ohio, began to hold prayer meetings in front of the town's saloons, appealing to owners to close their doors and end the misery of families of hard-drinking fathers. Thus began a spontaneous uprising—the "Woman's Crusade"—that spread across the country. From this agitation came the Woman's Christian Temperance Union (WCTU), which, under the guidance of Frances Willard, blossomed into the leading women's organization in the country.

Frances Willard and Women's Politics. Willard was a suffragist, but no admirer of Susan B. Anthony or Lucy Stone. "The clamor for 'rights,'" she felt, was the wrong approach. Better to offer "only prayerful, persistent pleas for the opportunity of duty"—that is, to link the vote to women's concerns as wives and mothers. Willard's political motto was "Home Protection." In 1879, after carefully laying the groundwork, she defeated the antisuffragist incumbent and became national president of the WCTU.

The liquor evil, while genuinely felt by Willard, was not why she abandoned a promising career as an educator; she had been president of the Evanston College for Ladies, and when it was folded into Northwestern, the first dean of women there. She regarded the WCTU essentially in political terms, a vehicle uniquely suited for converting womanly virtue into political power. Willard understood her middle-class members. Like herself, they were "literary-minded," evangelical Christian, with a

Wanted, Sober Men

This drawing appeared in a magazine in 1899, twenty-five years after the women of Hillsboro, Ohio, rose in revolt against the town's saloonkeepers and launched the Woman's Christian Temperance Union (WCTU). But the emotion it expresses had not changed — that the saloon was the enemy of the family. Culver Pictures.

vocation for service. She intended to mold them into a political force. With men excluded, the WCTU gave the natural leaders among the women space to hone their skills. And for the others, there was Willard's "Do-Everything" program, an ever-widening array of issues—labor conditions, prostitution, public health, international peace—that introduced these sheltered women to the ills of the world.

On the liquor front, the WCTU made some headway, mainly by local-option ordinances but also, as in Iowa, by statewide prohibition. Finding a way into men's political realm, however, was more challenging. Willard's own preference was for third-party politics. In the early 1880s, she led the WCTU into the Prohibition Party, a pretty moribund operation until the women came in, but even then, significant only in a handful of midwestern states. Willard had her reasons. In a small pond, she could be a big fish, as indeed she quickly became in the Prohibition Party. She was also something of a maverick, disdainful of the mainstream parties and supportive of the Knights of Labor. Finally, Willard got the coveted endorsement of woman suffrage by

the Prohibition Party. But of course that did nothing to advance the suffrage cause. And, in truth, the third-party gambit was a misstep, causing friction in the WCTU and mostly failing to wean members from their traditional party loyalties.

The major parties, in fact, were not as antifemale as their manly facades might have suggested. Understanding all too well that womenfolk influenced their men, both parties in their different ways campaigned for the women's "vote." In this competition, the Republicans had the advantage of their ideological roots in antebellum evangelical reform. Willard's motto "Home Protection" was not hers alone. Republicans had used the term, or a variant, against slavery, and in Willard's time they even used it to defend the tariff: Protection from cheap foreign goods meant higher American wages and hence "protection" for the family. In advancing this pro-family line, the Republicans recruited female party operatives and found a pool of them in, of all places, the WCTU. So, despite herself, Willard contributed to the expanding role of women in mainstream politics.

Not much changed in the short run. At the national level Republicans remained against prohibition and against woman suffrage. For its part, the WCTU abandoned Willard's political activism and dropped out of the suffrage struggle. But the link it established between women's social concerns and political participation helped lay the groundwork for fresh attacks on male electoral politics. In the meantime, even without the vote, the WCTU demonstrated how potent a force women might be in the public arena and how vibrant a political culture they could build.

➤ Who were the Mugwumps? Do you regard them as important players in post-Reconstruction politics? If so, why?

➤ What do we mean by "ethnocultural" politics, and why is it important for an understanding of late-nineteenth-century American politics?

➤ Why was it that women, although they mostly couldn't vote, nevertheless became important political actors in this era?

Race and Politics in the New South

When Reconstruction ended in 1877, so did the hopes of African Americans that they would enjoy the equal rights promised them by the Fourteenth and Fifteenth Amendments. Southern schools were segregated. Access to jobs, the courts, and social services was racially determined and unequal. No laws segregated public accommodation, however, and practices varied across the South. Only on the railroads, as rail travel became common, did whites demand that blacks be excluded from first-class cars, with the result that southern railroads became, after 1887, the first public accommodation legally segregated.

In politics the situation was still more fluid. Redemption had not driven blacks out of politics (see Chapter 15). On the contrary, their turnout at elections in the post-Reconstruction years was not far behind the turnout by whites. But blacks did not participate on equal terms with whites. In the black belt areas, where African Americans sometimes outnumbered whites, **gerrymandered** voting districts ensured that, while blacks got some offices, political control remained in white hands. Blacks were routinely intimidated during political campaigns. Even so, an impressive majority remained staunchly Republican, refusing, as the last black congressman from Mississippi told his House colleagues in 1882, "to surrender their honest convictions, even upon the altar of their personal necessities."

Whatever hopes blacks entertained for better days, however, faded during the 1880s and then, in the next decade, expired in a terrible burst of racial terrorism.

Biracial Politics

No democratic society can survive if it does not allow competing economic and social interests to be heard. In the United States the two-party system performs that role. The sectional crisis severely tested the two-party system because, in both the North and the South, opposing the dominant party came to be seen as treasonable. In the victorious North, despite the best efforts of the Republicans, the Democrats shed their disgrace after the war and reclaimed their status as a major party. In the defeated South, however, the scars of war cut deep, and Reconstruction cut even deeper. The struggle for "**home rule**" empowered southern Democrats. They had "redeemed" the South from Republican domination — hence the name they adopted: Redeemers. Cloaked in the mantle of the Lost Cause, the Redeemers claimed a monopoly on political legitimacy.

The Republican Party in the South did not fold up, however. On the contrary, it soldiered on, sustained by tenacious black loyalty, by a hard core of white support, by patronage from Republican national administrations, and by a key Democratic vulnerability. This was the gap between the universality

the Democrats claimed as the party of Redemption and its actual domination by a single interest — the South's economic elite.

Class antagonism, though masked by sectional patriotism, was never absent from southern society. The Civil War had brought out long-smoldering differences between planters and hill-country farmers, who felt called on to shed blood for a slaveholding system in which they had no part. Afterward, class tensions were exacerbated by the spread of farm tenancy and by the emergence of low-wage industrial labor. Unable to make their grievances heard, economically distressed southerners broke with the Democratic Party in the early 1880s and mounted insurgent movements across the region. Most notable were the Readjusters, who briefly gained power in Virginia over the issue of Reconstruction debt: They opposed repayment to bond-holding speculators that would have left the state destitute. After subsiding briefly, this agrarian discontent revived mightily in the late 1880s, as tenant farmers joined farmers' alliances and helped create the Populist Party (see p. 602).

As this insurgency accelerated, the question of black participation became critical. Racism cut through southern society and, so some thought, most infected the lowest rungs. "The white laboring classes here," wrote an Alabamian in 1886, "are separated from the Negroes, working all day side by side with them, by an innate consciousness of race superiority," which "excites a sentiment of sympathy and equality with the classes above them." Yet when times got bad enough, hard-pressed whites could also see blacks as fellow victims. "They are in the ditch just like we are," asserted one white Texan. Southern Populists never fully reconciled these contradictory impulses. They did not question the racist conventions of social inequality. Nor were the interests of white farmers and black tenants always in concert. But once agrarian protest turned political, the logic of interracial solidarity became hard to deny.

In the meantime, black farmers had developed a political structure of their own. The Colored Farmers' Alliance operated much less openly than its white counterparts — it could be worth a black man's life to make too open a show of his independence — but nevertheless gave black voters a voice at the table with white Populists. The demands of partisan politics, once the break with the Democrats came, clinched the argument for interracial unity. Where the Populists fused with the Republican Party, as in North Carolina and Tennessee, they automatically became allies of black leaders. Where the Populists fielded separate third-party tickets, they needed to appeal directly to black voters. "The accident of

Map 19.2   Disfranchisement in the New South

In the midst of the Populist challenge to Democratic one-party rule in the South, a movement to deprive blacks of the right to vote spread from Mississippi across the South. By 1910 every state in the region except Tennessee, Arkansas, Texas, and Florida had made constitutional changes designed to prevent blacks from voting, and these four states accomplished much the same result through poll taxes and other exclusionary methods. For the next half century, the political process in the South would be for whites only.

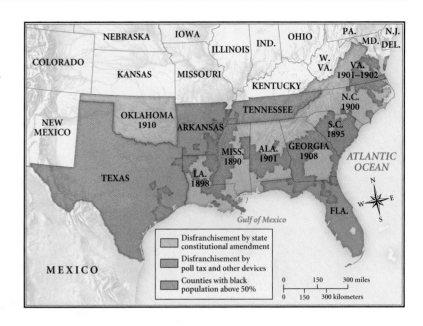

color can make no difference in the interest of farmers, croppers, and laborers," argued the Georgian Tom Watson. "You are kept apart that you may be separately fleeced of your earnings." This interracial appeal, even if not always wholehearted, put at risk the foundations of elite southern politics.

One-Party Rule Triumphant

The Democrats struck back with all their might. They played the race card, parading as the "white man's party" while denouncing the Populists for promoting "Negro rule." Yet they shamelessly competed for the black vote. In this they had many advantages: money, control of the local power structures, and a paternalistic relationship to the black community. When all else failed, mischief at the polls enabled the Democrats to beat back the Populists. Across the South in the 1892 elections, the Democrats snatched victory from defeat by a miraculous vote count—including the votes of many long dead or gone. Thus the Mississippian Frank Burkitt's bitter attack on the conservatives: They were "a class of corrupt office-seekers" who had "hypocritically raised the howl of white supremacy while they debauched the ballot boxes . . . disregarded the rights of the blacks . . . and actually dominated the will of the white people through the instrumentality of the stolen negro vote."

Black Disfranchisement. In the midst of these deadly struggles, the Democrats decided to settle matters once and for all. The movement to disfranchise the blacks, hitherto tentative, swiftly gathered steam (Map 19.2). In 1890 Mississippi adopted a literacy test that effectively drove the state's blacks out of politics. The motives behind it were cynical, but the literacy test could be dressed up as a reform for white Mississippians tired of electoral fraud and violence. Their children and grandchildren, argued one influential figure, should not be left "with shotguns in their hands, a lie in their mouths and perjury on their lips in order to defeat the negroes." Better, a Mississippi journalist wrote, to devise "some legal defensible substitute for the abhorrent and evil methods on which white supremacy lies." This logic even persuaded some weary Populists: Frank Burkitt, for example, was arguing *for* the Mississippi literacy test in the words quoted in the previous paragraph.

The race question had helped bring down the Populists; now it helped reconcile them to defeat. Embittered whites, ambivalent all along about interracial cooperation, turned their fury on the blacks. Insofar as disfranchising measures asserted militant white supremacy, poor whites approved. Of course, it was important that their own vulnerability—their own lack of education—be partially offset by lenient enforcement of the literacy test. Thus, to take a blatant instance, Louisiana's grandfather clause exempted from the test those entitled to vote on January 1, 1867 (before the Fifteenth Amendment gave freedmen that right), together with their sons and grandsons. But poor whites were not protected from property and poll-tax requirements, and many stopped voting.

Poor whites might have objected more had their spokesmen not been conceded a voice in southern politics. A new brand of demagogic politician came forward to speak for them, appealing not to their economic interests but to their racial prejudices. Tom Watson, the Georgia Populist, rebuilt his political career as a spellbinding

Disfranchisement

This political drawing that appeared in *Judge* magazine on July 30, 1892, shows members of the Ku Klux Klan barring black voters from the polls. By 1892, in fact, this drawing was behind the times. Literacy tests and poll taxes were beginning to disfranchise blacks with less menace and more likelihood of evading the constitutional requirement (note the sign behind the Klansmen) under the Fifteenth Amendment that the right to vote not be denied "on account of race, color, or previous condition of servitude." Museum of American Political Life.

race-baiter (see Comparing American Voices, "'Negro Domination!'" pp. 600–601). In South Carolina "Pitchfork" Ben Tillman, more of a mainstream Democratic politician, adeptly manipulated images of white manhood. What bound southerners together, no matter their class, was their sturdy independence, their defense of the virtue of white womanhood, and their resistance to outside meddling in southern affairs. A U.S. senator for many years, Tillman was as fiery as Tom Watson at condemning blacks as "an ignorant and debased and debauched race."

The Ascendancy of Jim Crow. A brand of white supremacy emerged that was more virulent than anything blacks had faced since Reconstruction. The color line, hitherto incomplete, became rigid and comprehensive. Segregated seating in trains, first adopted in the late 1880s, provided a precedent for the legal separation of the races. The enforcing legislation, known as **Jim Crow** laws, soon applied to every type of public facility—restaurants, hotels, streetcars, even cemeteries. In the 1890s the South became a region fully segregated by law for the first time.

The U.S. Supreme Court soon ratified the South's decision. In *Plessy v. Ferguson* (1896), the Court ruled that segregation was not discriminatory—that is, it did not violate the Fourteenth Amendment—provided that blacks received accommodations equal to those of whites. The "separate but equal" doctrine ignored the realities of southern life. Segregated facilities were rarely if ever "equal" in any material sense, and segregation was itself intended to underscore the inferiority of blacks (as was also the case in the Southwest, where Hispanics and Asian were segregated under cover of *Plessy v. Ferguson*). With a similar disregard for reality, the Supreme Court in *Williams v. Mississippi* (1898) validated the disfranchising devices of the southern states on the grounds that, if race was not a specified criterion for disfranchisement, the rights of blacks to vote under the Fifteenth Amendment were not being violated.

The Case of Grimes County. What this counterrevolution meant is perhaps best captured locally by the events in Grimes County, a cotton-growing area in east Texas, where African Americans composed more

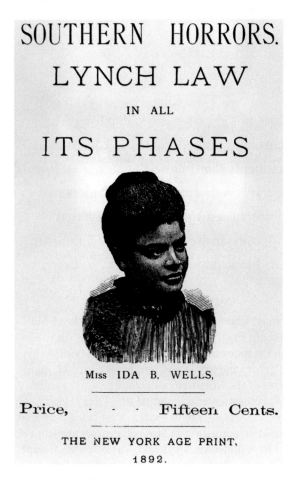

SOUTHERN HORRORS.
LYNCH LAW
IN ALL
ITS PHASES

Miss IDA B. WELLS,

Price, · · · Fifteen Cents.

THE NEW YORK AGE PRINT,
1892.

Miss Ida B. Wells

In 1887 Ida Wells (Wells-Barnett after she married in 1895) was thrown bodily from a train in Tennessee for refusing to vacate her seat in a section reserved for whites, launching her into a lifelong crusade for racial justice. Her mission was to expose the evil of lynching in the South. This portrait is from the title page of a pamphlet she published in 1892 entitled, "Southern Horrors. Lynch Law in All Its Phases."
Miriam and Ira D. Wallach Division of Art, Prints and Photographs, The New York Public Library. Astor, Lenox and Tilden Foundations.

than half of the population. They kept the local Republican Party going after Reconstruction and regularly sent black representatives to the Texas legislature during the 1870s and 1880s. More remarkably, the local Populist Party that appeared among white farmers proved immune to Democrats' taunts of "black rule." A Populist-Republican coalition swept the county elections in 1896 and 1898, a surprising remnant of the southern Populist movement.

In 1899 defeated Democratic candidates and prominent citizens organized the secret White Man's Union. Blacks were forcibly prevented from voting in town elections that year. The two most important black leaders were shot down in cold blood. Night riders terrorized both white Populists and black Republicans. When the Populist sheriff

proved incapable of enforcing the law, the game was up. Reconstituted as the White Man's Party, the Union became the local Democratic Party in a new guise. The Democrats carried Grimes County by an overwhelming vote in 1900. The day after the election, gunmen laid siege to the sheriff's office. They killed his brother and a friend and drove him, badly wounded, out of the county forever.

The White Man's Party ruled Grimes County for the next fifty years. The whole episode was the handiwork of the county's "best citizens," suggesting how respectable terror had become in the service of white supremacy. Grimes County, as a leading citizen grimly said, intended to "force the African to keep his place." After Populism was crushed in that corner of Texas, blacks could survive only if they stayed out of politics and avoided trouble with whites.

Like the blacks of Grimes County, southern blacks in many places resisted as best they could. When Georgia adopted the first Jim Crow law applying to streetcars in 1891, Atlanta blacks declared a boycott, and over the next fifteen years blacks boycotted segregated streetcars in at least twenty-five cities. "Do not trample on our pride by being 'jim crowed,'" the Savannah *Tribune* urged its readers: "Walk!" Ida Wells-Barnett emerged as the most outspoken black crusader against lynching, so enraging the Memphis white community by the editorials in her newspaper, *Free Speech*, that she was forced in 1892 to leave the city.

Some blacks were drawn to the Back-to-Africa movement, abandoning all hope that they would ever find justice in America. But for most Africa was not a real choice. They were Americans, and they had to bend to the raging forces of racism and find a way to survive.

➤ The Redeemers imposed a system of one-party rule on the South after Reconstruction. Why was this system initially vulnerable to attack?

➤ How do you explain the disfranchisement of southern blacks during the 1890s? What measures did whites enact to prevent blacks from voting?

➤ What was "Jim Crow"? Would the answer to question 1 serve also to explain Jim Crow's establishment in the South?

The Crisis of American Politics: The 1890s

Populism was a catalyst for political crisis not only in the South but also across the entire nation. But while in the South the result was preservation of

"Negro Domination!"

The title of this feature—Comparing American Voices—does not always mean comparing what different Americans have said. It's also possible, taking a chronological approach, to compare what a single individual said at different times. In the two documents that follow, the author is Tom Watson, the fiery Georgia Populist. In both, he was addressing the "everlasting and overshadowing Negro Question" that he thought distinguished the South and obstructed the radical, class-based politics he advocated. The two documents offer diametrically opposite answers and thereby illuminate how it came to be that the race-obsessed South disfranchised its black population.

TOM WATSON: 1892

In 1892, when Watson wrote the essay below, he had recently been elected to Congress on a third-party ticket and had high hopes that Populism would break the grip of the conservative Democrats and bring a new day for the South's oppressed tenant farmers, black and white.

The white tenant lives adjoining the colored tenant. Their houses are almost equally destitute of comforts. Their living is confined to bare necessities. . . . They pay the same enormous prices for farm supplies. Christmas finds them both without any satisfactory return for a year's toil. Dull and heavy and unhappy, they both start the plows again when "New Year's" passes.

Now the People's Party says to these two men, "You are kept apart that you may be separately fleeced of your earnings. You are made to hate each other because upon that hatred is rested the keystone of the arch of financial despotism which enslaves you both. You are deceived and blinded that you may not see how this race antagonism perpetuates a monetary system which beggars both."

This is so obviously true it is no wonder both these unhappy laborers stop to listen. No wonder they begin to realize that no change of law can benefit the white tenant which does not benefit the black one likewise; that no system which now does injustice to one of them can fail to injure both. Their every material interest is identical. The moment this becomes a conviction, mere selfishness, the mere desire to better their conditions, escape onerous taxes, avoid usurious charges, lighten their rents, or change their precarious tenements into smiling, happy homes, will drive these two men together, just as their mutual inflamed prejudices now drive them apart.

. . . Why should the colored man always be taught that the white man of his neighborhood hates him, while a Northern man, who taxes every rag on his back, loves him? Why should not my tenant come to regard me as his friend rather than the manufacturer who plunders us both? Why should we perpetuate a policy which drives the black man into the arms of the Northern politician?

. . . To the emasculated individual who cries "Negro supremacy!" there is little to be said. . . . Not being prepared to make any such admission in favor of any race the sun ever shone on, I have no words which can portray my contempt for the white men, Anglo-Saxons, who can knock their knees together, and through their chattering teeth and pale lips admit they are afraid the Negroes will "dominate us." The question of social equality does not enter into the calculation at all. That is a thing each citizen decides for himself. No statute ever yet drew the latch of the humblest home—or ever will. Each citizen regulates his visiting list—and always will.

The conclusion, then, seems to me this: They will become political allies, and neither can injure the one without weakening both. It will be in the interest of both that each should have justice. And on these broad lines of mutual interest, mutual forbearance, and mutual support the present will be made the stepping-stone to future peace and prosperity.

SOURCE: "The Negro Question in the South," *Arena*, vol. VI (1892), in *A More Perfect Union: Documents in U.S. History*, 2 vols., ed. Paul F. Boller and Ronald Story (Boston: Houghton Mifflin, 1984), 2: 83–85.

TOM WATSON: 1904

After the 1896 election and the collapse of Populism, Watson withdrew from politics. In 1904, however, he returned to head a Populist presidential ticket, in part as a protest against the rightward drift of the national Democratic Party. Although he had no illusions about how he would do nationwide (he got a total of 117,000 votes), he was chagrined by his poor showing in his native state, which he attributed to the race-baiting of the conservative Democratic machine. Two weeks later, on November 19, 1904, he delivered the following address to a partisan crowd at the courthouse in Thomson, Georgia. *

There never was a time when the greedy corporations, the soulless combinations of sordid wealth, has so nearly got the industrial world by the throat. . . . There never was a time when the avarice of the few so monopolized the wealth created by the laborers of this republic as to-day. . . .

The time has come when we must act for the best interests for our homes and firesides. Negroes may call themselves Republicans, or call themselves Democrats, or call themselves Methodists, or call themselves Baptists, but when you touch them on any subject that concerns their color they are all just negroes. They run together, they stand as one man representing the colored race. So with the whites in the South. . . . When any question comes up in the South that concerns us as a race then every distinction falls down and we stand together. . . . Every man ought to know that; every man does know it.

And yet we allow these small politicians [to frighten] us, year after year, into voting for men whom we know nothing about and for a platform we utterly detest. . . . Our task from the beginning has been peculiarly difficult in the South because of the belief if the white people divide the negro would be the balance of power and would rule the South. That has been our stumbling block. . . . Now, no Southern man wanted negro domination . . . no Anglo-Saxon man anywhere ever wanted it. No. The white race has made civilization what it is, and the white race intends to keep it what it is. We told those colored people whenever we spoke to them that "when we took hold of you, you were savages from Africa; we taught you everything you know. . . . You have had the best example of civilization and to the extent that you have copied it you have become good citizens, farmers, carpenters, black-smiths—Christians, because our God has become your God." And we said to those people, "Follow us and we will guarantee you"—what? Social equality? No. Political equality?—No. We said, "We will give you equality as a citizen, under the law that will protect your life, your limb, your property, your home and your

fire-side, just as it protects ours." That is as far as we ever went, and I am willing to go that far to-day. [Applause.] And the man who does not believe in going that far is not a man who believes in Jeffersonian democracy. [Applause.]

But the Democrats said, "You will divide the white people and the negro will have the balance of power. We will have negro domination." . . . We wept; and bowed down in sack-cloth and ashes. That is all we could do. Our Party was swept out of existence. Then what? The Southern states began to disfranchise the negro, and in almost every state the negro has been taken out of politics. And why hasn't he been taken out of politics in Georgia? . . . [The Democrats] were using the fear of negro domination to hold your votes. . . . Now what? What! They were afraid of the negro, weren't they? They were afraid of the negro and negro domination (They say) and here they had had almost a generation to put him out but he is in as big as life. The negro is an old sinner 364 days of the year, but the 365th, which is on election day, he is "sugar in the gourd." [Applause, laughter and cheers.]

At the very opening of this campaign, I threw at their feet the challenge—"If you are earnest in what you say, if you are afraid of the negro, if you are really afraid of the negro, you miserable coward [applause], if you really mean it, then we are ready to help you out of your scrape, you pusillanimous political coward, we will come up and help you pass any kind of law that you yourself say was necessary to keep the white man on top." [Applause and cheers.]

*NOTE: In 1907, with Watson's backing, the Georgia legislature passed a law disfranchising blacks.

SOURCE: "Speech of Hon. Thomas E. Watson, Delivered at Thomson, Ga., November 19th, 1904," unpublished ms., Watson Papers, University of North Carolina. Printed by permission.

ANALYZING THE EVIDENCE

➤ In his 1904 speech, Watson claimed that his views on black participation in politics had not changed. Is that correct?

➤ Do you think Watson became more of a racist between 1892 and 1904? In what ways?

➤ The "Negro Question" had to do with the relations between the races. In what ways did Watson redefine those relations between 1892 and 1904?

one-party rule, in national politics the result was a revitalized two-party system.

Ever since Reconstruction, national politics had been stalemated by the even balance between the parties. In the late 1880s the equilibrium began to break down. Benjamin Harrison's election to the presidency in 1888 was the last close election of the era (Democrat Grover Cleveland actually got a larger popular vote). Thereafter, the tide turned against the Republicans, saddled by the lackluster Harrison administration and by Democratic charges that the protectionist McKinley Tariff of 1890 was a giveaway to the business interests. That year Democrats took the House of Representatives decisively and won a number of governorships in normally Republican states. In 1892 Cleveland regained the presidency by the largest margin in twenty years (the only president to be elected to two nonconsecutive terms).

Had everything else remained equal, the events of 1890 and 1892 might have initiated an era of Democratic supremacy. But everything else did not remain equal. By the time of Cleveland's inauguration, farm foreclosures and railroad bankruptcies signaled economic trouble. On May 3, 1893, the stock market crashed. In Chicago 100,000 jobless workers walked the streets; nationwide the unemployment rate soared above 20 percent.

As depression set in, which party would prevail—and on what platform—became an open question. The first challenge to the status quo arrived from the West and South, where falling grain and cotton prices were devastating farmers.

The Populist Revolt

Farmers were of necessity joiners. They needed organization to overcome their social isolation and provide economic services—hence the appeal of the Granger movement, which had spread across the Midwest after 1867 (see Chapter 16), and after the Grange's decline, the emergence of a new movement of farmers' alliances in many rural districts. From diffuse organizational beginnings, two dominant groups emerged. One was the Farmers' Alliance of the Northwest, which was confined mainly to the midwestern states. More dynamic was the National (or Southern) Farmers' Alliance, which in the mid-1880s spread rapidly from Texas onto the Great Plains and eastward into the cotton South as "traveling lecturers" extolled the virtues of cooperative activity and reminded farmers of "their obligation to stand as a great conservative body against the encroachments of monopolies and . . . the growing corruption of wealth and power." While thus recapitulating Granger resentment against railroads and merchants, the alliances initially re-

sisted the temptation of third-party politics, preferring instead self-help and institution-building.

A prime example was the Texas Exchange, a huge cooperative that marketed the crops of cotton farmers and provided them with cheap loans. When cotton prices fell in 1891, the Texas Exchange failed. The Texas Alliance then proposed a new scheme— a **"subtreasury" system**, which would enable farmers to store their crops in public warehouses and borrow against the unsold crops from a public fund until the cotton could be profitably sold. The subtreasury plan provided the same credit and marketing functions as the defunct Texas Exchange, but with a crucial difference: The federal government would be the underwriter. When the Democratic Party declared the scheme too radical, the Texas Alliance decided to strike out in politics independently.

These events in Texas revealed, with special clarity, a process of politicization that rippled through the Alliance movement. Rebuffed by the major parties, Alliance men more or less reluctantly abandoned their Democratic and Republican allegiances, and as state Alliances grew stronger and more impatient, they began to field independent slates. The confidence gained at the state level led to the formation of the national People's (Populist) Party in 1892. In the elections that year, with the veteran antimonopoly campaigner James B. Weaver as their presidential candidate, the Populists captured a million votes and carried four western states (Map 19.3). For the first

Map 19.3   The Heyday of Western Populism, 1892

This map shows the percentage of the popular vote won by James B. Weaver, the People's Party candidate, in the presidential election of 1892. Except in California and Montana, the Populists won broad support across the West and genuinely threatened the established parties in that region.

Mary Elizabeth Lease

As a political movement the Populists were short on cash and organization but long on rank-and-file zeal and tub-thumping oratory. No one was more rousing on the stump than Mary Elizabeth Lease, who came from a Kansas homestead and pulled no punches. "What you farmers need to do," she proclaimed in her speeches, "is to raise less corn and more Hell!" The photograph shows her as a nineteenth-century lady. The cartoonist's drawings show her in action. Kansas Historical Society.

MRS. MARY ELIZABETH LEASE AS SHE APPEARED IN 1895 WHEN SHE WAS AT THE HEIGHT OF HER POLITICAL ACTIVITIES IN KANSAS.

time agrarian protest truly challenged the national two-party system.

One Populist advantage was the many women in the movement. They had gotten in on the ground floor, when the alliances were just networks of local clubs that had formed for largely social purposes. The women had come along with their men. Although prominent as speakers and lecturers, women rarely became alliance leaders, and their role diminished with the shift into politics. In deference to the southern wing, the Populist platform was silent on woman suffrage. Still, neither Democrats nor Republicans would have countenanced a spokeswoman such as the fiery Mary Elizabeth Lease, who became famous for calling on farmers "to raise less corn and more hell." The profanity might have been a reporter's invention, but the passion was all hers. Mrs. Lease insisted just as strenuously on Populism's "grand and holy mission . . . to place the mothers of this nation on an equality with the fathers."

Populist Ideology. "There are but two sides," proclaimed a Populist manifesto. "On the one side are the allied hosts of monopolies, the money power, great trusts and railroad corporations. . . . On the other are the farmers, laborers, merchants and all the people who produce wealth. . . . Between these two there is no middle ground."

By this reasoning farmers and workers formed a single producer class. The claim was not merely rhetorical. The national platform contained strong labor planks, and party leaders earnestly sought union support. Texas railroad workers and Colorado miners cooperated with the farmers' alliances, got their support in strikes, and actively participated in forming state Populist parties. The attraction of Populism, in fact, pulled the labor movement to the left. Inside the American Federation of Labor Samuel Gompers briefly lost control to a faction that advocated independent labor politics in alliance with the Populists. The center of this agitation was Chicago, where the radical reformer Henry Demarest Lloyd envisioned a farmer-labor movement that might actually prevail in America.

In its explicit class appeal — in recognizing that "the irrepressible conflict between capital and labor is upon us" — Populism parted company from the two mainstream parties. Indeed, it had the makings of an American version — a farmer-labor version — of the social democratic parties emerging in Europe at this time, although Populism lacked the Marxist component. But, like the European parties, it favored a strong state. In the words of the Populist platform: "We believe that the power of government — in other words, of the people — should be expanded as rapidly and as far as the good sense of an intelligent people and the teachings of experience shall justify, to the end that oppression, injustice and poverty should eventually cease in the land." Spokesmen such as Lorenzo Dow

Lewelling, Populist governor of Kansas, considered it to be "the business of the government to make it possible to live and sustain the life of my family."

At the founding Omaha convention in 1892, Populists called for nationalization of the railroads and communications; protection of the land, including natural resources, from monopoly and foreign ownership; a graduated income tax; and the free and unlimited coinage of silver. From this array of issues, the last—free silver—emerged as the cardinal demand of the Populist Party.

Free Silver. Reeling from rock-bottom prices, embattled farmers gravitated in the early 1890s to the unlimited coinage of silver because they hoped that an increase in the money supply would raise farm prices and give them some relief. In addition, the party's slim resources would be fattened by hefty contributions from silver-mining interests. Wealthy mine operators, scornful though they might be of Populist radicalism, yearned for the day when the government would buy at a premium all the silver they could produce.

Free silver triggered a debate for the soul of the Populist Party. Henry Demarest Lloyd voiced labor's objection. He called free silver the "cowbird of reform," stealing in and taking over the nest that others had built. Free silver, if it became the defining party issue, would undercut the broader Populist program and alienate wage earners, who had no enthusiasm for inflationary measures. The bread-and-butter appeal of free silver, however, was simply too great.

But once Populists made that choice, they fatally compromised their party's identity as an independent movement. For free silver was not an issue over which Populists held a monopoly. It was, on the contrary, a question at the very center of mainstream American politics.

Money and Politics

In a rapidly developing economy, the money supply is bound to be a hotly contested issue. The volume of money has to increase rapidly enough to meet the economy's needs or growth will be stifled. How fast the money supply should grow, however, is a divisive question. More money in circulation inflates prices and reduces the real cost of borrowing, to the benefit of debtors and commodity producers. The "sound money" people—creditors, individuals on fixed incomes, established businessmen—have an opposite interest.

Before the Civil War the main source of the nation's money supply had been state-chartered banks, several thousand of them, all issuing banknotes to borrowers that then circulated as money.

The economy's need for money was amply met by the state banks, although the soundness of the banknotes—the ability of the issuing banks to stand behind their notes and redeem them at face value—was always uncertain. This freewheeling activity was sharply curtailed by the U.S. Banking Act of 1863, which prohibited state banks from issuing banknotes not backed by U.S. government bonds. However, because the Lincoln administration was printing paper money—**greenbacks**—to pay for the Civil War, in effect the U.S. Treasury replaced the state banks as the source of easy money.

Once the war ended, the question became: Should the federal government continue in that role? No, argued the sound money interests. Washington had no business printing paper money and should restore the traditional practice of limiting the national currency to the amount of *specie*—gold and silver—held by the U.S. Treasury. The issue was hotly contested for a decade, but in 1875 the sound money interests prevailed, and the circulation of greenbacks as legal tender—that is, backed by nothing more than the good faith of the federal government—came to an end. With state banknotes also in short supply, the country entered an era of chronic **deflation**.

This was the context out of which the silver question emerged. Since the colonial era, both gold and silver had served as specie, but as the supply of silver tightened, it became more valuable as metal than as money and in 1873 was officially dropped as a medium of exchange. Soon silver mining in the West surged, and the price of silver suddenly fell. The greenback supporters began agitating for a resumption of the bimetallic policy. If the federal government resumed buying at the fixed ratio prevailing before 1873—16 ounces of silver equaling 1 ounce of gold—silver would flow into the treasury and greatly expand the volume of money.

With so much at stake for so many people, the currency question became one of the staples of post-Reconstruction politics. Twice the pro-silver coalition in Congress won modest victories. First, the Bland-Allison Act of 1878 required the U.S. Treasury to purchase and coin between $2 million and $4 million worth of silver each month. Then, in the more sweeping Sherman Silver Purchase Act of 1890, an additional 4.5 million ounces of silver bullion was to be purchased monthly, to serve as the basis for new issues of U.S. Treasury notes.

These legislative battles, although hard fought, cut across party lines, in the familiar fashion of post-Reconstruction politics. But in the early 1890s, as hard times set in, silver suddenly became a defining issue between the parties; in particular, it radicalized the Democrats.

Climax: The Election of 1896

As the party in power, the Democrats bore the brunt of responsibility for the economic crisis. Any Democratic president would have been hard pressed, but the man who actually held the job, Grover Cleveland, could hardly have made a bigger hash of it. When jobless marchers—the so-called Coxey's army—arrived in Washington in 1894 to demand federal relief, Cleveland dispersed them forcibly and arrested their leader, Jacob S. Coxey, for trespassing on the Capitol grounds. Cleveland's brutal handling of the Pullman strike (see Chapter 17) further alienated the labor vote. Nor did he live up to his reputation as a tariff reformer. Cleveland lost control of the battle when the protectionist McKinley Tariff of 1890 came up for revision in Congress. The resulting Wilson-Gorman Tariff of 1894, which Cleveland allowed to pass into law without his signature, caved in to special interests and left many rates unchanged.

Cleveland and Free Silver. Most disastrous, however, was Cleveland's stand on the silver question. Cleveland was a committed sound-money man. Nothing that happened after the depression set in—not collapsing prices, not the suffering of farmers, not the groundswell of support for free silver within his own party—budged Cleveland. Economic pressures, in fact, soon forced him to abandon a silver-based currency altogether. With the government's gold reserves dwindling, Cleveland persuaded Congress in 1893 to repeal the Sherman Silver Purchase Act, in effect sacrificing the country's painfully crafted program for maintaining a limited bimetallic policy. Then, as his administration's problems deepened, Cleveland turned in 1895 to a syndicate of private bankers led by J. P. Morgan to arrange the gold purchases needed to replenish the treasury's depleted reserves. The administration's secret negotiations with Wall Street, once discovered, enraged Democrats and completed Cleveland's isolation from his party.

William Jennings Bryan and the Cross of Gold. At their Chicago convention in 1896, the Democrats repudiated Cleveland and turned left. The leader of the triumphant silver Democrats was William Jennings Bryan of Nebraska. Bryan was a political phenomenon. Only thirty-six years old, he had already served two terms in Congress and had become a passionate advocate of free silver. Bryan, remarked the journalist Frederic Howe, was "preeminently an evangelist," whose zeal sprang from "the Western self-righteous missionary mind." With biblical fervor Bryan swept up his audiences when he joined the debate on free silver at the

The Candidates, 1896

The 1896 presidential campaign marked one small step in the technology of electioneering—the introduction of the celluloid campaign button, which a party supporter could pin on his lapel. It is doubtful, however, that this innovation made any difference in the outcome of the election. Collection of Janice L. and David J. Frent.

Democratic convention. He locked up the presidential nomination with a stirring attack on the gold standard: "You shall not press down upon the brow of labor this crown of thorns, you shall not crucify mankind on a cross of gold."

Bryan's nomination meant that the Democrats had become the party of free silver; his "cross of gold" speech meant that the money question would be a national crusade. No one could be neutral on this defining issue. Silver Republicans bolted their party; gold Democrats went for a splinter Democratic ticket or supported the Republican Party; even the Prohibition Party split into gold and silver wings. The Populists, meeting after the Democratic convention, accepted Bryan as their candidate. The free-silver issue had become so vital that they could not do otherwise. Although they nominated their own vice presidential candidate, Tom Watson of Georgia, the Populists found themselves for all

practical purposes absorbed into the Democratic silver campaign.

The Republicans took up the challenge. Their party leader was the wealthy Cleveland iron maker Mark Hanna, a brilliant political manager and an exponent of the new industrial capitalism. Hanna orchestrated an unprecedented money-raising campaign among America's corporate interests. His candidate, William McKinley of Ohio, personified the virtues of Republicanism, standing solidly for high tariffs, sound money, and prosperity. While Bryan broke with tradition and crisscrossed the country by railroad in a furious whistle-stop campaign, the dignified McKinley received delegations at his home in Canton, Ohio. Bryan orated with moral fervor; McKinley talked of economic progress and a full dinner pail.

Not since 1860 had the United States witnessed so hard-fought an election over such high stakes. For

THE SACRILEGIOUS CANDIDATE.

No man who drags into the dust the most sacred symbols of the Christian world is fit to be president of the United States.

The Cross of Gold

Bryan's Cross of Gold speech was one of the great orations in American political history. Republican critics, however, were not so keen on it and did their best to puncture its Christian aura. In this cartoon by Grant Hamilton, Bryan is accused of cynically using the cross and crown of thorns for political purposes. What Bryan's really up to, the cartoon suggests, is revolution, hence in the background a pillaged city and the little man, right out of the French revolution. Library of Congress/ Picture Research Consultants & Archives.

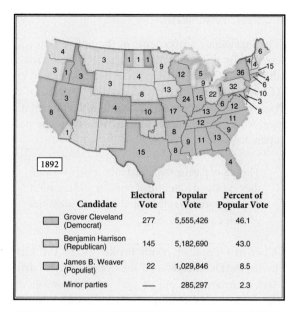

Candidate	Electoral Vote	Popular Vote	Percent of Popular Vote
Grover Cleveland (Democrat)	277	5,555,426	46.1
Benjamin Harrison (Republican)	145	5,182,690	43.0
James B. Weaver (Populist)	22	1,029,846	8.5
Minor parties	—	285,297	2.3

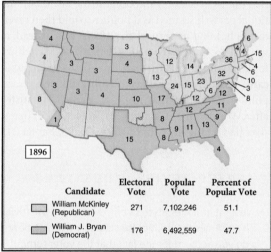

Candidate	Electoral Vote	Popular Vote	Percent of Popular Vote
William McKinley (Republican)	271	7,102,246	51.1
William J. Bryan (Democrat)	176	6,492,559	47.7

Map 19.4   Presidential Elections of 1892 and 1896

In the 1890s the age of political stalemate came to an end. Students should compare the 1892 map with Map 19.1 (p. 586) and note especially Cleveland's breakthrough in the normally Republican states of the upper Midwest. In 1896 the pendulum swung in the opposite direction, with McKinley's consolidation of Republican control over the Northeast and Midwest far overbalancing the Democratic advances in the thinly populated western states. The 1896 election marked the beginning of forty years of Republican dominance in national politics.

the middle class, sound money stood symbolically for the soundness of the social order. With jobless workers tramping the streets and bankrupt farmers up in arms, Bryan's fervent assault on the gold standard struck fear in many hearts. Republicans denounced the Democratic platform as "revolutionary and anarchistic" and Bryan's supporters as "social

misfits who have almost nothing in common but opposition to the existing order and institutions."

Though little noticed at the time, ethnocultural influences figured strongly in the campaign. In their bid for electoral dominance in 1890 and 1892, the Democrats had turned to their advantage the Republican reputation as the party of temperance and religious intolerance. Now, in 1896, the Republicans beat a strategic retreat from the politics of morality. McKinley himself had represented an ethnically mixed district of northeastern Ohio. In appealing to his immigrant and working-class constituents, he had learned the art of easy tolerance, expressed in his words, "Live and let live." Of the two candidates, the prairie orator Bryan, with his biblical language and moral righteousness, presented the more alien image to traditional Democratic voters in the big cities.

McKinley won handily, with 271 electoral votes to Bryan's 176. He kept the ground Republicans had regained in the 1894 midterm elections and pushed into Democratic strongholds, especially in the cities. Boston, New York, Chicago, and Minneapolis, all taken by Cleveland in 1892, went for McKinley in 1896. Bryan ran strongly only in the South, in silver-mining states, and in the Populist West (Map 19.4). But the gains his evangelical style brought him in some Republican rural areas did not compensate for his losses in traditionally Democratic urban districts.

The paralyzing equilibrium in American politics ended in 1896. The Republicans skillfully turned both economic and cultural challenges to their advantage. They persuaded the nation that they were the party of prosperity, and they persuaded many traditionally Democratic urban voters that they were sympathetic to ethnic diversity. In so doing the Republicans became the nation's majority party, notwithstanding the Demcratic lock on the South. In 1896, too, electoral politics regained its place as an arena for national debate, setting the stage for the reform politics of the Progressive era.

➤ Farmers, like other Americans, had strong ties to the established parties, yet many of them became Populists anyway. Why was that?

➤ Cleveland is rated as a pretty good president for his first term and a bad one for his second term. How do you explain that reversal?

➤ It would be hard to imagine American voters today getting excited about the money supply (and hard, no doubt, for students to get excited about it in this chapter). So how do you account for the fact that free silver was the hot topic of the 1896 election?

SUMMARY

This chapter is about late nineteenth-century politics. We start with the period 1877–1892, when the great politics of sectional crisis gave way to an age of political quiescence. Except for the judicial branch, governmental institutions were weak, the national parties avoided big issues, and laissez-faire was the prevailing philosophy. And yet, while little seemed at stake, politics engendered extraordinarily high levels of popular participation. This was partly because of the entertainment value, but more importantly because politics was the arena in which the nation's ethnic and religious conflicts were fought out and because organizationally the parties were strongly developed and highly active. Finally, while still lacking voting rights, women carved out for themselves, in their guise as defenders of the family, an increasingly prominent place in politics.

In the South, post-Reconstruction politics followed a different, less settled course because the emergent one-party system was resisted by poor whites and Republican blacks. Biracial southern Populism flared briefly in the late 1880s and then failed, triggering a grim reaction that disfranchised African Americans, completed a rigid segregation system, and let loose a terrible cycle of racial hatred and violence. Blacks resisted, but had to bend to overwhelming power of white supremacy.

In this chapter's final section, we return to national politics, which in the 1890s again became an arena of principled debate. Galvanized by the rise of Populism, the Democratic Party committed itself to free silver, sidetracking the last great third-party challenge to mainstream politics and making the election of 1896 a moment of truth for the major parties. The Republicans won decisively, ending a paralyzing stalemate and assuring themselves of political dominance for the next thirty years.

Connections: Politics

The immediate antecedents of the political history covered by this chapter are in the sectional crisis of the 1850s (Chapter 13) and the Reconstruction era (Chapter 15), when fundamental questions of Union and slavery were resolved. In the aftermath, politics took a breather and, as we say in the part opener (p. 485):

> The major parties remained robust only because they exploited a culture of popular participation and embraced the ethnic and religious identities of their constituencies.

When the Populist revolt broke out in the early 1890s, the Democrats took the opportunity to drive African Americans out of politics and consolidate their grip on the South, while the Republicans carried the 1896 election and became the dominant national party. It seemed as if politics would then revert to the holding pattern of the 1880s, but instead, as we will see in Chapter 20, the demand for reform took hold and the two parties—first the Republicans, then the Democrats—embraced progressive politics. Although that impulse seemed exhausted after World War I (Chapter 23), in fact the Progressives had set the stage for the New Deal (Chapter 24).

CHAPTER REVIEW QUESTIONS

➤ In light of James Bryce's complaint about the triviality of American politics (see chapter opener), how do you account for the fact that the voter turnout in the 1880s was the highest in our history?

➤ How important do you think race was in explaining the failure of southern Populism?

➤ Why do historians regard the election of 1896 as one of the decisive elections in American history?

TIMELINE

1874	Woman's Christian Temperance Union founded
1877	Rutherford B. Hayes inaugurated as president, marking end of Reconstruction
1881	President James A. Garfield assassinated
1883	Pendleton Civil Service Act
1884	Mugwump reformers leave Republican Party to support Grover Cleveland, first Democrat-elected president since 1856
1887	Florida adopts first law segregating railroad travel
1888	James Bryce's *The American Commonwealth*
1890	McKinley Tariff
	Democrats sweep congressional elections, inaugurating brief era of Democratic Party dominance
	Mississippi becomes first state to adopt literacy test to disfranchise blacks
1892	People's (Populist) Party founded
1893	Panic of 1893 leads to national depression
	Repeal of Sherman Silver Purchase Act (1890)
1894	"Coxey's army" of unemployed fails to win federal relief
1896	Election of Republican president William McKinley; free-silver campaign crushed
	Plessy v. Ferguson upholds constitutionality of "separate but equal" segregation

FOR FURTHER EXPLORATION

The literature on late-nineteenth-century politics is a topic on which historians have had a field day. On the ideological underpinnings, an older book by Robert G. McCloskey, *American Conservatism in the Age of Enterprise* (1951), still retains its freshness. Mark Wahlgren, *Rum, Romanism & Rebellion: The Making of a President, 1884* (2000), is a fresh analysis of the first phase of post-Reconstruction national politics. The mass appeal of Gilded Age politics is incisively explored in Michael E. McGerr, *The Decline of Popular Politics: The American North, 1865–1928* (1986). Alexander Keyssar, *The Right to Vote: The Contested History of Democracy in the United States* (2000), is illuminating on the conservative assault on voting rights in this period. Kathryn Kish Sklar, *Florence Kelley and the Nation's Work* (1995), traces the emergence of women's political culture through the life of a leading reformer. Rebecca Edwards, *Angels in the Machinery: Gender in American Party Politics* (1997), reveals women's unexpectedly large role within the main parties. On southern politics the seminal book is C. Vann Woodward, *Origins of the New South, 1877–1913* (1951), which still defines the terms of discussion among historians. The most far-reaching revision is Edward L. Ayers, *The Promise of the New South* (1992). The process of sectional reconciliation is imaginatively treated in David W. Blight, *Race and Reunion: The Civil War in Memory* (2001). The most recent treatment of disfranchisement is Michael Perman, *Struggle for Mastery: Disfranchisement in the South, 1888–1908* (2001). Richard D. Hofstadter, *The Age of Reform* (1955), stresses the darker side of Populism, in which intolerance and paranoia figure heavily. Hofstadter's thesis, which once dominated debate among historians, has given way to a more positive assessment. The key book here is Lawrence Goodwyn, *Democratic Promise: The Populist Moment* (1976), which argues that Populism was a broadly based response to industrial capitalism. Peter H. Argesinger, *The Limits of Agrarian Radicalism* (1995), stresses the effectiveness of the party status quo to frustrate western Populism. Michael Kazin, *The Populist Persuasion* (1995), describes how the language of Populism entered the discourse of mainstream American politics. Much information on Gilded Age presidents can be found at the Web site **americanpresident.org/presidentialresources.htm**.

TEST YOUR KNOWLEDGE

To assess your command of the material in this chapter, see the Online Study Guide at **bedfordstmartins.com/henretta**.

For Web sites, images, and documents related to topics and places in this chapter, visit **bedfordstmartins.com/makehistory**.

20 The Progressive Era
1900–1914

O N THE FACE OF IT, the political tumult of the 1890s ended with William McKinley's election in 1896. After the bitter struggle over free silver, the victorious Republicans had no stomach for crusades. The main thing, as party chief Mark Hanna said, was to "stand pat and continue Republican prosperity."

Yet beneath the surface a deep unease had set in. Hard times had unveiled truths not acknowledged in better days—that a frightening chasm, for example, had opened between America's social classes. In Richard Olney's view the great Pullman strike of 1894 had brought the country "to the ragged edge of anarchy." As Cleveland's attorney general, it had been Olney's job to crush the strike (see Chapter 17). But he took little joy from his success. He asked himself, rather, how such repressive actions might be avoided in the future. His answer was that the government should regulate labor relations on the railroads so that crippling rail strikes would not happen. As a first step toward Olney's goal, Congress adopted the Erdman Railway Mediation Act in 1898. In such ways did the crisis of the 1890s turn the nation's thinking to reform.

The problems themselves, however, were of much older origin. For many decades Americans had been absorbed in building the world's most advanced industrial economy. At the beginning of the twentieth century, they paused, looked around, and began to add up the costs—a frightening concentration of corporate power, a rebellious working class, misery in the cities, and the corruption of machine politics.

◄ **Reba Owen, Settlement-House Worker**

The settlement house was a hallmark of progressive America. Columbus, Ohio, had five, including Godman Guild House, where Reba Owen served as a visiting nurse, tending the pregnant mothers and children of the neighborhood. LifeCare Alliance/Courtesy, Ohio Historical Society.

Now, with the strife-torn 1890s behind them, reform became an absorbing concern of many Americans. It was as if social awareness reached a critical mass around 1900 and set reform activity going as a major, self-sustaining phenomenon. For this reason the years from 1900 to World War I have come to be known as the Progressive era.

The Course of Reform

Historians have sometimes spoken of a progressive "movement." But progressivism was not a movement in any meaningful sense. There was no agreed-upon agenda, no unifying organization. Both the Republican and Democratic parties had progressive wings. And, at different times and places, different social groups became active. The term *progressivism* describes a widespread, many-sided effort after 1900 to build a better society. And yet, if progressivism was many-sided, it did have a center, and that was the urban middle class.

The Middle-Class Impulse

In 1889 Jane Addams and Ellen Gates Starr established Hull House on Chicago's West Side after visiting Toynbee Hall in the London slums. Flanked by saloons and "horrid little houses," in a neighborhood of mainly Italian immigrants, the dilapidated mansion that they called Hull House was the model for scores of settlement houses that sprang up in the ghettos of the nation's cities, serving as community centers and spark plugs for neighborhood betterment. At the Henry Street Settlement in New York City, Lillian Wald made visiting nurses a major service. Mary McDowell, head of the University of Chicago Settlement, installed a bathhouse, a children's playground, and a citizenship school for immigrants.

The settlement house was a hallmark of social progressivism, and for Jane Addams it meant a lifetime in ugly surroundings, endlessly battling for garbage removal, playgrounds, better street lighting, and police protection.

Why would she have made that choice? Addams was a daughter of the middle class. She might have lived a life of ease and personal cultivation, and that indeed was what her prosperous parents had intended for her when they sent her off to Rockford College. But Addams came home in 1881 sad and unfulfilled, feeling "simply smothered and sickened by advantages." Hull House became her salvation, enabling her to "begin with however small a group

to accomplish and to live." In retrospect, she realized that hers was not an individual crisis, but a crisis that afflicted her entire generation. In a famous essay, she spoke of the "subjective necessity" of the settlement house. Addams meant that it was as much for the young middle-class residents eager to serve as it was a response to the needs of slum dwellers.

The generational crisis was also a crisis of faith. Progressives like Jane Addams characteristically grew up in homes imbued with Christian piety, then found themselves incapable of sustaining the faith of their parents. Many went through a religious crisis, ultimately settling on careers in social work, education, or politics, where religious striving might be translated into secular action. Jane Addams, for one, took up settlement-house work believing that by uplifting the poor, she would herself be uplifted: She would experience "the joy of finding Christ" by acting "in fellowship" with the needy.

The Protestant clergy itself struggled with these issues, translating a long-felt concern for the plight of the poor into a major theological doctrine — the Social Gospel. The leading exponent was the Baptist cleric Walter Rauschenbusch, whose ideas had been forged by his ministry in the squalid Hell's Kitchen section of New York City. The churches must not wall themselves off from the misery and despair in their midst, said the Reverend Rauschenbusch. They had to embrace the "social aims of Jesus." The Kingdom of God on Earth would be achieved not by striving for personal salvation but in the cause of social justice.

What lent urgency to these inner callings was the discovery that there was no insulating middle-class Americans from the ills of industrial society. That was a truth borne painfully home to Jane Addams when her eldest sister lay ill in a hospital during the Pullman strike. Held up by the turmoil, her sister's distraught family failed to reach her bedside before she died. Addams feared that such painful episodes, inescapable whenever labor and capital came to blows, would inculcate "lasting bitterness" in middle-class homes. There was no denying that "the present industrial system is in a state of profound disorder," and no denying the stake of the middle class in "right[ing] it." It was up to reformers like herself, products of the middle class, to take up that task.

Progressive Ideas

Finding solutions, however, was easier said than done. Jane Addams wrote poignantly of her uncertainty, having launched Hull House, about just how to proceed. She "longed for . . . an explanation of the social chaos and the logical steps toward its better ordering." The answers that were forthcoming depended first of all on the emergence of a new intellectual style that we can call *progressive*.

If the facts could be known, everything else was possible. That was the starting point for progressive thinking. Hence the burst of enthusiasm for scientific investigation — statistical studies by the federal government of immigration, child labor, and economic practices; social research by privately funded foundations delving into industrial conditions; vice commissions in many cities looking into prostitution, gambling, and other moral ills of an urban society. Great faith was also placed in academic expertise. In Wisconsin the state university became a key resource for Governor Robert La Follette's reform administration — the reason, one supporter boasted, for "the democracy, the thoroughness, and the accuracy of the state in its legislation."

Similarly, progressives were strongly attracted to scientific management, which had originally been intended to rationalize work in factories (see Chapter 17). But its founder, Frederick W. Taylor, argued that his basic approach — the "scientific" analysis of human activity — offered solutions to waste and inefficiency in municipal government, schools and hospitals, even at home. Scientific management, said Taylor, could solve all the social ills that arise from "such of our acts as are blundering, ill-directed, or inefficient."

Scientific management was an American invention, but progressive intellectuals also felt themselves part of a transatlantic world. Ideas flowed in both directions, with the Americans, in fact, very much on the receiving end. Since the 1870s, they had flocked to German universities, absorbing the economics and political science that became key tools of progressive reform. On many fronts, social politics overseas seemed far in advance of the United States. The sense of having fallen behind — that "the tables are turned," as the young progressive Walter Weyl wrote, and that "America no longer teaches democracy to an expectant world, but herself goes to school in Europe and Australia" — was a spur to fresh ideas.

The main thing was to resist ways of thinking that discouraged purposeful action. Social Darwinists who had so dominated Gilded Age thought (see Chapter 19) were wrong in their belief that society developed according to fixed and unchanging laws. "It is folly," pronounced the Harvard philosopher William James, "to speak of the 'laws of history,' as of something inevitable, which science only has to discover, and which anyone can then foretell and observe, but do nothing to alter or avert." James denied the existence of absolute truths and advocated instead a philosophy he called **pragmatism**, which judged ideas by their consequences. Philosophy should be concerned with solving problems, James insisted, and not with contemplating ultimate ends.

Nowhere were the battle lines more sharply drawn than in the courts, where judges treated the law as if it had arisen from eternal principles. One such principle was liberty of contract, which the Supreme Court invoked in *Lochner v. New York* (1905) to strike down a state law limiting the hours of bakers. The Court contended it was protecting the contractual liberty of the bakers (as well as their employers). Nonsense, responded the dissenting Justice Oliver Wendell Holmes. If the choice was between working and starving, could it be said that bakers freely chose to work 14 hours a day?

Legal realism, as Justice Holmes's reasoning came to be known, rested on his conviction that "the life of the law has not been logic; it has been experience." Dean Roscoe Pound of the Harvard Law School called for "the adjustment of principles and doctrines to the human conditions they are to govern rather than assumed first principles." Nor should the law claim to be above the struggle, added Pound's student Felix Frankfurter; its proper role was to be "a vital agency for human betterment."

No practitioner of legal realism took this advice more to heart than the brilliant Boston lawyer Louis D. Brandeis, the son of Jewish emigrants from Austria-Hungary. He became known as "the people's lawyer" because, on behalf of the little guy, he regularly took on and beat the mightiest vested interests in town. An admirer of Frederick W. Taylor, Brandeis won a famous railroad rate case by demonstrating that the railroads operated inefficiently and didn't deserve to charge their customers more money. In fact, it was Brandeis who coined the term *scientific management*. Always ready to enlist in a good cause, Brandeis embodied progressivism's greatest strength — its capacity for uniting the brainpower of progressive intellectuals with the high-mindedness of social reformers.

The Muckrakers. The progressive mode of action — idealistic in intent, tough-minded in practice — nurtured a new kind of reform journalism. During the 1890s bright new magazines like *Collier's* and *McClure's* began to find an urban audience for lively, fact-filled reporting. Almost by accident, editors discovered that what most interested middle-class readers was the exposure of mischief in American life. Investigative reporters fanned out on the trail of evildoers.

Who Said Muck Rake?
The Smile That Won't Come Off.)

Lincoln Steffens's article "Tweed Days in St. Louis" in the October 1902 issue of *McClure's* is credited with starting the trend. In a riveting series Steffens wrote about "the shame of the cities" — the corrupt ties between business and political machines. Ida M. Tarbell attacked the Standard Oil monopoly, and David Graham Phillips told how money controlled the Senate. William Hard exposed industrial accidents in "Making Steel and Killing Men" (1907) and child labor in "De Kid Wot Works at Night" (1908). Hardly a sordid corner of American life escaped the scrutiny of these tireless reporters.

Theodore Roosevelt, among many others, thought they went too far. In a 1906 speech, he compared them to the man with a muckrake in *Pilgrim's Progress* (by the seventeenth-century English preacher John Bunyan) who was too absorbed with raking the filth on the floor to look up and accept a celestial crown. Thus the term **muckraker** became attached to journalists who exposed the underside of American life. Their efforts were in fact health-giving. More than any other group, the muckrakers called the people to arms.

Women Progressives

When she started out, Jane Addams did not regard Hull House as a specifically woman's enterprise. But of course, in her personal odyssey, it had mattered that she was a daughter, not a son. And while men were welcome, the settlement houses were overwhelmingly led and staffed by women. Over time, as the reform impulse quickened, the settlement-house movement became a nodal point for the distinctively feminine cast of social progressivism.

This was in keeping with women's long-established role as the nation's "social housekeepers," those who traditionally shouldered the burden of humanitarian work in American cities. Middle-class women were the foot soldiers for charity organizations, visiting needy families, assessing their problems, and referring them to relief agencies. After many years of such dedicated labor, Josephine Shaw Lowell of New York City concluded that giving assistance to the poor was not enough. "If the working people had all they ought to have, we should not have the paupers and criminals," she declared. "It is better to save them before they go

Saving the Children

In the early years at Hull House, Jane Addams recalled, toddlers sometimes arrived for kindergarten tipsy from a breakfast of bread soaked in wine. To settlement-house workers, the answer to such ignorance was in child-care education, and so began the program to send visiting nurses into immigrant homes. They taught mothers the proper methods of caring for children — including, as this photograph shows, the daily infant bath, given in a dishpan if necessary. Chicago Historical Society.

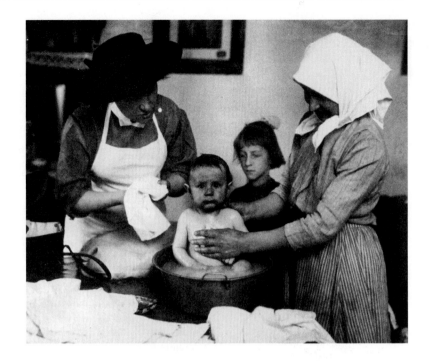

under, than to spend your life fishing them out afterward." Lowell founded the New York Consumers' League in 1890. Her goal was to improve the wages and working conditions of female clerks in the city's stores by issuing a "White List" — a very short list at first — of cooperating shops.

From these modest beginnings Lowell's organization spread to other cities and blossomed into the National Consumers' League in 1899. At its head stood a feisty, outspoken woman, Florence Kelley, an early resident of Hull House and then chief factory inspector of Illinois. Investigating the sweated trades of Chicago, Kelley and Jane Addams quickly lost faith in voluntary reform: The exploited garment workers could be rescued only by state factory legislation. When she joined the National Consumers' League, Kelley brought that focus to its work. Under her crusading leadership, the Consumers' League became a powerful advocate for protective legislation for women and children.

Among its achievements, none was more important than the Supreme Court's *Muller v. Oregon* decision in 1908, which upheld an Oregon law limiting the workday for women to ten hours. The Consumers' League recruited Louis Brandeis, whose brief before the Court devoted a scant two pages to the narrow constitutional issue — whether, under its police powers, Oregon had the right to regulate women's working hours. Instead, Brandeis rested his case on data gathered by the Consumers' League describing the toll that long hours took on women's health and family duties. The *Muller* decision was a triumph for legal realism

and, by approving an expansive welfare role for the states, cleared the way for a mighty lobbying effort by women's organizations, whose victories included the first law providing public assistance for mothers with dependent children in Illinois in 1911; the first minimum wage law for women in Massachusetts in 1912; more effective child-labor laws in many states; and, at the federal level, the Children's and Women's bureaus in the Labor Department in 1912 and 1920, respectively (Table 20.1). The **welfare state**, insofar as it arrived in America in these years, was what women progressives had made of it; they erected a "maternalist" welfare system.

Revival of Woman's Suffrage. Women reformers like Jane Addams and Florence Kelley breathed new life into the suffrage movement. Why, they asked, should a woman who was capable of running a settlement house or lobbying a bill be denied the right to vote? And why should only women like themselves be making that fight? By asking that question, they opened the way for working-class women to join the suffrage struggle and, just as important, revealed the capacity of social reformers to expand beyond their middle-class base.

Believing that working women should be encouraged to help themselves, New York reformers in 1903 founded the National Women's Trade Union League. Financed by wealthy supporters, the league organized women workers, played a considerable role in their strikes, and trained working-class leaders. One such leader was Rose Schneiderman, who became a union organizer among New York's

TABLE 20.1	Progressive Legislation and Supreme Court Decisions
State Laws	
1903	Wisconsin primary law
	Oregon ten-hour law for women
1910	New York Bureau of Industries and Immigration
	Washington State adopts woman suffrage
1911	Illinois law providing aid for mothers with dependent children
	New York State Factory Commission
1912	Massachusetts minimum-wage law for women and children
Federal Laws	
1898	Erdman Railway Mediation Act
1902	Newlands Reclamation Act
1903	U.S. Bureau of Corporations
	Elkins Act
1906	Hepburn Railway Act
	Pure Food and Drug Act
	Meat Inspection Act
1909	Payne-Aldrich Tariff Act
1913	Underwood Tariff Act
	Federal Reserve Act
1914	Federal Trade Commission Act
	Clayton Antitrust Act
1916	Seamen's Act
	Federal Farm Loan Act
Supreme Court Decisions	
1895	*U.S. v. E. C. Knight* shelters manufacturing from antitrust law
1897	*U.S. v. Trans-Missouri* quashes "rule of reason" in antitrust suits
1904	*U.S. v. Northern Securities* orders dissolution of a company ruled a monopoly under Sherman Act
1905	*Lochner v. New York* invalidates a state law limiting hours of bakers
1908	*Muller v. Oregon* approves a state law limiting working hours of women
	Loewe v. Lawlor (Danbury Hatters case*)* finds a labor boycott to be a conspiracy in restraint of trade
1911	*U.S. v. Standard Oil* restores rule of reason as guiding principle in antitrust cases

garment workers; another was Agnes Nestor, who led Illinois glove workers. Although often resenting the patronizing ways of their well-to-do sponsors, such trade-union women identified their cause with the broader struggle for women's rights. When New York State held suffrage referenda in 1915 and 1917, strong support came from Jewish and Italian precincts inhabited by unionized garment workers.

Around 1910, suffrage activity began to quicken, and tactics shifted. In Britain suffragists had begun to picket Parliament, assault politicians, and stage hunger strikes while in jail. Inspired by their example, Alice Paul, a young Quaker once a resident of

Suffragists on Parade, 1913

After 1910 the suffrage movement went into high gear. Suffragist leaders decided that a constitutional amendment was a more effective route than battling for the vote state by state. The impressive women's parade in Washington, D.C., at Woodrow Wilson's inauguration served notice on the incoming administration that the suffragists meant business. The new president was not pleased with his uninvited guests. Brown Brothers.

Britain, applied similar confrontational tactics to the American struggle. Although woman suffrage had been won in six western states since 1910, Paul rejected the state-by-state route as too slow (Map 20.1). She advocated a constitutional amendment that in one stroke would grant women everywhere the right to vote. In 1916 Paul organized the militant National Woman's Party.

The mainstream National American Woman Suffrage Association (NAWSA), from which Paul had split off, was also rejuvenated. Carrie Chapman Catt, a skilled organizer from the New York movement, took over as national leader in 1915. Under her guidance NAWSA brought a broad-based organization to the campaign for a federal amendment.

Feminism. In the midst of this suffrage struggle, something new and more fundamental began to happen. A younger generation — college-educated, self-supporting women — refused to be hemmed in by the social constraints of women's "separate sphere." "Breaking into the Human Race" was the aspiration they proclaimed at a mass meeting in New York in 1914. "We intend simply to be ourselves," declared the chair Marie Jenny Howe, "not just our little female selves, but our whole big human selves."

The women at this meeting called themselves **feminists**, a term that was just coming into use. In this, its first incarnation, *feminism* meant freedom for full personal development. Thus did Charlotte Perkins Gilman, famous for her advocacy of communal kitchens as a means of liberating women from homemaking, imagine the new woman: "Here she comes, running, out of prison and off the pedestal; chains off, crown off, halo off, just a live woman."

Feminists were militantly pro-suffrage, but unlike their more traditional suffragist sisters, not on the basis that women would uplift American politics. Rather, they demanded the right to vote because they considered themselves just as good as men. At the moment the reviving suffrage movement was about to triumph, it was overtaken by a larger revolution that redefined the struggle for women's rights as a battle against all the constraints that prevented women from achieving their potential as human beings.

This feminist revolution also challenged women's social progressivism, which was premised on the belief that women were the weaker sex. It was just this argument, at the very heart of Brandeis's brief in the landmark *Muller* case, that rang true with the Supreme Court. "The two sexes differ in structure of body, in the functions to be performed by each, in the amount of physical strength," the Court agreed. "This difference justifies . . . legislation . . . designed to compensate for some of the burdens which rest upon her." But feminists wanted no such

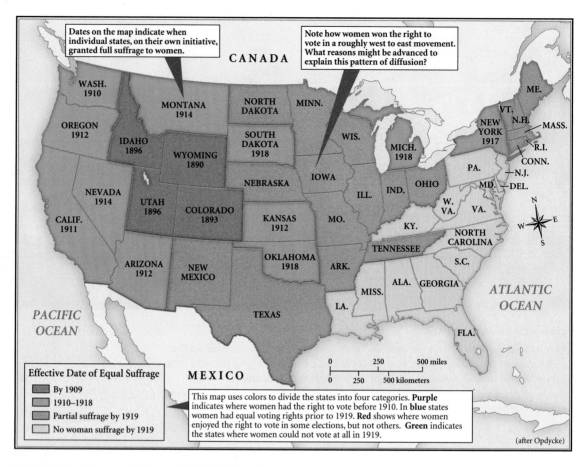

Dates on the map indicate when individual states, on their own initiative, granted full suffrage to women.

Note how women won the right to vote in a roughly west to east movement. What reasons might be advanced to explain this pattern of diffusion?

Effective Date of Equal Suffrage
- By 1909
- 1910–1918
- Partial suffrage by 1919
- No woman suffrage by 1919

This map uses colors to divide the states into four categories. **Purple** indicates where women had the right to vote before 1910. In **blue** states women had equal voting rights prior to 1919. **Red** shows where women enjoyed the right to vote in some elections, but not others. **Green** indicates the states where women could not vote at all in 1919.

(after Opdycke)

MAP 20.1 Woman Suffrage, 1890–1919

By 1909, after more than sixty years of agitation, only four lightly populated western states had granted women full voting rights. A number of other states offered partial suffrage, limited mostly to voting for school boards and such issues as taxes. Between 1910 and 1918, as the effort shifted to the struggle for a constitutional amendment, eleven states joined the list granting full suffrage. The most stubborn resistance was in the South.

compensation. Thus, to the surprise of Maryland's progressive governor Charles J. Bonaparte, some feminists objected to his 1914 women's minimum wage bill because it implied that "women need some special care, protection and privilege." A wedge was surfacing that would ultimately fracture the women's movement, dividing an older generation of progressives from feminists who prized gender equality more highly than any social benefit.

Urban Liberalism

The evolution of the women's movement—in particular, the recruitment of working-class women to what had been a middle-class struggle—was entirely characteristic of how progressivism evolved more generally.

When the Republican Hiram Johnson ran for California governor in 1910, he was the reform candidate of the state's middle class. Famous as prosecutor of the corrupt San Francisco boss Abe Ruef, Johnson pledged to purify California politics and curb the Southern Pacific Railroad—the dominating economic power in the state. By his second term, Johnson was championing social and labor legislation. His original base in the middle class had eroded, and he had become the champion of California's working class.

Johnson's career reflected a shift in the center of gravity of progressivism, which had begun as a movement of the middle class but then took on board America's working people. A new strain of progressive reform emerged that historians have labeled *urban liberalism*. To understand this phenomenon, we have to begin with city machine politics.

Thirty minutes before quitting time on Saturday afternoon, March 25, 1911, fire broke out at the

The Triangle Tragedy

This drawing, by the artist John Sloan, captures better than any photograph the horror of the Triangle fire. The image of the two women clinging to each other as they fell is accurate. According to observers, a number of young workers, with no other way to escape the flames, chose to fall to their deaths in each other's arms. The fireman who can't bear to watch is probably a product of Sloan's imagination, but the anguish he felt is true enough, because when the fire trucks arrived, they didn't have the equipment to save anyone. The ladders were too short, and the nets the firemen spread too weak. The bodies simply shot right through to the ground. *Harper's Weekly,* May 8, 1915.

Triangle Shirtwaist Company in downtown New York. The flames trapped the workers, who were mostly young immigrant women. Many leapt to their deaths; the rest never reached the windows. The dead, 146 of them, averaged nineteen years of age.

In the wake of the tragedy, the New York State Factory Commission developed a remarkable program of labor reform: fifty-six laws dealing with fire hazards, unsafe machines, industrial homework, and wages and hours for women and children. The chairman of the commission was Robert F. Wagner; the vice chairman was Alfred E. Smith. Both were Tammany Hall politicians, serving at the time as leaders in the state legislature. They established the commission, participated fully in its work, and marshaled the party regulars to pass the proposals into law — all with the approval of the Tammany machine. The labor code that resulted was the most advanced in the country.

Tammany's response to the Triangle fire meant that it was conceding that social problems had outgrown the powers of party machines. Only the state could bar industrial firetraps or alleviate sweatshop work and slum life. And if that meant weakening grass-roots loyalty to Tammany, so be it. Al Smith and Robert Wagner absorbed the lessons of the Triangle investigation. They formed durable ties with such progressives as the social worker Frances Perkins, who sat on the commission as the representative of the New York Consumers' League, and became urban liberals — advocates of active intervention by the state in uplifting the laboring masses

of America's cities (see Comparing American Voices, "The Triangle Fire," pp. 620–621).

It was not only altruism that converted seasoned politicians like Smith and Wagner. The city machines faced strong competition from a new breed of middle-class, skilled urban reformers such as Mayor Brand Whitlock of Toledo, Ohio, whose administration not only attacked city-hall corruption but also provided better schools, cleaner streets, and more social services for Toledo's needy. Combining campaign magic and popular programs, Whitlock and similarly progressive mayors in Cleveland, Jersey City, and elsewhere won over the urban masses and challenged the rule of the machines.

Also confronting the bosses was a challenge from the left. The Socialist Party was making headway in the cities, electing Milwaukee's Victor Berger as the nation's first Socialist congressman in 1910 and winning municipal elections across the country. In the 1912 presidential election, the Socialist candidate Eugene Debs (see Chapter 17) garnered a record 6 percent of the vote. The political universe of the urban machines had changed, and they had to pay closer attention to opinion in the precincts.

Cultural Pluralism Embattled. Urban liberalism was driven not only by the plight of the economically downtrodden but by a sharpening nativist attack on immigrants. Old-stock evangelical Christians had long agitated for laws that would reinforce

The Triangle Fire

Entire books have been written about the tragic Triangle Shirtwaist Company fire, which was a defining event of the Progressive era. On the previous page, we can offer only a brief account. In the space below, however, we offer documents by four contemporaries who in one way or another played some part in the Triangle tragedy and its aftermath. In reading these documents, ask yourself in what ways they tell you things you didn't learn or couldn't have learned from the text.

WILLIAM G. SHEPARD, REPORTER

Following is an eyewitness account that appeared in newspapers across the country. It was filed by a reporter for the United Press, who phoned it in to his editor as he watched the unfolding tragedy.

I was walking through Washington Square when a puff of smoke issuing from a factory building caught my eye. I reached the building before the alarm was turned in. I saw every feature of the tragedy visible from outside the building. I learned a new sound—a more horrible sound than description can picture. It was the thud of a speeding, living body on a stone sidewalk. . . . I looked up—saw that there were scores of girls at the windows. The flames from the floor below were beating in their faces. Somehow I knew that they, too, must come down, and something within me—something I didn't know was there—steeled me.

I even watched one girl falling. Waving her arms, trying to keep her body upright until the very instant she struck the sidewalk, she was trying to balance herself. Then came the thud—then a silent, unmoving pile of clothing and twisted, broken limbs. . . .

On the sidewalk lay heaps of broken bodies. A policeman later went about with tags, which he fastened with wire to the wrists of the dead girls, and I saw him fasten no. 54 to the wrist of a girl who wore an engagement ring. . . .

The floods of water from the firemen's hose that ran into the gutter were actually stained red with blood. I looked upon the heap of dead bodies and I remembered these girls were shirtwaist makers. I remembered their great strike of last year in which these same girls had demanded more sanitary conditions and more safety precautions in the shops. These dead bodies were the answer.

STEPHEN S. WISE, RABBI

A week after the fire, on April 2, 1911, a memorial meeting was held at the Metropolitan Opera House. One of the speakers was Rabbi Stephen S. Wise, a prominent figure in New York reform circles. Following is what he said.

This was not an inevitable disaster which man could neither foresee nor control. We might have foreseen it, and some of us did; we might have controlled it, but we chose not to do so. . . . It is not a question of enforcement of law nor of inadequacy of law. We have the wrong kind of laws and the wrong kind of enforcement. Before insisting upon inspection and enforcement, let us lift up the industrial standards so as to make conditions worth inspecting, and, if inspected, certain to afford security to workers. . . . And when we go before the legislature of the state, and demand increased appropriations in order to ensure the possibility of a sufficient number of inspectors, we will not forever be put off with the answer: We have no money.

The lesson of the hour is that while property is good, life is better; that while possessions are valuable, life is priceless. The meaning of the hour is that the life of the lowliest worker in the nation is sacred and inviolable, and, if that sacred human right be violated, we shall stand adjudged and condemned before the tribunal of God and history.

ROSE SCHNEIDERMAN, TRADE UNIONIST

Rose Schneiderman was another speaker at the Opera House meeting. At age thirteen, she had gone to work in a garment factory like Triangle Shirtwaist's and, under the tutelage of the Women's Trade Union League, had become a labor organizer. The strike she mentions in her speech was popularly known as the Uprising of the 30,000, a nearly spontaneous walkout in 1909 that launched the union movement in the women's garment trades.

I would be a traitor to these poor burned bodies if I came here to talk good fellowship. We have tried you good people of the public and we have found you wanting. The old Inquisition had its rack and its thumbscrews and its instruments of torture with iron teeth. We know what these things are today; the iron teeth are our necessities, the thumbscrews are the high-powered and swift machinery close to which we must work, and the rack is here in the firetrap structures that will destroy us the minute they catch on fire.

This is not the first time girls have been burned alive in the city. . . . Every year thousands of us are maimed. The life of men and women is so cheap and property is so sacred. There are so many of us for one job it matters little if 146 of us are burned to death.

We have tried you citizens; we are trying you now, and you have a couple of dollars for the sorrowing mothers, brothers, and sisters by way of a charity gift. But every time the workers come out in the only way they know to protest against conditions which are unbearable the strong hand of the law is allowed to press down heavily upon us . . . [and] beats us back, when we rise, into the conditions that make life unbearable.

I can't talk fellowship to you who are gathered here. Too much blood has been spilled. I know from my experience it is up to the working people to save themselves. The only way they can save themselves is by a strong working-class movement.

MAX D. STEUER, LAWYER

After finding physical evidence of the locked door that had blocked escape from the fire, the district attorney brought manslaughter charges against the Triangle proprietors, Max Blanck and Isaac Harris, who hired in their defense the best, highest-priced trial attorney in town, Max D. Steuer. In this talk, delivered some time later to a rapt audience of lawyers, Steuer described how he undermined the testimony of the key witness for the prosecution.

There are many times, many times when a witness has given evidence very hurtful to your cause and you say, "No questions," and dismiss him or her in the hope that the jury will dismiss the evidence too. [*Laughter.*] But can you do that when the jury is weeping, and the little girl witness is weeping too? [*Laughter.*] . . . . There is one [rule] that commands what not to do. Do not attack the witness. Suavely, politely, genially, toy with the story.

In the instant case, about half an hour was consumed by the examiner [Steuer]. . . . Very little progress was made; but the tears had stopped. And then she was asked, "Now, Rose,

in your own words, and in your own way will you tell the jury everything you did, everything you said, and everything you saw from the moment you first saw flames."

The question was put in precisely the same words that the District Attorney had put it, and little Rose started her answer with exactly the same word that she had started it to the District Attorney . . . and the only change in her recital was that Rose left out one word. And then Rose was asked, "Didn't you leave out a word that you put it in when you answered it before?" . . . So Rose started to repeat to herself the answer [*laughter*], and as she came to the missing word she said, Oh, yes!" and supplied it; and thereupon the examiner went on to an entirely different subject . . . when again he [asked her to repeat her story]. . . . And Rose started with the same word and finished with the same word, her recital being identical with her first reply to the same question.

The jurymen were not weeping. Rose had not hurt the case, and the defendants were acquitted; there was not word of reflection at any time during that trial upon poor little Rose.

SOURCE: Leon Stein, ed., *Out of the Sweatshop* (New York: Quadrangle Books, 1977), 188–98.

ANALYZING THE EVIDENCE

➤ The hardest task of the historian is to conjure up the reality of the past — "this is what it was really like." That's where eye-witness evidence like the reporter Shepard's comes in. What is there in his account that you could not reasonably expect a historian to capture?

➤ Both Rabbi Wise and Rose Schneiderman are incensed at the Triangle carnage. Yet their speeches are quite different. In what ways? And with what implications for alternate paths to progressive reform?

➤ Max Steuer and Rose Schneiderman came from remarkably similar backgrounds. They were roughly the same age, grew up in poverty on the Lower East Side, and started out as child workers in the garment factories. So consider how differently they ended up! That of course speaks to the varieties of immigrant experience in America. But is there anything in their statements that helps account for their differing life paths? Would Steuer have been as effective had he been questioning Schneiderman?

their cultural and moral norms. After 1900 this movement strongly revived, cloaking itself now in the mantle of progressive reform. The Anti-Saloon League—"the Protestant church in action"—became a formidable advocate for prohibition in many states, skillfully attaching Demon Rum to other reform targets: The saloon made for dirty politics, poverty, and bad labor conditions.

The moral reform agenda expanded to include a new goal: restricting the immigration of southern and eastern Europeans into the United States. Edward A. Ross of the University of Wisconsin denounced "the pigsty mode of life" of Italian and Polish immigrants. The danger, respected social scientists said, was that America's Anglo-Saxon population would be "mongrelized" and its civilization swamped by "inferior" Mediterranean and Slavic cultures. Feeding on this fear, the Immigration Restriction League spearheaded a campaign to end America's historic open-door policy. Like prohibition, immigration restriction was considered by its proponents to be a progressive reform.

Urban liberals thought otherwise. They denounced prohibition and immigration restriction as attacks on the personal liberty and worthiness of urban immigrants. The Tammany politician Martin McCue accused the Protestant ministry "of seeking to substitute the policeman's nightstick for the Bible."

Organized Labor. City machines, always pragmatic, adopted urban liberalism without much ideological struggle. The same could not be said of the trade unions, the other institution that spoke for American working people. In its early years the American Federation of Labor (AFL) had strongly opposed state interference in labor's affairs. Samuel Gompers preached that workers should not seek from government what they could accomplish by their own economic power and self-help. **Voluntarism**, as trade unionists called this doctrine, did not die out, but it weakened substantially during the progressive years.

The AFL, after all, claimed to speak for the entire working class. When muckrakers exposed exploitation of workers and middle-class progressives came forward with solutions, how could the labor movement fail to respond? Thus began a retreat from labor's commitment to voluntarism. In state after state, organized labor joined the battle for progressive legislation and increasingly became its strongest advocate, including most particularly workers' compensation for industrial accidents.

Maimed Factory Worker

Lewis Hine, a great photographer of immigrant life, took this undated picture of a disabled factory worker. Two of his four children are in the background. How was he to support them? If his accident occurred before the passage of workers' compensation laws, they were probably out of luck. George Eastman House.

Industrial hazards took an awful toll at the workplace. Two thousand coal miners were killed every year, dying from cave-ins and explosions at a rate 50 percent higher than in German mines. Liability rules, based on **common law**, so heavily favored employers that victims of industrial accidents rarely got more than token compensation. The tide turned quickly once the labor movement got on board; between 1910 and 1917 all the industrial states enacted insurance laws covering on-the-job accidents.

Social Insurance Deferred. The United States hesitated, however, to broaden the attack on the hazards of modern industrial life. Health insurance and unemployment compensation, although popular in Europe, scarcely made it onto the American political agenda. Old-age pensions, which Britain adopted in 1908, got a serious hearing, only to come up against an odd barrier: The United States already had a pension system of a kind, for Civil War veterans. Easy access—as many as half of all native-born men over sixty-four or their survivors were collecting veterans' benefits in the early twentieth century—reinforced fears of state-induced dependency. Clarence J. Hicks, an industrial-relations expert, recalled Civil War pensioners idling away the hours around the wood stove in the grocery store in his Wisconsin town. They had decided "that the country owed them a living," lost their initiative, and "retreated from the battle of life."

Not until a later generation experienced the ravages of the Great Depression (see Chapter 23) would the country be ready for social insurance. A secure old age, unemployment insurance, health benefits—these human needs of a modern industrial order were beyond the reach of urban liberals in the Progressive era.

Reforming Politics

Like the Mugwumps of the Gilded Age (see Chapter 19), progressive reformers attacked corrupt party rule, but more adeptly and aggressively. Indeed, what distinguished political reform after 1900 was that it was no longer an amateurs' project. In the

Progressive era, political reformers understood the levers of power as well as did the scoundrels they were trying to throw out, and that was why, once the smoke cleared, the political reforms of this era proved enduring. In this, as in other realms, progressivism was a potent mix of idealism and tough-mindedness.

Robert M. La Follette and the Wisconsin Idea.
Born in 1855, Robert M. La Follette started as a conventional politician, rising from the Republican ranks in Wisconsin to serve in Congress for three terms. He was a party regular, never doubting that he was in honorable company until, by his own account, a Republican boss offered him a bribe to fix a judge in a railroad case. Awakened by this "awful ordeal," La Follette broke with the Wisconsin machine in 1891 and became a tireless advocate of political reform, which for him meant restoring America's democratic ideals. "Go back to the first principles of democracy; go back to the people," he told his audience when he launched his campaign against the state Republican machine. In 1900, after

Robert M. La Follette

La Follette was transformed into a political reformer when a Wisconsin Republican boss attempted to bribe him in 1891 to influence a judge in a railway case. As he described it in his *Autobiography*, "Out of this awful ordeal came understanding; and out of understanding came resolution. I determined that the power of this corrupt influence … should be broken." This photograph captures him at the top of his form, expounding his progressive vision to a rapt audience of Wisconsin citizens at an impromptu street gathering. Library of Congress.

battling for a decade, La Follette won the Wisconsin governorship on a platform of higher taxes for corporations, stricter utility and railroad regulation, and political reform.

The key to party reform, La Follette felt, was denying bosses the power to choose the party's candidates. This could be achieved by state legislation requiring that nominations be decided not in party conventions but by popular vote. Enacted in 1903, the **direct primary** expressed La Follette's democratic idealism, but it also suited his particular political talents. The party regulars opposing him were insiders, more comfortable in the caucus room than out on the stump. But that was where La Follette, a superb campaigner, excelled. The direct primary gave La Follette an iron grip on Republican politics in Wisconsin that lasted until his death twenty-five years later.

What was true of La Follette was more or less true of all successful progressive politicians. They typically described their work as political restoration, frequently confessing that they had converted to reform after discovering how far party politics had drifted from the ideals of representative government. Like La Follette, Albert B. Cummins of Iowa, William S. U'Ren of Oregon, and Hiram Johnson of California all espoused democratic ideals and all skillfully used the direct primary as the stepping stone to political power. They practiced a new kind of popular politics, which in a reform age could be a more effective way to power than the backroom techniques of the old-fashioned machine politicians.

Even the most democratizing of reforms espoused by the progressives — the initiative and recall — were really exercises in power politics. The *initiative* enabled citizens to have issues placed on the ballot; *recall* empowered them to remove officeholders who had lost the public's confidence. It soon became clear, however, that direct democracy did not supplant organized politics. Initiative and recall campaigns required organization, money, and expertise, and these were attributes not of the people at large but of well-financed interests. Like the direct primary, the initiative and recall had as much to do with power relations as with political reform.

Racism and Reform

The direct primary was the flagship of progressive politics — the crucial reform, as La Follette said, for defeating the party bosses and returning politics to "the people." The primary originated not in Wisconsin, however, but in the South, and by the time La Follette got his primary law in 1903, primaries were already operating in seven southern states. In the South, however, the primary was a *white* primary. Since by 1900 the Democratic nomination in the South was tantamount to election, barring African Americans from the party primary effectively barred them from political participation.

How could this exercise in white supremacy be justified as democratic reform? By the racism that pervaded even the progressive ranks. In a 1902 book on Reconstruction, Professor John W. Burgess of Columbia University pronounced the Fifteenth Amendment "a monstrous thing" for granting blacks the vote after the Civil War. Burgess was southern born, but he was confident that his northern audience saw the "vast differences in political capacity" between blacks and whites. Even the Republican Party offered no rebuttal. Indeed, as president-elect in 1908, William Howard Taft applauded southern disfranchising laws as necessary to "prevent entirely the possibility of domination by . . . an ignorant electorate." Taft assured southerners that "the federal government has nothing to do with social equality." Taft's successor, Woodrow Wilson, was prepared to go even further, signaling after he entered the White House in 1913 that he favored segregation of the U.S. civil service.

Booker T. Washington and Black Accommodation.

The black leader of the day was Booker T. Washington, who in a famous speech in Atlanta in 1895 had retreated from the defiant stand of an older generation of black abolitionists such as Frederick Douglass. Conciliatory toward the South, Washington considered "the agitation of the question of social equality the extremest folly." The Atlanta Compromise, as his stance became known, was "accommodationist," in the sense that it avoided a direct assault on white supremacy. Despite the conciliatory face he put on before white audiences, however, Washington did not concede the struggle. Behind the scenes he lobbied hard against Jim Crow laws and disfranchisement. In an age of severe racial oppression, no black dealt more skillfully with the elite of white America or wielded greater influence inside the Republican Party. What Washington banked on was black economic progress. When they had grown dependent on black labor and black enterprise, white men of property would recognize the justice of black rights. As Washington put it, "There is little race prejudice in the American dollar."

Black leaders knew Washington as a hard taskmaster, jealous of his authority and not disposed to regard opposition kindly. Even so, opposition surfaced, especially among younger, educated

Booker T. Washington

In an age of severe racial oppression, Washington emerged as the acknowledged leader of black people in the United States. He was remarkable both for his ability as spokesman to white Americans and for his deep understanding of the aspirations of black Americans. Born a slave, Washington suffered the indignities experienced by all blacks after emancipation. But having been befriended by several whites as he grew to manhood, he also understood what it took to gain white support — and maneuver around white hostility — in the black struggle for equality. Library of Congress.

blacks. They thought Washington was conceding too much. He instilled black pride, but of a narrowly middle-class and utilitarian kind. What about the special genius of blacks that W. E. B. Du Bois, a Harvard-educated African American sociologist, celebrated in his collection of essays, *The Souls of Black Folk* (1903)? And what of the "talented tenth" of the black population, whose promise could be stifled by manual education? Moreover, the situation for blacks was deteriorating, even in the North. Over 200,000 blacks migrated from the South between 1900 and 1910, sparking white resentment in northern cities. Attacks on blacks became widespread, capped by a bloody race riot in Springfield, Illinois, in 1908. In the face of all this, many black activists lost patience with Booker T. Washington's silence.

The Civil Rights Struggle Revived. The key figure was William Monroe Trotter, the pugnacious editor of the *Boston Guardian*. "The policy of compromise has failed," Trotter argued. "The policy of resistance and aggression deserves a trial." In 1906, after breaking with Washington, Trotter and Du Bois called a meeting at Niagara Falls — but on the Canadian side because no hotel on the U.S. side would admit blacks. The Niagara Movement that resulted had an impact far beyond the scattering of members and local bodies it organized. The principles it affirmed would define the struggle for the rights of African Americans: first, encouragement of black pride; second, an uncompromising demand for full political and civil equality; and above all, the resolute denial "that the Negro-American assents to inferiority, is submissive under oppression and apologetic before insults."

Going against the grain, a handful of white reformers rallied to the African American cause. Among the most devoted was Mary White Ovington, who grew up in an abolitionist family. Like Jane Addams, Ovington became a settlement-house worker, but among urban blacks in New York rather than in immigrant Chicago. News of the Springfield race riot of 1908 changed her life. Convinced that her duty was to fight racism, Ovington called a meeting of sympathetic white progressives, which led to the formation of the National Association for the Advancement of Colored People (NAACP) in 1909. Most of the members of the strife-torn Niagara Movement moved over to the NAACP. The organization's national leadership was dominated by whites, with one crucial exception. Du Bois became the editor of the NAACP's journal, *The Crisis*. With a passion that only a black voice could provide, Du Bois used that platform to demand equal rights. The NAACP scored its first success in helping beat back the Wilson administration's effort at segregating the federal civil service.

On social welfare the National Urban League took the lead, uniting in 1911 the many agencies serving black migrants arriving in northern cities. Like the NAACP, the Urban League was interracial, including both white reformers such as Ovington and black welfare activists such as William Lewis Bulkley, a New York school principal who was the league's main architect. In the South welfare work was very much the province of black women, who to some extent filled the vacuum left by black disfranchisement. Mostly working in the churches and schools, they also utilized the southern branches of the National Association of Colored Women's Clubs, which had started in 1896. And because their

Colored Women's League of Washington, D.C.

At a time when black men were being driven from politics in the South, their wives and sisters organized themselves and became an alternative voice of black conscience. Sara Iredell Fleetwood, superintendent of the Freedman's Hospital Training School for Nurses, founded the Colored Women's League of Washington, D.C., in 1892 for purposes of "racial uplift." This picture of the league was taken on the steps of Frederick Douglass's home in Anacostia, Washington. Mrs. Fleetwood is seated at the far right, third row from the bottom. The notations are by someone seeking to identify the other members, a modest effort to save for posterity these women, mostly teachers, who did their best for the good of the race. Library of Congress.

activities seemed unthreatening to white supremacy, black women were able to reach across the color line and find allies among white southern women.

Progressivism was a house of many chambers. Most were infected by the racism of the age, but not all. A saving remnant of white progressives rallied to the cause of racial justice. In alliance with black civil-rights advocates, they defined the issues and established the organizations that would spur the struggle for a better life for African Americans over the next half century.

➤ How do you account for the revival of the woman's suffrage movement during the Progressive era?

➤ In what ways did political reformers of the Progressive era (like Robert La Follette) differ from the Mugwump reformers of the late nineteenth century?

➤ What is the relationship between progressive reform and the struggle for racial equality?

Progressivism and National Politics

In its origins, progressivism was a local phenomenon, spurred by immediate and visible problems. But reformers soon realized that many social problems, like child labor and industrial safety, were best handled by Washington and that, so far as concerned the overweening power of big business, there was no place else to turn. Seasoned reformers like Robert La Follette, ambitious for a wider stage, migrated to Washington and ultimately formed a progressive bloc on Capitol Hill. Progressivism burst on the national stage, however, not via Congress, but by way of the presidency. This was partly because the White House provided a "bully pulpit" — to use Theodore Roosevelt's phrase. But just as important was the twist of fate that brought Roosevelt to the White House on September 14, 1901.

The Making of a Progressive President

Like many other budding progressives, Theodore Roosevelt was motivated by a high-minded, Christian upbringing. Born in 1858, he always identified himself — loudly — with the cause of righteousness. But Roosevelt did not scorn power and its uses. To the amazement of his socially prominent family, he plunged into Republican politics after Harvard and maneuvered himself into the New York State legislature. Contemptuous of the gentlemen Mugwumps, he much preferred the company of party professionals. Roosevelt rose in the New York party because he skillfully developed broad popular support and thus forced himself on reluctant state Republican bosses.

Safely back from the Spanish-American War as the hero of San Juan Hill (see Chapter 21), Roosevelt won the New York governorship in 1898. During his term in office he signaled his progressivism by pushing through civil service reform and a tax on corporations. He discharged the corrupt superintendent of insurance over the Republican Party's objections and asserted his confidence in the government's capacity to improve the life of the people.

Hoping to neutralize him, the party chieftains chose Roosevelt in 1900 for what seemed a dead-end job as William McKinley's running mate. Roosevelt accepted reluctantly. But on September 6, 1901, an anarchist named Leon F. Czolgosz shot the president. When McKinley died eight days later, Roosevelt became president, to the dismay of party regulars.

Roosevelt in fact moved cautiously, attending first to politics. Anxious to rein in the formidable conservative bloc in Congress, he adroitly used the patronage powers of his office to gain control of the Republican Party. But Roosevelt was also uncertain about how to proceed. At first the new president might have been described as a progressive without a cause.

Regulating the Marketplace

Most troubling to Roosevelt was the threat posed by big business to competitive markets. The drift toward large-scale enterprise was itself not new; for many years industrialists had been expanding their operations because of the efficiencies that vertical integration offered (see Chapter 17). But the bigger the business, the greater the power over markets. And when, in the aftermath of the depression of the 1890s, promoters scrambled to merge rival firms, the primary motive was not lower costs but the elimination of competition. These mergers — **trusts**, as they were called — greatly increased business concentration. By 1910, 1 percent of the nation's manufacturers accounted for 44 percent of the nation's industrial output (see Voices from Abroad, "James Bryce: America in 1905: 'Business Is King,' " p. 628).

J. Pierpont Morgan

J. P. Morgan was a giant among American financiers. He had served an apprenticeship in investment banking under his father, a leading Anglo-American banker in London. A gruff man of few words, Morgan had a genius for instilling trust and the strength of will to persuade others to follow his lead and do his bidding — qualities the great photographer Edward Steichen captured in this portrait. Courtesy, George Eastman House, reprinted with permission of Joanna T. Steichen.

James Bryce

America in 1905: "Business Is King"

James Bryce, British author of The American Commonwealth *(1888), a great treatise on American politics, visited the United States regularly over many years. In an essay published in 1905, Lord Bryce took stock of the changes he had seen during the previous quarter century. What most impressed him, beyond the sheer growth of material wealth, was the loss of individualism and the intensifying concentration of corporate power. In this he was at one with his old friend Theodore Roosevelt, who at that very time was gearing up to do battle with the trusts.*

That which most strikes the visitor to America today is its prodigious material development. Industrial growth, swift thirty or forty years ago, advances more swiftly now. The rural districts are being studded with villages, the villages are growing into cities, the cities are stretching out long arms of suburbs, which follow the lines of road and railway in every direction. The increase of wealth, even more remarkable than the increase of population, impresses the European more than ever before because the contrast with Europe is greater. The huge fortunes, the fortunes of those whose income reaches or exceeds a million dollars a year, are of course far more numerous than in any other country. . . . With this extraordinary material development it is natural that in the United States, business, that is to say, industry, commerce, and finance, should have more and more come to overshadow and

dwarf all other interests, all other occupations. . . . Business is king.

Commerce and industry themselves have developed new features. Twenty-two years ago there were no trusts. . . . Even then, however, corporations had covered a larger proportion of the whole field of industry and commerce in America than in Europe, and their structure was more flexible and efficient. Today this is still more the case; while as for trusts, they have become one of the most salient phenomena of the country. They fix the attention, they excite the alarm of economists and politicians as well as of traders in the Old World, while they exercise and baffle the ingenuity of American legislators. Workingmen follow, though hitherto with unequal steps, the efforts at combination which the lords of production and distribution have been making. The consumer stands, if not with folded hands, yet so far with no clear view of the steps he may make for his own protection. Perhaps his prosperity — for he is prosperous — helps him to be quiescent.

The example of the United States, the land in which individualism has been most conspicuously vigorous, may seem to suggest that the world is passing out of the stage of individualism and returning to that earlier stage in which groups of men formed the units of society. The bond of association was, in those early days, kinship, real or supposed, and a servile or quasi-servile dependence of the weak upon the strong. Now it is the power of wealth which enables the few to combine so as to gain command of the sources of wealth. . . . Is it a paradox to observe that it is because the Americans have been the most individualistic of peoples that they are now the people among whom the art of combination has reached its

maximum? The amazing keenness and energy, which were stimulated by the commercial conditions of the country, have evoked and ripened a brilliant talent for organization. This talent has applied new methods to production and distribution and has enabled wealth, gathered into a small number of hands, to dominate even the enormous market of America.

SOURCE: Allan Nevins, ed., *America through British Eyes* (Gloucester, MA: Peter Smith, 1968), 384–87.

ANALYZING THE EVIDENCE

➤ In what ways does it seem to Bryce that America's economic development stands in contrast to Europe's?

➤ How does he explain the "paradox" that the Americans — "the most individualistic of peoples" — should be leaders in developing business forms that will stifle individualism?

➤ Do Bryce's observations as a foreigner shed any special light on why an antitrust movement was building up in the country?

As early as his first annual message, Roosevelt acknowledged the nation's uneasiness with the "real and grave evils" of economic concentration. But what weapons could the president use in response?

Under long-established common law, anyone injured by monopoly or illegal restraint of trade could sue for damages. With the passage of the Sherman Antitrust Act of 1890, these common-law rights entered the U.S. statute books and could be enforced by the federal government when offenses involved interstate commerce. Neither Presidents Cleveland nor McKinley showed much interest, but the Sherman Act was there waiting to be deployed against abusive economic power.

Trust-Busting. Roosevelt's opening move was to create a Bureau of Corporations (1903) empowered to investigate business practices and bolster the Justice Department's capacity to mount antitrust suits. The department had already filed such a suit against the Northern Securities Company, a combine of the railroad systems of the Northwest. In a landmark decision the Supreme Court ordered Northern Securities dissolved in 1904.

That year Roosevelt handily defeated a weak conservative Democratic candidate, Judge Alton B. Parker. Now president in his own right, Roosevelt stepped up the attack on the trusts. He took on many of the nation's giant firms, including Standard Oil, American Tobacco, and DuPont. His rhetoric rising, Roosevelt became the nation's trust-buster, a crusader against "predatory wealth" (see Reading American Pictures, "Reining in Big Business? Cartoonists Join the Battle," p. 630).

But Roosevelt was not antibusiness. He regarded large-scale enterprise as a natural tendency of modern industrialism. Only firms that abused their power deserved punishment. But how to identify those companies? Under the Sherman Act, following common-law practice, the courts decided whether an act in restraint of trade was "unreasonable" — that is, harmful of the public interest — on a case-by-case basis. In the *Trans-Missouri* decision (1897), however, the Supreme Court abandoned this discretionary "rule of reason," holding now that actions that restrained or monopolized trade, regardless of the public impact, automatically violated the Sherman Act.

Little noticed at first, *Trans-Missouri* placed Roosevelt in a quandary. He had no desire to hamstring legitimate business activity, but he could not rely on the courts to distinguish between "good" and "bad" trusts. So Roosevelt assumed this task himself, which he could do because as chief executive it was up to him to initiate — or not initiate — antitrust prosecutions by the Justice Department.

In November 1904, with a government suit looming, the United States Steel Corporation's chairman Elbert H. Gary approached Roosevelt with a deal — cooperation in exchange for preferential treatment. The company would open its books to the Bureau of Corporations; if it found evidence of wrongdoing, the company would be warned privately and given a chance to set matters right. Roosevelt accepted this "gentlemen's agreement" because it met his interest in accommodating the modern industrial order while maintaining his public image as slayer of the trusts.

Railroad Regulation. The railroads posed a different problem. As quasi-public enterprises, they had never been free of oversight by the states; in 1887 they became subject to federal regulation by the Interstate Commerce Commission (ICC). As with the Sherman Act, this assertion of federal authority was mostly symbolic at first. Then Roosevelt got started, pushing through in 1903 the Elkins Act that prohibited discriminatory railway rates unfairly favoring preferred or powerful customers — a practice, Ida Tarbell reminded Americans with her muckraking articles on Standard Oil, that had given Rockefeller a leg-up in building his oil monopoly. With the 1904 election behind him, Roosevelt launched a drive for real railroad regulation. In 1906, after nearly two years of wrangling, Congress passed the Hepburn Railway Act, which empowered the ICC to set maximum shipping rates and prescribe uniform methods of bookkeeping. As a concession to the conservative Republican bloc, however, the courts retained broad powers to review the ICC's rate decisions.

Passage of the Hepburn Act was a triumph of Roosevelt's skills as a political operator. Despite grumbling by Senate progressives, Roosevelt was satisfied. He had achieved a landmark expansion of the government's regulatory powers over business.

The Environment. Another target was the West's natural resources. Although an ardent outdoorsman, Roosevelt was not a wilderness **preservationist** in the mold of John Muir (see Chapter 16). Having shaken off the illusions of his youthful days as a tenderfoot rancher, Roosevelt accepted the grim reality that the West's abundance, far from being limitless, was a finite and rapidly disappearing resource. Roosevelt was a **conservationist**. He believed in efficient use and sustainability, so that "we will hand . . . the water, the wood, the grasses . . . on to our children . . . in better and not worse shape than we got them."

Reining in Big Business? Cartoonists Join the Battle

For many years Americans had been troubled by the increasing scale of business enterprise. But after 1900 that concern boiled over with amazing and unexpected force. Almost overnight, curbing the trusts became the dominating political issue of the Progressive era. In the text we ascribe that development to a sudden speeding up of merger activity and a President uniquely gifted at crystallizing national sentiment. Is anything more to be learned abut this political phenomenon from scrutinizing the political cartoon below that appeared in humor magazine *Puck*?

ANALYZING THE EVIDENCE

➤ Historians value political cartoons in part because they are a gauge of what the public knows; the cartoonist's assumption is that readers will understand the content without being told. If that's so, what does the *Puck* cartoon reveal about the public's familiarity with the great tycoons of the time?

➤ Why is the location important? If the issue is business power, why are we being shown Wall Street rather than, say, the headquarters of U.S. Steel in Pittsburgh?

➤ Cartoons are also a kind of shorthand, stripping an issue to its barest elements and saying: "This is what it's really about." So in this cartoon, with Jack (Theodore Roosevelt) confronting the Wall Street Giants (Morgan, Rockefeller, the railroad tycoon James J. Hill), what's regulating big business really about?

"Jack and the Wall Street Giants," *Puck,* January 13, 1904. Library of Congress.

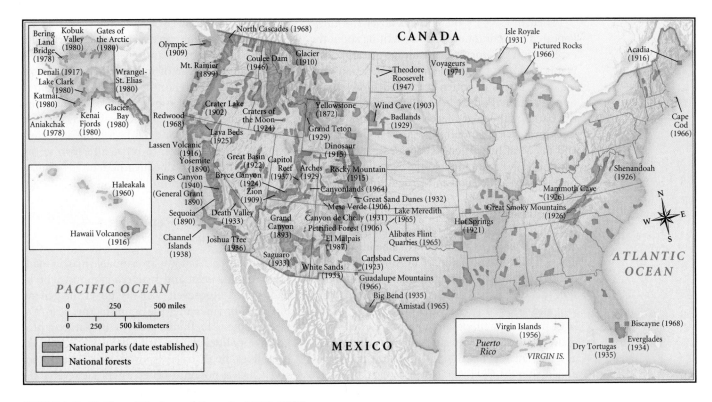

MAP 20.2 National Parks and Forests, 1872–1980

Close inspection of this map reveals that the national park system did not begin with the Progressive era. Indeed, Yellowstone, the first park, dates from 1872. In 1893, the federal government began the protection of national forests. Without Roosevelt, however, the national forest program might have languished, and during his presidency he added 125 million acres to the forest system plus six national parks. More importantly, Roosevelt endowed these systems with a progressive, public-spirited stamp that has remained a principle resource of environmentalists striving to preserve the nation's natural heritage. In the list of progressive triumphs, a robust national park and forest system is one of the most enduring.

In this endeavor, Roosevelt's guiding principle was, as his Public Lands Commission (1903) stated it, "public ownership"—the primacy of federal authority over the public domain for purposes of efficient management. This meant, first of all, vigorously deploying Roosevelt's executive powers, which he did by tripling the number of national forests, removing additional millions of acres of coal lands from private development, and adding national parks and (a new category authorized in 1906) many national monuments (Map 20.2). Equally significant were advances in federal administration, most importantly in an expanded Forest Service headed by an expert forester, Gifford Pinchot. That this ambitious program did not mean opposition to development was evident in Roosevelt's support for the Newland Reclamation Act (1902), which authorized irrigation projects for reclaiming and settling arid western lands.

Although mindful of western interests, federal bureaucrats like Pinchot infuriated ranchers and loggers unaccustomed to interference from Washington. They rebelled against grazing fees and logging restrictions, and their representatives in Washington eventually fought Roosevelt to a draw. Nowhere, in fact, did progressivism face fiercer resistance. Even so, there was no turning back. Roosevelt had reversed a century of heedless exploitation and imprinted conservation on the nation's public agenda (Map 20.2).

Consumer Protection. The protection of consumers, another signature issue for progressives, was very much the handiwork of muckraking journalism. What sparked the issue was a riveting series of articles in *Collier's* by Samuel Hopkins Adams exposing the patent-medicine business as "undiluted fraud," dangerous to the nation's health.

Then, in 1906, Upton Sinclair's novel *The Jungle* appeared. Sinclair thought he was writing about the exploitation of workers in Chicago meatpacking plants, but what caught the nation's attention were his descriptions of rotten meat and filthy conditions. President Roosevelt, weighing into the legislative battle, authorized a federal investigation of the stockyards. Within months the Pure Food and Drug and the Meat Inspection Acts passed, and another administrative agency joined the expanding federal bureaucracy — the Food and Drug Administration.

The Square Deal. During the 1904 presidential campaign, Roosevelt had taken to calling his program the Square Deal. This kind of labeling was new and would become a hallmark of American politics in the twentieth century, emblematic of a political style that dramatized issues, mobilized public opinion, and asserted presidential leadership. But the label meant something of substance as well. After many years of passivity and weakness, the federal government was reclaiming the role it had abandoned after the Civil War. Now, however, the target was the business economy. When companies abused their powers, the government would intercede to assure ordinary Americans a "square deal."

Campaigning for the Square Deal

When William McKinley ran for president in 1896, he sat on his front porch in Canton, Ohio, and received delegations of voters. That was not Theodore Roosevelt's way. He considered the presidency a "bully pulpit," and he used the office brilliantly to mobilize public opinion and to assert his leadership. The preeminence of the presidency in American public life begins with Roosevelt's administration. Here, at the height of his crusading power, Roosevelt stumps for the Square Deal in the 1904 election. Library of Congress.

Roosevelt was well aware, however, that his Square Deal was built on nineteenth-century foundations. In particular, antitrust doctrine seemed inadequate in an age of industrial concentration. Better, Roosevelt felt, for the federal government to regulate big business than try to break it up. In his final presidential speeches, Roosevelt dwelled on the need for a reform agenda for the twentieth century. Having chosen to retire after two terms, this was the task he bequeathed to his chosen successor, William Howard Taft.

The Fracturing of Republican Progressivism

William Howard Taft was an estimable man in many ways. An able jurist and a superb administrator, he had served Roosevelt well as governor-general of the Philippines after the Spanish-American War (see Chapter 21). But he was not by nature a progressive politician. He disliked the give-and-take of politics, he distrusted power, and, unlike Roosevelt, he was not one to cut corners. He revered the processes of law and was, in fundamental ways, a conservative.

Taft's Democratic opponent in the 1908 campaign was William Jennings Bryan. This was Bryan's last hurrah, his third attempt at the presidency, and he made the most of it. Eloquent as ever, Bryan attacked the Republicans as the party of the "plutocrats" and outdid them in urging tougher antitrust legislation, stricter railway regulation, and advanced labor legislation. Almost single-handedly, Bryan moved the Democratic Party into the mainstream of national progressive politics. But his robust campaign was not enough to offset Taft's advantages as Roosevelt's candidate. Taft won comfortably, entering the White House with a mandate to pick up where Roosevelt left off.

Taft's Troubles. By 1909 reform politics had unsettled the Republican Party. On the right, conservatives were girding themselves against further losses. Led by the formidable Senator Nelson W. Aldrich of Rhode Island, they were still a force to be reckoned with. On the left, progressive Republicans were rebellious. They felt that Roosevelt had been too easy on business, and with him gone from the White House, they intended to make up for lost time. Reconciling these conflicting forces within the Republican Party would have been a daunting task for a master politician. For Taft it spelled disaster.

First there was the tariff. Progressives considered protective tariffs a major reason why competition had declined and the trusts had taken hold. Although Taft had campaigned for tariff reform, he was won over by the conservative Republican bloc and ended up approving the protectionist Payne-Aldrich Tariff Act of 1909, which critics charged sheltered eastern industry from foreign competition.

Next came the Pinchot-Ballinger affair, which pitted Chief Forester Gifford Pinchot against Secretary of the Interior Richard A. Ballinger. Pinchot, a chum of Roosevelt's, accused Ballinger of plotting to transfer resource-rich Alaskan land to a private business group. When Pinchot aired these charges, Taft fired him for insubordination. Despite Taft's strong conservationist credentials, the Pinchot-Ballinger affair marked him among progressives as a friend of the "interests," bent on plundering the nation's resources.

Taft found himself propelled into the conservative Republican camp, an ally of "Uncle Joe" Cannon, the dictatorial Speaker of the House of Representatives. When a House revolt finally broke Cannon's power in 1910, it was regarded as a defeat for the president as well. Galvanized by Taft's defection, the reformers in the Republican Party became a dissident faction, calling themselves "Insurgents."

The Taft-Roosevelt Split. Home from a year-long safari in Africa, Roosevelt yearned to reenter the political fray. Taft's dispute with the Insurgents gave Roosevelt the cause he needed. But Roosevelt was a loyal party man, too astute a politician not to recognize that a party split would benefit the Democrats. He could be spurred into rebellion only by a true clash of principles. On the question of the trusts, just such a clash materialized.

Taft's legalistic mind rebelled at Roosevelt's practice of choosing among trusts when it came to antitrust prosecutions. The Sherman Act was on the books. "We are going to enforce that law or die in the attempt," Taft promised grimly. But he was held back until the Supreme Court reasserted the rule of reason in the *Standard Oil* decision (1911), which meant that, once again, the courts themselves undertook to distinguish between good and bad trusts. With that burden lifted, Taft's attorney general George W. Wickersham stepped up the pace of antitrust actions, immediately targeting the United States Steel Corporation. One of the charges was that the steel trust had illegally acquired the Tennessee Coal and Iron Company in 1907. Roosevelt had personally approved the transaction, believing it was necessary—so U.S. Steel representatives had told him—to prevent a financial collapse on Wall Street. Taft's suit against U.S. Steel thus amounted to a personal attack that Roosevelt could not, without dishonor, ignore.

The New Nationalism. Ever since leaving the White House, Roosevelt had been pondering the trust problem. Between breaking up big business and submitting to corporate rule, lay another alternative. The federal government could be empowered to oversee the nation's industrial corporations to make sure they acted in the public interest. They would be regulated by a federal trade commission as if they were natural monopolies or public utilities.

In a speech in Osawatomie, Kansas, in August 1910, Roosevelt made the case for what he called the New Nationalism. The central issue, he argued, was human welfare versus property rights. In modern society, property had to be controlled "to whatever degree the public welfare may require it." The government would become "the steward of the public welfare."

This formulation unleashed Roosevelt. He took up the cause of social justice, adding to his program a federal child labor law, regulation of labor relations, and a national minimum wage for women. Most radical, perhaps, was Roosevelt's attack on the legal system. Insisting that the courts stood in the way of reform, Roosevelt proposed sharp curbs on their powers, even raising the possibility of popular recall of court decisions.

Early in 1912 Roosevelt announced his candidacy for the presidency, immediately sweeping the Insurgent faction into his camp. A bitter party battle ensued. Roosevelt won the states that held primary elections, but Taft controlled the party caucuses elsewhere. Dominated by party regulars, the Republican convention chose Taft. Considering himself cheated out of the nomination, Roosevelt led his followers into a new Progressive Party, soon nicknamed the "Bull Moose" Party. In a crusading campaign Roosevelt offered the New Nationalism to the people.

Woodrow Wilson and the New Freedom

While the Republicans battled among themselves, the Democrats were on the move. The scars caused by the free-silver battle had faded, and William Jennings Bryan's 1908 campaign established the party's progressive credentials. The Democrats made dramatic electoral gains in 1910. And Bryan, after fourteen years as the party's standard-bearer, made way for a new generation of leaders.

The ablest was Woodrow Wilson of New Jersey, a noted political scientist who, as university president, had brought Princeton into the front rank of

HARPER'S WEEKLY

EDITED BY GEORGE HARVEY

July 13 1912　　THE NEW RIDER　　Price 10 Cents

American universities. In 1910, with no political experience, he accepted the Democratic nomination for governor of New Jersey and won. Wilson compiled a sterling reform record, including the direct primary, workers' compensation, and utility regulation. Wilson went on to win the Democratic presidential nomination in 1912 in a bruising battle.

Wilson possessed, to a fault, the moral certainty that was common among progressive leaders. The product of a family of Presbyterian clerics, he instinctively assumed the mantle of righteousness. Only gradually, however, did Wilson hammer out, in reaction to Roosevelt's New Nationalism, a coherent reform program, which he called the New Freedom. As he warmed to the debate, Wilson cast his differences with Roosevelt in fundamental terms of slavery and freedom. "This is a struggle for emancipation," he proclaimed in October 1912. "If America is not to have free enterprise, then she can have freedom of no sort whatever." The New Nationalism represented a future of collectivism, Wilson warned, whereas the New Freedom would preserve political and economic liberty.

Wilson actually had much in common with Roosevelt. "The old time of individual competition is probably gone by," Wilson admitted. He even agreed that preventing the abuse of private power required a strong federal government. He parted company from Roosevelt over means, not ends, confident that the government's existing powers were adequate, with some tinkering, to the task of restraining big business.

Despite all the rhetoric, the 1912 election fell short as a referendum on the New Nationalism

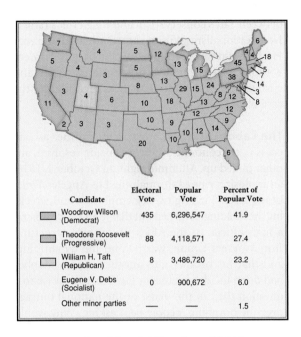

Candidate	Electoral Vote	Popular Vote	Percent of Popular Vote
Woodrow Wilson (Democrat)	435	6,296,547	41.9
Theodore Roosevelt (Progressive)	88	4,118,571	27.4
William H. Taft (Republican)	8	3,486,720	23.2
Eugene V. Debs (Socialist)	0	900,672	6.0
Other minor parties	—	—	1.5

MAP 20.3 Presidential Election of 1912

The 1912 election reveals why the two-party system is so strongly rooted in American politics. The Democrats, though a minority party, won an electoral landslide because the Republicans divided their vote between Roosevelt and Taft. This result indicates what is at stake when major parties splinter. The Socialists, despite a record vote of 900,000, received no electoral votes. To vote Socialist in 1912 meant in effect to throw away one's vote.

versus the New Freedom. The outcome turned on a more humdrum reality: Wilson won because he kept the Democratic vote, while the Republicans split between Roosevelt and Taft. Despite a landslide in the electoral college, Wilson received only 42 percent of the popular vote (Map 20.3).

Yet the 1912 election proved a turning point for economic reform. The debate between Roosevelt and Wilson had brought forth, in the New Freedom, a program capable of finally resolving the decade-long crisis over corporate power. Just as important, the election created a rare legislative opportunity. With Congress in Democratic hands, the time was ripe to act on the New Freedom.

The First Phase: Tariffs and the Federal Reserve. Long out of power, the Democrats were hungry for tariff reform. The Underwood Tariff Act of 1913 pared rates down to 25 percent, targeting especially the trust-dominated industries. Democrats confidently expected the Underwood Tariff to spur competition and reduce prices for consumers.

Wilson then turned to the nation's banking system, whose key weakness was the absence of a central bank, or federal reserve. The main function of central banks at that time was to regulate commercial banks and back them up in case they could not meet their obligations to depositors. In the past this backup role had been assumed by the great New York banks that handled the accounts of outlying banks. If the New York banks weakened, the entire system could collapse. This had nearly happened in 1907, when the Knickerbocker Trust Company failed and panic swept the nation's financial markets.

But if the need for a central bank was clear, the form it should take was hotly disputed. President Wilson, initially no expert, learned quickly and reconciled the reformers and bankers. The resulting Federal Reserve Act of 1913 gave the nation a banking system that was resistant to financial panic. The act delegated operational functions to twelve district reserve banks funded and controlled by their member banks. The Federal Reserve Board imposed public regulation on this regional structure. One crucial new power granted the Federal Reserve was authority to issue currency — federal reserve notes based on assets within the system — that resolved the paralyzing cash shortages experienced during runs on the banks. Another was authority by the Federal Reserve Board to set the discount rate (the interest rate) charged by the district reserve banks to the member banks and thereby the flow of credit to the general public. In one stroke the act strengthened the banking system and reined in Wall Street.

Settling the Trust Problem. Wilson now turned to the big question of the trusts. He relied heavily on a new advisor, Louis D. Brandeis, the celebrated "people's lawyer." Brandeis denied that bigness meant efficiency. On the contrary, he argued, firms that vigorously competed in a free market ran most efficiently. The main thing was to prevent the trusts from unfairly using their power to curb free competition.

Strengthening the Sherman Act, the obvious course, proved hard to do. Was it feasible to say exactly when company practices like overlapping boards of directors, discriminatory pricing, or exclusive contracts became illegal? Brandeis decided that it was not, and Wilson assented. In the Clayton Antitrust Act of 1914, amending the Sherman Act, the definition of illegal practices was left flexible, subject to the test of whether an action "substantially lessen[ed] competition or tend[ed] to create a monopoly."

This retreat from a definitive antitrust prescription meant that a federal trade commission would be needed to back up the Sherman and Clayton Acts. Wilson was understandably hesitant, given his opposition during the campaign to Roosevelt's powerful trade commission. At first Wilson favored an advisory, information-gathering agency. But ultimately, under the 1914 law establishing it, the Federal Trade Commission (FTC) received broad powers to investigate companies and issue "cease and desist" orders against unfair trade practices that violated antitrust law.

Despite a good deal of commotion, this arduous legislative process was actually an exercise in consensus building. Wilson opened the debate in a conciliatory way. "The antagonism between business and government is over," he said, and the time ripe for a program representing the "best business judgment in America." Afterward, Wilson felt he had brought the long controversy to a successful conclusion, and in fact he had. Steering a course between Taft's conservatism and Roosevelt's radical New Nationalism, Wilson carved out a middle way. He brought to bear the powers of government without shattering the constitutional order and curbed corporate abuses without threatening the capitalist system.

The Labor Question. In the meantime, as one crisis over economic power was being resolved, another boiled up. After midnight on October 1, 1910, an explosion ripped through the Los Angeles *Times* headquarters, killing twenty employees and wrecking the building. It turned out that John J. McNamara, a high official of the AFL's Bridge and Structural Iron Workers Union, was behind the dynamiting, and that his brother and another union member had done the deed. Lincoln Steffens gave voice to a question that, in the midst of the national outrage over the bombing, people kept asking. Why would

The Ludlow Massacre, 1914

Like John Sloan's drawing on page 619, this is one in a series expressing Sloan's outrage at social injustice in progressive America. It appears on the cover of *The Masses,* a popular socialist magazine. The drawing memorializes a tragic episode during a miners' strike at Ludlow, Colorado — the asphyxiation of many women and children when the state militia torched the tent city of evicted miners — and the aftermath, an armed revolt by enraged miners. University of Michigan Library.

"healthy, good-tempered boys like these McNamara boys . . . believe . . . that the only recourse they have for improving the conditions of the wage earner is to use dynamite against property and life?"

Steffens's question resonated ever more urgently as a wave of violent strikes swept the country—New York garment workers in 1910; railroad workers on the Illinois Central and Harriman lines in 1911; and textile workers, led by the Industrial Workers of the World (see Chapter 17), in Lawrence, Massachusetts, in 1912, and Paterson, New Jersey, in 1913. The IWW presence compounded middle-class anxieties that the country was in the grip of class war because the Wobblies did indeed invoke the violent language of class war. Finally, in a ghastly climactic episode in 1914, state militia during a bitter Colorado coal miners' strike torched a tent city at Ludlow and asphyxiated many strikers' wives and children. Infuriated miners took up arms and plunged Colorado into a civil war that ended only with arrival of the U.S. Army.

The "labor question" was suddenly on the progressive agenda. President Wilson appointed a blue ribbon U.S. Commission on Industrial Relations, whose job it would be, as the youthful journalist Walter Lippmann wrote, to explain "why America, supposed to become the land of promise, has become the land of disappointment and deep-seated discontent." In its majority report, the Commission took note that workers earning $10 or less a week lived at poverty levels, that they were ground down by repeated spells of unemployment, and that "an almost universal conviction [prevailed] that they, both as individuals and as a class, are denied justice." The core reason for industrial violence, including the McNamara bombing, was the fierce anti-unionism of American employers, which left workers with no voice and no hope for justice at the workplace. In its most important recommendation, the majority report called for federal legislation to protect the right of workers to organize and engage in collective bargaining. If this seemed, in 1915, too radical a proposal, it was in fact the opening shot in a battle for labor rights that would end triumphantly in the New Deal (see Chapter 24).

The immediate effect was to push President Wilson to the left. Having denounced Roosevelt's paternalism, he had at first been unreceptive to what he saw as special-interest demands by organized labor. On the leading issue—that unions be exempt from antitrust prosecutions that spiked their boycott weapon—the most Wilson was willing to accept was cosmetic language in the Clayton Act that did not grant them the immunity they

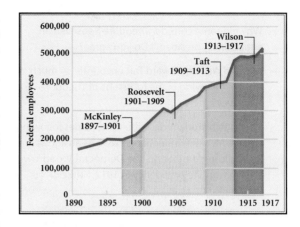

FIGURE 20.1   The Federal Bureaucracy, 1890–1917

The surge in federal employment after 1900 mirrored the surge in government authority under Theodore Roosevelt's progressive leadership. Not even Wilson, although he ran on a platform of limited government, could stem the tide.

sought. But now, instructed by the revelations of his Commission on Industrial Relations—and by labor's increasing clout at the polls—Wilson warmed up to the AFL. As his second presidential campaign drew near, Wilson lost some of his scruples about the paternalism of pro-labor legislation. In 1915 and 1916 he championed a host of bills beneficial to American workers: a federal child-labor law; the Adamson eight-hour law for railroad workers; and the landmark Seamen's Act, which eliminated age-old abuses of sailors aboard ship. Nor was it lost on observers that, his New Freedom rhetoric notwithstanding, Wilson presided over an ever more active federal government and an ever-expanding federal bureaucracy (Figure 20.1).

Wilson encountered the same dilemma that confronted all successful progressives—the clash of moral principle against the unyielding realities of political life. Progressives were high-minded but not radical. They saw evils in the system, but they did not consider the system itself to be evil. They also prided themselves on being realists as well as moralists. So it stood to reason that Wilson, like other progressives who achieved power, would find his place at the center.

But it would be wrong to underestimate their achievement. Progressives made presidential leadership important again, they brought government back into the nation's life, they laid the foundation for twentieth-century social and economic policy. And, as we shall see, they put an enduring stamp on America's self-definition as a world power.

➤ Why did some consider Theodore Roosevelt an antibusiness president? Do you agree?

➤ Why did William Howard Taft encounter so much trouble following in the footsteps of Theodore Roosevelt?

➤ Although historians describe the decades following William McKinley's election in 1896 as an age of Republican domination, the Democrat Woodrow Wilson won the presidency in 1912. How do you account for that?

SUMMARY

In this chapter we turn to the period, between 1900 and World War I, that is distinguishable by the prominence of reform activity — hence its designation as the Progressive era. In these years America gave its full attention to the problems resulting from industrialization and urban growth. We can discern the common elements of progressivism: first, a middle-class impulse for improving society; second, a tough-minded intellectual outlook confident of society's problem-solving capacity; third, muckraking journalism adept at exposing the problems for the nation's inspection. The reform activity that ensued, however, cannot be confined within a single mold because it was many-sided and always evolving.

American women took the lead on social welfare, and that effort reinvigorated the struggle for voting rights. Suffragists divided over tactics, however, and the rise of feminism generated further strains within the women's movement. In the cities working people and immigrants became reform-minded and set in motion a new political force — urban liberalism. Fighting the boss system, once the province of Mugwumps, now fell to seasoned professionals like Robert La Follette, who simultaneously democratized the political parties and seized power for themselves. When it came to race relations, most progressives were not progressive, but a saving remnant overcame the endemic racism of the age and joined with black activists to forge the major institutions that would fight for black rights in the twentieth century: the NAACP and the Urban League.

At the national level, progressivism arrived via the accidental presidency of Theodore Roosevelt. Accidental or not, Roosevelt used the "bully pulpit" of the presidency against the economic power of corporate business. This overriding problem led to Roosevelt's Square Deal, then to his New Nationalism, and finally to Woodrow Wilson's New Freedom. The role of the federal government expanded dramatically but, despite the rhetoric, in service to a cautious and pragmatic handling of the country's problems.

Connections: Politics

Reform is a recurring theme in American history. The sectional crisis of the 1850s was preceded, as readers of Chapter 11 will recall, by reform ferment that sparked both the antislavery and women's rights movements. In this chapter, we treat a second great age of reform, when, as the part opener (p. 485) notes,

> political reformers, women progressives, and urban liberals went about the business of cleaning up machine politics and making life better for America's urban masses.

The Progressive era was cut short by World War I (Chapter 22), and in the aftermath, as the good times of the Roaring Twenties flowed, Americans lost interest in reform (Chapter 23). But not for long. We will see in Chapter 24 how the Great Depression brought forth the New Deal and an era of sweeping reform that still structures, despite powerful countercurrents, our public life today.

CHAPTER REVIEW QUESTIONS

➤ Class matters in America. But in what specific ways did class matter in the development of progressivism?

➤ Why was it that the women's movement was so central to social reform during the Progressive era?

➤ Define the Square Deal, the New Nationalism, and the New Freedom, and explain why these programs are keys to understanding national politics during the Progressive era.

TIMELINE

1889	Jane Addams and Ellen Gates Starr found Hull House
1893	Panic of 1893 starts depression of the 1890s
1899	National Consumers' League founded
1900	Robert M. La Follette elected Wisconsin governor
1901	President McKinley assassinated; Theodore Roosevelt succeeds him
1903	National Women's Trade Union League founded
1904	Supreme Court dissolves the Northern Securities Company
1906	Upton Sinclair's *The Jungle* is published
	Hepburn Railway Act
1908	*Muller v. Oregon* upholds regulation of working hours for women
	William Howard Taft elected president
1909	NAACP formed
1910	Roosevelt announces the New Nationalism
	Woman suffrage movement revives
1911	*Standard Oil* decision restores "rule of reason"
	Triangle Shirtwaist Company fire
1912	Progressive Party formed
	Woodrow Wilson elected president
1913	Federal Reserve Act
	Underwood Tariff Act
1914	Clayton Antitrust Act

FOR FURTHER EXPLORATION

The historical literature on the Progressive era offers an embarrassment of riches. A good entry point is Michael McGerr, *A Fierce Discontent: The Rise and Fall of the Progressive Movement in America, 1870–1920* (2003). Richard Hofstadter, *Age of Reform* (1955), is an elegantly written interpretation that remains worth reading despite its disputed central arguments. The following books are a sampling of the best that has been written about progressivism: John D. Buenker, *Urban Liberalism and Progressive Reform* (1973), on the politics of urban liberalism; Nancy F. Cott, *The Grounding of Modern Feminism* (1987); Robert M. Crunden, *Ministers of Reform, 1889–1920* (1982), on the religious underpinnings; Nancy S. Dye, *As Equals and Sisters* (1980), on working women in the movement; Naomi Lamoreaux, *The Great Merger Movement in American Business, 1895–1904* (1985); Martin J. Sklar, *The Corporate Reconstruction of American Capitalism, 1890–1916* (1988), on the progressive struggle to fashion a regulatory policy for big business; David P. Thelen, *The New Citizenship* (1972), on La Follette and Wisconsin progressivism. Among the stimulating recent books, see Nancy Cohen, *The Reconstruction of American Liberalism* (2002), on the intellectual origins; Glenda Elizabeth Gilmore, *Gender and Jim Crow: Women and the Politics of White Supremacy in North Carolina, 1869–1920* (1996), on black women's political activity in the Progressive era; Linda Gordon, *Pitied But Not Entitled: Single Mothers and the History of Welfare, 1890–1935* (1994), which uses the modern debate over welfare reform as a lens for probing the tangled origins of the American welfare system; Sara Hunter Graham, *Woman Suffrage and the New Democracy* (1996), which treats the battle for the vote as a precocious exercise in modern single-issue politics; Julie Greene, *Pure and Simple Politics: The A.F. of L., 1881–1915* (1997), on labor's increasing political involvement; Elizabeth Lasch-Quinn, *Black Neighbors* (1993), on the racial conservatism of settlement-house progressives; Daniel T. Rodgers, *Atlantic Crossings: Social Democracy in a Progressive Age* (1998), a brilliant exploration of progressivism as an international phenomenon; and, as a sparkling narrative, David Von Dreier, *Triangle: The Fire that Changed America* (2003). "Votes for Women: Selections from the National American Woman Suffrage Association Collection, 1848–1921" at **lcweb2.loc.gov/ammem/naw/nawshome.html** is a searchable archive of over 160 documents from the NAWSA collection. "Theodore Roosevelt: Icon of the American Century" at **www.npg.si.edu/exh/roosevelt/roocat.htm** presents pictures from the National Portrait Gallery, a biographical narrative, and information on Roosevelt's family and friends. "The Evolution of the Conservation Movement, 1850–1920" at **memory.loc.gov/ ammem/amrvhtml/conshome.html** offers a timeline and archive of materials on the development of the conservation movement from 1850 to 1920.

TEST YOUR KNOWLEDGE

To assess your command of the material in this chapter, see the Online Study Guide at **bedfordstmartins.com/henretta**.

For Web sites, images, and documents related to topics and places in this chapter, visit **bedfordstmartins.com/makehistory**.

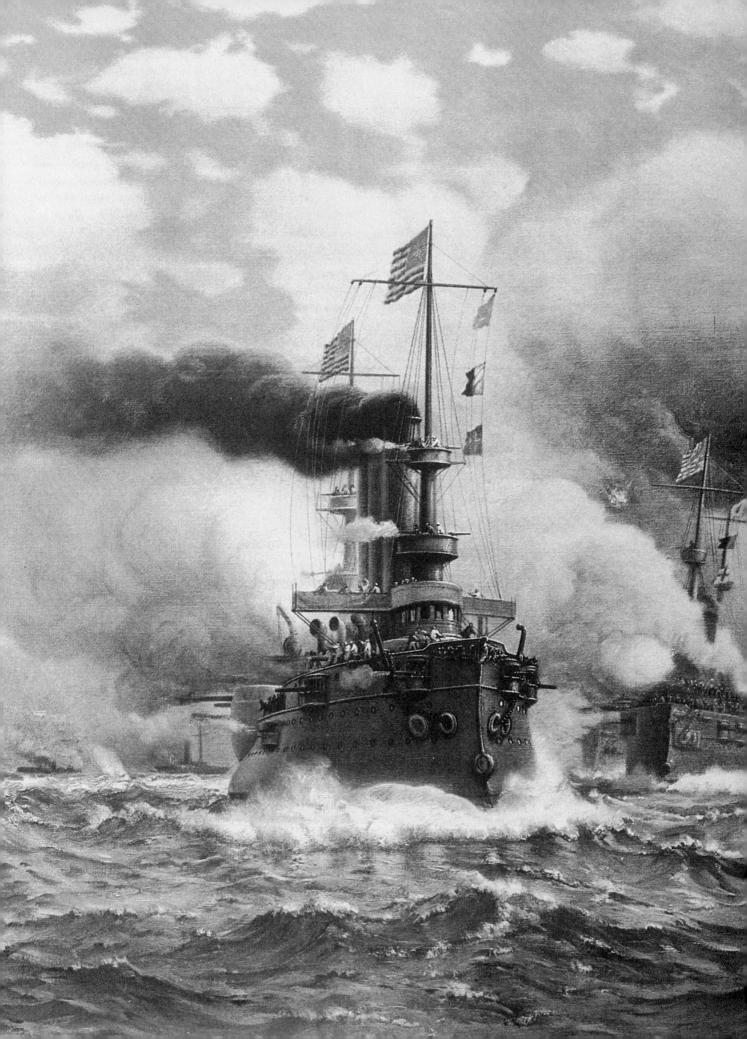

21 An Emerging World Power, 1877–1914

I N 1881 GREAT BRITAIN SENT a new envoy to Washington. He was Sir Lionel Sackville-West, son of an earl and brother-in-law of the Tory leader Lord Denby, but otherwise distinguished only as the lover of a celebrated Spanish dancer. His well-connected friends wanted to park Sir Lionel somewhere comfortable, but out of harm's way. So they made him minister to the United States.

Twenty years later such an appointment would have been unthinkable. All the European powers staffed their missions in Washington with top-of-the-line ambassadors. And they treated the United States, without question, as a fellow Great Power.

In Sir Lionel's day the United States scarcely cast a shadow on world affairs. America's army was smaller than Bulgaria's; its navy ranked thirteenth in the world and was a threat mainly to the crews manning its rickety ships. By 1900, however, the United States was flexing its muscles. It had just made short work of Spain in a brief but decisive war and acquired an empire stretching from Puerto Rico to the Philippines. America's standing as a rising naval power was manifest, and so was its muscular assertion of national interest in the Caribbean and the Pacific.

The Europeans could not be sure what America's role would be, since the United States retained its traditional policy against entangling alliances.

◀ **Battle of Santiago de Cuba, 1898**

James G. Tyler's dramatic painting of the final sea battle of the Spanish-American War showcased America's newest weapon of war, the battleship. Franklin D. Roosevelt Library.

But foreign offices across the Continent acknowledged the importance of the United States and carefully assessed its likely response to every event.

The Roots of Expansion

With a population of fifty million, the United States already ranked with the great European powers in 1880. In industrial production the nation stood second only to Britain and was rapidly closing the gap. Anyone who doubted the military prowess of Americans needed only to recall the ferocity with which they had fought one another in the Civil War. The great campaigns of Lee, Sherman, and Grant had entered the military textbooks and were closely studied by army strategists everywhere, as was evident in the skirmishing lines and massed charges employed by the German infantry against the French in the Franco-Prussian War of 1870.

And when vital interests were at stake, the United States had not shown itself lacking in diplomatic vigor. The Civil War had put the United States at odds with both France and Britain. The dispute with France involved Mexico. The United States regarded a French-sponsored regime set up there under Archduke Maximilian in 1863 as threatening to the security of the Southwest, whose seizure in 1848 still rankled Mexico. Once the Civil War ended, the United States responded forcefully. In 1867, as American troops under General Philip Sheridan massed on the border, the French military withdrew, abandoning Maximilian to a Mexican firing squad.

With Britain, the thorny issue involved damages to Union shipping by the *Alabama* and other Confederate sea raiders operating from English ports. American hopes of taking Canada as compensation were dashed by Britain's grant of dominion status to Canada in 1867. But four years later, after lengthy negotiations, Britain expressed regret and agreed to the arbitration of the *Alabama* claims, settling to America's satisfaction the last outstanding diplomatic issue of the Civil War.

Diplomacy in the Gilded Age

In the years that followed, the United States lapsed into diplomatic inactivity, not out of weakness but for lack of any clear national purpose in world affairs. The business of building the nation's industrial economy absorbed Americans and turned their attention inward. And while telegraphic cables provided the country with swift overseas communication after the 1860s, wide oceans still kept the world at a distance and gave Americans a sense of isolation and security.

European affairs, which centered on Franco-German rivalry and on bewildering Balkan enmities, hardly concerned the United States. As far as President Cleveland's secretary of state, Thomas F. Bayard, was concerned, "we have not the slightest share or interest [in] the small politics and backstage intrigues of Europe."

In these circumstances, why maintain a big navy? After the Civil War, the fleet gradually deteriorated. Of the 125 ships on the navy's active list, only about 25 were seaworthy at any one time, mainly sailing ships and obsolete ironclads modeled on the *Monitor* of Civil War fame. The administration of Chester A. Arthur (1881–1885) began a modest upgrading program, commissioning new ships, raising the standards for the officer corps, and founding the Naval War College. But the fleet remained small, without a unified naval command, and deployed mainly for coastal defense.

The conduct of diplomacy was likewise of little account. Appointment to the Foreign Service was mostly through the spoils system. American envoys and consular officers were a mixed lot, with many idlers and drunkards among the hardworking and competent. For its part the State Department tended to be inactive, exerting little control over either policy or its missions abroad. In Asia, Africa, and the Pacific islands the American presence was likely to be Christian missionaries, many of them women, and as women's social activism intensified at home, that too made itself felt in distant lands. As part of its do-everything program, the Woman's Christian Temperance Union began sending emissaries abroad to proselytize among the natives and convey the message that women's rights were an American cause.

Latin American Diplomacy. In the Caribbean, the expansionist enthusiasms of the Civil War era subsided. William H. Seward, Lincoln and Andrew Johnson's secretary of state, had dreamed of an American empire extending from the Caribbean across Mexico to Hawaii. Nothing came of his grandiose plans, nor of President Grant's efforts to purchase Santo Domingo (the future Dominican Republic) in 1870. The Senate regularly blocked later moves to acquire bases in Haiti, Cuba, and Venezuela. The long-cherished interest in a canal across Central America also faded. Despite its claim to exclusive rights, the United States stood by when a French company headed by the builder of Egypt's Suez Canal, Ferdinand de Lesseps, started to dig across the Panama isthmus in 1880. That project failed after a decade, but because of bankruptcy, not American opposition.

Diplomatic activity quickened when the energetic James G. Blaine became secretary of state in 1881. He got involved in a border dispute between Mexico and Guatemala, tried to settle a war Chile was waging against Peru and Bolivia, and called the first Pan-American conference. Blaine's interventions in Latin American disputes went badly, however, and his successor canceled the Pan-American conference after Blaine left office in late 1881. This was a characteristic example of Gilded Age diplomacy, driven largely by partisan politics and carried out without any clear sense of national purpose.

Pan-Americanism — the notion of a community of states of the Western Hemisphere — took root, however, and Blaine, returning in 1889 for a second stint at the State Department, approved the plans of the outgoing Cleveland administration for a new Pan-American conference. But little came of it, except for an agency in Washington that became the Pan-American Union. Any South American goodwill won by Blaine's efforts was soon blasted by the humiliation the United States visited upon Chile because of a riot against American sailors in the port of Valparaiso in 1891. Threatened with war, Chile apologized to the United States and paid an indemnity of $75,000. It was not lost upon South Americans that the United States, for all its fine talk about a community of nations, regarded itself as the hemisphere's dominating power, and acted accordingly.

Pacific Episodes. In the Pacific, American interest centered on Hawaii, where sugarcane had attracted a horde of American planters. Nominally an independent nation, Hawaii fell under American dominance. An 1875 treaty gave Hawaiian sugar duty-free entry into the American market and declared the islands off limits to other powers. A second treaty in 1887 granted the United States naval rights at Pearl Harbor.

When Hawaii's favored access to the American market was abruptly canceled by the McKinley Tariff of 1890, sugar planters began to plot an American takeover of the islands so that Hawaiian sugar would be treated as a domestic product. They organized a revolt in January 1893 against Queen Liliuokalani and quickly negotiated a treaty of annexation with the Harrison administration. Before the Senate could approve it, however, Grover Cleveland returned to the presidency and withdrew the treaty. To annex Hawaii, he declared, would violate America's "honor and morality" and an "unbroken tradition" against acquiring territory far from the nation's shores.

Meanwhile, the American presence elsewhere in the Pacific was growing. In 1867 the United States purchased Alaska from Imperial Russia for 7.2 million dollars. The initiative had come from St. Petersburg, which was anxious to unload an indefensible, treasury-draining possession. Secretary of State Seward, ever the expansionist, was happy to oblige, although it took some doing to persuade a dubious Congress. Alaska gave the United States not only a windfall of vast natural resources but also an unlooked-for presence stretching across the northern Pacific. Far to the south, in the Samoan Islands, the United States secured rights in 1878 to a coaling station for its steamships at Pago Pago harbor — a key link on the route to Australia — and established an informal protectorate there. In 1889, after some jostling with Germany and Britain, the rivalry over Samoa ended in a tripartite protectorate, with America retaining its rights in Pago Pago.

Sugarcane Plantation, Hawaii

Over 300,000 Asians from China, Japan, Korea, and the Philippines came to work in the Hawaiian cane fields between 1850 and 1920. The hardships they endured are reflected in plantation work songs, such as this one by Japanese laborers:
But when I came what I saw was Hell
The boss was Satan
The lunas [overseers] his helpers.
© Curt Teich Postcard Archives, Lake County Museum.

Cutting Sugar Cane. Hawaii.

American diplomacy in these years has been characterized as a series of incidents, not the pursuit of a foreign policy. Many things happened, but intermittently and without any well-founded conception of national objectives. This was possible because, as the Englishman James Bryce remarked in 1888, America still sailed "upon a summer sea." In the stormier waters that lay ahead, a different kind of diplomacy would be required.

The Economy of Expansionism

"A policy of isolation did well enough when we were an embryo nation," remarked Senator Orville Platt of Connecticut in 1893. "But today things are different. . . . We are 65 million people, the most advanced and powerful on earth, and regard to our future welfare demands an abandonment of the doctrines of isolation." What especially demanded that Americans look outward was their prodigious economy.

The Search for Foreign Markets. America's gross domestic product (GDP)—the total value of goods and services—quadrupled between 1870 and 1900. But was American demand big enough to absorb this multiplying output? Over 90 percent

was consumed at home. Even so, foreign markets mattered. Roughly a fifth of the nation's agricultural output was exported, and as the industrial economy expanded, so did the export of manufactured goods. Between 1880 and 1900, the industrial share of total exports jumped from 15 percent to over 30 percent.

American firms began to plant themselves overseas. As early as 1868 the Singer Sewing Machine Company established a factory in Glasgow, Scotland. The giant among American firms doing business abroad was Rockefeller's Standard Oil, with European branches operating tankers and marketing kerosene across the Continent. In Asia, Standard Oil cans, converted into utensils and roofing tin, became a visible sign of American market penetration. Brand names like Kodak (cameras), McCormick (agricultural equipment) and Ford (the Model T) became household words around the world.

Foreign trade was important partly for reasons of international finance. As a developing economy the United States attracted a lot of foreign capital. The result was a heavy outflow of dollars to pay interest and dividends to foreign investors. To balance this account, the United States needed to export more goods than it imported. In fact, a favorable

The Singer Sewing Machine

The sewing machine was an American invention that swiftly found markets abroad. The Singer Company, the dominant firm, not only exported large quantities but also produced 200,000 machines annually at a Scottish plant that employed 6,000 workers. Singer's advertising rightly boasted of its prowess as an international company and of a product that was "The Universal Machine." New-York Historical Society.

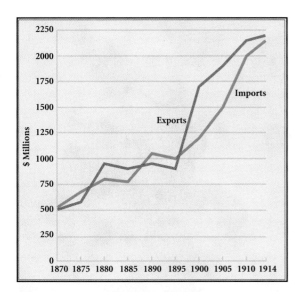

FIGURE 21.1 Balance of U.S. Imports, 1870–1914

By 1876 the United States had become a net exporting nation. The brief reversal after 1888 aroused fears that the United States was losing its foreign markets and helped fuel the expansionist drive of the 1890s.

import-export balance was achieved in 1876 (Figure 21.1). But because of its dependence on foreign capital, America had to be constantly vigilant about its export trade.

Even more important, however, was the relationship that many Americans perceived between foreign markets and the nation's social stability. Hard times always sparked agrarian unrest and labor strife. The problem, many thought, was that the nation's capacity to produce was outrunning its capacity to consume. When the economy slowed, cutbacks in domestic demand drove down farm prices and caused layoffs across the country. The answer was to make sure there would always be enough buyers for America's surplus products, and this meant buyers in foreign markets.

Trade and Diplomacy. How did these concerns about overseas trade relate to America's foreign policy? The bulk of American exports in the late nineteenth century — over 80 percent — went to Europe and Canada (Table 21.1). In these countries the normal practice of diplomacy sufficed to protect the nation's economic interests, although normal practice included close cooperation with big international players like Standard Oil. Rockefeller was thankful for the "ambassadors and ministers and consuls [who] have aided to push our way into new markets to the utmost corners of the world." In these places — in Asia, Latin America, and other regions that Americans considered "backward" — a tougher brand of intervention was required because there the United States was competing with other industrial powers.

Asia and Latin America represented only a modest part of America's export trade. Still, this trade was growing — it was worth $200 million in 1900 — and parts of it mattered a great deal to specific industries — for example, the Chinese market for American textiles. The real importance of these non-Western markets, however, was not so much their current value as their future promise. China especially exerted a powerful grip on the American mercantile imagination. Many felt that the China trade, although quite small at the time, would one day be the key to American prosperity. Therefore, China and other beckoning markets must not be closed to the United States.

In the mid-1880s the pace of European imperialism picked up. After the Berlin Conference of 1884, Africa was rapidly carved up by the European powers. In a burst of modernizing energy, Japan transformed itself into a major power and began to

	TABLE 21.1 Exports to Canada and Europe Compared with Exports to Asia and Latin America, 1875–1900			
Year	**Exports to Canada and Europe ($)**	**Percentage of Total**	**Exports to Asia and Latin America ($)**	**Percentage of Total**
1875	494,000,000	86.1	72,000,000	12.5
1885	637,000,000	85.8	87,000,000	11.7
1895	681,000,000	84.3	108,000,000	13.4
1900	1,135,000,000	81.4	200,000,000	14.3

SOURCE: Compiled from information in *Historical Statistics of the United States* (1960); U.S. Department of Commerce, *Long Term Growth, 1860–1965* (1966); National Bureau of Economic Research, *Trends in the American Economy in the Nineteenth Century* (1960).

challenge China's claims to Korea. In the Sino-Japanese War (1894–1895), Japan won an easy victory and started a scramble among the Great Powers, including Russia, to divide China into spheres of influence. In Latin America, U.S. interests began to be challenged more aggressively by Britain, France, and Germany.

On top of all this came the Panic of 1893, setting in motion industrial strikes and agrarian protests that Cleveland's secretary of state, Walter Q. Gresham, like many other Americans, took to be "symptoms of revolution." With the nation's social stability seemingly at risk, securing the markets of Latin America and Asia became an urgent matter.

The Making of a "Large" Foreign Policy

"Whether they will or no, Americans must now begin to look outward. The growing production of the country requires it." So wrote Captain Alfred T. Mahan, voicing an opinion many others held by 1890. What he added, however, was uniquely his — a strategy of American expansionism. Mahan's argument was that control of the seas was the key to imperial power, and from this insight emerged an American expansionist strategy.

Alfred T. Mahan and the Strategy of Naval Power.
Mahan was a naval officer in an age when the navy was no place for an ambitious young man. Posted to a rickety ship cruising Latin America, he spent his spare time reading history. In a library in Lima, Peru, he hit upon the idea that great empires — Rome in ancient times, Britain in his own day — had derived their power from control of the seas. This insight became the basis for his *The Influence of Seapower upon History* (1890), the celebrated book that shaped America's strategic thinking about its role in the world.

The United States should regard the oceans not as barriers, Mahan wrote, but as "a great highway . . . over which men pass in all directions." Traversing that highway required a robust merchant marine (America's had fallen on hard times since its heyday in the 1850s), a powerful navy to protect American commerce, and overseas bases. Having converted from sail to steam, navies required coaling stations far from home. Without such stations, Mahan warned, warships were "like land birds, unable to fly far from their own shores."

Mahan advocated the construction of a canal across Central America connecting the Atlantic and Pacific Oceans. Such a canal would enable the eastern United States to "compete with Europe, on

Alfred T. Mahan

Mahan's theory about the influence of sea power on history came to him while he was killing time on a tour of naval duty, reading Roman history in a library in Lima, Peru, in 1885. His insight was personal as well as intellectual: Embarrassed by the decrepit ships on which he served, Mahan thought the United States should have a modern fleet in which officers like himself could serve with pride (and with some hope of professional advancement). U.S. Naval Historical Foundation.

equal terms as to distance, for the markets of East Asia." The canal's approaches would need to be guarded by bases in the Caribbean Sea. Hawaii would have to be annexed to extend American power into the Pacific. What Mahan envisioned was a form of colonialism different from Europe's — not rule over territories and populations, but control of strategic points around the globe in defense of America's trading interests.

Other enthusiasts of a powerful America flocked to Mahan, including such up-and-coming politicians as Theodore Roosevelt and Henry Cabot Lodge. The influence of these men, few in number but well connected, increased during the 1890s. Lodge became a senator, while Roosevelt became McKinley's assistant secretary of the navy. They pushed steadily for what Lodge called a "large policy."

Rebuilding the Navy. Mahan proposed a battle-ship fleet capable of striking a decisive blow against an enemy far from America's shores. In 1890 Congress appropriated funds for three battleships as the first installment on a two-ocean navy. Battle-ships might be expensive, said Benjamin F. Tracy, Harrison's ambitious secretary of the navy, but they were "the premium paid by the United States for the insurance of its acquired wealth and its growing industries." The battleship took on a special aura for those—like the young Roosevelt—who had grand dreams for the United States. "Oh, Lord! If only the people who are ignorant about our Navy could see those great warships in all their majesty and beauty, and could realize how [well fitted they are] to uphold the honor of America!"

The incoming Cleveland administration was less spread-eagled and, by canceling Harrison's scheme for annexing Hawaii, established its antiexpansionist credentials. But after hesitating briefly Cleveland picked up the naval program of his Republican predecessor, pressing Congress just as forcefully for more battleships (five were authorized) and making the same basic argument. The nation's commercial vitality—"free access to all markets," in the words of Cleveland's second secretary of state, Richard Olney—depended on its naval power.

While rejecting the territorial aspects of Mahan's thinking, Cleveland absorbed the underlying strategic arguments about where America's vital interests lay. This explains the remarkable crisis that suddenly blew up in 1895 over Venezuela.

The Venezuela Crisis. For years a border dispute simmered between Venezuela and British Guiana. Now the United States demanded that the dispute be resolved. The European powers were carving up Africa and Asia. How could the United States be sure that Europe did not have similar designs on Latin America? Secretary of State Olney made that point in a bristling note to London on July 25, 1895, insisting that Britain accept arbitration or face the consequences. Invoking the Monroe Doctrine, Olney warned that the United States would brook no challenge to its vital interests in the Caribbean. These vital interests were America's, not Venezuela's; Venezuela was not consulted during the entire dispute.

Once the British realized that Cleveland meant business, they backed off and agreed to arbitration of the boundary dispute. Afterward, Olney remarked with satisfaction that, as a great industrial nation, the United States needed "to accept [a] commanding position" and take its place "among the Powers of the earth." Other countries would have to accommodate America's need for access to "more markets and larger markets for the consumption and products of the industry and inventive genius of the American people."

The Ideology of Expansionism

As policymakers hammered out a new foreign policy, a sustaining ideology took shape. One source of expansionist dogma was the Social Darwinist theory that dominated the political thought of this era (see Chapter 19). If, as Charles Darwin had shown, animals and plants evolved through the survival of the fittest, so did nations. "Nothing under the sun is stationary," warned the American social theorist Brooks Adams in *The Law of Civilization and Decay* (1895). "Not to advance is to recede." By this criterion the United States had no choice; if it wanted to survive, it had to expand.

Linked to Social Darwinism was a spreading belief in the inherent superiority of the Anglo-Saxon "race." In the late nineteenth century, Great Britain basked in the glory of its representative institutions, industrial prosperity, and far-flung empire—all ascribed to the supposed racial superiority of its people and, by extension, of their American cousins as well. On both sides of the Atlantic, **Anglo-Saxonism** was in vogue. Thus did John Fiske, an American philosopher and historian, lecture the nation on its future responsibilities: "The work which the English race began when it colonized North America is destined to go on until every land on the earth's surface that is not already the seat of an old civilization shall become English in its language, in its religion, in its political habits, and to a predominant extent in the blood of its people."

Fiske entitled his lecture "Manifest Destiny." A half century earlier this term had expressed the sense of national mission—America's "manifest destiny"—to sweep aside the Native American peoples and occupy the continent. In his widely read book *The Winning of the West* (1896), Theodore Roosevelt drew a parallel between the expansionism of his own time and the assault on the Indians. To Roosevelt, what happened to "backward peoples" mattered little because their conquest was "for the benefit of civilization and in the interests of mankind." More than historical parallels, however, linked the Manifest Destiny of past and present.

In 1890 the U.S. Census reported the end of the continental movement westward: there was no longer a frontier beyond which land remained to be conquered. The psychological impact of that news was profound, spawning among other things a new historical interpretation that said the nation's character was shaped by the frontier. In a landmark essay setting out this thesis — "The Significance of the Frontier in American History" (1893) — the young historian Frederick Jackson Turner suggested a link between the closing of the frontier and overseas expansion. "He would be a rash prophet who should assert that the expansive character of American life has now entirely ceased," Turner wrote. "Movement has been its dominant fact, and, unless this training has no effect upon a people, the American energy will continually demand a wider field for its exercise." As Turner predicted, Manifest Destiny did turn outward.

Thus a strong current of ideas, deeply rooted in American experience and traditions, justified the new diplomacy of expansionism. The United States was eager to step onto the world stage. All it needed was the right occasion.

➤ What is the relationship between America's economic interests abroad and the expansionist impulse of the late nineteenth century?

➤ Describe Alfred T. Mahan's impact on American strategic thinking in the late nineteenth century.

➤ What were the intellectual currents that encouraged Americans to believe that their country should be an imperial power?

An American Empire

Ever since Spain had lost most of its American empire in the early nineteenth century, Cubans had yearned to join their mainland brothers and sisters in freedom. Movements for independence had sprung up repeatedly, most recently in a rebellion in the late 1860s. In February 1895, inspired by the poet José Martí, Cuban patriots rebelled again. Although Martí died in an early skirmish, his followers persisted and mounted a stubborn guerrilla war. The Spaniards controlled the towns, the insurgents much of the countryside. In early 1896 the newly appointed Spanish commander, Valeriano Weyler, adopted a harsh policy of *reconcentration*, forcing entire populations into guarded camps. Because no aggressive pursuit followed, this ruthless strategy only inconvenienced the guerrilla fighters. The toll on civilians, however, was devastating. Out of a population of 1,600,000, as many as 200,000 died of starvation, exposure, or dysentery.

The Cuban Crisis

Rebel leaders shrewdly saw that they could tip the balance by drawing the United States into their struggle. A key group of exiles, the Junta, set up shop in New York to make the case for *Cuba Libre*. By itself, their cause might not have attracted much interest. The Spaniards were behaving no more dishonorably than any other colonial power; nor were atrocities in short supply elsewhere in the world. The Cuban exiles, however, arrived at a lucky moment.

William Randolph Hearst had just purchased the *New York Journal*, and he was in a hurry to build readership. Locked in a circulation war with Joseph Pulitzer's *New York World*, Hearst elevated Cuba's agony into flaming front-page headlines. Not much actual news could be extracted from Cuba, for the sporadic fighting took place in the remote interior, beyond the reach of Hearst's correspondents in Havana. It did not matter. Rebel claims were good enough for Hearst, and a drumbeat of superheated articles began to appear about mostly nonexistent battles and about Spanish atrocities.

Across the country powerful sentiments stirred: humanitarian concern for the suffering Cubans, sympathy with their aspirations for freedom, and, as anger against Spain rose, a fiery patriotism soon tagged **jingoism**. These sentiments were often entwined with American anxieties over the perceived effeminacy of modern life (see Chapter 18). A gendered language infused much of the debate, with rebels portrayed as chivalric defenders of Cuban women against the "lustful bondage" of the Spaniards. It would be good for the nation's character, jingoists argued, for Americans to ride to the rescue. The government should not pass up this opportunity, said Senator Albert J. Beveridge, to "manufacture manhood." In this emotion-laden atmosphere, Congress began calling for Cuban independence.

Presidential Politics. Grover Cleveland, still in office when the rebellion broke out, took a cooler view of the situation. His concern was with America's vital interests, which, he told Congress, were "by no means of a wholly sentimental or philanthropic character." The Cuban civil war was disrupting trade and destroying American property, especially Cuban sugar plantations. Cleveland also was worried that Spain's troubles might draw in other European powers. A chronically unstable Cuba was incompatible with America's strategic interests, in particular, the planned inter-oceanic canal whose Caribbean approaches would have to be safeguarded.

If Spain could put down the rebellion, that was fine with Cleveland. But there was a limit, he felt, to how long the United States could tolerate Spain's impotence.

The McKinley administration, on taking office in March 1897, adopted much the same pragmatic line. Like Cleveland, McKinley was motivated by a conception of the United States as the dominant Caribbean power, with vital interests that had to be protected. McKinley, however, was inclined to be tougher on the Spaniards. He was upset by their "uncivilized and inhumane conduct" in Cuba. And he had to contend with rising jingoism in the Senate. But the notion, long held by historians, that McKinley was swept along against his better judgment by popular opinion and by congressional pressure was wrong. McKinley was very much his own man—a skilled politician and a canny, if undramatic, president. In particular, McKinley was sensitive to business fears of any rash action that might disrupt an economy just recovering from depression.

The Road to War. On September 18, 1897, the American minister in Madrid informed the Spanish government that it was time to "put a stop to this destructive war." Either ensure an "early and certain peace" or the United States would step in. At first America's hard line seemed to work. The conservative regime fell, and a liberal government, upon taking office in October 1897, moderated its Cuban policy. Spain recalled General Weyler, backed away from reconcentration, and offered Cuba a degree of self-rule but not independence. Madrid's incapacity soon became clear, however. In January 1898 Spanish loyalists in Havana rioted against the offer of autonomy. The Cuban rebels, encouraged by the prospect of American intervention, demanded full independence.

On February 9, 1898, Hearst's *New York Journal* published a private letter by Dupuy de Lôme, the Spanish minister to the United States. In it de Lôme called President McKinley "weak" and "a bidder for the admiration of the crowd." Worse, his letter suggested that the Spanish government was not taking the American demands seriously. De Lôme immediately resigned, but the damage had been done.

A week later the U.S. battle cruiser *Maine* blew up and sank in Havana harbor, with the loss of 260 seamen. "Whole Country Thrills with the War Fever," proclaimed the *New York Journal*. From that moment onward popular passions against Spain became a major factor in the march toward war.

"Remember the Maine!"

In late January 1898 the *Maine* entered Havana harbor on a courtesy call. On the evening of February 15, a mysterious blast sent the U.S. warship to the bottom. This dramatic lithograph conveys something of the impact of that event on American public opinion. Although no evidence ever linked the Spanish authorities to the explosion, the sinking of the *Maine* fed the emotional fires that prepared the nation for war with Spain. Granger Collection.

McKinley kept his head. He assumed that the sinking had been accidental. A naval board of inquiry, however, issued a damaging report. Disagreeing with a Spanish investigation, the American board concluded improbably that the sinking had been caused by a mine. (A 1976 naval inquiry disagreed: The more likely cause was faulty ship design that placed explosive munitions too close to coal bunkers prone to spontaneous fires.) No evidence linked the Spanish to the purported mine. But if a mine did sink the ship, then the Spanish were responsible for not protecting a peaceful American vessel within their jurisdiction.

President McKinley had no stomach for the martial spirit engulfing the country. He was not swept along by the calls for blood to avenge the *Maine*. But he could not ignore an aroused public opinion. Hesitant business leaders now also became impatient for the dispute with Spain to end. War was preferable to the unresolved Cuban crisis. On March 27, McKinley cabled to Madrid what was in effect an ultimatum: an immediate armistice for six months, abandonment of the practice of reconcentration, and, with the United States as mediator, peace negotiations with the rebels. Desperate to avoid war, the Spanish government was prepared to concede on all these points, but balked at McKinley's added demand that mediation had to result in Cuban independence. That would have meant the Madrid regime's downfall and, indeed, might have jeopardized the Crown itself.

On April 11, McKinley informed Congress that further negotiation was useless and asked for authority to intervene in Cuba. His motives were as he described them: "In the name of humanity, in the name of civilization, in behalf of endangered American interests which give us the right and the duty to speak and to act, the war in Cuba must stop." The War Hawks in Congress—a mixture of empire-minded Republicans like Henry Cabot Lodge and western Democrats espousing Cuban self-determination—chafed under McKinley's cautious progress. But the president did not lose control, and he defeated their demand for recognition of the rebel republican government, which would have reduced the administration's freedom of action in dealing with Spain.

The resolutions authorizing intervention in Cuba contained an amendment by Senator Henry M. Teller of Colorado disclaiming any intention by the United States to take possession of Cuba. No European government should say that "when we go out to make battle for the liberty and freedom of Cuban patriots, that we are doing it for the purpose of aggrandizement." This had to be made clear with regard to Cuba, "whatever," Senator Teller added, "we may do as to some other islands."

Did McKinley have in mind "some other islands"? Was this really a war of aggression, secretly motivated by a desire to seize strategic territory from Spain? In a strict sense, almost certainly no. It was not *because* of expansionist ambitions that McKinley forced Spain into a corner. But once war came McKinley saw it as an opportunity. As he wrote privately after hostilities began: "While we are conducting war and until its conclusion, we must keep all we get; when the war is over we must keep what we want." Precisely what would be forthcoming, of course, depended on the fortunes of battle.

The Spoils of War

Hostilities formally began when Spain declared war on the United States on April 24, 1898. Across the country regiments began to form. Theodore Roosevelt immediately resigned as assistant secretary of the navy, ordered a fancy uniform, and accepted a commission as lieutenant colonel of a volunteer cavalry regiment soon to become famous as the Rough Riders. Raw recruits poured into makeshift bases around Tampa, Florida. Confusion reigned. Tropical uniforms did not arrive; the food was bad, the sanitation worse; and rifles were in short supply. No provision had been made for getting the troops to Cuba; the government hastily began to collect a miscellaneous fleet of yachts, lake steamers, and commercial boats. Fortunately, the small regular army was a disciplined, highly professional force: Its 28,000 seasoned troops provided a nucleus for the 200,000 civilians who had to be turned into soldiers inside of a few weeks.

The navy was in better shape. Spain had nothing to match America's seven battleships and armored cruisers, and the ships it did have were undermanned and ill-prepared for battle. The Spanish admiral, Pascual Cervera, gloomily expected that his fleet would "like Don Quixote go out to fight windmills and come back with a broken head."

The Pacific Campaign. The decisive engagement of the war took place in the far Pacific, not in Cuba. This was the handiwork of Theodore Roosevelt, who, while still in the Navy Department, had gotten the intrepid Commodore George Dewey appointed commander of the Pacific fleet, with instructions that, in the event of war, he was to set sail immediately against the Spanish fleet in the Philippines. When hostilities began, Roosevelt confronted his surprised superior, John Long, and pressured him into validating the instructions to Dewey. On May 1, American ships cornered the Spanish fleet in Manila Bay and destroyed it. The victory produced euphoria in the United States. Immediately, part of the army being trained for the Cuban campaign was diverted to the Philippines. Manila, the Philippine capital, fell on August 13, 1898.

With Dewey's naval victory, American strategic thinking clicked into place. "We hold the other side of the Pacific and the value to this country is almost beyond imagination," declared Senator Lodge. "We must on no account let the [Philippine] Islands go." President McKinley agreed, and so did his key advisors. Naval strategists had long coveted an anchor in the western Pacific. At this time, too, the Great Powers were carving up China into spheres of influence. If American merchants wanted a crack at that glittering market, the United States would have to project its power into Asia.

Once the decision for a Philippine base had been made, other decisions followed almost automatically. The question of Hawaii was quickly resolved. After stalling the previous year, Hawaiian annexation went through Congress by joint resolution

in July 1898. Hawaii had suddenly acquired a crucial strategic value: It was a halfway station on the way to the Philippines. The navy pressed for a coaling base in the central Pacific; that meant Guam, a Spanish island in the Marianas. There was need also for a strategically located base in the Caribbean; that meant Puerto Rico. By July, before the assault on Cuba, the full scope of McKinley's war aims had crystallized.

The Cuban Front. And so had the strategic objective in the Cuban campaign: a quick and decisive victory forcing Spain to fulfill America's imperial requirements. The Spanish forces were already depleted by the long guerrilla war. Tied down by the rebels, they permitted the landings at Daiquiri to go uncontested. Santiago, where the Spanish fleet was anchored, became the key to the military campaign (Map 21.1). Half-trained and ill-equipped, the American forces moving on the city might have been checked by a determined opponent. The Spaniards fought to maintain their honor, but they had no stomach for a real war against the Americans.

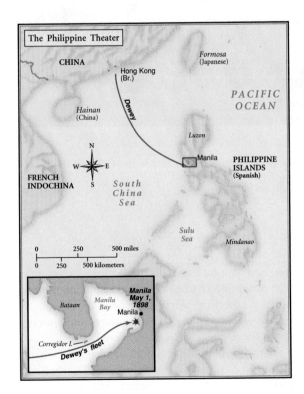
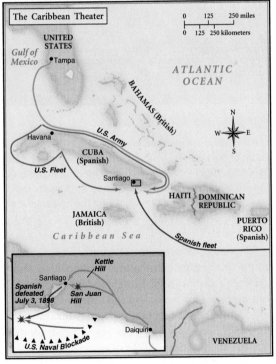

MAP 21.1   The Spanish-American War of 1898

The swift American victory in the Spanish-American War resulted from overwhelming naval superiority. Dewey's destruction of the Spanish fleet in Manila harbor doomed the Spaniards in the Philippines. In Cuba, American ground forces won a hard victory on San Juan Hill, for they were ill equipped and poorly supplied. With the United States in control of the seas, the Spaniards saw no choice but to give up the battle for Cuba.

The Battle of San Juan Hill

On July 1, 1898, the key battle for Cuba took place on heights overlooking Santiago. African American troops bore the brunt of the fighting. Although generally overlooked, the black role in the San Juan battle is done justice in this contemporary lithograph, without the demeaning stereotypes by which blacks were normally depicted in an age of intensifying racism. Even so, the racial hierarchy is maintained. The blacks are the foot soldiers; their officers are white. Library of Congress.

The main battle, on July 1, occurred near Santiago on the heights commanded by San Juan Hill. Roosevelt's dismounted Rough Riders (there had been no room for horses on the transports) seized Kettle Hill. Then the frontal assault against the San Juan heights began. Four black regiments took the brunt of the fighting. White observers grudgingly credited much of the victory to the "superb gallantry" of the black soldiers. In fact it was not quite a victory. The Spaniards, driven from their forward positions, retreated to a well-fortified second line. The exhausted Americans had suffered heavy casualties; whether they could have mounted a second assault was questionable. They were spared this test, however, by the Spanish. On July 3 Cervera's fleet in Santiago harbor made a daylight attempt to run the American blockade and was destroyed. A few days later, convinced that Santiago could not be saved, the Spanish forces surrendered.

The two nations signed an armistice in which Spain agreed to liberate Cuba and cede Puerto Rico and Guam to the United States. American forces occupied Manila pending a peace treaty.

The Imperial Experiment

The big question was the Philippines, an archipelago of 7,000 islands populated — as William R. Day,

McKinley's secretary of state, put it in the racist language of that era — by "eight or nine millions of absolutely ignorant and many degraded people." Not even avid American expansionists advocated colonial rule over subject peoples — that was European-style imperialism, not the strategic bases that Mahan and his followers had in mind. Mahan and Lodge initially advocated keeping only Manila. It gradually became clear, however, that Manila was not defensible without the whole of Luzon, the large island on which the city was located.

Taking the Philippines. McKinley and his advisors surveyed the options. One possibility was to return most of the islands to Spain, but the reputed evils of Spanish rule made that a "cowardly and dishonorable" solution. Another possibility was to partition the Philippines with one or more of the Great Powers. But, as McKinley observed, to turn over valuable territory to "our commercial rivals in the Orient — that would have been bad business and discreditable."

Most plausible was Philippine independence. As in Cuba, Spanish rule had already stirred up a rebellion, led by the ardent patriot Emilio Aguinaldo. An arrangement might have been possible like the one being extracted from the Cubans over Guantanamo Bay: the lease of a naval base to the Americans as the price of freedom. But after some hesitation McKinley concluded that "we could not leave [the Filipinos] to themselves — they were unfit for self-rule — and they would soon have anarchy and misrule over there worse than Spain's was."

Emilio Aguinaldo

At the start of the war with Spain, U.S. military leaders brought the Filipino patriot Emilio Aguinaldo back from Singapore because they thought he would stir up a popular uprising that would help defeat the Spaniards. Aguinaldo came because he thought the Americans favored an independent Philippines. These differing intentions — it has remained a matter of dispute what assurances Aguinaldo received — were the root cause of the Filipino insurrection that proved far costlier in American and Filipino lives than the war with Spain that preceded it. Corbis-Bettmann.

As for the Spaniards, they had little choice against what they considered "the immoderate demands of a conqueror." In the Treaty of Paris they ceded the Philippines to the United States for a payment of $20 million. The treaty encountered harder going at home and was ratified by the Senate (requiring a two-thirds majority) on February 6, 1899, with only a single vote to spare.

The Anti-Imperialists.

The administration's narrow margin signaled the revival of an antiexpansionist tradition that had been briefly silenced by the passions of a nation at war. In the Senate opponents of the treaty invoked the country's republican principles. Under the Constitution, argued the conservative Republican George F. Hoar, "no power is given to the Federal Government to acquire territory to be held and governed permanently as colonies" or "to conquer alien people and hold them in subjugation." The alternative — making eight million Filipinos American citizens — was equally unpalatable to the anti-imperialists, who were no more champions of "these savage people" than were the expansionists.

Leading citizens enlisted in the anti-imperialist cause, including the steel king Andrew Carnegie, who offered a check for $20 million to purchase the independence of the Philippines; the labor leader Samuel Gompers, who feared the competition of cheap Filipino labor; and Jane Addams, who believed that women should stand for peace. The key group was a social elite of old-line Mugwumps, reformers such as Carl Schurz, Charles Eliot Norton, and Charles Francis Adams. In November 1898 a Boston group formed the first of the Anti-Imperialist Leagues that began to spring up around the country.

Although skillful at publicizing their cause, the anti-imperialists never became a popular movement. They shared little but their anti-imperialism and, within the Mugwump core, lacked the common touch. Moreover the Democrats, their natural allies, waffled on the issue. Although an outspoken anti-imperialist, William Jennings Bryan, the Democratic standard-bearer, confounded his friends by favoring ratification of the treaty. He hesitated to stake his party's future on a crusade against a national policy he privately believed to be irreversible. Still, if it was an accomplished fact, Philippine annexation exacted a higher moral cost than anyone had expected.

War in the Philippines.

On February 4, 1899, two days before the Senate ratified the treaty, fighting broke out between American and Filipino patrols on the edge of Manila. Confronted by American annexation, the rebel leader Aguinaldo asserted his nation's independence and turned his guns on the occupying American forces.

The ensuing conflict far exceeded in ferocity the war just concluded with Spain. Fighting tenacious guerrillas, the U.S. Army resorted to the same tactics the Spaniards had employed in Cuba, moving people into towns, carrying out indiscriminate attacks beyond the perimeters, and burning crops and villages. Atrocities became commonplace on both sides. In three years of warfare, 4,200 Americans and many thousands of Filipinos died. The fighting ended in 1902, and William Howard Taft, who had been appointed governor-general, set up a civilian administration. He intended to make the Philippines a model of American road-building and sanitary engineering.

McKinley's convincing victory over William Jennings Bryan in the 1900 election, though by no means a referendum on American expansionism, suggested popular satisfaction with America's overseas adventure. Yet a strong undercurrent of misgivings was evident (see Comparing American Voices, "Debating the Philippines," pp. 656–657). Americans had not anticipated the brutal methods needed to subdue the Filipino guerrillas. "We are destroying these islanders by the thousands, their villages and cities," protested the philosopher William James. "No life shall you have, we say, except as a gift from our philanthropy after your unconditional surrender to our will. . . . Could there be any more damning indictment of that whole bloated ideal termed 'modern civilization'?"

There were, moreover, disturbing constitutional issues to be resolved. The Treaty of Paris, while guaranteeing them freedom of religion, specifically withheld from the inhabitants of the ceded Spanish territories any promise of citizenship. It would be up to Congress to decide their "civil rights and political status." Did this treatment conform to the Constitution? In 1901 the Supreme Court said that it did. The Constitution did not automatically extend citizenship to the acquired territories. Whether the inhabitants would be granted citizenship, or even the constitutional protections available to aliens in the United States, was up to Congress. A line was thus drawn between overseas expansion and the nation's continental expansion, marking the new territories as colonies, not future states, and marking the United States irrefutably as a colonial power. In 1916, in accordance with a recommendation by a special commission set up by McKinley, the Jones Act committed the United States to Philippine independence but set no date (the Philippines formally achieved independence in 1946).

The brutal war in the Philippines rubbed off some of the moralizing gloss but left undeflected America's global aspirations. In a few years the United States had assembled an overseas empire: Hawaii, Puerto Rico, Guam, the Philippines, and finally, in 1900, several of the Samoan islands that had been jointly administered with Germany and Britain (Map 21.2). The United States, remarked the legal scholar John Bassett Moore in 1899, had moved "from a position of comparative freedom from entanglements into a position of what is commonly called a world power" (see Reading American Pictures, "Imperial Dilemmas," p. 658)."

➤ Why should a rebellion in Cuba — after all, an internal affair of Spain's — have become a cause for war with the United States?

➤ If America's quarrel with Spain was over Cuba, why was the most important engagement of the Spanish-American War Dewey's naval victory in the Philippines?

➤ If, as Americans repeatedly said, they had fought Spain to help the Cuban people gain independence, how did the United States find itself fighting the Filipino people for just the opposite reason, that is, to prevent them from having independence?

Onto the World Stage

In Europe the flexing of America's muscles against Spain caused a certain amount of consternation. The major powers had tried before war broke out to intercede on Spain's behalf — but tentatively, because no one was looking for trouble with the Americans. President McKinley had listened politely to their envoys and then proceeded with his war.

The decisive outcome confirmed what the Europeans already suspected. After Dewey's naval victory, the semiofficial French paper *Le Temps*

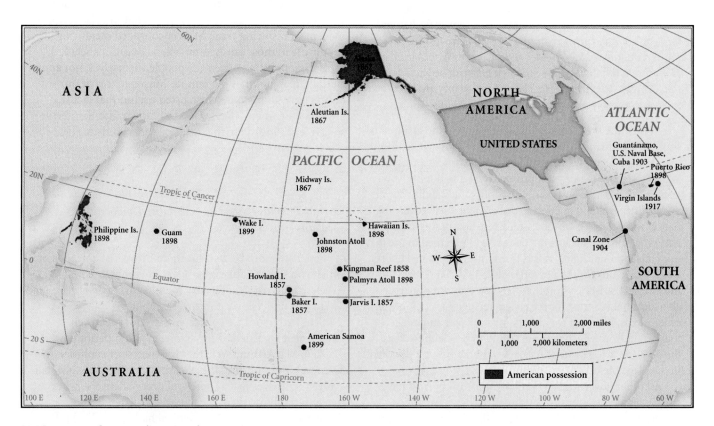

MAP 21.2   The American Empire, 1917

In 1890 Alfred T. Mahan wrote that the United States should regard the oceans as "a great highway" across which America would carry on world trade. That was precisely what resulted from the empire the United States acquired after the Spanish-American War. The Caribbean possessions, the strategically located Pacific islands, and, in 1903, the Panama Canal Zone, gave the United States commercial and naval access to a wider world.

Debating the Philippines

As we know from President McKinley's musings, seizing the Philippines was an act of national self-interest. Of the alternatives, it was the one that seemed best calculated to serve America's strategic aims in Asia. But McKinley's geopolitical decision had unintended consequences. For one, it provoked a bloody insurrection. For another, it rubbed up against the nation's democratic principles. As these consequences hit home, a divided Senate set up a special committee and held closed hearings. Congressional testimony is a source much prized by historians. Some of it, of course, is prepared testimony. But once the questioning begins, the testimony becomes unscripted and can be especially revealing. The documents below are taken from the 1902 testimony before the Senate Committee on the Philippines.

IDEALS

General Arthur MacArthur was in on the action in the Philippines almost from the start. He commanded one of the first units to arrive there in 1898 and in 1900 was reassigned back as military governor and general commander of the troops. His standing as a military man — holder of the Congressional Medal of Honor from the Civil War — was on a par with his more famous son, Douglas MacArthur. Here he explains in prepared testimony his vision of America's mission to the Philippines.

At the time I returned to Manila [May 1900] to assume the supreme command it seemed to me that . . . our occupation of the island was simply one of the necessary consequences in logical sequence of our great prosperity, and to doubt the wisdom of [occupation] was simply to doubt the stability of our own institutions and in effect to declare that a self-governing nation was incapable of successfully resisting strains arising naturally from its own productive energy. It seemed to me that our conception of right, justice, freedom, and personal liberty was the precious fruit of centuries of strife . . . [and that] we must regard ourselves simply as the custodians of imperishable ideas held in trust for the general benefit of mankind. In other words, I felt that we had attained a moral and intellectual height from which we were bound to proclaim to all as the occasion arose the true message of humanity as embodied in the principles of our own institutions. . . .

All other governments that have gone to the East have simply planted trading establishments; they have not materially affected the conditions of the people. . . . There is not a single establishment, in my judgment, in Asia to-day that would survive five years if the original power which planted it was withdrawn therefrom.

The contrasting idea with our idea is this: In planting our ideas we plant something that can not be destroyed. To my mind the archipelago is a fertile soil upon which to plant republicanism. . . . We are planting the best traditions, the best characteristics of Americanism in such a way that they can never be removed from that soil. That in itself seems to me a most inspiring thought. It encouraged me during all my efforts in those lands, even when conditions seemed most disappointing, when the people themselves, not appreciating precisely what the remote consequences of our efforts were going to be, mistrusted us; but that fact was always before me — that going deep down into that fertile soil were the indispensable ideas of Americanism.

SKEPTICISM

At this point, the general was interrupted by Colorado Senator Thomas Patterson, a Populist-Democrat and a vocal anti-imperialist.

Sen. Patterson: Do you mean that imperishable idea of which you speak is the right of self-government?

Gen. MacArthur: Precisely so; self-government regulated by law as I understand it in this Republic.

Sen. Patterson: Of course you do not mean self-government regulated by some foreign and superior power?

Gen. MacArthur: Well, that is a matter of evolution, Senator. We are putting these institutions there so they will evolve themselves just as here and everywhere else where freedom has flourished. . . .

Sen. Patterson: [after the General had concluded his formal statement] Do I understand your claim of right and duty to retain the Philippine Islands is based upon the proposition that they have come to us upon the basis of our morals, honorable dealing, and unassailable international integrity?

Gen. MacArthur: That proposition is not questioned by

anybody in the world, excepting a few people in the United States. . . . We will be benefited, and the Filipino people will be benefited, and that is what I meant by the original proposition—

Sen. Patterson: Do you mean the Filipino people that are left alive?

Gen. MacArthur: I mean the Filipino people. . . .

Sen. Patterson: You mean those left alive after they have been subjugated?

Gen. MacArthur: I do not admit that there has been any unusual destruction of life in the Philippine Islands. The destruction is simply the incident of war, and of course it embraces only a very small percentage of the total population. . . . I doubt if any war—either international or civil, any war on earth—has been conducted with as much humanity, with as much careful consideration, with as much self-restraint, as have been the American operations in the Philippine Archipelago. . . .

REALITIES

Brigadier General Robert P. Hughes, a military district commander, testified as follows:

Q: In burning towns, what would you do? Would the entire town be destroyed by fire or would only the offending portions of the town be burned?—A. I do not know that we have ever had a case of burning what you would call a town in this country, but probably a barrio or a sitio; probably half a dozen houses, native shacks, where the insurrectos would go in and be concealed, and if they caught a detachment passing they would kill some of them.

Q: What did I understand you to say would be the consequences of that?—A. They usually burned the village.

Q: All the houses in the village?—A. Yes, every one of them.

Q: What would become of the inhabitants?—A. That was their lookout. . . .

Q: If these shacks were of no consequence what was the utility of their destruction?—A. The destruction was a punishment. They permitted these people to come in there and they gave no sign. It is always—

Q: The punishment in that case would fall, not upon the men, who could go elsewhere, but mainly upon the women and the little children.—A. The women and children are part of the family, and where you wish to inflict punishment you can punish the man probably worse in that way than in any other.

Q: But is that within the ordinary rules of civilized warfare? . . .—A. These people are not civilized.

Daniel J. Evans, Twelfth Infantry, describes the "water cure"

Q: The committee would like to hear . . . whether you were the witness to any cruelties inflicted upon the natives of the Philippine Islands; and if so, under what circumstances.—A. The case I had reference to was where they gave the water cure to a native in the Ilicano Province at Ilocos Norte . . . about the month of August 1900. There were two native scouts with the American forces. They went out and brought in a couple of insurgents. . . . They tried to get from this insurgent . . . where the rest of the insurgents were at that time. . . . The first thing one of the Americans—I mean one of the scouts for the Americans—grabbed one of the men by the head and jerked his head back, and then they took a tomato can and poured water down his throat until he could hold no more. . . . Then they forced a gag into his mouth; they stood him up . . . against a post and fastened him so that he could not move. Then one man, an American soldier, who was over six feet tall, and who was very strong, too, struck this native in the pit of the stomach as hard as he could. . . . They kept that operation up for quite a time, and finally I thought the fellow was about to die, but I don't believe he was as bad as that, because finally he told them he would tell, and from that on he was taken away, and I saw no more of him.

SOURCE: Henry F. Graff, ed., *American Imperialism and the Philippine Insurrection* (Boston: Little, Brown, 1969), 64–65, 80–81, 137–39, 144–45.

ANALYZING THE EVIDENCE

➤ In the text we offer an account of the reasons the United States decided to hold the Philippines. In what ways does General MacArthur's testimony add to our account? Confirm it? Contradict it?

➤ In the same vein: The text tells you about the anti-imperialist movement. In what ways does Senator Patterson's cross-examination of General MacArthur provide you with a better sense of what was eating the anti-imperialists?

➤ Does the clash of ideas in the documents you have just read strike you as dated, in the sense, for example, that the Model T or the nickelodeon are dated? Or does that debate remain relevant for our own time, reminding you of what you today might read about in a paper or hear in a newscast?

Imperial Dilemmas

When nations go to war, patriotic fervor—jingoism—takes hold and critics speak out at their peril. That's a moment when political cartoonists really earn their pay, because criticism is their stock in trade. It's in their clever drawings, if anywhere, that the historian will spy second thoughts as the nation marches on to war and glory. Here we have two examples of cartoonists at work just as the United States was plunging into what Senator Lodge called our "Splendid Little War," the Spanish-American War of 1898.

ANALYZING THE EVIDENCE

➤ The date on the *Life* magazine cover—June 16, 1898—is significant. Commodore Dewey has won his smashing victory in Manila Bay, opening the path to an overseas empire, and U.S. troops are preparing for the assault on Cuba. At this important moment, what is the *Life* cartoon's message?

➤ The United States went to war with Spain ostensibly to secure Cuban independence. What second thoughts about that objective are raised in the cartoon "Free Cuba?" Does it give you an inkling of the policy the United States would pursue with Cuba and the Philippines once their independence from Spain had been secured?

➤ In recent years, historians have become sensitive to the role of gender in many aspects of American life, even aspects seemingly remote—like international relations. Can you find any evidence in either of these cartoons that gendered thinking helped shape America's imperial adventure? In what ways?

Free Cuba? 1898, Granger Collection.

Hurrah for Imperialism! *Life,* 1898. Newbury Library.

observed that "what passes before our eyes is the appearance of a new power of the first order." And the *London Times* concluded: "This war must . . . effect a profound change in the whole attitude and policy of the United States. In the future America will play a part in the general affairs of the world such as she has never played before" (see Voices from Abroad, "Jean Hess, Émile Zola, and Ruben Dario: American Goliath," p. 660).

A Power among Powers

The politician most ardently agreeing with the *London Times'* vision of America's future was the man who, with the assassination of William McKinley, became president on September 14, 1901. Unlike his predecessors in the White House, Theodore Roosevelt was an avid student of world affairs, widely traveled and acquainted with many European leaders. He had no doubt about America's role in the world.

It was important, first of all, to uphold the country's honor in the community of nations. The country should never shrink from righteous battle. "All the great masterful races have been fighting races," Roosevelt declared. But when he spoke of war, Roosevelt had in mind actions by the "civilized" nations against "backward peoples." Roosevelt felt "it incumbent on all the civilized and orderly powers to insist on the proper policing of the world." That was why Roosevelt sympathized with European imperialism and how he justified American dominance in the Caribbean.

As for the "civilized and orderly" policemen of the world, the worst thing that could happen was for them to fall to fighting among themselves. Roosevelt had an acute sense of the fragility of world peace, and he was farsighted about the likelihood—in this he was truly exceptional among Americans—of a catastrophic world war. He believed in American responsibility for helping to maintain the balance of power.

Anglo-American Friendship. After the Spanish-American War, the European powers had been uncertain about how to deal with the victor. Only Great Britain had a clear view of what it wanted, as its position in Europe steadily worsened in the face of a rising challenge from Germany and soured relations with France and Russia over clashing imperial interests. In its growing isolation Britain turned increasingly to the United States. In the Hay-Pauncefote Agreement (1901), Britain gave up its treaty rights to participate in

any Central American canal project, clearing the way for a canal under exclusive U.S. control. And two years later the last of the vexing U.S.-Canadian border disputes—this one involving British Columbia and Alaska—was settled, again to American satisfaction.

No formal alliance was forthcoming, but Anglo-American friendship had been placed on such a firm basis that after 1901 the British admiralty designed its war plans on the assumption that America was "a kindred state with whom we shall never have a parricidal war." Roosevelt heartily agreed. "England and United States, beyond any other two powers, should be friendly." In his unflagging efforts to maintain a global balance of power, the cornerstone of Roosevelt's policy was the English relationship.

The Big Stick. Among nations, however, what counted was strength, not merely goodwill. Roosevelt wanted "to make all foreign powers understand that when we have adopted a line of policy we have adopted it definitely, and with the intention of backing it up with deeds as well as words." As Roosevelt famously said, "Speak softly and carry a big stick." By a "big stick" he meant, above all, naval power.

The battleship program went on apace under Roosevelt. In 1904 the U.S. Navy stood fifth in the world; by 1907 it was third. At the top of Roosevelt's agenda, however, was a canal across Central America. The Spanish-American War had graphically demonstrated the strategic need: The entire country had waited anxiously while the battleship *Oregon* steamed at full speed from the Pacific around the tip of South America to join the final action against the Spanish fleet in Cuba.

The Panama Canal. Freed by Britain's surrender of its joint canal rights in 1901, Roosevelt turned to the delicate task of leasing from Colombia the needed strip of land across Panama, a Colombian province. Furious when the Colombian legislature voted down the proposed treaty, Roosevelt contemplated outright seizure of Panama but settled on a more devious solution. With an independence movement brewing in Panama, the United States lent covert assistance that ensured the success of a bloodless revolution against Colombia. On November 6, 1903, the United States recognized Panama and two weeks later got a perpetually renewable lease on a canal zone. Roosevelt never regretted the victimization of Colombia, although the United States, as a kind of conscience money, paid Colombia $25 million in 1922.

Jean Hess, Émile Zola, and Ruben Dario

American Goliath

Until the 1890s, foreign commentary was mostly about the strange habits of Americans. It was, one might say, an anthropological approach to America. But once the United States flexed its muscles internationally, a different kind of foreign commentary emerged, as is evident in the three documents below. None of them resulted from a visit to the United States. There was plenty to say from afar. Moreover, the commentary now mirrored the commentators as much as what they commented on. America was no longer merely an object of curiosity. What the Goliath did mattered. That's what came from being a Great Power.

Jean Hess, a Frenchman well traveled in East Asia, questioned American motives for intervening in the Philippines (1899).

Nowhere, in my opinion, better than in the Philippines, has it been shown that modern wars are simply "deals." The American intervention in the struggle engaged in by the revolutionary Tagals against the Spanish government has turned out to be nothing but a speculation of "business men," and not the generous effort of a people paying a debt in procuring for others the liberty that it concedes belongs to all. . . . Back of all these battles, this devastation and mourning, in spite of the newly-born Yankee imperialism, there was only, there is only, what the people of the Bourse [stock market] call a deal.

Émile Zola, the great French novelist, feared that America's military adventurism was dealing a blow to the cause of world peace (1900).

I know that, for belief in peace and future disarmament, the time is scarcely auspicious, as we are now beholding an alarming recrudescence of militarism. Nations which till now seem to have held aloof from the contagion, to have escaped this madness so prevalent in Europe, now appear to be attacked. Thus, since the Spanish war, the United States seems to have become a victim of the war fever. . . . I can see in that great nation a dangerous inclination toward war. I can detect the generation of vague ideas of future conquest. Until the present time that country wisely occupied itself with its domestic affairs and let Europe severely alone, but now it is donning plumes and epaulets, and will be dreaming of possible campaigns and be carried away with the idea of military glory — notions so perilous as to have been responsible for the downfall of nations.

In 1905, a year after the promulgation of the Roosevelt Corollary, the acclaimed Nicaraguan poet Ruben Dario issued an impassioned challenge from a small Central American country under the shadow of the Goliath. (Nicaragua was in fact occupied by U.S. Marines four years later.) Dario addressed his poem "To Roosevelt."

You are primitive and modern, simple
  and complex;
you are one part George Washington
  and one
part Nimrod.
You are the United States,
future invader of our naive America
with its Indian blood, an America
that still prays to Christ and still
  speaks Spanish.
. . . .
The United States is grand and
  powerful.
. . . A wealthy country,
joining the cult of Mammon to the
  cult of Hercules;
while Liberty, lighting the path

to easy conflict, raises her torch in
  New York.

But our own America . . .
has lived, since the earliest moments
  of its life,
in light, in fire, in fragrance, and in
  love —
the America of Moctezuma and
  Atahuelpa. . . .
O men with Saxon eyes and barbarous souls,
our America lives. And dreams. And
  loves.
And it is the daughter of the Sun. Be
  Careful.
Long live Spanish America!

SOURCES: Philip S. Foner and Robert C. Winchester, eds., *The Anti-Imperialist Reader: A Documentary History of Anti-Imperialism in the United States,* 2 vols. (New York: Holmes and Meier, 1984), 1: 98–99, 417–18; Thomas G. Paterson and Dennis Merrill, eds., *Major Problems in American Foreign Relations,* 2 vols. (Lexington, MA: D. C. Heath, 1995), 1: 508–9; *Selected Poems of Ruben Dario,* trans. Lysander Kemp (Austin: University of Texas Press, 1965).

ANALYZING THE EVIDENCE

➤ The theme of this chapter is the emergence of the United States as a Great Power. What evidence is there in these documents that foreigners actually saw the United States that way?

➤ In world affairs Americans generally had a pretty good opinion of themselves — better, certainly, than of the corrupt Europeans. Do these documents suggest that Europeans took the Americans at their own word?

➤ Ruben Dario says that Americans have "barbarous souls." Does his poem suggest why he might say a mean thing like that? Does the fact that he's a Nicaraguan matter? Is his judgment shared by the Frenchmen Hess and Zola?

The Panama Canal: Excavating the Culebra Cut

The Canal Zone was acquired through devious means from which Americans could take little pride (and which led in 1978 to the U.S. Senate's decision to restore the property to Panama). But the building of the Panama Canal itself was a triumph of American ingenuity and drive. Dr. William C. Gorgas cleaned out the malarial mosquitoes that had earlier stymied the French. Under Colonel George W. Goethals, the U.S. Army overcame formidable obstacles in a mighty feat of engineering. This photograph shows the massive effort under way in December 1904 to excavate the Culebra Cut so that oceangoing ships would be able to pass through. Corbis-Bettmann.

Building the canal, one of the heroic engineering feats of the century, involved a vast swamp-clearing project, the construction of a series of great locks, and the excavation of 240 million cubic yards of earth. It took the U.S. Army Corps of Engineers and the digging by thousands of hired laborers eight years to finish the huge project. When the Panama Canal opened in 1914, it gave the United States a commanding commercial and strategic position in the Western Hemisphere (Map 21.3).

Policeman of the Caribbean. Next came the task of making the Caribbean basin secure. The countries there, said Secretary of State Elihu Root, had been placed "in the front yard of the United States" by the Panama Canal. Therefore, as Roosevelt put it, they had to "behave themselves."

In the case of Cuba, good behavior was readily managed by the settlement following the Spanish-American War. Before withdrawing in 1902 the United States reorganized Cuban public finances and concluded a swamp-clearing program that eliminated yellow fever, a disease that had ravaged Cuba for many years. As a condition for gaining independence, Cuba accepted a proviso in its constitution called the Platt Amendment, which gave the United States the right to intervene if Cuban independence was threatened or if internal order broke down. Cuba also granted the United States a lease on Guantanamo (which is still in effect), where the U.S. Navy built a large base. It was a bitter pill for the Cubans, who thought they had made their own revolution, only to find their hard-won independence poisoned at birth. Mutual incomprehension — Americans expected gratitude, Cubans felt mainly

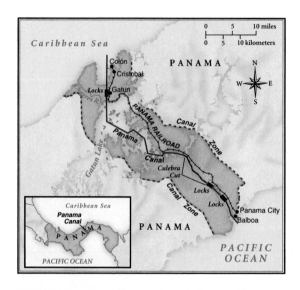

MAP 21.3   The Panama Canal: The Design

The forty-mile-long canal route zigzags to take maximum advantage of the regional topography, including an existing internal waterway via Gatun Lake. The lake is situated 85 feet above sea level, necessitating the use of locks to raise and lower ships as they approach the lake and the section known as the Culebra Cut, pictured on the previous page.

resentment — sowed the seeds of a new revolutionary movement and Fidel Castro's future triumph in 1959. Of that, of course, Theodore Roosevelt was oblivious.

Claiming that instability in the Caribbean invited the intervention of European powers, he announced in 1904 that the United States would act as "policeman" of the region, stepping in, "however reluctantly, in flagrant cases . . . of wrong-doing or impotence" (Map 21.4). This so-called Roosevelt Corollary to the Monroe Doctrine transformed its broad principle against European interference in Latin America into an unrestricted American right to regulate Caribbean affairs. The Roosevelt Corollary was not a treaty with other states; it was a unilateral declaration sanctioned only by American power and national interest.

Citing the Roosevelt Corollary, the United States intervened regularly in the internal affairs of Caribbean states. In 1905 American personnel took over the customs and debt management of the Dominican Republic and, similarly, the finances of Nicaragua in 1911 and Haiti in 1916. When domestic order broke down, the U.S. Marines occupied Cuba in 1906, Nicaragua in 1909, and Haiti and the Dominican Republic in later years.

The Open Door in Asia

Commercial interest dominated American policy in East Asia, especially the prospect of the huge China market. By the late 1890s Japan, Russia,

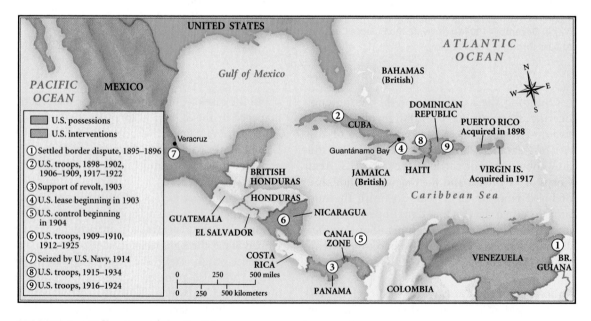

MAP 21.4   Policeman of the Caribbean

After the Spanish-American War, the United States vigorously asserted its interest in the affairs of its neighbors to the south. As the record of interventions shows, the United States truly became the "policeman" of the Caribbean.

Germany, France, and Britain had all carved out spheres of influence in China. Fearful of being frozen out, U.S. Secretary of State John Hay in 1899 sent them an Open Door note claiming the right of equal trade access—an open door—for all nations that wanted to do business in China. Despite its Philippine bases, the United States lacked real leverage in East Asia and elicited only noncommittal responses from the occupying powers. But Hay chose to interpret them as accepting the American open-door position.

When a secret society of Chinese nationalists, the Boxers, rebelled against the foreigners in 1900, the United States sent 5,000 troops from the Philippines and joined the multinational campaign to break the Boxers' siege of the diplomatic missions in Peking (Beijing). America took this opportunity to assert a second principle of the Open Door: that China would be preserved as a "territorial and administrative entity." As long as the legal fiction of an independent China survived, so would American claims to equal access to the China market.

In the Caribbean the European powers had acceded to American dominance. But Britain, Germany, France, and Russia were strongly entrenched in East Asia and not inclined to defer to American interests (Map 21.5). The United States also confronted a powerful Asian nation—Japan—that had its own vital interests. Although the open-door policy was important to him, Roosevelt sensed that higher stakes were at risk in the Pacific.

Japan had unveiled its military strength in the Sino-Japanese War of 1894–1895, which began the division of China into spheres of influence—not colonies, but regions marked off by the Great Powers over which they asserted informal dominance. A decade later, provoked by Russian rivalry in Manchuria and Korea, Japan suddenly attacked the tsar's fleet at Port Arthur, Russia's leased port in China. In a series of brilliant victories, the Japanese smashed the Russian forces in Asia. Anxious to restore a balance of power, Roosevelt mediated a settlement of the Russo-Japanese War at Portsmouth, New Hampshire, in 1905. Japan emerged as the dominant power in East Asia.

Contemptuous of other Asian nations, Roosevelt respected the Japanese—"a wonderful and civilized people . . . entitled to stand in absolute equality with all the other peoples of the civilized world." He conceded that Japan had "a paramount interest in what surrounds the Yellow Sea, just as

MAP 21.5 The Great Powers in East Asia, 1898–1910

The pattern of foreign dominance over China was via "treaty ports," where the powers based their naval forces, and "spheres of influence" extending from the ports into the hinterland. This map reveals why the United States had a weak hand; it lacked a presence on this colonized terrain. The Boxer rebellion in 1900, by bringing an American expeditionary force to Peking, gave the United States a chance to insert itself onto the Chinese mainland, and American diplomats made the most of the opportunity to defend U.S. commercial interest in China.

the United States has a paramount interest in what surrounds the Caribbean." But American strategic and commercial interests in the Pacific had to be accommodated. The United States approved of Japan's protectorate over Korea in 1905, and then of its declaration of full sovereignty six years later. However, a surge of anti-Asian feeling in California complicated Roosevelt's efforts. In 1906 San Francisco's school board placed all Asian students in a segregated school, infuriating Japan. The "Gentlemen's Agreement" of 1907, in which Japan agreed to restrict immigration to the United States, smoothed matters over, but periodic racist slights by Americans made for continuing tensions with the Japanese.

Roosevelt meanwhile moved to balance Japan's military power by increasing American naval strength in the Pacific. American battleships visited Japan in 1908 on a global tour that impressively displayed U.S. sea power. Late that year, near the end of his administration, Roosevelt achieved a formal accommodation with Japan. The Root-Takahira Agreement confirmed the status quo in the Pacific, as well as the principles of free oceanic commerce and equal trade opportunity in China.

William Howard Taft, however, entered the White House in 1909 convinced that the United States had been short-changed. He pressed for a larger role for American investors, especially in the railroad construction going on in China. An exponent of **dollar diplomacy** — the aggressive coupling of American political and economic interests abroad — Taft hoped that American capital would counterbalance Japanese power and pave the way for increased commercial opportunities. When the Chinese Revolution of 1911 toppled the ruling Manchu dynasty, Taft supported the victorious Chinese Nationalists, who wanted to modernize their country and liberate it from Japanese domination. The United States thus entered a long-term rivalry with Japan that would end in war thirty years later.

The United States had become embroiled in a distant struggle heavy with future liabilities but little by way of the fabulous profits that had lured Americans to Asia.

Wilson and Mexico

When Woodrow Wilson became president in 1913, he was bent on reform in American foreign policy no less than in domestic politics. Wilson did not really differ with his predecessors on the importance of America's economic interests overseas. He applauded the "tides of commerce" that would arise from the Panama Canal. But he opposed dollar diplomacy, which he believed bullied weaker countries financially and gave undue advantage to American business. It seemed to Wilson "a very perilous thing to determine the foreign policy of a nation in terms of material interest."

The United States, Wilson insisted, should conduct its foreign policy in conformity with its democratic principles. He intended to foster "constitutional liberty in the world," especially among the nation's neighbors in Latin America. In a major foreign-policy speech in 1913, Wilson promised that the United States would "never again seek one additional foot of territory by conquest." He was committed to advancing "human rights, national integrity, and opportunity" abroad. To do otherwise would make "ourselves untrue to our own traditions."

Mexico became the primary object of Wilson's ministrations. A cycle of revolution had begun there in 1911. The dictator Porfirio Díaz was overthrown by Francisco Madero, who spoke much as Wilson did about liberty and constitutionalism. But before Madero got very far with his reforms, he was deposed and murdered in February 1913 by one of his generals, Victoriano Huerta. Other powers recognized Huerta's provisional government but not the United States, despite a longstanding tradition of granting quick recognition to new governments. Wilson abhorred Huerta, called him a murderer, and pledged "to force him out."

By intervening in this way, Wilson insisted, "we act in the interest of Mexico alone. . . . We are seeking to counsel Mexico for its own good." Wilson meant that he intended to put the Mexican Revolution back on the constitutional path started by Madero. Wilson was not deterred by the fact that American business interests, with big investments in Mexico, favored Huerta.

The emergence of armed opposition in northern Mexico under Venustiano Carranza strengthened Wilson's hand. But Carranza's Constitutionalist movement was ardently nationalist and had no desire for American intervention. Carranza angrily rebuffed Wilson's efforts at bringing about elections by means of a compromise with the Huerta regime. He also vowed to fight any intrusion of U.S. troops in his country. All he wanted from Wilson, Carranza asserted, was recognition of the Constitutionalists' belligerent status, so that they could purchase arms in the United States. In exchange for vague promises to respect property rights and "fair" foreign concessions, Carranza finally got his way in 1914. American weapons began to flow to his troops.

When it became clear that Huerta was not about to fall, the United States threw its own forces into the conflict. On the pretext of a minor insult to the U.S. Navy at Tampico, Wilson ordered the occupation of the port of Veracruz on April 21, 1914, at the cost of 19 American and 126 Mexican lives. At that point the Huerta regime began to crumble. Carranza nevertheless condemned the United States, and his forces came close to engaging the Americans. When he entered Mexico City in triumph in August 1914, Carranza had some cause to thank the Yankees. But if any sense of gratitude existed, it was overshadowed by the anti-Americanism inspired by Wilson's insensitivity to Mexican pride and revolutionary zeal.

No sooner had the Constitutionalists triumphed than Carranza was challenged by his northern general, Pancho Villa, with some encouragement by American interests in Mexico. Defeated and driven northward, Villa began to stir up

Pancho Villa, 1914

This photograph captures General Villa at the height of his powers, at the head of Carranza's northern army in 1914. The next year, he broke with Carranza and, among other desperate tactics, began to attack Americans. Much admired in the United States, Villa overnight became Public Enemy No. 1. He evaded General Pershing's punitive expedition of 1916, however, demonstrating the difficulties even modern armies have against a guerilla foe who knows the terrain and can melt away into a sympathetic population. Brown Brothers.

trouble along the border, killing sixteen American civilians taken from a train in January 1916 and two months later raiding the town of Columbus, New Mexico. Wilson sent 11,000 troops under General John J. Pershing across the border after the elusive Villa. Soon Pershing's force resembled an army of occupation more than a punitive expedition. Mexican public opinion demanded that Pershing withdraw, and armed clashes with Mexican troops began. At the brink of war, the two governments backed off, and U.S. forces began to withdraw in early 1917. Soon after, with a new constitution ratified and elections completed, the Carranza government finally received official recognition from Washington.

The Gathering Storm in Europe

In the meantime Europe had begun a drift toward war. There were two main sources of tension. One was the rivalry between Germany, the new superpower of Europe, and the European states threatened by its might—above all France, which had been humiliated in the Franco-Prussian War of 1870. The second danger zone was the Balkans, where the Ottoman Empire was disintegrating and where, in the midst of explosive ethnic rivalries, Austria-Hungary and Russia were maneuvering for dominance. Out of these conflicts an alliance system had emerged, with Germany, Austria-Hungary, and Italy (the Triple Alliance) on one side and France and Russia (the Dual Alliance) on the other.

The tensions in Europe were partially released by European imperial adventures, especially by France in Africa and by Russia in Asia. These activities put France and Russia at odds with imperial Britain, effectively excluding Britain from the European alliance system. Fearful of Germany, however, Britain in 1904 resolved its differences with France, and the two countries reached a friendly understanding, or *entente*. When Britain came to a similar understanding with Russia in 1907, the basis was laid for the Triple Entente. A deadly confrontation between two great European power blocs became possible.

In these European quarrels Americans had no obvious stake nor any inclination, in the words of a cautionary Senate resolution, "to depart from the traditional American foreign policy which forbids participation . . . [in] political questions which are entirely European in scope." But on becoming president, Theodore Roosevelt took a lively interest in European affairs and was eager, as the head of a Great Power, to make a contribution to the cause of peace. In 1905 he got his chance.

The Anglo-French entente of the previous year was based partly on a deal about territory in North Africa: The Sudan went to Britain, Morocco to France. Then Germany suddenly challenged France over Morocco—a disastrous move, conflicting with Germany's self-interest in keeping France's attention diverted from Europe. The German ruler, Kaiser Wilhelm II, turned to Roosevelt for help. Roosevelt arranged an international conference, which was held in January 1906 at Algeciras, Spain. With U.S. diplomats playing a key role, the crisis was defused. Germany got a few token concessions, but France's dominance over Morocco was sustained.

Algeciras marked an ominous turning point—the first time the power blocs fated to come to blows in 1914 squared off against one another. But in 1906 the outcome of the conference seemed a diplomatic triumph. Roosevelt's secretary of state, Elihu Root, boasted of America's success in "preserv[ing] world peace because of the power of our detachment." Root's words prefigured how the United States would define its role among the Great Powers. It would be the apostle of peace, distinguished by its "detachment," by its lack of selfish interest in European affairs.

Opposing this internationalist impulse, however, was America's traditional suspicion of foreign entanglements. In principle, Americans were all in favor of world peace; organizations like the American Peace Society flourished during the Progressive era. But the country grew nervous when it came to translating principle into practice. Thus Americans embraced the international movement for the peaceful resolution of disputes among nations. They enthusiastically greeted the Hague Peace Conference of 1899, which established the International Court of Arbitration. Making use of the Court, however, required bilateral treaties with other nations defining the arbitration ground rules. Roosevelt carefully excepted all matters affecting "the vital interests, the independence, or the honor" of the United States. Even so, the Senate shot down Roosevelt's arbitration treaties. Taft's efforts met a similar fate.

So, when he became Wilson's secretary of state, William Jennings Bryan took a milder route. An apostle of world peace, Bryan devoted himself to negotiating a series of "cooling off" treaties with other countries—so called because the parties agreed to wait for one year while disputed issues were submitted to a conciliation process.

Algeciras, 1906

When President Roosevelt intervened in the Moroccan crisis, he was intent only on resolving
a dangerous dispute between European powers. That Morocco, a formally independent
Muslim nation with its own king, was also a party to the dispute was of little interest to him.
In this photograph, El-Hadj el-Mokri, the Moroccan ambassador to Spain, signs an agreement
at Algeciras on April 7, 1906, allowing France to police his country's borders. In so doing, he
helped resolve France's dispute with Germany, but of course at his own country's expense.
Unnoticed in the general congratulations was the humiliation visited upon Morocco, one
among innumerable such humiliations that seeded the bitterness the Muslim world today
feels against the West. Copyright Hulton-Deutsch Collection/CORBIS.

Although admirable, these bilateral agreements
had no bearing on the explosive power politics of
Europe. As tensions there reached the breaking
point in 1914, the United States remained effectively on the sidelines.

Yet at Algeciras Roosevelt had correctly anticipated what the future would demand of America.
So did the French journalist Andre Tardieu, who
remarked in 1908:

> The United States is . . . a world power. . . . Its
> power creates for it . . . a duty — to pronounce
> upon all those questions that hitherto have
> been arranged by agreement only among
> European powers. . . . The United States inter-
> venes thus in the affairs of the universe. . . . It

is seated at the table where the great game is
played, and it cannot leave it.

➤ What did Roosevelt mean when he said the
United States had to be the "policeman" of the
Caribbean?

➤ Why did the United States find it so much more
difficult to work its will in the Far East than in the
Caribbean?

➤ Woodrow Wilson believed the United States should
be true to its democratic principles in dealing with
Latin America. How would you rate Wilson's approach
when he applied it to the Mexican Revolution?

SUMMARY

In this chapter, we explore how the United States emerged as a Great Power in the late nineteenth century. By any economic or population standard, the country already ranked with the major European powers. But America's orientation was inward-looking, and that was reflected in the lax conduct of its foreign policy and the neglect of its navy. America's swift economic growth, however, and the resulting need for outlets for its surplus products, forced the country to look outward. By the early 1890s strategists like Alfred T. Mahan were calling for a battleship navy, an inter-ocean canal, and overseas bases. Accompanying this expansionist thinking were legitimating ideas drawn from Social Darwinism, Anglo-Saxon racism, and America's tradition of Manifest Destiny.

The Spanish-American War provided the opportunity for acting on these imperialist inclinations. Swift victory enabled the United States to seize from Spain the key possessions it wanted. In taking the Philippines, however, the United States overstepped the colonialism palatable to the country — strategic bases, not control over alien populations. The result was a bitter Filipino insurrection, and a resurgence of anti-imperialist sentiment at home. Even so, the McKinley administration realized the strategic goals it had set, and the United States entered the twentieth century poised to take its place as a Great Power.

In Europe, the immediate consequences were few. Only in its growing ties with Britain and by Roosevelt's involvement in the Moroccan crisis did the United States depart from its traditional avoidance of European entanglements. In the Caribbean and Asia, however, the United States moved aggressively, building the Panama Canal, asserting its dominance over the nearby states, and pressing for the Open Door in China. When Woodrow Wilson became president, he tried to bring the conduct of foreign policy more into conformity with the nation's political ideals, only to have the limitations of that approach revealed by his intervention in the Mexican Revolution. Although world peace was an increasingly popular cause in America, that sentiment did not translate into diplomatic action. The United States stood on the sidelines as a great war engulfed Europe in 1914.

Connections: Diplomacy

The events related in this chapter mark a turning point in the nation's relations with the larger world. For nearly a century, American diplomacy had dealt mostly with the lingering effects of its colonial origins (Chapter 8) and with the territorial claims arising from Manifest Destiny (Chapter 13). Even as its population and economy grew prodigiously, America was content to remain on the diplomatic sidelines until it finally burst onto the world stage at the end of the 1890s. As we say in the part opener (p. 485):

> In short order, the United States went to war with Spain, acquired an overseas empire, and became actively engaged in Latin America and Asia. There was no mistaking America's standing as a Great Power. . . .

In the next chapter we will see how the United States handled that challenge as a participant in World War I, and, again, in Chapter 25, how it learned from its mistakes and tried to do better in World War II. From then on, American diplomacy becomes a dominant theme in this text, but the dilemma the country first faced in 1900 — how to define its role as a Great Power — remains as current and unresolved today as it was a hundred years ago.

CHAPTER REVIEW QUESTIONS

➤ Why did it become untenable for the United States to adhere to its traditional isolation from world affairs?

➤ By 1899 the United States had acquired an overseas empire. How did that happen?

➤ How did Roosevelt, Taft, and Wilson differ as architects of American imperialism?

TIMELINE

1875	Treaty brings Hawaii within U.S. orbit
1876	United States achieves favorable balance of trade
1881	Secretary of State James G. Blaine inaugurates Pan-Americanism
1889	Conflict with Germany in Samoa
1890	Alfred Thayer Mahan's *The Influence of Seapower upon History*
1893	Annexation of Hawaii fails
	Frederick Jackson Turner's "The Significance of the Frontier in American History"
1894	Sino-Japanese War begins breakup of China into spheres of influence
1895	Venezuela crisis
	Cuban civil war
1898	Spanish-American War
	Hawaii annexed
	Anti-imperialist movement launched
1899	Treaty of Paris
	Guerrilla war in the Philippines
	Open-door policy in China
1901	Theodore Roosevelt becomes president; diplomacy of the "big stick"
1902	United States withdraws from Cuba; Platt Amendment gives United States right of intervention
1903	United States recognizes Panama and receives grant of Canal Zone
1904	Roosevelt Corollary to the Monroe Doctrine
1906	United States mediates Franco-German crisis over Morocco at Algeciras
1907	Gentlemen's Agreement with Japan
1908	Root-Takahira Agreement
1913	Intervention in the Mexican Revolution
1914	Panama Canal opens
	World War I begins

FOR FURTHER EXPLORATION

Walter LaFeber, *The American Search for Opportunity, 1865–1913* (1993), is an excellent, up-to-date synthesis. LaFeber emphasizes economic interest—the need for overseas markets—as the source of American expansionism. His immensely influential *The New Empire, 1860–1898* (1963) initiated the scholarly debate on this issue. A robust counterpoint is Fareed Zakaria's *From Wealth to Power* (1998), which asks why the United States was so slow (compared to other imperial nations) to translate its economic power into international muscle. The debate can be explored at greater depth in Michael Hunt, *Ideology and U.S. Foreign Policy* (1987); Thomas J. McCormick, *China Market: America's Quest for Informal Empire, 1893–1901* (1967); and Mark R. Shulman, *Navalism and the Emergence of American Sea Power, 1882–1893* (1995). On the war with Spain the liveliest narrative is still Frank Freidel, *A Splendid Little War* (1958). Ivan Musicant, *Empire by Default* (1998), offers a fuller, up-to-date treatment. The overlooked role of the Cuban rebels is brought to light by Louis S. Perez, *The War of 1898: The United States and Cuba* (1998). Lewis Gould, *The Spanish-American War and President McKinley* (1982), emphasizes McKinley's strong leadership. Ernest R. May, *Imperial Democracy: The Emergence of America as a Great Power* (1961), exemplifies the earlier view that McKinley was a weak figure driven to war by jingoistic pressures. One source of the raging jingoism of this era is uncovered in Kristin L. Hoganson, *Fighting for American Manhood: How Gender Provoked the Spanish-American and Philippine-American Wars* (1998). On the Mexican involvement see John S. D. Eisenhower, *Intervention! The United States and the Mexican Revolution* (1993). The revolution as experienced by the Mexicans is brilliantly depicted in John Womack, *Zapata and the Mexican Revolution* (1968). Michael J. Hogan and Thomas G. Patterson, eds., *Explaining the History of American Foreign Relations*, 2d ed. (2004) is a useful collection of new essays on historical writings on American diplomacy, much of it pertinent to the period covered by this chapter.

The Library of Congress maintains an excellent Web site, "The World of 1898: The Spanish-American War," at **www.loc.gov/rr/hispanic/1898/**, with separate sections on the war in Cuba, the Philippines, Puerto Rico, and Spain. "American Imperialism" at **www.boondocksnet.com** includes an extensive collection of stereoscopic images, political cartoons, maps, photographs, and documents from the period.

TEST YOUR KNOWLEDGE

To assess your command of the material in this chapter, see the Online Study Guide at **bedfordstmartins.com/henretta**.

For Web sites, images, and documents related to topics and places in this chapter, visit **bedfordstmartins.com/makehistory**.

PART FIVE

The Modern State and Society

1914–1945

	GOVERNMENT	DIPLOMACY	ECONOMY	SOCIETY	CULTURE
	The Rise of the State	**From Isolation to World Leadership**	**Prosperity, Depression, and War**	**Nativism, Migration, and Social Change**	**The Emergence of a Mass National Culture**
1914	▶ Wartime agencies expand power of federal government ▶ High taxes on the wealthy and on corporations	▶ United States enters World War I (1917) ▶ Wilson's Fourteen Points (1918)	▶ Shift from debtor to creditor nation ▶ Agricultural prosperity	▶ Southern blacks migrate to factory work in North ▶ Attacks against German Americans ▶ "Red Scare" (1919–1920)	▶ Wartime promotion of national unity ▶ Americanization campaign ▶ Silent screen; Hollywood becomes movie capital of the world
1920	▶ Republican ascendancy ▶ Prohibition (1920–1933) ▶ Business-government partnership ▶ Nineteenth Amendment gives women the vote	▶ Treaty of Versailles rejected by U.S. Senate (1920) ▶ Washington Conference sets naval limits (1921) ▶ Dawes Plan (1924)	▶ Economic recession (1920–1921) ▶ Booming prosperity (1922–1929) ▶ Automobile age begins ▶ Rise of welfare capitalism	▶ Rise of nativism and revival of KKK ▶ National Origins Act (1924) ▶ Mexican American immigration grows ▶ Harlem Renaissance	▶ Advertising promotes consumer culture ▶ New media — radio, movies — create national popular culture ▶ Image of "Roaring Twenties"
1930	▶ Franklin Roosevelt becomes president (1933) ▶ The New Deal: vast government intervention in economy ▶ Social welfare liberalism	▶ Good Neighbor Policy toward Latin America (1933) ▶ Isolationism grows ▶ U.S. neutrality proclaimed (1939)	▶ Great Depression (1929–1941) ▶ TVA aids development ▶ Rise of CIO and organized labor	▶ Farming families migrate from dust bowl states to California ▶ Indian New Deal ▶ Reverse migration to Asia and Mexico	▶ Documentary impulse in arts ▶ Works Project Administration assists artists
1940	▶ Government mobilizes industry for war output ▶ Massive war budgets and debt ▶ Universal income tax system	▶ United States enters World War II (1941) ▶ Allies defeat fascist powers ▶ Atomic bombing of Japan (1945) ▶ United Nations created (1945)	▶ War spending ends depression ▶ Business executives join government ▶ Labor unions prosper ▶ Married women enter workforce	▶ Internment of Japanese Americans ▶ Segregation in armed forces ▶ Rural whites and blacks migrate to war jobs in cities	▶ Movie industry expands and aids war effort ▶ Rationing limits consumer culture

In the 1930s journalist Mark Sullivan described World War I as a "fundamental alteration, from which we would never go back." Sullivan was correct in viewing the war as a pivotal point in world history, but many of the important factors that were transforming America were in place before the war. By 1914 industrialization, massive immigration, and the growth of cities had set the foundations for distinctly *modern* American society: diverse, prosperous, and urban. This new society was also more organized, more bureaucratic, and more complex. And by 1945, after having mobilized its resources to fight two world wars and the Great Depression, it was more wealthy and powerful, with a much larger national government. The edifice of the new society was largely complete.

GOVERNMENT An essential feature of modern American society was a strong national state. This state came late and haltingly to the United States compared with those of the industrialized countries of western Europe. American participation in World War I called forth an unprecedented mobilization of the domestic economy, but policymakers quickly dismantled the centralized wartime bureaucracies in 1919. During the 1920s the Harding and Coolidge administrations embraced a philosophy of business-government partnership, believing that corporate capitalism would provide for the welfare of the American people. It took the Great Depression, with its countless business failures and unprecedented levels of unemployment, to overthrow that long-cherished idea. Franklin D. Roosevelt's New Deal dramatically expanded federal responsibility for the economy and the welfare of ordinary citizens. An even greater expansion of the national state resulted from the massive mobilization following America's entry into World War II. Unlike the experience after World War I, the new state apparatus remained in place when the war ended.

DIPLOMACY A second defining feature of modern America was its slow but steady movement toward a position of world political leadership, which it continues to hold today. World War I provided the first major impetus: Before 1914 the world had been dominated by European nations, but from that point on the United States grew increasingly influential in international economic and political affairs. In 1918 American troops provided the margin of victory for the Allies, and President Wilson helped to shape the treaties that ended the war. Although the United States refused to join the League of Nations, its dominant economic position meant that it played an active role in world affairs in the 1920s and 1930s. America's global presence accelerated in 1941, when the nation threw all its energies into a second world war waged against fascist nations in Europe and Asia. Of all the major powers, only the United States emerged physically unscathed from that devastating global conflagration. The country was also the only one to possess a dangerous new weapon—the atomic bomb. Within wartime decisions and strategies lay the roots of the Cold War that followed.

ECONOMY The dominant world position of modern America was the result of a robust domestic economy. Between 1914 and 1945 the nation boasted the world's most productive economic system. Even the Great Depression, which hit the United States harder than any other industrialized nation, did not permanently undermine America's global economic standing. American businesses successfully competed in world markets, and American financial institutions played the leading role in international economic affairs. Large-scale corporate organizations replaced smaller family-run businesses. The automobile industry symbolized the ascendancy of mass-production techniques. Many workers shared in the general prosperity but also bore the brunt of economic downturns. These uncertainties fueled the dramatic growth of the labor movement in the 1930s.

SOCIETY The character of modern American society was shaped by the great wave of European immigration between 1880 and 1914 and the movement of native-born Americans from farms to cities. The growth of metropolitan areas gave the nation an increasingly urban tone, and geographical mobility broke down regional differences. Many old-stock white Americans viewed these processes with alarm; in 1924 they secured legislation limiting immigration to countries in the Western Hemisphere. Migration across the border from Mexico continued to shape the West and Southwest. And the internal movement of people continued: African Americans moved north and west to take factory jobs, dust bowl farmers migrated to the Far West, and Applachian whites took jobs in World War II defense plants around the country.

CULTURE Finally, modern America saw the emergence of a mass national culture. By the 1920s advertising and the new entertainment media— movies, radio, and magazines— disseminated the new values of consumerism, and the Hollywood movie industry exported this vision of the American experience worldwide. Not even the Great Depression could divert Americans from their desire for leisure, self-fulfillment, and consumer goods. The emphasis on consumption and a quest for a rising standard of living would define the American experience for the rest of the twentieth century.

SEPT 29th 1917

Price 10 Cents
In Canada, 15 Cents

Leslie's

Illust___ ___kly Newspaper

Paul Stahr

Be Patriotic
sign your country's pledge to save the food

★

22

War and the American State

1914–1920

WHEN THE UNITED STATES ENTERED the Great War in 1917, President Wilson and his administration led the country with the same idealistic rhetoric they had brought to domestic concerns during the Progressive era. "It's Up to You—Protect the Nation's Honor—Enlist Now." "Rivets Are Bayonets—Drive Them Home!" "Women! Help America's Sons Win the War: Buy U.S. Government Bonds." "Food Is Ammunition—Don't Waste It." At every turn during the eighteen months of U.S. participation in the Great War—at the movies, in schools and libraries, in shop windows and post offices, at train stations and factories—Americans encountered dramatic posters urging them to do their share. These posters, although now often displayed as colorful reminders of a bygone era, had the serious goal of unifying the American people in voluntary, self-sacrificing service to the nation.

As symbols of the increased presence of the federal government in the lives of Americans, the posters had an even broader significance. The new federal bureaucracies created to coordinate the war effort began the process that led to the emergence, during the New Deal of the 1930s, of a national administrative state. Finally, these patriotic placards underlined the fact that modern warfare was waged by citizens as well as armies. The war effort required a mobilization of the entire population and opened

◄ **American Women and the War Effort**

Popular magazines like *Leslie's Illustrated Weekly Newspaper* teamed up with the federal government to promote food conservation. Here an idealized woman draped in the Stars and Stripes encourages voluntary sacrifice on her fellow citizens. Eager to avoid food rationing, government officials mobilized 500,000 volunteers to go door to door to secure housewives' signatures on cards that pledged them to follow food conservation guidelines. *Leslie's,* September 29, 1917 / Picture Research Consultants & Archives.

up new employment opportunities for white women and for members of ethnic minorities. The passions of war also sharpened old ethnic and ideological differences and turned them into crusades of hate, first against those of German origin or descent and then of "Bolshevik" Reds or communists. In aggravating latent class, racial, and ethnic divisions among the American people, the war on the home "front" foreshadowed the social confrontations of the 1920s and 1960s.

The Great War likewise transformed the nation's position in the world. Before the conflict began in 1914, European nations had dominated international politics and trade. Four years of costly and bloody warfare shattered European supremacy. When the war ended, the United States was no longer a regional power — it was now seated at the table of the "great game" of international politics and committed, in Woodrow Wilson's words, to making the world "safe for democracy." Even as American leaders ceased to pursue this idealistic goal during the 1920s, the nation spread its political, economic, and cultural influence across the globe.

The Great War, 1914–1918

When war erupted in August 1914, most Americans saw no reason to involve themselves in the struggle among Europe's imperialistic powers. No vital U.S. interests were at stake. Indeed, the United States had good economic relationships with both the Allied Powers of Great Britain, France, and Russia and the Central Powers of Germany and Austria-Hungary. For many citizens, the war confirmed their faith in what historians call *American exceptionalism* — the belief that their democratic values and institutions allowed the country to avoid corrupting foreign alliances and warfare. But a combination of factors — economic interests, neutrality rights, cultural ties with Great Britain, and German miscalculations — would finally draw the United States into the war on the Allied side in 1917.

War in Europe

Almost from the moment France, Russia, and Britain formed the Triple Entente in 1907 to counter the Triple Alliance of Germany, Austria-Hungary, and Italy (see Chapter 21), European leaders began to prepare for what they saw as an inevitable conflict. The spark that ignited the war came in Europe's perennial tinderbox, the Balkans,

where Austria-Hungary and Russia were competing for power and influence as the Ottoman Empire slowly disintegrated. Austria's seizure in 1908 of the Ottoman provinces of Bosnia and Herzegovina, with their substantial Slavic populations, had enraged Slavic ideologues in Russia and its ally, the independent Slavic state of Serbia. In response, Serbian terrorists recruited Bosnians to resist Austrian rule. In June 1914 in the town of Sarajevo, a nineteen-year-old Bosnian student, Gavrilo Princip, assassinated Franz Ferdinand, the heir to the Austro-Hungarian throne, and his wife, the Duchess of Hohenberg.

The complex system of European diplomatic alliances, which for years had maintained a fragile peace, now quickly pulled all the major powers into war. Blaming Serbia for the assassination, Austria-Hungary declared war on Serbia on July 28. Russia, which had a secret treaty with Serbia, mobilized its armies; Germany responded by declaring war on Russia and its French ally. To attack France, the Germans launched a brutal invasion of the neutral country of Belgium, which prompted Great Britain to declare war on Germany on August 4. In less than a week, nearly all of Europe was at war.

The combatants formed two large rival blocs. The Allied Powers — Great Britain, France, Russia — were pitted against the Central Powers — Germany and Austria-Hungary, joined by Turkey in 1914 (Map 22.1). Two major battle zones emerged. The British and French (and later the Americans) battled on the Western Front against the Germans, who also fought against the Russians on the Eastern Front. Because most of the warring nations held colonial empires, the conflict spread to parts of the world far beyond Europe, including the Middle East, Africa, and China. Indeed, by 1915, Italy and Japan had joined the Allied side and Bulgaria linked up with the Central Powers — hoping to use the war to secure valuable colonies or adjacent territories. Because of its worldwide scope, the conflict soon became known as the Great War and, following a second global conflict during the 1940s, as World War I.

The term *Great War* also suggested its terrible devastation, both to armies and civilians. New military technology, much of it from the United States, made warfare more deadly than ever before. Every soldier carried a long-range, high-velocity rifle that could hit a target at 1,000 yards — a vast technical improvement over the 300-yard range of the rifle-musket used in the American Civil War. The machine gun was an even more deadly technological innovation. Its American-born inventor, Hiram Maxim, moved to Great Britain in the 1880s to follow a friend's advice: "If you want to make your

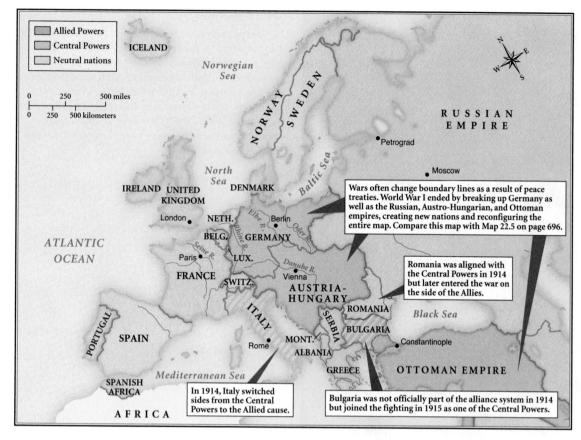

MAP 22.1   European Alliances in 1914

In early August 1914 a complex set of interlocking alliances drew all of the major European powers into war. At first the United States avoided the conflict, which did not directly threaten its national interests. Not until April 1917 did America enter the war on the Allied side.

---

fortune, invent something which will allow those fool Europeans to kill each other more quickly." The concentrated fire of rifles, machine guns, and artillery gave a tremendous advantage to defensive positions. For four bloody years, the Allies and the Central Powers fought over a narrow swath of territory that cut across Belgium and northern France. Millions of soldiers lived for months in 25,000 miles of heavily fortified trenches. One side and then the other would mount an attack across "no man's land," only to be caught in a sea of barbed wire or mowed down by machine guns and artillery fire. Trying to break the stalemate, the Germans launched an attack at Ypres in April 1915 that used deadly poison gas, yet another technological nightmare that inflated the number of casualties. As the Germans tried to break through the French lines at Verdun between February and December 1916, they suffered 450,000 casualties; the French fared even worse, with 550,000 dead or wounded soldiers. All to no avail. From 1914 to 1918, the Western Front barely moved.

The Perils of Neutrality

As the stalemate continued, the United States grappled with its role in the international conflagration. Two weeks after the outbreak of war in Europe, President Wilson called on Americans to be "neutral in fact as well as in name, impartial in thought as well as in action." If he kept America out of the European conflict, Wilson reasoned, he could arbitrate — and influence — its ultimate settlement, much as Theodore Roosevelt had helped to end the Russo-Japanese War of 1905.

Domestic Divisions. The nation's divided loyalties also influenced Wilson's policy. Many Americans, including Wilson, felt deep cultural ties to the Allies, especially Britain and France. Yet most Irish Americans resented Britain's centuries-long occupation of their homeland and the cancellation of Irish Home Rule in 1914. Moreover, more than ten million immigrants had come to the United States from Germany and Austria-Hungary, and many of

Trench Warfare

Millions of soldiers lived for months at a time in trenches that stretched for hundreds of miles across northern France. This photograph captures a moment of peace, when an exhausted soldier could catch some sleep or scribble a letter to his wife or family. Life in the trenches profoundly scarred many men and created a raft of new psychological ailments: "gas neurosis," "burial-alive neurosis," and "soldier's heart" — all symptoms of shell shock. Imperial War Museum, London.

them lived in German-speaking rural communities or belonged to German cultural organizations. Whatever his personal sympathies, Wilson could not easily have rallied the nation to the Allied side in 1914.

Many politically active Americans refused to support either side. Progressive Republican senators, such as Robert La Follette of Wisconsin and George Norris of Nebraska, vehemently opposed American participation in the European conflict. Virtually the entire political left, led principally by Eugene Debs and the Socialist Party, condemned the war as a conflict among greedy capitalist and imperialist nations. A. Philip Randolph and other African American leaders wanted no part in a struggle among white nations. Newly formed pacifist groups, among them the American Union against Militarism and the Women's Peace Party, both founded in 1915, mobilized popular opposition to the war. So too did two giants of American industry, Andrew Carnegie and Henry Ford. In December 1915 Ford spent half a million dollars to send one hundred men and women to Europe on a "peace ship" in an attempt to negotiate an end to the war.

Conflict on the High Seas. Such sentiments might have kept the nation neutral if the conflict had not spread to the high seas. The United States wished to trade peacefully with all the warring nations, but the combatants would not grant America this luxury. By September 1914, the British had imposed a naval blockade on the Central Powers in the hope of cutting off vital supplies of food, raw materials, and military armaments. The United States complained strongly at this infringement of its rights as a "neutral carrier" but did not take punitive action. The war had produced a spectacular increase in trade with the Allies that more than made up for the lost commerce with the Central Powers. American trade with Britain and France grew from $824 million in 1914 to $3.2 billion in 1916. By 1917, U.S. banks had lent the Allies $2.5 billion. In contrast, American trade and loans to Germany totaled only $29 million and $27 million, respectively, by 1917. This imbalance in commerce and credit translated into closer U.S. ties with the Allies, despite the nation's official posture of neutrality.

To challenge British control of the seas, the German navy launched a devastating new weapon, the U-boat (short for *Unterseeboot,* the "undersea" boat or submarine). In April 1915 the German embassy in the United States issued a warning to civilians that all ships flying the flags of Britain or its allies were liable to destruction. A few weeks later, a German U-boat off the coast of Ireland torpedoed the British luxury liner *Lusitania,* killing 1,198 people, 128 of them Americans. The attack on the unarmed passenger vessel (which was later revealed to have been carrying munitions) incensed Americans — newspapers branded it a "mass murder" — and prompted President Wilson to send a series of strongly worded protests to Germany. Mounting tension between the two nations temporarily subsided in September 1915, when Germany announced its U-boats would no longer attack passenger ships without warning.

The *Lusitania* crisis prompted Wilson to rethink his opposition to military preparedness. The president was further discouraged by the failure of his repeated attempts in 1915 and 1916 to mediate an end to the European conflict through his aide, Colonel Edward House. With neither side apparently interested in serious peace negotiations, in the fall of 1915 Wilson endorsed a $1 billion buildup of the army and the navy.

Nonetheless, American public opinion still ran strongly against entering the war, a factor that profoundly shaped the election of 1916. The reunited Republican Party passed over the belligerently prowar Theodore Roosevelt in favor of Supreme Court Justice Charles Evans Hughes, a former progressive governor of New York. The Democrats renominated Wilson, who campaigned both on his record

The 1916 Campaign

The Women's Bureau of the Democratic National Committee sponsored this campaign van. It reminded Americans of President Woodrow Wilson's progressive program of reform and his recent support for the eight-hour workday and a farm loan program. To clinch the case for reelection, it asked: "WHO KEEPS US OUT OF WAR?" Corbis-Bettmann.

as a progressive (see Chapter 20) and as the president who "kept us out of war." Wilson eked out a narrow victory; winning California by 4,000 votes, he secured a slim majority in the Electoral College.

Moving Toward War. Whatever Wilson's campaign slogan, the events of early 1917 diminished his lingering hopes of staying out of the conflict. On January 31 Germany announced the resumption of unrestricted submarine warfare, a decision dictated by the impasse in the land war. In response, Wilson broke off diplomatic relations with Germany on February 3. A few weeks later, newspapers published an intercepted communication from Germany's foreign secretary, Arthur Zimmermann, to the German minister in Mexico City. Zimmermann urged Mexico to join the Central Powers and, in the event the United States entered the war, promised to help Mexico recover "the lost territory of Texas, New Mexico, and Arizona." This threat to the territorial integrity of the United States jolted both congressional and public opinion. During 1916, the civil warfare sparked by the Mexican Revolution had spilled over the border. When raids led by Pancho Villa resulted in the deaths of sixteen U.S. citizens, a U.S. army force commanded by General John J. Pershing occupied parts of northern Mexico (see Chapter 21) and the two nations edged toward war. Given these tensions along the border, American policymakers took the German threat seriously.

The resumption of unrestricted submarine warfare and the Zimmermann telegram inflamed anti-German sentiment throughout the nation. German U-boats were now attacking American ships without warning, sinking three on March 18 alone. On April 2, 1917, Wilson appeared before a special session of Congress to ask for a declaration of war. The rights of the nation had been trampled, and its trade and citizens' lives imperiled, he told the legislators, but America should not enter the war for selfish or material motives. Rather, reflecting his Christian zeal and progressive idealism, Wilson justified the war as a moral crusade: "We desire no conquest, no dominion. We seek no indemnities for ourselves, no material compensation for the sacrifices we shall freely make. We are but one of the champions of the rights of mankind." In a memorable phrase intended to ennoble the nation's role, Wilson proposed that U.S. participation in the war would make the world "safe for democracy."

Four days later, on April 6, 1917, the United States declared war on Germany. Reflecting the divided feelings of the country, the vote was far from unanimous. Six senators and fifty members of the

House voted against the action, including Representative Jeannette Rankin of Montana, the first woman elected to Congress. "I want to stand by my country," she declared, "but I cannot vote for war."

"Over There"

To native-born Americans, Europe seemed a great distance away—literally "over there," as the lyrics of George M. Cohan's popular song described it. After the declaration of war, many citizens were surprised to learn that the United States planned to send troops to Europe—they had assumed that the nation's participation would be limited to military and economic aid. In May 1917, General John J. Pershing traveled to London and Paris to determine how the United States could best support the war effort. The answer was clear; as Marshal Joseph Joffre of France put it: "Men, men, and more men."

Conscription. The problem was that the United States had never maintained a large standing army; in 1917, the U.S. army consisted of fewer than 200,000 men. To field a fighting force, the government turned to conscription—a compulsory military draft. The Selective Service Act in May 1917 underlined the increasing power of the state over ordinary citizens. Unlike the Civil War, when resistance to the military draft was common, conscription went smoothly. By combining central direction by military authorities in Washington with local civilian-run draft boards, the Selective Service System respected the nation's tradition of individual freedom and local autonomy. Still, the process of draft registration demonstrated the bureaucratic potential of the American state. On a single day, June 5, 1917, more than 9.5 million men between the ages of twenty-one and thirty were processed for military service in their local voting precincts. By the end of the war, almost 4 million men, popularly known as "doughboys," plus a few thousand female navy clerks and army nurses, were in uniform. Another 300,000 men (labeled as "slackers") evaded the draft, and another 4,000 received classification as conscientious objectors.

President Wilson chose General Pershing to head the American Expeditionary Force (AEF). Before the new army could fight, it had to be trained and outfitted and transported across the submarine-infested Atlantic. The nation's first significant contribution to the Allied war effort was to secure the safety of the seas. When the U.S. entered the war, German U-boats were sinking 900,000 tons of Allied ships each month. By sending merchant and troop ships in armed convoys, the U.S. Navy cut that rate to

400,000 tons by the end of 1917. More important, no American soldiers were killed on the way to Europe.

Allied Victory on the Western Front. Meanwhile, trench warfare on the Western Front continued its deadly grind. Allied commanders pleaded for American reinforcements, but Pershing was reluctant to put his soldiers under foreign commanders, preferring to delay introducing American troops until the AEF could be brought up to full strength. Thus, until May 1918, the brunt of the fighting continued to fall on the French and British. Their burden increased when the Eastern Front collapsed following the Bolshevik (Communist) Revolution in Russia in November 1917. To consolidate its power at home, the Bolshevik regime, led by Vladimir Ilych Lenin, sought peace with the Central Powers. In the Treaty of Brest-Litovsk in March 1918, the new Russian government surrendered its sovereignty over vast territories in central Europe, including Russian Poland, the Ukraine, and the Baltic provinces. Freed from warfare with Germany, Lenin's Communist government emerged victorious after a three-year civil war against supporters of the ousted tsar, Nicholas II, and other counterrevolutionaries.

When the war with Russia ended in March 1918, the Germans launched a major offensive on the Western Front. By May the German army had advanced to within 50 miles of Paris and was bombarding the city with long-range artillery. As Allied leaders intensified their calls for American troops, Pershing committed about 60,000 Americans to help the French repel the Germans in the battles of Château-Thierry and Belleau Wood (Map 22.2). Augmented by American troops, who now began to arrive in massive numbers, the Allied forces brought the German offensive to a halt in mid-July. By mid-September 1918 American and French troops, led by General Pershing, had forced the Germans to retreat at St. Mihiel. The last major assault of the war began on September 26, when Pershing pitted over a million American soldiers against vastly outnumbered and exhausted German troops. The Meuse-Argonne campaign pushed the enemy back across the Selle River near Verdun and broke the German defenses, at a cost of over 26,000 American lives.

World War I ended on November 11, 1918, when German and Allied representatives signed an **armistice** in the railway car of Marshal Ferdinand Foch of France. The flood of American troops and supplies during the last six months of the war had helped secure the Allied victory. The nation's decisive contribution signaled a shift in international power as European diplomatic and economic dominance declined, and the United States emerged as a world leader.

MAP 22.2   U.S. Participation on the Western Front, 1918

When American troops reached the European front in significant numbers in 1918, the Allied and Central Powers had been fighting a deadly **war of attrition** for almost four years. The influx of American troops and supplies helped to break the stalemate. Successful offensive maneuvers by the American Expeditionary Force included those at Belleau Wood and Château-Thierry and the Meuse-Argonne campaign.

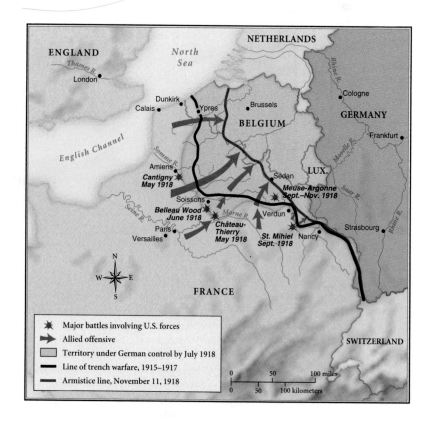

The American Fighting Force

About 2 million American soldiers were in France at the war's end. Two-thirds of them had seen some military action, but most American soldiers escaped the horrors of sustained trench warfare. Still, during the eighteen months that the United States was at war, 53,000 American servicemen were killed in action, and another 203,000 suffered wounds. Another 63,000 died from other causes, mainly the devastating influenza pandemic that swept the world in 1918 and 1919 and killed at least 50 million people. However, the nation's military casualties were a mere speck as compared with the 8 million soldiers lost by the Allies and the Central Powers and the 500,000 American civilians who died in the influenza epidemic.

Eddie Rickenbacker: Flying Ace. Although individual bravery was increasingly anachronistic in modern warfare, the war generated its share of American heroes. The best known were Sergeant Alvin York, who single-handedly killed 25 Germans and took 132 prisoners in the battle of Châtel-Chéhéry in the Meuse-Argonne campaign, and Edward Vernon Rickenbacker, a former professional racecar driver. When the war began in 1914, Rickenbacker added an English-sounding middle name to disguise his German ancestry and enlisted immediately once the United States entered the war. Sent to France as a driver, he quickly learned to fly and, in March 1918, joined the 94th Aero Pursuit Squadron. Eddie soon demonstrated his skills, dueling in the skies with the German "Flying

Fighting the Flu

The influenza epidemic of 1918 to 1919 traversed the globe, making it a pandemic that killed as many as 50 million people. According to recent research, the flu began as a virus native to wild birds and then mutated into a form that passed easily from one human to another. In the United States, one-fifth of the population was infected and more than 500,000 civilians died — ten times the number of American soldiers who died in combat during World War I. The epidemic spread with frightening speed and strained the resources of a public-health system already fully mobilized for the war effort. In October 1918 alone, 200,000 Americans died. Here doctors, army officers, and reporters don surgical masks and gowns before touring hospitals that treat influenza patients. Corbis-Bettmann.

Flying Aces

As millions of men suffered and died in the trenches, a few hundred pilots did battle in the sky. America's best-known fighting pilot was Eddie Rickenbacker (middle) of the Ninety-fourth Aero Pursuit Squadron, who was credited with twenty-six "victories" over enemy aircraft. The Ninety-fourth was known as the hat-in-the-ring squadron for the American custom of throwing a hat into the ring as an invitation to fight. Note the hat insignia on the plane. Corbis-Bettmann.

Circus" led by Manfred von Richthofen, the famous "Red Baron." By the war's end, Rickenbacker had fought in 134 air battles, downed 26 German planes, and become a national hero. Although air pilots played only a minor role in the war, they captivated the popular imagination — as their daredevil aerial exploits provided a vivid contrast to the monotony of deadly trench warfare.

Rickenbacker's more important contribution to history came later. In 1935 he joined Eastern Airlines, one of the pioneering flagships of commercial aviation, and soon became its president. Until his death in 1973, Rickenbacker was a leading figure in the development of commercial aviation, which in the years after World War II revolutionized world travel.

Diversity and Racism in the Armed Forces.

Most American soldiers were not heroes like York and Rickenbacker, but rather ordinary men from rural farms and crowded cities. The army taught them about venereal disease, issued them condoms, and gave them safety razors — changing the sexual outlook and shaving habits of a generation. The recruits reflected the heterogeneity of the nation's population. About one-fifth of the American soldiers had been born in another country, leading some people to call the AEF the American Foreign Legion. Army censors had to be able to read forty-nine languages to check letters written home by American servicemen. Although this diversity worried some observers, most predicted that service in the armed forces would promote the Americanization of the nation's immigrants.

The "Americanization" of the army remained imperfect at best, with African American soldiers receiving the worst treatment. Over 400,000 black men served in the military, accounting for 13 percent of the armed forces; 92 percent were draftees, a far higher rate than that of whites. Blacks were organized into rigidly segregated units, almost always under the control of white officers. In addition, blacks were assigned to the most menial tasks, such as kitchen and clean-up details. Although the policy of segregation minimized contact between black and white recruits, racial violence erupted at several camps. The worst incident occurred in Houston in August 1917, when black members of the Twenty-fourth Infantry's Third Battalion killed fifteen white soldiers and police officers in retaliation for a string of racial incidents. Sixty-four soldiers were tried in military courts, and nineteen were hanged. The army quickly disbanded the battalion, but the legacy of racial mistrust lingered throughout the rest of the war (see Voices from Abroad, "A German Propaganda Appeal to Black Soldiers," p. 682).

In contrast to the segregation of African Americans, Native Americans served in integrated combat units. Ironically, racial stereotypes about the natural abilities of Native American men as warriors, adroit tacticians, and camouflage experts enhanced their military reputations and meant that officers gave them hazardous duties as advance scouts, messengers, and snipers. Approximately 13,000, or 25 percent, of the adult male Native American population served in the military, often with distinction. Roughly 5 percent died, compared to 2 percent for the military as a whole.

After the armistice, American troops came home and quickly readjusted to civilian life. Spared the trauma of sustained battle, many members of the AEF had experienced the war "over there"

A German Propaganda Appeal to Black Soldiers

In an effort to undermine morale, both the Allied Powers and the Central Powers distributed propaganda tracts among the opposing troops. This piece of German propaganda was directed toward black soldiers in France. According to Charles Williams—who, with the cooperation of the secretary of war, the Federal Council of Churches, and the Phelps-Stokes Fund, investigated conditions for black recruits—the reaction of African American soldiers who read the propaganda was clear: "We know what they say is true, but don't worry; we're not going over."

To the Colored Soldiers of the U.S. Army,

September, 1918, Vosges Mountains.

Hello, boys, what are you doing over there? Fighting the Germans? Why? Have they ever done you any harm? Of course, some white folks and the lying English-American papers told you that the Germans ought to be wiped out for the sake of humanity and democracy. What is democracy? Personal freedom, all citizens enjoying the same rights socially and before the law. Do you enjoy the same rights as the white people do in America, the land of freedom and democracy? Or aren't you rather rated over there as second class citizens? Can you go to a restaurant where white people dine, can you get a seat in a theatre where white people sit, can you get a pullman seat or berth in a railroad car, or can you ride in the South in the same street car with white people? And how about the law? Is lynching and the most horrible cruelties connected therewith a lawful proceeding in a democratic country?

Now all of this is entirely different in Germany, where they do like colored people, where they do treat them as gentlemen and not as second class citizens. They enjoy exactly the same social privileges as every white man, and quite a number of colored people have mighty fine positions in Berlin and other big German cities.

Why, then, fight the Germans only for the benefit of the Wall Street robbers to protect the millions they have lent to the English, French, and Italians? You have been made the tool of the egotistic and rapacious rich in England and America, and there is nothing in the whole game for you but broken bones, horrible wounds, broken health or — death. No satisfaction whatever will you get out of this unjust war. You have never seen Germany; so you are fools if you allow people to teach you to hate it. Come over and see for yourself. Let those do the fighting who make profit out of this war; don't allow them to use you as cannon food. To carry the gun in their defense is not an honor but a shame. Throw it away and come over to the German lines. You will find friends who will help you along.

SOURCE: Charles H. Williams, *Sidelights on Negro Soldiers* (Boston: B. J. Brimmer Co., 1923), 70–71.

ANALYZING THE EVIDENCE

➤ Are there any statements in this tract that are not true? If it makes truthful claims, is it accurate to call it "propaganda"?

➤ According to Williams, black soldiers accepted the validity of this harsh description of African American life in the United States. How do you explain their decision to remain loyal to a country that oppressed them and their people?

more as tourists than as soldiers. Before joining the army, most recruits had barely traveled beyond their hometowns, and for them the journey across the ocean to Europe was a once-in-a-lifetime event. Their letters described "old cathedrals, chateaux and ancient towns . . . quite wonderful . . . to eyes so accustomed to the look of the New World." In 1919, a group of former AEF officers formed the American Legion "to preserve the memories and incidents of our association in the great war." The word *legion* perfectly captured the romantic, almost chivalric memories that many veterans held of their wartime service. Only later did disillusionment set in over the contested legacy of World War I.

➤ What were the causes of World War I? Why is the conflict considered a "world" war?

➤ Why did America become involved in the war? How did President Wilson justify his decision to enter the war in 1917? How did Americans respond?

➤ How did the fighting in Europe differ from previous wars? What was the experience like for soldiers on the front lines?

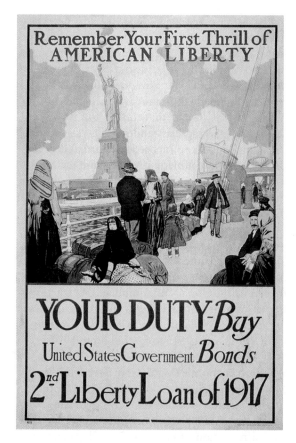

"Remember Your First Thrill of American Liberty"

U.S. government officials were eager to enlist all Americans in the battle against the Central Powers. They carefully crafted patriotic advertising campaigns that urged Americans to buy bonds, conserve food, enlist in the military, and join in the war effort in countless other ways. This poster targeted recent immigrants to the United States, reminding them that "American Liberty" carried with it the "Duty" to buy war bonds. Library of Congress.

War on the Home Front

Fighting World War I required an extraordinary economic effort on the home front. At the height of mobilization, one-fourth of the gross national product went for war production. Although the federal government expanded its power and presence during the emergency, the watchword was voluntarism — and it worked. Corporations, workers, and the general public did their part to win the war. Business and government proved especially congenial partners, a collaboration that typified the pattern of state building in America. Similarly, the rapid dismantling of the federal bureaucracy after the war reflected the longstanding preference for limited government. Still, during the war many progressives continued their efforts to use governmental policies to improve American society.

Mobilizing Industry and the Economy

Even before the formal declaration of war, the United States had become the arsenal of the Allied Powers. As hundreds of tons of American supplies —

grain, guns, and manufactured goods — crossed the Atlantic and the Allies paid for them in gold, the United States became a leading creditor nation. Moreover, as the cost of the war drained British economic reserves, U.S. financial institutions began to provide capital for investments around the globe. America's shift from debtor to creditor status, which would last until the 1980s, guaranteed the nation a major role in the international financial affairs and world politics.

Paying for the War. Wars are expensive, and World War I was no exception. The Wilson administration spent $33 billion fighting the war — about eight times more than Union government expended during the Civil War. Because the disruption of international trade reduced tariff revenues, a major source of federal income, Treasury Secretary William McAdoo turned for revenue to the income taxes permitted by the Sixteenth Amendment (1913). Working with Democrats in Congress, he secured passage of War Revenue Bills in 1917 and 1918 that embodied progressive principles of economic justice. Rather than taxing the wages and salaries of working-class and middle-class Americans, this legislation imposed substantial levies on the income of wealthier individuals and the excess-profits of business corporations. Because of this unprecedented intrusion of the state into the workings of corporate capitalism, by 1918 U.S. corporations were paying over $2.5 billion in taxes per year — more than half of all federal taxes.

In all, the United States raised about one-third of the cost of the war from taxes. The rest came from loans, especially the popular Liberty Loans that encouraged public support for the war effort. Because of these loans, the federal debt increased from $1 billion in 1915 to $20 billion in 1920.

Wartime Economic Regulation: Bernard Baruch. Mobilization required the coordination of economic production. To the dismay of many progressives who had hoped that the war emergency would increase federal regulation of business, the Wilson administration suspended antitrust laws to encourage output and turned to nation's business executives for economic expertise. Corporate officials flocked to Washington, where they served with federal officials on the boards of war-related agencies. The agencies usually sought a middle ground between state control of the economy and total freedom for business, a compromise that had mixed results.

The central agency for directing military production was the War Industries Board (WIB), established in July 1917. After a fumbling start that showed the limits of voluntarism, the Wilson administration reorganized the board under the direction of Bernard Baruch, a Wall Street financier. Born in 1870 to a family of German Jewish immigrants, Baruch began as an office boy in a Wall Street firm and quickly achieved success as a stockbroker, speculator, and member of the New York Stock Exchange. An immensely wealthy man, he supported Wilson's bid for the presidency in 1912 and came to his aid in 1917. (He also served President Franklin D. Roosevelt as a member of his "Brain Trust"; see

Bernard Baruch in 1919

When this photograph was taken, Baruch was forty-nine years old and had just served as chairman of the War Industries Board and as an advisor to President Woodrow Wilson at the Versailles Peace Conference. Copyright Bettmann/Corbis.

Chapter 24). Baruch was a superb administrator. Under his direction, the War Industries Board greatly expanded the federal government's economic powers: It gathered economic data and statistics, allocated scarce resources among industries, ordered factories to convert to war production, set prices, and standardized procedures. Although the WIB had the authority to compel compliance, Baruch preferred to win voluntary cooperation from industry. A man of immense charm, he usually succeeded — helped along by the lucrative military contracts at his disposal. Despite higher taxes, corporate profits soared because of guaranteed profits on military production and the war-driven economic boom that continued without interruption until 1920.

In some instances, the new federal agencies took dramatic, decisive action. When the severe winter of 1917–1918 led to coal shortages in northeastern cities, the Fuel Administration ordered all factories east of the Mississippi River to shut down for four days; then it artificially raised the price of coal to increase production. The Railroad War Board, which coordinated the nation's sprawling transportation system, took even more aggressive action. To ensure the rapid movement of troops and equipment, in December 1917 it seized control of private railroads. The Board guaranteed railroad shareholders a "standard return" equal to their average earnings between 1915 and 1917 and promised to return the carriers to private control following the end of the war. Although progressive reformers wanted to assist railroad workers and shippers by continuing federal control, the government fulfilled its pledge.

Perhaps the most successful wartime agency was the Food Administration, created in August 1917 and led by Herbert Hoover, an engineer who had managed major projects around the world. Using the slogan "Food will win the war," Hoover convinced farmers to expand production of wheat and other grains from 45 million acres in 1917 to 75 million in 1919. The increased output not only supplied Americans with food but also allowed a threefold rise in food exports to war-torn Europe. Rather than ration items in short supply, the Food Administration mobilized "the spirit of self-denial and self-sacrifice." Hoover sent women volunteers from door to door to persuade housewives to observe "Wheatless" Mondays, "Meatless" Tuesdays, and "Porkless" Thursdays and Saturdays. Hoover, a Republican in politics, emerged from the war as one of the nation's most admired public figures.

With the signing of the armistice in November 1918, the United States scrambled to dismantle wartime controls. Wilson disbanded the WIB on January 1, 1919, resisting suggestions that the board would stabilize the economy during demobilization. Like most Americans, Wilson could tolerate government planning during an emergency but not as a permanent feature of the economy.

Although the nation's participation in the war lasted just eighteen months, it left an enduring legacy: the modern bureaucratic state. Entire industries were organized as never before, linked to a maze of government agencies and executive departments. A modern and progressive system of income taxation was established, with the potential for vastly increasing federal revenue. Finally, the collaboration between business and government was mutually beneficial, a lesson both partners would put to use in state building in the 1920s and afterward.

Mobilizing American Workers

Modern wars are never won solely by armies and business and government leaders. Farmers, factory workers, and other civilians played crucial roles in the America's World War I victory, thanks in part to government propaganda posters that constantly exhorted citizens "to do their bit for Uncle Sam." However, World War I produced fewer rewards for workers than for owners and managers.

Organized Labor. The position of labor unions improved during the war, although they remained junior partners to business and government. Samuel Gompers, leader of the American Federation of Labor (AFL), traded the union's support for the war for a voice on government policy; he sat on the National Defense Advisory Commission. The National War Labor Board (NWLB), formed in April 1918, also improved the working lives of laboring men and women. Composed of representatives of labor, management, and the public, the NWLB established an eight-hour day for war workers, with time and a half for overtime, and endorsed equal pay for women workers. In return for a no-strike pledge, the NWLB supported the workers' right to organize unions and required employers to deal with shop committees. When executives at a Smith and Wesson arms plant in Springfield, Massachusetts, discriminated against union employees, the NWLB took over the firm.

After years of federal hostility toward labor, the NWLB's actions brought a dramatic change in labor's status and power. From 1916 to 1919 AFL membership grew by almost one million workers, reaching over three million at the end of the war. Few of the wartime gains lasted, however. Like

other agencies, the NWLB was quickly disbanded at war's end. Wartime inflation ate up most of the wage hikes, and a virulent postwar antiunion movement caused a decline in union membership that lasted into the 1930s.

Black and Mexican American Workers. The war emergency created job opportunities for ethnic and racial minorities. For the first time northern factories actively recruited African Americans, spawning a "Great Migration" from southern farms to the nation's industrial heartland (Map 22.3). During the war, more than 400,000 African Americans moved northward to St. Louis, Chicago, New York, and Detroit. The rewards were great. Black workers in Henry Ford's Detroit auto works took home $5 day, the same high pay as white workers. Other African Americans looked forward to working in northern meatpacking plants; as one migrant from Mississippi recalled, "You could not rest in your bed at night for thoughts of Chicago." African Americans encountered discrimination in the North — in jobs, housing, and education — but most celebrated their escape from the repressive racism and low pay of the southern agricultural system (see Comparing American Voices, "The Great Migration," pp. 686–687).

Mexican Americans in California, Texas, New Mexico, and Arizona also found new opportunities. Wartime labor shortages prompted many Mexican Americans to leave farm labor for industrial jobs in rapidly growing southwestern cities, where they mostly settled in segregated neighborhoods (barrios). Continuing political instability in Mexico combined with a demand for agricultural laborers in the U.S. encouraged more Mexicans to move across the border. Between 1917 and 1920 at least 100,000 Mexicans entered the United States, and, despite meeting discrimination because of their dark skins and Catholic religion, many of them stayed.

Women and the War Effort. Women were the largest group to take advantage of new wartime opportunities. White women and, to a lesser degree, black and Mexican American women, took factory jobs usually filled by men. About one million women joined the labor force for the first time, and another eight million women gave up low-wage jobs as teachers and domestic servants for higher-paying industrial work. Americans soon got used to the sight of female streetcar conductors, train engineers, and defense workers. But everyone — including most working women — believed that those jobs would return to men after the war (see Reading American Pictures, " 'Over Here': Women's Wartime Opportunities," p. 689).

The Great Migration

The Great Migration of African Americans from the rural South to the cities of the North marked a pivotal point in twentieth-century African American history and one that scholars have explored extensively. To capture this black experience, historians have drawn on a variety of primary sources, including black newspapers such as the *Chicago Defender* and the *Atlanta Journal*; records of the Chicago Urban League, an organization that helped southern migrants adjust to their new environment; and the report of the Chicago Commission on Race Relations, which interviewed many African Americans following the devastating race riot of 1919 (see p. 698). Other newspaper and magazine articles reveal the responses of southern whites to the departure of their agricultural labor force and of northern whites to the influx of African Americans.

ANONYMOUS AFRICAN AMERICAN MIGRANTS
Letters Home to the South

Particularly evocative sources on the Great Migration are the letters written by the migrants. African American historian Emmett J. Scott recognized their historical value as early as 1919 and published a collection of "letters from Negroes of all conditions in almost all parts of the South," in the Journal of Negro History. *Given that many migrants spoke "black English," Scott may have edited these letters for grammar and style. As you read these letters, consider why they were important to the migrants and their families. What insights do they offer as to the reasons for African American migration? When Scott published these letters, he omitted the names of writers and recipients. What factors might have influenced his decision?*

CHICAGO, ILLINOIS.

My dear Sister: I was agreeably surprised to hear from you and to hear from home. I am well and thankful to say I am doing well. The weather and everything else was a surprise to me when I came. I got here in time to attend one of the greatest revivals in the history of my life — over 500 people joined the church. We had a Holy Ghost shower. You know I like to have run wild. It was snowing some nights and if you didnt hurry you could not get standing room. Please remember me kindly to any who ask of me. The people are rushing here by the thousands and I know if you come and rent a big house you can get all the roomers you want. You write me exactly when you are coming. I am not keeping house yet I am living with my brother and his wife. My sone is in California but will be home soon. He spends his winter in California. I can get a nice place for you to stop until you can look around and see what you want. I am quite busy. I work in Swifts packing Co. in the sausage department. My daughter and I work for the same company — We get $1.50 a day and we pack so many sausages we dont have much time to play but it is a matter of a dollar with me and I feel that God made the path and I am walking therein.

Tell your husband work is plentiful here and he wont have to loaf if he want to work. . . . Well goodbye from your sister in Christ.

CHICAGO, ILLINOIS, 11/13/17.
Mr. H———
Hattiesburg, Miss.
Dear M———: Yours received sometime ago and found all well and doing well. hope you and family are well.

I got my things alright the other day and they were in good condition. I am all fixed now and living well. I certainly appreciate what you done for us and I will remember you in the near future.

M, old boy, I was promoted on the first of the month I was made first assistant to the head carpenter when he is out of the place I take everything in charge and was raised to $95. a month. You know I know my stuff.

Whats the news generally around H'burg? I should have been here 20 years ago. I just begin to feel like a man. It's a great deal of pleasure in knowing that you have got some privilege My children are going to the same school with the

whites and I dont have to umble to no one. I have registered—
Will vote the next election and there isnt any "yes sir" and
"no sir"—its all yes and no and Sam and Bill.

Florine says hello and would like very much to see you.

All joins me in sending love to you and family. How is
times there now? Answer soon, from your friend and bro.

SOURCE: *Journal of Negro History* 4, no. 4 (1919): 457, 458–459.

DWIGHT THOMPSON FARNHAM
Making Efficient Use of Migrant Black Workers

*As the migrants' letters suggest, African Americans felt opti-
mistic about the opportunities available in the North. But the
"promised land" often fell short of expectations. In Chicago
and other cities, African Americans lived in run-down houses
and often had to take the roughest and most dangerous jobs. As
the following excerpt from an* Industrial Management *article
of 1918 indicates, blacks did not escape racism when they
moved north. As you read Dwight Thompson Farnham's advice to factory employers, consider the significance of his reference to the "ancestor's environment" of the black workers.
What other clues does this document provide as to the racist
underpinnings of Farnham's approach to managing black
workers?*

Last year some of our more progressive corporations
awoke to the fact that there was a vast reservoir of labor—
amounting to over 10,000,000 souls—nearly 11 per cent of
the country's population—as yet practically untapped for
manufacturing purposes. With true American initiative
these corporations sent agents into the South. Negro settlements were placarded with notices setting forth the high
wages and the ideal living conditions prevailing in the
North. Trainloads of negro mammies, pickaninnies and all
that miscellaneous and pathetic paraphernalia of mysterious
bundles and protesting household pets which accompanies
our colored citizen on his pilgrimages moved into St. Louis,
Kansas City and Chicago, and from there were distributed to
the industrial centers of the country. . . .

The really serious problem which confronts the would-
be user of negro labor is that of handling his negroes in such
a way as to avoid disastrous loss of operating efficiency. . . .
The mistake most foremen make is that they use the same
method with the negro that they use with white labor. . . .

Once the plant executives, the foremen who come in
contact with the workmen, realize that the negro is different
physically, temperamentally and psychologically from any of
the white races, the battle is half won. . . . The man who

hates the negro very seldom ever gets on with him. The
darky is as quick to feel dislike as a child and resents it accordingly. The man who regards his antics at first with
amused toleration is much more likely to eventually control
him, although there will be a great many periods of discouragement when the amateur overseer will feel very much as
did A. B. Frost's dominie who rescued the bull calf and undertook to lead him to safety with the latter tied about his
waist. Sympathy and understanding are necessary but senti-
mentality is fatal, as experience demonstrates. . . .

The rank and file of negroes require more supervision
than the rank and file of whites. By this I do not mean more
"driving" nor more "watching," I mean constructive supervision in the sense of thinking for and looking ahead for. We
must provide the negro with the foresight of which his ancestor's environment has largely deprived him. . . .

A certain amount of segregation is necessary at times to
preserve the peace. This is especially true when negroes are
first introduced into a plant. It is a question if it is not always best to have separate wash rooms and the like. In
places where different races necessarily come into close contact and in places where inherited characteristics are especially accentuated, it is better to keep their respective
folkways from clashing wherever possible. . . .

SOURCE: Dwight Thompson Farnham, "Negroes a Source of Industrial
Labor," *Industrial Management* 56, no. 2 (August 1918): 123–128, from Eric
Arnesen, *Black Protest and the Great Migration: A Brief History with
Documents* (Boston: Bedford/St. Martin's, 2003), 74–78.

ANALYZING THE EVIDENCE

➤ When historians analyze historical events, they seek to uncover their causes. What explanation do the migrants' letters
give for the Great Migration? Is it the same as that given by
Farnham? How do you explain the difference?

➤ In addition to the violence of the postwar race riots discussed
on page 698, urban African Americans suffered from unemployment as factories cut back production. After reading Farnham's selection, suggest several reasons why southern black
migrants were often "the last hired and the first fired."

➤ Do the migrants' letters give any clues as to why migration out
of the South continued after World War I, despite the problems blacks encountered in the North?

German Beer, Mexican Workers

Immigrants from Germany owned and managed most of the breweries in the United States. But the workers at the Maier and Zoblein Brewery in Los Angeles circa 1900 came from many nations, including Mexico. About four thousand Mexicans lived in Los Angeles County in 1900 (about 4 percent of the population); by 1930, there were 150,000 Mexicans in Los Angeles, about 7 percent of the rapidly growing city. Los Angeles Public Library.

Wartime Reform: Woman Suffrage and Prohibition

Many progressive reformers used the war effort to push for improvements in women's lives. Mary Van Kleek, an industrial sociologist, joined the Department of Labor to lobby for equal pay for women workers, and Pauline Goldmark, a social reformer from the National Consumer's League, advocated more employment opportunities for women in her role as a railroad administrator. More important, women's groups used the war ef-

fort to secure two constitutional amendments: woman suffrage and **Prohibition.**

Suffrage Victory: Alice Paul. When the war began, the National American Woman Suffrage Association (NAWSA) threw the support of its two million members behind the Wilson administration. Its president, Carrie Chapman Catt, argued that women had to prove their patriotism to advance the cause of the suffrage movement. In response, NAWSA women in communities all over the country labored exhaustively to promote food

"Over Here": Women's Wartime Opportunities

Working Women at the Puget Sound Navy Yard, Washington, 1919. National Archives.

Women took on new jobs during World War I by working as mail carriers, police officers, heavy machinery operators, and farm laborers attached to the Women's Land Army. Black women, who were customarily limited to employment as domestic servants or agricultural laborers, found that the war opened up new opportunities and better wages in industry. When the war ended, black and white women alike usually lost jobs deemed to be men's work. However, in 1919, when an anonymous photographer took this picture, these women riveters were still hard at work at the Puget Sound Navy Yard near Seattle, Washington.

ANALYZING THE EVIDENCE

➤ Look carefully at the picture. What had the women been doing when asked by the photographer to pose for this shot? What clues indicate the work activities of the women?

➤ Why do you imagine that the photograph was taken? If this photograph had been published in a Seattle newspaper, how might viewers have responded to it?

➤ Although the women are posed, the men in the background seem to be acting in a spontaneous fashion.

How might we interpret their behavior?

➤ What does the photograph suggest about the women's attitude about their work as ship-builders?

➤ The presence of black women indicates diversity in the wartime Seattle workforce. Does anything in the photo tell us about the relationship between white and black women in the shipyards?

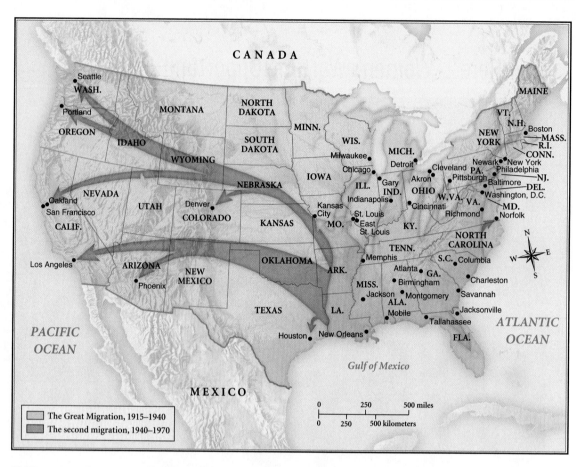

MAP 22.3 The Great Migration and Beyond

Employment opportunities that opened up during World War I and World War II served as catalysts for the Great Migration of African Americans out of the rural South. In the first migration, which began in 1915, blacks headed primarily to industrial cities of the North and Midwest, such as Chicago, New York, and Pittsburgh (see Comparing American Voices, "The Great Migration," pp. 686–687). During World War II, blacks' destinations expanded to include the West, especially Los Angeles, the San Francisco Bay Area, and Seattle. This map simplifies a complex process of movement by individuals and families, who often moved several times and retained close ties with kinfolk in the South.

conservation, to protect children and women workers, and to distribute emergency relief through organizations like the Red Cross.

Alice Paul and the National Woman's Party (NWP) took a more militant tack to win the vote. Born and raised as a Quaker, whose ranks had produced some of the leading women reformers of the nineteenth century, Paul graduated from Swarthmore College, worked in the settlement house movement, and in 1912 earned a Ph.D. in political science at the University of Pennsylvania. Inspired by the militant British suffragist Christabel Pankhurst, Paul became a congressional lobbyist for NAWSA. Increasingly frustrated by the refusal of political leaders to support woman suffrage, in 1916 she founded the NWP, which immediately undertook an activist campaign of mass meetings and parades. In July 1917, Paul and other NWP militants began picketing the White House, standing as "Silent Sentinels" and holding woman suffrage banners—perhaps the first instance of group nonviolent civil disobedience in American history. Arrested for "obstructing traffic" and sentenced to seven months in jail, Paul and the women protestors went on a hunger strike, which prison authorities met with forced feeding. Public shock at the women's treatment drew renewed attention to the issue of woman suffrage and put new pressure on the Wilson administration.

Alice Paul, Suffragist and Politician

Taking advantage of the newest technology, Alice Paul goes on the radio in 1922 to announce plans for the dedication of the Washington headquarters of the National Women's Party. Despite her success in winning the vote for women, Paul was unable to mobilize support for a separate political party to represent their interests. Copyright Bettmann/Corbis.

Impressed by the patriotism of the NAWSA and worried by the militancy of Paul and the NWP, President Wilson sensed that his campaign to make the world safe for democracy had to begin at home. In January 1918, he urged support for woman suffrage as a "war measure." The constitutional amendment quickly passed the House of Representatives but took eighteen months to get through the Senate and another year to win ratification by the states. Finally, on August 26, 1920, Tennessee gave the Nineteenth Amendment the last vote it needed. The goal that had first been declared publicly at the Seneca Falls convention in 1848 was finally achieved seventy-two years later, thanks in part to the war emergency.

Moral Reform, Family Welfare, and Prohibition. Other activists used the war to advance their agendas. Moral reformers concerned with vice and prostitution joined with military officials to keep the army "fit to fight." They encouraged the government to educate soldiers about sexually transmitted diseases and to shut down "red-light" districts near military training camps. With the assistance of two Protestant Christian organizations, the Young Men's Christian Association and the Young Women's Christian Association, government officials warned young men and women about the dangers of sexual activity and celebrated the value of "social purity."

Other reformers pressed for measures to protect the families of army recruits. Responding to re-

ports of economic hardship among working-class military families, Congress enacted the War Risk Insurance Act in 1917. The act required enlisted men and noncommissioned officers to allot $15 of their monthly military pay to their dependents; the federal government contributed an additional allowance to the dependents of servicemen, disbursing almost $570 million between 1917 and 1921. This program of federal regulation and assistance was unprecedented; although short-lived, these wartime family assistance programs would shape the welfare programs established in the New Deal era (see Chapter 24).

An even more dramatic intrusion of the federal government into people's private lives resulted from the efforts of prohibitionists. On the eve of World War I, nineteen states had passed prohibition laws, and many other states allowed local communities to regulate liquor sales. Generally, only industrial states with large immigrant populations, such as Massachusetts, New York, Rhode Island, Illinois, and California, had resisted the trend toward restricting the sale and consumption of alcoholic beverages.

Many progressives supported prohibition. Urban reformers, worried about alcoholic husbands, impoverished families, and public morality, considered a ban on drinking as a benefit to society rather than a repressive denial of individual freedom. In rural communities many people equated liquor with the sins of the city: prostitution, crime, immigration, machine politics, and public disorder. The churches with the greatest

Safe Sex, Vintage 1919

To teach young American men how to avoid venereal diseases, the War Department used posters, pep talks, and films. There were no effective treatments for venereal infections until 1928, when Alexander Fleming discovered penicillin, and so the army urged soldiers to avoid prostitutes or use condoms. *Fit to Fight* starred handsome Ray McKee, who had already appeared in eighty films, and was directed by E. H. Griffith, who would go on to direct sixty Hollywood films between 1920 and 1946. Social Welfare History Archives Center, University of Minnesota / Picture Research Consultants & Archives.

strength in rural areas, including Methodists, Baptists, and Mormons, also strongly condemned drinking. Protestants from rural areas dominated the membership of the Anti-Saloon League, which had supplanted the Woman's Christian Temperance Union as the leading proponent of prohibition.

Temperance advocates knew their enemies. The liquor industry flourished in cities, especially among recent immigrants from Europe and citizens of German and Irish descent. Most saloons were located in working-class neighborhoods and served as gathering places for workers. Machine politicians conducted much of their business in bars. Consequently, many immigrants and working-class people opposed prohibition; they demanded the freedom to drink what they pleased and resented the attempt of progressive reformers and religious zealots to destroy their ethnic cultures.

However, the fervor of World War I gave political momentum to the prohibitionist cause. Intense anti-German hysteria was one spur to action. Because many major breweries—Pabst, Busch, Schlitz—had been founded by German immigrants, many Americans felt that it was unpatriotic to drink beer. Beer consumption also declined because Congress undertook to conserve scarce food supplies by prohibiting the use of barley, hops, and other grains in breweries and distilleries. The national prohibition campaign culminated in December 1917, when Congress passed the Eighteenth Amendment. Ratified by nearly every state by 1919 and effective on January 16, 1920, the amendment prohibited the "manufacture, sale, or transportation of intoxicating liquors" anywhere in the United States (Map 22.4).

The Eighteenth Amendment was the most striking example of the wartime success of a progressive reform. It also stood as yet another example of the widening influence of the national state on matters of economic policy and personal behavior. Unlike woman suffrage, the other constitutional amendment that won wartime passage, Prohibition never gained general acceptance and was repealed with the Twenty-first Amendment in 1933.

Promoting National Unity

The progressive educator and philosopher John Dewey, a staunch supporter of American involvement in World War I, argued that wars represented a "plastic juncture" when societies became open to reason and new ideas. Rudolph Bourne, a one-time pupil of Dewey's and an outspoken pacifist, strongly disagreed. "If the war is too strong for you to prevent," Bourne asked, how can you "control and mold [it] to your liberal purposes?"

MAP 22.4   Prohibition on the Eve of the Eighteenth Amendment, 1919

Well before the adoption of the Eighteenth Amendment in 1919, the temperance crusade had won bans on the legal sale of alcoholic beverages in many states. Maine, North Dakota, and Kansas had been dry since the nineteenth century; a few southern states joined the movement during the Progressive era; but the rush to prohibition came only during World War I, when it became unpatriotic to distill scarce grain into alcohol or to buy beer from German American brewers. Most states that resisted prohibition were heavily urban and industrial or had large numbers of immigrants and German Americans.

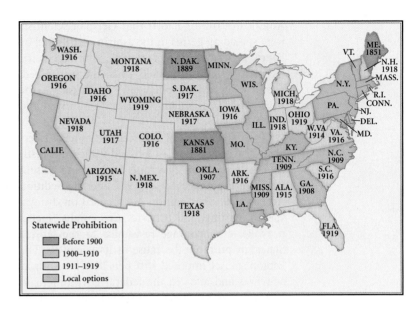

President Wilson shared Bourne's pessimism about the effect of wartime passions: "Once lead this people into war, and they'll forget there ever was such a thing as tolerance." But the president also recognized the need to create support for the war. "It is not an army we must shape and train for war, it is a nation." By backing the campaign to promote "One Hundred Percent Americanism," Wilson undermined the spirit of reform that had elevated him to the highest office in the land.

George Creel and Wartime Propaganda. In April 1917 Wilson formed the Committee on Public Information (CPI) to promote public support for the war. This government propaganda agency, headed by the journalist George Creel, attracted progressive reformers and muckraking journalists such as Ida Tarbell and Ray Stannard Baker. Professing lofty goals — educating citizens about democracy, promoting national unity, assimilating immigrants, and breaking down the isolation of rural life — the committee acted as a nationalizing force by promoting the development of a common ideology.

The CPI touched the lives of practically every American. It distributed seventy-five million pieces of patriotic literature and, by enlisting thousands of volunteers — "four-minute men" — to deliver short pro-war speeches at local movie theaters, reached a huge audience. Creel called the CPI "the world's greatest adventure in advertising" and hoped it would "inspire" patriotism without in-

flaming passions. However, by 1918 the committee was encouraging its speakers to use inflammatory stories of alleged German atrocities to build support for the war effort.

Curbing Dissent. As a spirit of conformity pervaded the home front, many Americans found themselves the targets of suspicion. Businesses took out newspaper ads instructing citizens to report to the Justice Department "the man who spreads pessimistic stories, cries for peace, or belittles our efforts to win the war." Posters warned Americans to look out for German spies. A quasi-vigilante group, the American Protective League, mobilized about 250,000 self-appointed "agents," furnished them with badges issued by the Justice Department, and told them to spy on neighbors and coworkers. In 1918, the members of the League staged violent raids against draft evaders and opponents of the war.

The CPI urged recent immigrants and long-established ethnic groups to become "One Hundred Percent Americans" by giving up their Old World customs and ties. German Americans bore the brunt of this Americanization campaign. German music and operas — Beethoven, Bach, Wagner — were banished from the concert halls, and many communities prohibited the teaching of the German language in their schools. Sauerkraut was renamed "liberty cabbage," and hamburgers became "liberty sandwiches" or Salisbury steaks. When the influenza epidemic struck down thousands of

Americans, rumor had it that German scientists were spreading germs in the aspirin distributed by Bayer, a German drug company. Although anti-German hysteria dissipated when the war ended, hostility toward "hyphenated" Americans—the Irish-, Polish-, or Italian-American—survived into the 1920s.

During the war, law enforcement officials tolerated little criticism of established values and institutions. The main legal tools for curbing dissent were the Espionage Act of 1917 and the Sedition Act of 1918. The Sedition Act focused on disloyal speech, writing, and behavior that might "incite, provoke, or encourage resistance to the United States, or promote the cause of its enemies." The Espionage Act imposed stiff penalties for antiwar activities and allowed the federal government to ban treasonous materials from the mails. The postmaster general revoked the mailing privileges of groups considered to be radical, virtually shutting down their publications.

Individuals also felt the long arm of the state. Because the Espionage and Sedition acts defined treason and sedition loosely, they led to the conviction of more than a thousand people. The Justice Department focused particularly on Socialists, who criticized the war and the draft, and on radicals like the Industrial Workers of the World (the IWW, see Chapter 17), whose attacks on militarism threatened to disrupt war production in the western lumber and copper industries. In September 1917 the Justice Department arrested 113 IWW leaders and charged them with interfering with the war effort. Socialist Party leader Eugene Debs was sentenced to ten years in jail for stating that the master classes declared war while the subject classes fought the battles. Victor Berger, a Milwaukee Socialist who had been jailed under the Espionage Act, was twice prevented from taking the seat to which he had been elected in the U.S. House of Representatives.

The courts rarely resisted these wartime excesses. In *Schenck v. United States* (1919), the Supreme Court upheld the conviction of Charles T. Schenck, the general secretary of the Socialist Party. Schenck had not been jailed for violent acts but for mailing pamphlets urging draftees to resist induction into the army. Writing for a unanimous court, Justice Oliver Wendell Holmes declared that the freedom of speech guaranteed by the First Amendment did not extend to words that constituted "a clear and present danger to the safety of the country." The legal restrictions on free speech imposed during World War I became a permanent feature of American life. Well into the twentieth century, the courts used Holmes's "clear and present danger" test to curb individual freedom in the name of national security.

> ➤ How did the nation mobilize its industrial base and manpower to fight World War I? What were the main challenges?

> ➤ What was the impact of World War I on racial and ethnic minorities? On women?

> ➤ In what ways did the government limit civil liberties during the war, and with what justification?

An Unsettled Peace, 1919–1920

The end of the war created a new set of problems. The Wilson administration had to demobilize the troops, return war plants to civilian use, and, most important, negotiate a peace treaty. President Wilson made peacemaking his highest goal and, from December 1918 to June 1919, went to Europe to achieve it. As Wilson bargained and fought with Allied leaders to achieve a moral international order, he ignored urgent domestic issues. Ethnic and racial tensions that had smoldered during the war erupted in controversy and strife. And fears of domestic radicalism boiled over in America's first Red Scare.

The Treaty of Versailles

In January 1917 Woodrow Wilson had proposed a "peace without victory" on the grounds that only a peace among equals could last. His goal was not a "balance of power, but a community of power; not organized rivalries, but an organized common peace." The keystone of Wilson's postwar plan was a permanent League of Nations that would prevent future wars.

The Fourteen Points. President Wilson approached the peace negotiations in France with the zeal of a missionary. Determined to win approval for his vision of a new world order, he was prepared to appeal to "the peoples of Europe over the heads of their rulers." And well he might. Wildly enthusiastic European crowds greeted the American president as a hero; in Paris two million people lined the Champs-Élysées to pay tribute to "Wilson the Just." The president scored a diplomatic victory in January 1919 when the Allies accepted his **Fourteen Points** as the basis for the peace negotiations. In this blueprint for the postwar world, the president called for open diplomacy, "absolute freedom of navigation upon the seas," arms reduction, the removal of trade barriers, and an international commitment to **national self-determination** for the peoples of the Austro-Hungarian, Russian, and German empires. Essential to Wilson's vision was the creation of a multinational organization "for the purpose of affording mutual guarantees of political independence and territorial integrity to great and small States alike." The League of Nations became Wilson's obsession.

The Fourteen Points expressed the spirit of progressivism. Widely distributed as propaganda during the final months of the war, Wilson's plan would extend American ideals — democracy, freedom, and peaceful economic expansion — to the rest of the world. The League of Nations, acting as an international regulatory body (akin to the Federal Trade Commission in the United States), would mediate disputes among nations, supervise

arms reduction, and — according to the crucial Article X of its covenant — curb aggressor nations through collective military action. Wilson hoped that the presence of the League would prevent future wars and thus ensure that the Great War would be "the war to end all wars." By emphasizing these lofty goals, the American president set the stage for disappointment: His ideals for world reformation proved too far-reaching to be practical or attainable.

Negotiating the Treaty. Twenty-seven countries and peoples sent representatives to the peace conference at Versailles, near Paris, many of them hoping the Allied Powers would recognize their claims to national sovereignty. Distrustful of the new Bolshevik regime in Russia and its call for a worker-led revolution against capitalism and imperialism, the Allies deliberately excluded its representatives. That action was hardly surprising; in 1918, the United States, Britain, and Japan had

The Peace at Versailles

This painting by Sir William Orpen of the signing of the peace treaty in the Hall of Mirrors at Versailles in June 1919 captures the solemnity and grandeur of the occasion. Wilson holds a copy of the treaty, with British Prime Minister David Lloyd George to his right and French Premier Georges Clemenceau to his left. The president was justifiably proud of his role in the peace negotiations, but his refusal to compromise doomed the treaty in the U.S. Senate. Imperial War Museum, London.

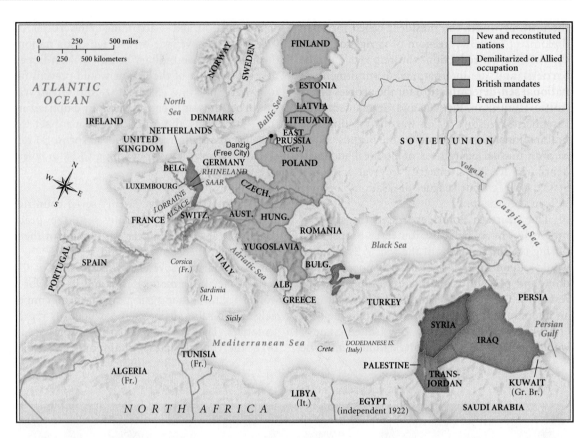

MAP 22.5   Europe and the Middle East after World War I

World War I and its aftermath dramatically altered the landscape of Europe and the Middle East. In central Europe, the collapse of the German, Russian, and Austro-Hungarian empires brought the reconstitution of Poland and the creation of a string of new states based on the principle of national (ethnic) self-determination. The demise of the Ottoman Empire resulted in the appearance of the quasi-independent territories of Iraq, Syria, Lebanon, and Palestine, whose affairs were supervised by one of the Allied Powers under a mandate of the League of Nations.

deployed thousands of troops in Russia to support anti-Bolshevik forces. The victorious Allies also barred Germany from the peace conference, choosing instead to work out the details and impose the completed treaty on their defeated foe.

The Big Four — Wilson, Prime Minister David Lloyd George of Great Britain, Premier Georges Clemenceau of France, and Prime Minister Vittorio Orlando of Italy — did most of the negotiating. The three European leaders sought a peace that differed radically from Wilson's plan. They wanted to punish Germany by demanding heavy reparations and treat themselves to the spoils of war. Indeed, Britain, France, and Italy had already made

secret agreements to divide up German colonies in Africa.

Given the existence of such schemes, it is a tribute to Wilson that he managed to influence the peace settlement as much as he did. The president intervened repeatedly to soften harsh demands for reprisal against Germany. Moreover, he won support for national self-determination, a fundamental principle of the Fourteen Points. In accord with that precept, the Big Four fashioned the independent states of Austria, Hungary, Poland, Yugoslavia, and Czechoslovakia in central Europe and established four new nations along the Baltic Sea: Finland, Estonia, Lithuania, and Latvia (Map 22.5). This string of states, which stretched from the Baltic to the Mediterranean, not only embodied the Wilsonian principle of national self-determination but also served as a *cordon sanitaire*—a sanitary zone protecting the peoples of western Europe from direct exposure to the Communist ideology of Soviet Russia.

Wilson had less success in achieving other goals. The diplomats at Versailles dismantled the empires of the Central Powers but, instead of creating independent states, assigned the colonies to the victorious Allied nations to administer as mandates. France and England received parts of the old Turkish and German empires in the Middle East and Africa, and Japan assumed responsibility for the former German colonies and spheres of influence in the Far East. Still, some of the Allied Powers received less than they wanted. Japan lost face when it failed to win a treaty provision that affirmed racial equality, and Italy protested bitterly when it was denied lands along its border with Yugoslavia and a colony in Africa. Moreover, representatives of colonized peoples, such as Ho Chi Minh, the future revolutionary leader of Vietnam, were generally ignored when they sought freedom for their nations—a decision that had grave consequences for France and the United States in the second half of the twentieth century (see Chapter 29). The resistance of Allied leaders likewise meant that important issues, such as freedom of the seas and free trade, never even appeared on the agenda. Most important, Wilson was unable to deter French and British demands that Germany accept a "war guilt" clause and pay enormous war reparations. In a draconian settlement that left lasting resentment, the Allies forced Germany to give up valuable territories, coal supplies, merchant ships, and valuable patents—and to pay $33 billion in monetary reparations.

The Fate of the Treaty. In the face of these disappointments, Wilson consoled himself with the hope that the League of Nations, which was authorized by the peace treaty, would moderate the terms of the settlement and secure a peaceful resolution of other international disputes. For the United States to participate in the League, he would have to persuade the Senate to ratify the Treaty of Versailles. The outlook was not promising. Although major newspapers and the important religious denominations supported the treaty, the Republican Party had a majority in the Senate and was openly hostile to the agreement.

Opposition to the treaty and the League came from several sources. One group, called the "irreconcilables," consisted of western Republican progressives such as William Borah of Idaho, Hiram Johnson of California, and Robert La Follette of Wisconsin. Isolationist in outlook, they opposed U.S. involvement in European affairs and membership in the League of Nations. Less dogmatic, but more influential, was a group of Republicans led by Senator Henry Cabot Lodge of Massachusetts. Lodge and his allies wanted amendments to Article X of the treaty—the provision for collective security—to ensure that the treaty would not infringe on Congress's constitutional authority to declare war. Beyond that, they worried that Article X would prevent the United States from pursuing an independent foreign policy. Wilson refused to compromise, especially to placate Lodge, a hated political rival. "I shall consent to nothing," he told the French ambassador. "The Senate must take its medicine."

To mobilize popular and political support for the treaty, the president embarked on an extensive and exhausting speaking tour. His impassioned defense of the League of Nations brought large audiences to tears, but the strain proved too much for the sixty-two-year-old president. In late September 1919 in Pueblo, Colorado, Wilson collapsed; a week later, back in Washington, he suffered a severe stroke that left him paralyzed on one side of his body. Wilson still refused to compromise. From his sickbed, the president ordered Democratic senators to vote against all Republican amendments. Brought up for a vote in November 1919, the treaty failed to win the required two-thirds majority; a second attempt, in March 1920, fell seven votes short.

The treaty was dead and so was Wilson's leadership of the nation. Although the president slowly recovered from his stroke, he was never the same. When Wilson died in 1924, David Lloyd George remarked, he was "as much a victim of the war as any soldier who died in the trenches." During the final eighteen months of the Wilson administration, the president's wife, Edith Bolling Galt Wilson, his physician, and the various cabinet heads oversaw the routine business of government.

The United States never ratified the Versailles treaty or joined the League of Nations. Many wartime issues remained partially resolved, notably the enormous reparations demanded from Germany and the fate of Europe's colonial empires amidst rising demands for national self-determination.

These problems played a major role in the coming of World War II; some, like the competing ethnic nationalisms in the Balkans, remain unresolved today (see Chapters 25 and 30).

Racial Strife, Labor Unrest, and the Red Scare

"The World War has accentuated all our differences," a journalist in the popular periodical *World's Work* acutely observed. "It has not created those differences, but it has revealed and emphasized them." In the aftermath of the war, race riots revealed white resistance to the rising expectations of African Americans. Thousands of strikes exposed class tensions, and an obsessive government-led hunt for foreign radicals reflected deep-seated anxieties about social order and the nation's ethnic pluralism.

Race Riots. Many African Americans emerged from the war determined to insist on their rights as American citizens. Thousands had fought for their country; millions of others had loyally supported the war effort. Black demands for equal treatment simply exacerbated white racism and violence. In the South, the number of lynchings rose from forty-eight in 1917 to seventy-eight in 1919, including several of African American soldiers in their military uniforms. In the northern states, now home to tens of thousands of southern-born blacks, race riots broke out in more than twenty-five cities. One of the first and most deadly riots occurred in 1917 in East St. Louis, Illinois; nine whites and more than forty blacks died in a conflict sparked by competition over jobs at a defense plant. In Chicago, five days of rioting in July 1919 left twenty-three blacks and fifteen whites dead. By the end of that summer, the death toll from racial violence had reached 120.

The causes of the Chicago riot were similar to those in other cities. The arrival of fifty thousand African American newcomers during the war years had strained the city's social fabric and increased racial tensions. Blacks competed with whites — many of them recent arrivals from central Europe — for scarce housing and jobs. Unionized white workers

Chicago Race Riot

Racial violence exploded in Chicago during the summer of 1919, and photographer Jun Fujita was on the scene to capture it. As one of the few Japanese immigrants in Chicago at the time, Fujita was probably no stranger to racism, and it took personal courage to put himself in the midst of the escalating violence. When the riot finally ended, thirty-eight people were dead and more than five hundred were injured. Chicago Historical Society / Photo by Jun Fujita.

General Strike in Seattle

Seattle was a strong union town, and 110 local unions took part in the 1919 general strike that paralyzed the city. Although the strike was peaceful, city officials deputized local citizens for police duty, such as this ragtag group of volunteers being issued guns. Museum of History and Industry, Seattle, WA.

deeply resented blacks who served as strikebreakers; indeed, in some stockyards and packing plants, white workers considered the words *Negro* and *scab* to be synonymous. In close elections, black voters often held the balance of power, which allowed their leaders to demand political favors and patronage positions.

Ethnic conflicts over jobs and patronage had long been part of the urban scene, but racism turned them into violent confrontations. When gangs of young white men bombed or burned houses in African American neighborhoods or attacked their residents, blacks fought back in self-defense and for their rights as citizens. Wilson's rhetoric about democracy and self-determination had raised their expectations, too.

A Year of Strikes, 1919. Workers also had higher expectations. The economic prosperity and government regulations of the war years had brought them higher pay, shorter hours, and better working conditions. As workers tried to maintain and advance these gains, employers tried to cut high wartime wages and root out unions. Consumers and native-born Americans generally sided with management. They blamed workers for the rapidly rising cost of living, which jumped nearly 80 percent between 1917 and 1919, and remained suspicious of unions, which they identified with radicalism and foreigners.

These developments set the stage for a massive confrontation between employers and workers. In 1919 more than four million wage laborers—one

in every five—went on strike, a proportion never since equaled. The year began with a walkout by shipyard workers in Seattle, a strong union town, and spread into a general strike that crippled the city. Another major strike disrupted the steel industry; 350,000 workers demanded union recognition and an end to twelve-hour shifts and the seven-day workweek. Elbert H. Gary, the head of the United States Steel Corporation, refused to negotiate; he hired Mexican and African American strikebreakers, maintained substantial production, and eventually broke the strike. Public employees fared no better. Late in the year, the Boston police force shocked many Americans by demanding union representation and going on strike to get it. Governor Calvin Coolidge of Massachusetts propelled himself into the political spotlight by declaring, "There is no right to strike against the public safety by anybody, anywhere, any time." Coolidge fired the entire police force, and the strike failed. The public supported the governor's decisive action, and the Republican Party rewarded Coolidge by nominating him in 1920 as its vice presidential candidate. The impressive gains made by workers and unions during the war swiftly melted away. Inflation cut workers' purchasing power, corporate managers attacked workers' unions, and judges issued coercive injunctions against picketers and strikers. Lacking public support, unions declined in numbers and strength throughout the 1920s.

The Red Scare and the Palmer Raids. A majority of white Americans opposed unions because they feared radicalism. The socialist outlook of many recent immigrants frightened native-born citizens, and the communist ideology of the Russian Bolsheviks terrified them. President Wilson shared these concerns. Embarking for Europe in 1919, he warned of "a flood of ultraradicalism, that will swamp the world." When the Bolsheviks founded the Third International (or Comintern) in 1919, an organization intended to export Communist ideology and foster revolutions throughout the world, Americans began to see radicals everywhere. Hatred of the German "Huns" was quickly replaced by hostility toward the Bolshevik "Reds."

Ironically, as public concern about domestic Bolshevism increased, radicals were rapidly losing members and political power. Of the fifty million adults in the United States in 1920, no more than 70,000 belonged to either the fledgling U.S. Communist Party or the Communist Labor Party in 1919. Both the International Workers of the World and the Socialist Party had been weakened by wartime repression and internal dissent. Yet the public and the press continued to blame almost every disturbance, especially labor conflicts, on alien radicals. "REDS DIRECTING SEATTLE STRIKE—TO TEST CHANCE FOR REVOLUTION," warned a typical newspaper headline.

Political tensions mounted amid a series of terrorist threats and bombings in the spring of 1919. In April, alert postal workers discovered and defused thirty-four mail bombs addressed to prominent government officials. In June a bomb detonated outside the Washington townhouse of the recently appointed attorney general, A. Mitchell Palmer. Palmer and his family escaped unharmed, but the bomber was blown to bits. Angling for the presidential nomination, Palmer capitalized on the event by fanning fears of domestic radicalism.

With President Wilson virtually incapacitated, Palmer had a free hand. He set up an antiradicalism division in the Justice Department and appointed J. Edgar Hoover to direct it. Hoover's division shortly became the Federal Bureau of Investigation (FBI). Then the attorney general staged the first of what became known as "Palmer raids." In November 1919, on the second anniversary of the Russian Revolution, Palmer's agents stormed the headquarters of radical organizations. The dragnet pulled in thousands of aliens who had committed no crime but were suspect because of their anarchist or revolutionary beliefs or their immigrant backgrounds. Lacking the protection of U.S. citizenship, they could be deported without a formal indictment or trial. In December 1919 the USS *Buford*, nicknamed the "Soviet Ark," sailed to Russia with a cargo of 294 deported radicals—including the famous anarchists Emma Goldman and Alexander Berkman.

The peak of Palmer's power came with his New Year's raids in January 1920. In one night, with the greatest possible publicity, federal agents rounded up six thousand radicals. They invaded private homes, union headquarters, and meeting halls—arresting citizens and aliens alike and denying them access to legal counsel. Palmer was riding high in his ambitions for the presidency, but then he overstepped himself. He predicted that on May Day 1920 an unnamed radical conspiracy would attempt to overthrow the U.S. government. State militia units and police went on twenty-four-hour alert to guard the nation against the threat of revolutionary violence, but not a single incident occurred. As the summer of 1920 passed without major labor strikes or renewed bombings, the hysteria of the Red Scare began to abate, and Palmer faded from view.

The Sacco and Vanzetti Case. The wartime legacy of antiradicalism and anti-immigrant sentiment persisted well into the next decade. At the height of the Red Scare in May 1920, police in South Braintree, Massachusetts, arrested Nicola Sacco, a shoemaker, and Bartolomeo Vanzetti, a fish peddler, for the robbery and murder of a shoe company's paymaster. Sacco and Vanzetti were self-proclaimed anarchists and Italian aliens who had evaded the draft; both were armed at the time of their arrest. Convicted of the paymaster's murder and sentenced to death in 1921, Sacco and Vanzetti sat on death row for six years while supporters appealed their verdicts. Although evidence suggesting their innocence surfaced, Judge Webster Thayer denied a motion for a new trial. Scholars still debate the question of their guilt, but most agree that the two anarchist immigrants did not receive fair handling by the judicial system. As the future Supreme Court justice Felix Frankfurter said at the time, "The District Attorney invoked against them a riot of political passion and patriotic sentiment."

The war—with its nationalistic emphasis on patriotism and traditional cultural values—left ugly racial, ethnic, and class tensions in its wake. Still, the United States emerged from World War I as a much stronger nation than when it entered. Unlike its European allies and enemies, it had suffered relatively few casualties and no physical destruction to its lands or cities. Indeed, thanks to the war, the

The Passion of Sacco and Vanzetti by Ben Shahn
(1931–1932)

Ben Shahn (1898–1969) came to the United States from Lithuania as a child and achieved fame as a social realist painter and photographer. Shahn used his art to advance his belief in social justice. In this painting, Sacco and Vanzetti lie dead and pale, hovered over by four distinguished Massachusetts citizens. Judge Webster Thayer, who presided at their trial in 1921, stands in a window in the background; the grim-faced men holding lilies, a symbol of death, are President A. Lawrence Lowell of Harvard and the two other members of a commission appointed by the governor in 1927 to review the case. The commission concluded that the men were guilty, a finding that led to their execution. Copyright Geoffrey Clements / CORBIS, Copyright Estate of Ben Shahn/VAGA, New York.

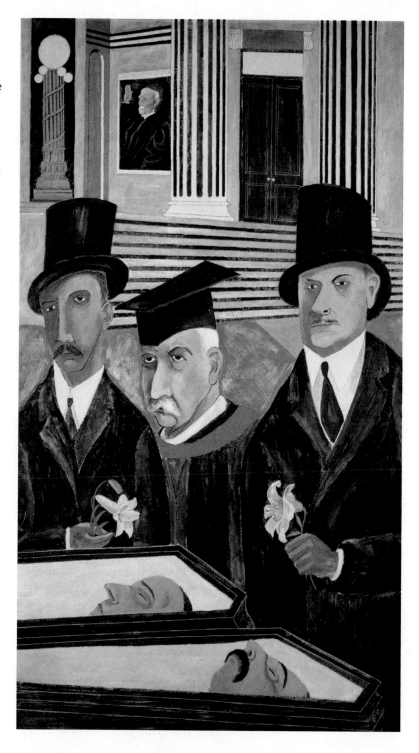

United States had become a major international power, both economically and politically.

➤ Describe the peace conference at Versailles. What nations attended? What nations did not? Who became the primary decision makers?

➤ What was President Wilson's vision of the postwar world, and how specifically did he propose to

achieve it? How did other participants at the peace conference react to Wilson's ideas?

➤ What were the main components of the final treaty, and how do you explain the refusal of the United States to ratify it?

➤ What were the main causes and results of postwar social conflicts within the United States?

SUMMARY

In this chapter, we saw that the United States entered the war in 1917 for a variety of reasons: German violations of American neutral rights at sea, cultural and economic ties to the Allied powers, and Wilson's progressive goal of using the power and influence of the United States to end the conflict and create a just world order.

In tracing mobilization on the home front, we explored the problems facing the federal government as it created an army from scratch, boosted agricultural and industrial production, and recruited workers and raw materials for the defense industry. Some reformers — women suffragists, labor organizers, and prohibitionists — successfully used the war emergency to advance their goals. But we also saw how the passions and disruptions of wartime undercut the spirit of progressive reform and increased social tensions. As the fighting in Europe ended, race riots, strikes, and police raids brought violence to American factories and cities.

We also explored the challenges facing Wilson as he sought a just and lasting peace. The Versailles treaty embodied only some of the president's Fourteen Points, and his postwar hopes suffered another blow when the U.S. Senate refused to ratify the treaty, which would have authorized American participation in the League of Nations. Nonetheless, American participation in World War I — first economically and then militarily — set in motion a major shift in international power. The United States emerged from the war as a dominant world power, a position it would retain throughout the twentieth century.

Connections: Diplomacy

As noted in the Summary, during and after World War I the United States was in a position to play a powerful role in international affairs. But the nation lacked both a strong diplomatic tradition and a respected foreign policy bureaucracy. Moreover, the American public and many members of Congress were unwilling to support active engagement in international politics. As a result, during the 1920s and 1930s the United States retreated from diplomatic involvement in European and Asian affairs, except with respect to financial matters. As we stated in the essay that opened Part Five (p. 671), the "dominant economic position" of privately owned American banks and corporations pulled the nation into the world economy.

Our discussion in Chapter 23 will show how American bankers financed the international economic system during the 1920s, assisting Germany to pay war reparations and the Allied Powers to pay their war debts. Chapter 24 will then explain how the collapse of international economy during the Great Depression prompted Americans to question the wisdom of the nation's intervention in World War I and encouraged a further retreat into political isolationism. Only the threat to democracy posed by fascist governments in Germany, Japan, and Italy in the late 1930s allowed President Franklin Roosevelt to persuade a reluctant nation to prepare for a new war. The story of Roosevelt's political and diplomatic initiatives appears in Chapter 25, which also charts the crucial contribution of the United States to the war against the Axis Powers. Coming in quick succession, the First and Second World Wars thrust the United States into world affairs. This diplomatic revolution is one of the central themes of Part Five.

CHAPTER REVIEW QUESTIONS

➤ How did World War I change America — both its standing in the world and at home? Why is the war important enough for the authors of this textbook to give it a full chapter?

➤ Is it fair to say that progressivism shaped America's involvement in World War I — why the United States entered the war, how the nation fought, and Wilson's plan for peace? Why or why not?

➤ In what ways did World War I contribute to the growth of the American state?

TIMELINE

1914	Outbreak of war in Europe
	United States declares neutrality
1915	German submarine sinks *Lusitania*
1916	Woodrow Wilson reelected president
	Revenue Act of 1916 raises taxes
1916–1919	Great Migration of African Americans to North
1917	United States enters World War I
	Selective Service Act initiates draft
	War Risk Insurance Act protects soldiers' families
	War Industries Board established
	Militant demands for woman suffrage
	East St. Louis race riot
	Espionage Act
	Bolsheviks come to power in Russia
	Committee on Public Information established
1918	Wilson proposes Fourteen Points peace plan
	Meuse-Argonne campaign tests U.S. soldiers
	Eugene Debs imprisoned under Sedition Act
	Armistice ends war
	U.S. and Allied troops intervene in Russia
1919	Treaty of Versailles
	Chicago race riot
	Major wave of labor strikes
	Red Scare and Palmer raids
	Schenck v. United States limits free speech
	League of Nations defeated in Senate
	Eighteenth Amendment (Prohibition) ratified
	War Industries Board disbanded
1920	Nineteenth Amendment (woman suffrage) ratified
	Sacco and Vanzetti arrested

FOR FURTHER EXPLORATION

A recent definitive military history of World War I is Hew Strachan, *The First World War* (2004). "The Great War and the Shaping of the 20th Century" at **www.pbs.org/greatwar/index.html** accompanies the PBS documentary series of the same name. The BBC site on World War I contains excellent memoirs, animations, and maps at **www.bbc.co.uk/history/war/wwone**. "The World War I Document Archive" at **www.lib.byu.edu/~rdh/wwi** provides extensive primary documents and Web links. Frank Freidel, *Over There: The Story of America's First Great Overseas Crusade* (1990), offers soldiers' vivid firsthand accounts. Meirion and Susie Harries, *The Last Days of Innocence: America at War, 1917–1918* (1997), captures America's war experience at home and abroad. "Newspaper Pictorials: World War I Rotogravures" at **memory.loc.gov/ammem/collections/rotogravures** uses the Sunday sections of two prominent New York newspapers to chronicle American life and attitudes toward the war. For the war in fiction, begin with William March, *Company K* (1993), and Ernest Hemingway's *In Our Time* (1925) and *A Farewell to Arms* (1929). For the home front, see *Pale Horse, Pale Rider* (1939) by Katherine Anne Porter.

"The Deadly Virus: The Influenza Epidemic of 1918" at **www.archives.gov/exhibits/influenza-epidemic/index.html** describes the outbreak that infected one-fifth of the world's population. See also "Influenza 1918," the PBS companion site at **www.pbs.org/wgbh/amex/influenza**. Leo Robert Klein's "Red Scare" at **newman.baruch.cuny.edu/digital/redscare** explores strikes, race riots, deportations, and various social movements from 1918 to 1920. The Authentic History Center at **www.authentichistory.com/1900s.html** documents racial stereotypes and the movements for suffrage and prohibition. On prohibition, see "Alcohol, Temperance, and Prohibition" at **dl.lib.brown.edu/temperance**. For the Anti-Saloon League, go to the collection of documents, fliers, cartoons, and songs at the Westerville (Ohio) Public Library, **www.wpl.lib.oh.us/AntiSaloon/index.html**. William M. Tuttle Jr., *Race Riot: Chicago in the Red Summer of 1919* (1970), provides analysis of that devastating riot, as well as a summary of the Great Migration of African Americans.

The Library of Congress Web site "American Leaders Speak: Recordings from World War I and the 1920 Election" at **memory.loc.gov/ammem/nfhtml**, offers voice recordings of key figures of the World War I era. "The South Texas Border, 1900–1920" at **memory.loc.gov/ammem/award97/txuhtml/runyhome.html** is a collection of over eight thousand items pertaining to the Lower Rio Grande Valley. Of particular interest is the material on the years surrounding World War I.

TEST YOUR KNOWLEDGE

To assess your command of the material in this chapter, see the Online Study Guide at **bedfordstmartins.com/henretta**.

For Web sites, images, and documents related to topics and places in this chapter, visit **bedfordstmartins.com/makehistory**.

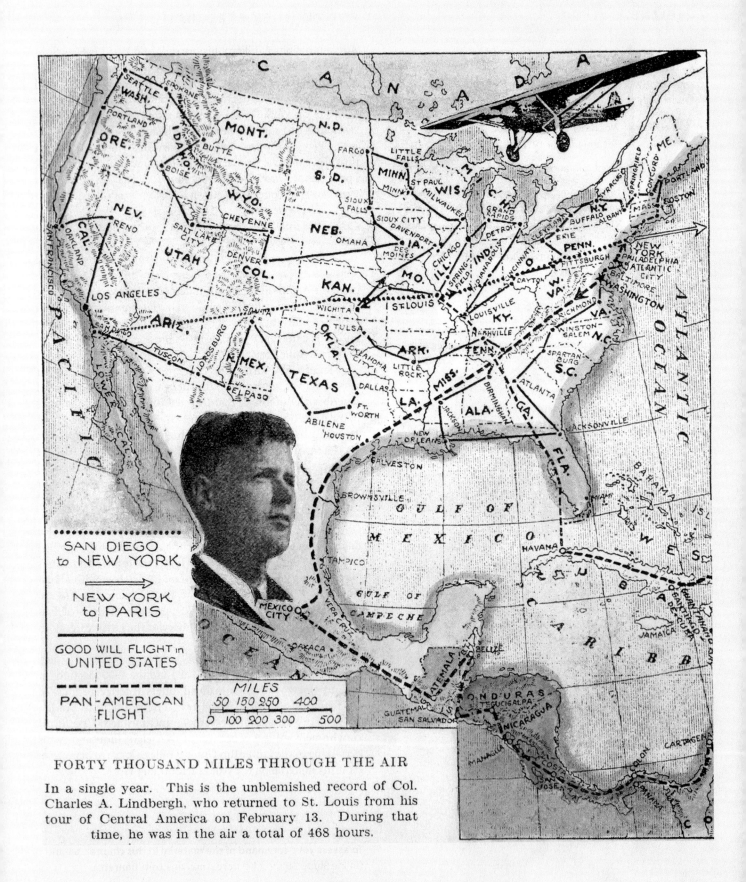

SAN DIEGO to NEW YORK

→ NEW YORK to PARIS

GOOD WILL FLIGHT in UNITED STATES

PAN-AMERICAN FLIGHT

MILES
50 150 250 400
0 100 200 300 500

FORTY THOUSAND MILES THROUGH THE AIR

In a single year. This is the unblemished record of Col. Charles A. Lindbergh, who returned to St. Louis from his tour of Central America on February 13. During that time, he was in the air a total of 468 hours.

23

Modern Times
1920–1932

THE 1920S WAS A DECADE filled with sharp contrasts—between Prohibition laws and speakeasy nightclubs, modern science and fundamentalist religion, economic boom and financial bust, popular heroes and social villains. Charles Lindbergh was one of the heroes. In May 1927, Lindbergh flew his small plane, *The Spirit of St. Louis*, from New York to Paris, a distance of 3,620 miles. He did it alone and without stopping—a tense journey that stretched over 33 hours. Nobody had ever done this before. Returning home to tickertape parades, Lindbergh became *Time* magazine's first Man of the Year in 1928. The handsome young aviator captivated the nation by blending a mastery of modern technological expertise with the middle-class virtues of hard work and individualism. Amidst the grinding routine of life in a modern industrial society, Lindbergh showed that an adventurous individual could make a difference.

The life of Samuel Insull taught Americans the same lesson—with a twist. A financial entrepreneur who was more important than Lindbergh and almost as well known, Insull began the decade as a hero and ended it as a villain. Insull was born in England and came to New York to work as the personal secretary to the great inventor Thomas Edison. In 1892, he moved to Chicago, where he built a small electrical power company into

◄ **Charles Lindbergh (1902–1974), Famous Aviator**

Lindbergh's trans-Atlantic flight instantly made him a celebrity with the catchy nicknames of "Lucky Lindy" and "The Lone Eagle." Financed by Harry Guggenheim, scion of a wealthy mining family interested in promoting aviation, Lindbergh flew the *Spirit of St. Louis* on a goodwill tour in 1928. He touched down in all 48 states, stopped in 92 cities, delivered 147 speeches, and was feted in dozens of parades. Granger Collection.

a giant enterprise. By 1907, Insull's Commonwealth Edison Company was providing electrical power for the entire city; by 1924 his Chicago Rapid Transit Company was offering transportation to many of its residents as well. At the peak of his power in 1929, Insull controlled electric utility companies in five thousand communities in thirty-two states. To finance this utility empire, Insull used the tools of modern capitalism: He created a pyramid of holding companies that allowed him to manage companies valued at $500 million with a personal investment of only $27 million. He funded much of the rest by issuing low-priced stocks and bonds, which nearly one million Americans eagerly snapped up.

As Insull's career shows, many characteristics of modern America were in place by the end of World War I. The war had made the United States a major player in the world and solidified the foundations of the modern American corporate economy. But it was the 1920s that saw the coming of a mass national culture. Thanks to entrepreneurs like Insull and automobile manufacturer Henry Ford, millions of Americans could embrace the new consumer culture with its plethora of assembly-line-produced goods: cars, refrigerators, phonographs, and radios. The economic innovations and prosperity of the 1920s gave Americans the highest standard of living in the world. The values of the nineteenth-century middle classes — the Protestant ethic of hard work, self-denial, and frugality — gave way to a fascination with consumption, leisure, and self-realization, some of the essential features of modern life.

Then, suddenly and unexpectedly, the collapse of the stock market in 1929 and the coming of the Great Depression threw the nation and its political and business leaders into disarray. By 1932, the holding company pyramid built by Samuel Insull had collapsed in bankruptcy, and 600,000 investors had lost their life savings. The Chicago financier fled to Greece and then to Paris, not — like Lindbergh — in triumph but in disgrace. At home, Americans faced silent factories and massive unemployment; the optimism of the 1920s about the promise of American life would now be put to a severe test.

The Business-Government Partnership of the 1920s

The business-government partnership fostered by World War I expanded throughout the 1920s. As the *Wall Street Journal* enthusiastically proclaimed, "Never before, here or anywhere else, has a government been so completely fused with business." And, the *Journal* might have added, so successfully fused. The nation's prosperity from 1922 to 1929 seemed to confirm the wisdom of allowing corporate interests to manage economic life. Gone, or at least submerged, was the reform impulse of the Progressive era (see Chapter 20). Middle-class Americans no longer viewed business leaders as rapacious robber barons; they were now respected — even sacred — public figures. President Calvin Coolidge captured the prevailing public mood when he solemnly declared, "The man who builds a factory builds a temple. The man who works there worships there."

Politics in the Republican "New Era"

With the ailing Woodrow Wilson out of the presidential picture in 1920, the Democrats nominated Governor James M. Cox of Ohio for president and Assistant Secretary of the Navy Franklin D. Roosevelt as vice president. The Democratic platform called for U.S. participation in the League of Nations and a continuation of Wilson's progressivism. The Republicans, now led by the conservative, pro-business wing of the party, selected Ohio Senator Warren G. Harding and Vermont Governor Calvin Coolidge as their candidates. Sensing the desire of many Americans to put the war and the stresses of 1919 behind them, Harding promised "not heroics but healing, not nostrums but normalcy." On election day, he won in a landslide, beginning a Republican dominance that would last until 1932.

Warren Harding had been neither an outstanding state politician in Ohio nor an influential figure in the U.S. Senate. But with victory nearly certain in 1920, Republican Party leaders wanted a candidate they could dominate. Genial, loyal, and mediocre, "Uncle Warren" fit the bill. Harding knew his limitations and assembled a strong cabinet, composed of progressives as well as conservatives, to help him guide the government. Charles Evans Hughes, former reform governor, Supreme Court justice, and presidential candidate, took firm control of the State Department. As secretary of agriculture, Henry C. Wallace created new links with farm organizations while Attorney General Harlan Fiske Stone, a future chief justice, cleaned up the mess at the Department of Justice left by the Palmer Raids. Financier Andrew W. Mellon ran the Treasury Department and quickly reduced the high wartime tax rates, freeing up money for private investment.

The "Associated State." The most active member of the Harding administration was Secretary of Commerce Herbert Hoover, who had successfully headed the Food Administration during the war.

Under Hoover's direction, the Commerce Department fostered the creation of two thousand trade associations representing companies in almost every major industry. Government officials worked closely with the associations, providing them with statistical research, assisting them to devise industry-wide standards, and urging them to stabilize prices and wages. By creating informal governmental ties between government and industry — an "associated state" — Hoover hoped to promote the public interest. His goal was to achieve through voluntary cooperation what Progressive era reformers had sought through governmental regulation.

Unfortunately, not all government-business cooperation served all of the interests of the public. The Republican-dominated Federal Trade Commission (FTC) ignored antitrust laws that forbade restraints on trade, such as collusion among companies on prices. Similarly the Supreme Court, now headed by the former conservative Republican president William Howard Taft, refused to break up the mammoth United States Steel Corporation; as long as there was some competition in the steel industry, the Court ruled, the company's dominant position and ability to set prices were within the law.

The same could not be said about many of President Harding's political associates, who turned out to be dishonest and corrupt. When Harding died suddenly of a heart attack in San Francisco in August 1923, evidence of widespread fraud and corruption in his administration was just coming to light. The worst scandal concerned the secret leasing to private companies of government oil reserves in Teapot Dome, Wyoming, and in Elk Hills, California. Secretary of the Interior Albert Fall was eventually convicted of taking $300,000 in bribes and became the first cabinet officer in American history to serve a prison sentence.

The 1924 Election. Following Harding's death, Vice President Calvin Coolidge moved to the White House. In contrast to his predecessor's political cronyism and outgoing style, Coolidge personified the austere rectitude of a Vermont Yankee. Coolidge's taciturn personality and unimpeachable morality reassured Republican voters, who were drawn primarily from the native-born Protestant middle classes, small business owners, skilled workers, farmers, northern blacks, and wealthy industrialists. To win their backing, Coolidge affirmed his support for business and limited government and announced his candidacy for the presidency in 1924.

When the Democrats gathered to nominate a candidate, they were even more divided than usual. Traditionally the party drew its strength from white voters in the Jim Crow South and immigrant-dominated urban political machines in the North, two constituencies whose interests often collided. Throughout the 1920s, the two groups of Democrats disagreed mightily over Prohibition, immigration restriction, and, most seriously, the mounting power of the racist and anti-immigrant Ku Klux Klan (Map 23.1). These conflicts produced a hopeless

Warren Harding and Calvin Coolidge

The political careers of New Era political leaders Warren G. Harding (1865–1923) and Calvin Coolidge (1872–1933) present a study in contrasts. Harding (left), a small-town politician from Marion, Ohio, was prone to cronyism and mediocrity. Calvin Coolidge (right), of Vermont, was cut from a different cloth: taciturn, upright, stern, and capable. In the wake of the Harding scandals, Coolidge reassured citizens' faith in Republican government by his unimpeachable ethics. © Bettmann/Corbis.

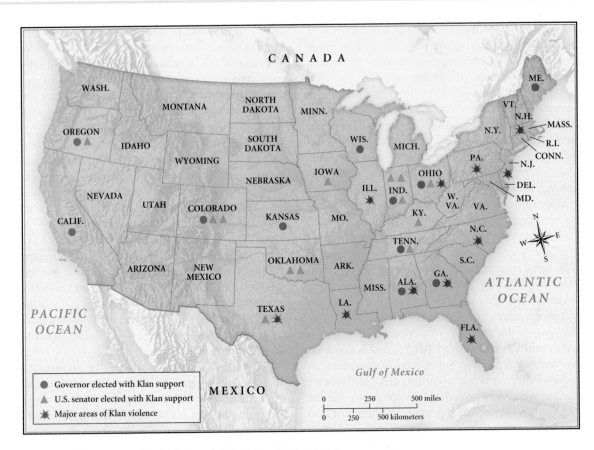

MAP 23.1 Ku Klux Klan Politics and Violence in the 1920s

Unlike the Reconstruction-era Klan, the Klan of the 1920s was geographically dispersed and had substantial strength in the West and Midwest as well as the South. Although the Klan is often thought of as a rural movement, some of its strongest "klaverns" were in Chicago, Los Angeles, Atlanta, Detroit, and other large cities. The organization's members operated as vigilantes in areas where they were strong; elsewhere, their aggressive tactics triggered riots between Klansmen and their ethnic and religious targets.

deadlock between northern supporters of Governor Al Smith of New York and southern and western advocates of former Treasury Secretary William A. McAdoo of California. After 103 ballots, the delegates compromised on John W. Davis, a wealthy and influential Wall Street lawyer who hailed from West Virginia.

The 1924 campaign also featured a third-party challenge by Senator Robert M. La Follette of Wisconsin, who ran on the Progressive Party ticket. La Follette's candidacy mobilized reformers and labor leaders as well as disgruntled farmers. His progressive-minded platform called for nationalization of railroads, public ownership of utilities, and the right of Congress to overrule Supreme Court decisions.

The Republicans won an impressive victory, with Coolidge receiving 15.7 million votes to Davis's 8.4 million and La Follette's 4.9 million. Perhaps the most significant aspect of the election was the low voter turnout. Only 52 percent of the

electorate cast ballots in 1924, compared to more than 70 percent in presidential elections of the late nineteenth century. Newly enfranchised women voters were only partially to blame; a long-term drop in voting by men, rather than apathy among women, caused most of the decline.

Women in Politics. After achieving the suffrage in 1920, women expanded their political activism. Partisan women tried to break into party politics, but Democrats and Republicans granted them only token positions. African American women were equally unsuccessful as they struggled for voting rights in the South and a federal antilynching law. Women were more influential as lobbyists. The Women's Joint Congressional Committee, a Washington-based coalition of ten major white women's organizations, including the newly formed League of Women Voters, lobbied actively for reform legislation. Its major accomplishment was the passage in 1921 of the

The League of Women Voters

The League was the brainchild of Carrie Chapman Catt, the president of the National American Woman Suffrage Association. Formed in 1920, as the Nineteenth Amendment was about to give women the vote, the League undertook to educate Americans to be responsible citizens and to win enactment of legislation favorable to women. The League helped to secure passage of the Sheppard-Towner Act of 1921, which provided federal aid for maternal and child-care programs. In the 1930s, members campaigned for the enactment of the Social Security and other social welfare legislation. Library of Congress.

Sheppard-Towner Federal Maternity and Infancy Act. The first federally funded health-care legislation, the act aimed to lower high rates of infant mortality by funding medical clinics, prenatal educational programs, and visiting nurse projects. The act was controversial. Conservatives charged that it was both a Communist plot to socialize American medicine and an attack on the rights of the states, which traditionally handled public health measures. Indeed, many men in Congress voted for the Sheppard-Towner Act only because they feared that otherwise newly enfranchised women would vote

them out of office. By the late 1920s, when it became clear that women did not vote as a bloc, Congress cut off appropriations for the program.

As support for progressive reform languished on the national level, some state leaders pursued ambitious agendas. In New York, where urban social-welfare liberalism was coalescing under the leadership of Al Smith and Robert Wagner (see Chapter 20), new legislation expanded aid to public schools, added benefits to workers' compensation programs, and created new state forests, scenic parks, and automobile parkways. However, the dominant motif of the 1920s was limited government. Responsibility for the well-being of the country lay increasingly in the hands of its corporate business leaders.

Corporate Capitalism

The revolution in business management that began in the 1890s finally triumphed in the 1920s. Large-scale corporate bureaucracies headed by chief executive officers (CEOs) replaced individual- or family-run enterprises as the major form of business organization. Few CEOs owned a significant part of their enterprises; the owners — thousands of stock shareholders — no longer controlled daily operations. Moreover, many corporations were so large that they dominated their markets; what the famous eighteenth-century economist Adam Smith had called the "invisible hand" of market forces gave way to the "visible hand" of managers who controlled output and prices.

Business Consolidation. Indeed, by 1930 a handful of managers stood at the center of American economic life. As a result of a vigorous pattern of consolidation, the two hundred largest corporations controlled almost half the nonbanking corporate wealth in the United States. During the 1920s businesses combined at a rapid rate, with the largest number of mergers occurring in rapidly growing industries such as chemicals (Dupont), electrical appliances and machinery (Westinghouse and General Electric), and automobiles (General Motors). Rarely did any single corporation monopolize an entire industry; rather, an **oligopoly** of a few major producers dominated the market and controlled prices. The nation's financial institutions expanded and consolidated along with its corporations. Total banking assets rose from $48 billion in 1919 to $72 billion in 1929. Mergers between Wall Street banks enhanced the role of New York as the financial center of the United States and, increasingly, the world. In 1929 almost half the nation's banking resources were controlled by 1 percent of American banks, a mere 250 depositories.

The Economy during the 1920s. Many Americans benefited from the success of corporate enterprise, particularly after 1921. Immediately after World War I, the nation experienced a series of economic shocks. In 1919, Americans spent their wartime savings, causing rampant inflation: Prices jumped by a third in a single year. Then came a sharp two-year recession that raised unemployment to 10 percent and cut prices more than 20 percent. Finally, in 1922 the economy began to grow smoothly and almost continuously. Between 1922 and 1929 the gross domestic product grew from $74.1 billion to $103.1 billion, approximately 40 percent, and per capita income rose impressively from $641 to $847.

An abundance of new consumer products, particularly the automobile, sparked economic growth during the 1920s. Manufacturing output expanded 64 percent during the decade, as factories churned out millions of cars, refrigerators, stoves, and radios. To produce these goods, basic industries supplied huge quantities of raw materials: steel, copper, chemicals, natural gas, electrical power, oil and gasoline. More efficient machinery and new methods of mass production increased workers' productivity by 40 percent. Scientific management, first introduced in 1895 by Frederick W. Taylor (see Chapter 20), also boosted productivity. Widely implemented in the 1920s, these techniques allowed managers to extract greater output from workers.

The economy had some weaknesses. Agriculture — which still employed one-fourth of all workers — never fully recovered from the postwar recession. During the war, American farmers had borrowed heavily to expand production, but as European farmers returned to their fields, the world market was glutted with goods. Prices for wheat dropped by 40 percent, corn by 32 percent, and hogs by 50 percent. As their income plunged, farmers looked to Congress for help. The McNary-Haugen bills of 1927 and 1928 proposed a system of federal price supports for a slew of agricultural products — wheat, corn, cotton, rice, and tobacco. President Coolidge opposed the bills as "class" (special-interest) legislation and vetoed both of them. Between 1919 and 1929, the farmers' share of the national income plummeted from 16 percent to 8.8 percent.

Other "sick industries," particularly coal and textiles, also missed out on the prosperity of the 1920s. Like farmers, these businesses had expanded output during the war and now faced overcapacity and falling prices. This underside of American economic life foreshadowed the Great Depression of the 1930s.

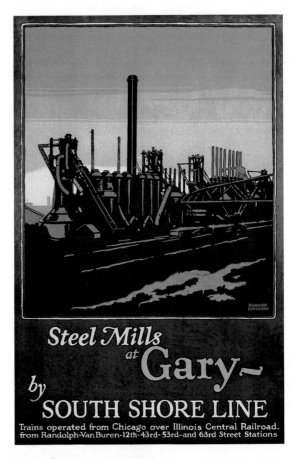

Modern Industry/Modern Art

This dramatic poster, executed by artist Norman Erickson in 1928, promotes the United States Steel Corporation's mills of Gary, Indiana, as a tourist attraction on a par with Yellowstone National Park. And it reflects a new interest in industrial landscapes by serious artists. The Gary experienced by steelworkers had less beauty than Erickson's poster and more soot, grime, and hard work. Yet the artist's eerie orange background captured the color of the heavily polluted sky around Gary's steel mills. Chicago Historical Society.

Welfare Capitalism. Unlike farmers and miners, industrial workers and white-collar employees shared in the prosperity of the 1920s. Henry Ford and other major corporate employers paid their workers well to increase their buying power as consumers. Many industries went to a shorter workweek (five full days and a half day on Saturday), giving their employees more leisure time. Profitable firms, such as International Harvester, offered workers two weeks of paid vacation every year.

The 1920s were also the heyday of **welfare capitalism**, a system of labor relations that stressed management's responsibility for employees' well-being. At a time when unemployment compensation and government-sponsored pensions did not exist, General Electric, U.S. Steel, and other large corporations offered workers health insurance, old-age pension plans, and the opportunity to buy stock in the company at below-market prices. Other firms subsidized mortgages or contributed to employee savings plans. Their goal was to create a loyal and long-serving workforce, particularly among salaried employees, mostly managers and office workers, and important wage workers, such as shop foremen.

Welfare capitalism had a second goal of deterring production-line workers from joining labor unions. In addition to providing ample benefits, some companies set up employee committees to voice workers' complaints and to consult regularly with managers over working conditions. Other corporations attacked unions as un-American because they forced workers to become members; they celebrated the "American Plan" of an open, nonunion shop. Decisions by the conservative-minded Supreme Court undercut union activism and government regulation of the labor market. In *Colorado Coal Company v. United Mine Workers,* the Court ruled that a striking union could be penalized for illegal restraint of trade. The Court also stuck down federal legislation regulating child labor, and in *Atkins v. Children's Hospital,* it voided a minimum wage for women workers in the District of Columbia. Such decisions and aggressive anti-union campaigns caused membership in labor unions to fall from 5.1 million in 1920 to 3.6 million in 1929 — about 10 percent of the nonagricultural workforce. Welfare capitalism seemed to represent the wave of the future in industrial relations.

Economic Expansion Abroad

The growing power of U.S. corporations was clearly apparent in the international arena. American manufacturers actively promoted foreign sales of consumer products: radios, telephones, automobiles, and sewing machines. To supply these markets, firms built factories in foreign countries and bought up existing businesses. General Electric set up production facilities in Latin America, China, Japan, and Australia; General Motors expanded its sales in Europe by taking over the Vauxhall Motor Company in Britain and Opel in Germany. Other American firms invested abroad in new sources of supply. Attracted by lower livestock prices, three major American meatpackers — Swift, Armour, and Wilson — built plants in Argentina. The United Fruit Company developed plantations in Costa Rica, Honduras,

and Guatemala; other American companies set up sugar plantations in Cuba and rubber plantations in the Philippines and Malaya. Standard Oil of New Jersey acquired oil reserves in Mexico and Venezuela (a precursor to American oil investments in the Middle East after World War II). During the 1920s foreign investments by U.S. corporations more than doubled, to a total of $15.2 billion.

American banks were equally active in providing funds to European countries that were rebuilding their war-torn economies. American banks also emerged as key players in the postwar debt system. The banks lent money to Germany, enabling it to pay reparations to the Allied Powers. Britain and France then used these funds to pay off their wartime loans from the United States. While American political leaders insisted on payment of these debts ("They hired the money, didn't they?" scoffed President Coolidge), they made it very difficult to do. The Fordney-McCumber Tariff of 1922 followed the long-standing Republican policy of using high tariffs to exclude foreign-made goods. Unable to sell their goods in the United States, European nations could not easily earn the dollars needed to pay their debts.

In 1924, U.S. diplomats and bankers met with their counterparts from France, Great Britain, and Germany to address the debt situation and to promote European financial stability. The meeting produced the Dawes Plan, named for Charles G. Dawes, the Chicago banker who negotiated the agreement; it reduced the reparations that Germany owed to the Allies and provided substantial American bank loans to assist the Germans to keep up with the payments. The success of the Dawes Plan depended on the continuing flow of American capital to Germany and the ability of the Allies to pay their debts to the United States.

This fragile and unstable system of international finance collapsed in the wake of the American stock market crash in October 1929. The outflow of capital from the United States to Europe slowed and then stopped, undermining the flow of reparation payments. The stock market crisis also increased congressional support for a policy of economic nationalism; the Hawley-Smoot Act of 1930 raised tariffs on imports to an all-time high and made it nearly impossible for the Allied Powers to pay off the remaining $4.3 billion in war loans. Even as American corporations successfully extended their sales and investments to the corners of the earth, American politicians and bankers failed to create a stable structure of international finance.

Bananas
... a good mixer
with every fruit that grows

Oranges, apples, grapefruit, pineapples, pears, melons, grapes—all these and many others—blend perfectly with bananas. The distinctive flavor of the banana, when added to a fruit cup, a fruit salad, or any fruit combination, brings out the flavor of the other fruits and makes them taste better.

"E AT plenty of fresh fruits" is now an accepted principle of diet—and the mere sight of mellow, luscious bananas is an invitation to serve many delicious and nourishing fruit combinations.

All year round from the tropics . . . Easter, Fourth of July, Thanksgiving, Christmas—every season, every day—bananas are available. Thanks to the nearness and all-year-round productiveness of the tropics, they always can be had at your grocery or fruit store.

Children crave the temptingly flavored banana instinctively. And it is well that they do, for bananas are one of the most important energy-producing foods. Doctors and dietitians consider the banana not only one of the most *valuable* foods, but also one of the most *easily digested* . . . as beneficial for grown-ups as for children.

Serve bananas with other fruits, with cereals, with milk or cream . . . or serve them plain. But always be sure they are fully ripe (generously flecked with brown spots). If they are not at the proper stage of ripeness when you buy them, let them ripen at room temperature. Never place them in the ice-box.

UNIFRUIT   BANANAS
Reg. U. S. Pat. Off.
A United Fruit Company Product
Imported and Distributed by Fruit Dispatch Company
17 Battery Place, New York, N. Y.

"Ripe bananas are good for little children."

Foreign Policy in the 1920s

American foreign policy during the 1920s and 1930s was both **isolationist** and internationalist. By refusing to join the League of Nations or the Court of International Justice (the World Court), the United States declined to play an active role in international politics; in this regard, the nation's stance was clearly isolationist. However, as the efforts of American diplomats to shore up the international financial system suggest, the United States pursued a vigorous, internationalist economic policy. Moreover, officials in the Department of State and the Department of Commerce worked constantly to open up new foreign markets for American manufacturers and bankers and to protect existing American interests in other countries.

These initiatives were particularly important in the Caribbean and Latin America, where the United States had a long history of economic activity and military intervention. Both continued during the 1920s. To quell civil unrest and exclude European intervention, the U.S. government dispatched troops to the Dominican Republic from 1916 and 1924. American military forces likewise remained in Nicaragua almost continuously from 1912 to 1933 and in Haiti from 1915 to 1934. Relations with Mexico remained tense, a legacy of U.S. intervention during the Mexican Revolution (see Chapter 21) and of the Mexican government's efforts to **nationalize** its oil and mineral deposits — a policy that alarmed Standard Oil of New Jersey (owned primarily by the Rockefeller family) and other U.S. petroleum companies with investments in Mexico.

The Washington Conference and the Kellogg-Briand Pact. As the United States continued to seek a dominant position in the Western Hemisphere, it sought to reduce its political and military commitments in East Asia and in Europe. The Washington Naval Arms Conference of 1921 revealed American strategy in the Pacific. Secretary of State Charles Evans Hughes won acceptance of a bold plan that placed strict limits on naval expansion. His goal was to deter both excessive expenditures on arms and the buildup of Japanese naval power, which would give Japan a dominant position in East Asia. The major naval powers agreed to scrap some warships, to halt the construction of large battleships for ten years, and to maintain the tonnage of naval vessels among Britain, the United States, Japan, France, and Italy at a fixed ratio. As one commentator quipped, in a short speech Hughes had sunk "more ships than all the admirals of the world have sunk in a cycle of centuries."

Seven years later, American Secretary of State Frank Kellogg devised another low-cost solution to a European problem. Rather than sign an agreement committing the United States to guarantee the territorial integrity of France, Kellogg persuaded French foreign minister Aristide Briand to support a broader pact condemning militarism. Fifteen nations signed the pact in Paris in 1928; forty-eight more approved it later. The signatories agreed to "condemn recourse to war for the solution of international controversies, and renounce it as an instrument of national policy." U.S. peace groups enthusiastically supported the pact, and the U.S. Senate ratified it eighty-five to one. Critics correctly pointed out that the agreement lacked mechanisms for enforcement and was little more than an "international kiss."

In the end, fervent hopes and pious declarations were no cure for the massive economic, political, and territorial problems created by World War I. U.S. policymakers vacillated, as they would in the 1930s, between wanting to play a larger role in world events and fearing that treaties and responsibilities would limit their ability to act unilaterally. Their diplomatic efforts would ultimately prove inadequate to the mounting international crises of the 1930s that led to World War II.

➤ How do you explain the resurgent popularity of business leaders during the 1920s? What changed from the Progressive era, when corporate executives were held in contempt?

➤ In what ways did government and business work together during the "new era"? What were the sources of this relationship?

➤ Describe American foreign policy — both political and economic — during the 1920s. Is it best characterized as "isolationist" or "internationalist"?

A New National Culture

The 1920s represented an important watershed in the development of a mass national culture. A new emphasis on leisure, consumption, and amusement characterized the era. Automobiles, paved roads, the parcel post service, movies, radios, telephones, mass-circulation magazines, brand names, and chain stores linked Americans — in the mill towns in the southern Piedmont, outposts on the Oklahoma plains, and ethnic enclaves in states along the Atlantic and Pacific coasts — in an expanding web of national experience. In fact, as consumerism spread around the world, American products and culture achieved global influence.

A Consumer Society

In homes across the country during the 1920s, Americans sat down to breakfasts of Kellogg's corn flakes and toast from a General Electric toaster. Then they got into Ford Model Ts to go to work or go shopping at Safeway, A&P, or Woolworths, one of the chain stores that had sprung up across the country. In the evening the family gathered to listen to radio programs like *Great Moments in History,* to catch up on events in the latest issue of *Reader's Digest,* or to enjoy the melodramatic tales in *True Story;* on weekends they might see the newest Charlie Chaplin film at the local theater. Millions of Americans now shared similar daily experiences.

Yet many Americans — blacks, working-class families, and many farmers — did not participate fully in the new commercial culture or accept its middle-class values. As one historian puts it, "Buying an electric vacuum cleaner did not turn Josef Dobrowolski into *True Story*'s Jim Smith." Moreover, the unequal distribution of income limited many consumers' ability to buy the enticing new products. At the height of prosperity in the 1920s, the average annual income for the bottom 40 percent of American families was only $725 (about $8,200 today); after meeting the cost of food, housing, and clothing, they had only $135 to spend on everything else. Many Americans stretched their incomes by buying on the newly devised installment plan that allowed people to purchase cars, radios, refrigerators, and sewing machines "on time." "Buy now, Pay later," said the ads, and millions did. By 1927, two-thirds of American cars were financed through monthly payments, and consumer lending grew to $7 billion a year — the tenth-largest business in the United States.

Electric appliances — refrigerators, radios, fans, irons, vacuum cleaners — were among the most important of the new products and had a dramatic impact on women's lives. While unmarried women increased their participation in the workforce, the primary roles for most married women remained those of housewives and mothers. Electric appliances made housewives' chores less arduous but did not greatly increase their leisure time. More middle-class housewives began to do their own housework and laundry, replacing human servants with electric ones. The new gadgets also raised standards of cleanliness, encouraging women to spend more time doing household chores.

To encourage consumers to view the new products as "necessities" rather than "luxuries," manufacturers were spending no less than $2.6 billion a year on advertising by 1929. A new advertising industry (centered on New York City's Madison Avenue) devised sophisticated ways to spur sales, often aided by experts in the growing academic field of psychology. Some ads featured white-coated doctors to imply scientific approval of their products. Others appealed to people's social aspirations by depicting elegant men and women who smoked certain brands of cigarettes or drove recognizable makes of cars. Ad writers also preyed on people's insecurities, coming up with a variety of socially unacceptable "diseases," such as the dreaded "B.O." (body odor).

Most consumers were not the passive victims of manipulative advertising agencies but willing participants in a new culture. For many middle-class Americans, the traditional criteria for judging self-worth — personal character, religious commitment, and social standing — now had a powerful rival: the gratification of personal desires through the acquisition of more and better possessions.

The World of the Automobile

No possession typified the new consumer culture better than the automobile. "Why on earth do you need to study what's changing this country?" a Muncie, Indiana, resident asked sociologists Robert and Helen Lynd. "I can tell you what's happening in just four letters: A-U-T-O!" The showpiece of modern capitalism, the automobile revolutionized American economic and social life.

Mass production of cars stimulated the prosperity of the 1920s. Before the introduction of the moving assembly line in 1913, Ford workers took

twelve and a half hours to put together an auto; on an assembly line they took only ninety-three minutes. By 1927 Ford was producing a car every twenty-four seconds. Auto sales climbed from 1.5 million in 1921 to 5 million in 1929, a year in which Americans spent $2.58 billion on cars. By the end of the decade, Americans owned 23 million cars — about 80 percent of the world's automobiles — an average of one car for every five people.

The expansion of the auto industry had a ripple effect on the American economy. It stimulated the steel, petroleum, chemical, rubber, and glass industries and, directly or indirectly, provided jobs for 3.7 million workers. Highway construction became a billion-dollar-a-year enterprise, financed by federal subsidies and state gasoline taxes. Car ownership broke down the isolation of rural life, spurred the growth of suburbs, and, in 1924, spawned the first suburban shopping center, Country Club Plaza outside Kansas City.

The auto also changed the way Americans spent their leisure time. Although gasoline was not cheap (about $2.30 a gallon in 2006 prices), they took to the roads, becoming a nation of tourists. The American Automobile Association, founded in 1902, reported that in 1929 about 45 million people — almost a third of the population — took vacations by automobile, patronizing the "autocamps" and tourist cabins that were the forerunners of post–World War II motels. Like the movies, cars changed the dating patterns of young Americans. Contrary to many parents' views, premarital sex was not invented in the backseat of a Ford, but a Model T offered more privacy than did the family living room or the front porch and contributed to increased sexual experimentation among the young.

The Movies and Mass Culture

The new mass media — glossy magazines, radio, and especially movies — did more than anything else to involve Americans in a common national culture. American movies had their roots in turn-of-the-century nickelodeons, where for a nickel a mostly working-class audience could see one-reel silent films such as *The Great Train Robbery*. By 1910 the moviemaking industry had concentrated in southern California, which had cheap land, plenty of sunshine, and varied scenery — mountains, deserts, cities, and the Pacific Ocean — within easy reach. By the end of World War I, the United States was producing 90 percent of all films, and Hollywood reigned as the movie capital of the world.

As directors turned to feature films and began exhibiting them in large, ornate theaters, movies drew their audiences from the middle class as well as the working class. Early movie stars, including Buster Keaton, Charlie Chaplin, Mary Pickford, and Douglas Fairbanks, became idols who helped to set national trends in clothing and hairstyles. Then a new cultural icon, the flapper, burst on the scene to represent emancipated womanhood.

Clara Bow: The "It" Girl. Clara Bow was Hollywood's favorite flapper, a bobbed-hair "jazz baby" who rose to stardom almost overnight. Born into an extremely poor family in Brooklyn, New York, in 1905, Bow dropped out of school in the eighth grade and set her sights on a career as an actress. At the age of eighteen she won a Hollywood contract; three years later she was a star— the lead character in *It*, one of the first movies to gross $1 million. Whatever "It" was, Clara had it. With her boyish figure and shock of red hair, she had a strikingly sensual presence; "she could

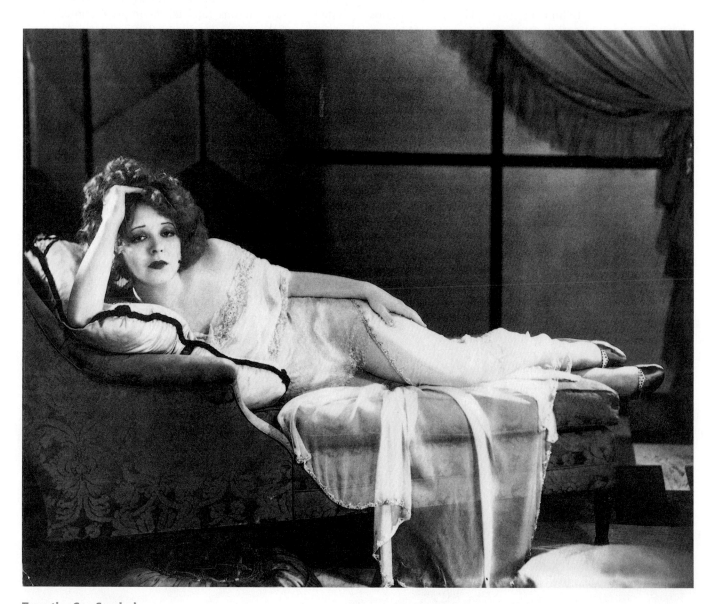

Twenties Sex Symbol

Clara Bow was not the girl next door, as this seductive film still from *Her Wedding Night* (1930) confirms. "I've never taken dope," gushed one seventeen-year-old boy, "but it was like a shot of dope when you looked at this girl." Bow's career was cut short by several nervous breakdowns, some unhappy love affairs, and the arrival of "talkies," which did not suit her style. She left Hollywood in 1931 to marry a Nevada rancher and made her last film in 1932. Culver Pictures.

flirt with the grizzly bear," wrote one reviewer. Thousands of young women took Bow as their model. Decked out in short skirts and rolled-down silk stockings, flappers wore makeup, smoked, danced to jazz, and flaunted their liberated lifestyle. Like so many cultural icons, the flappers represented only a tiny minority of women but, thanks to the movies and advertising industry, they become the symbol of women's sexual and social emancipation.

The movies were big business, grossing $1.6 billion in 1926. The large studios — United Artists, Paramount, and Metro-Goldwyn-Mayer — dominated the industry and were run mainly by eastern European Jewish immigrants such as Samuel Goldfish (later Goldwyn). Movies became even more profitable and culturally powerful with the advent of the "talkies." Warner Brothers' *The Jazz Singer* (1927), starring Al Jolson, was the first

feature-length film to offer sound. Despite the enormous expense — some $300 million — all the major studios quickly made the transition to "talkies." By 1929, the nation's 23,000 movie theaters were selling 90 million tickets a year.

Jazz. That the first talkie was *The Jazz Singer* was not a coincidence. Jazz music captured important aspects of the culture of the 1920s, especially its creative excitement and sensual character. As a word, *jazz* was originally a vulgar term for the sex act; as music, it was (and is) an improvisational form whose notes are rarely written down. Jazz began in the dance halls and bordellos of turn-of-the century New Orleans and was a thoroughly American — indeed, African American — art form. Most of the early jazz musicians were black, and they carried its rhythms to Chicago, New York, Kansas City, and Los Angeles. The best-known performers were

All That Jazz

The phonograph machine dramatically expanded the popularity of jazz music, which now could be heard at home as well as in a city jazz joint. The success of "Crazy Blues" by Mamie Smith and her Jazz Hounds, which sold a million records in 1920, convinced record companies that there was an African American market for what were called "race records." Composer Perry Bradford plays the piano; Bradford was also the composer of "Keep A Knockin," which Little Richard made into a major rock 'n' roll hit in 1957. Division of Political History, Smithsonian Institution, Washington, D.C.

composer-pianist Ferdinand "Jelly Roll" Morton, trumpeter Louis "Satchmo" Armstrong, composer-bandleader Edward "Duke" Ellington, and singer Bessie Smith, "the empress of the Blues."

Phonograph records increased the appeal of jazz and the blues by capturing their spontaneity and distributing it to a wide audience; jazz, in turn, boosted the infant recording industry. Soon this uniquely American art form had caught on in Europe, especially in France. Because jazz often expressed black dissent to the straightforward, optimistic rhythms of white music, it became popular among certain groups of American whites — young people, intellectuals, social outcasts — who felt stifled by middle-class culture. Later in the century, other African American musical forms — notably rhythm-and-blues and hip-hop — would again subvert middle-class values and inject themes of sex and violence into American popular culture.

Journalism and Radio. Mass-circulation magazines and the radio were also key factors in the cre-ation of a national culture. In 1922 ten magazines claimed a circulation of at least 2.5 million, including the *Saturday Evening Post,* the *Ladies' Home Journal,* and *Good Housekeeping.* Tabloid newspapers, which highlighted crime, sports, comics, and scandals, also became part of the national scene, as did news services such as the Associated Press. Thanks to the AP, people across the United States read the same articles.

The newest instrument of mass culture, professional radio broadcasting, was truly a child of the 1920s. It began in November 1920 when station KDKA in Pittsburgh carried the presidential election returns; a mere nine years later, eight hundred stations, most affiliated with the Columbia Broadcasting Service (CBS) or the National Broadcasting Company (NBC), were on the air and nearly ten million American households (40 percent of the total) owned a radio (Map 23.2). Unlike Europe, where radio was a government monopoly, American radio stations were government licensed but privately owned; they drew their revenue from advertisers and corporate sponsors. One of the most

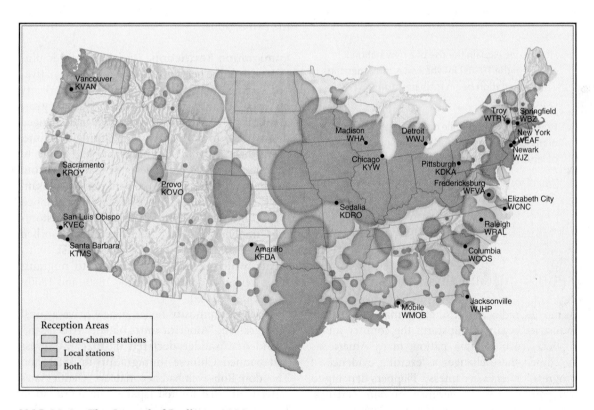

MAP 23.2 The Spread of Radio, to 1939

In 1938 about three-quarters of the U.S. population — approximately 26 million households — owned radios. Four national networks dominated broadcasting, transmitting news and entertainment programs on local stations across the country. Powerful clear-channel stations located in major cities reached listeners hundreds of miles away. By 1939, only sparsely populated areas were beyond radio's reach.

popular radio shows of all time, *Amos 'n' Andy*, which premiered on the NBC network in 1928, featured two white actors playing stereotypical black characters. Stock phrases from the weekly show, like "Check and double check," quickly became part of everyday speech. So many people "tuned in" (a new phrase of the 1920s, similar to "log in" today) to *Amos 'n' Andy* that other activities came to a halt during the show's airtime.

Leisure and Sports. As the workweek shrank and paid vacations increased, Americans had more time and energy to expend on recreation. Cities and suburbs built baseball diamonds, tennis courts, swimming pools, and golf courses. Sports became a big business as private entrepreneurs built huge football and baseball stadiums and formed professional teams to play in them. Fans could attend games, listen to them on the radio, or catch highlights in the movie newsreels. Star athletes — boxer Jack Dempsey, golfer Bobby Jones, baseball slugger Babe Ruth — became national celebrities. Excluded from the white teams, outstanding black athletes like baseball pitcher Satchel Paige played on teams in the Negro National League and the Southern Negro League.

> ➤ How do we explain the rise of a new national culture in the 1920s? In what ways did Americans across the nation begin to share common experiences?
>
> ➤ How did the automobile epitomize the new values of mass consumption and the changing patterns of leisure in America?
>
> ➤ What facets of cultural change does the example of Clara Bow help us to understand?

Redefining American Identity

As movies, radio, advertising, and mass-production industries began to transform the country into a modern, cosmopolitan nation, many Americans welcomed these changes as exciting evidence of progress. Others were uneasy. Flappers dancing to jazz, youthful sexual experimentation in Model Ts, hints of a decline in religious values: These harbingers of a new era worried rural folk and city dwellers who had been born and raised in small towns. They were also troubled by the powerful presence in American cities of millions of Catholic and Jewish immigrants from Europe and African

American migrants from the South. Beneath the clichés of the Jazz Age and the Roaring Twenties were deeply felt tensions that surfaced in conflicts over immigration, religion, Prohibition, and race relations. At stake was no less than the definition of what it meant to be an American.

The Rise of Nativism

Tensions between city dwellers and rural folk escalated sharply during the 1920s. For the first time in the nation's history, more people lived in urban areas — ranging from small towns of 2,500 people to large cities — than in rural areas. And there was no mistaking the trend. During the 1920s about 6 million American left farms for the cities. By 1929, ninety-three cities had populations over 100,000. New York City exceeded 7 million; Chicago boasted almost 3 million, and the population of Los Angeles exploded to 1.2 million. Because political districts did not reflect this population shift, rural areas still controlled most state legislatures. Sharp battles over the use of tax dollars, especially for city services, intensified the growing cultural conflict between the two regions.

Immigration Restriction. Racial and ethnic pluralism lay at the heart of this conflict. When native-born white Protestants — both farmers and city dwellers — looked at their society in 1920, they saw a nation of 105 million people that had changed dramatically in only forty years. During that time, more than 23 million immigrants had come to America, many of them Jews or Catholics from southern and eastern Europe and many of peasant stock. Senator William Bruce of Maryland branded them "indigestible lumps" in the "national stomach," implying that they might never be absorbed into the dominant culture. Such **nativist** sentiments, which recalled the reaction to migrants from Ireland and German in the 1840s and 1850s, were widely shared.

Nativist animosity fueled a new drive against immigration. "America must be kept American," President Coolidge declared in 1924. Congress had banned Chinese immigration in 1882, and Theodore Roosevelt had negotiated a "Gentleman's Agreement" that limited Japanese immigration in 1907 (see Chapter 21). Now nativists charged that there were too many European migrants and certainly too many who were anarchists, socialists, and radical labor organizers. Responding to these concerns, Congress passed an emergency immigration act in 1921 and a more restrictive measure, the

National Origins Act, in 1924. The act cut immigration quotas to 2 percent of each nationality, as reflected in the 1890 census—which had included few people from southeastern Europe and Russia. In 1929 an even more restrictive quota went into effect, setting a cap of 150,000 immigrants per year from Europe and continuing to ban most migrants from Asia.

The new laws continued to permit unrestricted immigration from countries in the Western Hemisphere, and Latin Americans arrived in increasing numbers. Over a million Mexicans entered the United States between 1900 and 1930.

Some fled the chaos of the Mexican Revolution of 1910; many more Mexicans migrated in response to American labor shortages during World War I. Nativists lobbied Congress to cut this flow, and so too did the leaders of labor unions, who pointed out that a flood of impoverished migrants would lower wages for all American workers. But Congress heeded the pleas of American employers, especially large-scale farmers in Texas and California, who wanted cheap labor. Only the coming of the Great Depression cut off migration from Mexico (see Reading American Pictures, "Patrolling the Texas Border," p. 720).

Ku Klux Klan Women Parade in Washington, D.C.
During the 1920s the antiblack and anti-Catholic Ku Klux Klan was a powerful force in American life. Perhaps as many as 500,000 women joined the Women of the Ku Klux Klan (WKKK), including these women who paraded down Pennsylvania Avenue in Washington, D.C., in 1928. The organization was so deeply rooted in the daily lives of many southern and midwestern white Protestants that one woman from rural Indiana remembered her time in the KKK as "just a celebration . . . a way of growing up." National Archives at College Park, MD.

Patrolling the Texas Border

The United States Border Patrol, Laredo, Texas, 1926. University of Texas at Austin.

In 1926, San Antonio photographer Eugene Omar Goldbeck took this photograph of Border Patrol officers in Laredo, Texas. Since 1917, Mexicans, like other immigrants, had been subject to a head tax and a literacy test. However, because of pressure from southwestern employers eager for cheap Mexican labor, the U.S. government had not enforced these provisions and migrant laborers moved back and forth across the border. Following the passage of the National Origins Act of 1924, the federal government established the Border Patrol to prevent Europeans from entering the United States illegally through Canada and Mexico. The Border Patrol focused its enforcements efforts on the Southwest and then mainly to stem the tide of Mexican immigration. In addition to the Border Patrol, new procedures, including bathing, delousing, and medical inspections at key points of entry, "hardened" the border and ended the casual movement of Mexican workers in and out of the United States.

ANALYZING THE EVIDENCE

➤ Goldbeck's photograph is clearly a posed one. What do you suppose was the intent of presenting the Border Patrol in this fashion?

➤ What is the significance of the type of uniforms the officers are wearing?

➤ What aspects of their methods might potentially exacerbate the illegal immigrant problem?

➤ If you were an immigrant worker, how might you read this image?

The New Klan. Another expression of nativism in the 1920s was the revival of the Ku Klux Klan (see Chapter 15). Shortly after the premiere in 1915 of *Birth of a Nation,* a popular film glorifying the Reconstruction-era Ku Klux Klan, a group of southerners gathered on Stone Mountain outside Atlanta to revive the racist organization. Taking as its motto "Native, white, Protestant supremacy," the modern Klan appealed to both urban and rural folk, though its largest "klaverns" were in urban areas. The KKK found significant support in the Far West, the Southwest, and the Midwest, especially Oregon, Indiana, and Oklahoma. The Klan of the 1920s did not limit its harassment to blacks but targeted Catholics and Jews as well. Its tactics remained the same: arson, physical intimidation, and economic boycotts. The new Klan also turned to politics; hundreds of Klansmen won election to local offices and state legislatures (see Map 23.1, p. 708). At the height of its power in 1925, the Klan had over three million members—including a strong contingent of women who pursued a political agenda that combined racism, nativism, and equal rights for white Protestant women.

After 1925 the Klan declined rapidly, undermined by internal rivalries and rampant corruption. Especially damaging was the revelation that Grand Dragon David Stephenson, the Klan's national leader, had kidnapped and sexually assaulted his former secretary, driving her to suicide. In addition, the passage of the National Origins Act in 1924 robbed the Klan of a potent issue. Nonetheless, the Klan remained strong in the Jim Crow South, and during the 1930s, some northern Klansmen supported the American Nazi movement, which shared its antiblack and anti-Jewish beliefs.

Legislating Values: Evolution and Prohibition

Other cultural conflicts erupted over religion and alcoholic beverages. The debate between modernist and revivalist Protestants, which had been simmering since the 1890s (see Chapter 18), came to a boil in the 1920s. Modernists, or liberal Protestants, found ways to reconcile their religious beliefs with Charles Darwin's theory of evolution and other scientific principles. Revivalist Protestants, who were strongly rooted in **fundamentalist** Baptist and Methodist churches, insisted on a literal reading of the Bible. So too did popular evangelical preachers such as Billy Sunday and Aimee Semple McPherson, who used storefront churches and open air revivals to popularize their own blends of charismatic fundamentalism.

The Scopes Trial. Religious controversy entered the political arena when fundamentalists wrote their beliefs into law. In 1925 the Tennessee state legislature made it "unlawful . . . to teach any theory that denies the story of the Divine creation of man as taught in the Bible, and to teach instead that man has descended from a lower order of animals." The American Civil Liberties Union (ACLU), which had been formed during the Red Scare to protect free speech rights, challenged the constitutionality of the law. It intervened in the trial of John T. Scopes, a high school biology teacher, who had taught the principles of evolution to his class and faced a jail sentence

The First Modern Evangelist: Aimee Semple McPherson (1890–1944)

Aimee McPherson founded the Four Square Gospel Church, which now claims a worldwide membership of two million. Born as Beth Kennedy in Ontario, Canada, she married missionary Robert Semple in 1907. After his death in China, she married Harold McPherson and eventually settled in Los Angeles. By 1923, she was preaching to a radio audience and to crowds of 5,000 at her massive Angelus Temple. In 1926 McPherson attracted national attention by disappearing for a month and claiming she was kidnapped. Many suspected she was at a romantic hideaway with the Temple's radio operator, but her preaching career flourished into the 1930s. She died of an overdose of sedatives in 1944.
Copyright Bettmann / Corbis.

for doing so. The case attracted national attention because Clarence Darrow, a famous criminal lawyer, defended Scopes, and William Jennings Bryan, three-time presidential candidate and ardent fundamentalist, spoke for the prosecution.

The press dubbed the Scopes trial the "monkey trial." The label referred both to Darwin's argument that human beings and primates share a common ancestor and to the circus atmosphere at the trial, which was broadcast live over Chicago radio station WGN. The jury took only eight minutes to deliver its verdict: guilty. Though the Tennessee Supreme Court overturned Scopes's conviction, the controversial law remained on the books for more than thirty years (see Comparing American Voices, "The Scopes Trial," pp. 724–725). As the 1920s ended, science and religion were locked in a standoff; beginning in the 1980s, fundamentalists would launch a new attack against Darwin and modern science (see Chapter 32).

The "Noble Experiment." Like the dispute over evolution, Prohibition — the "noble experiment," as it was called — involved the power of the state to enforce social values (see Chapter 22). Americans drank less after the Eighteenth Amendment took effect in January 1920, but those who continued to drink gave the decade its reputation as the Roaring Twenties. Urban ethnic groups — German, Irish, Italian — had long opposed restrictions on drinking and refused to comply with the new law. Some brewed their own beer or distilled "bathtub gin." Many others patronized illegal saloons and clubs, called speakeasies, that sprang up everywhere; there were more than 30,000 speakeasies in New York City alone. Liquor smugglers operated with ease

Defining Beer

The Eighteenth (Prohibition) Amendment banned "intoxicating liquors." Over the strong objections of the beer industry, the Volstead Act of 1919 outlawed beverages with an alcoholic content of more than 0.5 percent. As support for Prohibition declined in the early 1930s, former brewery owners and workers campaigned for the legalization of beer, as in this march. In March 1933, nine months before the repeal of the Prohibition amendment, Congress amended the Volstead Act to allow the manufacture of beer with an alcoholic content of 3.2 percent. Library of Congress.

along Canadian and Mexican borders and used speedboats to land cargoes of wine, gin, and liquor along the Atlantic Coast. Organized crime (the "Mob"), which already had a presence among Italians and Jews in major cities, took over the bootleg trade and grew wealthy from its profits. The "noble experiment" turned out to be a dismal failure.

Those Americans who favored repeal of the Eighteenth Amendment — the "wets" — slowly built support for their cause in Congress and the state legislatures. The coming of the Great Depression hastened the process, as politicians looked for ways to create jobs and raise tax revenue. With the ratification of the Twenty-first Amendment on December 5, 1933, nationwide Prohibition came to an inglorious end.

Intellectual Crosscurrents

As millions of Americans celebrated the military victory in World War I and their peacetime prosperity, influential writers and intellectuals rendered bitter dissents. The novelist John Dos Passos railed at the obscenity of "Mr. Wilson's war" in *The Three Soldiers* (1921) and again in *1919* (1932). Ernest Hemingway's novels *In Our Time* (1924), *The Sun Also Rises* (1926), and *A Farewell to Arms* (1929) also powerfully described the dehumanizing consequences and the futility of war. In his despairing poem *The Waste Land* (1922), T. S. Eliot portrayed a fragmented civilization in ruins.

Influenced by Eliot's dark vision, writers offered stinging critiques of what they saw as the complacent, moralistic, and anti-intellectual tone of American life. In *Babbitt* (1922), the novelist Sinclair Lewis satirized the stifling conformity of a middle-class businessman. In 1925 Theodore Dreiser wrote his naturalistic masterpiece *An American Tragedy* and F. Scott Fitzgerald published *The Great Gatsby,* both probing indictments of the mindless pursuit of material goods and wealth.

Harlem Renaissance. More affirmative works of art and literature emanated from Harlem, the center of African American life in New York City. During the 1920s, Harlem stood as "the symbol of liberty and the Promised Land to Negroes everywhere," as an influential black minister put it. Talented African American artists and writers flocked to Harlem, where they broke with older genteel traditions of black literature to reclaim a cultural identity with their African roots.

The Harlem Renaissance championed racial pride. Authors such as Claude McKay, Jean Toomer,

The Harlem Renaissance

The Crisis, edited by the leading black intellectual W. E. B. Du Bois, was the magazine of the National Association for the Advancement of Colored People (NAACP). With its dramatic use of modern architecture and art, this cover from 1929 suggests the cultural and political awakenings associated with the Harlem Renaissance. Henry Lee Moon Library and Civil Rights Archive, NAACP, Washington, DC.

and Jessie Fauset explored the black experience and represented the "New Negro" in fiction. Countee Cullen and Langston Hughes turned to poetry, and Augusta Savage used sculpture to draw attention to black accomplishments. Zora Neale Hurston spent a decade collecting folklore in the South and the Caribbean and incorporated that material into her short stories and novels. This creative work embodied the ongoing African American struggle to find a way, as the influential black intellectual W. E. B. Du Bois explained, "to be both a Negro and an American."

The poet Langston Hughes, who became a leading exponent of the Harlem Renaissance, captured its affirmative spirit when he asserted, "I am a Negro — and beautiful." Hughes drew on the black artistic forms of blues and jazz in *The Weary Blues* (1926), a groundbreaking collection of poems. Considered the most original black poet and the most representative African American writer of the time, Hughes also wrote novels, plays, and essays.

The Scopes Trial

In 1925, the Tennessee legislature passed a law prohibiting the teaching of the scientific theory of evolution in the state's public schools. The law resulted in the trial of John Scopes in Dayton, Tennessee, and triggered a much broader debate about science and religion, free speech and government power. As the following passages suggest, the participants in these debates began from different premises and came to different conclusions.

JOHN ROACH STRATON
Preserving a Christian Worldview

John Roach Straton was a prominent Protestant minister who, for religious reasons, strongly supported the Tennessee law. He published these remarks in the American Fundamentalist *in 1925.*

The real issue at Dayton and everywhere today is: "Whether the religion of the Bible shall be ruled out of the schools and the religion of evolution, with its ruinous results shall be ruled into the schools by law." The issue is whether the taxpayers — the mothers and fathers of the children — shall be made to support the false and materialistic religion, namely evolution, in the schools, while Christianity is ruled out, and thereby denied their children.

That is the exact issue in this country today. And that it is a very real and urgent issue is proved by the recent invasion of the sovereign state of Tennessee by a group of outside agnostics, atheists, Unitarian preachers, skeptical scientists, and political revolutionists. . . . They left New York and Chicago, where real religion is being most neglected, and . . . went to save from itself a community . . . where man is still regarded, not as a descendant of the slime and beasts of the jungle, but as a child of God. . . .

THE AMERICAN CIVIL LIBERTIES UNION (ACLU)
Defending Free Inquiry in the Classroom

The American Civil Liberties Union (ACLU) was founded during World War I to oppose governmental suppression of free speech and individual rights. The ACLU assisted Scopes's defense and, in a later pamphlet entitled The Gag on Teaching *(1931), condemned the attempts by various private interest groups to use state power to control the content of education.*

The great essential to education is freedom — freedom in presenting and studying all the facts, and freedom of teachers to believe as they see fit and to express their beliefs like other citizens. It holds that, when for any reason this freedom is curtailed, real education itself is crippled.

The professed objects of our educational system have always been freedom from propaganda for private interests, liberty for teachers outside their classrooms, and the training of children without reference to any economic dogma. . . .

During the hysteria of war [World War I], the pattern for interference with education was set, and majority dogmas became firmly entrenched. The dogmas of conventional patriotism developed first as part of the war propaganda, evidenced in the laws for the teaching of the Constitution, flag-saluting, special oaths of loyalty from teachers, and the revision of history textbooks. Then came the efforts of the Ku Klux Klan and the Fundamentalists in the name of Protestantism to outlaw evolution, compel the reading of the Bible (Protestant version) and, in one state [Oregon], to ban all private (meaning Catholic) schools. . . .

The tendencies to restrict freedom of teaching can be fought only by constant agitation, repeal of the present restrictive laws, opposition to specific measures and cases of discrimination and by the growth of teachers' unions to protect teachers' liberties.

THE AMERICAN FEDERATION OF TEACHERS
Freedom: The Key to Knowledge

The American Federation of Teachers joined the ACLU in criticizing political interference and censorship in education. In this Resolution of 1925, the AFT defends the professional expertise of American educators.

In certain states of the union teaching as a constructive social function has been menaced, and may be menaced again, by misguided legislative authority that fears to trust the intelligence, the public spirit and the devotion to duty of the profession whose obligation it is, and whose desire it is, to serve the people by training the children for intelligent citizenship. The reactionary Lusk school laws in the state of New York [which required that teachers subscribe to loyalty oaths] . . . as well as the numerous bills in several states that have been designed to censor the writing and the teaching of history in the schools all reflect the same unfortunate suspicion and mistrust of educational intelligence which the Tennessee anti-evolution law betrays. . . .

Without freedom in the intellectual life, and without the inspiration of uncensored discovery and discussion, there could ultimately be no scholarship, no schools at all and no education. . . .

WILLIAM JENNINGS BRYAN
Let the Sovereign People Decide

William Jennings Bryan endorsed the biblical story of creation, but his defense of the Tennessee law reflected his deep belief in democratic government and the legitimacy of majority rule. In "Who Shall Control" (1925), Bryan offers a robust defense of the law and of his political philosophy.

The first question to be decided is: Who shall control our public schools? . . . Four sources of control have been suggested. The first is the people, speaking through their legislatures. That would seem to be the natural source of control. The people are sovereigns and governments derive their just powers from the consent of the governed. . . . Legislatures regulate marriage and divorce, property rights, descent of property, care of children, and all other matters between citizens. Why are our legislatures not competent to decide what kind of schools are needed, the requirements of teachers, and the kind of instruction that shall be given?

If not the legislatures, then who shall control? Boards of Education? It is the legislature that authorizes the election of boards and defines their duties, and boards are elected by the people or appointed by officials elected by the people. All authority goes back at last to the people; they are the final source of authority.

Some have suggested that the scientists should decide what shall be taught. How many scientists are there? . . . The American Society for the Advancement of Science has about

eleven thousand members. . . . [That] makes about one scientist for every ten thousand people—a pretty little oligarchy to put in control of the education of all the children. . . .

The fourth source suggested is the teacher. Some say, let the teacher be supreme and teach anything that seems best to him. The proposition needs only be stated to be rejected as absurd. The teacher is an employee and receives a salary; employees take directions from their employers. . . . [A] teacher must respect the wishes of his employers on all subjects upon which the employers have a deep-seated conviction. . . .

The Tennessee case is represented by some as an attempt to stifle freedom of conscience and freedom of speech, but the charge is seen to be absurd when the case is analyzed. Professor Scopes, the defendant in the Tennessee case, has a right to think as he pleases—the law does not attempt to regulate his thinking. . . .

Professor Scopes was not arrested for doing anything as an individual. He was arrested for violating a law as a representative of the state and as an employee in a school. . . . The right of free speech cannot be stretched as far as Professor Scopes is trying to stretch it. A man cannot demand a salary for saying what his employers do not want said.

SOURCE: Jeffrey P. Moran, *The Scopes Trial: A Brief History with Documents* (Boston: Bedford/St. Martins, 2002), 211–212, 192–194, 189–191.

ANALYZING THE EVIDENCE

➤ Was the Tennessee battle really a conflict between modern urban values and traditional rural beliefs?

➤ Are there any limits to legislative power? What constitutional provisions might restrict political censorship or the suppression of scientific knowledge?

➤ Does the prescribed teaching of the Christian Bible violate the First Amendment to the Constitution, which forbids the "establishment" of religion?

➤ Is there an inherent conflict between a democratic polity and freedom of intellectual and scientific inquiry?

➤ In recent years, the Japanese government has censored textbooks to exclude information about the "rape of Nanking" in the 1930s (see Chapter 25). How might that controversy be used in debates over the Scopes trial?

The vitality of the Harlem Renaissance was short-lived. During the Jazz Age, when Harlem was in vogue, the wealthy white patrons and influential publishers courted its writers. But white interest and black creativity waned as the depression of the 1930s cut incomes and sparked riots over jobs and living conditions in Harlem and other black districts. However, the writers of the Harlem Renaissance found a new popularity in the 1960s, when their works were rediscovered by black intellectuals during the civil rights movement.

Marcus Garvey and the UNIA. As the Harlem Renaissance built racial pride among artists, the Universal Negro Improvement Association (UNIA) did the same among the black working classes. Led by Jamaican-born Marcus Garvey and based in Harlem, the UNIA championed black separatism. Garvey urged blacks to return to Africa, arguing that peoples of African descent would never be treated justly in countries dominated by whites. The UNIA grew rapidly in the early 1920s and soon claimed four million followers, many of whom were recent migrants to northern cities. It published a newspaper, *Negro World*; opened "liberty halls" in northern cities; and solicited funds for the Black Star Line steamship company, which would trade with the West Indies and carry African Americans back to Africa.

The UNIA declined as quickly as it had arisen. In 1925, Garvey was convicted of mail fraud in connection with his solicitations for the Black Star Line; two years later President Coolidge commuted his sentence but ordered his deportation to Jamaica. Without Garvey's charismatic leadership, his movement quickly collapsed.

Culture Wars: The Election of 1928

Cultural issues — the emotionally charged questions raised by Prohibition, Protestant fundamentalism, and nativism — set the agenda for the presidential election of 1928. The national Democratic Party, now controlled by its northern urban wing, nominated Governor Alfred E. Smith of New York. Smith was the first presidential candidate to reflect the aspirations of the urban working classes and of European Catholic immigrants. The grandson of Irish peasants and a Catholic, Smith began his political career as a Tammany Hall ward heeler, became a dynamic state legislative leader and reformer, and matured as an effective four-term governor of the nation's most populous state.

But Smith had liabilities. He spoke in a heavy New York accent and sported a brown derby that underlined his ethnic working-class origins. Middle-class reformers questioned his ties to the political bosses of Tammany Hall; temperance advocates knew he was a "wet" and opposed his election. Smith's most damaging handicap was his religion. In 1928, Protestant Americans were not ready for a Catholic president. Although Smith insisted that his religion would not affect his duties as president, most Protestants opposed his candidacy. "No Governor can kiss the papal ring and get within gunshot of the White House," declared a Methodist bishop from Buffalo.

The Republican nominee, Secretary of Commerce Herbert Hoover, was also a new breed of candidate. Hoover had never run for any political office and did not run very hard for the presidency, delivering only seven campaign speeches. His candidacy rested on his outstanding career as an engineer and professional administrator; indeed, for many Americans, he embodied the managerial and technological promise of the Progressive era. Beyond that, Hoover had the benefit of eight years of Republican prosperity and strong support from the business community. He promised voters that his vision of individualism and cooperative endeavor would promote prosperity and banish poverty from the United States.

Hoover won a stunning victory. He received 58 percent of the popular vote to Smith's 41 percent and 444 electoral votes to Smith's 87. Because many southern Protestants refused to vote for a Catholic, Hoover carried Texas, Virginia, and North Carolina — breaking the Democratic "Solid South" for the first time since Reconstruction. Equally significant, Smith won the industrialized states of Massachusetts and Rhode Island and carried the nation's twelve largest cities (Map 23.3). The Democrats were on their way to fashioning a new identity as the party of the urban masses, a reorientation the New Deal would complete in the 1930s.

Ironically, Herbert Hoover's victory put him in the unenviable position of leading the United States when the Great Depression struck in 1929. Having claimed credit for the prosperity of the 1920s, the Republicans could not escape blame for the Depression.

➤ What changes in American society prompted the dissent expressed by nativist activists, the Ku Klux Klan, and religious fundamentalists? How did these groups voice their outrage?

➤ How do you explain the simultaneous appearance of the new Klan, the Harlem Renaissance, and Marcus Garvey's UNIA movement?

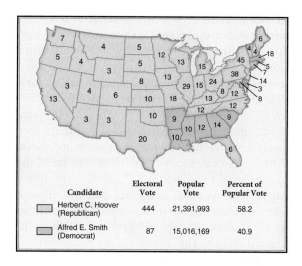

Candidate	Electoral Vote	Popular Vote	Percent of Popular Vote
Herbert C. Hoover (Republican)	444	21,391,993	58.2
Alfred E. Smith (Democrat)	87	15,016,169	40.9

MAP 23.3 Presidential Election of 1928

Historians still debate the extent to which 1928 was a critical election — an election that produced a significant realignment in voting behavior. Although the Republican Herbert Hoover swept the popular and the electoral votes, Democrat Alfred E. Smith won majorities not only in the South, his party's traditional stronghold, but also in Rhode Island, Massachusetts, and (although it is not evident on this map) all of the large cities of the North and Midwest. In subsequent elections, the Democrats won even more votes among African American and European ethnic groups and, until 1980, were the nation's dominant political party.

The Onset of the Great Depression, 1929–1932

Booms and busts are characteristic features of the **business cycle** in capitalist economies, and they were familiar features of the American landscape. Since the early nineteenth century, the United States had experienced recessions or panics about every twenty years. But none was as severe as the Great Depression of the 1930s, and none lasted as long.

Causes and Consequences

The economic downturn began slowly and almost imperceptibly in 1927. For five years Americans had spent at a faster pace than their wages and salaries had risen. As consumers ran out of cash and credit, spending declined and housing construction slowed. Soon inventories piled up; in 1928, manufacturers began to cut back production and lay off workers, reducing incomes and reinforcing the slowdown. By the summer of 1929, the economy was clearly in recession.

The Great Crash. Although a few commentators noted the slowdown in production, many more focused on the rapid rise in the stock market. Stock prices surged 40 percent in 1928 and 1929, as investors got caught up in speculative frenzy. On "Black Thursday," October 24, 1929, and again on "Black Tuesday," October 29, the bubble burst. On those two bleak days, more than 28 million shares changed hands in panic trading. Practically overnight, stock values fell from a peak of $87 billion to $55 billion.

The crash exposed long-standing weaknesses in the economy. Agriculture was in the worst shape because farm products sold at low prices throughout the 1920s. In 1929 the yearly income of a farmer averaged only $273, compared to $750 for other occupations. Because farmers accounted for a fourth of the nation's workers, their meager buying power dragged down the entire economy. Two other major industries — railroads and coal — had also fallen on hard times. As automobile and truck traffic increased, railroad revenues from passenger travel and freight shipments declined, forcing several railroads into bankruptcy. Coal mining companies experienced similar financial difficulties. Battered by overexpansion, obsolescent machinery, and bitter labor struggles, they faced sharp competition from other sources of energy: hydroelectric power, fuel oil, and natural gas. A final structural weakness was the unequal distribution of wealth. In 1929, the top 5 percent of American families received 30 percent of the aggregate income while the bottom 50 percent of American families received only about 20 percent — most of which was spent on food and housing. Once the depression began, a majority of the population lacked sufficient buying power to revive the economy.

The Great Crash had a massive social impact. It wiped out the savings of thousands of individual investors and dealt a severe blow to many banks, which had invested heavily in corporate stocks or lent money to speculators. Hundreds of banks failed, and because bank deposits were uninsured, depositors lost some or all of their money. Frightened customers withdrew their savings from solvent banks, which responded by closing their doors and thus deepening the crisis.

The Financial Panic Becomes a Depression. The American economy went rapidly downhill following the crash on Wall Street. Between 1929 and 1933, the U.S. gross domestic product fell almost by half, from $103.1 billion to $58 billion. Consumption dropped by 18 percent, construction by 78 percent, and

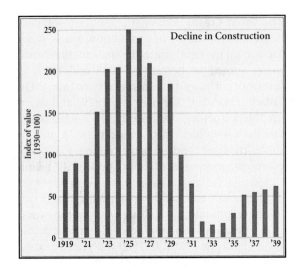

FIGURE 23.1 A Statistical Index of Boom and Bust

This graph shows the fluctuations in the construction industry between 1919 and 1939, as measured by the value of new building permits. The building boom reached its peak in 1925 and then slowly declined until 1930, when it plunged to record lows. Recovery was underway by 1936 and, because the prices of wages and materials had fallen, was more vigorous than the graph suggests. SOURCE: *Historical Statistics of the United States, Colonial Times to 1970* (Washington, D.C.: U.S. Government Printing Office, 1975), 626.

private investment by 88 percent. Nearly 9,000 banks went bankrupt or closed their doors and 100,000 businesses failed (Figure 23.1). The consumer price index declined by 25 percent, and corporate profits fell from $10 billion to $1 billion. Most tellingly, unemployment rose from 3.2 percent to 24.9 percent; 12 million people were out of work, and many who had jobs took wage cuts (Figure 23.2). "We didn't go hungry," said one family, "but we lived lean."

The economic downturn became self-perpetuating. The more the economy contracted, the longer people expected the decline to last; so corporations declined to invest in new plants and consumers refused to buy new cars or appliances. Economic stagnation solidified: "You could feel the depression deepen," recalled writer Caroline Bird.

The Worldwide Depression. President Hoover later blamed the severity of the American Depression on the international economic situation, and his analysis had considerable merit. During the 1920s the flow of international credit hinged on the willingness of American banks and corporations to make loans and investments in European countries, allowing them to pay reparations and war debts and to buy U.S. goods. As the domestic

economic crisis deepened, U.S. banks and companies reduced their foreign investments, disrupting the European financial system. As economic conditions in Britain, Germany, and France worsened, European demand for American exports fell drastically. When the Hawley-Smoot Tariff of 1930 raised rates to all-time highs, European governments retaliated by imposing their own trade restrictions. To protect its economy, Great Britain also abandoned the "gold standard," the system used to adjust the values of international currencies. As other countries quickly followed Britain's example, European markets for American goods, especially agricultural products, contracted sharply. The troubles of American farmers deepened.

As the crisis undermined the economies of the wealthy North Atlantic nations, it had a major impact on world trade. In 1929 the United States had produced 40 percent of the world's manufactured goods. When American companies cut back production, they also cut back purchases of raw materials and supplies abroad. Their decisions reverberated around the world—reducing the demand for Argentine cattle, Brazilian coffee, Chinese silk, Mexican oil, Indonesian rubber, and African minerals. The crash of 1929 undermined fragile economies around the globe and brought on a worldwide depression.

Herbert Hoover Responds

Campaigning for the presidency in 1928, Herbert Hoover looked forward to a "final triumph over poverty." Once elected, he foresaw an era of Republican prosperity and governmental restraint and, even after the Great Crash, stubbornly insisted that the downturn was temporary. "The Depression is over," he told a delegation of business executives in June 1930.

As the depression continued, the president adopted a two-pronged strategy. Reflecting his ideology of voluntarism and his reliance, as secretary of commerce, on the business community, the president turned first to corporate leaders. Hoover asked business executives to maintain wages and production levels and to work with the government to rebuild Americans' confidence in the capitalist economic system.

But Hoover recognized that voluntarism might not be enough, given the depth of the crisis, and so turned as well to government action. Soon after the stock market crash, he won cuts in federal taxes in an attempt to boost private spending and corporate investment, and he called on state and local governments to increase capital expenditures on public

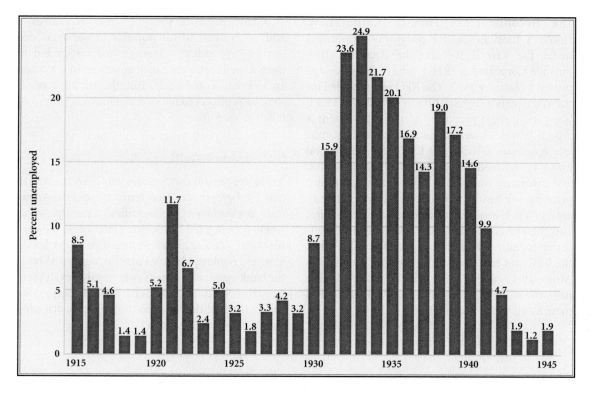

FIGURE 23.2 Unemployment, 1915–1945

During the 1920s, business prosperity and low rates of immigration resulted in historically low unemployment levels. The Great Depression threw millions of people out of work; by 1933 one in four American workers was unemployed, and the rate remained high until 1941, when the nation began to mobilize for war.

works. By 1932, the president had secured an unprecedented increase in federal spending for public works to $423 million. Some of his initiatives were misguided: The Revenue Act of 1932, which increased taxes to balance the budget and lower interest rates, choked both consumption and investment.

Similarly, his refusal to consider direct federal relief for unemployed Americans and to rely on private charity—the "American way," he called it—was a mistake; unemployment during the depression was too massive for private charities and state and local relief agencies to handle (Map 23.4).

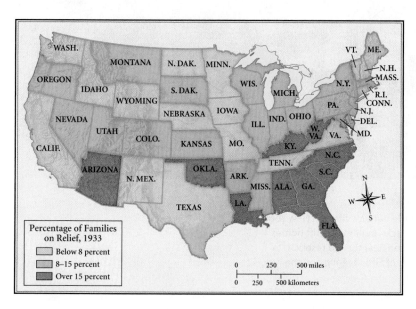

MAP 23.4 The Great Depression: Families on Relief, to 1933

Although the Great Depression was a nationwide crisis, some regions were hit harder than others. Economic hardship was widespread in the agricultural-based southern and Appalachian states and, to a lesser extent, in the industrial states of the Northeast and Midwest. As the depression worsened in 1931 and 1932, local and state governments, as well as charitable organizations, could not keep up with the demand for relief. After Franklin D. Roosevelt assumed the presidency in 1933, the national government began a massive program of aid through the Federal Emergency Relief Administration (FERA).

The Reconstruction Finance Corporation. Hoover's most innovative program—continued under the New Deal—was the Reconstruction Finance Corporation (RFC), which Congress approved in January 1932. The RFC was modeled on the War Finance Corporation of World War I and, like that agency, gave the federal government a crucial role in American economic life. To stimulate economic activity, the RFC provided federal loans to railroads, financial institutions, banks, and insurance companies. This strategy of **pump priming**—infusing funds into the major corporate enterprises—was designed to increase production and thereby create new jobs and invigorate consumer spending. This plan might have worked, but the RFC was too cautious in lending the money. Although Congress allocated $1.5 billion to the RFC, the agency had expended only 20 percent of these funds by the end of 1932.

Compared with previous chief executives—and in contrast to his popular image as a "do-nothing" president—Hoover had responded to the national emergency with government action on an unprecedented scale. But the nation's needs were also unprecedented, and Hoover's programs failed to meet them.

Rising Discontent

As the depression continued, many citizens came to hate Herbert Hoover. New terms entered the American vocabulary: "Hoovervilles" (shanty towns where people lived in packing crates) and "Hoover blankets" (newspapers). Rising discontent led to violence. Bankrupt farmers banded together to resist the bank agents and sheriffs who tried to evict them from their land. Thousands of other farmers joined the Farm Holiday Association; they barricaded

Hoovervilles

By 1930 homeless people had built shantytowns in most of the nation's cities. In New York City squatters camped out along the Hudson River railroad tracks, built makeshift homes in Central Park, or lived in the city dump. This photograph, taken near the old reservoir in Central Park, looks east toward the fancy apartment buildings of Fifth Avenue and the Metropolitan Museum of Art, at left. Grant Smith / Corbis.

local roads and, to protest low prices, dumped milk, vegetables, and other foodstuffs on the roadways. Layoffs and wage cuts led to violent industrial strikes. When coal miners in Harlan County, Kentucky, went on strike over a 10 percent wage cut in 1931, the mine owners and the National Guard crushed the union. A confrontation in 1932 between workers and security forces at the Ford Motor Company's giant River Rouge factory left three workers dead and fifty with serious injuries.

In 1931 and 1932 civil disorder appeared in the nation's cities. Unemployed citizens demanded jobs and bread from local authorities while hard-pressed wage earners staged rent strikes. Some of these crowd actions were the work of the Communist Party, which hoped to use the depression to undermine Americans' commitment to the capitalist system. Although these strikes and marches received broad support and often got results from city and state governments, they won few converts to communism. In the early 1930s, the Communist Party was a tiny organization with only 12,000 members.

Not radicals but veterans staged the most publicized — and most tragic — protest. In the summer of 1932, the "Bonus Army," a ragtag group of about 15,000 unemployed World War I veterans, hitchhiked to Washington to demand immediate payment of their bonuses, a pension payment that was due to be paid in 1945. "We were heroes in 1917, but we're bums now," one veteran complained bitterly. While their leaders lobbied Congress, the Bonus Army camped out a few miles from the U.S. Capitol building. When the marchers refused an order to leave their camp, Hoover called out regular army troops under the command of General Douglas MacArthur, who would become a leading general during World War II. MacArthur's troops burned the encampment to the ground and, in the fight that followed, injured more than a hundred marchers. When newsreel footage showing the U.S. Army attacking its veterans was shown in movie theaters across the nation, Hoover's popularity plunged.

The 1932 Election

Despite this discontent, the nation was not in a revolutionary mood as it neared the election of 1932. Many middle-class Americans had internalized the ideal of the **self-made man** and blamed themselves for their economic hardships. Despair and apathy, not anger, was their mood (see Voices from Abroad, "Mary Agnes Hamilton: Breadlines and Beggers," p. 732). The Republicans, who could find no credible way to dump an

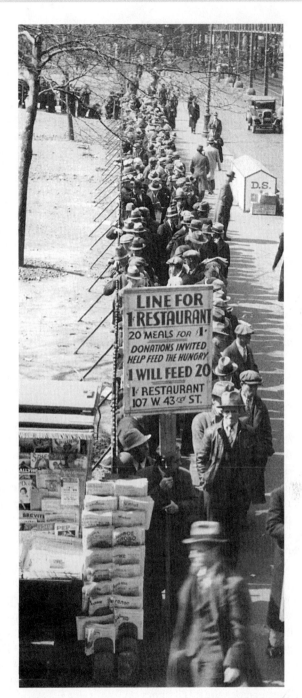

The Breadline

Some of the most vivid images from the depression appear in pictures of long breadlines and of respectable-looking men selling apples on street corners. All the people in this breadline are men; many women chose to endure deprivation rather than violate standards of respectable behavior by soliciting aid in public. Franklin D. Roosevelt Library, Hyde Park, NY.

Mary Agnes Hamilton

Breadlines and Beggars

British writer and Labor Party activist Mary Agnes Hamilton arrived in New York on a gloomy morning in December 1931. Following a lecture tour that took her as far west as Nebraska, Hamilton wrote a book conveying her impressions of American life. Her observations of conditions in New York City during the grim winter of 1931–1932 suggest the devastation and despair gripping urban America.

One does not need to be long in New York (or for that matter in Chicago, in Cleveland, in Detroit, in Kansas, or in Buffalo) to see that there are plenty of real tragedies, as well as plenty of not-so-real ones. . . . In New York, one has only to pass outside the central island bounded by Lexington and Sixth Avenues to see hardship, misery, and degradation, accentuated by the shoddy grimness of the shabby houses and broken pavements. Look down from the Elevated [railway], and there are long queues of dreary-looking men and women standing in "breadlines" outside the relief offices and the various church and other charitable institutions. Times Square, at any hour of the day and late into the evening, offers an exhibit for the edification of the theater-goer, for it is packed with shabby, utterly dumb and apathetic-looking men, who stand there, waiting for the advent of the coffee wagon run by Mr. W. R. Hearst of the *New York American*. . . . At every street corner, and wherever taxi or car has to pause, men try to sell one apples, oranges, or picture papers. Not matches — matches, in

book form, are given away with every fifteen-cent package of cigarettes, lie on every restaurant table, litter the street, half used, and exemplify how little, as yet, the depression has done to overcome the national habit of easy-going wastefulness. On a fine day, men . . . line every relatively open space, eager to shine one's shoes. It is perhaps because so many people are doing without this "shine," or attempting with unfamiliar hands and a sense of deep indignity to shine their own, that the streets look shabby and the persons on them so much less well-groomed than of yore. The well-shod feet of the States struck me forcibly on my first visit; the ill-cleaned feet of New York struck me as forcibly in January and April 1932. In 1930 an English friend, long domesticated in New England, told me that she hesitated to bring her children to London, since the sight of beggars would make so painful an impression on them; in 1932 there are more beggars to be met with in New York than in London. Yes, distress is there; the idle are there. How many, no one really knows. Ten million or more in the country; a million and a half in New York are reported. They are there; as is, admittedly a dark undergrowth of horrid suffering that is certainly more degraded and degrading than anything Britain or Germany knows. Their immense presence makes a grim background to the talk of depression: there is an obscure alarm as to what they may do "if this goes on." . . .

The American people, unfamiliar with suffering, with none of that long history of catastrophe and calamity behind it which makes the experience of European nations, is outraged and baffled by misfortune. Depression blocks its view: it cannot see round it. Misled in the onset by leaders who assured it, in every soothing term and

tone, that reverse was to last but for a little while; that it was the preliminary to recovery; that American institutions were immune to the ills that had laid the countries of the rest of the world upon their backs; that prosperity was native to the soil of the Union, and all that was needed was to wait till the clouds, blown up by the wickedness of other lands, rolled by, as they were bound to do, and that speedily; the nation now suffers from a despair of any and every kind of leadership. Every institution is assailed; even the sacred foundations of democracy are being undermined. The defeatism that has been so lamentably evidenced in Congress is not peculiar to Congressmen, any more than is the crude individualism of their reactions. It lies like a pall over the spirit of the nation. It is felt by most people to be, in fact, the greatest obstacle to recovery, to that restoration of confidence for which everybody pleads, which everybody sees as necessary. But how to break it nobody knows.

SOURCE: Mary Agnes Hamilton, "In America Today," in *America through British Eyes,* ed. Allan Nevins (Gloucester, MA: Peter Smith, 1968), 443–444.

ANALYZING THE EVIDENCE

➤ Why might Hamilton believe that the condition of the idle in America is "more degraded and degrading than anything Britain or Germany had experienced"?

➤ What is Hamilton's opinion of the reaction of America's political leaders to the depression? Is it a valid assessment?

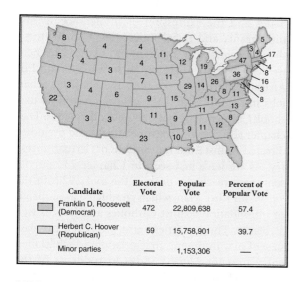

Candidate	Electoral Vote	Popular Vote	Percent of Popular Vote
Franklin D. Roosevelt (Democrat)	472	22,809,638	57.4
Herbert C. Hoover (Republican)	59	15,758,901	39.7
Minor parties	—	1,153,306	—

MAP 23.5 The Presidential Election of 1932

Franklin Roosevelt's convincing electoral victory over Herbert Hoover in 1932 reflected a political realignment among urban voters and mass dissatisfaction with Republican response to the depression. Strikingly, amid this grave crisis in capitalism, the Communist and Socialist presidential candidates received fewer than one million of the nearly forty million votes.

incumbent president, unenthusiastically renominated Hoover. The Democrats turned to Governor Franklin Delano Roosevelt of New York, who had persuaded his state's legislature to run up a budget deficit to finance innovative relief and unemployment programs.

Roosevelt was born into a wealthy New York family, a distant cousin to former president Theodore Roosevelt, whose career he emulated. After attending Harvard College and Columbia University, Roosevelt served as assistant secretary of the navy during World War I ("T.R." had done the same prior to the Spanish-American War). Franklin Roosevelt's service in the Wilson administration, in combination with his famous name and strong speaking abilities, earned him the vice presidential nomination on the Democratic ticket in

1920. Then, in 1921, a crippling attack of polio left both of his legs paralyzed for life. Strongly supported by his wife, Eleanor, he returned to public life and campaigned successfully for the governorship of New York in 1928 and again in 1930.

Roosevelt's campaign for the presidency in 1932 foreshadowed little of the New Deal. He pledged vigorous action but gave no indication as to what it might be: "The country needs and, unless I mistake its temper, the country demands bold, persistent experimentation." He won easily, receiving 22.8 million votes to Hoover's 15.7 million. Despite the nation's economic collapse, Americans remained firmly committed to the two-party system. The Socialist Party candidate, Norman Thomas, got fewer than a million votes, and the Communist nominee, party leader William Z. Foster, drew only 100,000 votes (Map 23.5).

Elected in November, Roosevelt would not begin his presidency until March 1933. (The Twentieth Amendment, ratified in 1933, set subsequent inaugurations for January 20.) As FDR waited, Americans suffered through the worst winter of the depression and hoped things would get better. Nationwide, the unemployment rate stood at 20 to 25 percent; in three major industrial cities in Ohio it was staggering: 50 percent in Cleveland, 60 percent in Akron, and 80 percent in Toledo. Public-welfare institutions were totally overwhelmed. Despite dramatic increases in their spending, private charities and public relief agencies reached only a fraction of the needy. The nation's banking system was so close to collapse that many state governors closed banks temporarily to avoid further withdrawals. By March 1933, the nation had hit rock bottom.

➤ What were the causes of the Great Depression? In what ways did foreign events affect the financial downturn?

➤ How did President Hoover respond to the economic emergency?

SUMMARY

By the 1920s the United States was on its way to becoming a modern, urban society based on corporate business enterprises and mass consumption. As we have seen, the Republican Party controlled the national government and fostered a close partnership between business and government. At home, Secretary of Commerce Herbert Hoover promoted industry-wide trade associations to coordinate economic policy; abroad, American diplomats encouraged economic expansion while avoiding direct involvement in international politics.

We also explored the ways in which movies, radio, and other mass media encouraged the development of a national culture. This emergent culture placed a new emphasis on leisure, consumption, and amusement. However, only a minority of Americans could take full advantage of the comfortable, even elegant, lifestyles promoted by the new advertising industry. Families needed a middle-class income to buy all of the conveniences of modern life: cars, radios, vacuum cleaners, and toasters. Most farmers were left outside the charmed circle of prosperity, as were most African Americans and many working-class immigrants from Europe and Mexico.

Not everyone welcomed the new secular values of the 1920s. Cultural disputes over drinking alcoholic beverages, teaching science, and forming immigration policies spilled over into politics, bringing the new Ku Klux Klan to prominence and disrupting the already fractured Democratic Party. Republican political ascendancy continued under President Herbert Hoover, who expected to extend the prosperity of the Twenties and lessen poverty.

Instead, Hoover had to deal with the worst depression in American history. As we have seen, the Great Depression had many causes: speculation in stocks, long-term weaknesses in major industries, and fragile international finances. When Hoover's policies proved unavailing, voters turned to Democrat Franklin D. Roosevelt. The new president entered office faced with massive unemployment, a banking crisis, and a citizenry on the verge of despair.

Connections: Society

As we noted in the essay that began Part Five (p. 671), two central themes of the years between 1914 and 1945 are the migration of people within the United States and the expression of intolerance against immigrants and racial minorities. Both of these themes were clearly apparent in Chapter 22. There we described the migration during World War I of African Americans from the rural South to urban jobs in the North and the postwar race riots that shook Chicago, East St. Louis, and other cities. That chapter also detailed wartime attacks and prejudice directed against American citizens of German ancestry. As we have just seen in Chapter 23, nativist sentiment reached a peak in the mid-1920s in the "new" Ku Klux Klan, which conducted a campaign of intimidation against Catholics and Jews as well as blacks. This sentiment also prompted the passage of new immigration legislation, which limited entry into the United States to residents of the Western Hemisphere. Chapter 24 will continue that story by explaining how the Great Depression of the 1930s prompted the "reverse" migration of people back to Mexico, Asia, and Europe. It will also discuss the movement of hundreds of thousands of farmers from the "dust bowl" states of the Great Plains to California and explain how New Deal agricultural programs prompted a new migration of African Americans from the rural South. Finally, in Chapter 25, we will see that in World War II, as in World War I, internal migration and wartime passions triggered race riots and, in an extreme example of racial prejudice, the internment of more than 100,000 Japanese Americans.

CHAPTER REVIEW QUESTIONS

➤ What were the main cultural conflicts of the 1920s? Are they the same or different from the "culture wars" of the present?

➤ This chapter is titled "Modern Times." What was especially "modern" about the 1920s that made the decade stand out from previous years?

➤ Describe the continuing process of state building in the 1920s. In what ways did the government become more or less active in society, the economy, and American culture?

➤ What problems in the American economy were exposed by the crisis of the Great Depression? To what extent did those economic problems reflect social problems, especially social inequality?

TIMELINE

1920	Eighteenth Amendment outlaws alcoholic beverages First commercial radio broadcast Warren G. Harding elected president Census reveals shift in population from farms to cities
1920–1921	Economic recession cuts jobs
1921	Sheppard-Towner Act assists maternal care Washington Conference supports naval disarmament
1922–1929	Record economic growth expands consumption Automobile Age begins
1922	T. S. Eliot, *The Waste Land*
1923	President Harding dies in office; succeeded by Calvin Coolidge *Time* magazine founded
1924	Dawes Plan reduces German reparation payments Teapot Dome scandal U.S. troops withdrawn from Dominican Republic National Origins Act limits immigration
1925	F. Scott Fitzgerald, *The Great Gatsby* Height of Ku Klux Klan's power Scopes trial over free speech and the teaching of science
1927	First "talkies" in movie industry Charles Lindbergh's solo flight
1928	Herbert Hoover elected president Kellogg-Briand Pact condemning militarism signed
1929	Ernest Hemingway, *A Farewell to Arms* Stock market crash
1930	Hawley-Smoot Tariff cuts imports
1931	Miners strike in Harlan County, Kentucky
1932	Reconstruction Finance Corporation created Bonus Army rebuffed in Washington Communist-led hunger marches in cities Farm Holiday Association dumps produce Franklin D. Roosevelt elected president

FOR FURTHER EXPLORATION

Lynn Dumenil, *The Modern Temper: American Culture and Society in the 1920s* (1995), offers an overview, while Loren Baritz, ed., *The Culture of the Twenties* (1970), provides a collection of documents. For politics and the state, consult Ellis W. Hawley, *The Great War and the Search for a Modern Order: A History of the American People and Their Institutions, 1917–1933* (1979), and Lee Nash, ed., *Understanding Herbert Hoover: Ten Perspectives* (1987). For fiction, see Sinclair Lewis's classics, *Main Street* (1920) and *Babbitt* (1922), and Sherwood Anderson's *Winesburg, Ohio* (1919). The Library of Congress's "Prosperity and Thrift: The Coolidge Era and the Consumer Economy, 1921–1929" at **memory.loc.gov/ammem/coolhtml/coolhome.html** contains original documents, film footage, and scholarly insights.

Harlem Renaissance authors appear in Alain Locke, ed., *The New Negro* (1925). See also the Circle Association's "Web Links to the Harlem Renaissance" at **www.math.buffalo.edu/~sww/circle/harlem-ren-sites.html**. "Marcus Garvey: Look for Me in the Whirlwind" at **www.pbs.org/wgbh/amex/garvey** contains images and materials on other African American leaders. Kevin Boyle, *Arc of Justice: A Saga of Race, Civil Rights, and Murder in the Jazz Age* (2004), and David Levering Lewis, *W. E. B. Du Bois: The Fight for Equality and the American Century 1919–1963* (2000), describe the racial tensions beneath the surface of the Roaring Twenties.

The SUNY-Binghamton's Web site, "Women and Social Movements in the United States, 1830–1930," at **womhist.binghamton.edu**, is especially rich on the 1920s. "Flapper Station" at **home.earthlink.net/~rbotti** details the youth culture of the 1920s. See also "Music of the Roaring Twenties" at **www.authentichistory.com/audio/1920s/1920smusic01.html**. For an exhaustive history of jazz from 1880 to 1930, see "Jazz Roots" at **www.jass.com** and "The Red Hot Jazz Archive: A History of Jazz Before 1930" at **www.redhotjazz.com**. "Ad Access" at **scriptorium.lib.duke.edu/adaccess** contains images of a wide variety of U.S. advertisements between 1911 and 1955. To gain insight into America's first media superstar, see "Charles Lindbergh: An American Aviator" at **www.charleslindbergh.com**. The conflict over creationism and evolution during the 1920s is detailed in "Tennessee vs. John Scopes: The 'Monkey Trial'" at **www.law.umkc.edu/faculty/projects/ftrials/scopes/scopes.htm**.

See the Web site accompanying "The Crash of 1929," an American Experience production for PBS, at **www.pbs.org/wgbh/amex/crash**.

TEST YOUR KNOWLEDGE

To assess your command of the material in this chapter, see the Online Study Guide at **bedfordstmartins.com/henretta**.

For Web sites, images, and documents related to topics and places in this chapter, visit **bedfordstmartins.com/makehistory**.

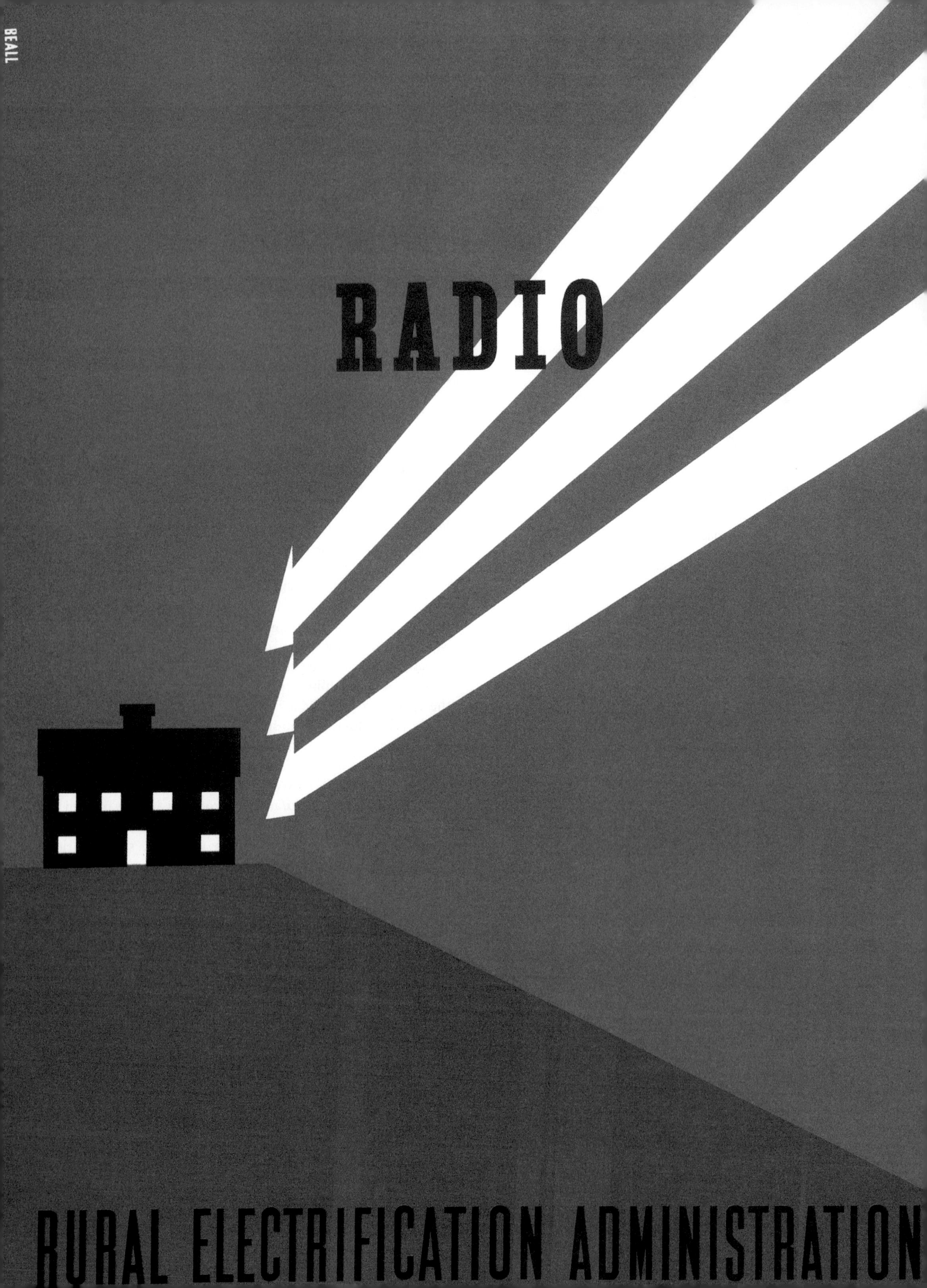
BEALL
RADIO
RURAL ELECTRIFICATION ADMINISTRATION

24 Redefining Liberalism: The New Deal

1933–1939

"**W**HAT IS GOING TO BECOME OF US?" asked an Arizona man. "You can't sleep, you know. You wake up at 2 A.M. and you lie and think." Many Americans went sleepless in 1933, as the nation entered the fourth year of the worst economic contraction in its history. Times were hard — very hard — and there was no end in sight.

In his inaugural address in March 1933, President Franklin Delano Roosevelt tried to dispel the gloom and despondency that gripped the nation. "The only thing we have to fear is fear itself," Roosevelt declared. His demeanor grim and purposeful, Roosevelt issued a ringing call "for action, and action now," and promised strong presidential leadership. He would ask Congress for "broad Executive power to wage a war against the emergency, as great as the power that would be given to me if we were in fact invaded by a foreign foe." With these words, Roosevelt launched a program of federal activism — which he called the *New Deal* — that would change the nature of American government.

The New Deal represented a new form of liberalism, the ideology of individual rights that had long shaped the character of American society and politics. To protect those rights, "classical" nineteenth-century liberals had sought to keep governments small and relatively powerless. Their successors, the "regulatory" liberals of the Progressive era, had

◄ **New Deal Art**

The Rural Electrification Administration used this poster, designed by Lester Beall in 1937, to celebrate the power of radio and to encourage farmers to form cooperatives to bring electric power to their localities. The radio gave rural folk immediate access to news of farm prices and world events, soap operas, and advertising — making them part of modern American life. The Wolfsonian-Florida International University, Miami Beach, Florida, The Mitchell Wolfson, Jr. Collection.

safeguarded the liberty of individuals by bolstering the authority of the state and federal governments to oversee and, if necessary, to control large business corporations. The New Deal activists went much further—their **"social welfare" liberalism** expanded individual rights. Beginning in the 1930s and continuing until the 1970s, they increased the amount and scope of national legislation; created an increasingly centralized federal administrative system; and instituted new programs, such as Social Security, that gave the national government responsibility for the welfare of every American citizen. Their efforts did not go unchallenged. Critics of the New Deal charged that its program of "big government" and "social welfare" directly repudiated traditional **classical liberal** principles and, beginning with the "Reagan Revolution" of the 1980s, would seek to undo many of its programs.

The New Deal Takes Over, 1933–1935

The Great Depression destroyed Herbert Hoover's political reputation and boosted that of Franklin Delano Roosevelt. Although some Americans, especially wealthy conservatives, hated the new Democratic president, he was immensely popular; millions called him by his initials—FDR—which became his nickname. Ironically, the ideological differences between Hoover and Roosevelt were not vast. Both were committed to maintaining the nation's basic social and institutional structures. Both believed in the morality of a balanced budget and extolled the values of hard work, cooperation, and sacrifice. But Roosevelt's personal charm, his political savvy, and his willingness to experiment made all the difference. Above all, his New Deal programs put people to work, instilling hope for the nation's future.

Roosevelt's Leadership

Roosevelt immediately established a close rapport with the American people. More than 450,000 letters poured into the White House in the week after his inauguration, and they continued to come at a rate of 5,000 a week throughout the 1930s. Whereas one person had handled public correspondence under Hoover, a staff of fifty was required by the new administration. Roosevelt's masterful use of the new medium of radio, especially the "fireside chats" during his first two terms, bolstered his relationship with the people. Many citizens thanked him personally for their successes, saying "He gave me a job" or "He saved my home" (see Comparing American Voices, "Ordinary People Respond to the New Deal," pp. 740–741).

FDR

Franklin Delano Roosevelt was a successful politician partly because he loved to mix with a crowd. Despite Roosevelt's upper-class background, he had a knack for relating easily to those from all occupations. Although a well-dressed crowd turned out to greet him in Elm Grove, West Virginia, as he campaigned for the presidency in 1932, Roosevelt took care to be photographed shaking hands with coal miner Zeno Santanella. *Courtesy of the Franklin D. Roosevelt Library.*

Roosevelt's charisma allowed him to continue the expansion of presidential powers begun in the administrations of Theodore Roosevelt and Woodrow Wilson. He dramatically enlarged the role of the executive branch in setting the budget and initiating legislation. For policy formulation, he relied heavily on his "Brain Trust" of professors from Columbia and Harvard universities: Raymond Moley, Rexford Tugwell, Adolph A. Berle, and Felix Frankfurter. He turned as well to his talented cabinet, which included Secretary of the Interior Harold L. Ickes, Frances Perkins at Labor, Henry A. Wallace at Agriculture, and Henry Morgenthau, Jr., the secretary of the Treasury. Financier Bernard Baruch was also influential. This array of intellectual and administrative talent attracted hundreds of highly qualified recruits to Washington. Young professors and newly trained lawyers streamed out of Ivy League law schools into the expanding federal bureaucracy, where they had a direct hand in shaping legislation. Inspired by the idealism of the New Deal, many of them would devote their lives to public service and the principles of social welfare liberalism.

The Hundred Days

Roosevelt promised "action now," and he kept his promise. The first months of his administration produced a whirlwind of activity in Congress, which was controlled by Democrats elected with Roosevelt in 1932. In a legendary legislative session, known as the "Hundred Days," Congress enacted fifteen major bills. This legislation focused primarily on four major problems — banking failures, agricultural overproduction, the business slump, and soaring unemployment.

The Emergency Banking Act. The president and Congress first addressed the banking crisis. Since the stock market crash, bank failures had cut into the savings of nearly nine million families; to prevent more failures, dozens of states had closed their banks. On March 5, the day following his inauguration, FDR declared a national "bank holiday" — a euphemism for closing all the banks — and called Congress into special session. Four days later Congress passed the Emergency Banking Act — the debate in the House took only thirty-eight minutes — which permitted banks to reopen if a Treasury Department inspection showed they had sufficient cash reserves.

The act worked because Roosevelt convinced the public that it would. In his first Sunday night

fireside chat, to a radio audience estimated at 60 million, the president reassured citizens that federal scrutiny would ensure the safety of their deposits. When the banking system reopened on March 13, deposits exceeded withdrawals, restoring stability to one of the nation's prime financial institutions. "Capitalism was saved in eight days," quipped Roosevelt's advisor Raymond Moley. A second banking law of 1933, the Glass-Steagall Act, further restored public confidence; it created the Federal Deposit Insurance Corporation (FDIC), which insured deposits up to $2,500. Four thousand banks had collapsed in the months prior to Roosevelt's inauguration, but only sixty-one closed their doors in all of 1934 (Table 24.1).

The avalanche of legislation now began. Congress created the Home Owners Loan Corporation to refinance home mortgages threatened by foreclosure. It then established the Civilian Conservation Corps (CCC), which mobilized 250,000 young men to do reforestation and conservation work. Two controversial measures also won quick approval. One set up the Tennessee Valley Authority (TVA), a government-owned corporation that would produce cheap hydroelectric power and encourage economic development in the flood-prone river valley (see Map 24.3 on p. 760); critics assailed it as creeping socialism. The second act legalized the sale of beer, offending moral reformers; but full repeal of Prohibition, by constitutional amendment, was already in the works and came eight months later, in December 1933.

The Agricultural Adjustment Act. Because farmers formed more than a quarter of the workforce, Roosevelt considered effective agricultural legislation

TABLE 24.1	American Banks and Bank Failures, 1920–1940		
Year	Total Number of Banks	Total Assets ($ billion)	Bank Failures
1920	30,909	53.1	168
1929	25,568	72.3	659
1931	22,242	70.1	2,294
1933	14,771	51.4	4,004
1934	15,913	55.9	61
1940	15,076	79.7	48

SOURCE: *Historical Statistics of the United States: Colonial Times to 1970* (Washington, D.C.: U.S. Government Printing Office, 1975), 1019, 1038–1039.

Ordinary People Respond to the New Deal

Franklin Roosevelt's fireside chats and his relief programs prompted thousands of ordinary Americans to write directly to the president and his wife Eleanor. Taken together, they offer a vivid portrait of depression-era America and of popular support for, and opposition to, the New Deal.

MRS. M.H.A.

Mrs. M.H.A. worked in the County Court House in Eureka, California.

June 14, 1934
Dear Mrs. Roosevelt:

I know you are overburdened with requests for help and if my plea cannot be recognized, I'll understand it is because you have so many others, all of them worthy....

My husband and I are a young couple of very simple, almost poor families. We married eight years ago on the proverbial shoe-string but with a wealth of love.... We managed to build our home and furnish it comfortably.... Then came the depression. My work has continued and my salary alone has just been sufficient to make our monthly payments on the house and keep our bills paid.... But with the exception of two and one-half months work with the U.S. Coast and Geodetic Survey under the C.W.A. [Civil Works Administration], my husband has not had work since August, 1932.

My salary could continue to keep us going, but I am to have a baby.... I can get a leave of absence from my job for a year. But can't you, won't you do something so my husband can have a job, at least during that year? ...

As I said before, if it were only ourselves, or if there were something we could do about it, we would never ask for help. We have always stood on our own feet and been proud and happy. But you are a mother and you'll understand this crisis.

Very sincerely yours,
Mrs. M. H. A.

UNSIGNED LETTER

This unsigned letter came from a factory worker in Paris, Texas.

November 23, 1936
Dear President,

[N]ow that we have had a land Slide [in the election of 1936] and done just what was best for our country ... I do believe you Will Strain a point to help the ones who helped you mostly & that is the Working Class of People I am not smart or I would be in a different line of work & better up in ever way yet I will know you are the one & only President that ever helped a Working Class of People....

I am a White Man American age, 47 married wife 2 children in high School am a Finishing room foreman I mean a Working foreman & am in a furniture Factory here in Paris Texas where thaire is 175 to 200 Working & when the NRA [National Recovery Administration] came in I was Proud to See my fellow workmen Rec 30 Per hour in Place of 8 cents to 20 cents Per hour....

I can't see for my life President why a man must toil & work his life out in Such factories 10 long hours ever day except Sunday for a small sum of 15 cents to 35 cents per hour & pay the high cost of honest & deason living expences....

please see if something can be done to help this one Class of Working People the factories are a man killer not venelated or kept up just a bunch of Republickins Grafters 90/100 of them Please help us some way I Pray to God for relief. I am a Christian ... and a truthful man & have not told you wrong & am for you to the end.

[not signed]

R.A.

R.A. was 69 years old and an architect and builder in Lincoln, Nebraska.

May 19/34
Dear Mrs Roosevelt:

In the Presidents inaugural address delivered from the capitol steps the afternoon of his inauguration he made mention of The Forgotten Man, and I with thousands of others am wondering if the folk who was borned here in America some 60 or 70 years a go are this Forgotten Man, the President had in mind, if we are this Forgotten Man then we are still Forgotten.

We who have tried to be diligent in our support of this most wonderful nation of ours boath social and other wise, we in our younger days tried to do our duty without complaining....

And now a great calamity has come upon us and seemingly no cause of our own it has swept away what little savings we had accumulated and we are left in a condition that is imposible for us to correct, for two very prominent reasons if no more.

First we have grown to what is termed Old Age, this befalls every man.

Second, . . . we are confronted on every hand with the young generation, taking our places, this of corse is what we have looked forward to in training our children. But with the extra ordinary crises which left us helpless and placed us in the position that our fathers did not have to contend with. . . .

We have been honorable citizens all along our journey, calamity and old age has forced its self upon us please do not send us to the Poor Farm but instead allow us the small pension of $40.00 per month. . . .

Mrs. Roosevelt I am asking a personal favor of you as it seems to be the only means through which I may be able to reach the President, some evening very soon, as you and Mr. Roosevelt are having dinner together privately will you ask him to read this. And we American citizens will ever remember your kindness.

Yours very truly.

R. A.

M.A.

M.A. was a woman who held a low-level salaried position in a corporation.

Jan. 18, 1937

[Dear Mrs. Roosevelt:]

I . . . was simply astounded to think that anyone could be nitwit enough to wish to be included in the so called social security act if they could possibly avoid it. Call it by any name you wish it, in my opinion, (and that of many people I know) is nothing but downright stealing. . . .

I am not an "economic royalist," just an ordinary white collar worker at $1600 per [year — about $21,700 in 2007]. Please show this to the president and ask him to remember the wishes of the forgotten man, that is, the one who dared to vote against him. We expect to be tramped on but we do wish the stepping would be a little less hard.

Security at the price of freedom is never desired by intelligent people.

M. A.

M.A.H.

M.A.H. was a widow who ran a small farm in Columbus, Indiana.

December 14, 1937

Mrs. Roosevelt:

I suppose from your point of view the work relief, old age pensions, slum clearance and all the rest seems like a perfect remedy for all the ills of this country, but I would like for you to see the results, as the other half see them.

We have always had a shiftless, never-do-well class of people whose one and only aim in life is to live without work. I have been rubbing elbows with this class for nearly sixty years and have tried to help some of the most promising and have seen others try to help them, but it can't be done. We cannot help those who will not try to help themselves and if they do try a square deal is all they need, . . . let each paddle their own canoe, or sink. . . .

I live alone on a farm and have not raised any crops for the last two years as there was no help to be had. I am feeding the stock and have been cutting the wood to keep my home fires burning. There are several relievers around here now who have been kicked off relief but they refuse to work unless they can get relief hours and wages, but they are so worthless no one can afford to hire them. . . . They are just a fair sample of the class of people on whom so much of our hard earned tax money is being squandered and on whom so much sympathy is being wasted. . . .

You people who have plenty of this worlds goods and whose money comes easy have no idea of the heart-breaking toil and self-denial which is the lot of the working people who are trying to make an honest living, and then to have to shoulder all these unjust burdens seems like the last straw. . . . No one should have the right to vote theirself a living at the expense of the tax payers.

M. A. H.

SOURCES (IN ORDER): Robert S. McElvaine, *Down and Out in the Great Depression* (Chapel Hill: University of North Carolina Press, 1983), 54–55; Michael P. Johnson, ed., *Reading the American Past*, 3rd ed., 2 vols. (Boston: Bedford/St. Martin's, 2005), 2: 166–167; Robert D. Marcus and David Burner, eds., *America Firsthand*, 7th ed. (Boston: Bedford/St. Martin's, 2007), 184, 182–184.

ANALYZING THE EVIDENCE

➤ How do you explain the personal, almost intimate, tone of these letters to the Roosevelts?

➤ How have specific New Deal programs helped or hurt the authors of these letters?

➤ What are the basic values of the authors? Do they differ between those who support and oppose the New Deal?

"the key to recovery." The federal government had long assisted farmers: through cheap prices for land, the extension services of the Department of Agriculture, and the Federal Farm Loan Act of 1916. But the Agricultural Adjustment Act (AAA), a measure jointly developed by administration officials and major farm organizations, represented a new level of government involvement in the farm economy. To solve the problem of overproduction, which resulted in low prices for farm crops, the AAA set up an allotment system for seven major commodities (wheat, cotton, corn, hogs, rice, tobacco, and dairy products). The act provided cash subsidies to farmers who cut their production of these crops; to pay these subsidies, the act imposed a tax on the processors of these commodities, which they in turn passed on to consumers. New Deal policymakers hoped that farm prices would rise as production (and supply) fell, spurring consumer purchases by farmers and assisting a general economic recovery.

By dumping cash in farmers' hands (a special-interest policy that continues to this day), the AAA stabilized the farm economy. But the act's benefits were not evenly distributed. Subsidies went primarily to the owners of large- and medium-sized farms, who often cut production by reducing the amount of land they rented to tenants and sharecroppers. In the South, where many sharecroppers were black and the landowners and government administrators were white, such practices forced 200,000 black families off the land. Some black farmers tried to protect themselves by joining the Southern Tenant Farmers Union (STFU), a biracial organization founded in 1934. "The same chain that holds you hold my people, too," an elderly black farmer reminded his white colleagues. But landowners had such economic power and such support from local politicians and sheriffs that the STFU could do little. Dispossessed of access to land and denied government aid, hundreds of thousands of black sharecroppers and white smallholders moved to the cities.

The National Recovery Act. The New Deal's initial response to depressed levels of business activity was the National Industrial Recovery Act. The act drew on the regulatory approaches of Bernard Baruch's War Industries Board during World War I and Herbert Hoover's trade associations of the 1920s. It also reflected "corporatist" theories of a government-planned economy popular in Europe and implemented in Italy by Benito Mussolini. The government agency charged with implementing the act, the National Recovery Administration (NRA), established a system of self-government in more than six hundred industries. Each industry — ranging from large businesses such as coal, cotton, and steel to small ones such as dog food and costume jewelry — regulated itself by hammering out a government-approved code of prices and production quotas, similar to those for farm products. These agreements had the force of law and covered workers as well as employers. The codes outlawed child labor and set minimum wages and maximum hours for adult workers. One of the most far-reaching provisions, Section 7(a), guaranteed workers the right to organize and bargain collectively "through representatives of their own choosing." This right to union representation was an important spur to the growth of the labor movement in the 1930s.

In many instances the trade associations set by Hoover in the 1920s, which were controlled by large companies, dominated the code-drafting process. As a result, the NRA solidified the power of large businesses at the expense of smaller enterprises, labor unions, and consumer interests. To sell the program to skeptical consumers and businesspeople, the NRA launched an extensive public relations campaign, complete with plugs in Hollywood films and "Blue Eagle" stickers with the NRA slogan, "We Do Our Part."

Unemployment Legislation. The early New Deal also addressed the critical problem of unemployment and impoverished working families. By 1933, local governments and private charities had exhausted their resources and looked to Washington for assistance. Roosevelt responded reluctantly because he feared a budget deficit. Nonetheless, he asked Congress to fund relief for millions of unemployed Americans. In May, Congress established the Federal Emergency Relief Administration (FERA). Directed by Harry Hopkins, a hard-driving social worker from New York, the FERA provided federal funds to the states for relief programs. In his first two hours in office, Hopkins distributed $5 million. Over the program's two-year existence, FERA spent $1 billion.

Roosevelt and his advisors had strong reservations against the "dole," the popular name for these government welfare payments. As Hopkins worried, "I don't think anybody can go year after year, month after month, accepting relief without affecting his character. . . . It is probably going to undermine the independence of hundreds of thousands of families." To maintain a commitment to individual initiative, the New Deal tried to put people to work. Early in 1933, Congress appropriated $3.3 billion

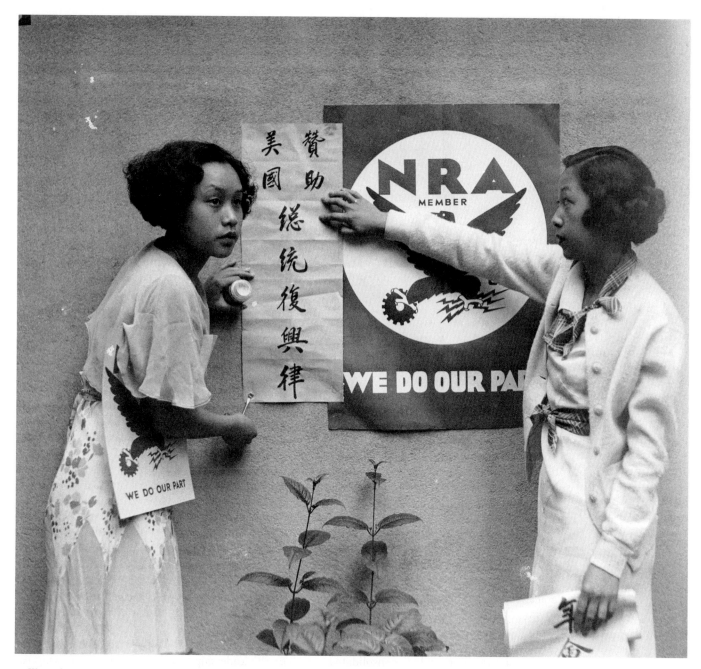

Selling the NRA in Chinatown

To mobilize support for its program, the National Recovery Administration (NRA) distributed millions of posters to businesses and families, urging them to display the "Blue Eagle" in shops, factories, and homes. Here Constance King and Mae Chinn of the Chinese Y.M.C.A. affix a poster (and a Chinese translation) to a shop in San Francisco that is complying with the NRA codes. Copyright Bettmann / Corbis.

for the Public Works Administration (PWA), a construction program directed by Secretary of the Interior Harold L. Ickes. However, Ickes's cautious approach to approving public works projects limited the agency's effectiveness in providing jobs or spurring recovery. So in November 1933 Roosevelt established the Civil Works Administration (CWA), named Harry Hopkins as its head, and gave it $400 million in PWA funds. Within thirty days, Hopkins had put 2.6 million men and women to work; at its peak in January 1934, the CWA funded the employment of 4 million Americans in public works' projects: repairing bridges, building highways, constructing public buildings, and setting up community projects. The CWA, a stopgap measure to get the country through the winter of 1933–1934, lapsed the next spring after spending all its funds.

When an exhausted Congress recessed in June 1933, it had accomplished much: banking reform, recovery programs for agriculture and industry, unemployment relief, and a host of other measures. Few presidents had so dominated a legislative session and won the passage of so many measures (the only future president to do so would be Lyndon Baines Johnson in 1965; see Chapter 28). A mass of "alphabet" agencies (the CCC, CWA, FERA, AAA, NRA), as the New Deal programs came to be known, began to flow from Washington. But if the avalanche of new laws and programs halted the downward psychological spiral of the Hoover years, they had yet to break the grip of the depression.

Financial Reform. As Roosevelt waited anxiously for the economy to revive, he turned his attention to the reform of Wall Street, where insider trading, fraud, and reckless speculation had triggered the financial panic of 1929. In 1934, Congress established the Securities and Exchange Commission (SEC) to regulate the stock market. The commission had broad powers to regulate companies that issued stock and bonds to the public, set rules for margin (credit) transactions, and prevent stock sales by those with inside information on corporate plans. The Banking Act of 1935 authorized the president to appoint a new Board of Governors of the Federal Reserve System, placing control of interest rates and other money-market policies at the federal level rather than with regional banks.

The New Deal under Attack

As Congress and the president consolidated the New Deal, their work came under attack from many quarters. Roosevelt saw himself as the savior of the American system of democratic capitalism, declaring simply: "To preserve we had to reform." Many bankers and business executives disagreed. To them, FDR became "That Man," a traitor to his class. In 1934, Republican business leaders joined with conservative Democrats in a "Liberty League" that lobbied against the "reckless spending" and "socialist" reforms of the New Deal. Reflecting their outlook, Herbert Hoover condemned the NRA as a "state-controlled or state-directed social or economic system"; and that, the former president declared, is "tyranny, not liberalism."

The Supreme Court likewise repudiated many New Deal measures. In May 1935, the Court unanimously ruled that the National Industrial Recovery Act represented an unconstitutional delegation of Congress's legislative power to a code-writing agency in the executive branch of the government. The case, *Schechter v. United States,* arose when a firm in Brooklyn, New York, sold diseased chickens to local storekeepers in violation of NRA codes. In addition to the delegation issue, the Court declared that the NRA unconstitutionally extended federal authority to *intrastate* (as opposed to *interstate*) commerce. Roosevelt publicly protested that the Court's narrow interpretation would return the Constitution "to the horse-and-buggy definition of interstate commerce," but he could only watch helplessly as the Court also struck down a raft of New Deal legislation in 1935: the Agricultural Adjustment Act, a Railroad Retirement Act, and the Frazier-Lemke debt relief act.

Challenges from the Left. If business executives and the Supreme Court thought the New Deal had gone too far, other Americans believed it had not gone far enough. Francis Townsend, a Long Beach, California, doctor, spoke for the nation's elderly, most of whom had no pension plans and feared poverty in their old age. In 1933 Townsend proposed the Old Age Revolving Pension Plan, which would give $200 a month (about $3,000 today) to citizens over the age of sixty. To receive payments the elderly would have to retire from their jobs, thus opening their positions to younger workers, and agree to spend the money within a month. Townsend Clubs soon sprang up across the country, particularly in the Far West. These clubs mobilized mass support for old-age pensions and helped win passage of the far less ambitious Social Security Act of 1935 (see p. 746).

Father Charles Coughlin also challenged Roosevelt's leadership and attracted a large following, especially in the Midwest. A priest in a Catholic parish in Detroit, Coughlin had turned to the radio in the mid-1920s to enlarge his pastorate. By 1933, about forty million Americans listened regularly to the Radio Priest's broadcasts. Coughlin initially supported the New Deal but turned against it when Roosevelt refused to nationalize the banking system and expand the money supply. To promote these programs, which resembled the proposals of the Populist Party of the 1890s (see Chapter 19), Coughlin organized the National Union for Social Justice and continued to attack the administration's policies.

The most direct political threat to Roosevelt came from Senator Huey Long. As the Democratic governor of Louisiana, the flamboyant Long had achieved stunning popularity by lowering utility bills, increasing taxes on corporations, and building new highways, bridges, hospitals, and schools. Long's accomplishments came at a price: To push through these measures, he had seized almost dictatorial control of the state government. In 1934, Long broke with the New Deal and, like Townsend and Coughlin, established a national movement. His "Share Our Wealth Society," which boasted over four million followers, argued that the depression did not stem from overproduction but from underconsumption. The unequal distribution of wealth prevented ordinary families from buying goods and stimulating economic activity. To put money in the hands of millions of consumers, the Society advocated a tax of 100 percent of all income over $1 million and all inheritances over $5 million. Long hoped that this program would carry him into the White House.

Although somewhat simplistic, the economic proposals offered by Townsend, Coughlin, and Long were no more radical than the NIRA or the AAA. Like the New Deal measures, they were plausible responses to the depression; in fact, some of them were subsequently endorsed by social welfare liberals. It was the constitutional views of Coughlin and Long that separated them from most politically engaged Americans: Neither man had much respect for representative government. "I'm the Constitution around here," Long declared during his governorship, while Coughlin suggested that dictatorial rule might be necessary to preserve democracy. Voters seemed not to mind. As their policies won increasing popularity, Roosevelt and his advisors feared that Long might join forces with Coughlin and Townsend to form a third party that would appeal to many Democratic voters. This prospect encouraged Republicans, who hoped that a split among between New Dealers and other reformers might return their party, and its ideology of small government and free enterprise, to political power in the 1936 election.

The Kingfish

Huey Long, the Louisiana governor and senator, called himself "the Kingfish" because, he said, "I'm a small fish here in Washington. But I'm the Kingfish to the folks down in Louisiana." An exceptionally charismatic man and a brilliant campaigner, he attracted a significant following with his "Share Our Wealth" plan, which aimed to redistribute the nation's wealth. Democrats worried that he might run for president in 1936 on a third-party ticket, threatening Franklin Roosevelt's reelection. But in September 1935 Long was killed (apparently by his bodyguard) during an assassination attempt by a young doctor over a Louisiana political dispute. Long is seen here shaking hands with a Louisiana supporter. Louisiana State Museum.

➤ What were the major differences between the approaches of Herbert Hoover and Franklin D. Roosevelt to the crisis of the depression?

➤ What were the main programs of the New Deal's "Hundred Days"? Why did FDR and the Democrats believe that these programs would work?

➤ Define the criticism of the New Deal from the political right and left. Who were the New Deal's major critics, and what were their alternative programs?

The Second New Deal, 1935–1938

As attacks on the New Deal from the conservative right and the liberal left mounted, Roosevelt and his advisors abandoned the middle ground and moved to the left. Historians have labeled this new course the Second New Deal. Acknowledging his inability to win the support of big business, Roosevelt openly criticized the "money classes," proudly stating: "We have earned the hatred of entrenched greed." And he moved decisively to counter the rising popularity of Townsend, Coughlin, and Long by stealing parts of their programs and, he hoped, much of their thunder. The administration's Revenue Act of 1935 proposed a substantial tax increase on corporate profits and higher income and estate taxes on wealthy citizens. Conservatives called the legislation an attempt to "soak the rich," and Congress moderated its rates, so that it boosted revenue only by $250 million a year. But FDR was happy. He had met Huey Long's Share Our Wealth plan with a plan of his own.

Legislative Accomplishments

The Revenue Act symbolized the administration's new outlook. Unlike the First New Deal, which focused on economic recovery, the Second New Deal emphasized social justice: the use of national legislation to enhance the power of working people and the security and welfare of the old, the disabled, and the unemployed.

The Wagner Act. The first beneficiary of Roosevelt's move to the left was the labor movement. The rising number of strikes in 1934 — about 1,800 job actions involving a total of 1.5 million workers — reflected the dramatic growth of rank-and-file militancy. When the Supreme Court voided the

NIRA in 1935, thereby invalidating Section 7(a), labor unions demanded new legislation that would protect workers' rights to organize and bargain collectively. Named for its sponsor, Senator Robert F. Wagner of New York, the Wagner Act (1935) upheld the right of industrial workers to join unions; because of the opposition of southern Democrats, who represented the interest of planters and landlords, it did not apply to farm workers. The act outlawed many practices used by employers to squelch unions, such as firing workers for organizing activities. It also established the National Labor Relations Board (NLRB), a federal agency with the authority to protect workers from employer coercion, supervise elections for union representation, and guarantee the process of collective bargaining.

The Social Security Act. A second initiative, the Social Security Act of 1935, had an even greater impact. Other industrialized societies, such as Germany and Britain, had created national old-age pension systems around 1900, but American Progressives had failed to muster political support for a similar program in the United States. But now millions of citizens had joined the Townsend and Long movements; their demands gave political muscle to pension advocates within the administration, such as Grace Abbott, head of the Children's Bureau, and Secretary of Labor Frances Perkins. They won the president's support for a Social Security Act that provided old-age pensions for most privately employed workers and established a joint federal-state system of compensation for unemployed workers. Because of southern Democratic opposition in Congress, farm workers and domestic servants were excluded from both programs.

Roosevelt had his own concerns. Knowing that compulsory pension and unemployment legislation would be controversial, he refused to include a provision for national health insurance because that would make it more difficult to get the measure through Congress. A firm believer in personal responsibility, the president also insisted that workers bear part of the cost of the new pension and unemployment plans. Consequently, the act was not funded out of general tax revenues but by mandatory contributions paid by workers and their employers. Decades later, this funding mechanism protected the Social Security system from the attempt of "New Right" conservatives to abolish it; having contributed to the pension fund, millions of workers demanded that they receive its benefits (see Chapter 30).

The Social Security Act was a milestone in the creation of an American welfare state. Never before had the federal government assumed such responsibility for the well-being of a substantial majority of the citizenry. In addition to pension and unemployment coverage, the act mandated aid to various categories of Americans: the blind, deaf, and disabled as well as dependent children. These categorical assistance programs to the so-called "deserving poor" grew dramatically after the 1930s. Aid to Dependent Children covered only 700,000 youngsters in 1939; by 1994, its successor, Aid to Families with Dependent Children (AFDC), enrolled 14.1 million Americans, 60 percent of whom were African American or Hispanic. A minor program during the New Deal, AFDC had become one of the central facets of the American welfare system and one of the most controversial (see Chapter 30).

The Works Progress Administration. Roosevelt was never enthusiastic about public relief programs. But with the election of 1936 on the horizon and 10 million Americans still out of work, FDR won funding for the Works Progress Administration (WPA). Under the energetic direction of Harry Hopkins, the WPA became the main federal relief agency. Whereas the Federal Emergency Relief Administration of 1933–1934 had supplied grants to state relief programs, the WPA put workers directly onto the federal payroll. Between 1935 and 1943 the WPA spent $10.5 billion and employed 8.5 million Americans. The agency's workers constructed or repaired 651,087 miles of roads; 124,087 bridges; 125,110 public buildings; 8,192 parks; and 853 airports. Though the WPA was an extravagant operation by the standards of the 1930s, it reached only about one-third of the nation's unemployed. Wages were low — on average $55 a month ($800 today) — so as not to compete with private-sector jobs. But most WPA workers were thankful for any job that allowed them to eke out a living.

The 1936 Election

As the 1936 election approached, new voters joined the Democratic Party. Many had personally benefited from New Deal programs or knew those who had (Table 24.2). Roosevelt could count on a potent coalition of organized labor, midwestern farmers, white ethnic groups, northern blacks, and middle-class families concerned about unemployment and old-age dependence.

In addition, he commanded the support of Jews, intellectuals, and progressive Republicans. The Democrats also held on, though with some difficulty, to their traditional constituency of white southerners.

The Republicans realized that the New Deal was too popular to oppose directly. So they chose as their candidate the progressive governor of Kansas, Alfred M. Landon. Landon accepted the legitimacy of most New Deal programs but stridently criticized their inefficiency and expense.

TABLE 24.2	Major New Deal Legislation
Agriculture	
1933	Agricultural Adjustment Act (AAA)
1935	Resettlement Administration (RA) Rural Electrification Administration
1937	Farm Security Administration (FSA)
1938	Agricultural Adjustment Act of 1938
Finance and Industry	
1933	Emergency Banking Act Glass-Steagall Act (created the FDIC) National Industrial Recovery Act (NIRA)
1934	Securities and Exchange Commission (SEC)
1935	Banking Act of 1935 Revenue Act (wealth tax)
Conservation and the Environment	
1933	Tennessee Valley Authority (TVA) Civilian Conservation Corps (CCC) Soil Conservation and Domestic Allotment Act
Labor and Social Welfare	
1933	Section 7(a) of NIRA
1935	National Labor Relations Act (Wagner Act) National Labor Relations Board (NLRB) Social Security Act
1937	National Housing Act
1938	Fair Labor Standards Act (FLSA)
Relief and Reconstruction	
1933	Federal Emergency Relief Administration (FERA) Civil Works Administration (CWA) Public Works Administration (PWA)
1935	Works Progress Administration (WPA) National Youth Administration (NYA)

The Republican candidate also pointed to authoritarian regimes in Italy and Germany, directed by Benito Mussolini and Adolf Hitler respectively, and hinted that FDR harbored similar dictatorial ambitions.

These charges fell on deaf ears. Roosevelt's victory in 1936 was one of the biggest landslides in American history. The assassination of Huey Long in September 1935 had deflated the threat of a serious third-party challenge; the candidate of the combined Long-Townsend-Coughlin camp, Congressman William Lemke of North Dakota, garnered fewer than 900,000 votes (1.9 percent) for the Union Party ticket. Roosevelt received 60.8 percent of the popular vote and carried every state except Maine and Vermont. The New Deal was at high tide.

Stalemate

"I see one-third of a nation ill-housed, ill-clad, ill-nourished," the president declared in his second inaugural address in January 1937. But any hopes that FDR had for expanding the liberal welfare state were quickly dashed. Within a year, staunch opposition to New Deal initiatives arose in Congress and the South, and a sharp recession undermined confidence in Roosevelt's economic leadership.

The Fight over the Supreme Court. Roosevelt's first setback came when he stunned Congress and the nation by asking for fundamental changes in the Supreme Court. In 1935 the Court had struck down a series of New Deal measures and a minimum wage law in New York State by the narrow margin of 5 to 4. With the Wagner Act, the TVA, and Social Security coming up on appeal, the future of the New Deal lay in the hands of a few elderly, conservative-minded judges. To diminish their influence, the president proposed to add a new justice for every member over the age of seventy. Roosevelt's opponents protested that he was trying to "pack" the Court; concerned by this blatant attempt to alter a traditional institution, Congress rejected the proposal after a bitter months-long debate.

If Roosevelt lost the battle, he won the war. Swayed by FDR's overwhelming election victory in 1936, the Court upheld a California minimum wage law and the Wagner and Social Security Acts. Moreover, a series of resignations allowed Roosevelt to reshape the Supreme Court; his new appointees, who included Hugo Black, Felix Frankfurter, and William O. Douglas, viewed the Constitution as a "living document" that had to be interpreted in the light of present conditions and generally supported New Deal measures.

Nonetheless, the court-packing fiasco revealed Roosevelt's vulnerability and energized congressional conservatives. Throughout Roosevelt's second term a conservative coalition composed mainly of southern Democrats and rural Republicans blocked or impeded social legislation. The president did win passage of the National Housing Act of 1937, which mandated the construction of low-cost public housing, and the Fair Labor Standards Act of 1938, which made permanent the minimum wage, maximum hours, and anti-child labor provisions in the NRA codes. But Congress rejected or modified other administration initiatives, including a far-reaching plan for reorganizing the executive branch of the federal government.

The Roosevelt Recession. The "Roosevelt recession" of 1937–1938 dealt the most devastating blow to the president. From 1933 to 1937 the gross domestic product had grown at a yearly rate of about 10 percent; by 1937 industrial output and real income had finally returned to 1929 levels. Unemployment had declined from 25 percent to 14 percent. "The emergency has passed," remarked Senator James F. Byrnes of South Carolina.

Acting on this assumption, Roosevelt slashed the federal budget, which had been running a modest deficit. Congress cut the WPA's funding in half, causing layoffs of about 1.5 million workers; the Federal Reserve, fearing inflation, raised interest rates. The results halted the economic recovery. The stock market dropped sharply, and unemployment soared to 19 percent. Quickly reversing course, Roosevelt spent his way out of the recession by boosting funding for the WPA and resuming public works projects. Although improvised, this spending program accorded with the theories advanced by John Maynard Keynes, a British economist who proposed that governments use **deficit spending** (funds obtained by borrowing rather than through taxation) to stimulate the economy when private spending proved insufficient. Untested and sharply criticized by Republicans and conservative Democrats in the 1930s, **Keynesian economics** gradually won wider acceptance as defense spending during World War II ended the Great Depression. Beginning in the 1940s, Democratic administrations endorsed Keynesian principles and after 1980, Republican administrations engaged in massive deficit spending, both to stimulate the economy and offset the effects of tax cuts (see Chapters 26 and 30).

To restore the vitality of the New Deal, Roosevelt decided to "purge" the Democratic Party of some of his most conservative opponents. During the primary elections in 1938, the president campaigned against members of his own party who had been hostile to New Deal initiatives. His purge failed abysmally and opened the door for a Republican resurgence. Profiting from the "Roosevelt recession" and court-packing fiasco, Republicans picked up eight seats in the Senate, eighty-one in the House, and thirteen state governorships.

The New Deal had run out of steam. Roosevelt's political mistakes were partly responsible for this outcome, but so too were his successes. By 1939, the challenge posed by the Great Depression to American capitalist and democratic institutions had been met. The economy was back on course and so too was normal party politics; Americans had rejected the simplistic solutions proposed by demagogic politicians and the allure of fascist and communist alternatives to the American tradition of liberal individualism. A reformer rather than a revolutionary, Roosevelt had done his part to save capitalism and democracy. He lacked a new domestic agenda and the political power to enact it. Had it not been for the outbreak of a major war in Europe, FDR probably would have served out his second term and retired from the scene. In any event, by 1939 the New Deal was over.

➤ How did the Second New Deal differ from the first? What were FDR's reasons for changing course?

➤ Why did the New Deal reach a stalemate?

➤ Describe Keynesian economics. How important was it to the New Deal?

The New Deal's Impact on Society

Whatever the limits of the New Deal, it had a tremendous impact on the nation. Its ideology of social welfare liberalism fundamentally altered Americans' relationship to their government, providing assistance to a wide range of groups: the unemployed, the elderly, white ethnic workers, women, and racial minorities. To serve these diverse constituencies, New Dealers created a sizeable federal bureaucracy; the number of civilian federal employees increased by 80 percent between 1929 and 1940 and reached a total of one million. The expenditures—and deficits—of the federal government grew at an even faster rate. In 1930 the Hoover administration spent $3.1 billion and had a surplus of almost $1 billion; in 1939 New Dealers expended $9.4 billion and ran a deficit of nearly $3 billion. But the real step toward major government spending came with World War II (and later military buildups), when federal outlays routinely totaled $95 billion and deficits grew to $50 billion. In peace or in war, power increasingly centered in the nation's capital, not in the states.

The Rise of Labor

Exploiting their dominant position in national politics, Democrats used legislation and tax dollars to cement the allegiance of blocs of voters to their party. One of their prize targets were the millions of workers with ties to the labor movement. Demoralized and shrinking organizations at the end of the 1920s, labor unions rose to influence as they took advantage of increased worker militancy and New Deal legislation. Thanks to Section 7(a) of the National Industrial Recovery Act and the Wagner Act, unions found it easier to organize workers, to win recognition from management, and to bargain for higher wages, seniority systems, and grievance procedures. By the end of the decade, the number of unionized workers had tripled to almost nine million, or 23 percent of the nonfarm workforce.

The Congress of Industrial Organizations (CIO) served as the cutting edge of the union movement. It did so by promoting "industrial unionism"— that is, it organized all the workers in an industry, both skilled and unskilled, into one union. John L. Lewis, leader of the United Mine Workers (UMW), was the foremost exponent of industrial unionism. By 1935, Lewis had rejected the philosophy of the American Federation of Labor (AFL), which favored organizing workers on a craft-by-craft basis, and helped to create the CIO.

The CIO scored its first major victory in the automobile industry. On December 31, 1936, General Motors workers in Flint, Michigan, staged a sit-down strike, vowing to stay at their machines until management agreed to collective bargaining. The workers lived in the factories and machine shops for forty-four days before General Motors recognized their union, the United Automobile Workers (UAW). Shortly thereafter the CIO won another major victory at the U.S. Steel Corporation. Despite a history of bitter opposition to unionization, as demonstrated in the 1919 steel strike (see Chapter 22),

"Big Steel" executives capitulated without a fight in March 1937 and recognized the Steel Workers Organizing Committee (SWOC). Another group of companies, "Little Steel," refused to negotiate, sparking a protest at the Republic Steel Corporation in Chicago that took the lives of ten strikers; only in 1941 did workers in Little Steel win union recognition.

The 1930s constituted one of the most active periods of labor solidarity in American history (Map 24.1). The sit-down tactic spread rapidly and reached a high point in March 1937, when a total of 167,210 workers staged 170 sit-down strikes. Labor unions called nearly 5,000 strikes that year and won favorable terms in 80 percent of them. Large numbers of middle-class Americans opposed the sit-down tactics, which they considered a violation of private property. In 1939, the Supreme Court accepted this argument and upheld a law that banned the sit-down tactic.

Organize

The Steel Workers Organizing Committee was one of the most vital labor organizations contributing to the rise of the CIO during the late 1930s. Note that artist Ben Shahn chose a man who might be of either European or African ancestry to represent the steel workers, part of a conscious effort to build a labor movement across racial and ethnic lines. This iconography also reinforced the notion that the typical worker was male, despite the large number of women who joined the CIO. Library of Congress.

The CIO welcomed new groups to the labor movement. Unlike the AFL, which had long excluded or segregated African American workers, the CIO actively organized blacks in the steel and meatpacking industries. In California, its organizers set out to win equal pay for Mexican American women who worked in the canning industry. Corporate giants such as Del Monte, McNeill, and Libby paid women around $2.50 a day, while their male counterparts received $3.50 to $4.50. These differentials shrank following the formation in 1939 of the United Cannery, Agricultural, Packing, and Allied Workers, an unusually democratic union in which women played leading roles. Altogether, some 800,000 women workers joined CIO unions.

Labor's new vitality spilled over into political action. The AFL generally had stood aloof from partisan politics, but the CIO quickly allied itself with the Democratic Party, hoping to persuade the Party to nominate candidates sympathetic to labor. The CIO gave $770,000 (about $12 million today) to Democratic campaigns in 1936, and its Political Action Committee became a major Democratic contributor during the 1940s.

Despite its successes during the 1930s, the labor movement did not develop into a dominant force in American life. Roosevelt never made the growth of the labor movement a high priority, and many workers remained suspicious of unionization, especially as New Deal programs provided unemployment assistance and pension benefits. And while the Wagner Act helped unions to achieve better working conditions for their members, it did not redistribute power in American industry. Managers retained authority over most corporate affairs. In fact, business executives found that unions could be used as a buffer against rank-and-file militancy; likewise, National Labor Relation Board officials, concerned about rising consumer prices, pressed unions to moderate their demands for higher wages and benefits. The road to union power, even with New Deal protection, continued to be a rocky and uncertain one.

Women and Blacks in the New Deal

Although the New Deal did not directly challenge gender inequities and racial injustice, its programs generally enhanced the welfare of women and African Americans.

Women in Government. Women won the vote in 1920, but only with the New Deal did they enter the higher ranks of government in significant numbers.

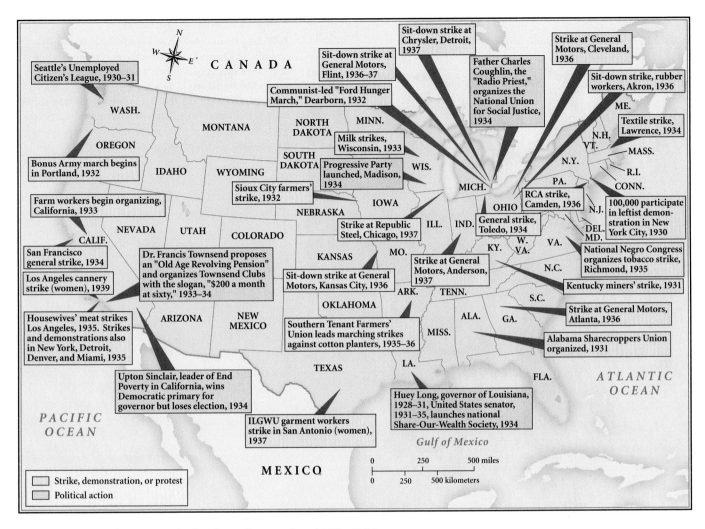

MAP 24.1 Popular Protest in the Great Depression, 1933–1939

The depression forced Americans to look closely at their society, and many of them did not like what they saw. Some citizens expressed their discontent through popular movements, and this map suggests the geography of discontent. The industrial Midwest witnessed union movements, strikes, and Radio Priest Charles Coughlin's demands for social reform. Simultaneously, farmers' movements — tenants in the South, smallholders in the agricultural Midwest — engaged in strikes and dumping campaigns, and rallied behind the ideas of progressives in Wisconsin and Huey Long in the South. Protests took diverse forms in California, which was home to strikes by farmworkers, women, and — in San Francisco — all wage workers. The West was also the seedbed of two important reform proposals: Upton Sinclair's "End Poverty in California" movement and Francis Townsend's "Old Age Revolving Pension" clubs.

Frances Perkins, the first woman named to a cabinet post, served as secretary of labor throughout Roosevelt's presidency. Molly Dewson, a social reformer turned politician, headed the Women's Division of the Democratic National Committee, where she pushed an issue-oriented program that supported New Deal reforms. Roosevelt's women appointees also included the first female director of the mint, the head of a major WPA division, and a judge on a circuit court of appeals. Many of those women were close friends as well as professional colleagues and cooperated in an informal network to advance feminist and reform causes.

Eleanor Roosevelt exemplified the growing prominence of women in public life. In the 1920s she had worked closely with other reformers to expand positions for women in political parties, labor unions, and education. During her years in the

A First Lady without Precedent

Reflecting Eleanor Roosevelt's tendency to turn up in odd places, a famous 1933 *New Yorker* cartoon has one coal miner saying to another, "For gosh sakes, here comes Mrs. Roosevelt." Life soon imitated art. In this photograph from 1935, the first lady emerges from a coal mine in Dellaire, Ohio, still carrying her miner's cap in her left hand and talking to mine supervisor Joseph Bainbridge. Wide World Photos, Inc.

White House, Mrs. Roosevelt emerged as an independent and influential public figure. She held press conferences for women journalists, wrote a popular syndicated news column called "My Day," and traveled extensively throughout the country. By descending deep into coal mines to view working conditions and meeting with African American antilynching advocates, she became the conscience of the New Deal, pushing her pragmatically minded husband to do more for the disadvantaged. "I sometimes acted as a spur," Mrs. Roosevelt later reflected, "even though the spurring was not always wanted or welcome." And she knew the limits of her power with the president: "I was one of those who served his purposes."

Without the vocal support of Eleanor Roosevelt, Frances Perkins, and other prominent women, New Deal policymakers might have completely overlooked the needs of women. Despite their efforts, a fourth of the NRA codes set a lower minimum wage for women than for men performing the same jobs; only 7 percent of the workers in the Civil Works Administration were female; and the Civilian Conservation Corps excluded women entirely. Women fared better under the Works Progress Administration; at its peak, 405,000 women were on the job rolls. Still, most policymakers and most Americans viewed the depression primarily as a crisis for male breadwinners and gave priority to their needs. When asked in a 1936 Gallup poll whether wives should work when their husbands had jobs, 82 percent of those interviewed said no. Reflecting such sentiments, many state legislatures enacted laws that prohibited married women from working. Not until the 1970s would women's quest for equal rights begin to be addressed.

Blacks Join the New Deal Coalition. Especially in the South, African Americans remained in the lowest paying jobs and faced harsh social and political discrimination. In a celebrated 1931 case in

Scottsboro, Alabama, nine young black men were accused of rape by two white women who had been riding a freight train. The women's stories contained many inconsistencies, but in interracial matters a southern white woman was usually taken at her word. Within two weeks, a white jury convicted all nine defendants of rape; eight received the death sentence. After the U.S. Supreme Court overturned the sentences on grounds that the defendants had been denied adequate legal counsel, five of the men were again convicted and sentenced to long prison terms. The Scottsboro case received wide coverage in black communities across the country, as did the rise in the number of lynchings; white mobs lynched twenty blacks in 1930 and twenty-four in 1934.

This violence, and the dispossession of sharecroppers by the AAA, prompted a renewal of the "Great Migration" of African Americans to the cities of the North and Midwest. One destination was Harlem, where housing was already at a premium because of the black influx during the

1920s. Because residential segregation kept African Americans from moving to many sections of New York, they had to pay high rents to live in crowded and deteriorating buildings. Jobs were scarce. White-owned stores in Harlem would not employ blacks; elsewhere in New York City hard-pressed whites took over the menial jobs traditionally held by blacks — as waiters, domestic servants, elevator operators, and garbage collectors. Unemployment in Harlem rose to 50 percent, twice the national rate. These conditions triggered a major race riot in March 1935 as blacks went on a rampage. Before order was restored, four rioters were killed and millions of dollars in property was destroyed.

For the majority of white Americans, the events in Scottsboro and Harlem reinforced their beliefs that blacks were a "dangerous class." Consequently, there was little support for federal intervention to secure the civil rights of African Americans. In fact, many New Deal programs reflected prevailing racist attitudes. CCC camps segregated blacks and whites, and many NRA codes did not protect black

Scottsboro Defendants

The 1931 trial in Scottsboro, Alabama, of nine black youths accused of raping two white women became a symbol of the injustices African Americans faced in the South's legal system. Denied access to an attorney, the defendants were found guilty, and eight were sentenced to death. When the U.S. Supreme Court overturned their convictions in 1932, the International Labor Defense organization hired the noted criminal attorney, Samuel Leibowitz, who eventually won the acquittal of four defendants and jail sentences for the rest. This photograph, taken in a Decatur jail, shows Leibowitz conferring with Haywood Patterson, in front of the other eight defendants. Brown Brothers.

Mary McLeod Bethune

This 1943 painting by Betsy Graves Reyneau captures the strength and dignity of one of the twentieth century's most important African Americans. Behind Bethune is a picture of the first building at the Daytona Literary and Industrial School for Training of Negro Girls, which later became Bethune-Cookman College. National Portrait Gallery, Smithsonian Institution / Art Resource, NY.

workers from discrimination. Most tellingly, Franklin Roosevelt repeatedly refused to support legislation to make lynching a federal crime, arguing it would antagonize southern Democrats whose support he needed to pass New Deal measures.

Nevertheless, blacks received significant benefits from New Deal relief programs directed toward poor Americans. Reflecting their poverty, African Americans made up about 18 percent of the WPA's recipients, although they constituted only 10 percent of the population. The Resettlement Administration, established in 1935 to help small farmers and tenants buy land, fought for the rights of black tenant farmers until angry southerners in Congress drastically cut its appropriations. Such help from New Deal agencies, and a belief that the White House—or at least Eleanor Roosevelt—cared about their plight, caused blacks to change their political allegiance. Since the Civil War, African Americans had staunchly supported the party of Abraham Lincoln, the Great Emancipator; even in the dark depression year of 1932, black voters in

northern cities overwhelmingly supported Republican candidates. But in 1936 black Americans outside the South (where few blacks were allowed to vote) gave Roosevelt 71 percent of their votes. In Harlem, where state and federal relief dollars increased dramatically in the wake of the 1935 riot, African American support for the president was an extraordinary 81 percent. Black voters have remained strongly Democratic ever since.

Mary McLeod Bethune: Black New Dealer. African Americans supported the New Deal in part because the Roosevelt administration appointed many blacks to federal office. Among the most important of these was Mary McLeod Bethune. Born in 1875 in South Carolina, Bethune was the child of former slaves who founded a school that eventually became the prestigious Bethune-Cookman College. Becoming an educator herself, Bethune served during the 1920s as president of the National Association of Colored Women (NACW)—a leading black women's organization. In 1935 she organized the National Council of Negro Women (NCNW), a coalition of the major associations of black women.

Bethune joined the New Deal in 1935, serving first as a member of the advisory committee of the National Youth Administration and then as director of the NYA's Division of Negro Affairs. In that position she emerged as the leader of the Federal Council of Negro Affairs, a group of black administrators who met on Sunday nights at her home in Washington. Along with NAACP general secretary Walter White, she had access to the White House and pushed continually, though often without success, for New Deal programs that would directly assist African Americans.

The Indian Reorganization Act. The New Deal had a greater direct impact on Native Americans. Indian peoples had long made up one of the nation's most disadvantaged and powerless minorities. Their average annual income in 1934 was only $48, and their unemployment rate was three times the national average. The plight of Native Americans won the attention of Secretary of the Interior Harold Ickes and Commissioner of the Bureau of Indian Affairs John Collier. They pushed for an Indian Section of the Civilian Conservation Corps and earmarked FERA and CWA work relief projects for Indian reservations.

More ambitious was the Indian Reorganization Act of 1934, sometimes called the "Indian New Deal." That law reversed the Dawes Act of 1887 by promoting Indian self-government through formal constitutions and democratically elected tribal

A Bitter Harvest

In the early 1930s California was rocked by strikes, and one of the largest was the cotton pickers' strike of 1933. Demanding higher wages and better working conditions, the predominantly Mexican American workforce set up camps for the duration of the strike. While the men stood on the picket line, their wives and daughters took care of the cooking, cleaning, and child care. Bancroft Library, University of California, Berkeley.

councils. A majority of Indian peoples—some 174—accepted the reorganization policy, but 78 refused to participate, primarily because they preferred traditional consensus-seeking methods of making decisions. New Deal administrators accepted their decision. Influenced by academic anthropologists, who celebrated the unique character of native cultures, government officials no long attempted to assimilate Native Americans into mainstream society. Instead, they embraced a policy of **cultural pluralism** and pledged to preserve Indian languages, arts, and traditions.

Migrants and Minorities in the West

Over the course of the late nineteenth and twentieth centuries, the American West—and especially California—grew dramatically in population and wealth (see Chapter 16). During the 1920s and 1930s, agriculture in California became a big business—large scale, intensive, and diversified. Corporate-owned farms produced specialty crops—lettuce, tomatoes, peaches, grapes, and cotton—whose staggered harvests required lots of transient labor during picking seasons. Thousands of workers, initially migrants from Mexico and Asia and later from the midwestern states, trooped from farm to farm harvesting those crops for shipment to eastern markets. Some of these migrants also settled in the rapidly growing cities along the West Coast, especially the sprawling metropolis of Los Angeles. Until the Great Depression, many foreign migrants viewed California as the promised land.

Mexicans and Asians. The economic downturn brought dramatic changes to the lives of thousands of Mexican Americans. The 1930 census reported 617,000 Mexican Americans; by 1940 the number had dropped to 377,000. A formal deportation

A New Deal for Indians

John Collier, the New Deal's commissioner for Indian affairs, was a former social worker who had become interested in Native American tribal cultures in the 1920s. A longtime opponent of the assimilationist policies of the Dawes Act of 1887, Collier led successful efforts to provide Native American peoples with communally controlled lands and self-government. Here, Collier speaks with Chief Richard of the Blackfoot Nation, one of the Indian leaders attending the Four Nation celebration at historic Old Fort Niagara, New York, in 1934. Corbis-Bettmann.

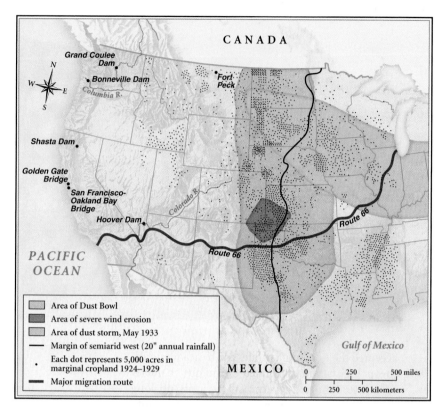

MAP 24.2 The Dust Bowl and Federal Building Projects in the West, 1930–1941

A U.S. Weather Bureau scientist called the drought of the 1930s "the worst in the climatological history of the country." Conditions were especially severe in the southern plains, where farming on marginal land threatened the environment even before the drought struck. As farm families migrated west on U.S. Route 66, the federal government began a series of massive building projects that provided flood control, irrigation, electric power, and transportation facilities to residents of the states of the Far West.

policy for illegal immigrants instituted by the Hoover administration was partly responsible for the decline in numbers, but even more Mexicans left voluntarily in the first years of the depression. Working as migrant laborers, they knew that local officials would ship them back to Mexico rather than support them on relief during the winter.

Under the New Deal, the situation of Mexican Americans improved. Those migrants living in Los Angeles, El Paso, and other cities qualified for relief more easily, and there was more relief to go around. New Deal initiatives supporting labor unions indirectly encouraged the acculturation of Mexican immigrants; joining the CIO was an important stage in becoming Americans for many Mexicans. Other immigrants heeded the call of the Democratic Party to join the New Deal coalition. Los Angeles activist Beatrice Griffith noted, "Franklin D. Roosevelt's name was the spark that started thousands of Spanish-speaking persons to the polls."

The farm union organizer César Chavez grew up in such a family. In 1934, when Chavez was ten, his father lost his farm near Yuma, Arizona, and the family became part of the migrant workforce in California. They experienced continual discrimination, even in restaurants where signs proclaimed "White Trade Only." César's father joined several bitter strikes in the Imperial Valley, part of a wave of job actions across the state. All of the strikes failed, including one in the San Joaquin Valley that

mobilized 18,000 cotton pickers. But these strikes set the course for the young Chavez, who founded the United Farm Workers, a successful union of Mexican American workers, in 1962 (see pp. 886–887).

Men and women of Asian descent—mostly from China, Japan, and the Philippines—formed a tiny minority of the American population but were a significant presence in some western cities and towns. Immigrants from Japan and China had long faced discrimination; for example, a California law of 1913 prohibited immigrants from owning land. Japanese farmers, who specialized in fruit and vegetable crops, circumvented this restriction by putting land titles in the names of their American-born children. As farm prices declined during the depression and racial discrimination undermined the prospects of rising generation for nonfarm jobs, about 20 percent of the migrants returned to Japan.

Chinese Americans were even less prosperous than their Japanese counterparts were. Only 3 percent of Chinese Americans worked in professional and technical occupations, and discrimination kept them out of most industrial jobs. In San Francisco, most Chinese worked in small ethnic businesses—restaurants, laundries, and firms that imported textiles and ceramics. In the hard times of the depression, they turned for assistance both to traditional Chinese social organizations such as *huiguan* (district associations) and to local authorities; in 1931, about one-sixth of San Francisco's Chinese population

Drought Refugees

Like the Joad family in John Steinbeck's powerful novel *The Grapes of Wrath* (1939), many thousands of poor people hit hard by the drought, dust, and debt of farm life in the Great Plains loaded their possessions into pickup trucks and hoped for brighter futures in the West. This photograph, shot in 1937 by Dorothea Lange, shows a family of Missouri drought refugees taking a break on Highway 99 near Tracy, California. Library of Congress.

was receiving public welfare aid. Few benefited from the New Deal. Until the repeal of the Chinese Exclusion Act in 1943, Chinese immigrants were classified as "aliens ineligible for citizenship" and therefore excluded from most federal programs.

Because Filipino immigrants came from a U.S. territory, they were not affected by the ban on Asian immigration passed in 1924 (see Chapter 23). During the 1920s their numbers swelled to about 50,000, many of whom worked as laborers on large corporate-owned farms. As the depression cut wages, Filipino immigration slowed to a trickle and was virtually cut off by the Tydings-McDuffie Act of 1934. The act granted independence to the Philippines (which since 1898 had been an American dependency), classified all Filipinos in the United States as aliens, and restricted immigration to fifty persons per year.

Dust Bowl Migration to California. Even as California lost its dazzle for Mexicans and Asians, it became the destination of tens of thousands of displaced farmers from the "dust bowl" of the Great Plains. Between 1930 and 1941, a severe drought afflicted farmers in the semiarid states of Oklahoma,

Texas, New Mexico, Colorado, Arkansas, and Kansas. But the dust bowl was primarily a human creation. Farmers had pushed the agricultural frontier beyond its natural limits, stripping the land of its native vegetation and destroying the delicate ecology of the plains (Map 24.2). When the rains dried up and the winds came, nothing remained to hold the soil. Huge clouds of thick dust rolled over the land, turning the day into night.

This ecological disaster prompted a mass exodus. Their crops ruined and their debts unpaid, at least 350,000 "Okies" (so-called whether or not they were from Oklahoma) loaded their meager belongings into beat-up Fords and headed to California. Many were drawn by handbills distributed by commercial farmers that promised good jobs and high wages; instead, they found low wages and terrible living conditions. Before the depression, white native-born workers made up 20 percent of the migratory farm labor force of 175,000; by the late 1930s, Okies accounted for 85 percent of the workers. John Steinbeck's novel *The Grapes of Wrath* (1939) immortalized them and their journey, and New Deal photographer Dorothea Lange's haunting images of migrant camps in California gave a

Odette Keun

A Foreigner Looks at the Tennessee Valley Authority

In 1936 French writer Odette Keun visited the United States and was so impressed by the Tennessee Valley Authority (TVA) that she wrote a book about it. Keun was struck not only by the vast size of the TVA but also by its imaginative scope. By promoting such projects, she argued, democratic governments could ward off popular support for fascist solutions to the Great Depression.

The vital question before democracy is, therefore, not how to bring back an economic freedom which is irretrievably lost, but how to prevent the intellectual freedom, which is still our heritage, from being submerged. It is already threatened. It will be threatened more and more strongly in the years ahead — and the menace, of course, is dictatorship. But to fight dictatorship it is necessary first to understand in what circumstances it arises, and then to think out the counterattack which democracy can launch against its approaching force.

Dictatorship springs from two very clear causes. One is the total incapacity of parliamentary government: total, as in Germany in 1933 and in Spain in 1935. To such a breakdown neither the democratic nations of Europe nor America have yet been reduced, although everywhere there are very ominous creaks and cracks, and the authority and prestige of parliamentary institutions have greatly and perilously diminished. The other cause, infinitely closer to us and more

dynamic, is the failure of the economic machine to function properly, and by functioning properly I mean ensuring a livelihood for the entire population. No system can survive if it cannot procure food and wages for the people who live under it. Man has to get subsistence from his rulers, for the most immediate and the most imperious law of our nature is that the belly must be filled. It is perfectly futile to orate on fine, high, and abstract principles to human beings who are permanently hungry, permanently harassed, permanently uncertain, who hear their wives begging for the rent and their children crying out for nourishment. . . .

One of the main tenets of liberalism — I reiterate this like a gramophone, but I must get it to sink in — is that all necessary overhauling and adjustment ought to be done in a manner which will minimize the shock to the greatest number, and soften as much as possible the unavoidable human suffering which these changes entail. This opposition to extremes, this practice of a graduated change, we can call "the middle of the road in time and space." But it is not nearly enough to conceive it and to bestow upon it a name. We must reach it. It is unutterably foolish to look at the middle of the road, to talk of the middle of the road, to hope for the middle of the road — and never get there.

Now I have tried to show that the middle of the road is already being laid down in America. The Tennessee Valley Authority is laying it down. Handicapped and restricted though it is in all sorts of ways, it is the noblest, the most intelligent, and the best attempt made in this country or in any other democratic country to economize, marshal, and integrate the actual assets of a region, plan its development and future, ameliorate its standards of living, establish it in a

more enduring security, and render available to the people the benefits of the wealth of their district, and the results of science, discovery, invention, and disinterested forethought. In its inspiration and its goal there is goodness, for goodness is that which makes for unity of purpose with love, compassion, and respect for every life and every pattern of living. The economic machine, bad though it is, has not been smashed in the Tennessee Watershed; it is being very gradually, very carefully, very equitably reviewed and amended, and the citizens are being taught and directed, but not bullied, not coerced, not regimented, not frightened, within the constitutional frame the nation itself elected to build. It is not while the Tennessee Valley Authority has the valley in its keeping that despair or disintegration can prepare the ground for a dictatorship and the loss of freedom. The immortal contribution of the TVA to liberalism, not only in America but all over the world, is the blueprint it has drawn, and that it is now transforming into a living reality, of the road which liberals believe is the only road mankind should travel.

SOURCE: Odette Keun, "A Foreigner Looks at the TVA," in *This Was America,* ed. Oscar Handlin (Cambridge, MA: Harvard University Press, 1949), 547–549.

ANALYZING THE EVIDENCE

➤ According to Keun, why has dictatorship come to Germany and Spain? Why might the TVA prevent such an outcome in the United States?

➤ What does the term *liberalism* mean to Keun, and why does she consider the TVA an example of that ideology?

personal face to some of the worst suffering of the depression.

A New Deal for the Environment

Concern for the land was one of the dominant motifs of the New Deal, and the shaping of the public landscape was among its most visible legacies. Franklin Roosevelt and Interior Secretary Harold Ickes were avid conservationists and used public concern over the drought and devastation in the dust bowl to spread "the gospel of conservation." Their national resources policy stressed scientific management of the land and the often aggressive use of public authority to preserve or improve the natural environment.

The Tennessee Valley Authority. The most extensive New Deal environmental undertaking was the Tennessee Valley Authority (TVA). Since World War I, experts had recommended the building of dams to control severe flooding and erosion in the Tennessee

The Human Face of the Great Depression

Migrant Mother by Dorothea Lange is one of the most famous documentary photographs of the 1930s. Lange spent only ten minutes in the pea-picker's camp in California where she captured this image and did not even get the name of the woman whose despair and resignation she so powerfully recorded. She was later identified as Florence Thompson, a full-blooded Cherokee from Oklahoma. Library of Congress.

River Basin, a seven-state area with some of the country's heaviest rainfall (Map 24.3). But when progressive reformers in the 1920s proposed a series of flood-control dams that would also generate cheap electricity, private utility companies blocked the project. As governor of New York, FDR had waged a similar unsuccessful battle to develop public power in the Niagara region. So in 1933 he encouraged Congress to fund the Tennessee project. The TVA was the ultimate watershed demonstration area, integrating flood control, reforestation, electricity generation, and agricultural and industrial development, including the production of chemical fertilizers. The dams and their hydroelectric plants provided cheap electric power for homes and industrial plants and ample recreational opportunities for the valley's residents. The project won praise around the world (see Voices from Abroad, "Odette Keun: A Foreigner Looks at the Tennessee Valley Authority," p. 758).

The TVA also contributed to the efforts of the Roosevelt administration to keep farmers on the land by enhancing the quality of rural life. The Rural Electrification Administration (REA), established in 1935, was central to that goal. Fewer than one-tenth of the nation's 6.8 million farms had electricity, and private utilities balked at the expense of running lines to individual farms. The REA addressed this problem by promoting the creation of nonprofit farm cooperatives. For a $5 down payment, local farmers could join the coop and apply for low-interest federal loans covering the cost of installing power lines. By 1940, 40 percent of the nation's farms had electricity; a decade later, 90 percent did.

Electricity brought relief from the drudgery and isolation of farm life. Electric milking machines and water pumps saved hours of manual labor. Electric irons, vacuum cleaners, and washing machines eased women's burdens, and radios enlivened the lives of the entire family. Electric lights extended the time children could read, women could sew, and families could eat their evening meals. One farm woman remembered, "I just turned on the light and kept looking at Paw. It was the first time I'd ever really seen him after dark." Along with the automobile, electricity probably did more than any other technological innovation to break down the barriers between urban and rural life in twentieth-century America.

Still, the dust bowl disaster focused the attention of urban dwellers and government planners on rural issues of land management and ecological balance. Agents from the Soil Conservation Service in the Department of Agriculture taught farmers to prevent soil erosion by tilling hillsides among the contours of the land. Government

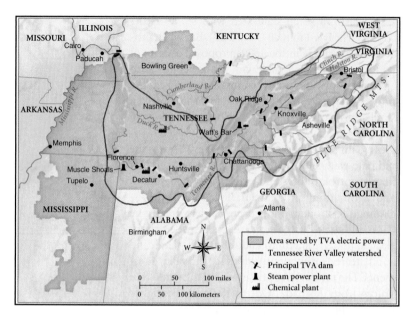

MAP 24.3   The Tennessee Valley Authority, 1933–1952

The Tennessee Valley Authority was one of the New Deal's most far-reaching environmental projects. Between 1933 and 1952, the TVA built twenty dams and improved five others, taming the flood-prone Tennessee River and its main tributaries. The cheap hydroelectric power generated by the dams brought electricity to hundreds of thousands of area residents, and artificial lakes provided extensive recreational facilities. Widely praised at the time, the TVA came under attack in the 1970s for its practice of strip mining and the pollution caused by its power plants and chemical factories.

agronomists also tried to remove marginal farms from cultivation. One of their most widely publicized programs was the Shelterbelts, the planting of 220 million trees running north along the ninety-ninth meridian from Abilene, Texas, to the Canadian border. Planted as a windbreak, the trees also prevented soil erosion.

New Deal projects that enhanced people's enjoyment of the natural environment can be seen today throughout the country. CCC and WPA workers built the famous Blue Ridge Parkway, which connects the Shenandoah National Park in Virginia with the Great Smoky Mountain National Park in North Carolina. In the West, government workers built the San Francisco Zoo, Berkeley's Tilden Park, and the canals of San Antonio. The CCC helped to complete the East Coast's Appalachian Trail and the West Coast's Pacific Crest Trail through the Sierra Nevada. In state parks across the country, cabins, shelters, picnic areas, lodges, and observation towers stand as monuments to the New Deal ethos of recreation coexisting with nature.

The New Deal and the Arts

Many American artists redefined their relationship to society in response to the Great Depression, and many became politically engaged. Never had there been a decade, critic Malcolm Cowley noted in 1939, "when literary events followed so closely on the flying coat-tails of social events." Because the New Deal funded many arts projects, the link between politics and the arts was both close and controversial.

Federal Arts Projects. As the economic downturn dried up traditional sources of private patronage, creative artists, like other Americans, turned to Washington. A WPA project known as "Federal One" put unemployed artists, actors, and writers to work, but its spirit and purpose extended far beyond relief. New Deal administrators encouraged artists to create projects of interest to the entire community, not just the cultured elite. "Art for the millions" became a popular New Deal slogan and encouraged the painting of murals in hundreds of public buildings (see Reading American Pictures, "Interpreting the Public Art of the New Deal," p. 761).

The Federal Art Project (FAP) gave work to many young artists who would become the twentieth century's leading painters, muralists, and sculptors. Jackson Pollock, Alice Neel, Willem de Kooning, and Louise Nevelson all received support. The Federal Music Project employed fifteen thousand musicians, and government-sponsored orchestras toured the country, presenting free concerts of both classical and popular music. Like many New Deal programs, the Music Project emphasized American themes. The composer Aaron Copland wrote his ballets *Billy the Kid* (1938) and *Rodeo* (1942) for the WPA, basing the compositions on western folk motifs. The federal government also employed the musicologist Charles Seeger and his wife, the composer Ruth Crawford Seeger, to catalog hundreds of American folk songs.

The Federal Writers' Project (FWP) gave work to five thousand writers and produced more than a thousand publications. It collected the oral histories

Interpreting the Public Art of the New Deal

"The Promise of the New Deal," Ben Shahn (1938). Roosevelt Arts Project.

Murals are perhaps the most pervasive artistic legacy of the New Deal. They decorate federal buildings throughout the nation today. The goals of the agencies that commissioned murals were to give employment to artists, bring art to the masses, and celebrate the American people and their nation. All murals were "realistic" in style and many embodied the decade's emphasis on regionalism by depicting the history of a locality and its people at work and play. This image comes from a large, three panel mural by well-known artist Ben Shahn that adorns a public school in Roosevelt, New Jersey.

Originally called the Jersey Homesteads, the town was created by the Farm Security Administration as a planned community for poor immigrant Jewish garment workers from New York City. The first two panels of the mural depict Jewish immigrants and their work. The third panel, pictured here, features in the left corner a teacher instructing workers about the history of unions. Seated at the right are New Deal planners and labor leaders. The figures behind them are the prospective residents of the new community. For the full mural, go to **www.scc.rutgers.edu/njh/ homesteads/mural.htm.**

ANALYZING THE EVIDENCE

➤ What does this third panel of Shahn's mural tell us about the character and the goals of the New Deal?

➤ Note the blueprint of the street plan and the houses depicted on the mural (top center). Then turn to the cartoon in Chapter 27 (p. 837) which depicts Levittown, a famous housing development built by a private corporation in the late 1940s. What does a comparison of those two images suggest?

➤ How does this mural fit with the discussion of the documentary impulse discussed in this chapter?

of many Americans, including two thousand narratives by former slaves, and published a set of popular state guidebooks. Young FWP employees who later achieved fame included Saul Bellow, Ralph Ellison, Tillie Olsen, and John Cheever. The black folklorist and novelist Zora Neale Hurston finished three novels while in the Florida FWP, among them *Their Eyes Were Watching God* (1937). And Richard Wright won the 1938 *Story* magazine prize for the best tale by a WPA writer. Wright used his spare time to complete *Native Son* (1940), a novel that took a bitter look at racism.

Of all the New Deal arts programs, the Federal Theatre Project (FTP) was the most ambitious. Under the gifted direction of Hallie Flanagan, the FTP reached an audience of 25 to 30 million people in the four years of its existence. Talented directors, actors, and playwrights, including Orson Welles, John Huston, and Arthur Miller, offered their services. Because many FTP productions took a critical look at American social problems, it was attacked in Congress as sympathetic to communism and its funding was cut off in 1939.

The Documentary Impulse. The WPA arts projects reflected a broad artistic trend called the "documentary impulse." Documentary artists focused on actual events that were relevant to people's lives and presented them in ways that aroused the interest and emotions of the audience. It influenced practically every aspect of American culture — literature, photography, art, music, film, dance, theater, and radio. It is evident in John Steinbeck's *Grapes of Wrath* and in John Dos Passos's *USA* trilogy, which used actual newspaper clippings and headlines in its fictional story. *The March of Time* newsreels, which movie audiences saw before feature films, presented images of world events for a pre-television age. New photojournalism magazines, including *Life* and *Look*, carried this documentary approach into millions of living rooms.

The federal government played a leading role in compiling the documentary record of the 1930s. It sent journalist Lorena Hickok, writer Martha Gellhorn, and many other investigators into the field to report on the conditions of people on relief. And the Historical Section of the Farm Security Administration compiled a remarkable series of photographs of the American scene. Under the direction of Roy Stryker, a talented group of photographers — Dorothea Lange, Walker Evans, Ben Shahn, and Margaret Bourke-White — produced haunting images of sharecroppers, dust bowl migrants, and urban homeless, permanently shaping the image of the Great Depression.

Building the American Future

Margaret Bourke-White's photograph of the Fort Peck Dam in Montana, with the two human figures in the foreground establishing its huge scale, graced the inaugural cover of *Life* magazine in 1936. Fort Peck was one of a series of dams built by the Works Projects Administration to control floods on the Missouri River. *Life*'s first issue also contained a photo essay about the town nearest to the Fort Peck Dam, which was named, appropriately, New Deal, Montana. Margaret Bourke-White, *Life Magazine,* copyright 1936 Time Warner, Inc.

The Legacies of the New Deal

The New Deal did much more than simply reinforce and extend the "regulatory" liberalism of the Progressive era. By creating a powerful national bureaucracy and laying the foundation of a social welfare state, it redefined the meaning of American liberalism. For the first time the federal government became an ongoing part of everyday life. During the 1930s, millions of people began to pay taxes directly to the Social Security Administration and the Internal Revenue Service, and more than a third of the population received direct government assistance from new federal programs, including old-age pensions, unemployment compensation, farm loans, relief work, and mortgage guarantees. Furthermore, the government stood ready to intervene in the economy when private enterprise failed to produce economic stability. New legislation regulated the stock market, reformed the Federal Reserve System, and subjected business corporations to federal regulation.

Like all major social transformations, the New Deal was criticized by those who thought it did too much and those who protested that it did too little. "Classical" liberals, who gave high priority to small government and individual freedom, pointed out that the New Deal state intruded deeply into the personal and financial lives of the citizenry. The Social Security Act, for example, imposed compulsory taxes on workers and forced families to comply with ever more complicated bureaucratic regulations. As one historian has written, the act instigated a "mercantilist regulation of family life not seen since the eighteenth century." Conversely, advocates of social welfare liberalism complained that the New Deal's safety net had many holes, especially in comparison with the far more extensive welfare systems provided by the governments of western Europe. These critics pointed out that there was no provision for a national health-care system; that domestic workers and farm laborers were excluded from most welfare programs; and that, in the many New Deal programs administered by state governments, benefits were often low.

Despite recurring debate about the increased presence of the state in American life, the New Deal set a pattern of government involvement in the life of the society that would persist for the rest of the twentieth century. There was a significant expansion of social welfare programs in the 1960s during the "Great Society" initiative of President Lyndon Johnson, and most of those programs remained intact in the wake of the "Reagan Revolution" of the 1980s (see Chapters 28 and 30).

The New Deal Coalition. Whatever the fate of the depression-era social welfare liberalism, there is no question that it was brilliant politics. The Democratic Party courted and won the allegiance of citizens who benefited from New Deal programs. Organized labor aligned itself with the administration that had made it a legitimate force in modern industrial life. Blacks voted Democratic as economic aid began to flow into their communities. The Women's Division of the Democratic National Committee elicited grassroots political support from 80,000 women who praised what the New Deal had done for their communities. The unem-

ployed also looked kindly on the Roosevelt administration. According to one of the earliest Gallup polls, 84 percent of those on relief voted the Democratic ticket in 1936.

Roosevelt's magnetic personality and the New Deal's farm relief and social security programs also brought millions of middle-class voters into the Democratic fold. Many were first- or second-generation immigrants from southern and central Europe — Italians, Poles, Slovaks, and Jews — who had now found a secure place in American life. The New Deal completed the transformation of the Democratic Party that had begun in the 1920s. Its coalition of ethnic groups, city dwellers, organized labor, blacks, and a broad cross-section of the middle class formed the nucleus of the northern Democratic Party for decades to come, and provided support for additional liberal reforms.

From its inception, the New Deal coalition also contained a potentially fatal contradiction involving the issue of race. Roosevelt and the Democratic Party depended heavily on white voters in the South, who strongly preferred to keep African Americans poor and powerless. Such policies faced increasing opposition not only from northern liberals but also from the increasing number of northern black Democrats. As the struggle over civil rights for African Americans entered the national agenda beginning in the late 1940s, it would gradually destroy the Roosevelt coalition. Even in the late 1930s, southern Democrats refused to support the expansion of federal power, fearing it would undermine white rule in the South. Thanks in part to this southern Democratic opposition, the New Deal, as we have seen, ground to a halt. The darkening international scene was also important. As Europe moved toward war and Japan flexed its muscles in the Far East, Roosevelt became increasingly preoccupied with international relations and pushed domestic reform further and further into the background.

➤ What impact did the New Deal have on organized labor, women, and racial and ethnic minorities?

➤ Under the New Deal, the government's involvement in the environment and in the arts was unprecedented. What were the major components of this new departure?

➤ What were the most significant long-term results of the New Deal? What were its limitations?

SUMMARY

We have seen the ways in which Franklin Delano Roosevelt's First New Deal concentrated on stimulating economic recovery, providing jobs and relief to the unemployed, and reforming banks and other financial institutions. His goal was to restore Americans' confidence in their society and institutions. The Second New Deal was different. Influenced by the persistence of the depression and the popularity of Huey Long's Share Our Wealth Society, FDR promoted social welfare legislation that would provide economic security for American citizens.

We also explored the impact of the New Deal on various groups of citizens, especially blacks, women, and unionized workers. Our survey focused on the depression-era experiences of migrants in the West, particularly the Mexicans, Asians, and Okies who worked in the farms and factories of California. Because New Deal legislation and programs assisted such groups, they gravitated to the Democratic Party. Its coalition of white southerners, ethnic urban workers, farmers, and a cross-section of the middle classes gave the party overwhelming majorities in Congress and provided FDR with a landslide presidential victory in 1936.

Finally, we examined the accomplishments and legacies of the New Deal. In the short run, it pulled the nation out of the crisis of 1933, provided relief, and preserved capitalist economic institutions and a democratic political system. Over the longer run, it expanded the size and power of the federal government and, through the Social Security system, farm subsidy programs, and public works projects, extended its presence into the lives of nearly every American. Great dams and electricity projects sponsored by the Tennessee Valley Authority in the Southeast, the Works Project Administration in the West, and the Rural Electrification Administration made permanent contributions to the quality of national life.

Connections: Economy

As we noted in the essay that opened Part Five (p. 671), between 1914 and 1945 the United States "boasted the world's most productive economic system." But the performance of the American economy varied widely over the decades. In Chapter 22 we saw how spending for military mobilization during World War I invigorated the industrial sector and food shortages in Europe ushered in a boom time for American farmers. But after the war, the farm economy fell into a two-decades-long crisis. As Chapter 23 explained, during the 1920s food surpluses cut farm prices and farm income, and Presidents Coolidge and Hoover vetoed farm relief legislation. Chapter 24 described the farm policies of the New Deal, which both subsidized farm owners and forced many tenant and sharecropping families off the land. As we will see in Chapter 25, new shortages of goods during World War II restored the prosperity of the farm sector, which was now increasingly dominated by the operators of large-scale farms.

The evolution of the industrial economy followed a roughly similar pattern. As we saw in Chapter 23, there was a sharp postwar economic recession in the early 1920s but then a quick recovery, thanks to the demand for new consumer goods: automobiles and many kinds of electrical goods. However, the wages paid to workers were not sufficient to sustain the boom, which collapsed in 1929. As this chapter explained, the various economic policies of the New Deal preserved the capitalist system and demonstrated the crucial importance of government intervention in smoothing out the business cycle and maintaining prosperity. Chapter 25 will show how massive government spending ended the Great Depression and, in the process, confirmed the economic theories of John Maynard Keynes.

CHAPTER REVIEW QUESTIONS

➤ Some historians have seen the New Deal as an evolution of Progressivism, but others have argued that it represented a revolution in social values and government institutions. What do you think?

➤ In what ways did Roosevelt's personality, values, and political style affect the policies and programs of the New Deal?

➤ What changes took place during the depression era with respect to the lives of women, workers, and racial and ethnic minorities? What role did the New Deal play?

TIMELINE

1931–1937	Scottsboro case: trials and appeals
1933	FDR's inaugural address and first fireside chats
	Emergency Banking Act begins the Hundred Days
	Civilian Conservation Corps (CCC) created
	Agricultural Adjustment Act (AAA)
	National Industrial Recovery Act (NIRA)
	Tennessee Valley Authority (TVA) established
	Townsend Clubs promote Old Age Revolving Pension Plan
	Twenty-first Amendment repeals Prohibition
1934	Securities and Exchange Commission (SEC) created
	Southern Tenant Farmers Union (STFU) founded
	Indian Reorganization Act
	Senator Huey Long promotes Share Our Wealth Society
	Father Charles Coughlin founds National Union for Social Justice
1935	Harlem race riot
	Supreme Court voids NRA in *Schechter v. United States*
	National Labor Relations (Wagner) Act
	Social Security Act creates old-age pension system
	Works Progress Administration (WPA) created
	Huey Long assassinated
	Rural Electrification Administration (REA) established
	Supreme Court voids Agricultural Adjustment Act
	Congress of Industrial Organizations (CIO) formed
1936	General Motors sit-down strike
	Landslide reelection of FDR marks peak of New Deal power
1937	FDR's Supreme Court plan fails
1937–1938	"Roosevelt recession" raises unemployment
1938	Fair Labor Standards Act (FLSA)
1939	Federal Theatre Project terminated

FOR FURTHER EXPLORATION

Robert S. McElvaine, *The Great Depression* (1984), provides a general treatment of the New Deal. Blanche Wiesen Cook's *Eleanor Roosevelt* (vol. 1, 1992; vol. 2, 1999) and Katie Loucheim, ed., *The Making of the New Deal: The Insiders Speak* (1983), portray important New Dealers. For popular reaction to Roosevelt's fireside chats, see Lawrence W. Levine and Cornelia R. Levine, *The People and the President* (2002). Robert S. McElvaine's *Down and Out in the Great Depression* (1983) contains letters written by ordinary people, while Studs Terkel's *Hard Times: An Oral History of the Great Depression* (1970) offers their memories. For audio versions of Terkel's interviews, go to the Chicago Historical Society at **www.studsterkel.org/index.html**. James Agee and Walker Evans's *Let Us Now Praise Famous Men* (1941) is a compelling portrait of southern poverty. For a memoir of a depression-era childhood, see Russell Baker's *Growing Up* (1982). John Steinbeck, *The Grapes of Wrath* (1939); Josephine Herbst, *Pity Is Not Enough* (1933); and Richard Wright, *Native Son*, (1940) are classic novels. See also Harvey Swados, *The American Writer and the Great Depression* (1966).

For two extensive collection of 1930s materials, see the "New Deal Network" at **newdeal.feri.org** and "America in the 1930s" at **xroads.virginia.edu/~1930s/home_1.html**, which includes clips of radio programs. See also the University of Utrecht's "American Culture in the 1930s" at **www.let.uu.nl/ams/xroads/ 1930proj.htm** and the wonderful collection of government-commissioned art at **www.archives.gov/exhibits/new_deal_ for_the_arts/index.html**. The Library of Congress has a multimedia presentation, "Voices from the Dust Bowl," at **memory .loc.gov/ammem/afctshtml/tshome.html** and a superb collection of photographs covering the years 1935–1945 at **lcweb2. loc.gov/ammem/fsowhome.html**. For music, listen to **www.authentichistory.com/1930s.html**. The political cartoons of the day are available in the "FDR Cartoon Archive" at **www.nisk.k12. ny.us/fdr**.

For the impact of the depression and the New Deal on African Americans, go to **memory.loc.gov/ammem/aaohtml/ exhibit/aopart8.html**. For the "'The Scottsboro Boys' Trials: 1931–1937," log on to **www.law.umkc.edu/faculty/projects/ FTrials/scottsboro/scottsb.htm**. For audio reminiscences about racial segregation during this and later decades, listen to "Remembering Jim Crow" at **americanradioworks.publicradio .org/features/remembering**.

TEST YOUR KNOWLEDGE

To assess your command of the material in this chapter, see the Online Study Guide at **bedfordstmartins.com/henretta**.

For Web sites, images, and documents related to topics and places in this chapter, visit **bedfordstmartins.com/makehistory**.

25

The World at War

1939–1945

THE SECOND WORLD WAR WAS "the largest single event in human history, fought across six of the world's seven continents and all of its oceans. It killed fifty million human beings, left hundreds of millions of others wounded in mind or body and materially devastated much of the heartland of civilization" both in Europe and East Asia. So concluded the noted military historian John Keegan, in a grim judgment that still rings true. The war was so vast and so destructive because it was waged both with technologically advanced weapons and with massive armies. The military conflict began in 1939 with a *blitzkrieg* ("lightning war") attack by wonderfully engineered German tanks across the plains of Poland. It ended in 1945 when American planes dropped two atomic bombs, the product of even more breathtaking scientific breakthroughs, on the Japanese cities of Hiroshima and Nagasaki. In between these demonstrations of technological prowess and devastating power, huge armies confronted and destroyed one another on the steppes of Russia, the river valleys of China, and the sandy deserts of North Africa.

Well might soldiers and civilians "jive in the streets" around Times Square in New York City on August 1945, celebrating V-J (Victory over Japan) Day. World War II was finally over. Many American lives had been lost or forever damaged, but the country emerged from the war intact

◄ **One City (and Island) at a Time**

By late 1944, the victory of the United States and its allies was nearly certain, but Japanese and German troops continued to fight with great courage and determination. Many European cities and every Pacific island had to be taken foot by foot. Here, American troops from the 325th Regiment of the 82nd Airborne Division advance slowly through the rubble-filled street of a German city in early 1945. Collection of Jeff Ethell.

and prosperous. As one man told journalist Studs Terkel, "Those who lost nobody at the front had a pretty good time." In fact, many Americans viewed the brutal conflict as the "good war," a successful defense of democratic values from the threat posed by German and Japanese fascism. When evidence of the grim reality of the Jewish Holocaust came to light, U.S. participation in the war seemed even more just.

Although it was not fully apparent at the time, World War II changed the nation's government in fundamental ways. The power of the federal government, which had been increasing since the Progressive era and World War I, grew exponentially during the conflict. Equally important, the government remained powerful after the war ended. Federal laws, rules, and practices put in place during the war — universal taxation of incomes, nationwide antidiscrimination employment standards, a huge military establishment, and multibillion dollar budgets, to name but a few — became part of American life. So too did the active participation of the United States in international politics and diplomacy, a participation all the more important because of the unresolved issues of the wartime alliance with the Soviet Union. A powerful American state, the product of a long "hot" war, would remain in place to fight an even longer, more expensive, and more dangerous Cold War.

The Road to War

The Great Depression disrupted economic life and political life around the world, everywhere endangering traditional institutions. An antidemocratic movement known as fascism, which had developed in Italy during the 1920s, spread to Japan, Germany, and Spain. By the mid-1930s, these states had forsaken their democratic institutions and instituted authoritarian, militaristic governments led by powerful dictators: Adolf Hitler in Nazi Germany, Benito Mussolini in Italy, Francisco Franco in Spain, and, after 1940, Hideki Tojo in Japan. As early as 1936, President Roosevelt warned Americans that other peoples had "sold their heritage of freedom for the illusion of a living" and called on them to work for "the survival of democracy" both at home and abroad. Hampered at first by the pervasive isolationist sentiment in the country, by 1939 FDR was leading the nation toward war against the Fascist powers.

The Rise of Fascism

World War II had its roots in the settlement of World War I (see Chapter 22). Germany deeply resented the harsh terms imposed on it by the Treaty of Versailles, and Japan and Italy revived their dreams of overseas empires that had been thwarted by the treaty makers. The League of Nations, the collective security system established at Versailles, proved unable to maintain the existing international order.

The first challenge came from Japan. In 1930, that small island nation was controlled by a militaristic regime with an expansionist agenda. To become a major industrial power, Japan needed raw materials and overseas markets for its goods. To get them, Japan embarked on a program of military expansion. In 1931, its troops occupied Manchuria, the northernmost province of China, and in 1937 it launched a full-scale invasion of China. In both instances the League of Nations condemned Japan's action but took no action to stop the military invasion.

Hitler

In 1933, Adolph Hitler seized power in Germany, intent on restoring its status as a major power. His ambitions grew steadily: overturning the Versailles treaty, asserting German control of central Europe, dominating Europe and the world. Here, dressed as usual in a military uniform, he salutes army troops and brown-suited members of his National-Socialist German Workers Party (NSDAP or Nazi) at the party's annual meeting in Nuremberg in 1938. Note the swastika — the symbol of his Nazi Party — prominently displayed on the *führer's* sleeve. Time Life Pictures / Getty Images.

Japan's defiance of the League encouraged a fascist dictator half a world away: Italy's Benito Mussolini who had come to power in 1922 and introduced a fascist political system. Fascism in Italy and, later, in Germany rested on an ideology of a powerful state that directed economic and social affairs. It disparaged parliamentary government, independent labor movements, and individual rights and celebrated authoritarian rule; Mussolini called for "a dictatorship of the state over many classes cooperating."

The Italian dictator had long been unhappy with the Versailles treaty, which had not awarded Italy any of the former German or Turkish colonies in Africa or the Middle East. So in 1935 he invaded Ethiopia, one of the few independent countries left in Africa. The Ethiopian emperor, Haile Selassie, appealed to the League of Nations, which condemned the invasion but imposed only limited sanctions. By 1936 the Italians had subjugated Ethiopia and were now an imperial nation.

Hitler and National Socialism. But it was Germany, not Italy, that presented the gravest threat to the world order in the 1930s. There, huge World War I reparation payments, economic depression, fear of communism, labor unrest, and rising unemployment fueled the rise of Adolf Hitler and his National Socialist (Nazi) Party. In 1933 Hitler became chancellor of Germany, and the legislature, the *Reichstag*, granted him dictatorial powers to deal with the crisis. He soon took the title of *führer* (leader) and outlawed other political parties.

Hitler's goal was nothing short of European domination and world power, as he made clear in his book *Mein Kampf* (*My Struggle*). Hitler's plan was to overturn the territorial settlements of the Versailles treaty, unite Germans living throughout central and eastern Europe in a great German fatherland, and annex large areas of eastern Europe. The "inferior races" who lived in these lands—Jews, Gypsies, and Slavs—would be removed or subordinated to the German "master race." A virulent anti-Semite, Hitler had long blamed Jews for Germany's problems. Once in power, he began a sustained and brutal persecution of Jews, which expanded to a campaign of extermination when the war began.

Hitler's strategy for restoring Germany's lost territories and military power was to provoke a series of minor crises—daring Britain and France to go to war to stop him. In 1935, Hitler announced that he planned to rearm the nation in violation of the Versailles treaty. No one stopped him. In 1936 Germany sent troops into the Rhineland, a region that had been declared a demilitarized zone under the treaty; once again, France and Britain took no

action. Later that year, Hitler and Mussolini joined forces in the Rome-Berlin Axis, a political and military alliance. Also in 1936, Germany signed an Anti-Comintern Pact with Japan. Its announced purpose was to oppose the Comintern, a Soviet-backed worldwide organization that spread communist ideology, but the pact was really a military alliance between Japan and the Axis Powers.

Isolationists versus Interventionists

While these events were taking place in Europe, the Roosevelt administration focused its energies on restoring the American economy and, diplomatically, on consolidating American influence in the Western Hemisphere. Secretary of State Cordell Hull implemented a Good Neighbor Policy, under which the United States voluntarily renounced the use of military force and armed intervention in Latin America. As part of this effort, in 1934 Congress repealed the Platt Amendment, a relic of the Spanish-American War, which asserted the U.S. right to intervene in Cuba's affairs (see Chapter 21). However, the United States kept (and still maintains) a major naval base at Cuba's Guantanamo Bay, and its diplomats continued to intervene in various Latin American countries on behalf of American business interests there.

Congress and the American public accepted such economic intervention, but they were increasingly resistant to diplomatic initiatives that might result in political entanglements. In part, the growing support for political isolationism reflected disillusionment with American participation in World War I. In 1934 Gerald P. Nye, a progressive Republican senator from North Dakota, began a congressional investigation into the profits of munitions makers during World War I and then widened the investigation to determine their influence (and that of the banks that lent millions to the Allies) on America's decision to declare war. Nye's committee concluded that war profiteers, whom it called "merchants of death," had maneuvered the nation into World War I for financial gain.

Although the Nye committee failed to prove this charge, its factual findings gave momentum to the isolationist movement and resulted in the passage of a series of legislative acts. All were explicitly designed to prevent a recurrence of the events that helped to pull the nation into World War I. Thus, the Neutrality Act of 1935 imposed an embargo on arms trading with countries at war and declared that American citizens traveled on the ships of belligerent nations at their own risk. In 1936 Congress expanded the act to ban loans to belligerents, and in

1937 it adopted a "cash-and-carry" provision: If a country at war wanted to purchase nonmilitary goods from the United States, it had to pay for them in cash and pick them up in its own ships.

The Popular Front. Other Americans, especially writers, intellectuals, and progressive social activists, responded to the rise of fascism in Europe by advocating interventionist policies. Some of them joined the American Communist Party, which had taken the lead in organizing opposition to fascism and which was also gaining supporters as the depression revealed deep flaws in the capitalist system. Between 1935 and 1938, Communist party membership peaked at about 100,000, from a wide range of social groups: African American farmers in Alabama, white electrical workers in New York, union organizers, even a few New Deal administrators. Many intellectuals did not join the party, but considered themselves "fellow travelers." They sympathized with the party's objectives, wrote for the *Daily Worker*, and supported organizations sponsored by the party.

The courting of intellectuals, union members, and liberal organizations reflected a shift in the strategy of the Communist Party. Fearful of German and Japanese aggression, the Soviet Union instructed its followers in western Europe and the United States to join in a Popular Front with other opponents of fascism. The Popular Front strategy became even more urgent with the outbreak of the Spanish Civil War in 1936. Armed forces led by Generalissimo Francisco Franco, strongly supported by the Fascist regimes in Germany and Italy, led a rebellion against Spain's democratically elected Republican government. Backed only by the Soviet Union and Mexico, the Republicans, or Loyalists, relied heavily on military volunteers from other countries, including the 3,200-strong American Abraham Lincoln Brigade. The governments of the United States, Great Britain, and France, despite their Loyalist sympathies, remained neutral — a policy that ensured a Fascist victory. American intellectuals strongly supported the Spanish Loyalists but grew increasingly uneasy with the Popular Front because of the rigidity of their Communist associates and the cynical brutality and political repression of Soviet leader Joseph Stalin.

The Failure of Appeasement. Further encouraged by the passivity of the Allied Powers during the Spanish Civil War, Hitler expanded his aggression in 1938. He sent troops to annex German-speaking Austria, while simultaneously scheming to seize a part of Czechoslovakia. Because Czechoslovakia had an alliance with France, war seemed imminent. But at the Munich Conference in September 1938, Britain and France again capitulated, agreeing to let Germany annex the Sudetenland — the German-speaking border areas of Czechoslovakia — in return for Hitler's pledge to seek no more territory. The agreement, declared British Prime Minister Neville Chamberlain, guaranteed "peace for our time."

Within six months, however, Hitler's forces had overrun the rest of Czechoslovakia and were threatening to march into Poland. Britain and France, realizing that their policy of appeasement had been disastrous, now prepared to take a stand. Then in August 1939 Hitler and Stalin shocked the world by signing a Nonaggression Pact. The pact had advantages for both sides. It protected Russia from a German invasion but only at the cost of destroying the Popular Front and severely weakening support for the Communist Party in western Europe and the United States. For Germany, the results of the pact were all positive. It assured Hitler that he would not have to wage a two-front war. Now protected in the east, on September 1, 1939, Hitler launched a *blitzkrieg* ("lightning war") against Poland; two days later Britain and France declared war on Germany. World War II had begun.

Retreat from Isolationism

Because the United States had become a major world power, its response would affect the course of the European conflict. Two days after the European war started, the United States officially declared its neutrality. Roosevelt made no secret of his sympathies and pointedly rephrased Woodrow Wilson's declaration of 1914 (see p. 675): "This nation will remain a neutral nation, but I cannot ask that every American remain neutral in thought as well." The overwhelming majority of Americans — some 84 percent, according to a poll in 1939 — supported Britain and France rather than Nazi Germany, but most Americans did not want to be drawn into another war.

At first the need for American intervention seemed remote. After the German conquest of Poland in September 1939, a false calm settled over Europe. But then on April 9, 1940, Nazi tanks overran Denmark. Norway fell to the Nazi *blitzkrieg* next, and the Netherlands, Belgium, and Luxembourg followed. Finally, on June 22, 1940, France fell. Britain stood alone against Hitler's plans for domination of Europe.

Support for Intervention Grows. What *Time* magazine would later call America's "thousand-step road to war" had already begun. After a bitter battle in Congress in 1939, Roosevelt won a change in the neutrality laws to allow the Allies to buy arms on a cash-and-carry basis. Interventionists, led by the journalist William Allen White and his Committee to Defend America by Aiding the Allies, became increasing vocal. In response, isolationists, including the aviator Charles Lindbergh and Senator Gerald Nye, formed the America First Committee to keep the nation out of the war; they attracted strong support in the Midwest and from conservative newspapers.

Despite the efforts of the America Firsters, in 1940 the United States moved closer to involvement in the war. In May Roosevelt created the National Defense Advisory Commission and laid the basis for a bipartisan defense effort by bringing two prominent Republicans, Henry Stimson and Frank Knox, into his cabinet as secretaries of war and the navy, respectively. During the summer, the president traded fifty World War I destroyers to Great Britain in exchange for the right to build military bases on British possessions in the Atlantic, thus circumventing the nation's neutrality law by executive order. In October, a bipartisan vote in Congress approved a large increase in defense spending and instituted the first peacetime draft registration and conscription in American history.

While the war expanded from Europe to its colonial possessions in North Africa and the oil-rich Middle East, the United States was preparing for the 1940 presidential election. The conflict had convinced Roosevelt that he should seek an unprecedented third term. Overcoming strong opposition from conservative Democrats, Roosevelt chose the liberal secretary of agriculture, Henry A. Wallace, as his running mate. The Republicans nominated Wendell Willkie of Indiana, a former Democrat who supported many New Deal policies. The two parties' platforms differed only slightly. Both parties pledged aid to the Allies, and both candidates pledged not to send "one American boy into the shambles of another war," as Willkie put it. Willkie's spirited campaign resulted in a closer election than those of 1932 or 1936; nonetheless, Roosevelt and the Democrats won 55 percent of the popular vote and a lopsided total in the Electoral College.

Lend-Lease and the Atlantic Charter. With the election behind him, Roosevelt concentrated on persuading the American people to increase aid to Britain, whose survival he viewed as the key to American security. In an address to Congress in January 1941, he outlined "four essential freedoms" (freedom of speech and of religion, freedom from want and fear) that he believed it was necessary to protect. Two months later, with Britain no longer able to pay cash for arms, Roosevelt convinced Congress to pass the Lend-Lease Act. The legislation authorized the president to "lease, lend, or otherwise dispose of" arms and other equipment to any country whose defense was considered vital to the security of the United States. When Hitler abandoned his Nonaggression Pact with Stalin and invaded the Soviet Union in June 1941, the United States promptly extended lend-lease to the Soviets, who became part of the Allied coalition. The implementation of lend-lease marked the unofficial entrance of the United States into the European war.

Roosevelt underlined his support for the Allied cause by meeting in August 1941 with Winston Churchill, who had become Britain's prime minister. Their joint press release, which became known as the Atlantic Charter, provided the ideological foundation of the Western cause. Like Wilson's Fourteen Points and Roosevelt's Four Freedoms, the charter called for economic collaboration and guarantees of political stability after the war to ensure that "all men in all the lands may live out their lives in freedom from fear and want." The charter also supported free trade, national self-determination, and the principle of collective security.

As in World War I, when Americans started supplying the Allies, Germany attacked U.S. and Allied ships. By September 1941 Nazi submarines and American vessels were fighting an undeclared naval war in the Atlantic, unknown to the American public (Map 25.1). Without a dramatic enemy attack, however, and with the public reluctant to enter the conflict, Roosevelt hesitated to ask Congress for a declaration of war.

The Attack on Pearl Harbor

The final provocation came not from Germany but from Japan. Throughout the 1930s, Japanese military advances in China had upset the balance of political and economic power in the Pacific, where the United States had long enjoyed the benefits of the open-door policy (see Chapter 21). After Japan's invasion of China in 1937, Roosevelt denounced "the present reign of terror and international lawlessness," suggesting that aggressors be "quarantined" by peace-loving nations. Despite such rhetoric, the United States refused to intervene when Japanese troops sacked the city of Nanking, massacred 300,000 Chinese residents and raped thousands of women, and sank an American gunboat in the Yangtze River.

As Japan pacified coastal areas of China, its imperial ambitions expanded. In 1940 Japan signed a formal military alliance with Germany and Italy, and its troops occupied the northern section of the French colony of Indochina (present-day Vietnam). Its goal was to create and dominate a Greater East

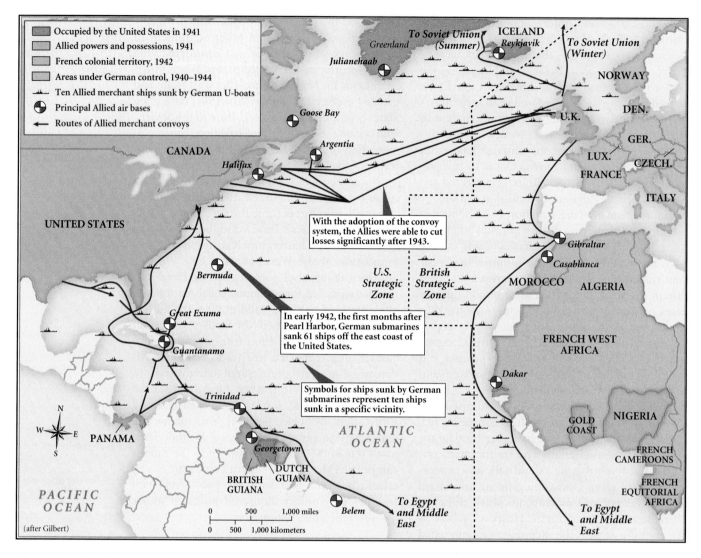

Map 25.1   World War II in the North Atlantic, 1939–1943

After the start of the war in Europe in September 1939, Germany escalated its submarine attacks on Allied and American merchant shipping in the Atlantic. Continued German advances spurred Congress to pass the Lend-Lease Act in March 1941 and President Roosevelt and Prime Minister Churchill to issue the Atlantic Charter in August. A pivotal factor in the Allied victory in Europe would be countering the German submarine threat in the Atlantic. With the establishment of the convoy system — the protection of merchant vessels with destroyers armed with sonar and depth charges — the Atlantic shipping lanes became safer, allowing the transport of troops and materials to Great Britain and North Africa.

Asia Co-Prosperity Sphere stretching from Indonesia to Korea. The United States responded to the invasion of Indochina by restricting trade with Japan, especially aviation-grade gasoline and scrap metal. Roosevelt hoped these economic sanctions would deter Japanese aggression. But in July 1941 Japanese troops occupied the rest of Indochina. Roosevelt now froze Japanese assets in the United States and instituted an embargo on all trade with Japan, including vital oil shipments that accounted for almost 80 percent of Japanese consumption.

In September 1941 the government of Prime Minister Hideki Tojo began secret preparations for war against the United States. By November American military intelligence knew that Japan was planning an attack but did not know where it would come. Early on Sunday morning, December 7, 1941, Japanese bombers attacked Pearl Harbor in Hawaii, killing more than 2,400 Americans. They destroyed or heavily damaged eight battleships, three cruisers, three destroyers, and almost two hundred airplanes.

Pearl Harbor, December 7, 1941

Sailors at the Naval Air Station stare in disbelief as a huge explosion rocks the battleship USS *Arizona*, anchored at Pearl Harbor. The Japanese bombed both the American fleet and the nearby military airfields to prevent a counterattack against the aircraft carriers that had launched the strike. U.S. Naval Historical Foundation.

Although the assault was devastating, it united the American people (as the September 11, 2001, terrorist attacks would do some sixty years later). The next day Roosevelt went before Congress. Calling December 7 "a date which will live in infamy," he asked for a declaration of war against Japan. The Senate voted unanimously for war, and the House concurred by a vote of 388 to 1. The lone dissenter was Jeannette Rankin of Montana, who had also opposed American entry into World War I. Three days later Germany and Italy declared war on the United States, and the United States in turn declared war on those nations.

➤ Compare the impact of the depression on the politics and political institutions of the United States, Italy, and Germany. What are the similarities and differences?

➤ As the world edged toward war in the late 1930s, many Americans were committed to political isolationism. What were the sources of this isolationism, and how was it manifest?

➤ Why did the United States join the fight in World War II? What are the key events leading to America's involvement?

Organizing for Victory

The task of fighting a global war greatly accelerated the influence of the federal government on all aspects of American life. Coordinating the changeover from civilian to war production, raising an army, and assembling the necessary workforce required a vast increase in the scope and size of government agencies. Mobilization on such a scale also demanded close cooperation between business executives in major corporations and political leaders in Washington, solidifying a partnership that had been growing since World War I. But the most dramatic expansion of power occurred at the presidential level when Congress passed the War Powers Act of December 18, 1941, giving President Roosevelt unprecedented authority over all aspects of the conduct of the war. This act marks the beginning of what historians call the Imperial Presidency—the far-reaching use (and abuse) of executive authority during decades of American world dominance, from 1945 to the present.

Financing the War

Defense mobilization definitively ended the Great Depression. In 1940, the gross national product stood at $99.7 billion; in 1945 it reached $211 billion. After-tax profits of American businesses nearly doubled, and farm output grew by a third. Federal spending of $186 billion on war production powered this advance; by late 1943, two-thirds of the economy was directly involved in the war effort (Figure 25.1). The government paid for these military expenditures by raising taxes and borrowing money. The Revenue Act of 1942 dramatically expanded the number of people paying income taxes from 3.9 million to 42.6 million; the annual revenue rose to $35.1 billion, facilitated by a payroll deduction system instituted in 1943. Most citizens willingly paid their income taxes as an expression of patriotism. Thanks to this revolutionary—and apparently permanent—

change in government financing, taxes on personal incomes and business profits paid for half the cost of the war, compared with 30 percent of the cost of World War I. The government borrowed the rest, both from wealthy Americans and ordinary citizens, who invested some of their wartime wages in long-term Treasury bonds. The **national debt** grew steadily, topping out at $258.6 billion in 1945.

The war also brought a significant expansion in the federal bureaucracy. The number of civilians employed by the government increased almost fourfold, to 3.8 million—a far more dramatic growth than during the New Deal. Leadership of federal agencies also changed as the Roosevelt administration turned from New Deal reformers to business executives. These executives became known as "dollar-a-year men" because they accepted only a token government salary and remained on the payroll of their corporations. Donald Nelson, a former executive at the Sears, Roebuck Company headed the powerful War Production Board (WPB). The Board awarded defense contracts, evaluated military and civilian requests for scarce resources, and oversaw the conversion of industry to military production. To encourage businesses to convert to war production, the board granted generous tax write-offs for plant construction and approved contracts with "cost-plus" provisions that guaranteed a profit and promised that businesses could keep the new factories after the war.

Henry J. Kaiser: "Miracle Man." In the interest of maximum production, the WPB preferred to deal with major corporations rather than with small businesses. America's fifty-six largest corporations received three-fourths of the war contracts; the top ten received a third. The best-known contractor was Henry J. Kaiser. Already highly successful from building roads in California and the Hoover and Grand Coulee dams, Kaiser turned to industrial production. At his Richmond, California, shipyard, he revolutionized ship construction by applying

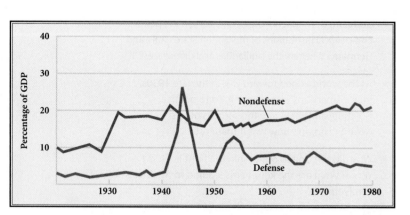

Figure 25.1 Government Military and Civilian Spending as a Percentage of GDP, 1920–1980.

Government military spending was about 3 percent of the gross domestic product (GDP) in the 1920s and 1930s, but it ballooned to more than 25 percent during World War II, to 13 percent during the Korean War, and to nearly 10 percent during the Vietnam War. Federal government spending for civilian purposes doubled during the New Deal and has remained at about 17 to 20 percent of GDP ever since.

The Miracle Man

Henry Kaiser knew how to run a business with no-nonsense efficiency. He built towns to house his workers, provided them with superior medical care, and organized them to build ships in record time. Here Kaiser uses an 81-piece, 14-foot-long model to show ship owners and Navy brass how his workers built a 10,400-ton Liberty freighter in the amazing time of 4 days, 15 hours, and 26 minutes. Corbis-Bettmann.

Henry Ford's techniques of mass production. Previously, most shipbuilding had been done by skilled workers who had served lengthy apprenticeships. To meet wartime production schedules, Kaiser broke the work process down into small, specialized tasks that newly trained workers could do quickly. Soon each of his work crews was building a "Liberty Ship," a huge vessel to carry cargo and troops to the war zone, every five days. The press dubbed him the "Miracle Man."

The Kaiser shipyards were also known for their corporate welfare programs, which boosted workers' productivity almost as much as his efficient assembly system. Kaiser offered his workers day care for their children, financial counseling, subsidized housing, and low-cost health care. The Kaiser Permanente Medical Care Program, founded in 1942, provided subsidized, prepaid health care for the shipyard workers and their families (and lives on today, as one of the nation's largest and most successful health maintenance organizations).

Central to all of Kaiser's business miracles was a close relationship with the federal agencies. The government financed the great dams he built during the depression and, through the Reconstruction Finance Corporation, lent him $300 million to build shipyards and manufacturing plants during the war. One historian has aptly called Kaiser a "government entrepreneur," the model for a new breed of business executive that prospered because of government contracts (and continue to do so, today). As Secretary of War Henry Stimson put it, in capitalist countries at war "you had better let business make money out of the process or business won't work."

Working together, American business and government turned out a prodigious supply of military hardware: 86,000 tanks; 296,000 airplanes; 15 million rifles and machine guns; 64,000 landing craft; and 6,500 cargo ships and naval vessels. The system of allotting contracts, along with the suspension of the antitrust prosecutions during the war, hastened the trend toward large corporate structures. In 1940, the largest one hundred companies produced 30 percent of the industrial output; by 1945, their share had soared to 70 percent. These same corporations formed the core of the nation's military-industrial complex of the Cold War era (see Chapters 26 and 27).

Mobilizing the American Fighting Force

Going to war meant mobilizing human resources, both on the battlefield and the home front (see Reading American Pictures, "U.S. Political Propaganda on the Home Front During World War II," p. 776). During World War II, the armed forces of the United States numbered more than 15 million men and women. The draft boards registered about 31 million men between the ages of eighteen and forty-four, but more than half the men failed to meet the physical standards, many because of defective teeth. The military tried to screen out homosexuals but had little success. Once in the services, homosexuals found opportunities to participate in a gay culture more extensive than that in civilian life.

Racial discrimination was part of military life, directed mainly against the approximately 700,000 blacks in uniform. The National Association for the Advancement of Colored People (NAACP) and other civil rights groups chided the government with reminders such as "A Jim Crow army cannot fight for a free world," but the military continued to segregate African Americans and to assign them the most menial duties. In contrast, Native Americans and Mexican Americans were never officially segregated and usually welcomed into combat units.

U. S. Political Propaganda on the Homefront during World War II

Why We Fight. National Museum of American Art, Smithsonian Institution, Washington, D.C.

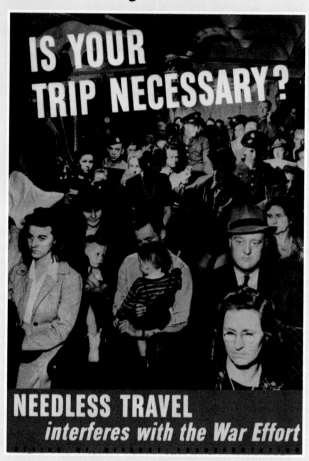

Please Stay Home. Picture Research Consultants & Archives.

In times of war, governments use visual imagery to motivate the public and frame the meaning of the war both at home and abroad. During World War II, as we point out in the text, the United States government made every effort to convince the American people to understand and support the war. But what can visual imagery tell us about the nature of World War II? These two pictures—produced in the U.S. during the war—provide some answers. The first is a 1942 lithograph by two artists, Karl Koehler and Victor Ancona, de-

picting a Nazi officer. The second is a poster of bus travelers produced by the Office of Defense Transportation.

ANALYZING THE EVIDENCE

▶ How might these images affect a viewer? What visual cues or elements do the image-makers employ to create an impact? List some of these items and compare them across the two images. Is one image more convincing than the other? Why?

▶ What kind of message does each image convey? Are these messages consistent with each other? Can you combine the messages into a larger statement explaining the U.S. perspective on fighting the war?

Approximately 350,000 American women enlisted in the armed services. About 140,000 served as army WACS (Women's Army Corps) and 100,000 as naval WAVES (Women Accepted for Volunteer Emergency Service). One-third of the nation's registered nurses, almost 75,000 overall, volunteered for military duty. In addition, about 1,000 WASPs (Women's Airforce Service Pilots) ferried planes and supplies in noncombat areas. The armed forces limited the types of duty assigned to women, as it did with blacks. Women officers could not command men, and WACS and WAVES were barred from combat duty, although female as well as male nurses served close to the front lines, risking capture or death. Most of the jobs women did in the military—clerical work, communications, and health care—reflected stereotypes of women's roles in civilian life.

Workers and the War Effort

As millions of working age citizens joined the military, the nation faced a critical labor shortage. The backlog of depression-era unemployment quickly disappeared, as defense industries alone provided jobs for about seven million new workers. Substantial numbers of women and blacks joined the industrial workforce; unions, benefiting from the demand for their members, negotiated higher wages and improved conditions for America's workers.

Rosie the Riveter. Government and corporate recruiters drew on patriotism as they urged women to take jobs in defense industries. "Longing won't bring him back sooner . . . GET A WAR JOB!" one poster beckoned, while the artist Norman Rockwell's famous "Rosie the Riveter" beckoned to women from the cover of the *Saturday Evening Post.* The government directed its publicity at housewives, but many working women gladly abandoned low-paying "women's" jobs as domestic servants or file clerks for higher-paying work in the defense industry. Suddenly the nation's factories were full of women working as airplane riveters, ship welders, and drill-press operators. Women made up 36 percent of the labor force in 1945, compared with 24 percent at the beginning of the war. Women war workers often faced sexual harassment on the job and usually received lower wages than men did. In shipyards women with the most seniority and responsibility earned $6.95 a day, whereas the top men made as much as $22.

When the men came home from war and the nation's plants returned to peacetime operations, Rosie the Riveter was out of a job. But many married women refused to put on aprons and stay home, and women's participation in the labor force rebounded steadily for the rest of the 1940s. The wartime expansion of the female workforce, especially among married women, began a trend that would continue for the rest of the twentieth century and change the character of family life (see Comparing American Voices, "Women in the Wartime Workplace," pp. 778–779).

Organized Labor. Workers used wartime mobilization to extend the gains in unionization and

A Real "Rosie" at Work

Elegant posters by artists J. Howard Miller (1942) and Norman Rockwell (1943) celebrated the work of the six million women who worked in the defense industry during World War II, as did the song that gave them a generic name: Rosie the Riveter. As this photograph suggests, the work itself had more grease and grime than elegance. This young woman operates a high-powered lathe, a boring machine that makes engine parts to precise specifications. Library of Congress.

Women in the Wartime Workplace

During World War II, millions of men served in the armed forces and millions of women worked in war-related industries. A generation later, some of these women workers recounted their wartime experiences to historians in oral interviews.

EVELYN GOTZION
Becoming a Union Activist

Evelyn Gotzion went to work at Rayovac, a battery company in Madison, Wisconsin, in 1935; she retired in 1978. While at Rayovac, Gotzion and her working husband raised three children.

I had all kinds of jobs. [During the war] we had one line, a big line, where you'd work ten hours and you'd stand in one spot or sit in one spot. It got terrible, all day long. So I suggested to my foreman, the general foreman, that we take turns of learning everybody's job and switching every half hour. Well, they [the management] didn't like it, but we were on the side, every once in a while, learning each other's job and learning how to do it, so eventually most all of us got so we could do all the jobs, [of] which there were probably fifteen or twenty on the line. We could do every job so we could go up and down the line and rotate. And then they found out that that was really a pretty good thing to do because it made the people happier. . . .

[O]ne day I was the steward, and they wouldn't listen to me. They cut our rates, so I shut off the line, and the boss came up and he said, "What are you doing?" I said, "Well, I have asked everybody that I know why we have gotten a cut in pay and why we're doing exactly the same amount of work as we did. . . . So, anyhow, we wrote up a big grievance and they all signed it and then I called the president of the union and then we had a meeting. . . . At that point the president decided that I should be added to the bargaining committee so that I would go in and argue our case, because I could do it better than any of the rest of them because I knew what it was. . . . We finally got it straightened out, and we got our back pay, too. From then on I was on the bargaining committee all the years that I worked at Rayovac.

SOURCE: Michael E. Stevens and Ellen D. Goldlust, eds., *Women Remember the War, 1941–1945* (Madison: State Historical Society of Wisconsin Press, 1993), 26–29.

FANNY CHRISTINA (TINA) HILL
War Work: Social and Racial Mobility

After migrating to California from Texas and working as a domestic servant, Tina Hill, an African American, got a wartime job at North American Aircraft. After time off for a pregnancy in 1945, Hill worked there until 1980.

Most of the men was gone, and . . . most of the women was in my bracket, five or six years younger or older. I was twenty-four. There was a black girl that hired in with me. I went to work the next day, sixty cents an hour. . . . I could see where they made a difference in placing you in certain jobs. They had fifteen or twenty departments, but all the Negroes went to Department 17 because there was nothing but shooting and bucking rivets. You stood on one side of the panel and your partner stood on this side and he would shoot the rivets with a gun and you'd buck them with the bar. That was about the size of it. I just didn't like it . . . went over to the union and they told me what to do. I went back inside and they sent me to another department where you did bench work and I liked that much better. . . .

Some weeks I brought home twenty-six dollars . . . then it gradually went up to thirty dollars [about $400 in 2007]. . . . Whatever you make you're supposed to save some. I was also getting that fifty dollars a month from my husband and that was just saved right away. I was planning on buying a home and a car. . . . My husband came back [from the war, and] . . . looked for a job in the cleaning and pressing place, which was just plentiful. . . . That's why he didn't bother to go out to North American. But what we both weren't thinking about was that they [North American] have better benefits because they did have an insurance plan and a union to back you up. Later he did come to work there, in 1951 or 1952. . . .

When North American called me back [after she left to have a baby] was I a happy soul! . . . It made me live better. It really did. We always say that Lincoln took the bale off of the Negroes. I think there is a statue up there in Washington, D.C., where he's lifting something off the Negro. Well, my sister always said — that's why you can't interview her because she's so radical — "Hitler was the one that got us out of the white folks' kitchen."

SOURCE: Excerpted from Sherna B. Gluck, *Rosie the Riveter Revisited* (Boston: G. K. Hall & Co., 1987), 37–42.

PEGGY TERRY
War: Wider Horizons and Personal Tragedies

Peggy Terry was born in Oklahoma, grew up in Paducah, Kentucky, and worked in defense plants in Kentucky and Michigan before settling in Chicago.

The first work I had after the Depression was at a shell-loading plant in Viola, Kentucky. It is between Paducah and Mayfield. They were large shells: anti-aircraft, incendiaries, and tracers. . . . We made the fabulous sum of thirty-two dollars a week [about $445 in 2007]. To us it was just an absolute miracle. Before that, we made nothing.

You won't believe how incredibly ignorant I was. I knew vaguely that a war had started, but I had no idea what it meant. . . . I was eighteen. My husband was nineteen. We were living day to day. When you are involved in stayin' alive, you don't think about big things like a war. It didn't occur to us that we were making these shells to kill people. It never entered my head. . . . We were just a bunch of hillbilly women laughin' and talkin'. . . .

I worked in building number 11. I pulled a lot of gadgets on a machine. The shell slid under and powder went into it. Another lever you pulled tamped it down. Then it moved on a conveyer belt to another building where the detonator was dropped in. You did this over and over.

Tetryl was one of the ingredients and it turned us orange. Just as orange as an orange. Our hair was streaked orange. Our hands, our face, our neck just turned orange, even our eyeballs. We never questioned. None of us ever asked, What is this? Is this harmful? . . . The only thing we worried about was other women thinking we had dyed our hair. Back then it was a disgrace if you dyed your hair. . . .

I think of how little we knew of human rights, union rights. We knew Daddy had been a hell-raiser in the mine workers' union, but at that point it hadn't rubbed off on any of us women. Coca-Cola and Dr. Pepper were allowed in every building, but not a drop of water. You could only get a drink of water if you went to the cafeteria, which was about two city blocks away. Of course you couldn't leave your machine long enough to go get a drink. . . .

The war just widened my world. Especially after I came up to Michigan. . . . We made ninety dollars a week [about $1,000 in 2007]. We did some kind of testing for airplane radios. Ohh, I met all those wonderful Polacks. They were the first people I'd ever known that were any different from me. A whole new world just opened up. I learned to drink beer like crazy with 'em. They were all very union-conscious. I learned a lot of things that I didn't even know existed. . . .

My husband was a paratrooper in the war, in the 101st Airborne Division. He made twenty-six drops in France, North Africa, and Germany. . . . Until the war he never drank. He never even smoked. When he came back he was an absolute drunkard. And he used to have the most awful nightmares. He'd get up in the middle of the night and start screaming. I'd just sit for hours and hold him while he just shook. We'd go to the movies, and if they'd have films with a lot of shooting in it, he'd just start to shake and have to get up and leave. He started slapping me around and slapped the kids around. He became a brute.

SOURCE: Studs Terkel, *"The Good War": An Oral History of World War II* (New York: Pantheon, 1984), 102–111.

ANALYZING THE EVIDENCE

➤ What common themes appear in the working lives of these three women? For example, how do labor unions affect their conditions of employment?

➤ How did the war change the lives of these women?

➤ These interviews occurred long after the events they describe. How might that long interval have affected the women's accounts of those years?

working conditions made in the New Deal. By 1945 almost 15 million workers belonged to a union, up from 9 million in 1939. These gains stemmed in part from organized labor's embrace of patriotism. In December 1941, representatives of the major unions made a "no-strike" pledge—nonbinding in character—for the duration of the war. In January 1942 Roosevelt set up the National War Labor Board (NWLB), composed of representatives of labor, management, and the public. The NWLB established wages, hours, and working conditions and had the authority to order government seizure of plants that did not comply. Forty plants were seized during the war.

During its tenure the NWLB handled 17,650 disputes affecting 12 million workers. It resolved the controversial issue of mandatory union membership through a compromise. New hires did not have to join a union, but those who already belonged had to maintain their union membership over the life of a contract. Agitation for wage increases caused a more serious disagreement. Because managers wanted to keep production running smoothly and profitably, they were willing to pay higher wages. However, pay raises conflicted with the government's efforts to combat inflation, which drove up prices dramatically in the early war years. Incomes rose as much as 70 percent during the war because workers earned pay for overtime work, which was not covered by wage ceilings and greatly increased output.

Despite higher incomes, many union members felt cheated as they watched corporate profits soar in relation to wages. Dissatisfaction peaked in 1943 when a nationwide railroad strike was narrowly averted. Then, John L. Lewis led more than half a million United Mine Workers out on strike, demanding an increase in wages over that recommended by the NWLB. Lewis's tactics won concessions, but they also alienated many Americans and made him one of the most disliked public figures of the 1940s. Congress responded by passing (over Roosevelt's veto) the Smith-Connally Labor Act of 1943, which required a thirty-day cooling-off period before a strike and prohibited strikes in defense industries. The legacy of this public and congressional hostility would hamper the union movement in the postwar years.

African American and Mexican American Workers.

During the war, a new mood of militancy swept through the African American community. "A wind is rising throughout the world of free men everywhere," Eleanor Roosevelt wrote during the war, "and they will not be kept in bondage." Black leaders pointed out parallels between anti-Semitism

Fighting for Freedom at Home and Abroad, 1941

This protester from the Negro Labor Relations League pointedly drew the parallel between blacks serving in the armed forces and winning access to jobs at the Bowman Dairy Company, a Chicago bottler, dried milk producer, and distributor that employed three thousand workers. Library of Congress.

in Germany and racial discrimination in America and pledged themselves to a "Double V" campaign: victory over Nazism abroad and victory over racism and inequality at home.

Even before Pearl Harbor, black labor activism was on the rise. In 1940 only 240 of the nation's 100,000 aircraft workers were black, and most of them were janitors. African American leaders demanded that the government require defense contractors to hire more blacks. When the government took no action, A. Philip Randolph, head of the Brotherhood of Sleeping Car Porters, the largest black union, announced plans for a "March on Washington" in the summer of 1941. Roosevelt was not a strong supporter of civil rights, but he feared the embarrassment of a massive public protest and he worried about a disruption of the nation's war preparations.

In June 1941, in exchange for Randolph's cancellation of the march, Roosevelt issued Executive Order 8802. It prohibited "discrimination in the employment of workers in defense industries or government because of race, creed, color, or national origin," and established the Fair Employment Practices Commission (FEPC). This federal commitment to minority employment rights was both unprecedented and limited: For example, it did not affect segregation in the armed forces, and the FEPC could not require compliance with its orders. Still, the committee resolved about a third of the more than eight thousand complaints it received.

Encouraged by the ideological climate of the war years, the League of United Latin American Citizens (LULAC)—the Latino counterpart to the NAACP—challenged long-standing patterns of discrimination and exclusion. In Texas, where it was still common to see signs reading, "No Dogs or Mexicans Allowed," the organization protested limited job opportunities and the segregation of schools and public facilities. The NAACP itself grew ninefold to 450,000 members by 1945, and in Chicago James Farmer helped to found the Congress of Racial Equality (CORE), a group known nationwide for protesting through direct action, such as rallies and sit-ins. These wartime developments—both federal intervention in the form of the FEPC and resurgent African American militancy—laid the groundwork for the civil rights revolution of the 1960s.

Politics in Wartime

The federal government expanded dramatically during the war years, but there was little attempt to use the state to promote progressive social reform on the home front, as in World War I. Many people, including business leaders, believed that an enlarged federal presence was justified only insofar as it assisted war aims. Moreover, in the 1942 elections Republicans had picked up ten seats in the Senate and forty-seven seats in the House, bolstering conservatives in Congress and cutting back prospects for new social initiatives. As war mobilization brought full employment, Roosevelt ended several popular New Deal programs, such as the Civilian Conservation Corps and the National Youth Administration.

As the war dragged on, Roosevelt began to lay the ideological foundations for new federal social welfare measures. In his State of the Union address in 1944, he called for a second bill of rights, which would guarantee that Americans had jobs, adequate food and clothing, decent homes, medical care, and education. There was some public support for such welfare measures, but Congress was less enthusiastic and extended benefits only to military veterans or GIs (short for "government issue"). The Servicemen's Readjustment Act (1944), popularly known as the "GI Bill of Rights," provided education, job training, medical care, pensions, and mortgage loans for men and women who had served in the armed forces. An extraordinarily influential program, particularly in expanding access to higher education, it distributed almost $4 billion in benefits to nine million veterans between 1944 and 1949; in the 1950s, it was extended to veterans of the Korean War.

The Election of 1944. Roosevelt's call for social legislation was part of a plan to reinvigorate the New Deal political coalition. In the election of 1944, Roosevelt once again headed the Democratic ticket. Party leaders, aware of FDR's health problems and anxious to find a middle-of-the-road successor, dropped Vice President Henry Wallace from the ticket. They feared that Wallace's outspoken support for labor, civil rights, and domestic reform would alienate southern Democrats. In his place they chose Senator Harry S Truman of Missouri. A direct-speaking, no-nonsense politician, Truman won his seat because of the sponsorship of Thomas Pendergast, the Democratic boss in Kansas City. Truman rose to prominence for heading a Senate investigation of government efficiency in awarding wartime defense contracts.

The Republicans nominated Governor Thomas E. Dewey of New York. Only forty-two years old, Dewey had won fame fighting organized crime as a U.S. attorney. Like drug smuggling today, the bootlegging of liquor during Prohibition generated huge profits and highly organized criminal "families" that subsequently turned to prostitution and the "protection" racket. Dewey took on the mobs in New York and, despite his use of controversial "third-degree" interrogation tactics, won the admiration of many Americans. Because Dewey accepted the general principles of welfare state liberalism domestically and internationalism in foreign affairs, he attracted some of Roosevelt's supporters. But a majority of voters preferred political continuity. Roosevelt received 53.5 percent of the nationwide vote and 60 percent in cities of more than 100,000 people, where ethnic minorities and labor unions strongly supported Democratic candidates. The continuing strength of the New Deal coalition after the economic emergency of the Great Depression had passed indicated that the long era of Republican political dominance (1896–1932) had come to an end.

> ➤ In what ways did World War II contribute to the growth of the federal government? How did it foster what historians now call the "military-industrial complex"?

> ➤ What impact did war mobilization have on women, racial minorities, and organized labor? What legislation or government rules affected their lives as workers, and what effect did it have on their political allegiance?

Life on the Home Front

The United States did not suffer the physical devastation that ravaged much of Europe and East Asia, but the war deeply affected the lives of millions of civilians, in ways good and bad. Americans welcomed the return of prosperity but shuddered every time they saw a Western Union boy on his bicycle, fearing he carried a telegram from the War Department reporting the death of someone's son, husband, or father. Many citizens also grumbled about the annoying government regulations that were a constant fact of life, but accepted that things would be different "for the duration."

"For the Duration"

Just like the soldiers in uniform, people on the home front had jobs to do. They worked on civilian defense committees, recycled old newspapers and scrap material, and served on local rationing and draft boards. About twenty million home "Victory gardens" produced 40 percent of the nation's vegetables. Various federal agencies encouraged these efforts, especially the Office of War Information (OWI), which disseminated news and promoted patriotism. The OWI urged advertising agencies to link their clients' products to the war effort, arguing that patriotic ads would not only sell goods but also "invigorate, instruct and inspire" the citizenry.

Popular Culture. Popular culture, especially the movies, reinforced the connections between the home front and the war effort. Hollywood producers, directors, and actors offered their talent to the War Department. Director Frank Capra created a series of "Why We Fight" documentaries to explain war aims to conscripted soldiers. Movie stars such as John Wayne, Anthony Quinn, and Spencer Tracy portrayed the heroism of American fighting men in many films, including *Wake Island* (1942), *Guadalcanal Diary* (1943), and *Thirty Seconds over Tokyo* (1945). Other movies, such as *Watch on the Rhine* (1943), warned of the danger of fascism at home and abroad, while the Academy Award–winning *Casablanca* (1943) demonstrated the heroism and patriotism of an ordinary American in German-occupied North Africa.

Average weekly movie attendance soared to over 100 million. Demand was so high that many theaters operated around the clock to accommodate defense workers on the swing and night shifts. Many movies had patriotic themes. In the box-office hit *Since You Went Away* (1943), Claudette Colbert starred as a wife who took a defense job after her husband left for war, while Oscar-winning Greer Garson played a courageous British housewife in *Mrs. Miniver* (1942). In this pre-television era, newsreels accompanying the feature films kept the public up-to-date on the war, as did on-the-spot radio broadcasts by Edward R. Murrow and other well-known commentators.

Wartime Prosperity and Rationing. Perhaps the major source of Americans' high morale was wartime prosperity. Federal defense spending had ended the depression, unemployment had disappeared, and per capita income doubled in real terms from $595 in 1939 to $1,237 in 1945. Despite geographical dislocations and shortages of many items, about 70 percent of Americans admitted midway through the war that they had personally experienced "no real sacrifices." A Red Cross worker put it bluntly: "The war was fun for America. I'm not talking about the poor souls who lost sons and daughters. But for the rest of us, the war was a hell of a good time."

For many Americans the major inconveniences of the war were the limitations placed on their consumption. In contrast to the largely voluntaristic approach used during World War I, federal agencies such as the Office of Price Administration subjected almost everything Americans ate, wore, or used during World War II to rationing or regulation. The first major scarcity was rubber. The Japanese conquest of Malaya and the Netherlands Indies cut off 97 percent of America's imports of natural rubber, an essential raw material. An entire new industry, synthetic rubber, was born and by late 1944 was producing 762,000 tons a year. To conserve rubber for the war effort, the government rationed tires, and so many of the nation's thirty million car owners put their cars up on blocks for the duration. As more people walked, they wore out their shoes. In 1944 shoes were rationed to two pairs per person a year, half the prewar average.

The government also rationed fuel oil, so schools and restaurants shorted their hours, and homeowners lowered their thermostats to 65 degrees. To cut domestic gasoline consumption, the government rationed supplies and imposed a nationwide speed limit of 35 miles per hour, which cut highway deaths dramatically. By 1943, the government was regulating the amount of meat, butter, sugar, and other foods Americans could buy. Most people cooperated with the complicated system of rationing points and coupons, but almost a fourth occasionally bought items on the black market, especially meat, gasoline, cigarettes, and nylon stockings. Manufacturers of automobiles, refrigerators, and radios, who had been forced to switch to military production, told consumers to save their money now and buy products once the war ended.

Migration and Social Conflict

The war and government policies determined where many people lived. When men entered the armed services, their families often followed them to training bases or points of debarkation. The lure

of high-paying defense jobs encouraged others — Native Americans on reservations, white southerners in the hills of Appalachia, farmers on marginal lands — to move. About fifteen million Americans changed residences during the war years, half of them moving to another state.

As a major center of defense production for the Pacific war, California was affected more than any other state by wartime migration. The state welcomed nearly three million new residents and grew by 53 percent during the war. "The Second Gold Rush Hits the West," headlined the *San Francisco Chronicle* in 1943. A tenth of all federal dollars flowed into California, and the state's factories turned out one-sixth of all war materials. People went where the defense jobs were — to Los Angeles, San Diego, and the San Francisco Bay area. Some towns grew practically overnight: Within two years of the opening of

A Family Effort

After migrating from the Midwest to Portland, Oregon, fifteen members of the family of John R. Brauckmiller (sixth from left) found jobs at Henry Kaiser's Swan Island shipyard. From 1943 to 1945, the shipyard turned out 152 T-2 Tankers, mostly for use by the U.S. Navy to carry fuel oil. A local newspaper pronounced the Brauckmillers as "the shipbuildingest family in America," and because of the importance of shipbuilding to the war effort, *Life* magazine featured the family in its issue of August 16, 1943. Ralph Vincent, *The Journal*, Portland, OR.

Zoot Suit Youth in Los Angeles

During a four-day riot in June 1943, servicemen in Los Angeles attacked young Latino men wearing distinctive "zoot suits," which were widely viewed as emblems of gang membership and a delinquent youth culture. The police response was to arrest scores of zoot-suiters. Here, a group of handcuffed young Latino men is about to board a Los Angeles County Sheriff's bus to make a court appearance. Note the wide-legged pants that taper at the ankle, a hallmark of the zoot suit. Library of Congress.

the huge Kaiser Corporation shipyard in Richmond, California, the town's population had quadrupled.

The growth of war industries prompted the migration of more than a million African Americans from the rural South to California, Illinois, Michigan, Ohio, and Pennsylvania—a continuation of the "Great Migration" earlier in the century (see Chapter 22). As migrant blacks and whites competed for jobs and housing, racial conflicts broke out in forty-seven cities during 1943. The worst violence took place in the Detroit area. In June 1943, a major race riot erupted, with Polish Americans and southern white migrants on one side and African Americans on the other. It left thirty-four people dead and hundreds injured.

Racial conflict struck the West as well. In Los Angeles, male Hispanic teenagers organized *pachuco* (youth) gangs. Many dressed in "zoot suits"— broad-brimmed felt hats, pegged trousers, and clunky shoes; they wore their long hair slicked down and carried pocket knives on gold chains. The young women who partied with them favored long coats, huarache sandals, and pompadour hairdos. Some blacks and working-class white teenagers in Los Angeles and eastern cities took up the zoot suit style to indicate both their group identity and their rejection of white, middle-class values. To many adults, the zoot suit symbolized wartime juvenile delinquency. When rumors circulated in June 1943 that a *pachuco* gang had beaten a white sailor, it set off a four-day riot. White servicemen roamed through Mexican American neighborhoods and attacked zoot-suiters,

taking special pleasure in slashing their pegged pants. Some attacks occurred in full view of white police officers, who did nothing to stop the violence.

Civil Rights during Wartime

These outbreaks of social violence were sharp but limited. Unlike World War I, which evoked intense prejudice and widespread harassment of German Americans, the mood on the home front was generally calm in the 1940s. Federal officials interned about five thousand potentially dangerous German and Italian aliens during the war. But leftists and Communists, prime targets of government repression at the end of World War I, experienced few problems, in part because the Soviet Union and the United States were allies in the fight against right-wing fascist nations.

Japanese Internment. The internment of Japanese aliens and Japanese American citizens was a glaring exception to this record of tolerance. Immediately after the attack on Pearl Harbor, the West Coast remained calm. Then, as residents began to fear attacks, spies, and sabotage, California's long history of racial antagonism toward Asian immigrants came into play (see Chapters 16, 21, and 24). Local politicians and newspapers whipped up sentiment against Japanese Americans, who numbered only about 112,000, had no political power, and clustered together in ethnic communities in the three West Coast states.

Early in 1942 Roosevelt responded to West Coast fears by issuing Executive Order 9066. The order, and

Behind Barbed Wire

As part of the forced relocation of 112,000 Japanese Americans, Los Angeles photographer Toyo Miyatake and his family were sent to Manzanar, a camp in the California desert east of the Sierra Nevada. Miyatake secretly began shooting photographs of the camp with a handmade camera. Eventually, Miyatake received permission from the authorities to document life in the camp — its births, weddings, deaths, and high school graduations. To communicate the injustice of internment, he also took staged photographs, such as this image of three young boys behind barbed wire with a watchtower in the distance. For Miyatake, it gave new meaning to the phrase "prisoners of war." *Toyo Miyatake.*

a subsequent act of Congress, gave the War Department the authority to evacuate Japanese Americans from the West Coast and intern them in relocation camps for the rest of the war. Despite the lack of any evidence of disloyalty or sedition activity among the evacuees, few public leaders opposed the plan. "A Jap's a Jap," snapped General John DeWitt, the officer charged with defense of the West Coast. "It makes no difference whether he is an American citizen or not."

The relocation plan shocked Japanese Americans, more than two-thirds of whom were native-born American citizens. (They comprised the Nisei generation, the children of the immigrant Issei

generation.) Army officials gave families only a few days to dispose of their property. Businesses that took a lifetime to build were liquidated overnight, and speculators snapped up Japanese real estate for a fraction of its value (see Voices from Abroad, "Monica Itoi Sone: Japanese Relocation," p. 786). The War Relocation Authority moved the internees to hastily built camps in desolate areas in California, Arizona, Utah, Colorado, Wyoming, Idaho, and Arkansas (Map 25.2). Ironically, the Japanese Americans who made up one-third of the population of Hawaii, and presumably posed a greater threat because of their numbers and proximity to Japan,

Map 25.2 Japanese Relocation Camps

In 1942, the government ordered 112,000 Japanese Americans living on the West Coast into internment camps in the nation's interior because of their supposed threat to public safety. Some of the camps were as far away as Arkansas. The federal government rescinded the mass evacuation order in December 1944, but when the war ended in August 1945, 44,000 people still remained in the camps.

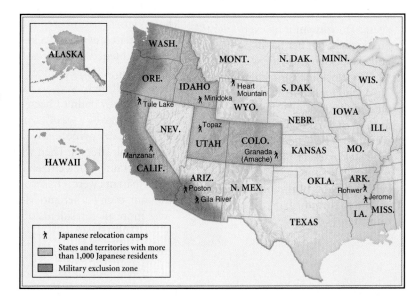

Monica Itoi Sone

Japanese Relocation

As Monica Itoi Sone discovered, her legal status as an American citizen did not keep her from being treated like an unwelcome foreigner. Her autobiography, Nisei Daughter *(1953), tells the story of the relocation and internment of Japanese Americans during World War II. In 1942 Sone was a young woman who had been born and raised in Seattle; she saw herself as an "American." In this selection, Sone ponders the question of national identity as she describes the Itoi family's forced evacuation by the U.S. Army. Her family spent the entire war in an internment camp in Idaho, but in 1943 Sone was allowed to attend college in Indiana.*

We felt fortunate to be assigned to a room at the end of the barracks because we had just one neighbor to worry about. The partition wall separating the rooms was only seven feet high with an opening of four feet at the top, so at night, Mrs. Funai next door could tell when Sumi was still sitting up in bed in the dark, putting her hair up. "Mah, Sumi-chan," Mrs. Funai would say through the plank wall, "are you curling your hair tonight again? Do you put it up every night?" Sumi would put her hands on her hips and glare defiantly at the wall.

The block monitor, an impressive Nisei who looked like a star tackle with his crouching walk, came around the first night to tell us that we must all be inside our room by nine o'clock every night. At ten o'clock, he rapped at the door again, yelling, "Lights out!" and Mother rushed to turn the light off not a second later.

Throughout the barracks, there were a medley of creaking cots, whimpering infants and explosive night coughs. Our attention was riveted on the intense little wood stove which glowed so violently I feared it would melt right down to the floor. We soon learned that this condition lasted for only a short time, after which it suddenly turned into a deep freeze. Henry and Father took turns at the stove to produce the harrowing blast which all but singed our army blankets, but did not penetrate through them. As it grew quieter in the barracks, I could hear the light patter of rain. Soon I felt the "splat! splat!" of raindrops digging holes into my face. The dampness on my pillow spread like a mortal bleeding, and I finally had to get out and haul my cot toward the center of the room. In a short while Henry was up. "I've got multiple leaks, too. Have to complain to the landlord first thing in the morning."

All through the night I heard people getting up, dragging cots around. I stared at our little window, unable to sleep. I was glad Mother had put up a makeshift curtain on the window for I noticed a powerful beam of light sweeping across it every few seconds. The lights came from high towers placed around the camp where guards with Tommy guns kept a twenty-four hour vigil. I remembered the wire fence encircling us, and a knot of anger tightened in my breast. What was I doing behind a fence like a criminal? If there were accusations to be made, why hadn't I been given a fair trial? Maybe I wasn't considered an American anymore. My citizenship wasn't real, after all. Then what was I? I was certainly not a citizen of Japan as my parents were. On second thought, even Father and Mother were more alien residents of the United States than Japanese nationals for they had little tie with their mother country. In their twenty-five years in America, they had worked and paid their taxes to their adopted government as any other citizen.

Of one thing I was sure. The wire fence was real. I no longer had the right to walk out of it. It was because I had Japanese ancestors. It was also because some people had little faith in the ideas and ideals of democracy. They said that after all these were but words and could not possibly insure loyalty. New laws and camps were surer devices. I finally buried my face in my pillow to wipe out burning thoughts and snatch what sleep I could.

SOURCE: Monica Itoi Sone, *Nisei Daughter* (Boston: Little, Brown & Co., 1953), 176–178.

ANALYZING THE EVIDENCE

➤ What was the difference between Sone's legal status and that of her parents? Why were they treated the same, given their different legal statuses?

➤ Based on the information in the text, what answer would the Supreme Court have given to Sone's claim that she deserved a "fair trial" before being imprisoned "like a criminal"?

were not interned. They provided much of the un-skilled labor in the island territory and the Hawaiian economy could not function without them.

Cracks soon appeared in the relocation policy. A labor shortage in farming led the government to furlough seasonal agricultural workers from the camps as early as 1942. About 4,300 college students were allowed to resume their education outside the West Coast military zone. Another route out of the camps was enlistment in the armed services. The 442nd Regimental Combat Team, a segregated unit composed almost entirely of Nisei volunteers, served with distinction in Europe.

Gordon Hirabayashi: Constitutional Rights.
Nisei Gordon Hirabayashi was among the few Japanese Americans who actively resisted incarceration. A student at the University of Washington, Hirabayashi was a religious pacifist who had registered with his draft board as a conscientious objector. He challenged internment by refusing to register for evacuation; instead, he turned himself in to the FBI. "I wanted to uphold the principles of the Constitution," Hirabayashi later stated, "and the curfew and evacuation orders which singled out a group on the basis of ethnicity violated them." Tried and convicted in 1942, he appealed his case to Supreme Court in *Hirabayashi v. United States* (1943). In that case, and also in *Korematsu v. United States* (1944), the Court allowed the removal of Japanese Americans from the West Coast on the basis of "military necessity," but avoided ruling on the constitutionality of the internment program. But in *Ex Parte Endo* (1944), the Court held that American citizens of undoubted loyalty could not be confined by government authorities.

The Court's refusal to rule directly on the relocation program underscored the fragility of civil liberties in wartime. Although Congress in 1988 issued a public apology and $20,000 in cash to each of the 80,000 surviving Japanese American internees, it once again gave the government sweeping powers of arrest and detention in the PATRIOT Act of 2001 (see Chapter 32).

➤ What impact did World War II have on everyday life for the majority of Americans?

➤ What distinguished the internal migration of Americans during World War II from that of the World War I era? Who moved and why?

➤ How do you explain the decision to intern Americans of Japanese birth or ancestry?

Fighting and Winning the War

World War II was, literally, a war for control of the world. Had the Axis Powers triumphed, Germany would have dominated, either directly or indirectly, all of Europe and much of Africa; Japan would have controlled most of East Asia. To prevent this outcome, which would have crippled democracy worldwide, destroyed the British and French empires, and restricted American power to the Western Hemisphere, the Roosevelt administration took the United States to war. The United States extended aid to the Allied Powers in the late 1930s, resorted to economic warfare against Germany and Japan in 1940 and 1941, and then fully committed its industrial might and armed forces from 1942 to 1945. Its intervention, and that of the Soviet Union, decided the outcome of conflict and shaped the character of the postwar world.

Wartime Aims and Tensions

Great Britain, the United States, and the Soviet Union were the key actors in the Allied coalition. China, France, and other nations played lesser roles. The "Big Three," consisting of President Franklin Roosevelt, Prime Minister Winston Churchill of Great Britain, and Premier Joseph Stalin of the Soviet Union, set military strategy and diplomatic policy. The Atlantic Charter, which Churchill and Roosevelt had drafted in August 1941, set out the Anglo-American vision of the postwar international order. It called for free trade, national self-determination, and collective security. Stalin had not participated in that agreement and disagreed fundamentally with some of its precepts, such as a capitalist-run international trading system. Moreover, he hoped to protect the USSR from invasion from the West by setting up a band of Soviet-controlled buffer states along his border with Germany and western Europe.

The first major conflict among the Allies concerned military strategy and timing. While they agreed that defeating Germany (rather than Japan) was the top military priority, they argued over how best to do it. In 1941 the German army had invaded the Soviet Union and advanced to the outskirts of Leningrad and Moscow before being halted by hard-pressed Russian forces in early 1942. To relieve pressure on the Soviet army, Stalin wanted the British and Americans to attack Germany in western Europe, opening this "second front" with a major invasion through France. Roosevelt informally assured Stalin that the Allies would open a second front in 1942, but the British opposed an early invasion and American war production was not yet sufficient to support it. For the next eighteen months, Stalin's pleas went unanswered, and the Soviet Union bore the brunt of the fighting. Then, at a conference of the "Big Three" in Tehran, Iran, in November 1943, Churchill and Roosevelt agreed to open a second front in France within six months in return for Stalin's promise to join the fight against Japan. Both sides adhered to this agreement, but the long delay in creating a second front angered Stalin, who became increasingly suspicious about American and British intentions.

The War in Europe

Following the attack on Pearl Harbor, the Allies suffered one defeat after another. German armies pushed deep into Soviet territory in the south; advancing through the wheat fields of the Ukraine and the rich oil fields of the Caucasus, they moved toward the major city of Stalingrad. Simultaneously the Germans began an offensive in North Africa aimed at seizing the Suez Canal. In the Atlantic, German submarines relentlessly and successfully damaged American convoys carrying oil and other vital supplies to Britain and the Soviet Union.

The Allied Advance. Then, in the winter of 1942–1943, the tide began to turn in favor of the Allies. In the epic Battle of Stalingrad, Soviet forces decisively halted the German advance, killing or capturing 330,000 German soldiers, and began to push westward (Map 25.3). By early 1944, Stalin's troops had driven the German army out of the

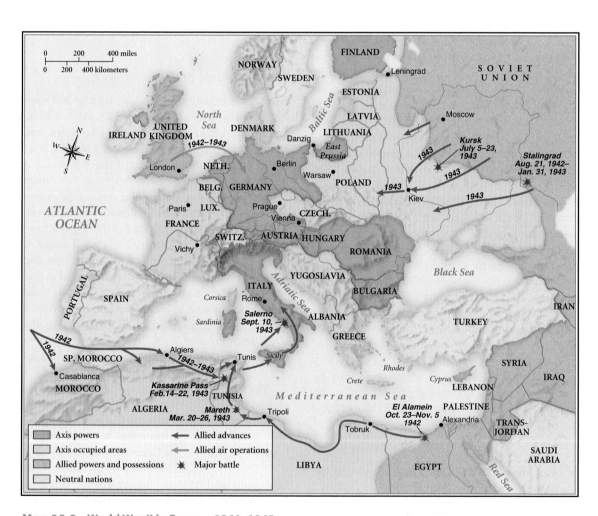

Map 25.3 World War II in Europe, 1941–1943

Hitler's Germany reached its greatest extent in 1942 when Nazi forces had occupied Norway, France, North Africa, central Europe, and much of western Russia. The tide of battle turned in late 1942 when the German advance stalled at Leningrad and Stalingrad. By early 1943, the Soviet army had launched a massive counterattack at Stalingrad, and Allied forces had driven the Germans from North Africa and launched an invasion of Sicily and the Italian mainland.

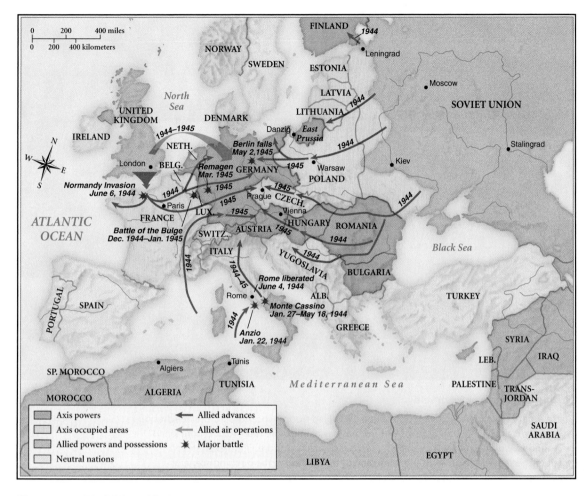

Map 25.4 World War II in Europe, 1944–1945

By the end of 1943, the Russian army had nearly pushed the Germans out of the Soviet Union, and by June 1944, when the British and Americans finally invaded France, the Russians had liberated eastern Poland and most of southeastern Europe. By the end of 1944, British and American forces were ready to invade Germany from the west, and the Russians were poised to do the same from the east. Germany surrendered on May 8, 1945.

Soviet Union. Meanwhile, the Allies launched a major offensive in North Africa, Churchill's substitute for a second front in France. Between November 1942 and May 1943, Allied troops under the leadership of General Dwight D. Eisenhower and General George S. Patton defeated Germany's *Afrika Korps,* led by General Erwin Rommel.

From Africa, the Allied command followed Churchill's strategy of attacking the Axis through its "soft underbelly": Sicily and the Italian peninsula. Faced with an Allied invasion, the Italian king ousted Benito Mussolini's Fascist regime in July 1943. German troops occupied Italy, restored Mussolini, and resisted the invasion. American and British troops took Rome only in June 1944 and were still fighting German forces in northern Italy when the European war ended in May 1945

(Map 25.4). Churchill's southern strategy proved a time-consuming and costly failure.

The long-promised invasion of France came on "D-Day," June 6, 1944. That morning, after an agonizing delay caused by bad weather, the largest armada ever assembled moved across the English Channel under the command of General Dwight D. Eisenhower. When American, British, and Canadian soldiers hit the beaches of Normandy, they suffered terrible casualties but secured a beachhead. Over the next few days, more than 1.5 million soldiers and thousands of tons of military supplies and equipment flowed into France. In August Allied troops liberated Paris; by September they had driven the Germans out of most of France and Belgium. Meanwhile, long-range Allied bombers had attacked German cities as well as military and

Hitting the Beach at Normandy

These American soldiers were among the 156,000 Allied troops who stormed the beaches of Normandy, France, on D-Day, June 6, 1944; on that day alone, more than 10,000 were killed or wounded. Within a month, one million Allied troops came ashore. Filmmaker Steven Spielberg recreated the carnage and confusion of the landing in the opening scene of *Saving Private Ryan* (1998). Library of Congress.

industrial targets. The air campaign killed some 305,000 civilians and soldiers and wounded another 780,000.

The Germans were not yet ready to give up, however. In December 1944 they mounted a final offensive in Belgium, the so-called Battle of the Bulge, before being pushed back across the Rhine River into Germany. As American and British troops drove toward Berlin from the west, Soviet troops advanced from the east through Poland. On April 30, as Russian troops massed outside Berlin, Hitler committed suicide; on May 8, Germany formally surrendered.

The Holocaust. As Allied troops advanced into Poland and Germany in the spring of 1945, they came face to face with Adolf Hitler's "final solution of the Jewish question": the extermination camps where six million Jews had been put to death, along with another six million Poles, Slavs, Gypsies, homosexuals, and other "undesirables." Photographs of the Nazi death camps at Buchenwald, Dachau, and Auschwitz showed bodies stacked like cordwood

and survivors so emaciated they were barely alive. Quickly published in *Life* and other mass-circulation magazines, the photographs horrified the American public.

The Nazi persecution of German Jews in the 1930s was widely known in the United States. But when Jews began to flee from Germany, the United States refused to relax its strict immigration laws to take them in. American officials, along with those of most other nations, continued this exclusionist policy during World War II, as the Nazi regime extended its control over millions of east European Jews. Among the various factors that combined to inhibit American action, the most important was widespread anti-Semitism: in the State Department, Christian churches, and the public at large. The legacy of the immigration restriction legislation of the 1920s and the isolationist attitudes of the 1930s also discouraged policymakers from assuming responsibility for the fate of the refugees. As later American administrations would learn (as "ethnic cleansing" killed millions in India in the 1940s and Bosnia

The Living Dead

When Allied troops advanced into Germany in the spring of 1945, they came face to face with what had long been rumored — concentration camps, Adolf Hitler's "final solution of the Jewish question." In this picture from Wobbelin concentration camp — liberated by the 82nd Airborne Division of the 9th U.S. Army — emaciated inmates are being taken to a hospital. In the days before the camp was liberated, one thousand of the five thousand prisoners had been allowed to starve to death. U.S. Holocaust Memorial Museum.

and Rwanda in the 1990s), such political considerations often conflict with humanitarian values. Taking a narrow view of the national interest, the State Department allowed only 21,000 Jewish refugees to enter the United States during the war. But the War Refugee Board, established by President Roosevelt in 1944, following a plea by Secretary of the Treasury Henry Morganthau, helped to move 200,000 European Jews to safe havens in various countries.

The War in the Pacific

Winning the war against Japan was as arduous as the campaign against Germany in Europe. After crippling the American battle fleet at Pearl Harbor, the Japanese quickly expanded their military presence in the South Pacific, with seaborne invasions of Hong Kong, Wake Island, and Guam. Japanese forces then advanced into Southeast Asia, conquering the Solomon Islands, Burma, and Malaya and threatening Australia and India. By May 1942, they had forced the surrender of American forces in the Philippine Islands and, in the Bataan "death march," callously allowed the deaths of 10,000 prisoners of war.

At that dire moment, American naval forces scored two crucial victories. In the Battle of the Coral Sea near southern New Guinea in May 1942, they halted the Japanese offensive against Australia. In June, at the Battle of Midway Island, the American navy inflicted serious damage on the Japanese fleet. In both battles dive bombers and fighters launched from American aircraft carriers provided the margin of victory.

The American military command, led by General Douglas MacArthur and Admiral Chester W. Nimitz, then took the offensive in the Pacific (Map 25.5). For the next eighteen months, American forces advanced slowly toward Japan, taking one island after another in the face of bitter Japanese resistance. In October 1944, MacArthur and Nimitz began the reconquest of the Philippines by winning the Battle of Leyte Gulf, a massive naval encounter in which the Japanese lost practically their entire fleet (Map 25.6).

By early 1945, victory over Japan was in sight. Japanese military forces had suffered devastating losses, and American bombing of the Japanese homeland had killed about 330,000 civilians and crippled its economy. But the closer U.S. forces got to the Japanese home islands, the more fiercely the Japanese fought. On the small island of Iwo Jima, 21,000 Japanese soldiers fought to the death, killing 6,000 American marines and wounding 14,000 more. On Okinawa, the American toll reached 7,600 dead and 32,000 wounded. Desperate to halt the American advance and short of ammunition, Japanese pilots flew *kamikaze* (suicidal) missions, crashing their bomb-laden planes into American ships. Based on the fighting on Okinawa and Iwo Jima, American military commanders grimly predicted millions of casualties in the upcoming invasion of Japan.

Planning the Postwar World

As Allied forces moved toward victory in the Pacific and Europe, Roosevelt, Churchill, and Stalin met in February 1945 at Yalta, a resort on the Black Sea. Roosevelt focused on maintaining Allied unity, which he saw as the key to postwar peace and stability. But two sets of issues, the fate of the British and French colonial empires and of central and eastern Europe, threatened to divide

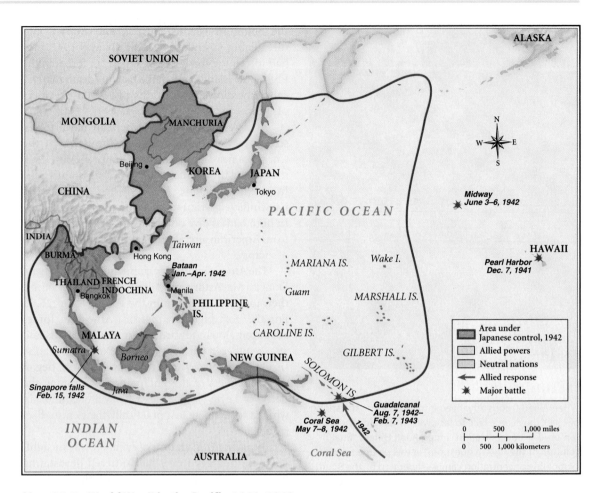

Map 25.5   World War II in the Pacific, 1941–1942

After the attacks on Pearl Harbor in December 1941, the Japanese rapidly extended their domination in the Pacific. The Japanese flag soon flew as far east as the Marshall and Gilbert islands and as far south as the Solomon Islands and parts of New Guinea. Japan also controlled the Philippines, much of Southeast Asia, and parts of China, including Hong Kong. By mid-1942, American naval victories at the Coral Sea and Midway stopped further Japanese expansion.

the Big Three. An independence movement in British India, led by Mahatma Gandhi, had already gathered strength and caused friction between Roosevelt and Churchill. A more serious source of conflict was Stalin's insistence that Russian national security demanded the installation of pro-Soviet governments in central and eastern Europe. Roosevelt pressed for an agreement that guaranteed self-determination and democratic elections in Poland and neighboring countries but, given the presence there of Soviet troops, had to accept a pledge from Stalin to hold "free and unfettered elections" at a future time. The three leaders agreed to divide Germany into four administrative zones, each controlled by one of the four powers (the United States, Great

Britain, France, and the Soviet Union) and also to partition the capital city, Berlin, which lay in the middle of the Soviet zone, among the four powers.

Creating the United Nations. To continue and expand their alliance, the Big Three agreed to establish an international body to replace the discredited League of Nations. They decided that the new United Nations organization would have a Security Council composed of the five major Allied powers — the United States, Britain, France, China, and the Soviet Union — and six other nations elected on a rotating basis. They also agreed that the five permanent members of the Security Council should have veto power over decisions of the

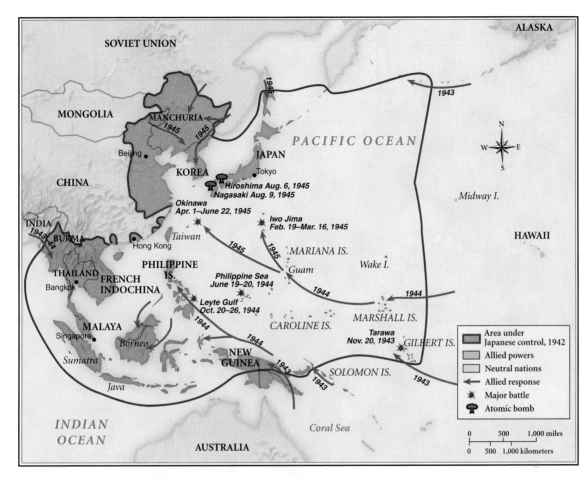

Map 25.6 World War II in the Pacific, 1943–1945

Allied forces retook the islands in the central Pacific in 1943 and 1944 and ousted the Japanese from the Philippines early in 1945. The capture of Guam, Iwo Jima, and Okinawa allowed American bombers to attack Japan itself. On August 6 and 9, the United States dropped atomic bombs on Hiroshima and Nagasaki; on August 9 the Soviet Army invaded Japanese-occupied Manchuria. The Japanese offered to surrender on August 10.

General Assembly, in which all nations would be represented. Roosevelt, Churchill, and Stalin announced that the United Nations would convene in San Francisco on April 25, 1945.

Roosevelt returned to the United States in February, visibly exhausted by his 14,000-mile trip. The sixty-three-year-old president was a sick man, suffering from heart failure and high blood pressure. On April 12, 1945, during a short visit to his vacation home in Warm Springs, Georgia, Roosevelt suffered a cerebral hemorrhage and died.

The Atom Bomb. When Harry S Truman assumed the presidency, he learned for the first time about the top-secret Manhattan Project,

charged with developing a new weapon—an atomic bomb. European physicists, many of them Jewish, had achieved the theoretical breakthroughs that foreshadowed the atomic age during the first decades of the twentieth century. By the 1930s scientists knew that the tiny nuclei of atoms could be split into yet smaller particles, a process called fission. They also knew that the fission of highly processed uranium would produce a chain reaction and unleash tremendous amounts of energy. Working at the University of Chicago in December 1942, Enrico Fermi and Leo Szilard, refugees from Fascist Italy and Nazi Germany, produced the first controlled chain reaction. With the aid of Albert Einstein, the greatest theorist of modern physics and a refugee

The Big Three at Yalta

With victory in Europe at hand, Roosevelt journeyed in 1945 to Yalta, on the Black Sea, and met for the final time with Churchill and Stalin. The leaders discussed the important and controversial issues of the treatment of Germany, the status of Poland, the creation of the United Nations, and Russian entry into the war against Japan. The Yalta agreements mirrored a new balance of power and set the stage for the Cold War. Franklin D. Roosevelt Library.

scholar at Princeton, they persuaded Franklin Roosevelt to develop an atomic weapon, warning that German scientists were also working on such nuclear reactions.

The Manhattan Project cost $2 billion, employed 120,000 people, and involved the construction of thirty-seven installations in nineteen states—all of this activity hidden from Congress, the American people, and even Vice President Truman. Directed by General Leslie Graves and scientist Robert Oppenheimer, the nation's top physicists assembled the first bomb in Los Alamos, New Mexico, and successfully tested it on July 16, 1945. Overwhelmed by its frightening power, Oppenheimer recalled the words from the *Bhagavad Gita,* the Hindu bible: "I am become Death, Destroyer of Worlds."

Three weeks later, President Truman ordered the dropping of atomic bombs on two Japanese cities, Hiroshima on August 6 and Nagasaki on August 9. Truman was not a reflective man, and he did not question the morality of using such a revolutionary weapon. Administration officials were convinced that Japan's military leaders would never surrender unless their country was utterly devastated, and they knew that an American invasion would cost hundreds of thousands of lives. Truman may also have hoped that use of the bomb would intimidate Stalin and ease his objections to American plans for the postwar world. Whatever the long-range intention or result, atomic bombs achieved the immediate goal. The deaths of 100,000 people at Hiroshima and 60,000 at Nagasaki prompted the Japanese government to offer to surrender on August 10 and to sign a formal agreement on September 2, 1945.

Hiroshima

This aerial view of Hiroshima after the dropping of an atomic bomb on August 6, 1945, shows the terrible devastation of the city. A U.S. Army report prepared in 1946 describes the bomb exploding "with a blinding flash in the sky, and a great rush of air and a loud rumble of noise extended for many miles around the city; the first blast was soon followed by the sounds of falling buildings and of growing fires, and a great cloud of dust and smoke began to cast a pall of darkness over the city." Except for fifty concrete-reinforced buildings designed to withstand earthquakes, every structure within one mile of the center of the bomb blast was reduced to rubble. The physical destruction was second to the human cost: With a population estimated at between 300,000 and 400,000 people, Hiroshima lost 100,000 in the initial explosion, and many thousands more died slowly of radiation poisoning. U.S. Air Force.

Fascism had been defeated, thanks to a strange alliance between the capitalist nations of the West and the communist government of the Soviet Union. The coming of peace would strain, and then destroy, the victorious coalition.

> ➤ Describe the course of the war in Europe and the Pacific. What factors led to the Allied victory in World War II?

> ➤ Explain why the United States used atomic weapons in Japan. Why was the Americans' use of these weapons controversial?

SUMMARY

As we have seen, the rise of fascism and expansionism in Germany, Italy, and Japan led to the outbreak of World War II. Initially, the American public preferred a policy of noninvolvement. But by 1940 President Roosevelt had begun mobilizing public opinion for intervention and converting the economy to war production. The Japanese attack on Pearl Harbor on December 7, 1941, brought the nation into World War II, a global conflict that involved massive military campaigns in both Europe and the Pacific.

As with World War I, mobilization led to a dramatic expansion of the size and power of the federal government. It also increased geographical and social mobility as new defense plants in California and elsewhere created job opportunities for women, rural whites, southern blacks, and Mexican Americans. Government intervention in the economy assisted the labor movement to consolidate its gains during the 1930s. In addition, the ideological climate of fighting Nazism aided the cause of civil rights for African Americans. At the same time, religious and racial animosity blocked the admission of Jewish refugees and prompted the forced internment of 112,000 Japanese Americans, a devastating denial of civil liberties.

As our account makes clear, the prospects of an American and Allied victory were bleak during much of 1942. By 1943 the Allies had taken the offensive, thanks to advances by the Soviet army in Europe and the American navy in the Pacific; by the end of 1944 victory was all but certain. Among the major powers, only the United States emerged physically unharmed from the war, and it alone possessed the atomic bomb, the most lethal weapon of mass destruction ever created. But the most vexing result of World War II was the onset of the Cold War between the United States and the Soviet Union. This conflict would dominate American foreign policy for the next four decades.

Connections: Government

The "Rise of the State" has been a central theme of Part Five. As we stated in the essay that opened Part Five (p. 671), "American participation in World War I called forth an unprecedented mobilization of the domestic economy" by government institutions, a process we described in Chapter 22. Chapter 23 then explained how that wartime collaboration continued in the 1920s. Herbert Hoover and other government officials promoted polices of the "associated state" and "welfare capitalism," which encouraged large corporate businesses to assume broad economic and social responsibilities. When the Great Depression revealed the flaws in these policies and ideologies, Franklin Roosevelt's New Deal instituted a variety of new government programs to spur economic recovery and social welfare. As Chapter 24 made clear, the National Recovery Association, the Agricultural Adjustment Act, the Works Project Administration, and similar measures represented unprecedented levels of government supervision of American economic life. Likewise, the ideology of social welfare liberalism and its partial realization in the Social Security Act of 1935 gave the federal government major responsibility for the welfare of a substantial majority of American citizens. As we saw in Chapter 25, these links between the state and its citizenry grew even closer and more pervasive during World War II, with the creation of universal income taxation and the enactment of the GI Bill of Rights. Moreover, as we noted in the Part Opener, "Unlike the experience after World War I, the new state apparatus remained in place when the war ended." In Part Six, which covers the period from 1945 to 1980, we will explain how the federal government grew in size and power as it both armed the nation to fight a Cold War abroad and worked to end poverty and expand prosperity at home.

CHAPTER REVIEW QUESTIONS

> ➤ According to the oral historian Studs Terkel, World War II was a "good war." Do you agree with this assessment?

> ➤ Overall, what sort of impact — positive or negative — did World War II have on women and minority groups in the United States?

> ➤ Why was there tension among the Allies during the war, and what long-term impact did it have?

TIMELINE

1933	Adolf Hitler becomes chancellor of Germany
1935	Italy invades Ethiopia
1935–1937	U.S. Neutrality Acts
1936	Germany reoccupies Rhineland demilitarized zone
	Rome-Berlin Axis established
	Japan and Germany sign Anti-Comintern Pact
1937	Japan invades China
1938	Munich agreement between Germany, Britain, and France
1939	Nazi-Soviet Nonaggression Pact
	Germany invades Poland
	Britain and France declare war on Germany
1940	American conscription reinstated
	Germany, Italy, and Japan sign Tri-Partite Pact
1941	Roosevelt promulgates Four Freedoms
	Germany invades the Soviet Union
	Lend-Lease Act passed
	Fair Employment Practices Commission created
	Atlantic Charter promulgated
	Japanese attack Pearl Harbor
1942	Allies suffer severe defeats in Europe and Asia
	Executive Order 9066 leads to Japanese internment camps
	Battles of Coral Sea and Midway halt Japanese advance
	Women recruited for war industries
1942–1945	Rationing of scarce goods
1943	Race riots in Detroit and Los Angeles
	Fascism falls in Italy
1944	D-Day: Allied landing in France
	GI Bill of Rights enacted
	Supreme Court avoids issue of the constitutionality of Japanese American internment
1945	Yalta Conference
	Battles of Iwo Jima and Okinawa
	Germany surrenders
	Harry S Truman becomes president after Roosevelt's death
	United Nations convenes
	Atomic bombs dropped on Hiroshima and Nagasaki
	Japan surrenders

FOR FURTHER EXPLORATION

The standard military history of World War II is Henry Steele Commager, *The Story of World War II*, as expanded and revised by Donald L. Miller (1945; revisions 2001). Fifty-three personal stories of war appear in *War Stories: Remembering World War II* (2002), edited by Elizabeth Mullener. An engaging overview of war on the home front is John Morton Blum, *V Was for Victory* (1976). See also "Cents and Sacrifice" at **www.nauticom.net/ www/harts/homefront.html**, a comprehensive site with many links to other valuable resources. The National Archives Administration at **www.archives.gov/exhibit_hall/index.html** has two World War II sites: "A People at War" and "Powers of Persuasion: Poster Art from World War II." An anthology that focuses on popular culture and the wartime experience is Lewis A. Erenberg and Susan E. Hirsch, eds., *The War in American Culture* (1996). Powerful novels inspired by the war include John Hersey, *A Bell for Adano* (1944); James Jones, *From Here to Eternity* (1951); and Norman Mailer, *The Naked and the Dead* (1948).

The Library of Congress exhibit "Women Come to the Front: Journalists, Photographers, and Broadcasters During World War II" at **lcweb.loc.gov/exhibits/wcf/wcf0001.html** and "Rosie Pictures: Select Images Relating to American Women Workers During World War II" at **www.loc.gov/rr/ print/list/126_rosi.html** record the contributions of women during World War II. Sherna B. Gluck, *Rosie the Riveter Revisited* (1988), offers compelling accounts by women war workers.

Many sites cover the Japanese internment, including the interesting one at the University of Washington on Seattle's Japanese American community: **www.lib.washington.edu/exhibits/ harmony/default.htm**. For interviews with detainees and thousands of images, go to **www.densho.org/densho.asp**. The Library of Congress site "Suffering Under a Great Injustice" at **memory.loc.gov/ammem/aamhtml** presents a haunting exhibition of Ansel Adams's photographs of the Manzanar camp.

For "'Man on the Street Interviews' Following the Attack on Pearl Harbor," go to **lcweb2.loc.gov/ammem/afcphhtml/ afcphhome.html**. See also the "Rutgers Oral History Archive of World War II" at **oralhistory.rutgers.edu**.

The decision to drop the bomb remains controversial. An excellent site is Lehigh University Professor Edward J. Gallagher's "*The Enola Gay* Controversy: How Do We Remember a War That We Won?" at **www.lehigh.edu/~ineng/ enola**. See also the masterful biography of the bomb's principal architect: Kai Bird and Martin J. Sherwin, *American Prometheus: The Triumph and Tragedy of J. Robert Oppenheimer* (2005).

TEST YOUR KNOWLEDGE

To assess your command of the material in this chapter, see the Online Study Guide at **bedfordstmartins.com/henretta**.

For Web sites, images, and documents related to topics and places in this chapter, visit **bedfordstmartins.com/makehistory**.

PART SIX

The Age of Cold War Liberalism

1945–1980

DIPLOMACY	POLITICS	ECONOMY	SOCIETY	CULTURE
The Cold War	**Decline of the Liberal Consensus**	**Ups and Downs of U.S. Economic Dominance**	**Social Movements and Demographic Diversity**	**Consumer Culture and Its Critics**

	DIPLOMACY	POLITICS	ECONOMY	SOCIETY	CULTURE
1945	▶ Truman Doctrine (1947) ▶ Marshall Plan (1948) ▶ Berlin blockade ▶ NATO founded (1949)	▶ Truman's Fair Deal liberalism ▶ Taft-Hartley Act (1947) ▶ Truman reelected (1948)	▶ Reconversion ▶ Strike wave (1946) ▶ Bretton Woods system established: World Bank, IMF	▶ Migration to cities accelerates ▶ Armed forces desegregated (1948)	▶ End of wartime rationing ▶ Rise of television ▶ First Levittown (1947)
1950	▶ Permanent mobilization: NSC-68 (1950) ▶ Korean War (1950–1953) ▶ U.S replaces France in Vietnam	▶ McCarthyism ▶ Eisenhower's modern Republicanism ▶ Warren Court activism	▶ Rise of military-industrial complex ▶ Industrial economy booms ▶ Labor-management accord	▶ *Brown v. Board of Education* (1954) ▶ Montgomery bus boycott (1955) ▶ Urban crisis emerges	▶ Growth of suburbia ▶ Sun Belt emerges ▶ Religious revival ▶ Baby boom ▶ Youth culture develops
1960	▶ Cuban missile crisis (1962) ▶ Vietnam War escalates (1965) ▶ Tet offensive (1968); peace talks begin	▶ Kennedy's New Frontier ▶ Kennedy assassinated ▶ Great Society, War on Poverty ▶ Nixon's election (1968) ushers in conservative era	▶ Kennedy-Johnson tax cut, military expenditures fuel economic growth	▶ March on Washington (1963) ▶ Civil rights legislation (1964, 1965) ▶ Student activism ▶ Black Power	▶ Shopping malls spread ▶ Baby boomers swell college enrollment ▶ Hippie counterculture
1970	▶ Nixon visits China (1972); SALT initiates détente (1972) ▶ Paris Peace accords (1973) end Vietnam War ▶ Carter brokers Camp David accords between Egypt and Israel (1978) ▶ Iranian revolution; hostage crisis	▶ Watergate scandal; Nixon resigns (1974) ▶ Weak presidencies of Ford and Carter	▶ Arab oil embargo (1973–1974); inflation surges, while income stagnates ▶ Onset of deindustrialization	▶ Revival of feminism ▶ *Roe v. Wade* (1973) ▶ New Right urges conservative agenda	▶ Consumer and environmental protection movements ▶ Deepening social divide over ERA and gay rights

"What Rome was to the ancient world," proclaimed the influential journalist Walter Lippmann in 1945, "America is to be for the world of tomorrow." Lippmann's remark captures America's sense of triumphant confidence at the end of World War II. What he underestimated were the challenges, both global and domestic, confronting the United States. In this Part Six, covering the years 1945–1980, we track how the United States fared in its quest to become the Rome of the twentieth century.

DIPLOMACY Hardly had Lippmann penned his triumphant words in 1945 than the Soviet Union challenged America's plans for postwar Europe. The Truman administration responded by crafting the policies and alliances that came to define the Cold War. That struggle spawned two "hot" wars in Korea and Vietnam and fueled a terrifying nuclear arms race. By the early 1970s, as the bi-polar assumptions of the Cold War broke down, the Nixon administration got on better terms with both the Soviet Union and China. The high hopes for détente, however, fell short, and during Carter's tenure Soviet-U.S. relations lapsed into a state of anxious stalemate. The hostage crisis in Iran revealed that, beyond the Cold War, other big challenges, especially from the aggrieved Muslim world, faced the United States.

POLITICS Lippmann's confidence in America's future in part stemmed from his sense of a nation united on the big domestic questions. Except for a brief postwar reaction, which brought forth the Taft-Hartley Act (1947), the liberal consensus prevailed. And while not much headway was made by Truman's Fair Deal, neither did Republicans under Eisenhower attempt any dismantling of the New Deal. Johnson's ambitious Great Society, however, did provoke a conservative response and, beginning with the debacle of the Democratic convention of 1968, the country moved to the right. The interaction of the domestic and global — the links between liberalism and the Cold War — was especially clear at this juncture because it was Vietnam that, more than anything, undermined the Great Society and the liberal consensus. By the end of the 1970s, with a big assist from the Carter administration, the Democrats had lost the grip they had won under FDR as the nation's dominant party.

ECONOMY In no realm did America's supremacy seem so secure in the postwar years as in economics. While the war-torn countries of Europe and Asia were picking through the rubble, the American economy boomed, fed both by the military-industrial complex and by a high-spending consumer culture. Real income grew, and collective bargaining became well entrenched. In the 1950s, no country was competitive with America's economy. By the 1970s, however, American industry had been overtaken, and a sad process of dismantling, of deindustrialization, began. At the same time, the inflationary spiral that had begun during the Vietnam War speeded up under the impact of the oil embargo of 1973. A decade of "stagflation" set in, and with it a suspicion that America's vaunted economic powerhouse had seen its best days.

SOCIETY The victory over Nazism in World War II spurred demands for America to make good on its promise of equality for all. In great waves of protests beginning in the 1950s, African Americans — and then women, Latinos, and other minorities — challenged the status quo. Starting with the Supreme Court's landmark *Brown v. Board of Education* (1954) decision, the country began to outlaw the practices of segregation, discrimination, and disfranchisement that had held minorities down. In the 1970s, however, reaction set in, fueled in part by the growing militancy of blacks and others, in part by the discovery of a resentful "silent majority" by conservative politicians. Achieving equality, it turned out, was easier said than done.

CULTURE America's economic power in the postwar years accelerated the development of a consumer society that cherished the tract house, the car, and television set. As millions of Americans moved into suburban subdivisions, the birth-rate speeded up, spawning a baby boom generation whose social influence would be felt for the next seventy-five years. Under the surface calm of the 1950s, a mood of cultural rebellion took hold. In the 1960s, it would burst forth in the hippie counterculture and the antiwar movement. Although both subsided in the early 1970s, they left a lasting impact on the country's politics, in particular, as fuel that fed the resurgence of American conservatism.

Walter Lippmann died in 1974. He had lived long enough to see his high hopes of 1945 blasted by the Cold War, by economic troubles, and by the collapse of the liberal consensus.

26

Cold War America
1945–1960

O N MAY 1, 1950, THE RESIDENTS OF Mosinee, Wisconsin, staged a
mock Communist takeover of their small papermill town. Secret
police interrogated citizens. The mayor was carted off to jail. The local
paper reappeared as a mini-*Pravda*. And restaurants served only potato
soup and black bread. Dreamed up by the American Legion, Mosinee's
"Day Under Communism" was a sensational media event that conveyed
a chilling message: America's way of life was under siege by the Communist menace.

The Mosinee episode captured a towering irony of the postwar
period. Americans in 1945 had indeed been anxious over what would
follow victory. But their anxiety was not directed at the Soviet Union.
Weren't we all part of the Grand Alliance? No, what worried Americans
was closer to home. Defense plants were shutting down, war workers
being laid off, and twelve million job-seeking veterans on the way home.
Might the country slide back into the Great Depression? In short order,
those fears dissipated. Home building picked up. Cars flowed from the
assembly lines. Consumers began to spend like crazy the savings they had
piled up during the war. The economy was in fact entering the strongest
boom in American history. But instead of being able to settle back and
enjoy their prosperity, the good people of Mosinee worried about a
Soviet coup in their town. They had exchanged one fear — of economic
hard times — for another: the Communist menace.

◄ **The Perils of the Cold War**

In this detail of a 1948 Pulitzer Prize–winning cartoon, Rube Goldberg depicts the perilous
nature of America's postwar peace — one that was based largely on the threat of nuclear
annihilation. University of California at Berkeley, Bancroft Library.

The conflict that emerged between the Soviet Union and the United States, while not leading to any direct engagement on the battlefield, inaugurated a long twilight era of international tension — a Cold War — when either side, armed with nuclear weapons, might have tipped the entire world into oblivion.

The impact of the Soviet-American confrontation on domestic affairs was far-reaching. The Cold War fostered a climate of fear and suspicion of "subversives" in government, education, and the media. It boosted military expenditures, fueling a growing arms race between the two superpowers, creating a "military-industrial complex" in the United States, and undergirding an amazing era of economic expansion (see Chapter 27). That prosperity helped to expand federal power, perpetuating the New Deal state in the postwar era. But the Cold War also now held liberal politics hostage because the ability of the New Deal coalition to advance its agenda at home depended on its prowess as a Cold Warrior abroad. In all these ways, the line between the international and the domestic blurred. That was an enduring legacy of the Cold War.

The Cold War

The Cold War began in 1946. It ended forty-five years later with the collapse of the Soviet Union. In that intervening period, a vast amount was written by historians about why the Cold War had happened. By no means did all blame the Soviets. Eventually, indeed, those holding the opposite view — the "revisionist" historians, so-called — often held the upper hand. But in truth, the debate was ultimately inconclusive because the scholarly conditions that prevailed really precluded definitive history. The Soviet archives, for one thing, were completely closed. More important, perhaps, historians were trying to capture an event that was still happening. Only now that it is over can historians look back and gain the perspective needed for understanding why the Cold War occurred.

Descent into Cold War, 1945–1946

World War II itself set the basic conditions for Cold War rivalry. With Germany and Japan defeated and America's British and French allies exhausted, only the two superpowers remained standing in 1945. Even had nothing else divided them, the United States and the USSR would have jostled against each other as they moved to fill the vacuum. But, of course, the two countries *were* divided — by ideology, by history, by geography and strategic interest, even by relative power (with the advantage, both militarily and economically, heavily on the American side). FDR understood that bridging the divide and maintaining the U.S.-Soviet alliance were essential conditions for postwar stability. But he also believed that permanent peace depended on adherence to the Wilsonian principles of collective security, self-determination, and free trade (see Chapter 22). The challenge was to find a way of reconciling Wilsonian principles with U.S.-Soviet power realities.

Yalta. That was what Roosevelt, Churchill, and Stalin had undertaken at the Yalta Conference of February 1945. They agreed there to go forward with the United Nations, committing themselves to a new international forum for resolving future conflicts and fostering world peace. The realist side of that noble arrangement, demanded by the U.S. and the USSR, was that permanent seats with veto rights be reserved for them (and their three major allies) on the Security Council. The paramount problem at Yalta, however, was eastern Europe. Roosevelt and Churchill agreed that Poland and its neighbors would fall under the Soviet "sphere of influence" — thus meeting Stalin's demand for secure western borders. But Yalta also called for "free and unfettered" elections — thus upholding the essential principle of democratic self-determination. Implicit in Yalta's details was an expectation — the nub of the deal — that freely elected governments would consent to Soviet domination.

That actually had happened in Finland and, after Yalta, briefly in Czechoslovakia. It could not happen in Poland. For that, Stalin had himself to blame. With war impending in 1939, he made his infamous secret pact with Hitler for the partition of Poland. When the Nazis invaded, the Soviet Union seized its apportioned share (and reclaimed much of it as sovereign territory when the Nazis retreated in 1944). Then Stalin ordered the execution of the entire Polish officer corps in Russian hands in the Katyn forest, a deed that, when exposed by the Nazis in 1943, caused a rift with the Polish government-in-exile in London. Equally unforgivable was Stalin's betrayal of the Poles of Warsaw late in the war. When they rose against the Germans, the Red Army halted on the outskirts so that any potential anti-Communist opposition could be finished off by the Nazis. Evidently blind to the resentment of his victims, Stalin — American observers reported — was taken aback by the fear and loathing that greeted his approaching armies. So there would be no free elections, a conclusion Stalin had already arrived at before Yalta. He got the puppet regime he required, but never the consent of the Poles, or the Hungarians, Romanians, and other subject peoples of eastern Europe. Stalin's unwillingness—his *inability,* if he was to fulfill his ambitions—to hold free elections was the precipitating event of the Cold War.

Truman Takes Command. Historians doubt that, had he lived, even the resourceful Roosevelt could have preserved the Grand Alliance. With Harry Truman, no such possibility existed. Truman was inexperienced in foreign affairs. As vice president, he had been kept in the dark about Roosevelt's negotiations (or even about the atomic bomb). His blunt instinct was to stand up to Stalin. At a meeting held shortly after he took office, the new president berated the Soviet foreign minister, V. M. Molotov, over the Soviets' failure to honor their Yalta agreements. He abruptly halted lend-lease shipments that the Soviets desperately needed and denied their request for $6 billion in credits. Truman used what he called "tough methods" that July at the Potsdam Conference, which had been called to take up postwar planning. After learning of the successful test of America's atomic bomb, Truman "told the Russians just where they got off and generally bossed the whole meeting," recalled Winston Churchill.

Stalin was not taken by surprise. He had been kept informed by his spy network about the Manhattan Project virtually from its inception in 1942—far earlier than Truman himself knew about it. Nor was Stalin intimidated. His spies assured him that the small American arsenal posed no immediate threat to the Soviet Union. And his own scientists were on a crash course to producing a Soviet bomb, their efforts much eased by plutonium bomb blueprints stolen from the Manhattan Project. It was a time, as Stalin said, for strong nerves. But the atomic issue did enflame tensions, requiring extra displays of toughness by the Soviets, deepening their suspicions of the West, and, on the American side, encouraging a certain swagger. It was unwise, warned Secretary of War Stimson, for the United States to try to negotiate with "this weapon rather ostentatiously on our hip."

In early 1946, the United States made an effort to head off the impending nuclear race, proposing in the Baruch Plan (after its sponsor, the financier Bernard Baruch) that all weapons-related development and production be placed under the control of a special U.N. atomic agency and that a strict system of inspections and punishments (not subject to Security Council veto) be instituted to prevent violations by individual nations. Once international controls were fully in place, the United States would dispose of its stockpile of atomic bombs. Hot on the trail of their own bomb, the Soviets, although they went through the motions of negotiation, regarded the Baruch Plan as an American trick to dominate them. Its failure foreshadowed a frenzied nuclear arms race between the two superpowers.

By then, Truman's instinctive toughness was being seconded by his more seasoned advisors, a distinguished group known collectively as the Establishment for their elite pedigrees and high-placed public service. Close students of diplomacy, some of them, like Averell Harriman and George F. Kennan, experts on Soviet affairs, concluded that Stalin's actions in eastern Europe were not an aberration, but truly reflective of Stalin's despotic regime. A cogent summary of their views came, ironically, from a former Russian foreign minister, Maxim Litvinoff, who had negotiated America's recognition of the Soviet Union with FDR in 1933. Lamenting the end of wartime cooperation, Litvinoff told a CBS Moscow correspondent that the USSR had returned "to the outmoded concept of security in terms of territory—the more you've got, the safer you are." This was because "the ideological concept prevailing here [is] that conflict between Communist and capitalist worlds is inevitable." The Soviet Union was at that time, in early 1946, expanding its reach, maintaining troops in northern Iran, pressing Turkey for access to the Mediterranean, sponsoring a guerrilla war in Greece. If the current Soviet demands were satisfied, the CBS man asked, what then? "It would lead to the West's being faced, after a more or less short time, with the next set of demands," replied Litvinoff.

George Kennan and the Containment Strategy

Just how the West should respond was crystallized in February 1946 by George F. Kennan in an eight-thousand-word cable, dubbed the "Long Telegram," from his post at the U.S. embassy in Moscow. Kennan argued that the Soviet Union was an "Oriental despotism" and Communism just "the fig-leaf" justifying its crimes. For Soviet leaders, hostility to the West provided the essential excuse "for the dictatorship without which they do not know how to rule." The West had no way of altering this perverse internal dynamic. Its only recourse, Kennan wrote in a famous *Foreign Affairs* article a year later, was to meet the Soviets "with unalterable

George F. Kennan

As a diplomat, foreign policy theorist, and historian, George F. Kennan (1904–2005) enjoyed a long and distinguished career spanning more than seventy years. This portrait by Guy Rowe dates from 1955. National Portrait Gallery, Smithsonian Institution/Art Resource, N.Y.

counter-force at every point where they show signs of encroaching upon the interests of a peaceful and stable world." Kennan called for "long-term, patient but firm and vigilant *containment* of Russian expansive tendencies." Containment, the key word, defined America's evolving strategic stance against the Soviet Union, and Kennan, its author, became one of the most influential advisors in the Truman administration.

On its face, containment seemed a counsel of despair, dooming the United States to a draining, inconclusive struggle without end. In fact, Kennan was more optimistic than that. The Soviet system, he argued with notable foresight, was inherently unstable, and eventually — not in Stalin's time, but eventually — it would collapse. Moreover, the Soviets were not reckless. "If . . . situations can be created in which [conflict] is not to [their] advantage," they would pull back. So it was up to the West to create those situations, avoiding an arms race, picking its fights carefully, exercising patience.

Kennan's attentive readers included Stalin, who had quickly obtained a copy of the classified Long Telegram. To keep things even, Stalin ordered his

ambassador in Washington to prepare his own Long Telegram, and got back an eerie mirror image of Kennan's analysis, with the United States cast as imperialist aggressor, driven by the crisis of monopoly capitalism, and spending "colossally" on arms and overseas bases. Like Kennan, the Soviet ambassador was confident of the adversary's instability, only in his case, from a rather shorter-term perspective. America's problem was its British alliance, which was "plagued with great internal contradictions" and bound to explode, probably over differences in the Middle East.

The Truman Doctrine. The alliance, in fact, was in some difficulty, not out of conflicting interests, however, but because of British exhaustion. In February 1947 London informed Truman that it could no longer afford to support the anti-Communists in Greece, where a bitter guerrilla war was going on. If the Communists won in Greece, Truman worried, that would embolden the Communist parties in France and Italy and, of more immediate concern, threaten Soviet domination of the eastern Mediterranean. In response the president announced what

Postwar Devastation

Berlin, Germany, was reduced to rubble during World War II. Allied bombing, followed by brutal fighting in April 1945 when Soviet troops entered Berlin, devastated the once impressive capital city. Here, in a telling statement about the collapse of Hitler's Third Reich, German refugees walk in front of what was once Goebbels's Propaganda Ministry. U.S. policymakers feared that the economic disorder following this type of destruction would make many areas of postwar Europe vulnerable to Communist influence. National Archives.

came to be known as the Truman Doctrine. In a speech to the Republican-controlled Congress on March 12, he asserted an American responsibility "to support free peoples who are resisting attempted subjugation by armed minorities or by outside pressures." To that end, Truman requested large-scale assistance for Greece and Turkey. "If we falter in our leadership, we may endanger the peace of the world," Truman declared, and "we shall surely endanger the welfare of our own nation." Despite the open-endedness of this military commitment, Congress quickly approved Truman's request for $300 million in aid to Greece and $100 million for Turkey.

The Marshall Plan. In the meantime, Europe was sliding into economic chaos. Devastated by the war, it was hit by the worst winter in memory in 1947. People were starving, and European credit was near-

ing zero. At Secretary of State George C. Marshall's behest, Kennan's small team of advisers came up with a remarkable proposal: a massive infusion of American capital to help get the European economy back on its feet. Speaking at the Harvard commencement in June 1947, Marshall urged the nations of Europe to work out a comprehensive recovery program and then ask the United States for aid, which would be forthcoming.

Truman's pledge of financial aid to European economies met with significant opposition in Congress. Republicans castigated the Marshall Plan as a huge "international W.P.A." But in the midst of the congressional stalemate, on February 25, 1948, came a Communist coup in Czechoslovakia. A stark reminder of Soviet ruthlessness, the coup rallied congressional support for the Marshall Plan. In March 1948 Congress voted overwhelmingly to approve funds for the program. Like most other foreign-policy initiatives of the 1940s and 1950s, the Marshall Plan won bipartisan support.

Over the next four years, the United States contributed nearly $13 billion to a highly successful recovery effort. Western European economies revived, industrial production increased 64 percent, and the appeal of the local Communist parties waned. The Marshall Plan was actually a good deal for the United States, providing stronger markets for American goods and fostering the economic multilateralism and interdependence it wanted to encourage in Europe (see Voices from Abroad, "Jean Monnet: Truman's Generous Proposal," p. 807). And, most notably, the Marshall Plan was a strategic masterstroke. The Soviets had been invited to participate. At first they did, then Stalin, sensing a trap, ordered his delegation home and, on

further reflection, ordered the satellite delegations home as well. It was a clumsy performance, placing the onus for dividing Europe on the Soviets and depriving their threadbare partners of assistance they sorely needed.

The Berlin Crisis. The flashpoint for a hot war, if it existed anywhere, was Germany. This was because the stakes were so high for both sides and the German situation initially so fluid. At Yalta, Germany's future had been left undecided, except that it would be made to pay heavy reparations and be permanently demilitarized. For the time being, a defeated Germany would be divided into four zones of occupation controlled by the Soviet Union, the United States, Britain, and France. A similar arrangement later applied to Berlin (Map 26.1). As it happened, Anglo-American

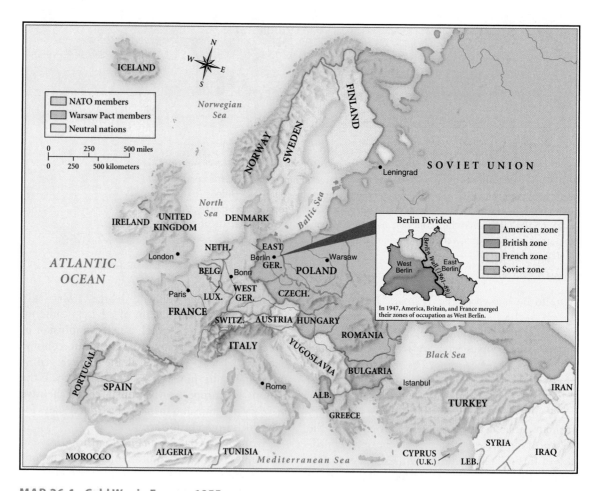

MAP 26.1 Cold War in Europe, 1955

This map vividly shows the Cold War division of Europe as it was in 1955. In green are the NATO countries, allied to the United States; in purple, the Warsaw Pact countries, allied to the USSR. At that point, in 1955, West Germany had just been admitted to NATO, completing Europe's stabilization into two rival camps. But Berlin, Germany's traditional capital, remained divided, and one can see, from its location deep in East Germany, why it was always a flashpoint in Cold War controversies.

Jean Monnet

Truman's Generous Proposal

Jean Monnet was an eminent French statesman and a tireless promoter of postwar European union. As head of a French postwar planning commission, he helped oversee the dispersal of Marshall Plan funds, the importance of which he describes in his memoirs.

So we had at last concerted our efforts to halt France's economic decline; but now, once more, everything seemed to be at risk. Two years earlier [1947], we thought that we had plumbed the depths of material poverty. Now we were threatened with the loss of even basic essentials. . . . Our dollar resources were melting away at an alarming rate, because we were having to buy American wheat to replace the crops we had lost during the winter. . . . A further American loan was soon exhausted.

Nor was this grim situation confined to France. Britain too had come to the end of her resources. In February 1947 she had abruptly cancelled her aid to Greece and Turkey, whose burdens she had seemed able to assume in 1945. Overnight, this abrupt abdication gave the United States direct responsibility for part of Europe. Truman did not hesitate for a moment: with the decisiveness that was to mark his actions as President, he at once asked for credits and arms for both Turkey and Greece. . . . [Soon after], he announced the Truman Doctrine of March 12, 1947. Its significance was general: it meant that the United States would prevent Europe from becoming a depressed area at the mercy of Communist advance. On the very same day, the Four-Power Conference began in Moscow. There, for a whole month, George Marshall, Ernest Bevin, and Georges Bidault argued with Vyacheslav Molotov about all the problems of the peace, and above all about Germany.

When Marshall returned to Washington, he knew that for a long time there would be no further genuine dialogue with Stalin's Russia. The "Cold War," as it was soon to be known, had begun. . . . Information from a number of sources convinced Marshall and his Under-Secretary Dean Acheson that once again, as in 1941, the United States had a great historic duty. And once again there took place what I had witnessed in Washington a few years earlier: a small group of men brought to rapid maturity an idea which, when the Executive gave the word, turned into vigorous action. This time, it was done by five or six people, in total secrecy and at lightning speed. Marshall, Acheson, [William] Clayton, Averell Harriman, and George Kennan worked out a proposal of unprecedented scope and generosity. It took us all by surprise when we read the speech that George Marshall made at Harvard on June 5, 1947. Chance had led him to choose the University's Commencement Day to launch something new in international relations: helping others to help themselves.

SOURCE: Jean Monnet, *Memoirs*, trans. Richard Mayne (New York: Doubleday, 1978), 264–266.

ANALYZING THE EVIDENCE

➤ Why, according to Monnet, did Europe need massive economic assistance, and fast?

➤ Monnet was writing as an embattled Frenchman about the Marshall Plan. If you compare his account with the textbook's account, what is missing from Monnet's account?

➤ Can you explain, on the basis of Monnet's account of the Marshall Plan, why the North Atlantic Treaty Organization, which was established the following year, proved so durable?

forces, encountering much less German resistance than did the Soviets, could have occupied virtually all of Germany, including Berlin. Churchill pleaded for this, but Roosevelt said no. Even so, Eisenhower's troops ended up a hundred miles inside the Soviet zone at war's end, only to be withdrawn—again over Churchill's protests—at Truman's order. These goodwill gestures proved of no account as tensions mounted and the two sides jockeyed for advantage in Germany. When no agreement for a unified state was forthcoming in 1947, the western allies consolidated their zones and prepared to establish an independent federal German republic, supported by an infusion of Marshall Plan money.

Some of that money was slated for West Berlin, in hopes of making it a capitalist showplace deep inside the Soviet zone. On its face, of course, the Allied presence in Berlin was anomolous, an accident of interim wartime arrangements, and indefensible against the Soviets. That, at any rate, was the way Stalin saw it. In June 1948 he halted all Allied traffic to West Berlin. Instead of giving way, as he had expected, Truman and the British were galvanized into action. They improvised an airlift. For nearly a year American and British pilots, who had been dropping bombs on Berlin only four years earlier, flew in 2.5 million tons of food and fuel—nearly a ton for each resident. The Berlin crisis was the closest the two sides came to actual war, and probably the closest America came—since it had no other military option at the time—to using the atomic bomb against the USSR. But

Stalin backed down. On May 12, 1949, he lifted the blockade. West Berlin became a symbol of resistance to Communism.

The crisis in Berlin persuaded western European nations that they needed a collective security pact with the United States. In April 1949, for the first time since the end of the American Revolution, the United States entered into a peacetime military alliance, the North Atlantic Treaty Organization (NATO). Under the NATO pact, twelve nations—the United States, Canada, Britain, France, Italy, Belgium, the Netherlands, Luxembourg, Denmark, Norway, Portugal, and Iceland—agreed that "an armed attack against one or more of them in Europe or North America shall be considered an attack against them all." In May 1949 those nations also agreed to the creation of the Federal Republic of Germany (West Germany), which joined NATO in 1955. In response, the Soviet Union set up the German Democratic Republic (East Germany) in 1949; an economic association, the Council for Mutual Economic Assistance (COMECON), in 1949; and a military alliance for eastern Europe, the Warsaw Pact, in 1955. In these parallel steps, the two superpowers were institutionalizing the Cold War and thereby translating tense uncertainty into permanent stalemate.

Nuclear Stalemate. The final stage in that process came in September 1949, when American military intelligence detected a rise in radioactivity in the atmosphere—proof that the Soviet Union

The Berlin Airlift

For 321 days American planes like this one flew missions to bring food and other supplies to Berlin after the Soviet Union had blocked all surface routes into the former German capital. The blockade was finally lifted on May 12, 1949, after the Soviets conceded that it had been a failure. AP Images.

Testing the Bomb

After World War II, the development of nuclear weapons went on apace, requiring frequent testing of the more advanced weapons. This photograph shows members of the 11th Airborne division viewing the mushroom cloud from one such A-bomb test at the Atomic Energy Commission's proving grounds at Yucca flats in Nevada, November 1, 1951. Finally acknowledging the dangers to the atmosphere (and the people in the vicinity or downwind), the United States and the Soviet Union signed a treaty in 1963 banning above-ground testing. J. R. Eyerman/Time Life Pictures/Getty Images.

had detonated an atomic bomb. With America's brief tenure as sole nuclear power over, there was a pressing need for a major reassessment of the nation's strategic planning. Truman turned to the National Security Council (NSC), an advisory body established by the National Security Act of 1947 that also created the Department of Defense and the Central Intelligence Agency (CIA). In April 1950 the NSC delivered its report, known as "NSC-68." Bristling with alarmist rhetoric, the document urged a crash program to maintain America's nuclear edge, including stepped-up production of atomic bombs and the development of a hydrogen bomb, a thermonuclear device a thousand times more destructive than the atomic bombs that had destroyed Hiroshima and Nagasaki. What American intelligence did not know was that Soviet scientists, unlike their American counterparts, had been working on

both tracks all along and were making headway toward a hydrogen bomb. The United States got there first, exploding its first hydrogen bomb in November 1952; the Soviet Union followed in 1953.

Although he accepted the NSC-68 recommendation, Truman had grave misgivings about the furies he was unleashing. This was apparent in his decision to lodge control over nuclear weapons in a civilian agency, not with the military. Truman did not want nuclear weapons incorporated into military planning and treated as a functional part of the nation's arsenal (as they had been at Hiroshima and Nagasaki). Evidence suggests that Stalin, in fact, had similar misgivings. And with the advent of the hydrogen bomb, the utility of nuclear devices as actual weapons shrank to zero. No political objective could possibly be worth the destructiveness of a thermonuclear exchange. One effect was to reinforce the grudging stalemate that had taken hold in Europe. A "balance of terror" now prevailed.

The other, paradoxically, was to magnify the importance of conventional forces. The United States, having essentially demobilized its wartime army, had relied on the atomic bomb as the equalizer against the vast Soviet army. Now, if it wanted a credible deterrent, the only option was a stronger conventional military. To that end, NSC-68 called for increased taxes to finance "a bold and massive program of rebuilding the West's defensive potential to surpass that of the Soviet world." Truman was reluctant to commit to a major defense buildup, fearing that it would overburden the budget. Two months after NSC-68 was completed, events in Asia took that decision out of his hands.

Containment in Asia

Containment aimed primarily at preventing Soviet expansion in Europe. But as tensions built up in Asia, Cold War doctrines began to influence the American position there as well. At first America's attention centered on Japan. After dismantling Japan's military, American occupation forces under General Douglas MacArthur drafted a democratic constitution and oversaw the rebuilding of the economy, paving the way for the restoration of Japanese sovereignty in 1951. Considering the scorched-earth war just ended, this was a remarkable achievement, thanks partly to the imperious MacArthur, but mainly to the Japanese, who put their militaristic past behind them and embraced peace. Trouble on the mainland then drew America's attention, and the Cold War mentality kicked in.

The "Fall" of China. A civil war had been raging in China since the 1930s, as Communist forces led by Mao Zedong (Mao Tse-tung) contended for power with Nationalist forces under Jiang Jieshi (Chiang Kai-shek). Although dissatisfied with the corrupt Jiang regime, American officials did not see Mao as a good alternative, and they resigned themselves to supporting the Nationalists. Between 1945 and 1949 the United States provided more than $2 billion to Jiang's forces, but in August 1949 the Truman administration gave up on the Nationalists and cut off aid. By then their fate was sealed. The People's Republic of China was formally established under Mao on October 1, 1949, and the remnants of Jiang's forces fled to Taiwan.

Initially, the American response was muted. Both Stalin and Truman expected Mao to take an independent line, as the Communist Tito had recently done in Yugoslavia. Mao, however, aligned himself with the Soviet Union, partly out of exaggerated fears that the United States would rearm the Nationalists and send them back to the mainland. As attitudes hardened, many Americans viewed Mao's success as a defeat for the United States. A pro-Nationalist "China lobby" accused Truman's State Department of being responsible for the "loss" of China. Sensitive to these charges, the Truman administration refused to recognize "Red China," and also blocked China's admission to the United Nations, treating the world's most populous country as an international pariah. But the United States pointedly refused to guarantee Taiwan's independence, and in fact accepted the outcome on the mainland. It had not, however, taken account of a country few Americans had ever heard of, Korea, which had been a part of the Japanese Empire since 1910 and whose future now had to be decided.

The Korean War. In Korea, as in Germany, Cold War confrontation grew out of interim arrangements made at the end of the war. The United States and the Soviet Union, both with troops in Korea, had agreed to occupy the nation jointly, dividing their sectors at the thirty-eighth parallel, pending Korea's unification. As tensions rose in Europe, the thirty-eighth parallel hardened into a permanent demarcation line. The Soviets supported a Communist government, led by Kim Il Sung, in North Korea; the United States backed a long-time Korean nationalist, Syngman Rhee, in South Korea. Both were spoiling for a fight, but neither could launch an all-out offensive without the backing of his sponsor. Washington repeatedly said no, and so did Moscow — until Stalin, reading a speech by Secretary of State Dean Acheson declaring South Korea outside America's "defense perimeter," concluded that the United States would not intervene.

On June 25, 1950, the North Koreans launched a surprise attack across the thirty-eighth parallel (Map 26.2). Truman immediately asked the U.N. Security Council to authorize a "police action" against the invaders. Because the Soviet Union was temporarily boycotting the Security Council to protest China's exclusion from the United Nations, it could not veto Truman's request. With the Security Council's approval of a "peacekeeping force," Truman ordered U.S. troops to Korea.

Though fourteen other non-Communist nations sent troops, the rapidly assembled U.N. army in Korea was overwhelmingly American, with General

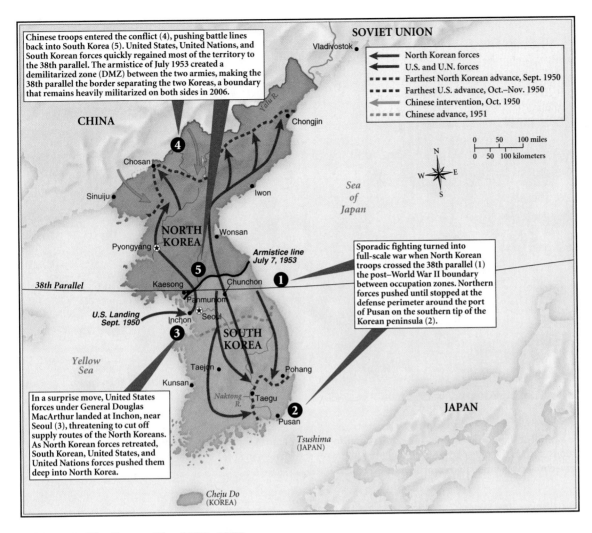

Chinese troops entered the conflict (4), pushing battle lines back into South Korea (5). United States, United Nations, and South Korean forces quickly regained most of the territory to the 38th parallel. The armistice of July 1953 created a demilitarized zone (DMZ) between the two armies, making the 38th parallel the border separating the two Koreas, a boundary that remains heavily militarized on both sides in 2006.

North Korean forces	
U.S. and U.N. forces	
Farthest North Korean advance, Sept. 1950	
Farthest U.S. advance, Oct.–Nov. 1950	
Chinese intervention, Oct. 1950	
Chinese advance, 1951	

Sporadic fighting turned into full-scale war when North Korean troops crossed the 38th parallel (1) the post–World War II boundary between occupation zones. Northern forces pushed until stopped at the defense perimeter around the port of Pusan on the southern tip of the Korean peninsula (2).

In a surprise move, United States forces under General Douglas MacArthur landed at Inchon, near Seoul (3), threatening to cut off supply routes of the North Koreans. As North Korean forces retreated, South Korean, United States, and United Nations forces pushed them deep into North Korea.

MAP 26.2 The Korean War, 1950–1953

The Korean War, which the United Nations officially deemed a "police action," lasted three years and cost the lives of over 36,000 U.S. troops. South and North Korean deaths were estimated at over 900,000. Although hostilities ceased in 1953, the U.S. military and the North Korean army faced each other across the demilitarized zone for the next fifty years.

Douglas MacArthur placed in charge. At first, the North Koreans held an overwhelming advantage, occupying the entire peninsula except for the southeast area around Pusan. But on September 15, 1950, MacArthur launched a surprise amphibious attack at Inchon, far behind the North Korean lines, while U.N. forces staged a breakout from Pusan. Within two weeks the U.N. forces controlled Seoul, the South Korean capital, and almost all the territory up to the thirty-eighth parallel. Although the Chinese government in Beijing warned repeatedly against further incursions, MacArthur's troops crossed the thirty-eighth parallel on October 9, reaching the Chinese border at the Yalu River by the end of the month. Just after Thanksgiving a massive Chinese counterattack of almost 300,000 "volunteers" forced MacArthur's

forces into headlong retreat back down the Korean penninsula. On January 4, 1951, Communist troops reoccupied Seoul.

Two months later American forces and their allies counterattacked, regained Seoul, and pushed back to the thirty-eighth parallel. Then stalemate set in. With public support in the United States for a prolonged war waning, Truman and his advisors decided to work for a negotiated peace.

MacArthur disagreed. Arrogant and brilliant, the general fervently believed that America's future lay in Asia, not Europe. In an inflammatory letter to the House minority leader, Republican Joseph J. Martin of Massachusetts, he denounced the Korean stalemate, declaring "There is no substitute for victory." The strategy backfired. On

The Korean War

As a result of Harry Truman's 1948 executive order, for the first time in the nation's history, all troops, such as the men of the Second Infantry Battalion, shown here in Korea in 1950, served in racially integrated combat units (see p. 853). National Archives.

April 11 Truman relieved MacArthur of his command, accusing him of insubordination. Truman's decision was highly unpopular, but he had the last word. After failing to win the Republican presidential nomination in 1952, MacArthur faded from public view.

The war dragged on for more than two years after MacArthur's dismissal. An armistice was not signed until July 1953, leaving Korea divided at the original demarcation line at the thirty-eighth parallel. North Korea remained firmly allied with the Soviet Union; South Korea signed a mutual defense treaty with the United States in 1954.

The Impact of the Korean War. The Korean War had lasting consequences. Truman's decision to commit troops to Korea without congressional approval set a precedent for future undeclared wars. His refusal to unleash atomic bombs, even when American forces were reeling under a massive Chinese attack, set limiting ground rules for Cold War conflict. The war also expanded American involvement in Asia, transforming containment

into a truly global policy. Finally, it ended Truman's resistance to a major military buildup. Overall defense expenditures grew from $13 billion in 1950, roughly one-third of the federal budget, to $50 billion in 1953, nearly two-thirds of the budget. Although military expenditures dropped briefly after the Korean War, defense spending remained at over $35 billion annually throughout the 1950s. American foreign policy had become more global, more militarized, and more expensive (Figure 26.1). Even in times of peace, the United States now functioned in a state of permanent mobilization.

➤ Why was the United States unable to avoid entering a Cold War with the Soviet Union?

➤ How are the ideas of George F. Kennan reflected in Truman's Cold War policies?

➤ What was the long-term significance of the Korean War?

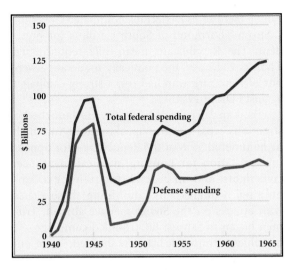

FIGURE 26.1 National Defense Spending, 1940–1965

In 1950 the defense budget was $13 billion, less than a third of total federal outlays. In 1961 defense spending reached $47 billion, fully half of the federal budget and almost 10 percent of the gross domestic product.

The Truman Era

Harry Truman never intended to be a caretaker president. On September 16, 1945, just fourteen days after Japan surrendered and six months after FDR's death, Truman staked his claim to domestic leadership with a plan that called for a dramatic expansion of the New Deal. He intended to fulfill the expansive Economic Bill of Rights that Roosevelt had famously proclaimed in his State of the Union Address in 1944. Truman phrased his proposals in just that way, as rights expected by all Americans— to a "useful and remunerative" job, good housing, "adequate medical care," "protection from the economic fears of old age," and a "good education." Truman had no way of foreseeing on V-J day the confounding forces lying in wait. In the end, his high hopes were crushed, and Truman went down in history not, as he hoped, as FDR's worthy successor, but as a Cold Warrior.

Reconversion

No sooner had Truman finished laying out his ambitious domestic program than he was waylaid by cascading problems over converting the wartime economy to peacetime. Left in the dark about the atomic bomb, government planners had assumed that reconversion would be phased in while Japan

was being subdued. So when the war suddenly ended, no reconversion plan was in place. The hasty dismantling of the vast wartime machine frustrated liberal planners, who had hoped to give small business a headstart in the peacetime market while the big manufacturers were still in war production. What worried Truman, however, was runaway inflation. He wanted to keep the wartime Office of Price Administration (OPA) in place while domestic production caught up with pent-up demand. His efforts at price control were overwhelmed by consumers impatient to spend money and businesses eager to take it from them, with the result that consumer prices soared by 33 percent in the immediate postwar years.

Postwar Strikes and the Taft-Hartley Act.

Organized labor was far stronger than it had ever been. Union membership had swelled to over fourteen million by 1945, including two-thirds of all workers in mining, manufacturing, construction, and transportation. Determined to make up for their wartime sacrifices, workers mounted crippling strikes in the automobile, steel, and coal industries. General strikes effectively brought normal life to a halt in half a dozen cities in 1946.

Truman responded erratically. In some cases, he gave way, as, for example, when he lifted price controls on steel in early 1946 so that the industry could grant the wage demands of the strikers. In other instances, Truman tried to show union leaders who was boss. Faced by a devastating railway strike, he threatened to place the nation's railroad system under federal control and asked Congress for the power to draft striking workers into the army—moves that infuriated union leaders but got the strikers back to work. In November 1946, when coal miners called a strike as winter approached, Truman secured a sweeping court order against the union. When its imperious leader John L. Lewis, having been slapped with a huge fine, tried to negotiate, Truman turned him away. He was not going to have "that son of a bitch" in the White House.

If Truman outraged organized labor, an important partner in the Democratic coalition, his display of toughness did little to placate the Republicans, who, having gained control of both houses of Congress in 1946, moved quickly to curb labor's power. In alliance with conservative southern Democrats, they passed the Taft-Hartley Act (1947), a sweeping overhaul of the 1935 National Labor Relations Act. Some of the new provisions aimed at perceived abuses—the **secondary boycott**, crippling national strikes, unionization of supervisory employees. Ultimately of greater significance, however, were skillfully crafted changes in procedures and language that over time eroded the law's stated purpose of protecting the right of workers to organize and engage in collective bargaining. Unions especially disliked Section 14b, which allowed states to pass "right-to-work" laws prohibiting the **union shop**. Truman issued a ringing veto of the Taft-Hartley bill in June 1947, but Congress easily overrode the veto.

The 1948 Election. By 1947, most observers wouldn't have bet a nickel on Truman's future. His popularity ratings had plummeted, and "To err is Truman" had entered the political language. Democrats would have dumped him for 1948 had they found a better candidate. As it was, the party fell into disarray. The left wing split off and formed the Progressive Party, nominating as its candidate Henry A. Wallace, an avid New Dealer whom Truman had fired as secretary of commerce in 1946 because of his vocal opposition to the Cold War. The right-wing challenge came from the South. When northern liberals such as Mayor Hubert H. Humphrey of Minneapolis pushed through a strong civil rights platform at the Democratic convention, the southern delegations bolted and,

calling themselves Dixiecrats, nominated Governor J. Strom Thurmond of South Carolina for president. The Republicans meanwhile renominated Thomas E. Dewey, the politically moderate governor of New York who had run a strong campaign against FDR in 1944.

Truman surprised everyone. He launched a strenuous cross-country speaking tour in which he hammered away at the Republicans for opposing legislation for housing, medical insurance, civil rights, and, in general, for running a "do-nothing" Congress. By combining these issues with attacks on the Soviet menace abroad, Truman began to salvage his troubled campaign. At his rallies enthusiastic listeners shouted, "Give 'em hell, Harry!"

Truman won a remarkable victory, receiving 49.6 percent of the vote to Dewey's 45.1 percent (Map 26.3). The Democrats also regained control of both houses of Congress. Strom Thurmond carried only four southern states, while Henry Wallace failed to win any electoral votes. Truman retained the support of organized labor, Jewish and Catholic voters in the big cities, and black voters in the North. Most important, he appealed effectively to people like himself from the farms, towns, and small cities in the nation's heartland.

Truman Triumphant

In one of the most famous photographs in American political history, Harry S Truman gloats over a headline in the *Chicago Daily Tribune*. Pollsters had predicted an easy victory for Thomas E. Dewey. Their primitive techniques, however, missed the dramatic surge in support for Truman during the last days of the campaign. © Bettmann/Corbis.

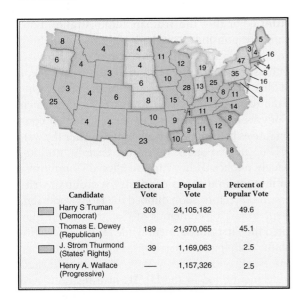

Candidate	Electoral Vote	Popular Vote	Percent of Popular Vote
Harry S Truman (Democrat)	303	24,105,182	49.6
Thomas E. Dewey (Republican)	189	21,970,065	45.1
J. Strom Thurmond (States' Rights)	39	1,169,063	2.5
Henry A. Wallace (Progressive)	—	1,157,326	2.5

MAP 26.3 Presidential Election of 1948

Truman's electoral strategy in 1948 was to concentrate his campaign in areas where the Democrats had their greatest strength. In an election with a low turnout, Truman held onto enough support from Roosevelt's New Deal coalition of blacks, union members, and farmers to defeat Dewey by more than two million votes.

The Fair Deal

In his 1949 State of the Union address, Truman rechristened his program the Fair Deal. It incorporated the goals he had set out initially—national health insurance, aid to education, a housing program, expansion of Social Security, a higher minimum wage, and a new agricultural program—but also struck out in some new directions. In its attention to civil rights (see Chapter 27), the Fair Deal reflected the growing importance of African Americans to the Democratic Party's coalition of urban voters. And the desire to raise the living standards of an ever-greater number of citizens reflected a new liberal vision of the role of the state.

Truman was inspired by the renown English economist, John Maynard Keynes, who had argued that government was capable by means of its fiscal powers of preventing economic depressions. In bad times, deficit spending would "prime the pump," re-igniting consumer spending and private investment and restoring prosperity. The Employment Act of 1946, which asserted the government's responsibility and established a Council of Economic Advisers to assist the president, embodied this Keynesian policy. Truman wanted the Employment Act reinforced by raising its goal to "full" employment and by expanding welfare programs that would undergird consumer purchasing power.

Among the opportunities that came and went, most notable, in light of the nation's current health-care crisis, was the proposal for national health insurance. This was a popular idea, with strong backing from organized labor, but it was denounced as "socialized medicine" by the American Medical Association; the insurance industry (which had spotted a new profit center); and big corporations, which (to their everlasting regret) preferred providing health coverage directly to employees. Lobbying groups were equally effective at defeating Truman's agricultural reforms, which aimed at helping small farmers, and federal aid to education. In the end, the only significant breakthrough, other than improvements in the minimum wage and Social Security, was the National Housing Act of 1949, which authorized the construction of 810,000 low-income units.

Despite Democratic majorities, Congress remained a huge stumbling block. The same conservative coalition that had blocked Roosevelt's initiatives in his second term and dismantled or cut New Deal programs during wartime continued the fight against the Fair Deal. On top of this came the Cold War. The outbreak of fighting in Korea in 1950 was especially damaging, diverting national attention and federal funds from domestic affairs. Another potent diversion was the nation's growing paranoia over internal subversion, the most dramatic manifestation of the Cold War's effect on American life.

The Great Fear

Was there any significant Soviet penetration of the American government? Historians had mostly debunked the idea and so, in earlier editions, did this textbook. But we were wrong. Records opened up since 1991—intelligence files in Moscow and, among U.S. sources, most importantly the Venona intercepts of Soviet cables—name among American suppliers of information FDR's assistant secretary of the Treasury Department (Harry Dexter White); FDR's administrative aide (Laughlin Currie); a mid-level, strategically placed group in the State Department (including Alger Hiss, who was with FDR at Yalta); and several hundred more, some identified only by code name, working in a range of government departments and agencies.

What are we to make of this? Many of these enlistees in the Soviet cause were bright young New Dealers in the mid-1930s, when Moscow's Popular Front suggested—to the uninformed, at any rate—that the lines between liberal, progressive, and Communist were blurred and permeable (see Chapter 25). At that time, in the mid-1930s, the United States was not at war, nor ever expected to be. And when war did come, the Soviet Union was an American ally. The flow of stolen documents speeded up and kept Soviet intelligence privy to all aspects of the American war effort. What most interested Stalin was U.S. intentions about a second front and—an obsessive fear of his—a separate deal with Hitler. And, of course, the atomic bomb. Even here, people turned a blind eye to Soviet espionage. Many Los Alamos scientists, indeed, thought it a mistake not to tell the Soviets about the bomb. J. Robert Oppenheimer, the director of the Manhattan Project, was inclined to agree. He just didn't like "the idea of having the [secrets] moved out the back door."

Once the Cold War set in, of course, Oppenheimer's indulgent view of Soviet espionage became utterly inadmissible, and the government moved with great fanfare to crack down. In March 1947 President Truman issued an executive order launching a comprehensive loyalty program for federal employees. Of the activities deemed to be "disloyal," the operative one was membership in any of a list of "subversive" organizations compiled by the attorney general. On that basis, federal loyalty boards mounted witch hunts that wrecked the careers of about ten thousand public servants, not one of whom was ever tried and convicted of espionage.

As for the actual suppliers of information to the Soviets, they seem mostly to have left off spying once the Cold War began. For one thing, the professional apparatus of Soviet agents running them was dismantled or disrupted by stepped-up American counterintelligence work. After the war, moreover, most of these well-connected amateur spies moved on to other careers. The State Department official Alger Hiss, for example, was serving as head of the prestigious Carnegie Endowment for International Peace when he was accused in 1948 by a Communist-turned-informant, Whittaker Chambers, of having passed classified documents to him in the 1930s. Skepticism by historians about internal subversion—that it was insignificant—seems justified if we start in 1947, just when the hue-and-cry about internal subversion was blowing up into a second Red Scare (for the first, see Chapter 22).

HUAC. For this, the Truman administration bore some responsibility. It had legitimized making "disloyalty" the proxy for subversive activity. Others, however, were far more ruthless and adept at this technique, beginning with the House Un-American Activities Committee (HUAC), which Congressman Martin Dies of Texas and other conservatives had launched back in 1938. After the war, HUAC helped spark the Great Fear by holding widely publicized hearings on alleged Communist infiltration in the movie industry. A group of writers and directors, soon dubbed the Hollywood Ten, went to jail for contempt of Congress when they cited the First Amendment while refusing to testify about their past associations. Hundreds of other actors, directors, and writers whose names had been mentioned in the HUAC investigation were unable to get work, victims of an unacknowledged but very real **blacklist** honored by industry executives.

Following Washington's lead, many state and local governments, universities, political organizations, churches, and businesses undertook their own antisubversion campaigns, which often included the requirement that employees take loyalty oaths. In the labor movement, where Communists had been active as organizers in the 1930s, charges of Communist domination led to the expulsion of a number of industrial unions by the CIO in 1949. Civil rights organizations such as the NAACP and the National Urban League also expelled Communists or "fellow travelers"—words used to describe people viewed as Communist sympathizers although not members of the Communist Party. Thus the Great Fear spread from the federal government to the farthest reaches of American associational, cultural, and economic life.

Here, too, however, revelations from the Soviet archives have complicated the picture. Historians have mostly regard the American Communist Party as a "normal" organization, acting in America's home-grown radical tradition and playing by the rules of the game. Soviet archives clearly show otherwise. The American party was taking money and instructions from Moscow. It was in no way independent, so that, when Communists joined other organizations, not only red-baiters found their participation problematic. Consider the expulsion of the Communist-led industrial unions mentioned above. In 1948 the CIO had gone all-out for Truman's reelection, which was the only hope it had of reversing the hated Taft-Hartley Act. The Communist line was to support Wallace's Progressive Party, and that's what the Communist-led unions did, thereby

The Army-McCarthy Hearings

These 1954 hearings contributed to the downfall of Senator Joseph McCarthy by exposing his reckless accusations and bullying tactics to the huge television audience that tuned in each day. Some of the most heated exchanges took place between McCarthy (center) and Joseph Welch (seated, left), the lawyer representing the army. When the gentlemanly Welch finally asked, "Have you no decency left, sir?" he fatally punctured McCarthy's armor. The audience broke into applause because someone had finally had the courage to stand up to the senator from Wisconsin. © Bettmann/Corbis.

demonstrating that they were Communists first, trade unionists second — a cardinal sin for the labor movement. The expulsions left in their wake the wrecked lives of many innocent, high-minded trade unionists, and that was true wherever anti-Communism took hold, whether in universities, school boards, or civil rights organizations.

McCarthyism. The finale of the Great Fear opened with the meteoric rise of Senator Joseph McCarthy of Wisconsin. In February 1950 McCarthy delivered a bombshell during a speech in Wheeling, West Virginia: "I have in my hand 57 cases of individuals who would appear to be either card-carrying members or certainly loyal to the Communist Party, but who nevertheless are still helping to shape our foreign policy [in the State Department]." McCarthy later reduced his numbers, and he never released any names or proof, but he had gained the attention he sought. For the next four years, he was

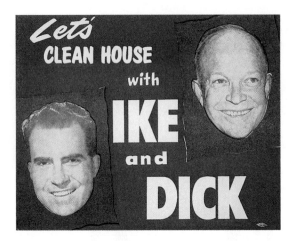

The 1952 Presidential Campaign

The Republican campaign capitalized on scandals involving bribery and influence-peddling that engulfed the Truman administration's second term and on Dwight Eisenhower's popularity. Everyone knew him as "Ike." They didn't particularly know his running mate Richard M. Nixon as "Dick." That was just thrown in for good measure. Collection of Janice L. and David J. Frent.

the central figure in a virulent smear campaign. Critics who disagreed with him exposed themselves to charges of being "soft" on Communism. Truman called McCarthy's charges "slander, lies, character assassination," but could do nothing to curb them. The Republicans, for their part, refrained from publicly challenging their most outspoken senator and, on the whole, were content to reap the political benefits (see Comparing American Voices, "Hunting Communists and Liberals," pp. 820–821).

In early 1954 McCarthy overreached himself by launching an investigation into possible subversion in the U.S. Army. When lengthy hearings — the first of its kind broadcast on the new medium of television — brought McCarthy's smear tactics into the nation's living rooms, support for him declined. In December 1954 the Senate voted 67 to 22 to censure McCarthy for unbecoming conduct. He died from an alcohol-related illness three years later at the age of forty-eight, his name forever attached to a period of political repression of which he was only the most flagrant manifestation.

➤ Why did Harry Truman seem a failure during his first term in the White House?

➤ How does the Fair Deal differ from the New Deal?

➤ Why have historians revised their views about the significance of espionage in American government? Does this make any difference about how we evaluate McCarthyism?

Modern Republicanism

As election day 1952 approached, America seemed ready for change. The question was, How much? With the Republican victory, the country got its answer: Very little. The new president, Dwight D. Eisenhower, set the tone for what his supporters called "modern Republicanism" — an updated GOP approach that aimed at moderating, not dismantling, the New Deal state. Eisenhower and his supporters were — despite themselves — successors of FDR, not Herbert Hoover. Foreign policy revealed a similar continuity. Like their predecessors, Republicans saw the world in Cold War polarities. They embraced the defense buildup begun during the Korean War and pushed containment to the far reaches of the world.

They Liked Ike

The Republicans' problem was that, after twenty years of Democratic rule, they were the minority party. Only one in three registered voters was Republican. The party faithful gave their hearts to Robert A. Taft of Ohio, the Republican leader in the Senate since 1939, but their heads told them that only a moderate, less-well-defined candidate was likely to attract the independent vote. General Eisenhower filled the bill. He was an immensely popular figure, widely admired as the architect of D-Day and victory in Europe. Eisenhower was a man without a political past. Believing that democracy required that the military stand aside, he had never voted. Democrats and Republicans courted him, but it turned out that Eisenhower was a Republican, a believer in balanced budgets and individual responsibility. For regional balance, Eisenhower asked Senator Richard M. Nixon of California to be his running mate. Nixon was youthful, tirelessly partisan, and strongly anti-Communist. He had won his spurs by leading HUAC's investigation of Alger Hiss's espionage past.

The Democrats never seriously considered renominating Harry Truman, who by 1952 was a thoroughly discredited leader, primarily because of the unpopularity of the Korean War, but also because of a series of scandals that Republicans dubbed "the mess in Washington." With a certain relief, the Democrats turned to Governor Adlai E. Stevenson of Illinois, who enjoyed the support of respected liberals, such as Eleanor Roosevelt, and of organized labor. To appease conservative southern voters, the Democrats nominated Senator John A. Sparkman of Alabama for vice president.

Throughout the campaign Stevenson advocated New Deal-Fair Deal policies with an almost literary eloquence. But Eisenhower's artfully unpretentious speeches and "I Like Ike" slogan were more effective with voters. Eager to win the support of the broadest electorate possible, Eisenhower played down specific questions of policy. Instead, he attacked the Democrats with the "K_1C_2" formula—"Korea, Communism, and Corruption."

That November Eisenhower won 55 percent of the popular vote, carrying all the northern and western states and four southern states. His triumph did not translate, however, into a new Republican majority. Republicans regained control of Congress on his coattails, but lost it 1954 and did not recover when Eisenhower easily won reelection over Adlai Stevenson in 1956. For most of his tenure, Eisenhower had to work with a Democratic Congress.

The Hidden-Hand Presidency

Although supremely confident as an international leader, Eisenhower started out a novice in domestic affairs. He did his best to set a quieter national mood after the rancorous Truman years. Disliking confrontation, he was reluctant to speak out against Joe McCarthy, and he was not a leader on civil rights. Yet Eisenhower was no stooge as president. Political scientists have characterized his leadership style as the "hidden-hand presidency." They point out that Eisenhower maneuvered deftly behind the scenes while maintaining a public demeanor of being above the fray. If he sometimes seemed inarticulate and bumbling, that was often a studied effect to mask his real intentions. He in fact ran a tight ship and was always in command.

After 1954, when the Democrats took control over Congress, the Eisenhower administration accepted legislation promoting social welfare. Federal outlays for veterans' benefits, housing, and Social Security were increased, and the minimum wage was raised from 75 cents an hour to $1. The creation of the new Department of Health, Education, and Welfare (HEW) in 1953 consolidated government administration of social welfare programs, confirming federal commitments in that area. Welfare expenditures went steadily upward during Eisenhower's tenure, consuming an ever larger share of the federal budget. Like Truman, Eisenhower accepted the government's responsibility for economic performance and, despite his faith in a balanced budget, engaged in deficit spending whenever employment dipped. He intervened even more vigorously when it came to holding in check the inflation sparked by the Korean War.

More striking was the expanded scope of federal activity. In a move that drastically altered America's landscape and driving habits, the National Interstate and Defense Highways Act of 1956 authorized $26 billion over a ten-year period for the construction of a nationally integrated highway system (see Map 27.2, p. 839). To link the Great Lakes with the Atlantic Ocean, the United States and Canada cosponsored in 1959 the construction of the St. Lawrence Seaway. These enormous public works programs surpassed anything undertaken during the New Deal. And when the Soviet Union launched the first satellite, *Sputnik*, in 1957, the startled country went into high gear to catch up in this new Cold War space competition (see Reading American Pictures, "Why a Cold War Space Race?," p. 823). Eisenhower authorized the National Aeronautics and Space Administration (NASA) the following year, and, alarmed that the United States was falling behind in science and technology, he persuaded Congress to appropriate additional money for college scholarships and university research.

Only in the area of natural resources did the Eisenhower administration actually reduce federal activity—turning over offshore oil to the states and private developers, and authorizing privately financed hydroelectric dams on the Snake River. In most other ways—New Deal welfare programs, Keynesian intervention in the economy, new departures in public works, scientific research, higher education—the Eisenhower Republicans had become part of a broad **liberal consensus** in American politics. That was the view of a true conservative, Senator Barry Goldwater of Arizona, who remarked sourly that Ike had run a "Dime Store New Deal."

Eisenhower and the Cold War

Every incoming administration likes to proclaim itself a grand departure from its predecessor.

Hunting Communists and Liberals

The onset of the Cold War created an opportunity for some conservatives to seize on anti-Communism as a weapon to attack the Truman administration. In Senator McCarthy's case, the charge was that the Truman administration was harboring Soviet spies within the government. There was also a broader, more amorphous attack on people not accused of spying but of having Communist sympathies and thus being "security risks" and unsuitable for government positions. For this targeted group, the basis of suspicion was generally membership in organizations that supported policies that overlapped with or seemed similar to policies supported by the Communist Party.

McCARTHYISM
Senator Joseph McCarthy, Speech Delivered in Wheeling, West Virginia, February 9, 1950

Senator McCarthy was actually late getting on board the anti-Communist rocket ship. This was the speech that launched him into orbit. No one ever saw the piece of paper he waved about with the names of fifty-seven spies in the State Department. Over time, the number fluctuated, and never materialized into a single indictable spy. Still, McCarthy had an extraordinary talent for whipping up anti-Communist hysteria. His downfall came in 1954, when the U.S. Senate formally censured McCarthy for his conduct; three years later, he died of alcoholism at the age of 48.

Today we are engaged in a final, all-out battle between communistic atheism and Christianity. The modern champions of communism have selected this as the time. And, ladies and gentlemen, the chips are down — they are truly down. . . .

The reason why we find ourselves in a position of impotency is not because our only powerful potential enemy has sent men to invade our shores, but rather because of the traitorous actions of those who have been treated so well by this Nation. It has not been the less fortunate or members of minority groups who have been selling this Nation out, but rather those who have had all the benefits that the wealthiest nation on earth has had to offer — the finest homes, the finest college education, and the finest jobs in Government we can give. . . .

I have in my hand 57 cases of individuals who would appear to be either card carrying members or certainly loyal to the Communist Party, but who nevertheless are still helping to shape our foreign policy. . . .

THE ORDEAL OF FRANK P. GRAHAM
Fulton Lewis Jr.'s Radio Address, January 13, 1949

The groundwork for McCarthy's anti-Communist crusade was laid by the House Un-American Activities Committee (HUAC), which had been formed in 1938 by conservative southern Democrats seeking to investigate alleged Communist influence around the country. One of its early targets had been Dr. Frank P. Graham, the distinguished president of the University of North Carolina. A committed southern liberal, Graham was a leading figure in the Southern Conference on Human Welfare, the most prominent southern organization supporting the New Deal, free speech, organized labor, and greater rights for southern blacks — causes that some in the South saw as pathways for Communist subversion. After the war, HUAC stepped up its activities and kept a close eye on Dr. Graham.

Among Dr. Graham's duties, one was to serve as the head of the Oak Ridge Institute of Nuclear Studies, a consortium of fourteen southern universities designed to undertake joint research with the federal government's atomic energy facility at Oak Ridge, Tennessee. To enable him to carry on his duties, the Atomic Energy Commission (AEC) granted Dr. Graham a security clearance, overriding the negative recommendation of the AEC's Security Advisory Board. That was the occasion for the following statement by Fulton Lewis Jr., a conservative radio commentator with a nationwide following.

. . . About Dr. Frank P. Graham, president of the University of North Carolina, and the action of the Atomic Energy Commission giving him complete clearance for all atomic secrets despite the fact that the security officer of the commission flatly rejected him . . .

President Truman was asked to comment on the matter today at his press and radio conference, and his reply was that he has complete confidence in Dr. Graham. . . . The defenders of Dr. Graham today offered the apology that during the time he joined the various subversive and Communist front organizations [like the Southern Conference for Human Welfare] — organizations so listed by the Attorney General of the United States — this country was a co-belligerent with Soviet Russia, and numerous people joined such groups and causes. That argument is going to sound very thin to most American citizens, because the overwhelming majority of us would have no part of any Communist or Communist front connections at any time. . . .

Frank Porter Graham's Telegram to Fulton Lewis Jr., January 13, 1949

One can imagine Graham's shock at hearing himself pilloried on national radio. (He had not even been aware of the AEC's investigation of him.) Following is his response to Lewis.

. . . In view of your questions and implications I hope you will use my statement to provide for my answers. . . . I have always been opposed to Communism and all totalitarian dictatorships. I opposed both Nazi and Communist aggression against Czechoslovakia and the earlier Russian aggression against Finland and later Communist aggression against other countries. . . .

During the period of my active participation, the overwhelming number of members of the Southern Conference were to my knowledge anti-Communists. There were several isolationist stands of the Conference with which I disagreed. The stands which I supported as the main business of the Conference were such as the following: Federal aid to the states for schools; abolition of freight rate discrimination against Southern commerce, agriculture, and industry; anti-poll tax bill; anti-lynching bill; equal right of qualified Negroes to vote in both primaries and general elections; the unhampered lawful right of labor to organize and bargain collectively in our region; . . . minimum wages and social security in the Southern and American tradition. . . .

I have been called a Communist by some sincere people. I have been called a spokesman of American capitalism by Communists and repeatedly called a tool of imperialism by the radio from Moscow. I shall simply continue to oppose Ku Kluxism, imperialism, fascism, and Communism whether in America . . . or behind the "iron curtain."

HOUSE UN-AMERICAN ACTIVITIES COMMITTEE
Report on Frank Graham, February 4, 1949

Because of the controversy, HUAC released this report on Dr. Graham.

A check of the files, records and publications of the Committee on Un-American Activities has revealed the following information:

Letterheads dated September 22, 1939, January 17, 1940, and May 26, 1940, as well as the "Daily Worker" of March 18, 1939, . . . reveal that Frank P. Graham was a member of the American Committee for Democracy and Intellectual Freedom. . . . In Report 2277, dated June 25, 1942, the Special Committee on Un-American Activities found that "the line of the American Committee for Democracy and Intellectual Freedom has fluctuated in complete harmony with the line of the Communist Party." The organization was again cited by the Special Committee . . . as a Communist front "which defended Communist teachers." . . .

A letterhead of February 7, 1946, a letterhead of June 4, 1947 . . . and an announcement of the Third Meeting, April 19–21, 1942, at Nashville, Tennessee, reveal that Frank P. Graham was honorary President of the Southern Conference for Human Welfare. . . .

In a report on the Southern Conference for Human Welfare, dated June 16, 1947, the Committee on Un-American Activities found "the most conclusive proof of Communist domination of the Southern Conference for Human Welfare is to be found in the organization's strict and unvarying conformance to the line of the Communist Party in the field of foreign policy. It is also a clear indication of the fact that the real purpose of the organization was not 'human welfare' in the South, but rather to serve as a convenient vehicle in support of the current Communist Party line." . . .

SOURCES: *Congressional Record*, U.S. Senate, 81st Cong., 2d Sess. (Washington, D.C.: GPO, 1950); Frank Porter Graham Papers, University of North Carolina at Chapel Hill Library.

ANALYZING THE EVIDENCE

➤ On what grounds do Fulton Lewis Jr. and HUAC assert that Frank Graham was a security risk? Do they charge that he was a Communist? Is there any evidence in these documents that he might have been a security risk?

➤ How does Graham defend himself? Are you persuaded by his defense?

➤ Do you see any similarity between McCarthy's famous speech at Wheeling, West Virginia, and the suspicions voiced against Dr. Graham by Fulton Lewis Jr. and HUAC a year earlier?

Eisenhower's gesture in this direction was his secretary of state, John Foster Dulles, a lawyer highly experienced in world affairs, but ill-suited by his self-righteous temperament for the craft of diplomacy. Dulles despised "atheistic Communism," and, rather than settling for the status quo, he argued for the "liberation" of the "captive countries" of eastern Europe. This was bombast. The power realities that had called forth containment still applied, as was evident in Eisenhower's first important act as president. Redeeming his campaign pledge to resolve the Korean war, Eisenhower went to Korea. More importantly he stepped up the negotiations that led to an agreement essentially fixing in place the military stalemate at the thirty-eighth parallel.

The Khrushchev Era. Stalin's death in March 1953 precipitated an intraparty struggle in the Soviet Union, which lasted until 1956, when Nikita S. Khrushchev emerged as Stalin's successor. He soon startled Communists around the world by denouncing Stalin and detailing his crimes and blunders. Khrushchev also surprised Westerners by calling for "peaceful coexistence." But any hopes of a thaw evaporated when Hungarians rose up in 1956 and demanded that the country leave the Warsaw Pact. Soviet tanks moved into Budapest and crushed the rebellion—an action the United States condemned but could not realistically resist. Some of the blood was on Dulles's hands because he had embolded the Hungarians with his rhetoric of "rolling back" the Iron Curtain—a pledge that the reality of nuclear weapons made impossible to fulfill.

With no end to the Cold War in sight, Eisenhower turned his attention to containing the cost of containment. Like Truman before him, he hoped to economize by relying on a nuclear arsenal as an alternative to expensive conventional forces. Nuclear weapons delivered "more bang for the buck," explained Defense Secretary Charles E. Wilson. Under the "New Look" defense policy, the Eisenhower administration stepped up production of the hydrogen bomb, approved extensive atmospheric testing, developed the long-range bombing capabilities of the Strategic Air Command, and installed the Distant Early Warning line of radar stations in Alaska and Canada. The Soviets, however, matched the United States weapon for weapon in an escalating arms race. By 1958 both nations had intercontinental ballistic missiles (ICBMs). When an American nuclear submarine launched an atomic-tipped Polaris missile in 1960, Soviet engineers raced to produce an equivalent weapon.

Eisenhower had second thoughts about a nuclear policy aptly named MAD (Mutually Assured Destruction)—based on the premise of annihilitating the enemy even if one's own country was destroyed. Eisenhower tried to negotiate an arms-limitation agreement with the Soviet Union. Progress along those lines was cut short, however, when on May 5, 1960, the Soviets shot down an American U-2 spy plane over their territory. Eisenhower at first denied that the plane was engaged in espionage, but when the Soviet Union produced the captured pilot, Francis Gary Powers, Eisenhower admitted that he had authorized secret flights over the Soviet Union. In the midst of the dispute, a proposed summit meeting with Khrushchev was canceled, and Eisenhower's last chance to negotiate an arms agreement evaporated.

Containment in the Post-Colonial World

Containment policy had been devised in response to Soviet threats in Europe but, as intervention in Korea suggested, it was an infinitely expandable concept. The early Cold War era was a time when new nations were emerging across the **Third World**, inspired by powerful anticolonialist movements that went back before World War II. Between 1947 and 1962 the British, French, Dutch, and Belgian empires in the Middle East, Africa, and Asia all but disintegrated. Committed to national self-determination, FDR had favored these developments, often to the fury of his British and French allies. He expected democracies to emerge, new partners in an American-led, free-market world system. But as the Cold War intensified, that confidence began to wane. Both the Truman and Eisenhower administrations often failed to recognize that indigenous nationalist or socialist movements in emerging nations had their own goals and were not necessarily pawns of the Soviet Union.

Believing that nations had to choose sides, the United States tried to draw them into collective security agreements, with the NATO alliance in Europe as a model. Dulles orchestrated the creation of the Southeast Asia Treaty Organization (SEATO), which in 1954 linked America and its major European allies with Australia, Pakistan, Thailand, New Zealand, and the Philippines. An extensive system of defense alliances eventually tied the United States to more than forty other countries (Map 26.4). The United States also signed

Why a Cold War Space Race?

Satellite Space Race. The Michael Barson Collection / Past Perfect.

"Wonder Why We're Not Keeping Pace?" © 1957 by Herblock in *The Washington Post.*

At the center of the Cold War was science—big science, evidenced most dramatically by the continuous development of nuclear weapons and advances in rocket technology. In the 1950s, the physicists who created the first atomic (and then thermonuclear) weapons—Robert Oppenheimer, Edward Teller, and others—became household names and part of the collective face of America's scientific superiority. Then, in 1957, the United States was startled when the Soviets successfully launched *Sputnik,* the first man-made satellite to orbit the earth. Almost overnight, the United States embarked on a "space race" aimed at catching up with and surpassing the Soviet Union, at a cost of billions of dollars and with far-reaching consequences for American education, science, and space exploration. The two illustrations above say something about America's initial reaction to the news about *Sputnik.*

ANALYZING THE EVIDENCE

➤ Few scientific or technological achievements spark a card game, yet *Sputnik* did. Under the rules of the game, anyone dealt the *Sputnik* card lost two turns. What does that tell you?

➤ Herblock was perhaps the most influential and widely syndicated political cartoonist of the Cold War era. What does his cartoon suggest are the reasons the United States didn't beat the Soviets into space?

➤ The Cold War was far more than geopolitical conflict. It was also a competition between rival economic and cultural systems. How is that battle to demonstrate superiority revealed by the *Sputnik* episode? And by the "space race" that followed?

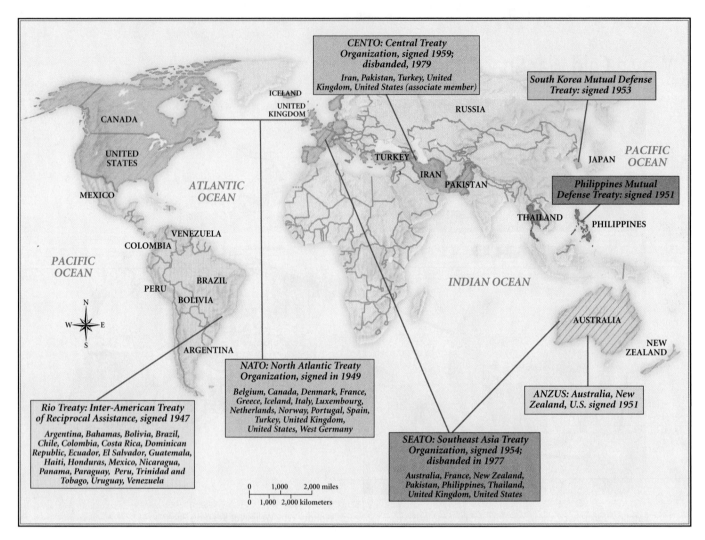

CENTO: Central Treaty Organization, signed 1959; disbanded, 1979

Iran, Pakistan, Turkey, United Kingdom, United States (associate member)

South Korea Mutual Defense Treaty: signed 1953

Philippines Mutual Defense Treaty: signed 1951

NATO: North Atlantic Treaty Organization, signed in 1949

Belgium, Canada, Denmark, France, Greece, Iceland, Italy, Luxembourg, Netherlands, Norway, Portugal, Spain, Turkey, United Kingdom, United States, West Germany

ANZUS: Australia, New Zealand, U.S. signed 1951

Rio Treaty: Inter-American Treaty of Reciprocal Assistance, signed 1947

Argentina, Bahamas, Bolivia, Brazil, Chile, Colombia, Costa Rica, Dominican Republic, Ecuador, El Salvador, Guatemala, Haiti, Honduras, Mexico, Nicaragua, Panama, Paraguay, Peru, Trinidad and Tobago, Uruguay, Venezuela

SEATO: Southeast Asia Treaty Organization, signed 1954; disbanded in 1977

Australia, France, New Zealand, Pakistan, Philippines, Thailand, United Kingdom, United States

MAP 26.4 American Global Defense Treaties in the Cold War Era

The advent of the Cold War led to a major shift in American foreign policy — the signing of mutual defense treaties. Dating back to George Washington's call "to steer clear of permanent alliances with any portion of the foreign world," the United States had avoided treaty obligations that entailed the defense of other nations. As late as 1919, the U.S. Senate had rejected the principle of "collective security," the centerpiece of the League of Nations established by the Treaty of Versailles that ended World War I. But after World War II, in response to fears of Soviet expansion globally, the United States entered defense alliances with much of the non-Communist world, as this map vividly reveals.

bilateral defense treaties with South Korea and Taiwan, and sponsored a strategically valuable defensive alliance between Iran and Iraq on the southern flank of the Soviet Union.

The Eisenhower administration, less concerned about democracy than stability, tended to support governments, no matter how repressive, that were overtly anti-Communist. Some of America's staunchest allies — the Philippines, Korea, Iran, Cuba, and Nicaragua — were governed by dictatorships or right-wing regimes that lacked broad-based support. Moreover, Dulles often resorted to covert operations against governments that, in his opinion, were too closely aligned with the Soviets.

For such tasks he used the Central Intelligence Agency (CIA), which had moved beyond its original mandate of intelligence-gathering into active, albeit covert, involvement in the internal affairs of foreign countries, even to the extent of overthrowing several governments. When Iran's nationalist premier, Muhammad Mossadegh, seized British oil properties in 1953, CIA agents helped depose him and installed the young Muhammad Reza Pahlavi as Shah of Iran. In 1954 the CIA engineered a coup in Guatemala against the popularly elected Jacobo Arbenz Guzman, who had expropriated land owned by the American-owned United Fruit Company and accepted arms from Czechoslovakia. Eisenhower specifically approved those CIA efforts. "Our traditional ideas of international sportsmanship," he confessed privately, "are scarcely applicable in the morass in which the world now [1955] flounders."

Vietnam. How Eisenhower's confession might entangle America was already unfolding on a distant stage, in a country of no strategic interest and utterly unknown to most Americans. This was Vietnam, part of French Indochina. When the Japanese occupiers surrendered in August 1945, the nationalist movement that had led the resistance, the Vietminh, seized control, with American encouragement. Their leader, Ho Chi Minh, admired the United States, and when he proclaimed an independent republic, he did so with words drawn from the American Declaration of Independence. But Ho was also a Communist, and as the Cold War took hold, being Communist outweighed America's commitment to self-determination. The next year, when France moved to restore its control over the country, Truman rejected Ho's plea for support in the Vietnamese struggle for independence and sided with France.

Eisenhower picked up where Truman left off. If the French failed, Eisenhower argued, the **domino theory**—a notion that would henceforth bedevil American strategic thinking—would one after the next lead to the collapse of all non-Communist governments in the region. Although the United States eventually provided most of the financing, the French still failed to defeat the tenacious Vietminh. After a fifty-six-day siege in early 1954, the French went down to stunning defeat at the huge fortress of Dienbienphu. The result was the 1954 Geneva Accords, which partitioned Vietnam temporarily at the seventeenth parallel (see Map 28.6, p. 877), committed France to withdraw from north of that line, and called for elections within two years that would lead to a unified Vietnam.

The United States rejected the Geneva Accords and immediately set about undermining them. With the help of the CIA, a pro-American government took power in South Vietnam in June 1954. Ngo Dinh Diem, an anti-Communist Catholic residing in the United States, returned as premier. The next year, in a rigged election, Diem became president of an independent South Vietnam. Facing certain defeat by the popular Ho Chi Minh, Diem called off the reunification elections that were scheduled for 1956. As the last French soldiers left in March 1956, the United States took over, with South Vietnam now the front line in the American battle to contain Communism in Southeast Asia. To prop him up, the Eisenhower administration sent Diem an average of $200 million a year in aid and stationed approximately 675 American military advisors in Saigon, the capital. Few Americans, including probably Eisenhower himself, had any inkling where this might lead.

The Middle East. If Vietnam was still of minor concern, the same could not be said for the Middle East, an area rich in oil and complications. The Zionist movement had long encouraged Jews to return to their ancient homeland of Israel (Palestine). After World War II, many survivors of the Nazi extermination camps resettled in Palestine, which

Future Israelis

In 1945 these survivors of the Buchenwald concentration camp, like many other Jewish survivors of Hitler's gas ovens, resettled in Palestine. International guilt over the Holocaust was one of the factors that led the United Nations in 1947 to the acceptance of a Jewish state and to the partition of Palestine making such a state possible. National Archives.

was still controlled by Britain under a World War I mandate (see Chapter 22). On November 29, 1947, the U.N. General Assembly voted to partition Palestine, between Jewish and Arab sectors. When the British mandate ended, Zionist leaders proclaimed the state of Israel. The Arab League nations invaded, but Israel survived. Many Palestinians fled or were driven from their homes during the fighting. The Arab defeat, which meant they could not return, left them permanently stranded in refugee camps. President Truman quickly recognized the new state, winning crucial support from Jewish voters in the 1948 election, but alienating the Arabs.

Long dominant in the Persian Gulf, Britain began a general withdrawal after giving up the mandate in Palestine. Two years after gaining independence from Britain, Egypt in 1954 came under the rule of Gamal Abdel Nasser, who pro-

claimed a form of pan-Arab socialism that aimed at leading the entire Middle East out of its dependent, colonial relationship with the West. When Nasser obtained promises of help from the Soviet Union in building the Aswan Dam on the Nile, Secretary of State Dulles countered with an offer of American assistance. Nasser refused to distance himself from the Soviets, however, and Dulles abruptly withdrew his offer in July 1956. A week later Nasser retaliated, nationalizing the Suez Canal, through which three-quarters of western Europe's oil was transported. After several months of fruitless negotiation, Britain and France, in alliance with Israel, attacked Egypt and retook the canal. The attack came just as Eisenhower was condemning the Soviet invasion of Hungary. The president demanded that France and Britain pull back. Egypt retook the Suez Canal and built the Aswan Dam with Soviet support.

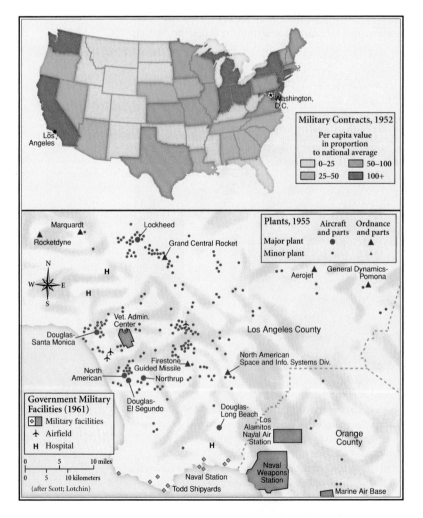

MAP 26.5 The Military-Industrial Complex

Defense spending gave a big boost to the Cold War economy, but, as the upper map suggests, the benefits were by no means equally distributed. The big winners were the Middle Atlantic states, the industrialized upper Midwest, Washington State (with its aircraft and nuclear plants), and California. The epicenter of California's military-industrial complex was Los Angeles, which, as is evident in the lower map, was studded with military facilities and major defense contractors like Douglas Aircraft, Lockheed, and General Dynamics. There was work a-plenty for engineers and rocket scientists.

The Suez Crisis, 1956

In this photograph, Egyptian President Gamal Abdel Nasser is greeted ecstatically by Cairo crowds after he nationalized the Suez Canal. Nasser's gamble paid off. Thanks to American intervention, military action by Britain, France, and Israel failed, and Nasser emerged the triumphant voice of Arab nationalism across the Middle East. The popular emotions he unleashed against the West survived his death in 1970 and are more potent today than ever, although now expressed more through Islamic fundamentalism than Nasser's brand of secular nationalism. Getty Images.

In early 1957, concerned that the USSR might step into the vacuum left by the British, the president announced the Eisenhower Doctrine, which stated that American forces would assist any nation in the region "requiring such aid, against overt armed aggression from any nation controlled by International Communism." Later that year, Eisenhower invoked the doctrine when he sent the U.S. Sixth Fleet to the Mediterranean Sea to aid King Hussein of Jordan against a Nasser-backed revolt. A year later he landed 14,000 troops to back up a pro-American government in Lebanon. The Eisenhower Doctrine was further proof of the global reach of containment, in this instance, accentuated by the strategic need to protect the West's access to steady supplies of oil.

Eisenhower's Farewell Address

In his final address to the nation, Eisenhower warned against the power of what he called the **"military-industrial complex,"** which by then was employing 3.5 million Americans (Map 26.5). Its pervasive influence, he said, "is felt in every city, every statehouse, every office of the federal government." Even though his administration had fostered this growing defense establishment, Eisenhower was gravely concerned about its implications for a democratic people: "We must guard against the acquisition of unwarranted influence, whether sought or unsought, by the military-industrial complex," he warned. "We must never let the weight of this combination endanger our liberties or democratic processes." With those words Dwight Eisenhower showed how well he understood the impact of the Cold War on American life. Only by vigilance could the democratic values of a free people be preserved in an age of constant global struggle.

> Why do we say that Eisenhower was heir to FDR, not Herbert Hoover?

> Was Eisenhower an adherent to the concept of containment? How so?

> Why was America's deepening involvement in the Third World a phenomenon of the 1950s rather than the 1940s?

SUMMARY

We have seen how the Cold War began as a conflict between the United States and the Soviet Union over eastern Europe. Very early in the conflict the United States adopted a strategy of containment, and although initially intended only for Europe, the strategy quickly expanded to Asia when China was "lost" to Mao's Communists. The first effect of that expansion was the Korean War, after which, under Eisenhower, containment of Communism became America's guiding principle across the Third World. Cold War imperatives meant a major military buildup, a scary nuclear arms race, and unprecedented entanglements across the globe.

We have also seen how, on the domestic front, Truman started out with high hopes for an expanded New Deal, only to be stymied by the problems of reconversion, by resistance from Congress, and by competing spending demands of the Cold War. The greatest Cold War–inspired distraction, however, was a climate of fear over internal subversion by Communists that gave rise to McCarthyism. Truman's successor, Dwight Eisenhower, brought the Republicans back into power. Although personally conservative, Eisenhower actually proved a New Dealer in disguise.

He declined to cut back on social welfare programs and broke new ground in federal spending on highways, scientific research, and higher education. When he left office, it seemed that a "liberal consensus" prevailed, with old-fashioned, laissez-faire conservativism mostly marginalized.

Connections: Diplomacy and Politics

In the essay opening Part Six, we started with Walter Lippmann's boast at the close of World War II that "what Rome was to the ancient world . . . America is to be for the world of tomorrow." His confidence in America's future rested in part on his expectation that the Grand Alliance described in Chapter 25 would be durable. Had he gone further back to World War I (see Chapter 21), Lippmann might not have been so optimistic. Woodrow Wilson's hostile response to the Russian revolution had assumed that the two systems were irreconcilable, a belief that the Soviets fully shared. Once the Cold War began after 1945, it became the dominant event in American diplomatic history for the next half-century. In the case of the liberal consensus, its roots in the New Deal (Chapter 24) are entirely clear. Between 1945 and 1960, the liberal consensus held sway, even during Eisenhower's presidency, but after peaking in the mid-1960s with Johnson's Great Society (Chapter 28), it went into decline. The New Deal structure itself remained durable, despite the reaction against the War on Poverty, but the Democratic Party's grip on the country began to fail, and by the close of the Carter administration, conservatism and the Republican Party were clearly in the ascendancy (Chapter 29).

CHAPTER REVIEW QUESTIONS

> What factors gave rise to the Cold War between the United States and the Soviet Union?

> In what ways were President Truman's and Eisenhower's foreign policies similar? How did they differ?

> What was the domestic impact of the anti-Communist crusade of the late 1940s and 1950s?

TIMELINE

1945	Yalta and Potsdam conferences
	Harry S Truman succeeds Roosevelt
	End of World War II
	Senate approves U.S. participation in United Nations
1946	George Kennan outlines containment policy
	Baruch Plan for international control of atomic weapons fails
	War begins between French and Vietminh over control of Vietnam
1947	Taft-Hartley Act limits union power
	House Un-American Activities Committee (HUAC) investigates film industry
	Truman Doctrine promises aid to governments resisting Communism
	Marshall Plan aids economic recovery in Europe
1948	Communist coup in Czechoslovakia
	Truman signs executive order desegregating armed forces
	State of Israel created
	Stalin blockades West Berlin; Berlin airlift begins
1949	North Atlantic Treaty Organization (NATO) founded
	Soviet Union detonates atomic bomb
	Mao Zedong establishes People's Republic of China
1950–1953	Korean War
1950	Joseph McCarthy's "list" of Communists in government
	NSC-68 calls for permanent mobilization
1952	Dwight D. Eisenhower elected president
1953	Stalin dies
1954	Army-McCarthy hearings on army subversion
	French defeat at Dienbienphu in Vietnam
	Geneva Accords partition Vietnam at seventeenth parallel
1956	Crises in Hungary and at Suez Canal
	Interstate Highway Act
1957	Soviet Union launches *Sputnik*
1958	National Aeronautics and Space Administration (NASA) established
1960	U-2 incident leads to cancellation of U.S.-USSR summit meeting
1961	Eisenhower warns nation against military-industrial complex

FOR FURTHER EXPLORATION

James T. Patterson, *Grand Expectations: The United States, 1945–1974* (1996), offers a detailed, comprehensive account of this period. For a reconsideration of the Cold War from a post–Cold War perspective, see especially John Lewis Gaddis, *We Now Know: Rethinking Cold War History* (1997), and, for a more wide-ranging analysis, *The Cold War: A New History* (2005). On the Fair Deal, the best treatment is Alonso Hamby, *Beyond the New Deal: Harry S. Truman and American Liberalism* (1973). Jennifer Klein, *For All These Rights* (2003), is a probing analysis of why the United States failed to develop a national healthcare system. On McCarthyism, David Oshinsky, *A Conspiracy So Immense: The World of Joe McCarthy* (1983), is excellent. Key books containing documents and analysis of Soviet espionage are John E. Haynes and Harvey Klehr, *The Secret World of American Communism* (1995), and *Venona: Decoding Soviet Espionage in America* (1999). On the 1950s, see J. Ronald Oakley, *God's Country: America in the Fifties* (1986). David Halberstam's *The Fifties* (1993) offers a brief but searing account of CIA covert activities in Iran and Guatemala.

The Woodrow Wilson International Center for Scholars has established the Cold War International History Project at **www.wilsoncenter.org/index.cfm?topic_id=1409&fuseaction=topics.home**, an exceptionally rich Web site offering documents on the Cold War, including materials from former Communist-bloc countries. The Center for the Study of the Pacific Northwest's site, "The Cold War and Red Scare in Washington State," at **www.washington.edu/uwired/outreach/cspn/curcan/main.html**, provides detailed information on how the Great Fear operated in one state. Its bibliography includes books, documents, and videos. Project Whistlestop: Harry Truman at **www.trumanlibrary.org/whistlestop/student_guide.htm**, a program sponsored by the U.S. Department of Education, is a searchable collection of images and documents from the Harry S Truman Presidential Library. The site is organized into categories such as the origins of the Truman Doctrine, the Berlin airlift, the desegregation of the armed forces, and the 1948 presidential campaign. Users can also browse through the president's correspondence. "Korea + 50: No Longer Forgotten" is cosponsored by the Harry S Truman and Dwight D. Eisenhower Presidential Libraries, at **www.trumanlibrary.org/korea**. It offers official documents, oral histories, and photographs connected to the Korean War. It also features an audio recording of President Truman's recollections of his firing of General MacArthur in 1951.

TEST YOUR KNOWLEDGE

To assess your command of the material in this chapter, see the Online Study Guide at **bedfordstmartins.com/henretta**.

For Web sites, images, and documents related to topics and places in this chapter, visit **bedfordstmartins.com/makehistory**.

The Saturday Evening
POST
June 4, 1955 • 15¢
America's Mighty Mile:
THE SOO
LOOK, MOM—NO WHEELS!
The Vehicle That Floats
on Land
Sargent

27

The Age of Affluence
1945–1960

I N 1959, VICE PRESIDENT RICHARD NIXON traveled to Moscow to open the American National Exhibit. It was the height of the Cold War. After sipping Pepsi-Cola, Nixon and Soviet Premier Nikita Khrushchev got into a heated debate about the relative merits of Soviet and American societies. Standing in the kitchen of a model American home, they talked dishwashers, toasters, and televisions, not rockets, submarines, and missiles. Images of the "kitchen debate" flashed across TV screens around the world.

What was so striking about the Moscow exhibition was the way its American planners enlisted affluence and mass consumption in service to Cold War politics. The suburban lifestyle trumpeted at the exhibition symbolized the superiority of capitalism over Communism.

During the postwar era, Americans did enjoy the highest standard of living in the world. But behind the affluence, everything was not as it seemed. The suburban calm masked contradictions in women's lives and cultural rebelliousness among young people. Suburban growth often came at the expense of urban life, sowing the seeds of inner-city decay and exacerbating racial tensions. Nor was prosperity ever as widespread as the Moscow exhibit implied. The suburban lifestyle was beyond the reach of the working poor, Spanish-speaking immigrants, and most African Americans. And in the South, a civil rights revolution was in the making.

.

◄ **Life in the Suburbs**

In the 1950s the *Saturday Evening Post* celebrated the suburban ideal: family, leisure, and a nurturing wife and mother.

Economic Powerhouse

The United States enjoyed overwhelming political and economic advantages at the end of World War II. Unlike the Soviet Union, western Europe, and Japan, America emerged physically unscathed from the war and poised to take advantage of the postwar boom. Dominated by giant corporations, the American economy benefited from stable internal markets, heavy investment in research and development, and the rapid diffusion of new technology. For the first time, employers generally accepted collective bargaining, which for workers translated into rising wages, expanding benefits, and a growing rate of home ownership. At the heart of this postwar prosperity lay the involvement of the federal government. Federal outlays for defense and domestic programs gave a huge boost to the economy. Not least, the federal government recognized that prosperity rested on global foundations.

Engines of Economic Growth

By the end of 1945, war-induced prosperity launched the United States into an era of unprecedented economic growth. Pent-up demand after years of wartime mobilization made Americans eager to spend. Business applied scientific and technological innovations developed for military purposes, such as plastics and synthetic fibers, to the production of consumer goods. Over the next two decades, the gross domestic product (GDP) tripled, benefiting a wider segment of society than anyone would have dreamed possible in the dark days of the Depression.

The Bretton Woods System. American global supremacy rested in part on economic institutions created at a United Nations conference at Bretton Woods, New Hampshire, in July 1944. The International Bank for Reconstruction and Development (known commonly as the World Bank) provided private loans for the reconstruction of war-torn Europe as well as for the development of Third World countries. A second institution, the International Monetary Fund (IMF), was set up to stabilize the value of currencies and provide a predictable monetary environment for trade, with the U.S. dollar serving as the benchmark for other currencies. The United States dominated the World Bank and the IMF because it contributed the most capital and the strongest currency. In 1947, multinational trade negotiations resulted in the first General Agreement on Tariffs and Trade (GATT), which led to the establishment of an international body to oversee trade rules and practices.

The World Bank, the IMF, and GATT were the cornerstones of the so-called Bretton Woods system that guided the world economy after the war. These international organizations encouraged stable prices, the reduction of tariffs, flexible domestic markets, and international trade based on fixed exchange rates. The Bretton Woods system effectively served America's conception of the global economy, paralleling America's ambitious diplomatic aims in the Cold War.

The Kitchen Debate

At the Moscow Fair in 1959, the United States put on display the technological wonders of American home life. When Vice President Richard Nixon visited, he and Soviet Premier Nikita Khrushchev got into a heated debate over the relative merits of their rival systems, with the up-to-date American kitchen as a case in point. This photograph shows the debate in progress. Khrushchev is the bald man pointing his finger at Nixon. On the other side of Nixon stands Leonid Brezhnev, who would be Khrushchev's successor. Getty Images.

The Military-Industrial Complex. A second linchpin of postwar prosperity was defense spending. The military-industrial complex that President Eisenhower identified in his 1961 Farewell Address had its roots in the business-government partnerships of the world wars. But unlike after 1918, the massive commitment of government dollars for defense continued after 1945. Even though the country was technically at peace, the economy and the government operated practically on a war footing—in a state of permanent mobilization.

Based at the sprawling Pentagon in Arlington, Virginia, the Defense Department evolved into a massive bureaucracy. Defense-related industries entered into long-term relationships with the Pentagon in the name of national security. Some companies did so much business with the government that they became dependent on Defense Department orders. Over 60 percent of the income of Boeing, General Dynamics, and Raytheon eventually came from military contracts, while Lockheed received 81 percent and Republic Aviation 100 percent. All of them were giant enterprises, made even bigger by the Pentagon's inclination to favor the largest firms.

As permanent mobilization took hold, science, industry, and the federal government became increasingly intertwined. According to the National Science Foundation, federal money underwrote 90 percent of the cost of research on aviation and space, 65 percent of that on electricity and electronics, 42 percent of that on scientific instruments, and 24 percent of that on automobiles. With the government footing part of the bill, corporations transformed new ideas into useful products with amazing speed. After the Pentagon backed IBM's investment in integrated circuits in the 1960s, those new devices, which were crucial to the computer revolution, entered commercial production within three years.

The growth of this military-industrial establishment had a dramatic impact on national priorities. Between 1900 and 1930, excepting World War I, the country spent less than 1 percent of GDP on the military. By the early 1960s the figure had risen to nearly 10 percent. The defense buildup created jobs, and lots of them. Taking into account the indirect benefits (the additional jobs created to serve and support defense workers), perhaps one worker in seven nationally owed his or her job to the military-industrial complex. But increased military spending also limited the resources for domestic social needs. Critics of military spending calculated the trade-offs: The cost of a nuclear aircraft carrier and support ships equaled that of a subway system

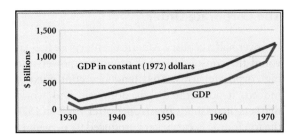

FIGURE 27.1 Gross Domestic Product, 1930–1972

After a sharp dip during the Great Depression, the GDP rose steadily in both real and constant dollars in the postwar period.

for Washington, D.C.; the money spent on one Huey helicopter could have built sixty-six units of low-income housing.

The Economic Record. America's annual GDP jumped from $213 billion in 1945 to more than $500 billion in 1960; by 1970, it exceeded $1 trillion (see Figure 27.1). To working Americans, this sustained economic growth meant a 25 percent rise in real income between 1946 and 1959. Postwar prosperity also featured low inflation. After the postwar reconversion period, inflation slowed to 2 to 3 percent annually during the 1950s, and it stayed low until the escalation of the Vietnam War in the mid-1960s. Low inflation meant stable and predictable prices. Feeling secure about the present and confident about the future, most Americans rightly felt that they were better off than they had ever been before. In 1940, 43 percent of American families owned their homes; by 1960, 62 percent did. Prosperity, as measured by the rate of income growth at different income levels, was quite equally distributed. Families in the 95th percentile did no better than lower-income families; the fastest rate of income growth, in fact, was at the 60th percentile.

Even so, the picture was not entirely rosy. The distribution of income remained stubbornly skewed, with the top 10 percent of Americans earning more than the bottom 50 percent. Moreover, the economy was plagued by periodic recessions, damaging especially to the most disadvantaged Americans. In *The Affluent Society* (1958) the economist John Kenneth Galbraith argued that the poor were only an "afterthought" in the minds of economists and politicians. Yet, as Galbraith noted, one in thirteen families at the time earned less than $1,000 a year.

The Corporate Order

For over half a century, American enterprise had favored the consolidation of economic power into big corporate firms. That tendency continued—indeed, it accelerated—as domestic and world markets increasingly overlapped after 1945. In 1970 the top four U.S. carmakers produced 91 percent of all motor vehicles sold in the country; the top four in tires produced 72 percent, in cigarettes 84 percent, and in detergents 70 percent. Despite laws restricting branch banking to a single state, in 1970 the four largest banks held 16 percent of the nation's banking assets; the top fifty banks held 48 percent.

The classic, vertically integrated corporation of the early twentieth century had produced a single line of products that served a national market (see Chapter 17). This strategy worked even better in the 1950s, when sophisticated media advertising enabled large corporations to break into hitherto resistant markets, for example, beer, where loyalty to local brews in their infinite variety was legendary. To erode that preference, Anheuser-Busch and other national producers sponsored televised sports, parlaying the aura of championship games into national acceptance of their standardized, "lighter" beers. "Bud, the King of Beers"—just as good for the little guy as for the big-league star. By 1970, big multiplant brewers controlled 70 percent of the beer market.

To this well-honed approach, national firms now added a new strategy of diversification. CBS, for example, hired the Hungarian inventor Peter Goldmark, who perfected color television during the 1940s, long-playing records in the 1950s, and a video recording system in the 1960s. As the head of CBS Laboratories, Goldmark patented more than a hundred new devices and created multiple new markets for his happy employer. Because big outfits like CBS had the deepest pockets, they were the firms best able to diversify through investment in industrial research.

More revolutionary was the sudden rise of the conglomerates, giant enterprises comprised of firms in unrelated industries. Conglomerate-building resulted in the nation's third great merger wave (the first two had taken place in the 1890s and the 1920s). Because of their diverse holdings, conglomerates shielded themselves from instability in any single market and seemed better able to compete globally. International Telephone and Telegraph transformed itself into a conglomerate by acquiring Continental Baking (famous for Wonder Bread), Sheraton Hotels, Avis Rent-a-Car, Levitt and Sons home builders, and Hartford Fire Insurance. Ling-Temco-Vought, another conglomerate, produced steel, built ships, developed real estate, and brought cattle to market.

Expansion into foreign markets also spurred corporate growth. At a time when "made in Japan" still meant shoddy workmanship, U.S. products were considered the best in the world. American firms expanded into foreign markets when domestic demand became saturated or when recessions cut into sales. During the 1950s U.S. exports nearly doubled, giving the nation a trade surplus of close to $5 billion in 1960. By the 1970s, Gillette, IBM, Mobil, and Coca-Cola made more than half their profits from abroad.

In their effort to direct such giant enterprises, managers placed more emphasis on planning. Companies recruited top executives who had business-school training, the ability to manage information, and skills in corporate planning, marketing, and investment. A new generation of corporate chieftains emerged, operating in a complex environment that demanded long-range forecasting and close coordination with investment banks, law firms, the federal government, the World Bank, and the IMF.

The New Managerial Class. To man their bureaucracies, the postwar corporate giants required a huge supply of white-collar foot soldiers. They turned to the universities, which, fueled partly by the GI Bill, grew explosively after 1945. Better educated than their elders, the members of the new managerial class advanced more quickly, and at a younger age, into responsible jobs. As one participant-observer remarked: "If you had a college diploma, a dark suit, and anything between the ears, it was like an escalator; you just stood there and moved up." (He was talking about men; few women gained entrance to the managerial ranks.)

Corporations offered lifetime employment, but they also expected lifetime loyalty. Atlas Van Lines, in the business of moving them, estimated that corporate managers were transferred an average of fourteen times—once every two and a half years—during their careers. Perpetually mobile IBM managers joked that the company's initials stood for "I've Been Moved."

Climbing the corporate ladder rewarded men without hard edges—the "well adjusted." In *The Lonely Crowd* (1950) the sociologist David Reisman contrasted the independent businessmen and professionals of earlier years with the managerial class of the postwar world. He concluded that the new corporate men were "other-directed," more attuned

Organization Men (and a Few Women)

What happened when the 5:57 P.M. discharged commuters in Park Forest, Illinois, a suburb of Chicago? This was the subject of William H. Whyte's *The Organization Man* (1956). Were these hordes of commuters thinking about their stressful workdays at the office or the martinis waiting for them when they walked in the doors of their suburban homes? Photo by Dan Weiner, Courtesy Sarah Weiner.

to their associates than driven by their own goals. The sociologist William Whyte painted a somber picture of "organization men" who left the home "spiritually as well as physically to take the vows of organization life." A recurring theme of the 1950s, in fact, was that the conformity demanded of the man in the gray flannel suit (the title of Sloan Wilson's popular novel) was stifling creativity and blighting lives.

Labor-Management Accord

For blue-collar workers, collective bargaining became for the first time the normal means for determining how their labor would be rewarded. Anti-union employers had fought long and hard against collective bargaining, confining organized labor to a narrow band of craft trades and a few industries, primarily coal mining, railroading, and stove manufacture. The power balance shifted during the Great Depression (see Chapter 24), and by the time

the dust settled after World War II, labor unions overwhelmingly represented America's industrial work force (Figure 27.2). The question then became: How would labor's power be used?

In late 1945, Walter Reuther of the United Auto Workers (UAW) challenged General Motors in a fundamental way. The youthful Reuther was thinking big, beyond a single company, or even a single industry. He aimed at nothing less than a reshaped, high-employment economy. To jumpstart it, he demanded a 30 percent wage hike with no price increase for GM cars, and when General Motors said no, it couldn't afford that, Reuther demanded that the company "open the books."

General Motors implacably resisted this "opening wedge" into the rights of management. The company took a 113-day strike, rebuffed the government's intervention, and soundly defeated the UAW. Having made its point, General Motors laid out the terms for a durable relationship. It would accept the UAW as its bargaining partner

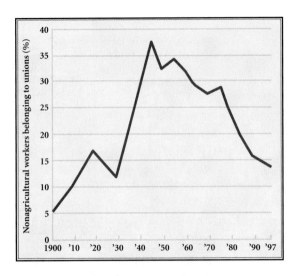

FIGURE 27.2 Labor Union Strength, 1900–1997

Labor unions reached their peak strength immediately after World War II, when they represented close to 40 percent of the nonfarm workforce. Although there was some decline after the mid 1950s, unions still represented nearly 30 percent in 1973. Thereafter, their decline was precipitous. SOURCE: AFL-CIO Information Bureau, Washington, D.C.

and guarantee GM workers an ever higher living standard. The price was that the UAW abandon its assault on the company's "right to manage." On signing the five-year GM contract of 1950 — the Treaty of Detroit, it was called — Reuther accepted the company's terms.

The Treaty of Detroit opened the way for a more broadly based "labor-management accord" — not industrial peace, because the country still experienced many strikes, but general acceptance of collective bargaining as the method for setting the terms and conditions of employment. For industrial workers, the result was rising real income, from $54.92 a week in 1949 to $71.81 (in 1947–1949 dollars) in 1959. The average worker with three dependents gained 18 percent in spendable real income in that period. In addition, collective bargaining delivered greater leisure (more paid holidays and lengthier vacations) and, in a startling departure, a social safety net.

In postwar Europe, America's allies were constructing welfare states. That was the preference of American unions as well. But having lost the bruising battle in Washington for national health care, the unions turned to the bargaining table. By the end of the 1950s, union contracts commonly provided defined-benefit pension plans (supplementing Social Security); company-paid health insurance; and, for two million workers, mainly in steel and

auto, a guaranteed annual wage (via supplementary unemployment benefits). Collective bargaining had become, in effect, the American alternative to the European welfare state.

The sum of these union gains was a new sociological phenomenon, the "affluent" worker — as evidenced by relocation to the suburbs, by homeownership, by increased ownership of cars and other durable goods, and, an infallible sign of rising expectations, by installment buying. For union workers, the contract became, as Reuther boasted, the passport into the middle class. Generally overlooked, however, were the many unorganized workers with no such passport — those consigned to casual labor or low-wage jobs in the service sector. In retrospect, economists recognized that America had developed a two-tiered, inequitable labor system.

The labor-management accord that generated the good life for so many workers seemed in the 1950s absolutely secure. The union rivalries of the 1930s abated. In 1955 the industrial-union and craft-union wings joined together in the AFL-CIO, representing 90 percent of the nation's 17.5 million union members. At its head stood George Meany, a cigar-chomping former New York plumber who, in his blunt way, conveyed the reassuring message that organized labor had matured and was management's fit partner.

The labor-management accord, impressive though it was, never was as durable as it seemed. Vulnerabilities lurked, even in the accord's heyday. For one thing, the sheltered markets — the essential condition for passing on the costs of collective bargaining — were in fact quite fragile. In certain industries, the leading firms were already losing market share — for example, in meatpacking and steel — and nowhere, not even in auto, was their dominance truly secure. A second, more obvious vulnerability, was the non-union South, which, despite a strenuous postwar drive, the unions failed to organize. The South's success at attracting companies pointed to a third, most basic vulnerability, namely, the abiding anti-unionism of American employers. At heart, they regarded the labor-management accord as a negotiated truce, not a permanent peace. It was only a matter of time, and the onset of a more competitive environment, before the scattered anti-union forays of the 1950s turned into a full-scale counteroffensive.

The postwar labor-management accord, it turns out, was a transitory event, not a permanent condition of American economic life. And, in a larger sense, that was true of the postwar boom. It was a transitory event, not a permanent condition.

Lost in Levittown

This 1954 *New Yorker* cartoon humorously reflected what critics saw as the stifling uniformity of the new suburbs. Suburbanites didn't seem to mind. They understood that Levitt's houses were so cheap because he built them all alike. But, admittedly, Mrs. Barnes's confusion was a downside. The New Yorker Collection, 1954, Robert J. Day, from cartoonbank.com. All Rights Reserved.

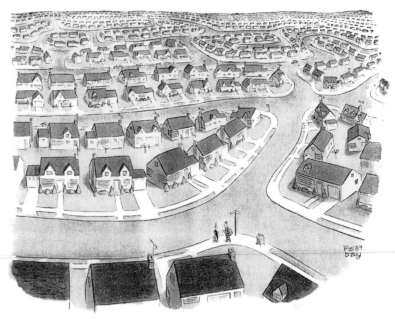

"I'm Mrs. Edward M. Barnes. Where do I live?"

➤ In what ways is the prosperity of the 1950s explained by the Cold War?

➤ Why is "the man in the gray flannel suit" the representative businessman of the 1950s?

➤ What do we mean by the "labor-management accord"?

The Affluent Society

Prosperity is more easily measured — how much an economy produces, how much people earn — than the good life that prosperity actually buys. For the 1950s, however, the contours of the American good life emerged with exceptional distinctness: a preference for suburban living, a high valuation on consumption, and a devotion to family and domesticity. In this section we ask, why those particular choices? And with what — not necessarily happy — consequences?

The Suburban Explosion

Suburban migration had been ongoing ever since the nineteenth century, but never on the explosive scale that the country experienced after World War II. Within a decade or so, developers filled up farmland on the outskirts of cities with tract housing and shopping malls. Entire counties once rural, like San Mateo, south of San Francisco, or Prince Georges, outside Washington, D.C., were built up. By 1960, more people lived in suburbs than in cities.

The Housing Boom. Home construction had virtually ended during the Great Depression, and returning veterans, dreaming of home and family, faced a critical housing shortage. After the war, construction surged to meet pent-up demand. A fourth of the country's entire housing stock in 1960 had not even existed a decade earlier.

An innovative Long Island building contractor, William J. Levitt, revolutionized the suburban housing market by applying mass-production techniques and turning out new homes at dizzying speed. Levitt's basic four-room house, complete with kitchen appliances, was priced at $7,990 in 1947. Levitt did not need to advertise; word of mouth brought buyers flocking to his developments in New York, Pennsylvania, and New Jersey (all called, naturally, Levittown). Dozens of other developers, including California's shipping magnate Henry J. Kaiser, were soon snapping up cheap farmland and building subdivisions around the country.

Even at $7,990, Levitt's homes were beyond the means of young families, or would have been, had the traditional home-financing standard — half down and ten years to pay off the balance — still prevailed. That's where the Federal Housing Administration (FHA) and the Veterans Administration (VA) came in. After the war, the FHA insured 30-year mortgages with as little as 5 percent down and interest at 2 or 3 percent. The VA was even more lenient, requiring only a token $1 down for qualified ex-GI's. FHA and VA mortgages best explain why, after hovering around 45 percent for the previous half-century, home ownership jumped to 60 percent by 1960.

What purchasers of Levitt's houses got, in addition to a good deal, were homogeneous communities. The developments contained few old people or unmarried adults. Even the trees were young. Owners agreed to cut their lawns once a week and not to hang out laundry on the weekends. Then there was the matter of race. Levitt's houses came with **restrictive covenants** prohibiting occupancy "by members of other than the Caucasian Race." (Covenants often applied to Jews and Catholics as well.)

Levitt, a marketing genius, knew his customers. The UAW learned the hard way. After the war, the CIO union launched an ambitious campaign for open-housing ordinances in the Detroit area. White auto workers rebelled, rebuking the union leadership by voting for racist politicans who promised to keep white neighborhoods white. A leading advocate of racial equality nationally, the UAW quietly shelved the fight at the local level. In *Shelley v. Kraemer* (1948) the Supreme Court outlawed restrictive covenants, but the practice persisted informally long afterward. Among America's bastions of racial segregation, the suburb was probably the last to fall.

The Sun Belt. Suburban living, although a nationwide phenomenon, was most at home in the Sun Belt, where taxes were low, the climate mild, and open space allowed for sprawling subdivisions (Map 27.1). Fueled by World War II, the South and

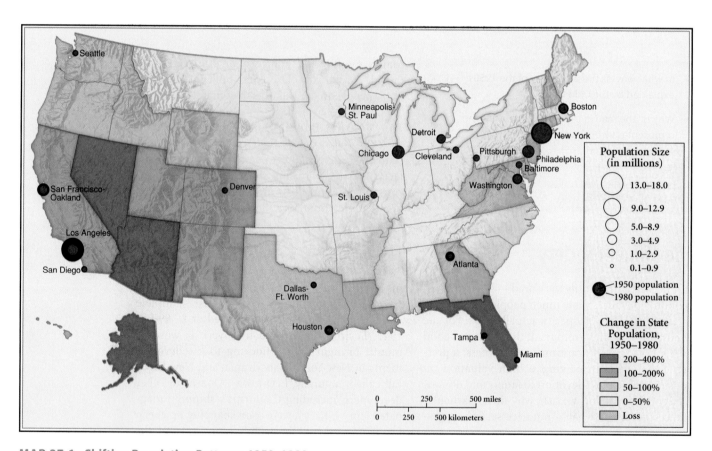

MAP 27.1 Shifting Population Patterns, 1950–1980

This map shows the two major, somewhat overlapping, patterns of population movement between 1950 and 1980. Most striking is the rapid growth of the Sun Belt states. All the states experiencing increases of over 100 percent in that period are in the Southwest, plus Florida. The second pattern involves the growth of metropolitan areas, defined as a central city or urban area and its suburbs. The central cities were themselves mostly not growing, however. The metropolitan growth shown in this map was accounted for by the expanding suburbs. And because Sun Belt growth was primarily suburban growth, that's where we see the most rapid metropolitan growth, with Los Angeles the clear winner.

West began to boom. Florida added 3.5 million people, many of them retired, between 1940 and 1970. Texas profited from an expanding petrochemical industry and profitable agriculture. Most dramatic was California's growth, spurred especially by lots of work in the state's defense-related aircraft and electronics industries. California's climate and job opportunites acted as magnets pulling people from all parts of the country. By 1970, California contained a tenth of the nation's population and surpassed New York as the most populous state.

Boosters heralded the booming development of the Sun Belt. But growth came at a price. In the arid Southwest, increasing demands for water and energy made for environmental and health problems. As cities competed for scarce water resources, they depleted underground acquifers and dammed scenic rivers. The proliferation of coal-burning power plants increased air pollution, and so did traffic. The West's nuclear industry, while good for the economy, also brought nuclear waste, uranium mines, and atomic test sites. And growth had a way of consuming the easy, uncongested living that attracted people to the Sun Belt in the first place. Still, for folks occupying those ranch-style houses, with their nice lawns, barbecues, and air-conditioning, suburban living seemed at its best in sunny California or Arizona.

Cars and Highways. Without automobiles, suburban growth on such a massive scale would have been impossible. Planners laid out subdivisions on the assumption that everybody would drive. And they did—to get to work, to take the children to Little League, to shop at the mall. With gas plentiful at 15 cents a gallon, no one cared about fuel efficiency, or seemed to mind the elaborate tail fins and chrome detail that weighed down their V-eights. In 1945 Americans owned twenty-five million cars; by 1965 the number had tripled to seventy-five million (see Voices from Abroad, "Hanoch Bartov: Everyone Has a Car," p. 840).

More cars required more highways, and the federal government obliged. In 1947 Congress authorized the construction of 37,000 miles of highways; major new legislation in 1956 increased this commitment by another 42,500 miles (Map 27.2). One of the largest civil-engineering projects in history, the new interstate system linked the entire country, with far-reaching effects on both the cities and the countryside. The interstate highways rerouted traffic away from small towns, bypassed well-traveled main roads like Route 1 on the East Coast and the cross-country Route 66, and cut wide swaths through old neighborhoods in the cities. Excellent mass transit systems, like those of Los Angeles and the San Francisco Bay Area, gave way to freeways. Federal highway funding specifically excluded mass transit, and the auto industry

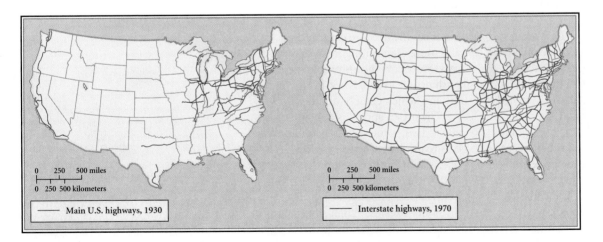

0   250   500 miles

0 250 500 kilometers

—— Main U.S. highways, 1930

0   250   500 miles

0 250 500 kilometers

—— Interstate highways, 1970

MAP 27.2   Connecting the Nation: The Interstate Highway System, 1930 and 1970

The 1956 Interstate and Defense Highways Act paved the way for an extensive network of federal highways throughout the nation. The act pleased American drivers and enhanced their love affair with the automobile, and also benefited the petroleum, construction, trucking, real estate, and tourist industries. The new highway system promoted the nation's economic integration, facilitated the growth of suburbs, and contributed to the erosion of America's distinct regional identities.

Hanoch Bartov

Everyone Has a Car

One of Israel's foremost writers and journalists, Hanoch Bartov spent two years in the United States working as a correspondent for the newspaper Lamerchav. *As a newcomer to Los Angeles in the early 1960s, he was both fascinated and appalled by Americans' love affair with the automobile.*

Our immediate decision to buy a car sprang from healthy instincts. Only later did I learn from bitter experience that in California, death was preferable to living without one. Neither the views from the plane nor the weird excursion that first evening hinted at what I would go through that first week.

Very simple—the nearest supermarket was about half a kilometer south of our apartment, the regional primary school two kilometers east, and my son's kindergarten even farther away. A trip to the post office—an undertaking, to the bank—an ordeal, to work—an impossibility.

Truth be told: the Los Angeles municipality . . . does have public transportation. Buses go once an hour along the city's boulevards and avenues, gathering all the wretched of the earth, the poor and the needy, the old ladies forbidden by their grandchildren to drive, and other eccentric types. But few people can depend on buses, even should they swear never to deviate from the fixed routes. . . . There are no tramways. No one thought of a subway. Railroads—not now and not in the future. Why? Because everyone has a car. A man invited me to his house, saying, "We are neighbors, within ten minutes of each other." After walking for an hour

and a half I realized what he meant—"ten minute drive within the speed limit." Simply put, he never thought I might interpret his remark to refer to the walking distance. The moment a baby sees the light of day in Los Angeles, a car is registered in his name in Detroit. . . .

At first perhaps people relished the freedom and independence a car provided. You get in, sit down, and grab the steering wheel, your mobility exceeding that of any other generation. No wonder people refuse to live downtown, where they can hear their neighbors, smell their cooking, and suffer frayed nerves as trains pass by bedroom windows. Instead, they get a piece of the desert, far from town, at half price, drag a water hose, grow grass, flowers, and trees, and build their dream house. . . .

The result? A widely scattered city, its houses far apart, its streets stretched in all directions. Olympic Boulevard from west to east, forty kilometers. Sepulveda Boulevard, from Long Beach in the south to the edge of the desert, forty kilometers. Altogether covering 1,200 square kilometers. As of now.

Why "as of now"? Because greater distances mean more commuting, and more commuting leads to more cars. More cars means problems that push people even farther away from the city, which chases after them.

The urban sprawl is only one side effect. Two, some say three, million cars require an array of services. . . .

. . . Why bother parking, getting out, getting in, getting up and sitting down, when you can simply "drive in"? Mailboxes have their slots facing the road, at the level of the driver's hand. That is how dirty laundry is deposited, electricity and water bills paid. That is how love is made, how children are taken to school. That is how the anniversary wreath is laid on

the graves of loved ones. There are drive-in movies. And, yes, we saw it with our own eyes: drive-in churches. Only in death is a man separated from his car and buried alone. . . .

SOURCE: Oscar and Lilian Handlin, eds., *From the Outer World* (Cambridge, MA: Harvard University Press, 1997), 293–296.

ANALYZING THE EVIDENCE

➤ From Bartov's observations, what are the pluses and minuses of America's car culture? In what ways was the automobile changing American society?

➤ Why did Bartov find owning a car was necessary, especially in southern California?

➤ Everyone, of course, didn't have a car. Who, according to Bartov, used public transportation?

LIFE BELTS AROUND CITIES WOULD PROVIDE   A PLACE FOR BOMBED-OUT REFUGEES TO GO

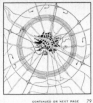

CONTINUED ON NEXT PAGE ▶

City Life Belts

What to do in case of nuclear attack? That was the problem Norbert Wiener, a renown cyberneticist at MIT, was thinking about when he and his colleagues came up with this design for an eight-lane "Life-Belt" around the country's major cities. Citizens who made it out would find safety at camp sites beyond the targeted areas. *Life* magazine, December 18, 1950.

was no friend either. General Motors made it a practice of buying up mass transit systems and scrapping them. By 1960 two-thirds of Americans drove to work each day. In Sun Belt cities like Los Angeles and Phoenix, the proportion came closer to 100 percent.

The postwar suburban explosion was distinctively American. In war-ravaged European cities, home construction was centered on high-density neighborhoods and along mass transit lines. Not until twenty years later did Europeans experiment with low-density suburban housing, and never with the disastrous effect, as in America, of gutting the central cities.

The Search for Security

There was a reason why Congress called the 1956 legislation creating America's modern freeway system

the National Interstate and *Defense* Highways Act. The four-lane freeways, used every day by commuters, might some day, in a nuclear war, evacuate them to safety. That captured as well as anything the underside of postwar life, when suburban living abided side by side with the shadow of annihilation.

The Cold War, reaching as it did across the globe, was omnipresent at home as well, permeating domestic politics, intruding on the debate over racial injustice, and creating an atmosphere that stifled dissent. For the first time, America had a peacetime draft. In every previous war, the country had quickly demobilized. But when World War II ended, the draft remained in place. Every neighborhood seemed to have a boy in the armed forces.

Most alarming was the nuclear standoff with the Soviet Union. Bomb shelters and civil defense drills

Duck and Cover

The nation's Civil Defense Agency's efforts to prepare Americans for a nuclear attack extended to children in schools, where repeated drills taught them to "duck and cover" when the alarm went off. Variations of this 1954 scene at Franklin Township School in Quakertown, New Jersey, were repeated all over the nation. Paul F. Kutta. Courtesy *Reminisce Magazine.*

provided a daily reminder of mushroom clouds. In the late 1950s a small but growing number of citizens raised questions about radioactive fallout from above-ground bomb tests. Federal investigators later documented illnesses, deaths, and birth defects among "downwinders"—people who lived near nuclear test sites. The most shocking revelations, however, came in 1993, when the Department of Energy released previously classified documents on human radiation experiments conducted in the late 1940s and 1950s under the auspices of the Atomic Energy Commission and other federal agencies. Many of the experiments were undertaken with little concern for or understanding of the adverse effects on the subjects.

By the late 1950s, public concern over nuclear testing had become a high-profile issue, and new antinuclear groups such as SANE (the National Committee for a Sane Nuclear Policy) and Physicians for Social Responsibility called for an international test ban.

Returning to the Church. In an age of anxiety, Americans yearned for a reaffirmation of faith. Church membership jumped from 49 percent of the population in 1940 and to 70 percent in 1960. People flocked especially into the evangelical Protestant denominations, who benefited from a remarkable new crop of preachers. Most notable was the young Reverend Billy Graham, who made brilliant use of television, radio, and advertising to spread the gospel. The religious reawakening meshed, in a time of Cold War, with Americans' view of themselves as a righteous people opposed

to "godless Communism." In 1954 the phrase "under God" was inserted into the Pledge of Allegiance, and after 1956 U.S. coins carried the words, "In God We Trust."

The resurgence of religion, despite its evangelical bent, had a distinctly moderate tone. An ecumenical movement bringing Catholics, Protestants, and Jews together flourished, and so did a concern for the here-and-now. In his popular television program, Catholic Bishop Fulton J. Sheen asked, "Is life worth living?" He and countless others answered that it was. None was more affirmative than Norman Vincent Peale, whose best-selling book *The Power of Positive Thinking* (1952) embodied the trend toward the therapeutic use of religion, an antidote to the stresses of modern life.

Consumer Culture

In some respects, postwar consumerism seemed like a return to the 1920s—an abundance of new gadgets and appliances, more leisure time, the craze for automobiles, and new types of mass media. Yet there was a significant difference. In the 1950s consumption became associated with citizenship. Buying things, once a sign of personal indulgence, now meant fully participating in American society and, moreover, fulfilling a social responsibility. By spending, Americans fueled a high-employment economy. What the suburban family consumed, asserted *Life* magazine in a photo essay featuring one such family, would help assure "full employment

Billy Graham, Evangelist

Billy Graham was the first great revival preacher of the postwar era, a worthy successor to Billy Sunday and Aimee Semple McPherson. In this photograph, the Reverend Graham is preaching to more than thirty thousand people jammed into Wall Street on July 10, 1957. In what he termed the "greatest service" of his New York Crusade, the evangelist gave a twenty-minute extemporaneous sermon from an improvised pulpit on the steps of the Federal Memorial Hall. In the foreground is the foot of the George Washington statue. At rear is the New York Stock Exchange.
© Bettmann/Corbis.

and improved living standards for the rest of the nation."

Advertising. As in the past, product makers sought to stimulate consumer demand through aggressive advertising. More money was spent in 1951 on advertising ($6.5 billion) than on primary and secondary education ($5 billion). The 1950s gave Americans the Marlboro Man; M&Ms that melt in your mouth, not in your hand; Wonder Bread to build strong bodies in twelve ways; and the "does she or doesn't she?" Clairol hair-coloring woman. Motivational research delved into the subconscious to suggest how the messages should be pitched. Like other features of the consumer culture, this one got its share of muckraking condemnation in Vance Packer's best-selling *The Hidden Persuaders* (1957).

Advertising heavily promoted the appliances that began to fill the suburban kitchen, many of them unavailable during the war, others new to the postwar market. In 1946 automatic washing machines replaced the old machines with hand-cranked wringers, and clothes dryers also came on the market. Commercial laundries across the country struggled to stay in business. Another new item was the home freezer, encouraging the dramatic growth of the frozen-food industry. Partly because of all the electrical appliances, consumer use of electricity doubled during the 1950s.

Television. TV's leap to cultural prominence was swift and overpowering. There were only 7,000 sets in American homes in 1947, yet a year later the CBS and NBC radio networks began offering regular programming, and by 1950 Americans owned 7.3 million TV sets. Ten years later, 87 percent of American homes had at least one television set.

Although licensed by the Federal Communications Commission (FCC), television stations, like radio, depended entirely on advertising for profits. Soon television supplanted radio as the chief diffuser of popular culture. Movies, too, lost the cultural dominance they had once enjoyed. Movie attendance shrank throughout the postwar period, and movie studios increasingly relied on overseas distribution to earn a profit.

What Americans saw on television, besides the omnipresent commercials, was an overwhelmingly white, Anglo-Saxon world of nuclear families, suburban homes, and middle-class life. A typical show was *Father Knows Best,* starring Robert Young and Jane Wyatt. Father left home each morning wearing a suit and carrying a briefcase. Mother was a full-time housewife, always tending to her three children, but, as a sterotypical female, prone to bad driving and tears. The children were sometimes rebellious, but family conflicts were invariably resolved. *The Honeymooners,* starring Jackie Gleason as a Brooklyn bus driver, and *Life of Reilly,* a situation comedy featuring a California aircraft worker, were rare in their treatment of working-class lives. Black characters such as Rochester in Jack Benny's comedy show appeared mainly as sidekicks and servants.

The types of television programs developed in the 1950s built on older entertainment genres but also pioneered new ones. Taking its cue from the movies, television offered some thirty westerns by 1959, including *Gunsmoke, Wagon Train,* and

Advertising in the TV Age

Aggressive advertising of new products, such as the color television, helped fuel the surge in consumer spending during the 1950s. Marketing experts emphasized the role of television in promoting family togetherness, while interior designers offered decorating tips that placed the television at the focal point of living rooms and the increasingly popular "family rooms." Here, the family watches a variety program starring singer Dinah Shore, who was the television spokeswoman for Chevrolet cars. Every American probably could hum the tune of the little song she sang in praise of the Chevy. Motorola.

Bonanza. Professional sports became big-time television — far exceeding the potential of radio. Programming geared to children, such as Walt Disney's *Mickey Mouse Club, Howdy Doody,* and *Captain Kangaroo,* created the first generation of children glued to the tube.

Although the new medium did offer some serious programming, notably live theater and documentaries, FCC Commissioner Newton Minow concluded in 1963 that television was "a vast wasteland." But it did what it intended, which was to sell products and fill America's leisure hours with reassuring entertainment.

The Baby Boom

A popular 1945 song was called "Gotta Make Up for Lost Time," and Americans did just that. Two things were noteworthy about the families they formed after World War II. First, marriages were remarkably stable. Not until the mid-1960s did the divorce rate begin to rise sharply. Second, married couples were intent on having babies. Everyone expected to have two or more children — it was part of adulthood, almost a citizen's responsibility. After a century and a half of decline, the birthrate shot up: More babies were born between 1948 and 1953 than were born in the previous thirty years (Figure 27.3).

Among reasons for this baby boom, one was that everyone was having children at the same time. A second was a drop in the marriage age — down to twenty-two for men, twenty for women. Younger parents meant a bumper crop of children. Women who came of age in the 1930s averaged 2.4 children; their counterparts in the 1950s, 3.2 children. The baby boom peaked in 1957 and remained at a high level until the early 1960s. Thereafter, the

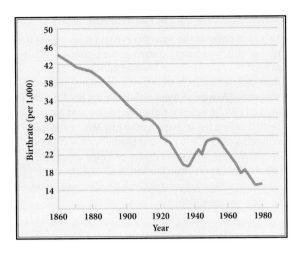

FIGURE 27.3   The American Birthrate, 1860–1980

When birthrates are viewed over more than a century, the postwar baby boom is clearly only a temporary reversal of the longterm downward trend in the American birthrate.

birthrate declined, returning to earlier long-term patterns.

"Scientific" Child Rearing. To keep all those baby-boom children healthy and happy, middle-class parents increasingly relied on the advice of experts. Dr. Benjamin Spock's best-selling *Baby and Child Care* sold a million copies a year after its publication in 1946. Spock urged mothers to abandon the rigid feeding and baby-care schedules of an earlier generation. New mothers found Spock's commonsense approach liberating, but it did not totally soothe their insecurities. If mothers were too protective, Spock and others argued, they might hamper their children's preparation for adult life. Mothers who wanted to work outside the home felt guilty because Spock recommended that they be constantly available for their children.

Less subject to fashion were the very real advances in diet, public health, and medical practice that made for healthier children. Serious illness turned routine after the introduction of such "miracle drugs" as penicillin (introduced in 1943), streptomycin (1945), and cortisone (1946). When Dr. Jonas Salk perfected a polio vaccine in 1954, he became a national hero. The free distribution of Salk's vaccine in the nation's schools, followed in 1961 by Dr. Albert Sabin's oral polio vaccine, demonstrated the potential of government-sponsored public health programs. The conquest of polio made the children of the 1950s the healthiest generation ever.

The baby boom had a vast impact on American society. All those babies fueled the economy as families bought food, diapers, toys, and clothing for their expanding broods. The nation's educational system also got a boost. The new middle class, America's first college-educated generation, placed a high value on education. Suburban parents approved 90 percent of proposed school bond issues during the 1950s. By 1970 school expenditures accounted for 7.2 percent of the gross national

Polio Pioneers

These Provo, Utah, children each received a "Polio Pioneer" souvenir button for participating in the trial of the Salk vaccine in 1954. Dr. Jonas Salk's announcement the next year that the vaccine was safe and effective made him a national hero. March of Dimes Birth Defect Foundation.

A Woman's Dilemma in Postwar America

This 1959 cover of the *Saturday Evening Post* depicts the no-win situation facing women in the postwar era. But at least they could dream. Women consigned to low-paid, dead-end jobs in the service sector imagined suburban life with Mr. Wonderful helping do the dishes. In reality, Mr. Wonderful turned out to be that guy settled before the television set while Mrs. Homemaker scoured a dirty frying pan and the baby fussed. But of course Mrs. Homemaker's dream of a nice office job just was just as much an illusion. A no-win situation. 1959 SEPS: Licensed by Curtis Publishing Company, Indianapolis, IN. All rights reserved. www.curtispublishing.com.

product, double the 1950 level. In the 1960s the baby-boom generation swelled college enrollments and, not coincidentally, the ranks of student protesters (see Chapter 28). The passage of time did not diminish the impact of the baby boom. When baby boomers competed for jobs during the 1970s, the labor market became tight. When career-oriented baby boomers belatedly began having children in the 1980s, the birthrate jumped. And in our own time, as baby boomers begin retiring, huge funding problems threaten to engulf Social Security and Medicare. Who would have thought that the intimate decisions of so many couples after World War II would be affecting American life well into the twenty-first century?

Contradictions in Women's Lives

"The suburban housewife was the dream image of the young American woman," the feminist Betty Friedan wrote of the 1950s. "She was healthy, beautiful, educated, concerned only about her husband, her children, and her home." Friedan gave up a psychology fellowship and a career as a journalist to marry, move to the suburbs, and raise three children. "Determined that I find the feminine fulfillment that eluded my mother . . . I lived the life of a suburban housewife that was everyone's dream at the time," she said.

The Feminine Mystique. The idea that a woman's place was in the home was, of course, not new. What Betty Friedan called the "feminine mystique" of the 1950s — that "the highest value and the only commitment for women is the fulfillment of their own femininity" — bore remarkable similarities to the nineteenth-century's cult of true womanhood.

The updated version drew on new elements of twentieth-century science and culture, even Freudian psychology. Psychologists equated motherhood with "normal" female identity and berated mothers who worked outside the home. Television and film depicted career women as social and sexual misfits, the heavies in movies like *Mildred Pierce.* The postwar consumer culture also emphasized women's domestic role as purchasing agents for home and family. "Love is said in many ways," ran an ad for toilet paper. Another asked, "Can a woman ever feel right cooking on a dirty range?"

Although the feminine mystique held cultural sway, it by no means was as all-encompassing as Friedan implied in her 1963 best-seller, *The Feminine Mystique.* Indeed, Friedan herself resisted the stereotype, doing freelance journalism while at home, and, as a result of that work, stumbling on the subject and writing the book that made her famous. Middle-class wives often found constructive outlets for their energy in the League of Women Voters, the PTA, and the Junior League. As in earlier periods, some women used the rhetoric of domesticity to justify political activism, which in this period involved community improvement, racial integration, and nuclear disarmament. As for working-class women, many of them doubtless would have loved to embrace domesticity, if only they could. The economic needs of their families demanded otherwise.

Women at Work. The feminine mystique notwithstanding, more than one-third of American women in the 1950s held jobs outside the home. As the service sector expanded, so did the demand for workers in jobs traditionally filled by women.

Occupational segmentation still haunted women. Until 1964 the classified sections of most newspapers separated employment ads into "Help Wanted Male" and "Help Wanted Female." More than 80 percent of all employed women did stereotypical "women's work" as salespersons, health-care technicians, waitresses, stewardesses, domestic servants, receptionists, telephone operators, and secretaries. In 1960 women represented only 3.5 percent of lawyers (many top law schools did not admit women at all) and 6.1 percent physicians, but 97 percent nurses, 85 percent librarians, and 57 percent social workers. Along with women's jobs went women's pay, which averaged 60 percent of men's pay in 1963.

What was new was the range of women at work. At the turn of the century, the typical female worker was young and unmarried. By midcentury she was in her forties, married, and with children in school. In 1940 only 15 percent of wives had worked. By 1960, 30 percent did, and by 1970 it was 40 percent.

Married women worked to supplement family income. Even in the prosperous 1950s, the wages of many men could not pay for what middle-class life demanded: cars, houses, vacations, and college educations for the children. Poorer households needed more than one wage earner just to get by.

How could American society so steadfastly uphold the domestic ideal when so many wives and mothers were out of the house and at work? In many ways the contradiction was hidden by the women themselves. Fearing public disapproval, women usually justified their work in family-oriented terms: "Of course I believe a woman's place is at home, but I took this job to save for college for our children." Moreover, when women took jobs outside the home, they still bore full responsibility for child care and household management. As one overburdened woman noted, she now had "two full-time jobs instead of just one — underpaid clerical worker and unpaid housekeeper."

Youth Culture

In 1956, only partly in jest, the CBS radio commentator Eric Sevareid questioned "whether the teenagers will take over the United States lock, stock, living room, and garage." Sevareid was grumbling about American youth culture, a phenomenon first noticed in the 1920s, that had its roots in lengthening years of education, the role of peer groups, and the consumer patterns of teenagers. Like so much else in the 1950s, the youth culture came down to having money.

Market research revealed a distinct teen market to be exploited. A 1951 *Newsweek* story noted with awe that the $3 weekly spending money of the average teenager was enough to buy 190 million candy bars, 130 million soft drinks, and 230 million sticks of gum. In 1956 advertisers projected an adolescent market of $9 billion for transistor radios (first introduced in 1952), 45-rpm records, clothing, and fads such as Silly Putty (1950) and Hula Hoops (1958). Increasingly, advertisers targeted the young, both to capture their spending money and to exploit their influence on family purchases. Note the changing slogans for Pepsi-Cola: "Twice as much for a nickel" (1935), "Be sociable — have a Pepsi" (1948), "Now it's Pepsi for those who think young" (1960), and finally "the Pepsi Generation" (1965).

Hollywood movies played a large role in fostering a teenage culture. At a time when Americans were being lured by television, young people made up the largest audience for motion pictures. Soon Hollywood studios catered to them with films like *The Wild One* (1951), starring Marlon Brando, and *Rebel without a Cause* (1955), starring James Dean. "What are you rebelling against?" a waitress asks Brando in *The Wild One*. "Whattaya got?" he replies.

What really defined this generation, however, was its music. Rejecting the romantic ballads of the 1940s, teenagers discovered rock 'n' roll, an amalgam of white country and western music and black-inspired rhythm and blues. The Cleveland disc jockey Alan Freed played a major role in introducing white America to the black-influenced sound by playing what were called "race" records. "If I could find a white man who had the Negro sound and the Negro feel I could make a billion dollars," said the owner of a record company. The performer fitting that bill was Elvis Presley, who rocketed into instant celebrity in 1956 with his hit records "Hound Dog" and "Heartbreak Hotel." Between 1953 and 1959 record sales increased from $213 million to $603 million, with rock 'n' roll as the driving force.

Many adults were not happy. They saw in rock 'n' roll music, teen movies, and magazines such as *Mad* (introduced in 1952) an invitation to race mixing, rebellion, and disorder. The media featured hundreds of stories on problem teens, and in 1955 a Senate subcommittee headed by Estes Kefauver conducted a high-profile investigation of juvenile delinquency and its origins in the popular media. Denunciations of the new youth culture, if anything, only increased its popularity.

Cultural Dissenters

Youth rebellion was only one aspect of a broader discontent with the conformist culture of the

Elvis Presley

The young Elvis Presley, shown here on the cover of his first album in 1956, embodied cultural rebellion against the drabness of adult life in the 1950s. 1956 BGM Music.

1950s. Artists, jazz musicians, and writers expressed their alienation in a remarkable flowering of intensely personal, introspective art forms. In New York, Jackson Pollock and other painters developed an inventive style that became known as abstract expressionism. Swirling and splattering paint onto giant canvases, Pollock emphasized self-expression in the act of painting.

A similar trend characterized jazz, where black musicians developed a hard-driving improvisational style known as bebop. Whether the "hot" bebop of saxophonist Charlie Parker or the more subdued "cool" West Coast sound of the trumpeter Miles Davis, postwar jazz was cerebral, intimate, and individualistic. As such, it stood in stark contrast to the commercialized, dance-oriented "swing" bands of the 1930s and 1940s.

Black jazz musicians found eager fans not only in the African American community but among young white Beats, a group of writers and poets centered in New York and San Francisco who disdained middle-class conformity and suburban materialism. In his poem "Howl" (1956), which became a manifesto of the Beat generation, Allen Ginsberg lamented: "I saw the best minds of my generation destroyed by madness, starving hysterical naked, dragging themselves through the angry streets at dawn looking for an angry fix." In works such as Jack Kerouac's novel *On the Road* (1957), the Beats glorified spontaneity, sexual adventurism, drug

FIGURE 27.4 Legal Immigration to the United States by Region, 1931–1984

Historically, immigrants to the United States had come primarily from Europe. This figure shows the dramatic shift that began after 1960, as Latinos and Asians began to arrive in increasing numbers. Asians, who represented nearly 50 percent of all immigrants by the 1980s, especially benefited from the liberalization of U.S. immigration laws. SOURCE: Robert W. Gardner, Bryant Robie, and Peter C. Smith, "Asian Americans: Growth, Change, and Diversity," *Population Bulletin* 40, no. 4 (Washington, D.C.: Population Reference Bureau, 1985): 2.

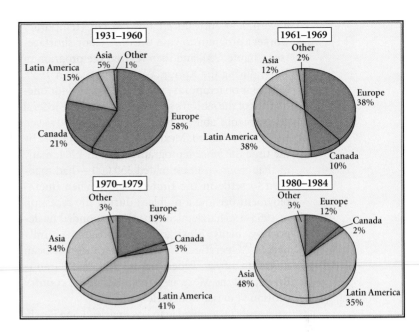

use, and spirituality. Like other members of the postwar generation, the Beats were apolitical; their rebellion was strictly cultural. In the 1960s, however, the Beats would inspire a new generation of young rebels angry at both the political and cultural status quo.

➤ In what ways does the growth of the Sun Belt reflect key themes of the suburban explosion?

➤ What was the relationship between consumer culture and the emphasis on family life in the postwar era?

➤ Is it correct to say that the 1950s was exclusively a time of cultural conformity?

The Other America

While middle-class whites flocked to the suburbs, an opposite stream of poor and working-class migrants, many of them southern blacks, moved into the cities. What these urban newcomers inherited was a declining economy and a decaying environment. To those enjoying prosperity, "the Other America" — as the social critic Michael Harrington called it in 1962 — remained largely invisible. Only in the South, where African Americans organized to combat segregation, did the stain of social injustice catch the nation's attention.

Immigrants and Migrants

Ever since the passage of the National Origins Act of 1924 (see Chapter 23), U.S. immigration policy had aimed mainly at keeping foreigners out.

Anti-immigrant sentiment intensified during the Great Depression, hardly budging even to rescue Jews fleeing Nazi persecution. World War II caused the bar to be lowered slightly, enabling returning servicemen to bring home their war brides and, under the Displaced Persons Act (1948), permitting the entry of approximately 415,000 Europeans, among them former Nazis like Werner von Braun, the rocket scientist. The overt anti-Asian bias of America's immigration laws also became untenable. In a gesture to an important ally, the Chinese Exclusion Act was repealed in 1943. More far-reaching was the 1952 McCarran-Walter Act, which (in addition to barring Communists and other radicals) ended the exclusion under the 1924 act of Japanese, Koreans, and southeast Asians.

Although not many came until later, the immediate impact on Asian immigrant communities was considerable. On the eve of World War II, Chinatowns were populated primarily by men. Although largely married, their wives remained in China. The repeal of the Chinese Exclusion Act, and the granting of naturalization rights, encouraged those men to bring their wives to America. The result was a more normal, family-oriented community, a development also seen in the Filipino American and Japanese American communities. Approximately 135,000 men and 100,000 women of Chinese origin were living in the United States in 1960, mostly in New York State and California (Figure 27.4).

Latino Immigration. After the national-origins quota system went into effect in 1924, Mexico replaced eastern and southern Europe as the nation's labor reservoir. During World War II, the federal government introduced the *bracero* (temporary worker) program to ease wartime labor shortages (see Chapter 25), and then revived the program in 1951, during the Korean War. At its peak in 1959, Mexicans on temporary permits accounted for one-quarter of the nation's seasonal workers. The federal government's ability to control the flow, however, was strictly limited. Mexicans came illegally, and by the time the *bracero* program ended in 1964, many of that group—an estimated 350,000—had managed to settle in the United States. When unemployment became a problem during the recession of 1953–1954, federal authorities responded by deporting many Mexicans in a program grimly named "Operation Wetback" (because Mexican migrants often waded across the Rio Grande River), but the Mexican population in the country continued to rise nonetheless.

Mostly they settled in to Los Angeles, Long Beach, El Paso, and other southwestern cities, following the crops during the harvest season or working in the expanding service sector. But many also went north, augmenting well-established Mexican American communites in Chicago, Detroit, Kansas City, and Denver. Although still important for American agriculture, more Mexican Americans by 1960 were employed as industrial and service workers.

Another major group of Spanish-speaking migrants came from Puerto Rico. American citizens since 1917, Puerto Ricans enjoyed an unrestricted right to move to the mainland. Migration increased dramatically after World War II, when mechanization of the island's sugarcane industry pushed many Puerto Ricans off the land. Airlines began to offer cheap direct flights between San Juan and New York City. With the fare at about $50, two weeks' wages, Puerto Ricans became America's first immigrants with the luxury of arriving by air.

Most Puerto Ricans went to New York, where they settled first in East ("Spanish") Harlem and then scattered in neighborhoods across the city's five boroughs. This massive migration, which increased the Puerto Rican population to 613,000 by 1960, transformed the ethnic composition of the city. More Puerto Ricans now lived in New York City than in San Juan. They faced conditions common to all recent immigrants: crowded and deteriorating housing, segregation, menial jobs, poor schools, and the problems of a bilingual existence.

Cuban refugees constituted the third largest group of Spanish-speaking immigrants. In the six years after Fidel Castro's seizure of power in 1959 (see Chapter 28), an estimated 180,000 people fled Cuba for the United States. The Cuban refugee community grew so quickly that it turned Miami into a cosmo-

politan, bilingual city almost overnight. Unlike other migrants to urban America, Miami's Cubans quickly prospered, in large part because they had arrived with money and middle-class skills.

Indian Relocation. In western cities, an influx of Native Americans also contributed to the rise in the nonwhite urban population. In 1953, Congress passed a resolution authorizing a program to terminate the autonomous status of the Indian tribes and empty the reservations. The Bureau of Indian Affairs encouraged voluntary migration by subsidizing moving costs and establishing relocation centers in San Francisco, Denver, Chicago, and other cities. Despite the program's stated goal of assimilation, the 60,000 Native Americans who migrated to the cities mostly settled together in ghetto neighborhoods, with little prospect of adjusting successfully to an urban environment.

Black Migration. African Americans came in large number to cities from the rural South, continuing the "Great Migration" that had begun during World War I (see Chapter 22). Black migration was hastened by the transformation of southern agriculture. Synthetic fabrics cut into the demand for cotton, while mechanization cut into the demand for farm labor. The mechanical cotton picker, introduced in 1944, effectively destroyed the sharecropper system. Cotton acreage declined from 43 million acres in 1930 to less than 15 million in 1960, while the southern farm population fell from 16.2 million to 5.9 million. Although both whites and blacks left the land, the starkest decline was among blacks. By 1990 only 69,000 black farmers remained nationwide, a tiny fraction of the country's farmers.

Where did these displaced farmfolk go? White southerners from Appalachia moved north to "hillbilly" ghettos, such as Cincinnati's Over the Rhine neighborhood and Chicago's Uptown. As many as 3 million blacks headed to Chicago, New York, Washington, Detroit, Los Angeles, and other cities between 1940 and 1960. Certain sections of Chicago seemed like the Mississippi Delta transplanted, so pervasive were the migrants. By 1960 about half the nation's black population was living outside the South, compared with only 23 percent before World War II.

The Urban Crisis

Migration to American cities, whether from Europe or rural America, had always been attended by hardship—by poverty, slum housing, and cultural dislocation. So severe had these problems seemed

West Side Story
The influx of Puerto Rican immigrants after World War II inspired Leonard Bernstein's 1957 Broadway hit *West Side Story*. The plot recast Shakespeare's *Romeo and Juliet* in a Puerto Rican neighborhood on New York's West Side in the 1950s. Confrontations between members of youth gangs and adult figures of authority, as pictured here in a still from the movie version, were set to highly stylized song and dance routines. The Kobal Collection.

half a century earlier that they had helped spark the reform wave of the Progressive era (see Chapter 20). But hardship then had been temporary, a kind of waystation on the path to a better life. That had been true initially of the post-1941 migration, when blacks had found jobs in defense industry and, in the postwar boom, in Detroit auto plants and Chicago packing houses. Later migrants were not so lucky. By the 1950s, the economy was changing. The manufacturing sector was contracting, and technological advances — what people then called "automation" — hit unskilled and semiskilled jobs especially hard — "jobs in which Negroes are disproportionately concentrated," noted the civil rights activist Bayard

Rustin. Black migrants, Rustin warned, were becoming economically superfluous, and in that respect their situation was fundamentally different, far bleaker than anything faced by earlier immigrants.

A second difference involved race. Every immigrant wave — Irish, Italian, Slavic, Jewish — had been greeted by hostility, but none so virulent as that experienced by black migrants. In the 1950s, a more tolerant era, they were spared the race rioting that had afflicted their predecessors. But racism in its more covert forms held them back at every turn — by housing restrictions, by schools increasingly segregated, by an urban infrastructure underfunded and decaying because whites were fleeing to the suburbs.

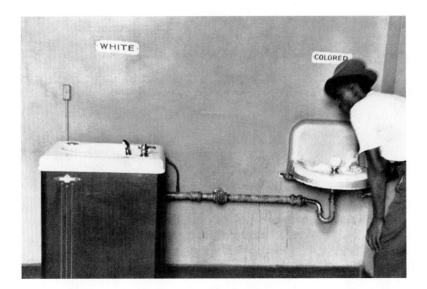

Racial Segregation, North Carolina, 1950
Until as recently as forty years ago, separate drinking fountains like the ones in this picture could be seen across the South. It was the resulting humiliation visited on blacks every day of their lives that explains why the Greensboro Four finally decided to sit down at that Woolworth's lunch counter in 1959 (see p. 855). Elliot Erwitt/Magnum Photos, Inc.

In the 1950s, the nation's twelve largest cities lost 3.6 million whites while gaining 4.5 million nonwhites.

Urban Renewal. As if joblessness and discrimination were not enough, black ghettoes were hit during the 1950s by a frenzy of urban renewal. Seeking to revitalize city centers, urban planners, politicians, and real-estate developers proposed razing blighted neighborhoods to make way for modern construction projects. Local residents were rarely consulted about whether they wanted their neighborhoods "renewed." In Boston, almost a third of the old city was demolished — including the historic West End, a long-established Italian neighborhood — to make way for a new highway, high-rise housing, and government and commercial buildings. In San Francisco some 4,000 residents of the Western Addition, a predominantly black neighborhood, lost out to an urban renewal program that built luxury housing, a shopping center, and an express boulevard. Between 1949 and 1967 urban renewal demolished almost 400,000 buildings and displaced 1.4 million people.

The urban experts knew what to do with these people. They would be relocated to federally funded housing projects, an outgrowth of New Deal housing policy, now much expanded and combined with generous funding for slum clearance. However well intentioned, these grim projects had a disastrous impact on black community life, destroying neighborhoods and relegating the inhabitants to social isolation. The notorious Robert Taylor Homes in Chicago, a huge complex of 28 sixteen-story buildings and 20,000 residents, almost all black, became a breeding ground for crime and hopelessness.

In 1962, the Swedish sociologist Gunnar Myrdal (author of *An American Dilemma,* a pioneering book about the country's race relations) wondered whether shrinking economic opportunity in the United States might not "trap an 'under-class' of unemployed and, gradually, unemployable and underemployed persons and families at the bottom of a society." Myrdal's term *underclass* — referring to a population permanently mired in poverty and dependency — would figure centrally in future American debates about social policy. In 1962, however, *underclass* was a newly coined word, describing a phenomenon not yet noticed but already well under way in the inner cities of 1950s America.

The Emerging Civil Rights Struggle

In the South, segregation prevailed. In most southern states, blacks could not eat in restaurants patronized by whites or use the same waiting rooms and toilets at bus stations. All forms of public transportation were rigidly segregated by custom or by law. Even drinking fountains were labeled "White" and "Colored."

Blacks understood that segregation would never be abolished without grassroots struggle. But that was not their only weapon. They also had the Bill of Rights and the great Reconstruction amendments to the Constitution. In this respect, fighting segregation was different from fighting poverty. Blacks had no constitutional right not to be poor, but they did have constitutional rights not to be discriminated against, if only these rights could be exercised. The Cold War, moreover, gave civil rights advocates added leverage because America's reputation in the world now counted to America's leaders. So the battle against racial injustice, as it took shape after World War II, proceeded on two tracks — on the ground, where blacks began to stand up for their rights, and in the courts and corridors of power, where words sometimes mattered more than action.

Civil Rights under Truman. During World War II, the National Association for the Advancement of Colored People (NAACP) redoubled its efforts to combat discrimination in housing, transportation, and other areas. Black demands for justice continued into the postwar years, spurred by symbolic victories, as when Jackie Robinson broke through the color line in major league baseball by joining the Brooklyn Dodgers in 1947. African American leaders also had hopes for President Truman. Although capable of racist language, Truman supported civil rights on moral grounds. He understood, moreover, the growing importance of the black vote in key northern states, a fact driven home by his surprise 1948 victory. Truman also worried about America's image abroad. It didn't help that the Soviet Union often compared the South's treatment of blacks with the Nazis' treatment of the Jews.

Lacking support in Congress, Truman turned to executive action. In 1946 he appointed a National Civil Rights Commission, whose 1947 report called for robust federal action on behalf of civil rights. In 1948, under pressure from A. Phillip Randolph's Committee Against Jim Crow in Military Service, Truman signed an executive order desegregating the armed forces. And then, with his hand strengthened by the victory for civil rights at the 1948 Democratic convention, Truman went on the offensive, pushing legislation on a variety of fronts, including voting rights and equal employment opportunity. Invariably, his efforts were defeated by filibustering southern Senators.

With Dwight Eisenhower as president, civil rights no longer had a champion in the White House. But in the meantime, NAACP lawyers Thurgood Marshall and William Hastie had been preparing the legal ground in a series of test cases challenging racial discrimination, and in 1954 they hit pay dirt.

Brown v. Board of Education. The case involved Linda Brown, a black pupil in Topeka, Kansas, who had been forced to attend a distant segregated school rather than the nearby white elementary school. The NAACP's chief counsel, Thurgood Marshall, argued that such segregation, mandated by the Topeka Board of Education, was unconstitutional because it denied Linda Brown the "equal protection of the laws" guaranteed by the Fourteenth Amendment. In a unanimous decision on May 17, 1954, the Supreme Court agreed, overturning the "separate but equal" doctrine of *Plessy v. Ferguson* (see Chapter 19). Speaking for the Court, the new Chief Justice Earl Warren wrote:

> To separate Negro children . . . solely because of their race generates a feeling of inferiority as to their status in the community that may affect their hearts and minds in a way unlikely ever to be undone. . . . We conclude that in the field of public education the doctrine of "separate but equal" has no place. Separate educational facilities are inherently unequal.

In an implementing 1955 decision known as *Brown II,* the Court declared simply that integration should proceed "with all deliberate speed."

In the South, however, the call went out for "massive resistance." A Southern Manifesto signed in 1956 by 101 members of Congress denounced the *Brown* decision as "a clear abuse of judicial power" and encouraged their constituents to defy it. That year 500,000 southerners joined White Citizens' Councils dedicated to blocking school integration. Some whites revived the old tactics of violence and intimidation, swelling the ranks of the Ku Klux Klan to levels not seen since the 1920s.

President Eisenhower accepted the *Brown* decision as the law of the land, but he thought it was a mistake and was not happy about committing federal power to enforce it. A crisis in Little Rock, Arkansas, finally forced his hand. In September 1957 nine black students attempted to enroll at the all-white Central High School. Governor Orval Faubus called out the National Guard to bar them. Then the mob took over. Every day the nine students had to run a gauntlet of angry whites chanting "Go back to the jungle." As the vicious scenes played out on television night after night, Eisenhower acted. He sent 1,000 federal troops to Little Rock and nationalized the Arkansas National Guard, ordering them to protect the black students. Eisenhower thus became the first president since Reconstruction to use federal troops to enforce the rights of blacks (see Reading American Pictures, "The Cold War and the Civil Rights Movement," p. 854).

The *Brown* decision validated the NAACP's legal strategy, but white resistance also revealed that winning in court was not enough. Prompted by one small act of defiance, southern black leaders embraced nonviolent protest.

The Montgomery Bus Boycott. On December 1, 1955, Rosa Parks, a seamstress in Montgomery, Alabama, refused to give up her seat on a city bus to a white man. She was arrested and charged with violating a local segregation ordinance. Parks's act was not the spur-of-the-moment decision that it seemed. A woman of sterling reputation and a long-time NAACP member, she had been chosen to play that part. Rosa Parks fit the bill perfectly for the challenge the local NAACP intended against segregated buses.

The Cold War and the Civil Rights Movement

"Careful, the Walls Have Ears." *Oakland Tribune,* September 11, 1957.

"Right Into Their Hands." *Arkansas Democrat-Gazette,* September 11, 1957.

In 1957, in the far-off African nation of Mozambique, an official at the U.S. embassy worried that the school desegregation crisis in Little Rock, Arkansas, had "become a symbol of Negro-White relations in the United States." Similar worries about the impact of the Arkansas crisis on the Cold War struggle with the Soviet Union surfaced in many American newspapers and magazines, often in the form of political cartoons. The first cartoon above appeared in the *Oakland Tribune* on September 11, 1957, two weeks before President Eisenhower intervened by federalizing the Arkansas National Guard. The second cartoon appeared on the same day in the local newspaper, the *Arkansas Democrat-Gazette.*

ANALYZING THE EVIDENCE

▶ How has the artist's drawing for the *Arkansas Democrat-Gazette* depicted Little Rock segregationists? Are they the kind of people that the cartoonist thinks should be representing America before the world?

▶ Why do you suppose the *Oakland Tribune's* artist omitted African Americans and depicted the crisis as a battle between two groups of whites? Why is "The Whole Wide World" paying such close attention?

▶ Do both cartoons convey the same message, or do they suggest different perspectives on the issue?

▶ As historical evidence, how useful do you think these cartoons are at explaining why Americans began to take the civil rights struggle seriously in the 1950s?

The Greensboro Four

Pictured here are the four African American students who, entirely on their own, decided to demand service at the Woolworth's whites-only lunch counter in Greensboro, North Carolina, and started a sit-down protest movement across the South. Second from the left is Franklin McCain, whose interview appears in Comparing American Voices, "Challenging White Supremacy," on the following pages. © Bettmann/Corbis.

Once the die was cast, the black community turned for leadership to the Reverend Martin Luther King Jr., the recently appointed pastor of Montgomery's Dexter Street Baptist Church. The son of a prominent black minister in Atlanta, King embraced the teachings of Mahatma Gandhi, whose campaigns of passive resistance had led to India's independence from Britain in 1947. After Rosa Parks's arrest, King endorsed a plan by a local black women's organization to boycott Montgomery's bus system until it was integrated.

For the next 381 days Montgomery blacks formed car pools or walked to work. The bus company neared bankruptcy, and downtown stores complained about the loss of business. But only after the Supreme Court ruled in November 1956 that bus segregation was unconstitutional did the city of Montgomery finally comply. "My feets is tired, but my soul is rested," said one satisfied woman boycotter.

The Montgomery bus boycott catapulted King to national prominence. In 1957, along with the Reverend Ralph Abernathy, he founded the Southern Christian Leadership Conference (SCLC), based in Atlanta. The black church, long the center of African American social and cultural life, now lent its moral and organizational strength to the civil rights movement. Black churchwomen were a tower of strength, transferring the skills honed by years of church work to the fight for civil rights. Soon the SCLC joined the NAACP as one of the main advocacy groups for racial justice.

Greensboro. The battle for civil rights entered a new phase in Greensboro, North Carolina, on February 1, 1960, when four black college students

Challenging White Supremacy

No problem is more challenging to the historian than figuring out how long-oppressed, ordinary people finally rise up and demand justice. During the 1950s that liberating process was quietly under way among southern blacks, first bursting forth dramatically in the Montgomery bus boycott of 1955 and then, by the end of the decade, emerging across the South. Here we take the testimony of two individuals who stepped forward and took the lead in those struggles.

FRANKLIN McCAIN
Desegregating Lunch Counters

Franklin McCain was one of the four African American students at North Carolina A&T College in Greensboro, North Carolina, who sat down at the Woolworth's lunch counter on February 1, 1960, setting off by that simple act a wave of student sit-ins that rocked the South and helped initiate a national civil rights movement. In the following interview, McCain describes how he and his pals took that momentous step.

The planning process was on a Sunday night, I remember it quite well. I think it was Joseph who said, "It's time that we take some action now. We've been getting together, and we've been, up to this point, still like most people we've talked about for the past few weeks or so — that is, people who talk a lot but, in fact, make very little action." After selecting the technique, then we said, "Let's go down and just ask for service." It certainly wasn't titled a "sit-in" or "sit-down" at that time. "Let's just go down to Woolworth's tomorrow and ask for service, and the tactic is going to be simply this: we'll just stay there."

. . . Once getting there . . . we did make purchases of school supplies and took the patience and time to get receipts for our purchases, and Joseph and myself went over to the counter and asked to be served coffee and doughnuts. As anticipated, the reply was, "I'm sorry, we don't serve you here." And of course we said, "We just beg to disagree with you. We've in fact already been served.". . . The attendant or waitress was a little bit dumbfounded, just didn't know what to say under circumstances like that. . . .

At that point there was a policeman who had walked in off the street, who was pacing the aisle . . . behind us, where we were seated, with his club in his hand, just sort of knocking it in his hand, and just looking mean and red and a little bit upset and a little bit disgusted. And you had the feeling that he didn't know what the hell to do. . . . Usually his defense is offense, and we've provoked him, yes, but we haven't provoked outwardly enough for him to resort to violence. And I think this is just killing him; you can see it all over him.

If it's possible to know what it means to have your soul cleansed — I felt pretty clean at that time. I probably felt better on that day than I've ever felt in my life. Seems like a lot of feelings of guilt or what-have-you suddenly left me, and I felt as though I had gained my manhood. . . . Not Franklin McCain only as an individual, but I felt as though the manhood of a number of other black persons had been restored and had gotten some respect from just that one day.

The movement started out as a movement of nonviolence and a Christian movement. . . . It was a movement that was seeking justice more than anything else and not a movement to start a war. . . . We knew that probably the most powerful and potent weapon that people have literally no defense for is love, kindness. That is, whip the enemy with something that he doesn't understand. . . . The individual who had probably the most influence on us was Gandhi . . . . Yes, Martin Luther King's name was well-known when the sit-in movement was in effect, but . . . no, he was not the individual we had upmost in mind when we started the sit-in movement.

SOURCE: Howell Raines, *My Soul Is Rested*. Copyright ©1977 by Howell Raines. Originally published by Penguin Putnam, 1977. Reprinted with permission of PFD, Inc.

JOHN McFERREN
Demanding the Right to Vote

In this interview, given about ten years after the events he describes, John McFerren tells of the battle he undertook in 1959 to gain the vote for the blacks of Fayette County, Tennessee. By the time of the interview, he had risen in life and become a grocery-store owner and property holder, thanks, he says, to the economic boycott imposed on him by angry whites. Unlike Greensboro, the struggle in Fayette County never made national headlines. It was just one of many local struggles that signaled the beginning of a new day in the South.

My name is John McFerren. I'm forty-six years old. I'm a Negro was born and raised in West Tennessee, the county of Fayette, District 1. My foreparents was brought here from North Carolina five years before the Civil War . . . because the rumor got out among the slaveholders that West Tennessee was still goin to be a slaveholdin state. And my people was brought over here and sold. And after the Civil War my people settled in West Tennessee. That's why Fayette and Haywood counties have a great number of Negroes.

Back in 1957 and '58 there was a Negro man accused of killin a deputy sheriff. This was Burton Dodson. He was brought back after he'd been gone twenty years. J. F. Estes was the lawyer defendin him. Myself and him both was in the army together. And the stimulation from the trial got me interested in the way justice was bein used. The only way to bring justice would be through the ballot box.

In 1959 we got out a charter called the Fayette County Civic and Welfare League. Fourteen of us started out in that charter. We tried to support a white liberal candidate that was named L. T. Redfearn in the sheriff election and the local Democrat party refused to let Negroes vote.

We brought a suit against the Democrat party and I went to Washington for a civil-rights hearing. Myself and Estes and Harpman Jameson made the trip. It took us twenty-two hours steady drivin. . . . I was lookin all up—lotsa big, tall buildins. I had never seen old, tall buildins like that before. After talkin to [John Doar] we come on back to the Justice Department building and we sat out in the hall while he had a meetin inside the attorney general's office. And when they come out they told us they was gonna indict the landowners who kept us from voting. . . .

Just after that, in 1960, in January, we organized a thousand Negroes to line up at the courthouse to register to vote. We started pourin in with big numbers—in this county it was 72 percent Negroes—when we started to register to vote to change the situation.

In the followin . . . October and November they started puttin our people offa the land. Once you registered you had to move. Once you registered they took your job. Then after they done that, in November, we had three hundred people forced to live in tents on Shepard Towles's land. And when we started puttin em in tents, then that's when the White

Citizens Council and the Ku Klux Klan started shootin in the tents to run us out.

Tent City was parta an economic squeeze. The local merchants run me outa the stores and said I went to Washington and caused this mess to start. . . . They had a blacklist . . . And they had the list sent around to all merchants. Once you registered you couldn't buy for credit or cash. But the best thing in the world was when they run me outa them stores. It started me thinkin for myself. . . .

The southern white has a slogan: "Keep em niggers happy and keep em singin in the schools." And the biggest mistake of the past is that the Negro has not been teached economics and the value of a dollar. . . . Back at one time we had a teacher . . . from Mississippi—and he pulled up and left the county because he was teachin the Negroes to buy land, and own land, and work it for hisself, and the county Board of Education didn't want that taught in the county. And they told him, "Keep em niggers singin and keep em happy and don't teach em nothin."

. . . You cannot be free when you're beggin the man for bread. But when you've got the dollar in your pocket and then got the vote in your pocket, that's the only way to be free. . . . And I have been successful and made good progress because I could see the only way I could survive is to stay independent. . . . The Negro is no longer goin back. He's goin forward.

SOURCE: Stanley I. Kutler, ed., *Looking for America*, 2d ed., 2 vols. (New York: Norton, 1979), 2: 449–453.

ANALYZING THE EVIDENCE

➤ McCain took a stand on segregated lunch counters. McFerren took a stand on the right to vote. Why did they choose different targets? Does it matter that they did?

➤ McCain speaks of the sense of "manhood" he felt as he sat at that Woolworth counter. Would that feeling have been enough to satisfy McFerren?

➤ Almost certainly, McCain and McFerren never met. Suppose they had. What would they have had in common? Would what they had in common have been more important than what separated them?

➤ McCain speaks knowingly of the figures and ideas that influenced him. Why do you suppose McFerren is silent about such matters? If he had spoken up, do you suppose he would have—or should have—mentioned Booker T. Washington (see Chapter 20)?

took seats at the "whites-only" lunch counter at the local Woolworth's. They were determined to "sit in" until they were served (see Comparing American Voices, "Challenging White Supremacy," pp. 856–857). Although they were arrested, the sit-in tactic worked—the Woolworth lunch counter was desegregated—and sit-ins quickly spread to other southern cities. A few months later Ella Baker, an administrator with the SCLC, helped to organize the Student Non-Violent Coordinating Committee (SNCC, known as "Snick") to facilitate student sit-ins. By the end of the year, about 50,000 people had participated in sit-ins or other demonstrations, and 3,600 of them had been jailed. But in 126 cities across the South blacks were at last able to eat at Woolworth lunch counters.

The victories so far had been limited, but the groundwork had been laid for a civil rights offensive that would transform the nation's race relations.

> ➤ What were the most significant migration trends in this era?

> ➤ What were the key components of the urban crisis?

> ➤ What is the significance of the *Brown v. Board of Education of Topeka* decision?

SUMMARY

We have explored how, at the very time it became mired in the Cold War, the United States entered an unparalleled era of prosperity. Indeed, the Cold War was one of the engines of prosperity. The postwar economy was marked especially by the dominance of big corporations. Corporate dominance in turn helped make possible the labor-management accord that spread the benefits of prosperity to workers beyond the dreams of earlier generations.

After years of depression and war-induced insecurity, Americans turned inward toward religion, home, and family. Postwar couples married young, had several children, and—if they were white and middle class—raised their children in a climate of suburban comfort and consumerism. The pro-family orientation of the 1950s celebrated social conformity and traditional gender roles, even though millions of women entered the workforce in those years. Cultural conformity, however, provoked resistance, both by the burgeoning youth culture and by a remarkably inventive generation of painters, musicians, and writers.

Not everyone, moreover, shared the postwar prosperity. Postwar cities increasingly became places of last resort for the nation's poor. Black migrants, unlike earlier immigrants, encountered an urban economy that had little use for them. Without opportunity, and faced by pervasive racism, they were on their way to becoming, many of them, an American underclass. In the South, however, discrimination produced a civil rights uprising that white America could not ignore. Many of the smoldering contradictions of the postwar period—Cold War anxiety in the midst of suburban domesticity, tensions in women's lives, economic and racial inequality—helped spur the protest movements of the 1960s.

Connections: Economy

"In the 1950s," we noted in the essay opening Part Six, "no country was competitive with America's economy." The roots of that supremacy went back into the late nineteenth century when, as we discussed in Chapter 17, heavy industry, mass-production technology, and corporate business structure emerged. In the 1920s (Chapter 23) this industrial economy was refined and, after the hiatus of the Great Depression, became the basis for the post–World War II economic boom. In Chapter 29, we describe the first stages in the decline of this manufacturing economy during the 1970s. The postwar consumer culture had roots that went back into the 1920s (Chapter 23), while the accompanying suburbanization went back even earlier, into the nineteenth century (Chapter 18). Similarly, we can trace back to earlier discussions the migratory patterns (to Chapters 17 and 22) and the decay of the cities (to Chapter 18).

CHAPTER REVIEW QUESTIONS

> ➤ How do you acount for the economic prosperity of the postwar era?

> ➤ Why did the suburb achieve paramount significance for Americans in the 1950s?

> ➤ Who were the people who occupied "the Other America"? Why were they there rather than in mainstream America?

TIMELINE

1944	Bretton Woods economic conference World Bank and International Monetary Fund (IMF) founded
1946	First edition of Dr. Spock's *Baby and Child Care*
1947	First Levittown built Jackie Robinson joins the Brooklyn Dodgers
1948	Beginning of network television
1950	Treaty of Detroit initiates labor-management accord
1953	Operation Wetback
1954	*Brown v. Board of Education of Topeka*
1955	Montgomery bus boycott begins AFL and CIO merge
1956	National Interstate and Defense Highways Act Elvis Presley's breakthrough records
1957	Peak of postwar baby boom Eisenhower sends U.S. troops to enforce integration of Little Rock Central High School Southern Christian Leadership Conference (SCLC) founded
1960	Student sit-ins in Greensboro, North Carolina

FOR FURTHER EXPLORATION

Two engaging introductions to postwar society are Paul Boyer, *Promises to Keep* (1995), and David Halberstam, *The Fifties* (1993). John K. Galbraith, *The Affluent Society* (1958), is a lively and influential contemporary analysis of the postwar economy. Nelson Lichtenstein, *State of the Union: A Century of American Labor* (2002), offers a searching account of the labor-management accord. The best book on the consumer culture, wide-ranging in perspective, is Lizabeth Cohen, *A Consumers' Republic: The Politics of Mass Consumption in Postwar America* (2003). Elaine Tyler May, *Homeward Bound* (1988), is the classic introduction to postwar family life. For insightful essays on the impact of television, see Karal Ann Marling, *As Seen on TV* (1996). An excellent, award-winning memoir of the Beat generation is Joyce Johnson, *Minor Characters* (1983). For youth culture, see William Graebner, *Coming of Age in Buffalo* (1990), and, a classic of the period, Paul Goodman, *Growing Up Absurd* (1960). On the urban crisis, see especially Nicholas Lemann, *The Promised Land: The Great Migration and How It Changed America* (1991), and Thomas J. Sugrue, *The Origins of the Urban Crisis: Race and Inequality in Postwar Detroit* (1996). Taylor Branch's biography of Martin Luther King Jr., *Parting the Waters: America in the King Years, 1954–1963* (1988), while focusing on King's leadership, provides an engaging account of the early civil rights movement.

Literary Kicks: The Beat Generation, at **www.litkicks.com/BeatPages/msg.jsp?what=BeatGen**, is an independent site created by New York writer Levi Asher devoted to the literature of the Beat generation. The site includes writings by Jack Kerouac, Allen Ginsberg, Neal Cassady, and others; material on Beats, music, religion, and film; an extensive bibliography; biographical information; and photographs.

The Arkansas *Democrat Gazette* has compiled materials from two Arkansas newspapers covering the Central High School crisis in Little Rock in 1957 at **www.ardemgaz.com/prev/central**. Editorials and daily news coverage, including photographs, are featured, as well as later commentary by such diverse political figures as former president and Arkansas governor Bill Clinton and former Arkansas governor Orval Faubus.

TEST YOUR KNOWLEDGE

To assess your command of the material in this chapter, see the Online Study Guide at **bedfordstmartins.com/henretta**.

For Web sites, images, and documents related to topics and places in this chapter, visit **bedfordstmartins.com/makehistory**.

28 The Liberal Consensus: Flaming Out

1960–1968

O N INAUGURATION DAY, 1961, STANDING bare-headed in the wintry January brightness, the freshly sworn-in president issued a ringing declaration: "Let the word go forth from this time and place, to friend and foe alike, that the torch has passed to a new generation of Americans, born in this century, tempered by war, disciplined by a hard and bitter peace, proud of our ancient heritage." John F. Kennedy challenged Americans everywhere: "Ask not what your country can do for you, ask what you can do for your country." And, more than anyone might have expected, Americans responded. "There's a moral wave building among today's youth," said a civil rights volunteer in 1964, "and I intend to catch it." Kennedy's politics of expectation might have been initially mostly a matter of atmospherics, but over time it built into the greatest burst of liberal reform since the New Deal—landmark civil rights laws, Medicare, the War on Poverty, and much else. All this—the triumph of the liberal consensus—starts with the indelible image of the youthful Kennedy exhorting the country on that Inauguration Day, 1961.

Fast forward to 1968, to the Democratic National Convention in Chicago. Kennedy is dead, assassinated. His civil rights mentor, Martin Luther King Jr., is dead, assassinated. His younger brother and heir apparent, Bobby, is dead, assassinated. And his successor in the White

◄ **Peace Demonstrators**

Antiwar demonstrators wave a red flag bearing the peace sign near the Washington Monument where thousands gathered for a Moratorium Day rally in Washington, D.C., November 15, 1969. © Bettmann/Corbis.

House, Lyndon B. Johnson, is so discredited that he has withdrawn his name from nomination. On the streets the Chicago police teargassed and clubbed demonstrators, who screamed (as the TV cameras rolled), "The whole world is watching!" Some of them had once been the idealistic young people of Kennedy's exhortation. Now they detested everything that Kennedy's liberalism stood for. Inside the convention hall, the proceedings were chaotic, the atmosphere poisonous, the delegates bitterly divided over Vietnam. As expected, Johnson's vice president, Hubert Humphrey, easily won the nomination, but he hadn't been done any favors. He acknowledged going home feeling not triumphant, but "heartbroken, battered, and defeated." The Chicago convention had been "a disaster."

In this chapter we undertake to explain how Kennedy's stirring Inauguration metamorphosed into the searing Democratic National Convention of 1968. Between those two events, indelible in America's memory, the liberal consensus flamed out.

John F. Kennedy and the Politics of Expectation

Since the days of FDR and the New Deal, Americans had come increasingly to look to Washington and the president for answers to the nation's prob-

lems. Few presidents were happier to oblige than John Kennedy. He came to Washington primed for action, promising that his "New Frontier" would get America moving again. The British journalist Henry Fairley called this activist impulse "the politics of expectation." Soon enough, expectation came up against unyielding reality, but Kennedy's can-do style nevertheless left a lasting impression on American politics.

The New Politics

Charisma, style, and personality — these, more than platforms and issues — were hallmarks of a new brand of politics that we associate with John F. Kennedy. With the power of the media in mind, a younger generation of politicians saw in television a new way to reach directly to the voters. Candidates drifted away from traditional party organizations, with their ward bosses, state committees, and party machines that had once delivered the votes on election day. By using the media, campaigns could bypass the party structures and touch, if only with a 30-second commercial, the ordinary citizen.

The new politics was Kennedy's natural environment. A Harvard alumnus, World War II hero, senator from Massachusetts, he had inherited his love of politics from his grandfathers, both colorful Irish-Catholic politicians in Boston. Ambitious, hard-driving, and deeply aware of style, the forty-three-year-old Kennedy made full use of his many

The Kennedy Magnetism

John Kennedy, the Democratic candidate for president in 1960, used his youth and personality to attract voters. Here the Massachusetts senator draws an enthusiastic crowd on a campaign stop in Elgin, Illinois. AP Images.

advantages to become, as novelist Norman Mailer put it, "our leading man." His one disadvantage — that he was Catholic in a country that had never elected a Catholic president — he masterfully neutralized. His family's wealth and his energetic fund-raising financed an exceptionally expensive campaign. And thanks to media advisers and his youthful, attractive personality, he projected a superb television image.

His Republican opponent, Eisenhower's vice president Richard M. Nixon, was a more seasoned politician, but personally awkward and ill-endowed for combat in the new politics. The great innovation of the 1960 campaign was a series of four nationally televised debates. Nixon, less photogenic than Kennedy, looked sallow and unshaven under the intense studio lights. Polls showed that television did sway political perceptions: Voters who heard the first debate on the radio concluded that Nixon had won, but those viewing it on television favored Kennedy.

Despite the edge Kennedy enjoyed in the debates, he won only the narrowest of electoral victories, receiving 49.7 percent of the popular vote to Nixon's 49.5 percent. Kennedy attracted Catholics, black voters, and the labor vote; his vice presidential running mate, Lyndon Johnson from Texas, brought in southern Democrats. Yet only 120,000 votes separated the two candidates, and the shift of a few thousand votes in key states such as Illinois (where Chicago Mayor Richard Daley's machine miraculously generated the needed margin) would have reversed the outcome. Despite his razor-thin margin, Kennedy won 303 electoral votes, compared to Nixon's 219, revealing once again the distorting effect of the electoral college on the people's choice.

The Kennedy Administration

Unlike Eisenhower, Kennedy believed in a federal government that was visibly active and a presidency that set the tone for bold leadership. Kennedy's vigor attracted unusually able and ambitious people, including Robert McNamara, a renowned systems analyst and former head of Ford, at Defense, and C. Douglas Dillon, a highly admired Republican banker, as secretary of the Treasury. A host of trusted advisers and academics — "the best and the brightest," the journalist David Halberstam called them — flocked to Washington to join the New Frontier. Included on the team as attorney-general was Kennedy's kid brother, Robert, a trusted adviser who had made a name as a hard-hitting investigator of organized crime. Not everyone was enchanted.

Kennedy's people "might be every bit as intelligent as you say," House Speaker Sam Rayburn told his old friend Lyndon Johnson, "but I'd feel a whole lot better about them if just one of them had run for sheriff once." Sure enough, the new administration immediately got into hot water.

The Bay of Pigs. In January 1961 Soviet Premier Nikita Khrushchev announced that the USSR intended to support "wars of national liberation" wherever in the world they occurred. Kennedy took Khrushchev's words as a challenge, especially as they applied to Cuba, where in 1959 Fidel Castro had overthrown the dictator Fulgencio Batista and declared a revolution. Determined to keep Cuba out of the Soviet orbit, Kennedy took up plans by the Eisenhower administration to dispatch Cuban exiles from Nicaragua to foment an anti-Castro uprising. The invaders had been trained by the Central Intelligence Agency, but they were ill prepared for their task and betrayed by the CIA's inept planning. Upon landing at Cuba's Bay of Pigs on April 17, the force of 1,400 was apprehended and crushed by Castro's troops. The anticipated rebellion never happened. Kennedy had the good sense to reject CIA pleas for a U.S. air strike. And he was gracious in defeat. He went before the American people and took full responsibility for the fiasco.

Peace Corps, Foreign Aid, Astronauts. Kennedy redeemed himself with a series of bold initiatives. One was the Peace Corps, which embodied his call to public service in his inaugural address. Thousands of men and women agreed to devote two or more years to programs teaching English to Filipino schoolchildren or helping African villagers obtain adequate supplies of water. Exhibiting the idealism of the early 1960s, the Peace Corps was also a Cold War weapon intended to show developing countries of the so-called Third World that there was a better way than Communism (Map 28.1). Also embodying this aim were ambitious programs of economic assistance. The State Department's Agency for International Development coordinated foreign aid for the Third World, and its Food for Peace program distributed surplus agricultural products. In 1961 the president proposed a "ten-year plan for the Americas" called the Alliance for Progress, a $20 billion partnership between the United States and the republics of Latin America, to reverse the cycle of poverty and stimulate economic growth.

Kennedy was also keen on space exploration. Early in his administration, Kennedy proposed that the nation commit itself to landing a man on the

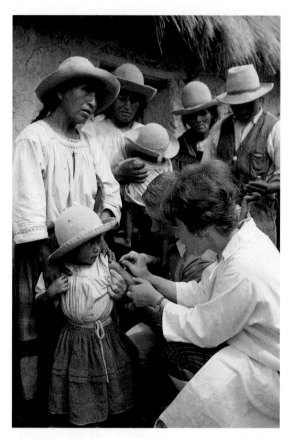

The Peace Corps

The Peace Corps, a New Frontier program initiated in 1961, attracted thousands of idealistic young Americans, including these volunteers who worked in a vaccination program in Bolivia. David S. Boyer/National Geographic Society Image Collection.

moon within the decade. Two weeks later, on May 5, 1961, Alan Shepard became the first American in space (beaten there by the Soviet cosmonaut Yuri Gagarin's 108-hour flight). The following year, John Glenn manned the first space mission to orbit the earth. Capitalizing on America's fascination with space flight, Kennedy persuaded Congress to greatly increase funding for the National Aeronautics and Space Administration (NASA), enabling the United States to pull ahead of the Soviet Union. (Kennedy's men on the moon arrived in 1969.)

Domestic Agenda. Kennedy's most striking domestic achievement — another of his bold moves — was the application of modern economic theory to government **fiscal policy**. New Dealers had lost faith in a balanced budget, turning instead to the Keynesian approach of deliberate deficit spending to stimulate economic growth. Now, in addition to deficit spending, Kennedy and his economic advisers proposed a reduction in income taxes. A tax

cut, they argued, would put money in the hands of consumers, thereby generating more demand, more jobs, and ultimately higher tax revenues. Congress balked at this unorthodox proposal, but it made its way through in 1964, marking a milestone in the use of tax cuts to encourage economic growth, an approach later embraced by Republican fiscal conservatives (see Chapter 30).

But Kennedy was less engaged by the more humdrum matters of social policy, notwithstanding that he had given lip service to an ambitious agenda during his presidential campaign. In part, he was stymied by the lack of a strong popular mandate in the election's outcome. He was also a cautious politician, unwilling to expend capital where the odds were against him. Kennedy managed to push through legislation raising the minimum wage and expanding Social Security, but on other emerging issues — federal aid to education, mass transportation, medical insurance for the elderly — he gave up in the face of conservative opposition in Congress.

The Civil Rights Movement Stirs

Kennedy was equally cautious about civil rights. Despite his campaign commitment, in his first two years he failed to deliver on a civil rights bill. The opposition in Congress, where segregationist southern Democrats dominated key committees, just seemed too formidable. But civil rights was not like other domestic issues. Its fate was going to be decided not in the halls of Congress, but on the streets of southern cities.

Freedom Riders. Emboldened by the success of SNCC's sit-in tactics at integrating lunch counters (see Chapter 27), the interracial Congress of Racial Equality (CORE) organized a series of "freedom rides" in 1961 on interstate bus lines throughout the South. The aim was to call attention to blatant violation of recent Supreme Court rulings against segregation in interstate commerce. The activists who signed on, mostly young, both black and white, knew they were taking their lives in their hands. In Anniston, Alabama, club-wielding Klansmen attacked one of the buses with stones and set it on fire. The freedom riders escaped only moments before the bus exploded. Other riders were brutally beaten in Montgomery and Birmingham. State authorities refused to intervene. "I cannot guarantee protection for this bunch of rabble rousers," declared Governor John Patterson. That left it up to Washington. Although Kennedy discouraged the freedom rides, films of beatings and burning buses

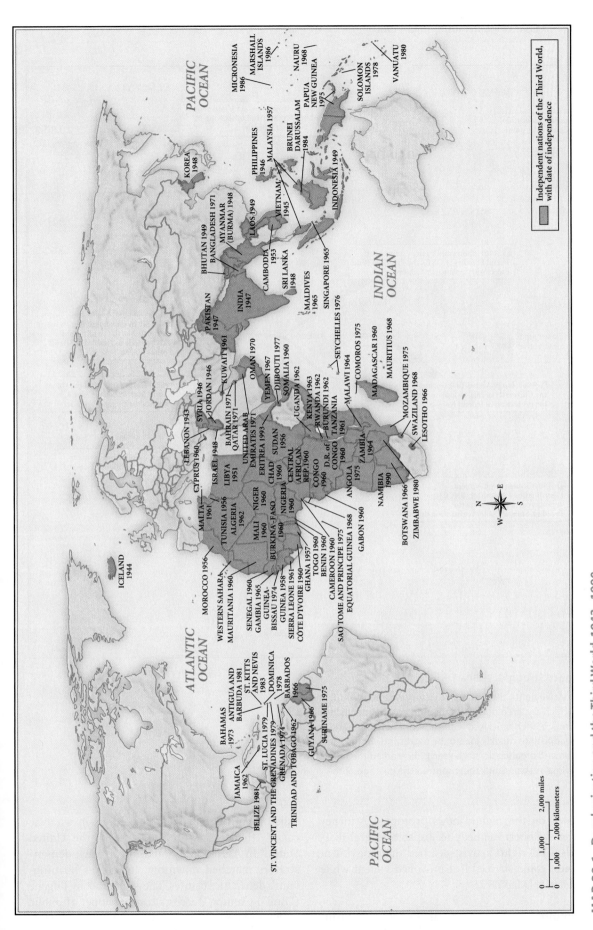

MAP 28.1 Decolonization and the Third World, 1943–1990

At the end of World War II, the colonial empires built up over the previous centuries by European countries were still formally intact. After 1945, movements for national self-determination swept across Africa, India, and Southeast Asia. This map shows the many nations carved out of that struggle, all of them parts of the "Third World," a Cold War term designating countries not formally aligned either with the Western or the Soviet blocs. Courted by both the United States and the Soviet Union, some Third World nations like Vietnam and Angola became key battlegrounds of the Cold War, often with disastrous results for the local populations.

Map legend:
☐ Independent nations of the Third World, with date of independence

PACIFIC OCEAN

ATLANTIC OCEAN

INDIAN OCEAN

PACIFIC OCEAN

MICRONESIA 1986
MARSHALL ISLANDS 1986
NAURU 1968
PAPUA NEW GUINEA 1975
SOLOMON ISLANDS 1978
VANUATU 1980

KOREA 1948
PHILIPPINES 1946
MALAYSIA 1957
BRUNEI DARUSSALAM 1984
VIETNAM 1945
INDONESIA 1949

BHUTAN 1949
BANGLADESH 1971
MYANMAR (BURMA) 1948
LAOS 1949
CAMBODIA 1953
SRI LANKA 1948
MALDIVES 1965
SINGAPORE 1965

PAKISTAN 1947
INDIA 1947

KUWAIT 1961
OMAN 1970
YEMEN 1967
DJIBOUTI 1977
ERITREA 1993
SOMALIA 1960
SEYCHELLES 1976
COMOROS 1975
MADAGASCAR 1960
MAURITIUS 1968

LEBANON 1943
SYRIA 1946
JORDAN 1946
BAHRAIN 1971
QATAR 1971
UNITED ARAB EMIRATES 1971

CYPRUS 1960
ISRAEL 1948
LIBYA 1951
SUDAN 1956
CHAD 1960
CENTRAL AFRICAN REP. 1960
UGANDA 1962
KENYA 1963
RWANDA 1962
BURUNDI 1962
TANZANIA 1961
MALAWI 1964
MOZAMBIQUE 1975
SWAZILAND 1968
LESOTHO 1966

MALTA 1961
TUNISIA 1956
ALGERIA 1962
NIGER 1960
NIGERIA 1960
CONGO 1960
D.R. of CONGO 1960
ANGOLA 1975
ZAMBIA 1964
NAMIBIA 1990
ZIMBABWE 1980
BOTSWANA 1966

MOROCCO 1956
WESTERN SAHARA
MAURITANIA 1960
SENEGAL 1960
GAMBIA 1965
GUINEA-BISSAU 1974
GUINEA 1958
SIERRA LEONE 1961
CÔTE D'IVOIRE 1960
MALI 1960
BURKINA FASO 1960
GHANA 1957
TOGO 1960
BENIN 1960
CAMEROON 1960
SAO TOME AND PRINCIPE 1975
EQUATORIAL GUINEA 1968
GABON 1960

ICELAND 1944

BAHAMAS 1973
ANTIGUA AND BARBUDA 1981
ST. KITTS AND NEVIS 1983
DOMINICA 1978
ST. LUCIA 1979
ST. VINCENT AND THE GRENADINES 1979
GRENADA 1974
BARBADOS 1966
TRINIDAD AND TOBAGO 1962
JAMAICA 1962
BELIZE 1981
GUYANA 1966
SURINAME 1975

N
W E
S

0   1,000   2,000 miles
0   1,000   2,000 kilometers

865

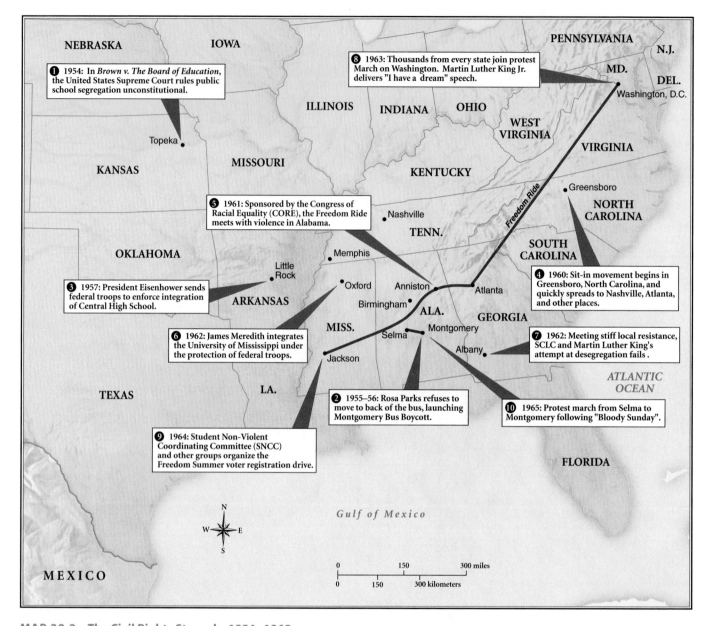

MAP 28.2 The Civil Rights Struggle, 1954–1965

In the postwar battle for black civil rights, the first major victory was the NAACP litigation of *Brown v. Board of Education*, which declared public school segregation unconstitutional. As indicated on this map, the struggle then quickly spread, raising other issues and seeding new organizations. Other organizations quickly joined the battle and shifted the focus away from the courts to mass action and organization. The year 1965 marked the high point, when violence against the Selma, Alabama, marchers spurred the passage of the Voting Rights Act (see p. 872).

shown on the nightly news prompted Attorney General Robert Kennedy to dispatch federal marshals. Civil rights activists learned that nonviolent protest could succeed if it provoked violent white resistance (Map 28.2).

Birmingham. This lesson was confirmed in Birmingham, Alabama, when Martin Luther King Jr.

called for protests against conditions in what he called "the most segregated city in the United States." In April 1963 thousands of black demonstrators marched downtown to picket Birmingham's department stores. They were met by Eugene ("Bull") Connor, the city's commissioner of public safety, and his police, who used snarling dogs, electric cattle prods, and high-pressure fire hoses to

Racial Violence in Birmingham

When thousands of blacks marched through downtown Birmingham, Alabama, to protest racial segregation in April 1963, they were met with fire hoses and attack dogs unleashed by Police Chief "Bull" Connor. The violence, which was televised on the national evening news, shocked many Americans and helped build sympathy for the civil rights movement among northern whites. AP Images/Bill Hudson.

break up the crowds. Television cameras captured the scene for the evening news.

Outraged by the brutality, President Kennedy decided it was time to step in. On June 11, 1963, after Alabama Governor George Wallace barred two black students from the state university, Kennedy went on television and delivered a passionate speech denouncing racism and announcing a new civil rights bill. Black leaders hailed the speech as a "Second Emancipation Proclamation." That night Medgar Evers, president of the Mississippi chapter of the NAACP, was shot in the back and killed in his driveway in Jackson. The martyrdom of Evers became a spur to further action.

The March on Washington. To marshal support for Kennedy's bill, civil rights leaders adopted a tactic that A. Philip Randolph had first advanced in 1941 (see Chapter 25): a massive demonstration in

Washington. Although the planning was not primarily Martin Luther King's, he was truly the public face of the March on Washington on August 28, 1963. It was King's dramatic "I Have a Dream" speech, ending with the exclamation from an old Negro spiritual—"Free at last! Free at last! Thank God Almighty, we are free at last!"—that captured the nation's imagination. The sight of 250,000 blacks and whites marching solemnly together marked the high point of the civil rights movement and confirmed King's position, especially among white liberals, as the leading spokesperson for the black cause.

Although the March on Washington galvanized public opinion, it changed few congressional votes. Southern senators continued to block Kennedy's legislation by threatening a filibuster. In September a Baptist church in Birmingham was bombed and four black Sunday school students were killed,

The March on Washington

The Reverend Martin Luther King Jr. (1929–1968) was the most eloquent advocate of the civil rights movement. For many, his "I Have a Dream" speech of the 1963 March on Washington was the high point of the day, and, for some, of the entire civil rights struggle. The focus on the charismatic King, however, meant that the importance of other civil rights leaders was frequently overlooked. Bob Adelman/Magnum Photos, Inc.

shocking the nation and bringing the civil rights demonstrations to a boiling point.

Kennedy, Cold Warrior

Foreign affairs gave greater scope for Kennedy's fertile mind. A resolute cold warrior, Kennedy took a hard line against Communism. In contrast to Eisenhower, whose cost-saving New Look program had built up the American nuclear arsenal at the expense of conventional weapons, Kennedy proposed a new policy of "flexible response," stating that the nation must be prepared "to deter all wars, general or limited, nuclear or conventional, large or small." Congress quickly granted Kennedy's military requests, and by 1963 the defense budget reached its highest level as a percentage of total federal expenditures in the Cold War era.

Already strained by the Bay of Pigs invasion, U.S.-Soviet relations deteriorated further in June 1961 when Soviet Premier Khrushchev deployed soldiers to isolate Communist-controlled East Berlin from the western sector controlled by West Germany. With congressional approval, Kennedy responded by adding 300,000 troops to the armed forces and promptly dispatching 40,000 of them to Europe. In mid-August, to stop the exodus of East Germans, the Soviets ordered construction of the Berlin Wall, and East German guards began policing the border. Until it was dismantled in 1989, the Berlin Wall remained the supreme symbol of the Cold War.

The climactic confrontation of the Cold War came in October 1962. In a somber televised address,

Kennedy revealed that reconnaissance planes had spotted Soviet-built bases for intermediate-range ballistic missiles in Cuba. Some of those weapons had already been installed, and more were on the way. Kennedy announced that the United States would impose a "quarantine on all offensive military equipment" intended for Cuba (Map 28.3). As the two superpowers went on full military alert, people around the world feared an imminent nuclear war. But as the world held its breath, the ships carrying Soviet-made missiles turned back. After a week of tense negotiations, both Kennedy and Khrushchev made concessions: Kennedy pledged not to invade Cuba, and Khrushchev promised to dismantle the missile bases.

The risk of nuclear war, greater during the Cuban missile crisis than at any other time in the postwar period, led to a slight thaw in U.S.-Soviet relations. As national security advisor McGeorge Bundy put it, both sides were chastened by "having come so close to the edge." Kennedy softened his Cold War rhetoric and Soviet leaders, similarly chastened, agreed to talk. In August 1963 the three principal nuclear powers—the United States, the Soviet Union, and Great Britain—announced a ban on the testing of nuclear weapons in the atmosphere, although underground testing was allowed to continue. The new emphasis on peaceful coexistence also led to the establishment of a Washington-Moscow telecommunications "hotline" in 1963 so that leaders could contact each other quickly in a crisis.

But no matter how much American leaders talked about opening channels of communication with Moscow, relations with the Soviet Union

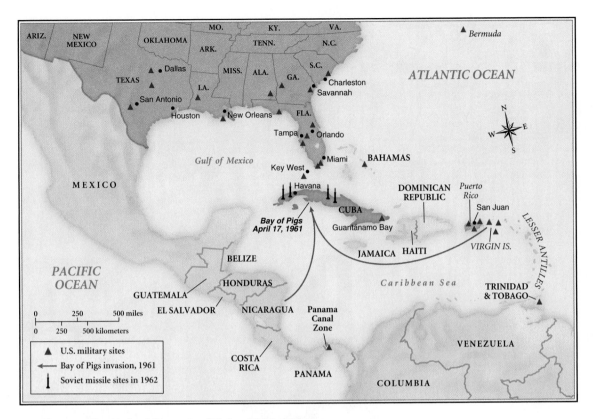

MAP 28.3   The United States and Cuba, 1961–1962

Fidel Castro's takeover in Cuba in 1959 brought Cold War tensions to the Caribbean. In 1961 the United States tried unsuccessfully to overthrow Castro's regime by supporting the Bay of Pigs invasion of Cuban exiles launched from Nicaragua and other points in the Caribbean. In 1962 a major confrontation with the Soviet Union occurred over Soviet construction of nuclear missile sites in Cuba. The Soviets removed the missiles after President Kennedy ordered a naval blockade of the island. Despite the fall of the Soviet Union in 1991 and the official end of the Cold War, the United States continues to view Cuba, still governed in 2006 by Fidel Castro, as an enemy nation.

remained tense, and containment remained the cornerstone of U.S. policy.

The Vietnam Puzzle. When Kennedy became president, he inherited Eisenhower's involvement in Vietnam. Kennedy saw Vietnam in very much the same Cold War terms. But what really grabbed him was the chance to test the counterinsurgency doctrine associated with his "flexible response" military strategy. The army was training U.S. Special Forces, called Green Berets for their distinctive headgear, to engage in unconventional, small-group warfare. Kennedy and his advisers wanted to try out the Green Berets in the Vietnamese jungles.

Despite American aid, the corrupt and repressive Diem regime installed by Eisenhower in 1954 was losing ground (see Chapter 26). By 1961 Diem's opponents, with backing from North Vietnam, had formed a revolutionary movement known as the National Liberation Front (NLF). The NLF's guerrilla forces—the Vietcong—found a receptive audience among peasants alienated by Diem's "strategic hamlet" program, which uprooted whole villages and moved them into barbed-wire compounds. Buddhists charged Diem, a Catholic, with religious persecution. Starting in May 1963, militant Buddhists staged dramatic demonstrations, including several self-immolations recorded by American television crews. Losing patience with Diem, Kennedy let it be known in Saigon that the United States would support a military coup. On November 1, 1963, Diem was overthrown and assassinated—an eventuality evidently not anticipated by Kennedy. At that point, there were about 16,000 American "advisers" (an elastic term that included helicopter crews and Special Forces) in Vietnam.

In a CBS interview, Kennedy had remarked that it was up to the South Vietnamese whether "their war"

The Berlin Wall

A West Berlin resident walks alongside a section of the Berlin Wall in 1962, a year after its construction. Note the two border guards on the East Berlin side, plus the numerous loud speakers, which East German Communists used to broadcast propaganda over the barricade that divided the city. © Bettmann/Corbis.

would be won or lost. Advisers close to the president later argued that, had he run strongly in the 1964 election, he would have felt emboldened to cut America's losses and leave. But that argument downplays the geopolitical issues at stake in Vietnam. The United States was now engaged in a global war against Communism. Giving up in Vietnam would be weakening America's "credibility" in that struggle. And, under the prevailing "domino theory," other pro-American states would topple after Vietnam's loss. Kennedy subscribed to these received Cold War tenets. Whether he might have surmounted them down the road is, like how Lincoln might have handled Reconstruction after the Civil War had he lived, an unanswerable historical question.

The Kennedy Assassination

On November 22, 1963, Kennedy went to Texas on a political trip. As he and his wife, Jacqueline, rode in an open car past the Texas School Book Depository in Dallas, he was shot through the head and neck by a sniper. Kennedy died within the hour. (The accused killer, Lee Harvey Oswald, a twenty-four-year-old loner, was himself killed while in custody a few days later.) Before Air Force One left Dallas to take the president's body back to Washington, a grim-faced Lyndon Johnson was sworn in as president. Kennedy's stunned widow, still wearing her bloodstained pink suit, looked on.

Kennedy's youthful image, the trauma of his assassination, and the nation's sense of loss contributed to a powerful Kennedy mystique. His canonization after death actually capped an extraordinarily successful effort at stage-managing the presidency. An admiring country saw in Jack and Jackie Kennedy an ideal American marriage (he was in fact an obsessive womanizer); in Kennedy the man the epitome of robust good health (although he was actually afflicted by Addison's disease and

Buddhist Protest, 1966

Buddhist nun Thich Nu Thanh Quang burns to death at the Dieu de Pagoda in Hue, South Vietnam, in a ritual act of suicide in protest against the Catholic Saigon regime on May 29, 1966. Its inability to win over the Buddhist population was a major source of weakness for the South Vietnamese government. AP Images.

kept going by potent medications); and in the Kennedy White House a glamorous world of high fashion and celebrity. No presidency ever matched the Kennedy aura of "Camelot"—after the mythical realm of King Arthur in the hit musical of that title—but every president after him embraced the idea, with greater or lesser success, that image mattered as much as reality—maybe more—in conducting a politically effective presidency. In Kennedy's case, the ultimate irony was that his image as martyred leader produced grander legislative results than anything he might have achieved as a live president in the White House.

➤ Why was Kennedy an effective politican?

➤ Why did civil rights become a big issue during the Kennedy years?

➤ What were the results of Kennedy's foreign policy?

Lyndon B. Johnson and the Great Society

Lyndon Johnson was a seasoned politician from Texas, a longtime Senate leader at his best negotiating in the back rooms of power. Compared to Kennedy, Johnson was a rough-edged character who had scrambled his way up, without too many scruples, to wealth and political eminence. But unlike other bootstrap successes, he never forgot his hill-country origins or lost his sympathy for the down-

trodden. Johnson was no match for the Kennedy style, but he capitalized on Kennedy's assassination, applying his astonishing energy and negotiating skills to bring to fruition many of Kennedy's stalled programs and more than a few of his own in an ambitious program he called the "Great Society."

The Momentum for Civil Rights

On assuming the presidency, Lyndon Johnson promptly pushed for civil rights legislation as a memorial to his slain predecessor. His motives were a combination of the political and the personal. As a politician, he wanted the Democratic Party to benefit from the national groundswell for civil rights, although he was too shrewd an operative not be aware of the price the party would pay in the South. It was more important to him, as a president from the South, to reach across regional lines and appeal to a broad national audience. Achieving historic civil rights legislation would, he hoped, place his mark on the presidency.

The Civil Rights Act of 1964. Overcoming a southern filibuster, Congress approved in June 1964 the most far-reaching civil rights legislation since Reconstruction. The keystone of the Civil Rights Act, Title VII, outlawed discrimination in employment on the basis of race, religion, national origin, or sex. Another section guaranteed equal access to public accommodations and schools. The law granted new enforcement powers to the U.S. attorney general and established the Equal Employment Opportunity Commission (EEOC) to implement

Freedom Summer, 1964

In the summer of 1964 — "Freedom Summer" — hundreds of civil rights volunteers converged on Mississippi and Alabama to conduct voter registration drives. In this photograph, college students in Oxford, Ohio, sing and hold hands before their departure for Mississippi. They knew that rough days were ahead of them. Shapiro/Black Star/Stockphoto.com.

the prohibition against job discrimination. It was a law with real teeth. But it left untouched obstacles to black voting rights.

Freedom Summer. So protesters went back into the streets. In 1964 black organizations and churches mounted a major civil rights campaign in Mississippi. Known as "Freedom Summer," the effort drew several thousand volunteers from across the country, including many idealistic white college students. Freedom Summer workers established freedom schools, which taught black children traditional subjects as well as their own history; conducted a major voter registration drive; and organized the Mississippi Freedom Democratic Party, a political alternative to the all-white Democratic organization in Mississippi. Some southerners reacted swiftly and violently. Fifteen civil rights workers were murdered; only about 1,200 black voters were registered that summer.

The need for federal action became even clearer in March 1965, when Martin Luther King Jr. and other black leaders called for a massive march from Selma, Alabama, to the state capitol in Montgomery to protest the murder of a voting-rights activist. As soon as the marchers left Selma, mounted state troopers attacked them with tear gas and clubs. The scene was shown on national television that night. Calling the episode "an American tragedy," President Johnson redoubled his efforts to persuade Congress to pass the pending voting-rights legislation.

The Voting Rights Act. The Voting Rights Act, which passed on August 6, 1965, outlawed the literacy tests and other measures most southern states used to prevent blacks from registering to vote and

authorized the attorney general to send federal examiners to register voters in any county where less than 50 percent of the voting-age population was registered. Together with the Twenty-fourth Amendment (1964), which outlawed the poll tax in federal elections, the Voting Rights Act enabled millions of blacks to register and vote for the first time since after Reconstruction.

In the South the results were stunning. In 1960 only 20 percent of blacks of voting age had been registered to vote; by 1964 the figure had risen to 39 percent, and by 1971 it was 62 percent (Map 28.4). As Hartman Turnbow, a Mississippi farmer who risked his life to register in 1964, later declared, "It won't never go back where it was."

Enacting the Liberal Agenda

Johnson's success in pushing through the Voting Rights Act had stemmed in part from the 1964 election, when he had faced the Republican Barry Goldwater of Arizona. An arch-conservative, Goldwater ran on a anti-Communist, anti-government platform, offering "a choice, not an echo." There would be no Republican "Dime Store New Deal" this time around. The voters didn't buy it. Johnson and his running mate Hubert H. Humphrey of Minnesota won in a landslide (Map 28.5). In the long run, Goldwater's candidacy marked the beginning of a grassroots conservative revolt that would eventually transform the Republican Party and American politics. In the short run, however, Johnson's sweeping victory enabled him to bring to fruition the legislative programs of the "Great Society."

Like most New Deal liberals, Johnson held an expansive view of the role of government. Now he

MAP 28.4 Black Voter Registration in the South, 1964 and 1975

After passage of the Voting Rights Act of 1965, black registration in the South increased dramatically. The bars on the map show the number of blacks registered in 1964, before the act was passed, and in 1975, after it had been in effect for ten years. States in the Deep South, such as Mississippi, Alabama, and Georgia, had the biggest increases.

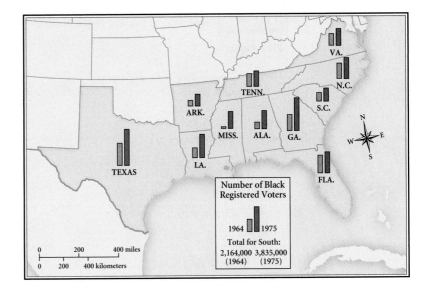

had a popular mandate and, equally important, the filibuster-proof majority he needed to push his programs forward (see Table 28.1).

One of Johnson's first successes was breaking the congressional deadlock on aid to education. Passed in April 1965, the Elementary and Secondary

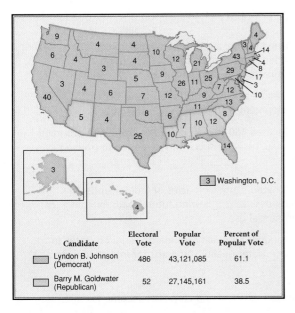

MAP 28.5 Presidential Election of 1964

This map reveals how one-sided Lyndon Johnson's victory was over Barry Goldwater in 1964. Except for Arizona, his home state, Goldwater won only five states in the deep South — not of much immediate consolation to him, but a sure indicator that the South was cutting its historic ties to the Democratic Party. Moreover, although soundly rejected in 1964, Goldwater's Far Right critique of "big government" laid the foundation for a Republican resurgence in the 1980s.

Education Act authorized $1 billion in federal funds, sidestepping the religious issue by dispensing aid to public and parochial schools alike on the basis of the number of needy children in attendance. Six months later, Johnson signed the Higher Education Act, providing federal scholarships for college students.

The Eighty-ninth Congress also gave Johnson the votes he needed to achieve some form of national health insurance. Realizing the game was up, the American Medical Association fell back to a demand that services be provided through the existing private system of doctors and hospitals. On that basis, two new programs came forth: Medicare, a health plan for the elderly funded by a surcharge on Social Security payroll taxes, and Medicaid, a health plan for the poor paid for by general tax revenues and administered by the states.

Johnson's programs targeted not only the disadvantaged; the middle class benefited, too. Federal urban renewal and home mortgage assistance helped those who could afford to live in single-family homes or modern apartments. Medicare covered every elderly person eligible for Social Security, regardless of need. Much of the federal aid to education went to the children of the middle class.

And everyone benefited from the Great Society's environmental reforms. President Johnson pressed for expansion of the national park system, improvement of the nation's air and water, protection for endangered species and the wilderness, and stronger land-use planning. At the insistence of his wife, Lady Bird Johnson, he promoted the Highway Beautification Act of 1965. His approach marked a break with past conservation efforts, which had concentrated on husbanding the nation's natural

TABLE 28.1	Major Great Society Legislation

Civil Rights

1964	Twenty-fourth Amendment	Outlawed poll tax in federal elections
	Civil Rights Act	Banned discrimination in employment and public accommodations on the basis of race, religion, sex, or national origin
1965	Voting Rights Act	Outlawed literacy tests for voting; provided federal supervision of registration in historically low-registration areas

Social Welfare

1964	Economic Opportunity Act	Created Office of Economic Opportunity (OEO) to administer War on Poverty programs such as Head Start, Job Corps, and Volunteers in Service to America (VISTA)
1965	Medical Care Act	Provided medical care for the poor (Medicaid) and the elderly (Medicare)
1966	Minimum Wage Act	Raised hourly minimum wage from $1.25 to $1.40 and expanded coverage to new groups

Education

1965	Elementary and Secondary Education Act	Granted federal aid for education of poor children
	National Endowment for the Arts and Humanities	Provided federal funding and support for artists and scholars
	Higher Education Act	Provided federal scholarships for postsecondary education

Housing and Urban Development

1964	Urban Mass Transportation Act	Provided federal aid to urban mass transit
	Omnibus Housing Act	Provided federal funds for public housing and rent subsidies for low-income families
1965	Housing and Urban Development Act	Created Department of Housing and Urban Development (HUD)
1966	Metropolitan Area Redevelopment and Demonstration Cities Acts	Designated 150 "model cities" for combined programs of public housing, social services, and job training

Environment

| 1964 | Wilderness Preservation Act | Designated 9.1 million acres of federal lands as "wilderness areas," barring future roads, buildings, or commercial use |
| 1965 | Air and Water Quality Acts | Set tougher air quality standards; required states to enforce water quality standards for interstate waters |

Miscellaneous

1964	Tax Reduction Act	Reduced personal and corporate income tax rates
1965	Immigration Act	Abandoned national quotas of 1924 law, allowing more non-European immigration
	Appalachian Regional and Development Act	Provided federal funding for roads, health clinics, other public works projects in economically depressed regions

resources. Secretary of the Interior Stewart Udall emphasized quality of life, battling the problem "of vanishing beauty, of increasing ugliness, of shrinking open space, and of an overall environment that is diminished daily by pollution and noise and blight." In a similar vein, the National Endowment for the Arts and the Humanities was established in 1965 to support the work of artists, writers, and scholars.

In the prevailing reform climate, it even became possible to tackle the nation's discriminatory immigration policy, which since 1924 had used a national-origins quota system that favored northern Europeans. The Immigration Act of 1965 abandoned the quota system, replacing it with more equitable numerical limits on immigration from all nations. To promote family reunification, the law also provided that close relatives of individuals already legally resident in the United States could be admitted outside the numerical limits, an exception that especially benefited Asian and Latin American immigrants. The ethnic diversity of our nation today—and of our campuses—goes back to that 1965 Immigration Act.

The War on Poverty. What drove Johnson hardest, however, was his determination to "end poverty in our time." The president called it a national disgrace that, in the midst of plenty, a fifth of all Americans—hidden from sight in Appalachia, in urban ghettos, in migrant labor camps, on Indian reservations—lived in poverty. Many had fallen through the cracks and were not served by New Deal welfare programs.

The "Johnson Treatment"

Lyndon B. Johnson, a shrewd and adroit politician, learned many of his legislative skills while serving as majority leader of the Senate from 1953 to 1960. Here he zeroed in on Senator Theodore Francis Green of Rhode Island. After assuming the presidency, Johnson remarked, "They say Jack Kennedy had style, but I'm the one who got the bills passed." *George Tames, The New York Times.*

So one tactic was shoring up those programs. The Great Society broadened Social Security to include waiters and waitresses, domestic servants, farmworkers, and hospital employees. Social welfare expenditures increased rapidly, especially for Aid to Families with Dependent Children (AFDC), as did public housing and rent subsidy programs. Food stamps, begun in 1964 mainly to stabilize farm prices, grew into a major source of assistance to low-income families.

The Office of Economic Opportunity (OEO), established by the Economic Opportunity Act of 1964, was the Great Society's showcase in the War on Poverty. Built around the twin principles of equal opportunity and community action, OEC advanced programs so numerous and diverse that they recalled the alphabet agencies of the New Deal. Head Start provided free nursery schools to prepare disadvantaged preschoolers for kindergarten. The Job Corps and Upward Bound provided young people with training and jobs. Volunteers in Service to America (VISTA), modeled on the Peace Corps, provided technical assistance to the urban and rural poor. An array of regional development programs aimed, like foreign aid, at spurring economic growth in impoverished areas. The Community Action Program encouraged its clients to demand "maximum feasible participation" in decisions that affected them. Community Action organizers worked closely with lawyers employed by the Legal Services Program to provide the poor with access to the legal system.

The Limits of the Great Society. By the end of 1965, the Johnson administration had compiled the most impressive legislative record since the New Deal and put issues of poverty, justice, and access at the center of national political life. Yet the Great Society never quite measured up to the extravagant promises made for it.

The proportion of Americans living below the poverty line dropped from 20 percent to 13 percent between 1963 and 1968 (Figure 28.1). African Americans did even better. In the 1960s the black poverty rate fell by half as millions of blacks moved into the middle class. Critics, however, credited the decade's booming economy more than government programs. Moreover, distribution of wealth remained highly skewed. In relative terms, the bottom 20 percent remained as far behind as ever.

An inherent problem was the limited funding, which was set at less than $2 billion annually. It also proved impossible to hold together the extraordinarily diverse political coalition first forged by Franklin Roosevelt in the 1930s—middle-class and poor; white and nonwhite; Protestant, Jewish, and Catholic; urban and rural—that Johnson rallied for the Great Society. Inevitably, the demands of certain groups—such as blacks' demands for civil rights and the urban poor's demands for increased political power—conflicted with the interests of other Democrats. In the end Johnson's coalition was not strong enough to withstand a growing challenge by conservatives who resisted expanded civil rights and social welfare benefits.

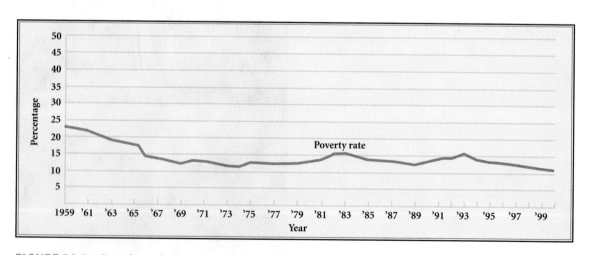

FIGURE 28.1 Americans in Poverty, 1959–2000

Between 1959 and 1973 the poverty rate among American families dropped by more than half—from 23 percent to 11 percent. There was, however, sharp disagreement about the reasons for that notable decline. Liberals credited the War on Poverty, while conservatives favored the high-performing economy, with the significant poverty dip of 1965–1966 caused by military spending, not Johnson's domestic programs.

Democrats were themselves plagued by disillusionment over the shortcomings of their reforms. In the early 1960s the lofty rhetoric of the New Frontier and the Great Society had raised people's expectations. But competition for federal largesse was keen, and the shortage of funds left many promises unfulfilled, especially after 1965 when the Vietnam War siphoned funding away from domestic programs. In 1966 the government spent $22 billion on the Vietnam War and only $1.2 billion on the War on Poverty. Ultimately, as Martin Luther King Jr. put it, the Great Society was "shot down on the battlefields of Vietnam."

➤ Why, after years of resistance, did Congress pass the great civil rights acts of 1964 and 1965?

➤ What were the key components of the Great Society?

➤ What factors limited the success of the War on Poverty?

Into the Quagmire, 1963–1968

Just as Kennedy inherited Vietnam from Eisenhower, so Lyndon Johnson inherited Vietnam from Kennedy. Only the inheritance was now more burdensome, for it became clear that only massive American intervention could prevent the collapse of South Vietnam (Map 28.6). Johnson was a subscriber, like Kennedy, to the Cold War tenets of global containment—that America's credibility was at stake in Vietnam and that the domino effect would have devastating consequences. But whereas, in Kennedy's case, second thoughts might have prevailed, that was an impossibility with Johnson. "I am not going to lose Vietnam," he vowed upon taking office. "I am not going to be the President who saw Southeast Asia go the way China went."

Escalation

Johnson was unwilling to level with the American people. For one thing, he doubted that they had the

MAP 28.6 The Vietnam War, 1968

The Vietnam War was a guerrilla war, fought in skirmishes rather than set-piece battles. Despite repeated airstrikes, the United States was never able to halt the flow of North Vietnamese troops and supplies down the Ho Chi Minh Trail, which wound through Laos and Cambodia. In January 1968 Vietcong forces launched the Tet offensive, a surprise attack on cities and provincial centers across South Vietnam. Although the attackers were pushed back with heavy losses, the Tet offensive revealed the futility of American efforts to suppress the Vietcong guerrillas and marked a turning point in the war.

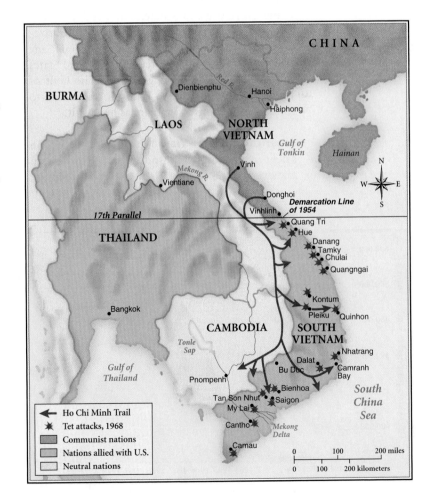

stomach for the course he was contemplating. And he did not want to endanger his grand domestic agenda. He felt he "had no choice but to keep my foreign policy in the wings" because "the day it exploded into a major debate on the war, that day would be the beginning of the end of the Great Society." So he ran in 1964 on the pledge that there be no escalation—no American boys fighting Vietnam's fight—although he intended to do exactly that. And while he wanted congressional approval, perhaps even a declaration of war, Johnson needed a good excuse, which he found even before the 1964 campaign was over.

The Gulf of Tonkin Resolution. During the summer, while American naval forces were conducting reconnaissance missions off the North Vietnamese coast, Johnson got reports that North Vietnamese torpedo boats had fired on the destroyer *Maddox* in international waters. In the first attack, on August 2, the damage inflicted was limited to a single bullet hole; a second, on August 4, later proved to be only misread radar sightings. It didn't matter. In a national emergency—real or imagined—the president's call to arms is hard to resist. In the entire Congress, House and Senate, only two lone Senators voted against Johnson's request for authorization to "take all necessary measures to repel any armed attack against the forces of the United States and to prevent further aggression." The Gulf of Tonkin resolution handed Johnson a mandate to conduct operations in Vietnam as he saw fit.

Americanizing the War. With the 1964 election safely behind him, Johnson began an American takeover of the war in Vietnam. The escalation, which was accomplished in the early months of 1965, took two forms: deployment of American ground troops and the intensification of bombing against North Vietnam.

On March 8, 1965, the first Marines waded ashore at Da Nang, ostensibly to protect the huge American air base there. Soon they were skirmishing with the enemy. Over the next three years, the number of American troops in Vietnam grew dramatically (Figure 28.2). By 1966 more than 380,000 American soldiers were stationed in Vietnam; by 1967, 485,000; and by 1968, 536,000. The escalating demands of General William Westmoreland, the commander of U.S. forces, confirmed a fear Kennedy had expressed before his death that requesting troops was like taking a drink: "The effect wears off and you have to take another."

In the meantime, in an operation called Rolling Thunder, Johnson unleashed a bombing campaign against North Vietnam. A special target was the Ho Chi Minh Trail, an elaborate network of trails, bridges, and shelters that stretched from North Vietnam through Cambodia and Laos into South Vietnam. By 1968 a million tons of bombs had fallen on North Vietnam, 800 tons a day for three-and-a-half years. Twice that tonnage was dropped on the jungles of South Vietnam as U.S. forces tried to flush out the Vietcong fighters.

To the surprise of American planners, the bombing had little effect on the Vietcong's ability to wage war. The flow of troops and supplies continued unabated as the North Vietnamese quickly rebuilt roads and bridges, moved munitions plants underground, and constructed a network of tunnels and shelters. Instead of destroying North Vietnamese morale, Operation Rolling

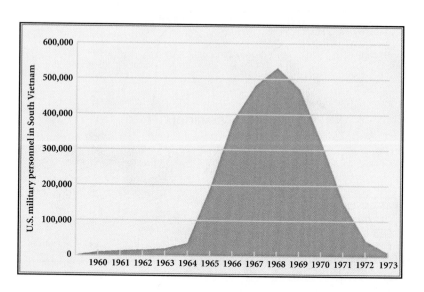

FIGURE 28.2   U.S. Troops in Vietnam, 1960–1973

This figure graphically tracks America's involvement in Vietnam. After Lyndon Johnson decided on escalation in 1964, troop levels jumped from 23,300 to a peak of 543,000 personnel in 1968. Under Richard Nixon's Vietnamization program, beginning in the summer of 1969, levels drastically declined; the last U.S. military forces left South Vietnam on March 29, 1973.

Thunder intensified their nationalism and hardened their will to fight.

The massive commitment of troops and air power devastated Vietnam's countryside. After one harsh but not unusual engagement, a commanding officer reported, using the logic of the time, "It became necessary to destroy the town in order to save it." Besides the bombing, a defoliation campaign began to deprive guerrillas of cover, destroying crops and undercutting the economic and cultural base of Vietnamese society. (In later years defoliants such as Agent Orange were found to have highly toxic effects on humans, including the G.I.s serving in Vietnam.) In Saigon and other South Vietnamese cities, the influx of American soldiers and dollars distorted local economies, fostered corruption and prostitution, and triggered uncontrollable inflation and black-market activity.

In Washington the debate intensified about why the increased American presence was failing to turn the tide of the war. Some advisors argued that military action could accomplish little without reform in Saigon. Other critics claimed that the United States never fully committed itself to a "total victory" (see Comparing American Voices, "The Toll of War," pp. 880–881). Military strategy was inextricably tied to political considerations. For domestic reasons policymakers often searched for an elusive "middle ground" between all-out invasion of North Vietnam (and the possibility of war with China) and the politically unacceptable alternative of disengagement. Hoping to win a war of attrition, the Johnson administration gambled that American superiority in personnel and weaponry would ultimately triumph.

Public Opinion on Vietnam

A big part of Johnson's gamble was that he could retain the support of the American people. He had reason for confidence on that score: A broad, steady consensus had formed in earlier years favorable to Washington's conduct of the Cold War. Both Democrats and Republicans approved Johnson's escalation in Vietnam, and so did public opinion polls in 1965 and 1966. But then public opinion began to shift.

In July 1967 a Gallup poll revealed that for the first time a majority of Americans disapproved of Johnson's Vietnam policy and believed the war had reached a stalemate. Every night Americans saw on television U.S. soldiers advancing steadily and heard about staggering Vietcong "body counts," but increasingly television screens showed the carnage of war and dead and wounded Americans. Journalists

began to warn that the Johnson administration suffered from a "credibility gap." The administration, they charged, was concealing discouraging information about the war's progress. In February 1966 television coverage of hearings by the Senate Foreign Relations Committee (chaired by J. William Fulbright, an outspoken critic of the war) raised further questions about the administration's policy.

The Rise of the Antiwar Movement. Out of these troubling developments an antiwar movement began to crystallize. Its core was, in addition to longstanding pacifist groups, a new generation of peace activists like SANE (the National Committee for a Sane Nuclear Policy) that in the 1950s had protested atmospheric nuclear testing. After the escalation in 1965, they were joined by student groups, clergy, civil rights advocates, even Dr. Spock. The antiwar coalitions were soon capable of mounting mass demonstrations in Washington, bringing out 20,000 to 30,000 people at a time. Although they were a diverse lot, participants in these rallies shared a common skepticism about U.S. policy in Vietnam. They charged variously that intervention was morally wrong and antithetical to American ideals; that an independent, anti-Communist South Vietnam was unattainable; and that no American objective justified the suffering inflicted on the Vietnamese people (see Voices from Abroad, "Che Guevara: Vietnam and the World Freedom Struggle," p. 883).

Economic developments put Johnson even more on the defensive. The Vietnam War cost the taxpayers $27 billion in 1967, and the deficit jumped from $9.8 billion to $23 billion. The cost of the war nudged the inflation rate upward. Only in the summer of 1967 did Johnson ask for a 10 percent surcharge on income taxes, an increase that Congress did not approve until 1968. By then the inflationary spiral that would plague the U.S. economy throughout the 1970s was well under way.

Student Activism

No group was more visible in these antiwar protests than college students. Many of them had been inspired by the black college students of Greensboro, North Carolina, who had sparked the wave of sit-ins that did so much to challenge segregation in the South (see Chapter 27). Galvanized by the struggle for racial justice, white students—many of whom had been raised in a privileged environment and inculcated with faith in American goodness—began to question U.S. foreign and domestic policy and middle-class conformity.

The Toll of War

The Vietnam War produced a rich and graphic literature: novels, journalists' reports, interviews, and personal letters. These brief selections suggest the war's profound impact on those Americans who experienced it firsthand.

DONALD L. WHITFIELD

Donald L. Whitfield was a draftee from Alabama, who was interviewed some years after the war.

I'm gonna be honest with you. I had heard some about Vietnam in 1968, but I was a poor fellow and I didn't keep up with it. I was working at a Standard Oil station making eight dollars a day. I pumped gas and tinkered a little with cars. I had a girl I saw every now and then, but I still spent most of my time with a car. When I got my letter from the draft lady, I appealed it on the reason it was just me and my sister at home. We were a poor family and they needed me at home, but it did no good.

My company did a lot of patrolling. We got the roughest damn deal. Shit, I thought I was going to get killed every night. I was terrified the whole time. We didn't have no trouble with the blacks. I saw movies that said we done the blacks wrong, but it wasn't like that where I was. Let's put it like this: they make pretty good soldiers, but they're not what we are. White Americans, can't nobody whip our ass. We're the baddest son of a bitches on the face of this earth. You can take a hundred Russians and twenty-five Americans, and we'll whip their ass....

I fly the Rebel flag because this is the South, Bubba. The American flag represents the whole fifty states. That flag represents the southern part. I'm a Confederate, I'm a Southerner....

I feel cheated about Vietnam, I sure do. Political restrictions — we won every goddamned battle we was in, but didn't win the whole goddamn little country.... Before I die, the Democratic-controlled Congress of this country — and I blame it on 'em — they gonna goddamn apologize to the Vietnam veterans.

SOURCE: James R. Wilson, *Landing Zones: Southern Veterans Remember Vietnam* (Durham, NC: Duke University Press, 1990), 203, 204, 207, 209, 210.

GEORGE OLSEN

George Olsen served in Vietnam from August 1969 to March 1970, when he was killed in action. He wrote this letter to his girlfriend.

31 Aug '69
Dear Red,
Last Monday I went on my first hunter-killer operation....

The frightening thing about it all is that it is so very easy to kill in war. There's no remorse, no theatrical "washing of the hands" to get rid of nonexistent blood, not even any regrets. When it happens, you are more afraid than you've ever been in your life — my hands shook so much I had trouble reloading.... You're scared, really scared, and there's no thinking about it. You kill because that little SOB is doing his best to kill you and you desperately want to live, to go home, to get drunk or walk down the street on a date again. And suddenly the grenades aren't going off any more, the weapons stop and, unbelievably fast it seems, it's all over....

I have truly come to envy the honest pacifist who honestly believes that no killing is permissible and can, with a clear conscience, stay home and not take part in these conflicts. I wish I could do the same, but I can't see letting another take my place and my risks over here.... The only reason pacifists such as the Amish can even live in an orderly society is because someone — be they police or soldiers — is taking risks to keep the wolves away.... I guess that's why I'm over here, why I fought so hard to come here, and why, even though I'm scared most of the time, I'm content to be here.

SOURCE: Bernard Edelman, ed., *Dear America: Letters Home from Vietnam* (New York: Pocket Books, 1985), 204–205.

ARTHUR E. WOODLEY JR.

Arthur E. Woodley Jr. was a Special Forces Ranger and gave this interview a decade after his return.

You had to fight to survive where I grew up. Lower east Baltimore. . . . It was a mixed-up neighborhood of Puerto Ricans, Indians, Italians, and blacks. Being that I'm light-skinned, curly hair, I wasn't readily accepted in the black community. I was more accepted by Puerto Ricans and some rednecks. They didn't ask what my race classification was. I went with them to white movies, white restaurants, and so forth. But after I got older, I came to the realization that I was what I am and came to deal with my black peers. . . .

I figured I was just what my country needed. A black patriot who could do any physical job they could come up with. Six feet, one hundred and ninety pounds, and healthy. . . .

I didn't ask no questions about the war. I thought communism was spreading, and as an American citizen, it was my part to do as much as I could to defeat the Communist from coming here. Whatever America states is correct was the tradition that I was brought up in. And I thought the only way I could possibly make it out of the ghetto was to be the best soldier I possibly could. . . .

Then came the second week of February of '69. . . . We recon this area, and we came across this fella, a white guy, who was staked to the ground. His arms and legs tied down to stakes. . . . He had numerous scars on his face where he might have been beaten and mutilated. And he had been peeled from his upper part of chest to down to his waist. Skinned. Like they slit your skin with a knife. And they take a pair of pliers or a instrument similar, and they just peel the skin off your body and expose it to the elements. . . .

And he start to cryin', beggin' to die.

He said, "I can't go back like this. I can't live like this. I'm dying. You can't leave me here like this dying." . . .

It took me somewhere close to 20 minutes to get my mind together. Not because I was squeamish about killing someone, because I had at that time numerous body counts. Killing someone wasn't the issue. It was killing another American citizen, another GI. . . . We buried him. We buried him. Very deep. Then I cried. . . .

When we first started going into the fields, I would not wear a finger, ear, or mutilate another person's body. Until I had the misfortune to come upon those American soldiers who were castrated. Then it got to be a game between the Communists and ourselves to see how many fingers and ears that we could capture from each other. After a kill we would cut his finger or ear off as a trophy, stuff our unit patch in his mouth, and let him die.

With 89 days left in country, I came out of the field. What I now felt was emptiness. . . . I started seeing the atrocities that we caused each other as human beings. I came to the realization that I was committing crimes against humanity and myself. That I really didn't believe in these things I was doin'. I changed.

SOURCE: Wallace Terry, *Bloods: An Oral History of the Vietnam War by Black Veterans* (New York: Ballantine, 1984), 243–263.

GAYLE SMITH

Gayle Smith was a nurse in a surgical unit in Vietnam in 1970–1971 and gave this interview a few years later.

I objected to the war and I got the idea into my head of going there to bring people back. I started thinking about it in 1966 and knew that I would eventually go when I felt I was prepared enough. . . .

Boy, I remember how they came in all torn up. It was incredible. The first time a medevac came in, I got right into it. I didn't have a lot of feeling at that time. It was later on that I began to have a lot of feeling about it, after I'd seen it over and over and over again. . . . I turned that pain into anger and hatred and placed it onto the Vietnamese. . . . I did not consider the Vietnamese to be people. They were human, but they weren't people. They weren't like us, so it was okay to kill them. It was okay to hate them. . . .

I would have dreams about putting a .45 to someone's head and see it blow away over and over again. And for a long time I swore that if the Vietnamese ever came to this country I'd kill them.

It was in a Vietnam veterans group that I realized that all my hatred for the Vietnamese and my wanting to kill them was really a reflection of all the pain that I had felt for seeing all those young men die and hurt. . . . I would stand there and look at them and think to myself, "You've just lost your leg for no reason at all." Or "You're going to die and it's for nothing." For nothing. I would never, never say that to them, but they knew it.

SOURCE: Albert Santoli, ed., *Everything We Had* (New York: Random House, 1981), 141–148.

ANALYZING THE EVIDENCE

➤ Why did these four young people end up in Vietnam?

➤ How would you describe their experiences there?

➤ How were they changed by the war? What do their reflections suggest about the war's impact on American society?

In June 1962 forty students from Big Ten and Ivy League universities met in Port Huron, Michigan, to found Students for a Democratic Society (SDS). Tom Hayden wrote a manifesto, the Port Huron Statement, which expressed their disillusionment with the consumer culture and the gulf between rich and poor. These students rejected Cold War foreign policy, including but not limited to the Vietnam conflict. The founders of SDS referred to their movement as the "New Left" to distinguish themselves from the "Old Left"— Communists and Socialists of the 1930s and 1940s. Consciously adopting the activist tactics pioneered by the civil rights movement, they turned to grassroots organizing in cities and on college campuses.

The Free Speech Movement. The first major student demonstrations erupted in the fall of 1964 at the University of California at Berkeley, after administrators banned political activity in Sproul Plaza, where student groups had traditionally distributed leaflets and recruited members. In protest, the major student organizations formed the Free Speech Movement (FSM) and organized a sit-in at the administration building. Some students had just returned from Freedom Summer in Mississippi, radicalized by their experience. Mario Savio spoke for many of them when he compared the conflict in Berkeley to the civil rights struggle in the South: "The same rights are at stake in both places—the right to participate as citizens in a democratic society and to struggle against the same enemy." Emboldened by the Berkeley movement, students across the nation were soon protesting their universities' academic policies and then, more passionately, the Vietnam War.

The Draft. A spur to student protest was a change in the military's Selective Service system, which in January 1966 abolished automatic student deferments. To avoid the draft, young men enlisted in the National Guard, or declared themselves conscientious objectors, or became draft dodgers. Some left the country, most often for Canada or Sweden. In public demonstrations, opponents of the war burned their draft cards, picketed induction centers, and on a few occasions broke into Selective Service offices and destroyed records.

As antiwar and draft protests multiplied, students realized that their universities were deeply implicated in the war effort. In some cases as much as 60 percent of a university's research budget came from government contracts. Protesters blocked recruiters from the Dow Chemical Company, the producer of napalm and Agent Orange. Arguing that universities should not train students for war, they demanded that the Reserve Officer Training Corps (ROTC) be removed from college campuses.

After 1967, nationwide student strikes, mass demonstrations, and other organized protests became commonplace. In October 1967 more than 100,000 antiwar demonstrators marched on Washington, D.C., as part of "Stop the Draft Week." The event culminated in a "siege of the Pentagon," in which protesters clashed with police and federal marshals. Hundreds of people were arrested and several demonstrators beaten. Lyndon Johnson, who had once dismissed antiwar protesters as "nervous Nellies," rebellious children, or Communist dupes,

Free Speech at Berkeley, 1964

Students at the University of California's Berkeley campus protested the administration's decision to ban political activity in the school plaza. Free speech demonstrators, many of them active in the civil rights movement, relied on tactics and arguments that they learned during that struggle. University of California at Berkeley, Bancroft Library.

Che Guevara

Vietnam and the World Freedom Struggle

*C*he Guevara was a middle-class, medically trained Argentinian who enlisted in Castro's Cuban Revolution and became a world icon of guerrilla resistance. In 1965 he left Cuba in order to foment revolutionary struggle in Africa and Latin America. Two years later he was captured in Bolivia and executed. Between his departure from Cuba and his death in Bolivia in 1967, he made only one public statement, which he titled "Vietnam and the World Freedom Struggle."

This is the painful reality: Vietnam, a nation representing the aspirations and the hopes for victory of the entire world of the disinherited, is tragically alone. . . .

And — what grandeur has been shown by this people! What stoicism and valor in this people! And what a lesson for the world their struggle holds!

It will be a long time before we know if President Johnson ever seriously thought of initiating some of the popular reforms necessary to soften the sharpness of the class contradictions that are appearing with explosive force and more and more frequently.

What is certain is that the improvements announced under the pompous label of the Great Society have gone down the drain in Vietnam.

The greatest of the imperialist powers feels in its own heart the drain caused by a poor, backward country;

and its fabulous economy feels the effect of the war. . . .

And for us, the exploited of the world, what should our role be in this? . . .

Our part, the responsibility of the exploited and backward areas of the world, is to eliminate the bases sustaining imperialism — our oppressed peoples, from whom capital, raw materials, technicians and cheap labor are extracted, and to whom new capital, means of domination, arms and all kinds of goods are exported, submerging us in absolute dependence.

The fundamental element of this strategic goal will be, then, the real liberation of the peoples, a liberation that will be obtained through armed struggle in the majority of cases, and which, in the Americas, will have almost unfailingly the property of becoming converted into a socialist revolution.

In focusing on the destruction of imperialism, it is necessary to identify its head, which is none other than the United States of North America. . . .

The adversary must not be underestimated; the North American soldier has technical ability and is backed by means of such magnitude as to make him formidable. He lacks the essential ideological motivation which his most hated rivals of today have to the highest degree — the Vietnamese soldiers. . . .

Over there, the imperialist troops encounter the discomforts of those accustomed to the standard of living which the North American nation boasts. They have to confront a hostile land, the insecurity of those who cannot move without feeling that they are walking on enemy territory; death for those who go outside of fortified redoubts; the permanent hostility of the entire population.

All this continues to provoke repercussions inside the United States; it is going to arouse a factor

that was attenuated in the days of the full vigor of imperialism — the class struggle inside its own territory.

SOURCE: Ernesto C. Guevara, *Che Guevara Speaks* (New York: Pathfinder Press, 1967), 144–159.

ANALYZING THE EVIDENCE

➤ Guevara was a Latin American. He had never been to Southeast Asia. So why was he interested in Vietnam?

➤ How does Guevara define the struggle going on in Vietnam? How does he describe the two warring sides? Can you see, on the basis of that description, why Guevera was confident the United States couldn't win the Vietnam war?

➤ Why would Guevara have bothered to speak about Johnson's Great Society program?

➤ Can you explain, based on this document, why Guevara was an inspirational figure to many student antiwar protesters?

now had to face the reality of large-scale public opposition to his policies.

> ➤ What difficulties did the United States face in fighting a war against North Vietnam and the Vietcong in South Vietnam?
>
> ➤ Why did President Johnson suffer a "credibility gap" over Vietnam?
>
> ➤ What was the student role in the antiwar movement? How can we explain students' willingness to protest the war?

Coming Apart

In the student protests, in the SDS, and in the Berkeley Free Speech Movement, more obviously was at stake than Vietnam. Indeed, antiwar protest merged into a variegated, broad-based attack on the status quo — "the Movement," to its participants — that not only challenged Cold War assumptions, but blasted America's liberal consensus.

The roots of this assault go back to the 1950s, back to when the Beats denigrated capitalism, teenagers defied their elders, and African American sit-ins protested racial injustice. By the mid-1960s this angry disaffection had broadened into a many-sided attack on mainstream America.

The Counterculture

While the New Left plotted against the political and economic "system," a growing number of young Americans embarked on a general revolution against authority and middle-class respectability. The "hippie" — attired in ragged blue jeans, tie-dyed T-shirts, beads, and army fatigues, with long, unkempt hair — symbolized the new counterculture.

Not surprisingly, given the importance of rock 'n' roll in the 1950s, popular music helped define the counterculture. Folk singer Pete Seeger set the tone for the era's political idealism with songs such as the antiwar ballad "Where Have All the Flowers Gone?" In 1963, the year of the Birmingham demonstrations and President Kennedy's assassination, Bob Dylan's "Blowin' in the Wind" reflected the impatience of people whose faith in America was wearing thin.

Other winds of change in popular music came from the Beatles, four working-class Brits who burst onto the American scene early in 1964. The Beatles' music, by turns lyrical and driving, was remarkably successful, spawning a commercial and cultural phenomenon called "Beatlemania." American youths' eager embrace of the Beatles deepened the generational divide between teenagers and their elders. The Beatles also helped to pave the way for the more rebellious, angrier music of other British groups, notably the Rolling Stones.

Drugs intertwined with music in the rituals of the youth culture. The recreational use of drugs — especially marijuana and the hallucinogenic popularly known as LSD or "acid" — was celebrated in popular music. San Francisco bands such as the Grateful Dead and Jefferson Airplane and musicians like guitarist Jimi Hendrix developed a musical style known as "acid rock," which was characterized by long, heavily amplified guitar solos accompanied by psychedelic lighting effects. In August 1969, 400,000 young people journeyed to Bethel, New York, to "get high" on music, drugs, and sex at the three-day Woodstock Music and Art Fair.

Jimi Hendrix at Woodstock

The three-day outdoor Woodstock concert in August 1969 was a defining moment in the rise of the counterculture. The event attracted 400,000 young people, who journeyed to Bethel, New York, for a weekend of music, drugs, and sex. Jimi Hendrix closed the show early Sunday morning with an electrifying version of "The Star-Spangled Banner." More overtly political than most counterculture music, Hendrix's rendition featured sound effects that seemed to evoke the violence of the Vietnam War. Michael Wadleigh, who directed the documentary *Woodstock*, called Hendrix's performance "his challenge to American foreign policy." Allan Koss/The Image Works.

For a brief time adherents of the counterculture believed a new age was dawning. They experimented in communal living and glorified uninhibited sexuality. In 1967 the "world's first Human Be-In" drew 20,000 people to Golden Gate Park in San Francisco. The Beat poet Allen Ginsberg "purified" the site with a Buddhist ritual, and the LSD advocate Timothy Leary, a former Harvard psychology teacher, urged the gathering to "turn on to the scene, tune in to what is happening, and drop out." That summer — dubbed the "Summer of Love" — San Francisco's Haight-Ashbury, New York's East Village, and Chicago's Uptown neighborhoods swelled with young dropouts, drifters, and teenage runaways dubbed "flower children." Their faith in instant love and peace quickly turned sour, however, as they suffered bad drug trips, sexually transmitted diseases, loneliness, and violence. Although many young people kept their distance, media cov-

erage made it seem as if all of American youth was rejecting the nation's social and cultural norms.

Beyond Civil Rights

Among young blacks, knocking the mainstream meant something else. It meant rejecting the established civil rights leadership, with its faith in the courts and legislative change. It meant an eye-for-an-eye, not Martin Luther King's nonviolence. It meant wondering why blacks wanted to be integrated with whites anyway. Above all, it expressed fury at the poverty of blacks and at white racism that was beyond the reach of civil rights laws.

Malcolm X. Black rage had expressed itself historically in demands for racial separation, espoused in the late nineteenth century by the Back-to-Africa movement and in the 1920s by Marcus Garvey (see

Malcolm X (1925–1965)

Malcolm X has an assistant hold up the picture of a fallen black as he addresses a Harlem rally on May 14, 1963, in support of civil rights demonstrations in Birmingham, Alabama. The photograph was not in fact related to the brutal police attack on Birmingham demonstrators, but it represented what Malcolm X considered to be the norm for how blacks were treated in America. From a Birmingham jail, Martin Luther King Jr. warned that if his appeal for racial justice went unheeded, African Americans would turn to "people who have lost faith in America ... and who have concluded that the white man is an incurable 'devil.'" He had Malcolm X in mind. © Bettmann/Corbis.

Chapter 23). In the 1960s the leading exponent of black separatism was the Nation of Islam, which fused a rejection of Christianity with a strong dose of self-improvement. Black Muslims, as they were known, adhered to a strict code of personal behavior, with the men always recognizable by their dark suits and white shirts, the women by their long dresses and head coverings. Black Muslims preached an apocalyptic brand of Islam, anticipating the day when Allah would banish the white "devils" and give the black nation justice. Although its full converts numbered only about 10,000, the Nation of Islam had a wide popular following in urban ghettoes.

The most charismatic Black Muslim was Malcolm X (the X stood for his African family name lost under slavery). A spellbinding speaker, Malcolm X preached a philosophy of militant protest and separatism, though he advocated violence only for self-defense. Hostile to the traditional civil rights organizations, he caustically referred to the 1963 March on Washington as the "Farce on Washington." In 1964, after a power struggle with the founder, Elijah Muhammad, Malcolm X broke with the Nation of Islam. While remaining a black nationalist, his anti-white views moderated, and he began to talk in terms of class struggle uniting poor whites and blacks. But he got no further. On February 21, 1965, Malcolm X was assassinated while delivering a speech in Harlem. Three Black Muslims were later convicted of his murder.

Black Power. A more secular brand of black nationalism emerged in 1966 when young black SNCC and CORE activists, following the lead of Stokely Carmichael, began to call for black self-reliance and racial pride under the banner of "Black Power." Amid growing distrust of whites, SNCC declared itself a blacks-only organization and ejected its white members. In the same year Huey Newton and Bobby Seale, two college students in Oakland, California, founded the Black Panthers, a militant self-defense organization dedicated to protecting blacks from police violence. The Panthers' organization quickly spread to other cities, where members undertook a wide range of community organizing projects. Their rhetoric, however, declared their affinity for Third World revolutionary movements and armed struggle.

Among the most significant legacies of Black Power was the assertion of racial pride. Rejecting white society, blacks wore African clothing and hairstyles and awakened interest in black history, art, and literature. By the 1970s many colleges and universities were offering programs in black studies.

Urban Riots. The rage expressed by Black Power boiled over, in inchoate form, in a wave of riots that struck the nation's cities. The first "long hot summer" began in July 1964 in New York City, when police shot a black criminal suspect in Harlem. Angry youths looted and rioted there for a week. Over the next four years, the volatile issue of police brutality set off riots in dozens of cities. In August 1965 the arrest of a young black motorist in the Watts section of Los Angeles sparked six days of rioting that left thirty-four dead. The riots of 1967 were the most serious, engulfing twenty-two cities in July and August. The most devastating outbreaks occurred in Newark and Detroit. Forty-three people were killed in Detroit alone, nearly all of them black, and $50 million worth of property was destroyed.

The Assassination of Martin Luther King Jr. Stirred by this turmoil, and by disappointment with his civil rights achievements, Martin Luther King began to confront the deep-seated problems of poverty and racism facing American blacks. He spoke out eloquently against the Vietnam War and planned a poor people's campaign to fight economic injustice and inequality. In support of that cause, he went to Memphis, Tennessee, to support a strike by predominantly black sanitation workers, and there, on April 4, 1968, he was assassinated. King's death set off a further round of urban rioting, with major violence breaking out in many cities.

Although King died unfulfilled, he had set in motion permanent, indeed revolutionary, changes in American race relations. He had helped end Jim Crow segregation, won federal legislation ensuring black Americans' most basic civil rights, and broke the white monopoly on political power in the South. And not least, his example inspired other oppressed groups in America to enter the struggle for equal rights.

César Chavez and the Chicano Movement. For Mexican Americans, the counterpart to Martin Luther King was César Chavez, although, in Chavez's case, the conversion to economic struggle came much earlier. He and Dolores Huerta had begun in the Community Service Organization, a California group founded in the 1950s to promote Mexican political participation and civil rights. Leaving that organization in 1962, Chavez concentrated on the agricultural region of Delano, California, and with Huerta, organized the United Farm Workers (UFW), a union for migrant workers. While Huerta, a brilliant organizer, was crucial

César Chavez

Mexican American labor leader César Chavez, seen here addressing a rally in Guadalupe, California, won national attention in 1965 during a strike of migrant farmworkers, most of them Mexican Americans, against California grape growers. Drawing on tactics from the civil rights movement, Chavez called for nonviolent action and effectively mobilized nationwide support for a boycott of nonunion table grapes. FPG/Getty Images.

to the movement, it was Chavez, with his deep spirituality and commitment to nonviolent protest, who became the symbol for what was popularly called *La Causa*. A 1965 grape pickers' strike led the UFW to call a nationwide boycott of table grapes, bringing Chavez huge publicity and backing from the AFL-CIO. In a bid for attention to the struggle, Chavez staged a hunger strike in 1968, which ended dramatically after twenty-eight days with Senator Robert F. Kennedy at his side to break the fast. Victory came in 1970 when California grape growers signed contracts recognizing the UFW.

On a parallel track, Mexican Americans had since the 1930s (see Chapter 24) actively worked to surmount the poverty, uncertain legal status, and language barriers that made political mobilization difficult. That situation began to change when the Mexican American Political Association (MAPA)

mobilized support for John F. Kennedy. Over the next four years, MAPA and other organizations worked successfully to elect Mexican American candidates such as Edward Roybal of California and Henry González of Texas to Congress.

Younger Mexican Americans grew impatient with MAPA, however. The barrios of Los Angeles and other western cities produced the militant Brown Berets, modeled on the Black Panthers (who wore black berets). Rejecting the assimilationist approach of their elders, 1,500 Mexican American students met in Denver in 1969 to hammer out a new political and cultural agenda. They proclaimed a new term, *Chicano*, to replace Mexican American, and later organized a new political party, La Raza Unida (The United Race), to promote Chicano interests and candidates. In California and other southwestern states, students staged demonstrations

Wounded Knee Revisited

In 1973 members of the American Indian Movement staged a seventy-one-day protest at Wounded Knee, South Dakota, site of the 1890 massacre of two hundred Sioux by U.S. soldiers (see Chapter 16). The takeover was sparked by the murder of a local Sioux by a group of whites but quickly expanded to include demands for basic reforms in federal Indian policy and tribal governance. © Bettmann/Corbis.

to press for bilingual education, the hiring of more Chicano teachers, and the creation of Chicano studies programs. By the 1970s dozens of such programs were offered at universities throughout the region.

The Native American Movement. American Indians also found a model in black struggles for equality. Numbering nearly 800,000 in the 1960s, they were exceedingly diverse, divided by language, tribal history, region, and degree of integration into American life. As a group, they shared a staggering unemployment rate (ten times the national average), the worst housing, the highest disease rates, and the least access to education of any group in the United States.

Since World War II, the National Congress of American Indians had lobbied for reform. In the 1960s the prevailing spirit of protest swept through Indian communities. Young militants, like their counterparts in the black civil rights movement, challenged the accommodationist approach of their elders. Proposing a new name for themselves — Native Americans — they embraced the concept of "Red Power." Beginning in 1968 with the formation of the militant American Indian Movement (AIM), young Native Americans staged escalating protests, occupying the deserted federal penitentiary on Alcatraz Island in San Francisco Bay and sitting-in at the headquarters of the hated Federal Bureau of Indian Affairs in Washington, D.C. In February 1973, a siege at Wounded Knee, South Dakota, the site of the infamous 1890 massacre of the Sioux, ended in a gun battle with the FBI.

Although upsetting to many white onlookers, Native American protest did spur government action on tribal issues.

➤ What are the elements in the counterculture of the 1960s?

➤ How do you account for the Black Power movement?

➤ How do you explain the spillover of the black civil rights struggle into the Mexican American and Native American communities?

1968: A Year of Shocks

By 1968, a sense of crisis gripped the country. Riots in the cities, campus unrest, and a nose-thumbing counterculture seemed on the verge of tearing America apart. What crystallized the crisis was the fact that 1968 was an election year.

The Politics of Vietnam

President Johnson had gambled in 1965 on a quick victory, before the political cost of escalation at home came due. But there was no quick victory. North Vietnamese and Vietcong forces fought on, the South Vietnamese government enjoyed little popular support, and American casualties mounted. By early 1968, the death rate reached several hundred a week. Johnson and his generals kept insisting that there was "light at the end of the tunnel." Facts on the ground showed otherwise.

The Tet Offensive. On January 30, 1968, the Vietcong unleashed a massive, well-coordinated assault in South Vietnam. Timed to coincide with Tet, the lunar Vietnamese new year holiday, the offensive struck thirty-six of the forty-four provincial capitals and five of the six major cities, including Saigon, where Vietcong nearly overran the supposedly impregnable U.S. embassy. In strictly military terms, the Tet offensive was a failure, with very heavy Vietcong losses and the South Vietnamese government still intact. But psychologically, the effect was devastating. Television brought into American homes the shocking images — the American embassy under siege, with a pistol-wielding staff member peering warily from a window, the Saigon police chief placing a pistol to the head of a Vietcong suspect and, live on TV, executing him.

The Tet offensive made a mockery of official pronouncements that the United States was winning the war. Just before, a Gallup poll found that 56 percent of Americans considered themselves "hawks" (supporters of the war), while only 28 percent identified with the "doves" (war opponents). Three months later doves outnumbered hawks 42 to 41 percent. Without embracing the peace movement, many Americans simply concluded that the war was unwinnable (see Reading American Pictures, "War and Its Aftermath: Images of the Vietnam Conflict, 1968 and 1982," p. 890).

So did a growing faction within the Democratic Party. Even before Tet, Senator Eugene J. McCarthy of Minnesota had entered the Democratic primaries as an antiwar candidate. A core of student activists "went clean for Gene" by cutting their hair and putting away their jeans. President Johnson won the early New Hampshire primary, but McCarthy received a stunning 42.2 percent of the vote. To make matters worse for the president, McCarthy's showing propelled Senator Robert Kennedy, a far more formidable opponent, into the race.

Johnson realized that his political support was evaporating. At the end of an otherwise routine televised address on March 31, he stunned the nation by announcing that he would not seek reelection. He also called a partial halt to the bombing and vowed to devote his remaining months in office to the search for peace. On May 10, 1968, preliminary peace talks between the United States and North Vietnam opened in Paris.

Political Turmoil. Just four days after Johnson's withdrawal from the presidential race, Martin Luther King Jr. was assassinated in Memphis. The ensuing riots in cities across the country left forty-three people dead. Soon afterward, students protesting Columbia University's plans for expanding into a neighboring ghetto occupied several campus buildings. The brutal response of the New York City police helped to radicalize even more students.

Then came the final tragedy of the year. On June 5, 1968, as he celebrated his victory in the California primary over Eugene McCarthy, Robert Kennedy was shot dead by a young Palestinian. Robert Kennedy's assassination was a calamity for the Democratic Party because only he had seemed able to surmount the party's Vietnam problem. In his brief but dramatic campaign, Kennedy had reached beyond the antiwar elements to traditional members of the New Deal coalition, including blue-collar workers, who were becoming susceptible to patriotic appeals from the right.

With Kennedy gone, the energy went out of the antiwar Democrats. McCarthy's campaign limped along, while Senator George S. McGovern of South Dakota entered the Democratic race in an effort to keep the Kennedy forces together. Meanwhile, Vice President Hubert H. Humphrey lined up pledges from traditional Democratic constituencies — unions, urban machines, and state political organizations. Democrats found themselves on the verge of nominating not an antiwar candidate but a public figure closely associated with Johnson's war policies.

The Siege of Chicago. At the August Democratic convention, the political divisions generated by the war consumed the party. Most of the drama occurred not in the convention hall but outside on the streets of Chicago. Thousands of protesters descended on the city. The most visible group, led by Jerry Rubin and Abbie Hoffman, a remarkable pair of troublemakers, claimed to represent the Youth International Party. To mock those inside the convention hall, these "Yippies" nominated a pig, Pigasus, for president. Their stunts, geared for maximum media exposure, diverted attention from the more serious, far more numerous activists who had come to Chicago to protest the war.

Richard J. Daley, the Democratic mayor, increasingly angry as protesters disrupted his convention, ordered the police to break up the demonstrations. Several nights of skirmishes between protesters and police culminated on the evening of the nominations. In what an official report later described as a "police riot," police officers attacked protesters with Mace, tear gas, and clubs. As the nominating speeches proceeded, television networks broadcast films of the riot, cementing a popular impression of the Democrats as the party of disorder. Inside the hall the Democrats dispiritedly nominated Hubert

War and Its Aftermath:
Images of the Vietnam Conflict, 1968 and 1982

America's Longest War. Copyright Tim Page.

The Vietnam Veterans Memorial. Peter Marlow / Magnum Photos, Inc.

The Vietnam War ended in 1975, but it remains a painful and contested event in the American memory. Images of both combat and remembrance continue to shape our understanding not only of the conflict itself, but also of the meaning of U.S. participation in wars abroad today. The first photograph shows the brutal aftermath of a combat operation by U.S. soldiers in Vietnam during the war. The second photo captures a group of U.S. veterans embracing in front of the Vietnam Veterans' Memorial in Washington, D.C. Dedicated in 1982, the monument, designed by architect Maya Ling, contains the names of over 58,000 U.S. servicemen and -women killed in the war.

ANALYZING THE EVIDENCE

➤ What does the first photo, "America's Longest War," reveal about how the war was fought and experienced by ordinary soldiers?

➤ Given the political climate of the late 1960s, what effect on their feelings about the war do you think this image of carnage and others like it had on those who viewed it?

➤ Why are the veterans embracing in front of the memorial? What is the significance of the clothing and items they are wearing?

➤ Traditionally, war memorials featured statues of combatants or generals in heroic poses; this one has only the names of those killed in combat. Yet the Vietnam monument is widely seen as being emotionally evocative. What does this suggest about the American view of the Vietnam War? See **www.nps.gov/vive** for more information about the memorial.

H. Humphrey, who chose Senator Edmund S. Muskie of Maine as his running mate. The delegates approved a middle-of-the-road platform that endorsed continued fighting in Vietnam while urging a diplomatic solution to the conflict.

Backlash

Political realignments are infrequent in American history. The last one had been 1932, when many Republicans, despairing over the Great Depression, had switched sides and voted for FDR. The year 1968 was another such pivotal moment. Consider a forty-seven-year-old machinist's wife from Dayton, Ohio, described by the social scientists Ben J. Wattenberg and Richard Scammon in their book, *The Real Majority* (1970):

> That lady in Dayton is afraid to walk the streets alone at night . . . she has a mixed view about blacks and civil rights because she lived in a neighborhood that became all black . . . her brother-in-law is a policeman [and] she is deeply distressed that her son is going to a community junior college where LSD was found on campus.

Growing up in the Great Depression, she was likely a great admirer of FDR, maybe with his picture on her living room wall. Such working-class people were the heart and soul of the New Deal democracy. But now, in the sour aftermath of the Chicago convention, their votes were up for grabs. And as always, politicians with their noses to the wind were eager to oblige.

Governor George C. Wallace of Alabama, a third-party candidate, skillfully exploited working-class anxieties over student protests and urban riots. He called for "law and order" in the streets and denounced welfare mothers who, thanks to Johnson's Great Society, were "breeding children as a cash crop." Wallace skewered "overeducated, ivory-towered folks with pointed heads looking down their noses at us." Although no longer overtly a racist, Wallace traded on his fame as the segregationist governor who had stood up to the federal government during the Selma crisis of 1965. His hope was that, by carrying the South, he could deny the major parties an electoral majority and force the 1968 election into the House of Representatives. That strategy failed, and Wallace's political star faded after a near-fatal shooting in 1972 left him paralyzed, but he had defined hot-button issues — liberal elitism, welfare queens, law and order — of immense

utility to the next generation of mainstream conservatives.

The Republican candidate, Richard Nixon, offered a more sophisticated version of Wallace's populism. After losing the presidential campaign in 1960, and after losing again in the California gubernatorial race in 1962, Nixon had seemed finished, but he engineered an amazing political comeback and in 1968 won the Republican presidential nomination. As part of what his advisers called the "southern strategy," he chose Spiro Agnew, the conservative governor of Maryland, as his running mate. Nixon hoped to attract southern voters still smarting over Democratic civil rights legislation. Nationally, Nixon appealed to people who came to be known as the "silent majority." He pledged to represent the "quiet voice" of the "great majority of Americans, the forgotten Americans, the nonshouters, the nondemonstrators."

Despite the Democratic debacle in Chicago, the election actually proved to be close. In the last weeks of the campaign, Humphrey rallied by disassociating himself from Johnson's war policies. When on October 31 President Johnson announced a complete halt to the bombing of North Vietnam, Nixon countered by intimating that he had his own plan to end the war (in reality no such plan existed). On election day Nixon received 43.4 percent of the vote to Humphrey's 42.7 percent, defeating him by a scant 500,000 votes out of the 73 million that were cast (Map 28.7). Wallace finished with 13.5 percent of the popular vote.

The closeness of the outcome masked the fact that 1968 really was a pivotal election. Humphrey received almost 12 million fewer votes than had Johnson in 1964. The South, except for Texas, abandoned the Democratic Party, never to return. Nixon's "southern strategy" had worked. In the North, he and Wallace made significant inroads among traditionally Democratic voters. And while party divisions over Vietnam had been briefly patched up, the underlying ideological differences — signified by the rivalry of Hubert Humphrey and George McGovern — persisted, with corrosive effect on the party's effectiveness. New Deal Democrats would never again have the unity of purpose that had served them for thirty years. Assaulted from both left and right, the liberal consensus was coming apart.

➤ What were the critical events of 1968 that have led historians to describe it as a "watershed year"?

➤ Why did the Democrats lose their grip as the majority party in the late 1960s?

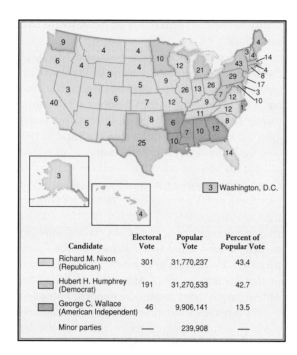

MAP 28.7   Presidential Election of 1968

With Lyndon B. Johnson's surprise withdrawal and the assassination of the party's most charismatic contender, Robert Kennedy, the Democrats faced the election of 1968 in disarray. Governor George Wallace of Alabama, who left the Democrats to run as a third-party candidate, campaigned on the backlash against the civil rights movement. As late as mid-September Wallace held the support of 21 percent of the voters. But in November he received only 13.5 percent of the vote, winning five southern states. Republican Richard M. Nixon, who like Wallace emphasized "law and order" in his campaign, defeated Hubert H. Humphrey with only 43.4 percent of the popular vote, but it was now clear, given that Wallace's southern support would otherwise have gone to Nixon, that the South had shifted decisively to the Republican side.

SUMMARY

In this chapter, we saw how the liberal consensus — agreement about a New Deal approach to the nation's social and economic ills — peaked in the mid-1960s and then, under the combined pressure of the Vietnam War and cultural conflict, flamed out. John F. Kennedy opened the politics of expectation in the 1960 campaign, although the domestic accomplishments of the New Frontier were limited. Following John Kennedy's assassination in 1963, Lyndon Johnson advanced the most ambitious liberal reform program since the New Deal, securing not only civil rights legislation, but an array of programs in education, medical care, transportation, and, above all, his War on Poverty. But the Great Society fell short of its promise as Johnson escalated the American involvement in Vietnam.

The war bitterly divided Americans. Galvanized by the carnage of war and the draft, the antiwar movement spread rapidly among young people. The spirit of rebellion spilled beyond the antiwar movement. The New Left challenged the corporate dominance of society, while the more apolitical counterculture preached personal liberation through sex, drugs, music, and spirituality. Moving beyond civil rights, the Black Power movement encouraged racial pride and assertiveness, serving also as a model for Mexican Americans and Native Americans.

In 1968, the nation was rocked by the assassinations of Martin Luther King and Robert F. Kennedy and a wave of urban riots, fueling a growing popular desire for law and order. Adding to the national disquiet was a Democratic convention that summer, divided by the Vietnam war and under siege by rioting in the streets. A new wave of conservatism took hold of the country, contributing to the resurgence of the Republican Party under Richard Nixon.

Connections: Diplomacy and Politics

In the Part Six opening essay, we remark that "the interaction of domestic and global — the links between liberalism and the Cold War — was especially clear [in the 1960s] because it was Vietnam that, more than anything else, undermined the Great Society and the liberal consensus." In Chapter 26, we showed how that link between liberalism and the Cold War was forged during the Truman and Eisenhower administrations. Unlike in earlier periods, anti-Communism in its McCarthyite phase was not regarded as an attack on liberal reform. In the wake of Vietnam this changed, and prosecution of the Cold War increasingly became an attack on the liberal consensus, a development that, as we shall see in Chapter 30, culminated under the leadership of Ronald Reagan in the 1980s.

CHAPTER REVIEW QUESTIONS

➤ How do you explain the preeminence of civil rights in the politics of the 1960s?

➤ What are the differences between Kennedy's New Frontier and Johnson's Great Society?

➤ Why is the United States' involvement in the Vietnam War so often called a "quagmire"?

TIMELINE

1960	John F. Kennedy elected president
1961	Peace Corps established
	Bay of Pigs invasion
	Berlin Wall erected
1962	Cuban missile crisis
	Students for a Democratic Society (SDS) founded
	César Chavez and Dolores Huerta organize the United Farm Workers (UFW)
1963	Betty Friedan's *The Feminine Mystique*
	Civil rights protest in Birmingham, Alabama
	March on Washington
	Nuclear test-ban treaty
	John F. Kennedy assassinated; Lyndon B. Johnson assumes presidency
1964	Freedom Summer; Civil Rights Act
	Economic Opportunity Act inaugurates War on Poverty
	Free Speech Movement at Berkeley
	Gulf of Tonkin Resolution authorizes military action in Vietnam
1965	Immigration Act abolishes national quota system
	Voting Rights Act
	Medicare and Medicaid programs established
	Malcolm X assassinated
	Operation Rolling Thunder escalates bombing campaign
	First U.S. combat troops arrive in Vietnam
	Race riot in Watts district of Los Angeles
1966	Stokely Carmichael proclaims black power
1967	Hippie counterculture's "Summer of Love"
	100,000 march in antiwar protest in Washington, D.C.
1968	Tet offensive dashes American hopes of victory
	Martin Luther King Jr. and Robert F. Kennedy assassinated
	Riot at Democratic National Convention in Chicago
	Richard Nixon elected president
	American Indian Movement (AIM) organized

FOR FURTHER EXPLORATION

Good starting points for understanding Kennedy's presidency are W. J. Rorabaugh, *Kennedy and the Promise of the Sixties* (2002), and David Halberstam, *The Best and the Brightest* (1972). Arthur M. Schlesinger Jr., *A Thousand Days* (1965), offers a detailed insider's account. For Lyndon Johnson, see Robert Dallek, *Flawed Giant* (1998).

Henry Hampton and Steve Fayer's oral history, *Voices of Freedom* (1991), and Harvard Sitkoff, *The Struggle for Black Equality*, 2nd ed. (1993), offer engaging accounts of the civil rights movement. On Martin Luther King Jr., see Taylor Branch's three-part biography, *Parting the Waters: 1954–1963* (1988), *Pillar of Fire: 1963–1965* (1998), and *At Canaan's Edge: 1965–1968* (2005). On Vietnam, the basic history is George Herring, *America's Longest War: The United States and Vietnam* (1986). Vivid accounts of dissent in the 1960s are Todd Gitlin, *The Sixties: Years of Hope, Days of Rage* (1987), and Maurice Isserman and Michael Kazin, *America Divided: The Civil War of the 1960s* (1999).

The period is unusually rich in compelling primary accounts. *Takin' It to the Streets* (1995), edited by Alexander Bloom and Wini Breines, offers an impressive array of documents that encompass the war, counterculture, civil rights, feminism, gay liberation, and other issues. Henry Hampton and Steve Fayer's oral history, *Voices of Freedom* (1991), and *The Autobiography of Malcolm X* (1965), cowritten with Alex Haley, provide insight into black struggle. Memoirs of Vietnam are numerous. Secretary of Defense Robert McNamara offers an insider's view and belated apologia in his *In Retrospect* (1995). Ron Kovic's *Born on the Fourth of July* (1976) is one soldier's powerful account of the war experience and its aftermath.

The John F. Kennedy Library and Museum's site at **www.jfklibrary.org** provides a large collection of records from Kennedy's presidency, including transcripts and recordings of JFK's speeches, a database of his executive orders, and a number of other resources. Civil Rights in Mississippi Digital Archive, at **www.lib.usm.edu/~spcol/crda/oh/index.html**, offers 150 oral histories relating to the civil rights movement in Mississippi. Audio clips are also included, as are short biographies, photographs, newsletters, FBI documents, and arrest records. A useful Vietnam site that includes state papers and official correspondence from 1941 to the fall of Saigon in 1975 is at **www.mtholyoke.edu/acad/intrel/vietnam.htm**.

TEST YOUR KNOWLEDGE

To assess your command of the material in this chapter, see the Online Study Guide at **bedfordstmartins.com/henretta**.

For Web sites, images, and documents related to topics and places in this chapter, visit **bedfordstmartins.com/makehistory**.

29

The 1970s: Toward a Conservative America

"THE UNITED STATES STEEL CORPORATION announced yesterday that it was closing 14 plants and mills in 8 states. About 13,000 production and white-collar workers will lose their jobs." "Weyerhaeuser Co. may trim about 1,000 salaried employees from its 11,000 member workforce over the next year." "Philadelphia: Food Fair Inc. plans to close 89 supermarkets in New York and Connecticut." Imagine a citizen of the 1950s emerging from a time capsule into the 1970s. She is bewildered by these gloomy newspaper headlines. What happened to America's vaunted economic supremacy? Equally bewildering is the sight of the all-powerful United States withdrawing from Vietnam, defeated by a third-tier country this citizen has probably never heard of. And she is utterly stunned, as one whose notion of an American president is Dwight D. Eisenhower, to be told that the current president, charged with obstruction of justice, has resigned in disgrace and left the White House.

Yet it's not all bad news. Who would have imagined Americans, in a time of joblessness and runaway inflation, mounting robust consumer and environmental movements? Yet that's what happened in the 1970s. Or the struggle for civil rights, far from pausing after the strenuous 1960s, intensifying and, in the case of women's and gay rights, breaking

◀ **No Gas**

During the energy crisis of 1973, American motorists faced widespread gasoline shortages for the first time since World War II. Although gas was not rationed, gas stations were closed on Sundays, and some communities instituted further restrictions such as creating systems by which motorists with license plates ending in even numbers could purchase gas on certain days, with alternate days being reserved for odd numbers. Tom Ebenhoh/Black Star/Stockphoto.com.

new ground? Or a grassroots conservative movement, rising up in the millions in defense of traditional values?

If the historian is hard put making sense of the 1970s, it's because these crosscurrents suggest a country in the throes of change. But with Ronald Reagan's election in 1980, Americans better understood what was happening. They were leaving the liberal America behind and entering an age of political conservatism.

The Nixon Years

Richard Nixon was a master of the subtle art of politics. In the 1968 campaign his "southern strategy" and appeal to the "silent majority" had worked wonders at undermining the New Deal coalition. But Nixon was not, in fact, prepared to offer a genuine alternative. And insofar as he tried, he came up against a Democrat-controlled Congress — itself a stubborn legacy of the liberal age. Like Kennedy, moreover, Nixon much preferred foreign affairs. But here, too, while more adept a strategist, he was enmeshed by his inheritance of Vietnam. So we have to put Nixon down as a transitional figure — with one foot in the liberal past, the other in the conservative future — except in one respect. His departure was not transitional. He left with a big bang.

Nixon's Domestic Agenda

As a Republican candidate, it was incumbent on Nixon to run on an antigovernment platform. He called his approach the "New Federalism," vowing to "reverse the flow of power and resources from the states and communities to Washington and start power and resources flowing back . . . to the people." Nixon's particular take on this pledge was his revenue-sharing program, which distributed a portion of federal tax revenues to the states as block grants to be spent as state officials saw fit — an approach that became a fixture on the Republican agenda. Nixon also scaled back government programs that had grown dramatically during the Johnson administration. War on Poverty programs were reduced and the Office of Economic Opportunity entirely dismantled in 1971. Nixon also refused to spend billions of dollars appropriated by Congress for urban renewal, pollution control, and other environmental initiatives, and vetoed a 1971 bill to establish a comprehensive national child-care system on the grounds that such "communal approaches to child rearing" endangered the American family.

Yet Nixon could be imaginative, even daring, when it came to social welfare. He was much influenced by a key White House adviser, Daniel Moynihan, a Democrat and an independent-minded expert on urban affairs. In 1969 Nixon proposed a Family Assistance Plan, which would guarantee a family of four an income of $1,600 a year, plus $600 in food stamps. The appeal of this proposal lay in its simplicity: It would eliminate multiple layers of bureaucracy and pare down the nation's jerry-built welfare system. Attacked in the Senate both by conservatives and liberals, however, Nixon's plan failed. Welfare reform was postponed for another day. And so was national health insurance, another of Nixon's failed initiatives, in which he proposed a public/private system that would guarantee universal coverage.

No enemy of the major **entitlement programs**, Nixon approved generous advances in Medicare, Medicaid, and Social Security. And his administration expanded the regulatory apparatus of the modern state. New government agencies — the Environmental Protection Agency (EPA) in 1970, the Occupational Safety and Health Administration (OSHA), and the Consumer Products Safety Commission in 1972 — brought the federal government deep into areas hitherto only lightly regulated or not regulated at all.

Nixon's mixed record reflected the political crosscurrents of his time. His conservative base pushed in one direction; the Democratic Congress pushed in another. Consumer and environmental protections loomed large for the middle class. Social Security and Medicare mattered to working-class voters he was appealing to. But Nixon was himself not a laissez-faire conservative, and — what especially distinguished him — he had a zest for experimenting with the mechanics of government.

Détente

Richard Nixon regarded himself a "realist" in foreign affairs. That meant, above all, advancing the national interest. Everything else — commitments to allies, extending democracy abroad, championing human rights — came second, if that. Nixon's realism was fervently seconded by his national security adviser, Henry Kissinger, although Kissinger had arrived at Nixon's view by a more scholarly route. As a Harvard professor, he had closely studied the nineteenth-century diplomat Metternich, who at the Vienna Congress of 1815 crafted a balance-of-power system that stabilized Europe for an entire century.

Conducting foreign affairs Metternich's way, however, required a degree of secrecy that was antithetical to America's constitutional system. Nixon and Kissinger did the best they could. They bypassed Congress, cut out the State Department (including the secretary of state, William Rogers), and established "back channels" to agencies whose expertise they needed. It was a dangerous game, but for a time, a game they played successfully. Nixon and Kissinger were preparing to take advantage of international conditions ripe for change.

For one thing, all the major players faced significant internal unrest. It was not only the United States that was rocked by student protesters. Street rioting almost brought down the French government in May 1968. German universities were hotbeds of protest. On the Communist side, it had taken Russian tanks to put down a reformist challenge — the "Prague Spring" — in Czechoslovakia. But tanks only put down people; they couldn't put down dissident ideas, which seeped even into the Soviet Union. And in China, Mao Zedong's Cultural Revolution had gotten out of hand, with young Red Guards turning on the regime. A shared sense of internal fragility made all the major powers receptive to an easing of international tensions.

Ultimately of greater importance, however, was an upheaval in the original arrangement of the Cold War. The notion of a bipolar world no longer held. Once the Cold War stalemated around 1950, neither superpower found it possible to keep its side in line. In America's case, the most difficult partner was France, which under the imperious Charles de Gaulle, thumbed its nose at the United States and walked away from NATO. That, however, was nothing compared to Soviet relations with China, which by 1969 had deteriorated from eternal friendship into outright border warfare, with the possibility of a nuclear exchange not excluded.

Nixon saw his chance. In 1971 he sent Kissinger secretly to Beijing (Peking) to explore an accommodation. Mao was actually thinking along the same lines. So an arrangement was not difficult to arrive at. The United States would back away from the Chinese Nationalists on Taiwan, permit China's admission to the United Nations (with a permanent seat on the Security Council), and eventually grant recognition (in 1978). In February 1972, President Nixon arrived in Beijing in a blaze of publicity to ratify the deal. This was the man who had clawed his

Nixon in China

When President Nixon arrived in China in February 1972 to ratify détente with Mao Zedong, a required part of the visit was a tour of the Great Wall. In this photograph, Mao's Vice Premier Li Hsien-nien is on the president's right, Secretary of State William Rogers on his left.
@ Bettmann/Corbis.

way into prominence by railing against the Democrats for "losing" China and hounding Alger Hiss into prison. Nixon's credentials as an anti-Communist were impeccable. That was why he felt free to come to Beijing, he remarked genially to Mao. "Those on the right can do what those on the left only talk about." Mao responded: "I like rightists."

Nixon then turned to the Soviet Union. He had already reached a secret understanding with Leonid Brezhnev, the Soviet premier, about Cuban issues left hanging after the missile crisis of 1962. In exchange for an American promise not to invade, the Soviets agreed to dismantle a submarine base and withhold offensive missiles from Castro. Three months after the Beijing summit, Nixon journeyed in another blaze of publicity to Moscow to sign the first Strategic Arms Limitations Treaty (SALT I) limiting the production and deployment of intercontinental ballistic missiles (ICBMs) and antiballistic missile systems (ABMs). SALT I, while technically modest, was intended only as a first step toward comprehensive arms limitation.

The summits in Beijing and Moscow inaugurated what came to be known as **détente** (in French: "relaxation of tensions"). Although the agreements themselves were quite limited, and rocky times lay ahead, the fact was the Cold War had reached a turning point. Nixon had parlayed a strategic advantage—the dangerous rift in the Communist world—into a new tripartite balance of power. The world had become a less dangerous place. And Nixon hoped for a dividend over Vietnam.

Nixon's War

Vietnam became an American project in the 1950s on the assumption that containing Communism was a global struggle, East against West, with Vietnam on the front line. The concept of a bipolar world, already outmoded in Lyndon Johnson's time, was utterly refuted by Richard Nixon's embrace of détente. Yet, when it came to Vietnam, Nixon picked up where Johnson had left off. Abandoning Vietnam, Nixon insisted, would damage America's "credibility" and make it seem "a pitiful, helpless giant." And, like Johnson, Nixon had himself to consider. He was not going to be the first American president to lose a war. Nixon wanted peace, but only "peace with honor."

The North Vietnamese were not about to oblige him. The only outcome acceptable to them was a unified Vietnam under their control. What remained negotiable were the details, the terms of surrender, and that, plus the wiliness of the North Vietnamese negotiators, enabled the Paris talks

begun by Johnson to continue, intermittently. But on the essentials, North Vietnam was immovable. So Nixon fashioned a two-pronged response.

To damp down criticism at home, he began withdrawing American troops while delegating the ground fighting to the South Vietnamese. Under this new policy of "Vietnamization," American troop levels dropped from 543,000 in 1968, to 334,000 in 1971, to barely 24,000 by early 1973. American casualties, and the political liabilities they entailed, dropped correspondingly. But the killing in Vietnam continued. As the U.S. ambassador to Vietnam, Ellsworth Bunker, noted cynically, it was just a matter of changing "the color of the bodies."

The companion policy called for an intensified bombing campaign, concealed from the war-weary American public. To step up the pressure, Nixon in March 1969 ordered secret air attacks on neutral Cambodia, through whose territory the North Vietnamese had been moving supplies and reinforcements. The secret war on Cambodia culminated on April 30, 1970, in an "incursion" into Cambodia to destroy enemy havens there. In late 1971, as American troops withdrew from the region, Communist forces infiltrated back in and stepped up their attacks. The next spring North Vietnamese forces launched a major offensive against South Vietnam. In April, as the fighting intensified, Nixon ordered B-52 bombing raids against North Vietnam, and a month later he approved the mining of North Vietnamese ports, something Johnson had never dared do. Nixon had a freer hand because, in the "spirit" of détente, China no longer threatened to intervene. Nor was Brezhnev deterred from welcoming Nixon in May 1972 at the height of the B-52 bombing onslaught (causing some Soviet casualties). The North Vietnamese might have felt more isolated, but supplies from China and the USSR continued, and they fought on.

At home, Nixon's war exacted a huge toll. Far from abating, the antiwar movement intensified. On November 16, 1969, Mobilization Day brought a record half a million protesters to Washington. A secret war, moreover, could be kept secret only for so long. When news of the invasion of Cambodia came out, American campuses exploded in outrage and, for the first time, students died. On May 4, 1970, at Kent State University in Ohio, panicky National Guardsmen fired into an antiwar rally, killing four students and wounding eleven. At Jackson State College in Mississippi, Guardsmen stormed a dormitory, killing two black students. More than 450 colleges closed in protest; across the country the spring semester was essentially canceled.

Pro-War Rally

Under a sea of American flags, construction workers in New York City march in support of the Vietnam War. Tens of thousands of them wearing "hard hats" jammed Broadway for four blocks opposite City Hall, and the overflow crammed the side streets. Working-class patriotism became a main source of support for Nixon's war. Paul Fusco/Magnum Photos, Inc.

The Vietnam poison infected even the military. In November 1969, the story of the My Lai Massacre broke, revealing the slaughter of 350 Vietnamese villagers by U.S. troops in retaliation for earlier casualties they had taken. The young lieutenant in command, William Calley, was court-martialed, sentenced to life imprisonment, then released to his barracks at Nixon's order, and eventually paroled. As the war dragged on, morale sank. Troops refused to go into combat; thousands deserted or turned to drugs. Many sewed peace symbols on their uniforms. In the heat of battle, overbearing junior officers were sometimes "fragged" — killed or wounded by grenades of their own soldiers. At home, a group called Vietnam Veterans against the War turned in their combat medals at demonstrations outside the U.S. Capitol.

Despite everything, Nixon persevered, hunkering down in the White House, castigating student protesters as "bums," and rallying a potent backlash against them. "Hardhat" became a patriotic symbol after New York construction workers beat demonstrators at a peace rally in May 1970. Slowly, Vietnamization eroded the antiwar opposition. With the army's manpower needs reduced, the draft was cut back (and ended entirely in 1973), deflating the ardor of many antiwar students. And militant groups, like the SDS, splintered and became ineffective, while the SDS's violent offshoot, the Weathermen, were arrested or driven underground. In the end, Nixon outlasted his critics. What he couldn't outlast was North Vietnam.

With the 1972 election approaching, Nixon sent Henry Kissinger back to the Paris peace talks. In a key concession, Kissinger accepted the continued

The Fall of Saigon

After the 1973 U.S. withdrawal from Vietnam, the South Vietnamese government lasted another two years. In March 1975 the North Vietnamese forces launched a final offensive and by April they had surrounded the capital of Saigon. Here, panicked Vietnamese seek sanctuary at the U.S. embassy compound. Nik Wheeler/Sipa Press.

presence of North Vietnamese troops in South Vietnam. North Vietnam then agreed to an interim arrangement whereby the Saigon government would stay in power while a tripartite commission arranged elections and a final settlement. American prisoners of war would be returned, and the remaining U.S. troops withdrawn. With Kissinger's announcement that "peace is at hand," Nixon got the election lift he wanted, but the agreement was then sabotaged by General Nguyen Van Thieu, the South Vietnamese president. So Nixon, in one final spasm of blood-letting, unleashed the two-week "Christmas bombing," the most savage of the entire war. On January 27, 1973, the two sides signed the Paris Peace Accords, essentially restating the cease-fire agreement of the previous October. The United States might have achieved that agreement four years earlier had it been willing to accept North Vietnamese troops in the South.

Nixon hoped that, with massive U.S. aid, the Thieu regime might survive. But Congress was in revolt. It refused appropriations for bombing Cam-

bodia after August 15, 1973, and gradually cut back aid to South Vietnam. In March 1975 North Vietnamese forces launched a final offensive. On television, horrified American viewers watched as South Vietnamese officials and soldiers battled American embassy personnel to board the last helicopters out of Saigon. On April 29, 1975, Vietnam was reunited. Saigon was renamed Ho Chi Minh City, after the founding father of the Communist regime.

Did this sad outcome matter? Yes, certainly, for America's Vietnamese allies, who lost jobs and property, spent years in "re-education" camps, or fled the country. Yes, for next-door Cambodia, where the maniac Khmer Rouge took over, murdered 1.7 million people, and drove the country nearly back to the Stone Age. For the United States, yes, for the wasted lives (58,000 dead, 300,000 wounded), the $150 billion spent, the slow-to-heal internal wounds, the lost confidence in America's political leaders. But in geopolitical terms? Not really. Defeat in South Vietnam did not mean, as successive American administrations had feared, victory for the Communist side because there no longer was a Communist "side." The Hanoi regime called itself Communist, but never intended to be anybody's satellite, least of all China's, an ancient enemy. (Within a few years the two countries fell to fighting over disputed borders.) Today, after twenty years of embargo, America's relations with the People's Republic of Vietnam are normal, with diplomatic recognition granted in 1995. That event would hardly be worth mentioning but for the fact that it is a postscript to America's most disastrous military adventure of the twentieth century.

The 1972 Election

The Democrats had fallen into disarray after 1968. Swept up by reform enthusiasms, followers of George McGovern took over the party, adopting new rules intended to encourage grassroots participation and assure that women, blacks, and young people held delegate seats "in reasonable relation to their presence in the population." Benefiting from these guidelines, McGovern's army of antiwar activists blitzed the precinct-level caucuses, winning delegate commitments far beyond McGovern's actual party support. Fresh faces filled the 1972 convention—38 percent women, 15 percent black, 23 percent under thirty (compared to 2.6 percent in 1968)—bursting with enthusiasm, but mostly innocent of national politics. In the past, an alliance of urban machines, labor unions, and ethnic groups—the heart of the New Deal coalition—would almost certainly have rejected an upstart candidate like McGovern. But few of the party faithful qualified as delegates under the changed rules. The crowning insult came when the convention rejected the credentials of Chicago Mayor Richard Daley and his delegation, seating instead an Illinois delegation led by Jesse Jackson, a firebrand young black minister and former aide of Martin Luther King.

Capturing the party was one thing; winning a national election quite another. McGovern was, in fact, a weak campaigner. He started badly at the convention, which was in bedlam when he finally delivered his acceptance speech at 2:30 A.M. His running mate, Senator Thomas Eagleton of Missouri, turned out to have a history of mental illness and had to be replaced. And McGovern failed to mollify key party backers like the AFL-CIO, which, for the first time in memory, refused to endorse the Democratic ticket.

McGovern was no match for Nixon, who pulled out all the stops. Using the advantages of incumbency, he gave the economy a well-timed lift and proclaimed (prematurely) a cease-fire in Vietnam. Nixon's appeal to the "silent majority"—people who "care about a strong United States, about patriotism, about moral and spiritual values"—was by now well-honed, with added wrinkles about "forced" busing and law and order.

Nixon won in a landslide, receiving nearly 61 percent of the popular vote and carrying every state except Massachusetts and the District of Columbia. The returns revealed how fractured traditional Democratic voting blocs had become. McGovern received only 38 percent of the big-city Catholic vote, and overall lost 42 percent of self-identified Democrats. The 1972 election marks a pivotal moment in the country's shift to the right. The full effect of that shift was delayed, however, by the president's soon-to-be-discovered self-inflicted wounds.

Watergate

On June 17, 1972, a funny thing happened at the Watergate complex in Washington, D.C. Early that morning, five men carrying wiretapping equipment were apprehended breaking into the Democratic National Committee's (DNC) headquarters. The arrest of two accomplices soon followed. Queried by the press, a White House spokesman dismissed the episode as "a third-rate burglary attempt." Wiretap equipment? At the DNC headquarters? Pressed further, Nixon himself denied any White House involvement in "this very bizarre incident."

In fact, the two kingpins, G. Gordon Liddy and E. Howard Hunt, were former FBI and CIA agents currently working for Nixon's Committee to Re-elect the President (CREEP). Earlier they had been on the White House payroll, hired in 1971 after the publication by the *New York Times* of the Pentagon Papers, a classified history of American involvement in Vietnam up to 1967, before Nixon's time. Even so, Nixon was enraged at the leak by Daniel Ellsberg, one of Washington's "best and brightest" and a trusted Pentagon insider. In response, the president set up a clandestine squad, known as the "plumbers" because their job was to plug administration leaks and do other nasty jobs. Hunt and Liddy, two of the plumbers, burglarized Ellsberg's psychiatrist's office in an unsuccessful effort to discredit him. Now, as CREEP operatives, they were arranging illegal wiretaps at DNC headquarters, part of a campaign of "dirty tricks" against the Democrats.

The Watergate burglary was no isolated incident. It was part of a broad pattern of illegality and misuse of power by a White House obsessed with the antiwar movement and prepared to fight its critics by any means, fair or foul. That siege mentality best explains why Nixon took a fatal misstep. He could have dissociated himself from the break-in by dismissing his guilty aides, or even just by letting justice take its course. But it was election time, and Nixon hung tough. He arranged hush money for the burglars and instructed the CIA to stop an FBI investigation into the affair. This was obstruction of justice, a criminal offense.

The Wheels of Justice. Nixon kept the lid on until after the election, but then, as the wheels of justice turned, the lid came off. In January 1973, the Watergate burglars were found guilty. One of them, the security chief for CREEP, began to talk. In the meantime, two tenacious reporters at the *Washington Post,* Carl Bernstein and Bob Woodward, uncovered CREEP's illegal "slush fund" and its links to key White House aides. (Their informant, famously known as Deep Throat, was finally revealed in 2005 to be the second-in-command at the FBI, W. Mark Felt.) In May a Senate investigating committee began holding nationally televised hearings, at which Assistant Secretary of Commerce Jeb Magruder confessed his guilt and implicated former Attorney General John Mitchell, White House Counsel John Dean, and others. Dean, in turn, implicated Nixon. Just as startling, a former White House aide revealed that Nixon had installed a secret taping system in the Oval Office.

Citing executive privilege, Nixon refused to surrender his tapes. Under enormous pressure, he eventually released sanitized transcripts and some of the tapes, but with a highly suspicious eighteen-minute gap. Finally, on June 23, 1974, the Supreme Court ordered Nixon to release the unexpurgated tapes. Lawyers were astounded to find in them incontrovertible evidence that the president had ordered the cover-up six days after the break-in. By then, the House Judiciary Committee was already considering articles of impeachment. Certain that he would be convicted by the Senate, on August 9, 1974, Nixon became the first U.S. president to resign his office.

The next day Vice President Gerald Ford was sworn in as president. Ford, the Republican minority leader in the House of Representatives, had replaced Vice President Spiro Agnew, who had himself resigned in 1973 for accepting kickbacks while governor of Maryland. The transfer of power proceeded smoothly. A month later, however, Ford stunned the nation by granting Nixon a "full, free, and absolute" pardon "for all offenses he had committed or might have committed during his presidency." Ford took that action, he said, to spare the country the agony of Nixon's criminal prosecution.

Aftermath. In Moscow, puzzled Kremlin leaders suspected a giant right-wing conspiracy against Nixon. They could not understand, recalled the Soviet ambassador to Washington at the time, "how a powerful president could be forced to resign . . . because of what they saw as a minor breach of conduct. Soviet history knew no parallel." That was one meaning of Watergate — that, in America, the rule of law prevailed (just barely; Nixon likely would have survived had he destroyed the tapes). A second meaning involved the constitutional separation of powers. As commander-in-chief, Nixon asserted unlimited authority, including wiretapping or worse, in the name of national security and, like the Kremlin leaders, he was perplexed at being brought down by a "pigmy-sized" incident like Watergate.

Congress pushed back, passing a raft of laws against the abuses of the Nixon administration — the War Powers Act (1973), reining in the president's ability to deploy U.S. forces without congressional approval; the Freedom of Information Act (1974), protecting privacy and access to federal records; the Fair Campaign Practices Act (1974), limiting and regulating contributions in presidential campaigns; and the Federal Intelligence Surveillance Act (1978), prohibiting domestic wiretapping without a warrant. Only in the short run, however, can it be said that these measures curbed America's tendency to embrace an imperial presidency.

▶ Why is the Nixon presidency considered a transitional one between the liberalism of the preceding decades and the conservatism that emerged in the 1980s?

▶ What do we mean when we say that Nixon was a "realist" in foreign affairs?

▶ Why did it take Nixon four years to reach a settlement with North Vietnam?

▶ How do you account for the Watergate scandal? What was its significance?

Battling for Civil Rights: The Second Stage

In the midst of Nixon's travail, the civil rights struggle continued, now entering a second, more complicated stage. In the first stage, the landmark achievements—*Brown v. Board of Education* (1954), the Civil Rights Act of 1964, and the Voting Rights Act of 1965—had been bitterly resisted, but once those battles ended, the moral atmosphere shifted. In principle, at any rate, Americans no longer defended segregation, or racial discrimination, or the denial of voting rights. But now the time came for enforcing those rights, sometimes, it turned out, at the expense of other Americans—and that meant strife. In the 1970s, moreover, the battle lines shifted from race to gender, as women, and then gays, mobilized and demanded equal rights. For many Americans, that was a great deal harder to handle because equality of the sexes hit closer to home than did racial equality. The effect was galvanizing. If the battle for equal rights had entered a second stage, so did the evolution of the conservative movement, increasingly driven as it now was by moral values and religious faith.

The Revival of Feminism

In the postwar years feminism was a languishing movement, with few advocates and no burning issues. That changed dramatically during the 1960s, initially sparked by the black civil rights movement, and then by the decade's broader social upheaval. But the revival of feminism also sprang from the deeply felt needs of many women at this juncture in their lives.

One spark was Betty Friedan's indictment of suburban domesticity, *The Feminine Mystique*, which appeared in 1963 (see Chapter 27). White, college-educated, middle-class women read Friedan's book and thought, "She's talking about me." *The Feminine Mystique*, after a slow start, became a runaway best seller. It gave women a vocabulary with which to express their dissatisfaction and made them believe that self-realization was attainable through jobs, education, and escape from mind-deadening domesticity.

Paradoxically, *The Feminine Mystique* was a bit out of date by the time it appeared. The domesticity it described was already crumbling. More and more women were working, including married women (40 percent by 1970) and mothers with preschool children (30 percent by 1970). After the postwar baby boom, women were again having fewer children, aided now by the birth control pill, first marketed in 1960, and the intrauterine device (IUD). At the same time the divorce rate, on the rise for the past century, speeded up as the states liberalized divorce laws. Educational levels were also rising; by 1970 women made up 42 percent of the college population. All these changes undermined traditional gender roles and enabled women, as they read *The Feminine Mystique*, to embrace its liberating prescriptions.

Budding feminists also received positive signals from Washington. In 1961, Kennedy appointed a Presidential Commission on the Status of Women, which issued a 1963 report documenting employment and educational discrimination against women. The result was some minor legislation, but, more importantly, a rudimentary network of activist women in public life that had formed in the course of the commission's work. A bigger breakthrough resulted by sheer inadvertence. Hoping to derail the pending Civil Rights Act of 1964, a key conservative, Representative Howard Smith of Virginia, mischievously added "sex" to the categories protected against discrimination under Title VII. The act passed anyway, and, to everyone's surprise, women suddenly had a powerful tool for fighting sex discrimination—provided, of course, that the Equal Employment Opportunity Commission (EEOC) could be prodded into doing its job.

With that objective in mind, Friedan and others founded the National Organization for Women (NOW) in 1966. Modeled on the NAACP, NOW intended to be a civil rights organization for women, with the aim of bringing "women into full participation in . . . American society now, exercising all the privileges and responsibilities thereof in truly equal partnership with men"—a classic statement of feminism. Under Friedan, who served as NOW's first president, membership grew from 1,000 in 1967 to 15,000 in 1971, and NOW became, like the NAACP, a powerful voice for equal rights.

The 1960s spawned another branch of feminists, the women's liberationists, primarily younger, college-educated women who had earned their spurs in the civil rights, New Left, and the antiwar movements. To their chagrin, they discovered that the male leaders of these movements were no better than the frat boys they had known in college. Women who tried to raise feminist issues were shouted off the platform with jeers like "Move on, little girl, we have more important issues to talk about here than women's liberation."

Fed up with this treatment, women radicals broke away and began their own movement. Unlike NOW, women's liberation had little formal structure and was best described as an alliance of loose collectives that had formed in New York, San Francisco, and other big cities. "Women's lib," as it was dubbed by a skeptical media, went public in 1968 at the Miss America pageant. Most eye-catching was a "freedom trash can" into which women were invited to fling false eyelashes, hair curlers, brassieres, and girdles—all

branded as symbols of female oppression. Women's liberation was a phenomenon of the 1960s, mirroring the identity politics of Black Power activists and the self-dramatization of the counterculture.

An activity more broadly experienced was "consciousness raising"—group sessions in which women shared their experiences. Swapping stories about being passed over for a promotion, needing a husband's signature on a credit card application, or enduring whistles and leers on the streets, participants began to realize that their individual problems were part of a wider pattern of oppression.

Feminism at High Tide. Before 1969 most women heard about NOW and other feminist organizations by word of mouth. After that, the media brought women's issues to a wider audience. New terms such as *sexism* and *male chauvinism* became part of the national vocabulary. As converts flooded in, the two branches of the women's movement began to converge. Radical women realized that key feminist goals—child care, equal pay, and abortion rights—could best be achieved in the political arena. At the same time, more traditional activists developed a broader view of women's oppression. Although still largely white and middle class, feminists began to think of themselves as part of a broad and growing social crusade. Only later did the movement grapple with the fact that as much divided women—race, class, age, sexual preference—as united them.

Women's opportunities expanded dramatically in higher education. Formerly all-male bastions, such as Yale, Princeton, and the U.S. Military Academy, admitted women undergraduates for the first time. Hundreds of colleges started women's studies programs, and the proportion of women attending graduate and professional schools rose markedly. With the adoption of Title IX in 1972, Congress broadened the 1964 Civil Rights Act to include educational institutions, prohibiting colleges and universities that received federal funds from discriminating on the basis of sex. By requiring comparable funding for sports programs, Title IX made women's athletics a real presence on college campuses.

Women also became increasingly visible in public life. The National Women's Political Caucus, founded in 1971, actively promoted the election of women to public office. Bella Abzug, Elizabeth Holtzman, Shirley Chisholm, Patricia Schroeder, and Geraldine Ferraro served in Congress; Ella T. Grasso became Connecticut's governor in 1974, as did Dixie Lee Ray in Washington State in 1976. Women's political mobilization produced significant legislative and administrative gains. Congress authorized child-care tax deductions for working parents in 1972, and in 1974 passed the Equal Credit Opportunity Act, which enabled married women to get credit, including credit cards and mortgages, in their own names. In 1977, 20,000 women went to Houston for the first National Women's Conference. Their "National Plan of Action" represented a hard-won consensus on topics ranging from violence against women to homemakers' rights, the needs of older women, and, most controversially, abortion and other reproductive issues.

Phyllis Schlafly: The Equal Rights Amendment, Defeated. Buoyed by its successes, the women's movement renewed the fight for an Equal Rights Amendment (ERA) to the Constitution. First introduced in Congress in 1923, the ERA stated in its entirety, "Equality of rights under the law shall not be denied or abridged by the United States or any State on the basis of sex." In the early days, the ERA had split the women's movement, with social reformers fearing that the amendment would jeopardize protective legislation for women. That fear, while not wholly gone, no longer prevented feminists of all varieties from favoring the amendment. As much as anything, the ERA became a symbolic statement of women's equality. Congress enthusiastically adopted the amendment in 1972, and within two

years thirty-four states ratified it. But then progress abruptly halted (Map 29.1).

For this, credit goes chiefly to a remarkable woman, Phyllis Schlafly, a lawyer, outspoken anti-Communist, and long-time activist in conservative causes. Despite her own flourishing career, Schlafly advocated traditional roles for women. She liked to bait feminists by opening her speeches with "I'd like to thank my husband for letting me be here tonight." The ERA, she proclaimed, would create an unnatural "unisex society," with women drafted into the army and forced to use single-sex toilets and locker rooms. Her STOP ERA organization galvanized a "silent" population of conservative Americans. Grassroots networks mobilized, showing up at statehouses with home-baked bread and apple pies. As labels on baked goods at one anti-ERA rally expressed it, "My heart and hand went into this dough / For the sake of the family please vote no." It was a message that

Phyllis Schlafly

Phyllis Schlafly, leader of the Stop ERA movement, talks with reporters during a rally at the Illinois State Capitol on March 4, 1975, at a time when the state legislature was considering whether to ratify the Equal Rights Amendment. Schlafly described herself as a housewife and called her strenuous political career a "hobby." © Bettmann/Corbis.

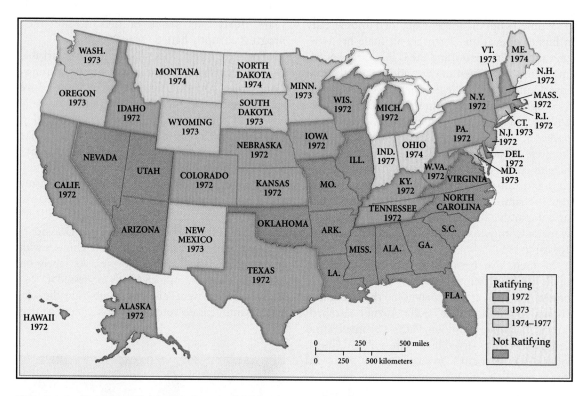

Map 29.1 States Ratifying the Equal Rights Amendment, 1972–1977

The ratifying process for the Equal Rights Amendment (ERA) went smoothly in 1972 and 1973 but then stalled. The turning point came in 1976, when ERA advocates lobbied extensively, particularly in Florida, North Carolina, and Illinois, but failed to sway the conservative legislatures in those states. After Indiana ratified in 1977, the amendment still lacked three votes toward the three-fourths majority needed for adoption. Efforts to revive the ERA in the 1980s were unsuccessful, and it became a dead issue.

resonated widely, especially among those troubled by the rapid pace of social change (see Comparing American Voices, "Debating the Equal Rights Amendment," pp. 908–909). The ERA never was ratified, despite a congressional extension of the deadline until June 30, 1982.

Gays and Lesbians. Parallel to, and inspired by, the feminist movement, homosexual men and women launched their own protest movement. The crystallizing event was the "Stonewall riot" of 1969 in New York City, when patrons of a gay bar fought back against police harassment. In the assertion of pride that followed, activists began to call themselves *gay* rather than homosexual; founded advocacy groups, newspapers, and political organizations; and offered emotional support to those who "came out" and publicly affirmed their homosexuality. In New York's Greenwich Village, San Francisco's Castro district, and other urban enclaves, vibrant gay communities emerged. In 1973 the National Gay Task Force launched a campaign to make gay men and lesbians a

protected group under laws covering employment and housing rights. These efforts succeeded mostly at the local level. During the 1970s Detroit, Boston, Los Angeles, Miami, San Francisco, and other cities passed laws barring discrimination on the basis of sexual preference.

Like the ERA, gay rights came under attack from conservatives. When the Miami city council passed a measure banning discrimination against gay men and lesbians in 1977, the singer Anita Bryant led a campaign to repeal the law by popular referendum. Later that year voters overturned the measure by a two-to-one majority, prompting similar antigay campaigns around the country. Once again, the country was witnessing the clash between equal rights for an oppressed minority and the moral values of a conservative majority.

Enforcing Civil Rights

The Equal Rights Amendment provoked a *political* struggle. Supporters and opponents mobilized and lobbied their legislators. The losing side, bitter though it might be, could not say its voice had been unheard. But to a large degree the civil rights struggle bypassed this democratic process. For one thing, under the American constitutional system fundamental rights trumped majority rule — which was, for example, the basis on which *Brown v. Board of Education* had struck down state-mandated segregated schooling. For another thing, and perhaps more important, *enforcing* civil rights was a judicial and/or executive function. Courts and federal agencies did the heavy lifting. And that — the unaccountability of the key actors — fed the outrage of many Americans already feeling adversely affected by the gains of protected minorities.

Affirmative Action. When Congress banned job discrimination in the Civil Rights Act (1964), all that it intended was that employers hire on a merit basis and without regard to race, religion, ethnicity, or sex. The wave of urban riots made the Johnson administration think again. The Kerner Commission (1968), after investigating the causes behind the rioting, strongly urged a massive federal effort at countering the white racism that held blacks back and deprived them of hope. One result was *affirmative action* — procedures designed to take into account the disadvantaged position of minorities after centuries of discrimination. First advanced by the Labor Department in 1968, affirmative action was refined by a series of court rulings that identified acceptable procedures, including hiring and enrollment goals, special recruitment and training programs, and *set-asides* (specially reserved slots).

Aided by affirmative action, African Americans enrolled in colleges and universities doubled between and 1970 and 1977, to 1.1 million, or 9.3 percent of total student population. Blacks moved into white-collar professions, found new opportunities in civil service, or got better access to union jobs. Latinos did as well, and white women far better.

Affirmative action, however, did not sit well with many whites, who felt the deck was being stacked against them. Complaints began to be heard about "reverse discrimination." Especially troubling were quotas because they were easily abused, tempting employers and college administrators to shoot for the numbers, without too much concern about whether the minorities hired or admitted really merited affirmative action.

In 1978 Allan Bakke, a white man, sued the University of California at Davis Medical School for rejecting him in favor of less qualified minority candidates. The Supreme Court rejected the medical school's quota system, which set aside 16 of 100 places for "disadvantaged" students. The Court ordered Bakke admitted, but indicated that a more flexible approach, in which racial factors could be considered along with other factors, would still pass muster. *Bakke v. University of California* thus upheld affirmative action, but by rejecting straightforward implementation, also called it into question. "Reverse discrimination" had become a rallying cry for conservatives.

Busing. The other main civil rights objective — desegregating the schools — produced far more fireworks. For fifteen years southern states, by a variety of stratagems, had fended off court directives that they move to integration "with all deliberate speed" (see Chapter 27). In 1968, hardly a third of all black children in the South attended schools with whites. At that point, the federal courts got serious and, in a series of stiff decisions, ordered an end to "dual school systems." Where this did not happen, the courts intervened directly. In 1971, in a landmark decision, the Supreme Court imposed a county-wide busing plan on Charlotte-Mecklenberg, North Carolina. In this case, integration went smoothly, and, in fact, the South as a whole essentially gave up the fight. By the mid-1970s, 86 percent of black children were attending school with whites.

But in the North, where segregated schooling was also a fact of life — arising, however, from residential patterns, not legally mandated separation — busing orders sparked intense and sometimes violent opposition. In South Boston, a strongly Irish-Catholic working-class neighborhood, mobs attacked African American students bused in from Roxbury. Armed police were required to keep South Boston High School open.

As a solution to segregation, busing came up against cherished attachments to neighborhood schooling. Busing also had the perverse effect of speeding up "white flight" to the suburbs. The result was egregiously evident in Detroit, where a black city was encircled by white suburbs. To integrate Detroit schools would have required merging city and suburban districts, which in fact was what a lower court ordered in 1971. But in *Milliken v. Bradley* (1974) the Supreme Court overruled the lower court. Thereafter, busing as a means of achieving racial balance fell out of favor. But in the meantime "forced busing," much touted by Nixon in the 1972 campaign, added to the grievances of conservatives, not least by reminding them of how much they hated what they perceived as the arrogance of unelected judges.

Debating the Equal Rights Amendment

Fifty years after it had first been introduced, Congress in 1972 finally approved the Equal Rights Amendment ("Equality of rights under the law shall not be denied or abridged by the United States or by any State on account of sex") and sent it off to the states for ratification. The amendment set off a furious debate, especially in the South and Midwest. Following are four of the voices in that debate.

J. MARSE GRANT

J. Marse Grant was the editor of the Biblical Recorder *and Chairman of the Baptist State Convention of North Carolina. He delivered these remarks to the Constitutional Amendments Committee of the state legislature.*

Recently I received a letter in which the writer told me to pick up my Bible. . . . He told me to read what God would have me do about ERA. I told him that this is exactly what I had done. And from my Bible I learned long ago that God loves all His children. That He gave them talents and abilities, and that in Him there is no male or female. . . .

The New Testament reveals countless ways in which women are an integral art of Jesus' ministry. He gave them new respect and dignity. He forsook the old traditions of his day—He talked to women in public—He visited in their homes—and it's little wonder, and not just accidentally, in my opinion, that women were the last ones at the cross. They were the first ones at the Resurrection, too. How anyone can distort the teachings of Christ and try to say that Christ was against equality and freedom for all people is hard for me to understand. . . .

It is unfortunate that I am here to apologize today that some here in the church oppose this amendment, but some in the church also opposed the Civil Rights Act in 1964. Some in the church defended slavery and quoted scripture to try to prove it. Some opposed the right of women to vote using many of the fallacious arguments that they are now using against ERA, but they were wrong. Dead wrong.

SOURCE: William A. Link and Marjorie Spruill Wheeler, eds. *The South in the History of the Nation* (Boston: Bedford/St. Martin's, 1999), 293–294.

JERRY FALWELL

Jerry Falwell was a fundamentalist Baptist preacher in Virginia, a television evangelist, and the founder of the Moral Majority (see p. 929 for his photograph).

I believe that at the foundation of the women's liberation movement there is a minority core of women who were once bored with life, whose real problems are spiritual problems. Many women have never accepted their God-given roles. . . . God Almighty created men and women biologically different and with differing needs and roles. He made men and women to complement each other and to love each other. . . . Women who work should be respected and accorded dignity and equal rewards for equal work. But this is not what the present feminist movement and equal rights movement are all about.

The Equal Rights Amendment is a delusion. I believe that women deserve more than equal rights. And, in families and in nations where the Bible is believed, Christian women are honored above men. Only in places where the Bible is believed and practiced do women receive more than equal rights. Men and women have differing strengths. The Equal Rights Amendment can never do for women what needs to be done for them. Women need to know Jesus Christ as their Lord and Savior and be under His Lordship. They need a man who knows Jesus Christ as his Lord and Savior, and they need to be part of a home where their husband is a godly leader and where there is a Christian family. . . . ERA is not merely a political issue, but a moral issue as well. A definite violation of holy Scripture, ERA defies the mandate that "the husband is the head of the wife, even as Christ is the head of the church" (Ep. 5:23). In 1 Peter 3:7 we read that husbands are to give their wives honor as unto the weaker vessel, that they are both heirs together of the grace of life. Because a woman is weaker does mean that she is less important.

SOURCE: Jerry Falwell, *Listen America* (New York: Doubleday, 1980), 150–151.

SAM ERVIN JR.

Sam Ervin Jr. represented North Carolina in the U.S. Senate from 1954 to 1974 and was a key figure in the Watergate investigation. In 1971, he inserted these remarks into the Congressional Record.

Let us consider for a moment whether there be a rational basis for reasonable distinctions between men and women in any of the relationships or undertakings of life.

When He created them, God made physiological and functional differences between men and women. These differences confer upon men a greater capacity to perform arduous and hazardous physical tasks. Some wise people even profess the belief that there may be psychological differences between men and women. To justify their belief, they assert that women possess an intuitive power to distinguish between wisdom and folly, good and evil.

To say these things is not to imply that either sex is superior to the other. It is simply to state the all important truth that men and women complement each other in the relationships and undertakings on which the existence and development of the race depend. . . . The physiological and functional differences between men and women constitute the most important reality. Without them human life could not exist.

For this reason, any country which ignores these differences when it fashions its institutions and makes its laws is woefully lacking in rationality. . . .

The Congress and the legislatures of the various states have enacted certain laws based upon the conviction that the physiological and functional differences between men and women make it advisable to exempt or exclude women from certain arduous and hazardous activities in order to protect their health and safety. . . . Among federal laws of this nature are the Selective Service Act, which confines compulsory military service to men. . . . Among the state laws of this kind are laws which limit hours during which women can work, and bar them from engaging in occupations particularly arduous and hazardous such as mining.

If the Equal Rights Amendment should be interpreted by the Supreme Court to forbid any legal distinctions between men and women, all existing and future laws of this nature would be nullified.

SOURCE: *Congressional Record*, 15 February 1972 (Washington, D.C.: GPO, 1972).

ELIZABETH DUNCAN KOONTZ

Elizabeth Duncan Koontz was a distinguished educator, the first black woman to head the National Education Association and the U.S. Women's Bureau. At the time she made this statement at state legislative hearings on the ERA in 1977, she was assistant state superintendent for public instruction in North Carolina.

A short time ago I had the misfortune to break my foot. . . . The pain . . . did not hurt me as much as when I went into the emergency room and the young woman upon asking me my name, the nature of my ailment, then asked me for my husband's social security number and his hospitalization number. I asked her what did that have to do with my emergency. And she said, "We have to be sure of who is going to pay your bill." I said, "Suppose I'm not married, then." And she said, "Then give me your father's name."

I did not go through that twenty years ago when I was denied the use of that emergency room because of my color. I went through that because there is an underlying assumption that all women in our society are protected, dependent, cared for by somebody who's got a social security number and hospitalization insurance. Never once did she assume I might be a woman who might be caring for my husband, instead of him by me, because of some illness. She did not take into account the fact that one out of almost eight women heading families in poverty today [is] in the same condition as men in families and poverty. . . .

My greater concern is that so many women today . . . oppose the passage of the ERA very sincerely and . . . tell you without batting an eye, "I don't want to see women treated that way." And I speak up, "What way is that?" . . . Women themselves have been a bit misguided. We have mistaken present practice for law, and women have . . . assumed too many times that their present condition cannot change. The rate of divorce, the rate of desertion, the rate of separation, and the death rate of male supporters is enough for us to say: "Let us remove all legal barriers to women and girls making their choices—this state cannot afford it."

SOURCE: Link & Wheeler, *op cit.*, 295–296.

ANALYZING THE EVIDENCE

➤ J. Marse Grant and Jerry Falwell were both southern Baptists. Both appealed to the Bible in discussing the ERA. Yet they came to opposite conclusions. How do you explain that?

➤ Senator Ervin characterizes his opposition to the ERA as being based on "rational" grounds. What does he mean by that? Would he agree with Falwell that the ERA was "not merely a political issue, but a moral issue as well"?

➤ Falwell speaks of women as "the weaker vessel." Why does Elizabeth Duncan Koontz disagree with that characterization? And what does her disagreement suggest to you about the social divisions underlying the debate over the ERA?

An Antibusing Confrontation in Boston

Tensions over court-ordered busing ran high in Boston in 1976. When a black lawyer tried to cross the city hall plaza during an antibusing demonstration, he became a victim of Boston's climate of racial hatred and violence. This Pulitzer Prize–winning photograph by Stanley Forman for the Boston *Herald American* shows a protester trying to impale the man with a flagpole. Stanley Forman.

Judicial Activism. The decision that initiated the tumult over busing — *Brown v. Board of Education* (1954) — also triggered a larger judicial revolution. Traditionally, it was liberals, not conservatives, who favored *judicial restraint,* which roughly meant that courts defer to legislatures. After many years, the liberal espousal of judicial restraint finally triumphed in 1937, when the Supreme Court reversed itself and let stand key New Deal laws — to the shock and outrage of conservatives.

That history explains why many respected liberal jurists and legal scholars, while favoring racial equality, objected to the *Brown* decision. They felt it violated principles of judicial restraint they had spent lifetimes defending. What ultimately persuaded them was a shift in the big issues coming before the Court. When property rights had been at stake, conservatives favored activist courts willing to curb antibusiness legislatures. Now that personal rights came to the fore, it was liberals' turn to celebrate activist judges and, preeminently, the man whom President Eisenhower appointed chief justice of the Supreme Court in 1953, Earl Warren. A popular Republican governor of California, Warren surprised many, including Eisenhower, by his robust advocacy of civil rights and civil liberties issues. If conservatives found reason to bewail judicial activism, there was no one they blamed more than Chief Justice Warren.

Consider these landmark Warren Court decisions. On the treatment of criminals: that they had a constitutional right to counsel, including at initial interrogations (1963, 1964), and to be informed by arresting officers of their right to remain silent (1966). On indecency: that pornography was protected by freedom of the press unless shown to be "utterly without redeeming social importance" (1964). On prayers and Bible reading in the schools: that religious ritual of any kind violated the constitutional separation of church and state (1962, 1963). In *Griswold v. Connecticut* (1965), the Supreme Court struck down an 1879 state law prohibiting the purchase and use of contraceptive devices by couples as a violation of their constitutional right of privacy.

Griswold opened the way for *Roe v. Wade* (1973), which declared the anti-abortion laws of Texas and Georgia unconstitutional. Abortions performed during the first trimester were protected by the right of privacy (following *Griswold*). At the time, and afterward, some legal authorities questioned whether the Constitution recognized any such privacy right (which the Court extracted from the Third and Eighth Amendments). Moreover, individual states were already legalizing abortion. Nevertheless, the Supreme Court chose to move forward, translating a policy matter traditionally state-regulated into a national, constitutionally protected right. For the women's movement and liberals generally, *Roe v. Wade* was a great, if unanticipated, victory; for evangelical Christians, Catholics, and conservatives generally, it was a bitter pill. Other rights-creating issues — "coddling" criminals, prohibiting school prayer, protecting pornography — had a polarizing effect. But *Roe v. Wade* was in a class by itself. In 1976 opponents convinced Congress to deny Medicaid funds for abortions, an opening round in a protracted campaign against *Roe* that continues to this day.

➤ What were the sources of growth for the women's rights movement?

➤ Why did enforcing civil rights prove more controversial than passing civil rights legislation?

➤ Why did the conservative/liberal alignment on judicial restraint change after 1954?

Lean Years

On top of everything else, the economy went into a tailspin. Oil supplies suddenly fell short, disrupting industry and sending gas prices sky-high. At the same time the United States found itself challenged by foreign competitors making better and cheaper products. All the economic indicators — inflation, employment, productivity, growth — turned negative. In such times, quality-of-life concerns normally get short shrift. Not in the 1970s, when, along side economic distress, environmental and consumer movements began to flourish.

Energy Crisis

Modern economies run on oil. And if the oil stops, woe follows. Something like that happened to the United States in the 1970s. Once the world's leading producer, the United States by the late 1960s was heavily dependent on imported oil, which mostly came from the Persian Gulf (Figure 29.1). American and European oil companies had discovered and developed the Middle Eastern fields, but control had been wrested away by the emerging Muslim states as they threw off the remnants of European colonialism. Foreign companies still extracted and marketed the oil — only they had the expertise at the time — but under profit-sharing agreements that recognized ownership by the Persian Gulf states. In 1960, they and other oil-rich developing countries formed the Organization of Petroleum

Exporting Countries (OPEC). OPEC was a cartel, and had it been a domestic enterprise, it would have been treated as an unlawful conspiracy in restraint of trade. But nothing prevented independent countries from conspiring in restraint of trade. During the 1960s, with the world awash in oil, the OPEC cartel was in fact ineffective.

That changed in 1973, when Egypt and Syria invaded Israel, initiating the Yom Kippur War. Israel prevailed, but only after being resupplied by an emergency American airlift. Already resentful of Western support for Israel (and encouraged by the Soviets), the Arab states declared an oil embargo against the United States, western Europe, and Japan. The effect was devastating, forcing Americans to spend long hours in line at the pumps and pushing gas prices up by 40 percent. Oil had become a political weapon. And the West's vulnerability stood revealed. In 1979, after a second shortage caused by the Iranian revolution, oil prices peaked at $34 a barrel, $31 dollars more than in 1973.

The United States scrambled to meet its energy needs. A national speed limit of 55 miles an hour was imposed to conserve fuel. Americans began to buy smaller, more fuel-efficient cars, only not from Detroit, which was tooled up to produce "gas guzzlers." Pretty soon VWs, Toyotas, and Datsuns (Nissans at a later date) dotted American highways, while sales of American cars slumped. The effect on the economy was considerable because one of every six jobs in the country was generated directly or indirectly by the auto industry. Even worse was the

FIGURE 29.1 U.S. Energy Consumption, 1900–2000

Coal was the nation's primary source of energy until the 1950s, when it was surpassed by oil and natural gas. The revival of coal consumption after 1960 stemmed from new open-pit mining in the West that provided cheaper fuel for power plants. The decline in oil consumption in 1980 reflects the nation's response to the oil crisis of the 1970s, including, most notably, fuel-efficient automobiles. Nuclear energy became an important new fuel source, but after 1990 its contribution leveled off as a result of the safety concerns triggered by the Three Mile Island incident (see pp. 913–914). SOURCE: *World Almanac 2002.*

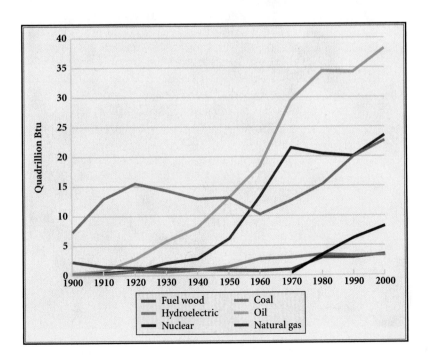

raging inflation set off by the oil shortage. Worst of all perhaps was the psychic shock to Americans at the discovery that their well-being was hostage to forces beyond their control.

Environmentalism

The energy crisis — and the realization it drove home that the earth's resources were not limitless — gave a huge boost to the environmental movement. In some ways, environmentalism was an offshoot of the 1960s counterculture. Activists talked about the "rights of nature," just as they had about the rights of women or blacks. Civil rights and antiwar activism readily translated into protest tactics against polluters and wilderness destroyers. More fundamentally, however, environmentalism was a feature of America's advanced consumer society. Now that they had the basic necessities, and then some, Americans wanted a quality of life defined by a healthy environment and by access to unspoiled nature.

The modern movement began in 1962 when Rachel Carson published *Silent Spring,* a stunning analysis of the impact of pesticides, most especially DDT, on the food chain. There followed a succession of galvanizing issues — concern over an environmentally destructive Alaskan oil pipeline, a proposed airport in the Florida Everglades, and a huge oil spill in January 1969 off the coast of Santa Barbara, California. Environmentalism became certifiably a mass movement on the first Earth Day, April 22, 1970, when 20 million citizens gathered in communities across the country to express their support for the endangered planet.

Earth Day, 1970

No single event better encapsulated the growing environmental awareness of Americans than the nationwide celebration of the first Earth Day on April 22, 1970. In this photograph, young people in Dallas have just hoisted their placard on a heap of garbage swept up from the city streets. *TimeLife Pictures/Getty Images.*

Nuclear Energy. The mother of environmental wars in the 1970s was the controversy over nuclear power. Electricity from the atom—what could be better? That was how Americans had greeted the arrival of power-generating nuclear technology in the 1950s. By 1974, utility companies were operating forty-two nuclear power plants, with a hundred more planned. Given the oil crisis, nuclear energy might have seemed a godsend. Besides, unlike coal- or oil-driven plants, nuclear operations produced no air pollutants. But environmentalists saw only the dangers. A meltdown would be catastrophic and so, in slow motion, might be the unsolved problem of radioactive wastes. These fears seemed to be confirmed in March 1979 when the reactor core at a nuclear plant at Three Mile Island near Harrisburg, Pennsylvania, came close to meltdown. A prompt shutdown saved the plant, but the near-catastrophe enabled environmentalists to win the battle over nuclear energy (see Reading American Pictures, "A Near Meltdown at Three Mile Island, 1979," p. 914). After Three Mile Island, the utility industry backed down and stopped building nuclear-powered plants.

The Consumer Movement. Environmentalism helped rekindle a consumer movement that had languished since the Progressive era (see Chapter 20). The key figure was Ralph Nader, a young Harvard-educated lawyer whose book, *Unsafe at Any Speed* (1965), attacked General Motors for putting flashy styling ahead of safety in the engineering of the rear-engine Chevrolet Corvair. Buoyed by his success, Nader in 1969 launched a Washington-based consumer protection organization that spawned a national network of activists fighting everything from consumer fraud to dangerous toys. Staffed largely by student volunteers known as "Nader's Raiders," the organization pioneered such legal tactics as the class-action suit, which enabled lawyers to represent an entire pool of grievants in a single litigation. In Nader's wake, dozens of other groups emerged in the 1970s and afterward to combat the tobacco industry, unethical insurance and credit practices, and a host of other consumer problems.

Environmental Legislation. Environmentalists proved remarkably adept at sparking governmental action. In 1969 Congress passed the National Environmental Policy Act, which required the developers to file environmental impact statements assessing the impact of their projects on particular ecosystems. The next year Nixon established the Environmental Protection Agency (EPA) and signed the Clean Air Act, which established standards for auto emissions that caused air pollution. Following the lead of several states, Congress banned the use of DDT in 1972, and in 1980 created the Superfund to finance the cleanup of toxic waste sites. The Endangered Species Act (1973) expanded the scope of the Endangered Animals Act of 1964, granting species such as snail darters and spotted owls protected status. On the consumer front, a big victory was the establishment of the federal Consumer Products Safety Commission in 1972.

These environmental successes were not, however, universally appreciated. Fuel-economy standards for cars was said to hinder the auto industry as it struggled to keep up with foreign competitors. Corporations resented environmental regulations, but so did many of their workers, who believed that tightened standards threatened their jobs. "IF YOU'RE HUNGRY AND OUT OF WORK, EAT AN ENVIRONMENTALIST" read one labor union's bumper sticker. In a time of rising unemployment, activists clashed head-on with proponents of economic growth and global competitiveness.

Economic Woes

While the energy crisis had dealt a hard blow, the economy was also beset by a host of longer-term problems. The high cost of the Vietnam War and the Great Society contributed to a growing federal deficit and spiraling inflation. In the industrial sector, the country faced growing competition from Germany and Japan. America's share of world trade dropped from 32 percent in 1955 to 18 percent in 1970, and was headed down. As a result, in 1971 the value of the dollar fell to its lowest level since World War II, and the United States posted its first trade deficit in almost a century.

In the 1970s, the country's economic performance turned dismal. Gross domestic product (GDP), which had been increasing at a sizzling 4.1 percent per year in the 1960s, dropped after 1970 to 2.9 percent. In a blow to national pride, nine western European countries surpassed the United States in per capita GDP by 1980. The economy was also characterized by stagnating wages, unemployment, and galloping inflation (Figure 29.2). The devastating combination of unemployment and inflation—*stagflation,* so-called—contradicted a basic principle taught by economists: Prices were not supposed to rise in a stagnant economy. In the 1970s, they did. For ordinary Americans, the reality of

A Near Meltdown at Three Mile Island, 1979

Goldsboro, PA. National Archives.

Crisis Management. Jimmy Carter Presidential Library.

Hardly had atomic bombs devastated Japan in 1945 than American leaders began touting the "peaceful" uses of atomic technology, especially the generation of electrical power by nuclear-powered steam turbines. By 1979, nuclear plants were producing 11 percent of the nation's electricity. At that point, dreams of a nuclear-powered America suddenly ended, punctured by a nearly catastrophic accident at the Three Mile Island plant near Harrisburg, Pennsylvania.

On March 28, 1979, the pumps for the Unit 2 reactor shut down, stopping the flow of cooling water and initiating a meltdown of the radioactive core. Had a full meltdown occurred, it would have breached the walls of the containment building and released huge amounts of radiation into the atmosphere. Fortunately, a full meltdown at Three Mile Island was averted. But for several days it was touch-and-go.

ANALYZING THE EVIDENCE

➤ When talk about nuclear energy began, not a lot was said about the fact that the huge plants would have to be placed in somebody's backyard. The first photo shows the neighborhood abutting the Three Mile Island facility. Look carefully at the houses. What sort of people might live there? Would you be happy to live there? What are the social implications of your answer?

➤ The second photograph shows President Carter and his wife Rosalynn inspecting the facility on April 1, 1979, just as the crisis was ending. Carter had been a nuclear engineer. Do you suppose he was there to offer his expertise? If not, what was he doing there?

Nervous Humor. © Batom. North American Syndicate.

➤ The cartoon is a commentary on Carter's visit. What does it portend about the future of nuclear energy in America? What details in the cartoon can you point to that support your answer?

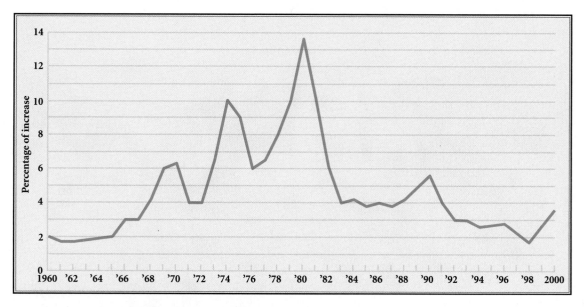

FIGURE 29.2   The Inflation Rate, 1960–2000

The impact of the oil crisis of 1973 on the inflation rate appears all too graphically in Figure 29.2. The dip in 1974 reflects the sharp recession that began that year, after which the inflation rate zoomed up to a staggering 14 percent in 1980. The return to normal levels after 1980 stemmed from very harsh measures by the Federal Reserve Board, which, while they succeeded, came at the cost of a painful slowdown in the economy. SOURCE: *Statistical Abstract of the United States, 2000.*

stagflation was a noticeable decline in the standard of living, as discretionary income per worker dropped 18 percent between 1973 and the early 1980s. Many families were kept afloat only by the second income brought in by working wives.

Deindustrialization. America's economic woes struck hardest in the industrial sector, which suddenly — shockingly — began to be dismantled. Worst hit was the steel industry, which for seventy-five years had been the economy's crown jewel. Its problems were, ironically, partly a product of good fortune. Only the American steel industry had been left unscathed by the devastation of World War II. In the postwar years, that gave U.S. producers an open, hugely profitable field, but it also saddled them with outdated plants and equipment.

When the German and Japanese industries rebuilt — with the aid of American funding and technology — they incorporated the latest and best of everything. Moreover, the American industry's natural advantages were eroding. With its abundant iron-ore reserves exhausted, the industry competed for raw materials on global markets like everyone else. Meanwhile, advances in international shipping deprived it of the comparative advantage of location. Distant from

markets and with no natural resources, Japan built a powerhouse of an industry. When Japanese steel flooded in during the 1970s, the American industry was simply overwhelmed. A massive dismantling began, including the entire Pittsburgh district. By the time the smoke cleared in the mid-1980s, the American industry was competitive again, but it was a shadow of its former self.

The steel industry was the prime example of what became known as *deindustrialization*. The country was in the throes of an economic transformation that left it largely stripped of its industrial base. A swath of the Northeast and Midwest, the country's manufacturing heartland, became the nation's "Rust Belt" (Map 29.2), strewn with abandoned plants and dying communities.

Many thousands of blue-collar workers lost well-paid union jobs. What they faced is revealed by the 4,100 steelworkers left jobless by the shutdown of the Campbell Works of the Youngstown Sheet & Tube Co. in 1977. Two years later, a third had retired early, at half pay. Ten percent had moved, mostly to the Sun Belt. Fifteen percent were still jobless, with unemployment benefits long gone. Forty percent had found local work, but mostly in low-paying, service-sector jobs. Most of these Ohio

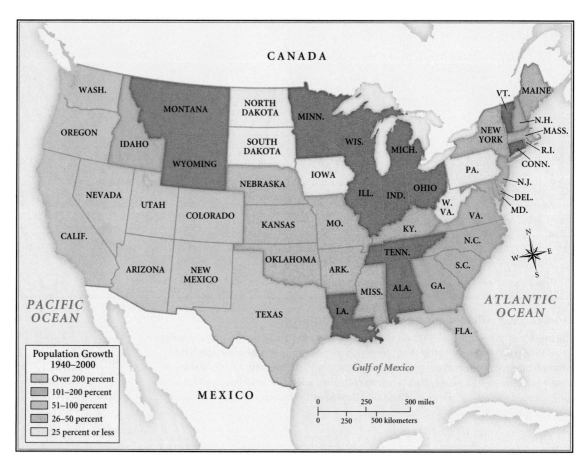

Map 29.2 From Rust Belt to Sun Belt, 1940–2000

One of the most significant developments of the post–World War II era was the growth of the Sun Belt. Sparked by federal spending for military bases, the defense industry, and the space program, states of the South and Southwest experienced an economic boom in the 1950s (see Map 27.1 on page 838). This growth was further enhanced in the 1970s, as the heavily industrialized regions of the Northeast and Midwest declined, and migrants from what was quickly dubbed the "Rust Belt" headed to the South and West in search of jobs.

steelworkers had fallen from their perch in the middle class.

Organized Labor in Decline. Deindustrialization dealt harshly with the labor movement. In the early 1970s, as inflation hit, the number of strikes surged; 2.4 million workers participated in work stoppages in 1970 alone. Challenged by foreign competition, industry became more resistant to union demands, and labor's bargaining power waned. In these hard years, the much-vaunted labor-management accord of the 1950s went bust. Instead of higher wages, unions now mainly fought to save jobs. In the 1970s union membership dropped sharply, with industrial unions — the Rust Belt unions — especially hard hit. By the end of the 1980s, only 16 percent of American workers were organized (See Figure 27.2, p. 836).

The impact on liberal politics was huge. With labor's decline, a main buttress of the New Deal coalition was coming undone.

Taxpayer Revolts. The economic crisis also hardened anti-tax sentiment, reversing a postwar spirit of generous public investment. The premier example was California, which after World War II created, among other achievements, an unrivaled system of higher education. With stagflation, real estate values rocketed upward, and so did property taxes. Especially hard hit were retirees and others on fixed incomes. Into this dire situation stepped Howard Jarvis, an anti-New Dealer cut to the same cloth as the ERA-hating Phyllis Schlafly and, like her, a genius at mobilizing a grassroots movement. Despite opposition by virtually the entire state establishment, Californians in 1978 voted overwhelmingly

Symbol of the Rust Belt

A padlock on the gate of Youngstown, Ohio's United States Steel mill symbolizes the creation of the Rust Belt in the 1970s. Economic hard times caused widespread plant closures in the industrial areas of the Midwest and Northeast and an exodus to the booming Sun Belt (see Map 29.2). © Bettmann/Corbis.

for Proposition 13, which rolled back property taxes, capped future increases, and harnessed all tax measures, state or local, to a two-thirds voting requirement. As a vehicle for hobbling public spending, Prop 13 was extraordinarily effective. Per capita funding of California public schools plunged from the top tier to the bottom (next to Mississippi). Prop. 13 also pulled off the neat trick of hugely benefiting, under the shelter of California's elderly, wealthy homeowners and businesses (commercial property got the same protection). More broadly, Prop. 13 inspired tax revolts across the country and gave conservatives an enduring issue: No New Taxes.

➤ Why did the United States enter an energy crisis in the 1970s?

➤ What were the major concerns of the environmentalist movement?

➤ What were the causes and effects of deindustrialization?

Politics in the Wake of Watergate

Nixon's resignation in 1974 left American politics in limbo. Popular disdain for politicians, already evident in declining voter turnout, deepened. "Don't vote. It only encourages them," read one bumper stick in 1976. Watergate damaged short-term Republican prospects, but also created an opening for the party's right wing. It was telling

that Gerald Ford, in advance of his 1976 reelection bid, dumped his vice president, Nelson Rockefeller, a liberal Republican, for a conservative running mate, Senator Robert Dole of Kansas. As for the Democrats, Watergate granted them a reprieve, a second chance at recapturing their eroding base. But that required leadership, not something the party's freewheeling rules for choosing a candidate could guarantee. Any governor with a nice head of hair, a winning manner, some money in the bank, and a semblance of organization had a shot at the party's nomination.

Jimmy Carter: The Outsider as President

"Jimmy Who?" was how journalists first responded when James E. Carter, governor of Georgia and self-styled peanut farmer, emerged from the pack and went on to win the Democratic nomination. Trading on Watergate, Carter pledged to restore morality to the White House. "I will never lie to you," he promised voters. Carter played up his credentials as a Washington outsider, although he made sure, in selecting Senator Walter F. Mondale of Minnesota, to have a running mate with ties to traditional Democratic voting blocs. Ford, still wounded by his pardon of Nixon and with little to boast about as a caretaker president, was a fairly easy mark. Carter won with 50 percent of the popular vote to Ford's 48 percent.

For a time, Carter got some mileage out of casting himself as an outsider, the common man who walked back to the White House after the Inauguration, delivered fireside chats in a cardigan sweater,

A Framework for Peace

After two weeks of intense personal diplomacy, President Jimmy Carter persuaded President Anwar el-Sadat of Egypt (left) and Prime Minister Menachem Begin of Israel (right) to sign a peace treaty in 1978. The signing of the Camp David Accords marked an important first step in constructing a framework for peace in the Middle East. This was Carter's greatest foreign-policy achievement. David Rubinger/TimeLife Pictures/Getty Images.

and carried his own bags. The fact that he was a born-again Christian also played well. But Carter's inexperience began to tell. His outsider strategy distanced him from established congressional leaders. Shying away from the Democratic establishment, Carter relied heavily on inexperienced advisers and friends from Georgia. And he himself, a prodigious worker, was an inveterate micromanager, exhausting himself over details best left to subordinates.

Economic Policy. On the domestic front, Carter's big challenge was managing the economy. The problems he faced defied easy solution. Most confounding was stagflation. If the government focused on the inflation side — forcing prices down by increasing taxes or raising interest rates — unemployment became worse. If the government tried to stimulate employment, inflation became worse. Seeking to cut through this conundrum, Nixon had imposed price and wage controls in 1971, a brave try, but one that created more problems than it solved.

Carter lacked Nixon's daring. At heart, in fact, he was an economic conservative. He toyed with the idea of an "industrial policy" to bail out the ailing manufacturing sector, but moved instead in a free-market direction by lifting the New Deal–era regulation of the airline, trucking, and railroad industries. **Deregulation** stimulated competition and cut prices, but also drove firms out of business and hurt unionized workers.

Taking office after a sharp mid-1970s downturn, Carter offered a stimulus package that was at cross-purposes with his Federal Reserve Board's program of attacking inflation by raising interest rates. Then turmoil in the Middle East in 1979 curtailed oil supplies, and gas prices jumped again. In a major TV address, Carter lectured Americans about the nation's "crisis of confidence" and "crisis of the spirit." He called energy conservation "the moral equivalent of war" — or, in the media's shorthand, "MEOW," aptly capturing the nation's assessment of Carter's homily. By then, his approval rating had fallen below 30 percent. And no wonder: an inflation rate over 11 percent, failing

Fei Xiaotong

America's Crisis of Faith

Fei Xiaotong, a Chinese anthropologist and sociologist, wrote influential books on the United States during World War II and the 1950s. Despite his criticism of U.S. foreign policy, his often sympathetic treatment of America contributed to twenty years of political ostracism in China. Regaining prominence in the late 1970s, he joined an official delegation to the United States in 1979. When he returned to China, Fei wrote a series of essays entitled "Glimpses of America." In this passage, he responds to President Jimmy Carter's assertion in his famous "malaise" speech of 1979 that Americans faced a spiritual crisis.

I read in the newspaper that the energy crisis in the United States is getting worse and worse. I hear that after spending several days of quiet thought in his mountain retreat, President Carter decided that America's real problem is not the energy crisis but a "crisis of faith." The way it is told is that vast numbers of people have lost their faith in the present government and in the political system, and do not believe that the people in the government working with current government methods can solve the present series of crises. Even more serious, he believes that the masses have come to have doubts about traditional American values, and if this continues, in his opinion, the future of America is terrible to imagine. He made a sad and worried speech. I have not had an opportunity to read the text of his speech, but if he

has truly realized that the present American social system has lost popular support, that should be considered a good thing because at least it shows that the old method of just treating the symptoms will no longer work.

In fact, loss of faith in the present social system on the part of the broad masses of the American people did not begin with the energy crisis. The spectacular advances in science and technology in America in the last decade or two and the unceasing rise in the forces of production are good. But the social system remains unchanged, and the relations of production are basically the same old capitalism. This contradiction between the forces of production and the relations of production has not lessened but become deeper. The ruling class, to be sure, still has the power to keep on finding ways of dealing with the endless series of crises, but the masses of people are coming increasingly to feel that they have fallen unwittingly into a situation where their fate is controlled by others, like a moth in a spiderweb, unable to struggle free. Not only the blacks of Harlem—who are clearly able to earn their own living but still have to rely on welfare to support themselves without dignity—but even well-off families in gardenlike suburban residences worry all day that some accident may suddenly rob them of everything. As the dependence of individuals on others grows heavier and heavier, each person feels in his heart that this society is no longer to be relied on.... No wonder people complain that civilization was created by humans, but humans have been enslaved by it. Such a feeling is natural in a society like America's. Carter is right to call this feeling of helplessness a "crisis of faith," for it is a doubting of the present culture.

Only he should realize that the present crisis has been long in the making and is already deep....

These "Glimpses of America" essays may be brought to a close here, but to end with the crisis of faith does violence to my original intention. History is a stream that flows on and cannot be stopped. Words must be cut off, but history goes bubbling on. It is inconceivable that America will come to a standstill at any crisis point. I have full faith in the great American people and hope that they will continue to make even greater contributions to the progress of mankind....

SOURCE: R. David Arkush and Leo O. Lee, trans. and eds., *Land Without Ghosts: Chinese Impressions of America from the Mid-Nineteenth Century to the Present* (Berkeley: University of California Press, 1989).

ANALYZING THE EVIDENCE

➤ Xiaotong is writing about America as someone schooled in Marxist (or Communist) analysis. Can you point to elements in his essay that indicate that perspective?

➤ Xiaotong agrees with Carter that America's problem is not the energy crisis, but a "crisis of faith." Does that mean he agrees with the president about the nature of the crisis?

➤ As a historical document, what value, if any, do you think a historian would find in Xiaotong's essay?

Afghanistan, 1980

Afghani fighters stand in triumph on a destroyed Soviet helicopter. The weapon that brought it down might well have been a shoulder-launched missile from the American-supplied arsenal, courtesy of the CIA. When the defeated Soviets left Afghanistan, the CIA congratulated itself on its smart moves, only to experience what experts call "blow back," as empowered mujahaddin such as those depicted here turned on the United States and made Afghanistan under the Taliban a haven for Al Qaeda. As for those shoulder-launched missiles, they have become a major headache for the West in the battle against Islamic terrorism. © Alain DeJean/Sygma/Corbis.

industries, long lines at the pumps. It seemed the worst of all possible economic worlds (see Voices from Abroad, "Fei Xiaotong: America's Crisis of Faith," p. 919).

Carter and the World

In foreign affairs, President Carter had a firmer sense of what he was about. He was the anti-Nixon, a world leader who rejected Kissinger's "realism" in favor of human rights and peacemaking. Carter established the Office of Human Rights in the State Department and withdrew economic and military aid from repressive regimes in Argentina, Uruguay, and Ethiopia, although he was unable to budge equally repressive U.S. allies like the Philippines, South Korea, and South Africa. In Latin America, Carter punctured an enduring symbol of Yankee imperialism by signing a treaty on September 7,

1977, turning control over the Panama Canal to Panama (effective December 31, 1999). Despite a conservative outcry, the Senate narrowly approved the treaty.

President Carter scored his greatest success by tackling the intractable Arab-Israeli conflict. In 1978 he invited Israel's prime minister Menachem Begin and Egyptian president Anwar el-Sadat to Camp David, the presidential retreat in Maryland. For two weeks, Carter kept the discussions going and finally, after promising additional economic aid, persuaded Sadat and Begin to adopt a "framework for peace," under which Egypt recognized Israel and received back the Sinai Peninsula, which Israel had occupied since 1967.

Though deploring "inordinate fear of Communism," Carter's efforts at improving relations with the Soviet Union foundered. He caused resentment by criticizing the Kremlin's record on

American Hostages in Iran

Images of blindfolded, handcuffed American hostages seized by Iranian militants at the American embassy in Tehran in November 1979 shocked the nation and created a foreign-policy crisis that eventually cost President Carter his chance for reelection. Alain Mingam/ Gamma Press Images.

human rights. Negotiations for arms reductions went slowly, and when the SALT II agreement limiting bombers and missiles was finally signed in 1979, Senate hawks objected. Hopes for Senate ratification collapsed when the Soviet Union invaded Afghanistan that December. Treating the invasion as a major crisis, Carter placed an embargo on wheat shipments to the USSR, called for increased defense spending, and declared an American boycott of the 1980 summer Olympics in Moscow (in return the USSR boycotted the 1984 games in Los Angeles). In a fateful decision, Carter began providing covert assistance to anti-Soviet fighters in Afghanistan, some of whom metamorphosed into anti-American Islamic radicals in later years.

Carter's undoing, however, came in Iran. The Shah, Muhammad Reza Pahlavi, was an American client, installed by the CIA in 1953 (see Chapter 26) to prevent the nationalization of Iran's oil industry. Thereafter, the United States counted Iran as a faithful ally, a bulwark in the troubled Middle East, and a steady source of oil. Notwithstanding his fine words, Carter followed the same path as his Cold War predecessors, overlooking the crimes of Iran's CIA-trained secret police, SAVAK, the growing fragility of the Shah's regime, and mounting popular enmity toward the United States. Early in 1979, the Shah was driven into exile, overthrown by

an Iranian revolution that brought the Shiite cleric Ayatollah Ruhollah Khomeini to power.

In October 1979, the United States admitted the deposed Shah, who was suffering from cancer, for medical treatment. In response, Iranian students seized the U.S. embassy in Teheran, taking sixty-six Americans hostage. The captors demanded that the Shah be returned to Iran for trial, but the United States refused. Instead, President Carter suspended arms sales to Iran and froze Iranian assets in American banks.

For the next fourteen months, the hostage crisis paralyzed Jimmy Carter's presidency. Night after night, humiliating pictures of blindfolded hostages appeared on television newscasts. An attempt to mount a military rescue in April 1980 had to be aborted because of equipment failures in the desert. During the withdrawal, one of the helicopters collided with a transport plane, setting off ammunition explosions and causing multiple American casualties. After this fiasco, the torturous negotiations, simplified by the Shah's death, finally succeeded. As a parting shot, the Iranians waited until the day Carter left office to deliver the hostages.

Every war president in the twentieth century — Wilson, FDR, Truman, Johnson — had been a Democrat. So Carter performed a remarkable feat. Single-handedly, he marked the Democrats indelibly as the party of wimps. All the elements were now in place for the triumph of the conservatives. All they needed was a leader.

> ➤ Why did Jimmy Carter have so much trouble managing the economy?

> ➤ What distinguished Carter's conduct of foreign policy from Nixon's? Which foreign policy would you say was more successful? Nixon's or Carter's?

SUMMARY

As we have seen, the 1970s constitute a transitional period, with one foot in the liberal past, the other foot in the conservative future. This was evident in Richard Nixon's presidency, which tried to consolidate a new Republican majority, yet also accepted, and in some ways expanded, an activist state. In foreign policy, similarly, Nixon moved in two directions, capitalizing on Communist divisions to move toward détente, yet adhering to Cold War assumptions in Vietnam. The drift toward Republican supremacy was cut short by the Watergate scandal, which forced Nixon to resign in 1974.

For much of the 1970s, Americans struggled with economic problems, including inflation, energy shortages, stagnation of income, and deindustrialization. Despite diminishing expectations, Americans actively supported movements for environmental and consumer protection. The battle for civil rights entered a second stage, expanding to encompass women's and gay rights and, in the realm of racial justice, focusing more on problems of enforcement. One effect, however, was a new, more conservative social mood that began to challenge liberal values in politics and society more generally.

The presidencies of Gerald Ford and Jimmy Carter did little to restore Americans' faith in their political leaders. Carter failed to resolve the economic crisis besetting the nation, and his foreign policy, while high-minded, ran into comparable difficulties, topped off by the Iranian hostage crisis of 1979.

Connections: Society

In this chapter, we discussed the "second stage" of the civil rights revolution, which, like the first stage, prompted strong opposition. In the 1960s, however, the resistance was regional, limited to the South, whereas in the 1970s, the resistance became national and, as compared to the defense of racial segregation, touched concerns that many Americans considered legitimate and important. In the case of women's rights, we can trace back to the battle over woman suffrage (see Chapter 19) how strongly felt the belief had historically been about the proper role of women. In the case of enforcement of civil rights, the roots of resistance cannot be located in a single chapter, but are embedded in traditions of individual rights, going back to the Revolutionary era, that made Americans uncomfortable with arguments that favored affirmative action or court-mandated busing. Historically, the obligations of citizenship had not entailed parting with rights or privileges to advance the rights or privileges of others. As we will see in Chapter 30, the potency of these conservative views fueled a political revolution in the age of Ronald Reagan.

CHAPTER REVIEW QUESTIONS

> ➤ What impact did the Nixon administration have on American politics?

> ➤ Why are the 1970s considered an era of "declining expectations" for Americans?

> ➤ What were the major causes of the apparent weakening of the United States as a superpower during this period?

TIMELINE

1966	National Organization for Women (NOW) founded
1968	Richard Nixon elected president
1969	Stonewall riot leads to gay liberation movement Mobilization Day climaxes Vietnam war protests
1970	Earth Day first observed Environmental Protection Agency established Nixon orders invasion of Cambodia; renewed antiwar protests Killings at Kent State and Jackson State
1971	Pentagon Papers published
1972	Watergate break-in; Nixon reelected Nixon visits People's Republic of China SALT I Treaty with Soviet Union
1973	*Roe v. Wade* legalizes abortion Endangered Species Act Paris Peace Accords War Powers Act Arab oil embargo; gas shortages
1974	Nixon resigns over Watergate; Ford becomes president and pardons Nixon Busing controversy in Boston
1975	Fall of Saigon
1976	Jimmy Carter elected president
1978	Carter brokers Camp David accords between Egypt and Israel Proposition 13 reduces California taxes *Bakke v. University of California* limits affirmative action
1979	Three Mile Island nuclear accident Soviet Union invades Afghanistan Hostages seized at American embassy in Tehran, Iran
1980	"Superfund" created to clean up toxic land sites

FOR FURTHER EXPLORATION

Peter N. Carroll, *It Seemed Like Nothing Happened* (1982), provides a general overview of the period. Gary Wills, *Nixon Agonistes,* rev. ed. (1990), judges Nixon to be a product of his times. For Watergate, a starting point is the books by the *Washington Post* journalists who broke the scandal, Carl Bernstein and Bob Woodward: *All the President's Men* (1974) and *The Final Days* (1976). Stanley Kutler, *The Wars of Watergate* (1990), is the definitive history. Gary Sick, a Jimmy Carter White House advisor on Iran, offers an insider's account of the hostage crisis in *All Fall Down: America's Tragic Encounter with Iran* (1986). For documents on the Carter presidency and his "malaise" speech, see Daniel Horowitz, *Jimmy Carter and the Energy Crisis of the 1970s* (2005). Thomas Byrne Edsall with Mary D. Edsall, *Chain Reaction: The Impact of Race, Rights, and Taxes on American Politics* (1991), examines some of the divisive social issues of the 1970s. J. Anthony Lukas, *Common Ground* (1985), tells the story of the Boston busing crisis through the biographies of three families. Barbara Ehrenreich examines the backlash against feminism in *Hearts of Men* (1984).

For the Watergate scandal, see the National Archives and Record Administration's Watergate Trial Tapes and Transcripts at **nixon.archives.gov/index.php**, which provides transcripts of the infamous tapes as well as other useful links to archival holdings concerning Richard Nixon's presidency. Watergate, at **watergate.info**, is a textual, visual, and auditory survey of the scandal. Created by Australian political science professor Malcolm Farnsworth, the site's materials include a Nixon biography with speech excerpts, a Watergate chronology, an analysis of the significance of the "Deep Throat" informant, and an assessment of the Watergate legacy. Relevant links provide access to primary documents. The Oyez Project at Northwestern University, at **www.oyez.org/oyez/frontpage**, is an invaluable resource for over one thousand Supreme Court cases, with audio transcripts, voting records, and summaries. For this period, see, for example, its materials on *Roe v. Wade*, *Bakke v. University of California*, and *Griswold v. Connecticut*. Documents from the Women's Liberation Movement, culled from the Duke University Special Collections Library, emphasize the women's movement of the late 1960s and early 1970s. This searchable site, at **scriptorium.lib.duke.edu/wlm**, includes books, pamphlets, and other written materials on categories that include theoretical writings, reproductive health, women of color, and women's work and roles.

TEST YOUR KNOWLEDGE

To assess your command of the material in this chapter, see the Online Study Guide at **bedfordstmartins.com/henretta**.

For Web sites, images, and documents related to topics and places in this chapter, visit **bedfordstmartins.com/makehistory**.

PART SEVEN

Entering a New Era: Conservatism, Globalization, Terrorism

1980–2006

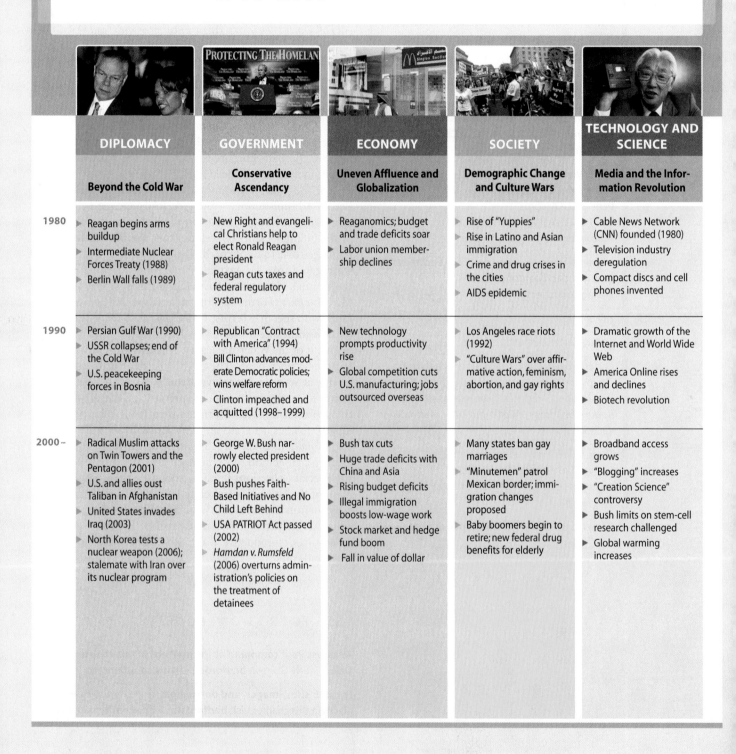

	DIPLOMACY	GOVERNMENT	ECONOMY	SOCIETY	TECHNOLOGY AND SCIENCE
	Beyond the Cold War	**Conservative Ascendancy**	**Uneven Affluence and Globalization**	**Demographic Change and Culture Wars**	**Media and the Information Revolution**
1980	▸ Reagan begins arms buildup ▸ Intermediate Nuclear Forces Treaty (1988) ▸ Berlin Wall falls (1989)	▸ New Right and evangelical Christians help to elect Ronald Reagan president ▸ Reagan cuts taxes and federal regulatory system	▸ Reaganomics; budget and trade deficits soar ▸ Labor union membership declines	▸ Rise of "Yuppies" ▸ Rise in Latino and Asian immigration ▸ Crime and drug crises in the cities ▸ AIDS epidemic	▸ Cable News Network (CNN) founded (1980) ▸ Television industry deregulation ▸ Compact discs and cell phones invented
1990	▸ Persian Gulf War (1990) ▸ USSR collapses; end of the Cold War ▸ U.S. peacekeeping forces in Bosnia	▸ Republican "Contract with America" (1994) ▸ Bill Clinton advances moderate Democratic policies; wins welfare reform ▸ Clinton impeached and acquitted (1998–1999)	▸ New technology prompts productivity rise ▸ Global competition cuts U.S. manufacturing; jobs outsourced overseas	▸ Los Angeles race riots (1992) ▸ "Culture Wars" over affirmative action, feminism, abortion, and gay rights	▸ Dramatic growth of the Internet and World Wide Web ▸ America Online rises and declines ▸ Biotech revolution
2000–	▸ Radical Muslim attacks on Twin Towers and the Pentagon (2001) ▸ U.S. and allies oust Taliban in Afghanistan ▸ United States invades Iraq (2003) ▸ North Korea tests a nuclear weapon (2006); stalemate with Iran over its nuclear program	▸ George W. Bush narrowly elected president (2000) ▸ Bush pushes Faith-Based Initiatives and No Child Left Behind ▸ USA PATRIOT Act passed (2002) ▸ *Hamdan v. Rumsfeld* (2006) overturns administration's policies on the treatment of detainees	▸ Bush tax cuts ▸ Huge trade deficits with China and Asia ▸ Rising budget deficits ▸ Illegal immigration boosts low-wage work ▸ Stock market and hedge fund boom ▸ Fall in value of dollar	▸ Many states ban gay marriages ▸ "Minutemen" patrol Mexican border; immigration changes proposed ▸ Baby boomers begin to retire; new federal drug benefits for elderly	▸ Broadband access grows ▸ "Blogging" increases ▸ "Creation Science" controversy ▸ Bush limits on stem-cell research challenged ▸ Global warming increases

In a 1972 interview, President Richard M. Nixon remarked, "History is never worth reading until it's fifty years old. It takes fifty years before you're able to come back and evaluate a man or a period of time." Nixon's comments remind us that writing recent history poses a particular challenge; not knowing the future course of events, we can't say for certain which present-day trends will prove to be the most important. Part Seven is therefore a work-in-progress; its perspective will change as events unfold. At this point, it focuses on five broad themes: the ascendancy in American politics of the New Right, the impact of economic globalization, social conflicts stemming from cultural diversity, the revolution in information technology, and the end of the Cold War and the rise of Muslim terrorism.

DIPLOMACY In a surprising development in the late 1980s, the Soviet Union and its satellite Communist regimes in Eastern European suddenly collapsed. The Soviet demise produced, in the words of President George H. W. Bush, a "new world order" and left the United States as the only military superpower. Accepting that role, the United States worked to counter civil wars, terrorist activities, and military aggression in many parts of the world and especially in the Middle East. In 1991, it fought the Persian Gulf War in response to Iraq's invasion of Kuwait and, in the late 1990s, led military action and peacekeeping efforts in Serbia and Bosnia. In 2001, in response to terrorist attacks on New York and Washington by the radical Islamic group Al Qaeda, President George W. Bush attacked Al Qaeda's bases in Afghanistan. He then ordered an invasion of Iraq in 2003 that quickly toppled the regime of dictator Saddam Hussein but triggered civil chaos and a violent insurgency that is still ongoing.

GOVERNMENT With Ronald Reagan's election in 1980, "New Right" conservatism began its ascendancy. The conservative agenda was to roll back the social welfare state created by liberal Democrats during the New Deal and the Great Society. Presidents Reagan, George H. W. Bush, and George W. Bush cut taxes, limited the regulatory activities of federal agencies, transferred some powers and resources to state governments, and appointed conservative-minded judges to the federal courts. The most important change in the federal welfare system, however, came during the Clinton administration in 1996, with new legislation designed to shift families from dependency on welfare payments to employment in the labor market. Evangelical Christians and conservative lawmakers brought abortion, gay rights, and other cultural issues into the political arena, setting off controversies that revealed sharp divisions among the American people.

ECONOMY The American economy grew substantially during the quarter century beginning in 1980, thanks to the increased productivity of workers and the controversial tax and spending policies of the federal government. Tax cuts spurred investment and government spending for military purposes boosted production; these policies also created huge budget deficits, a dramatic increase in the national debt, and a widening gap between rich and poor Americans. Equally significant, the end of Cold War allowed the spread of capitalist enterprise around the globe. As multinational corporations set up manufacturing facilities in China and other low-wage countries, they undercut industrial production and wage rates in the United States and helped to create a massive American trade deficit. Because of the trade and budget deficits, American prosperity rested on an increasingly shaky foundation.

SOCIETY The increasing heterogeneity of American society—in demographic composition and in cultural values—was yet another characteristic of life in the first decade of the twenty-first century. Increased immigration from Latin America and Asia added to cultural tensions and produced a new nativist movement. Continuing battles over affirmative action, abortion, sexual standards, homosexuality, feminism, and religion in public life took on an increasingly passionate character, inhibiting the quest for politically negotiated solutions.

TECHNOLOGY AND SCIENCE One effect of faith-based politics was a significant challenge to scientific evidence and research, most especially against the claims of evolution and the advent of stem-cell research. Even the dramatic changes in technology, which boosted economic productivity and provided easy access to information and entertainment, posed new challenges. Would cable technology, with its multitude of choices, further erode a common American culture? Would the World Wide Web facilitate the outsourcing of American middle-class jobs? Would computer technology allow corporations—and government agencies—to track the lives and limit the freedom of American citizens? Like any revolution, the innovations in computer technology had an increasingly significant impact on many spheres of American life.

A "new world order," a New Right ascendancy, a new global economy, massive new immigration, and a technological revolution: We live in a time of rapid political and social changes and continuing diplomatic and technological challenges that will test the resiliency of American society and the creativity of American leaders.

30

The Reagan Revolution and the End of the Cold War

1980–2001

O N NOVEMBER 9, 1989, MILLIONS of television viewers worldwide watched jubilant Germans knock down the Berlin Wall. The wall, which had divided the city since 1961, was a vivid symbol of Communist repression and the Cold War division of Europe. More than four hundred East Germans had lost their lives trying to escape to freedom on the other side. Now East and West Berliners, young and old, danced on the remains of the forbidding wall. Two years later, in 1991, the Soviet Union itself dissolved, ending the Cold War. A new world order was in the making.

The end of the Cold War was the result, in part, of a dramatic change in American political life. The election of President Ronald Reagan began a conservative political ascendancy that continues to the present. Supported by the Republican Party's New Right, Reagan declared political war against both the Soviet Union and the liberal ideology that had informed American public policy since the New Deal of Franklin D. Roosevelt (1933–1945). However, the Republicans' domestic agenda was complicated by a split between religious conservatives, who demanded strong government action to implement their faith-based agenda, and economic conservatives, who favored limited government and free markets. Moreover, the Democratic Party remained a potent — and flexible — political force. Acknowledging the rightward shift in the country's mood,

◄ **The Wall Comes Down**

As the Communist government of East Germany collapsed, West Berliners showed their contempt for the wall dividing the city by defacing it with graffiti. Then, in November 1989, East and West Berliners destroyed huge sections of the wall with sledgehammers, an act of psychic liberation that symbolized the end of the Cold War. Alexandria Avakian / Woodfin Camp & Associates.

Democrat Bill Clinton trod a centrist path that led him to the White House in 1992 and again in 1996. "The era of big government is over," Clinton declared. At home as well as abroad, a new order emerged during the last decades of the century.

The Rise of Conservatism

The Great Depression of the 1930s and World War II had discredited the traditional conservative program of limited government at home and an isolationist-oriented foreign policy. Although the conservatives' crusade against communism revived their political fortunes during the height of the Cold War in the 1950s, they failed to articulate an ideology and a set of policies that would command the support of a majority of American voters. Then, in the late 1970s, conservative Republicans took advantage of serious blunders by liberal Democrats and built a formidable political coalition.

Reagan and the Emergence of the New Right

The personal odyssey of Ronald Reagan embodies the story of "New Right" Republican conservatism. Before World War II, Reagan was a well-known movie actor — and a New Deal Democrat and admirer of Franklin Roosevelt. He turned away from the New Deal partly out of self-interest (he disliked paying high taxes) and partly out of principle. As head of the Screen Actors Guild from 1947 to 1952, he had to deal with communist union organizers — the left wing of the liberal New Deal. Dismayed by their hard-line tactics and goals, he became a militant anti-communist and a conservative. Giving up his fading movie career, Reagan became a well-known spokesperson for the General Electric Corporation. By the early 1960s, he had become a Republican and threw himself into California politics, speaking for conservative causes and candidates.

Ronald Reagan came to national prominence in 1964. Speaking to the Republican convention on national television, he delivered a powerful speech supporting the presidential nomination of archconservative Barry Goldwater (see Chapter 28). Just as the "Cross of Gold" speech elevated William Jennings Bryan to fame in 1896, so Reagan's address — titled "A Time for Choosing" and delivered again and again throughout the mid-1960s — secured his political future. With the financial backing of wealthy southern California business interests, he won the governorship of California in

1968 and again in 1972. His impassioned rhetoric supporting limited government, low taxation, and law and order won broad support among citizens of the most populous state and made him a force in national politics. Narrowly defeated in his bid for the Republican presidential nomination in 1976, Reagan counted on his growing popularity to make him the party's candidate in 1980.

Liberal Decline and Conservative Resurgence. In 1964, the conservative message preached by Ronald Reagan and Barry Goldwater appealed to few American voters. Then came the series of events that mobilized opposition to the Democratic Party and its liberal agenda: a stagnating economy, the failed war in Vietnam, African American riots, a judiciary that legalized abortion and enforced school busing, and an expanded federal regulatory state. By the mid-1970s, conservatism commanded greater popular support. In the South, long a Democratic stronghold, whites hostile to federal support of civil rights for African Americans voted Republican in increasing numbers. Simultaneously, middle-class suburbanites and migrants to the Sun Belt states endorsed the conservative agenda of combating crime, limiting social welfare spending, and increasing expenditures on military defense.

Strong "New Right" grassroots organizations spread the message. In 1964, 3.9 million volunteers had campaigned for Barry Goldwater, twice as many as worked for Lyndon B. Johnson; in the late 1970s, they swung their support to Ronald Reagan. Skilled conservative political operatives such as Richard Viguerie, a Louisiana-born Catholic and antiabortion activist, applied new computer technology to political campaigning. They used computerized mailing lists to solicit campaign funds, drum up support for conservative causes and candidates, and get out the vote on election day.

Other organizational support for the New Right came from think tanks funded by wealthy conservatives. The Heritage Foundation, American Enterprise Institute, and the Cato Institute issued policy proposals and persistently attacked both liberal social policy and the permissive culture they claimed it spawned. These organizations blended the traditional conservative themes of unrestrained individualism and a free-market economy with the hot-button "social issues" of affirmative action, the welfare state, and changing gender and sexual values. They also fostered the growth of a cadre of conservative intellectuals. For decades, William F. Buckley, the founder and editor of the *National*

Review, and Milton Friedman, the Nobel Prize–winning laissez-faire economist at the University of Chicago, were virtually the only prominent conservative intellectuals. Now they were joined on the public stage by the so-called neoconservatives—well-known intellectuals such as Jeane Kirkpatrick, Nathan Glazer, and Norman Podhoretz, editor of *Commentary* magazine. Many neoconservatives had once advocated radical and liberal causes; vehemently recanting their former views, they provided intellectual respectability to the Republican Right. As liberal New York Senator Daniel Moynihan remarked, suddenly "the GOP has become a party of ideas."

The Religious Right. The most striking new entry into the conservative coalition was the Religious Right. Drawing its membership from conservative Catholics and Protestant evangelicals, the Religious Right condemned growing public acceptance of divorce, abortion, premarital sex, and feminism. Charismatic television evangelists, such as Pat Robertson, the son of a U.S. senator, and Jerry Falwell, the founder of the Moral Majority, emerged as the champions of a faith-based political agenda. As these cultural and moral conservatives attacked Democratic liberals for supporting lenient punishments for criminals, permissive sexuality, and welfare payments to unmarried mothers with multiple children, economic conservatives called for cuts in taxes and government regulations. Ronald Reagan endorsed the programs of both groups and, with their support, captured the Republican nomination for president in 1980 (see Comparing American Voices, "Christianity and Public Life," pp. 930–931). To win the votes of more moderate Republicans, Reagan chose former CIA director George H. W. Bush as his running mate.

The Election of 1980

In the election of 1980, President Jimmy Carter's sinking popularity virtually doomed his campaign. When the Democrats renominated him over his liberal challenger, Edward (Ted) Kennedy of Massachusetts, Carter's approval rating was stunningly low—a mere 21 percent of Americans believed he was an effective president. The reasons were readily apparent. Economically, millions of citizens were feeling the pinch from stagnant wages, high inflation, crippling mortgage rates, and an unemployment rate of nearly 8 percent (see Chapter 29). Diplomatically, the nation blamed Carter for failing to respond strongly to Soviet expansion and to the Iranian hostage crisis.

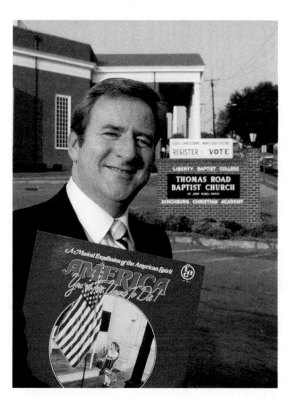

Jerry Falwell

The resurgence of evangelical religion in the 1970s was accompanied by a conservative movement in politics known as the New Right or the Christian Right. Founded in 1979 by televangelist Jerry Falwell, the Moral Majority was one of the earliest New Right groups, committed to promoting "family values" and (as the title to the record album suggests) patriotism in American society and politics. Wally McNamee/Corbis.

The incumbent president found himself constantly on the defensive, while Reagan remained upbeat and decisive. "This is the greatest country in the world," Reagan reassured the nation in his warm baritone voice, "we have the talent, we have the drive. . . . All we need is the leadership." To emphasize his intention to be a formidable international leader, Reagan hinted that he would take strong action to win the hostages' return. To signal a rejection of the Democrats' liberalism, the California governor declared his opposition to affirmative action and forced busing, and promised to get "the government off our backs." Most important, Reagan effectively appealed to the many Americans who felt financially insecure. In a televised debate between the candidates, Reagan emphasized the economic plight of working- and middle-class Americans in an era of "stagflation"—stagnant wages amidst rapidly rising prices. He posed the rhetorical question, "Are you better off today than you were four years ago?"

Christianity and Public Life

Modern social welfare liberalism embodies an ethic of moral pluralism and favors the separation of church and state. Conservative Christians challenge the legitimacy of pluralism and secularism and seek, through political agitation and legal action, to make religion an integral part of public life.

PRESIDENT RONALD REAGAN
"The Rule of Law under God"

Reagan's candidacy was strongly supported by Christian conservatives. He delivered these remarks to the National Association of American Evangelicals in 1983.

I want you to know that this administration is motivated by a political philosophy that sees the greatness of America in you, her people, and in your families, churches, neighborhoods, communities—the institutions that foster and nourish values like concern for others and respect for the rule of law under God.

Now, I don't have to tell you that this puts us in opposition to, or at least out of step with, a prevailing attitude of many who have turned to a modern-day secularism, discarding the tried and time-tested values upon which our very civilization is based. No matter how well intentioned, their value system is radically different from that of most Americans. And while they proclaim that they're freeing us from superstitions of the past, they've taken upon themselves the job of superintending us by government rule and regulation. Sometimes their voices are louder than ours, but they are not yet a majority....

Freedom prospers when religion is vibrant and the rule of law under God is acknowledged. When our Founding Fathers passed the First Amendment, they sought to protect churches from government interference. They never intended to construct a wall of hostility between government and the concept of religious belief itself.

Last year, I sent the Congress a constitutional amendment to restore prayer to public schools. Already this session, there's growing bipartisan support for the amendment, and I am calling on the Congress to act speedily to pass it and to let our children pray....

SOURCE: Ronald Reagan, *Speaking My Mind: Selected Speeches* (New York: Simon & Schuster, 1989), 169–180.

DONALD E. WILDMON
Network Television as a Moral Danger

Wildmon is a Christian minister and a grassroots religious activist. This selection comes from The Home Invaders *(1985).*

One night during the Christmas holidays of 1976, I decided to watch television with my family.... Not far into the program was a scene of adultery. I reacted to the situation in the manner as I had been taught. I asked one of the children to change channels. Getting involved in the second program, we were shocked with some crude profanity....

As I sat in my den that night, I became angry. I had been disturbed by the deterioration of morals I had witnessed in the media and society during the previous twenty-five years. This was accompanied by a dramatic rise in crime, a proliferation of pornography, increasingly explicit sexual lyrics in music, increasing numbers of broken homes, a rise in drug and alcohol use among the youth, and various other negative factors. I had managed to avoid those unpleasant changes to a large degree by staying away, turning my head, justifying my actions with the reasons most commonly expressed: freedom of speech, pluralism, tolerance....

Realizing that these changes were being brought into the sanctity of my home, I decided I could and would no longer remain silent.... Out of that decision came the National Federation for Decency (and out of the NFD came the Coalition for Better Television).... But the more I dealt with the problems, the more I realized that I was dealing only with symptoms not the disease....

This great struggle is one of values, particularly which ones will be the standard for our society and a base for our system of justice in the years to come. For 200 years our country has based its morals, its sense of right and wrong, on the Christian view of man. The Ten Commandments and the Sermon on the Mount have been our solid foundation ... the most perfect system ever devised in the history of mankind.

Television is the most pervasive and persuasive medium we have. At times it is larger than life. It is our only true national medium. Network television is the greatest educator we have.... It is teaching that adultery is an acceptable and approved lifestyle.... It is teaching that hardly anyone goes to church, that very few people in our society are Christian or live by Christian principles. How? By simply censoring Christian characters, Christian values, and Christian culture from the programs.

If within the next five years we fail to turn the tide of this humanist value system which seeks to replace our Christian heritage, then we have ... lost the battle.

SOURCE: Donald E. Wildmon, *The Home Invaders* (Elgin, IL: Victor Books, 1985), 3–7.

A. BARTLETT GIAMATTI
The Moral Majority as a Threat to Liberty

A. Bartlett Giamatti was the president of Yale University (1978–1986) and subsequently president of the National (Baseball) League. He offered these remarks to the entering class of Yale undergraduates in 1981.

A self-proclaimed "Moral Majority," and its satellite or client groups, cunning in the use of a native blend of old intimidation and new technology, threaten the values [of pluralism and freedom]. . . .

From the maw of this "morality" come those who presume to know what justice for all is; come those who presume to know which books are fit to read, which television programs are fit to watch. . . . From the maw of this "morality" rise the tax-exempt Savonarolas who believe they, and they alone, possess the "truth." There is no debate, no discussion, no dissent. They know. . . . What nonsense.

What dangerous, malicious nonsense. . . .

We should be concerned that so much of our political and religious leadership acts intimidated for the moment and will not say with clarity that this most recent denial of the legitimacy of differentness is a radical assault on the very pluralism of peoples, political beliefs, values, forms of merit and systems of religion our country was founded to welcome and foster.

Liberty protects the person from unwarranted government intrusions into a dwelling or other private places. In our tradition the State is not omnipresent in the home. And there are other spheres of our lives and existence, outside the home, where the State should not be a dominant presence. Freedom extends beyond spatial bounds. Liberty presumes an autonomy of self that includes freedom of thought, belief, expression, and certain intimate conduct.

SOURCE: Yale University Archives.

ANTHONY KENNEDY
The Constitution Protects Privacy

Kennedy, a Roman Catholic, was named to the Supreme Court by Ronald Reagan in 1988. In Lawrence v. Texas *(2003), he wrote the opinion for five of the six justices in the majority; Sandra Day O'Connor wrote a concurring opinion.*

The question before the Court is the validity of a Texas statute making it a crime for two persons of the same sex to engage in certain intimate sexual conduct.

In Houston, Texas, officers of the Harris County Police Department were dispatched to a private residence in response to a reported weapons disturbance. They entered an apartment where one of the petitioners, John Geddes Lawrence, resided. . . . The officers observed Lawrence and another man, Tyron Garner, engaging in a sexual act. The two petitioners were arrested, held in custody over night, and charged and convicted before a Justice of the Peace.

The complaints described their crime as "deviate sexual intercourse, namely anal sex, with a member of the same sex (man)." . . .

We conclude the case should be resolved by determining whether the petitioners were free as adults to engage in the private conduct in the exercise of their liberty under the Due Process Clause of the Fourteenth Amendment to the Constitution.

[The Texas statute in question seeks] to control a personal relationship that, whether or not entitled to formal recognition in the law, is within the liberty of persons to choose without being punished as criminals. . . . The liberty protected by the Constitution allows homosexual persons the right to make this choice. . . .

The present case does not involve minors. It does not involve persons who might be injured or coerced or who are situated in relationships where consent might not easily be refused. It does not involve public conduct or prostitution. It does not involve whether the government must give formal recognition to any relationship that homosexual persons seek to enter. The case does involve two adults who, with full and mutual consent from each other, engaged in sexual practices common to a homosexual lifestyle. The petitioners are entitled to respect for their private lives. The State cannot demean their existence or control their destiny by making their private sexual conduct a crime. Their right to liberty under the Due Process Clause gives them the full right to engage in their conduct without intervention of the government. "It is a promise of the Constitution that there is a realm of personal liberty which the government may not enter."

SOURCE: *Lawrence v. Texas*, 539 U.S. 558, 562–563, 567, 571, 579 (2003).

ANALYZING THE EVIDENCE

➤ What would Ronald Reagan think of the opinion written by Justice Kennedy, his appointee? Would Reagan agree with it, given his condemnation of those who are intent on "subordinating us to government rule and regulation"?

➤ According to Wildmon and Giamatti, what should be shown on television, and who should make those decisions?

➤ When should the government police private conduct? Consider the criteria outlined in the final paragraph of Justice Kennedy's opinion.

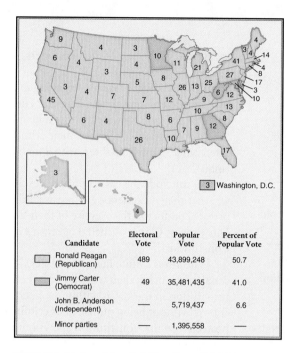

MAP 30.1 Presidential Election of 1980

Ronald Reagan easily defeated Democratic incumbent Jimmy Carter, taking 51 percent of the popular vote to Carter's 41 percent and winning the electoral vote in all but six states and the District of Columbia. Reagan cut deeply into the traditional Democratic coalition by wooing many southern whites, urban ethnics, and blue-collar workers. More than five million Americans expressed their discontent with Carter's ineffectiveness and Reagan's conservatism by voting for Independent candidate John Anderson, a longtime Republican member of the House of Representatives.

In November, the voters gave a clear answer. They repudiated Carter, giving him only 41 percent of the vote. Independent candidate John Anderson garnered 7 percent, and Reagan won easily, with 51 percent of the popular vote nationwide and higher percentages in the South (Map 30.1). Equally important, the Republicans elected thirty-three new members of the House of Representatives and twelve new senators, which gave them control of the U.S. Senate for the first time since 1954.

Superior financial resources contributed to the Republican success: Two-thirds of all corporate donations to political action committees went to conservative Republican candidates. While the Democratic Party saw its key constituency—organized labor—dwindle in size and influence, the GOP used its ample funds to reach voters through a sophisticated campaign of television and direct-mail advertisements. "Madison Avenue" advertising techniques—long used to sell commercial products—had begun to shape political

campaigns in the 1960s. Now they became the primary means of trumpeting the virtues of a political candidate and attacking the credentials of his or her opponent.

Political Realignment. This aggressive campaigning continued the realignment of the American electorate that had begun during the 1970s. The core of the Republican Party remained the relatively affluent, white, Protestant voters who supported balanced budgets, opposed government activism, feared crime and communism, and believed in a strong national defense. But "Reagan Democrats" had now joined the Republican cause; prominent among these formerly Democratic voters were southern whites, who opposed civil rights legislation, and Catholic blue-collar workers, who were alarmed by antiwar protestors, feminist demands, and welfare expenditures. Reagan Republicanism also struck a responsive note among young voters, who increasingly identified themselves as "moderates" or "conservatives," and among the socially mobile residents of rapidly growing suburban communities in Texas, Arizona, and California.

The Religious Right was another significant contributor to the Republican victory. The Moral Majority claimed that it registered two million new voters for the 1980 election, and the Republican Party's platform reflected its influence. The platform called for a constitutional ban on abortion, voluntary prayer in public schools, and a mandatory death penalty for certain crimes. The Republicans also demanded an end to court-mandated busing and, for the first time in forty years, opposed the Equal Rights Amendment. Within the Republican Party, conservatism had triumphed.

Reagan's victory led some observers to predict a long-lasting alteration in American voting patterns. As *U.S. News & World Report* proclaimed, "A Massive Shift . . . Right." Other commentators offered more cautious assessments. They noted that Reagan won a bare majority of the votes cast and that turnout was unusually low because many working-class voters—disillusioned Democrats—stayed home. Rather than an endorsement of conservatism, one analyst called the election a "landslide vote of no confidence in an incompetent administration." Whatever the verdict, Ronald Reagan's victory raised the possibility of a dramatic shift in government policies and priorities. As he entered office, the new president claimed the American public had given him a mandate for sweeping change. His success—or failure—would determine the significance of the election and the New Right.

➤ What were the key groups of the new Republican coalition? Were their goals complementary? Contradictory?

➤ What factors led to Ronald Reagan's election in 1980?

The Reagan Presidency, 1981–1989

Ronald Reagan's personality was as important as his policies. Frayed by the cultural turmoil of the 1960s and the economic malaise of the 1970s, the majority of voters embraced the former movie actor's optimistic message of national pride and purpose. Even when major scandals threatened his administration, Reagan maintained his popularity, leading critics to dub him "the Teflon president" since nothing damaging seemed to stick. More sympathetic observers called him "the Great Communicator"; they praised his ability to address the anxieties of Americans and to win support for the Republicans' conservative economic and cultural agenda.

Reaganomics

First elected at age sixty-nine, Ronald Reagan was the oldest man ever to serve as president. His appearance and demeanor belied his age. Concerned since his acting days with his physical fitness, the president conveyed a sense of vigor and purpose (see Reading American Pictures, "Image Warfare: Fighting to Define the Reagan Presidency," p. 934). His folksy humor endeared him to millions, who overlooked his frequent misstatements and indifference to details of public policy. He kept his political message clear and simple. "Government is not the solution to our problem," Reagan declared. "Government is the problem."

In his first year of office, Reagan and his chief advisor, James A. Baker III, moved quickly to set new government priorities. To roll back the expanded liberal state, they launched a coordinated three-pronged assault on federal taxes, social welfare spending, and the regulatory bureaucracy. To win the Cold War, they advocated a vast increase in defense spending. And, to match the resurgent economies of Germany and Japan, whom the United States had defeated in World War II and then helped to rebuild, they set out to restore American leadership of the world's capitalist societies.

"Supply-Side" Theory. To achieve this goal, the new administration advanced a new set of economic and tax policies. Quickly dubbed "Reaganomics," these policies sought to boost the economy by increasing the supply of goods. The theory underlying "supply-side economics," as this approach was called, emphasized the need to increase investment in productive enterprises. According to George Gilder, a major supply-side theorist, the best way to bolster investment was to reduce the taxes paid by business corporations and wealthy Americans, who could then use these funds to expand production. Supply-siders maintained that the resulting economic expansion would increase government revenues and offset the loss of tax dollars stemming from the original tax cuts.

Taking advantage of Republican control of the Senate and his personal popularity following a failed assassination attempt, Reagan won congressional approval of the Economic Recovery Tax Act (ERTA). The act reduced income tax rates paid by most Americans by 23 percent over three years. For the wealthiest Americans — those with millions to invest — the highest marginal tax rate dropped from 70 to 50 percent. The act also slashed estate taxes, the levies on inheritances instituted around 1900 to prevent the transmission of huge fortunes from one generation to the next. Finally, the new legislation trimmed the taxes paid by business corporations by $150 billion over a period of five years. As a result of ERTA, by 1986 the annual revenue of the federal government had been cut by $200 billion.

Shifts in Spending. David Stockman, Reagan's budget director, hoped to match this sizable reduction in tax revenue with a comparable cutback in federal expenditures. To meet this ambitious goal, he proposed substantial cuts in Social Security and Medicare. But Congress — and the president — rejected such efforts because they were not willing to antagonize middle-class and elderly voters who viewed these government entitlements as sacrosanct. As neoconservative columnist George Will noted ironically, "Americans are conservative. What they want to conserve is the New Deal." This contradiction between Republican ideology and practical politics would frustrate the GOP into the twenty-first century.

In a futile attempt to balance the budget, Stockman advocated spending cuts on programs for food stamps, unemployment compensation, and welfare assistance such as Aid to Families with Dependent Children (AFDC). In the administration's view, these programs represented the worst features of Lyndon Johnson's Great Society — a huge

Image Warfare: Fighting to Define the Reagan Presidency

As might be expected, U.S. presidents and their staffs attempt to project a positive image of the chief executive and the administration's policies. But contradictions often arise between the image and values cultivated by a president and the actual policies pursued by the White House. The presidency of Ronald Reagan is a case in point. As the text points out, Reagan helped to stimulate a conservative movement in American politics and society during the 1980s. Images of Reagan quickly became vital for the White House to deliver its message of conservative reform to the American people. As the cartoon published by the *Arkansas Gazette* illustrates, powerful imagery could also be wielded by Reagan's political opponents.

ANALYZING THE EVIDENCE

➤ Examine the photo of Reagan at his ranch in California. This image was taken by a White House photographer. What message does the image convey about Reagan as a person? How does this message reinforce the policies created by Reagan that you read about in the text?

➤ What message does the cartoon convey about Reagan policies? How does this differ from the official White House message expressed in the photo of Reagan?

➤ Together, what do these two images tell us about the image and reality of the Reagan presidency? Do you think that cartoons or photographs are a more accurate source of information for understanding the historical meaning of a particular president and his administration? Why or why not?

President Reagan at His Ranch in Southern California. Ronald Reagan Presidential Library.

Presidential Landscaping. Courtesy *Arkansas Gazette*, 1984.

FIGURE 30.1 The Annual Federal Budget Deficit (or Surplus), 1940–2005

During World War II, the federal government incurred an enormous budget deficit. But between 1946 and 1965, it ran either an annual budget surplus or incurred a relatively small debt. As measured in 2005 dollars, the accumulated national debt increased by about $50 billion during that twenty-year period or about $2.5 billion a year. The annual deficits rose significantly during the Vietnam War and the stagflation of the 1970s, but they really exploded between 1982 and 1994, in the budgets devised by the Ronald Reagan and George H. W. Bush administrations, and again between 2002 and 2005, in those prepared by George W. Bush. The Republican presidents increased military spending while cutting taxes, an "enjoy-it-now" philosophy that transferred the cost to future generations of Americans.

SOURCE: National Priorities Project. See also *U.S. Budget for Fiscal Year 2007*, Historical Tables, Table 15.6.

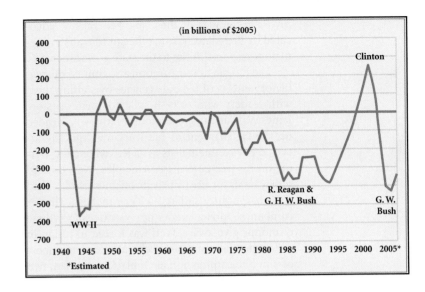

handout to economic drones at the expense of hardworking taxpayers. Congress approved some cutbacks but preserved most of these welfare programs because of their importance; in 1980, some 21 million people relied on the food stamp program. It likewise continued to lavish huge subsidies and tariff protection on wealthy farmers and business corporations — "welfare for the rich," as some critics put it. As the administration's spending cuts fell far short of its goal, the federal budget deficit increased dramatically.

Military spending accounted for the bulk of the growing federal deficit, and President Reagan was its strongest supporter. "Defense is not a budget item," he declared, "you spend what you need." To "make America number one again," Reagan and Defense Secretary Caspar Weinberger pushed through Congress a five-year, $1.2 trillion military spending program that accelerated an arms buildup begun in 1978 by President Carter after the emergence of a pro-Soviet government in Afghanistan. The administration revived the B-1 bomber, which Carter had canceled because of its great expense and limited usefulness, and continued development of the MX, a new missile system approved by Carter. Reagan's most ambitious and controversial weapons plan, proposed in 1983, was the Strategic Defense Initiative (SDI). Popularly known as "Star Wars" because of its science-fiction-like features, SDI would consist of a system of laser-equipped satellites that would detect and destroy incoming ballistic missiles carrying atomic weapons. Would it work? Most scientists were dubious; Secretary of State George Shultz thought

it was "lunacy," and even Weinberger, who liked every weapons system he saw, dismissed the idea. Nonetheless, Congress approved initial funding for the controversial — and enormously expensive — project. During Reagan's presidency military spending accounted for nearly one-fourth of all federal expenditures.

The combination of lower taxes and higher defense spending led to a skyrocketing national debt (Figure 30.1). By the time Reagan left office, the federal deficit had tripled — rising from $930 billion in 1981 to $2.8 trillion in 1989. Every American citizen — from small baby to senior citizen — now owed a hidden debt of $11,000.

Regulatory Cutbacks. Advocates of Reaganomics also asserted that excessive regulation by federal government agencies impeded economic growth. Some of these bureaucracies, such as the U.S. Department of Labor, had risen to prominence during the New Deal; others, such as the Environmental Protection Agency (EPA) and the Occupational Safety and Health Administration (OSHA), were created by Democratic Congresses during the Great Society and the Nixon administration (see Chapters 24, 28, and 29). Although these agencies provided many services to business corporations, they also increased their costs — by assisting labor unions to organize, ordering safety improvements in factories, and requiring expensive equipment to limit the release of toxic chemicals into the environment. To reduce the reach of federal regulatory agencies, the Reagan administration cut their budgets — by an average of 12 percent. And, invoking the idea of the "New Federalism" advocated by President Nixon, it began to transfer regulatory responsibilities to the state governments.

The Reagan administration also limited the regulatory efforts of federal agencies by staffing them with leaders who were hostile to their mission. James Watt, an outspoken conservative who headed up the Department of the Interior, explicitly attacked environmentalists as "a left-wing cult." Acting on his free-enterprise principles, Watt opened public lands for use by private businesses—oil and coal corporations, large-scale ranchers, timber companies. Already under heavy criticism for these economic give-aways, Watt was forced to resign in 1983 when he dismissively characterized members of a public commission as "a black, a woman, two Jews, and a cripple." Anne Gorsuch Buford, whom Reagan appointed to head the EPA, likewise resigned when she was implicated in a money scandal and was cited for contempt of Congress for refusing to provide documents regarding the Superfund program, which cleans up toxic waste sites.

The Sierra Club and other environmental groups roused enough public outrage about these appointees and their policies that the administration changed its position. During President Reagan's second term, he significantly increased the EPA's budget, created new wildlife preserves, and added acreage to the National Wilderness Preservation System and animals and plants to the endangered species lists.

Reaganomics Stalled. Ultimately, politics in a democracy is "the art of the possible," and savvy politicians know when to advance and when to retreat. Having attained two of his prime goals—a major tax cut and a dramatic increase in defense spending—Reagan did not carry through on his promises to scale back big government and the welfare state. When Reagan left office in 1989, federal spending stood at 22.1 percent of the gross domestic product (GDP) and federal taxes at 19 percent of GDP, both virtually the same as in 1981. In the meantime, the federal deficit had tripled in size, and the number of civilian government workers had increased from 2.9 to 3.1 million. This outcome—so different from the president's lofty rhetoric—elicited harsh criticism from conservative commentators. As one of them angrily charged, there was no "Reagan Revolution."

That verdict was too narrow. Despite its failed promises, the presidency of Ronald Reagan set the nation on a new political and ideological path. Social welfare liberalism, ascendant since 1933, was now thoroughly on the defensive. Moreover, the Reagan presidency restored popular belief that America—and individual Americans—could enjoy increasing prosperity.

Reagan's Second Term

As Ronald Reagan campaigned in 1984 for a second term in the White House, he claimed credit for a resurgent economy. On coming into office in 1981, he had supported the "tight" money policy implemented by the Federal Reserve Board headed by Paul Volker. By raising interest rates to the extraordinarily high level of 18 percent, Volker had quickly cut the high inflation rates of the Carter years. But this deflationary policy caused an economic recession that put some ten million Americans out of work. President Reagan's approval rating plummeted, and in the elections of 1982, Democrats picked up twenty-six seats in the House of Representatives and seven state governorships.

The economy—and the president's popularity—quickly revived. During the 1984 election campaign, Reagan hailed his tax cuts as the reason for the economic resurgence. His campaign theme, "It's Morning in America," suggested that a new day of prosperity and pride had dawned. The Democrats nominated former vice president Walter Mondale of Minnesota. With strong ties to labor unions, ethnic groups, and party leaders, Mondale epitomized the New Deal coalition that had dominated the Democratic Party since Franklin Roosevelt. To appeal to women voters, Mondale selected Representative Geraldine Ferraro of New York as his running mate—the first woman to run on the presidential ticket of a major political party. Neither Ferraro's presence nor Mondale's credentials made a difference. The incumbent president carried the entire nation except for Minnesota and the District of Columbia and won a landslide victory. Still, Democrats retained their majority in House and, in 1986, regained control of the Senate.

The Iran-Contra Affair. A major scandal marred Reagan's second term. Early in 1986 news leaked out that the administration had negotiated an "arms-for-hostages" deal with the revolutionary Islamic government of Iran. For years the president had denounced Iran as an "outlaw state" and a supporter of terrorism. Now he wanted its help. To win Iran's assistance in freeing some American hostages held by Hezbollah, a pro-Iranian Shiite terrorist group in Lebanon, the administration covertly sold arms to the "outlaw state." While this secret Iranian arms deal was diplomatically suspect and politically controversial, the use of resulting profits in

Nicaragua was patently illegal. In 1981, the Reagan administration had suspended aid to the Sandinista government of Nicaragua. It charged that the Sandinistas, a left-wing movement that had overthrown dictator Anastasio Somoza Debayle, were pursuing socialist policies detrimental to American interests, forming a military alliance with Fidel Castro in Cuba, and supporting a leftist rebellion in neighboring El Salvador (Map 30.2). To overthrow the Sandinista government, President Reagan ordered the Central Intelligence Agency (CIA) to aid an armed Nicaraguan opposition group called the Contras. Although Reagan praised the Contras as "freedom fighters," Congress worried that the pres-

ident and other executive branch agencies were assuming war-making powers that the Constitution reserved to the legislature. In 1984 it strengthened the Boland Amendment, thereby banning the CIA and other government officials from providing any military support to the Contras.

Oliver North, a lieutenant colonel in the U.S. Marines and an aide to the National Security Council, consciously defied that ban. With the tacit or explicit consent of high-ranking administration officials, including the president, he used the profits from the Iranian arms deal to assist the Contras. When asked if he knew of North's illegal actions, Reagan replied, "I don't remember." Still swayed by

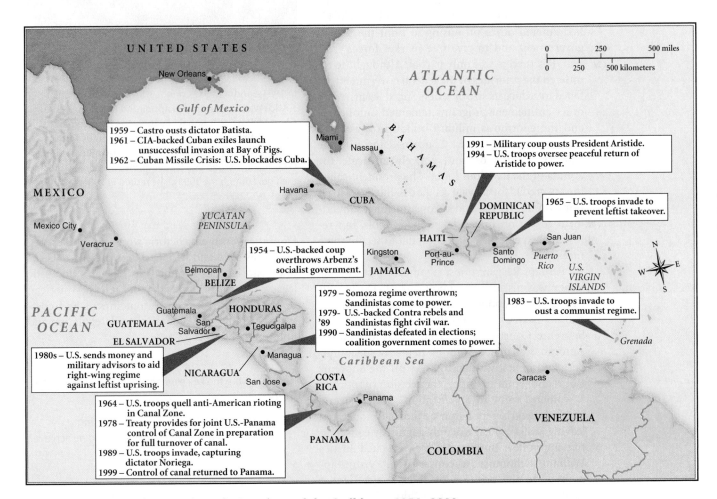

MAP 30.2 U.S. Involvement in Latin America and the Caribbean, 1954–2000

Ever since the Monroe Doctrine (1823), the United States has claimed a special interest in Latin America. During the Cold War, U.S. foreign policy throughout Latin America focused on containing instability and the appeal of communism in a region plagued by poverty and military dictatorships. Providing foreign aid was one approach to addressing social and economic needs, but the United States frequently intervened with military forces (or by supporting military coups) to remove unfriendly or socialist governments. The Reagan administration's support of the Contra rebels in Nicaragua, some of which was contrary to U.S. law, was one of those interventions.

Reagan's charm, the public accepted this convenient loss of memory. Nonetheless, the Iran-Contra affair resulted in the prosecution of Colonel North and several other officials and jeopardized the president's historical reputation. It was not only that administration officials (as Lawrence Walsh, the special prosecutor appointed to investigate the scandal, concluded) carried out "two programs contrary to congressional policy and contrary to national policy [and] . . . broke the law," but also that President Reagan — of all people — had bribed terrorists. Most Americans were shocked by Reagan's dealings with Iran and its terrorist allies.

The Reagan Legacy. Deeply stung by the Iran-Contra scandal, Reagan proposed no bold domestic policy initiatives in his last two years in office. He had entered office promising to limit the federal government and to give free-market forces freer rein. His success was only partial. Although he re-ordered the priorities of the federal government, he failed to reduce its size or scope. Social Security and other entitlement programs remained untouched, and the enormous military buildup outweighed cuts in other programs. Concerned to unite the country, Reagan did not actively advocate the agenda of the Religious Right. The president called for tax credits for private religious schools, restrictions on abortions, and a constitutional amendment to permit prayer in public schools, but refused to expend his political capital to secure these measures.

Perhaps Reagan's most significant institutional legacy was his judicial appointments. During his two terms, he appointed 368 federal court judges, many of them with conservative credentials, and three Supreme Court justices, Sandra Day O'Connor, Antonin Scalia, and Anthony Kennedy. O'Connor became the first woman to serve on the Supreme Court and wrote an important decision supporting a woman's right to an abortion. Both she and Kennedy won a reputation as judicial moderates, leaving Scalia as Reagan's only genuinely conservative appointee. But Reagan also elevated Justice William Rehnquist, a conservative Nixon appointee, to the position of chief justice. Under Rehnquist's conservative leadership (1986–2005), an often-divided court watered down, but did not usually overturn, the liberal rulings of the Warren Court (1954–1967) with respect to individual liberties, abortion rights, affirmative action, and the rights of criminal defendants.

Reagan failed to roll back the social welfare and regulatory state of the New Deal-Great Society era, but he did change the dynamic of American politics.

Another Barrier Falls

In 1981, Sandra Day O'Connor, shown here with Chief Justice Warren Burger, was appointed to the Supreme Court by President Ronald Reagan, the first woman to serve on that body. In 1993, she was joined by Ruth Bader Ginsburg, an appointee of President Bill Clinton. O'Connor emerged as a leader of the "moderate" bloc on the Court during the 1990s; she retired in 2006. Fred Ward/Black Star/Stockphoto.com.

His antigovernment rhetoric won many adherents, as did his bold and fiscally dangerous tax cuts. As one historian has summed up Reagan's domestic legacy, "For the next twenty years at least, American policies would focus on retrenchment and cost-savings, budget cuts and tax cuts, deregulation and policy redefinitions."

➤ What were the key elements of Reagan's domestic policy?

➤ What limits did Reagan face in promoting conservative goals? What successes did he achieve?

Defeating Communism and Creating a New World Order

Ronald Reagan entered office determined to confront the Soviet Union diplomatically and militarily. Backed by Republican hard-liners, Reagan unleashed some of the harshest Cold War rhetoric since

Reagan and Gorbachev: Fellow Political Revolutionaries

Both Ronald Reagan and Mikhail Gorbachev changed the political outlook of their nations. As Reagan undermined social welfare liberalism in the United States, Gorbachev challenged the rigidity of the Communist Party and state socialism in the Soviet Union. Although they remained ideological adversaries, by the mid-1980s the two leaders had established a personal rapport, which helped to facilitate agreement on a series of arms reduction measures. © Bettmann/Corbis.

the 1950s, labeling the Soviet Union an "evil empire" and vowing to make certain it ended up "on the ash heap of history." By his second term Reagan had decided that this goal was best achieved by actively co-operating with Mikhail Gorbachev, its young and reform-minded leader. The collapse of the Soviet Union in 1991 ended the nearly fifty-year-long Cold War, but a new set of foreign challenges quickly appeared: the creation of a viable new world order (see Voices from Abroad, "Zhu Shida: China and the United States: A Unique Relationship," p. 940).

The End of the Cold War

The collapse of the Soviet Union and the end of the Cold War were the most dramatic developments in foreign affairs during the 1980s and early 1990s. The fall of the Soviet regime was the result of external pressure from the United States and the internal weaknesses of the Communist economy and soci-

ety. To defeat the Soviets, the administration pursued a two-pronged strategy. First, it abandoned the policy of "détente" and set about to rearm America. This buildup in American military strength, reasoned Secretary of Defense Caspar Weinberger, a determined hard-liner, would force the Soviets into an arms race that would strain their economy and undermine support for the Communist regime. Second, the president supported the policy of CIA Director William Casey to fund guerrillas who were trying to overthrow pro-Communist governments in Angola, Mozambique, Afghanistan, and Central America—and thereby roll back Soviet influence in the Third World.

The Weaknesses of the Soviet Union. These strategies succeeded because they exploited the internal weaknesses and policy mistakes of the Communist regime. Its system of state socialism and central economic planning had transformed Russia

Zhu Shida

China and the United States: A Unique Relationship

To understand the dynamics of American society and American foreign policy, the government-funded Chinese Academy of Social Sciences created an Institute of American Studies. Zhu Shida is a research associate at the Institute; in 2002, he published this piece on a semiofficial Chinese government Web site.

The relationship between China, one of the oldest civilizations with the biggest population, and the United States, one of the youngest civilizations with the strongest economy, is significant not only for the two peoples but also for the future of the whole world.

The factors influencing the Sino-US relationship include economic, strategic, diplomatic and cultural elements. Undoubtedly, among them the economic factor is the most important one. Economic interests are at the heart of China-US relations. In 2001, trade volume between the two nations hit US $8.4 billion, 8.1 percent higher than the previous year. Tempted by the colossal Chinese market, the US has become China's biggest investor with an investment of US $4.8 billion in 2001 and an accumulated investment of US $35.5 billion. . . .

Strategically, China and the US have common interests. The White House needs China's assistance and influence to handle North Korea and non-proliferation issues. America also needs China's cooperation in fighting terrorism. On the Taiwan question that remains the most sensitive issue, China asks the United States to abide by the three joint communiqués and pursue the one-China policy. . . .

To handle the Sino-US relationship appropriately, both sides should realize the necessity to further understanding and respect for each other's cultures, which, unfortunately, often has been neglected.

The origins of American culture lie in a combination of Puritanism, liberalism, individualism and republicanism. Reflected in politics, American culture takes the form of hegemonism with a strong religious flavor and labeled by its self-defined freedom, democracy and human rights standard. . . . Beginning with the original immigrating Puritans, Americans have regarded themselves as the chosen people, superior to any other peoples in the world. Meanwhile, in free and open America, there is no room for the strict consensus system characteristic of traditional societies. Therefore, without a unified attitude and consistent account in all fields of its political culture, discordant voices can be heard from time to time in American society, which is unimaginable and almost impossible in China.

The essence of Chinese culture is family affection and attachment. Any individual behavior damaging national dignity and group honor is not encouraged in Chinese society that thinks highly of collective benefits and reputation, which is beyond the understanding of American people.

In addition to the cultural differences between the two nations, we also need to realize the inherent discrepancies in American culture that influence American politics and foreign policies frequently. On the one hand, in terms of Puritanism, one of the origins of the American culture, since the earliest Puritans came to the New World due to the religious persecutions they suffered in England, the freedom and right for individuals to pursue welfare have occupied a special position in Puritanism. Naturally, Puritans harbor religious fervor for human rights. On the other, the protracted existence of racial discrimination and segregation did not change until after the Civil Rights movement during the 1950s and 1960s. Even today, the deep-rooted barrier between whites and minorities is still hard to be removed completely in the United States. The cultural contradictions are the source of America's double standards on the human rights issue.

The aggressive American culture with a short history of a little more than 200 years is built on the basis of individualism and liberalism, while the introversive Chinese culture with a 5000 years' tradition lays stress on collectivism and cultural consensus at the expense of individual voices. Obviously, the essences of these two cultures are contradictory. This cultural contradiction is the main reason for the constant Sino-US clashes. Nevertheless, mutual complementarities in economy magnetize the two nations, forcing them to compromise for their cultural discrepancies.

SOURCE: China Internet Information Center, www.china.org.cn/english/2002/Mar/29138.htm.

ANALYZING THE EVIDENCE

➤ Ronald Reagan frequently evoked Puritan John Winthrop's image of America as a shining "city on a hill" and a beacon for mankind. How does Zhu Shida interpret the impact of Puritan ways of thinking on American foreign policy? Based on your reading in this textbook, how accurate is his understanding of American culture?

➤ Given the institutional status of the writer and the essay's place of publication, how should we interpret it?

➤ According to the author, what factors pull China and the United States together? Which ones push them apart?

Pope John Paul II in Poland, 1979

Polish-born Karol Joseph Wojtyla (1920–2005) was named a cardinal of the Roman Catholic Church in 1967 and was selected as pope in 1978. The following year he visited Poland, where he reiterated his opposition to Communist rule. His visit sparked the formation of the Solidarity workers' movement and, as its founder Lech Walesa put it, "started this chain of events that led to the end of communism." © Martin Athenstaedt/DPA/Corbis.

from an agricultural to an industrial society. But it had done so very inefficiently; lacking the discipline and opportunities of a market economy, most enterprises hoarded raw materials, employed too many workers, and did not develop new products. Except in military weaponry and space technology, the Russian economy fell farther and farther behind those of capitalist societies in the post–World War II years, and most people in the Soviet bloc endured a low standard of living. Moreover, the Soviet invasion of Afghanistan, like the American war in Vietnam, turned out to be major blunder—an unwinnable war that cost vast amounts of money, destroyed military morale, and undermined popular support of the Communist government.

Mikhail Gorbachev, a younger Russian leader who became general secretary of the Communist Party in 1985, recognized the need for internal economic reform, technological progress, and an end to the Afghanistan war. His policies of *glasnost* (openness) and *perestroika* (economic restructuring) spurred widespread criticism of the rigid institutions and authoritarian controls of the Communist regime. To lessen tensions with the United States, Gorbachev met with Reagan in 1985, and the two leaders established a warm personal rapport. By 1987, they agreed to eliminate all intermediate-range nuclear missiles based in Europe. A year later, Gorbachev ordered Soviet troops out of Afghanistan, and Reagan replaced many of his hard-line advisors with policymakers who favored a renewal of détente.

The Collapse of Communism in Europe. As Gorbachev's reforms revealed the flaws of the Soviet system, the peoples of eastern and central Europe demanded the ouster of their Communist governments. In Poland, the Roman Catholic Church and its pope—Polish-born John Paul II—joined with Solidarity, the trade union movement led by Lech Walesa, to push for the overthrow of the pro-Soviet regime. In 1956, 1964, and 1968, Russian troops had quashed popular uprisings in Hungary, East Germany, and Czechoslovakia. Now they did not intervene, and a series of peaceful uprisings — "Velvet Revolutions" — created a new political order throughout the region. The destruction of the Berlin Wall in November 1989 symbolized the end of the Communist rule in central Europe. Two years later, the Soviet Union collapsed. Alarmed by Gorbachev's reforms, Soviet military leaders seized the premier in August 1991. But widespread popular opposition led by Boris Yeltsin, the president of the Russian Republic, thwarted their efforts to oust him from office. Their failure broke the dominance of the Communist Party. On December 25, 1991, the Union of Soviet Socialist Republics formally dissolved to make way for an eleven-member Commonwealth of Independent States (CIS). The Russian Republic assumed leadership of the CIS, but the USSR was no more (Map 30.3).

In 1956 Nikita Khrushchev had told the United States, "We will bury you," but now the tombstone read, "The Soviet Union, 1917–1991." For more than forty years the United States fought a bitter economic and ideological battle against its Communist foe, a struggle that had an enormous impact on American society. By linking the campaign for African American rights to the diplomatic competition with the Soviet Union in the Third World, liberal politicians advanced the cause of racial equality in the United States; conversely, by labeling social welfare legislation as "communistic," conservative politicians limited its extent, as did the staggering cost of Cold War. American taxpayers spent some *$4 trillion* on nuclear weapons and trillions more on conventional arms. The physical and psychological costs were equally high: radiation from atomic weapons tests, anti-Communist witch-hunts, and — most pervasive of all — a constant fear of nuclear annihilation. "Nobody — no country, no party, no person — 'won' the cold war," concluded George Kennan, the architect in 1947 of the American policy of "containment," because both sides paid such a heavy price to wage the war and both benefited greatly from its end. Of course, many

MAP 30.3 The Collapse of the Soviet Union and the Creation of Independent States, 1989–1991

The collapse of Soviet Communism dramatically altered the political landscape of central Europe and central Asia. The Warsaw Pact, the USSR's answer to NATO, vanished. West and East Germany reunited, and the nations created by the Versailles Treaty of 1919 — Estonia, Latvia, Lithuania, Poland, Czechoslovakia, Hungary, and Yugoslavia — reasserted their independence or split into smaller ethnically defined nations. The Soviet republics bordering Russia, from Belarus in the west to Kyrgyzstan in the east, also became independent states, while remaining loosely bound with Russia in the Commonwealth of Independent States (CIS).

Americans had no qualms about proclaiming victory, and advocates of free-market capitalism, particularly conservative Republicans, celebrated the outcome. The collapse of Communism in Eastern Europe and the disintegration of the USSR itself, they argued, demonstrated that they had been right all along. Thus, Ronald Reagan's role in facilitating the end of the Cold War, for reasons both international and domestic, was his most important achievement.

The Presidency of George H. W. Bush

George H. W. Bush, Reagan's vice president and successor, was a man of intelligence, courage, and ambition. Born to wealth and high status, he served with great distinction as a naval aviator during World War II and then graduated Phi Beta Kappa from Yale University. Bush prospered as a Texas oil developer and Member of Congress, and then served, under Richard Nixon, as ambassador to the United Nations and head of the CIA. Although Bush lacked Reagan's extraordinary charisma and commanding presence, he had many other strengths that his predecessor lacked.

George Bush won the Republican nomination in 1988 and chose as the vice presidential candidate a young conservative Indiana senator, Dan Quayle. In the Democratic primaries, Governor Michael Dukakis of Massachusetts easily outpolled the charismatic civil rights leader Jesse Jackson, whose populist Rainbow Coalition brought together minority and liberal groups within the party. Dukakis chose Senator Lloyd Bentsen of Texas as his running mate.

The election campaign had a harsh tone as brief television "attack ads" took precedence over a thoughtful discussion of policy issues. The Republican's mantra was "Read My Lips: No New Taxes," a sound bite drawn from a Bush speech. The Bush campaign charged that Dukakis was "a card-carrying member" of the American Civil Liberties Union and was "soft on crime." Bush supporters repeatedly ran TV ads focused on Willie Horton, a convicted African American murderer who had raped a woman while on furlough from a prison in Dukakis's state of Massachusetts. Placed on the defensive by these attacks, Dukakis failed to unify the liberal and moderate factions within Democratic Party and to mount an effective campaign. Bush carried thirty-eight states, winning the popular vote by 53.4 percent to 45.6 percent, but Democrats retained control of the House of Representatives and the Senate.

Democratic Legislative Initiatives. Faced with a Democratic Congress and personally interested in foreign affairs, George H. W. Bush proposed few distinctive domestic initiatives. Rather, congressional Democrats took the lead. They enacted legislation allowing workers to take leave for family and medical emergencies, a measure that Bush vetoed. Then, over the president's opposition, they secured legislation enlarging the rights of workers who claimed discrimination because of their race or gender. With the president's support, congressional liberals also won approval of the Americans with Disabilities Act, a major piece of legislation that significantly enhanced the legal rights of physically disabled people in employment, public transportation, and housing.

Activist Republican Judges. As Democratic politicians seized the initiative in Congress, conservative Republican judges made their presence known in the courts. In *Webster v. Reproductive Health Services* (1989), the Supreme Court upheld the authority of state governments to limit the use of public funds and facilities for abortions. The following year, the justices approved a regulation that prevented federally funded health clinics from discussing abortion with their clients. Then, in the important case of *Planned Parenthood of Southeastern Pennsylvania v. Casey* (1992), the court upheld a Pennsylvania law requiring a twenty-four-hour waiting period prior to an abortion. Surveying these and other decisions, a reporter suggested that 1989 was "The Year the Court Turned Right," with a conservative majority ready and willing to limit or invalidate liberal legislation and legal precedents.

This observation was only partly correct. While the Court was no longer a bastion of liberal jurisprudence, it was not yet firmly conservative in character. Although the *Casey* decision, written by Reagan appointee Sandra Day O'Connor, upheld certain restrictions on abortions, it affirmed the "essential holding" in *Roe v. Wade* that women had a constitutional right to control their bodies. Justice David Souter, appointed to the Court by Bush in 1990, voted with O'Connor to uphold *Roe* and, like her, emerged as an ideologically "moderate" justice on a range of issues.

Bush's other appointment to the Court was Clarence Thomas, an African American conservative with little judicial experience or legal expertise. Thomas's nomination proved controversial; he was opposed by leading black organizations, such as the NAACP and the Urban League, and accused of sexual harassment by Anita Hill, a black law professor. Hill told the all-male Senate Judiciary Committee that Thomas had sexually harassed her when they were colleagues at a federal agency. Despite these charges, Republicans in the Senate won Thomas's

Anita Hill Challenges a Supreme Court Nominee
University of Oklahoma law professor Anita Hill accused
Clarence Thomas, an African American nominated to the
Supreme Court by President George H. W. Bush, of sexual
harassment. Hill's charges sparked controversy during
Thomas's confirmation hearings, but the Senate, voting
largely on party lines, narrowly approved his
appointment by a vote of 52 to 48. Subsequently,
women's rights activists embarked on a campaign to
elect more women to Congress. Brad Markel/Getty Images.

confirmation by a narrow margin. Once on the
bench, Thomas took his cues from his conservative
colleagues, Chief Justice William Rehnquist and
Justice Antonin Scalia.

"Read My Lips." The controversy over Clarence
Thomas hurt Bush at the polls. Politically minded
women accused Republicans of ignoring sexual harassment—an issue of concern to many men and
women—and vowed to mobilize voters. In the
election of 1992, the number of women, mostly
Democrats, elected to the Senate increased from
three to seven, and in the House it increased from
thirty to forty-eight.

Bush's main political problems stemmed from
the huge budget deficit bequeathed to his administration by Ronald Reagan. In 1985 Congress had
enacted the Gramm-Rudman Act, which mandated
automatic cuts in government programs in 1991 if
the budget remained wildly out of balance. That
moment had now come. Unless Congress and the

president acted, there would be a shutdown of all
nonessential government departments and the lay-
off of thousands of employees. To resolve the crisis,
Congress enacted legislation that cut spending and
significantly increased taxes. Abandoning his pledge
of "No New Taxes," Bush signed the legislation,
earning the enmity of conservative Republicans and
diminishing his chances for reelection in 1992.

Bush also struggled with an economic recession
that began in 1990 and stretched into the middle of
1991. As unemployment mounted, the president
could do little because the funding for many federal
programs—including housing, public works, and
social services—had been shifted to state and local
governments during the Reagan administration.
The states faced problems of their own because the
economic slowdown sharply eroded their tax revenues. Indeed, to balance their budgets, as required
by their constitutions, they laid off workers and cut
social spending. The combination of the tax increase, which alienated Republican conservatives,
and a tepid federal response to the recession, which
turned independent voters against the administration, became crucial factors in denying George H. W.
Bush reelection in 1992.

Reagan, Bush, and the Middle East, 1980–1991

The end of the Cold War left the United States as the
only military superpower and raised the prospect of
a "new world order" dominated by the United States
and its European and Asian allies. But there were
problems. American diplomats now confronted an
array of regional, religious, and ethnic conflicts that
defied easy solutions. Those in the Middle East—
the oil-rich lands stretching between Afghanistan
and Morocco—remained the most pressing and
the most threatening to American interests.

Israel and the Palestinians. Like previous presidents, Ronald Reagan had little success in resolving
the conflicts between the Jewish state of Israel and
its Muslim Arab neighbors. In 1982 the Reagan administration initially supported Israel's invasion of
Lebanon to attack forces of the Palestine Liberation
Organization (PLO), which had taken over part
of that country. As the violence escalated in 1984,
the administration urged an Israeli withdrawal
and dispatched an American military force as
"peacekeepers," a decision it quickly regretted.
Lebanese Muslim militants, angered by U.S. support
for Israel, targeted American marines with a truck
bomb, killing 241 soldiers; rather than confront the
bombers, the administration withdrew American
forces. Three years later, Palestinians in the Gaza

Men — and Women — at War

Women played visible roles in the Persian Gulf War, comprising approximately 10 percent of the American troops. In the last decades of the twentieth century, increasing numbers of women chose military careers and, although prohibited from most fighting roles, were increasingly assigned to combat zones. *Luc Delahaye/ Sipa Press.*

Strip and along the West Bank of the Jordan River — territories occupied by Israel since 1967 — mounted an *intifada,* a civilian uprising against Israeli authority. In response, American diplomats stepped up their efforts to persuade the PLO and Arab nations to accept the legitimacy of Israel and to convince the Israelis to allow the creation of a Palestinian state. Neither initiative met with much success.

Iran and Iraq. American policymakers faced a second set of problems in the oil-rich nations of Iran and Iraq. In September 1980 the revolutionary Islamic government of Iran, headed by Ayatollah Khomeini, found itself at war with Iraq, a secular state headed by the ruthless dictator Saddam Hussein and his Sunni Muslim followers. The war started over a series of boundary disputes, in particular, access to deep water ports in the Persian Gulf essential to shipping oil. Fighting quickly escalated into a war of attrition that claimed a million casualties. The Reagan administration ignored Hussein's brutal repression of his political opponents in Iraq and the murder (using poison gas) of tens of thousands of Iraqi Kurds and Shiite Muslims. Anxious to preserve a balance of power in the Middle East, the administration provided Hussein with military intelligence and other aid. Finally, in 1988, an armistice ended the inconclusive war, with both sides still claiming the territory that sparked the conflict.

The Gulf War, 1990–1991. Two years later, in August 1990, Saddam Hussein again went to war to expand Iraq's boundaries. His troops quickly conquered Kuwait, Iraq's small oil-rich neighbor and threatened Saudi Arabia, the site of one-fifth of the world's known oil reserves and an informal ally of the United States. In response, President George H. W. Bush quickly sponsored a series of resolutions in the United Nations Security Council condemning Iraq, calling for its withdrawal from Kuwait, and imposing an embargo and trade sanctions. When Hussein refused to withdraw, Bush successfully prodded the UN to authorize the use of force against "the butcher of Baghdad" if Iraq did not withdraw by January 15. Demonstrating great diplomatic finesse, the president organized a military coalition of thirty-four nations. The House of Representatives authorized American participation by a vote of 252 to 182; dividing mostly along party lines, the Senate voted for war by the close vote of 52 to 47.

The war for the "liberation of Kuwait" was quickly won by the coalition forces led by the United States. A month of American air strikes crushed the communication network of the Iraqi army, destroyed its air forces, and weakened the morale of its soldiers. A land offensive then quickly forced the withdrawal of Iraqi forces from Kuwait (see Map 32.2, p. 1001). To avoid a protracted war and retain French and Russian support for the UN coalition, President Bush did not try to occupy Iraq and remove Saddam Hussein from power. Instead, he won the passage of United Nations Resolution 687, which imposed economic sanctions against Iraq unless it allowed unfettered inspection of its weapons systems, destroyed all biological and chemical arms, and unconditionally pledged not to develop nuclear weapons.

The military victory, low incidence of American casualties, and quick withdrawal produced a euphoric reaction at home. "By God, we've kicked the Vietnam syndrome once and for all," Bush gloated, as his approval rating shot up precipitously. The president spoke too soon. Throughout the 1990s, Saddam Hussein would remain a problem for American policymakers. Indeed, his secretive policies were one factor that, in March 2003, caused Bush's son, President George W. Bush, to initiate another war in Iraq—one that was much more protracted, expensive, and bloody for Americans and Iraqis alike (see Chapter 32).

Thus, the end of the Cold War resulted not in an era of peace but rather two very hot wars in the Middle East. For half a century, the United States and the USSR had tried to divide the world into two rival commercial and ideological blocs—Communist and capitalist. The next half century promised a new set of struggles, one of them between a Western-led agenda of economic and cultural globalization and an anti-Western ideology of Muslim and Arab regionalism.

➤ What factors led to the end of the Cold War?

➤ How did the composition and decisions of the Supreme Court change during the Reagan-Bush administrations?

➤ Why did the United States intervene in the conflicts between Iraq and Iran and Iraq and Kuwait? What were American goals in each case?

The Clinton Presidency, 1993–2001

The election of 1992 brought a Democrat, Arkansas Governor Bill Clinton, to the White House. A profound admirer of John F. Kennedy, Clinton hoped to rekindle the idealistic vision of the slain president. Like Kennedy, Clinton was a political pragmatist; distancing himself from party liberals and special-interest groups, he styled himself as a "New Democrat" who would bring "Reagan Democrats" and middle-class voters back to the party.

Clinton's Early Record

Raised in Hope, Arkansas, by an alcoholic stepfather who abused his mother, Clinton left home to study at Georgetown University. He won a Rhodes scholarship to Oxford and earned a law degree at Yale, where he married a classmate, Hillary Rodham. Returning to Arkansas, he entered politics and won election to six 2-year terms as governor. In 1991 at age forty-five, he was energetic, ambitious, and a policy "wonk"—extraordinarily well informed about political issues.

The Election of 1992. Clinton became the Democratic candidate, but only after surviving charges that he dodged the draft to avoid service in Vietnam, smoked marijuana, and cheated repeatedly on his wife. Although all of those stories had an element of truth, Clinton adroitly talked his way into the presidential nomination—he had charisma and a way with words. For his running mate he chose Al Gore, a second-term senator from Tennessee. At age forty-four, Gore was about the same age as Clinton, making them the first baby-boom national ticket, as well as the first all-southern ticket.

President Bush easily won renomination over his lone opponent, the conservative columnist Pat Buchanan. But Bush allowed the Religious Right to dominate the Republican convention and write a conservative platform that alienated many political moderates. The Bush campaign also suffered from the independent candidacy of Texas billionaire H. Ross Perot, whose condemnation of the rising federal deficit and the influence of corporate lobbyists on Congress appealed to many middle-class voters.

The Democrats mounted an aggressive campaign that focused on Clinton's domestic agenda: He promised a tax cut for the middle classes, universal health insurance, and a reduction of the huge Republican budget deficit. Freed from the demands of the Cold War, Democrats hoped that an emphasis on domestic issues where they traditionally ran strong would sweep them to victory. They were right. On election day, Bush could not overcome voters' discontent over the weak economy and conservatives' disgust at his tax hikes. He received only 37 percent of the popular vote, as millions of Republicans cast their ballots for Ross Perot, who won more votes (19 percent) than any independent candidate since Theodore Roosevelt in 1912. With 44 percent of the vote, Clinton won the election handily (Map 30.4). Moreover, the Democratic Party retained control of both houses of Congress, ending twelve years of divided government. Still, even as

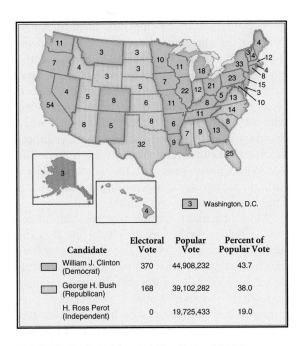

MAP 30.4 Presidential Election of 1992

The first national election after the end of the Cold War focused on the economy, which had fallen into a recession in 1991. The first-ever all-southern Democratic ticket of Bill Clinton (Arkansas) and Al Gore (Tennessee) won support across the country but won the election with only 44 percent of the popular vote. The Republican candidate, Vice President George H. W. Bush, ran strongly in his home state of Texas and the South, an emerging Republican stronghold. Independent candidate H. Ross Perot, a wealthy technology entrepreneur, polled an impressive 19 percent of the popular vote by capitalizing on voter dissatisfaction with the huge federal deficits of the Reagan-Bush administrations.

Candidate	Electoral Vote	Popular Vote	Percent of Popular Vote
William J. Clinton (Democrat)	370	44,908,232	43.7
George H. Bush (Republican)	168	39,102,282	38.0
H. Ross Perot (Independent)	0	19,725,433	19.0

the sun again shown on the Democrats, dark clouds appeared on the horizon. Bill Clinton entered the White House supported by a minority of voters and opposed by political enemies who considered him "a pot-smoking, philandering, draft-dodger" unqualified for the highest office in the land. He would need great political skills and more than a little good fortune to lead the country successfully, especially since he longed to go down in history as a great president.

The Failure of Health-Care Legislation. Clinton's ambition exceeded his abilities. The first year of his administration was riddled by mistakes — failed nominations of two attorney generals, embarrassing patronage revelations about the White House travel office, and an unsuccessful attempt to end a ban on homosexuals in the military. The president looked like a political amateur, out of his depth. He

compounded these minor errors by selecting health reform, an enduring liberal cause since the Truman administration but also an enormously complex issue, as the major objective of his first year in office.

Clinton's goal was to provide a system of health care that would cover all Americans. Though the United States spent a higher percentage of its GNP on medical care than any other nation, it was the only major industrialized country that did not provide government-guaranteed health insurance to all citizens. With medical costs and insurance premiums spiraling out of control, the president designated his wife, attorney Hillary Rodham Clinton, to head a task force to draft new legislation. This appointment was controversial because no First Lady had ever played a formal role in policymaking, but it also suited the times: In many American families, both husbands and wives held responsible positions in the workforce.

The recommendations of the task force were even more controversial. Recognizing the potency of Reagan's attack on "big government," the task force proposed a system of "managed competition": Market forces and private insurance companies, not government bureaucrats, would control health-care costs. The cost of the new system would fall heavily on employers, who had to pay 80 percent of their workers' health benefits, and many smaller businesses and insurance companies campaigned strongly against it. By September 1994, congressional Democratic leaders admitted that the Clintons' liberal health-care proposal was dead. Its failure left about forty million Americans, or 15 percent of the population, without health coverage.

Addressing other concerns of social welfare Democrats, Clinton appointed two pro-choice liberal jurists, Ruth Bader Ginsburg and Stephen Breyer, to the Supreme Court. He also placed women and racial minorities in cabinet positions. Janet Reno became attorney general, the first woman to head the Department of Justice; Donna E. Shalala headed the Department of Health and Human Services; and, in Clinton's second term, Madeleine Albright served as secretary of state. Clinton chose an African American, Ron Brown, as secretary of commerce, and two Latinos, Henry Cisneros and Frederico Peña, to head the Department of Housing and Urban Development (HUD) and the Department of Transportation, respectively.

The Clinton administration's policies toward social welfare, abortion, and crime likewise appealed to liberal Democrats. In 1993, Clinton signed the Family and Medical Leave Act, which had twice been

A Forceful and Controversial First Lady and Senator

Drawing inspiration from Eleanor Roosevelt, Hillary Rodham Clinton hoped the country was ready for a First Lady who actively shaped policy. It wasn't, or at least it wasn't ready for her health-care plan. Subsequently, Hillary Rodham Clinton assumed a less visible role in administration policymaking. In 2000, and again in 2006, she won election to the U.S. Senate from New York.

Robert Trippet/Sipa Press.

vetoed by President Bush, and the Clinic Entrance Act, which made it a federal crime to obstruct people entering hospitals or abortion clinics. Clinton's administration also won approval of two gun-control measures, on handguns and assault weapons, though neither had much affect on gun sales or the murder rate. To counter criticism from conservatives, Clinton "got tough on crime" and included funding in this legislation for 100,000 new police officers in local communities across the nation.

Clinton's Centrist Agenda. The president was more successful with the "centrist" New Democrat elements of his political agenda. Shortly before he left office, George H. W. Bush had signed the North American Free Trade Agreement (NAFTA), an arrangement among the United States, Canada, and Mexico to create a free-trade zone covering all of North America. The Clinton administration presided over Congress's consideration of the agreement, which was bitterly fought. Manufacturers looking for new markets or hoping to move their plants to Mexico, where workers' wages were much lower, strongly supported NAFTA. Labor

unions — a traditional Democratic constituency — opposed the agreement because it cut American jobs. Environmentalists likewise condemned the pact because antipollution laws were weak (and even more weakly enforced) south of the border. However, the Clinton administration was filled with advocates of free trade, including Treasury Secretary Lloyd Bentsen, Labor Secretary Robert Reich, and Economic Policy adviser Robert Rubin. With Clinton's support, they pushed NAFTA through Congress by assembling a coalition of free-trade Democrats and Republicans.

More important, Clinton took meaningful action to reduce the budget deficits of the Reagan-Bush presidencies. In 1993 Clinton secured a five-year budget package that would reduce the federal deficit by $500 billion. Republicans unanimously opposed the proposal because it raised taxes on corporations and individuals with high incomes, and liberal Democrats complained because it limited social spending. Clinton also paid a price because he had to abandon his campaign promise to lower taxes for the middle class. But shared sacrifice led to shared rewards. By 1998, Clinton's fiscal policies had balanced the federal budget and had begun to pay down the federal debt — at a rate of $156 billion a year between 1999 and 2001. As fiscal sanity returned to Washington, the economy boomed, thanks in part to the low interest rates stemming from deficit reduction. Ready access to cheap oil between 1986 and 2001 also fueled the growing economy. During Clinton's two terms in office, unemployment fell from 6 to 4 percent, the GNP increased at an annual rate of 3 percent (twice that of Japan), the stock market more than doubled in value, and home ownership rose to an all-time high.

The Republican Resurgence

The failure of health reform and the passage of NAFTA discouraged liberal Democrats even as Clinton's policies on homosexuals, guns, and abortion energized conservative Republicans in Congress and throughout the country. "Clinton-haters" — those who denied his fitness to be president — hammered away at his conduct as governor, and his participation in an allegedly fraudulent Arkansas real estate deal that became known as "Whitewater." Hoping to prove that the president and Hillary Clinton were free from any taint of fraud, the Clinton administration appointed an independent prosecutor to investigate the case.

In the meantime, the midterm election of 1994 became a referendum on Clinton and his presidency, and its results transformed the political

A Bipartisan Balanced Budget

Throughout his time in the White House, Bill Clinton worked to reduce federal deficits by increasing taxes and restraining spending. On August 5, 1997, a smiling President Clinton signed a balanced budget bill, surrounded by congressional leaders including Republican John Kasich of Ohio (front row, far right), Chair of the House Budget Committee, and Republican Newt Gingrich of Georgia (front row, second from right), the Speaker of the House. Also looking on with satisfaction was Vice President Al Gore, who already had hopes for the presidency in 2000. Ron Edmonds/AP Images.

landscape. In a well-organized and well-funded campaign strongly supported by the National Rifle Association and the Religious Right, Republicans gained 52 seats in the House of Representatives, giving them control for the first time in forty years; they also retook control of the Senate and captured eleven governorships.

The "Contract with America." Leading the Republican charge was Representative Newt Gingrich, an intellectually aggressive conservative from Georgia, who became the new Speaker of the House. During the campaign, Gingrich announced a Republican "Contract with America," a list of proposals that he vowed would be voted on in the first one hundred days of the new session. The contract included constitutional amendments to balance the budget and term limits for members of Congress. It also promised significant tax cuts, reductions in welfare and other entitlement programs, anticrime initiatives, and cutbacks in federal regulations. These initiatives, and Republican control of Congress after 1994, represented the completion of the conservative-backed Reagan Revolution of 1980. The president and the Democrats were now on the defensive. In his State of the Union message of 1996, Clinton suggested that "the era of big government is over." For the rest of his presidency, he eschewed expansive liberal social welfare policies and sought Republican support for a centrist, New Democrat program.

The Budget Struggle and Welfare Reform. Despite Clinton's acceptance of governmental restraint, the Republican-dominated Congress failed to make significant reductions in the size of the federal budget. Most big-budget items were politically or economically untouchable. The Treasury had to pay interest on the national debt; the military budget had to be met; the Social Security system had to be funded. When Republicans passed a government funding act in 1995 that included tax cuts to the wealthy and less money for Medicare, Clinton vetoed the legislation, thereby shutting down many government offices for three weeks. Depicted by Democrats and many independent observers as heartless opponents of aid for senior citizens, the Republicans admitted defeat and gave the president a bill he would sign.

Republicans had greater success in reforming the welfare system, a measure that saved relatively little money but carried a big ideological message. The program for Aid to Families with Dependent Children (AFDC) provided annual payments (including food stamps) to families earning less than $7,740, well below the established poverty line. Still, many taxpaying Americans believed, with some justification, that the AFDC program perpetuated poverty by encouraging women recipients to bear children and to remain on welfare rather than to seek productive employment. Various state legislatures — both Democrat- and Republican-run — had already imposed work requirements and denied benefits for additional children born to women who were already on AFDC. In August 1996, the federal government did the same. After vetoing two Republican-authored bills, President Clinton signed the Personal Responsibility and Work Opportunity Act. This historic overhaul of federal entitlements ended the guarantee of cash assistance by abolishing AFDC, required most adult recipients to find work within two years, and gave states wide discretion in running their welfare programs.

The 1996 Election. The Republican takeover of Congress had one unintended consequence: It united the usually fractious Democrats behind the president. Unopposed in the 1996 primaries, Clinton burnished his image as a moderate by endorsing welfare reform. He also benefited from the continuing strength of the economy. The Republicans settled on Senate Majority Leader Bob Dole of Kansas as their presidential candidate. A veteran of World War II, in which he lost the use of an arm, Dole was a safe but uninspiring candidate, lacking both personal charisma and innovative policies. He called for a 15 percent tax cut *and* a balanced budget, a fiscal combination that few Americans believed possible. On election day, Clinton took 49 percent of the popular vote to 41 percent for Dole. Ross Perot, who failed to build his independent movement of 1992 into a coherent political party, received 8 percent. By dint of great effort — dozens of risky vetoes, centrist initiatives, determined fundraising — Clinton had staged a heroic comeback from the electoral disaster of 1994. Still, Republicans remained in control of Congress and, angry at Clinton's reelection, returned to Washington eager to engage in partisan combat.

Clinton's Impeachment

Clinton's hopes for a distinguished place in history unraveled halfway through his second term when a sex scandal led to his impeachment. The impeachment charges stemmed from Clinton's sworn testimony in a lawsuit filed by Paula Jones, a former Arkansas state employee. In that testimony and later on national television, Clinton denied having sexually harassed Jones during his governorship. These denials may well have been truthful. But during the testimony Clinton also denied having a sexual affair with Monica Lewinsky, a former White House intern — a charge that was undoubtedly true. Kenneth Starr, a conservative Republican who had taken over as independent counsel in the Arkansas Whitewater land deal, now widened his probe to include the Jones affair. Starr's report of September 1998 concluded that Clinton had lied under oath regarding Lewinsky and obstructed justice, and that these actions were grounds for impeachment.

Viewed historically, Americans have usually defined "high crimes and misdemeanors" — the constitutional standard for impeachment — as involving a serious abuse of public trust that threatened the integrity of the republic. In 1998, many conservative Republicans favored a much lower standard because they had never accepted "Slick Willy" Clinton's legitimacy as president. In reply to the question, "Why do you hate Clinton so much?",

The Politics of Impeachment

As this cartoon shows, the Republicans caught President Clinton with his pants down. But they failed to persuade a majority of Americans that Clinton's sexual escapades with White House intern Monica Lewinsky (and his lies about it while under oath) were "high crimes and misdemeanors" that merited his removal from office. The episode is best seen as an expression of the harsh ideological politics of the 1990s and, in retrospect, as an unnecessary and dangerous diversion of the nation's energies away from the looming threat of terrorism.

Auth ©1998 *The Philadelphia Inquirer.* Reprinted with permission Universal Press Syndicate. All Rights Reserved.

one conservative declared, "I hate him because he's a womanizing, Elvis-loving, non-inhaling, truth-shading, war-protesting, draft-dodging, abortion-protecting, gay-promoting, gun-hating baby boomer. That's why." Seeing Clinton as an exemplar of the permissive social values of the 1960s, conservative Republicans vowed to use the sex scandal to oust him from office. On December 19 the House of Representatives narrowly approved two articles of impeachment against Clinton: one for perjury for lying to a grand jury about his liaison with Lewinsky, and a second for obstruction of justice by encouraging others to lie on his behalf. Most Americans did not applaud the House's action; according to a CBS news poll, 38 percent supported impeachment while 58 percent opposed it.

Lacking public support, Republicans in the Senate fell well short of the two-thirds majority they needed to remove the president. Like Andrew Johnson, the only other president to be tried by the Senate (see Chapter 15), Bill Clinton paid a high price for this victory. The president spent so much time in his defense that he was unable to fashion a coherent Democratic alternative to the Republicans' conservative domestic agenda and, equally important, to address important problems of foreign policy.

Foreign Policy at the End of the Twentieth Century

Unlike George H. W. Bush, Clinton claimed no expertise in international affairs and did not desire to develop one. "Foreign policy is not what I came here to do," he lamented as he faced a series of minor international crises. Neither of his main advisors, Secretary of State Warren Christopher and Secretary of Defense Les Aspin, had a strategic vision of America's role in the post–Cold War world. Consequently, Clinton pursued a cautious diplomatic policy. Unless important American interests were directly threatened, the president avoided a commitment of U.S. influence and troops.

"Peacekeeping" in Somalia and Haiti. Clinton's caution stemmed in part from a harrowing episode in the east African country of Somalia, where ethnic warfare had created political chaos and massive famine. President Bush had approved American participation in a UN peacekeeping force, and Clinton had added additional troops. When bloody fighting in October 1993 killed eighteen American soldiers and wounded eighty-four, Clinton gradually withdrew the troops. The United States had few economic and diplomatic interests in Somalia, and even a sizeable peacekeeping force would be unable to quell the factional violence and restore national unity. For similar reasons, Clinton refused in 1994 to dispatch American forces to the central African nation of Rwanda, where ethnic conflict had escalated to genocide—the killing by Hutu extremists of at least 800,000 people, mostly ethnic Tutsis.

The Caribbean was much closer to home, and Clinton consequently gave it closer attention. In 1991 a military coup in Haiti had deposed Jean-Bertrand Aristide, the democratically elected president. Then a candidate for president, Clinton had criticized President Bush's refusal to grant asylum to refugees from the oppressive new Haitian regime. Once in the White House, Clinton reversed his stance: To thwart a massive influx of impoverished Haitian "boat people" who would strain welfare services and increase racial tension, the new president called for Aristide's return to power. Threatening a U.S. invasion, Clinton forced Haiti's military rulers to step down. American troops maintained Aristide in power until March 1995, when the United Nations took over responsibility for keeping the peace.

Intervention in the Balkans. An even more intractable set of internal conflicts—based on ethnicity, religion, and nationality—led to the disintegration of the Communist nation of Yugoslavia in 1991. Initially, the Roman Catholic regions of Slovenia and Croatia declared independence from Yugoslavia, which was dominated by Russian Orthodox Serbians. In 1992, the heavily Muslim province of Bosnia and Herzegovina declared its independence, but its substantial Serbian population refused to live in a Muslim-run multiethnic state. Supported financially and militarily by Slobodan Milosevic, the uncompromisingly nationalistic leader of Yugoslavia, they formed their own breakaway state and, to make it an all-Serbian society, launched a ruthless campaign of "ethnic cleansing." They drove tens of thousands of Bosnian Muslims and Croats from their homes, executed tens of thousands of men, raped equal numbers of women, and forced the survivors into crowded refugee camps.

America's European allies, particularly Germany, had long-standing economic ties to the Balkans, and the United States had taken an active role in its affairs during the Cold War. However, both Clinton and NATO leaders feared that military action against the Serbs would result in a Vietnam-like quagmire. Finally, in November 1995, Clinton organized a NATO-led bombing campaign and peacekeeping effort, backed by twenty thousand American troops, that ended the Serbs' vicious expansionist drive. Four years later a new crisis emerged in Kosovo, another province of the Serbian-dominated Federal Republic of Yugoslavia. Most Kosovo residents were ethnic Albanian Muslims, whom the Russian Orthodox Serbs vowed to drive out of the region. Again led by the United States, NATO intervened with aircraft strikes and military forces to preserve Kosovo's autonomy (Map 30.5). While always acting prudently in defense of American interests, the Clinton administration had slowly developed a policy of active "engagement" in nations beset with internal conflict.

Islamic Radicalism. In the Middle East, Clinton was as unsuccessful as previous presidents in mediating the long-standing conflict between Jews and Arabs. In 1994 he arranged a meeting in Washington

MAP 30.5   Ethnic Conflict in the Balkans: The Breakup of Yugoslavia, 1991–1992

The collapse of the Soviet Union spurred the disintegration of the independent Communist state of Yugoslavia, a multiethnic and multireligious state held together after 1945 by the near-dictatorial authority of Josip Broz Tito (1892–1980). Fanned by ethnic and religious hatreds, Yugoslavia splintered into warring states. Slovenia and Macedonia won their independence in 1991, but Russian Orthodox Serbia, headed by president Slobodan Milosevic, tried to rule the rest of the Balkan peoples. Roman Catholic Croatia freed itself from Serb rule in 1995, and, after ruthless Serbian aggression against Muslims in Bosnia and later in Kosovo, the United States and NATO intervened militarily to create the separate states of Bosnia-Herzegovina (1995) and Montenegro (2006) and the autonomous Muslim province of Kosovo (1999).

between Israeli prime minister Yitzhak Rabin and Yasir Arafat, chairman of the Palestine Liberation Organization. Urged on by Clinton, they negotiated an agreement that allowed limited Palestinian self-rule in the Gaza Strip and Jericho. The hope that this breakthrough would lead to a general peace settlement was short lived. In 1995, a Jewish religious fanatic assassinated Rabin, and the new prime minister, Benjamin Netanyahu of the religious Likud Party, reverted to a hard-line policy against the Palestinians. Despite Clinton's continuing efforts, the "peace process" failed to produce substantial progress.

Terrorists Bomb USS *Cole*

On October 12, 2000, a radical Muslim group with ties to Al Qaeda detonated a powerful bomb near the USS *Cole,* which was refueling in the port of Aden in Yemen. The explosion killed seventeen American sailors and injured thirty-seven others. After repairs costing $250 million, the USS *Cole* returned to active duty in April 2002. © Corbis/Sygma.

Indeed, the rise of radical Muslim organizations undermined the prospects of a Middle Eastern peace and challenged security and stability throughout the world. During the 1990s, radical Islamic movements staged armed insurgencies in parts of Russia and China and threatened existing governments in the Muslim states of Algeria, Egypt, Pakistan, and Indonesia. These terrorist groups likewise mounted a series of attacks against the United States, which they condemned as the main agent of economic globalization and cultural imperialism. In 1993 radical Muslim immigrants set off a bomb in the World Trade Center in New York City. Five years later, Muslim terrorists used truck bombs to blow up the American embassies in Kenya and Tanzania, and in 2000 they bombed an American warship, the USS *Cole,* in the port of Aden in Yemen. The Clinton administration knew these attacks were the work of Al Qaeda, a network of terrorists organized by the wealthy Saudi exile Osama bin Laden, but no one — in the State Department, CIA, or Pentagon — had yet figured out how to deal with these Islamic extremists (see Chapter 32).

As the Soviet Union collapsed in 1991, the director of the CIA had seen little cause to celebrate. "We have slain a large dragon," he admitted, "but we live now in a jungle filled with a bewildering variety of poisonous snakes. And in many ways, the dragon was easier to keep track of." As the century ended, his assessment rang true. The Balkan and African crises, the Middle Eastern morass, and radical Islamic terrorist groups served as potent reminders of a world in conflict and the limits of American power. If not quite as dangerous as the Cold War era, the "new world order" was no less problematic.

➤ In what ways did Clinton's administration suggest that he was a "New Democrat"?

➤ What was the goal of the Republicans' "Contract with America"?

➤ What foreign policy challenges did Clinton face, and how did he address them?

SUMMARY

As we have seen, the concluding decades of the twentieth century were a time of momentous change. In the international arena, the collapse of the Soviet Union and the end of the Cold War diminished the prospect of nuclear war. Nonetheless, regional and ethnic conflicts continued to pose a serious challenge to U.S. foreign policy. Militarily dominant, the United States found its economy challenged by strong competitors in Europe and Asia and its security endangered by ruthless terrorist groups.

The shifting economic fortunes of the nation affected domestic politics. The "stagflation" of the 1970s helped to ensure the electoral triumph of Ronald Reagan in 1980, and his administration's massive expenditures on defense boosted the domestic economy while creating an enormous federal deficit. Rather than getting "the government off our backs," Reagan simply used its power in different ways. "Reaganomics" shifted wealth into the hands of military planners and affluent Americans, mostly at the expense of the poor. Middle-class Americans — the majority of the population — generally prospered during the 1980s but divided ever more sharply over cultural issues. Influenced by the powerful lobby of the Religious Right, the Republican Party vigorously attacked the welfare state and the liberal cultural values that it represented.

These economic and cultural issues played out in the politics of the 1990s. The economic recession of 1991 assisted the election of Bill Clinton in 1992, as did his centrist, "New Democrat" policies that reflected the conservative movement's call for limited government. The Republican congressional landslide of 1994 limited Clinton's options, as did his sexual misconduct, which in 1998 led to his impeachment and loss of political effectiveness. As the century ended, American society was experiencing a massive technological revolution that promised to transform many aspects of life.

Connections: Government and Politics

Far into the future historians will debate Ronald Reagan's personal impact on the two great events presented in this chapter — the triumph of the conservative movement in America and the end of the Cold War. Still, there is no doubt, as we observed in the opening essay for Part Seven (p. 925), that President Ronald Reagan and his conservative successors were determined to carry out a governmental revolution:

The conservatives' agenda was to roll back the social welfare state created by liberal Democrats during the New Deal and the Great Society. Presidents Reagan, George H. W. Bush, and George W. Bush cut taxes, reduced spending on social welfare programs, and limited the regulatory activities of federal agencies.

In previous chapters, we have watched the slow construction of the governmental system that the conservatives attacked. Although prefigured in the regulatory legislation of the Progressive era (Chapter 20), it had its origins in the New Deal of Franklin Roosevelt. As we saw in Chapter 24, in response to the Great Depression the Roosevelt administration created a phalanx of federal agencies to oversee the American economy and, in the Social Security Act of 1935, laid the groundwork of a system to ensure the welfare of all Americans. But the powerful federal government of today is also the product of World War II and the Cold War. Those conflicts, as we saw in Chapters 25 and 26, brought a massive increase in government spending, taxes, and employees, as well as an influential "military-industrial complex" of private corporations. In fact, as our discussion of the decades since 1945 suggests, many private-interest groups have become reliant on favorable legislation or outright government subsidies. Because the modern state is so deeply implicated in the social and economic welfare of the American people as well as in their military defense, conservative politicians — as we explained in this chapter — have been unable to shrink substantially the size or scope of governmental activity.

CHAPTER REVIEW QUESTIONS

➤ How did the domestic policies of Presidents Reagan, Bush, and Clinton reflect the rise of conservatism in American politics?

➤ What comparisons can you make between the Iran-Contra scandal of Ronald Reagan's administration and the impeachment crisis of Bill Clinton's?

➤ What new challenges did the end of the Cold War bring to American foreign policy?

TIMELINE

1970s	Rise of the New Right
1981	Ronald Reagan becomes president; Republicans win control of Senate Economic Recovery Tax Act (ERTA) cuts taxes Military expenditures increase sharply Reagan cuts budgets of regulatory agencies Sandra Day O'Connor appointed to the Supreme Court
1981–1989	National debt triples Emergence of New Right think tanks: Heritage Foundation, American Enterprise Institute, and the Cato Institute U.S. assists Iraq in war against Iran (1980–1988)
1983	Strategic Defense Initiative (Star Wars)
1985	Gramm-Rudman Budget Act Mikhail Gorbachev takes power in Soviet Union
1986	Iran-Contra scandal weakens Reagan presidency William Rehnquist named chief justice
1987	United States and USSR agree to limit missiles in Europe
1988	George H. W. Bush elected president
1989	Destruction of Berlin Wall; "Velvet Revolutions" in eastern Europe *Webster v. Reproductive Health Services* limits abortion services
1990–1991	Persian Gulf War Americans with Disabilities Act
1991	Dissolution of Soviet Union ends Cold War Clarence Thomas named to the Supreme Court
1992	Democratic moderate Bill Clinton elected president in three-way race *Planned Parenthood of Southeastern Pennsylvania v. Casey* upholds *Roe v. Wade*
1993	Congress passes Family and Medical Leave Act North American Free Trade Agreement (NAFTA)
1994	Clinton fails to win health insurance but reduces budget deficit and national debt Republicans gain control of Congress
1995	U.S. troops enforce peace in Bosnia
1996	Personal Responsibility and Work Opportunity Act reforms welfare system
1998–1999	Bill Clinton impeached and acquitted American intervention in Bosnia and Serbia Rise of radical Muslim movements and Al Qaeda terrorists

FOR FURTHER EXPLORATION

James T. Patterson, *Restless Giant: The United States from Watergate to Bush v. Gore* (2005), provides a solid analysis of the 1980s and 1990s. For evangelical politics, see Frances FitzGerald, *Cities on a Hill* (1986), which has a section on Jerry Falwell and the Moral Majority; William Martin, *With God on Our Side: The Rise of the Religious Right in America* (1996); and Lisa McGerr, *Suburban Warriors: The Origins of the New American Right* (2001). Two valuable overviews of the Reagan presidency are Lou Cannon, *President Reagan: The Role of a Lifetime* (2000), and Haynes Johnson, *Sleepwalking through History: America in the Reagan Years* (1992). John Greene, *The Presidency of George Bush* (2000), discusses the policies of the senior Bush.

On foreign policy, consult Richard A. Melanson, *American Foreign Policy since the Vietnam War* (2005), which covers the years from 1970 to 2000, and Raymond Garthoff, *The Great Transition: Russian-American Politics and the End of the Cold War* (1994). Two fine Web sites that document various Cold War incidents are The National Security Archive, at **www.gwu.edu/~nsarchiv**, and The Cold War International History Project, at **www.wilsoncenter.org/index.cfm?fuseaction= topics.home&topic_id=1409**. For the Gulf War, see Michael Gordon and Bernard Trainor, *The Generals' War: The Inside Story of the Conflict in the Gulf* (1995), and **www.pbs.org/ wgbh/pages/frontline/gulf**, a site with maps, documents, and interviews with decision makers and soldiers.

For the Clinton years, consult William Berman, *From the Center to the Edge: The Politics and Policies of the Clinton Presidency* (2001), and Joe Klein, *The Natural: The Misunderstood Presidency of Bill Clinton* (2002). Richard A. Posner, *An Affair of State: The Investigation, Impeachment, and Trial of President Clinton* (1999), probes the legal aspects of that affair. For online materials on Clinton's impeachment, consult Jurist, the Law Professors' Network, at **jurist.law.pitt.edu/impeach.htm**.

Other interesting political studies include Steven Gillon, *"That's Not What We Meant to Do": Reform and Its Unintended Consequences in Twentieth Century America* (2001); Fred Greenstein, *The Presidential Difference: Leadership Style from FDR to Clinton* (2000); and Ted Halstead and Michael Lind, *The Radical Center: The Future of American Politics* (2001). Information on all U.S. presidents is available at **www.ipl.org/div/potus**.

TEST YOUR KNOWLEDGE

To assess your command of the material in this chapter, see the Online Study Guide at **bedfordstmartins.com/henretta**.

For Web sites, images, and documents related to topics and places in this chapter, visit **bedfordstmartins.com/makehistory**.

31

A Dynamic Economy, A Divided People

1980–2000

As 1999 came to a close, a technological disaster threatened millions of computers around the world. For decades programmers had used a two-digit field to describe dates, recording 1950 as simply "50." What would happen when the clock flashed to "Y2K" — shorthand for the year 2000? Would millions of personal, corporate, and government computers clock it as 1900, magically shifting the world a century back in time? Or would the computers crash and wipe out the data of millions of users? As it turned out, the great "Y2K" fear proved unfounded, as thousands of software programmers managed to patch the world's computer systems and avoid a disaster.

The moment was nonetheless symbolic. As the world entered the third millennium of the Christian era, the fates of its many peoples were directly tied to one another electronically and in many other ways. In centuries past, periodic waves of epidemical diseases — the Black Death, cholera, and influenza — had joined the peoples of the world, and then only in death. Now millions of people across the globe were linked together on a daily basis — working in export-oriented factories, watching television programs created in distant nations, flying thousands of miles in jet planes to other continents, and — perhaps most amazing of all — having pictures of their towns and fields snapped by satellite cameras

◄ **www.TimBerners-Lee**

Nothing represents the globalization of the world's economy and culture better than the World Wide Web, which allows instant access to Web sites around the globe. The technology behind the Web was invented between 1989 and 1991 by Tim Berners-Lee, an English computer scientist working at the time at CERN, the European Particle Physics Laboratory in Geneva, Switzerland. This photomosaic picture of Berners-Lee, who presently teaches at MIT, is composed of 2,304 Web sites. Tim Berners-Lee.

high in the stratosphere and beamed instantly around the world. The globe was growing smaller.

But not necessarily more harmonious. "Globalization"—the movement of goods, ideas, and organizations across political boundaries—created as many conflicts as it solved. Likewise, increased contact among Americans through modern means of communications made them more conscious of their differences—racial, ethnic, religious, ideological—and sharpened cultural conflict at home. In particular, New Right conservatives, who had come into their own in the Reagan-Bush years, squared off against social welfare liberals, who adhered to many of the social values that had flourished from the 1930s through the 1960s. The resulting "culture wars" strained social harmony as the twentieth century drew to a close.

America in the Global Economy and Society

When Bill Clinton ran for president in 1992, a large sign in his campaign "war room" underlined the main issue: "THE ECONOMY, STUPID." Throughout the last quarter of the century, bread-and-butter issues loomed large in the minds of many Americans. The abrupt rise in global oil prices in the 1970s had triggered a corrosive "stagflation" that had heaped hardship on the poor, shrunk middle-class expectations, and shaken the confidence of policymakers and business executives. It would take time, ingenuity, and a bit of luck to restore America's self-confidence.

The Economic Challenge

The 1980s began on a depressing economic note. Unemployment remained above 7 percent, and the cost of living continued to soar at a rate of 8 percent a year. When the Federal Reserve jacked up interest rates (to nearly 20 percent) to combat inflation (see Chapter 30), the nation experienced a sharp recession in 1981–1982, with nearly 10 percent of the workforce without jobs.

However, the economy quickly revived and turned the rest of the decade into one of relative prosperity. The wealthiest one-fifth of Americans, the primary beneficiaries of President Reagan's tax

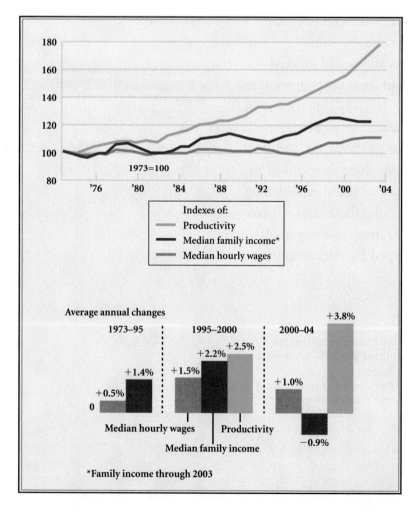

FIGURE 31.1 Productivity, Family Income, and Wages, 1970–2004

This chart tells a complex and not altogether happy story. The median hourly wages of American workers (adjusted for inflation) stagnated between 1970 and 1995. The rise in median family income reflected the increasing proportion of two-earner families, as more married women entered the workforce. The dramatic increases in productivity did not lead to higher wages for workers. Rather, businesses used those gains either to cut prices to compete in the global marketplace or to reward owners, shareholders, and, particularly, corporate executives.

Akio Morita and the Sony Corporation

In 1946 Akio Morita and Masaru Ibuka founded the Tokyo Telecommunications Engineering Corporation, which evolved into the Sony Corporation. Its first great sales success came in the mid-1950s with a pocket-sized transistor radio. Other innovative products followed in subsequent decades: in the 1960s, the popular Trinitron TV; in the 1970s, the Betamax video recorder and the Walkman radio; in the 1980s, the compact disc, the three-and-a-half inch diskette, and, shown here in a picture of Morita in 1985, the Handycam. In the 1990s, Sony devised the PlayStation, the memory stick, and many more electronic products. In 2005, Sony employed 150,000 workers and sold goods worth $18 billion in the United States and $67 billion worldwide. Photo by Bill Pierce/Time Life Pictures/Getty Images.

cuts and economic policies, did especially well. Many middle-class Americans also enjoyed a modest affluence, but the real wages of manufacturing and retail workers continued to stagnate (Figure 31.1). The poor — the thirty million citizens below the poverty line — struggled to survive.

Domestic Affluence and Foreign Debts. The fate of the poor was of little concern to the well-educated "baby boom" children who entered the labor force in the early 1980s. Many took high-paying jobs in the rapidly growing professional and technology sectors of the economy. These young urban professionals — the Yuppies, as they were called — set the tone for a strikingly materialistic culture. Yuppies (and Buppies, their black counterparts) dined at gourmet restaurants, enjoyed vacations at elaborate resorts, and lived in large suburban houses filled with expensive consumer goods. Their example shaped the outlook of the next generation. Surveys reported that 80 percent of college students in the 1980s placed a high value on individual economic success while only 40 percent gave importance to enlightened social values — an exact reversal of student attitudes during the 1960s. The majority of Americans who could not afford the new luxuries experienced them vicariously by watching *Lifestyles of the Rich and Famous,* a popular TV series that debuted in 1984. Every week, host Robin Leach took audiences into the mansions of people who enjoyed "champagne wishes and caviar dreams."

Tempering this enthusiasm, commentators warned of the nation's economic decline. Until the 1970s the United States had been the world's leading exporter of agricultural products, manufactured goods, and investment capital. Then, American exports began to fall, undercut in world markets by cheaper and often better designed products from Germany and Japan (see Chapter 29). By 1985, for the first time since 1915, the United States registered a negative balance of international payments. It now imported more goods than it exported, a trade deficit fueled by soaring imports of foreign oil, which increased between 1960 and 2000 from two to twelve million barrels per day. Moreover, America's earnings from foreign investments did not offset the imbalance in trade. The United States had become a debtor (rather than a creditor) nation; each year, it had to borrow money, in the form of credit or investment capital, to maintain the standard of living many Americans had come to expect.

Japan's Rise, America's Decline. The rapid ascent of the Japanese economy to the second largest in the world was a key factor in this historic reversal. Japan's Nikkei stock index tripled in value between 1965 and 1975, and then tripled again by 1985. Now more than a third of the American annual trade deficit of $138 billion was with Japan, whose corporations exported huge quantities of electronic goods (TVs, VCRs, microwave ovens) and other consumer products. Indeed, Japanese auto companies accounted for nearly a quarter of all cars bought in the United States. Using the profits of these sales, Japanese businesses bought up prime pieces of real estate, such as New York City's Rockefeller Center, and took over well-known American corporations. The purchase by Japan's Sony Corporation of two American icons, Columbia Pictures and CBS Records, frightened politicians and ordinary citizens. The post-1945 economic primacy of the United States was in rapid decline.

While Japan and Germany prospered, American businesses grappled with a worrisome decline in productivity. Between 1973 and 1992, the productivity of American workers grew at the meager rate of 1 percent a year, a far cry from the post–World War II rate of 3 percent annually. As a consequence, the wages of most employees stagnated and the number of high-paying, union-protected manufacturing jobs shrank. Unemployed industrial workers took whatever jobs they could find, usually minimum-wage positions as sales "associates" in fast-food franchises or in big-box stores, such as Wal-Mart or Home Depot. By 1985, more people in the United States worked for McDonald's slinging Big Macs than labored in the nation's steel industry, rolling out rails, girders, and sheet steel. Middle-class Americans—baby boomers included—also found themselves with less economic security. To remain competitive internationally, corporations reduced the number of middle-level managers and back-office accountants. Most laid-off middle managers eventually found new jobs, but many had to take sizeable cuts in pay.

As middle-class families struggled to make ends meet, poor Americans just held their own. The number remained stable, at about 31 million, and despite the Reagan-era budget cuts, Americans entitled to Medicare, food stamps, and Aid to Families with Dependent Children received about the same level of benefits in 1990 than they had in 1980. Still, the number of homeless citizens doubled. A Community Services Society report movingly described how thousands of people found themselves without a place to live: "Something happens—a job is lost, unemployment benefits run out, creditors and banks move in to foreclose, eviction proceedings begin—and quite suddenly the respectable poor find themselves among the disreputable homeless."

The Impact on Family Life. Challenging economic times accelerated changes already underway in family life and gender roles. As early as the 1960s, married women entered the paid workforce in increasing numbers, both to exercise their talents and to bolster their families' income (Figure 31.2). As men's wages stagnated during the 1970s, women increasingly sought paid employment—even though their pay averaged only about 70 percent of that paid to men. By 1994, 58 percent of adult women were in the labor force, up from 38 percent in 1962. Many women, especially those with young children, did double duty; as one working mother remarked, "You're on duty at work. You come home, and you're on duty" again.

Some women entered male-dominated fields, such as medicine, law, skilled trades, law enforce-

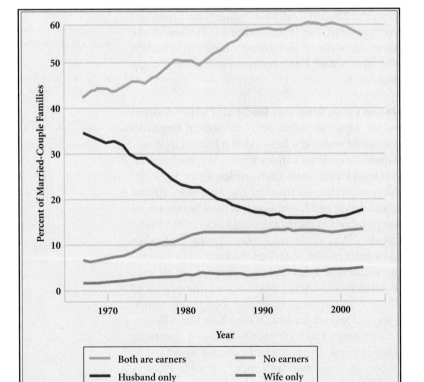

FIGURE 31.2 The Increase in Two-Worker Families

In 1968, about 43 percent of married couples sent both the husband and the wife into the workforce; thirty years later, 60 percent were two-earner families. The percentage of families in which the wife alone worked doubled (from 3 percent to 5 percent) during these years, while those with no earners (welfare recipients and, increasingly, retired couples) rose from 8 percent to 13 percent. Because these figures do not include unmarried persons and most illegal immigrants, they do not give a complete picture of the American workplace. But there is no doubt that women now play a major role in the workforce.

Barbie Goes to Work

Since 1959, the shapely Barbie doll has symbolized the "feminine mystique," the female as sexual object, and diffused this view of American womanhood around the nation and the globe. More than 500 million Barbies have been sold in 140 countries. But Barbie moves with the times. In 1985, she got her first computer, and in 1999, this doll and CD set transformed Barbie into a working woman, earning her own bread in the corporate workplace and, perhaps, with something intelligent to say! © Mattel.

ment, and the military, but the majority still labored in traditional fields, such as teaching, nursing, and sales work. In fact, one in five women held a clerical or secretarial job, the same proportion as in 1950. Still, as women flooded the labor force, cultural expectations and ideals began to change. Men learned to accept women as coworkers — and even as their bosses — and took responsibility for more household tasks. By the 1990s, only about 15 percent of U.S. households conformed to the model of the ideal American family depicted by the Hollywood script writers of the 1950s: employed father, homemaker wife, and young children.

The Turn to Prosperity

Between 1985 and 1990, American corporate executives and workers learned how to compete against their German and Japanese rivals. One key was technology and especially the use of information processing, which had been pioneered by Microsoft, Cisco, Sun, and other American companies. As corporations fitted out their plants and offices with computers, robots, and other "smart" machines, the productivity of the workforce rose. Bethlehem Steel, which invested $6 billion to modernize its operations during the late 1980s, soon doubled its productivity. Other firms retooled their corporate vision. Between 1980 and 1981, the Ford Motor Company lost $2.5 billion because of high expenses and stagnating sales. Responding to this desperate situation, Ford made fundamental reforms that improved the quality of its cars, enhanced the morale of assembly-line workers, and cut costs by adopting the Japanese system of rapid inventory resupply.

The stock market quickly reflected these initiatives, as ambitious and aggressive baby-boom brokers took control of Wall Street and government policy encouraged private investors. Prompted by the deregulation policies of the Carter administration, the Securities and Exchange Commission enacted new rules that made the financial industry more open and competitive (see Chapter 29). These measures encouraged the creation of discount brokerage firms, whose low fees prompted more small-scale investors to enter the stock market. Between 1980 and 2000, the percentage of American families owning some stock quadrupled from 13 to 51 percent. As the economic expansion gathered steam, stock prices spurted upward. In a six-month period in 1986, the value of stocks rose $400 billion. Even a major financial scandal in the savings and loan industry (which eventually cost taxpayers $132 billion) and a startling Wall Street crash in October 1987, in which stocks lost a fourth of their value, did not deter investors. Within two years, the market had regained its former level and continued to rise.

Goats and Heroes of the 1980s: Ivan Boesky, Lee Iacocca, and Donald Trump. The rise in stock values unleashed a wave of corporate mergers, as companies used stock to buy up competitors. As these deals multiplied, so too did the number of traders who profited illegally from insider knowledge. The most notorious of the white-collar criminals was Ivan Boesky, who acquired a fortune — and a reputation as an astute financier — as he arranged takeovers and buyouts. Invited to deliver the commencement address to graduates of the Business School at the University of California at Berkeley, Boesky said, "I think greed is healthy. You can be greedy and still feel good about yourself." At least until scandal strikes! Convicted of illegal trading, Boesky was sentenced to three-and-a-half years in prison (he served two years) and had to disgorge $50 million from his illicit profits and another $50 million in fines.

While sleazy financiers like Boesky gave corporate millionaires a bad name, successful business executives basked in the Reagan administration's adulation of wealth. When the president christened self-made entrepreneurs "the heroes for the eighties," he probably had Lee Iacocca in mind. The son of Italian immigrants, Iacocca personified the American Dream. Trained as an engineer, he rose through the ranks to become president of the Ford Motor Corporation; resigning from that position in 1978, he took over the ailing Chrysler auto company. Over the next decade, Iacocca turned Chrysler into a profitable company — securing a crucial $1.5 billion loan from the U.S. government and pushing the

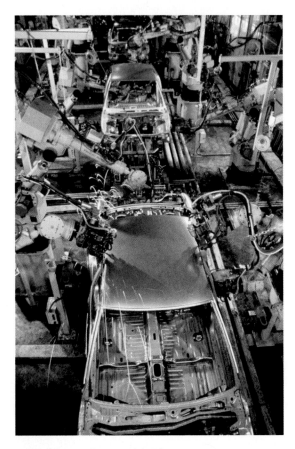

An Automated Assembly Line

Most basic manufacturing is now done by machines, like these robotic welders on an automobile assembly line. The use of these machines increases productivity, in part by eliminating the jobs traditionally done by welders. But this advance in technology also creates new jobs in making and servicing the robots and other automated machines. © Bettmann/Corbis.

development of new cars. To encourage Americans to buy improved Chrysler models, Iacocca starred in TV advertisements and echoed Reagan's rhetoric: "Let's make American mean something again."

Simultaneously, real estate entrepreneur Donald Trump revived the morale of many aspiring residents of New York City, whose government had long teetered on the brink of bankruptcy. In 1983, the flamboyant Trump built the equally flamboyant Trump Towers. At the entrance of the $200 million apartment building stood two enormous bronze "T's," a display of self-promotion reinforced by the media. Calling him "The Donald," a nickname used by his first wife, TV reporters and magazines commented relentlessly on his marriages and divorces and the extravagant lifestyle that his $3 billion real estate empire made possible.

Trump personified the materialistic values of the Reagan era. Accustomed to the elegance and extravagance of Hollywood, Ronald and Nancy Reagan created an affluent atmosphere in the White House that contrasted sharply with the austerity of the 1970s and Jimmy and Rosalynn Carter's subdued lifestyle. At Carter's inauguration in 1977, the Carter family dressed simply, walked to the ceremony, and led an evening of restrained merrymaking; four years later, Reagan and his wealthy Republican supporters racked up inauguration expenses of $16 million. Critics lambasted the extravagance of Trump and the Reagans, but many Americans joined with them in celebrating the return of American prosperity and promise.

The Boom Years of the 1990s. The economic resurgence of the late 1980s did not restore America's once dominant position in the international economy. The nation's heavy industries — steel, autos, chemicals — continued to lose market share, both because of weak executive leadership and because of the relatively high wages paid to American workers. Nonetheless, during the 1990s the economy of the United States grew at the impressive average rate of 3 percent per year. Moreover, its main international competitors were now struggling. In Germany, France, and other European industrial nations, high taxes and high wages stifled economic growth, while in Japan spectacular busts in the speculative-driven real estate and stock markets in 1989 crippled the economy. Its banking system burdened by billions of yen in bad debts, Japan limped though the 1990s with a meager growth rate of 1.1 percent a year.

Meanwhile, boom times came to the United States. During Bill Clinton's two terms in the White House (1993–2001), the stock market value of American companies nearly tripled. This boom, which was fueled by the flow of funds into high-tech and e-commerce firms, enriched American citizens and their governments. Middle-income families who were covered by pension plans saw their retirement savings suddenly double and felt good about the future. Simultaneously, the taxes collected on stock sales and profits provided a windfall for the state and federal governments. By 2000, the Clinton administration had paid off half of the enormous national debt created during the Reagan and Bush presidencies and was sending balanced budgets to Congress. Indeed, on the basis of recent events, the Congressional Budget Office projected an astonishing surplus of $4.6 trillion in governmental revenue during the coming decade.

As was the case during the Reagan era, the prosperity of the Clinton years was not equally distributed. By 1998 the income of the wealthiest 13,000 families in the United States was greater than the poorest 20 *million* families. Moreover, the good times did not last. A spectacular "bust" hit the over-inflated stock market in late 2000; within two years

Donald Trump

Some people are larger than life, and Donald Trump is certainly one of them. The beneficiary of an inheritance of $200 million from his father, "The Donald" built a series of spectacular hotels and condominiums, first in New York City and later in Atlantic City and Palm Beach. Trump's grandiose vision — of himself and his projects — has often placed him in vulnerable personal and financial situations. But neither a bitter divorce nor brushes with bankruptcy have dented his ego and ambition. He is pictured here in 1989 in the atrium of the Trump Tower in New York City.
Photo by Ted Thai/Time Life Pictures/Getty Images.

stock values fell about 40 percent (Figure 31.3). Their savings suddenly worth less, older Americans delayed their retirements. Faced by falling tax revenues, state governments cut services to balance their budgets, and the federal government again spent billions more than it collected.

Globalization

As Americans sought economic security, they recognized that their success depended in part on developments in the world economy. In one sense, this situation was not new. Over the centuries, Americans had depended on foreign markets for their tobacco, cotton, wheat, and industrial goods, and they had long received manufactures and millions of immigrants from other countries. But the *intensity* of international exchange varied over time, and it was again on the upswing. The end of the Cold War had shattered the political barriers that had restrained international trade and impeded capitalist development of vast areas of the world. Moreover, new communication systems — satellites, fiber optic cables, global positioning networks — would shrink

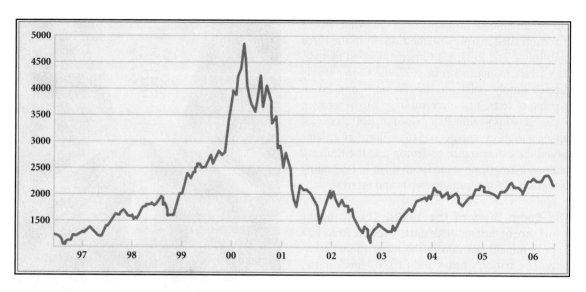

FIGURE 31.3   Boom and Bust in the Stock Market

In late 1999, the stock market took off. The rise of stocks listed on the NASDAQ (National Association of Security Dealers) Exchange was particularly rapid because of its heavy emphasis on technology companies. In little more than a year, the NASDAQ (pronounced *nass-dak*) index tripled in value. Its descent was equally quick. By mid-2002, the index was back where it started, and it continued to fall until early 2003. As in all booms and busts, fortunes were made — and lost — overnight.

the world to a degree unimaginable at the beginning of the twentieth century. The global economy was about to enter a new phase.

International Organizations. During the final decades of the Cold War, the leading capitalist industrial nations formed the Group of Seven (or G-7) to discuss — and manage — global economic policy. The G-7 nations — the United States, Britain, Germany, Italy, Japan, Canada, and France — largely controlled the activities of the major international financial organizations: the World Bank, the International Monetary Fund (IMF), and the General Agreement on Tariffs and Trade (GATT). During the 1990s these organizations became more inclusive. Russia joined the G-7, which became the Group of Eight (G-8), and in 1995 GATT evolved into the World Trade Organization (WTO), with nearly 150 member nations.

Working through the WTO, the promoters of freer global trade achieved many of their goals. They won reductions in tariff rates in many nations and removed many restrictions to the free international movement of capital investments (and profits). The WTO also negotiated agreements that facilitated international telecommunications, the settlement of contractual disputes, and (with less success) the protection of intellectual property rights. Many agreements benefited the wealthier nations; in return, the industrial nations agreed to

increase their imports of agricultural products, textiles, and raw materials from developing countries. Thanks to such measures, the value of American imports and exports rose from 17 percent of GNP in 1978 to 25 percent in 2000. By then, the worldwide volume of international exchange in goods and money had risen to about $1 trillion per day.

As globalization — the worldwide flow of capital, trade, and people — accelerated, so did the integration of regional economies. In 1991 the nations of western Europe created the European Union (EU) and began to move toward the creation of a single federal state (somewhat like the United States). Beginning as a free-trade zone, the EU subsequently promoted the free movement of its peoples among countries without passports and, in 2002, introduced a single currency, the euro (Map 31.1).

To offset the economic clout of the Euro-bloc, in 1993 the United States, Canada, and Mexico signed the North American Free Trade Agreement (NAFTA). This treaty, as ratified by the U.S. Congress, provides for the eventual creation of a free-trade zone covering all of North America; in 2005, some of its provisions were extended to the Caribbean and South America. In East Asia, the capitalist nations of Japan, South Korea, Taiwan, and Singapore consulted on matters of economic policy; as China gradually developed a quasi-capitalist economy, they included its Communist government in their deliberations.

MAP 31.1 Growth of the European Community, 1951–2005

The European Community (EU) began in the 1950s as a loose organization of western European nations. Over the course of the following decades, it created stronger common institutions, such as a European Parliament in Strasbourg, the EU Commission in Brussels, and a Court of Justice in Luxembourg. With the collapse of communism, the EU has expanded to include the nations of eastern and central Europe. It now includes twenty-five nations and 450 million people.

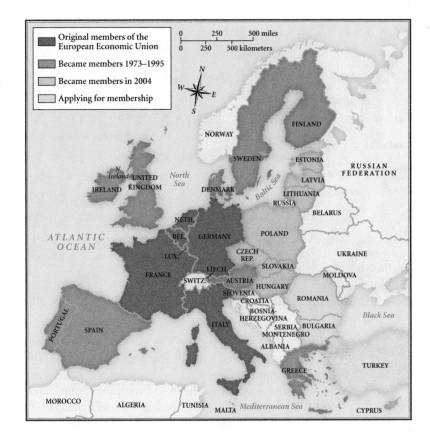

Multinational Corporations and American Labor. The growing number of multinational business corporations testified to the extent of globalization. In 1970, there were 7,000 corporations with offices and factories in multiple countries; by 2000, the number had exploded to 63,000. Many of the most powerful multinationals are American based. Wal-Mart, the biggest retailer in the United States, is also the world's largest corporation, with 1,200 stores in other nations and $32 billion in foreign sales. The McDonald's restaurant chain is equally pervasive. In 1980, McDonald's had 1,000 outlets outside the United States; twenty years later, there were nearly 13,000 and "McWorld" had become a popular short-hand term for globalization. While retaining its emphasis on American-style fast food, the company adapted its menu to local markets. In Finland, customers purchased a McRye; in Chile, a McNifica; and in India, Veg McCurry Pan.

The intensification of globalization dealt another blow to the fragile position of organized labor in the United States. In the 1950s, 33 percent of nonfarm American workers belonged to unions; by 1980, the number had fallen to 20 percent, and President Reagan helped to push it still lower. Shortly after coming into office, he crushed a major union of public employees. When federal workers represented by PATCO (the Professional Air Traffic Controllers' Or-

ganization) went on strike for higher pay and benefits, the president declared the strike to be illegal, fired 11,000 controllers who did not return to work, and broke the union. Heartened by Reagan's firm stance, corporate managers resisted the demands of labor unions at Eastern Airlines and Caterpillar Tractors. A few unions — such as the West Coast Longshoremen's Union and the Teamsters' Union — won important strikes, but their successes did not reverse the long decline of organized labor. By 1998, union members represented only 13.9 percent of the labor force, and by 2004, only 12.5 percent.

Globalization was partly responsible for the recent declines. To take advantage of low-cost labor, many multinational corporations closed their factories in the United States and "outsourced" manufacturing jobs to plants in Mexico, eastern Europe, and especially Asia. The athletic sportswear firm Nike was a prime example. Ignoring ideological boundaries, the company established manufacturing plants for its shoes and apparel in Communist Vietnam and China as well as capitalist Indonesia. By the mid-1990s, Nike had 150 factories in Asia that employed more than 450,000 workers, most of whom received low wages and endured harsh working conditions. Highly skilled jobs were outsourced as well. American corporations — Chase Manhattan Bank, Dell Computer, General Electric, and many

"McWorld" and Globalization in Saudi Arabia
Many of the leading multinational corporations transforming the world's economy are purveyors of American-style consumer goods like Nike and Disney products. So successful was McDonald's in extending its international markets with 13,000 foreign outlets that many critics refer to the results of globalization in general as "McWorld." AP Images.

others—hired English-speaking Indians to staff consumer call centers; and many American firms hired electrical engineers and computer technicians in Bangalore and other Indian high-tech centers.

From the standpoint of corporate profits, outsourcing made sense. In 2005 an American graduate of the California Institute of Technology could expect a starting salary of $56,000, while a graduate of the Indian Institute of Technology commanded only one-third as much. Viewed from a national economic perspective, the outsourcing of skilled American jobs seemed more problematic. Unlike the "brain drain" that brought tens of thousands of foreign-born doctors, engineers, scientists, and technicians to the United States, where they enriched its society, outsourcing undermined the wages of American workers and threatened the long-term vitality of its economy.

Outsourcing had a cultural as well as an economic impact. One of Nike's advertising campaigns, focused on American basketball superstar Michael Jordan, sold millions of pairs of shoes and made Jordan an international celebrity. It also spread American entrepreneurial values as Nike's ads urged people around the world to "Just Do It." Some of them took up the challenge. Yao Ming, a 7′6″ basketball star in China, joined the Houston Rockets, one of a dozen or more players from European and Asian countries who now played in the National Basketball Association. In professional sports, as in other businesses, owners now drew their employees from around the world. In the pursuit of productivity and profit in the new global economy, the political boundaries of nation-states became increasingly irrelevant.

Disease and Death in an Interconnected World.
An exponential growth in the movement of people and ideas across borders was yet another marker of a shrinking world. On any given day in the late twentieth century, an estimated two million travelers and immigrants crossed an international border. Ideas moved even faster. Communications satellites transmitted phone conversations, television programs, and business data through the air, while fiber optic cables instantaneously connected e-mail users and World Wide Web servers in distant continents.

As the globe shrank in size, certain dangers increased in magnitude. In 1918 and 1919, soldiers from distant lands spread a killer flu virus from the battlefields of Europe to most of the world (see Chapter 22). That vicious pandemic killed fifty million people. An equally deadly disease, the human immunodeficiency virus (HIV), spread from Africa to the United States during the 1970s. In 1981 American physicians recognized HIV as a new disease, one that was killing hundreds of gay males, who had become its main carriers. Within two decades HIV, which causes AIDS (acquired immune deficiency syndrome), had spread worldwide, infected over fifty million people of both sexes, and killed more than twenty million.

Within the United States, AIDS took thousands of lives—more than died in the Korean and Vietnam wars combined. Then, between 1995 and 1999, American deaths from HIV dropped 30 percent. This decline—the result of new treatment strategies using a combination of drugs, or a "cocktail"—led to cautious optimism about controlling the disease, for which there is no cure. The high cost of

A Nike Factory in China

In 2005, Nike produced its shoes and sportswear at 124 plants in China; additional factories were located in other low-wage countries. Most of the Chinese plants are run by subcontractors, who house the workers — mostly women between the ages of sixteen to twenty-five — in crowded dormitories. The wages are low, about $3 a day, but more than the women could earn if they remained in their rural villages. AP Images.

these drugs limited their availability, particularly in poor nations. In sub-Saharan Africa, the HIV crisis has reached epidemic proportions, with 30 million infections. South and Southeast Asia, as well as countries of the former Soviet Union, also have millions of infected people — five million in India alone.

Other life-threatening diseases have the potential to spread around the world in days. In February 2003, a viral respiratory illness called SARS (severe acute respiratory syndrome) appeared in China. Within a few months, the disease spread to more than two dozen countries in North America, South America, Europe, and Asia. Despite elaborate public health measures, the virus infected over eight thousand people and killed almost eight hundred of them. And in 2006 a bird virus infected — and killed — a few dozen people and raised the prospect

of a new pandemic, if the bird virus mutates to a form that easily spreads among humans.

The Endangered Environment. The expanding global economy also threatened the health of the world's peoples by polluting the environment. In some countries, the rapid rise in the number of mines, factories, and power plants destroyed irreplaceable natural resources or rendered them unusable. During the last three decades in Brazil, land-hungry peasants, lumber companies, and agribusinesses have cut down roughly a third of the region's ancient rain forests. In Taiwan and China, waste products from new industries and farms have polluted nearly every river — killing fish and rendering the water unsafe to drink.

The industrialized nations also threatened the environment. As millions of cars and thousands of

AIDS in Africa

AIDS (acquired immune deficiency syndrome) originated in Africa, where a chimpanzee virus jumped to humans in the 1960s, and it has taken its greatest toll on that continent. This man, from the Rakai province in southern Uganda, is dying — slowly wasting away — and is completely dependent for support on his twelve-year-old daughter. The Uganda government has implemented an AIDS-prevention program in Rakai and elsewhere and has reported a decline in the prevalence of HIV, the virus that causes AIDS. But it appears that the decline in the number of HIV-infected people is primarily the result of the deaths of many of them. In 2002 in Rakai, 200 people with long-standing HIV infections died, and 125 people became newly infected. Photo by Michael Jensen/www.world-photo.dk.

power plants in Europe and North America burned coal, oil, and other hydrocarbons, they raised the temperature of the atmosphere and the acidity of the oceans — a "greenhouse" effect with potentially momentous consequences. Similarly, the decades-long release into the atmosphere of chlorofluorocarbons (CFCs) — compounds used in industrial cleaning agents, refrigerators, and aerosol cans — significantly depleted the layer of ozone that protects humans from the sun's dangerous ultraviolet rays.

These dangers prompted thousands of Americans to join environmental-protection organizations, such as the Sierra Club and the Nature Conservatory. These groups, and officials of the Environmental Protection Agency, successfully curtailed some pollution. But they were unable to alter government policy on major issues or to convince their fellow citizens of the wisdom of conservation. Ignoring warnings of tightening of oil supplies, the Reagan and Bush administrations refused to support legislation raising mileage requirements for car manufacturers. General Motors and Ford likewise rejected such warnings because they wanted to sell more high-profit gas-guzzling SUV's and small trucks. Nor would most American consumers voluntarily change their lifestyles to reduce energy consumption and cut pollution.

Still, the United States supported a few environmental initiatives. In 1987 the United States was one of thirty-four nations that signed the Montreal Protocol, which banned the production of ozone-damaging CFCs by 1999. The American government likewise joined sixty-three other countries in the Basel Convention of 1994, which ended the export of hazardous wastes to developing countries. Still, American businesses and their political allies resisted efforts to prevent global warming. Although President Clinton signed the Kyoto Treaty of 1998, which committed industrialized countries to reduce greenhouse-gas emissions, the U.S. Senate refused to ratify the agreement. In 2001, the administration of George W. Bush rejected the Kyoto accord, both because it did not apply to underdeveloped countries — which were some of the worst polluters — and because it would restrict or raise the cost of American economic production.

Globalization and Its Critics. President George W. Bush has celebrated globalization as "the triumph of human liberty stretching across national borders . . . [and holding] the promise of delivering billions of the world's citizens from disease and hunger and want." Critics are less optimistic. Some see globalization as a new form of imperialism, whereby the industrialized nations exploit the peoples and natural resources of the rest of the world. Giving political form to these criticisms, Lori Wallach founded Public Citizens' Global Watch, an organization whose goal was to promote "democracy by challenging corporate globalization." Condemning multinational corporations for their failure to protect workers or the environment, Global Watch spearheaded a massive protest at the World Trade Organization meeting in Seattle in 1999. Thousands of activists, including union organizers, environmentalists, and concerned students, disrupted the city and prevented the WTO from convening. As one protestor explained, people "can't go to the

WTO Demonstration, Seattle, 1999

In November 1999, an estimated 75,000 people from many states and foreign nations staged an effective protest at a World Trade Organization (WTO) meeting in Seattle. The goals of the protesters were diffuse; many feared that the trend toward a system of free (capitalist-run) trade would primarily benefit multinational corporations and would hurt both developing nations and the working classes in the industrialized world. Protests have continued at subsequent meetings of the WTO and the World Bank. Hector Mata/AFP/Getty Images.

polls and talk to these big conglomerates. So they had to take to the streets and talk to them." Similar protests against globalization have occurred at meetings of the World Bank, International Monetary Fund, and the G-8 nations.

Indeed, on the occasion of a G-8 meeting in Scotland in 2005, critics mounted a worldwide protest against the financial impact of globalization on poor countries. "Live-8" assembled an international cast of music stars who gave free concerts at ten venues — stretching from London to Tokyo and from Philadelphia to Johannesburg. Broadcast on television and the World Wide Web, the concerts reached a huge audience. Although the concerts helped to persuade the G-8 nations to forgive billions of dollars of debts owned by African nations, they did little to address the internal corruption that has gravely hindered those countries' development. Still, by using the communication infrastructure of the global world, critics had forced a discussion of its effects.

➤ What were the sources of the American economic recovery of the 1980s and 1990s? Who were its heroes, and what were its shortcomings?

➤ What factors promoted "globalization"?

➤ Outline the arguments for and against globalization. Who is making these arguments? Why?

The New Technology

The technological advances that enabled Live-8 had already changed the character of everyday life for millions of Americans. Computers, cell phones, the Internet, and other electronic-based devices altered work, leisure, and access to knowledge in stunning ways.

The Computer Revolution

Scientists devised the first computers — information-processing machines that stored and manipulated data — for military purposes during World War II. Subsequently, the federal government funded computer research as part of the drive for American military superiority during the Cold War. Using this research, private companies began to build large "main frame" computers. In 1952, CBS News used UNIVAC (Universal Automatic Computer), the first commercial computer system, to predict the outcome of the presidential election.

Innovation and Miniaturization. The first computers were cumbersome and finicky machines. They used heat-emitting vacuum tubes for computation power and punched cards for writing programs and analyzing data. UNIVAC and other main-frame computers occupied an entire air-conditioned room, and programming them took several days. In 1947, scientists at Bell Labs invented the transistor, a tiny silicon device that amplifies a signal or opens or closes a circuit many times each second. The transistor revolutionized the electronics industry and allowed technicians to build a second generation of computers — smaller, more powerful, and much cheaper to manufacture. Then in 1959, scientists invented the integrated circuit — a silicon microchip composed of large numbers of interconnected transistors — and ushered in the third computer generation.

Progress continued at an unrelenting pace, as computer wizards devised smaller and more sophisticated chips. A great breakthrough came in 1971 with the development of the microprocessor, which placed the entire central processing unit (CPU) of a computer on a single silicon chip about the size of the letter "O" on this page. By the mid-1970s, a few chips provided as much processing power as a World War II–era computer.

The day of the personal computer (PC) had arrived. In 1977, the Apple Corporation offered a personal computer for $1,195 (about $3,300 today), a price middle-class Americans could afford. When the Apple II became a runaway success, other companies scrambled to get into the market. International Business Machines (IBM) offered its first personal computer in 1981. In three decades, the computer had moved from a few military research centers, to thousands of corporate offices, and then to millions of people's homes. In the process, it created huge entrepreneurial opportunities and a host of overnight millionaires.

Bill Gates and Microsoft. Making computers user-friendly was the major challenge of the PC revolution. In the early 1970s, two former high-school classmates, Bill Gates, aged nineteen, and Paul Allen, twenty-one, set a goal of putting "a personal computer on every desk and in every home." They perceived that the key was "software," the programs that would tell the electronic components (the "hardware") what to do. In 1975 they founded the Microsoft Corporation, which soon dominated the software industry. The phenomenal success of Microsoft's MS-DOS and Windows operating systems stemmed primarily from the company's ability to anticipate industry trends, develop products

Triumph of the Geeks: Microsoft Employees, 1978

This group portrait shows eleven of Microsoft's thirteen employees as the company was about to relocate from Albuquerque, New Mexico, to Seattle, Washington. The oldest member was Paul Allen (front row, far right), age twenty-five; Bill Gates (front row, far left) was twenty-three. A quarter of a century later, Allen was worth $20 billion, Gates was worth nearly $100 billion, and Microsoft had more than fifty thousand employees. Courtesy, Bob Wallace.

quickly, and market them relentlessly. As a Microsoft veteran described the corporate strategy: "See where everybody's headed, then catch up and go past them." And pass them it did. By 2000, the company's products ran nine out of every ten personal computers in the United States and a majority of those around the world. Bill Gates became a billionaire, and Microsoft exploded into a huge company with 57,000 employees and annual revenue of $38 billion. Indeed, Microsoft's near-monopoly of basic computer operating systems prompted government regulators in the United States and the European Union to lodge antitrust suits against the company and force changes in its business practices.

The Impact of the Internet. During the 1990s, personal computers grew even more significant with the spread of the Internet and the World Wide Web. Like the computer itself, the Internet was the product of military-based research. During the 1970s, the Pentagon set up a system of hundreds of computers (or "servers") that were widely dispersed across the United States and connected to each other by copper wires (and now by fiber optic cables). Designed to preserve military communications in the event of a Soviet nuclear attack, the system was soon used by government scientists, academic specialists, and military contractors to exchange text-based e-mail messages via their computers.

The debut in 1991 of the graphics-based World Wide Web, a vast collection of interconnected documents, enhanced the popular appeal and commercial possibilities of the Internet. By 2006, nearly 70 percent of all Americans and slightly more than one billion people worldwide used the Internet to send messages or to view material on the Web. The Web al-

lowed companies, organizations, and individuals to create their own "home pages," incorporating visual, audio, and textual information. Businesses used the Internet to sell their products and services; the volume of e-commerce transactions grew steadily, to $114 billion in 2003 and $172 billion in 2005. During his unsuccessful bid for the 2004 Democratic presidential nomination, Governor Howard Dean of Vermont demonstrated the political potential of the Internet, by using it to raise money and mobilize grassroots support for his campaign. Other politicians and social activists have followed his lead, using the Internet and the Web in ever more creative ways.

Already thousands of businesses were using networked computers—creating the modern electronic office. Small companies kept their records and did all their correspondence and billing on a few desktop machines; large corporations set up linked computers that shared a common database. Some employees no longer came physically to the office; some days they worked as "telecommuters" with their home computers and fax machines connected to the office network by telephone lines, fiber optic cables, and wireless relay systems.

Computers and the Internet transformed leisure as well as work. Millions of Americans took advantage of e-mail to stay in close touch with family and friends. More anonymously, they joined online chat rooms, dating services, and interactive games. Those with broadband connections to the Internet watched "streaming videos" of news events and downloaded music videos and feature films. Interestingly—and importantly—millions of users tried to persuade others to see the world as they do. In 1997 a few people began personal online diaries called Web logs or "blogs"; by 2004, the number of bloggers had grown to eight million, and they offered their authors' perspectives on a wide range of issues: politics, diplomacy, and consumer affairs.

More profoundly, the Web empowered people by providing easy access to knowledge. For nearly two centuries, local public libraries had served that function; now, much of the content of a library was instantly available in a home or office. Using powerful "search engines" such as Google and Yahoo!, people easily located information—some wonderfully accurate and some distressingly problematic—on nearly every subject under the sun. Millions of Americans regularly read newspapers online and used the Web to acquire medical information about diet, drugs, and disease. Students and scholars mined the Web's digital archives and online journals; lawyers used Lexis-Nexis programs for immediate access to hundreds of cases on specific legal issues. Many things that libraries did well, the Web did wonderfully.

Small Electronics. Advances in electronic technology fostered the rapid creation of new leisure and business products. The 1980s saw the introduction of videocassette recorders (VCRs), compact disc (CD) players, cellular telephones, and inexpensive fax machines. Hand-held video camcorders joined film-based cameras as instruments for preserving family memories; parents video-taped their children's lives—sports achievements, graduations, and marriages—and played them on the home television screen. By 2000, cameras took digital pictures that could be stored and transmitted on computers, digital video discs (DVDs) became the newest technology for viewing movies, and TiVo (a direct video recording system) gave television viewers enormous flexibility in watching programs. At the same time, higher resolution television sets, flat plasma screens, and home theater setups became more affordable and widely disseminated.

Wireless telephones (or cell phones), which became available in the 1980s, presaged a communications revolution. By 2003, two-thirds of American adults carried these portable devices, and people under thirty used them in an increasing variety of ways—to take pictures, play games, connect to the Internet, and send text messages. Building on wireless technology for computers, prosperous families created a home network of telephones, computers, and media/entertainment systems. In 2001, Apple Computer revolutionized the pop music industry with the iPod, a hand-sized unit that stored up to 5,000 songs, and iTunes, a system for downloading music from the Web. By 2006, iPods could store and play video. This revolution in technology, like the cultural revolution of the 1960s, was increasingly

the work of the young, who dragged their parents into the new information age.

Legal, Ethical, and Social Issues. Like all new technologies, the computers-Internet-electronics revolution raised a host of social issues and legal conflicts. Many disputes involved the "pirating" of intellectual property through the illegal reproduction of a computer program or a content file. Microsoft and other software companies devised a variety of technical and legal stratagems to protect their copyrighted products, which usually cost millions of dollars to develop. Similarly, the recording industry used lawsuits to shut down the NAPSTER program, which allowed music buffs to share songs through the Internet and burn their own CDs for virtually no cost. Yet intellectual piracy continues, both because of the refusal of governments in China and elsewhere to protect copyrights and because of the decentralized character of the new technology. Just as the Defense Department's system of hundreds of servers would "work around" a Soviet attack, so the existence of millions of personal computers (and skilled operators) has thwarted efforts to police their use.

Computers empowered scientists as well as citizens. Researchers in many scientific disciplines used powerful "supercomputers" to analyze complex natural and human phenomena ranging from economic forecasting to nuclear fusion to human genetics. In 1990, officials at the National Science Foundation allocated $350 million for the Human Genome Project. The Project's goal was to map the human genetic code and unravel the mysteries of DNA (deoxyribonucleic acid), the basic building block of all living things. In 1998, Celera Genomics, a private company backed by pharmaceutical corporations, launched a competing project in hopes of developing profitable drugs. Eventually the two groups pooled their efforts and, by 2003, had built a map of every human gene and posted it, free of charge, on the Web.

As scientists used computers and other technological innovations to probe the mysteries of life, they revived long-standing moral debates. Should employers or insurance companies be permitted to use genetic testing for purposes of hiring or health-care coverage? Should the stem cells from aborted (or in vitro produced) fetuses be used in the search for cures for Alzheimer's, AIDS, and other debilitating diseases (see Chapter 32)? As commentators debated these biomedical issues, other observers worried about the negative impact of the new computer-based technology. Would the use of automatic telephone menus, bank ATMs, and scanners in retail stores gradually create a machine-driven world in which people had little contact with each other? Would the use of the Web by children and

The Biotech Revolution

In 1953, scientists James Watson, Francis Crick, and Roslyn Franklin discovered the double helix structure of DNA (deoxyribonucleic acid), the molecule that carries the distinct genetic blueprint of specific living things. Once DNA's structure was understood, it became theoretically possible to isolate the genetic codes that control nearly every human characteristic — from height and hair color to inherited diseases and certain cancers. But the process would be enormously complicated, given that there are nearly three billion nucleic acid base pairs in just one set of human chromosomes. With the assistance of computer-linked, automated gene-sequencing machines (like these at the Whitehead Institute at MIT), scientists produced a genetic blueprint of the human species in 2003. The medical payoffs are still to come. © Sam Ogden, Photo Researchers.

youths expose them to sexual abuse? Could personal and financial privacy be preserved in a digital world in which businesses and governments could easily create an electronic "profile" of people's lives and hack into their computers?

Political questions were equally challenging. What were the implications of the Patriot Act of 2001 (see Chapter 32), which permits the federal government to monitor electronically citizens' telephone, e-mail, Web, and library usage? Is the loss of civil privacy and liberty an acceptable price to pay for increased security from terrorists? Such questions, debated throughout the twentieth century, acquired increased urgency in the electronic age.

Finally, would a "digital divide" accentuate existing class and racial divisions? Would affluent Americans who could afford computers and Internet access race ahead of poorer citizens? The evidence was contradictory. In 2005, fewer than half of the families with incomes of $30,000 or less had home access to the Internet. Yet most poorer children and adults had access to the new technology and the global communications network because the local, state, and federal governments have connected computers in schools and public libraries to the Internet and the Web.

Technology and the Control of Popular Culture

Americans have reveled in mass-consumer culture ever since the 1920s, when the spread of automobiles, electric appliances, movies, and radio enhanced the quality of everyday life and leisure. By exposing citizens to the same movies and radio programs, the new communication technologies also helped to forge a homogeneous national popular culture. During the 1950s, the spread of television — and its domination by three networks: ABC, CBS, and NBC — likewise encouraged the emergence of a uniform perspective among a majority of middle-class Americans.

Fragmentation in the Television Industry. During the 1970s, new technological developments reshaped the television industry and the cultural landscape. The advent of cable and satellite broadcasting brought more specialized networks and programs into American living rooms. People now got news round-the-clock from Ted Turner's CNN (Cable News Network), watched myriad sports events on the ESPN channels, and tuned into the Fox network for innovative entertainment. By the 1990s, millions of viewers had access to scores, sometimes hundreds, of specialized channels. They could watch old or new movies, golf tournaments, and cooking classes; view religious or African American or Hispanic programming; and buy goods on home-shopping channels. By 1998, such specialized programming had captured 53 percent of the prime-time TV audience.

One of the most successful niche channels was MTV (Music TV), which debuted in 1981. Initially, its main offerings were slickly made videos featuring popular vocalists, who sang and acted out the words of their songs. Essentially advertisements for CDs, these videos were extremely popular among teenagers, who often watched the channel for two hours a day. With its flashy colors, creative choreography, and rapid cuts, MTV popularized singers such as Michael Jackson and Madonna and pushed forward the creation of a culture based on visual and aural "stimulation."

As television became more competitive, network and cable programmers increasingly laced their shows with sexual stimulation. As a television executive explained, "In a cluttering environment where there are so many more media, you have to be more explicit and daring to stand out." In the 1980s network stations began to feature steamier plots on daytime and evening soaps, like *Dallas* and *Dynasty*, while in the 1990s cable shows, such as Home Box Office's (HBO) *Sex in the City*, aired partial nudity and explicit discussion of sexual relations. Talk-show hosts, ranging from the respectable Oprah Winfrey to the shocking Jerry Springer, recruited ordinary Americans to share the secrets of their personal lives—which often involved sexuality, drug abuse, and domestic violence. As the American pop-artist Andy Warhol had predicted, ordinary people eagerly embraced the opportunity to expose their lives and to be "world-famous for 15 minutes."

As TV became more "stimulating" and "reality" oriented, critics argued that it negatively shaped people's outlooks and actions. For evidence they cited violent television dramas, such as HBO's critically acclaimed series *The Sopranos*, which interweaved the personal lives of a Mafia family with the amoral and

Oprah Winfrey

Oprah Winfrey is an American success story. She was born in 1954 to unwed parents, lived first with her grandmother in rural Mississippi and then with her mother in Milwaukee and her father in Nashville. After graduating from Tennessee State University, she became a radio broadcaster and hit the big time in the mid-1980s, with a successful debut as a movie actress and as a national television daytime talk show host. Presently the *Oprah Winfrey Show* boasts a weekly audience of 21 million in 105 countries. Here she chats with author Toni Morrison, whose prize-winning novels Oprah has publicized on her Book Club. © Reuters / Corbis.

relentless violence of their business deals. Did the impact of the dozens of such violence-focused dramas, combined with the widespread availability of guns, increase the already high American murder rate? Did it play a role in a series of shootings by high school students, which culminated in 1999 with the murder of twelve students and one teacher at Columbine High School in Littleton, Colorado? Some lawmakers thought so. In a half-hearted effort to thwart youthful violence, Congress stipulated in the Telecommunication Reform Act of 1996 that manufacturers include a "V-chip" in new TV sets to allow parents to block specific programs.

Deregulation and Media Giants: Warner-AOL and Rupert Murdoch. As the controversy over TV violence indicates, technology never operates in a social and political vacuum. The expansion of cable television and specialized programming stemmed in part from policies set by the Federal Communications Commission (FCC) during the Reagan administration. Mark Fowler, the FCC chair, shared the president's disdain for government regulation of business. "Television is just another appliance. . . . It's a toaster with pictures," Fowler suggested, as the FCC eliminated requirements that stations provide extensive news programming and allow full debate on controversial political issues. Freed from such "public service" responsibilities, TV newscasts increasingly shunned serious coverage of political and economic events and focused on lurid events, such as floods, fires, murders, and scandals connected to celebrities. The troubled marriage and divorce of Prince Charles of England and Lady Diana—and her subsequent death—saturated the airwaves, and the distinction between news and entertainment became blurred.

Fowler's FCC also minimized controls over children's programming. Soon cartoon programs such as *G.I. Joe* and *Care Bears* became extended advertisements for licensed replicas of their main characters. Even the characters of the Public Broadcasting Service's popular *Sesame Street* joined the parade of licensed replicas, as consumer culture extended into the lives of the youngest Americans. Responding to complaints from parents and children's advocates, Congress enacted the Children's Television Act of 1990, which reinstated some restrictions, but the commercialization of virtually every aspect of childhood proceeded nonetheless.

Whatever the programming, the television stations that carried them were increasingly owned by a handful of large companies. In 1985, Congress raised the number of television stations a company could own from seven to twelve. Subsequent regulations promoted even more concentration in media ownership; by 2003, one company owned eight radio

stations and three television stations in a single city, in addition to a newspaper and a TV cable system. On the national level, there was a similar trend toward monopolization. In 1990 Warner Communications merged with Time/Life to create an enormous entertainment corporation that included the Warner Brothers film studio, HBO, TNT, Six Flags, the Atlanta Braves, Atlantic Records, and the magazines of Time, Inc. (*Time, Fortune, Sports Illustrated,* and *People*). In 1995, the company brought in $21 billion in revenues. Subsequently, Warner Communications merged with America Online (renamed simply "AOL" in 2006), the largest provider of Internet access. Although this merger turned out to be a poor business decision, it testified to the growing cultural influence of a few giant corporations.

Australian-born entrepreneur Rupert Murdoch stands as the exemplar of concentrated media ownership in the new global economy. As of 2004, Murdoch owned satellite TV companies in five countries and a worldwide total of 175 newspapers; in the United States, his holdings included Direct TV, the Fox TV Network, the Twentieth Century Fox Studio, the *New York Post,* and thirty-five television stations. A conservative ideologue as well as an entrepreneur, Murdoch has used his news empire to promote his political views. His career indicates not only the technological dimensions of globalization but also the influence of conservative individuals, institutions, and ideas at the beginning of the twenty-first century.

➤ What are the most important aspects of the computer revolution? What are the social consequences of this changing technology?

➤ How is the computer revolution related to globalization?

➤ How did the television industry change after 1980? Why does it matter?

Culture Wars

Times of economic affluence, like the 1950s, often encourage social harmony by damping down class conflict. Such was not the case in the 1980s and 1990s, a prosperous era that was marked by unrelenting warfare over cultural issues. Rooted in the social divisions of the 1960s, these "culture wars" generally pitted religious conservatives against secular liberals. Often instigated by politicians to advance their candidacies, they focused primarily on issues of racial and ethnic pluralism, on challenges to traditional "family values," and on the

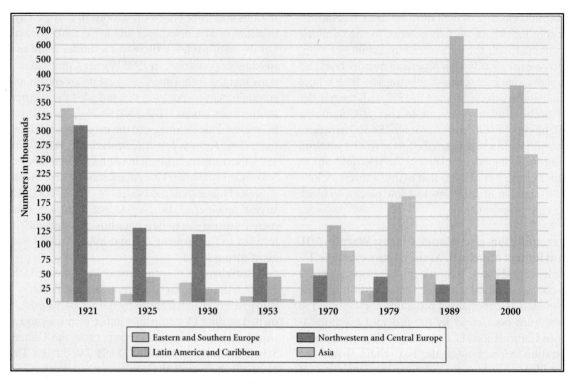

FIGURE 31.4 American Immigration, 1920–2000

Legislation inspired by nativism slowed the influx of immigrants after 1920, as did the dislocations brought on by economic depression and war in the 1930s and 1940s. Note the high rate of non-European immigration since the 1970s, the result of new eligibility rules in the Immigration Act of 1965 (see Chapters 27 and 28). The dramatic increase since 1980 in the number of migrants from Latin America and Asia reflects American economic prosperity, traditionally a magnet for migrants, and the rapid acceleration of illegal immigration.

rights of sexual minorities, especially gay men and women.

An Increasingly Pluralistic Society

In 1992, Republican presidential hopeful Patrick Buchanan warned Americans that their country was "undergoing the greatest invasion in its history, a migration of millions of illegal aliens a year from Mexico." A sharp-tongued cultural warrior, Buchanan exaggerated — but not by much. According to the Census Bureau, the population of the United States grew from 203 million people in 1970 to 280 million in 2000 (and topped 300 million in October 2006). Of that increase of 77 million, immigrants accounted for 28 million, with legal migrants numbering about 21 million and illegal entrants adding another 7 million (Figure 31.4). Relatively few migrants — legal or illegal — came from Europe (2 million), Africa (about 600,000), and Canada (250,000), the historical homelands of most American citizens. The overwhelming majority, some 25 million, came either from East Asia (9 million) or Latin America (16 million).

These immigrants and their children profoundly altered the demography of various states and the entire nation. By 2000, 27 percent of California's population was foreign-born; and Asians, Latinos, and native-born blacks constituted a majority of the residents. Nationally, there were now more Latinos (about 35 million) than African Americans (34 million), and Asians numbered over 12 million. Based on present rates of immigration and births, demographers predicted that by 2050 Americans of European descent would be a minority of the population. As Buchanan had pointed out, a "great invasion" was indeed changing the character — and the color — of American society. Small wonder that ethnic and racial diversity, long a source of conflict in American society, emerged as a prominent theme of the culture wars.

Latino and Asian Immigration. The massive inflow of *legal* immigrants was the unintended result of the Immigration Act of 1965, which allowed family members to join migrants already in the United States. Spanish-speaking Latinos took advantage of this provision; millions of Mexicans came to the United States, and hundreds of thousands arrived

MAP 31.2 Hispanic and Asian Populations, 2000

In 2000, people of Hispanic descent made up more than 11 percent of the American population, and now outnumber African Americans as the largest minority group. Asian Americans accounted for an additional 4 percent of the population. Demographers predict that by the year 2050 only about half of the U.S. population will be composed of non-Hispanic whites. Note the high percentage of Hispanics and Asians in California and certain other states.

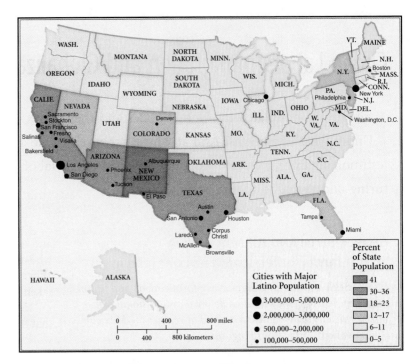

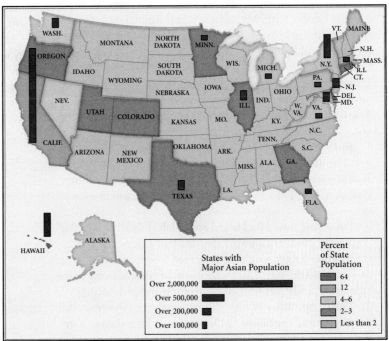

from El Salvador, Guatemala, and the Dominican Republic. Historically, most Latinos had lived in California, Texas, and New Mexico; now they settled in cities throughout the country—numbering 16 percent of the population in Florida and New York (see Map 31.2).

Most Latinos were poor men and women seeking a better life in the United States. They willingly worked for low wages—cleaning homes, tending lawns, servicing hotel rooms, painting houses,

working construction. Many labored "for cash, no questions asked"; as members of the "underground" economy, they did not pay income or Social Security taxes. Instead, many immigrants regularly sent funds to their families back home and urged them to migrate—legally or illegally. Their hopes lay in the future, especially in their American-born children, who could claim the rights of U.S. citizens (see Comparing American Voices, "Cheap Labor: Immigration and Globalization," pp. 978–979).

Cheap Labor: Immigration and Globalization

Immigrants populated the United States and they continue to remake it. But for whose benefit? Under what conditions? And at whose expense? Those are three of the questions raised by these testimonials from men and women employed in the labor-intensive industries of garment manufacturing and agricultural production.

GEORGE STITH AND JUANITA GARCIA

"Local farm workers could not get jobs at all"

George Stith and Juanita Garcia were farmworkers and union members. In 1952, they testified before a congressional committee considering whether to expand or restrict the Mexican "guest worker" (braceros) program.

STITH: Mr. Chairman and members of the committee, My name is George Stith. My address is Star Route Box 5, Gould, Ark. All my life I have worked on cotton plantations. When I was 4 years old my family moved to southern Illinois, near Cairo. We picked cotton in southeast Missouri, and west Tennessee nearly every year. We later moved across the river into Missouri and share-cropped. In 1930 we moved back to Arkansas. I don't know whether I am a migratory worker or not, but we certainly did a lot of migrating.

In 1936 when I was share cropping in Woodruff County, Ark. I joined the union which was then called the Southern Tenant Farmers Union. It is now the National Farm Labor Union, A. F. of L. I have been a member of the union ever since. . . .

For a long time I had heard about labor shortages in the West and how Mexican workers were being imported. I was sure that no people would be imported from Mexico to work on farms in Arkansas. There were too many people living in the little towns and cities who go out to chop and pick cotton. . . .

The importation of Mexican nationals into Arkansas did not begin until the fall of 1949. Cotton-picking wages in my section were good. We were getting $4 per 100 pounds for picking. As soon as the Mexicans were brought in the wages started falling. Wages were cut to $3.25 and $3 per 100 pounds. In many cases local farm workers could not get jobs at all. . . . The cotton plantation owners kept the Mexicans at work and would not employ Negro and white pickers. . . .

GARCIA: My name is Juanita Garcia. I live in Brawley, Calif. I work in the field and in the packing sheds. I lost my job in a packing shed about 2 weeks ago. I was fired because I belonged to the National Farm Labor Union. . . . My father, my brothers, and sisters also work on the farms. For poor people like us who are field laborers, making a living has always been hard. Why? Because the ranchers and companies have always taken over. . . .

In the Imperial Valley we have a hard time. It so happens that the local people who are American citizens cannot get work. . . . The wetbacks [illegal immigrants] and nationals from Mexico have the whole Imperial Valley. . . . The nationals and wetbacks take any wages the ranchers offer to pay them. The wages get worse every year. . . .

Last year they fired some people from the shed because they had nationals to take their jobs. There was a strike. . . . They took the nationals from the camps to break our strike. They had 5,000 scabs that were nationals. We told the Mexican consul about this. We told the Labor Department. They were supposed to take the nationals out of the strike. They never did take them away.

SOURCE: Migratory Labor, Hearings before Subcommittee on Labor and Labor-Management Relations, 82nd Congress, 2nd Session (Washington, D.C., Government Printing Office, 1952), 89–90, 93–94.

TRONG AND THANH NGUYEN

"We're political refugees. . . . We spend our money here."

Trong and Thanh Nguyen fled from Communist Vietnam in the mid-1970s.

TRONG: When my wife and I came to Chicago, our major concern was to feed our five small children. We had Vietnamese pride and did not want to take public aid. We wanted the American community and authorities to respect us.

Just trying to begin a new life here, we had so many difficulties. When I worked as a janitor at Water Tower Place, a co-worker told me, "Trong, do you know that America is overpopulated? We have more than two hundred million people. We don't need you. Go back where you belong." I was shocked to hear people trying to chase us out. . . .

THANH: When we first came to Chicago, I cried a lot. In the factory where I worked, there weren't many Americans. Most were Mexicans, some legal, but also many illegal aliens. . . . They cursed our people. Some Mexicans said, "You come here and take our jobs. Go back wherever you came from." . . . "You come here to make money, then go back home and live like kings." That was too much. I couldn't hold it in any more.

I told them in a very soft voice, "We are Vietnamese people. You don't have enough education to know where our country is. Vietnam is a small country, but we did not come to America to look for jobs. We're political refugees. We can't go back home." I didn't call them bad names or anything, but I said, "You are the ones who come here to make money to bring back to your country. We spend our money here." After that, they didn't bother us very much.

SOURCE: Paul S. Boyer, ed., *Enduring Voices*, 3rd ed. (Boston: Houghton Mifflin, 1996), 408–409.

PETRA MATA AND FEIYI CHEN

"Garment workers . . . made a decent living before free trade"

Petra Mata and Feiyi Chen are immigrants from low-wage countries who were "insourced"; on coming to the United States they worked as low-paid garment workers. Then, their jobs were "outsourced" — sent abroad to even lower-paid workers as a result of free trade and globalization.

MATA: My name is Petra Mata. I was born in Mexico. I have completed no more than the sixth grade in school. In 1969, my husband and I came to the U.S. believing we would find better opportunities for our children and ourselves. We first arrived without documents, then became legal, and finally became citizens. For years I moved from job to job until I was employed in 1976 by the most popular company in the market, Levi Strauss & Company. I earned $9.73 an hour and also had vacation and sick leave. Levi's provided me and my family with a stable situation, and in return I was a loyal employee and worked there for fourteen years.

On January 16, 1990, Levi's closed its plant in San Antonio, Texas, where I had been working, leaving 1,150 workers unemployed, a majority of whom were Mexican-American women. The company moved its factory to Costa Rica. . . .

As a result of being laid off, I personally lost my house, my method of transportation, and the tranquility of my home. My family and I had to face new problems. My husband was forced to look for a second job on top of the one he already had. He worked from seven in the morning to six at night. Our reality was very difficult. At that time, I had not the slightest idea what free trade was or meant. . . .

Our governments make agreements behind closed doors without participation from the working persons who are most affected by these decisions — decisions that to my knowledge only benefit large corporations and those in positions of power. . . .

CHEN: My name is Feiyi Chen. I immigrated to the United States in December 1998 from China. I began my working career as a seamstress in a garment factory because I did not speak English and the garment manufacturing industry was one of the few employment opportunities available to me. I typically worked ten hours a day, six days a week, at a backbreaking pace. Most garment bosses know that new immigrants have few choices when it comes to work and so they take advantage by paying workers less than the minimum wage with no overtime pay. . . . I learned from some of the older garment workers that garment workers in San Francisco actually made a decent living before free trade lured many of the better-paying garment factories over to other countries and forced the smaller and rule-abiding factories to shut down because they could not compete with the low cost of production from neighboring countries. . . .

Working as a seamstress and an assembly worker has always been hard, but with so many of the factories leaving the country in search of cheaper labor, life for immigrant workers like myself is getting worse. For example, many garment workers who were paid one dollar for sewing a piece of clothing are now only making fifty cents for the same amount of work. There are a lot of garment workers who still work ten hours a day but make less than thirty dollars a day.

SOURCE: Christine Ahn, *Shafted: Free Trade and America's Working Poor* (Oakland, CA: Food First Books, 2003), 32–38.

ANALYZING THE EVIDENCE

➤ Describe the experiences of the workers as related in their statements. What generalizations can you make about the impact of immigration on wages? On the relations among ethnic groups in the United States?

➤ How does "globalization," a major focus of this chapter, affect the lives of these workers? Provide some specific examples from the documents that show its impact.

➤ What role would these workers like the federal government to play? According to the discussion in this chapter, what is American policy with respect to globalization?

➤ Consider the questions raised in the introduction: Who benefits from immigration, legal or illegal? How does it affect working conditions? Is there a cost, and who pays it?

New Immigrants

In the 1980s, many Korean immigrants opened small grocery and fruit stores in urban neighborhoods. Their economic success was hard won — the result of disciplined saving and long hours of work — and often led to conflicts with poor blacks and Hispanics, who resented their rapid economic mobility. Kay Chernush.

Most Asian migrants came from China, the Philippines, South Korea, India, and Pakistan. In addition, 700,000 refugees migrated to the United States from Indochina (Vietnam, Laos, and Cambodia) after the Vietnam War. Some of these Asians were well educated or entrepreneurial; they adapted quickly and successfully to life in their new homeland. But a majority lacked professional or vocational skills and took low-paying jobs.

As in the past, the immigrants congregated in ethnic conclaves. In Los Angeles, Koreans created the thriving community of "Koreatown"; in Brooklyn, New York, Russian Jews settled in "Little Odessa"; Latino migrants took over entire sections of Chicago, the District of Columbia, Dallas, and Houston. As the number of immigrants grew, ethnic entrepreneurs catered to their tastes — establishing restaurants, food stores, clothing shops, and native-language newspapers — while mainstream department stores, car dealers, and politicians vied for their dollars and votes. Although many migrants worked and shopped outside their ethnic enclaves, they usually socialized, attended church, and married within the community.

Anti-immigrant Sentiment. While some native-born Americans celebrated this renewal of the nation's ethnic pluralism, many others worried about its massive size. Similar concerns had fueled nativist opposition to Irish Catholic immigrants in the 1840s and to Jews and Catholics from eastern

and southern Europe around 1900. As in the past, critics argued that immigrants assimilated slowly, depressed wages for all workers, and raised crime rates (see Voices from Abroad, "Janet Daley: A U.S. Epidemic," p. 981). They also sounded new and potent themes: that the rapidly rising population endangered the environment and burdened governments with millions of dollars in costs for schools, hospitals, police, and social services. Responding to such concerns, the Welfare Reform Act of 1996 curtailed the access of legal immigrants to food stamps and other welfare benefits.

The most far-reaching challenges to mass immigration emerged at the state level. In 1986, California voters overwhelmingly supported Proposition 63, which established English as the state's "official language," and seventeen other states followed suit. Eight years later, Californians approved Proposition 187, a ballot initiative forthrightly named "Save Our State," which barred illegal aliens from public schools, nonemergency care at public health clinics, and all other state social services. The initiative also required law enforcement officers, school administrators, and social workers to report suspected illegal immigrants to the Immigration and Naturalization Service. When a federal judge ruled that Proposition 187 was unconstitutional, supporters of the measure demanded that Congress take action to curtail legal migration and expel illegal entrants.

An unlikely coalition of politicians prevented the passage of such federal legislation. Heeding the pleas of business owners and large-scale farmers, who wanted a plentiful supply of low-wage workers, conservative Republicans refused to restrict immigration. Liberal Democrats also opposed such legislation because they supported ethnic pluralism and cultural diversity. Indeed, in 1986 Congress enacted (and President Reagan signed) a measure that granted amnesty to nearly two million illegal aliens and, in its lack of rigorous enforcement provisions, ensured that the flood of illegal migrants would continue, as indeed it has. By 2006, Congress was again debating this contentious issue.

African Americans. The dramatic increase in Asians and Latinos brought some benefits to African Americans. As immigrant workers took the lowest paid jobs in the construction, manufacturing, and hotel service industries, many blacks used their experience and facility in English to move into supervisory positions. Some of these African Americans joined the ranks of the middle classes and moved to better lives in the suburbs. Yet the poorer blacks who remained in the inner cities now paid more for housing because the demand from

Janet Daley

A U.S. Epidemic

Around 8:30 p.m. on April 19, 1989, marauding gangs of youths began to beat up joggers and bicyclists in New York City's Central Park. About the same time, Trisha Meilli, a twenty-nine-year-old American investment banker of Italian descent, was brutally raped, beaten, and left for dead in the park. In a coma for twelve days, Meilli did not remember any details of the attack. Five black and Latino young men from Harlem, arrested initially because of the gang attacks, confessed to the assault and served prison terms of seven to eleven years. In 2002, long after Daley's article appeared in an English newspaper, The Independent, *DNA tests pinned the attack on Matias Reyes, a convicted serial rapist and murderer. Reyes, who was born in Puerto Rico, told prison officials that he alone raped and beat the jogger.*

[London, August 29, 1990]
THE TRIAL in New York of the Central Park rapists has brought into focus two tacit assumptions that underpin conventional wisdom about America and the prognosis for our own [English] future.

The first is that everything wrong with American society is a result of its "system" (that is, its political and economic organisation). The second is that as our "system" becomes more like that of the United States (more free-market based), we shall inevitably suffer the same problems of a mindlessly violent underclass....

Both of these contentions seem to me wrong. To begin with, the notion that a country's social mores and attitudes are brought about entirely by the form of its government and econ-omy is a bit of Marxist theoretical baggage that ought to be thrown out. ... It is an absurd idea that whatever is wrong with our social relations, or even our family lives, must be accounted for by the structure of our national institutions. Juvenile crime is a plague in communist China and alcoholism—a more traditional kind of drug abuse—is endemic in the Soviet Union.

Many of the worst instances of anarchic violence in America—such as the attack on the Central Park jogger—do not arise from the underclass in the proper economic sense at all. These boys were not notably poor, or from families without aspirations.

Those aspects of American life that are most repugnant—its lunatic viciousness and criminality—can be accounted for by purely historical circumstances which the political system could influence in only the most marginal way. The United States is an enormous continental landmass which was settled in an ad hoc, opportunist fashion by disparate groups of people with different motivations and lifestyles. This Babel-like chaos was governed in the most minimal way. ... Each immigrant group created its own cohesiveness. The Irish, the East Europeans, the Jews all had their communities which gave them some sense of security. And when the geographical communities began to disperse, there were still networks of tribal feeling and attachment.

Into this mix early this century came a great wave of Sicilians who brought with them their own family industry. The Mafia gained a hold in America at a time when law enforcement was nominal and social insecurity was universal. Having had its roots in the Little Italy of New York, it now runs the gambling, prostitution and drug empires of America. It has had deep connections with whole swathes of the transport industry through its connections with certain unions. ...

This pervasive influence of organised crime which arose through a historical coincidence—the arrival of a particular subculture in a loosely organised country which, for separate historical reasons, had committed itself constitutionally to the citizen's right to bear arms—is more central to the current problems of the US than its capitalist economy or its political ideology.

To describe Britain as inevitably on the same road is simple historical ignorance. For a stable and deeply conservative society to come to grips with immigrant groups may present us with a challenge, but it can never lead to the conditions with which America is faced, and which are the result of attempting to build a society from scratch out of a diverse and discordant collection of peoples.

The oppressive conformity and intolerance of American life arise from this compulsion to create a homogeneous culture out of ethnic chaos. A society without a central historical axis breeds chronic anxiety.

SOURCE: *The Independent* (London), August 29, 1990, p. 18.

ANALYZING THE EVIDENCE

➤ According to Daley, why is violence so widespread in the United States? How convincing is her analysis?

➤ Does Daley's argument provide insight into the rape of the Central Park jogger?

➤ What are we to make of Daley's conclusion, given the bombing of the London subway system in 2005 by four Muslim youth, three of whom were born in England of Pakistani descent?

immigrants drove up rents. Massive immigration also adversely affected many inner-city black children because overcrowded and underfunded schools diverted scarce resources to bilingual education for Spanish- and Chinese-speaking students.

Still, government policy continued to provide African Americans (and Latinos and white women) with preferential treatment in areas such as hiring for public sector jobs, "set-aside" programs for minority-owned businesses, and university admissions. Conservatives had long argued that such programs were deeply flawed because they amounted to intrusive governmental "social engineering," promoted "reverse discrimination" against white men, and resulted in the selection and promotion of less-qualified applicants. During the 1990s, conservatives—along with many Americans who believed in "equal opportunity"—demanded an end to such legal privileges.

Once again, California stood at the center of the debate. In 1995, under pressure from the Republican governor, Pete Wilson, the regents of the University of California voted to scrap its twenty-year-old policy of affirmative action. A year later, California voters approved Proposition 209, which banished affirmative action privileges in state employment and public education. When the number of Latino and African Americans admitted to the flagship Berkeley campus of the University of California plummeted, conservatives hailed the result as proving that the previous admissions policy had lowered intellectual standards. Avoiding a direct reply to that charge, liberals maintained that state universities should educate potential leaders of all ethnic and racial groups.

Affirmative action remained controversial. In 2001, the California Regents devised a new admissions plan to assist minority applicants; two years later the U.S. Supreme Court invalidated an affirmative action plan at the University of Michigan, but allowed racial-preference policies that promoted a "diverse" student body. In the face of growing public and judicial opposition, the future of such programs was uncertain.

Race and Crime: Rodney King and O. J. Simpson.

While affirmative action programs assisted some African Americans to rise into the middle classes, they did not address the social problems of poorer blacks. Millions of African Americans lived in households headed by wage-earning single mothers, who had neither the time nor the energy to supervise their children's lives. Many of their daughters bore babies at an early age, while their sons ran with street gangs and dealt in illegal drugs. To address drug use and the crimes that it generated, the Reagan administration urged young people to "Just Say No." This campaign had some success in cutting

drug use among middle-class black and white teenagers, but did not staunch the dangerous flow of crack cocaine into poor African American neighborhoods. "The police are losing the war against crack," *Newsweek* noted grimly in 1986, "and the war is turning the ghettos of major cities into something like a domestic Vietnam." Indeed, the murderous competition among black drug dealers took the lives of thousands of young African American men, and police efforts to stop drug use and trafficking brought the arrest and imprisonment of tens of thousands more.

In April 1992, this seething underworld of crime and urban impoverishment erupted in five days of race riots in Los Angeles. The worst civil disorder since the 1960s, the violence took sixty lives and caused $850 million in damage. The riot was set off by the acquittal (on all but one charge) of four white Los Angeles police officers accused of using excessive force in arresting a black motorist, Rodney King, who had led them on a wild car chase. A graphic amateur video showing the policemen kicking and clubbing King did not sway the predominantly white jury, even as it highlighted police brutality and the harassment of minorities.

The riot exposed the fragility of urban America and acute rifts between urban blacks and their immigrant neighbors. Many Los Angeles blacks resented recent immigrants from Korea, who had set up successful small retail businesses. When they

To Live and Die in L.A.

As rioters looted stores in South-Central Los Angeles and burned over one thousand buildings, the devastation recalled that caused by the African American riots in Watts in 1965. But Los Angeles was now a much more diverse community. More than 40 percent of those arrested in 1992 were Hispanic, and the rioters attacked Koreans and other Asians as well as whites. Silvie Kreiss/Liason.

tried to loot and burn these businesses during the riot, the Koreans fought them off with guns. Frustrated by high unemployment and crowded housing conditions, Latinos joined in the rioting and accounted for more than half of those arrested and a third of those killed. The riots represented both an expression of black rage at white injustice and the class-based looting of property by poor African Americans and immigrant Latinos.

In 1995, Los Angeles police worried about another black-led riot as the trial of O. J. Simpson neared its end. A renowned African American college and professional football player and a well-paid representative for Hertz Rental Cars, Simpson was accused of the brutal murder of his ex-wife, Nicole Brown Simpson, a white woman. The prosecution produced damning evidence of Simpson's guilt, but black defense attorney Johnnie Cochran argued that a police detective tampered with the evidence. More important, Cochran played the "race card," encouraging the predominately black jury to view Simpson as a victim of racial prejudice and to acquit him. Although a substantial majority of whites, in Los Angeles and the nation, believed that Simpson was guilty, they peacefully accepted the jury's verdict of "not guilty." In the 1990s, unlike the 1920s and 1940s, whites no longer resorted to racial riots to suppress or take revenge against blacks. Now it was African Americans who took to the streets.

Multiculturalism. For most of the twentieth century, supporters of civil rights for African Americans and other ethnic groups advocated their "integration" into the wider society and culture. Integration had been the dream of Martin Luther King Jr. and César Chavez (see Chapter 28). Beginning in the 1970s, some blacks (and Latinos) rejected integration in favor of "multiculturalism" and set out to win political support for the creation of racially and ethnically distinct institutions. Some liberals supported this multicultural agenda, but Arthur Schlesinger Jr. (a well-known historian and advisor to President Kennedy) and many others opposed such separatist schemes. Conservative commentators, such as George F. Will, William Bennett, and Patrick Buchanan, uniformly condemned multiculturalism as a threat to core American values. Fearing the "balkanization," or fragmentation, of American culture, they opposed classroom instruction of immigrant children in their native languages and revisions of university curricula that deemphasized the importance of European culture.

This warfare over culture issues extended into Congress. Believing that the programs aired on public television and the grants awarded by the National Endowments for the Arts and the Humanities

promoted multiculturalism, conservative lawmakers tried to cut off their funding. When that effort failed, they drastically reduced the organizations' budgets. Conservatives also took aim at the antiracist and antisexist regulations and speech codes that had been adopted by many colleges. Demanding the protection of the First Amendment right of free speech, conservatives (along with liberals in the American Civil Liberties Union) opposed attempts to regulate "hate" speech.

Conflicting Values: Women's and Gay Rights

Conservatives were equally worried about the state of American families. They pointed to the 40 percent rate of divorce among whites and the 70 percent rate of out-of-wedlock pregnancies among blacks. The "abrasive experiments of two liberal decades," they charged, had eroded respect for marriage and family values. To members of the Religious Right, there were a wide range of culprits: legislators who enacted liberal divorce laws, funded child care, and allowed welfare payments to unmarried mothers, and judges who banished religious instruction from public schools. While their celebration of "traditional family values" evoked all these issues, religious conservatives were particularly intent on resisting the new freedoms and rights claimed by women and homosexuals.

Feminists, the Religious Right, and Abortion. In the 1980s, public opinion polls showed strong support for many feminist demands, including equal pay in the workplace, an equitable sharing of household and child-care responsibilities, and personal control of reproductive decisions. But in *Backlash: The Undeclared War on American Women* (1991), journalist Susan Faludi warned that conservative social groups had launched an all-out campaign against the feminist movement and its agenda of civic equality for women. To resist this conservative onslaught, the National Organization of Women (NOW) expanded its membership and agenda to include "Third Wave" feminists. These new feminists adopted a multicultural perspective and advanced the distinctive concerns of women of color, lesbians, and working women. Younger feminist women also felt more secure of their sexuality; many of them identified with the pop music star Madonna, whose outrageous sexualized style seemed to empower her rather than make her a sex object.

Abortion became a central issue in the cultural warfare between feminists and religious conservatives, and also a defining issue between Democrats and Republicans. Feminists viewed the issue from the perspective of the pregnant woman; they argued that the right to a legal, safe abortion was crucial to her control over her life. Conversely, religious conservatives maintained that legalized abortion improperly gave a higher value to the woman's individual rights than to her sacred vocation of motherhood. They also viewed abortion from the perspective of the unborn fetus — claiming that its rights trumped those of the living mother. Indeed, in cases of a difficult childbirth, some conservatives would sacrifice the life of the mother to save that of the fetus. To dramatize the larger issues at stake, the antiabortion movement christened itself as "pro-life," while proponents of abortion rights described themselves as "pro-choice." Both ideologies had roots in the American commitment to "life, liberty, and the pursuit of happiness." The question remained: Whose life? Whose liberty? Whose definition of happiness?

The hierarchy of the Catholic Church gave its answer to these questions in 1971, when it sponsored the formation of the National Right to Life Committee. Church leaders launched a sophisticated media campaign to build popular support for its antiabortion stance, distributing films of late-term fetuses in utero and photographs of tiny fetal hands. By the 1980s, fundamentalist Protestants assumed leadership of the antiabortion movement, which became increasingly confrontational and politically powerful.

Pressed by antiabortion interest groups, state legislatures passed laws that regulated the provision of abortion services. These laws required underage girls to obtain parental permission for abortions, denied public funding for abortions for poor women, and mandated waiting periods and elaborate counseling. These laws navigated between conflicting conservative beliefs. Religious conservatives demanded laws prohibiting abortions; "free enterprise" conservatives responded that abortion decisions were private matters and, like businesses, should be immune from government control. However, both groups of conservatives agreed that parents — and not the state — had the right to make important decisions for their minor children. As we saw in Chapter 30, in two decisions, *Webster v. Reproductive Health Services* (1989) and *Planned Parenthood of Southeastern Pennsylvania v. Casey* (1992), the Supreme Court accepted the constitutionality of many of these restrictions. But the federal courts continued to overturn state laws that prohibited late-term abortions when the life of the mother was in danger.

The debate over abortion stirred deep emotions (see Reading American Pictures, "The Abortion Debate Hits the Streets," p. 985). During the 1990s, evangelical Protestant activists mounted protests outside abortion clinics and harassed their staffs and clients. Pro-life extremists advocated killing the doctors and nurses who performed abortions, and a few carried out their threats. In 1994, an antiabortion activist killed a worker at two Massachusetts abortion clinics and wounded five others; other religiously motivated extremists murdered doctors in Florida and New York. Cultural warfare had turned deadly — resorting to terror to achieve its ends.

The Controversy over Gay Rights. The issue of homosexuality stirred equally deep feelings on both sides. As more gay men and women "came out of the closet" in the years after Stonewall (see Chapter 29), they formed groups that demanded a variety of protections and privileges. Defining themselves as a "minority" group, gays sought legislation that protected them from discrimination in housing, education, public accommodations, and employment. Public opinion initially opposed such initiatives, but by the 1990s, many cities and states banned discrimination on the basis of sexual orientation.

This legislation did not end the conflict. Gay groups asserted that civic equality included extensive legal rights for same-sex couples, such as eligibility for workplace health-care coverage on the same basis as married heterosexuals. Indeed, many homosexuals wanted their partnerships recognized as legal marriages and treated identically to opposite-sex unions. Proposals for gay marriage roused widespread opposition because they confounded traditional practices and would have immense implications for the American family system.

The Religious Right had long condemned homosexuality as morally wrong and a major threat to the traditional family. Pat Robertson, North Carolina senator Jesse Helms, and other conservatives campaigned vigorously against antidiscrimination measures for gays. Their arguments that such laws amounted to undeserved "special rights" struck a responsive chord in Colorado. In 1992, Colorado voters amended the state constitution to bar local jurisdictions from passing ordinances protecting gays and lesbians, a measure subsequently overturned as unconstitutional by the Supreme Court. In 1998, Congress entered the fray by enacting the Defense of Marriage Act, which allowed states to refuse to recognize gay marriages or civil unions formed in other jurisdictions. However, in *Lawrence v. Texas* (2003), the Supreme Court ruled that states may not prohibit private homosexual activity between consenting adults (see Chapter 30, Comparing American Voices, pp. 930–931). As the new century began, the debate over legal rights for gays and lesbians rivaled in fervor and importance those over immigration restriction, abortion, and affirmative action. Increasingly, these cultural issues shaped the dynamics of American politics.

The Abortion Debate Hits the Streets

Divided Women, Divided Public: Protesting in Washington, D.C., 2004. Declan McCullagh.

Few issues in U.S. history divided late-twentieth-century Americans as profoundly as abortion. Since the Supreme Court's *Roe v. Wade* decision (1973), protests and counterprotests have grown. As the text suggests, the issue intrudes constantly into the social, cultural, and political history of recent decades (see Chapters 29, 30, and 32). Because the battle involves a seemingly irreconcilable difference between conflicting moral principles, finding common ground for compromise has been difficult. Antiabortion activists sometimes compare their fight with that of the abolitionists in the pre–Civil War era (who argued that slavery was immoral) and liken *Roe v. Wade* to *Dred Scott*—the 1857 Supreme Court decision that protected slave property. Those who support abortion often stake their ground on the rights of the individual—a woman's right to control her life and her body—and invoke the Constitution's protection of individual freedom and privacy. The photograph above suggests the character of the resulting political confrontation. What do you see?

ANALYZING THE EVIDENCE

➤ Describe the people marching in the street. Who is protesting on the sidewalk? What does the composition of the two groups say about the abortion controversy?

➤ Next, look at how the police are positioned. From what you've read in the narrative, why might this sort of police deployment be necessary?

➤ Finally, look at the signs both groups are holding up. What messages do they convey? How do the slogans frame the debate? What principles do they invoke?

➤ Abortion was a significant political issue in the mid-nineteenth century, when many states first outlawed the practice, and again in the 1960s, when five states repealed antiabortion laws and eleven others reformed their restrictive legislation. Since the late 1970s, abortion has become an important issue in national politics and often divides Democrats and Republicans. From what you've read in the text and see in this picture, how can you explain the political importance of this issue?

➤ Who were the new immigrants? What were the sources of hostility to them?

➤ How do you account for the cultural conflict over issues relating to women and homosexuals? Who are the sides in conflict?

SUMMARY

As we have seen, a number of factors contributed to the revival of the American economy between 1980 and 2000. The defense buildup and the Reagan tax cuts poured billions of dollars into the economy, and American corporations invested heavily in research and new technologies. As the Japanese and German economies faltered, the United States reasserted its leading role in the global economy. The increase in the number of multinational firms, many of them U.S.-based, pushed forward the process of globalization. While nation-states remained immensely important, people, goods, and investment capital moved easily across political boundaries.

Technological innovations strengthened the American economy and transformed daily life. The computer revolution and the spread of the Internet changed the ways in which Americans shopped, worked, learned, and stayed in touch with family and friends. Technology likewise altered the character of television programming and viewing, as cable and satellite technology, along with government deregulation, provided Americans with a wider variety of entertainment choices.

As our account has suggested, globalization and technological change accentuated various cultural conflicts within the United States. Advances in biomedical science revived old moral debates, and globalization facilitated the immigration of millions of Asians and Latin Americans. The new immigrants increased the anxieties of many citizens about ethnic diversity and multiculturalism, while the poverty and crime that characterized the inner cities highlighted the nation's class and racial problems. Conservatives spoke out strongly, and with increasing effectiveness, against what they viewed as serious threats to "family values." Debates over women's rights, access to abortion, affirmative action, and the legal rights of homosexuals intensified. As the nation entered the twenty-first century, its people were sharply divided by cultural values as well as by economic class and racial identity.

Connections: Society and Technology

Cultural conflict has been a significant feature of recent American life. As we noted in the essay that opened Part Seven (p. 925):

> Increased immigration from Latin America and Asia added to cultural tensions and produced a new nativist movement. Continuing battles over affirmative action, abortion, sexual standards, homosexuality, feminism, and religion in public life took on an increasingly passionate character.

Neither set of issues was new. During the 1920s, as we explained in Chapter 23, powerful nativist sentiment forced the passage of a National Origins Act that severely restricted immigration from many countries. That decade also witnessed nationwide Prohibition, a failed attempt to impose a moral code by force of law. Both immigration and moral issues came to the fore again in the 1960s, but with a far different result. As we saw in Chapter 28, the Immigration Act of 1965 opened the way for a more diverse and more numerous flow of migrants, while the countercultural revolution challenged traditional social strictures and moral values and overthrew many of them. The battle was far from over, as we have discovered in Chapter 31. Beginning in the 1970s and gaining force in subsequent decades, moral and sexual conservatives launched a cultural offensive intended to encourage and, if possible, to legislate a return to the social arrangements and values that were dominant in the first half of the twentieth century.

That attempt at cultural control will take place in a world shaped by the technology of the computer chip and the Internet. In assessing possible outcomes, we might look back at earlier technological revolutions—the impact of electricity and the telephone in Chapter 18, of the radio and automobiles in Chapter 23, and of television in Chapter 27—all of which expanded the range of people's knowledge and choices. In such ways does technology influence, but not determine, cultural outcomes.

CHAPTER REVIEW QUESTIONS

➤ In what ways did the new technology affect the American economy? What was its relation to globalization?

➤ What was the outcome of the various cultural wars of the 1980s and 1990s?

TIMELINE

1980s	Rise of "Yuppies" (young urban professionals)
	Japan emerges as major economic power
	Women enter workforce in increasing numbers
	Lee Iacocca revives Chrysler Corporation
	Bill Gates builds Microsoft as computer use spreads
	Immigration of Latinos and Asians expands
	Conservatives challenge affirmative action programs
1981	Reagan crushes air traffic controllers' strike
	AIDS epidemic identified; begins worldwide spread
1985	United States becomes debtor nation
1987	Montreal environmental protocol cuts ozone loss
1989	Savings and Loan scandals and crises
1990s	Stock market boom continues after 1987 crash
	Globalization intensifies; American jobs outsourced
	Wal-Mart emerges as major economic force
	Decline of labor unions continues
	Personal computer and small electronics revolution
	Spread of World Wide Web (WWW)
	Human Genome Project unravels structure of DNA
	Deregulation of television industry; concentration of media ownership
	Opposition to immigration and multiculturalism grows
1991	European Union formed
1992	Los Angeles race riots
1993	North American Free Trade Agreement (NAFTA)
1995	World Trade Organization (WTO) created
1998	Battles over abortion, gay rights intensify; Congress passes Defense of Marriage Act
1999	Protests against WTO policies begin
2001	George W. Bush administration rejects Kyoto environmental treaty

FOR FURTHER EXPLORATION

Alfred Eckes Jr. and Thomas Zeilin, *Globalization and the American Century* (2003), link American prosperity during the twentieth century to participation in the global economy. For insight into the dynamics and character of American social classes, see David Brooks, *Bobos in Paradise: The New Upper Class and How They Got There* (2000); Barbara Ehrenreich, *Fear of Falling: The Inner Life of the Middle Class* (1989); and Nelson Lichtenstein, *State of the Union: A Century of American Labor* (2002). In *More Equal Than Others* (2004), Godfrey Hodgson points to increasing social inequality as a central theme of the United States in the late twentieth century. Two other authors put greater emphasis on ideological demands for equality: John Skrentny, *The Minority Rights Revolution* (2002), and Samuel Walker, *The Rights Revolution: Rights and Community in Modern America* (1998). Two fine studies of family life are Stephanie Coontz, *The Way We Never Were: American Families and the Nostalgia Trap* (1992), and Arlie Hochschild, *The Second Shift: Working Parents and the Revolution at Home* (2002). See also Susan Faludi, *Backlash: The Undeclared War against American Women* (1991).

Provocative studies of technology include Howard Segal, *Future Imperfect: The Mixed Blessings of Technology in America* (1994), and Edward Tenner, *Why Things Bite Back: Technology and the Revenge of Unintended Consequences* (1996). Mary Ann Watson, *Defining Visions: Television and the American Experience Since 1945* (1998), surveys the changing character of the TV era, while Leonard Downie Jr. and Robert G. Kaiser, *The News about the News: American Journalism in Peril* (2002), point to its impact on the press. For a discussion of environmental issues, consult Adam Rose, *The Bulldozer in the Countryside: Suburban Sprawl and the Rise of American Environmentalism* (2001). The course of the AIDS epidemic can be followed in the *New York Times* — go to **www.nytimes.com/ref/health/25years-aids.html**.

On the culture wars, see Gertrude Himmelfarb, *One Nation, Two Cultures* (1999), and James Hunter, *Culture Wars: The Struggle to Define America* (1991). For race relations, consult Terry Anderson, *The Pursuit of Fairness: A History of Affirmative Action* (2004), and Jennifer Hochschild, *Facing Up to the American Dream: Race, Class, and the Soul of America* (1996). In *Debating Immigration, 1882–Present* (2001), Roger Daniels and Otis Graham offer a historical perspective on a contemporary issue. For discussions of recent arrivals, consult Nicolaus Mills, ed., *Arguing Immigration* (1994) and "The New Americans" at **www.pbs.org/independentlens/newamericans**.

TEST YOUR KNOWLEDGE

To assess your command of the material in this chapter, see the Online Study Guide at **bedfordstmartins.com/henretta**.

For Web sites, images, and documents related to topics and places in this chapter, visit **bedfordstmartins.com/makehistory**.

32 Into the Twenty-First Century

JUST AS MEMORIES DEFINE INDIVIDUALS, so collective memories shape a nation. Few Americans ever forgot the moment when they learned of the Japanese attack on Pearl Harbor on December 7, 1941. "You wake up on a Sunday morning," one later reflected, "and the world as you know it ends." Sixty years later, on the bright morning of September 11, 2001, Americans felt exactly the same way as they watched live on television the collapse of the two 110-story towers of New York City's World Trade Center. They knew that the nation had at arrived another defining moment.

The attack by Al Qaeda terrorists, like that of the Japanese on Hawaii, caught the nation by surprise, and for good reason. As the world's only superpower, the United States faced significant challenges in many places: North Korea, Bosnia, Iraq, Iran, and Russia. Only in retrospect did the Al Qaeda threat come sharply into focus. Yes, Osama bin Laden, its wealthy Saudi-born leader, had called in 1998 for a *jihad*, a holy war, against America. Al Qaeda operatives had bombed American embassies in Kenya and Tanzania in 1998 and the USS *Cole*, an American warship visiting Yemen, in 2000. But no one, not the CIA, nor the Pentagon, nor Presidents Bill Clinton and George W. Bush, imagined suicidal terrorists ramming commercial jets into the World Trade Center and

◀ **A Poignant Symbol**

This striking photograph captures one of the nation's most revered symbols, the Statue of Liberty, against a backdrop of smoke from New York City's World Trade Center following the terrorist attacks of September 11, 2001. Daniel Hulshizer/AP Images.

Pentagon. Al Qaeda's brutal audacity simply exceeded American experience.

Once a minor annoyance, this band of terrorists became defined — no doubt to Osama bin Laden's great satisfaction — as an existential threat, on a par with the Nazis of 1941 and the nuclear-armed Soviets of 1950. America's global mission became the War on Terror. The cost of that effort, which is not finished, has been high — wars in Afghanistan and Iraq, $300 billion expended (as of 2006), tens of thousands of dead and wounded American soldiers and Iraqis, civil liberties in the United States at risk. However the War on Terror turns out, it has already left its mark on America. Gone are the high hopes inspired by victory in the Cold War. Instead, the United States enters the twenty-first century off its stride, somehow ill-equipped, despite its military and economic preeminence, for the challenges it now faces.

The Advent of George W. Bush

Less than a year before 9/11, Americans lived through a different kind of traumatic event. So closely contested was the presidential election of November 2000 that for a month the outcome remained in doubt. Only in mid-December, when the Supreme Court intervened, did Republican candidate George W. Bush's victory become certain. Having lost the popular vote, the new president might have been expected to govern in a moderate, bipartisan fashion. But, in fact, he proceeded as if he had won a popular mandate. In the process, he redefined conservatism. Traditionally, Republicans stood for limits on federal powers, balanced budgets, and individual rights. Now, these principles mostly went by the boards. The Bush administration tried simultaneously to cut taxes, expand entitlements, federalize public education, please the Religious Right, and expand America's global power. Where the Bush presidency stood on the political spectrum became an open question.

The Contested Election of 2000

George W. Bush's adversary was Al Gore, vice president in the Clinton administration. Both candidates came from privileged backgrounds. After a childhood in Midland, Texas, where his family had moved from Connecticut, Bush attended an elite New England private school and Yale University. Gore went to Harvard. Both men boasted impressive political pedigrees. Gore's father, a senator

from Tennessee, had long groomed his son for the presidency. Bush's paternal grandfather was a Connecticut senator and his father, George H. W. Bush, had recently served as president.

The Candidates. There the resemblance stopped. Where Al Gore was a straight arrow — divinity student, journalist, elected to Congress at the age of twenty-eight — Bush was at that age a bit of a hellraiser, going through what he himself described as a "nomadic" period of "irresponsible youth." Still, Karl Rove, his future political guru, saw something special even then in the happy-go-lucky Bush and became a steadfast ally. Bush became a Texas oil man, unsuccessfully, and ran for the House of Representatives in 1978, unsuccessfully, but he remained active in politics, mostly working for his father. After the elder Bush became president, George W. finally made it in business as managing partner of the Texas Rangers baseball franchise. In 1994, with Rove at his side, he was elected Texas governor and was on his way.

On the campaign trail against Gore, Bush presented himself as the genuine article, a regular guy. Unburdened by political baggage, he was free to position himself as he chose, and he chose the center. He ran as an outsider, deploring Washington partisanship and casting himself as a "uniter, not a divider," and promising to restore "honor and dignity" to the White House after the Clinton scandals. On domestic policy, he stood for "compassionate conservatism." Bush's campaign was orchestrated by Karl Rove, a supremely gifted strategist and political in-fighter. One of Rove's maxims was to find the right message and stick to it. That was George W. Bush, always "on message."

Al Gore, by contrast, never settled on a message. Vacillating between Clinton's centrism and his own liberalism, he gave the unfortunate impression of a man without fixed principles. His professorial demeanor — although well earned — came off badly against Bush's affability. If Bush was the superior campaigner, Vice President Gore was the beneficiary of the prosperity of the Clinton years. Affronted by the White House scandals, however, Gore distanced himself from Clinton — a decision that cost him crucial votes. Gore's real nemesis, however, was Ralph Nader, whose Green Party candidacy drew away the votes that certainly would have carried him to victory. As it was, Gore won the popular vote, amassing 50.9 million votes to 50.4 million for Bush, only to fall short in the Electoral College, 267 to 271.

The Mess in Florida. The Democrats immediately challenged the tally in Florida. In the heavily

The Contested Vote in Florida, 2000

When the vote recount got under way in Palm Beach, both sides brought out supporters to demonstrate outside the Supervisor of Elections Office, in hopes of influencing the officials doing the counting. In this photograph, supporters of George W. Bush and Al Gore clash after a rally on November 13, 2000, that had been addressed by Jesse Jackson, the dominant African American figure in the Democratic Party. ©Reuters/Corbis.

Democratic Miami area, confusing "butterfly" ballots caused elderly Gore supporters mistakenly to vote for Patrick Buchanan, the candidate of the conservative Reform Party. Elsewhere, election officials had to decide whether to count partially punched ballots registered by antiquated voting machines.

These problematic ballots turned the election into a partisan brawl. When Gore's campaign demanded hand recounts in several counties, Florida's Republican secretary of state halted the process and declared Governor Bush the winner. On appeal by the vice president's lawyers, Florida's Supreme Court ordered the recount to proceed. The Bush campaign immediately went to the U.S. Supreme Court. On December 12, the Court ruled, by a margin of 5 to 4, that recounting ballots in only selected counties violated the rights of other Floridians under the Fourteenth Amendment's equal protection clause. As if acknowledging the fragility of that argument, the Court declared *Bush v. Gore* a one-shot deal, not to be regarded as precedent in any future case. It surprised many legal experts that the Supreme Court had even accepted the case. The likeliest explanation for why it did was that cutting short the controversy seemed preferable to having it thrust into a bitterly divided U.S. House of Representatives, with unforeseeable consequences. But by making a transparently political decision, warned dissenting Justice Stephen G. Breyer, the majority was running "the risk of undermining the public's confidence in the Court itself." Still, the Court's ruling stuck. Gore had always played by the rules, and did so now, conceding the election to his Republican opponent.

The Bush Agenda

Although George Bush had positioned himself as a moderate, counter-tendencies drove his administration from the start. Foremost was the man he had chosen as his running mate, Richard Cheney, an uncompromising, conservative Republican. Ordinarily, the politics of vice presidents don't matter much, but Cheney was not an ordinary vice president. Offsetting the president's inexperience, the older Cheney was a seasoned Washington veteran, and, with Bush's consent, he became virtually a dual president, backed by a big staff and granted wide policymaking latitude. Equally determining was Bush's decision to bring his campaign advisor, Karl Rove, into the White House. Rove made a key strategic decision that Bush's political future required playing to the party's conservative base, foreclosing the easy-going centrism of Bush the campaigner.

On Capitol Hill, Rove's hard line was reinforced by Tom DeLay, the Republican whip and, after 2002, House majority leader. As Newt Gingrich's second-in-command in 1995, DeLay declared "all-out war" on the Democrats, and he was as good as his word. He masterminded the K Street Project (after the street housing Washington's lobbyists) that achieved a Republican lock on the big-money lobbying firms. Everything then fell into place. Lobbyists got access; House members got campaign funding; and, as paymaster, DeLay got a disciplined rank-and-file. Some of that money ended up underwriting a Republican takeover of the Texas legislature, which then gerrymandered five extra

Republican congressional districts. With that cushion, DeLay had a safe House majority, and no need to deal with Democrats. The Senate, although more collegial, went through a similar hardening process. After 2002, with Republicans in control of both Congress and the White House, any pretense of bipartisan lawmaking ended.

Out of these disparate elements—Bush's compassionate conservatism, Rove's political calculations, exceptionally combative allies—there emerged a hybrid brand of conservatism that defies easy classification.

Faith-Based Politics. After his wayward early years George W. Bush became, at the hands of the Rev. Billy Graham, a born-again Christian, the first to be president since Jimmy Carter. Bush let it be known that a prayer opened cabinet meetings and that a Bible study class met at the White House. On his first day in office, he banned foreign-aid funding for family-planning programs that offered abortion counseling.

As a sign of his commitment, Bush launched his "faith-based initiative" for federal support of church-related social-service programs. To this end, he created a special office in the White House, channeled federal money to a new Compassion Capital Fund, and persuaded Congress to authorize a Community-Based Abstinence Education program. Federal money began to flow to religiously based centers, many of them focusing on pregnancy services for unwed mothers and sexual abstinence for teenagers. Challenged that his faith-based

initiative violated the constitutional separation of church and state, Bush took a page from the playbook of civil rights advocates. The First Amendment, he argued, did not require "discriminating against religious institutions simply because they are religious." He was similarly audacious about discriminatory issues posed by his faith-based initiative. A 2002 executive order exempted religious groups receiving federal grants from the civil rights prohibition against hiring on the basis of religious affiliation.

Although the money involved was modest—a small fraction of total federal funding of social-service agencies—Bush's faith-based initiative demonstrated concretely his commitment to the Religious Right. To a unique degree, evangelical leaders had an ally in the White House, a true believer in their moral agenda.

The Politics of Inclusiveness. Bush's campaign had been blessedly free of Republican race-mongering, such as—to take a paternal example—his father's Willie Horton ad (featuring a black murderer) in the 1988 race against the hapless Michael Dukakis (see Chapter 30). By contrast, George W. was determinedly inclusive. Black speakers and entertainers featured prominently at the Republican convention, and of those most prominently featured, General Colin Powell, a former chair of the Joint Chiefs of Staff, became secretary of state, and Condoleezza Rice, a Stanford foreign-policy expert, became national security advisor and then, after Powell's retirement, secretary of state. Mexican Americans also

Colin Powell and Condoleezza Rice

Colin Powell, a distinguished army general, and Condoleezza Rice, a former Stanford academic, were leading figures in the Bush administration and powerful symbols of Bush's efforts at racial inclusiveness. Powell was secretary of state, and Rice national security advisor. Here they are seated side by side, attending a state dinner at the Grand Palace in Bangkok, Thailand, October 19, 2003. Paul J. Richards/AFP/Getty Images.

No Child Left Behind

President Bush was tireless at getting out into the country to drum up support for his programs. Here he chats with fourth graders on a visit to the Pierre Laclede Elementary School in St. Louis, Missouri, on January 5, 2004. The sign on the blackboard tells us why he was there. © Jason Reed/Reuters/Corbis.

figured prominently, and Bush, on easy terms with Texas's Latino community, was committed to finding a middle ground for resolving the increasingly contentious crisis over illegal immigrants.

On civil rights, the new administration hewed to a traditionally conservative line, routinely opposing affirmative action in cases coming before the courts. But when it came to equal opportunity, Bush was a crusader. He spoke feelingly of "the soft prejudice of low expectations," and that arresting phrase launched him into the thickets of educational reform.

No Child Left Behind. Fulfilling a campaign pledge, Bush in 2001 proposed the No Child Left Behind Act, which increased federal funding for primary and secondary education and funneled money to schools with a high percentage of students from disadvantaged backgrounds. Conservatives who favored school choice could take satisfaction from the provision that allowed students in underperforming schools to transfer to better institutions. But the main thrust of the law was hardly conservative. No civic responsibility in America was more distinctively local than the public schools, funded as they were by property taxes and controlled by locally elected school boards. No Child Left Behind overrode this precious autonomy, imposing federal standards for student performance as a means of disciplining a lagging educational system.

Local and state officials fought back. They argued that, because of inadequate congressional funding, the mandated programs ate into local budgets; that the emphasis on testing distorted good educational practice; and that a program emanating from Washington was bound to have unintended consequences (tempting school districts, for example, to encourage low-scoring students to drop out). By 2005 state governments were challenging the act in the courts.

Whatever its ultimate fate, there can be no denying the vaulting ambition of No Child Left Behind, or the degree to which it departed from conservative canons of states' rights and federal restraint.

Health Care. Equally confounding to conservative principles was Bush's response to the nation's festering health-care crisis. Despite hand-wringing by fiscal conservatives, the president did little to contain Medicare costs, which jumped from $433 billion to $627 billion during his first five years in office. What did grab his attention was a gaping hole in Medicare benefits. Without drug coverage, desperate seniors were surfing the Web and turning to Canada for more cheaply priced medicines. Preempting the Democrats, the Bush administration in 2003 muscled through Congress a drug-benefit bill that would cost $385 billion over the first five years. The conservative side of it was in the particulars: first, no negotiating by Medicare for bulk purchases, although that was how Canada and America's own Veterans Administration had cut drug costs; second, no direct provision by Medicare, but only via private insurers, who would compete for Medicare customers; and, third, substantial copayments, topping out at $3,600 for beneficiaries with big drug bills. In its solicitude for private business, market competition, and individual responsibility, Bush's drug program was soundly conservative, but with the government picking up the tab. No wonder that traditional conservatives were bewildered or that it had taken extraordinary steps by Tom DeLay's machine to wring out the final Republican votes to pass the bill in the House.

Included in the law was a provision enabling people to set up tax-free health savings accounts to pay for ordinary medical expenses. The central idea, generated by conservative think tanks, was to foster an "ownership society," in which individuals, rather than the state, took primary responsibility for their own welfare.

By 2005, the time seemed ripe to strike a bigger blow for Bush's ownership society. In the name of "reforming" Social Security, he proposed the diversion of a portion of its revenues into individual retirement accounts that account holders could invest in stocks and bonds. Despite a strenuous sales campaign and much support from conservatives, Bush's plan fell flat. It seemed that Americans preferred the comfort of the existing Social Security system to the adventure of an ownership society.

Embracing Business. The concern for private insurers and the drug companies shown in the Medicare drug bill faithfully reflected the administration's embrace of American business. As if to signal what was to come, Vice President Cheney—

himself the former head of the oil-equipment giant Halliburton—met with oil men as soon as the new administration was installed and hammered out an energy policy that, among other things, called for oil drilling in Alaska's Arctic National Wildlife Refuge and generous subsidies for Gulf of Mexico oil and gas operators (Map 32.1). In the case of electric utilities, the problem was the huge fines they faced for evading the requirement by the Clean Air Act that new or upgraded coal-burning equipment meet high air-quality standards. The Environmental Protection Agency (EPA), now run by Bush appointees, came to the rescue by issuing more accommodating rules (the most important of which exempted upgrades costing less than 20 percent of the replacement cost of the equipment). Better, the administration argued, to achieve regulatory goals voluntarily, a task best achieved, as with the EPA, by appointing industry people to do the regulating.

Life involved trade-offs, the administration argued: cheaper electricity or cleaner air? And, indeed, a whole host of issues—fuel economy standards for oversized SUVs, snowmobiles in Yellowstone, logging in the national forests—involved trade-offs. What struck Bush's critics was how consistently he came

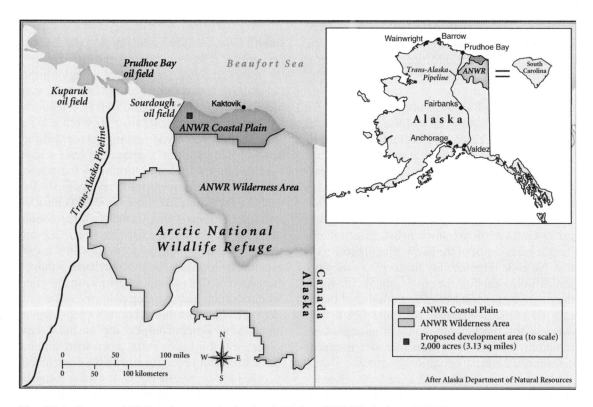

Map 32.1 Proposed Oil Development in the Arctic National Wildlife Refuge (ANWR)

Environmentalists fought the Bush administration to a standstill over the issue of opening Alaska's Arctic National Wildlife Refuge to oil exploration. This map shows the contested area, as well as the north slope of Alaska already producing oil and the pipeline bringing it to market.

down on the side of business. The president could speak with emotion about companies hit by the huge injury awards in cases involving medical malpractice and defective products. For him, legislation limiting company liability constituted a major achievement. He also supported a Republican-sponsored bill strongly advocated by credit card operators that tightened bankruptcy laws against delinquent borrowers. Bush kept a lower profile on organized labor, but his actions as employer — which, for the federal bureaucracy, he ultimately was — spoke loud and clear. He was adamant that the collective-bargaining rights of public employees not be applied to the new Department of Homeland Security. Adverse decisions by his appointees to the Labor Department and NLRB also began to have a cumulatively damaging effect on the labor movement.

Complicating the president's efforts was a cascade of corporate scandals triggered by the Wall Street plunge of 2000. Most spectacular was the collapse of Enron, a Houston-based energy giant and a big player in Republican politics. The first sign of trouble was a mysterious roiling of the California energy market, with sudden power shortages, rolling blackouts, and price spikes. When state officials appealed to Washington, they were rebuffed. Let the free market operate, said the administration. In fact, it was market rigging at work, and guilty traders eventually went to jail and disgorged illegal profits. For Enron, a major player, the scam was the least of its troubles. Enron fell into bankruptcy, a victim of astounding accounting frauds and insider dealing. Thousands of employees lost their jobs and retirement savings. The scandal spread to New York investment banks,

which had turned a blind eye while marketing Enron securities, and to its auditing firm, Arthur Andersen, which was driven out of business. Similar misconduct destroyed WorldCom, a major provider of telephone and telecommunications services; Global Crossing, a fiber optic cable company; and Adelphia Communications, a cable television conglomerate. As in the 1980s (see Chapter 31), these scandals cast a cloud over corporate America, with some of the nation's vaunted CEOs facing prison and business under heightened regulatory scrutiny.

Cutting Taxes. The domestic issue that most engaged President Bush, as it had Ronald Reagan, was taxes. Like Reagan, Bush acted immediately on taking office. His Economic Growth and Tax Relief Act of 2001 had something for everyone. It slashed income tax rates, extended the earned income credit for the poor, and phased out the estate tax by 2010 (when it would resume, unless Congress acted, at the original high rate). A second round of cuts in 2003 targeted dividend income and capital gains. By sheer magnitude, Bush's tax cuts exceeded Reagan's.

Bush denied Democratic accusations that his tax cuts favored the wealthy. If one looked at the rate of decline in a household's *tax bill*, the president was correct. The average low-income family got a whopping tax savings of 48 percent. But if measured by the effect on family *income*, Bush's cuts clearly favored the rich. His signature cuts — those favoring big estates and well-to-do owners of stocks and bonds — especially skewed the distribution upwards. Overall, low-income families (averaging $19,521 annually) got a tax break of $435; middle-income families (averaging $70,096) got

The Fall of Enron

Enron was an iconic corporation of the booming 1990s, widely touted as an example of how inspired business leadership could transform a stodgy company into a world leader — in Enron's case, as a trader in energy and other commodities. Its business turned out to be largely smoke and mirrors, kept aloft by fake accounting and financial manipulation. When the entire edifice came crashing down in 2001, Enron was overnight transformed from icon to villain. Symbolic of its fall from grace was the change in the name of the Houston Astros' baseball stadium — from Enron Field to Minute Maid Park. Brett Coomer/AP Images.

TABLE 32.1	Impact of the Bush Tax Cuts, 2001–2003					
Income in 2003	**Taxpayers**	**Gross Income**	**Total Tax Cut**	**% Change in Tax Bill**	**Tax Bill**	**Tax Rate**
Less than $50,000	92,093,452	$19,521	$435	−48%	$474	2%
$50,000 to 100,000	26,915,091	70,096	1,656	−21	6,417	9
$100,000 to 200,000	8,878,643	131,797	3,625	−17	18,281	14
$200,000 to 500,000	1,999,061	288,296	7,088	−10	60,464	21
$500,000 to 1,000,000	356,140	677,294	22,479	−12	169,074	25
$1,000,000 to 10,000,000	175,157	2,146,100	84,666	−13	554,286	26
$10,000,000 or more	6,126	25,975,532	1,019,369	−15	5,780,926	22

SOURCE: *New York Times,* April 5, 2006.

$1,656; and the very wealthy (averaging $2,146,100) got $84,666 (Table 32.1). Nor did everyone benefit equally. Taxpayers at the bottom and middle gained only 60 percent of the relative benefit—the ratio of money saved to income—enjoyed by those at the top.

No matter, the president suggested, because the main thing was that everyone benefited from the boost to the economy. Critics warned that because so little of the federal budget was discretionary, Bush's tax cuts were bound to plunge the federal government into debt. Bush was unperturbed. He was, in fact, not of the conservative school that favored tax cuts as a means of shrinking the government—"starving the beast," as Reaganites had called it—because, as it turned out, he was himself a champion spender. By 2006, federal expenditures had jumped 33 percent, at a faster clip than under any president since Lyndon Johnson. There followed a swift reversal of fiscal fortunes, with the Clinton-inherited federal surplus transformed into bulging deficits—estimated at over $300 billion for 2006. Over 60 percent of that shortfall was attributable to reduced tax revenues (see Reading American Pictures, "Conservatism at a Crossroads," p. 997).

Midway through Bush's second term the national debt stood at over $8 trillion, much of it owned by foreign investors, who also financed the nation's huge trade deficit. On top of that, staggering Social Security and Medicare obligations were coming due with the looming retirement of the baby boomers. It seemed that these burdens—in per capita terms, the national debt currently stands at $28,000 for every man, woman, and child—would be passed on to future generations.

How Bush's presidency might have fared in normal times is another of those unanswerable questions of history. In making his case as a candidate in 2000, George W. Bush had said little about foreign policy. He had assumed that his administration would rise or fall on the appeal of his domestic program. With 9/11, an altogether different political scenario unfolded.

➤ Explain why, if Bush lost the popular vote in 2000, he nevertheless became president.

➤ In what ways did Bush's policies depart from traditional conservatism?

➤ What were the main issues in the debate over tax cuts?

American Hegemony Challenged

The dictionary defines *hegemony* as "predominant influence exercised by one state over others." That was the United States in 2001, the hegemonic power in the world, unrivaled now that the Soviet Union was gone. It was therefore incumbent on the United States, George W. Bush often said, to be "humble" in its relations with other states. "If we're an arrogant nation," he warned, other peoples will "resent us." Bush's campaign words, however, bore little relation to his true bent. Once in office, he was much more inclined to take a muscular approach to foreign affairs. In this, Bush was heartily seconded by his vice president, a Cold Warrior of many years' standing. Cheney's key ally was the new secretary of defense, Donald Rumsfeld, who brought in a high-powered team of neoconservatives led by his deputy, Paul Wolfowitz. The neocons

Conservativism at a Crossroads

Since the New Deal of the 1930s, conservatives agreed on one thing—government needed to be small for American liberty to thrive. Small government meant, above all, fiscal restraint and minimal federal regulation, especially of the economy. The Republican Party won national power in 1980 by rejecting liberal Democratic programs and heeding Ronald Reagan's call to "get the government off our backs" (see Chapter 30). What do we make of conservatism today? Many conservatives today find themselves divided— whether to support the initiatives of the Bush administration or remain true to their core values. Throughout this text the authors have used political cartoons to illuminate where the American people stand on many different issues and, once again, the cartoonists haven't let us down.

Weighing the Return of Big Government. © Matson / *St. Louis Post-Dispatch* / caglecartoons.com.

ANALYZING THE EVIDENCE

➤ What does the first cartoon, published in the *St. Louis Post-Dispatch,* suggest are the causes of Uncle Sam's expanding waistline?

➤ In what ways does the second cartoon, from the *National Review,* offer a different explanation for the government's spending spree? Hint: The word "pork" for Washington insiders means spending bills favoring special interests or the pet projects of individual congressmen or senators.

➤ The *National Review* is a leading conservative journal, while the *St. Louis Dispatch* is generally regarded as a liberal newspaper. Can you tell that one is conservative and the other liberal from these two cartoons published in their pages? In what ways?

A National Shopping Spree. By permission of Gary Varvel / *The Indianapolis Star* / and Creator's Syndicate, Inc. This appeared in the *National Review,* May 22, 2006, p. 49.

disdained the idea of a "humble" foreign policy. On the contrary, they championed "benevolent hegemony" — the untrammeled use of America's power, military power if need be, to fashion a better, more democratic world.

In a striking display of unilateralism, the new administration walked away from an array of completed or pending diplomatic agreements. It repudiated the International Criminal Court and a UN convention banning biological weapons, and backed away from nuclear test bans, weapons reduction, and antiballistics missiles treaties. Most startling was its withdrawal from the Kyoto Protocol on global warming. When participating countries met in Bonn, Germany, in July 2001 to refine the Protocol and satisfy America's objections, the U.S. representative was instructed not to participate. All too soon, the United States would be looking for the world's support.

September 11, 2001

On that bright morning, nineteen Al Qaeda terrorists hijacked four commercial jets and flew two of them into New York City's World Trade Center, destroying its twin towers and killing over 2,600 people. A third plane plowed into the Pentagon, near Washington, D.C., and killed almost 200 passengers and Defense Department employees; the fourth, presumably headed for the White House, crashed in Pennsylvania when the passengers fought back and thwarted the hijackers.

How could it have happened? No fully satisfying answer was ever forthcoming, not even when the blue-ribbon 9/11 Commission issued its final report three years later. It was not as if the attack was unprecedented — the World Trade Center itself had been the target of an earlier truck bombing in 1993 — or even that the plot had gone wholly undetected. While attending flight schools, a few of the hijackers had drawn suspicions, and one suspect, Zacarias Moussoaui, had actually been taken into custody. Two of the hijackers had been flagged by the CIA, but it neglected to inform the FBI that they were in the country. The failure was not so much one of intelligence gathering, the 9/11 Commission concluded, but of an inability to "connect the dots" — much like the conclusion of the Senate committee that had looked into the Pearl Harbor attack of 1941. Although the incoming administration had been slow developing a counterterrorism program, the new president escaped blame for the disaster because the country's attention had turned to war.

On September 14, as soon as he got his bearings, President Bush headed for the World Trade Center ground zero, embraced rescue workers standing in the rubble, picked up a bullhorn and stirred the nation. As an outburst of patriotism swept the United States, Bush proclaimed a "War on Terror" and vowed to carry the battle to Al Qaeda.

Operating out of Afghanistan, where they had been given haven by the fundamentalist Taliban

September 11, 2001

Cameramen photographing the scene after a plane crashed into the north tower of New York City's World Trade Center found themselves recording a defining moment in the nation's history. When a second airliner approached and then slammed into the building's south tower at 9:03 A.M., the nation knew this was no accident. The United States was under attack. Of the 2,843 people killed on September 11, 2,617 died at the World Trade Center.
Robert Clark / AURORA.

Americans, Think!

While incomprehensible to Americans, the murderous attacks of 9/11 were greeted with satisfaction by many in the Muslim world. Their anti-Americanism was based in part on U.S. support for Israel, but also stemmed from their resentment of American wealth and power and of the corrosive effects that they felt Western capitalism and modernity exerted on their societies. Here, Pakistanis demonstrate at an anti-American rally in Islamabad on September 15, 2001. B. K. Bangash / AP Images.

regime, the elusive Al Qaeda at this moment offered a clear target. When the Taliban refused to turn over mastermind Osama bin Laden, the United States attacked, not with conventional forces, but by deploying military advisers, supplies, and special forces that bolstered anti-Taliban rebel forces. While Afghani allies carried the ground war, American planes and missiles rained destruction on the enemy. By early 2002, this lethal combination had ousted the Taliban government, destroyed the Al Qaeda training camps, and killed or captured many of its operatives. Bin Laden retreated to a mountain redoubt. Inexplicably, U.S. Special Forces failed to press the attack. Bin Laden evidently bought off the local war lords and escaped over the border into Pakistan.

The War on Terror: Iraq

At this point, the Bush administration could have declared victory and relegated the unfinished business — tracking down the Al Qaeda remnants, stabilizing Afghanistan, and shaking up the nation's security agencies — to a post-victory operational phase. President Bush had no such inclination. For him and his advisers, the War on Terror was not a metaphor, but the real thing, an open-ended war that required putting aside business-as-usual.

On the domestic side, Bush declared the terrorist threat too big to be contained by ordinary law-enforcement means. He wanted the government's powers of domestic surveillance placed on a wartime footing. With no hearings and little debate, Congress passed by virtual acclamation the USA PATRIOT Act (Uniting and Strengthening America by Providing Appropriate Tools Required to Intercept and Obstruct Terrorism), and, true to its title, the Patriot Act granted the administration sweeping authority to monitor citizens and apprehend suspected terrorists.

On the international front, the War on Terror called forth a policy of preventive war. International law recognized a nation's right to strike first if faced by an imminent threat from another state. The so-called Bush doctrine lowered the bar, declaring that the United States reserved the right to attack dangerous states even absent any imminent threat. Secretary of Defense Rumsfeld called it "anticipatory self-defense." In his State of the Union address in January 2002, President Bush singled out Iran, North Korea, and Iraq — "an axis of evil" — as the states most threatening to the United States.

Of the three, Iraq seemed the easiest mark, a pushover for Secretary Rumsfeld's lean, high-tech military. Neoconservatives in the Pentagon regarded Iraq as unfinished business, left over from the Gulf War of 1991 (see Chapter 30). They believed the elder Bush had been wrong, first, not to press on to Baghdad and, second, to have encouraged the Shiites, who constituted the Iraqi majority, to rise up against the tyrant Saddam Hussein and then to abandon them. Deputy Secretary of Defense Paul Wolfowitz, who had flown over the devastated rebel areas, vowed that there would be a reckoning. On a larger scale, Iraq represented for neoconservatives like Wolfowitz a chance to unveil the American mission to democratize the world. Iraqis would surely embrace democracy if given half a chance, and the democratizing effect would

The Search for Al Qaeda

After the terrorist attacks of 9/11, the United States succeeded in marshaling a multinational force to invade Afghanistan, where the Taliban regime harbored key elements of the Al Qaeda network. Here, Canadian infantrymen board a U.S. Army Chinook helicopter in the Shahi Kot mountains of Afghanistan in March 2002. By then, Taliban and Al Qaeda had mostly been cleared out of the country, but the Taliban regrouped in northern Pakistan and by 2006 had staged a comeback in the remote southern provinces of Afghanistan. © Jim Hollander / AFP / Corbis.

spread across the Middle East, reforming other unpopular Arab regimes and stabilizing the region. That in turn would secure the Middle East's oil supply, whose fragility Saddam's invasion of Kuwait in 1990 had made all too clear. And it was the oil, of course, that was of vital interest to the United States (Map 32.2).

None of these considerations, either singly or together, met Bush's declared threshold for preventive war. The administration, moreover, was sharply divided. The secretary of state, Colin Powell, although less influential than the Department of Defense hawks, was nevertheless a formidable voice. Powell and others, including America's anxious European allies, persuaded a reluctant President Bush that he needed international approval for any military action, and that meant going to the UN Security Council. The framework was already in place: Resolution 687 (and a succession of supporting resolutions) ordered Iraq after the Gulf War

to halt all work on weapons of mass destruction (WMD). UN inspectors had rooted out chemical and biological stockpiles and an unexpectedly advanced nuclear program, but in 1998 Iraq expelled the inspectors, and no one could be certain whether the WMD programs had resumed. At Secretary of State Powell's behest, the Security Council approved Resolution 1441, which demanded that Saddam Hussein allow the return of the UN weapons inspectors. Unexpectedly, he agreed.

Most of the nations supporting Resolution 1441 saw it as means of defusing the crisis: The main thing was to keep talking. The Bush administration saw Resolution 1441 as a prelude to war: The main thing was to get on with the invasion. Naturally, the diplomatic parrying became rancorous. Most mysterious was Saddam, who actually had no WMDs but by his obstructive efforts acted as if he did. Since he didn't, the UN inspectors came up empty-handed. Intelligence experts, both U.S.

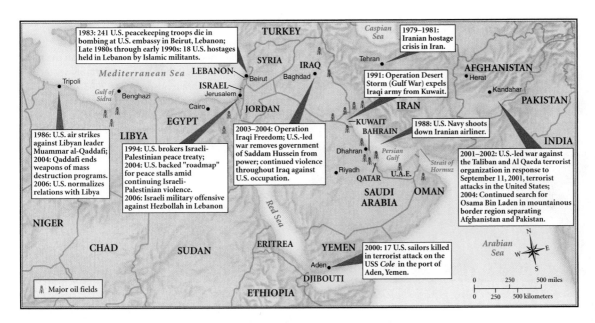

Map 32.2   U.S. Involvement in the Middle East, 1979–2006

The United States has long played an active role in the Middle East, driven by the strategic importance of that region and, most importantly, by America's need to ensure a reliable supply of oil from the Persian Gulf states. This map shows the highlights of that troubled involvement, from the Tehran embassy hostage-taking in 1979 to the invasion and current occupation of Iraq.

and European, were flummoxed. It seemed incredible that their estimates could be totally wrong. The Bush administration, gearing up for war, made the best intelligence case it could that Iraq constituted a "grave and gathering danger" and forged ahead.

Unable to secure a second Security Council resolution, the United States declared previous UN resolutions sufficient and invaded Iraq in March 2003. Its one major ally was Great Britain. A handful of other governments joined "the coalition of the willing," braving popular opposition at home to do so. Relations with France and Germany became poisonous. Even neighboring Mexico and Canada condemned the invasion, and Turkey, a key military ally, refused transit permission, ruining the army's plan for a northern thrust into Iraq. As for the Arab world, it exploded in anti-American demonstrations.

As in Afghanistan, the war began with massive air attacks intended to "shock and awe." *Time* magazine reported that targets around the capital city of Baghdad "got pulverized"; 130,000 U.S. and 30,000 British troops entered southern and central Iraq, accompanied by dozens of "embedded" reporters who broadcast events as they occurred. Within three weeks, the troops had taken Baghdad. The Iraqi regime collapsed, and its leaders went into hiding (Saddam Hussein was captured nine months later). On May 1, President Bush flew onto

the aircraft carrier *Abraham Lincoln* in a Navy jet dressed in fighter pilot's togs. Framed by a "Mission Accomplished" banner, Bush declared victory. But in fact the battle in Iraq had not ended; it was just beginning.

Despite meticulous preparations, the Pentagon had paid little attention to what the military called Phase IV, post-conflict operations. Pentagon planners simply assumed an easy transition, with a quick draw-down of forces by September. Early in the assault, however, Saddam's paramilitary—the *fedayeen*—began mounting attacks behind the lines. Field commanders wanted a pause so that the fedayeen could be dealt with. Rumsfeld ordered the advance onward, refusing to acknowledge that, as army commanders immediately recognized, the fedayeen signified an insurgency in the making. An opportunity to nip it in the bud was lost. The secretary of defense was similarly dismissive of the many well-respected, knowledgeable voices warning that the Iraqi occupation was going to be no picnic. So when, as the coalition forces arrived, the Iraqi police and civil authorities simply dissolved, the American military had no contingency plans and not enough troops to maintain order.

Thousands of poor Iraqis looted everything they could get their hands on—stores, shops, museums, industrial plants, government offices, and

Abu Ghraib

This is an image obtained by the Associated Press showing a detainee bent over with his hands on the bars of a cell while being watched by a comfortably seated soldier at the Abu Ghraib prison in late 2003. Although displaying one of the milder forms of torture, this Abu Ghraib photograph captured all too vividly the humiliating treatment of detainees that outraged the Muslim world. AP Images.

military arsenals filled with guns and tons of deadly explosives. The looting shattered the infrastructure of Baghdad and other Iraqi cities, leaving them without reliable supplies of electricity and water. In the midst of this turmoil, the insurgency got started, sparked by Sunni Muslims who had dominated Iraq under Saddam's Baathist regime. In a decision afterward regretted, the Coalition Provisional Authority disbanded the Iraqi army, turning loose thousands of armed, well-trained Baathists with nothing better to do than fight Americans. Insurgents began mounting daily attacks, employing increasingly effective IEDs (improvised explosive devices) to blow up Humvees and other troop carriers. On the Shiite side, the radical cleric Moqtada al-Sadr demanded immediate American withdrawal and twice unleashed his armed militia against U.S. forces. With the borders unguarded, Al Qaeda supporters flocked into Iraq from all over the Middle East, eager to do battle with the infidel Americans, bringing along a *jihadi* specialty, the suicide bomber (see Voices from Abroad, "Abu Musab al-Zarqawi: A Strategy for the Iraq Insurgency," p. 1003).

Popular insurgencies are a problem from hell for superpowers. Lyndon Johnson discovered this in Vietnam. Leonid Brezhnev discovered it in Afghanistan. And George W. Bush rediscovered it in Iraq. The intractable fact is that the superpower's troops are invaders. Although hard for Americans to believe, that was how Iraqis of all stripes viewed the U.S. troops — as an occupation army. From this, a dilemma followed. If the occupying forces cracked down hard, the civilian population suffered and became hostile. If the occupying forces relented, insurgents became bolder and took con-

trol as, for example, at the Sunni strongholds of Al Ramadi and Falluja (see Map 32.3, p. 1016). The one proven alternative was to pacify and hold insurgent areas, denying the guerrillas a base of support and forcing them to seek a political solution. But that required far more soldiers than the occupation authority had available, thanks to Rumsfeld's insistence on a lean military. Nor did planners reckon with the fact that, in a war against insurgents, no occupation force comes out with clean hands. In Iraq, that painful truth burst forth graphically in photographs showing American guards at Baghdad's Abu Ghraib prison abusing and torturing suspected insurgents. The ghastly images shocked the world. For Muslims, they offered final proof of American perfidy.

At that low point, in 2004, the United States had spent upwards of $100 billion. A thousand American soldiers had died, and ten thousand more had been wounded, many maimed for life. But if the U.S. pulled out, Iraq would descend into chaos. So, as Bush took to saying, the United States had to "stay the course."

The Election of 2004

The president had emerged from the 9/11 crisis looking invincible, with an approval rating approaching 90 percent. For party strategists, this was like money in the bank, only it proved to be a depleting resource, steadily drawn down as bad news from Iraq accumulated. Once the fruitless scouring for Iraqi WMDs ended, the administration came under relentless questioning. How had the United States gotten into this war? Was it a case of faulty intelligence? Or had the president misled the

Abu Musab al-Zarqawi

A Strategy for the Iraq Insurgency

From 2004 to June 2006, when he was killed by American forces, Abu Musab al-Zarqawi led the Al Qaeda-linked insurgency in Iraq. Born in Jordan in 1966, al-Zarqawi spent his youth as a petty criminal. During the 1980s, he fought as an Islamic jihadist against the Soviet occupation of Afghanistan. Al-Zarqawi then returned to Jordan, where he was imprisoned for seven years for conspiring to overthrow the monarchy and establish an Islamic caliphate. In this effort he was bent on expelling all Western influences from the Islamic world. But al-Zarqawi was also engaged in a struggle inside the Islamic world. He was Sunni, and he regarded the other main branch of Islam, the Shi'ite, as a heretical enemy as vile as the hated West. Early in 2004, as he was taking up his struggle in Iraq, al-Zarqawi wrote the following letter, which outlined the deadly strategy of bombings and sectarian violence he proposed to follow. The letter should be read for what it reveals of the mind of the figure who, until his death, was more responsible than any other for plunging Iraq into chaos.

God favored the [Islamic] nation with jihad on His behalf in the land of Mesopotamia [the ancient name for Iraq]. . . . The Americans, as you know well, entered Iraq on a contractual basis to create the State of Greater Israel from the Nile to the Euphrates and that this Zionized American Administration believes that accelerating the creation of the State of [Greater] Israel will accelerate the emergence of the Messiah. It came to Iraq with all its people, pride, and haughtiness toward God and his Prophet. It thought that the matter would be somewhat easy. . . . But it collided with a completely different reality. The operations of the brother mujahidin [fighters] began from the first moment. . . . This forced the Americans to conclude a deal with the Shi'a, the most evil of mankind. The deal was concluded on [the basis that] the Shi'a would get two-thirds of the booty for having stood in the ranks of the Crusaders against the mujahidin.

[The Shi'a are] the insurmountable obstacle, the lurking snake, the crafty and malicious scorpion, the spying enemy, and the penetrating venom. . . . Shi'ism is the looming danger and the true challenge. "They are the enemy. Beware of them. Fight them. By God, they lie." History's message is validated by the testimony of the current situation, which informs most clearly that Shi'ism is a religion that has nothing in common with Islam. . . .

[Among the Sunni mujahidin,] jihad here unfortunately [takes the form of] mines planted, rockets launched, and mortars shelling from afar. The Iraqi brothers still prefer safety and returning to the arms of their wives, where nothing frightens them. Sometimes the groups have boasted among themselves that not one of them has been killed or captured. We have told them in our many sessions with them that safety and victory are incompatible . . . that the [Islamic] nation cannot live without the aroma of martyrdom.

America did not come to leave, and it will not leave no matter how numerous its wounds become and how much of its blood is spilled. It is looking to the near future, when it hopes to disappear into its bases secure and at ease and put the battlefields of Iraq into the hands of the foundling government with an army and police that will bring [the terror] of Saddam . . . back to the people. There is no doubt that the space in which we can move has begun to shrink and that the grip around the throats of the [Arab and Sunni] mujahidin has begun to tighten. With the deployment of soldiers and police, the future has become frightening. . . .

The Shi'a . . . in our opinion are the key to change. I mean that targeting and hitting them in [their] religious, political, and military depth will provoke them to show the Sunnis their rabies . . . and bare the teeth of the hidden rancor working in their breasts. If we succeed in dragging them into the arena of sectarian war, it will become possible to awaken the inattentive Sunnis as they feel imminent danger and annihilating death at the hands of these [Shi'a]. . . .

I come back and again say that the only solution is for us to strike the religious, military, and other cadres among the Shi'a with blow after blow until they bend to the Sunnis. . . . God's religion is more precious than lives and souls. When the overwhelming majority stands in the ranks of truth, there has to be sacrifice for this religion. Let blood be spilled. . . .

SOURCE: Documents on Terrorist Abu Musab al-Zarqawi, 2004, www-personal.umich.edu/~jrcole/zarqawi/zarqawi.htm.

ANALYZING THE EVIDENCE

➤ According to al-Zarqawi, the Americans invaded Iraq "to create the State of Greater Israel from the Nile to the Euphrates." Why would he make a fantastic claim like that?

➤ If the Americans are the occupiers, why is his letter mostly about the Shi'ites? Why are they his primary target?

➤ Al-Zarqawi wrote this letter in early 2004. By mid-2006, at the time he was killed, how successful, based on your reading of the text, do you think he was in fulfilling the letter's aims?

Protecting the Homeland

One of the most potent results of the terrorist attacks of 9/11 was a universal call for heightened security at home. At a July 2002 speech in Washington, D.C., President Bush outlined his plan for an Office of Homeland Security, approved by Congress the following November, that was designed to strengthen the government's capacity to thwart terrorist threats and safeguard the country's borders. Images like this one of the president as the nation's defender had a long-lasting effect on public opinion and gave Bush a big boost against John Kerry in 2004. Paul J. Richards / AFP / Corbis.

country? The administration dug itself into a deeper hole by trying to discredit critics. One such misstep involved attacking Joseph C. Wilson, a retired diplomat who had challenged the White House's use of intelligence, by leaking that his wife, Valerie Plame, was a CIA agent. This potential violation of national security law led to a damaging investigation by a special prosecutor. Bush did better by changing the terms of the debate. His real objective, he now argued, was rescuing the Iraqi people from Saddam's oppressive regime or, in the grander neoconservative vein, giving them democracy. Even so, Iraq ate away at the president's ratings. As the bad news persisted, Bush's reelection became a race against time.

For Democrats, the Iraq quandary was even worse. How could they criticize the war without appearing unpatriotic? Some, like the early front runner Howard Dean of Vermont, had opposed the war. But the party couldn't run on what-might-have-been. And if being antiwar meant an immedi-

ate pullout, the party couldn't run on that either. Moreover, leading Democrats, including Dean's rivals, were themselves implicated. They had supported the resolution authorizing the president's use of force. So the party had no choice but to embrace the war and find a way of turning it against the Republicans, which meant, first, driving home the administration's mistakes and, second, knocking the president off his pedestal.

The obvious man for that job was Senator John Kerry of Massachusetts. In the early primaries, Kerry had run poorly and, but for an infusion of family cash, he would have been forced out. Kerry was, in fact, unengaging as a campaigner, except for one thing. He was a real Vietnam hero, twice wounded and decorated for bravery — in happy contrast to the president (who had spent the Vietnam years safely perched in the Texas Air National Guard). As the primary season wound down, an extraordinary thing happened. Democratic primary voters put aside their personal preferences and asked themselves that ineffably professional question: Who was electable? Kerry surged ahead and won the nomination. The Democratic convention in August was a tableau of patriotism, filled with waving flags, retired generals, Kerry's Vietnam buddies, and the candidate himself arriving on stage with a snappy salute: "Reporting for duty." Only the Republicans could have done it better, and when their turn came, with the Commander-in-Chief as their nominee, in fact they did.

The campaign that followed was at once inspiring and dispiriting. Dean's early surge had been driven by Web bloggers, a mobilizing strategy adopted by the Kerry campaign, and by proliferating political action committees like the liberal MoveOn.org that claimed to be independent and in effect ran parallel campaigns. For its part, the GOP outdid the Democrats at identifying and motivating its base, thanks especially to the church networks it had cultivated. For once, complaints about voter passivity did not apply. That was the inspiring part. The rest of it—the substance of the campaign—was a dispiriting exercise in attack ads and political choreography.

Democrats questioned Bush's Vietnam sinecure in the Air National Guard; Republicans challenged Kerry's patriotism for turning Vietnam peace activist. A sudden onslaught of slickly produced television ads by the "Swift Boat Veterans for Truth" charged that Kerry had lied to win his medals and fatally undercut his advantage. Nor did it help that Kerry, as a three-term senator, had a lengthy record easily mined for hard-to-explain votes, as, for example, why had he voted against, before he voted for, an Iraqi funding bill? Republicans tagged him a "flip-flopper," and the accusation, endlessly repeated, stuck. Bush, by contrast, got off easily. He adhered to his message: Iraq was "hard work," but America had to "stay the course." For all his debater's skills, Kerry failed to budge Bush in their televised debates. The strangest feature of the campaign was the distorting effect of the federal electoral system. In the forty or more states safely Democratic or Republican, people saw very little of the campaign, while voters in the few contested states (the most important being Florida, Pennsylvania, and Ohio) were inundated by attack ads and door-ringing volunteers.

These open states became the testing ground for Karl Rove's thesis that, given the nation's polarized politics, Republican victory in 2004 depended on the party's conservative, evangelical base. A year before, the Supreme Court of Massachusetts had issued a constitutional ruling in favor of same-sex marriages. In a blaze of media coverage, liberal officials around the country began to marry gay and lesbian couples. No issue—not even abortion—was better calculated to galvanize social conservatives, and Republicans knew it. President Bush called for a federal amendment restricting marriage to a man and a woman. In all eleven states considering constitutional bans on gay marriage, every one succeeded. That, commented the Associated Press, "showed the power of churchgoing Americans in this election and threw the nation's religious divide into stark relief."

On election day nearly 60 percent of eligible voters—the highest percentage since 1968—went to the polls. Bush beat Kerry by 286 electoral votes to 252. The crucial state was Ohio, where a gay marriage ban passed by 62 percent, probably drawing enough conservative voters to the polls to give the president his slim margin there. The president also did well, despite Iraq, on national security. Voters told interviewers that Bush made them feel "safer." Bush was no longer a minority president. He had won a clear, if narrow, popular majority. In the flush of victory, the president spoke confidently of newly won "capital" that he had big plans for expending.

➤ What is the connection between 9/11 and the war in Iraq?

➤ Why did the war in Iraq not go according to plan?

➤ Can you explain why President Bush was reelected in 2004?

Unfinished Business

When a presidential term ends, the historian who follows its course is prone to think, well, that's done. And with a political campaign, similarly: We know who won, so that's finished. This sense of finality, of course, is an illusion, conjured up by the natural form of historical narrative, which calls for beginnings and endings. The reality, in the case of President Bush's first term, was not of anything concluded, but on the contrary, as events continued to unfold, of a cascade of problems and uncertainties—what we might characterize as unfinished business. In this final section, we attempt a preliminary accounting of that post-2004 unfinished business.

The President's Travails

In the 2004 campaign, George W. Bush had outrun the clock on Iraq. Indeed, by use of his formidable presidential powers, he had slowed it a bit. At a critical moment, six weeks before the election, the recently installed Iraqi prime minister, Ayad Allawi, had visited the White House to say how well things were going in Iraq. But the problems kept coming. If the insurgency was bad news, civil war was worse. By 2006 Sunnis and Shiites were at each other's throats, and it became a race between insurgent efforts at fomenting civil war and American efforts at establishing a stable Iraqi government.

With no end in sight, recriminations over the Iraqi tangle kept bubbling up. In April 2006, half a dozen retired generals broke the military code of silence and called for Secretary Rumsfeld's resignation. "The commitment of our forces in this fight," charged Marine Lieutenant General Gregory Newbold in one widely quoted article, "was done with a casualness and swagger that are the special province of those who have never had to execute these missions—or bury the results." By the time General Newbold penned those searing words, 2,300 troops had died in Iraq, $300 billion had been spent, and public opinion had shifted decisively: 57 percent of Americans thought the war a mistake.

The political toll on Bush was enormous. His approval rating sank below 40 percent, and his committed base—those "strongly" approving—shrank calamitously to 20 percent. In effect, Bush had exhausted his windfall from the War on Terror; he would henceforth be governing from a position of political weakness.

Bush's vulnerability was revealed most graphically when he approved a contract for a Dubai-owned company to operate American seaports. So vociferous was the congressional opposition that the president backed down and scrapped the deal. Increasingly, he came under attack from his own base: from Christian conservatives who felt betrayed by Bush's post-election silence on the gay-marriage amendment, and from right wingers who, when serious debate began in mid-2006, preferred a punitive solution to the problem of illegal immigrants. Bush's biggest asset, his can-do aura, was punctured by his administration's slow response to Hurricane Katrina, which devastated New Orleans in August 2005, and then by the confused start of the Medicare drug benefit that left many elderly bewildered and without medication.

Meanwhile, Tom DeLay's K Street Project imploded. The lobbying scandals that brought it down cast a shadow on DeLay. Already under indictment for his role in the Texas gerrymandering scheme, he resigned from the House. His crony, the ace lobbyist Jack Abramoff, fingered other senior Republicans before heading off to jail and, to top things off, a sex scandal hit Capitol Hill in October 2006. Republican Congressman Mark Foley, a champion of family values, turned out to be a closeted gay who had harassed teenage Congressional pages. Foley immediately resigned, but damaging questions were raised about negligent oversight by the Republican leadership. As Democratic charges of a "culture of corruption" sank in, the approval ratings for the Republican-dominated Congress sank to record lows.

The bill came due in the midterm elections on November 7, 2006. The Democrats regained control of the House of Representatives and against all odds—they needed to take five out of six contested Republican seats—captured the Senate by a single seat. Gone was the heady talk sparked by the 2004 victory of a permanent Republican majority. Karl Rove's strategy, although it worked as intended, turned out not to be foolproof. The Republican base remained steadfast, comparable to 2004. The party's vaunted get-out-the-vote machinery did its job. And computer-aided redistricting gave Republican incumbents a big advantage. But the Democratic surge overwhelmed these defenses in key red states. Of the total votes cast in House races, Democrats won 55 percent, far exceeding Bush's winning margin in 2004. It was a dramatic shift in the independent vote—something like 25 percent of independents who had gone for Bush in 2004 voted Democratic in 2006—that did the trick. Moreover, Republicans lost control of six governorships and ten state legislatures, putting at risk their gerrymandered advantage in those states.

Only time will tell whether 2006 was a critical election, presaging a new political realignment, or just a temporary setback for the Republicans. Whatever the long-term consequences, the immediate impact on the political environment was evident, even before the returns were in. The Democrats, spooked by Iraq in 2004, had pressed the issue aggressively, and effectively made the midterm elections a referendum on the Iraq war. Finally acknowledging its unpopularity, President Bush began to give ground. He officially retired the phrase, "stay the course," lowered his sights from a democratic to a stable Iraq, and indicated that he was open to suggestions. The day after the election, Secretary of Defense Rumsfeld resigned. Bush was bowing to a new reality: The opposition party controlled Congress.

In the American political system, however, it is the president, not Congress, who bestrides the

Hurricane Katrina

When Hurricane Katrina bore down on New Orleans on August 29, 2005, officials thought at first that the city had avoided the brunt of the storm, but the impact was great enough to breach the surrounding earthen dams and flood New Orleans, hitting hardest the lower-lying neighborhoods where poor blacks lived. Two days later, the people on the roof of this apartment house were still stranded and desperately awaiting rescue. Images like this one of suffering ghetto-dwellers brought home a truth that many Americans had forgotten — that a black underclass still exists in this country. © Smiley N. Pool / Dallas Morning News / Corbis.

country. Presidents like Franklin D. Roosevelt and Ronald Reagan make a huge difference, indelibly marking and perhaps even redefining the country. But even the least of incumbents, because of the power of the office, leave the historian with a lot to think about, including, most notably, what has been left unresolved. Six years into his presidency, that seems likely to be a big part of George W. Bush's legacy — lots of unfinished business.

What Kind of America?

Terri Schiavo's tragedy could have happened in any family. She was a young woman who had fallen into a deep coma after a heart seizure. When her husband asked that her feeding tube be removed, her devoutly Catholic parents filed a lawsuit to stop him. On appeal, the Florida courts eventually ruled in the husband's favor. That normally would have concluded this family tragedy. Instead, conservative Republicans

intervened, transforming Schiavo's plight into a right-to-life crusade. Senate Majority Leader Bill Frist, a surgeon in private life, opined after viewing a videotape that Schiavo was alert. With much fanfare, Congress enacted emergency legislation on March 21, 2005, transferring the case to the Federal Courts, but to no avail. The Supreme Court turned down a final appeal, and Schiavo was allowed to die. An autopsy confirmed that she had indeed been in an irreversible vegetative state.

Faith against Science. What was essentially symbolic in the Schiavo case became hugely consequential in the controversy over stem-cell research. Medical researchers perceived in stem cells, the embryonic cells that develop into a baby's specialized body-building cells, the potential for regenerating damaged organs, offering hope for victims of heart attacks, spine injuries, and a host of degenerative diseases. The research requires a supply of stem cells, which can be harvested from frozen embryos left unused at fertility clinics. Destroying the embryos, however, provoked an outcry from right-to-life advocates. "There is no such thing as a spare embryo," the president told members of Nightlight Christian Adoptions, a group that arranges the adoption and implantation of frozen embryos left over after fertility treatments. Bush's opposition was not absolute. He proposed that federal funding be continued, but only for projects utilizing the handful of existing stem-cell lines.

In making that compromise, the president acknowledged the painful choices posed by stem-cell research. It was difficult, in truth, to deny the benefits, not only medically, but for America's scientific edge in the world (see Comparing American Voices, "The Stem-Cell Research Controversy," pp. 1010–1011). Challenging Bush, California voters in 2002 passed a major bond issue for state-financed stem-cell research. Other states followed California's example, even conservative Missouri, although in this case with no funding provision. The issue increasingly divided Republicans. In July 2006, Congress defied the president and passed a bill favoring stem-cell research, but lacked the votes to override Bush's veto.

On another front, the battle between science and faith raged over that old bugbear, Darwinism. In place of creationism, anti-evolutionists advanced a new theory, "intelligent design," which argued that some biological phenomena were too complex to be explained by random natural selection. In Kansas, the state school board provided a framework for this strategy: By its redefinition, science encompassed more than "natural explanations." The idea was not to abolish evolution, but to offer intelligent design as an alternative and then to "teach the controversy." The courts, however, were having none of it. In a case involving Dover, Pennsylvania, a federal judge declared intelligent design just a screen for creationism and, like creationism, an unconstitutional intrusion of religion into the public schools. And in the 2006 elections, Kansas voters rejected the creationist school board members.

In the nature of things, neither side ever completely prevails in value-laden conflicts like those over stem-cell research or evolution. In the ebb and flow, it appeared that, even with Bush behind them, faith-based conservatives had not gained the upper hand against science. An exception, probably temporary, was inside the federal government itself, where political appointees regularly stifled or ignored unwelcome scientific findings, such as on global warming and the morning-after birth control pill. Where science cannot be invoked—as,

for example, on gay marriage—social conservatives did better, and on abortion, their preeminent issue, the legal terrain shifted in their favor.

The Courts and Reproductive Rights. As a campaigner, Bush made no bones about his intentions; he meant to appoint conservative judges. In the first term, his lower court nominees provoked fierce, if ultimately futile, opposition from Senate Democrats. In 2005, with Justice Sandra Day O'Connor's retirement and Chief Justice William Rehnquist's death, two Supreme Court seats opened up. In finding replacements, President Bush was the beneficiary of a remarkable conservative project, dating back into the early 1980s, to prepare a future Supreme Court. Candidates were identified in law school (mainly through the student-run Federalist Society), awarded prestigious clerkships with conservative judges, brought into the Reagan administration for seasoning, and then appointed to the federal bench. Bush's nominees, John G. Roberts and Samuel Alito, both of them appellate federal judges, were graduates of that conservative project. They were superbly qualified jurists and hence, despite their avowed conservatism, invulnerable to Democratic attack.

Although much else was at stake, the litmus test for their appointments was abortion, as Bush discovered when, prior to Alito, he nominated his White House counsel, Harriet Miers, to the Supreme Court. Distrusting her pro-life bona fides, social conservatives erupted in fury and forced the president to withdraw her nomination. Even so, while well pleased with Roberts and Alito, they could not be confident of the impact on *Roe v. Wade*. For one thing, the Supreme Court was still one vote shy of a clear pro-life majority. Moreover, both appointees, under Senate questioning, expressed respect for settled precedent, which, for the present, applied to *Roe v. Wade*. But pro-life conservatives were likely to be emboldened in their current strategy, which was to chip away at *Roe v. Wade* by exploiting the "undue burden" standard in *Planned Parenthood v. Casey* (1992) that permits constraints, like informed consent for minors, on abortion.

The battle over reproductive rights, despite two new Supreme Court justices, remained unsettled. The same could not be said about the direction of the American judiciary, which was moving unambiguously to the right. It would take only one more Supreme Court appointment during Bush's remaining tenure for the conservative project, twenty years in the making, to be fully accomplished.

The New Supreme Court

When the president delivers his annual State of the Union Address each January before Congress, other leading federal officials show their respect by attending. In this photograph we see four of the nine justices of the Supreme Court assembled at President Bush's fifth Address on January 29, 2006, including the two newest members. Chief Justice John Roberts Jr. is at the left, Justice Samuel Alito on the right. In between are two older hands, Justices Clarence Thomas and Stephen Breyer. © Pablo Martinez Monsivais/Pool/CNP/Corbis.

Presidential Powers. Among the constitutional challenges facing the new Court, none was likely to be more consequential than adjudicating the limits on presidential powers in post–9/11 America. After the attack, Attorney General John Ashcroft advanced the proposition that fighting terrorism at home required a new "paradigm of prevention." In the first frantic months, a dragnet swept through Muslim communities, calling on eighty thousand immigrants to register and be fingerprinted and for eight thousand to undergo FBI interviews. About five thousand foreign nationals were imprisoned, held in a kind of preventive detention on minor charges or, failing that, as material witnesses. In another area, applying the Patriot Act aggressively, the Justice Department launched a massive information-gathering effort drawing on the customer records of financial firms, Internet providers, and telecommunications companies. Despite growing disquiet, Congress reauthorized the Patriot Act in early 2006 with only cosmetic changes.

The administration was not satisfied, however, with the antiterrorist powers granted it by Congress. In December 2005, the *New York Times* produced a bombshell: A report based on leaked information about a secret National Security Agency program that probably violated the Federal Information Surveillance Act by eavesdropping on telephone and e-mail traffic between domestic and foreign sites without court warrants. At congressional hearings, Ashcroft's successor, Attorney General Alberto Gonzales, was unrepentant. He refused to divulge any particulars about the NSA program on grounds of national security. And he invoked, as legal justification, the president's inherent powers as commander-in-chief. Presidents in every major war, Gonzales argued, had invoked the powers that Bush now claimed. But, in fact, Bush's secret NSA order rested on more far-reaching claims than emergency war powers. It expressed a bold effort to regain executive powers that leading members of the administration—especially Vice President

The Stem-Cell Research Controversy

When George W. Bush took office in 2001, the country was bitterly divided over whether or not the federal government should fund stem-cell research using frozen embryos. The following selections illuminate that debate and trace its course over the next five years.

GEORGE W. BUSH
"Human life is a sacred gift from our creator"

Himself a born-again Christian and politically aligned with the pro-life voter, President Bush sought a policy that would satisfy both opponents and advocates of stem-cell research. In a television address in August 2001, he presented the following rationale for his position.

My administration must decide whether to allow federal funds, your tax dollars, to be used for scientific research on stem cells derived from human embryos. A large number of these embryos already exist. They are the product of a process called in-vitro fertilization, which helps so many couples conceive children. When doctors match sperm and egg to create life outside the womb, they usually produce more embryos than are implanted in the mother. Once a couple successfully has children or if they are unsuccessful, the additional embryos remain frozen in laboratories. . . . A number have been donated to science and used to create privately funded stem-cell lines.

Based on preliminary work that has been privately funded, scientists believe further research using stem cells offers great promise that could help improve the lives of those who suffer from many terrible diseases, from juvenile diabetes to Alzheimer's, from Parkinson's to spinal cord injuries. . . .

Scientists further believe that rapid progress in this research will come only with federal funds. Federal dollars help attract the best and brightest scientists. They ensure new discoveries are widely shared at the largest number of research facilities. . . .

[But] research on embryonic stem cells raises profound ethical questions, because extracting the stem cell destroys the embryo, and thus destroys its potential for life.

As I thought through this issue I kept returning to two fundamental questions. First, are these frozen embryos human life and therefore something precious to be protected? And second, if they're going to be destroyed anyway, shouldn't they be used for a greater good, for research that has the potential to save and improve other lives? . . .

I've asked those questions and others of scientists, scholars, bioethicists, religious leaders, doctors, researchers, members of Congress, my Cabinet and my friends . . . and I have found widespread disagreement. I . . . believe human life is a sacred gift from our creator. I worry about a culture that devalues life, and believe as your president I have an important obligation to foster and encourage respect for life in America and throughout the world. . . .

As a result of private research, more than 60 genetically diverse stem cell lines already exist. They were created from embryos that have already been destroyed, and they have the ability to regenerate themselves indefinitely, creating ongoing opportunities for research.

I have concluded that we should allow federal funds to be used for research on these existing stem cell lines, where the life-and-death decision has already been made. . . .

This allows us to explore the promise and potential of stem-cell research without crossing a fundamental moral line by providing taxpayer funding that would sanction or encourage further destruction of human embryos that have at least the potential for life.

SOURCE: The White House, Office of the Press Secretary, "President Discusses Stem Cell Research," August 9, 2001, press release, www.whitehouse.gov/news/releases/2001/08/20010809-2.html.

CANDI CUSHMAN
"Uncommon Moms"

By 2004, public sentiment seemed to be tilting toward embryonic stem-cell research, with polls showing 60 percent of Americans in favor. In Congress, even some pro-life Republicans began to advocate overturning the restrictions President Bush had placed on federal funding. In this article, we see one element of the counterattack, described in the magazine of Focus on the Family, the leading conservative organization supporting the president's position.

Most credible scientists will admit that an embryo is a human being, with all of the DNA and chromosomes that a human being will ever need from birth to death. . . .

It might be easy for pro-life citizens who don't want their tax dollars supporting the destruction of human life to feel discouraged as this debate unfolds. Because it may seem difficult for embryos that look like microscopic masses to compete with emotionally compelling people pleading for cures.

They can take heart, however, because pro-life moms are walking the halls of Congress. And they're cutting through all that emotional hype by showing politicians the faces of the embryos they're proposing to kill.

One of those faces belongs to Mikayla Tesdall, a bouncy 3-year-old girl with blond pigtails who loves to sing worship songs to whoever will listen.

Mikayla is a Snowflake — the name given to six dozen adopted babies who began life as frozen embryos. Not too long ago, these crawling, talking toddlers were stored in the freezers of in-vitro fertilization clinics across the country. They were labeled by many politicians as mere "excess," worthy of destruction, until the Nightlight Christian Adoptions agency in California devised a way to rescue them by allowing infertile married couples to adopt them. Thus began an amazing process, in which Mikayla's adoptive mother, Sharon, had the little girl implanted in her womb as an embryo. . . .

And that personal experience has transformed Tesdall and other formerly apolitical moms into passionate pro-life warriors. They've been surprisingly effective, gaining access to places even some of the slickest lobbyists can't get into, like the White House. . . . They had a singular mission in mind: presenting Democrats and Republicans alike with undeniable proof that a human being is sacred and worth protecting at any stage — whether an embryo or a fully developed baby. . . .

And that's how, on the muggy morning of Sept. 22 [2004], Tesdall and Mikayla found themselves behind a podium in a U.S. House press room.

"I am two," Mikayla boldly announced to a roomful of reporters and legislators before her mother had a chance to speak. It was an unplanned moment, but no matter. The audience got the point: Mikayla is fully human and already full of self-will. As the little girl played at the foot of the podium with a princess tiara and plastic dolls, Tesdall told the room:

"No one questions that she is fully human today, so how can anyone disagree that she was fully human in her embryonic stage of development? After all, what did any of us adoptive moms, who have given birth to Snowflake babies, add to them? We added nothing — except love, nutrients, and a warm place to grow."

SOURCE: Candi Cushman, "Uncommon Moms," *Citizen Magazine.* Copyright © 2004 Focus on the Family, www.family.org/cforum/citizenmag/features/a0035021.cfm.

MICHAEL CHOROST
"The Promised Land"

Born in 1964, Michael Chorost was always hard of hearing; by his thirties, he was completely deaf. A writer and author, Chorost had a computer installed in his brain in 2001, which allowed him to hear again. In a blog posted on the Scientist *in February 2006, he suggests why millions of people with degenerative diseases support this research.*

I'm an obvious beneficiary of medical technology. Without the computer surgically embedded in my skull, I'd be totally deaf. The device, called a "cochlear implant," routes past my damaged inner ear by triggering my auditory nerves with sixteen tiny electrodes coiled up inside my cochlea.

It's not a cure, though, any more than glasses cure vision loss. It's a prosthesis, a workaround. Compared to the extraordinary delicacy and precision of naturally evolved organs, it's clumsy. . . .

But someday scientists may learn to coax the body into repairing its own damaged parts instead of creating technological fixes that require a constant supply of batteries. That's what makes stem-cell research so exciting. Forget prostheses. How about a cure? . . .

What makes stem cells exciting is that they are pluripotent: With the appropriate chemical triggers and physical nudges and pushes, they'll turn into any kind of cell there is. Several panelists noted that with the help of stem cells, the body is constantly remaking itself — skin, intestines, red blood cells. In many cases, the body degenerates and ages not because it has lost the ability to create stem cells, but because it has lost the ability to trigger the stem cells it has. Find those triggers, learn how to activate them, *et voila* [and there you have it].

SOURCE: Michael Chorost, "Risky Enough Business?" *The Scientist*, February 8, 2006, blog posting, www.thescientist.com/blog/display/23094.

ANALYZING THE EVIDENCE

➤ How would you characterize President Bush's stand on embryonic stem-cell research?

➤ Why is the two-year-old Mikayla Tesdall an important person for the opponents of embryonic stem-cell research? How about Michael Chorost? Is he the equivalent for the proponents?

➤ When many of his Republican allies in Congress changed their minds and voted in 2006 to lift the funding restrictions on stem-cell research, President Bush vetoed the measure. Can his veto — the very first of his administration — be explained by the documents you have read?

Cheney and Secretary of Defense Rumsfeld, both once Nixon appointees—believed had been lost after Watergate (see Chapter 29).

As time passed, concern over the rise of an imperial presidency became more palpable and bipartisan. The libertarian Cato Institute, a pillar of the conservative establishment, concluded, after surveying the record, that "far from defending the Constitution, President Bush has repeatedly sought to strip out the limits the document places on federal power." The question arose, as the ranking Democrat on intelligence in the House, Jane Harman, put it, whether violating the law for the sake of security "gives away the very values we are fighting for."

In the early summer of 2006, the answer to that question began to emerge. The defining issue involved the treatment of Al Qaeda and Taliban detainees at Guantanamo and other overseas sites. The administration had declared that, as "unlawful combatants," such detainees were not entitled to the rights either of prisoners of war or criminals under American law. Their treatment was strictly a matter of executive privilege and, indeed, in devising a policy, the administration acted irregularly, bypassing its own normal channels and delegating the task to a few lawyers operating out of the vice president's office. The abuses that crept in—of which Abu Ghraib was only the most notorious—blackened America's reputation abroad, while at home the detainee program became entangled in ever-mounting legal challenges.

On June 29, 2006, in the landmark *Hamdan v. Rumsfeld* decision, the Supreme Court struck down the military tribunals set up to try the Guantanamo detainees. The Court declared that international law on war prisoners applied to the detainees and that the tribunals fell far short of the Geneva Convention requirement that prisoners of war "receive all the judicial guarantees which are recognized as indispensable by all civilized peoples." Equally important, the Court ruled that such tribunals could not be established without congressional authorization. In declaring that President Bush did not have a "blank check," the Court went beyond the question of military tribunals. It potentially challenged the basic presumption underlying the administration's NSA eavesdropping program and other such secret antiterrorist activities. Faced with *Hamdan v. Rumsfeld*, the White House backed down, rescinding the executive order denying detainees Geneva Convention protections and entering hard bargaining with Congress about an appropriate judicial program for them.

In the short term, the president mostly prevailed. The legislation he signed on October 16, 2006 granted him the Congressional approval he needed, with only limited procedural protections

for defendants before military tribunals and a good deal of flexibility left in interrogating suspects. But there were certain to be further court challenges—especially over the denial of **habeas corpus** rights to foreign detainees—and the constitutional issues remained far from resolved.

Attorney General Gonzales was correct when he argued that other wartime presidents had also invoked the plenary powers that George Bush claimed after 9/11. It had usually taken the return of peace, but eventually all those prior wartime excesses had been followed by bitter regrets. The United States is still wiping out the stain of Japanese American internment in World War II (see Chapter 25). But, of course, the War on Terror was different from other wars. It had, as the president was fond of saying, no discernable end. So the country cannot wait for peace to restore constitutional protections. How Americans strike the balance between security and individual rights remains an open question in an unending War on Terror.

What Kind of World?

It has been said that no military strategy survives the first battle of war. The same might be said of diplomacy, certainly of President Bush's diplomacy. At the outset he operated on the presumption of America's world primacy: The United States would call the tune; everyone else would dance to it. Iraq swiftly exposed one fallacy. As an instrument of foreign policy, America's military power proved sorely wanting; it was a better diplomatic weapon held in reserve than unleashed. More fundamental, however, the administration overestimated its post–Cold War supremacy. Being the sole superpower, it turned out, was no picnic. Other nations did not submit gladly, and had they been so inclined, Bush's early unilateralism—his actions on global warming, arms reductions treaties, and Iraq—finished off that possibility. By the time he realized his mistake, in mid-2003, the harm had been done. Thereafter, the administration scrambled to rebuild coalitions, enlist the UN, and manage diplomatically problems once thought resolvable by force or bluster. In the realm of foreign affairs, the nation's unfinished business had mainly to do with a chastened superpower struggling to catch up with events that had spun out of its control.

A Multi-Polar World. Beyond anyone's expectations, the end of the Cold War altered the world's diplomatic landscape. The European Union (EU) expanded to the east, integrating the nations of central Europe into its ranks. The Communist government of China turned toward capitalism, seized the opportunities of globalization, and challenged Japan for the leadership of East Asia. Oil-rich Muslim nations, stretching across the Middle East to Kazakhstan and south to Indonesia, grew increasingly conscious of their wealth, religious identity, and potential geopolitical power. The old categories of the Cold War — Free World, Communist World, Third World — broke down and, despite America's military supremacy, a new multi-polar system was emerging.

The European Union now embraced twenty-five countries and 450 million people, with the third largest population in the world, behind China and India (see Map 31.1, p. 965). Because it included some of the world's most advanced economies, the EU accounted for a fifth of all global imports and exports. Its money — the euro — emerged as one of the world's preferred currencies for international exchange. Thanks to the euro, the American dollar was no longer supreme. The EU, however, was far from becoming a European version of the United States. Internal tensions ran deep — that became clear in the splintered response to Iraq — and resistance to a supranational EU authority in Brussels was, if anything, intensifying. The EU, moreover, preferred generous social programs to armies, and was militarily no challenge to the United States. Even so, the old commonality of interest was gone, and, on a variety of issues, Europe was as much a rival as an ally of the United States.

In China's case, the tilt was emphatically toward rivalry. A vast nation of 1.3 billion people, China became the fastest growing economy in the world. The Bush administration welcomed China's embrace of capitalism, and American consumers were beneficiaries of its cheap exports. But the economic tensions were many — over the enormous trade imbalance ($170 billion in 2004), over millions of American jobs lost, over an undervalued renminbi (the Chinese currency) that made Chinese goods artificially cheap, over rampant pirating of American intellectual property. China remained a one-party state, and that produced tension over human rights. And as China flexed its muscles, it threatened America's interests in East Asia and worldwide became an increasingly formidable rival.

As China's economy grew, so did its appetite for oil, and so, consequently, did an oil shortage that pushed up world oil prices. While American consumers grumbled about paying $3.50 a gallon for gasoline, policymakers worried about the empowering of oil-producing countries. This was most evident in the case of Russia, which, after reeling economically in the 1990s, revived on a surge of oil revenues. George Bush said he had looked into President Vladimir Putin's heart and found he was

a good guy. That was when Russia was down. Putin turned out not to be such a good guy when Russia got back on its feet. He took authoritarian control at home, threatened neighboring former Soviet republics, and, in various ways, stood up to the United States. He was, with some success, reasserting Russia's place in the world. In a lesser way, oil money emboldened Iran and even a bloc of South American countries led by rabidly anti-Yankee Hugo Chavez of Venezuela. For the United States, higher oil prices meant less global leverage.

Nuclear Proliferation. Where its weakened leverage counted most was in America's uphill struggle to contain the spread of atomic weapons. During the Cold War, only the Big Five — the United States, Britain, France, the Soviet Union, and China — plus Israel possessed nuclear arms. Most nations adhered to the Nuclear Non-Proliferation Treaty of 1968, which was policed by the International Atomic Energy Agency (IAEA).

Two of the nonsignatories, India and Pakistan, spurred by their bitter rivalry over Kashmir, secretly developed nuclear weapons during the 1990s. The Pakistani nuclear scientist Dr. A. Q. Khan, undoubtedly with the knowledge of high government officials, sold two other Muslim states, Libya and Iran, nuclear designs and equipment. The Pakistanis also traded the technology to Communist North Korea in exchange for missiles that could be used against India.

North Korea, a desperately poor, Stalinist country, bet the house on nuclear-weapons development, which it used variously as blackmail to extract aid and as insurance against real and imagined enemies. In 1994, the Clinton administration struck a deal, offering food, oil, and an advanced nuclear-power plant for an end to North Korea's atomic weapons program. In the late 1990s, the agreement broke down, amid bitter recriminations and well-founded charges of North Korean cheating. The Bush administration wanted to crack down, but, having failed to bring along China, Russia, and South Korea, it had to settle for ultimately fruitless negotiations. Evidently seeing the U.S. invasion of Iraq as an object lesson, North Korea rushed ahead with its nuclear program and early in 2005 announced that it possessed atomic bombs. In October 2006, it carried out an underground test of a nuclear device.

Iran played a more devious game. A signatory of the Non-Proliferation Treaty, Iran took the position that, while it did not want nuclear weapons, it intended to exercise its rights under the treaty to develop the technology for peaceful nuclear energy. Learning how to enrich plant-grade uranium, however, opens the path to producing weapons-grade

North Korea

Troops parade in Pyongyang, North Korea, in celebration of the seventieth anniversary of the founding of the Korean People's Army. One would have imagined that a country capable of fielding so splendid a military display would have been bursting with resources and wealth, but in fact North Korea was the most threadbare country in all of Asia, incapable of feeding its own people and held together by an extraordinarily dictatorial regime. No country was more nettlesome for the Bush administration as the United States struggled to keep nuclear proliferation in check. KOREAN NEWS SERVICE / AFP / Getty Images.

uranium. In 2002, dissidents alerted the IAEA to secret nuclear sites and, while Iranians adamantly denied it, everyone else concluded that they were bent on building atomic bombs. As with North Korea, the Bush administration took a tough line, including, until it became entangled in Iraq, a credible military threat. Since then, while refusing to take that threat "off the table," the United States has been reduced to playing a diplomatic game, which it appears to be losing because, as with North Korea, it cannot count on the support of other key nations. Its efforts at the UN Security Council have been frustrated by Russia and China, both with economic stakes in Iran. Meanwhile, Iranian elections unexpectedly produced a hard-line Islamic president, Mahmoud Ahmadinejad, who regularly threatened Israel's destruction. In April 2006, Ahmadinejad triumphantly announced that Iran had mastered the enrichment process for plant-grade uranium.

In a multi-polar world, the United States seemed impotent against the spread of nuclear weapons, even to an apocalyptic country like Iran.

Militant Islam. In Iran's case, at least, there was a state to hold responsible. Utterly beyond America's experience was the amorphous Islamic extremism that had no address. After 9/11, the global manhunt largely dismantled the Al Qaeda network. Thereafter, Osama bin Laden served far more as a symbolic than as an operational figure. But as a symbolic figure, he inspired the Muslim world. In its terrorist incarnation, Al Qaeda metastasized into amorphous cells, unknown in number, operating more or less independently but with equally murderous intent. Al Qaeda–inspired suicide bombings have taken a heavy toll in Madrid, London, Bali, and, increasingly, in Muslim countries. This violence was only the cutting edge of anti-Western rage that permeated the Muslim world, a fact brought shockingly home to Europeans in early 2006 in widespread rioting against mocking cartoons of the prophet Muhammad printed in a Danish newspaper.

In the past the United States had regarded Islamic extremism as an internal problem of its Middle Eastern allies. Earlier American administrations supported authoritarian regimes like that of the Shah in Iran (see Chapters 26 and 29) and generally turned a blind eye to their brutal repression of Islamic dissidents. In his second inaugural address, President Bush signaled a major policy shift. The United States, he proclaimed, was committed to ending tyranny around the world. In so doing, Bush was evoking the Wilsonian strain in American foreign policy — the conviction that the country's democratic principles should govern its dealings

with the rest of the world — but with a harder edge than President Wilson had ever imagined when he had called for a League of Nations after World War I (see Chapter 22).

Convinced that democracy was the answer to Islamic radicalism, Bush pressed for political reform in the Middle East. But when, as a result, Egypt's regime eased up in the 2005 elections, the militant Muslim Brotherhood gained strength, prompting another government crackdown. More shocking, early in 2006 Palestinians voted into power the hard-line Hamas, which the United States regarded as a terrorist organization. Hamas took office, but refused to disband its fighters or integrate them into the regular Palestinian military. In Lebanon, Hezbollah pursued a similar double-breasted strategy, participating in elections and

Chaos in Iraq

No figure was more adept at inciting chaos in Iraq than the young radical Shi'ite cleric Moqtada al-Sadr, who had a huge following among the Shi'ite poor, especially in the Baghdad slums. Here, he is pictured in the poster held aloft by a supporter celebrating the burning of a U.S. Army truck after an American action in the Shula neighborhood of Baghdad. Initially, al-Sadr aimed his ire at the invading Americans, but with the intensification of sectarian strife, he turned his death squads loose on the Sunnis, while also becoming in 2006 a powerful behind-the-scenes player in the new Iraqi government. Al-Sadr was emblematic of the subterranean complexities of Iraqi society that flummoxed the Bush administration when it undertook to bring democracy to Iraq.
© Ceerwan Aziz / Reuters / Corbis.

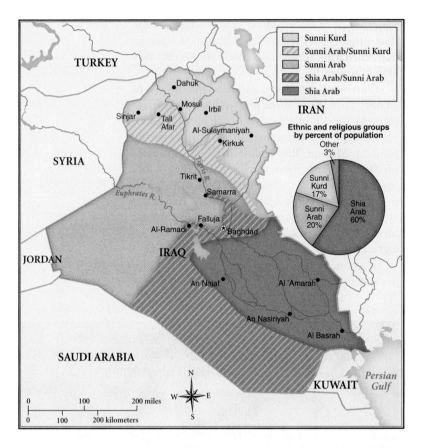

MAP 32.3 Ethnoreligious Groups in Iraq, 2006

Like other Middle Eastern countries, Iraq did not have a homogenous population. It was divided along religious lines between Sunni and Shi'ite Muslims (plus some Christians and, until they fled to Israel after 1948, many Jews) and ethnically among Arabs, Kurds, and Turkomen. When Iraq had been created under a League of Nations mandate after World War I, the British, who were in charge, installed the minority Sunni as the dominant political element, an arrangement that persisted until the United States toppled Saddam Hussein in 2003. The bitter internal strife that ensued stems from long-standing enthnoreligious divisions in Iraq and, among the possible outcomes, one is a de facto division of the country into autonomous Shiite, Sunni, and Kurdish regions.

joining the central government, but maintaining armed control of its own region. Hezbollah did not consult with the Beirut government in July 2006 before abducting two Israeli soldiers and precipitating a savage Israeli response that devastated much of Lebanon. Participating in elections, it seemed, was no antidote to Islamic extremism.

In Egypt, Palestine, and Lebanon, of course, the administration was just an anxious bystander. Iraq, however, was Bush's democratic project. Under American prodding, Iraqis held two national elections, wrote a constitution, established a parliament, and, in May 2006, after much wrangling, installed a prime minister. Beneath the formalities, however, Iraqi politics ran strictly along ethnic and sectarian lines. The dominant Shiite parties answered to their respective mullahs and, as with Hamas and Hezbollah, maintained their private militias, even while participating in the new government. Incessant insurgent attacks, capped by the bombing of a revered Samarra mosque in February 2006, finally pushed the Shiites over the edge. Their militias began in earnest to retaliate against Sunnis, utilizing death squads hardly distinguishable from the official police. As the carnage spread, a de facto partitioning began, with mass migrations from mixed Sunni-Shiite areas, and civil war became a real possibility (Map 32.3). That was the grim U.S. official finding three years after the Iraq invasion.

It remained unclear whether the warring sides would step back from the abyss of civil war. Or whether, if they did, the government would take hold. Or whether, if it did, the U.S-created Iraqi army could defeat the insurgency. Even if all these good things happened, if against the odds Iraq held together, in global terms America would still have failed because, in Islamic eyes, the Iraqi involvement had fatally tainted Western-style democracy. It had undercut Bush's global strategy for turning the tide against Islamic militancy, harmed America's leadership role in the world, and complicated its battle against nuclear proliferation. And if, as seemed evermore likely, Iraq went badly, the entire Middle East could go up in flames. The awful realization began to dawn that, beyond the cost in blood and treasure, Iraq had exacted a heavy toll on America's strategic interests in the world.

In an unguarded moment, President Bush remarked that Iraq would be a problem for the next administration. His admission is an apt epitaph for the Iraq involvement. Six months, and out. That was what the Pentagon hawks had expected. They never imagined that this sideshow—a quick victory on the way to bigger and better things—would bog down the Bush administration and become its defining, main event. They had misread the nature of global politics: Problems that force was meant to solve could turn around and bite you back.

TIMELINE

2000	George W. Bush wins contested presidential election
2001	September 11, Al Queda terrorists attack the World Trade Center and the Pentagon Military operations against the Taliban in Afghanistan begin Enron declares bankruptcy Congress passes the USA PATRIOT Act
2002	No Child Left Behind Act becomes law The United States defeats the Taliban in Afghanistan President Bush declares Iran, North Korea, and Iraq "an axis of evil"
2003	The United States invades Iraq in March; Iraqi regime quickly collapses The Bush administration promotes an "ownership society"
2004	Torture at the Abu Ghraib prison becomes public President Bush wins reelection
2005	Hurricane Katrina devastates the Gulf Coast John G. Roberts, Jr. is sworn in as Chief Justice of the United States The *New York Times* publishes reports about a domestic NSA eavesdropping program
2006	Samuel A. Alito is sworn in as an Associate Justice of the United States Supreme Court Congress reauthorizes the USA PATRIOT Act President Bush vetoes a stem-cell research bill passed by Congress North Korea tests a nuclear device Democratic Party regains control of Congress Continued sectarian violence in Iraq

FOR FURTHER EXPLORATION

A good starting point for learning about President Bush's background is Bill Minutaglia, *First Son: George W. Bush and the Bush Family Dynasty* (1999). Cass R. Sunstein and Richard A. Epstein, eds., *The Vote: Bush, Gore, and the Supreme Court* (2001), is an assessment by a range of legal scholars of the Supreme Court's decision resolving the disputed presidential election of 2000. Two sympathetic accounts of President Bush's style of leadership are David Frum, *The Right Man: The Surprise Presidency of George W. Bush* (2003), and Fred Barnes, *Rebel-in-Chief: Inside the Bold and Controversial Presidency of George W. Bush* (2006). Bush's domestic record is treated less kindly by Bruce Bartlett, *Impostor: How George W. Bush Bankrupted America and Betrayed the Reagan Administration* (2006); Douglas Brinkley, *The Great Deluge: Hurricane Katrina, New Orleans, and the Mississippi Gulf Coast* (2006); and Ron Suskind, *The Price of Loyalty: George W. Bush, the White House, and the Education of Paul O'Neill* (2004). O'Neill was Bush's first secretary of the Treasury.

On the administration's response to 9/11, see Richard A. Clarke, *Against All Enemies: Inside America's War on Terror* (2004); Seymour M. Hersh, *Chain of Command: The Road from 9/11 to Abu Ghraib* (2004); George Packer, *The Assassins' Gate: America in Iraq* (2004); and James Risen, *State of War: The Secret History of the CIA and Bush Administration* (2006). Especially informative about the prosecution of the war in Iraq is Michael R. Gordon and Bernard R. Trainor, *Cobra II: The Inside Story of the Invasion and Occupation of Iraq* (2006). Joseph Margulies, *Guantanamo and the Abuse of Presidential Power* (2006), is by a lawyer for one of the Guantanamo detainees. A scholarly treatment of critical constitutional issues facing the country is Bruce Ackerman, *Before the Next Attack: Preserving Civil Liberties in an Age of Terrorism* (2006).

The September 11 Digital Archive at **www.911digitalarchive .org** offers firsthand responses of Americans to the terrorist attack of September 11, 2001. The site includes oral histories, video and still images, and a valuable guide to Web sites on the topic.

On the Iraqi insurgency, **www.pbs.org/frontline/insurgency** contains interviews with U.S. military commanders and insurgency leaders, analysis by experts, and access to the *Frontline* documentary "Insurgency."

TEST YOUR KNOWLEDGE

To assess your command of the material in this chapter, see the Online Study Guide at **bedfordstmartins.com/henretta**.

For Web sites, images, and documents related to topics and places in this chapter, visit **bedfordstmartins.com/makehistory**.

The Declaration of Independence

**In Congress, July 4, 1776,
The Unanimous Declaration of the
Thirteen United States of America**

When in the Course of human events, it becomes necessary for one people to dissolve the political bands which have connected them with another, and to assume among the Powers of the earth, the separate and equal station to which the Laws of Nature and of Nature's God entitle them, a decent respect to the opinions of mankind requires that they should declare the causes which impel them to the separation.

We hold these truths to be self-evident, that all men are created equal, that they are endowed by their Creator with certain unalienable rights, that among these are Life, Liberty, and the pursuit of Happiness. That to secure these rights, Governments are instituted among Men, deriving their just powers from the consent of the governed. That whenever any Form of Government becomes destructive of these ends, it is the Right of the People to alter or to abolish it, and to institute new Government, laying its foundation on such principles and organizing its powers in such form, as to them shall seem most likely to effect their Safety and Happiness. Prudence, indeed, will dictate that Governments long established should not be changed for light and transient causes; and accordingly all experience hath shown, that mankind are more disposed to suffer, while evils are sufferable, than to right themselves by abolishing the forms to which they are accustomed. But when a long train of abuses and usurpations, pursuing invariably the same Object evinces a design to reduce them under absolute Despotism, it is their right, it is their duty, to throw off such Government, and to provide new Guards for their future security. — Such has been the patient sufferance of these Colonies; and such is now the necessity which constrains them to alter their former Systems of Government. The history of the present King of Great Britain is a history of repeated injuries and usurpations, all having in direct object the establishment of an absolute Tyranny over these States. To prove this, let Facts be submitted to a candid world.

He has refused his Assent to Laws, the most wholesome and necessary for the public good.

He has forbidden his Governors to pass Laws of immediate and pressing importance, unless suspended in their operation till his Assent should be obtained; and, when so suspended, he has utterly neglected to attend to them.

He has refused to pass other Laws for the accommodation of large districts of people, unless those people would relinquish the right of Representation in the Legislature, a right inestimable to them and formidable to tyrants only.

He has called together legislative bodies at places unusual, uncomfortable, and distant from the depository of their public Records, for the sole purpose of fatiguing them into compliance with his measures.

He has dissolved Representative Houses repeatedly, for opposing with manly firmness his invasions on the rights of the people.

He has refused for a long time, after such dissolutions, to cause others to be elected; whereby the Legislative powers, incapable of Annihilation, have returned to the People at large for their exercise; the State remaining in the mean time exposed to all the dangers of invasion from without and convulsions within.

He has endeavoured to prevent the population of these States; for that purpose obstructing the Laws of Naturalization of Foreigners; refusing to pass others to encourage their migrations hither, and raising the conditions of new Appropriations of Lands.

He has obstructed the Administration of Justice, by refusing his Assent to Laws for establishing Judiciary powers.

He has made Judges dependent on his Will alone, for the tenure of their offices, and the amount and payment of their salaries.

He has erected a multitude of New Offices, and sent hither swarms of Officers to harass our People, and eat out their substance.

He has kept among us, in times of peace, Standing Armies without the Consent of our legislature.

He has combined with others to subject us to a jurisdiction foreign to our constitution, and unacknowledged by our laws; giving his Assent to their Acts of pretended Legislation:

For quartering large bodies of armed troops among us:

For protecting them, by a mock Trial, from Punishment for any Murders which they should commit on the Inhabitants of these States:

For cutting off our Trade with all parts of the world:

For imposing taxes on us without our Consent:

For depriving us, in many cases, of the benefits of Trial by jury:

For transporting us beyond Seas to be tried for pretended offences:

For abolishing the free System of English Laws in a neighbouring Province, establishing therein an Arbitrary government, and enlarging its Boundaries so as to render it at once an example and fit instrument for introducing the same absolute rule into these Colonies:

For taking away our Charters, abolishing our most valuable Laws, and altering fundamentally the Forms of our Governments:

For suspending our own Legislatures, and declaring themselves invested with Power to legislate for us in all cases whatsoever.

He has abdicated Government here, by declaring us out of his Protection and waging War against us.

He has plundered our seas, ravaged our Coasts, burnt our towns, and destroyed the lives of our people.

He is at this time transporting large armies of foreign mercenaries to compleat the works of death, desolation, and tyranny, already begun with circumstances of Cruelty & perfidy scarcely paralleled in the most barbarous ages, and totally unworthy the Head of a civilized nation.

He has constrained our fellow Citizens taken Captive on the high Seas to bear Arms against their Country, to become the executioners of their friends and Brethren, or to fall themselves by their Hands.

He has excited domestic insurrections amongst us, and has endeavoured to bring on the inhabitants of our frontiers, the merciless Indian Savages, whose known rule of warfare, is an undistinguished destruction of all ages, sexes, and conditions.

In every stage of these Oppressions We have Petitioned for Redress in the most humble terms: Our repeated Petitions have been answered only by repeated injury. A Prince, whose character is thus marked by every act which may define a Tyrant, is unfit to be the ruler of a free people.

Nor have We been wanting in attention to our British brethren. We have warned them from time to time of attempts by their legislature to extend an unwarrantable jurisdiction over us. We have reminded them of the circumstances of our emigration and settlement here. We have appealed to their native justice and magnanimity, and we have conjured them by the ties of our common kindred to disavow these usurpations, which would inevitably interrupt our connections and correspondence. They too have been deaf to the voice of justice and of consanguinity. We must, therefore, acquiesce in the necessity, which denounces our Separation, and hold them, as we hold the rest of mankind, Enemies in War, in Peace Friends.

We, therefore, the Representatives of the United States of America, in General Congress, Assembled, appealing to the Supreme Judge of the world for the rectitude of our intentions, do, in the Name, and by Authority of the good People of these Colonies, solemnly publish and declare, That these United Colonies are, and of Right ought to be FREE AND INDEPENDENT STATES; that they are Absolved from all Allegiance to the British Crown, and that all political connection between them and the State of Great Britain, is and ought to be totally dissolved; and that as Free and Independent States, they have full Power to levy War, conclude Peace, contract Alliances, establish Commerce, and to do all other Acts and Things which Independent States may of right do. And for the support of this Declaration, with a firm reliance on the Protection of Divine Providence, we mutually pledge to each other our Lives, our Fortunes, and our sacred Honor.

John Hancock

Button Gwinnett	George Wythe	James Wilson	Josiah Bartlett
Lyman Hall	Richard Henry Lee	Geo. Ross	Wm. Whipple
Geo. Walton	Th. Jefferson	Caesar Rodney	Matthew Thornton
Wm. Hooper	Benja. Harrison	Geo. Read	Saml. Adams
Joseph Hewes	Thos. Nelson, Jr.	Thos. M'Kean	John Adams
John Penn	Francis Lightfoot Lee	Wm. Floyd	Robt. Treat Paine
Edward Rutledge	Carter Braxton	Phil. Livingston	Elbridge Gerry
Thos. Heyward, Junr.	Robt. Morris	Frans. Lewis	Step. Hopkins
Thomas Lynch, Junr.	Benjamin Rush	Lewis Morris	William Ellery
Arthur Middleton	Benja. Franklin	Richd. Stockton	Roger Sherman
Samuel Chase	John Morton	John Witherspoon	Sam'el Huntington
Wm. Paca	Geo. Clymer	Fras. Hopkinson	Wm. Williams
Thos. Stone	Jas. Smith	John Hart	Oliver Wolcott
Charles Carroll of Carrollton	Geo. Taylor	Abra. Clark	

The Articles of Confederation and Perpetual Union

Agreed to in Congress, November 15, 1777; Ratified March 1781

BETWEEN THE STATES OF NEW HAMPSHIRE, MASSACHUSETTS BAY, RHODE ISLAND AND PROVIDENCE PLANTATIONS, CONNECTICUT, NEW YORK, NEW JERSEY, PENNSYLVANIA, DELAWARE, MARYLAND, VIRGINIA, NORTH CAROLINA, SOUTH CAROLINA, GEORGIA.*

Article 1

The stile of this confederacy shall be "The United States of America."

Article 2

Each State retains its sovereignty, freedom and independence, and every power, jurisdiction, and right, which is not by this confederation expressly delegated to the United States, in Congress assembled.

Article 3

The said states hereby severally enter into a firm league of friendship with each other for their common defence, the security of their liberties and their mutual and general welfare; binding themselves to assist each other against all force offered to, or attacks made upon them, or any of them, on account of religion, sovereignty, trade, or any other pretence whatever.

Article 4

The better to secure and perpetuate mutual friendship and intercourse among the people of the different states in this union, the free inhabitants of each of these states, paupers, vagabonds, and fugitives from justice excepted, shall be entitled to all privileges and immunities of free citizens in the several states; and the people of each State shall have free ingress and regress to and from any other State, and shall enjoy therein all the privileges of trade and commerce, subject to the same duties, impositions, and restrictions, as the inhabitants thereof respectively; provided, that such restrictions shall not extend so far as to prevent the removal of property, imported into any State, to any other State of which the owner is an inhabitant; provided also, that no imposition, duties, or restriction, shall be laid by any State on the property of the United States, or either of them.

If any person guilty of, or charged with treason, felony, or other high misdemeanor in any State, shall flee from justice and be found in any of the United States, he shall, upon demand of the governor or executive power of the State from which he fled, be delivered up and removed to the State having jurisdiction of his offence.

Full faith and credit shall be given in each of these states to the records, acts, and judicial proceedings of the courts and magistrates of every other State.

Article 5

For the more convenient management of the general interests of the United States, delegates shall be annually appointed, in such manner as the legislature of each State shall direct, to meet in Congress, on the 1st Monday in November in every year, with a power reserved to each State to recall its delegates, or any of them, at any time within the year, and to send others in their stead for the remainder of the year.

No State shall be represented in Congress by less than two, nor by more than seven members; and no person shall be capable of being a delegate for more than three years in any term of six years; nor shall any person, being a delegate, be capable of holding any office under the United States, for which he, or any other for his benefit, receives any salary, fees, or emolument of any kind.

Each State shall maintain its own delegates in a meeting of the states, and while they act as members of the committee of the states.

In determining questions in the United States, in Congress assembled, each State shall have one vote.

Freedom of speech and debate in Congress shall not be impeached or questioned in any court or place out of Congress: and the members of Congress shall be protected in their

---

*This copy of the final draft of the Articles of Confederation is taken from the *Journals*, 9:907-25, November 15, 1777.

persons from arrests and imprisonments, during the time of their going to and from, and attendance on Congress, except for treason, felony, or breach of the peace.

Article 6

No State, without the consent of the United States, in Congress assembled, shall send any embassy to, or receive any embassy from, or enter into any conference, agreement, alliance, or treaty with any king, prince, or state; nor shall any person, holding any office of profit or trust under the United States, or any of them, accept of any present, emolument, office or title, of any kind whatever, from any king, prince, or foreign state; nor shall the United States, in Congress assembled, or any of them, grant any title of nobility.

No two or more states shall enter into any treaty, confederation, or alliance, whatever, between them, without the consent of the United States, in Congress assembled, specifying accurately the purposes for which the same is to be entered into, and how long it shall continue.

No state shall lay any imposts or duties which may interfere with any stipulations in treaties entered into by the United States, in Congress assembled, with any king, prince, or state, in pursuance of any treaties already proposed by Congress to the courts of France and Spain.

No vessels of war shall be kept up in time of peace by any State, except such number only as shall be deemed necessary by the United States, in Congress assembled, for the defence of such State or its trade; nor shall any body of forces be kept up by any State, in time of peace, except such number only as, in the judgment of the United States, in Congress assembled, shall be deemed requisite to garrison the forts necessary for the defence of such State; but every State shall always keep up a well regulated and disciplined militia, sufficiently armed and accoutred, and shall provide, and constantly have ready for use, in public stores, a due number of field pieces and tents, and a proper quantity of arms, ammunition and camp equipage.

No State shall engage in any war without the consent of the United States, in Congress assembled, unless such State be actually invaded by enemies, or shall have received certain advice of a resolution being formed by some nation of Indians to invade such State, and the danger is so imminent as not to admit of a delay till the United States, in Congress assembled, can be consulted; nor shall any State grant commissions to any ships or vessels of war, nor letters of marque or reprisal, except it be after a declaration of war by the United States, in Congress assembled, and then only against the kingdom or state, and the subjects thereof, against which war has been so declared, and under such regulations as shall be established by the United States, in Congress assembled, unless such State be infested by pirates, in which case vessels of war may be fitted out for that occasion, and kept so long as the danger shall continue, or until the United States, in Congress assembled, shall determine otherwise.

Article 7

When land forces are raised by any State for the common defence, all officers of or under the rank of colonel, shall be appointed by the legislature of each State respectively, by whom such forces shall be raised, or in such manner as such State shall direct; and all vacancies shall be filled up by the State which first made the appointment.

Article 8

All charges of war and all other expences, that shall be incurred for the common defence or general welfare, and allowed by the United States, in Congress assembled, shall be defrayed out of a common treasury, which shall be supplied by the several states, in proportion to the value of all land within each State, granted to or surveyed for any person, as such land and the buildings and improvements thereon shall be estimated according to such mode as the United States, in Congress assembled, shall, from time to time, direct and appoint.

The taxes for paying that proportion shall be laid and levied by the authority and direction of the legislatures of the several states, within the time agreed upon by the United States, in Congress assembled.

Article 9

The United States, in Congress assembled, shall have the sole and exclusive right and power of determining on peace and war, except in the cases mentioned in the 6th article; of sending and receiving ambassadors; entering into treaties and alliances, provided that no treaty of commerce shall be made, whereby the legislative power of the respective states shall be restrained from imposing such imposts and duties on foreigners as their own people are subjected to, or from prohibiting the exportation or importation of any species of goods or commodities whatsoever; of establishing rules for deciding, in all cases, what captures on land or water shall be legal, and in what manner prizes, taken by land or naval forces in the service of the United States, shall be divided or appropriated; of granting letters of marque and reprisal in times of peace; appointing courts for the trial of piracies and felonies committed on the high seas, and establishing courts for receiving and determining, finally, appeals in all cases of captures; provided, that no member of Congress shall be appointed a judge of any of the said courts.

The United States, in Congress assembled, shall also be the last resort on appeal in all disputes and differences now subsisting, or that hereafter may arise between two or more states concerning boundary, jurisdiction or any other cause whatever; which authority shall always be exercised in the manner following: whenever the legislative or executive authority, or lawful agent of any State, in controversy with another, shall present a petition to Congress, stating the matter in question, and praying for a hearing, notice thereof shall be given, by order of Congress, to the legislative or executive authority of the other State in controversy, and a day assigned for the appearance of the parties by their lawful agents, who shall then be directed to appoint, by joint consent, commissioners or judges to constitute a court for hearing and determining the matter in question; but, if they cannot agree, Congress shall name three persons out of each of the United States, and from the list of such persons each party shall alternately strike out one, the petitioners beginning, until the number shall be reduced to thirteen; and from that number not less than seven, nor more than nine names, as Congress shall direct, shall, in the presence of Congress, be drawn out by lot; and the persons whose names shall be so drawn, or any five of them, shall be commissioners or judges to hear and finally determine the controversy, so always as a major part of the judges who shall hear the cause shall agree in the determination; and if either party shall neglect to attend at the day appointed, without shewing reasons which Congress shall judge sufficient, or, being present, shall refuse to strike, the Congress shall proceed to nominate three persons out of each State, and the secretary of Congress shall strike in behalf of such party absent or refusing; and the judgment and sentence of the court to be appointed, in the manner before prescribed, shall be final and conclusive; and if any of the parties shall refuse to submit to the authority of such court, or to appear or defend their claim or cause, the court shall nevertheless proceed to pronounce sentence or judgment, which shall, in like manner, be final and decisive, the judgment or sentence and other proceedings begin, in either case, transmitted to Congress, and lodged among the acts of Congress for the security of the parties concerned: provided, that every commissioner, before he sits in judgment, shall take an oath, to be administered by one of the judges of the supreme or superior court of the State where the cause shall be tried, "well and truly to hear and determine the matter in question, according to the best of his judgment, without favour, affection, or hope of reward:" provided, also, that no State shall be deprived of territory for the benefit of the United States.

All controversies concerning the private right of soil, claimed under different grants of two or more states, whose jurisdictions, as they may respect such lands and the states which passed such grants, are adjusted, the said grants, or either of them, being at the same time claimed to have originated antecedent to such settlement of jurisdiction, shall, on the petition of either party to the Congress of the United States, be finally determined, as near as may be, in the same manner as is before prescribed for deciding disputes respecting territorial jurisdiction between different states.

The United States, in Congress assembled, shall also have the sole and exclusive right and power of regulating the alloy and value of coin struck by their own authority, or by that of the respective states; fixing the standard of weights and measures throughout the United States; regulating the trade and managing all affairs with the Indians not members of any of the states; provided that the legislative right of any State within its own limits be not infringed or violated; establishing and regulating post offices from one State to another throughout all the United States, and exacting such postage on the papers passing through the same as may be requisite to defray the expences of the said office; appointing all officers of the land forces in the service of the United States, excepting regimental officers; appointing all the officers of the naval forces, and commissioning all officers whatever in the service of the United States; making rules for the government and regulation of the said land and naval forces, and directing their operations.

The United States, in Congress assembled, shall have authority to appoint a committee to sit in the recess of Congress, to be denominated "a Committee of the States," and to consist of one delegate from each State, and to appoint such other committees and civil officers as may be necessary for managing the general affairs of the United States, under their direction; to appoint one of their number to preside; provided that no person be allowed to serve in the office of president more than one year in any term of three years; to ascertain the necessary sums of money to be raised for the service of the United States, and to appropriate and apply the same for defraying the public expences; to borrow money or emit bills on the credit of the United States, transmitting, every half year, to the respective states, an account of the sums of money so borrowed or emitted; to build and equip a navy; to agree upon the number of land forces, and to make requisitions from each State for its quota, in proportion to the number of white inhabitants in such State; which requisitions shall be binding; and thereupon, the legislature of each State shall appoint the regimental officers, raise the men, and cloathe, arm, and equip them in a soldier-like manner, at the expence of the United States; and the officers and men so cloathed, armed, and equipped, shall march to the place appointed and within the time agreed on by the United States, in Congress assembled; but if the United States, in Congress assembled, shall, on consideration of circumstances, judge proper that any State should not raise men, or should raise a smaller number than its quota, and that any other State should raise a greater number of men than the quota thereof, such extra number shall be raised, officered, cloathed, armed, and equipped in the same manner as the quota of such State, unless the legislature of such State shall judge that such extra number cannot be safely spared out of the same, in which case they shall raise, officer, cloathe, arm, and equip as many of such extra number as they judge can be safely spared. And the officers and men so cloathed, armed, and equipped, shall march to the place appointed and within the time agreed on by the United States, in Congress assembled.

The United States, in Congress assembled, shall never engage in a war, nor grant letters of marque and reprisal in time of peace, nor enter into any treaties or alliances, nor coin money, nor regulate the value thereof, nor ascertain the sums and expences necessary for the defence and welfare of the United States, or any of them: nor emit bills, nor borrow money on the credit of the United States, nor appropriate money, nor agree upon the number of vessels of war to be built or purchased, or the number of land or sea forces to be raised, nor appoint a commander in chief of the army or navy, unless nine states assent to the same; nor shall a question on any other point, except for adjourning from day to day, be determined, unless by the votes of a majority of the United States, in Congress assembled.

The Congress of the United States shall have power to adjourn to any time within the year, and to any place within the United States, so that no period of adjournment be for a longer duration than the space of six months, and shall publish the journal of their proceedings monthly, except such parts thereof, relating to treaties, alliances or military operations, as, in their judgment, require secrecy; and the yeas and nays of the delegates of each State on any question shall be entered on the journal, when it is desired by any delegate; and the delegates of a State, or any of them, at his, or their request, shall be furnished with a transcript of the said journal, except such parts as are above excepted, to lay before the legislatures of the several states.

Article 10

The committee of the states, or any nine of them, shall be authorized to execute, in the recess of Congress, such of the powers of Congress as the United States, in Congress assembled, by the consent of nine states, shall, from time to time, think expedient to vest them with; provided, that no power be delegated to the said committee, for the exercise of which, by the articles of confederation, the voice of nine states, in the Congress of the United States assembled, is requisite.

Article 11

Canada acceding to this confederation, and joining in the measures of the United States, shall be admitted into and entitled to all the advantages of this union; but no other colony shall be admitted into the same, unless such admission be agreed to by nine states.

The Constitution of the United States of America

**Agreed to by Philadelphia Convention,
September 17, 1787
Implemented March 4, 1789**

We the People of the United States, in Order to form a more perfect Union, establish Justice, insure domestic Tranquility, provide for the common defence, promote the general Welfare, and secure the Blessings of Liberty to ourselves and our Posterity, do ordain and establish this Constitution for the United States of America.

Article I

Section 1. All legislative Powers herein granted shall be vested in a Congress of the United States, which shall consist of a Senate and a House of Representatives.

Section 2. The House of Representatives shall be composed of Members chosen every second Year by the People of the several States, and the Electors in each State shall have the Qualifications requisite for Electors of the most numerous Branch of the State Legislature.

No Person shall be a Representative who shall not have attained to the Age of twenty-five Years, and been seven Years a Citizen of the United States, and who shall not, when elected, be an Inhabitant of that State in which he shall be chosen.

Representatives and direct Taxes shall be apportioned among the several States which may be included within this Union, according to their respective Numbers, *which shall be determined by adding to the whole Number of free Persons, including those bound to Service for a Term of Years, and excluding Indians not taxed, three fifths of all other Persons.** The actual Enumeration shall be made within three Years after the first Meeting of the Congress of the United States, and within every subsequent Term of ten Years, in such Manner as they shall by Law direct. The Number of Representatives shall not exceed one for every thirty Thousand, but each State shall have at Least one Representative; and *until such enumeration shall be made, the State of New Hampshire shall be entitled to chuse three, Massachusetts eight, Rhode Island and Providence Plantations one, Connecticut five, New York six, New Jersey four, Pennsylvania eight, Delaware one, Maryland six, Virginia ten, North Carolina five, South Carolina five, and Georgia three.*

When vacancies happen in the Representation from any State, the Executive Authority thereof shall issue Writs of Election to fill such Vacancies.

The House of Representatives shall chuse their Speaker and other Officers; and shall have the sole Power of Impeachment.

Section 3. The Senate of the United States shall be composed of two Senators from each State, *chosen by the Legislature thereof,*[†] for six Years; and each Senator shall have one Vote.

Immediately after they shall be assembled in Consequence of the first Election, they shall be divided as equally as may be into three Classes. The Seats of the Senators of the first Class shall be vacated at the Expiration of the second Year, of the second Class at the Expiration of the fourth Year, and of the third Class at the Expiration of the sixth Year, so that one-third may be chosen every second Year; and if Vacancies happen by Resignation, or otherwise, during the Recess of the Legislature of any State, the Executive thereof may make temporary Appointments until the next Meeting of the Legislature, which shall then fill such Vacancies.[‡]

No person shall be a Senator who shall not have attained to the Age of thirty Years, and been nine Years a Citizen of the United States, and who shall not, when elected, be an Inhabitant of that State for which he shall be chosen.

The Vice President of the United States shall be President of the Senate, but shall have no Vote, unless they be equally divided.

The Senate shall chuse their other Officers, and also a President pro tempore, in the absence of the Vice President, or when he shall exercise the Office of President of the United States.

The Senate shall have the sole Power to try all Impeachments. When sitting for that Purpose, they shall be on Oath or Affirmation. When the President of the United States is tried, the Chief Justice shall preside: And no Person shall be convicted without the Concurrence of two-thirds of the Members present.

Note: The Constitution became effective March 4, 1789. Provisions in italics are no longer relevant or have been changed by constitutional amendment.

*Changed by Section 2 of the Fourteenth Amendment.

[†]Changed by Section 1 of the Seventeenth Amendment.
[‡]Changed by Section 2 of the Seventeenth Amendment.

Judgment in Cases of Impeachment shall not extend further than to removal from Office, and disqualification to hold and enjoy any Office of honor, Trust or Profit under the United States: but the Party convicted shall nevertheless be liable and subject to Indictment, Trial, Judgment and Punishment, according to Law.

Section 4. The Times, Places and Manner of holding Elections for Senators and Representatives, shall be prescribed in each State by the Legislature thereof; but the Congress may at any time by Law make or alter such Regulations, except as to the Places of Chusing Senators.

The Congress shall assemble at least once in every Year, and such Meeting *shall be on the first Monday in December, unless they shall by Law appoint a different Day.**

Section 5. Each House shall be the Judge of the Elections, Returns and Qualifications of its own Members, and a Majority of each shall constitute a Quorum to do Business; but a smaller number may adjourn from day to day, and may be authorized to compel the Attendance of absent Members, in such Manner, and under such Penalties, as each House may provide.

Each House may determine the Rules of its Proceedings, punish its Members for disorderly Behavior, and, with the Concurrence of two-thirds, expel a Member.

Each House shall keep a Journal of its Proceedings, and from time to time publish the same, excepting such Parts as may in their Judgment require Secrecy; and the Yeas and Nays of the Members of either House on any question shall, at the Desire of one-fifth of those Present, be entered on the Journal.

Neither House, during the Session of Congress, shall, without the Consent of the other, adjourn for more than three days, nor to any other Place than that in which the two Houses shall be sitting.

Section 6. The Senators and Representatives shall receive a Compensation for their Services, to be ascertained by Law, and paid out of the Treasury of the United States. They shall in all Cases, except Treason, Felony and Breach of the Peace, be privileged from Arrest during their Attendance at the Session of their respective Houses, and in going to and returning from the same; and for any Speech or Debate in either House, they shall not be questioned in any other Place.

No Senator or Representative shall, during the Time for which he was elected, be appointed to any civil Office under the Authority of the United States, which shall have been created, or the Emoluments whereof shall have been increased, during such time; and no Person holding any Office under the United States, shall be a Member of either House during his Continuance in Office.

---

*Changed by Section 2 of the Twentieth Amendment.

Section 7. All Bills for raising Revenue shall originate in the House of Representatives; but the Senate may propose or concur with Amendments as on other Bills.

Every Bill which shall have passed the House of Representatives and the Senate, shall, before it becomes a Law, be presented to the President of the United States; If he approve he shall sign it, but if not he shall return it, with his Objections to that House in which it shall have originated, who shall enter the Objections at large on their Journal, and proceed to reconsider it. If after such Reconsideration two-thirds of that House shall agree to pass the Bill, it shall be sent, together with the Objections, to the other House, by which it shall likewise be reconsidered, and if approved by two-thirds of that House, it shall become a Law. But in all such Cases the Votes of both Houses shall be determined by Yeas and Nays, and the Names of the Persons voting for and against the Bill shall be entered on the Journal of each House respectively. If any Bill shall not be returned by the President within ten Days (Sundays excepted) after it shall have been presented to him, the Same shall be a Law, in like Manner as if he had signed it, unless the Congress by their Adjournment prevent its Return, in which Case it shall not be a Law.

Every Order, Resolution, or Vote to which the Concurrence of the Senate and the House of Representatives may be necessary (except on a question of Adjournment) shall be presented to the President of the United States; and before the Same shall take Effect, shall be approved by him, or being disapproved by him, shall be repassed by two-thirds of the Senate and House of Representatives, according to the Rules and Limitations prescribed in the Case of a Bill.

Section 8. The Congress shall have Power To lay and collect Taxes, Duties, Imposts and Excises, to pay the Debts and provide for the common Defence and general Welfare of the United States; but all Duties, Imposts and Excises shall be uniform throughout the United States;

To borrow money on the credit of the United States;

To regulate Commerce with foreign Nations, and among the several States, and with the Indian Tribes;

To establish an uniform Rule of Naturalization, and uniform Laws on the subject of Bankruptcies throughout the United States;

To coin Money, regulate the Value thereof, and of foreign Coin, and fix the Standard of Weights and Measures;

To provide for the Punishment of counterfeiting the Securities and current Coin of the United States;

To establish Post Offices and post Roads;

To promote the Progress of Science and useful Arts, by securing for limited Times to Authors and Inventors the exclusive Right to their respective Writings and Discoveries;

To constitute Tribunals inferior to the supreme Court;

To define and punish Piracies and Felonies committed on the high Seas, and Offenses against the Law of Nations;

To declare War, grant Letters of Marque and Reprisal, and make Rules concerning Captures on Land and Water;

To raise and support Armies, but no Appropriation of Money to that Use shall be for a longer Term than two Years;

To provide and maintain a Navy;

To make Rules for the Government and Regulation of the land and naval Forces;

To provide for calling forth the Militia to execute the Laws of the Union, suppress Insurrections and repel Invasions;

To provide for organizing, arming, and disciplining the Militia, and for governing such Part of them as may be employed in the Service of the United States, reserving to the States respectively, the Appointment of the Officers, and the Authority of training the Militia according to the discipline prescribed by Congress;

To exercise exclusive Legislation in all Cases whatsoever, over such District (not exceeding ten Miles square) as may, by Cession of particular States, and the acceptance of Congress, become the Seat of Government of the United States, and to exercise like Authority over all Places purchased by the Consent of the Legislature of the State in which the Same shall be, for the Erection of Forts, Magazines, Arsenals, dock-Yards, and other needful Buildings;—And

To make all Laws which shall be necessary and proper for carrying into Execution the foregoing Powers, and all other Powers vested by this Constitution in the Government of the United States, or in any Department or Officer thereof.

Section 9. The Migration or Importation of such Persons as any of the States now existing shall think proper to admit, shall not be prohibited by the Congress prior to the Year one thousand eight hundred and eight but a tax or duty may be imposed on such Importation, not exceeding ten dollars for each Person.

The privilege of the Writ of Habeas Corpus shall not be suspended, unless when in Cases of Rebellion or Invasion the public Safety may require it.

No Bill of Attainder or ex post facto Law shall be passed.

No capitation, or other direct, Tax shall be laid, unless in Proportion to the Census or Enumeration herein before directed to be taken.*

No Tax or Duty shall be laid on Articles exported from any State.

No Preference shall be given by any Regulation of Commerce or Revenue to the Ports of one State over those of another: nor shall Vessels bound to, or from, one State, be obliged to enter, clear, or pay Duties in another.

No Money shall be drawn from the Treasury, but in Consequence of Appropriations made by law; and a regular Statement and Account of the Receipts and Expenditures of all public Money shall be published from time to time.

No Title of Nobility shall be granted by the United States: And no Person holding any Office of Profit or Trust under them, shall, without the Consent of the Congress, accept of any present, Emolument, Office, or Title, of any kind whatever, from any King, Prince, or foreign State.

---

*Changed by the Sixteenth Amendment.

Section 10. No State shall enter into any Treaty, Alliance, or Confederation; grant Letters of Marque and Reprisal; coin Money; emit Bills of Credit; make any Thing but gold and silver Coin a Tender in Payment of Debts; pass any Bill of Attainder, ex post facto Law, or Law impairing the Obligation of Contracts, or grant any Title of Nobility.

No State shall, without the Consent of the Congress, lay any Imposts or Duties on Imports or Exports, except what may be absolutely necessary for executing its inspection Laws: and the net Produce of all Duties and Imposts, laid by any State on Imports or Exports, shall be for the Use of the Treasury of the United States; and all such Laws shall be subject to the Revision and Control of the Congress.

No State shall, without the Consent of the Congress, lay any duty of Tonnage, keep Troops, or Ships of War in time of Peace, enter into any Agreement or Compact with another State, or with a foreign Power, or engage in War, unless actually invaded, or in such imminent Danger as will not admit of delay.

Article II

Section 1. The executive Power shall be vested in a President of the United States of America. He shall hold his Office during the Term of four Years, and, together with the Vice President, chosen for the same Term, be elected, as follows:

Each State shall appoint, in such Manner as the Legislature thereof may direct, a Number of Electors, equal to the whole Number of Senators and Representatives to which the State may be entitled in the Congress; but no Senator or Representative, or Person holding an Office of Trust or Profit under the United States, shall be appointed an Elector.

The Electors shall meet in their respective States, and vote by Ballot for two Persons, of whom one at least shall not be an Inhabitant of the same State with themselves. And they shall make a List of all the Persons voted for, and of the Number of Votes for each; which List they shall sign and certify, and transmit sealed to the Seat of the Government of the United States, directed to the President of the Senate. The President of the Senate shall, in the Presence of the Senate and House of Representatives, open all the Certificates, and the Votes shall then be counted. The Person having the greatest Number of Votes shall be the President, if such Number be a Majority of the whole Number of Electors appointed; and if there be more than one who have such Majority, and have an equal Number of Votes, then the House of Representatives shall immediately chuse by Ballot one of them for President; and if no Person have a Majority, then from the five highest on the List the said House shall in like Manner chuse the President. But in chusing the President, the Votes shall be taken by States, the Representation from each State having one Vote; a quorum for this Purpose shall consist of a Member or Members from two thirds of the States, and a Majority of all the States shall be necessary to a Choice. In every Case, after the Choice of the President, the Person having the greatest Number of Votes of the

Electors shall be the Vice President. But if there should remain two or more who have equal Votes, the Senate shall chuse from them by Ballot the Vice President.*

The Congress may determine the Time of chusing the Electors, and the Day on which they shall give their Votes; which Day shall be the same throughout the United States.

No Person except a natural born Citizen, or a Citizen of the United States, at the time of the Adoption of this Constitution, shall be eligible to the Office of President; neither shall any Person be eligible to that Office who shall not have attained to the Age of thirty five Years, and been fourteen Years a Resident within the United States.

In Case of the Removal of the President from Office, or of his Death, Resignation, or Inability to discharge the Powers and Duties of the said Office, the same shall devolve on the Vice President, *and the Congress may by Law provide for the Case of Removal, Death, Resignation, or Inability, both of the President and Vice President, declaring what Officer shall then act as President, and such Officer shall act accordingly, until the Disability be removed, or a President shall be elected.*†

The President shall, at stated Times, receive for his Services a Compensation, which shall neither be increased nor diminished during the Period for which he shall have been elected, and he shall not receive within that Period any other Emolument from the United States, or any of them.

Before he enter on the Execution of his Office, he shall take the following Oath or Affirmation:—"I do solemnly swear (or affirm) that I will faithfully execute the Office of President of the United States, and will to the best of my Ability, preserve, protect and defend the Constitution of the United States."

Section 2. The President shall be Commander in Chief of the Army and Navy of the United States, and of the Militia of the several States, when called into the actual Service of the United States; he may require the Opinion, in writing, of the principal Officer in each of the executive Departments, upon any Subject relating to the Duties of their respective Offices, and he shall have Power to Grant Reprieves and Pardons for Offences against the United States, except in Cases of Impeachment.

He shall have Power, by and with the Advice and Consent of the Senate, to make Treaties, provided two thirds of the Senators present concur; and he shall nominate, and by and with the Advice and Consent of the Senate, shall appoint Ambassadors, other public Ministers and Consuls, Judges of the supreme Court, and all other Officers of the United States, whose Appointments are not herein otherwise provided for, and which shall be established by Law: but the Congress may by Law vest the Appointment of such inferior Officers, as they think proper, in the President alone, in the Courts of Law, or in the Heads of Departments.

The President shall have Power to fill up all Vacancies that may happen during the Recess of the Senate, by granting Commissions which shall expire at the End of their next Session.

Section 3. He shall from time to time give to the Congress Information of the State of the Union, and recommend to their Consideration such Measures as he shall judge necessary and expedient; he may, on extraordinary Occasions, convene both Houses, or either of them, and in Case of Disagreement between them, with Respect to the Time of Adjournment, he may adjourn them to such Time as he shall think proper; he shall receive Ambassadors and other public Ministers; he shall take Care that the Laws be faithfully executed, and shall Commission all the Officers of the United States.

Section 4. The President, Vice President and all civil Officers of the United States, shall be removed from Office on Impeachment for, and Conviction of, Treason, Bribery, or other high Crimes and Misdemeanors.

Article III

Section 1. The judicial Power of the United States, shall be vested in one supreme Court, and in such inferior Courts as the Congress may from time to time ordain and establish. The Judges, both of the supreme and inferior Courts, shall hold their Offices during good Behaviour, and shall, at stated Times, receive for their Services a Compensation, which shall not be diminished during their Continuance in Office.

Section 2. The judicial Power shall extend to all Cases, in Law and Equity, arising under this Constitution, the Laws of the United States, and Treaties made, or which shall be made, under their Authority;—to all Cases affecting Ambassadors, other public Ministers and Consuls;—to all Cases of admiralty and maritime Jurisdiction;—to Controversies to which the United States shall be a Party;—to Controversies between two or more States;—*between a State and Citizens of another State;*‡—between Citizens of different States;—between Citizens of the same State claiming Lands under Grants of different States, and between a State, or the Citizens thereof, and foreign States, Citizens or Subjects.

In all Cases affecting Ambassadors, other public Ministers and Consuls, and those in which a State shall be Party, the supreme Court shall have original Jurisdiction. In all the other Cases before mentioned, the supreme Court shall have appellate Jurisdiction, both as to Law and Fact, with such Exceptions, and under such Regulations as the Congress shall make.

---

*Superseded by the Twelfth Amendment.
†Modified by the Twenty-fifth Amendment.

‡Restricted by the Eleventh Amendment.

The trial of all Crimes, except in Cases of Impeachment, shall be by Jury; and such Trial shall be held in the State where said Crimes shall have been committed; but when not committed within any State, the Trial shall be at such Place or Places as the Congress may by Law have directed.

Section 3. Treason against the United States, shall consist only in levying War against them, or in adhering to their Enemies, giving them Aid and Comfort. No Person shall be convicted of Treason unless on the Testimony of two Witnesses to the same overt Act, or on Confession in open Court.

The Congress shall have Power to declare the Punishment of Treason, but no Attainder of Treason shall work Corruption of Blood, or Forfeiture except during the Life of the Person attainted.

Article IV

Section 1. Full Faith and Credit shall be given in each State to the public Acts, Records, and judicial Proceedings of every other State. And the Congress may by general Laws prescribe the Manner in which such Acts, Records, and Proceedings shall be proved, and the Effect thereof.

Section 2. The Citizens of each State shall be entitled to all Privileges and Immunities of Citizens in the several States.

A Person charged in any State with Treason, Felony, or other Crime, who shall flee from Justice, and be found in another State, shall on demand of the executive Authority of the State from which he fled, be delivered up, to be removed to the State having Jurisdiction of the Crime.

*No Person held to Service or Labour in one State, under the Laws thereof, escaping into another, shall, in Consequence of any Law or Regulation therein, be discharged from such Service or Labour, but shall be delivered up on Claim of the Party to whom such Service or Labour may be due.**

Section 3. New States may be admitted by the Congress into this Union; but no new State shall be formed or erected within the Jurisdiction of any other State; nor any State be formed by the Junction of two or more States, or parts of States, without the Consent of the Legislatures of the States concerned as well as of the Congress.

The Congress shall have Power to dispose of and make all needful Rules and Regulations respecting the Territory or other Property belonging to the United States; and nothing in this Constitution shall be so construed as to Prejudice any Claims of the United States, or of any particular State.

Section 4. The United States shall guarantee to every State in this Union a Republican Form of Government, and shall protect each of them against Invasion; and on Application of the Legislature, or of the Executive (when the Legislature cannot be convened) against domestic Violence.

Article V

The Congress, whenever two-thirds of both Houses shall deem it necessary, shall propose Amendments to this Constitution, or, on the Application of the Legislatures of two-thirds of the several States, shall call a Convention for proposing Amendments, which, in either Case, shall be valid to all Intents and Purposes, as Part of this Constitution, when ratified by the Legislatures of three-fourths of the several States, or by Conventions in three-fourths thereof, as the one or the other Mode of Ratification may be proposed by the Congress; Provided that no Amendment which may be made prior to the Year One thousand eight hundred and eight shall in any Manner affect the first and fourth Clauses in the Ninth Section of the first Article; and that no State, without its Consent, shall be deprived of its equal Suffrage in the Senate.

Article VI

All Debts contracted and Engagements entered into, before the Adoption of this Constitution, shall be as valid against the United States under this Constitution, as under the Confederation.

This Constitution, and the Laws of the United States which shall be made in Pursuance thereof; and all Treaties made, or which shall be made, under the Authority of the United States, shall be the supreme Law of the Land; and the Judges in every State shall be bound thereby, any Thing in the Constitution or Laws of any State to the Contrary notwithstanding.

The Senators and Representatives before mentioned, and the Members of the several State Legislatures, and all executive and judicial Officers, both of the United States and of the several States, shall be bound by Oath or Affirmation, to support this Constitution; but no religious Test shall ever be required as a Qualification to any Office or public Trust under the United States.

Article VII

The Ratification of the Conventions of nine States shall be sufficient for the Establishment of this Constitution between the States so ratifying the Same.

Done in Convention by the Unanimous Consent of the States present the Seventeenth Day of September in the Year of our Lord one thousand seven hundred and Eighty seven and of the Independence of the United States of America the Twelfth. In Witness whereof We have hereunto subscribed our Names.

---

*Superseded by the Thirteenth Amendment.

Go. Washington
President and deputy from Virginia

New Hampshire
John Langdon
Nicholas Gilman

Massachusetts
Nathaniel Gorham
Rufus King

Connecticut
Wm. Saml. Johnson
Roger Sherman

New York
Alexander Hamilton

New Jersey
Wil. Livingston
David Brearley
Wm. Paterson
Jona. Dayton

Pennsylvania
B. Franklin
Thomas Mifflin
Robt. Morris
Geo. Clymer
Thos. FitzSimons
Jared Ingersoll
James Wilson
Gouv. Morris

Delaware
Geo. Read
Gunning Bedford jun
John Dickinson
Richard Bassett
Jaco. Broom

Maryland
James McHenry
Dan. of St. Thos. Jenifer
Danl. Carroll

Virginia
John Blair
James Madison, Jr.

North Carolina
Wm. Blount
Richd. Dobbs Spaight
Hu Williamson

South Carolina
J. Rutledge
Charles Cotesworth Pinckney
Pierce Butler

Georgia
William Few
Abr. Baldwin

Amendments to the Constitution with Annotations (Including the Six Unratified Amendments)

In their effort to gain Antifederalists' support for the Constitution, Federalists frequently pointed to the inclusion of Article 5, which provides an orderly method of amending the Constitution. In contrast, the Articles of Confederation, which were universally recognized as seriously flawed, offered no means of amendment. For their part, Antifederalists argued that the amendment process was so "intricate" that one might as easily roll "sixes an hundred times in succession" as change the Constitution.

The system for amendment laid out in the Constitution requires that two-thirds of both houses of Congress agree to a proposed amendment, which must then be ratified by three-quarters of the legislatures of the states. Alternatively, an amendment may be proposed by a convention called by the legislatures of two-thirds of the states. Since 1789, members of Congress have proposed thousands of amendments. Besides the seventeen amendments added since 1791, only the six "unratified" ones included here were approved by two-thirds of both houses but not ratified by the states.

Among the many amendments that never made it out of Congress have been proposals to declare dueling, divorce, and interracial marriage unconstitutional as well as proposals to establish a national university, to acknowledge the sovereignty of Jesus Christ, and to prohibit any person from possessing wealth in excess of $10 million.*

Among the issues facing Americans today that might lead to constitutional amendment are efforts to balance the federal budget, to limit the number of terms elected officials may serve, to limit access to or prohibit abortion, to establish English as the official language of the United States, and to prohibit flag burning. None of these proposed amendments has yet garnered enough support in Congress to be sent to the states for ratification.

Although the first ten amendments to the Constitution are commonly known as the Bill of Rights, only Amendments 1 through 8 provide guarantees of individual rights. Amendments 9 and 10 deal with the structure of power within the constitutional system. The Bill of Rights was promised to appease Antifederalists who refused to ratify the Constitution without guarantees of individual liberties and limitations to federal power. After studying more than two hundred amendments recommended by the ratifying conventions of the states, Federalist James Madison presented a list of seventeen to Congress, which used Madison's list as the foundation for the twelve amendments that were sent to the states for ratification. Ten of the twelve were adopted in 1791. The first on the list of twelve, known as the Reapportionment Amendment, was never adopted (p. D-16). The second proposed amendment was adopted in 1992 as Amendment 27 (p. D-24).

Amendment I [1791]†

Congress shall make no law respecting an establishment of religion, or prohibiting the free exercise thereof; or abridging the freedom of speech, or of the press; or the right of the people peaceably to assemble, and to petition the Government for a redress of grievances.

• • •

The First Amendment is a potent symbol for many Americans. Most are well aware of their rights to free speech, freedom of the press, and freedom of religion and their rights to assemble and to petition, even if they cannot cite the exact words of this amendment.

The First Amendment guarantee of freedom of religion has two clauses: the "free exercise clause," which allows individuals to practice or not practice any religion, and the "establishment clause," which prevents the federal government from discriminating against or favoring any particular religion. This clause was designed to create what Thomas Jefferson referred to as "a wall of separation between church and state." In the 1960s the Supreme Court ruled that the First Amendment prohibits prayer and Bible reading in public schools.

Although the rights to free speech and freedom of the press are established in the First Amendment, it was not until the twentieth century that the Supreme Court began to explore the full meaning of these guarantees. In 1919 the Court ruled in Schenck v. United States that the government could suppress free expression only where it could cite a "clear and present danger." In a decision that continues to raise controversies, the Court ruled in 1990, in Texas v. Johnson, that flag burning is a form of symbolic speech protected by the First Amendment.

---

*Richard B. Bernstein, *Amending America* (New York: Times Books, 1993), 177–81.

---

†The dates in brackets indicate when the amendment was ratified.

Amendment II [1791]

A well regulated Militia, being necessary to the security of a free State, the right of the people to keep and bear Arms shall not be infringed.

. . .

Fear of a standing army under the control of a hostile government made the Second Amendment an important part of the Bill of Rights. Advocates of gun ownership claim that the amendment prevents the government from regulating firearms. Proponents of gun control argue that the amendment is designed only to protect the right of the states to maintain militia units.

In 1939 the Supreme Court ruled in United States v. Miller *that the Second Amendment did not protect the right of an individual to own a sawed-off shotgun, which it argued was not ordinary militia equipment. Since then, the Supreme Court has refused to hear Second Amendment cases, whereas lower courts have upheld firearm regulations. Several justices currently on the bench seem to favor a broader interpretation of the Second Amendment, which would affect gun-control legislation. The controversy over the impact of the Second Amendment on gun owners and gun-control legislation will certainly continue.*

Amendment III [1791]

No Soldier shall, in time of peace, be quartered in any house, without the consent of the Owner, nor in time of war, but in a manner to be prescribed by law.

. . .

The Third Amendment was extremely important to the framers of the Constitution, but today it is nearly forgotten. American colonists were especially outraged that they were forced to quarter British troops in the years before and during the American Revolution. The philosophy of the Third Amendment has been viewed by some justices and scholars as the foundation of the modern constitutional right to privacy.

Amendment IV [1791]

The right of the people to be secure in their persons, houses, papers, and effects, against unreasonable searches and seizures, shall not be violated, and no Warrants shall issue, but upon probable cause, supported by Oath or affirmation, and particularly describing the place to be searched, and the persons or things to be seized.

. . .

In the years before the Revolution, the houses, barns, stores, and warehouses of American colonists were ransacked by British authorities under "writs of assistance" or general warrants. The British, thus empowered, searched for seditious material or smuggled goods that could then be used as evidence against colonists who were charged with a crime only after the items were found.

The first part of the Fourth Amendment protects citizens from "unreasonable" searches and seizures. The Supreme Court has interpreted this protection as well as the words search and seizure *in different ways at different times. At one time, the Court did not recognize electronic eavesdropping as a form of search and seizure, although it does today. At times, an "unreasonable" search has been almost any search carried out without a warrant, but in the two decades before 1969 the Court sometimes sanctioned warrantless searches that it considered reasonable based on "the total atmosphere of the case."*

The second part of the Fourth Amendment defines the procedure for issuing a search warrant and states the requirement of "probable cause," which is generally viewed as evidence indicating that a suspect has committed an offense.

In Weeks v. U.S. *(1994) and* Mapp v. Ohio *(1962), the Court excluded evidence seized in violation of constitutional standards. The justification is that excluding such evidence deters violations of the amendment, but doing so may allow a guilty person to escape punishment.*

Amendment V [1791]

No person shall be held to answer for a capital or otherwise infamous crime, unless on a presentment or indictment of a Grand Jury, except in cases arising in the land or naval forces, or in the Militia, when in actual service in time of War or public danger; nor shall any person be subject for the same offence to be twice put in jeopardy of life or limb; nor shall be compelled in any criminal case to be a witness against himself, nor be deprived of life, liberty, or property, without due process of law; nor shall private property be taken for public use, without just compensation.

. . .

The Fifth Amendment protects people against government authority in the prosecution of criminal offenses. It prohibits the state, first, from charging a person with a serious crime without a grand-jury hearing to decide whether there is sufficient evidence to support the charge and, second, from charging a person with the same crime twice. The best-known aspect of the Fifth Amendment is that it prevents a person from being "compelled . . . to be a witness against himself." The last clause, the "takings clause," limits the power of the government to seize property.

Although invoking the Fifth Amendment is popularly viewed as a confession of guilt, a person may be innocent yet still fear prosecution. For example, during the cold war era of the late 1940s and 1950s, many people who had participated in legal activities that were associated with the Communist Party claimed the Fifth Amendment privilege rather than testify before the House Un-American Activities Committee because the mood of the times cast those activities in a negative light. Because "taking the Fifth" was viewed as an admission of guilt, those people often lost their jobs or became unemployable. Nonetheless, the right to protect oneself against self-incrimination plays an important role in guarding against the collective power of the state.

Amendment VI [1791]

In all criminal prosecutions, the accused shall enjoy the right to a speedy and public trial, by an impartial jury of the State and district wherein the crime shall have been committed, which district shall have been previously ascertained by law, and to be informed of the nature and cause of the accusation; to be confronted with the witnesses against him; to have compulsory process for obtaining witnesses in his favor, and to have the Assistance of Counsel for his defence.

. . .

The original Constitution put few limits on the government's power to investigate, prosecute, and punish crime. This process was of great concern to many Antifederalists, and of the twenty-eight rights specified in the first eight amendments, fifteen have to do with it. Seven rights are specified in the Sixth Amendment. These include the right to a speedy trial, a public trial, a jury trial, a notice of accusation, confrontation of opposing witnesses, testimony by favorable witnesses, and the assistance of counsel.

Amendment VII [1791]

In suits at common law, where the value in controversy shall exceed twenty dollars, the right of trial by jury shall be preserved, and no fact tried by a jury, shall be otherwise reexamined in any Court of the United States, than according to the Rules of the common law.

. . .

This amendment guarantees people the same right to a trial by jury as was guaranteed by English common law in 1791. Under common law, in civil trials (those involving money damages) the role of the judge was to settle questions of law and that of the jury was to settle questions of fact. The amendment does not specify the size of the jury or its role in a trial, however. The Supreme Court has generally held that those issues be determined by English common law of 1791, which stated that a jury consists of twelve people, that a trial must be conducted before a judge who instructs the jury on the law and advises it on facts, and that a verdict must be unanimous.

Amendment VIII [1791]

Excessive bail shall not be required, nor excessive fines imposed, nor cruel and unusual punishments inflicted.

. . .

The language used to guarantee the three rights in this amendment was inspired by the English Bill of Rights of 1689. The Supreme Court has not had a lot to say about "excessive fines." In recent years it has agreed that despite the provision against "excessive bail," persons who are believed to be dangerous to others can be held without bail even before they have been convicted.

Although opponents of the death penalty have not succeeded in using the Eighth Amendment to achieve the end of capital punishment, the clause regarding "cruel and unusual punishments" has been used to prohibit capital punishment in certain cases, such as minors and the mentally retarded.

Amendment IX [1791]

The enumeration in the Constitution, of certain rights, shall not be construed to deny or disparage others retained by the people.

. . .

Some Federalists feared that inclusion of the Bill of Rights in the Constitution would allow later generations of interpreters to claim that the people had surrendered all rights not specifically enumerated there. To guard against this, James Madison added language that became the Ninth Amendment. Interest in this heretofore largely ignored amendment revived in 1965 when it was used in a concurring opinion in Griswold v. Connecticut (1965). While Justice William O. Douglas called on the Third Amendment to support the right to privacy in deciding that case, Justice Arthur Goldberg, in the concurring opinion, argued that the right to privacy regarding contraception was an unenumerated right that was protected by the Ninth Amendment.

In 1980 the Court ruled that the right of the press to attend a public trial was protected by the Ninth Amendment. Although some scholars argue that modern judges cannot identify the unenumerated rights that the framers were trying to protect, others argue that the Ninth Amendment should be read as providing a constitutional "presumption of liberty" that allows people to act in any way that does not violate the rights of others.

Amendment X [1791]

The powers not delegated to the United States by the Constitution, nor prohibited by it to the States, are reserved to the States respectively, or to the people.

. . .

The Antifederalists were especially eager to see a "reserved powers clause" explicitly guaranteeing the states control over their internal affairs. Not surprisingly, the Tenth Amendment has been a frequent battleground in the struggle over states' rights and federal supremacy. Prior to the Civil War, the Jeffersonian Republican Party and Jacksonian Democrats invoked the Tenth

Amendment to prohibit the federal government from making decisions about whether people in individual states could own slaves. The Tenth Amendment was virtually suspended during Reconstruction following the Civil War. In 1883, however, the Supreme Court declared the Civil Rights Act of 1875 unconstitutional on the grounds that it violated the Tenth Amendment. Business interests also called on the amendment to block efforts at federal regulation.

The Court was inconsistent over the next several decades as it attempted to resolve the tension between the restrictions of the Tenth Amendment and the powers the Constitution granted to Congress to regulate interstate commerce and levy taxes. The Court upheld the Pure Food and Drug Act (1906), the Meat Inspection Acts (1906 and 1907), and the White Slave Traffic Act (1910), all of which affected the states, but it struck down an act prohibiting interstate shipment of goods produced through child labor. Between 1934 and 1935 a number of New Deal programs created by Franklin D. Roosevelt were declared unconstitutional on the grounds that they violated the Tenth Amendment. As Roosevelt appointees changed the composition of the Court, the Tenth Amendment was declared to have no substantive meaning. Generally, the amendment is held to protect the rights of states to regulate internal matters such as local government, education, commerce, labor, and business as well as matters involving families such as marriage, divorce, and inheritance within the state.

Unratified Amendment

Reapportionment Amendment (proposed by Congress September 25, 1789, along with the Bill of Rights)

After the first enumeration required by the first article of the Constitution, there shall be one Representative for every thirty thousand, until the number shall amount to one hundred, after which the proportion shall be so regulated by Congress, that there shall be not less than one hundred Representatives, nor less than one Representative for every forty thousand persons, until the number of Representatives shall amount to two hundred; after which the proportion shall be so regulated by Congress, that there shall not be less than two hundred Representatives, nor more than one Representative for every fifty thousand persons.

• • •

If the Reapportionment Amendment had passed and remained in effect, the House of Representatives today would have more than 7,000 members rather than 435 to reflect the current U.S. population.

Amendment XI [1798]

The Judicial power of the United States shall not be construed to extend to any suit in law or equity, commenced or prosecuted against one of the United States by Citizens of another State, or by Citizens or subjects of any foreign state.

• • •

In 1793 the Supreme Court ruled in favor of Alexander Chisholm, executor of the estate of a deceased South Carolina merchant. Chisholm was suing the state of Georgia because the merchant had never been paid for provisions he had supplied during the Revolution. Many regarded this Court decision as an error that violated the intent of the Constitution.

Antifederalists and many other Americans feared a powerful federal court system because they worried that it would become like the British courts of this period, which were accountable only to the monarch. Furthermore, Chisholm v. Georgia *prompted a series of suits against state governments by creditors and suppliers who had made loans during the war.*

In addition, state legislators and Congress feared that the shaky economies of the new states, as well as the country as a whole, would be destroyed, especially if Loyalists who had fled to other countries sought reimbursement for land and property that had been seized. The day after the Supreme Court announced its decision, a resolution proposing the Eleventh Amendment, which overturned the decision in Chisholm v. Georgia, *was introduced in the U.S. Senate.*

Amendment XII [1804]

The Electors shall meet in their respective States and vote by ballot for President and Vice-President, one of whom, at least, shall not be an inhabitant of the same State with themselves; they shall name in their ballots the person voted for as President, and in distinct ballots the person voted for as Vice-President, and they shall make distinct lists of all persons voted for as President, and of all persons voted for as Vice-President, and of the number of votes for each, which lists they shall sign and certify, and transmit sealed to the seat of government of the United States, directed to the President of the Senate; — the President of the Senate shall, in the presence of the Senate and House of Representatives, open all the certificates and the votes shall then be counted; — The person having the greatest number of votes for President, shall be the President, if such number be a majority of the whole number of Electors appointed; and if no person have such majority, then from the persons having the highest numbers not exceeding three on the list of those voted for as President, the House of Representatives shall choose immediately, by ballot, the President. But in choosing the President, the votes shall be taken by States, the representation from each State having one vote; a quorum for this purpose shall consist of a member or members from two-thirds of the States, and a majority of all the States shall be necessary to a choice. And if the House of Representatives shall not choose a President whenever the right of choice shall devolve upon them, before *the fourth day of March* next following, then the Vice-President shall act as

President, as in the case of the death or other constitutional disability of the President.*— The person having the greatest number of votes as Vice-President, shall be the Vice-President, if such number be a majority of the whole number of Electors appointed; and if no person have a majority, then from the two highest numbers on the list, the Senate shall choose the Vice-President; a quorum for the purpose shall consist of two-thirds of the whole number of Senators, and a majority of the whole number shall be necessary to a choice. But no person constitutionally ineligible to the office of President shall be eligible to that of Vice-President of the United States.

. . .

The framers of the Constitution disliked political parties and assumed that none would ever form. Under the original system, electors chosen by the states would each vote for two candidates. The candidate who won the most votes would become president, and the person who won the second-highest number of votes would become vice president. Rivalries between Federalists and Republicans led to the formation of political parties, however, even before George Washington had left office. In 1796 Federalist John Adams was chosen as president, and his great rival, Thomas Jefferson (whose party was called the Republican Party), became his vice president. In 1800 all the electors cast their two votes as one of two party blocs. Jefferson and his fellow Republican nominee, Aaron Burr, were tied with seventy-three votes each. The contest went to the House of Representatives, which finally elected Jefferson after thirty-six ballots. The Twelfth Amendment prevents these problems by requiring electors to vote separately for the president and vice president.

Unratified Amendment

Titles of Nobility Amendment
(proposed by Congress May 1, 1810)

If any citizen of the United States shall accept, claim, receive or retain any title of nobility or honor or shall, without the consent of Congress, accept and retain any present, pension, office or emolument of any kind whatever, from any emperor, king, prince or foreign power, such person shall cease to be a citizen of the United States, and shall be incapable of holding any office of trust or profit under them, or either of them.

. . .

This amendment would have extended Article I, Section 9, Clause 8 of the Constitution, which prevents the awarding of titles by the United States and the acceptance of such awards from foreign powers without congressional consent. Historians speculate that general nervousness about the power of the Emperor Napoleon, who was at that time extending France's empire throughout Europe, may have prompted the proposal. Though it

fell one vote short of ratification, Congress and the American people thought the proposal had been ratified, and it was included in many nineteenth-century editions of the Constitution.

The Civil War and Reconstruction Amendments (Thirteenth, Fourteenth, and Fifteenth Amendments)

In the four months between the election of Abraham Lincoln and his inauguration, more than two hundred proposed constitutional amendments were presented to Congress as part of a desperate attempt to hold the rapidly dissolving Union together. Most of these were efforts to appease the southern states by protecting the right to own slaves or by disfranchising African Americans through constitutional amendment. None were able to win the votes required from Congress to send them to the states. Ultimately, the Corwin Amendment seemed to be the only hope for preserving the Union by amending the Constitution.

The northern victors in the Civil War tried to restructure the Constitution just as the war had restructured the nation. Yet they were often divided in their goals. Some wanted to end slavery; others hoped for social and economic equality regardless of race; others hoped that extending the power of the ballot box to former slaves would help create a new political order. The debates over the Thirteenth, Fourteenth, and Fifteenth Amendments were bitter. Few of those who fought for these changes were satisfied with the amendments themselves; fewer still were satisfied with their interpretation. Although the amendments put an end to the legal status of slavery, it was nearly a hundred years after the amendments' passage before most of the descendants of former slaves could begin to experience the economic, social, and political equality the amendments were intended to provide.

Unratified Amendment

Corwin Amendment
(proposed by Congress March 2, 1861)

No amendment shall be made to the Constitution which will authorize or give to Congress the power to abolish or interfere, within any State, with the domestic institutions thereof, including that of persons held to labor or service by the laws of said State.

. . .

Following the election of Abraham Lincoln, Congress scrambled to try to prevent the secession of the slaveholding states. House member Thomas Corwin of Ohio proposed the "unamendable" amendment in the hope that by protecting slavery where it existed, Congress would keep the southern states in the Union. Lincoln indicated his support for the proposed amendment in his first inaugural address. Only Ohio and Maryland ratified the Corwin Amendment before the war caused it to be forgotten.

---

*Superseded by Section 3 of the Twentieth Amendment.

Amendment XIII [1865]

Section 1. Neither slavery nor involuntary servitude, except as a punishment for crime whereof the party shall have been duly convicted, shall exist within the United States, or any place subject to their jurisdiction.

Section 2. Congress shall have power to enforce this article by appropriate legislation.

• • •

Because the Emancipation Proclamation of 1863 abolished slavery only in the parts of the Confederacy still in rebellion, Republicans proposed a Thirteenth Amendment that would extend abolition to the entire South. In February 1865, when the proposal was approved by the House, the gallery of the House was newly opened to black Americans who had a chance at last to see their government at work. Passage of the proposal was greeted by wild cheers from the gallery as well as tears on the House floor, where congressional representatives openly embraced one another.

The problem of ratification remained, however. The Union position was that the Confederate states were part of the country of thirty-six states. Therefore, twenty-seven states were needed to ratify the amendment. When Kentucky and Delaware rejected it, backers realized that without approval from at least four former Confederate states, the amendment would fail. Lincoln's successor, President Andrew Johnson, made ratification of the Thirteenth Amendment a condition for southern states to rejoin the Union. Under those terms, all the former Confederate states except Mississippi accepted the Thirteenth Amendment, and by the end of 1865 the amendment had become part of the Constitution and slavery had been prohibited in the United States.

Amendment XIV [1868]

Section 1. All persons born or naturalized in the United States, and subject to the jurisdiction thereof, are citizens of the United States and of the State wherein they reside. No State shall make or enforce any law which shall abridge the privileges or immunities of citizens of the United States; nor shall any State deprive any person of life, liberty, or property, without due process of law; nor deny to any person within its jurisdiction the equal protection of the laws.

Section 2. Representatives shall be apportioned among the several States according to their respective numbers, counting the whole number of persons in each State, excluding Indians not taxed. But when the right to vote at any election for the choice of electors for President and Vice-President of the United States, Representatives in Congress, the Executive and Judicial officers of a State, or the members of the Legislature thereof, is denied to any of the male inhabitants of such State, being twenty-one years of age and citizens of the United States, or in any way abridged, except for participation in rebellion, or other crime, the basis of representation therein shall be reduced in the proportion which the number of such male citizens shall bear to the whole number of male citizens twenty-one years of age in such State.

Section 3. No person shall be a Senator or Representative in Congress, or Elector of President and Vice-President, or hold any office, civil or military, under the United States, or under any State, who, having previously taken an oath, as a member of Congress, or as an officer of the United States, or as a member of any State legislature, or as an executive or judicial officer of any State, to support the Constitution of the United States, shall have engaged in insurrection or rebellion against the same, or given aid or comfort to the enemies thereof. Congress may, by a vote of two-thirds of each house, remove such disability.

Section 4. The validity of the public debt of the United States, authorized by law, including debts incurred for payment of pensions and bounties for services in suppressing insurrection or rebellion, shall not be questioned. But neither the United States nor any State shall assume or pay any debt or obligation incurred in aid of insurrection or rebellion against the United States, or any claim for the loss or emancipation of any slave; but all such debts, obligations, and claims shall be held illegal and void.

Section 5. The Congress shall have power to enforce, by appropriate legislation, the provisions of this article.

• • •

Less than a year after Lincoln's assassination, Andrew Johnson was ready to bring the former Confederate states back into the Union and Confederate leaders back into Congress. Anxious Republicans drafted the Fourteenth Amendment to prevent that from happening. Moreover, most Southern states had enacted "Black Codes" that restricted the legal, political, and civil rights of former slaves. The most important provisions of this complex amendment made all native-born or naturalized persons American citizens and prohibited states from abridging the "privileges or immunities" of citizens; depriving them of "life, liberty, or property, without due process of law"; and denying them "equal protection of the laws." In essence, it made all former slaves citizens and protected the rights of all citizens against violation by their own state governments.

As occurred in the case of the Thirteenth Amendment, former Confederate states were forced to ratify the amendment as a condition of representation in the House and the Senate. The intentions of the Fourteenth Amendment, and how those intentions should be enforced, have been the most debated point of constitutional history. The terms due process *and* equal protection *have been especially troublesome. Was the amendment designed to outlaw racial segregation? Or was the goal simply to prevent the leaders of the rebellious South from gaining political power?*

The framers of the Fourteenth Amendment hoped Section 2 would produce black voters who would increase the power of the Republican Party. The federal government, however, never used its power to punish states for denying blacks their right to vote. Although the Fourteenth Amendment had an immediate impact in giving black Americans citizenship, it did nothing to protect blacks from the vengeance of whites once Reconstruction ended. In the late nineteenth and early twentieth centuries, Section 1 of the Fourteenth Amendment was often used to protect business interests and strike down laws protecting workers on the grounds that the rights of "persons," that is, corporations, were protected by "due process." More recently, the Fourteenth Amendment has been used to justify school desegregation and affirmative action programs, as well as to dismantle such programs.

Amendment XV [1870]

Section 1. The right of citizens of the United States to vote shall not be denied or abridged by the United States or by any State on account of race, color, or previous condition of servitude —

Section 2. The Congress shall have power to enforce this article by appropriate legislation.

• • •

The Fifteenth Amendment was the last major piece of Reconstruction legislation. Although earlier Reconstruction acts had already required black suffrage in the South, the Fifteenth Amendment extended black voting rights to the entire nation. Some Republicans felt morally obligated to do away with the double standard between the North and South because many northern states had stubbornly refused to enfranchise blacks. Others believed that the freedman's ballot required the extra protection of a constitutional amendment to shield it from white counterattack in the South. But partisan advantage also played an important role in the amendment's passage because Republicans hoped that by giving the ballot to blacks, they could lessen their party's political vulnerability.

Many women's rights advocates had fought for the amendment. They had felt betrayed by the inclusion of the word male *in Section 2 of the Fourteenth Amendment and were further angered when the proposed Fifteenth Amendment failed to prohibit denial of the right to vote on the grounds of sex as well as "race, color, or previous condition of servitude." In this amendment, for the first time, the federal government exerted its power to regulate the franchise, or vote. It was also the first time the Constitution placed limits on the power of the states to regulate access to the franchise. Although ratified in 1870, the amendment was not enforced until the twentieth century.*

The Progressive Amendments (Sixteenth– Nineteenth Amendments)

No amendments were added to the Constitution between the Civil War and the Progressive Era. America was changing, however, in fundamental ways. The rapid industrialization of the United States after the Civil War led to many social and economic problems. Hundreds of amendments were proposed, but none received enough support in Congress to be sent to the states. Some scholars believe that regional differences and rivalries were so strong during this period that it was almost impossible to gain a consensus on a constitutional amendment. During the Progressive Era, however, the Constitution was amended four times in seven years.

Amendment XVI [1913]

The Congress shall have power to lay and collect taxes on incomes, from whatever source derived, without apportionment among the several States, and without regard to any census or enumeration.

• • •

Until passage of the Sixteenth Amendment, most of the money used to run the federal government came from customs duties and taxes on specific items, such as liquor. During the Civil War the federal government taxed incomes as an emergency measure. Pressure to enact an income tax came from those who were concerned about the growing gap between rich and poor in the United States. The Populist Party began campaigning for a graduated income tax in 1892, and support continued to grow. By 1909 thirty-three proposed income tax amendments had been presented in Congress, but lobbying by corporate and other special interests had defeated them all. In June 1909 the growing pressure for an income tax, which had been endorsed by presidents Roosevelt and Taft, finally pushed an amendment through the Senate. The required thirty-six states had ratified the amendment by February 1913.

Amendment XVII [1913]

Section 1. The Senate of the United States shall be composed of two Senators from each State, elected by the people thereof, for six years; and each Senator shall have one vote. The electors in each State shall have the qualifications requisite for electors of [voters for] the most numerous branch of the State legislatures.

Section 2. When vacancies happen in the representation of any State in the Senate, the executive authority of such State shall issue writs of election to fill such vacancies: Provided, that the Legislature of any State may empower the executive thereof to make temporary appointments until the people fill the vacancies by election as the Legislature may direct.

Section 3. This amendment shall not be so construed as to affect the election or term of any Senator chosen before it becomes valid as part of the Constitution.

• • •

The framers of the Constitution saw the members of the House as the representatives of the people and the members of the Senate as the representatives of the states. Originally, senators were to be chosen by the state legislators. According to reform advocates, however, the growth of private industry and transportation conglomerates during the late nineteenth century had created a network of corruption in which wealth and power were exchanged for influence and votes in the Senate. Senator Nelson Aldrich, who represented Rhode Island in this period, for example, was known as "the senator from Standard Oil" because of his open support of special business interests.

Efforts to amend the Constitution to allow direct election of senators had begun in 1826, but because any proposal had to be approved by the Senate, reform seemed impossible. Progressives tried to gain influence in the Senate by instituting party caucuses and primary elections, which gave citizens the chance to express their choice of a senator who could then be officially elected by the state legislature. By 1910 fourteen of the country's thirty senators received popular votes through a state primary before the state legislature made its selection. Despairing of getting a proposal through the Senate, supporters of a direct-election amendment had begun in 1893 to seek a convention of representatives from two-thirds of the states to propose an amendment that could then be ratified. By 1905 thirty-one of forty-five states had endorsed such an amendment. Finally, in 1911, despite extraordinary opposition, a proposed amendment passed the Senate; by 1913 it had been ratified.

Amendment XVIII [1919; repealed 1933 by Amendment XXI]

Section 1. After one year from the ratification of this article the manufacture, sale, or transportation of intoxicating liquors within, the importation thereof into, or the exportation thereof from the United States and all territory subject to the jurisdiction thereof, for beverage purposes, is hereby prohibited.

Section 2. The Congress and the several States shall have concurrent power to enforce this article by appropriate legislation.

Section 3. This article shall be inoperative unless it shall have been ratified as an amendment to the Constitution by the legislatures of the several States, as provided by the Constitution, within seven years from the date of the submission thereof to the States by the Congress.

• • •

The Prohibition Party, formed in 1869, began calling for a constitutional amendment to outlaw alcoholic beverages in 1872. A prohibition amendment was first proposed in the Senate in 1876

and was revived eighteen times before 1913. Between 1913 and 1919 another thirty-nine attempts were made to prohibit liquor in the United States through a constitutional amendment. Prohibition became a key element of the Progressive agenda as reformers linked alcohol and drunkenness to numerous social problems, including the corruption of immigrant voters. Whereas opponents of such an amendment argued that it was undemocratic, supporters claimed that their efforts had widespread public support. The admission of twelve "dry" western states to the Union in the early twentieth century and the spirit of sacrifice during World War I laid the groundwork for passage and ratification of the Eighteenth Amendment in 1919. Opponents added a time limit to the amendment in the hope that they could thereby block ratification, but this effort failed. (See also Amendment XXI.)

Amendment XIX [1920]

Section 1. The right of citizens of the United States to vote shall not be denied or abridged by the United States or by any State on account of sex.

Section 2. Congress shall have the power to enforce this article by appropriate legislation.

• • •

Advocates of women's rights tried and failed to link woman suffrage to the Fourteenth and Fifteenth Amendments. Nonetheless, the effort for woman suffrage continued. Between 1878 and 1912 at least one and sometimes as many as four proposed amendments were introduced in Congress each year to grant women the right to vote. Although over time women won very limited voting rights in some states, at both the state and federal levels opposition to an amendment for woman suffrage remained very strong. President Woodrow Wilson and other officials felt that the federal government should not interfere with the power of the states in this matter. And many people were concerned that giving women the vote would result in their abandoning traditional gender roles. In 1919, following a protracted and often bitter campaign of protest in which women went on hunger strikes and chained themselves to fences, an amendment was introduced with the backing of President Wilson. It narrowly passed the Senate (after efforts to limit the suffrage to white women failed) and was adopted in 1920 after Tennessee became the thirty-sixth state to ratify it.

Unratified Amendment

Child Labor Amendment
(proposed by Congress June 2, 1924)

Section 1. The Congress shall have power to limit, regulate, and prohibit the labor of persons under eighteen years of age.

Section 2. The power of the several States is unimpaired by this article except that the operation of State laws shall be suspended to the extent necessary to give effect to legislation enacted by Congress.

. . .

Throughout the late nineteenth and early twentieth centuries, alarm over the condition of child workers grew. Opponents of child labor argued that children worked in dangerous and unhealthy conditions, that they took jobs from adult workers, that they depressed wages in certain industries, and that states that allowed child labor had an economic advantage over those that did not. Defenders of child labor claimed that children provided needed income in many families, that working at a young age helped to develop character, and that the effort to prohibit the practice constituted an invasion of family privacy.

In 1916 Congress passed a law that made it illegal to sell through interstate commerce goods made by children. The Supreme Court, however, ruled that the law violated the limits on the power of Congress to regulate interstate commerce. Congress then tried to penalize industries that used child labor by taxing such goods. This measure was also thrown out by the courts. In response, reformers set out to amend the Constitution. The proposed amendment was ratified by twenty-eight states, but by 1925 thirteen states had rejected it. Passage of the Fair Labor Standards Act in 1938, which was upheld by the Supreme Court in 1941, made the amendment irrelevant.

Amendment XX [1933]

Section 1. The terms of the President and Vice-President shall end at noon on the 20th day of January, and the terms of Senators and Representatives at noon on the 3rd day of January, of the years in which such terms would have ended if this article had not been ratified; and the terms of their successors shall then begin.

Section 2. The Congress shall assemble at least once in every year, and such meeting shall begin at noon on the 3rd day of January, unless they shall by law appoint a different day.

Section 3. If, at the time fixed for the beginning of the term of the President, the President-elect shall have died, the Vice-President-elect shall become President. If a President shall not have been chosen before the time fixed for the beginning of his term, or if the President-elect shall have failed to qualify, then the Vice-President-elect shall act as President until a President shall have qualified; and the Congress may by law provide for the case wherein neither a President-elect nor a Vice-President-elect shall have qualified, declaring who shall then act as President, or the manner in which one who is to act shall be selected, and such person shall act accordingly until a President or Vice-President shall have qualified.

Section 4. The Congress may by law provide for the case of the death of any of the persons from whom the House of Representatives may choose a President whenever the right of choice shall have devolved upon them, and for the case of the death of any of the persons from whom the Senate may choose a Vice-President whenever the right of choice shall have devolved upon them.

Section 5. Sections 1 and 2 shall take effect on the 15th day of October following the ratification of this article.

Section 6. This article shall be inoperative unless it shall have been ratified as an amendment to the Constitution by the Legislatures of three-fourths of the several States within seven years from the date of its submission.

. . .

Until 1933, presidents took office on March 4. Because elections are held in early November and electoral votes are counted in mid-December, this meant that more than three months passed between the time a new president was elected and when he took office. Moving the inauguration to January shortened the transition period and allowed Congress to begin its term closer to the time of the president's inauguration. Although this seems like a minor change, an amendment was required because the Constitution specifies terms of office. This amendment also deals with questions of succession in the event that a president- or vice-president-elect dies before assuming office. Section 3 also clarifies a method for resolving a deadlock in the electoral college.

Amendment XXI [1933]

Section 1. The eighteenth article of amendment to the Constitution of the United States is hereby repealed.

Section 2. The transportation or importation into any State, Territory, or Possession of the United States for delivery or use therein of intoxicating liquors, in violation of the laws thereof, is hereby prohibited.

Section 3. This article shall be inoperative unless it shall have been ratified as an amendment to the Constitution by conventions in the several States, as provided in the Constitution, within seven years from the date of the submission thereof to the States by the Congress.

. . .

Widespread violation of the Volstead Act, the law enacted to enforce prohibition, made the United States a nation of lawbreakers. Prohibition caused more problems than it solved by encouraging crime, bribery, and corruption. Further, a coalition of liquor and beer manufacturers, personal liberty advocates, and constitutional scholars joined forces to challenge the amendment. By 1929 thirty proposed repeal amendments had been introduced in Congress, and the Democratic Party made repeal part of its platform in the 1932 presidential campaign. The Twenty-first Amendment was proposed in February 1933 and ratified less than a year later. The failure of the effort to enforce prohibition through a constitutional amendment has often been cited by opponents of subsequent efforts to shape public virtue and private morality.

Amendment XXII [1951]

Section 1. No person shall be elected to the office of the President more than twice, and no person who has held the office of President, or acted as President, for more than two years of a term to which some other person was elected President shall be elected to the office of President more than once. But this article shall not apply to any person holding the office of President when this Article was proposed by the Congress, and shall not prevent any person who may be holding the office of President, or acting as President, during the term within which this Article becomes operative from holding the office of President or acting as President during the remainder of such term.

Section 2. This article shall be inoperative unless it shall have been ratified as an amendment to the Constitution by the legislatures of three-fourths of the several States within seven years from the date of its submission to the States by the Congress.

• • •

George Washington's refusal to seek a third term of office set a precedent that stood until 1912, when former president Theodore Roosevelt sought, without success, another term as an independent candidate. Democrat Franklin Roosevelt was the only president to seek and win a fourth term, though he did so amid great controversy. Roosevelt died in April 1945, a few months after the beginning of his fourth term. In 1946 Republicans won control of the House and the Senate, and early in 1947 a proposal for an amendment to limit future presidents to two four-year terms was offered to the states for ratification. Democratic critics of the Twenty-second Amendment charged that it was a partisan posthumous jab at Roosevelt.

Since the Twenty-second Amendment was adopted, two of the three presidents who might have been able to seek a third term, had it not existed, were Republicans Dwight Eisenhower and Ronald Reagan. Since 1826, Congress has entertained 160 proposed amendments to limit the president to one six-year term. Such amendments have been backed by fifteen presidents, including Gerald Ford and Jimmy Carter.

Amendment XXIII [1961]

Section 1. The District constituting the seat of Government of the United States shall appoint in such manner as the Congress may direct: A number of electors of President and Vice-President equal to the whole number of Senators and Representatives in Congress to which the District would be entitled if it were a State, but in no event more than the least populous State; they shall be in addition to those appointed by the States, but they shall be considered for the purposes of the election of President and Vice-President, to be electors appointed by a State; and they shall meet in the District and perform such duties as provided by the twelfth article of amendment.

Section 2. The Congress shall have the power to enforce this article by appropriate legislation.

• • •

When Washington, D.C., was established as a federal district, no one expected that a significant number of people would make it their permanent and primary residence. A proposal to allow citizens of the district to vote in presidential elections was approved by Congress in June 1960 and was ratified on March 29, 1961.

Amendment XXIV [1964]

Section 1. The right of citizens of the United States to vote in any primary or other election for President or Vice-President, for electors for President or Vice-President, or for Senator or Representative in Congress, shall not be denied or abridged by the United States or any State by reason of failure to pay any poll tax or other tax.

Section 2. The Congress shall have the power to enforce this article by appropriate legislation.

• • •

In the colonial and Revolutionary eras, financial independence was seen as necessary to political independence, and the poll tax was used as a requirement for voting. By the twentieth century, however, the poll tax was used mostly to bar poor people, especially southern blacks, from voting. Although conservatives complained that the amendment interfered with states' rights, liberals thought that the amendment did not go far enough because it barred the poll tax only in national elections and not in state or local elections. The amendment was ratified in 1964, however, and two years later the Supreme Court ruled that poll taxes in state and local elections also violated the equal protection clause of the Fourteenth Amendment.

Amendment XXV [1967]

Section 1. In case of the removal of the President from office or of his death or resignation, the Vice-President shall become President.

Section 2. Whenever there is a vacancy in the office of the Vice-President, the President shall nominate a Vice-President who shall take office upon confirmation by a majority vote of both Houses of Congress.

Section 3. Whenever the President transmits to the President pro tempore of the Senate and the Speaker of the House of Representatives his written declaration that he is unable to discharge the powers and duties of his office, and until he transmits to them a written declaration to the contrary, such powers and duties shall be discharged by the Vice-President as Acting President.

Section 4. Whenever the Vice-President and a majority of either the principal officers of the executive departments or of such other body as Congress may by law provide, transmit to the President pro tempore of the Senate and the Speaker of the House of Representatives their written declaration that the President is unable to discharge the powers and duties of his office, the Vice-President shall immediately assume the powers and duties of the office as Acting President.

Thereafter, when the President transmits to the President pro tempore of the Senate and the Speaker of the House of Representatives his written declaration that no inability exists, he shall resume the powers and duties of his office unless the Vice-President and a majority of either principal officers of the executive department[s] or of such other body as Congress may by law provide, transmit within four days to the President pro tempore of the Senate and the Speaker of the House of Representatives their written declaration that the President is unable to discharge the powers and duties of his office. Thereupon Congress shall decide the issue, assembling within forty-eight hours for that purpose if not in session. If the Congress, within twenty-one days after receipt of the latter written declaration, or, if Congress is not in session, within twenty-one days after Congress is required to assemble, determines by two-thirds vote of both Houses that the President is unable to discharge the powers and duties of his office, the Vice-President shall continue to discharge the same as Acting President; otherwise, the President shall resume the powers and duties of his office.

• • •

The framers of the Constitution established the office of vice president because someone was needed to preside over the Senate. The first president to die in office was William Henry Harrison, in 1841. Vice President John Tyler had himself sworn in as president, setting a precedent that was followed when seven later presidents died in office. The assassination of President James A. Garfield in 1881 posed a new problem, however. After he was shot, the president was incapacitated for two months before he died; he was unable to lead the country, and his vice president, Chester A. Arthur, was unable to assume leadership. Efforts to resolve questions of succession in the event of a presidential disability thus began with the death of Garfield.

In 1963 the assassination of President John F. Kennedy galvanized Congress to action. Vice President Lyndon Johnson was a chain-smoker with a history of heart trouble. According to the 1947 Presidential Succession Act, the two men who stood in line to succeed him were the seventy-two-year-old Speaker of the House and the eighty-six-year-old president of the Senate. There were serious concerns that any of these men might become incapacitated while serving as chief executive. The first time the Twenty-fifth Amendment was used, however, was not in the case of presidential death or illness, but during the Watergate crisis. When Vice President Spiro T. Agnew was forced to resign following allegations of bribery and tax violations, President Richard M. Nixon appointed House Minority Leader Gerald R. Ford vice president. Ford became president following Nixon's resignation eight months later and named Nelson A. Rockefeller as his vice president. Thus, for more than two years, the two highest offices in the country were held by people who had not been elected to them.

Amendment XXVI [1971]

Section 1. The right of citizens of the United States, who are eighteen years of age or older, to vote shall not be denied or abridged by the United States or by any State on account of age.

Section 2. The Congress shall have power to enforce this article by appropriate legislation.

• • •

Efforts to lower the voting age from twenty-one to eighteen began during World War II. Recognizing that those who were old enough to fight a war should have some say in the government policies that involved them in the war, Presidents Eisenhower, Johnson, and Nixon endorsed the idea. In 1970 the combined pressure of the antiwar movement and the demographic pressure of the baby-boom generation led to a Voting Rights Act lowering the voting age in federal, state, and local elections.

In Oregon v. Mitchell (1970), the state of Oregon challenged the right of Congress to determine the age at which people could vote in state or local elections. The Supreme Court agreed with Oregon. Because the Voting Rights Act was ruled unconstitutional, the Constitution had to be amended to allow passage of a law that would lower the voting age. The amendment was ratified in a little more than three months, making it the most rapidly ratified amendment in U.S. history.

Unratified Amendment

Equal Rights Amendment (proposed by Congress March 22, 1972; seven-year deadline for ratification extended to June 30, 1982)

Section 1. Equality of rights under the law shall not be denied or abridged by the United States or by any State on account of sex.

Section 2. The Congress shall have the power to enforce, by appropriate legislation, the provisions of this article.

Section 3. This amendment shall take effect two years after the date of ratification.

• • •

In 1923, soon after women had won the right to vote, Alice Paul, a leading activist in the woman suffrage movement, proposed an amendment requiring equal treatment of men and women. Opponents of the proposal argued that such an amendment would invalidate laws that protected women and would make women subject to the military draft. After the 1964 Civil Rights Act was adopted, protective workplace legislation was partially removed.

The renewal of the women's movement, as a by-product of the civil rights and antiwar movements, led to a revival of the Equal Rights Amendment (ERA) in Congress. Disagreements over language held up congressional passage of the proposed amendment, but on March 22, 1972, the Senate approved the ERA by a vote of 84 to 8, and it was sent to the states. Six states ratified the amendment within two days, and by the middle of 1973 the amendment seemed well on its way to adoption, with thirty of the needed thirty-eight states having ratified it. In the mid-1970s, however, a powerful "Stop ERA" campaign developed. The campaign portrayed the ERA as a threat to "family values" and traditional relationships between men and women. Although thirty-five states ratified the ERA, five of those state legislatures voted to rescind ratification, and the amendment was never adopted.

Unratified Amendment

D.C. Statehood Amendment
(proposed by Congress August 22, 1978)

Section 1. For purposes of representation in the Congress, election of the President and Vice President, and article V of this Constitution, the District constituting the seat of government of the United States shall be treated as though it were a State.

Section 2. The exercise of the rights and powers conferred under this article shall be by the people of the District constituting the seat of government, and as shall be provided by Congress.

Section 3. The twenty-third article of amendment to the Constitution of the United States is hereby repealed.

Section 4. This article shall be inoperative, unless it shall have been ratified as an amendment to the Constitution by the legislatures of three-fourths of the several states within seven years from the date of its submission.

• • •

The 1961 ratification of the Twenty-third Amendment, giving residents of the District of Columbia the right to vote for a president and vice president, inspired an effort to give residents of the district full voting rights. In 1966 President Lyndon Johnson appointed a mayor and city council; in 1971 D.C. residents were allowed to name a nonvoting delegate to the House; and in 1981 residents were allowed to elect the mayor and city council. Congress retained the right to overrule laws that might affect commuters, the height of District buildings, and selection of judges and prosecutors. The district's nonvoting delegate to Congress, Walter Fauntroy, lobbied fiercely for a congressional amendment granting statehood to the district. In 1978 a proposed amendment was approved and sent to the states. A number of states quickly ratified the amendment, but, like the ERA, the D.C. Statehood Amendment ran into trouble. Opponents argued that Section 2 created a separate category of "nominal" statehood. They argued that the federal district should be eliminated and that the territory should be reabsorbed into the state of Maryland. Most scholars believe that the fears of Republicans that the predominantly black population of the city would consistently elect Democratic senators constituted a major factor leading to the defeat of the amendment.

Amendment XXVII [1992]

No law varying the compensation for the services of the Senators and Representatives, shall take effect, until an election of Representatives shall have intervened.

• • •

Whereas the Twenty-sixth Amendment was the most rapidly ratified amendment in U.S. history, the Twenty-seventh Amendment had the longest journey to ratification. First proposed by James Madison in 1789 as part of the package that included the Bill of Rights, this amendment had been ratified by only six states by 1791. In 1873, however, it was ratified by Ohio to protest a massive retroactive salary increase by the federal government. Unlike later proposed amendments, this one came with no time limit on ratification. In the early 1980s Gregory D. Watson, a University of Texas economics major, discovered the "lost" amendment and began a single-handed campaign to get state legislators to introduce it for ratification. In 1983 it was accepted by Maine. In 1984 it passed the Colorado legislature. Ratifications trickled in slowly until May 1992, when Michigan and New Jersey became the thirty-eighth and thirty-ninth states, respectively, to ratify. This amendment prevents members of Congress from raising their own salaries without giving voters a chance to vote them out of office before they can benefit from the raises.

The American Nation

Admission of States into the Union

State	Date of Admission	State	Date of Admission	State	Date of Admission
1. Delaware	December 7, 1787	18. Louisiana	April 30, 1812	35. West Virginia	June 20, 1863
2. Pennsylvania	December 12, 1787	19. Indiana	December 11, 1816	36. Nevada	October 31, 1864
3. New Jersey	December 18, 1787	20. Mississippi	December 10, 1817	37. Nebraska	March 1, 1867
4. Georgia	January 2, 1788	21. Illinois	December 3, 1818	38. Colorado	August 1, 1876
5. Connecticut	January 9, 1788	22. Alabama	December 14, 1819	39. North Dakota	November 2, 1889
6. Massachusetts	February 6, 1788	23. Maine	March 15, 1820	40. South Dakota	November 2, 1889
7. Maryland	April 28, 1788	24. Missouri	August 10, 1821	41. Montana	November 8, 1889
8. South Carolina	May 23, 1788	25. Arkansas	June 15, 1836	42. Washington	November 11, 1889
9. New Hampshire	June 21, 1788	26. Michigan	January 26, 1837	43. Idaho	July 3, 1890
10. Virginia	June 25, 1788	27. Florida	March 3, 1845	44. Wyoming	July 10, 1890
11. New York	July 26, 1788	28. Texas	December 29, 1845	45. Utah	January 4, 1896
12. North Carolina	November 21, 1789	29. Iowa	December 28, 1846	46. Oklahoma	November 16, 1907
13. Rhode Island	May 29, 1790	30. Wisconsin	May 29, 1848	47. New Mexico	January 6, 1912
14. Vermont	March 4, 1791	31. California	September 9, 1850	48. Arizona	February 14, 1912
15. Kentucky	June 1, 1792	32. Minnesota	May 11, 1858	49. Alaska	January 3, 1959
16. Tennessee	June 1, 1796	33. Oregon	February 14, 1859	50. Hawaii	August 21, 1959
17. Ohio	March 1, 1803	34. Kansas	January 29, 1861		

Territorial Expansion

Territory	Date Acquired	Square Miles	How Acquired
Original states and territories	1783	888,685	Treaty of Paris
Louisiana Purchase	1803	827,192	Purchased from France
Florida	1819	72,003	Adams-Onís Treaty
Texas	1845	390,143	Annexation of independent country
Oregon	1846	285,580	Oregon Boundary Treaty
Mexican cession	1848	529,017	Treaty of Guadalupe Hidalgo
Gadsden Purchase	1853	29,640	Purchased from Mexico
Midway Islands	1867	2	Annexation of uninhabited islands
Alaska	1867	589,757	Purchased from Russia
Hawaii	1898	6,450	Annexation of independent country
Wake Island	1898	3	Annexation of uninhabited island
Puerto Rico	1899	3,435	Treaty of Paris
Guam	1899	212	Treaty of Paris
The Philippines	1899–1946	115,600	Treaty of Paris; granted independence
American Samoa	1900	76	Treaty with Germany and Great Britain
Panama Canal Zone	1904–1978	553	Hay–Bunau-Varilla Treaty
U.S. Virgin Islands	1917	133	Purchased from Denmark
Trust Territory of the Pacific Islands*	1947	717	United Nations Trusteeship

*A number of these islands have been granted independence: Federated States of Micronesia, 1990; Marshall Islands, 1991; Palau, 1994.

Presidential Elections

Year	Candidates	Parties	Percentage of Popular Vote	Electoral Vote	Percentage of Voter Participation
1789	**George Washington**	No party designations	*	69	
	John Adams[†]			34	
	Other candidates			35	
1792	**George Washington**	No party designations		132	
	John Adams			77	
	George Clinton			50	
	Other candidates			5	
1796	**John Adams**	Federalist		71	
	Thomas Jefferson	Democratic-Republican		68	
	Thomas Pinckney	Federalist		59	
	Aaron Burr	Democratic-Republican		30	
	Other candidates			48	
1800	**Thomas Jefferson**	Democratic-Republican		73	
	Aaron Burr	Democratic-Republican		73	
	John Adams	Federalist		65	
	Charles C. Pinckney	Federalist		64	
	John Jay	Federalist		1	
1804	**Thomas Jefferson**	Democratic-Republican		162	
	Charles C. Pinckney	Federalist		14	
1808	**James Madison**	Democratic-Republican		122	
	Charles C. Pinckney	Federalist		47	
	George Clinton	Democratic-Republican		6	
1812	**James Madison**	Democratic-Republican		128	
	De Witt Clinton	Federalist		89	
1816	**James Monroe**	Democratic-Republican		183	
	Rufus King	Federalist		34	
1820	**James Monroe**	Democratic-Republican		231	
	John Quincy Adams	Independent Republican		1	
1824	**John Quincy Adams**	Democratic-Republican	30.5	84	26.9
	Andrew Jackson	Democratic-Republican	43.1	99	
	Henry Clay	Democratic-Republican	13.2	37	
	William H. Crawford	Democratic-Republican	13.1	41	
1828	**Andrew Jackson**	Democratic	56.0	178	57.6
	John Quincy Adams	National Republican	44.0	83	
1832	**Andrew Jackson**	Democratic	54.5	219	55.4
	Henry Clay	National Republican	37.5	49	
	William Wirt	Anti-Masonic	8.0	7	
	John Floyd	Democratic	‡	11	
1836	**Martin Van Buren**	Democratic	50.9	170	57.8
	William H. Harrison	Whig		73	
	Hugh L. White	Whig		26	
	Daniel Webster	Whig	49.1	14	
	W. P. Mangum	Whig		11	
1840	**William H. Harrison**	Whig	53.1	234	80.2
	Martin Van Buren	Democratic	46.9	60	
1844	**James K. Polk**	Democratic	49.6	170	78.9
	Henry Clay	Whig	48.1	105	
	James G. Birney	Liberty	2.3		

Year	Candidates	Parties	Percentage of Popular Vote	Electoral Vote	Percentage of Voter Participation
1848	**Zachary Taylor**	Whig	47.4	163	72.7
	Lewis Cass	Democratic	42.5	127	
	Martin Van Buren	Free Soil	10.1		
1852	**Franklin Pierce**	Democratic	50.9	254	69.6
	Winfield Scott	Whig	44.1	42	
	John P. Hale	Free Soil	5.0		
1856	**James Buchanan**	Democratic	45.3	174	78.9
	John C. Frémont	Republican	33.1	114	
	Millard Fillmore	American	21.6	8	
1860	**Abraham Lincoln**	Republican	39.8	180	81.2
	Stephen A. Douglas	Democratic	29.5	12	
	John C. Breckinridge	Democratic	18.1	72	
	John Bell	Constitutional Union	12.6	39	
1864	**Abraham Lincoln**	Republican	55.0	212	73.8
	George B. McClellan	Democratic	45.0	21	
1868	**Ulysses S. Grant**	Republican	52.7	214	78.1
	Horatio Seymour	Democratic	47.3	80	
1872	**Ulysses S. Grant**	Republican	55.6	286	71.3
	Horace Greeley	Democratic	43.9		
1876	**Rutherford B. Hayes**	Republican	48.0	185	81.8
	Samuel J. Tilden	Democratic	51.0	184	
1880	**James A. Garfield**	Republican	48.5	214	79.4
	Winfield S. Hancock	Democratic	48.1	155	
	James B. Weaver	Greenback-Labor	3.4		
1884	**Grover Cleveland**	Democratic	48.5	219	77.5
	James G. Blaine	Republican	48.2	182	
1888	**Benjamin Harrison**	Republican	47.9	233	79.3
	Grover Cleveland	Democratic	48.6	168	
1892	**Grover Cleveland**	Democratic	46.1	277	74.7
	Benjamin Harrison	Republican	43.0	145	
	James B. Weaver	People's	8.5	22	
1896	**William McKinley**	Republican	51.1	271	79.3
	William J. Bryan	Democratic	47.7	176	
1900	**William McKinley**	Republican	51.7	292	73.2
	William J. Bryan	Democratic; Populist	45.5	155	
1904	**Theodore Roosevelt**	Republican	57.4	336	65.2
	Alton B. Parker	Democratic	37.6	140	
	Eugene V. Debs	Socialist	3.0		
1908	**William H. Taft**	Republican	51.6	321	65.4
	William J. Bryan	Democratic	43.1	162	
	Eugene V. Debs	Socialist	2.8		
1912	**Woodrow Wilson**	Democratic	41.9	435	58.8
	Theodore Roosevelt	Progressive	27.4	88	
	William H. Taft	Republican	23.2	8	
	Eugene V. Debs	Socialist	6.0		
1916	**Woodrow Wilson**	Democratic	49.4	277	61.6
	Charles E. Hughes	Republican	46.2	254	
	A. L. Benson	Socialist	3.2		

Year	Candidates	Parties	Percentage of Popular Vote	Electoral Vote	Percentage of Voter Participation
1920	**Warren G. Harding**	Republican	60.4	404	49.2
	James M. Cox	Democratic	34.2	127	
	Eugene V. Debs	Socialist	3.4		
1924	**Calvin Coolidge**	Republican	54.0	382	48.9
	John W. Davis	Democratic	28.8	136	
	Robert M. La Follette	Progressive	16.6	13	
1928	**Herbert C. Hoover**	Republican	58.2	444	56.9
	Alfred E. Smith	Democratic	40.9	87	
1932	**Franklin D. Roosevelt**	Democratic	57.4	472	56.9
	Herbert C. Hoover	Republican	39.7	59	
1936	**Franklin D. Roosevelt**	Democratic	60.8	523	61.0
	Alfred M. Landon	Republican	36.5	8	
1940	**Franklin D. Roosevelt**	Democratic	54.8	449	62.5
	Wendell L. Willkie	Republican	44.8	82	
1944	**Franklin D. Roosevelt**	Democratic	53.5	432	55.9
	Thomas E. Dewey	Republican	46.0	99	
1948	**Harry S Truman**	Democratic	49.6	303	53.0
	Thomas E. Dewey	Republican	45.1	189	
1952	**Dwight D. Eisenhower**	Republican	55.1	442	63.3
	Adlai E. Stevenson	Democratic	44.4	89	
1956	**Dwight D. Eisenhower**	Republican	57.6	457	60.6
	Adlai E. Stevenson	Democratic	42.1	73	
1960	**John F. Kennedy**	Democratic	49.7	303	64.0
	Richard M. Nixon	Republican	49.5	219	
1964	**Lyndon B. Johnson**	Democratic	61.1	486	61.7
	Barry M. Goldwater	Republican	38.5	52	
1968	**Richard M. Nixon**	Republican	43.4	301	60.6
	Hubert H. Humphrey	Democratic	42.7	191	
	George C. Wallace	American Independent	13.5	46	
1972	**Richard M. Nixon**	Republican	60.7	520	55.5
	George S. McGovern	Democratic	37.5	17	
1976	**Jimmy Carter**	Democratic	50.1	297	54.3
	Gerald R. Ford	Republican	48.0	240	
1980	**Ronald W. Reagan**	Republican	50.7	489	53.0
	Jimmy Carter	Democratic	41.0	49	
	John B. Anderson	Independent	6.6	0	
1984	**Ronald W. Reagan**	Republican	58.4	525	52.9
	Walter F. Mondale	Democratic	41.6	13	
1988	**George H. W. Bush**	Republican	53.4	426	50.3
	Michael Dukakis	Democratic	45.6	111**	
1992	**Bill Clinton**	Democratic	43.7	370	55.1
	George H. W. Bush	Republican	38.0	168	
	H. Ross Perot	Independent	19.0	0	
1996	**Bill Clinton**	Democratic	49	379	49.0
	Robert J. Dole	Republican	41	159	
	H. Ross Perot	Reform	8	0	
2000	**George W. Bush**	Republican	47.8	271	51.3
	Albert Gore	Democratic	48.4	267	
	Ralph Nader	Green	0.4	0	
2004	**George W. Bush**	Republican	50.7	286	60.3
	John Kerry	Democratic	48.3	252	
	Ralph Nader	Independent	.38	0	

*Prior to 1824, most presidential electors were chosen by state legislators rather than by popular vote.

†Before the Twelfth Amendment was passed in 1804, the Electoral College voted for two presidential candidates; the runner-up became vice president.

‡Percentages below 2.5 have been omitted. Hence the percentage of popular vote might not total 100 percent.

**One Dukakis elector cast a vote for Lloyd Bentsen.

Supreme Court Justices

Name	Terms of Service	Appointed by	Name	Terms of Service	Appointed by
John Jay, * N.Y.	1789–1795	Washington	Samuel Blatchford, N.Y.	1882–1893	Arthur
James Wilson, Pa.	1789–1798	Washington	Lucius Q. C. Lamar, Miss.	1888–1893	Cleveland
John Rutledge, S.C.	1790–1791	Washington	**Melville W. Fuller**, Ill.	1888–1910	Cleveland
William Cushing, Mass.	1790–1810	Washington	David J. Brewer, Kan.	1890–1910	B. Harrison
John Blair, Va.	1790–1796	Washington	Henry B. Brown, Mich.	1891–1906	B. Harrison
James Iredell, N.C.	1790–1799	Washington	George Shiras Jr., Pa.	1892–1903	B. Harrison
Thomas Johnson, Md.	1792–1793	Washington	Howell E. Jackson, Tenn.	1893–1895	B. Harrison
William Paterson, N.J.	1793–1806	Washington	Edward D. White, La.	1894–1910	Cleveland
John Rutledge, S.C.	1795	Washington	Rufus W. Peckham, N.Y.	1896–1909	Cleveland
Samuel Chase, Md.	1796–1811	Washington	Joseph McKenna, Cal.	1898–1925	McKinley
Oliver Ellsworth, Conn.	1796–1800	Washington	Oliver W. Holmes, Mass.	1902–1932	T. Roosevelt
Bushrod Washington, Va.	1799–1829	J. Adams	William R. Day, Ohio	1903–1922	T. Roosevelt
Alfred Moore, N.C.	1800–1804	J. Adams	William H. Moody, Mass.	1906–1910	T. Roosevelt
John Marshall, Va.	1801–1835	J. Adams	Horace H. Lurton, Tenn.	1910–1914	Taft
William Johnson, S.C.	1804–1834	Jefferson	Charles E. Hughes, N.Y.	1910–1916	Taft
Brockholst Livingston, N.Y.	1807–1823	Jefferson	**Edward D. White**, La.	1910–1921	Taft
Thomas Todd, Ky.	1807–1826	Jefferson	Willis Van Devanter, Wy.	1911–1937	Taft
Gabriel Duvall, Md.	1811–1835	Madison	Joseph R. Lamar, Ga.	1911–1916	Taft
Joseph Story, Mass.	1812–1845	Madison	Mahlon Pitney, N.J.	1912–1922	Taft
Smith Thompson, N.Y.	1823–1843	Monroe	James C. McReynolds, Tenn.	1914–1941	Wilson
Robert Trimble, Ky.	1826–1828	J. Q. Adams	Louis D. Brandeis, Mass.	1916–1939	Wilson
John McLean, Ohio	1830–1861	Jackson	John H. Clarke, Ohio	1916–1922	Wilson
Henry Baldwin, Pa.	1830–1844	Jackson	**William H. Taft**, Conn.	1921–1930	Harding
James M. Wayne, Ga.	1835–1867	Jackson	George Sutherland, Utah	1922–1938	Harding
Roger B. Taney, Md.	1836–1864	Jackson	Pierce Butler, Minn.	1923–1939	Harding
Philip P. Barbour, Va.	1836–1841	Jackson	Edward T. Sanford, Tenn.	1923–1930	Harding
John Cartron, Tenn.	1837–1865	Van Buren	Harlan F. Stone, N.Y.	1925–1941	Coolidge
John McKinley, Ala.	1838–1852	Van Buren	**Charles E. Hughes**, N.Y.	1930–1941	Hoover
Peter V. Daniel, Va.	1842–1860	Van Buren	Owen J. Roberts, Pa.	1930–1945	Hoover
Samuel Nelson, N.Y.	1845–1872	Tyler	Benjamin N. Cardozo, N.Y.	1932–1938	Hoover
Levi Woodbury, N.H.	1845–1851	Polk	Hugo L. Black, Ala.	1937–1971	F. Roosevelt
Robert C. Grier, Pa.	1846–1870	Polk	Stanley F. Reed, Ky.	1938–1957	F. Roosevelt
Benjamin R. Curtis, Mass.	1851–1857	Fillmore	Felix Frankfurter, Mass.	1939–1962	F. Roosevelt
John A. Campbell, Ala.	1853–1861	Pierce	William O. Douglas, Conn.	1939–1975	F. Roosevelt
Nathan Clifford, Me.	1858–1881	Buchanan	Frank Murphy, Mich.	1940–1949	F. Roosevelt
Noah H. Swayne, Ohio	1862–1881	Lincoln	**Harlan F. Stone**, N.Y.	1941–1946	F. Roosevelt
Samuel F. Miller, Iowa	1862–1890	Lincoln	James R. Byrnes, S.C.	1941–1942	F. Roosevelt
David Davis, Ill.	1862–1877	Lincoln	Robert H. Jackson, N.Y.	1941–1954	F. Roosevelt
Stephen J. Field, Cal.	1863–1897	Lincoln	Wiley B. Rutledge, Iowa	1943–1949	F. Roosevelt
Salmon P. Chase, Ohio	1864–1873	Lincoln	Harold H. Burton, Ohio	1945–1958	Truman
William Strong, Pa.	1870–1880	Grant	**Frederick M. Vinson**, Ky.	1946–1953	Truman
Joseph P. Bradley, N.J.	1870–1892	Grant	Tom C. Clark, Texas	1949–1967	Truman
Ward Hunt, N.Y.	1873–1882	Grant	Sherman Minton, Ind.	1949–1956	Truman
Morrison R. Waite, Ohio	1874–1888	Grant	**Earl Warren**, Cal.	1953–1969	Eisenhower
John M. Harlan, Ky.	1877–1911	Hayes	John Marshall Harlan, N.Y.	1955–1971	Eisenhower
William B. Woods, Ga.	1881–1887	Hayes	William J. Brennan Jr., N.J.	1956–1990	Eisenhower
Stanley Matthews, Ohio	1881–1889	Garfield	Charles E. Whittaker, Mo.	1957–1962	Eisenhower
Horace Gray, Mass.	1882–1902	Arthur	Potter Stewart, Ohio	1958–1981	Eisenhower

Name	Terms of Service	Appointed by	Name	Terms of Service	Appointed by
Bryon R. White, Colo.	1962–1993	Kennedy	Antonin Scalia, Va.	1986–	Reagan
Arthur J. Goldberg, Ill.	1962–1965	Kennedy	Anthony M. Kennedy, Cal.	1988–	Reagan
Abe Fortas, Tenn.	1965–1969	Johnson	David H. Souter, N.H.	1990–	Bush, G. H. W.
Thurgood Marshall, Md.	1967–1991	Johnson	Clarence Thomas, Ga.	1991–	Bush, G. H. W.
Warren E. Burger, Minn.	1969–1986	Nixon	Ruth Bader Ginsburg, N.Y.	1993–	Clinton
Harry A. Blackmun, Minn.	1970–1994	Nixon	Stephen G. Breyer, Mass.	1994–	Clinton
Lewis F. Powell Jr., Va.	1971–1987	Nixon	**John G. Roberts, Jr.**, Md.	2005–	Bush, G. W.
William H. Rehnquist, Ill.	1971–1986	Nixon	Samuel A. Alito Jr., N.J.	2006–	Bush, G. W.
John Paul Stevens, Ill.	1975–	Ford			
Sandra Day O'Connor, Ariz.	1981–2006	Reagan			
William H. Rehnquist, Va.	1986–2005	Reagan			

*Chief Justices are printed in bold type.

The American People: a Demographic Survey

A Demographic Profile of the American People

Year	Life Expectancy from Birth		Average Age at First Marriage		Number of Children Under 5 (per 1,000 Women Aged 22–24)	Percentage of Persons in Paid Employment		Percentage of Paid Workers Who Are Women
	White	Black	Men	Women		Men	Women	
1820					1,295		6.2	7.3
1830					1,145		6.4	7.4
1840					1,085		8.4	9.6
1850					923		10.1	10.8
1860					929		9.7	10.2
1870					839		13.7	14.8
1880					822		14.7	15.2
1890			26.1	22.0	716	84.3	18.2	17.0
1900	47.6	33.0	25.9	21.9	688	85.7	20.0	18.1
1910	50.3	35.6	25.1	21.6	643	85.1	24.8	20.0
1920	54.9	45.3	24.6	21.2	604	84.6	22.7	20.4
1930	61.4	48.1	24.3	21.3	511	82.1	23.6	21.9
1940	64.2	53.1	24.3	21.5	429	79.1	25.8	24.6
1950	69.1	60.8	22.8	20.3	589	81.6	29.9	27.8
1960	70.6	63.6	22.8	20.3	737	80.4	35.7	32.3
1970	71.7	65.3	22.5	20.6	530	79.7	41.4	38.0
1980	74.4	68.1	24.7	22.0	440	77.4	51.5	42.6
1990	76.1	69.1	26.1	23.9	377	76.4	57.4	45.2
2000	77.6	71.7	26.7	25.1	365	74.8	58.9	46.3
2004	78.2	73.4	27.4	25.8		73.3	59.2	46.5

SOURCE: U.S. Bureau of the Census, *Historical Statistics of the United States, Colonial Times to 1970 (1975); Statistical Abstract of the United States, 2001; Statistical Abstract of the United States, 2006.*

American Population

Year	Population	Percentage Increase	Year	Population	Percentage Increase
1610	350	—	1820	9,638,453	33.1
1620	2,300	557.1	1830	12,866,020	33.5
1630	4,600	100.0	1840	17,069,453	32.7
1640	26,600	478.3	1850	23,191,876	35.9
1650	50,400	90.8	1860	31,443,321	35.6
1660	75,100	49.0	1870	39,818,449	26.6
1670	111,900	49.0	1880	50,155,783	26.0
1680	151,500	35.4	1890	62,947,714	25.5
1690	210,400	38.9	1900	75,994,575	20.7
1700	250,900	19.2	1910	91,972,266	21.0
1710	331,700	32.2	1920	105,710,620	14.9
1720	466,200	40.5	1930	122,775,046	16.1
1730	629,400	35.0	1940	131,669,275	7.2
1740	905,600	43.9	1950	150,697,361	14.5
1750	1,170,800	29.3	1960	179,323,175	19.0
1760	1,593,600	36.1	1970	203,235,298	13.3
1770	2,148,100	34.8	1980	226,545,805	11.5
1780	2,780,400	29.4	1990	248,709,873	9.8
1790	3,929,214	41.3	2000	281,421,906	13.2
1800	5,308,483	35.1	2005	296,410,404	5.0
1810	7,239,881	36.4			

Note: These figures largely ignore the Native American population. Census takers never made any effort to count the Native American population that lived outside their reserved political areas and compiled only casual and incomplete enumerations of those living within their jurisdictions until 1890. In that year the federal government attempted a full count of the Indian population: The Census found 125,719 Indians in 1890, compared with only 12,543 in 1870 and 33,985 in 1880.

SOURCES: U.S. Bureau of the Census, *Historical Statistics of the United States, Colonial Times to 1970* (1975); *Statistical Abstract of the United States, 2001;* U.S. Bureau of the Census, Population Finder, http://factfinder.census.gov.

White/Nonwhite Population

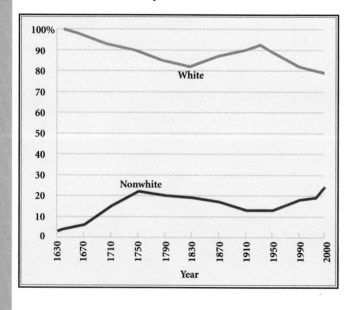

Urban/Rural Population

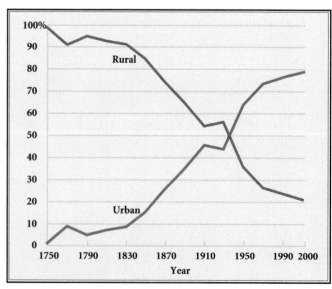

The Ten Largest Cities by Population, 1700–2000

		City	Population			City	Population
1700	1.	Boston	6,700	**1930**	1.	New York	6,930,446
	2.	New York	4,937*		2.	Chicago	3,376,438
	3.	Philadelphia	4,400†		3.	Philadelphia	1,950,961
1790	1.	Philadelphia	42,520		4.	Detroit	1,568,662
	2.	New York	33,131		5.	Los Angeles	1,238,048
	3.	Boston	18,038		6.	Cleveland	900,429
	4.	Charleston, S.C.	16,359		7.	St. Louis	821,960
	5.	Baltimore	13,503		8.	Baltimore	804,874
	6.	Salem, Mass.	7,921		9.	Boston	781,188
	7.	Newport, R.I.	6,716		10.	Pittsburgh	669,817
	8.	Providence, R.I.	6,380	**1950**	1.	New York	7,891,957
	9.	Marblehead, Mass.	5,661		2.	Chicago	3,620,962
	10.	Portsmouth, N.H.	4,720		3.	Philadelphia	2,071,605
1830	1.	New York	197,112		4.	Los Angeles	1,970,358
	2.	Philadelphia	161,410		5.	Detroit	1,849,568
	3.	Baltimore	80,620		6.	Baltimore	949,708
	4.	Boston	61,392		7.	Cleveland	914,808
	5.	Charleston, S.C.	30,289		8.	St. Louis	856,796
	6.	New Orleans	29,737		9.	Washington, D.C.	802,178
	7.	Cincinnati	24,831		10.	Boston	801,444
	8.	Albany, N.Y.	24,209	**1970**	1.	New York	7,895,563
	9.	Brooklyn, N.Y.	20,535		2.	Chicago	3,369,357
	10.	Washington, D.C.	18,826		3.	Los Angeles	2,811,801
1850	1.	New York	515,547		4.	Philadelphia	1,949,996
	2.	Philadelphia	340,045		5.	Detroit	1,514,063
	3.	Baltimore	169,054		6.	Houston	1,233,535
	4.	Boston	136,881		7.	Baltimore	905,787
	5.	New Orleans	116,375		8.	Dallas	844,401
	6.	Cincinnati	115,435		9.	Washington, D.C.	756,668
	7.	Brooklyn, N.Y.	96,838		10.	Cleveland	750,879
	8.	St. Louis	77,860	**1990**	1.	New York	7,322,564
	9.	Albany, N.Y.	50,763		2.	Los Angeles	3,485,398
	10.	Pittsburgh	46,601		3.	Chicago	2,783,726
1870	1.	New York	942,292		4.	Houston	1,630,553
	2.	Philadelphia	674,022		5.	Philadelphia	1,585,577
	3.	Brooklyn, N.Y.	419,921‡		6.	San Diego	1,110,549
	4.	St. Louis	310,864		7.	Detroit	1,027,974
	5.	Chicago	298,977		8.	Dallas	1,006,877
	6.	Baltimore	267,354		9.	Phoenix	983,403
	7.	Boston	250,526		10.	San Antonio	935,933
	8.	Cincinnati	216,239	**2000**	1.	New York	8,008,278
	9.	New Orleans	191,418		2.	Los Angeles	3,694,820
	10.	San Francisco	149,473		3.	Chicago	2,896,016
1910	1.	New York	4,766,883		4.	Houston	1,953,631
	2.	Chicago	2,185,283		5.	Philadelphia	1,517,550
	3.	Philadelphia	1,549,008		6.	Phoenix	1,321,045
	4.	St. Louis	687,029		7.	San Diego	1,223,400
	5.	Boston	670,585		8.	Dallas	1,188,580
	6.	Cleveland	560,663		9.	San Antonio	1,144,646
	7.	Baltimore	558,485		10.	Detroit	951,270
	8.	Pittsburgh	533,905				
	9.	Detroit	465,766				
	10.	Buffalo	423,715				

*Figure from a census taken in 1698.
†Philadelphia figures include suburbs.
‡Annexed to New York in 1898.
SOURCE: U.S. Census data.

Immigration by Decade

Year	Number	Percentage of Total Population	Year	Number	Percentage of Total Population
1821–1830	151,824	1.6	1921–1930	4,107,209	3.9
1831–1840	599,125	4.6	1931–1940	528,431	0.4
1841–1850	1,713,251	10.0	1941–1950	1,035,039	0.7
1851–1860	2,598,214	11.2	1951–1960	2,515,479	1.6
1861–1870	2,314,824	7.4	1961–1970	3,321,677	1.8
1871–1880	2,812,191	7.1	1971–1980	4,493,000	2.2
1881–1890	5,246,613	10.5	1981–1990	7,338,000	3.0
1891–1900	3,687,546	5.8	1991–2000	9,095,083	3.7
1901–1910	8,795,386	11.6	**Total**	**32,433,918**	
1911–1920	5,735,811	6.2			
Total	**33,654,785**		1821–2000 **GRAND TOTAL**	**66,088,703**	

SOURCES: U.S. Bureau of the Census, *Historical Statistics of the United States, Colonial Times to 1970* (1975), part 1, 105–106; *Statistical Abstract of the United States, 2001.*

Regional Origins

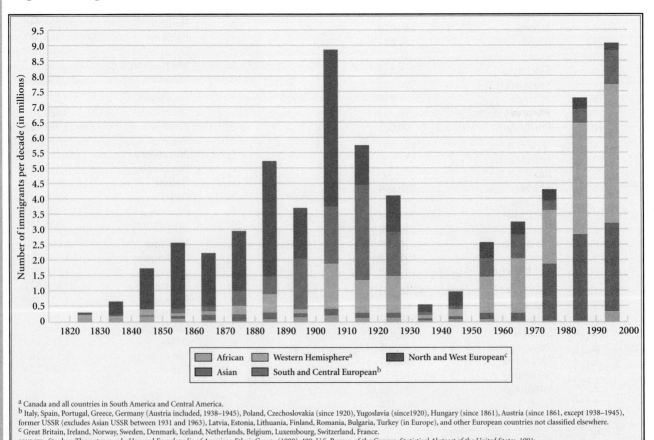

[a] Canada and all countries in South America and Central America.
[b] Italy, Spain, Portugal, Greece, Germany (Austria included, 1938–1945), Poland, Czechoslovakia (since 1920), Yugoslavia (since 1920), Hungary (since 1861), Austria (since 1861, except 1938–1945), former USSR (excludes Asian USSR between 1931 and 1963), Latvia, Estonia, Lithuania, Finland, Romania, Bulgaria, Turkey (in Europe), and other European countries not classified elsewhere.
[c] Great Britain, Ireland, Norway, Sweden, Denmark, Iceland, Netherlands, Belgium, Luxembourg, Switzerland, France.
SOURCES: Stephan Thernstrom, ed., *Harvard Encyclopedia of American Ethnic Groups* (1980), 480; U.S. Bureau of the Census, *Statistical Abstract of the United States, 1991;* U.S. Immigration and Naturalization Service, *Statistical Yearbook, 2000.*

The Labor Force (Thousands of Workers)

Year	Agriculture	Mining	Manufacturing	Construction	Trade	Other	Total
1810	1,950	11	75	—	—	294	2,330
1840	3,570	32	500	290	350	918	5,660
1850	4,520	102	1,200	410	530	1,488	8,250
1860	5,880	176	1,530	520	890	2,114	11,110
1870	6,790	180	2,470	780	1,310	1,400	12,930
1880	8,920	280	3,290	900	1,930	2,070	17,390
1890	9,960	440	4,390	1,510	2,960	4,060	23,320
1900	11,680	637	5,895	1,665	3,970	5,223	29,070
1910	11,770	1,068	8,332	1,949	5,320	9,041	37,480
1920	10,790	1,180	11,190	1,233	5,845	11,372	41,610
1930	10,560	1,009	9,884	1,988	8,122	17,267	48,830
1940	9,575	925	11,309	1,876	9,328	23,277	56,290
1950	7,870	901	15,648	3,029	12,152	25,870	65,470
1960	5,970	709	17,145	3,640	14,051	32,545	74,060
1970	3,463	516	20,746	4,818	15,008	34,127	78,678
1980	3,364	979	21,942	6,215	20,191	46,612	99,303
1990	3,223	724	21,346	7,764	24,622	60,849	118,793
2000	2,464	475	19,644	9,931	15,763	88,260	136,891

SOURCES: U.S. Bureau of the Census, *Historical Statistics of the United States, Colonial Times to 1970* (1975), 139; *Statistical Abstract of the United States, 1998*, table 675; *Statistical Abstract of the United States, 2006.*

Changing Labor Patterns

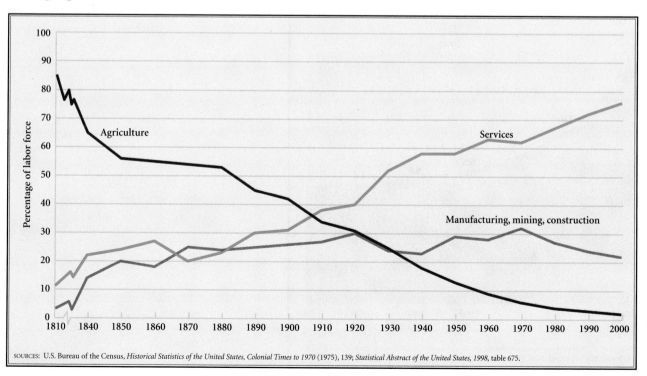

SOURCES: U.S. Bureau of the Census, *Historical Statistics of the United States, Colonial Times to 1970* (1975), 139; *Statistical Abstract of the United States, 1998*, table 675.

Birth Rate, 1820–2000

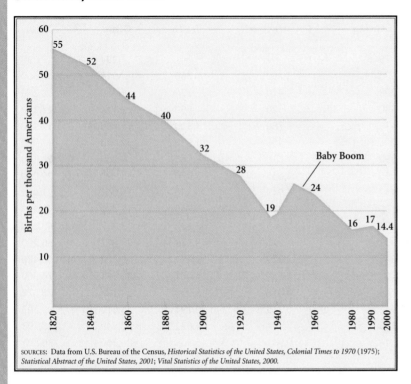

SOURCES: Data from U.S. Bureau of the Census, *Historical Statistics of the United States, Colonial Times to 1970* (1975); *Statistical Abstract of the United States, 2001; Vital Statistics of the United States, 2000.*

Death Rate, 1900–2000

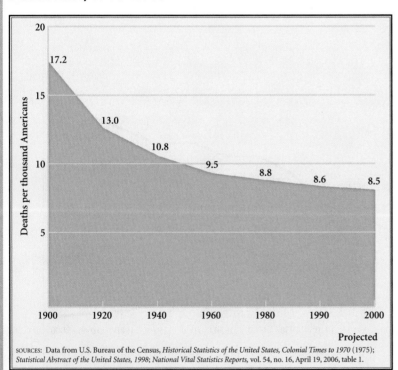

SOURCES: Data from U.S. Bureau of the Census, *Historical Statistics of the United States, Colonial Times to 1970* (1975); *Statistical Abstract of the United States, 1998; National Vital Statistics Reports,* vol. 54, no. 16, April 19, 2006, table 1.

Life Expectancy (at birth), 1900–2000

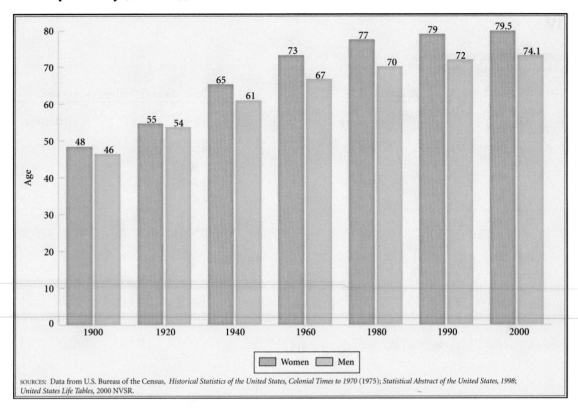

SOURCES: Data from U.S. Bureau of the Census, *Historical Statistics of the United States, Colonial Times to 1970* (1975); *Statistical Abstract of the United States, 1998*; *United States Life Tables*, 2000 NVSR.

The Aging of the U.S. Population, 1850–2000

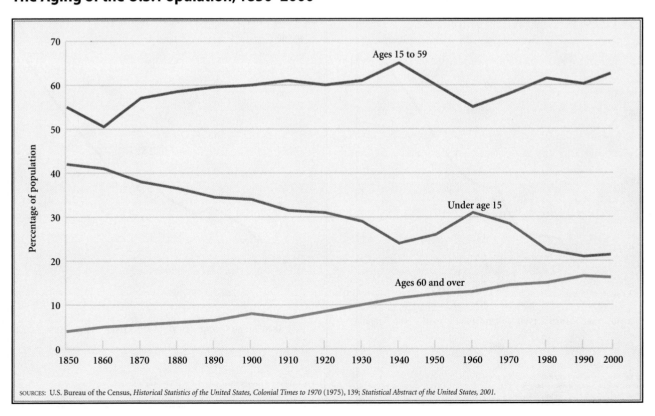

SOURCES: U.S. Bureau of the Census, *Historical Statistics of the United States, Colonial Times to 1970* (1975), 139; *Statistical Abstract of the United States, 2001.*

The American Government and Economy

The Growth of the Federal Government

Year	Employees (millions)		Receipts and Outlays ($ millions)	
	Civilian	Military	Receipts	Outlays
1900	0.23	0.12	567	521
1910	0.38	0.13	676	694
1920	0.65	0.34	6,649	6,358
1930	0.61	0.25	4,058	3,320
1940	1.04	0.45	6,900	9,600
1950	1.96	1.46	40,900	43,100
1960	2.38	2.47	92,500	92,200
1970	3.00	3.06	193,700	196,600
1980	2.99	2.05	517,112	590,920
1990	3.13	2.07	1,031,321	1,252,705
2000	2.88	1.38	2,025,200	1,788,800

SOURCES: *Statistical Profile of the United States, 1900–1980; Statistical Abstract of the United States, 2001.*

Gross Domestic Product, 1840–2000

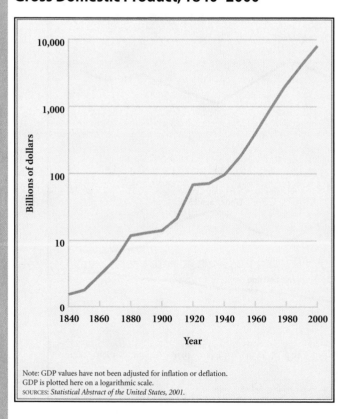

Note: GDP values have not been adjusted for inflation or deflation.
GDP is plotted here on a logarithmic scale.
SOURCES: *Statistical Abstract of the United States, 2001.*

GDP per Capita, 1840–2000

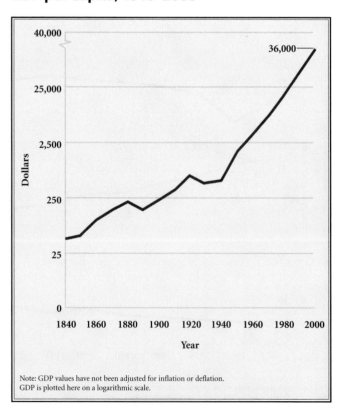

Note: GDP values have not been adjusted for inflation or deflation.
GDP is plotted here on a logarithmic scale.

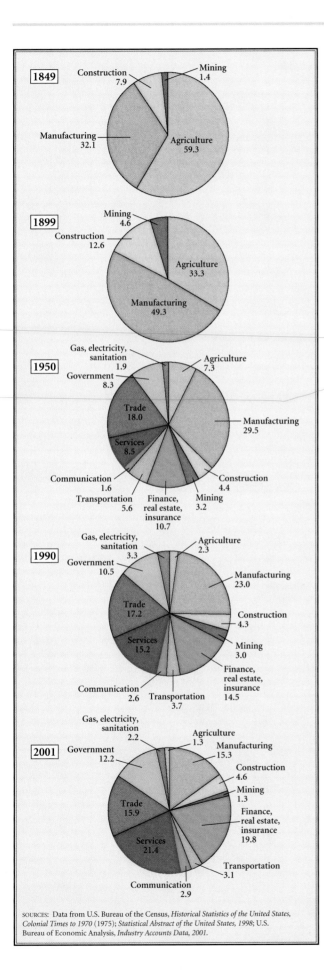

SOURCES: Data from U.S. Bureau of the Census, *Historical Statistics of the United States, Colonial Times to 1970* (1975); *Statistical Abstract of the United States, 1998*; U.S. Bureau of Economic Analysis, *Industry Accounts Data, 2001*.

Consumer Price Index

$100 in the year	1790 is equivalent to	$2,204 in 2005
	1800	1,605
	1810	1,640
	1820	1,720
	1830	2,185
	1840	2,330
	1850	2,580
Civil War Inflation	1860	2,425
	1870	1,540
	1880	1,970
$100 in the year	1890 is equivalent to	2,210 in 2005
	1900	2,400
World War I Inflation	1910	2,120
	1920	975
	1930	1,170
Post World War II	1940	1,400
Inflation	1950	810
	1960	660
	1970	500
	1980	240
$100 in the year	1990 is equivalent to	150 in 2005
	2000	115

This index provides a very rough guide to the purchasing power of $100 in various periods of American history. For example, in the early 1830s, day laborers earned about $1 a day or about $300 a year. This sum is the equivalent of about $6,555 a year in 2005 (3 × $2,185 = $6,555) or sixty percent of the gross income of a worker earing the federal government-designated minimum wage of $5.15 per hour. SOURCE: Lawrece H. Officer and Samuel H. Williamson, "Purchasing Power of Money…1774–2005," MeasuringWorth.com, August 2006. www.measuringworth.com/calcculators/ppowerus/

◀ **Main Sectors of the U.S. Economy: 1849, 1899, 1950, 1990, and 2001**

American Renaissance   A burst of American literature during the 1840s, highlighted by the novels of Herman Melville and Nathaniel Hawthorne; the essays of Ralph Waldo Emerson, Henry David Thoreau, and Margaret Fuller; and the poetry of Walt Whitman. (p. 252)

American System   A political program conceived in the early 1820s to expand economic development through a federally funded system of internal improvements (roads and canals), tariffs, and a national bank. Such policies marked a shift toward government involvement in the economy, reflecting the growing strength of commercial interests. (p. 304)

anarchism   The advocacy of a stateless society achieved by revolutionary means. Feared for their views, anarchists became the scapegoats for the 1886 Haymarket Square bombing. (p. 543)

Anglo-Saxonism   A theory widely held in the late nineteenth century that the English-speaking peoples were racially superior and, for that reason, justified in colonizing and dominating the peoples of less-developed areas of the world. Combined with Social Darwinism, Anglo-Saxonism fueled American expansionism in the late nineteenth century. (p. 647)

armistice   A temporary cession of military hostilities. World War I ended when the armistice of November 1918 simply continued because both sides had lost their will to fight further. (p. 679)

artisan republicanism   An ideology that celebrated small-scale producers, men and women who owned their own shops (or farms) and defined the ideal republican society as one constituted by, and dedicated to the welfare of, independent workers and citizens. (p. 280)

Benevolent Empire   A broad-ranging campaign of moral and institutional reforms inspired by evangelical Christian ideals and endorsed by upper-middle-class men and women in the 1820s. Ministers who promoted benevolent reform insisted that people who had experienced saving grace should provide moral guidance and charity to the less fortunate. (p. 290)

bills of exchange   Credit slips that British manufacturers, West Indian planters, and American merchants used in the eighteenth century in place of currency to settle transactions. (p. 90)

Black Codes   Laws passed by southern states after the Civil War denying ex-slaves the civil rights enjoyed by whites and intended to force blacks back to the plantations. (p. 459)

blacklist   Procedure used by employers throughout the nineteenth century to label and identify workers affiliated with unions. In the 1950s, blacklists were utilized to exclude alleged Communists from jobs in government service, the motion picture business, and many industries and unions. (p. 322)

business cycle   The periodic rise and fall of business activity that is characteristic of market-driven, capitalist economies. To increase profits, producers increase production and lower wages, which means workers cannot buy all the goods they produce. The surplus prompts a cutback in output and an economic recession. In the United States, major periods of expansion (1802–1818, 1824–1836, 1846–1856, 1865–1873, 1896–1914, and 1922–1928) were followed by either relatively short financial panics (1819–1822 and 1857–1860) or extended economic depressions (1837–1843, 1873–1896, and 1929–1939). (p. 239)

capitalism   A system of economic production based on the private ownership of property and the contractual exchange for profit of goods, labor, and money (capital). Although some elements of capitalism existed in the United States before 1820, a full-scale capitalist economy—and society—emerged only with the Market Revolution (1820–1850) and reached its pinnacle during the final decades of the century. *See* Market Revolution. (p. 237)

carpetbaggers   A derisive name given by Southerners to Northerners who moved to the South during Reconstruction. Former Confederates despised these Northerners as transient exploiters. Carpetbaggers actually were a varied group, including Union veterans who had served in the South, reformers eager to help the ex-slaves, and others looking for business opportunities. (p. 470)

caste system   A form of social organization that divides a society along relatively rigid lines of status based primarily on birth. (p. 28)

chattel slavery   A system of bondage in which a slave has the legal status of property and so can be bought and sold like property. (p. 52)

civic humanism   The belief that individuals owe a service to their community and its government. During the Renaissance, political theorists argued that selfless service was of critical importance in a republic, a form of government in which authority lies in the hands of some or all of the citizenry. (p. 20)

civil religion   A term used by historians to refer to a religious-like reverence for various political institutions and ideologies. An example is the belief in "republicanism" after the American Revolution. (p. 200)

clan   A group of related families that share a real or legendary common ancestor. Most Native peoples north of the Rio Grande organized their societies around clan groups, which combined to form a distinct people based on language and culture. (p. 9)

classical liberalism   The political ideology, dominant in England and the United States during the nineteenth century, that celebrated individual liberty, private property, a competitive market economy, free trade, and limited government. In the late twentieth-century United States, many economic conservatives embrace the principles of classical liberalism (and oppose the principles of social welfare liberalism). (p. 318)

closed shop   Workplace in which a job seeker had to be a union member to gain employment. In the nineteenth century, the closed shop was favored by craft unions as a method of keeping out incompetent and lower-wage workers and of strengthening the unions' bargaining position with employers. (p. 540)

closed-shop agreement   Labor agreement in which an employer agrees to hire only union members. Many employers viewed these agreements as illegal and worked to overturn them in the courts. Closed-shops became popular in the United States in the early part of the twentieth century. In 1947, under the Taft-Hartley Act, the closed-shop was declared illegal, but they continue to exist in practice. (p. 322)

collective bargaining   A process of negotiation between labor unions and employers, particularly favored by the American Federation of Labor (AFL). Led by Samuel Gompers, the AFL accepted the new industrial order, but fought for a bigger share of profits for the workers. (p. 540)

Columbian Exchange   The transfer in the sixteenth century of agricultural products and diseases from the Western Hemisphere to other continents, and from those other continents to the Western Hemisphere. (p. 25)

common law   Centuries-old body of English law based on custom and judicial interpretation, not legislation, and evolving case by case on the basis of precedent. The common law was transmitted to America along with English settlement and became the foundation of American law at the state and local levels. In the United States, even more than in Britain, the common law gave the courts supremacy over the legislatures in many areas of law. (p. 52)

companionate marriage   A marriage based on equality and mutual respect—both republican values. Although husbands in these marriages retained significant legal power, they increasingly came to see their wives as loving partners rather than as inferiors or dependents. (p. 245)

conscience Whigs   Whig politicians who opposed the Mexican War (1846–1848) on moral grounds. They maintained that the purpose of the war was to expand and perpetuate slavery. They feared that the addition of more slave states would ensure the South's control of the national government and undermine a society of yeomen farmers and "free labor" in the North. (p. 401)

conservationist   Advocacy for the protection of the natural environment for sustained use. As applied by Theodore Roosevelt at the start of the twentieth century, conservation accepted development of public lands, provided this was in the public interest and not wastefully destructive. In contrast, preservationists valued wilderness in its natural state and were more broadly opposed to development. (p. 629)

craft worker   An artisan or other worker who has a specific craft or skill. For example, a mason, a cabinetmaker, a printer, or a weaver. (p. 279)

cultural pluralism   A term coined in 1924 that posits that diversity, especially religious and ethnic diversity, can be a source of strength in a democratic nation and that cultural differences should be respected and valued. (p. 755)

deficit spending   High government spending in excess of tax revenues based on the ideas of British economist John Maynard Keynes, who proposed in the 1930s that governments should be prepared to go into debt to stimulate a stagnant economy. (p. 748)

deflation   The sustained decline of prices, generally accompanying an economic depression, but in the United States after the Civil War, the result of rapidly rising productivity, market competition, and a tight money supply. (p. 604)

deist, deism   The Enlightenment-influenced belief that the Christian God created the universe and then left it to run according to natural laws. (p. 117)

deregulation   Process of removing or limiting federal regulatory mechanisms, justified on the basis of promoting competition and streamlining government bureaucracy. President Carter began deregulation in the 1970s, starting with the airline, banking, and communications industries. The process continued under subsequent administrations. (p. 918)

détente   From the French word for "a relaxation of tension," this term was used to signify the new foreign policy of President Nixon, which sought a reduction of tension and hostility between the United States and the Soviet Union and China in the early 1970s. (p. 898)

direct primary   The selection of party candidates by a popular vote rather than by the party convention, this progressive reform was especially pressed by Robert La Follette, who viewed it as an instrument for breaking the grip of machines on the political parties. In the South, where it was limited to whites, the primary was a means of disfranchising blacks. (p. 624)

division of labor   A system of manufacture that assigns specific—and repetitive—tasks to each worker. The system was first implemented between 1800 and 1830 in the shoe industry and soon became general practice throughout the manufacturing sector of the U.S. economy. Although it improved productivity, it eroded workers' control and sense of achievement. (p. 272)

dollar diplomacy   Policy adopted by President Taft emphasizing the connection between America's economic and political interests overseas. The benefits would flow in both directions. Business would gain from diplomatic efforts in its behalf, while the strengthened American economic presence overseas would give added leverage to American diplomacy. (p. 664)

domino theory   An American Cold War concept associated with the containment policy that posited that in areas of East-West conflict, the loss of one country to communism would lead to the toppling of other non-Communist regimes. The term was first used by President Eisenhower, who warned of "falling dominos" in Southeast Asia if Vietnam became Communist. (p. 825)

dower, dower right   A legal right originating in Europe and carried to the American colonies that provided a widow with the use of one-third of the family's land and goods during her lifetime. (p. 16)

enclosure acts   Laws passed in sixteenth-century England that allowed landowners to fence in the open fields that surrounded many villages and use them for grazing sheep. This enclosure of the fields left peasants in those villages without land to cultivate, forcing them to work as wage laborers or as wool spinners and weavers. (p. 33)

encomiendas   Land grants in America given by the Spanish kings to privileged landholders (*encomenderos*) in the sixteenth century. *Encomiendas* also gave the landholders legal control over Native peoples who lived on or near their estates. (p. 25)

entitlement programs   Government programs that provide financial benefits to which recipients are entitled by law. Examples include Social Security, Medicare, unemployment compensation, and agricultural price supports. (p. 896)

established church   A church given privileged legal status by the government. Historically, established churches in Europe and America were supported by public taxes, and were often the only legally permitted religious institutions. (p. 258)

ethnocultural Refers to the distinctive social characteristics of immigrants and religious groups, especially in determining their party loyalties and stance on political issues touching personal behavior and public morality. (p. 590)

factory A structure first built by manufacturers in the early nineteenth century to concentrate all aspects of production — and the machinery needed to increase output — in one location. (p. 273)

Federalists Supporters of the Constitution of 1787, which created a strong central government, were called Federalists; those who feared that a strong central government would corrupt the nation's newly won liberty were called Antifederalists. (p. 195)

feminism, feminist Doctrine advanced in the early twentieth century by women activists that women should be equal to men in all areas of life. Earlier women activists and suffragists had accepted the notion of separate spheres for men and women, but feminists sought to overcome all barriers to equality and full personal development. (p. 617)

fiscal policy The range of decisions involving the finances of the federal government. These decisions include how much to tax, how much to spend, and what level of resulting deficit or surplus is acceptable. Such decisions — fiscal policy — have a big effect on a nation's allocation of economic resources, the distribution of income, and the level of economic activity. (p. 864)

Fourteen Points President Wilson proposed these principles as a basis for peace negotiations at Versailles in 1919. Included in the points were open diplomacy, freedom of the seas, free trade, territorial integrity, arms reduction, national self-determination, and establishment of the League of Nations. (p. 694)

franchise The right to vote. The franchise was gradually widened in the United States to include groups such as blacks and women, who had no vote in federal elections when the Constitution was ratified. In 1971, the Twenty-Sixth Amendment lowered the voting age from twenty-one to eighteen. (p. 302)

free market A system of economic exchange in which prices are determined by supply and demand and no producer or consumer dominates the market. The term also refers to markets that are not subject to government regulation. (p. 194)

free-soil movement A political movement of the 1840s that opposed the expansion of slavery. Motivating its members — mostly white yeomen farmers — was their belief that slavery benefited "aristocratic men." They wanted farm families to settle the western territories and install democratic republican values and institutions there. The short-lived Free-Soil Party (1848–1854) stood for "free soil, free labor, free men," which subsequently became the program of the Republican Party. (p. 402)

freehold, freeholder Property owned in its entirety, without feudal dues or landlord obligations. Freeholders have the legal right to improve, transfer, or sell their property. (p. 53)

fundamentalism, fundamentalist Any religious movement that adopts a "pure" and rigid belief system. In the United States, it usually refers to evangelical Protestants who interpret the Bible literally. In the 1920s, fundamentalists opposed modernist Protestants, who tried to reconcile Christianity with Darwin's theory of evolution by natural selection and other scientific discoveries. Fundamentalists' promotion of anti-evolution laws for public schools led to the famous Scopes trial of 1925; in recent decades, fundamentalists have strongly supported legislation to prohibit abortions and gay marriages. (p. 721)

gang-labor system A system of work discipline used on southern cotton plantations in the mid-nineteenth century. White overseers or black drivers constantly supervised gangs of enslaved laborers to enforce work norms and achieve greater productivity. (p. 373)

general strike A strike that draws in all the workers in a society, with the intention of shutting down the entire system. Radical groups like the Industrial Workers of the World (IWW), in the early twentieth century, saw the general strike as the means for initiating a social revolution. (p. 546)

gentility A refined style of living and elaborate manners that came to be highly prized among well-to-do English families after 1600. (p. 90)

gentry A class of Englishmen and -women who were substantial landholders but lacked the social privileges and titles of nobility. During the Price Revolution of the sixteenth century, the relative wealth and status of the gentry rose while those of the aristocracy fell. (p. 33)

gerrymander The political strategy (named after the early nineteenth-century politician Elbridge Gerry) of changing the boundaries of voting districts to give the dominant party an advantage. (p. 596)

ghetto Term describing an urban neighborhood composed of the poor, and occasionally used to describe any tight-knit community containing a single ethnic or class group. Ghettos came into being in the nineteenth century, in tandem with the enormous influx of immigrants to American cities. (p. 566)

Great American Desert The name given to the drought-stricken Great Plains by Euro-Americans in the early nineteenth century. Believing the region was unfit for cultivation or agriculture, Congress designated the Great Plains as permanent Indian country in 1834. (p. 392)

greenbacks Paper money issued by the U.S. Treasury during the Civil War to finance the war effort. Greenbacks had the status of legal tender in all public and private transactions. Because they were issued in large amounts and were not backed by gold or silver, the value of a greenback dollar fell during the war to 40 cents (but much less than the notes issued during the Revolutionary War, which became virtually worthless) and recovered only as the Union government won the war and proceeded to reduce its war-related debt. (p. 438)

guild An organization of skilled workers in medieval and early modern Europe that regulated the entry into and the practice of a trade. Guilds did not develop in colonial America because artisans generally were in short supply. (p. 20)

habeas corpus Latin for "bring forth the body," a legal writ forcing government authorities to justify their arrest and detention of an individual. Rooted in English common law, habeas corpus was given the status of a formal privilege in the U.S. Constitution (Article 1, Section 9), which also allows its suspension in cases of invasion or insurrection. During the Civil War, Lincoln suspended habeas corpus to stop protests against the draft and other anti-Union activities. The USA PATRIOT Act (2001) likewise suspends this privilege in cases of suspected terrorism, but the constitutional legitimacy of this and other provisions of the act have yet to be decided by the courts. (p. 434, 1012)

heresy A religious doctrine that is inconsistent with the teachings of a church. Some of the Crusades between 1096 and 1291 targeted groups of Christians whose beliefs the Roman Catholic Church judged to be heretical. (p. 16)

home rule   A rallying cry used by southern Democrats painting Reconstruction governments as illegitimate—imposed on the South—and themselves as the only party capable of restoring the South to "home rule." By 1876, northern Republicans were inclined to accept this claim. (p. 480)

homespun   Cloth spun and woven by American women and traditionally worn by poorer colonists. During the boycotts of British goods in the 1760s, wearing homespun clothes took on a political meaning, and even those who could easily afford finer clothing began wearing clothes made of homespun fabrics. Their work making homespun fabrics allowed women to contribute directly to the Patriot movement. (p. 148)

ideology   A systematic philosophy or political theory that purports to explain the character of the social world or to prescribe a set of values or beliefs. (p. 20)

impeachment   First step in the constitutional process for removing the president from office, in which charges of wrongdoing (articles of impeachment) are passed by the House of Representatives. A trial is then conducted by the Senate to determine whether the impeached president is guilty of the charges. (p. 468)

indenture, indentured servants   A seventeenth-century labor contract that required service for a period of time in return for passage to North America. Indentures were typically for a term of four or five years, provided room and board in exchange for labor, and granted free status at the end of the contract period. (p. 34)

indulgence   A certificate granted by the Catholic Church that claimed to pardon a sinner from punishment in the afterlife. In his *Ninety-five Theses*, written in 1517, Martin Luther condemned the sale of indulgences, a common practice among Catholic clergy. (p. 29)

industrial union   A group of workers in a single industry (for example, automobile, railroad, or mining) organized into a single association, regardless of skill, rather than into separate craft-based associations. The American Railway Union, formed in the 1880s, was one of the first industrial unions in the nation. (p. 544)

isolationism, isolationist   A foreign-policy stance supporting the withdrawal of the United States from involvement with other nations, especially an avoidance of entangling diplomatic relations. The common view of post–World War I U.S. foreign policy is that it was isolationist, but in fact the United States played an active role in world affairs, particularly in trade and finance. (p. 712)

Jim Crow   A term first heard in antebellum minstrel shows to designate black behavior and used in the age of segregation to designate facilities restricted to blacks, such as Jim Crow railway cars. (p. 598)

jingoism   This term came to refer to the super-patriotism that took hold in the mid-1890s during the American dispute with Spain over Cuba. Jingoes were enthusiastic about a military solution as a way of showing the nation's mettle and, when diplomacy failed, they got their wish with the Spanish-American War of 1898. (p. 648)

joint-stock corporation   A financial organization devised by English merchants around 1550 that subsequently facilitated the colonization of North America. In these companies, a number of investors pooled their capital and, in return, received shares of stock in the enterprise in proportion to their share of the total investment. (p. 56)

Keynesian economics   The theory, developed by British economist John Maynard Keynes in the 1930s, that purposeful government intention into the economy (through lowering or raising taxes, interest rates, and government spending) can affect the level of overall economic activity and thereby prevent severe depressions and runaway inflation. (p. 748)

"King Cotton"   A term used to describe the importance of raw cotton in the nineteenth-century economy. More specifically, the Confederate belief during the Civil War that their cotton was so important to the British and French economies that those governments would recognize the South as an independent nation and supply it with loans and arms. (p. 436)

labor theory of value   The belief that human labor produces value. Adherents argued that the price of a product should be determined not by the market (supply and demand) but by the amount of work required to make it, and that most of the price should be paid to the person who produced it. The idea was popularized by the National Trades' Union and other labor leaders in the mid-nineteenth century. (p. 280)

laissez-faire   The doctrine, based on economic theory, that government should not interfere in business or the economy. Laissez-faire ideas guided American government policy in the late nineteenth century and conservative politics in the twentieth. Business interests that supported laissez-faire in the late nineteenth century accepted government interference when it took the form of tariffs or subsidies that worked to their benefit. Broader uses of the term refer to the simple philosophy of abstaining from all government interference. (p. 318)

land bank   An institution, established by a colonial legislature, that printed paper money and lent it to farmers, taking a lien on their land to ensure repayment. (p. 99)

liberal, liberalism   The ideology of individual rights and private property outlined by John Locke (c. 1690) and embodied in many American constitutions, bills of rights, and institutions of government. *See also* classical liberalism *and* social welfare liberalism. (p. 479)

liberal consensus   Refers to widespread agreement among Americans in the decades after World War II that the pro-government policies of the New Deal were desirable and should be continued. In politics, the liberal consensus was reflected in the relatively small differences on economic and social policies between Republicans and Democrats until the advent of Ronald Reagan. (p. 819)

lien (crop lien)   A legal device enabling a creditor to take possession of the property of a borrower, including the right to have it sold in payment of the debt. Furnishing merchants took such liens on cotton crops as collateral for supplies advanced to sharecroppers during the growing season. This system trapped farmers in a cycle of debt and made them vulnerable to exploitation by the furnishing merchant. (p. 474)

literacy test   The requirement that an ability to read be demonstrated as a qualification for the right to vote. It was a device easily used by registrars to prevent blacks from voting, whether they could read or not, and was widely adopted across the South beginning with Mississippi in 1890. (p. 594)

machine tools   Cutting, boring, and drilling machines used to produce standardized metal parts that were assembled into products like sewing machines. The development of machine tools by American inventors in the early nineteenth century facilitated the rapid spread of the Industrial Revolution. (p. 278)

Manifest Destiny   A term coined by John L. O'Sullivan in 1845 to describe the idea that Euro-Americans were fated by God to settle the North American continent from the Atlantic to the Pacific Ocean. Adding geographical and secular dimensions to the Second Great Awakening, Manifest Destiny implied that the spread of American republican institutions and Protestant churches across the continent was part of God's plan for the world. In the late nineteenth century, the focus of the policy expanded to include overseas expansion. (p. 392)

manorial system   A quasi-feudal system of landholding in the Hudson River valley in which wealthy landlords leased out thousands of acres to tenant farmers in exchange for rent, a quarter of the value of all improvements (houses and barns, for example), and a number of days of personal service. (p. 70)

manumission   From the Latin *manumittere*, "to release from the hand," the legal act of relinquishing property rights in slaves. In 1782, the Virginia assembly passed an act allowing manumission; and within a decade, planters had freed ten thousand slaves. Worried that a large free black population would threaten the institution of slavery, the assembly repealed the law in 1792. (p. 252)

Market Revolution   The dramatic increase between 1820 and 1850 in the exchange of goods and services in market transactions. The Market Revolution resulted from the combined impact of the increased output of farms and factories, the entrepreneurial activities of traders and merchants, and the development of a transportation network of roads, canals, and railroads. (p. 272)

mass production   A system of factory production that often combines sophisticated machinery, a disciplined labor force, and assembly lines to turn out vast quantities of identical goods at low cost. In the nineteenth century, the textile and meatpacking industries pioneered mass production, which eventually became the standard mode for making consumer goods from cigarettes to automobiles, to telephones, radios, televisions, and computers. (p. 286)

matrilineal   Describes a system of family organization in which social identity and property descend through the female line. Children are usually raised in their mother's household, and her brother (their uncle) plays an important role in their lives. (p. 14)

mechanic   A term used in the nineteenth century to refer to a skilled craftsman and inventor who built and improved machinery and machine tools for industry. Mechanics developed a professional identity and established institutes to spread their skills and knowledge. (p. 274)

mercantilism   A set of parliamentary policies, first enacted in 1650 and constantly updated, that regulated colonial commerce and manufacturing for the enrichment of Britain. The policies ensured that the American colonies produced agricultural goods and raw materials for export to Britain, where they were sold to other European nations or made into finished goods. (p. 32)

mestizo   A person of mixed blood; specifically, the child of a European and a Native American. (p. 28)

middle class   In Europe, the class of traders and townspeople who were not part of either the aristocracy or the peasantry. The term was introduced in America in the early nineteenth century to describe both an economic group (of prosperous farmers, artisans, and traders) and a cultural outlook (of self-discipline, hard work, and social mobility). (p. 243)

Middle Passage   The brutal sea voyage from Africa to the Americas in the eighteenth and nineteenth centuries that cost nearly a million African slaves their lives. (p. 82)

military-industrial complex   A term first used by President Eisenhower in his farewell address in 1961, it refers to the interlinkage of the military and the defense industry that emerged with the arms buildup of the Cold War. Eisenhower particularly warned against the "unwarranted influence" that the military-industrial complex might exert on public policy. (p. 827)

Minutemen   Colonial militiamen who stood ready to mobilize on short notice during the imperial crisis of the 1770s. These volunteers formed the core of the citizens' army that met British troops at Lexington and Concord in April 1775. (p. 160)

muckrakers   Journalists in the early twentieth century whose stock-in-trade was exposure of the corruption of big business and government. Theodore Roosevelt gave them the name as a term of reproach. The term comes from a character in *Pilgrim's Progress*, a religious allegory by John Bunyan. (p. 614)

national debt   The financial obligations of the U.S. government for money borrowed from its citizens and foreign investors. Alexander Hamilton wanted wealthy Americans to invest in the national debt so that they would support the new national government. In recent decades, that same thinking has led the United States to encourage individuals and institutions in crucial foreign nations — Saudi Arabia and Japan, for example — to invest billions of dollars in the American national debt. (p. 206)

national self-determination   This concept holds that nations have the right to be sovereign states with political and economic autonomy. A central component of Woodrow Wilson's Fourteen Points for a World War I peace treaty, this concept challenged the existing colonial empires. The right of national self-determination continues to be invoked by nationalist, usually ethnic, groups, such as the Basques in Spain, the Kurds in Turkey and Iraq, and the Palestinians in Israel. (p. 695)

nationalize, nationalization   Government seizure and ownership of a business or natural resource. In the 1890s the Populist Party demanded nationalization of American railroads; in the 1950s the seizure by Cuba of American-owned sugar plantations and gambling casinos sparked a long-lasting diplomatic conflict. (p. 712)

nativist, nativism   Antiforeign sentiment in the United States that fueled drives against the immigration of Irish and Germans in the 1840s and 1850s, the Chinese and Japanese in the 1880s and 1890s, migrants from eastern and southern Europe in the 1910s and 1920s, and Mexicans in the 1990s and 2000s. Nativism prompted the Chinese Exclusion Act of 1882, the Immigration Restriction Act of 1924, and the interment of Japanese Americans during World War II. (p. 718)

nullification   Idea stating that a state convention could declare federal laws unconstitutional if they were seen to overstep Congressional powers. South Carolina politicians advanced this idea in 1828 as a response to Congress's so-called "Tariff of Abominations." After a heated confrontation, Congress passed a more moderate tariff in 1833. The question of federal power versus states' rights, however, was far from settled. The implied threat of nullification was secession and the South later acted upon this threat when they felt the federal government compromised their perceived right to slavery. (p. 309)

oligopoly In economics, the situation in which a given industry (steel making, automobile manufacturing) is dominated by a small number of large-scale companies. (p. 709)

outwork A system of manufacturing, also known as *putting out,* used extensively in the English woolen industry in the sixteenth and seventeenth centuries. Merchants bought wool and then hired landless peasants who lived in small cottages to spin and weave it into cloth, which the merchants would sell in English and foreign markets. (p. 32)

pagan A person whose spiritual beliefs center on the natural world. Pagans do not worship a supernatural God; instead, they pay homage to spirits and spiritual forces that dwell in the natural world. (p. 16)

party caucus An informal meeting of politicians held by political parties to make majority decisions and enforce party discipline. Traditionally members of Congress meet in party caucuses to select Congressional leaders. In the early history of America, small groups of party leaders chose candidates for office in party caucuses. Since the 1830s the major political parties have switched to using a national convention to nominate their candidates. (p. 303)

patronage The power of elected officials to grant government jobs. Beginning in the early nineteenth century, politicians systematically used—and abused—patronage to create and maintain strong party loyalties. After 1870, political reformers gradually introduced merit-based civil service systems in the federal and state governments. (p. 303)

peasant The traditional term for a farmworker in Europe. Some peasants owned land, while others leased or rented small plots from landlords. In some regions, peasants lived in compact communities with strong collective institutions. (p. 14)

peonage (debt peonage) As cotton prices declined during the 1870s, many sharecroppers fell into permanent debt. Merchants often conspired with landowners to make the debt a pretext for forced labor, or peonage. (p. 474)

personal-liberty laws Laws enacted in many northern states to protect free blacks and fugitive slaves from southern slave catchers. Early laws required a formal hearing before a local court. When these kinds of provisions were declared unconstitutional by the Supreme Court in *Prigg v. Pennsylvania* (1842), new laws prohibited state officials from helping slave catchers. (p. 407)

pocket veto Presidential way to kill a piece of legislation without issuing a formal veto. When congressional Republicans passed the Wade-Davis Bill in 1864, a harsher alternative to President Lincoln's restoration plan, Lincoln used this method to kill it by simply not signing the bill and letting it expire after Congress adjourned. (p. 458)

political machines Nineteenth-century term for highly organized groups operating within and intending to control political parties. Machines were regarded as antidemocratic by political reformers and were the target especially of Progressive era leaders such as Robert La Follette. The direct primary was the factored antimachine instrument because it made the selection of party candidates the product of a popular ballot rather than conventions that were susceptible to machine control. (p. 303)

poll taxes A tax paid for the privilege of voting, used in the South beginning during Reconstruction to disfranchise freedmen. Nationally, the northern states used poll taxes to keep immigrants and others deemed unworthy from the polls. (p. 469)

polygamy The practice of marriage by a man to multiple wives. Polygamy was customary among many African peoples and was practiced by many Mormons in the United States, particularly between 1840 and 1890. (p. 39)

popular sovereignty The republican principle that ultimate power resides in the hands of the electorate. Popular sovereignty dictates that voters directly or indirectly (through their elected representatives) ratify the constitutions of their state and national governments and amendments to those fundamental laws. During the 1850s, the U.S. Congress applied the principle to western lands by enacting legislation that gave residents there the authority to determine the status of slavery in their own territories. (p. 166)

pragmatism Philosophical doctrine developed primarily by William James that denied the existence of absolute truths and argued that ideas should be judged by their practical consequences. Problem solving, not ultimate ends, was the proper concern of philosophy, in James's view. Pragmatism provided a key intellectual foundation for progressivism. (p. 613)

praying town A Native American settlement in seventeenth-century New England supervised by a Puritan minister. Puritans used these settlements to encourage Indians to adopt English culture and Protestant Christianity. (p. 62)

predestination The idea that God chooses certain people for salvation even before they are born. Sixteenth-century theologian John Calvin was the main proponent of this doctrine, which became a fundamental tenet of Puritan theology. (p. 29)

preservationist, preservation Early-twentieth-century activists, like John Muir, who fought to protect the natural environment from commercial exploitation, particularly in the American West. (p. 629)

Price Revolution The impact of the high rate of inflation in Europe in the mid-1500s. American gold and silver, brought to Europe by Spain, doubled the money supply at a time when the population also was increasing. The increase in prices caused profound social changes—reducing the political power of the aristocracy and leaving many peasant families on the brink of poverty—setting the stage for substantial migration to America. (p. 32)

primogeniture The practice of passing family land, by will or by custom, to the eldest son. Republican-minded Americans of the Revolutionary era felt this practice was unfair, but they did not prohibit it. However, most state legislatures eventually passed laws providing that if a father dies without a will, all his children must receive an equal portion of his estate. (p. 16)

probate inventory An accounting of a person's property at the time of death, as recorded by court-appointed officials. Probate inventories are of great value to historians: These detailed lists of personal property, household items, and financial assets and debts tell us a good deal about people's lives. (p. 93)

Prohibition Law dictated by the Eighteenth Amendment of the Constitution that banned the manufacture and sale of alcoholic beverages. Prohibition took effect in January of 1920, but public resistance was intense. "Speakeasies" (illegal saloons) sprang up around the country and bootleggers (illegal providers) supplied alcoholic beverages smuggled from Canada and Mexico. Organized crime invested heavily in bootlegging and gang-war slayings generated much publicity. Public pressure led to the repeal of prohibition by the Twenty-First Amendment in 1933. (p. 688)

proprietors Groups of settlers who received land grants from the General Courts of Massachusetts Bay and Connecticut, mostly between 1630 and 1720. The proprietors distributed the land among themselves, usually based on social status and family need. This system encouraged widespread ownership of land in New England. (p. 61)

protective tariff A tax on imports levied to protect domestic products from foreign competition. A hot political issue throughout much of American history, protective tariffs became particularly controversial in the 1830s and again between 1880 and 1914, when Republicans (for protectionism) and Democrats (for free trade) centered their political campaigns on the issue. (p. 207)

pueblos Multistory and multiroom stone or mud-brick buildings built as residences by native peoples in the southwestern United States. (p. 11)

pump priming Term first used during the Great Depression of the 1930s to describe the practice of increased government spending in the hope that it would generate additional economic activity throughout the system. It is the beginning of a process that is supposed to lead to significant economic recovery. (p. 730)

Radical Whigs Eighteenth-century faction in Parliament that protested corruption in government, the growing cost of the British empire, and the rise of a wealthy class of government-related financiers. (p. 95)

reconquista The campaign by Spanish Catholics to drive North African Moors (Muslim Arabs) from the European mainland. After a centuries-long effort to recover their lands, the Spaniards defeated the Moors at Granada in 1492 and secured control of all of Spain. (p. 23)

republic A state without a monarch that is ruled by a representative system of government. In designing governments for the newly independent American states, Patriot leaders chose a republican form. They considered it an antidote to the poisonous corruption they had seen in the British monarchy. (p. 20)

republicanism A political ideology that repudiates rule by kings and princes and celebrates a representative system of government and a virtuous, public-spirited citizenry. Historically, most republics have limited active political participation to those with a significant amount of property. After 1800, the United States became a democratic republic, with widespread participation by white adult men of all social classes and, after 1920, by adult women. (p. 183)

republican motherhood The idea that the primary political role of American women was to instill a sense of patriotic duty and republican virtue in their children and mold them into exemplary republican citizens. (p. 248)

residual powers The constitutional principle that powers not explicitly granted to the federal government belong to the states. (p. 588)

restrictive covenants Limiting clauses in real estate transactions intended to prevent the sale or rental of properties to classes of the population considered "undesirable," such as African Americans, Jews, or Asians. Such clauses were declared unenforcable by the Supreme Court decision in *Shelley v. Kraemer* (1948), but continued to be instituted informally in spite of the ruling. (p. 838)

revenue tariff A tax on imports levied to raise money for the government. *See* protective tariff. (p. 207)

revival, revivalism An outburst of religious enthusiasm, often prompted by the preaching of a charismatic Baptist or Methodist minister. The Great Awakening of the 1740s was significant, but it was the revival that swept across the United States between the 1790s and 1850s that imparted a deep religiosity to the culture. Subsequent revivals in the 1880s and 1890s and in the late twentieth century helped maintain a strong evangelical Protestant culture in America. (p. 118)

rotten boroughs Tiny electoral districts for Parliament whose voters were controlled by wealthy aristocrats or merchants. In the 1760s, Radical Whig John Wilkes called for the elimination of rotten boroughs to make Parliament more representative of the property-owning classes. (p. 140)

rural ideal Concept advanced by the landscape architect Andrew Jackson Downing urging the benefits of rural life, it was especially influential among middle-class Americans making their livings in cities but attracted to the suburbs. (p. 557)

salutary neglect A term often used to describe British colonial policy during the reigns of George I (r. 1714–1727) and George II (r. 1727–1760). By relaxing their supervision of internal colonial affairs, royal bureaucrats contributed significantly to the rise of self-government in North America. (p. 94)

scalawags Southern whites who joined the Republicans during Reconstruction and were ridiculed by ex-Confederates as worthless traitors. They included ex-Whigs and yeomen farmers who had not supported the Confederacy and who believed that an alliance with the Republicans was the best way to attract northern capital and rebuild the South. (p. 470)

scientific management A system of organizing work, developed by Frederick W. Taylor in the late nineteenth century, designed to get the maximum output from the individual worker and reduce the cost of production, using methods such as the time-and-motion study to determine how factory work should be organized. The system was never applied in its totality in any industry, but it contributed to the rise of the "efficiency expert" and the field of industrial psychology. (p. 538)

secondary boycott (secondary labor boycott) Technique used by unions in labor disputes to exert pressure on an employer involved in the dispute by targeting other parties not involved but having a relationship to the employer, for example, as a supplier or as a customer. A secondary labor boycott was used in the Great Pullman Boycott of 1894 and failed when the government intervened. (p. 544)

secret ballot Before 1890, most Americans voted in "public." That is, voters either announced their vote to a clerk or handed in a ballot that had been printed by — and so was recognizable as the work of — a political party. Voting in "private" or in "secret" was first used on a wide scale in Australia. When the practice was adopted in the United States, it was known as the Australian ballot. (p. 376)

self-made man A nineteenth-century ideal that celebrated men who rose to wealth or social prominence from humble origins through self-discipline, hard work, and temperate habits. (p. 289)

sentimentalism A European cultural movement that emphasized emotions and a physical appreciation of God, nature, and people.

Sentimentalism came to the United States in the early nineteenth century and was a factor in the shift to marriages based on love rather than on financial considerations. (p. 244)

separate spheres Term used by historians to describe the nineteenth-century view that men and women have different gender-defined characteristics and, consequently, that the sexes inhabit — and should inhabit — different social worlds. Men should dominate the public sphere of politics and economics, while women should manage the private spheres of home and family. In mid-nineteenth-century America, this cultural understanding was both sharply defined and hotly contested. (p. 356)

separation of powers The constitutional arrangement that gives the three governmental branches — executive, legislative, and judicial — independent standing, thereby diffusing the federal government's overall power and reducing the chances that it might turn tyrannical and threaten the liberties of the people. (p. 458)

severalty Individual ownership of land. The term applied to the Dawes Severalty Act of 1890, which undertook to end tribal ownership and grant Indians deeds to individual holdings, i.e., severalty. (p. 503)

sharecropping The labor system by which freedmen agreed to exchange a portion of their harvested crops with the landowner for use of the land, a house, and tools. A compromise between freedmen and white landowners, this system developed in the cash-strapped South because the freedmen wanted to work their own land but lacked the money to buy it, while white landowners needed agricultural laborers but did not have money to pay wages. (p. 473)

Social Darwinism The application of Charles Darwin's biological theory of evolution by natural selection to the development of society, this late-nineteenth-century principle encouraged the notion that societies progress as a result of competition and the "survival of the fittest." Intervention by the state in this process was counterproductive because it impeded healthy progress. Social Darwinists justified the increasing inequality of late-nineteenth-century, industrial American society as natural. (p. 588)

"social welfare" liberalism The liberal ideology implemented in the United States during the New Deal of the 1930s and the Great Society of the 1960s. It uses the financial and bureaucratic resources of the state and federal governments to provide economic and social security to individual citizens, interest groups, and corporate enterprises. Social welfare programs include old age pensions, unemployment compensation, subsidies to farmers, mortgage guarantees, and tax breaks for corporations. (p. 738)

socialism A theory of social and economic organization based on the common ownership of goods. Utopian socialists of the early nineteenth century envisioned small planned communities; later socialists campaigned for state ownership of railroads and large industries. (p. 338)

Sons of Liberty Colonists — primarily middling merchants and artisans — who banded together to protest the Stamp Act and other imperial reforms of the 1760s. The group originated in Boston in 1765 but soon spread to all the colonies. (p. 145)

spoils system The widespread award of public jobs to political supporters following an electoral victory. Underlying this practice was the view that in a democracy rotation in office was preferable to a permanent class of officeholders. In 1829 Andrew Jackson began this practice on the national level, and it became a central, and corrupting, feature of American political life. (p. 303)

states' rights An interpretation of the Constitution that exalts the sovereignty of the states and circumscribes the authority of the national government. Expressed first by Antifederalists in the debate over the Constitution, and then in the Virginia and Kentucky resolutions of 1798, the ideology of states' rights became especially important in the South. It informed white southerners' resistance to the high tariffs of the 1820s and 1830s, to legislation to limit the spread of slavery, and to attempts by the national government in the mid-twentieth century to end Jim Crow practices. (p. 211)

subtreasury system A scheme deriving from the Texas Exchange, a cooperative in the 1880s, through which cotton farmers received cheap loans and marketed their crops. When the Texas Exchange failed in 1891, Populists proposed that the federal government take over these functions on a national basis through a "subtreasury," which would have the added benefit of increasing the stock of money in the country and thus push up prices for farm crops. (p. 602)

suburbanization The movement of the upper and middle classes beyond city limits to less crowded areas with larger homes that are connected to city centers by streetcar or subway lines. By 1910, 25 percent of the population lived in these new communities. The 1990 census revealed that the majority of Americans lived in the suburbs. (p. 560)

suffrage The right to vote. The classical republican ideology current before 1810 limited suffrage to those who held property and thus had "a stake in society." However, between 1810 and 1860, state constitutions extended the vote to virtually all adult white men and some free black men. Over the course of American history, suffrage has expanded as barriers of race, gender, and age have fallen. (p. 244, 466)

syndicalism A revolutionary movement that, like socialism, believed in the Marxist principle of class struggle and advocated the organization of society on the basis of industrial unionism. This approach was advocated by the Industrial Workers of the World (IWW) at the start of the twentieth century. (p. 546)

tariff A tax on imports, which has two purposes: raising revenue for the government and protecting domestic products from foreign competition. A hot political issue throughout much of American history, in the late nineteenth century the tariff became particularly controversial as protection-minded Republicans and pro-free-trade Democrats made the tariff the centerpiece of their political campaigns. (p. 585)

temperance, temperance movement A long-term series of activities by reform organizations to encourage individuals and governments to limit the consumption of alcoholic beverages. Leading temperance groups include the American Temperance Society of the 1830s, the Washingtonian Association of the 1840s, the Women's Christian Temperance Union of the late nineteenth century, and Alcoholics Anonymous, which was founded in the 1930s. (p. 293)

Third World This term came into use in the post–World War II era to describe developing or ex-colonial nations that were not aligned with either the Western capitalist countries led by the United States or the socialist states of eastern Europe led by the Soviet Union. It referred to developing countries in Asia, Africa, Latin America, and the Middle East. (p. 822)

total war A form of warfare, new to the nineteenth and twentieth centuries, that mobilized all of a society's resources — economic, political, and cultural — in support of the military effort. Governments now mobilized massive armies of conscripted civilians rather than small forces of professional soldiers. Moreover, they attacked civilians and industries that supported the war efforts of their enemies. Witness Sherman's march through Georgia in the Civil War, and the massive American bombing of Dresden, Hamburg, and Tokyo during World War II and of North Vietnam during the Vietnam War. (p. 434)

town meeting A system of local government in New England in which all male heads of households met regularly to elect selectmen, levy local taxes, and regulate markets, roads, and schools. (p. 61)

trade slaves West Africans who were sold by one African kingdom to another and who were not considered members of the society that had enslaved them. For centuries, Arab merchants carried trade slaves to the Mediterranean region; around 1440, Portuguese ship captains joined in this trade and began buying slaves from African princes and warlords. (p. 23)

transcendentalism A nineteenth-century intellectual movement that posited the importance of an ideal world of mystical knowledge and harmony beyond the world of the senses. As articulated by Ralph Waldo Emerson and Henry David Thoreau, transcendentalism called for the critical examination of society and emphasized individuality, self-reliance, and nonconformity. (p. 332)

trusts A term originally applied to a specific form of business organization enabling participating firms to assign the operation of their properties to a board of trustees, but by the early twentieth century, the term applied more generally to corporate mergers and business combinations that exerted monopoly power over an industry. It was in this latter sense that progressives referred to firms like United States Steel and Standard Oil as trusts. (p. 627)

union shop The requirement that, after gaining employment, a worker must join a union, as distinct from the closed shop, which requires union membership *before* gaining employment. (p. 814)

vaudeville A professional stage show composed of singing, dancing, and comedy routines that changed live entertainment from its seedier predecessors like minstrel shows to family entertainment for the urban masses. Vaudeville became popular in the 1880s and 1890s, the years just before the introduction of movies. (p. 574)

vice-admiralty court A tribunal presided over by a judge, with no jury. The Sugar Act of 1764 required that offenders be tried in a vice-admiralty court rather than in a common-law tribunal, where a jury decides guilt or innocence. This provision of the act provoked protests from merchant-smugglers accustomed to acquittal by sympathetic local juries. (p. 142)

virtual representation The claim made by British politicians that the interests of the American colonists were adequately represented in Parliament by merchants who traded with the colonies and by absentee landlords (mostly sugar planters) who owned estates in the West Indies. (p. 143)

voluntarism The view that citizens should themselves improve their lives, rather than rely on the efforts of state. Especially favored by Samuel Gompers, voluntarism was a key idea within the labor movement, but one gradually abandoned in the course of the twentieth century. (p. 622)

war of attrition A military strategy of small-scale attacks used, usually by the weaker side, to sap the resources and morale of the stronger side. Examples include the attacks carried out by Patriot militias in the South during the War of Independence, and the guerrilla tactics of the Vietcong and North Vietnamese during the Vietnam War. (p. 179)

welfare capitalism A system of labor relations that stresses management's responsibility for employees' well-being. Originating in the 1920s, welfare capitalism offered such benefits as stock plans, health care, and old-age pensions and was designed to maintain a stable workforce and undercut the growth of trade unions. (p. 710)

welfare state A nation that provides for the basic needs of its citizens, including such provisions as old-age pensions, unemployment compensation, child-care facilities, education, and other social programs. Major European countries began to provide such programs around 1900; the New Deal of the 1930s brought them to the United States. In the early twenty-first century, aging populations and the emergence of a global economy (the transfer of jobs to low-wage countries) threatens the economic foundation of the European and American welfare systems. (p. 615)

Whigs In the United States, a political party that began in 1834 with the opponents of Andrew Jackson, who they thought was treating the presidency like a monarchy. They took their name from a British political party with a reputation for supporting liberal principles and reform. The British Whigs rose in power during the Glorious Revolution of 1688 and favored "mixed government" in which the House of Commons would have a voice in shaping policies, especially the power of taxation, as opposed to a monarchy. The Whig party in the United States dissolved in the 1850s over the question of whether or not to extend slavery to the territories. (p. 318)

white-collar Middle-class professionals who are salaried workers as opposed to business owners or wage laborers; they first appeared in large numbers during the industrial expansion in the late nineteenth century. Their ranks were composed of lawyers, engineers, and chemists, as well as salesmen, accountants, and advertising managers. (p. 529)

yellow-dog contract An agreement by a worker, as a condition of employment, not to join a union. Employers in the late nineteenth century used this along with the blacklist and violent strikebreaking to fight unionization of their workforces. (p. 543)

yellow journalism Term that refers to newspapers that specialize in sensationalistic reporting. The name came from the ink used in Hearst's *New York Journal* to print the first comic strip to appear in color in 1895 and is generally associated with the inflammatory reporting leading up to the Spanish-American War of 1898. (p. 577)

yeoman In England between 1500 and 1800, a farmer who owned enough land to support his family in reasonable comfort. In America, Thomas Jefferson envisioned a nation of yeomen, of politically and financially independent farmers. (p. 14)

Chapter 1

Comparing American Voices: Friar Bernardino de Sahagun, "Aztec Elders Describe the Spanish Conquest." Excerpt from *The Florentine Codex: General History of the Things of New Spain*, translated by Arthur J.O. Anderson and Charles E. Dibble. Copyright © 1975 by the University of Utah Press and the School of American Research. Reprinted courtesy of the University of Utah Press.

Chapter 2

Table 2.3. "Environment, Disease, and Death in Virginia, 1618–1624." Adapted from table 3 in *The Chesapeake in the Seventeenth Century* by Thad W. Tate and David L. Ammerman, eds. Published by W.W. Norton (1979). © University of North Carolina Press. Reprinted by permission.

Chapter 4

Voices from Abroad: Gottlieb Mittelberger, "The Perils of Migration." Excerpt from "The Crossing to Pennsylvania" in *Journey to Pennsylvania* by Gottlieb Mittelberger, edited and translated by Oscar Handlin and John Clive, pp. 11–21: The Belknap Press of Harvard University Press. Copyright © 1960 by the President and Fellows of Harvard College. Reprinted by permission of the publisher.

Table 4.1: "Estimated European Migration to the British Mainland Colonies, 1700–1780."

Adapted (and altered from) *The Journal of Interdisciplinary History*, XXII (1992), 628, with the permission of the editors of *The Journal of Interdisciplinary History* and The MIT Press, Cambridge, Massachusetts. © 1992 by the Massachusetts Institute of Technology and The Journal of Interdisciplinary History, Inc.

Chapter 6

Fig. 6.1: "Middling Men Enter the Halls of Government, 1765–1790." Adapted from "Government by the People: The American Revolution and the Democratization of the Legislature" by Jackson T. Main. From *William and Mary Quarterly*, 3rd series, vol. 23 (1996). Reprinted by permission of the Omohundro Institute of Early American History and Culture.

Chapter 7

Voices from Abroad: William Cobbett, "Peter Porcupine Attacks Pro-French Americans." Excerpted from *Peter Porcupine in America: Pamphlets on Republicanism and Revolution* edited by David A. Wilson. Copyright © 1994 by Cornell University. Used by permission of the publisher, Cornell University Press.

Chapter 8

Comparing American Voices: Caroline Howard Gilman. "Female Submission in Marriage." Abridged version from *Major Problems in the History of American Families and Children* by Ayna Jabour, editor. Copyright © 2005 by Ayna Jabour. Reprinted with permission of Houghton Mifflin. All rights reserved.

Comparing American Voices: Martha Hunter Hitchcock. "Isolation, Unmentionable Sorrows and Suffering." Abridged versions from *Major Problems in the History of American Families and Children*. Copyright © 2005 by Ayna Jabour. Reprinted with permission of Houghton Mifflin. All rights reserved.

Comparing American Voices: Elizabeth Scott Neblett. "My Seasons of Gloom and Despondency." Abridged versions from Major *Problems in the History of American Families and Children* by Ayna Jabour, editor. Reprinted with the permission of Houghton Mifflin. All rights reserved.

Table 8.1. "African Slaves Imported into the United States, by Ethnicity, 1776–1809." Adapted from table A-6, "From Slaves, Convicts and Servants to Free Passengers" as published in the *Journal of American History* 85 (June 1998). Reprinted by permission.

Chapter 9

Voices from Abroad: German Immigrants in the Midwest. Excerpts from *News from the Land of Freedom: German Immigrants Write Home* by Walter D. Kamphoefner, Wolfgang Helbid, and Ulrike Sommer, ed. Translated by Susan Carter Vogel. Copyright © 1991 by Cornell University Press. Reprinted with permission of the publisher, Verlag C H Beck Press.

Table 9.1. "Leading Branches of Manufacture, 1860." Adapted from data (p.26) published in *Economic Growth of the U.S. 1790–1860* by Douglas C. North. © Douglas C. North. Reprinted by permission of Pearson Education, Inc. Upper Saddle River, NJ.

Chapter 10

Voices from Abroad: Alexis de Toqueville. "Parties in the United States." From *Democracy in America* by Alexis de Toqueville. Translated by Henry Reeve. Copyright © 1945 and renewed 1973 by Alfred A. Knopf, a division of Random House, Inc. Used by permission of Alfred A. Knopf, a division of Random House, Inc.

Chapter 11

Voices from Abroad: Noel Rae. "The Mystical World of the Shakers" from *Witnessing America* by Noel Rae. Copyright © by Noel Rae and The Stonesong Press, LLC. Used with permission Stonesong Press, LLC.

Comparing American Voices: David Brion Davis. American Temperance Magazine "You Shall Not Sell." From *Antebellum American Culture: An Interpretative Anthology* by David Brion Davis. Copyright © 1997 by David Brion Davis. Reprinted by permission of The Pennsylvania State University and the author.

Fig. 11.2. "The Surge in Immigration, 1842–1855." Adapted from *Division and the Stresses of Renunion 1845–1876* by David M. Potter. © David M. Potter. Reprinted by permission.

Chapter 21

Voices from Abroad: Robin Dario. "To Roosevelt." From *Selected Poems of Ruben Dario by Ruben Dario*. Translated by Lysander Kemp. Copyright © 1965, renewed 1993. By permission of the University of Texas Press.

Chapter 23

Comparing American Voices: John Roach Straton. From "The Most Sinister Movement in the United States," in *American Fundamentalist* 26, December 1925: 8–9. Reprinted in *Preachers, Pedagogues, and Politicians: The Evolution Controversy in North Carolina* by Willard B. Gatewood, Jr. Copyright © 1966 by the University of North Carolina at Chapel Hill. Used by permission of the publisher.

Voices from Abroad: Mary Agnes Hamilton. "Breadlines and Beggers." From *America Through British Eyes*, edited by Allan Nevins. Copyright © 1968 by Allan Nevins. Reprinted with permission of Peter Smith, publisher, Gloucester, MA.

Chapter 24

Voices From Abroad: Odette Keun. "A Foreigner Looks at the Tennessee Valley Authority." From *This Was America*, edited by Oscar Handlin. Copyright © 1949 by Harvard University Press. © 1960 by Oscar Handlin. Reprinted with the permission of the author.

Chapter 25

Comparing American Voices: Evelyn Gotzion. From *Women Remember the War 1941–1945*, by Michael E. Stevens and Ellen D. Goldlust, editors. Copyright © 1993 by Michael E. Stevens and Ellen D. Goldlust. Reprinted with the permission of the Wisconsin Historical Society.

Comparing American Voices: Fanny Christina Hill. Excerpted from interview on pp. 37–42 in *Rosie the Riveter Revisited* by Sherna Berger Gluck. Copyright © 1987 by Sherna B. Gluck. Reprinted with permission of the author.

Comparing American Voices: Peggy Terry. Excerpt from *The Good War* by Studs Terkel. Copyright 1984 by Studs Terkel. Reprinted by permission of Donadio & Olson, Inc.

Voices from Abroad: Monica Itoi Sone. "Japanese Relocation." From *Nisei Daughter* by Monica Sone. Copyright © 1953 by Monica Sone. Copyright © renewed 1981 by Monica Sone. By permission of Little, Brown, and Company, Inc.

Chapter 26

Voices from Abroad: Jean Monnet: Truman's Generous Proposal. Excerpt from *Memoirs* by Jean Monnet, translated by Richard Mayne. Translation copyright © 1978 by Doubleday, a division of Bantam, Doubleday Dell, a division of Random House, Inc. Used by permission of Doubleday, a division of Random House, Inc.

Comparing American Voices: Fulton Lewis, Jr's Radio Address, January 13, 1949. Manuscript Sept CB# 3926 Frank Porter Graham Papers #1819. Manuscript CB #3926 Wilson Library. Southern Historical Collection, University of North Carolina at Chapel Hill. Reprinted with permission.

Comparing American Voices: Frank Porter Graham's Telegram to Fulton Lewis Jr, January 13, 1949. Frank Porter Graham Papers #1819. Manuscript #3926 Wilson Library. Southern Historical Collection, Southern Historical Collection, Wilson Library, University of North Carolina at Chapel Hill. Reprinted with permission.

Comparing American Voices: House Un-American Activities Committee Report on Frank Graham. Frank Porter Graham Papers #1819. Manuscript Sept CB#3926 Wilson Library, University at Chapel Hill. Reprinted with permission.

Chapter 27

Voices from Abroad: Hanoch Bartov. Excerpt from "Measures of Influence" in Chapter 16 of *The Other World*, edited by Oscar and Lillian Handlin. Copyright © 1997. Published by Harvard University Press. Reprinted by permission of Oscar and Lillian Handlin.

Comparing American Voices: Franklin McCain. "Desegrating Lunch Counters." From *My Soul Is Rested: Movement Days in the Deep South Remembered*, by Howell Raines. Copyright © 1977 by Howell Raines. Originally published by Penguin Putnam, 1977. Reprinted with permission of PFD, Inc.

Comparing American Voices: John McFerren: "Demanding the Right to Vote." From *Looking for America*, Second Edition, Volume 1 by Stanley I. Kutler, editor. Copyright © 1979, 1976 by Stanley I. Kutler. Used by permission of W.W. Norton & Company, Inc.

Chapter 28

Comparing America Voices: James R. Wilson. Excerpts from *Landing Zones: Southern Veterans Remember Vietnam* by James R. Wilson. Copyright © 1990 Duke University Press. All rights reserved. Used by permission of the publisher.

Comparing American Voices: Arthur E. Woodley. Excerpt from *Bloods: An Oral History of the Vietnam War by Black Veterans* by Wallace Terry. Copyright © 1984 by Wallace Terry. Used by permission of Random House, Inc.

Comparing American Voices: Gayle Smith. Excerpt from *Everything We Had* by Albert Santoli. Copyright © 1981 by Albert Santoli and Vietnam Veterans of America. Used by permission of Random House.

Voices from Abroad: Che Guevara: "Vietnam and the World Freedom Struggle." From "Message to the Tricontinental" from *Che Guevara Speaks* by Ernesto Che Guevara. Copyright © 1967, 2000 by Pathfinder Press. Reprinted by permission.

Voices from Abroad: Fei Xiaotong. America's Crisis of Faith. From *Land Without Ghosts* by David Arkrush. Copyright © 1989 by the University of California Press Books. Reprinted by the permission of the California University of PressBooks in the format Textbook via Copyright Clearance Center.

Chapter 30

Comparing American Voices: Ronald Reagan. "The Rule of Law Under God." From *Speaking My Mind* by Ronald Reagan. Copyright © 1989 by Ronald Reagan. Reprinted with the permission of Simon & Schuster Adult Publishing Group.

Comparing American Voices: Donald E. Wildmon. "Network Television as a Moral Danger." Excerpt from *The Home Invaders* by Donald E. Wildmon. Copyright © 1985 by Donald E. Wildmon. Reprinted with permission.

Understanding History through Maps

Working with maps deepens your understanding of the basic issues of geography and how they relate to historical studies. Understanding these five themes — location, place, region, movement, and interaction — will enrich your readings of maps and the historical situation they depict.

Location "When?" and "where?" are the first questions asked by historians and cartographers. Every event happens somewhere and at some point in time, and maps are the best devices to show a particular location at a particular time.

Place Human activity creates places. Locations exist on their own without the presence of people, but they become places when people use the spots in some way. As human enterprise thickens and generation after generation use a place, it accumulates artifacts, develops layers of remains, and generates a variety of associations held in a society's history and memory.

Region A region highlights common elements, tying certain places together as a group distinguishable from other places. Perceiving regional ties helps the reader of historical maps because they suggest the forces binding individual interests together and encouraging people to act in common.

Movement All historical change involves movement. People move in their daily activities, in seasonal patterns, and in migration to new places of residence. To understand a map fully, the reader must always envision it as one part of a sequence, not unlike a "still" excerpted from a motion picture.

Interaction The interaction between people and the environment goes both ways. On the one hand, people change their environment to suit their needs. Human ingenuity has found ways to put almost all places to some use. On the other hand, climate and topography present constraints on how people use the land and force people to change their behavior and culture as they adapt to their natural surroundings.

See Guidelines for Reading a Map on the next page.

Guidelines for Reading a Map

Maps depend on an active reader, one who knows how to use maps and has some facility in connecting the maps and the narrative to each other into a meaningful educational experience. The ability to understand the strengths and limitations of maps is called cartographic literacy. Every time you encounter a map in America's History, Sixth Edition, ask yourself the following eight questions. With practice, you will improve your cartographic literacy, thereby deepening your historical understanding. Use these eight questions to consider the example map below.

1. What is the purpose of the map?

2. What date is represented on the map and why is this date historically significant?

3. How does the map help explain the narrative?

4. What additional information does the caption provide?

5. What elements are emphasized on the map?

6. How does the map represent the actual landscape?

7. In what ways does the map show change over time?

8. How do the basic themes of geography — location, place, region, movement, and human-environmental interaction — help unlock the theme of the map?

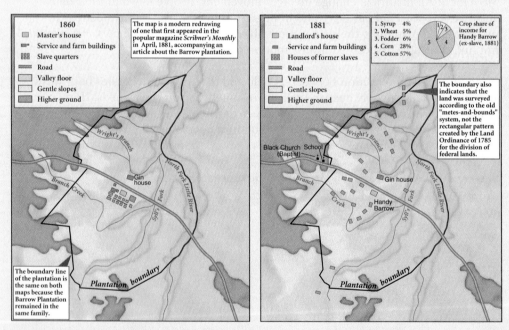

MAP 15.2 The Barrow Plantation, 1860 and 1881

Comparing the 1860 map of this central Georgia plantation with the 1881 map reveals the impact of sharecropping on patterns of black residence. In 1860 the slave quarters were clustered near the planter's house. In contrast, by 1881 the sharecroppers scattered across the plantation's 2,000 acres, building cabins on the ridges of land between the low-lying streams. The name Barrow was common among the sharecropping families, which means almost certainly that they had been slaves on the Barrow plantation who, years after emancipation, still had not moved on. For all the croppers freedom surely meant not only their individual lots and cabins, but also the school and church shown on the map.